THE
ART OF HERALDRY

PLATE I.

HERALDS IN OFFICIAL DRESS.

THE ART OF
HERALDRY

AN ENCYCLOPÆDIA
OF ARMORY

BY

ARTHUR CHARLES FOX-DAVIES

Bloomsbury Books
LONDON

Originally published 1904, this edition
Published 1986
© Bloomsbury Books 1986
A division of Godfrey Cave Associates Ltd
42 Bloomsbury Street, London WC1B 3QJ.

ISBN 0 906223 34 2

Printed and bound in Yugoslavia by
Mladinska Knjiga, Ljubljana

INTRODUCTION

TOO frequently it is the custom to consider the study of the science of Armory as the study of a subject which has passed beyond the limits of practical politics. Heraldry has been termed "The Shorthand of History," but nevertheless the study of that shorthand has been approached too often as if it were but the study of a dead language. The result has been that too much faith has been placed in the works of older writers, whose dicta have been accepted as both unquestionably correct at the date they wrote, and, as a consequence, equally binding at the present day.

Since Dame Juliana Berners wrote the "Boke of St. Albans," into which she managed to compress an unconscionable amount of rubbish, books and treatises on the subject of Armory have issued from the press in a constant succession. A few of them stand a head and shoulders above the remainder. The said remainder have already sunk into oblivion. Such a book as "Guillim" must of necessity rank in the forefront of any armorial bibliography; but any one seeking to judge the Armory of the present day by the standards and ethics adopted by that writer, would find himself making mistake after mistake, and led hopelessly astray. There can be very little doubt that the "Display of Heraldry" is an accurate representation of the laws of Armory which governed the use of Arms at the date the book was written; and it correctly puts forward the opinions which were then accepted concerning the past history of the science.

There are two points, however, which must be borne in mind.

The first is that the critical desire for accuracy which fortunately seems to have been the keynote of research during the nineteenth century, has produced students of Armory whose investigations into facts have swept away the fables, the myths, and the falsehood which had collected around the ancient science, and which in their preposterous assertions had earned for Armory a ridicule, a contempt, and a disbelief which the science itself, and moreover the active practice of the science, had never at any time warranted or deserved. The desire to gratify the vanity of illustrious patrons rendered the mythical traditions attached to Armory more difficult to explode than in the cases of those other sciences in which no one has a personal interest in upholding the wrong; but a study of the scientific works of bygone days, and the comparison, for example, of a sixteenth or seventeenth century medical book with a similar work of the present day, will show that all scientific knowledge during past centuries was a curious conglomeration of unquestionable fact, interwoven with and partly obscured by a vast amount of false information, which now can either be dismissed as utter rubbish or controverted and disproved on the score of being plausible untruth. Consequently, Armory, no less than medicine, theology, or jurisprudence, should not be lightly esteemed because our predecessors knew less about the subject than is known at the present day, or because they believed implicitly dogma and tradition which we ourselves know to be and accept as exploded. Research and investigation constantly goes on, and every day adds to our knowledge.

The second point, which perhaps is the most important, is the patent fact that Heraldry and Armory are not a dead science, but are an actual living reality. Armory may be a quaint

INTRODUCTION

survival of a time with different manners and customs, and different ideas from our own, but the word "Finis" has not yet been written to the science, which is still slowly developing and altering and changing as it is suited to the altered manners and customs of the present day. I doubt not that this view will be a startling one to many who look upon Armory as indissolubly associated with parchments and writings already musty with age. But so long as the Sovereign has the power to create a new order of Knighthood, and attach thereto Heraldic insignia, so long as the Crown has the power to create a new coronet, or to order a new ceremonial, so long as new coats of arms are being called into being,—for so long is it idle to treat Armory and Heraldry as a science incapable of further development, or as a science which in recent periods has not altered in its laws.

The many mistaken ideas upon Armory, however, are not all due to the two considerations which have been put forward. Many are due to the fact that the hand-books of Armory professing to detail the laws of the science have not always been written by those having complete knowledge of their subject. Some statement appears in a text-book of Armory, it is copied into book after book, and accepted by the outside world who study Armory as being correct; whilst all the time it is absolutely wrong, and has never been accepted or acted upon by the Officers of Arms. One instance will illustrate my meaning. There is scarcely a text-book of Armory which does not lay down the rule, that when a crest issues from a coronet it must not be placed upon a wreath. Now there is no rule whatever upon the subject; and instances are frequent, both in ancient and in modern grants, in which coronets have been granted to be borne upon wreaths; and the wreath should be inserted or omitted *according to the original grant of the crest.* Consequently, the so-called rule must be expunged.

Another fruitful source of error is the effort which has frequently been made to assimilate the laws of Armory prevailing in the three different Kingdoms into one single series of rules and regulations. Some writers have even gone so far as to attempt to assimilate with our own the rules and regulations which hold upon the Continent. As a matter of fact, many of the laws of Arms in England and Scotland are radically different; and care needs to be taken to point out these differences.

The truest way to ascertain the laws of Armory is by deduction from known facts. Nevertheless, such a practice may lead one astray, for the number of exceptions to any given rule in Armory is always great, and it is sometimes difficult to tell what is the rule, and which are the exceptions. Moreover, the Sovereign, as the fountain of honour, can over-ride any rule or law of Arms; and many exceptional cases which have been governed by specific grants have been accepted in times past as demonstrating the laws of Armory, when they have been no more than instances of exceptional favour on the part of the Crown.

In England no one is compelled to bear Arms unless he wishes; but, should he desire to do so, the Inland Revenue requires a payment of one or two guineas, according to the method of use. From this voluntary taxation the yearly revenue exceeds £70,000. This affords pretty clear evidence that Armory is still decidedly popular, and that its use and display are extensive; but at the same time it would be foolish to suppose that the estimation in which Armory is held, is equal to, or approaches, the romantic value which in former days was attached to the inheritance of Arms. The result of this has been—and it is not to be wondered at—that ancient examples are accepted and extolled beyond what should be the case. It should be borne in mind that the very ancient examples of Armory which have come down to us, may be examples of the handicraft of ignorant individuals; and it is not safe to accept unquestioningly laws of Arms which are deduced from Heraldic *handicraft* of other days. Most of them are correct, because as a rule such handicraft was done under supervision; but there is always the risk that it has not been; and *this risk should be borne in mind* when estimating the value of any particular example of Armory as proof or contradiction of any particular Armorial law. There were "heraldic stationers" before the present day.

A somewhat similar consideration must govern the estimate of the Heraldic art of a former day. To every action we are told there is a reaction; and the reaction of the present day, admirable and commendable as it undoubtedly is, which has taken the art of Armory back to the style in vogue in past centuries, needs to be kept within intelligent bounds. That the freedom of design and draughtsmanship of the old artists should be copied is desirable; but at the same time there is not the slightest necessity to copy, and to deliberately copy, the crudeness of execution which undoubtedly exists in much of the older work. The revulsion from what has been aptly styled "the die-sinker school of heraldry" has caused some artists to produce Heraldic drawings which (though doubtless modelled upon ancient examples) are grotesque to the last degree, and can be described in no other way.

INTRODUCTION

The genesis of "The Art of Heraldry" should be briefly stated. A work of a sumptuous character, "Heraldischer Atlas," by H. G. Ströhl, the talented and deservedly celebrated German Heraldic artist, was published in parts at Stuttgart, and was completed in 1899. This work, which far surpassed any previous Heraldic publication, attracted a great amount of attention. It then chiefly consisted of well-chosen and typical examples of Heraldic art at all periods, selected from all countries in Europe, and that portion of the work must naturally appeal to English readers equally with German, as will also the magnificent examples of Heraldic illustrations, which indeed form the outstanding feature of the great work referred to. Added to this was a lengthy section on the "Elements of Heraldry," which formed a valuable primer of Heraldry from the German point of view.

The work was brought to the notice of Messrs. T. C. and E. C. Jack, with a proposal that they should publish an English translation. But so large a portion of the text—particularly in the "Elements of Heraldry"—was essentially German, that in the form of a literal translation the work would not have stood much chance of success in this country. It was necessary, therefore, that Messrs. Jack, in arranging for the issue of an edition of the work in this country, should take care that it was adapted to the needs of British readers and scholars. After careful consideration they decided for the English edition,—

(1) To reproduce the series of Coloured Plates in their entirety.
(2) To reproduce the whole series of Illustration Blocks.
(3) To have the entire section relating to the Laws of Armory and to Examples of British Heraldry re-written.
(4) To add very considerably to the Illustrations from a British point of view.

The work was therefore placed in my hands for revision on the lines explained above, and consequently the entire responsibility for the English version is mine, as are the additional chapters essential to a British work on Armory, the subject matter of which was not included in the "Heraldischer Atlas."

A large proportion of the plates and blocks have been executed from the original work of Herr Ströhl, whose reputation as a master of Heraldic art is unsurpassed in his own country, the home of the choicest examples of Heraldic illustration in times past. The whole of the illustrations contained in the original work have been included in this edition. The necessity of devoting a larger proportion of the work to English Heraldry has afforded the Publishers the opportunity of adding some number of additional coloured plates and several hundred additional illustrations to those already included in the German version. Amongst these will be found examples of the work of G. W. Eve, R.E., Graham Johnston, C. W. Sherborn, R.E., J. Forbes Nixon, G. Scruby, J. Vinycomb, M.R.I.A., and Miss Helard, a list of names which includes the whole of the prominent Heraldic artists of the present day in this country. To the work of the above-mentioned have been added many reproductions taken from English sources which were overlooked or crowded out of the German version.

With regard to the literary portion of the volume I have no wish either to claim credit for work which is Herr Ströhl's, or to saddle him with a responsibility for my opinions. Each chapter therefore is signed. Those which are to all intents and purposes literal translations of the corresponding chapters in the German version bear Herr Ströhl's initials (H. S.). Chapters which are essentially mine are signed with my initials. Some chapters very properly carry the initials of us both. The order in which the initials are placed will afford some clue to the individual share of the work with which each should be credited. I may add that Herr Ströhl kindly offered to go over the proofs of that part of the book which was based upon his own work—an offer which I was delighted to accept, and I tender him my thanks therefor.

The fact of the practically simultaneous issue of the "Heraldischer Atlas" alone made it possible to include so large a number and so excellent a selection of coloured plates in the volume. There are some number of these which did not appear in the German version, but the majority did, and that the selection was already made when the work was put into my hands, has, I candidly admit, hampered me considerably in writing the earlier chapters of the book. But the point which has chiefly appealed to me in the production of an English version of another person's work has been the desire to import into British Heraldic art a fresh set of artistic models which may help in the development of the present revival in Heraldic art, and also to import into

INTRODUCTION

British minds a new set of Heraldic ideas, which possibly will tend to new departures, which perhaps may replace the "bedevilled" and overcrowded shields and crests into which our present system of differentiation, working upon a needlessly limited series of ideas and charges, was bound to result.

In the course of the pages which follow, many hundred coats of arms are illustrated or referred to as examples either of Heraldic art or of some point in the science of Armory. With few exceptions, the instances which may be quoted of Arms of other than British families have been selected by Herr Ströhl, except where otherwise stated. I have little acquaintance with the pedigrees of Continental families, and I must state plainly that I have no knowledge whatever as to the legal right of the various families to the Arms attributed to them. Nor can I give any guarantee upon the point as to the Arms of British families, although all which are illustrated and which are definitely attributed to specific individuals I believe to be correct. I have not deliberately chosen unauthorised Arms as examples without making this plainly apparent, but in hunting for instances to illustrate different points, I have sometimes been at a loss to supply these from Arms within my own knowledge, and have taken them from Papworth.

My sister, Miss Grace Muriel Fox-Davies, has very materially lightened my labours and assisted me by making for me a literal translation of Herr Ströhl's work, a task for which past residence in Germany had well qualified her. Nor can I omit to tender my best thanks to Miss Helard for the trouble she has undertaken on my behalf in making many drawings and collecting Heraldic examples for use in this book.

Amongst others to whom my grateful acknowledgments are due and are sincerely tendered, I must specially thank Sir James Balfour Paul, Lyon King of Arms, for his permission to reprint a lecture he delivered which covered the ground of one of my chapters far more adequately than I could have dealt with the matter myself. Mr. C. H. Athill, F.S.A., Richmond Herald, also; he has helped me most materially with his advice as to the selection of certain examples of Heraldic art, and from this and his aid towards the reproduction of these examples my book has greatly profited.

Mr. Cyril Davenport, F.S.A., very kindly helped me in the preparation of another of the chapters in the book which dealt with a subject on which he is admittedly an authority.

Mr. Albert Hartshorne, F.S.A., similarly undertook another chapter on a subject in which he has specialised, viz., Heraldic Effigies; and Mr. Walter J. Kaye, F.S.A., wrote the chapter on Heraldic Brasses, a subject in connection with which he is well known.

For assistance in connection with the production of some of the plates I am indebted to Mr. W. Rae Macdonald, Carrick Pursuivant of Arms, and other kindly help I acknowledge with pleasure from Captain Swinton, March Pursuivant; Mr. Everard Green, Rouge Dragon; and Mr. G. W. Eve, R.E.

I am also indebted to Mr. J. Vinycomb for a most excellent and very practical chapter, and to Rev. J. R. Crawford for another chapter.

To all whose names I have mentioned I offer my sincere thanks.

To the several others who promised me assistance, but have failed to carry out their promises, I can only say that I would gladly have accepted the will for the deed, had it been possible to put the will into type.

THE ART OF HERALDRY

CHAPTER I

THE ORIGIN OF ARMORY

RMORY is that science of which the rules and the laws govern the use, display, meaning, and knowledge of the pictured signs and emblems appertaining to shield, helmet, or banner. Heraldry has a wider meaning, for it comprises everything within the duties of a herald; and whilst Armory is undoubted Heraldry, the regulation of ceremonials and matters of pedigree, which are also within the scope of Heraldry, most decidedly are not Armory.

"Armory" relates only to the emblems and devices. "Armoury" relates to the weapons themselves as weapons of warfare, or to the place used for the storing of the weapons.

The word "Arms," like many other words in the English language, has several meanings, and at the present day is used in several senses. It may mean the weapons themselves; it may mean the limbs upon the human body. Even from the heraldic point of view it may mean the entire achievement, but it is usually intended only to refer to the device upon the shield.

Of the exact origin of arms and armory nothing whatever is definitely known, and it becomes difficult to point to any particular period as the period covering the origin of armory, for the very simple reason that it is much more difficult to decide what is or is not to be admitted as armorial.

Until comparatively recently heraldic books referred armory indifferently to the tribes of Israel, to the Greeks, to the Romans, to the Assyrians and the Saxons; and we are equally familiar with the "Lion of Judah" and the "Eagle of the Cæsars." In other directions we find the same sort of thing, for it has ever been the practice of semi-civilised nations to bestow or to assume the virtues and the names of animals and of deities as symbols of honour. We scarcely need refer to the North American Indians for proof of such a practice. They have reduced the subject almost to an exact science; and there cannot be the shadow of a doubt that it is to this semi-savage practice that armory is to be traced if its origin is to be followed out to its logical and most remote beginning. Equally is it certain that many recognised heraldic figures, and more particularly those mythical creatures of which the armorial menagerie alone has now cognisance, are due to the art of civilisations older than our own, and the legends of those civilisations which have called these mythical creatures into being.

The widest definition of armory would have it that any pictorial badge which is used by an individual or a family with the meaning that it is a badge indicative of that person or family, and adopted and repeatedly used in that sense, is heraldic. If such be your definition, you may ransack the Scriptures for the arms of the tribes of Israel, the writings of the Greek and Roman poets for the decorations of the armour and the persons of their heroes, mythical and actual, and you may annex numberless "heraldic" instances from the art of Nineveh, of Babylon, and of Egypt. Your heraldry is of the beginning and from the beginning. It *is* fact, but is it heraldry? Dame Juliana Berners' statement in the "Boke of St. Albans" that Christ was a gentleman of coat armour is a fable, and due distinction must be had between the fact and the fiction in this as in all other similar cases.

Mr. G. W. Eve in his "Decorative Heraldry" alludes to and illustrates many striking examples of figures of an embryonic type of heraldry, of which the best are one from a Chaldean bas-relief 4000 B.C., the earliest known device that can in any way be called heraldic, and another, a device from a Byzantine silk of the tenth century. Mr. Eve certainly seems inclined to follow the older heraldic writers in giving as wide an interpretation as possible to the word heraldic, but it is significant that none of these early instances which he gives appear to have any relation to a shield, so that, even if it be conceded that the figures are heraldic, they certainly cannot be said to be armorial. But doubtless the inclusion of such instances is due to an attempt, conscious or unconscious, on the part of the writers who have taken their stand on the side of great antiquity to so frame the definition of armory that it shall include everything heraldic, and due perhaps somewhat to the half unconscious reasoning that these mythical animals, and more especially the peculiarly heraldic positions they are depicted in, which nowadays we only know as part of armory, and which exist nowhere else within our knowledge save within the charmed circle of heraldry, must be evidence of the great antiquity of that science or art, call it which you will. But it is a false deduction, due to a confusion of premise and conclusion. We find certain figures at the present day purely heraldic—we find those figures fifty centuries ago. It certainly seems a correct conclusion that, therefore, heraldry must be of that age. But is not the real conclusion, that, our heraldic figures being so old, it is evident that the figures originated long before heraldry was ever thought of, and that instead of these mythical figures having been originated by the necessities of heraldry, and being part, or even the rudimentary origin of heraldry, they had existed—*for other reasons and purposes*—and that when the science of heraldry sprang into being, it found the *whole range* of its forms and charges already existing, and that *none* of these figures owe their being to heraldry? The gryphon is supposed to have *originated,* as is the double-headed eagle, from the dimidiation of two coats of arms resulting from impalement by reason of marriage. Both these figures were known ages earlier. Thus departs yet another of the little fictions which past writers on armory have fostered and perpetuated. Whether the ancient Egyptians and Assyrians knew they were depicting mythical animals, and did it, intending them to be symbolical of attributes of their deities, something beyond what they were familiar with in their ordinary life, we do not know; nor indeed have we any certain knowledge that there have never been animals of which their figures are but imperfect and crude representations.

But it does not necessarily follow that because an Egyptian artist drew a certain figure, which figure is now appropriated to the peculiar use of armory, that he knew anything whatever of the laws of armory. Further, where is this argument to end? There is nothing peculiarly heraldic about the lion passant, statant, dormant, couchant, or salient, and though heraldic artists may for the sake of artistic appearance distort the brute away from his natural figure, the rampant is alone the position which exists not in nature; and if the argument is to be applied to the bitter end, heraldry must be taken back to the very earliest instance which exists of any representation of a lion. The proposition is absurd. The ancient artists drew their lions how they liked, regardless of armory and its laws, which did not then exist; and, from decorative reasons, they evolved a certain number of methods of depicting the positions *e.g.* the lion and the eagle to suit their decorative purposes. When heraldry came into existence it came in as an adjunct of decoration, and it necessarily followed that the whole of the positions in which the craftsmen found the eagle or the lion depicted were appropriated with the animals for heraldry. That this appropriation for the exclusive purposes of armory has been silently acquiesced in by the decorative artists of

later days is simply proof of the intense power and authority which accrued later to armory, and which was in fact attached to anything relating to privilege and prerogative. To put it baldly, the dominating authority of heraldry and its dogmatic protection by the Powers that were, appropriated certain figures to its use, and then defied any one to use them for more humble decorative purposes not allied with armory. And it is the trail of this autocratic appropriation, and from the decorative point of view this arrogant appropriation, which can be traced in the present idea that a griffin or a spread eagle for example must be heraldic. Consequently the argument as to the antiquity of heraldry which is founded upon the discovery of the heraldic creature in the remote ages goes by the board. One practical instance may perhaps more fully demonstrate my meaning. There is one figure, probably the most beautiful of all of those which we owe to Egypt, which is now rapidly being absorbed into heraldry. I refer to the Sphinx. This, whilst strangely in keeping with the remaining mythical heraldic figures, for some reason or other escaped the exclusive appropriation of armorial use until within modern times. One of the earliest instances of its use in recognised armory occurs in the grant to Sir John Moore, K.B., the hero of Corunna, and another will be found in the augmentation granted to Admiral Sir Alexander Cochrane, K.B. (See Plate LXVIII.) Since then it has been used on some number of occasions. It has certainly remained, however, for the present Garter King of Arms to evolve from the depths of his imagination a position which no Egyptian sphinx ever occupied, when he granted two of them as supporters to Sir Edward Malet, G.C.B. (Fig. 1). The Sphinx has also been adopted as the badge of one of his Majesty's regiments, and I have very little doubt that now Egypt has come under our control the Sphinx will figure in some number of the grants of the future to commemorate fortunes made in that country, or lifetimes spent in the Egyptian services. If this be so, the dominating influence of armory will doubtless in the course of another century have given to the Sphinx, as it has to many other objects, a distinctly heraldic nature and character in the mind of the "man in the street" to which we nowadays so often refer the arbitrament

FIG 1.—The arms of Sir Edward Malet, G.C.B., G.C.M.G., and of his wife Lady Ermyntrude, with the supporters granted to the former arms: Quarterly, 1 and 4, azure, three escallops or (for Malet); 2 and 3, gules, two demi-lions passant guardant in pale or (for Hatche), the escutcheon being surrounded by the circle of the Order of the Bath, and by the collars and pendent therefrom the badges of a Knight Grand Cross of that Order, and of the Order of St. Michael and St. George; and impaling upon a second escutcheon the arms of Russell, namely: argent, a lion rampant gules, on a chief sable, three escallops of the field. Upon the escutcheon is placed a helmet befitting his degree, with a mantling azure and or; and for his crest, out of a ducal coronet or, an heraldic tiger's head ermine; and for his supporters, on either side of the escutcheon a sphinx, the upper part proper, the lower ermine, hooded and charged on the shoulder with an escallop or; with the motto, "Ma force de en hault."

between conflicting opinions. Perhaps in the even yet more remote future, when the world in general accepts as a fact that armory did not exist at the time of the Norman Conquest, we shall have some interesting and enterprising individual writing a book to demonstrate that because the Sphinx existed in Egypt long before the days of Cleopatra, heraldry must of necessity be equally antique.

I have no wish, however, to dismiss thus lightly the subject of the antiquity of heraldry, because there is one side of the question which I have not yet touched upon, and that is, the symbolism of these ancient and so-called heraldic examples. There is no doubt whatever that symbolism forms an integral part of armory; in fact there is no doubt that armory *itself* as a whole is nothing more or less than a kind of symbolism. I have no sympathy whatever with many of the ideas concerning this symbolism, which will be found in nearly all heraldic books before the day of the late J. R. Planché, Somerset Herald, who fired the train which exploded then and for ever the absurd ideas of former writers. That an argent field meant purity, that a field of gules meant royal or even martial ancestors, that a saltire meant the capture of a city, or a lion rampant noble and enviable qualities, I utterly deny. But that nearly every coat of arms for any one of the name of Fletcher bears upon it in some form or another an arrow or an arrow-head, because the origin of the name comes from the occupation of the fletcher, who was an arrowmaker, is true enough. Symbolism of that kind will be found constantly in armory, as in the case of the foxes and foxes' heads in the various coats of Fox, the lions in the coats of arms of Lyons, the horse in the arms of Trotter, and the acorns in the arms of Oakes; in fact by far the larger proportion of the older coats of arms, where they can be traced to their real origin, exhibit some such derivation. There is another kind of symbolism which formerly, and still, favours the introduction of swords and spears and bombshells into grants of arms to military men, that gives bezants to bankers and those connected with money, and that assigns woolpacks and cotton-plants to the shields of textile merchants; but that is a sane and reasonable symbolism, which the reputed symbolism of the earlier heraldry books was not.

It has yet to be demonstrated, however, though the belief is very generally credited, that all these very ancient Egyptian and Assyrian figures of a heraldic character had anything of symbolism about them. But even granting the whole symbolism which is claimed for them, we get but little further. There is no doubt that the eagle from untold ages has had an imperial symbolism which it still possesses. But that symbolism is not necessarily heraldic, and it is much more probable that heraldry appropriated both the eagle and its symbolism ready made, and together: consequently, if, as we have shown, the *existence* of the eagle is not proof of the coeval existence of heraldry, no more is the existence of the *symbolical* imperial eagle. For if we are to regard all symbolism as heraldic, where are we either to begin or to end? Church vestments and ecclesiastical emblems are symbolism run riot; in fact they are little else. But by no stretch of imagination can these be considered heraldic with the exception of the few (for example the crosier, the mitre, and the pallium) which heraldry has appropriated ready made. Therefore, though heraldry appropriated ready made from other decorative art, and from nature and handicraft, the whole of its charges, and though it is evident heraldry also appropriated ready made a great deal of its symbolism, neither the earlier existence of the forms which it appropriated, nor the earlier exist-

ence of their symbolism, can be said to weigh at all as determining factors in the consideration of the age of heraldry. Sloane Evans in his "Grammar of Heraldry" (p. ix.) gives the following instances as evidence of the greater antiquity, and they are worthy at any rate of attention if the matter is to be impartially considered.

"The antiquity of ensigns and symbols may be proved by reference to Holy Writ.

"1. 'Take ye the sum of all the congregation of the children of Israel, after their families, by the house of their fathers, with the number of their names. . . . And they assembled all the congregation together on the first day of the second month; and they declared their pedigrees after their families, by the house of their fathers, according to the number of the names, from twenty years old and upward. . . . And the children of Israel shall pitch their tents, every man by his own camp, and every man by his own standard, throughout their hosts' (Numbers i. 2, 18, 52).

"2. 'Every man of the children of Israel shall pitch by his own standard, with the ensign of their father's house' (Numbers ii. 2).

"3. 'And the children of Israel did according to all that the Lord commanded Moses: so they pitched by their standards, and so they set forward, every one after their families, according to the house of their fathers' (Numbers ii. 34)."

The Latin and Greek poets and historians afford numerous instances of the use of symbolic ornaments and devices. It will be sufficient in this work to quote from Æschylus and Virgil, as poets; Herodotus and Tacitus, as historians.

ÆSCHYLUS.

(*Septem contra Thebas.*)

The poet here introduces a dialogue between Eteocles, King of Thebes, the women who composed the chorus, and a herald (κηρυξ), which latter is pointing out the seven captains or chiefs of the army of Adrastus against Thebes; distinguishing one from another by the emblematical devices upon their shields.

1. *Tydeus.*

("Τοιαῦν αὐτῶν,—νυκτὸς ὀφθαλμὸς πρέπει."—Lines 380–386.)

" . . . Frowning he speaks, and shakes
The dark crest streaming o'er his shaded helm
In triple wave; whilst dreadful ring around
The brazen bosses of his shield, impress'd
With his proud argument:—'A sable sky
Burning with stars; and in the midst full orb'd
A silver moon;'—the eye of night o'er all,
Awful in beauty, forms her peerless light."

2. *Capaneus.*

("Ἔχει δὲ σῆμα,—ΠΡΗΣΩ ΠΟΛΙΝ."—Lines 428–430.)

" On his proud shield pourtray'd: 'A naked man
Waves in his hand a blazing torch;' beneath
In golden letters—'I will fire the city.'"

3. *Eteoclus.*

("Ἐσχημάτισται,—πυργωμάτων."—Lines 461–465.)

" . . . No mean device
Is sculptured on his shield: 'A man in arms,
His ladder fix'd against the enemies' walls,
Mounts, resolute, to rend their rampires down;'
And cries aloud (the letters plainly mark'd),
'Not Mars himself shall beat me from the Tow'rs.'"

4. *Hippomedon.*

("'Ο σηματουργὸς—φόβον βλέπων·"—Lines 487–494.)

" . . . On its orb, no vulgar artist
Expressed this image : ' A Typhæus huge,
Disgorging from his foul enfoulder'd jaws,
In fierce effusion wreaths of dusky smoke.
Signal of kindling flames ;. its bending verge
With folds of twisted serpents border'd round.'
With shouts the giant-chief provokes the war,
And in the ravings of outrageous valour
Glares terror from his eyes . . .''

5. *Parthenopæus.*

(" 'Ον μὴν ἀκόμπαστος—ἵαπτεσθαι Βέλη."—Lines 534–540.)

" . . . Upon his clashing shield,
Whose orb sustains the storm of war, he bears
The foul disgrace of Thebes :—' A rav'nous Sphynx
Fixed to the plates : the burnish'd monster round
Pours a portentous gleam : beneath her lies
A Theban, mangled by her cruel fangs : '—
'Gainst this let each brave arm direct the spear."

6. *Amphiaraus.*

(" Τοιαῦθ ὁ μάντις,—βλαστάνει βουλεύματα."—Lines 587–591.)

"So spoke the prophet ; and with awful port
Advanc'd his massy shield, the shining orb
Bearing no impress, for his gen'rous soul
Wishes to be, not to appear, the best ;
And from the culture of his modest worth
Bears the rich fruit of great and glorious deeds."

7. *Polynices.*

("῎Εχει δὲ—τἄ ξευρημ̄ατα."—Lines 639–646.)

" . . . His well-orb'd shield he holds,
New-wrought, and with a double impress charg'd :
' A warrior, blazing all in golden arms,
A female form of modest aspect leads ; '
Expressing justice, as th' inscription speaks,
' Yet once more to his country, and once more
To his Paternal Throne I will restore him '—
Such their devices . . .'"

VIRGIL.

(*The Æneid.*)

1. (" Atque hic exultans—insigne decorum."
—Lib. ii. lines 386–392.)

"Choræbus, with youthful hopes beguil'd,
Swol'n with success, and of a daring mind,
This new invention fatally design'd.
' My friends,' said he, ' since fortune shows the way,
'Tis fit we should the auspicious guide obey.
For what has she these Grecian arms bestowed,
But their destruction, and the Trojan's good ?
Then change we shields, and their devices bear :
Let fraud supply the want of force in war.
They find us arms.'—This said, himself he dress'd
In dead Androgeos' spoils, his upper vest,
His painted buckler, and his plumy crest."

2. (" Post hos insignem—serpentibus hydram.''
—Lib. vii. lines 655–658.)

" Next Aventinus drives his chariot round
The Latian plains, with palms and laurels crown'd.
Proud of his steeds, he smokes along the field ;
His father's hydra fills his ample shield ;
A hundred serpents hiss about the brims ;
The son of Hercules he justly seems,
By his broad shoulders and gigantic limbs."

4. (" Sequitur pulcherrimus Astur—insigne paternæ."
—Lib. x. lines 180–188.)

" Fair Astur follows in the wat'ry field,
Proud of his manag'd horse, and painted shield.
Thou muse, the name of Cinyras renew,
And brave Cupavo, follow'd but by few ;
Whose helm confess'd the lineage of the man,
And bore, with wings display'd, a silver swan.
Love was the fault of his fam'd ancestry,
Whose forms and fortunes in his Ensigns fly."

HERODOTUS.

1. *Clio,* § 171.

(" Καί σφι τριξὰ ἐξευρήματα ἔγένετο—τὰ σημήϊα ποιέεσθαι.")

" And to them is allowed the invention of three things,
which have come into use among the Greeks :—For the
Carians seem to be the first who put crests upon their helmets and sculptured devices upon their shields."

2. *Calliope,* § 74.

("'Ο δἔτερος τῶν λόγων—ἐπίσημον ἄγκυραν.")

" Those who deny this statement assert that he (Sophanes)
bare on his shield, as a device, an anchor."

TACITUS.

(*The Annals.*—Lib. i.)

1. (Tum redire paulatim—in sedes referunt."—Cap. 28.)

" They relinquished the guard of the gates ; and the
Eagles and other Ensigns, which in the beginning of the
Tumult they had thrown together, were now restored each
to its distinct station."

Potter, in his " Antiquities of Greece " (Dunbar's
edition, Edinburgh, 1824, vol. ii. page 79), thus speaks
of the ensigns or flags (σημεῖα) used by the Grecians in
their military affairs : " Of these there were different
sorts, several of which were adorned with images of
animals, or other things bearing peculiar relations to
the cities they belong to. The Athenians, for instance,
bore an *owl* in their ensigns (Plutarchus Lysandro), as
being sacred to Minerva, the protectress of their city ; the
Thebans a *Sphynx* (*idem* Pelopidas, Cornelius Nepos,
Epaminondas), in memory of the famous monster over-
come by Œdipus. The Persians paid divine honours
to the sun, and therefore represented him in their
ensigns " (Curtius, lib. 3). Again (in page 150), speaking of the ornaments and devices on their ships, he
says : " Some other things there are in the prow and
stern that deserve our notice, as those ornaments
wherewith the extremities of the ship were beautified,
commonly called ἀκρονεα (or νεῶν κορωνίδες), in Latin,
Corymbi. The form of them sometimes represented
helmets, sometimes living creatures, but most frequently
was winded into a round compass, whence they are
so commonly named *Corymbi* and *Coronæ.* To the
ἀκροστόλια in the prow, answered the ἄφλαστα in the
stern, which were often of an orbicular figure, or
fashioned like wings, to which a little shield called
ασπιδειον, or ἀσπιδίσκη, was frequently affixed ; sometimes a piece of wood was erected, whereon ribbons of
divers colours were hung, and served instead of a flag
to distinguish the ship. Χηνίσκος was so called from
Χὴν, à *Goose,* whose figure it resembled, because geese
were looked on as fortunate omens to mariners, for
that they swim on the top of the waters and sink not.
Παράσημον was the flag whereby ships were distinguished from one another ; it was placed in the prow,
just below the στόλος, being sometimes carved, and

THE ART OF HERALDRY

frequently painted, whence it is in Latin termed *pictura*, representing the form of a *mountain*, a *tree*, a *flower*, or any other thing, wherein it was distinguished from what was called *tutela*, or the safeguard of the ship, which always represented *some one of the gods*, to whose care and protection the ship was recommended; for which reason it was held sacred. Now and then we find the *tutela* taken for the Παράσημον, and perhaps sometimes the images of gods might be represented on the flags; by some it is placed also in the prow, but by most authors of credit assigned to the stern. Thus Ovid in his Epistle to Paris :—

'Accipit et pictos puppis adunca Deos.'

'The stern with painted deities richly shines.'

"The ship wherein Europa was conveyed from Phœnicia into Crete had a *bull* for its flag, and *Jupiter* for its tutelar deity. The Bœotian ships had for their tutelar god *Cadmus*, represented with a *dragon* in his hand, because he was the founder of Thebes, the principal city of Bœotia. The name of the ship was usually taken from the flag, as appears in the following passage of Ovid, where he tells us his ship received its name from the helmet painted upon it :—

' Est mihi, sitque, precor, flavæ tutela Minervæ,
   Navis et à pictâ casside nomen habit.'

' Minerva is the goddess I adore,
   And may she grant the blessings I implore ;
   The ship its name a painted helmet gives.'

"Hence comes the frequent mention of ships called *Pegasi, Scyllæ, Bulls, Rams, Tigers*, &c., which the poets took liberty to represent as living creatures that transported their riders from one country to another; nor was there (according to some) any other ground for those known fictions of Pegasus, the winged Bellerophon, or the Ram which is reported to have carried Phryxus to Colchos."

To quote another very learned author : "The system of hieroglyphics, or symbols, was adopted into every mysterious institution, for the purpose of concealing the most sublime secrets of religion from the prying curiosity of the vulgar; to whom nothing was exposed but the beauties of their morality. (See Ramsay's 'Travels of Cyrus,' lib. 3.) 'The old Asiatic style, so highly figurative, seems, by what we find of its remains in the prophetic language of the sacred writers, to have been evidently fashioned to the mode of the ancient hieroglyphics; for as in hieroglyphic writing the sun, moon, and stars were used to represent states and empires, kings, queens, and nobility—their eclipse and extinction, temporary disasters, or entire overthrow—fire and flood, desolation by war and famine; plants or animals, the qualities of particular persons, &c.; so, in like manner, the Holy Prophets call kings and empires by the names of the heavenly luminaries; their misfortunes and overthrow are represented by eclipses and extinction; stars falling from the firmament are employed to denote the destruction of the nobility; thunder and tempestuous winds, hostile invasions; lions, bears, leopards, goats, or high trees, leaders of armies, conquerors, and founders of empires; royal dignity is described by purple, or a crown; iniquity by spotted garments; a warrior by a sword or bow; a powerful man, by a gigantic stature; a judge by balance, weights, and measures—in a word, the prophetic style seems to be a speaking hieroglyphic.'"

It seems to me, however, that the whole of these are no more than symbolism, though they are undoubtedly symbolism of a high and methodical order, little removed from our own armory. Personally I do not consider them to be armory, but if the word is to be stretched to the utmost latitude to permit of their inclusion, one certain conclusion follows. That if the heraldry of that day had an orderly existence, it most certainly came absolutely to an end and disappeared. Armory as we know it, the armory of to-day, which as a system is traced back to the period of the Crusades, is no mere continuation by adoption. It is a distinct development and a re-development *ab initio*. Undoubtedly there is a period in the early development of European civilisation which is destitute alike of armory, or of anything of that nature. The civilisation of Europe is not the civilisation of Egypt, of Greece, or of Rome, nor a continuation thereof, but a new development, and though each of these in its turn attained a high degree of civilisation and may have separately developed a heraldic symbolism much akin to armory, as a natural consequence of its own development, as the armory we know is a development of its own consequent upon the rise of our own civilisation, nevertheless it is unjustifiable to attempt to establish continuity between the ordered symbolism of earlier but distinct civilisations, and our own present system of armory. The one and only civilisation which has preserved its continuity is that of the Jewish race. In spite of persecution they have preserved unchanged the minutest details of ritual law and ceremony, the causes of their suffering. Had heraldry, which is and has always been a matter of pride, formed a part of their distinctive life we should find it still existing. Yet the fact remains that no trace of Jewish heraldry can be found until quite recent times, when it has in a few cases been adopted from Christian civilisation. Consequently I accept unquestioningly the conclusions of the late J. R. Planché, Somerset Herald, who unhesitatingly asserted that armory did not exist at the time of the Conquest, basing his conclusions principally upon the entire absence of armory from the seals of that period, and the Bayeux tapestry.

The family tokens (*mon*) of the Japanese, however, fulfil very nearly all of the essentials of armory, although considered heraldically they may appear somewhat peculiar to European eyes. Though perhaps never forming the entire decoration of a shield, they do appear upon weapons and armour, and are used most lavishly in the decoration of clothing, rooms, furniture, and in fact almost every conceivable object, being employed for *decorative* purposes in precisely the same manners and methods that armorial devices are decoratively made use of in this country. A Japanese of the upper classes always has his *mon* in three places upon his *kimono*, usually at the back just below the collar and on either sleeve. The Japanese servants also wear their service badge in much the same manner that in olden days the badge was worn by the servants of a nobleman. The design of the service badge occupies the whole available surface of the back, and is reproduced in a miniature form on each lappel of the *kimono*. Unfortunately, like armorial bearings in Europe, but to a far greater extent, the Japanese *mon* has been greatly pirated and abused.

FIG. 2.—Kiku-non-hana-mon. State *Mon* of Japan.

Fig. 2, "Kiku - non - hana - mon," formed from the conventionalised bloom (*hana*) of the chrysanthemum, is the *mon* of the State. It is formed of sixteen petals arranged in a circle, and connected on the outer edge by small curves (see Plate CXV. Fig. 13).

5

Fig. 3, "Kiri-mon," is the personal *mon* of the Mikado, formed of the leaves and flower of the *Paulowna imperialis*, conventionally treated.

FIG. 3.—Kiri-mon. *Mon* of the Mikado.

FIG. 4.—Awoï-mon. *Mon* of the House of Minamoto Tokugawa.

Fig. 4, "Awoï-mon," is the *mon* of the House of Minamoto Tokugawa, and is composed of three sea-leaves (*Asarum*). The Tokugawa reigned over the country as *Shogune* from 1603 until the last revolution in 1867, before which time the Emperor (the Mikado) was only nominally the ruler.

Fig. 5 shows the *mon* of the House of Minamoto Ashikaya, which from 1336 until 1573 enjoyed the Shogunat.

FIG. 5.—*Mon* of the House of Minamoto Ashikaya.

FIG. 6.—Tomoye. *Mon* of the House of Arina.

Fig. 6 shows the second *mon* of the House of Arina, Tomoye, which is used, however, throughout Japan as a sign of luck.

FIG. 7.—Double eagle on a coin (*drachma*) under the Orthogide of Kaifa Naçr Edin Mahmud, 1217.

FIG. 8.—"Arms (!)" of the Mameluke Emir Toka Timur, Governor of Rahaba, 1350.

FIG. 9.—Lily on the Bab-al-Hadid gate at Damascus.

FIG. 10.—"Arms (!)" of the Emir Arkatây (a band between two keys).

FIG. 11.—"Arms (!)" of the Mameluke Emir Schaikhu.

FIG. 12.—Alleged Arms of Abu Abdallah, Mohammed ibn Naçr, King of Granada, said to be the builder of the Alhambra (1231-1272).

The Saracens and the Moors, to whom we owe the origin of so many of our recognised heraldic charges and the derivation of some of our terms (*e.g.* "gules," from the Persian *gul*, and "azure," from the Persian *lazurd*), had evidently on their part something more than the rudiments of armory, as Figs. 7 to 12 will indicate.

One of the best definitions of a coat of arms that I know, though this is not perfect, requires the twofold qualification that the design must be hereditary and must be connected with armour. And there can be no doubt that the theory of armory as we now know it is governed by those two ideas. The shields and the crests, if any decoration of a helmet is to be called a crest, of the Greeks and the Romans undoubtedly come within the one requirement. Also were they indicative of and perhaps intended to be symbolical of the owner. They lacked, however, heredity, and we have no proof that the badges we read of, or the decorations of shield and helmet, were continuous even during a single lifetime. Certainly as we now understand the term there must be both continuity of use, if the arms be impersonal, or heredity if the arms be personal. Likewise must there be their use as decorations of the implements of warfare.

If we exact these qualifications as essential, armory as a fact and as a science is a product of later days and is the evolution from the idea of tribal badges and tribal means and methods of honour applied to the decoration of implements of warfare. It is the conjunction and association of these two distinct ideas to which is added the no less important idea of heredity. The civilisation of England before the Conquest has left us no trace of any sort or kind that the Saxons, the Danes, or the Celts either knew or practised armory. So that if armory as we know it is to be traced to the period of the Norman Conquest, we must look for it as an adjunct of the altered civilisation and the altered law which Duke William brought into this country. Such evidence as exists is to the contrary, there is nothing that can be truly termed armorial in that marvellous piece of cotemporaneous workmanship known as the Bayeux tapestry.

Concerning the Bayeux tapestry and the evidence it affords, Woodward and Burnett's "Treatise on Heraldry," apparently following Planché's conclusions, remarks: "The evidence afforded by the famous tapestry preserved in the public library of Bayeux, a series of views in sewed work representing the invasion and conquest of England by WILLIAM the Norman, has been appealed to on both sides of this controversy, and has certainly an important bearing on the question of the antiquity of coat-armour. This panorama of seventy-two scenes is on probable grounds believed to have been the work of the Conqueror's Queen MATILDA and her maidens; though the French historian THIERRY and others ascribe it to the Empress MAUD, daughter of HENRY III. The latest authorities suggest the likelihood of its having been wrought as a decoration for the Cathedral of Bayeux, when rebuilt by WILLIAM's uterine brother ODO, Bishop of that See, in 1077. The exact correspondence which has been discovered between the length of the tapestry and the inner circumference of the nave of the Cathedral greatly favours this supposition. This remarkable work of art, as carefully drawn in colour in 1818 by Mr. C. STOTHARD, is reproduced in the sixth volume of the *Vetusta Monumenta;* and more recently an excellent copy of it from autotype plates has been published by the Arundel Society. Each of its scenes is accompanied by a Latin description, the whole uniting into a graphic history of the event commemorated. We see HAROLD taking leave of EDWARD THE CONFESSOR; riding to Bosham with his hawk and hounds; embarking for France; landing there and being captured by the Count of Ponthieu; redeemed by WILLIAM of Normandy, and in the midst of his Court aiding him against CONAN, Count of BRETAGNE; swearing on the sacred relics to recognise WILLIAM's claim of succession to the English throne, and then re-embarking for England. On his return, we have him recounting the incidents of his journey to EDWARD THE CONFESSOR, to whose funeral obsequies we are next introduced. Then we have HAROLD receiving the crown from the English people, and ascending the throne; and WILLIAM, apprised of what had taken place, consulting with his half-brother ODO about invading England. The war preparations of the Normans, their embarkation, their landing, their march to Hastings, and formation of a camp there, form the subjects of successive scenes; and finally we have the battle of Hastings, with the death of Harold, and the flight of the English. In this remarkable piece of work we have figures of more than six hundred persons, and seven hundred animals, besides thirty-seven buildings, and forty-one ships or boats. There are of course also numerous shields of warriors, of which some are round, others kite-shaped, and on some of the latter are rude figures, of dragons or other imaginary animals, as well as crosses of different forms, and spots. On one hand it requires little imagination to find the cross *patée* and the cross *botonnée* of heraldry prefigured on two of these shields. But there are several fatal objections to regarding these figures as incipient *armory*, namely, that while the most prominent persons of the time are depicted, most of them repeatedly, none of these is ever represented twice as bearing the same device, nor is there one instance of any resemblance in the rude designs described to the bearings actually used by the descendants of the persons in question. If a personage so important and so often depicted as the Conqueror had borne arms, they could not fail to have had a place in a nearly contemporary work, and more especially if it proceeded from the needle of his wife." Lower, in his "Curiosities of Heraldry," clinches the argument when he writes: "Nothing but disappointment awaits the curious armorist who seeks in this venerable memorial the pale, the bend, and other early elements of arms. As these would have been much more easily imitated with the needle than the grotesque figures before alluded to, we may safely conclude that personal arms had not yet been introduced." The "Treatise on Heraldry" proceeds: "The Second Crusade took place in 1147; and in MONTFAUCON'S plates of the no longer extant windows of the Abbey of St. Denis, representing that historical episode, there is not a trace of an armorial ensign on any of the shields. That window was probably executed at a date when the memory of that event was fresh; but in MONTFAUCON'S time, the beginning of the eighteenth century, the *Science héroïque* was matter of such moment in France that it is not to be believed that the armorial figures on the shields, had there been any, would have been left out."

Surely, if anywhere, we might have expected to have found it there. Neither the seals nor the coins of the period produced a shield of arms. Nor amongst the host of records and documents which have been preserved to us do we find any reference to armorial bearings. The intense value and estimation attached to arms in the fourteenth and fifteenth centuries, which has steadily though slowly declined since that period, would lead one to suppose that had arms existed as we know them at an earlier period, we should have found some definite record of them in the older chronicles. There are none, and no coat of arms in use at a later date can be relegated to the Conquest or any anterior period. Of arms, as we know them, there are *isolated examples* in the early part of the twelfth century, *perhaps* also at the end of the eleventh. At the period of the Third Crusade (1189) they were in actual existence as hereditary decorations of weapons of warfare.

Luckily, for the purposes of deductive reasoning,

human nature remains much the same throughout the ages, and, dislike it as we may, vanity now and vanity in olden days was a great lever in the determination of human actions. A noticeable result of civilisation is the effort to suppress any sign of natural emotion; and if the human race at the present day is not unmoved by a desire to render its appearance attractive, we may rest very certainly assured that in the twelfth and thirteenth centuries this motive was even more pronounced, and still yet more pronounced at a more remote distance of time. Given an opportunity of ornament, there you will find ornament and decoration. The ancient Britons, like the Maories of to-day, found their opportunities restricted to their skins. The Maories tattoo themselves in intricate patterns, the ancient Britons used woad, though history is silent as to whether they were content with flat colour or gave their preference to patterns. It is unnecessary to trace the art of decoration through the embroidery upon clothes, but there is no doubt that as soon as shields came into use they were painted and decorated, though I hesitate to follow practically the whole of the heraldic writers in the statement that it was *the necessity for distinction in battle* which accounted for the decoration of shields. Shields were painted and decorated, and helmets were adorned with all sorts of ornament, long *before* the closed helmet made it impossible to recognise a man by his facial peculiarities and distinctions. We have then this underlying principle of vanity, with its concomitant result of personal decoration and adornment. We have the relics of savagery which caused a man to be nicknamed from some animal. The conjunction of the two produces the effort to apply the opportunity for decoration and the vanity of the animal nickname to each other.

We are fast approaching armory. In those days every man fought, and his weapons were the most cherished of his personal possessions. The sword his father fought with, the shield his father carried, the banner his father followed would naturally be amongst the articles a son would be most eager to possess. Herein are the rudiments of the idea of heredity in armory; and the science of armory as we know it begins to slowly evolve itself from that point, for the son would naturally take a pride in upholding the fame which had clustered round the pictured signs and emblems under which his father had warred.

Another element then appeared which exercised a vast influence upon armory. Europe rang from end to end with the call to the Crusades. We may or we may not understand the fanaticism which gripped the whole of the Christian world and sent it forth to fight the Saracens. That has little to do with it. The result was the collection together in a comparatively restricted space of all that was best and noblest amongst the human race at that time. And the spirit of emulation caused nation to vie with nation, and individual with individual in the performance of illustrious feats of honour. War was elevated to the dignity of a sacred duty, and the implements of warfare rose in estimation. It is easy to understand the glory therefore that attached to arms, and the slow evolution which I have been endeavouring to indicate became a concrete fact, and to the Crusades is due the fact that the origin of armory as we now know it was practically coeval throughout Europe, and also the fact that a large proportion of the charges and terms and rules of heraldry are identical in all European countries.

The next dominating influence was the introduction, in the early part of the thirteenth century, of the closed helmet. This hid the face of the wearer from his followers and necessitated some means by which the latter could identify the man under whom they served. What more natural than that they should identify him by the decoration of his shield and the ornaments of his helmet, and by the coat or surcoat which he wore over his coat of mail ?

This surcoat had afforded another opportunity of decoration, and it had been decorated with the same signs that the wearer had painted on his shield, hence the term "coat of arms." This textile coat was in itself a product of the Crusades. The Crusaders went in their metal armour from the cooler atmospheres of Europe to the intolerable heat of the East. The surcoat and the lambrequin alike protected the metal armour and the metal helmet from the rays of the sun and the resulting discomfort to the wearer, and were also found very effective as a preventative of the rust resulting from rain and damp upon the metal. By the time that the closed helmet had developed the necessity of distinction and the identification of a man with the pictured signs he wore or carried, the evolution of armory into the science we know was practically complete.

A. C. F-D.

CHAPTER II

HERALDRY AND NUMISMATICS

By P. W. P. CARLYON-BRITTON, F.S.A.

IT is not with the heraldic and armorial devices found on mediæval and more recent coins that the following slight sketch will deal. "There is nothing new under the sun," and so, long before heraldry and the elaborated systems of armory arising from it issued from the events of the Crusades, objects, natural and fantastic alike, were adopted as symbols ofttimes of the god or goddess worshipped in the towns of ancient Greece, and so found place on the coins in honour of the deities alluded to, and as a guarantee of the genuineness and value of the precious media of commerce and exchange.

The invention of coins has been ascribed to Gyges, King of Lydia, about 700 B.C. At first these were mere lumps of metal of ascertained weight, bearing on one side a simple device, such as the head or forepart of a bull, and on the other the impress, in incuse form, of the punch that held the lump of metal in place while the necessary blows were struck. In course of time the preparation of the dies so much improved that devices of the highest artistic merit were impressed on the coins of gold, silver, and bronze.

To examine all these devices, and to speculate on all that such may well import, would be the work of very many years; but it may be taken that, prior to the great conquests of Alexander, the heads and symbols on the coins had reference to gods, and not to men. On the well-known coins of Athens the owl and olive branch—emblems of Athena—appear, and the use of this device was so constant that the coins were known as "owls," even as the Pegasos coins of Corinth were known as πῶλοι, or "colts." The Pegasos of Corinth (and later, Syracuse) had reference to the myth of Bellerophon and the winged steed caught by Athena's aid. To-day the same device adorns the Inner Temple by way of "arms," and the callow student of the musty inn may still, seeking wisdom's aid, perchance with woman's help, catch the coy steed, and mount to the woolsack's comfortable height. The tortoise or sea-turtle of Ægina was a symbol of the wave-born Aphrodite worshipped there, while sea-horses, sea-serpents, mermen, fish, and shells, betoken both the island or sea-shore dwellings of the issuers of the coins that bear them, and the worship of the ruler of the waves, Poseidon. On many coins appears a Nike standing on a prow, symbolic of victory in naval fight. The florin of our latest English King bears Britannia similarly placed.

The coins of ancient Greece draw ship and figure to a reasonable scale, but, looking at King Edward's new milled piece, one fears that with a change of steersman at the helm the huge Britannia may, all unwilling, slip from her narrow perch. The three human legs conjoined, or triskeles of the old Sicilian coins, still serve as modern "arms" for British Isle of Man. That symbols such as these in aftertime came to be regarded as symbolic of the town long using them cannot be doubted; an instance of this is the well-known badge of Eretria—a sepia or octopus, emblem of Poseidon. In reference to this symbol, Themistocles, in a passage quoted by Dr. Head in his *Historia Numorum*, slightingly compares the Eretrians to cuttle-fish : τοὺς δὲ Ἐρετριεῖς ἐπισκώπτων ἔλεγεν ὥσπερ τευθίδας μάχαιραν μὲν ἔχειν καρδίαν δὲ μὴ ἔχειν (Plut., Apophth. Reg. et Imp. (Themist.), xiv.). These coins were issued from about 480 B.C. The lion, stag, bull, boar, and most of the animals of modern heraldry, find a place on the old-world coins.

The eagle (sometimes with fulmen or thunderbolt) was a very favourite symbol of the lightning-giving Zeus, and finds a place on the ancient coins of Agrigentum, and later on those of Alexandria. The eagle came in after days to represent the might of Rome, later of Napoleon, and now the same noble bird, with double head, representing the empires of the East and West, does duty as the background and foundation supporting the arms of Austria and Russia, both claimants of the Imperator's ancient sway. The same device with single head most aptly represents the lofty and far-seeing views of Germania's present ruler, while the talons of that bird may well symbolise the clutching claws of war in the case of this modern claimant to the Roman eagle's power.

In addition to natural objects, however symbolical, the ancients represented on their coins bulls with human heads, the sphinx, griffin, chimæra, centaur, and other creatures not known to present-day zoology. The coins of Gela, in Sicily, have the device of a rushing man-headed bull, representing the personification of the rushing river Gelas. In present days the type would well represent the enthusiastic sort of antiquary who rushes headlong and bull-like in the direction he thinks he sees a point, but quite regardless of all things to be looked at on the way, ignorant of the past, and careless of the future. People such as these have argued that the griffin of our mediæval heraldry arose through the dimidiation of charges on one shield, yet the beast is found complete as now on coins of Teos and Abdera some five-and-twenty centuries ago!

The sphinx occurs on the coins of Chios, and, like the griffin at Teos, is supposed to indicate the cultus of Dionysos. In addition to types on coins signifying the local deity, others had chariots and other devices connected with the games· and festivals held in such high esteem by the ancients. Of a more heraldic character are the signs on ancient coins representing by a well-known attribute some idea or personage, the whole of which is not represented; thus the thunderbolt is the sign or symbol of Zeus, the trident of Poseidon, the club of Herakles, the lyre of Apollo, the bow of Artemis, the owl of Athena, and so forth. A second class wherein the ideals of modern heraldry are exactly anticipated are the symbols representing the personal signets or "arms" of the magistrates under whose authorities coins were from time to time issued. As an instance of this, the symbols on the later tetradrachms of Athens consist of small objects in the field of the coin, and change from year to year with the names of the magistrates, although there is no variation in the main type or device of the coins.

The coins of Abdera, in Thrace, bear the names of the annual Eponymi of the city, and the reverse type is in some cases a symbol representing the name of the magistrate. Thus, a coin bearing the name *ΝΙΚΟΣΤ-ΡΑΤΟΣ* has for type a warrior; *ΠΤΘΩΝ,* a tripod; *ΜΟΛΠΑΠΟΡΗΣ,* a dancing-girl, &c.

A third class of symbols has a strong analogy to canting or punning heraldry; thus, Ancona in Picenum derived its name from its situation in a bend of the coast (ἀγκών), and the coins have a bent arm upon them; the coins of Ancyra in Phrygia an anchor (ἄγκυρα). Again, the coins of Melitæa in Thessaly bore a bee (μέλιττα), and the coins of Rhodus in Rhodes have the head of Helios, the sun-god, and his emblem—a rose (ῥόδον). There are many instances of this punning symbolism, but the above instances of the "type parlant" will suffice.

As regards the attributes of modern heraldry, shield, helm, and coat of armour all find frequent place on the coins of the Greeks and Romans. Standards (with the numbers of the Roman legions, similar to the colours of our modern regiments), and after the conversion of Rome to the Christian faith, crosses and sacred monograms are represented on the coins. Coming a little nearer home, we find on the coins of the British King Cunobelin, struck at Colchester, an ear of corn, similar to that on the coins of Metapontum made some five or six centuries earlier. In the tenth century King Anlaf, a Dane ruling in Northumbria, had coins bearing the Danish raven, and other coins of Anlaf have a standard upon them. The Anglo-Saxon pennies from the earliest period of issue till the reign of Edward the Confessor have nearly all a cross upon them, but nothing truly heraldic occurs on an English coin prior to the reign of Edward III.

When in the time of Richard II. the heralds wished to assign arms to Edward the Confessor (St. Edward), they doubtless had reference to the reverse of one of the types of that King's coins known as the "sovereign" type. It is so called by reason of the King being represented on the obverse side seated on his throne, with sceptre in right hand and orb surmounted by a cross in the left. The reverse has in the angles of a voided cross four birds, which may be intended for doves, as the extant sceptre of King Edward the Confessor has a dove at the upper end. The heralds adopted this device, cross and birds complete, with slight variations. The cross voided became a cross *patonce*, the doves became martlets, and to the original number of four a fifth was added, perhaps as compensation for the original four being changed from doves to martlets, and being provided with only an apology for legs and feet.

It is clear that heraldry as now understood originated with the Crusades, but our ancient coins, gems, and other relics of a remote antiquity teach us that the language of symbolism, the hidden meaning, the type parlant and personal and civic sign, signet, badge, or identification, extend to an age as remote as when the thoughts of men were first capable of expression by the art of painter, sculptor, or engraver.

P. W. P. C-B.

CHAPTER III

THE STATUS AND THE MEANING OF A COAT OF ARMS IN GREAT BRITAIN

IT would be foolish and misleading to assert that the possession of a coat of arms at the present date has anything approaching the dignity which attached to it in the days of long ago; but one must trace this through the centuries which have passed in order to form a true estimate of it, and also to properly appreciate a coat of arms at the present day. It is necessary to go back to the Norman Conquest and the broad dividing lines of social life in order to obtain a correct knowledge. The Saxons had no armory, though they had a very perfect civilisation. This civilisation William the Conqueror upset, introducing in its place the system of feudal tenure with which he had been familiar on the Continent. Briefly, this feudal system may be described as the partition of the land amongst the barons and earls, in return for which, according to the land they held, they accepted a liability of military service for themselves and so many followers. These barons and earls in their turn sublet the land on terms advantageous to themselves, but nevertheless requiring from those to whom they sublet the same military service which the King had exacted from themselves proportionate with the extent of the sublet lands. Other subdivisions took place, but always with the same liability of military service, until we come to those actually holding and using the lands, enjoying them subject to the liability of military service attached to those particular lands. Every man who held land under these conditions—and it was impossible to hold land without them—was of the upper class. He was *nobilis* or *known*, and of a rank distinct, apart, and absolutely separate from the remainder of the population, who were at one time actually serfs, and for long enough afterwards, of no higher social position than they had enjoyed in their period of servitude. This wide distinction between the upper and the lower classes, which existed from one end of Europe to the other, was the very root and foundation of armory. It cannot be too greatly insisted upon. There were two qualitative terms, "gentle" and "simple," which were applied to the upper and lower classes respectively. Though now becoming archaic and obsolete, the terms "gentle" and "simple" are still occasionally to be met with used in that original sense; and the two adjectives "gentle" and "simple," in the everyday meanings of the words, are derived from, and are a *later* growth from the original usage with the meaning of the upper and lower classes; because the quality of being gentle was supposed to exist in that class of life referred to as gentle, whilst the quality of simplicity was supposed to be an attribute of the lower class. The word gentle is derived from the Latin word *gens* (*gentilis*), meaning a man, because those were *men* who were not serfs. Serfs and slaves were nothing accounted of. The word "gentleman" is a *derivative* of the word gentle, and a gentleman was a member of the gentle or upper class, and gentle qualities were so termed because they were the qualities supposed to belong to the gentle class. A man was not a gentleman, even in those days, because he happened to possess personal qualities usually associated with the gentle class; a man was a gentleman if he belonged to the gentle or upper class and not otherwise, so that "gentleman" was an identical term for one to whom the word *nobilis* was applied, both being names for members of the upper class. To all intents and purposes at that date there was no middle class at all. The kingdom was the land; and the trading community who dwelt in the towns were of little account save as milch kine for the purposes of taxation. The social position conceded to them by the upper class was little, if any, more than was conceded to the lower classes, whose life and liberties were held very cheaply. Briefly to sum up, therefore, there were but the two classes in existence, of which the upper class were those who held the land, who had military obligations, and who were noble, or in other words gentle. Therefore all who held land were gentlemen; because they held land they had to lead their servants and followers into battle, and they themselves were personally responsible for the appearance of so many followers, when the King summoned them to war. Now we have seen in the previous chapter that arms became necessary to the leader that his followers might distinguish him in battle. Consequently all who held land having, because of that land, to be responsible for followers in battle, found it necessary to use arms. The corollary is therefore evident, that all who held lands of the King were gentlemen or noble, and used arms; and as a consequence all who possessed arms were gentlemen, for they would not need or use arms, nor was their armour of a character upon which they could display arms, unless they were leaders. The leaders, we have seen, were the land-owning or upper class; therefore every one who had arms was a gentleman, and every gentleman had arms. But the status of gentlemen existed before there were coats of arms, and the later inseparable connection between the two was an evolution.

The preposterous prostitution of the word gentleman in these latter days is due to the almost universal attribute of human nature which declines to admit itself as of other than gentle rank; and in the eager desire to write itself gentleman, it has deliberately accepted and ordained a meaning to the word which it did not formerly possess, and has attributed to it and allowed it only such a definition as would enable almost anybody to be included within its ranks.

The word gentleman nowadays has become meaningless as a word in an ordinary vocabulary; and to use the word with its original and true meaning, it is necessary to now consider it as purely a technical term. We are so accustomed to employ the word nowadays in its unrestricted usage that we are apt to overlook the fact that such a usage is comparatively modern. The following extract from a well-known book, "The Right to Bear Arms," which has been published anonymously, will prove that its real meaning was understood and was decided by law so late as the seventeenth century to be "a man entitled to bear arms":—

"The following case in the Earl Marshal's Court, which hung upon the definition of the word, conclusively proves my contention:—

"'21st November 1637.—W. Baker, gent., humbly sheweth that having some occasion of conference with Adam Spencer of Broughton under the Bleane, co. Cant., on or about 28th July last, the said Adam did in most base and opprobrious tearmes abuse your petitioner, calling him a base, lying fellow, &c. &c. The defendant pleaded that Baker is noe Gentleman, and soe not capable of redresse in this court. Le Neve, Clarenceux, is directed to examine the point raised, and having done so, declared as touching the gentry of William Baker, that Robert Cooke, Clarenceux King of Arms, did make a declaration 10th May 1573, under his hand and seale of office, that George Baker of London, sonne of J. Baker of the same place, sonne of Simon Baker of Feversham, co. Cant., was a bearer of tokens of honour, and did allow and confirm to the said George Baker and to his posterity, and to the posterity of Christopher Baker, these Arms, &c. &c. And further, Le Neve has received proof that the petitioner, William Baker, is the son of William Baker of Kingsdowne, co. Cant., who was the brother of George Baker, and son of Christopher aforesaid.' The judgment is not stated. (The original Confirmation of Arms by Cooke, 10th May 1573, may now be seen in the British Museum.—*Genealogist* for 1889, p. 242.)"

It has been shown that originally practically all who held land bore arms. It has also been shown that armory was an evolution, and as a consequence it did not start, in this country at any rate, as a ready-made science with all its rules and laws completely known or promulgated. There is not the slightest doubt that, in the earliest infancy of the science, arms were assumed and chosen without the control of the Crown; and one would not be far wrong in assuming that, so long as the rights accruing from prior appropriation of other people were respected, a landowner finding the necessity of arms in battle, was originally at liberty to assume what arms he liked.

That period, however, was of but brief duration, for we find as early as 1390, from the celebrated Scrope and Grosvenor case, (1) that a man could have obtained at that time a definite right to his arms, (2) that this right could be enforced against another, and we find, what is more important, (3) that the Crown and the Sovereign had supreme control and jurisdiction over arms, and (4) that the Sovereign could and did grant arms. From that date down to the present time the Crown, both by its own direct action and by the action of the Kings of Arms to whom it delegates powers for the purpose, in Letters Patent under the Great Seal, specifically issued to each separate King of Arms upon his appointment, has continued to grant armorial bearings. Some number of early grants of arms direct from the Crown have been printed in the *Genealogical Magazine*, and some of the earliest distinctly recite that the recipients are made noble and created gentlemen, and that the arms are given them *as the sign of their nobility*. The class of persons to whom grants of arms were made in the earliest days of such instruments is much the same as the class which obtain grants of arms at the present day, and the successful trader or merchant is now at liberty, as he was in the reign of Henry VIII. and earlier, to raise himself to the rank of a gentleman by obtaining a grant of arms. A family must make its start at some time or other; let this start be made honestly, and not by the appropriation of the arms of some other man. The illegal assumption of arms began at an early date; and in spite of the efforts of the Crown, which have been continuous and repeated, it has been found that the use of "other people's" arms has continued. In the reign of Henry V. a very stringent proclamation was issued on the subject; and in the reigns of Queen Elizabeth and her successors, Heralds and Kings of Arms were commanded to make perambulations throughout the country for the purpose of pulling down and defacing improper arms, of recording arms properly borne by authority, and of compelling those who used arms without authority to obtain authority for them or discontinue their use. These perambulations were termed Visitations. The subject of Visitations, and in fact the whole subject of the right to bear arms, is dealt with at length in the book to which reference has been already made, namely, "The Right to Bear Arms."

The glory of a descent from a long line of armigerous ancestors, the glory and the pride of race inseparably interwoven with the inheritance of a name which has been famous in history, the fact that some arms have been designed to commemorate heroic achievements, the fact that the display of a particular coat of arms has been the method, which society has countenanced, of advertising to the world that one is of the upper class or a descendant of some ancestor who performed some glorious deed to which the arms have reference, the fact that arms themselves are the very sign of a particular descent or of a particular rank, have all tended to cause a false and fictitious value to be placed upon all these pictured emblems which as a whole they have never possessed, and which I believe they were never intended to possess. It is *because* they were the prerogative and the sign of aristocracy that they have been coveted so greatly, and consequently so often assumed improperly. Now aristocracy and social position are largely a matter of personal assertion. A man assumes and asserts for himself a certain position, which position is gradually and imperceptibly but continuously increased and elevated as its assertion is reiterated. There is no particular moment in a man's life at the present time, the era of the great middle class, at which he visibly steps from a plebeian to a patrician standing. And when he has fought and talked the world into conceding him a recognised position in the upper classes, he naturally tries to obliterate the fact that he or "his people" were ever of any other social position, and he hesitates to perpetually date his elevation to the rank of gentility by obtaining a grant of arms and thereby admitting that before that date he and his people were plebeian. Consequently he waits until some circumstance compels an application for a grant, and the consequence is that he thereby post-dates his actual gentility to a period long subsequent to the recognition by Society of his position in the upper classes.

Arms are the sign of the technical rank of gentility. The possession of arms is a matter of hereditary privilege, which privilege the Crown is willing should be obtained upon certain terms by any who care to possess it, who live according to the style and custom which is usual amongst gentle people. And so long as the possession of arms is a matter of privilege, even though this privilege is no greater than is consequent upon payment of certain fees to the Crown and its officers; for so long will that privilege possess a certain prestige and value, though this may not be very great. Arms have never possessed any greater value than attaches to a matter of privilege; and (with singularly few exceptions) in every case, be it

of a peer or baronet, of knight or of simple gentleman, this privilege has been obtained or has been regularised by the payment at some time or other of fees to the Crown and its officers. And the *only* difference between arms granted and paid for yesterday and arms granted and paid for five hundred years ago is the simple moral difference which attaches to the dates upon the patents.

Gentility is merely hereditary rank, emanating, with all other rank, from the Crown, the sole fountain of honour. It is idle to make the word carry a host of meanings it was never intended to. Arms being the sign of the technical rank of gentility, the use of arms is the advertisement of one's claim to that gentility. Arms mean nothing more. By coronet, supporters, and helmet can be indicated one's place in the scale of precedence; by adding arms for your wife you assert that she also is of gentle rank; your quarterings show the other gentle families you represent; difference marks will show your position in your own family (not a very important matter); augmentations indicate the deeds of your ancestors which the Sovereign thought worthy of being held in especial remembrance. *By the use of a certain coat of arms, you assert your descent from the person to whom those arms were granted, confirmed, or allowed.* That is the beginning and end of armory Why seek to make it mean more?

Of the growth of armory in Germany Herr H. G. Ströhl remarks in his *Heraldischer Atlas*, which is the real foundation of the present work:—

"The first heraldic designs were shown upon the flag, the *Zeichen* (mark, token, or sign), and the first step towards heraldry was the transfer of these designs to the shield. The shield design was still called *Zeichen*. About the middle of the twelfth century the use of heraldic decorations on armour had become universal. The thirteenth century ushered in an important and, especially for German heraldry, a characteristic addition to armorial decoration, through the introduction of a heraldic ornament on the helmet—the crest. In the same century armorial bearings commence to be regularly hereditary, at first in the higher, but also later in the lower ranks of the nobility. Single instances of hereditary coats of arms may already be pointed out as early as the end of the twelfth century.

"Those families who can trace their pedigree and their arms back to this first era of heraldry are called *Uradel* (old nobility), to distinguish them from the *Briefadel* (*i.e.* nobility by patent), who owe their origin to documentary grants (beginning as early as the fourteenth century), from the Emperor, or those in authority under him, the Court, Electors Palatini, or *Comites palatini cæsarei*. In the fourteenth century arms were granted without nobility by the Emperor, but more especially by those of his counts palatine to whom only a small county remained.[a] Those so invested were not noble, but only burghers bearing arms."[b]

However heraldry is looked upon, it must be admitted that from its earliest infancy armory possessed two essential qualities. It was the definite sign of hereditary nobility and rank, and it was practically an integral part of warfare; but also from its earliest infancy it formed a means of decoration. It would be a rash statement to assert that armory had lost its actual military character even now, but it certainly possessed it undiminished so long as tournaments took place, for the armory of the tournament was of a much

---

[a] There has never been any such distinction in arms recognised in England.

[b] The English analogy of this will be found in the "merchant marks" of former days, the precursors of our present trade marks.

higher standard than the armory of the battlefield, and the Eglinton tournament during the previous reign, which was a real tournament and no kind of theatrical mummery, makes one chary of asserting that even the day of the tournament is past. Armory as an actual part of warfare existed as a means of decoration for the implements of warfare, and as such it certainly continues to the present day.

Armory in that bygone age, although it existed as the symbol of the lowest hereditary rank, was worn and used in warfare, for purposes of pageantry, for the indication of ownership, for decorative purposes, for the needs of authenticity in seals, and for the purpose of memorialisation in records, pedigrees, and monuments. All those uses and purposes of armory can be traced back to a period coeval with that to which our certain knowledge of the existence of armory runs. Of all those usages and purposes, one only, that of the use of armorial bearings in actual battle, can be said to have come to an end, and even that not entirely so; the rest are still with us in actual and extensive existence. I am not versed in the minutiæ of army matters or army history, but I think I am correct in saying that there was no such thing as a regular standing army or a national army until the reign of Henry VIII. Prior to that time the methods of the feudal system supplied the wants of the country. The actual troops were in the employment, not of the Crown, but of the individual leaders. The Sovereign called upon, and had the right to call upon, those leaders to provide troops; but as those troops were not in the direct employment of the Crown, they wore the liveries and heraldic devices of their leaders. The leaders wore their own devices, originally for decorative reasons, and later that they might be distinguished by their particular followers: hence the actual use in battle in former days of private armorial bearings. And even yet the practice is not wholly extinguished, for the tartans of the Gordon and Cameron Highlanders are a relic of the usages of these former days. With the formation of a standing army, and the direct service of the troops to the Crown, the liveries and badges of those who had formerly been responsible for the troops gave way to the liveries and badges of the Crown. The uniform of the Beefeaters is a good example of the method in which in the old days a servant wore the badge and livery of his lord. The Beefeaters wear the scarlet livery of the Sovereign, and wear the badge of the Sovereign still. Many people will tell you, by the way, that the uniform of a Beefeater is identical now with what it was in the days of Henry VIII. It isn't. In accordance with the strictest laws of armory, the badge, embroidered on the front and back of the tunic, has

changed, and is now the triple badge—the rose, the thistle, and the shamrock—of the triple kingdom of Great Britain and Ireland. Every soldier who wears a scarlet coat, the livery of his Sovereign, every regiment that carries its colours, every saddle-cloth with a Royal emblem thereupon, is evidence that the use of armory in battle still exists in a small degree to the present day; but circumstances have altered. The troops no longer attack to the cry of "A Warwick! a Warwick!" they serve His Majesty the King and wear his livery and devices. They no longer carry the banner of their officer, whose servants and tenants they were; the regiment cherishes the banner of the armorial bearings of His Majesty. Within the last few years, probably within the lifetime of all my readers, there has been striking evidence of the manner in which circumstances alter everything. The Zulu War put an end to the practice of taking the colours of a regiment into battle; the South African War saw khaki substituted universally for the scarlet livery of His Majesty; and to have found upon a South African battlefield the last remnant of the armorial practices of the days of chivalry, one would have needed, I am afraid, to examine the buttons of the troopers. Still the scarlet coat exists in the army on parade: the Life Guards wear the Royal Cross of St. George and the Star of the Garter, the Scots Greys have the Royal Saltire of St. Andrew, and the Gordon Highlanders have the Gordon crest of the Duke of Richmond and Gordon; and there are many other similar instances.

There is yet another point. The band of a regiment is maintained by the officers of the regiment, and at the present day in the Scottish regiments the pipers have attached to their pipes banners bearing the various *personal* armorial bearings of the officers of the regiment. So that perhaps one is justified in saying that the use of armorial bearings in warfare has not yet come to an end. The other ancient usages of armory exist now as they existed in the earliest times. So that it is foolish to contend that armory has ceased to exist, save as an interesting survival of the past. It is a living reality, more *widely* in use at the present day than ever before.

Certainly the military side of armory has sunk in importance till it is now utterly overshadowed by the decorative, but the fact that armory still exists as the sign and adjunct of hereditary rank utterly forbids one to assert that armory is dead, and though this side of armory is now partly overshadowed by its decorative use, armory must be admitted to be still alive whilst its laws can still be altered. When, if ever, rank is finally swept away, and when the Crown ceases to grant arms, then armory will be dead, and can be treated as the study of a dead science.   A. C. F-D.

CHAPTER IV

THE HERALDS AND OFFICERS OF ARMS

THE Crown is the Fountain of Honour, having supreme control of coat-armour. This control in all civilised countries is one of the appanages of sovereignty, but from an early period much of the actual control has been delegated to the Heralds and Kings of Arms. The word Herald is derived from the Anglo-Saxon—*here*, an army, and *wald*, strength or sway—though it has probably come to us from the German word *Herold*. In the last years of the twelfth century there appeared at festal gatherings persons mostly

habited in richly coloured clothing, who delivered invitations to the guests and, side by side with the stewards, superintended the festivities. Many of them were minstrels, who, after tournaments or battle, extolled the deeds of the victors. These individuals were known in Germany as *Garzune*. The necessities of warfare required the existence of messengers whose position should be recognised, in order that communications of challenge and terms of surrender should pass between the combatants, and from an early date

THE ART OF HERALDRY

the duties above referred to devolved upon the same officers. And from the earliest times the persons of these messengers were recognised as inviolate.

In token of their office they wore the coats of arms of the leaders they served; and the original status of a herald was that of a non-combatant messenger. Originally every powerful leader had his own herald, and the dual character of minstrel and messenger led the herald to recount the deeds of his master, and, as a natural consequence, of his master's ancestors. When tournaments came into vogue it was natural that some one should examine the arms of those taking part, and from this the duties of the herald came to include a knowledge of coat-armour. As the Sovereign assumed or arrogated the control of arms, the right to grant arms, and the right of judgment in disputes concerning arms, it was but the natural result that the personal heralds of the Sovereign should be required to have a knowledge of the arms of his principal subjects, and should obtain something in the nature of a cognisance or control and jurisdiction over those arms; for doubtless the actions of the Sovereign would often depend upon the knowledge of his heralds.

under the King, who usually led his army in person, and to the Marshal was deputed the ordering and arrangement of the various bodies of troops, regiments, bands of retainers, &c., which ordering was at first facilitated and at length entirely determined by the use of various pictorial ensigns, such as standards, banners, crests, cognisances, and badges. The due arrangement and knowledge of these various ensigns became first the necessary study and then the ordinary duty of these officers of the Earl Marshal, and their possession of such knowledge, which soon in due course had to be written down and tabulated, secured to them an important part in mediæval life. The result was that at an early period we find them employed in semi-diplomatic missions, such as carrying on negotiations between contending armies on the field, bearing declarations of war, challenges from one sovereign to another, besides arranging the ceremonial not only of battles and tournaments, but also of coronations, Royal baptisms, marriages, and funerals.

From the fact that neither King of Arms nor herald is mentioned as officiating in the celebrated Scrope and Grosvenor case,

FIG. 13.—*Helmschau* or Helmet-Show. (From Konrad Grünenberg's *Wappencodex zu München*.) End of fifteenth century.

From being of the status of a personal servant of the King as a leader in battle, the office of herald came to appertain to the office of Sovereign, by virtue of which office the King claimed and exercised his control over the arms of his subjects.

The process of development in this country will be more easily understood when it is remembered that the Marshal or Earl Marshal was in former times, with the Lord High Constable, the first in *military* rank

of which very full particulars have come down to us, it is evident that the control of arms had not passed either in fact or in theory from the Crown to the officers of arms at that date. Konrad Grünenberg, in his *Wappencodex* ("Roll of Arms"), the date of which is 1483, to which reference will be made later when reproducing some number of examples of arms upon the roll, gives a representation of a *helmschau* (literally helmet-show), here reproduced (Fig. 13).

Long before that date, however, the position of a herald in England was well defined, for we find that on January 5, 1420, the King appointed William Bruges to be Garter King of Arms. It is usually considered in England that it would be found that in Germany armory reached its highest point of evolution. Certainly German heraldic art is in advance of our own, and it is curious to read in the latest and one of the best of German heraldic books (the original upon which the present work is based) that "from the very earliest times heraldry was carried to a higher degree of perfection and thoroughness in England than elsewhere, and that it has maintained itself at the same level until the present day. In other countries, for the most part, heralds no longer have any existence but in name." The initial figure which appears at the commencement of Chapter I. represents an English herald, John Smert, Garter King of Arms, and is taken from the grant of arms issued by him to the Tallow Chandlers' Company of London, which is dated September 24, 1456.

Long before there was any College of Arms, the Marshal, afterwards the Earl Marshal, had been appointed. The Earl Marshal is now head of the College of Arms, and to him has been delegated the whole of the control both of armory and of the College, with the exception of that part which the Crown has retained in its own hands. After the Earl Marshal come the Kings of Arms, the Heralds of Arms, and the Pursuivants of Arms.

The title of King of Arms, or, as it was more anciently written, King of Heralds, was no doubt originally given to the chief or principal officer, who presided over the heralds of a kingdom, or some principal province, which heraldic writers formerly termed *marches;* or else the title was conferred upon the officer of arms attendant upon some particular order of knighthood. The word *rex, roy,* or *king* has been often applied to the principal, the governor, the judge, the visitor, the supreme, the president, and the chief of some peculiar profession, art, or community, and the principal heralds were anciently denominated Kings of Heralds, a title which, in process of time, was further distinguished by the appellation of their different provinces. Garter, who is immediately attached to that illustrious order, is likewise principal King of Arms, and these, although separate and distinct offices, are and have been always united in one person. Upon the revival and new modelling of the Order of the Bath, in the reign of George the First, a King of Arms was created and attached to it, by the title of Bath King of Arms; and King George III., upon the institution of the Hanoverian Guelphic Order of Knighthood, annexed to that order a King of Arms, by the appellation of Hanover.

At the time of the creation of his office, Bath King of Arms was given Wales as his province, the intention being that he should rank with the others, granting

arms in his own province, but he was not, nor was Hanover, nor is the King of Arms of the Order of St. Michael and St. George, a member (as such) of the corporation of the College of Arms. The members of that corporation considered that the gift of the province of Wales, the jurisdiction over which they had previously possessed, to Bath King an infringement of their chartered privileges. The dispute was referred to the law officers of the Crown, whose opinion was in favour of the corporate body. Berry in his *Encyclopædia Heraldica* further remarks: "The Kings of Arms of the provincial territories have the titles of *Clarenceux* and *Norroy*, the jurisdiction of the former extending over the south, east, and west parts of England, from the river Trent southwards; and that of the latter, the remaining part of the kingdom northward of that river. Kings of Arms have been likewise assigned other provinces over different kingdoms and dominions, and besides Ulster King of Arms for Ireland, and Lyon King of Arms for Scotland, others were nominated for particular provinces abroad, when united to the Crown of England, such as *Aquitaine, Anjou,* and *Guyenne,* who were perhaps at their first creation intended only for the services of the places whose titles they bore, when the same should be entirely subdued to allegiance to the Crown of England, and who, till that time, might have had other provinces allotted to them, either provisionally or temporarily, within the realm of England.

There were also other Kings of Arms, denominated from the dukedoms or earldoms which our princes enjoyed before they came to the throne, as *Lancaster, Gloucester, Richmond,* and *Leicester,* the three first having marches, or provinces, and the latter a similar jurisdiction. Windsor, likewise, was a local title, but it is doubtful whether that officer was ever a King of Arms. *Marche* also assumed that appellation, from his provincial jurisdiction over a territory so called.

The badges of the Royal Family have at times given titles accordingly, as *Falcon,* &c., and the glorious victory of *Agincourt* was likewise given to one of the heralds, but whether merely nominally or provincially is uncertain; but it is doubtful whether the titles of *Ferrant, Volaunt,* and *Mushon,* Kings of Arms, were Christian or surnames, or the proper appellation of their respective officers.

But although anciently there were at different periods several Kings of Arms in England, only two provincial Kings of Arms have, for some ages, been continued in office, viz. Clarenceux and Norroy, whose provinces or marches are, as before observed, separated by the river Trent, the ancient limits of the escheaters, when there are only two in the kingdom, and the jurisdiction of the wardens of the forests.

Norroy is considered the most ancient title, being the only one in England taken from the local situation of his province, unless *Marche* should be derived from

FIG. 14.—Officers of Arms as represented in the famous Tournament Roll of Henry VIII., now preserved in the College of Arms.

the same cause. The title of *Norroy* was anciently written *Norreys* and *Norreis*, King of Arms of the people residing in the north; *Garter* being styled *Roy des Anglois*, of the people, and not *d'Angleterre*, of the kingdom, the inhabitants of the north being called *Norreys*,[a] as we are informed by ancient historians.

It appears that there was a King of Arms for the parts or people on the north of Trent as early as the reign of Edward I., from which, as Sir Henry Spelman observes, it may be inferred that the southern, eastern, and western parts had principal heralds, or Kings of Arms, although their titles at that early age cannot now be ascertained.

Norroy had not the title of King till after the reign of Edward II. It was appropriated to a King of Heralds, expressly called *Rex Norroy, Roy d'Armes del North, Rex Armorum del North, Rex de North*, and *Rex Norroy du North;* and the term *Roy Norreys* likewise occurs in the Pell Rolls of the 22nd Edward III.; but from that time till the 9th of Richard II. no farther mention is made of any such officer, from which it is probable a different person enjoyed the office by some other title during that interval, particularly as the office was actually executed by other Kings of Arms, immediately after that period. *John Otharlake, Marche King of Arms*, executed it in the 9th of Richard II. *Richard del Brugg, Lancaster King of Arms*, 1st Henry IV., and *Ashwell, Boys*, and *Tindal*, successively *Lancaster Kings of Arms*, until the end of that monarch's reign.

Edward IV. replaced this province under a King of Arms, and revived the dormant title of *Norroy*. But in the Statute of Resumptions, made 1st Henry VII., a clause was inserted that the same should not extend to *John Moore*, otherwise *Norroy*, chief Herald King of Arms of the north parts of this realm of England, so appointed by King Edward IV. by his Letters Patent, bearing date 9th July, in the eighteenth year of his reign. It has since continued without interruption.

Falcon King of Arms seems the next who had the title of King conferred upon him, and was so named from one of the Royal badges of King Edward III., and it was afterwards given to a herald and pursuivant, under princes who bore the falcon as a badge or cognisance, and it is difficult to ascertain whether this officer was considered a king, herald, or pursuivant. *Froissart*, in 1395, calls *Faucon* only a herald, and in 1364 mentions this officer as a King of Arms belonging to the King of England; but it is certain that in the 18th Richard II. there was a King of Arms by that appellation, and so continued until the reign of Richard III., if not later; but at what particular period of time the officer was discontinued cannot be correctly ascertained.

Windsor has been considered by some writers to have been the title of a King of Arms, from an abbreviation in some old records, which might be otherwise translated. There is, however, amongst the Protections in the Tower of London, one granted in the 49th Edward III. to *Stephen de Windesore, Heraldo Armorum rege dicto*, which seems to favour the conjecture, and other records might be quoted for and against this supposition, which might have arisen

a "Norreys and Surreis, that service aught the kyng,
     With horse and harneis at Carlele, made samning."

See Langtoft's Chronicle treating of the Wars of Edward I. against the Scots.

    " Bot Sir John de Waleis taken was, in a pleyne,
      Throgh spryng of Norreis men that were certeyn."

Ibid., *Australes se Norensibus opposuerunt.* M. Oaris, under the year 1237.

through mistake in the entries, as they contradict one another.

Marche seems the next in point of antiquity of creation; but although Sir Henry Spelman says that King Edward IV. descended from the *Earls of Marche*, promoted *Marche Herald* to be a King of Arms, giving him, perhaps, the marches for his province, it is pretty clearly ascertained that it was of a more early date, from the express mention of *March Rex Heraldorum* and *March Rex Heraldus* in records of the time of Richard II., though it may be possible that it was then only a nominal title, and did not become a real one till the reign of Edward IV., as mentioned by Spelman.

Lancaster King of Arms was, as the same author informs us, so created by Henry IV. in relation to his own descent from the Lancastrian family, and the county of Lancaster assigned to him as his province; but *Edmondson* contends "that that monarch superadded the title of Lancaster to that of Norroy, or King of the North, having, as it may be reasonably conjectured, given this province north of Trent, within which district Lancaster was situated, to him who had been formerly his officer of arms, by the title of that dukedom, and who might, according to custom, in some instances of former ages, retain his former title and surname of heraldship, styling himself *Lancaster Roy d'Armes del North.*"

Leicester King of Arms was a title similar to that of *Lancaster*, and likewise a creation to the same Sovereign, Henry IV., who was also Earl of Leicester before he assumed the crown, and was given to a person who was before that time a herald. It appears that *Henry Grene* was *Leicester Herald*, 9th King Richard II., and in the 13th of the same reign is called *a Herald of the Duke of Guyen and Lancaster*, but prior to the coronation of Henry IV. he was certainly a King of Heralds, and so styled in a privy seal dated antecedent to that ceremony. A similar instrument of the tenth year of that monarch's reign also mentions *Henry Grene*, otherwise *Leicester King of Arms*.

As it is evident that, during the reign of Henry IV., *Lancaster King of Arms* has under that title the province of the north, *Mr. Edmondson*, with good reason, supposes that the southern province, or part of that which is now under Clarenceux, might at that time be under this *Leicester*, especially as the title of *Clarenceux* was not in being till after the 3rd of Henry V., when, or soon after, the title of *Leicester* might have become extinct by the death of that officer; for although *Leicester King of Arms* went over into France with Henry V. in the third year of his reign, yet he is not mentioned in the constitutions made by the heralds at Roan in the year 1419–20.

Clarenceux, the next King of Arms in point of creation, is a title generally supposed to have been taken from *Clare*, in Suffolk, the castle at that place being the principal residence of the ancient Earls of Hereford, who were, from thence, though very improperly, called *Earls of Clare*, in the same manner as the Earls of Pembroke were often named *Earls of Strigoil and Chepstow;* the Earl of Hampshire, *Earl of Winchester;* the Earl of Derby, *Earl of Tuttebury;* the Earl of Sussex, *Earl of Chichester*, &c. King Edward III. created his third son Lionel *Duke of Clarence*, instead of the monosyllable *Clare* (from his marriage with the grand-daughter of the late Earl), but Lionel dying without issue male, Henry IV. created his younger son Thomas *Duke of Clarence*, who being slain without issue 9th of Henry V., the honour remained in the Crown, until King Edward IV. conferred it upon his own brother. Mr. Sandford tells us that *Clarence* is the country about the town, castle, and honour *of Clare*, from which duchy the name of *Clarenceux King of Arms* is derived. Spelman, however, contends that it is a mistake in attributing the institution of *Clarenceux* to King Edward IV. after the honour of *Clarence* devolved as an escheat to the Crown, upon the untimely death of his brother George, as he found William Horseley called by this title in the reign of Henry V. and also Roger Lygh, under King Henry VI.; and it is conjectured that the office of *Clarenceux King of Arms* is not more ancient than the reign of Edward III.

Gloucester Herald, frequently mentioned by historians, was originally the herald of the great Humphry, Duke of Gloucester, of whom mention is made upon record in the 10th of Henry VI.; and Richard, brother to Edward IV., who was created Duke of Gloucester, is said to have had a herald by that title during the reign of his brother, and who was attendant as such at the funeral of that monarch. In a manuscript in the Ashmolean collection, it is stated that Richard Champnay attended as Gloucester King of Arms at the coronation of Richard III. upon the 7th July following his usurpation of the crown; but it appears by more authentic record that this Richard Champnay was, by the style and title of Herald of Arms, on the 18th September, in the first year of his usurpation, by patent created a King of Arms and Principal Herald of the parts of Wales, by the style and title of Gloucester, giving him licence and authority to execute all and singular that by law or custom in former times belonged to the office of King of Arms. It is supposed that the office ceased upon his death, which in all probability took place before that of the usurper.

Richmond King of Arms.—A herald called *Richmond* is frequently mentioned, as well belonging to the Crown as of the nobility. But the records of the reign of King Henry VII., who had before his elevation to the throne been Earl of Richmond, contain many entries of *Richmond King of Arms;* but although somewhat vague in the description, sufficiently bear out the conjecture that Henry VII., previous to his coronation, created a new King of Arms by the title of *Richmond*, although no regular patent of creation has ever been found.

Sir Henry Spelman informs us that, in addition to the two Kings of Arms for the two heraldic provinces bounded north and south by the river Trent, there were also two provincial kings for the dominions of our Sovereign in France, styled *Guyenne* and *Agincourt* (omitting *Aquitaine* and *Anjou*, which were certainly in being at the same time), and another for *Ireland* by that name, altered by King Edward VI. into *Ulster*.

Ireland King of Arms first occurs upon record 6th Richard II., anno 1482, mentioned by *Froissart*, where he is called *Chandos le Roy d'Ireland*. A regular succession of officers, by the title of Ireland King of Arms, continued from that time till the reign of King Edward IV., but from the death of that monarch till the creation of Ulster by Edward VI. it is uncertain whether the title existed, or what became of the office.

Edward VI. altered the title of Ireland King of Arms into that of Ulster, or rather considered it as a new institution, from the words of his journal: "Feb. 2. There was a King of Arms made for Ireland, whose name was *Ulster*, and his province was all Ireland; and he was the fourth King of Arms, and the first Herald of Ireland." The patent passed under the Great Seal of England.

Guyenne, a part of Aquitaine, in France, a province belonging to the British Crown, gave title not only to a King of Arms, but to a herald likewise, and Sir Henry Spelman dates its creation in the time of Edward I., although it is somewhat doubtful, and thought to be in the reign of Edward III. Guyenne Herald appears upon record during the reign of Henry VI., and though Kings of Arms were frequently styled heralds in old records, it is more than probable both offices were in existence at the same time. From the time of Edward IV. no such officers belonging to the Crown of England seem to have been continued, and it is doubtful whether they ever held in constant succession from their first creation.

Aquitaine, which included what were afterwards called Guyenne, Xantoigne, Gascoigne, and some islands, gave title to a King of Heralds as early as the reign of Edward III., and it is conjectured to have been an officer belonging to the Black Prince, who had the principality of Aquitaine given to him by his father; but although this officer is mentioned in the reign of Richard II. and 3rd of Henry V., no record occurs after the latter period.

Agincourt was also a title conferred upon a herald, in memory of that signal victory; and lands were granted to him for life, 6th Henry V., as mentioned by Sir Henry Spelman; but whether the office was continued, or any particular province assigned to this officer, cannot be ascertained.

Anjou King of Arms was likewise an officer of King Henry VI., and attendant upon John, Duke of Bedford, when Regent of France, who assumed the title of Duke of Anjou, but upon the death of the Duke of Bedford, this officer was promoted to Lancaster King of Arms, and in all probability the title of Anjou, as a King of Heralds, was discontinued.

Volant also occurs upon record in the 28th Edward III., and *Vaillant, le Roy Vaillant Heraud*, and *le Roy Vailland*, are likewise mentioned in 1395.

Henry V. instituted the office of Garter King of Arms; but at what particular period is rather uncertain, although Mr. Anstis has clearly proved that it must have taken place after the 22nd May, and before the 3rd September, in the year 1417.

Stephen Martin Leake, Esq., who filled the office, sums up its duties in the following words: "*Garter* was instituted by King Henry V., A.D. 1417, for the service of the Most Noble Order of the Garter, which was made sovereign within the office of arms over all other officers, subject to the Crown of England, by the name of Garter King of Arms of England. In this patent he is styled Principal King of English Arms, and Principal Officer of Arms of the Most Noble Order of the Garter, and has power to execute the said office by himself or deputy, being an herald. By the constitution of his office, he must be a native of England, and a gentleman bearing arms. To him belongs the correction of arms, and all ensigns of honour, usurped or borne unjustly, and also to grant arms to deserving persons, and supporters to the nobility and Knights of the Bath; to go next before the sword in solemn proceeding, none interposing, except the constable and marshal; to administer the oath to all the officers of arms; to have a habit like the registrar of the order; baron's service in the court; lodgings in Windsor Castle; to bear his white rod with a banner of the ensigns of the order thereon before the Sovereign; also when any lord shall enter the Parliament chamber, to assign him his place, according to his dignity and degree; to carry the ensign of the order to foreign princes, and to do, or procure to be done, what the Sovereign shall enjoin, relating to the order; with other duties incident to his office of principal King of Arms, for the execution whereof he hath a salary of one hundred pounds a year, payable at the Exchequer, and an hundred pounds more out of the revenue of the order, besides fees."

Bath King of Arms was created 11th George I., in conformity with the statutes established by His Majesty for the government of the Order of the Bath, and in obedience to those statutes was nominated and created by the Great Master of the Order denominated *Bath,* and in Latin, *Rex armorum Honoratissimi Ordinis Militaris de Balneo.* These statutes direct that this officer shall, in all the ceremonies of the order, be habited in a white mantle lined with red, having on the right shoulder the badge of the order, and under it a surcoat of white silk, lined and edged with red; that he shall wear on his breast, hanging to a golden chain about his neck, an escocheon of gold, enamelled with the arms of the order, impaling the arms of the Sovereign, crowned with the Imperial crown. That at all coronations he shall precede the companions of the order, and shall carry and wear his crown as other Kings of Arms are obliged to do. That the chain, escocheon, rod, and crown, shall be of the like materials, value, and weight, with those borne and used by Garter Principal King of Arms, and of the like fashion, the before specified variations only excepted: and that besides the duties required of him in the several other articles of the statutes, he shall diligently perform whatever the Sovereign or Great Master shall further command. On the 14th January 1725, His Majesty was further pleased by his Royal sign-manual, to erect, make, constitute, and ordain the then Bath King of Arms, *Gloucester* King of Arms, and principal Herald of the parts of Wales, and to direct letters patent to be made out and pass the Great Seal, empowering him to grant arms and crests to persons residing within the dominions of Wales, either jointly with Garter, or singly by himself, with the consent and at the pleasure of the Earl Marshal, or his deputy for the time being, and for the future that the office of Gloucester should be inseparably annexed, united, and perpetually consolidated with the office of *Bath King of Arms, of the Most Honourable Military Order of the Bath, and Gloucester King of Arms, and principal Herald of the parts of Wales.* And also that he, for the dignity of the order, should in all assemblies and at all times have and take place and precedency above and before all other provincial Kings of Arms whatsoever. This armorial jurisdiction, however, was subsequently, as has been previously explained, annulled.

Concerning the heralds Berry remarks: "In former ages, when honour and chivalry were at their height, these officers were held in great estimation, as appears by the ceremonies which attended their creations, which was by the Sovereign himself or by special commission from him, and, according to Gerard Leigh, was after the following manner: The King asked the person to be so created whether he were a gentleman of blood or of second coat-armour; if he was not, the King gave him lands and fees, and assigned him and his heirs proper arms. Then, as the messenger was brought in by the herald of the province, so the pursuivant was brought in by the eldest herald, who, at the prince's command, performed all the ceremonies, as turning the coat of arms, setting the manacles thereof on the arms of the pursuivant, and putting about his neck the collar of SS, and when he was named, the prince himself took the cup from the herald, which was gilt, and poured the water and wine upon the head of the pursuivant, creating him by the name of *our herald,* and the King, when the oath was administered, gave the same cup to the new herald.

Upton sums up the business of a herald thus: That it was their office to create under officers, to number the people, to commence treaties of matrimony and of peace between princes, to visit kingdoms and regions, and to be present at martial exploits, &c., and they were to wear a coat of their master's arms, wearing the same in conflicts and tournaments, in riding through foreign countries, and at all great entertainments, coronations of kings and queens, and the solemnities of princes, dukes, and other great lords.

In the time of King Richard II. there belonged to the King of Arms and heralds the following fees, viz.: at the coronation of the King, a bounty of £100; when the King first displayed his banners, 100 marks; when the King's son was made a knight, 40 marks; when the prince and a duke first display their banners, £20; if it be a marquis, 20 marks; if an earl, £10; if a baron, 5 marks of silver crowns, of 15 nobles; and if a knight bachelor, newly made a banneret, 3 marks, or 10 nobles; when the King is married, the said Kings of Arms and heralds to have £50; when the Queen has a child christened, a largess at the Queen's pleasure, or of the lords of the council, which was sometimes £100, and at others 100 marks, more or less; and when she is churched, such another largess; when princesses, duchesses, marchionesses, countesses, and baronesses have a child christened, and when they are churched, a largess suitable to their quality and pleasure; as often as the King wears his crown, or holds Royal state, especially at the four great festivals of Christmas, Easter, Whitsuntide, and All Saints, to every one of the three Kings of Arms present when the King goes to the chapel to mass, a largess at the King's pleasure; when a maiden princess, or daughter of a duke, marquis, earl, or baron is married, there belongs to the said Kings of Arms, if present, the upper garment she is married in; if there be a combat within lists, there belong to the Kings of Arms, if present, and if not to the other heralds present, their pavilions; and if one of the combatants is vanquished, the Kings of Arms and heralds who are present shall have all the accoutrements of the person so vanquished, and all other armour that falls to the ground; when subjects rebel, and fortify any camp or place, and afterwards quit the same, and fly, without a battle, there appertain to the said Kings of Arms and heralds who are present all the carts, carriages, and tools left behind; and, at New Year's Tide, all the noblemen and knights of the court used to give the heralds New Year's gifts. Besides the King's heralds, in former times, divers noblemen had heralds and pursuivants, who went with their lords, with the King's heralds, when attending the King.

The fees of the King's heralds and pursuivants of arms have since varied, and, besides fees upon creations of peers, baronets, and knights, they have still donations for attendance at court upon the festivals of Christmas, Easter, Whitsuntide, All Saints, and St. George's Day; fees upon installation of Knights of the Garter and Bath, Royal marriages, funerals, public solemnities, &c., with small salaries paid from the Exchequer; but their ancient fees from the nobility, upon certain occasions, have been long discontinued, and their principal emolument arises from grants of arms, the tracing of genealogies, and recording the same in the Registers of the College of Arms.

The present *heralds* are six in number, viz.:—

Windsor Herald, which title was instituted 38th of Edward III., when that monarch was in France.

Chester Herald, instituted in the same reign.

Richmond Herald, instituted by King Edward IV.

Somerset Herald, instituted by King Henry VIII. about the time when that monarch created his son Henry Fitzroy Duke of Somerset.

THE ART OF HERALDRY

York Herald, instituted by King Edward III. in honour of his son, whom he created Duke of York.

Lancaster Herald, also instituted by Edward III. when he created his son Duke of Lancaster.

The heralds were first incorporated as a college by Richard III. They were styled the Corporation of King's Heralds and Pursuivants of Arms.

Concerning Pursuivants of Arms, Berry remarks that these officers, who are the lowest in degree amongst officers of arms, "were, as the name implies, followers, marshals, or messengers attendant upon the heralds. Pursuivants were formerly created by the nobility (who had, likewise, heralds of arms) with great ceremony in the following manner. One of the heralds, wearing his master's coat, leading the person to be created pursuivant by the left hand, and holding a cup full of wine and water in his right, came into the presence of the lord and master of him who was to be created, and of whom the herald asked by what name he would have his pursuivant called, which the lord having mentioned, the herald then poured part of the wine and water upon his head, calling him by the name so assigned to him. The herald then took the coat of his lord, and put it over his head athwart, so that part of the coat made for the arms before and behind, and the longer part of it on both sides of the arms of the person created, and in which way the pursuivant was always to wear it. This done, an oath of fidelity was administered to the new-made pursuivant, and the ceremony concluded." This curious method of the wearing of the tabard by a pursuivant has long since been discontinued, if indeed it was ever generally adopted, a point on which I have by no means been able to satisfy myself.

The appointment of heralds and pursuivants of arms by the nobility has long been discontinued, and there are now only four pursuivants belonging to the College of Arms, viz. :—

Rouge-Croix, the first, in point of antiquity of creation, is so styled from the red cross of St. George, the Patron Saint of England.

Blue-Mantle, so called by King Edward III., in honour of the French coat which he assumed, being blue.

Rouge-Dragon, so styled from the red dragon, one of the supporters of the Royal arms of King Henry VII. (who created this pursuivant), and also the badge of Wales, and

Portcullis, also instituted by Henry VII., and so named from that badge, or cognisance, used by him.

The duties of a pursuivant are similar to those of a herald; he assists in all public processions, or ceremonies, such as Royal marriages, funerals, installations, &c., and has certain fees for attendance upon such occasions. Pursuivants likewise receive fees upon creations of peers, baronets, and knights, and also donations for attending court upon the principal festivals of Christmas, Easter, Whit-Sunday, All Saints, and St. George's Day, and a small salary payable out of the Exchequer. They wear a tabard of damask silk, embroidered with the Royal arms, like the heralds, but no collar of SS.

Of the Heraldic Executive in Scotland, Lyon King of Arms (Sir James Balfour Paul), in his book "Heraldry in relation to Scottish History and Art," writes: "At one period the Lyon was solemnly crowned at his inauguration, and vested with his tabard and baton of office." The ceremony was a very elaborate one, and is fully described by Sir James Balfour in a MS., now in the Advocates' Library. There is also an account of the coronation of Sir Alexander Durham, when Laurie, the minister of the Tron Kirk, preached from the text, "What shall be done to the man whom the King delighteth to honour?" The crown was of gold,

and exactly similar to the Imperial crown of Scotland, save that it had no jewels. Now the Lyon's crown is the same as the English King of Arms. The crown is only worn at Royal coronations. At that of Charles I. at Edinburgh in 1633, the Lyon carried the vessel containing the sacred oil. In addition to his strictly armorial appointment, the Lyon is also a King of Arms of the Most Ancient and Most Noble Order of the Thistle.

Heralds and pursuivants formed an important part from very early times not only of the Royal Household, but also of those of the higher nobility, many of whom had private heralds. Of these officers there is a very full list given by Dr. Dickson in the preface to the Lord Treasurer's Accounts. Of heralds who were or ultimately became part of the King's Household we meet with Rothesay, Marchmont, Snowdon, Albany, Ross, and Islay; Ireland, Orkney, and Carrick are also mentioned as heralds, but it is doubtful whether the first and last were ever more than pursuivants. Of the latter class of officers the following were in the Royal establishment: Carrick, Bute, Dingwall, Kintyre, Ormonde, Unicorn; but we also find Aliszai or Alishay, Dragance, Diligens, Montrose, Falkland, Ireland, Darnaway, Garioch, Ettrick, Hales, Lindsay, Endure, Douglas, and Angus. Of the latter Garioch was created by James IV. for his brother John, Earl of Mar; Hailes in 1488, when Lord Hailes was made Earl of Bothwell; while Lindsay and Endure were both evidently attached to the Lindsay family, as were Douglas and Angus to the noblemen whose titles they bore. In 1403 Henry IV. of England granted a pursuivant under the title of Shrewsbury to George, Earl of March, for services rendered at the battle of that name, but we do not find that the office was continued.

In Scotland heralds appear at an early date, though none are mentioned as attending the coronation of Alexander III. in 1249; nor is there any account of any such officers accompanying that sovereign when he did homage to Edward I. at Westminster in 1278. In the next century, however, armorial bearings were quite well known in Scotland, and there is an entry in the Exchequer Rolls on 10th October 1337 of a payment of £32, 6s. Scots for the making of seventeen armorial banners, and in 1364 there is another to the heralds for services at the tournaments; while William Petilloch, herald, has a grant from David II. of three husbandlands in Bonjedward, and Allan Fawside gets a gift of the forfeited estate of one Coupland, a herald (*temp.* Edward Baliol).[b] The first mention of a herald, under his official designation, which I have met with in our records occurs in 1365, when there is a confirmation under the Great Seal by David II. of a charter by Dugal M'Dowille to John Trupour or Trumpour "*nunc dicto Carric heraldo.*" Sir James Balfour tells us that the Lyon and his heralds attended the coronation of Robert II. at Holyrood on 23rd May 1371, but whether or not this is true—and I have not been able to verify it—it is certain that a Lyon Herald existed very shortly after that date, as in the Exchequer Rolls mention is made of the payment of a certain sum to such an officer in 1377; in 1379 Froissart says that a herald was sent by Robert II. to London to explain that the truce had been infringed without his will and against his knowledge, and on 8th April 1381 a warrant was issued in London for a licence to "Lion Heraud" of the King of Scots, authorising him to take away a complete suit of armour which he had bought in that city. It is not, however, till 1388 that we find Lyon accorded the Royal style. In that year a payment is made "*Leoni regi heraldorum,*" but at the audit follow-

b Robertson's Index to "Missing Charters."

18

ing the battle of Otterburn he is called *defunctus*, which suggests that he had been slain on that well-fought field. The Lyon appears in several embassies

The initial letter on page 1 is a portrait of John Smert, Garter King of Arms, and is taken from the grant of arms to the Tallow Chandlers' Company,

FIG. 15.—The velvet tabard of Sir William Dugdale, Garter King of Arms from 26th April 1677 to 10th February 1686.

about this period both to England and France, and one Henry Greve, designed in the English Issue Rolls as "King of Scottish Heralds," was at the Tower of London in 1399, either at or immediately after the coronation of Henry IV. From 1391 onwards there is frequent mention of one Douglas, "Herald of the King," and in 1421 he is styled "Lyon Herald."

Of the German officers of arms they, like the English, are divided into three classes, known as *Wappenkönige, Herolde,* and *Persevanten.* These, like our own officers, had peculiar titles; for example, *Suchenwirt* (an Austrian ducal herald), *Lub-den-Frumen* (a Lichtenstein pursuivant), *Jerusalem* (a herald of the Limmer Palatinate), *Romreich* (an Imperial herald). About the middle of the sixteenth century, the official names of the heralds fell into disuse; they began to make use of their ancestral names with the title of *Edel* and *Ehrenvest* (noble and honourable), but this did not last long, and the heralds found themselves thrown back into the old ways, into which the knightly accoutrements had already wandered.

The official dress of an officer of arms as such in Great Britain is merely his tabard. This garment in style and shape has remained unchanged in this country from the earliest known period of which representations of officers of arms exist; but whilst the tabard itself has remained unaltered in its style, the arms thereupon have constantly changed, these always being the arms of the Sovereign for the time being. The costume worn with the tabard has naturally been subject to many changes, but it is doubtful if any attempt to regulate such costume was ever officially made prior to the reign of Queen Victoria. The tabard of a pursuivant is of damask silk; that of a herald, of satin; and that of a king of arms, of velvet.

FIG. 16.—William Bruges, the first Garter King of Arms, appointed 5th January 1420. (From an illuminated MS. in the Museum at Oxford.)

dated 24th September 1456. He is there represented as wearing beneath his tabard black breeches and coat, and a golden crown. But Fig. 16 is actually a representation of the first Garter King of Arms, William Bruges, appointed 5th January 1420. He is represented as carrying a white staff, a practice which has been recently revived, white wands being carried by all the heralds at the recent public funeral of the Right Hon. W. E. Gladstone. In Germany the wands of the heralds were later painted with the colours of the escutcheons of the Sovereign to whom they were attached. There was until recently no official hat for an officer of arms in England, and confirmation of this is to be found in the fact that Dallaway mentions a special licence to Wriothesley Garter giving him permission to wear a cap on account of his great age. Obviously, however, a tabard requires other clothing to be worn with it. The heralds in Scotland, until quite recently, when making public proclamations were content to appear in the ordinary elastic-side boots and cloth trousers of everyday life. This gave way for a brief period, in which Court dress was worn below the tabard, but now, as in England, the recognised uniform of a member of the Royal Household is worn. In England, owing to the less frequent ceremonial appearances of the heralds, and the more scrupulous control which has been exercised, no such anachronisms as were perpetuated in Scotland have been tolerated, and it has been customary for the officers of arms to wear their uniform as members of the Sovereign's Household (in which uniform they attend the levees) beneath the tabard when making proclamations at the opening of Parliament or on similar occasions. At a coronation and at some other full State ceremonies they wear knee-breeches, as will be seen in the portrait of Sir James Balfour Paul, Lyon King of Arms

(Fig. 20), or in that of Captain Swinton, March Pursuivant, on Plate III. All the heralds and Kings of Arms (but not the pursuivants) wear the curious collar of SS about which there has been so much discussion. The form has remained unchanged, save that the badge is the badge for the time being of the Sovereign. The heralds

FIG. 17.—Arms of Charles H. Athill, Esq., F.S.A., Richmond Herald, showing collar of SS.

have their collars of SS of silver, whilst those of a King of Arms are of silver gilt, and the latter have the further distinction that a portcullis is introduced on each shoulder (Fig. 21). The heralds and Kings of Arms usually place these collars round their shields in representations of their arms, as will be seen from Fig. 17, which is the coat of arms of Charles H. Athill, Esquire, F.S.A., Richmond Herald. This shows the usual method of depicting

FIG. 18.—Arms of the late J. W. Mitchell, Rothesay Herald and Lyon Clerk.

the collar. The arms are : Argent, on a chevron double cottised sable, three crescents or, the escutcheon being surrounded by his collar of SS. Mantling sable and argent. Crest, upon a wreath of the colours, three ostrich feathers argent, interlaced by as many annulets, also interlaced fessewise or; with the motto, "Crescam ut prosim." Fig. 18 also shows the badge which the Scottish heralds wear. The English Heralds have no

equivalent badge. The illustration is of the achievement of the late James William Mitchell, Rothesay Herald and Lyon Clerk, the arms depicted being in this case the coat recorded to him in the College of Arms (a different coat is registered in Lyon Office), as follows : Armorial bearings (as recorded in the Heralds' College, London) (see below)—Sable, a fess invected between an annulet and two mascles in chief and a mascle between two annulets in base or, within a bordure chequy of the last and first (and around the escutcheon is placed his collar of SS, and pendent by a blue riband edged with white is his badge, as a Herald of Scotland). Upon another escutcheon, charged with his arms as the foregoing, he bears, upon an escutcheon of pretence in right of his wife, the arms of Sykes, namely : Argent, on a chevron nebuly gules, between three fountains, as many eagles rising proper; and for his crest, upon a wreath of the colours, a mascle sable, interlaced with three ears of barley slipped or; with the motto, "Sapiens qui assiduus." An additional example of a collar of SS. is depicted in Fig. 19, which is a re-

FIG. 19.—The Arms of William Henry Weldon, Esq., Norroy King of Arms.

presentation of the arms of William Henry Weldon, Norroy King of Arms. The arms depicted are—Dexter, his official coat as Norroy King of Arms, namely : argent, a cross of St. George gules, on a chief per pale azure, and of the second a lion of England passant guardant or, crowned with an open crown, and between a fleur-de-lis on the dexter and a key on the sinister of the last, and impaling his family arms, namely : per fess argent and gules, on a pale a demi-lion rampant in chief and a cinquefoil in base all counterchanged, the escutcheon being encircled by his collar of SS. Mantling gules and argent. Crest : upon a wreath of the colours, a demi-lion rampant argent, gutté-de-sang, and resting his sinister paw upon two SS, as linked in a collar of SS argent ; with the motto, "Bien fait."

Collars of SS are also worn by Serjeants-at-Arms, and by the Lord Chief Justice.

In addition each King of Arms has his crown; the only occasion, however, upon which this is worn being at the ceremony of a coronation. The crown is of silver gilt, formed of a circle upon which is inscribed part of the first verse of the 51st Psalm, viz., "Miserere mei Deus secundum magnam misericordiam tuam": the rim is surmounted of sixteen leaves, in shape resembling the oak-leaf, every alternate one being somewhat higher than the remainder. Nine of these leaves are shown in a representation of it. The cap is of crimson

FIG. 20.—Sir James Balfour Paul, Lyon King of Arms.
(From a photograph by Kate Pragnell.)

satin, closed at the top by a gold tassel, and turned up with ermine. This will be seen in Figs. 19, 20, and 21.

Garter King of Arms has a baton or "sceptre" of silver gilt, about two feet in length, the top being of gold, of four sides of equal height, but of unequal breadth. On the two larger sides are the arms of St. George impaling the Sovereign's, and on the two lesser sides the arms of St. George surrounded by the Garter and motto, the whole ensigned with an Imperial crown. This has sometimes been placed in bend behind the arms of Garter King. Lyon King of Arms has a baton of blue enamel with gold extremities, the baton being powdered with roses, thistles, and fleurs-de-lis (see Fig. 20). Lyon (Sir James Balfour Paul) in his recently published work, "Heraldry in relation to Scottish History and Art," remarks that this is one of the few pieces of British official regalia which is still adorned with the ancient ensigns of France. But knowing how strictly all official regalia in England is required to have the armorial devices thereupon changed, as the Royal arms and badges change, there can be very little doubt that the appearance of the fleurs-de-lis in this case is due to an oversight. The baton happens to be that of a former Lyon King of Arms, which really should long since have been discarded and a new one substituted. Two batons are usually placed in saltire behind the arms of Lyon King of Arms, as will be seen in the illustration of the armorial bearings of Lyon King of Arms, which will be found on Plate IV.[c]

[c] Armorial bearings of Sir James Balfour Paul, Lyon King of Arms: Parted per pale, on the dexter side the official coat of Lyon King of Arms, namely: argent, a lion sejant full-faced gules, holding in the dexter paw a thistle slipped vert, and in the sinister a shield of the

Ulster King of Arms has a staff of office which, however, really belongs to his office as Knight Attendant on the Most Illustrious Order of St. Patrick. It will be seen in the photograph which we reproduce of the present Ulster King of Arms in his tabard (Fig. 758) and also in the reproduction of his bookplate (Fig. 21). The arms there represented are: Argent, on a cross sable, five estoiles of the field, impaled by the official coat of Ulster King of Arms, namely: or, a cross gules, on a chief of the last, a lion passant guardant between a harp and a portcullis, all of the field. Above the escutcheon is placed the coronet of a King of Arms, and thereupon a helmet befitting his degree, with a lambrequin azure and argent; and for his crest, upon a wreath of the colours, a dove holding in its bill an olive-branch all proper; with the motto, "Vincit omnia virtus."

The bookplate plainly shows the portcullis in the collar of SS, and also the harp (the badge of Ireland) which is attached to his collar, and the coronet or crown of a King of Arms.

The Scottish Heralds each have a rod of ebony (see Plate III.) tipped with ivory, which has been sometimes stated to be a rod of office. This, however, is not the case, and the explanation of their possession of it is very simple. They are constantly called upon by virtue of their office to make from the Market Cross in Edinburgh the Royal Proclamations. Now these Proclamations are read from printed copies which in size of type and paper are always of the nature of a poster. The

FIG. 21.—The Bookplate of Sir Arthur Vicars, K.C.V.O., Ulster King of Arms. (Designed and engraved by C. W. Sherborne.)

Herald would naturally find some difficulty in holding up a large piece of paper of this size on a windy day, in such a manner that it was easy to read from; consequently he winds it round his ebony staff, slowly unwinding it all the time as he reads.

Garter King of Arms, Lyon King of Arms, and

second, on a chief azure, a St. Andrew's Cross of the field, on the sinister his paternal coat, namely: or, a chevron indented sable between two lions rampant in chief and an escutcheon in base gules. Mantling sable, doubled or; and upon a wreath of his liveries is set for crest, a lion sejant guardant gules, his dexter paw resting upon an escutcheon as in the arms; and in an escroll over the same this motto, "Pro Rege et Republica."

THE ART OF HERALDRY

Ulster King of Arms all possess badges of their office which they wear about their necks.

The badge of Garter is of gold, having on both sides the arms of St. George, impaled with those of the Sovereign, within the Garter and motto, enamelled in their proper colours, and ensigned with the Royal crown.

The badge of Lyon King of Arms is oval, and is worn suspended by a broad green ribbon. The badge proper consists on the obverse of the effigy of St. Andrew bearing his cross before him, with a thistle beneath, all enamelled in the proper colours on an azure ground. The reverse contains the arms of Scotland, having in the lower parts of the badge a thistle, as on the other side; the whole surmounted with the Imperial crown. This is seen on the portrait of Lyon King of Arms.

The badge of "Ulster" is of gold, containing on one side the cross of St. Patrick, or as it is described in the statutes, "The cross gules of the Order upon a field argent, impaled with the arms of the Realm of Ireland," and both encircled with the motto, "Quis Separabit," and the date of the institution of the Order, MDCCLXXXIII. The reverse exhibits the arms of the office of Ulster, viz.: "Or, a cross gules, on a chief of the last a lion of England between a harp and portcullis, all of the first," placed on a ground of green enamel, surrounded by a gold border with shamrocks, surmounted by an Imperial crown, and suspended by a sky blue riband from the neck.

The Kings of Arms, the Heralds, and Pursuivants in England were incorporated by Charter 2 March, 1 Richard III., 1484, and the College of Arms at present consists of :—

FIG. 22.—The late J. W. Mitchell, Rothesay Herald and Lyon Clerk.

EARL MARSHAL.
The Duke of Norfolk, K.G., P.C.

KINGS OF ARMS.
Garter—Sir Albert William Woods, G.C.V.O., K.C.B., K.C.M.G., F.S.A.
Clarenceux—George Edward Cokayne, Esq., M.A., F.S.A.
Norroy—William Henry Weldon, Esq., C.V.O., F.S.A.

HERALDS.
Chester—Henry Murray Lane, Esq.
Lancaster—Edward Bellasis, Esq.
York—Alfred Scott Scott-Gatty, Esq., F.S.A.
Somerset—Henry Farnham Burke, Esq., C.V.O., F.S.A.
Richmond—Charles Harold Athill, Esq., F.S.A.
Windsor—William Alexander Lindsay, Esq., K.C., F.S.A.

PURSUIVANTS.
Rouge Croix—George William Marshall, Esq., LL.D., F.S.A.
Bluemantle—Gordon Ambrose De Lisle Lee.
Rouge Dragon—Everard Green, V.P.S.A.
Portcullis—Thomas Morgan Joseph-Watkin, F.S.A.

There is also at present one Extraordinary Herald—

Surrey (Extraordinary)—Charles Alban Buckler, Esq.

The arms of the Corporation of the College of Arms are : Argent, a cross gules between four doves, the dexter wing of each expanded and inverted azure. Crest: on a ducal coronet or, a dove rising azure. Supporters : two lions rampant guardant argent, ducally gorged or. The shield will be found on Plate II., Fig. 1.

The official arms of the English Kings of Arms are :—

Garter King of Arms. —Argent, a cross gules, on a chief azure, a ducal coronet encircled with a garter, between a lion passant guardant on the dexter and a fleur-de-lis on the sinister all or.

Clarenceux King of Arms.—Argent, a cross gules, on a chief of the second a lion passant guardant or, crowned of the last.

Norroy King of Arms.—Argent, a cross gules, on a chief of the second a lion passant guardant crowned of the first, between a fleur-de-lis on the dexter and a key on the sinister of the last.

Badges have never been officially assigned to the various Heralds; in fact badges have never been made the subject of grants, but from a remote period certain of the Royal badges relating to their titles have been used by various Heralds, viz. :—

Lancaster.—The red rose of Lancaster ensigned by the Royal crown.

York.—The white rose of York en soliel ensigned by the Royal crown.

Richmond.—The red rose of Lancaster impaled with the white rose en soliel of York, the whole ensigned with the Royal crown.

Windsor.—Rays of the sun issuing from clouds.

The four Pursuivants make use of the badges from which they derive their titles.

The present Officers of Arms for Scotland are :—

LYON KING OF ARMS.
Sir James Balfour Paul, Esq., V.P.S.A. (Scot.).

THE ART OF HERALDRY

Of these only Lyon King of Arms and Lyon Clerk are actively engaged with the control of armorial bearings.

The official arms of Lyon King of Arms and of Lyon Office are: Argent, a lion sejant full-faced gules, holding in the dexter paw a thistle slipped vert and in the sinister a shield of the second; on a chief azure, a St. Andrew's cross of the field (Plate IV.).

The only Officers of Arms in Ireland are:—

Athlone Pursuivant, however, is only an officer of the Order of St. Patrick. There are no official arms for Ulster's Office, that office, unlike the College of Arms, not being a corporate body, but the official arms of Ulster King of Arms are: Or, a cross gules, on a chief of the last a

FIG. 24.—A State Trumpeter. (*Temp.* Hen. VIII.)

lion passant guardant between a harp and a portcullis all of the field.

The portrait of the late J. W. Mitchell, Rothesay Herald and Lyon Clerk (Fig. 22), shows the head-dress formerly worn by the Scottish heralds.

At the late ceremony of the coronation of King Edward VII., a head-dress was designed for the officers of arms. This can be seen in the portrait of Captain Swinton, March Pursuivant (Plate III.). The caps are of black velvet embroidered at the side with a rose, a thistle, or a harp, respectively for the English, Scottish, and Irish officers of arms.

A great deal of confusion has arisen between the costume and the functions of a Herald and a Trumpeter, though the confusion has been confined to the minds of the uninitiated and the theatrical stage. The whole subject was very amusingly dealt with in the *Genealogical Magazine* in an article by Mr. G. Ambrose Lee, Bluemantle, and the illustrations which he gives of the relative dresses of the Heralds and the Trumpeters at different periods (see Figs. 23 to 26) are interesting. Briefly, the matter can be summed up in the statement that there never was a Trumpeter who made a proclamation, and there never was a Herald who blew a trumpet. The Trumpeters nearly always accompanied the Heralds to proclaim their presence and call attention to their proclamation.

In France the Heralds were formed into an incorporation by Charles VI. in 1406, their head being Mountjoye, King of Arms, with ten heralds and pursuivants under him. It will be noticed that this incorporation is earlier than that of the College of Arms in England. The Revolution played havoc with the French

FIG. 23.—A Herald. (*Temp.* Hen. VIII.)

Records, and no College of Arms now exists in France. But it is doubtful whether at any time it reached the

FIG. 25.—A State Trumpeter and a Herald at the coronation of James I.

dignity or authority which its English counterpart has enjoyed in former times.

Fig. 27 represents a French Herald of the early part of the fifteenth century. It is taken from a representation of the Rally of the Parisians against King Charles VI. in 1413, to be found in a MS. edition of Froissart, formerly in the Royal Library at Paris.

Whilst the official dress of the Heralds in England has undergone no change whatever, it is curious to note the varieties of costume which have been adopted in other countries, of which Plates I. and II. furnish examples.   A. C. F-D.

 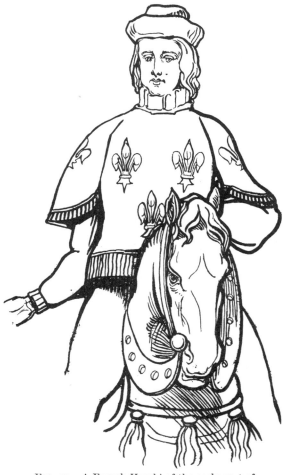

FIG. 26.—Peace proclaimed at the Royal Exchange after the Crimean War.

FIG. 27.—A French Herald of the early part of the fifteenth century.

THE ART OF HERALDRY

PLATE I

HERALDS IN OFFICIAL DRESS

The figures depicted upon Plate I. are as follows:—

Fig. 1.—The *Herald von Geldern*, known by the official name of *Gelre* or *Ghelre* (died *circa* 1372), from his *Wapenboeck au Armorial* (see Plate XXII.), taken from a copy by Victor Bouton, Paris, the publisher of the book.

The tabard shows the armorial bearings of the Duke von Geldern: Azure, a lion rampant or, queue-fourché, armed and langued gules.

The picture of the herald constitutes, in a manner, the closing feature of the book, and the broken chain *Gelre* holds in his hands seems to indicate that his duties as herald are at an end. The entries are continued until *circa* 1371, in which year, with the death of Duke Edward, the family of the Dukes von Geldern and Counts von Zütphen became extinct in the male line.

Fig. 2 is a representation of a *King of Arms* from a miniature in the *Tournois du roi René d'Anjou* (No. 2692 in the MSS. of the Paris National Library), fifteenth century.

The King of Arms, who is, as will be seen, mounted on horseback, bears on his tabard the arms of Grutuse (perhaps the coat of Louis de Bruges, Seigneur de Grutuse). These are: Quartered 1 and 4, or, a cross sable ; 2 and 3, gules, a saltire argent.

Fig. 3 shows the *King of Arms of the Order of the Golden Fleece* (Toison d'or), from Baron Reiffenberg's *Histoire de l'Ordre de la Toison d'or*, Brussels, 1830.

He is dressed entirely in red, and the pendant of his head-gear (the *cornette*) hangs down on the left side, as opposed to that of a knight, which was worn on the right side. *Toison d'or* wears over the shoulders a collar of gold, the *Potence*, composed of twenty-six enamelled plates, in two rows, ornamented with fifty-two coats of arms of Knights of the Order of the Golden Fleece (Fig. 28). The plates are fastened together in the centre with hinges, and closed underneath with the collar of the Order of the Golden Fleece. This peculiar ornament seems to be unique. In this costume "Messire Antoine de Beaulincourt, Chevalier, Seigneur de Beaulincourt, Vendeville, Bellenville et Lanson from 1549, the first King of Arms who was known as *Toison*

FIG. 28.—Emblem of the Order of the Golden Fleece in the Cathedral at Barcelona, 1518.

d'or, appeared in the 22nd Chapter of the Order, 1555, at Antwerp" (*Jahrbuch* "*Adler*," 1883). He died in 1559.

Fig. 4.—A *German Imperial Herald* of the first half of the sixteenth century, from a pen and ink drawing by Hans Holbein, in the Royal Collection of Engravings in Dresden. Fig. 29, the drawing of an Imperial Herald, from a woodcut by Michael Ostendorfer (*d.* 1559), belongs to the same period, but whereas Holbein's herald bears on his tabard the Imperial double-eagle, with the arms of Austria and Burgundy impaled, Ostendorfer's double-eagle bears the arms of Austria and Castile upon the inescutcheon.

Fig. 5 represents *Caspar Sturm*, a former Imperial Herald, his title being *Teutschland* (*i.e.* Deutschland—Germany). Previously to 1521 the Herald of the German Empire bore the official name of *Romreich* (*i.e.* Roman Empire). This representation is taken from a drawing executed by himself in his manuscript : " Kayser Karl des Fünfften vnd Irer Mt. Stathalter sampt der Achtzehen Churfursten vnd Fursten Auch des Kaiserlichen Regiments im heiligen Reich verordennter Rethe Namen vnd Wappen" ("Appointed Councillor of Names and Arms in the Holy Empire to the Emperor Charles V., and His Majesty's Lords of the State, together with the eighteen Electors and Princes, also to the Imperial Regiment"), in the possession of the "Herold" Society, Berlin. (See *Festschrift of the Herold*, 1894.) Sturm was appointed Herald of the Empire by Charles V. at Aix-la-Chapelle, October 27, 1521. "Der ernveste Herr Caspar Sturm, des Heiligen Reichs gewesner Allter Erenherold" ("The grave Herr Caspar Sturm, former Herald of the Holy Empire") leans upon the shields of the town of Nürnberg, and bears upon his tabard the Imperial eagle, and thereupon the impaled arms of Castile and Burgundy.

Fig. 6 represents a *Royal Hungarian Herald*, Johann von Francolin, the younger, 1560, from an engraving by Donat Hübschmann, in Vienna. His elder brother of the same name was likewise a herald. The Francolins, as also the greater number of the old heralds, came originally from Burgundy, and were ennobled by the Emperor Ferdinand I. at Regensburg, March 8, 1557.[d] The

arms depicted at the side of the figure are the personal achievement of Francolin, and though it is almost impossible to blazon the arms by the ordinary terms of English blazonry, they may perhaps be described : Party per chevron azure and or, two chevronels gules, the field between the chevronels paly of six of the first and second, in chief two heath-cocks (francolins) proper, crowned and gorged with coronets or, standing upon the upper chevronel, and in base an eagle displayed argent, charged with a saltire couped gules.

FIG. 29.—German Imperial Herald, from a woodcut by Michael Ostendorfer (*d.* 1559).

The helmet, with mantling azure, gules, and or, is crowned, and bears as a crest issuing from a coronet a heath-cock as in the arms. The tabard shows the new and the old arms of the kingdom of Hungary, the former being : Gules, a patriarchal cross argent issuing from three mounts vert ; the latter : Barry of eight gules and argent. Compare Plate II. Fig. 7. The figure of this herald is taken from the German edition of Francolin's *Thurnier Buchs* (Book of Tournaments), 1560, published by Raphael Hofhalter (Skrzetusky), Vienna.

Fig. 7 shows the costume of the *Electoral Herald of Brandenburg*, under the Great Elector, Frederick III., in the latter half of the seventeenth century. The colour of the fringed and gold-embroidered tabard refers to the blue shield and golden sceptre, which were the official arms of the *Archikamerarius* (Arch chamberlain) of the Holy Roman Empire, which dignity was enjoyed from 1415 by the Hohenzollerns, as Electors of Brandenburg. The shield, the Electoral crown upon the breast, and the shoulder-pieces, show the new arms of the Brandenburg margraviate, while the plain red eagle of the sceptre represents the older form.

PLATE II

HERALDS IN OFFICIAL DRESS

Plate II. gives examples of the *Heralds of the eighteenth and nineteenth centuries*, though, as has been already stated, Fig. 1 shows the shield of the English College of Arms, namely : Argent, a cross gules between four doves azure, the dexter wing of each expanded and inverted. Though always blazoned a dove azure, it is nevertheless usually depicted with the legs and beak gules.

Fig. 2, though not a good portrait, represents the present *Garter King of Arms* in his tabard, and in full dress, the tabard showing the Royal Arms of the United Kingdom of Great Britain and Ireland.

---

[d] In 1562 the Emperor Ferdinand I. presented to his herald Francolin, a piece of ground in front of the *Widmerthor* for the erection of windmills. It is still called *Windmühl gasse* (Windmill Lane),

and is situated in Circuit VI., Vienna: he received, moreover, among many other privileges, permission to display the Imperial eagle on the outside of his house.

THE ART OF HERALDRY

Fig. 3 is the *Herald of the Prussian Order of the Black Eagle* of the year 1890. The blue of the herald's dress, which is adorned with the small Prussian coat of arms, corresponds with the colour of the cross of the Order.

Fig. 4 is a *Herald* depicted as he officiated at the Coronation of King William I. of Prussia at Königsberg, October 18, 1861.

Fig. 5 is a *Royal Bavarian Herald* as he appeared at the Coronation of King Ludwig II. of Bavaria in the year 1864. He wears a sky-blue velvet tabard, richly embroidered with silver, and trimmed with silver bullion. Embroidered in front and behind is the Royal coat of arms of Bavaria. Below the tabard is worn an embroidered tunic of silver brocade, breeches of white satin with blue and white rosettes, while white silk stockings, and white leather shoes with blue and white rosettes, complete the official costume of the herald. A blue velvet cap, with a circlet embellished with silver and with three ostrich feathers, one blue and two white, serves as a head-covering. The herald's sceptre is of silver and is 80 centimetres in length. It is ensigned with a gold crown. When mounted the herald wears white kerseymere breeches and white leather boots, trimmed with silver fringe, and silver spurs; and in place of the sceptre, a silver truncheon 67 centimetres long is carried.

Fig. 6 represents a *Bavarian Pursuivant*. He wears a blue velvet tabard, bordered with silver edging, and an underdress of white satin with silver edges, breeches of white kerseymere, white leather boots trimmed with silver fringe, and with plated spurs, and a black hat turned up at the edge, with a blue and a white ostrich feather. (From information supplied by the Royal Bavarian Heralds' Office.)

Fig. 7 is the *Hungarian Provincial Herald* as he appeared at the Coronation of King Franz Joseph I. on the 8th June 1867. The tabard shows, in front and behind, the arms of Hungary. The *kalpak*, or hat, is adorned with overhanging ostrich feathers in the colours of the country, red, white, and green. The herald wears green underclothes laced with gold, and yellow *czismen* (boots). The white leather gauntlet gloves, fringed on the edges with the colours of the country, show on the backs of the hands the coat of arms of the country embroidered in their proper colours.

Fig. 8 is the *Herald of the Imperial Capital* and *City of Vienna.* He is dressed in the colours of the town, red and white, and bears on his breast the great coat of arms, and on the shoulder-pieces the lesser coat of arms, of the town.

Fig. 9 is a *Royal Swedish Herald* of the eighteenth century. He wears a purple-red velvet tabard, edged with the links of the collar of the Seraphin Order embroidered in gold. On the breast appears the monogram of Jesus Christ as upon the star of the Seraphin Order, and ensigned with the Royal crown. Around the neck are the ribbons of the Seraphin Order (blue), and the Wasa Order (green), with their badges. The herald is also wearing on the breast the knight's badge of the Order of the Sword (from a yellow ribbon), and of the Order of the North Star (from a black ribbon). Whether all or any of these Orders are part of his official costume, or whether they are worn by reason of the identity of the wearer, does not seem clear.

Fig. 10, another Swedish herald, is the *Herald of the Order of the Kingdom of Sweden,* otherwise the Order of the Seraphin. The tabard is of dark blue velvet, with gold embroidery similar to that of the Royal Herald. The inscription on the shoulder-pieces (sleeves) runs: "Jesvs Hominum Salvator."

Fig. 11 is the *Herald of the Swedish Order of the Sword.* The blue tabard bears on the breast the emblem of the Order, a naked sword ensigned by a crown. On the shoulder-pieces appears the inscription: "Pro Patria."

Fig. 12 represents the *Herald of the Swedish Order of the North Star.* The red tabard is decorated with the badge of this Order. The inscription on the shoulder-pieces is: "Nescit Occasum."

Fig. 13 is the *Herald of the Swedish Order of Wasa.* The green tabard is embroidered in front with the emblem of the Order, a golden sheaf of corn. Round the border runs the inscription: "Gvstaf. Den. III., Instiktare, MDCCLXXII. (Gustavus III., Founder, 1772). These Swedish costumes are no longer in use. The details were, however, supplied by the present Swedish herald, Major K. A. von Klingspor.
H. S.

CHAPTER V

ENGLISH HERALDIC EFFIGIES

By ALBERT HARTSHORNE, F.S.A.

THE value of monumental effigies as authentic pictures of armour and costume, and as furnishing accurate representations of ancient heraldry, has long been insisted upon and recognised. It must, however, be borne in mind that the carvers and the latteners of the memorials, which were for the most part only conventional representations of the soldiers, ladies, or ecclesiastics, could only imitate the armour or the costume up to a certain point, in consequence of the nature of their materials; and although the softer stones surrendered with greater freedom to the chisel, the study of such matters must be supplemented by reference to illuminated manuscripts, and to the actual examples of armour which present themselves for comparison by slow degrees, and, generally speaking, not until after the fourteenth century. But armour alone gives the least possible heraldry, and ancient tabards do not exist. With ecclesiastical vestments exhibiting heraldic charges the position is somewhat better; of ancient female costume, of course nothing remains earlier than of the time of Elizabeth, save fragments.

We fortunately have the real heraldic sleeved jupon, embroidered with the fourfold presentment of arms and the *cuir-bouilli* shield of the Black Prince at Canterbury—relics unique indeed for their period, and rare chivalric associations; but one would have been thankful for some actual examples of the small armorial shields of the middle of the fourteenth century, such as all the knights carried on the left arm, or for bouched pavises like those which the great Richard, Earl of Warwick, prepared at Calais when "he cast in his mynde, to do some new poynt of chevalry"; and still more grateful for original examples of fifteenth-century tabards or gorgeous late fifteenth and early sixteenth century ladies' heraldic mantles, such as are depicted on the effigies and brasses.

In the face of the great dearth of original examples of English heraldic shields and cognate remains, we may therefore turn with satisfaction to their accurate presentments on the monumental effigies and brasses, and not disregarding the equally valuable heraldic details upon the tombs when the figures heraldically fail us.

With regard specially to the heraldry associated with the effigies and brasses, whether sculptured or painted on the surcoats, jupons, tabards, or shields of the men, the mantles of the women, the orphreys of priestly vestments, or set forth in order upon the tombs, we are well situated. For in the sculptured heraldry of the earlier monuments, and more particularly in the delicate painted details in *gesso* upon them, the work leaves nothing to be desired; it is, in fact, exactly the same pictorial art that was applied to the real shields. No direct supplementary study is necessary, save the corroborative testimony of the Rolls of Arms. And in the use of these records some caution is necessary, because the compilers copied the mistakes of earlier Rolls, which were thus handed down and perpetuated. In the effigies and brasses of later times, though the arts have naturally deteriorated, there is still the same heraldic precision and accuracy in the representations that have so conspicuously *les défauts de leurs qualités.*

26

THE ART OF HERALDRY

A convincing proof of the care that was exercised in monumental heraldry is afforded by the tomb and relics of the Black Prince, the heraldic bearings on the real shield and jupon being precisely the same as are exhibited on the jupon of the *latten* effigy, save that in the latter the label is also shown. In this regard the real shield (Fig. 264) and jupon may have been originally made for Edward III.

This shield is formed of a light frame of wood, covered with *cuir-bouilli*, showing France and England quarterly in relief. For shields richly decorated with painting and gilding, a coat of *gesso* was first laid upon the outer surface, just as with the effigies. As time progressed, shields varied in form in accordance with the advance of architecture, which science, following perhaps at times the goldsmith's, gave impetus and character to the rest of the arts.

It does not appear that any definite rules were anciently observed respecting the selection and arrangement of arms on monuments. The effigy, of course, set forth the paramount coat, while on the sides of the tomb were naturally placed the arms of the nearest relations, and sometimes those of friends also. In cases where the Royal arms are shown on monuments of commoners, as on the Burghersh tomb at Lincoln, about 1350, and the brass of Sir Simon de Felbrigge, 1416, at Felbrig, Norfolk, the reasons are as obvious as the appearance of the SS collar on certain effigies and brasses. The Great Seals of England, and the wonderful series of ecclesiastical, official, and personal English seals form a very fertile source of study in relation to monumental heraldic shields, apart from their value as regards architecture, armour, and costume.

In the champlevé enamelled plate of Geoffrey Plantagenet, Earl of Anjou, 1150, a monumental memorial at Mans, he carries on a great curved shield: Azure, six lioncels rampant or (Fig. 41). He was father of Henry II., and such is the coat shown on the shield of William Longespée, 1227, son of Henry II., and Fair Rosamund, in his effigy at Salisbury, the earliest in England with armorial bearings. This is a remarkable and beautifully sculptured example of early heraldry, which might induce the consideration of the vexed and tempting question of Royal Arms in England before the time of Richard I. But we must pass on, merely recording that Longespée's surcoat has also been painted heraldically, and that the second Great Seal of Richard I. shows three lions passant.

The generality of the thirteenth-century effigies being carved in Purbeck, or in Sussex marble, hard, secondary fresh-water limestones, not readily lending themselves to minute sculpture, any heraldic accessories were painted upon the shields and surcoats, and have long since vanished. In rare and later cases the arms were sculptured on the shields. An effigy in the Temple Church, with a doubtful attribution to William Marshall, Earl of Pembroke, 1219, is an instance. The remarkable effigy of Sir Robert de Keynes, 1305, at Dodford, Northamptonshire, is in Purbeck marble, and shows him clad in banded mail, and carrying a kite-shaped shield, sculptured with his arms: Vair, two bars ——.

The comparatively limited use of Purbeck or of Sussex marble for effigies passed away early in the fourteenth century, the manufacture of effigies expanded, and freestones of various kinds, and worked in many localities, took their places. Sculptured arms on the shields only now became usual. An early instance in hard, red sandstone is the grand and martial figure at Hughenden, Buckinghamshire, apparently of a Welles. The shield of this remarkable memorial exhibits on a field of cross crosslets fitché a lion rampant double-queued, holding a child in its mouth, the surcoat being charged with a chief chequy, a griffin segreant holding a child in its paws. On the scabbard of the sword are a series of small shields, sculptured with bearings. There are now no indications of any tinctures on the figure, but the decoration of effigies was well established in the last years of the thirteenth century.

In the brass of Sir John D'Abernoun, 1277, at Abernoun, Surrey (Fig. 32), a small enamelled shield is carried on the left arm. Sir Roger de Trumpington, 1289, at Trumpington, Cambridgeshire (Fig. 33), and Sir Robert de Septvans, 1305, at Chartham, Kent (Fig. 37), have the shields on their brasses charged with their arms; the last-named knight's surcoat is powdered with winnowing-fans, and both he and Trumpington wear ailettes, heraldically charged. These odd decorations also occur on a few stone effigies, and often in painted glass and illuminated MSS. They were of very light construction, less for defence than display, and each was tied on the shoulder at right angles to it (Figs. 693 and 697).

Before passing into the fourteenth century we may touch upon a notable effigy in Westminster Abbey, although it is an exotic from Limoges. This is the wooden figure, covered with plates of copper, of William de Valence, son of Isabella of Angoulème, 1296. The monument consists of a stone altar-tomb, upon which is placed a wooden one sustaining the effigy. The upper tomb was originally covered with enamelled plates forming a background for a series of figures under canopies with shields above them. All these items are now gone, and the upper portion of the monument is reduced to a bare chest. The table of the tomb was covered with an enamelled lozengy diaper of the arms of England and Valence; a small portion remains. The pillow plates still exist and show an enamelled diaper of England and Valence armorials in rows alternating with rosettes, the work being of great delicacy and beauty. The surcoat was powdered with small scutcheons of Valence, according to a French custom. The shield of De Valence, happily remaining, represents the arms richly diapered; it is carried French-wise on the hip. On the stone tomb are the arms of England, repeated as having precedence, De Valence, and the same dimidiating Clermont, for his son Aylmer and his first wife.

The painting of effigies soon led to such elaborate decoration as was only possible upon a prepared surface of *gesso* laid upon the stone. From their costly and high art quality, rivalling in fact the refined efforts of the illuminators, it may be thought that only a comparatively small proportion were thus treated, yet we find in quite remote churches, indications on effigies of most elaborate work. Every effigy of the time was, in short, a heraldic text. For instance, in Rampton Church, Cambridgeshire, is the stone effigy of a De l'Isle of the beginning of the fourteenth century, on which the arms, or, a fess between two chevrons sable, cottised gules, have been most carefully painted, and the charges enriched and pencilled in pale grey arabesques, recalling the diapered fields in painted glass. Of the same time is the effigy of Stephen de Haccombe, Haccombe, Devonshire, which exhibits the remains of the rich decorations on the shield, and the flowing black arabesque pattern running over the painted links of the mail hauberk, perhaps a unique example.

While such work as this was being carried out, the practice of sculpturing the arms was still pursued. At Hatfield Broad Oak, Essex, an effigy of a De Vere has the quarterly shield carved alternately 1 and 4 with a diaper of lozenges, and 2 and 3 of circles. Sculptured and painted work on effigies was long carried out contemporaneously, the former emphasising the latter, or the artist enhancing the chisel of the carver as the nature of the stone and the circumstances of the production of the figures seemed to suggest or permit.

Having now arrived at a most attractive period of heraldic study, reference will be made to some examples of English armorial effigies which particularly illustrate it. In the Abbey is the noble canopied monument of Edmund Crouchback, Earl of Lancaster, 1296, second son of Henry III., and who married firstly Aveline, the great Fortibus heiress. The surcoat of the stone effigy has been painted with a diaper of England differenced by a label of France, and alternating with eagles displayed and quatrefoils. These are highly beautiful examples of heraldic ornamentation, painted in dark and light crimson, the charges most daintily pencilled in their colours. The shield is gone, but the trefoil in the upper spandril of the canopy shows the Earl of Lancaster on his barded horse, the shield, surcoat, and trappers painted with his arms. We are indebted to Charles Alfred Stothard for the decipherment and exquisite etchings illustrating the valuable painted details of this and many cognate memorials. At Minster in Kent is the effigy of Sir Robert de Shurland, who died after 1300, having been present at the siege of Caerlaverock in that year. His surcoat is powdered with lions rampant or, on a field azure, and his shield shows the enarmes. The freestone effigy of Sir Nicholas de Cogenhoe, 1281, at Cogenhoe, Northamptonshire, has the arms—a fess between three mascles—carved on his shield, the same coat occurring four times, with five others on the capitals of the nave arcade of his building—exceedingly rare features for the time. Aylmer de Valence, third and youngest son of William, succeeded his father in the earldom of Pembroke, and died in 1323. The entire surcoat of the stone effigy has been treated as a shield, and painted with the De Valence arms. In the spandril of the canopy the earl is shown on horseback, the barding and surcoat blazoned De Valence. As time advances, more importance is given to armorial shields on the tomb.

With the varied harness and fascinating costume of the knights of the time of Edward II. the small shield continued, carried on the arm, and always, whether in brasses or effigies, exhibiting the charges. Of the former kind, which are now becoming almost as numerous as effigies, we have many examples. John de Creke, 1325, Westley Waterless, Cambridgeshire, and John d'Abernoun, 1327, Stoke d'Abernoun, both wearing that strange and rare attire the cyclas—the transition garment between the surcoat and the jupon —are good types. In sculptured effigies of this time and style, armorial bearings were usually discontinued on the body garment, the cyclas, and appear only on the shield, carved or painted.

The introduction of the use of alabaster for monuments soon brought about retrogression by putting an end to the artistic gessoed and painted effigies, and introducing simpler modes of decoration. The earliest examples of alabaster statues, such as those of Edward II. at Gloucester, John of Eltham, 1334, in the Abbey, and William of Hatfield, 1335, at York, are most tenderly sculptured. The shield of John of Eltham is a real heraldic masterpiece, and the statuettes of his royal and noble relatives round the tomb leave nothing to be desired. The important brass of Sir Hugh Hastings, 1437, at Elsing, Norfolk, gives examples, in the small figures of the noble personages in the shafts of the canopy, of the transition in the heraldic decoration of military costume that was now taking place. Such was the harness of the heroes of Cressy and Poictiers. The shield on the arm has been abandoned, and the

armorials have returned to and appear only on the body of the close-fitting, short-skirted jupon, the immediate forerunner of the jupon proper. Of knightly brasses of the first half of the long reign of Edward III., showing the short-skirted jupon, very few remain. We have the Elsing examples, Sir John de Wantyng, 1347, at Wimbish, Essex, and Sir John Gifford, 1348, at Bowers Gifford, Essex, 1348, said to be the latest example carrying a shield.

From the end of the thirteenth to the middle of the fourteenth century the practice of placing shields of arms upon the sides of tombs had been gradually adopted, shields of arms and distressful "weepers" vying with or rivalling each other for precedence. In some cases we find nothing but "weepers," not necessarily in the exaggerated postures of grief that so many present—there are twenty-four on the tomb of a De Vere, about 1370, at Earls Colne, Essex, cheerfully exhibiting a variety of civil dress; in others only shields of arms; in others, again, mourners and panels and armorials share these honourable places with the best effect until far into the fifteenth century. Detailed reference to exquisite examples of heraldry more strictly architectural, such as the Abbey, Lincoln, and Beverley afford, seductive though it is, would be outside the limits of the present essay.

In the meantime the "marbelers" were setting up their alabaster effigies, first of the cyclas, and then of the camail and jupon type. In the latter—to pursue the subject chronologically—all the knights are now shown in tight jupons, and upon the swelling breasts the arms were delicately sculptured, as in the figure of Sir Thomas Cawne, about 1370, at Igtham, Kent; less frequently the arms were painted only. No class of effigy is more numerous than this one, and admirably as the heraldry and simple arming details are shown, these countless figures in alabaster, clunch, and other soft stones were mere conventional representations of knights *quelconques*, and not portraits. Thus stiffly accoutred they fought, for instance, at Agincourt on St. Crispin's day, 1415. Such "marble" and similar figures continued up to about 1418, and although a reaction had again arisen in favour of brasses, the felicitous medium which resigned itself with so much freedom to the sculptor's hand was not abandoned, and it continued in use until the middle of the seventeenth century. Great as is the value of works engraved in enduring brass, it is specially to alabaster transformed into a series of historical records that English heralds owe so much.

Conspicuous examples of armorials are the thirteen remaining of the original twenty shields on the tomb of Edmund of Langley, died 1402, at King's Langley, Hertfordshire. There never was an effigy. It is apparent that heraldic art in this case, as well as in others of the time, has somewhat declined since the death of John of Eltham; yet we may justly value these vigorous examples in alabaster. It is to be regretted that the latteners so seldom engraved armorial bearings on their camail and jupon figures; they were almost invariably sculptured or painted on the alabaster and other effigies. It is true that small shields laid apart in the Purbeck slabs are constantly found, but the interest of the paramount figure suffers by the personal deficiency, at least up to the death of Henry IV.

Now came the great change. The jupon, the lineal descendant of the armorial surcoat, was discarded; the man appears locked up in steel, and heraldry is banished for fully half a century to the tombs. Rows of rigid angels holding shields, generally alternating with flat and precise weepers, now coldly furnish the panelled monuments.

A few words are desirable about the mantles of the

ladies. That they were richly and heraldically embroidered we know from illuminated manuscripts, from early monuments, and from Chaucer's description of Riches in the "Romaunt of the Rose." In later centuries the effigies and brasses give complete evidence of the heraldic decoration of ladies' costume, and of the great amplitude of their embroidered gowns. The paintings on the robes of the Angevin queens at Fontevraud, the illuminations of the Loutterell Psalter, and the heraldic powderings on the dress of Ann of Bohemia, naturally occur to the mind. Monumental effigies and brasses furnish many instances of the heraldic mantle. An example on the effigy of Isabel, Dame Spencer, 1522, at Brington, Northamptonshire, is late but noteworthy. The brass of Margaret Percy, 1542, wife of Henry Clifford, first Earl of Cumberland, at Skipton, Yorkshire, exhibits in her mantle the quarters of two of the noblest of northern families (Fig. 31). This stately garment passed away soon after the middle of the sixteenth century.

With regard more particularly to the heraldic vestment *par excellence*—the tabard—it has been stated above, that the real jupon associated with the monument of the Black Prince displays the arms on its short tubular sleeves, as well as on the back and front, thus giving the earliest and the isolated fourteenth-century instance in England of the fourfold heraldic picture of the later tabards proper. It was not the custom with us for the jupon to be sleeved; its shape only allowed for the duplicate armorial representation, such as the surcoats and cyclases give. This is well shown by the very curious kneeling figure of Edward Despencer, 1375, at Tewkesbury.

The heraldic tabard, the light garment worn over the complete suits of steel, appears to have been introduced towards the end of the first quarter of the fifteenth century, and was the direct successor of the jupon. At first it had only elementary sleeves or wings—flappers—the armorials not appearing on them. The brass of John de Wantele, 1424, at Amberley, Sussex, seems to give the first form, and to be the earliest monumental representation of the new garment. This example is loose, with a full skirt, resembling, so far, the short-skirted jupons of the middle of the fourteenth century. It is apparent that for about fifty years the tabard formed no integral part of military costume, save when the display of armorials was imperative. Brasses do not indicate that it was in general use until about 1470, when it became not uncommon; but it is infrequently shown on these memorials, and rarely on effigies. In the last quarter of the fifteenth century, and the first of the sixteenth, knights were naturally averse to hiding their wonderful fluted suits of steel under a light silken tabard.

An early and striking example of this vestment on an effigy is shown by the figure of John Fitzalan, Earl of Arundel, 1434, at Arundel. This differs from that of Wantele in fitting to the waist, and represents the early settled shape. It has fully developed sleeves, or wings, charged, as on the body, with Arundel and Maltravers quarterly. In the last quarter of the century the waist was abandoned. Excellent and late examples are shown on the beautiful alabaster effigy of Edward Stafford, Earl of Wiltshire, 1499, at Lowick, in which a coat of eight quarters is four times presented; by the tabard of Sir John Spencer, 1522, at Brington; and by that of Sir Richard Knightley, 1534, at Fawsley, with a fourfold picture of twelve quarters, all in Northamptonshire. Many brasses of this time set forth, on somewhat stiff tabards, the arms of ancient houses; the Northamptonshire examples are shown as lightly embroidered, or painted, on linen or silk. They contrast very favourably with modern tabards, founded upon Dugdale, and utterly at variance with the style and character of ancient examples. The effigy of Sir John Spencer, 1599, also at Brington, exhibits a rigid tabard fitting to the waist, and embroidered with Spencer quarters. This is perhaps the latest example on an effigy in England. A reference to the manifold coats, sculptured and painted, on the striking array of Renaissance monuments of the Spencer family, may fittingly close this chapter, for we have left the ages of chivalry far behind, and the difference between the heraldry of the early fourteenth century—monumental in more than one sense—and that of the late sixteenth is very wide indeed. A. H.

CHAPTER VI

HERALDIC BRASSES

By WALTER J. KAYE, JUNR., B.A., F.S.A., F.S.A. SCOT.

Member of the Monumental Brass Society, London; Honorary Member of the Spalding Gentlemen's Society; Author of
"A Brief History of Gosberton, in the County of Lincoln."

MONUMENTAL brasses do not merely afford a guide to the capricious changes of fashion in armour, in ecclesiastical vestments (which have altered but little), and in legal, civilian, and feminine costume, but they provide us also with a vast number of admirable specimens of heraldic art. The vandal and the fanatic have robbed us of many of these beautiful memorials, but of those which survive to our own day the earliest on the continent of Europe marks the last resting-place of Abbot Ysowilpe, 1231, at Verden, in Hanover. In England there was once a brass, which unfortunately disappeared long ago, to an Earl of Bedford, in St. Paul's Church, Bedford, of the year 1208, leaving 1277 as the date of the earliest one.

Latten (Fr. *laiton*), the material of which brasses were made, was at an early date manufactured in large quantities at Cologne, whence plates of this metal came to be known as cullen (Köln) plates; these were largely exported to other countries, and the Flemish workmen soon attained the greatest proficiency in their engraving. Flemish brasses are usually large and rectangular, having the space between the figure and the marginal inscription filled either by diaper work or by small figures in niches. Brasses vary considerably in size: the matrix of Bishop Beaumont's brass in Durham Cathedral measures about 16 feet by 8 feet, and the memorial to Griel van Ruwescuere, in the chapel of the Lady Superior of the Béguinage at Bruges, is only about 1 foot square.

Brazen effigies are more numerous in England in the eastern and southern counties, than in parts more remote from the continent of Europe.

Armorial bearings are displayed in a great variety of ways on monumental brasses, some of which are exhibited in the rubbings selected for illustration. In most cases separate shields are placed above and below the figures. They occur also in the spandrils of canopies and in the shafts and finials of the same, as well as in the centre and at the angles of border-fillets. They naturally predominate in the memorials of warriors, where we find them emblazoned not only on shield

FIG. 30.—Brass in the Scarisbrick Chapel of Ormskirk Church, co. Lancs., to a member of the Scarisbrick family of that name. Arms: Gules, three mullets in bend between two bendlets engrailed argent. (From a rubbing by Walter J. Kaye.)

FIG. 31.—Brass of Margaret (daughter of Henry Percy, Earl of Northumberland), second wife of Henry, 1st Earl of Cumberland, in Skipton Parish Church. Arms: On the dexter side those of the Earl of Cumberland, on the sinister side those of Percy.

and pennon but on the scabbard and ailettes, and on the jupon, tabard, and cuirass also, while crests frequently occur on the tilting-helm. In one case (the brass of Sir Peter Legh, 1527, at Winwick, co. Lancaster) they figure upon the priestly chasuble. Walter Pescod, the merchant of Boston, Lincolnshire, 1398, wears a gown adorned with peascods—a play upon his name; and many a merchant's brass bears his coat of arms and merchant's mark beside, pointing a moral to not a few at the present day. The fifteenth and sixteenth centuries witnessed the greatest profusion in heraldic decoration in brasses, when the tabard and the heraldic mantle were evolved. A good example of the former remains in the parish church of Ormskirk, Lancashire, in the brass commemorating a member of the Scaris-

brick family, c. 1500 (Fig. 30). Ladies were accustomed at this time to wear their husbands' arms upon the mantle or outer garment and their own upon the kirtle, but the fashion which obtained at a subsequent period was to emblazon the husbands' arms on the dexter and their own on the sinister side of the mantle (Fig. 31).

The majority of such monuments, as we behold them now, are destitute of any indications of metals or tinctures, largely owing to the action of the varying degrees of temperature in causing contraction and expansion. Here and there, however, we may still detect traces of their pristine glory. But these matters received due attention from the engraver. To represent *or*, he left the surface of the brass untouched, except for gilding or perhaps polishing; this universal method has solved many heraldic problems. Lead or some other white metal was inlaid to indicate *argent*, and the various tinctures were supplied by the excision of a portion of the plate, thereby forming a depression, which was filled up by pouring in some resinous substance of the requisite colour. The various kinds of fur used in armory may be readily distinguished, with the sole exception of *vair* (*argent* and *azure*), which presents the appearance of a row of small upright shields alternating with a similar row reversed.

The earliest brass extant in England is that to Sir John D'Aubernoun, the elder (Fig. 32), at Stoke D'Abernon, in Surrey, which carries us back to the year 1277. The simple marginal inscription in Norman-French, surrounding the figure, and each Lombardic capital of which is set in its own matrix, reads: "Sire : John : Daubernoun : Chivaler : Gist : Icy : Deu : De : Sa : Alme : Eyt : Mercy : " [a] In the space between the inscription and the upper portion of the figure were two small shields, of which the dexter one alone remains, charged with the arms of the knight: "Azure, a chevron, or." Sir John D'Aubernoun is represented in a complete panoply of chain mail—his head being protected by a *coif de mailles*, which is joined to the *hauberk* or mailshirt, which extends to the hands, having apparently no divisions for the fingers, and being tightened by straps at the wrists. The legs, which are not crossed, are covered by long *chausses*, or stockings of mail, protected at the knees by *poleyns* or *genouillères* of *cuir bouilli* richly ornamented by elaborate designs. A surcoat, probably of linen, depends from the shoulders to a little below the knees, and is cut away to a point above the knee. This garment is tightly confined (as the creases in the surcoat show) at the waist by a girdle, and over it is passed a *guige* whereto the long sword is attached. "Pryck" spurs are fixed to the instep, and the feet rest upon a lion, whose mouth grasps the lower portion of a lance. The lance bears a pennon charged with a chevron, as also is the small heater-shaped shield borne on the knight's left arm. The whole composition measures about eight feet by three.

Heraldry figures more prominently in our second illustration, the brass to Sir Roger de Trumpington, 1289 (Fig. 33). This fine effigy lies under the canopy of an altar-tomb, so-called, in the church of St. Michael and All Angels, Trumpington, Cambridgeshire. It portrays the knight in armour closely resembling that already described, with these exceptions: the head rests upon a huge *heaume*, or tilting-helm, attached by a chain to the girdle, and the neck is here protected from side-thrusts by *ailettes* or oblong plates fastened behind the shoulders, and bearing the arms of Sir Roger. A dog here replaces the lion at the feet, the lance and pennon are absent, and the shield is rounded to the body. On

[a] Here lieth Sir John D'Aubernoun, knight. On his soul may God have mercy.

this brass the arms not only occur upon the shield, but also upon the ailettes, and are four times repeated on the scabbard. They afford a good example of "canting" arms: "Azure, crusilly and two trumpets palewise or, with a label of five points in chief, for difference." It is interesting also to notice that the engraver had not completed his task, for the short horizontal lines across the dexter side of the shield indicate his intention of cutting away the surface of the field.

Sir Robert de Setvans (formerly Septvans), whose

his arms: "Azure, a fess indented argent, between three crosslets botony, or." The first crosslet is charged with an annulet, probably as a mark of cadency. The engraver has omitted the indenture upon the fess, which, however, appears upon the shield. The knight's arms are protected by *epaulieres, brassarts, coutes,* and *vambraces;* his hands, holding a heart, by gauntlets of steel. An elaborate baldric passes round his waist, from which are suspended, on the left, a cross-hilted sword, in a slightly ornamented scabbard; on the right, a

FIG. 32.—Brass of Sir John D'Aubernoun at Stoke D'Abernon. Arms: Azure, a chevron or. (From a rubbing by Walter J. Kaye).

FIG. 33.—Brass of Sir Roger de Trumpington at Trumpington. Arms: Azure, crusilly and two trumpets palewise or. (From a rubbing by Walter J. Kaye.)

FIG. 34.—Brass of Sir William de Aldeburgh at Aldborough, Yorks. Arms: Azure, a fesse argent between three cross crosslets or. (From a rubbing by Walter J. Kaye.)

FIG. 35.—Brass of Elizabeth Knevet.

beautiful brass may be seen at Chartham, Kent, is habited in a surcoat whereon, together with the shield and ailettes, are seven winnowing fans—another instance of canting arms (Fig. 37). This one belongs to a somewhat later date, 1307.

Our next example is a mural effigy to Sir William de Aldeburgh, c. 1360, from the north aisle of Aldborough Church, near Boroughbridge, Yorkshire (Fig. 34). He is attired like the "veray parfite gentil knight" of Chaucer, in a *bascinet* or steel cap, to which is laced the *camail* or tippet of chain mail, and a hauberk almost concealed by a *jupon*, whereon are emblazoned

misericorde, or dagger of mercy. The thighs are covered by *cuisses*—steel plates, here deftly concealed probably by satin or velvet secured by metal studs—the knees by *genouillères,* the lower leg by *jambes,* which reveal chausses of mail at the interstices. Sollerets, or long, pointed shoes, whereto are attached rowel spurs, complete his outfit. The figure stands upon a bracket bearing the name "Will's de Aldeburgh."

The parish church of Eastington, Gloucestershire, contains a brass to Elizabeth Knevet, which is illustrated and described by Mr. Cecil T. Davis at p. 117 of his excellent work on the "Monumental Brasses of

THE ART OF HERALDRY

Gloucestershire." [b] The block (Fig. 35), which presents a good example of the heraldic mantle, has been very kindly placed at my disposal by Mr. Davis. To confine our description to the heraldic portion of the brass, we find the following arms upon the mantle:—

"Quarterly, 1. argent, a bend sable, within a bordure engrailed azure (Knevet); 2. argent, a bend azure, and chief, gules (Cromwell); 3. chequy or and gules, a chief ermine (Tatshall); 4. chequy or and gules, a bend ermine (De Cailly or Clifton); 5. paly of six within a bordure bezanté . . . 6. bendy of six, a canton . . ." [c]

A coat of arms occurs also at each corner of the slab: "Nos. 1 and 4 are on ordinary shields, and 2 and 3 on lozenges. Nos. 1 and 3 are charged with the same bearings as are on her mantle. No. 2, on a lozenge, quarterly, 1. Knevet; 2. Cromwell; 3. Tatshall; 4. Cailli; 5. De Woodstock; 6. paly of six within a bordure; 7. bendy of six, a canton; 8. or, a chevron gules (Stafford); 9. azure, a bend cottised between six

[b] "Monumental Brasses of Gloucestershire," by C. T. Davis. London: Phillimore & Co., 1899.
[c] The arms are quoted by Mr. Davis from Bigland's "Gloucestershire," p. 539.

lioncels rampant, or (de Bohun). No. 4 similar to No. 1, with the omission of 2 and 3."

In later times thinner plates of metal were employed a fact which largely contributed to preclude much of the boldness in execution hitherto displayed. A prodigality in shading, either by means of parallel lines or by cross-hatching, also tended to mar the beauty of later work of this kind. Nevertheless there are some good brasses of the Stuart period. These sometimes consist of a single quadrangular plate, with the upper portion occupied by armorial bearings and emblematical figures, the centre by an inscription, and the lower portion by a representation of the deceased, as at Forcett, in the North Riding of Yorkshire. Frequently, however, as at Rotherham and Rawmarsh, in the West Riding of the same county, the inscription is surmounted by a view of the whole family, the father kneeling on a cushion at a fald-stool, with his sons in a similar attitude behind him, and the mother likewise engaged with her daughters on the opposite side, while the armorial insignia find a place on separate shields above.

W. J. K.

CHAPTER VII

THE WEARING OF ARMS: PLATES V. AND VI.

BEFORE it is possible to pass to the consideration of heraldry, either as a science with its rules and regulations, or as an art or means of decoration with the various examples of the employment of armory for that purpose, it would be well to refer to the method in which armorial insignia were actually worn or carried in battle and tournament, and on Plates V. and VI. examples will be found taken from different sources. On Plate V. Fig. 1 is a representation of Lazarius Marcellinus Gerardini, head of the Genoese Government. The date is about 1248. (The representation is taken from *Cafari et continuatorum Annales Januæ a 1099–1294, Monumenta Germaniæ Historicæ*, by G. H. Pertz, xviii. B., 1863, Plate III.) Banner, surcoat, and the clothing of the horse, and even the knight's saddle, show the arms: "Argent, a lion rampant guardant azure." As crest appears "a peacock in pride."

Fig. 2 represents Herr Hartmann v. Owe, a Swabian Knight and Minnesinger, who had been the retainer of a baronial family. He was probably born somewhere about 1165, and died between 1210 and 1220. On his shield of sable he bears three eagles' heads erased argent, two and one, and the horsecloth is adorned with a repetition of the charges, which are not restricted in number. The crest on the helmet is likewise an eagle's head, but here it is of azure, collared and beaked or. In the Heidelberg Minnesinger MS. "Book of Songs" (see the letterpress accompanying Plate LXXIII.) the arms of von Owe are the same but with different tinctures, appearing as: Azure, three eagles' heads argent, armed or; crest, an eagle's head argent, armed or. The horsecloth shows the same eagles' heads as the shield, as does also the banner with which the knight is there equipped.

Fig. 3 is Herr Wahsmut v. Kunzich (Künzingen). The Künzingens, one of whom, this Wahsmut, was well known as a Minnesinger, were settled in Baden, where, to the S.W. of Donaueschingen, the Künsingen Castle stable still exists. He bears for arms: Vert, two trout, and on his pot helmet two red fish. On his green banner appear four trout in pale. The Heidelberg

Roll shows these arms in a different form, namely: "Azure, two fish argent," and on the helmet two fish argent, whilst on a blue banner are three silver fishes. Both of these equestrian figures are taken from the *Weingartner Liederhandschrift* (Weingarten "Book of Songs"), of which fuller details will be found later.

Fig. 4 is "Le Comte de Charolais le Téméraire." This is Charles the Bold (afterwards Duke of Burgundy), the son of Philip the Good of Burgundy, who during his father's lifetime, until his accession in 1467, bore the title of Count of Charolais, from the Lordship of Charolais purchased in 1390. The surcoat and horsecloths bear the arms of the ducal house, over which is placed a white label with three points. The coat of Burgundy is quartered, and charged with the shield of Flanders: Or, a lion rampant sable. The first and fourth quarters show the modern arms of Burgundy: Azure, semé-de-lis or, within a border compony gules and argent. The second quarter is party per pale, on the dexter the old arms of Burgundy: Bendy of six or and azure, within a bordure gules; and on the sinister the arms of the Duchy of Brabant: Sable, a lion rampant or, armed gules. The third quarter is also divided per pale and shows on the dexter the ancient arms of Burgundy again, and on the sinister the arms of the Duchy of Limburg: Argent, a lion rampant gules, crowned and armed or, langued azure. On his tilting helmet, over which the arms of New Burgundy are depicted, he bears the old crest of France (a fleur-de-lis or), and round his neck he wears the collar of the Order of the Golden Fleece. [The quarterings are numbered, and the terms dexter and sinister are used in the above description as would be correct if the coat of arms were depicted on a shield.]

Fig. 5 is the Duke of Brabant. In this case also, the surcoat and horsecloth are adorned with armorial bearings: Sable, a lion rampant or. The barred helmet with its ermine mantling bears a pair of wings, composed of peacocks' feathers and ermine, and between these wings is a peacock's tail.

The two last drawings (about 24.5 centimetres high)

32

THE ART OF HERALDRY

are taken from the publication *Ancien Armorial équestre de la Toison d'or et de l'Europe au xv. Siècle*, Paris, 1890, a manuscript of the fifteenth century belonging to the *Bibliothèque de l'Arsenal*, Paris, No. 4790, the author of which was probably a heraldic officer of Duke Philip the Good. His sketches conclude with the promotion of a Knight of the Golden Fleece in 1461. Fig. 4 is taken from the *Armorial de la Toison d'or*. Fig. 5 is from the *Armorial de l'Europe*.

On Plate VI. are representations of figures taken from Tournament Rolls, and these show the customary array worn at tournaments in the fifteenth century by those taking part. It will be noticed that all the figures are armed only with a sword, and perhaps it may be well to add a word of warning on the subject of tournaments. There were two distinct methods of encounter; the most familiar being the joust or tilting with spears; the other being the tourney with swords. In the figures which are reproduced the helmet is in each case barred, and the combatants sit raised up on a high saddle in order not to be hindered in the handling of their weapons by their own horses. The upper group shows the Duke of Brittany, Fig. 1 (arms: Ermine; crest, out of a coronet, a golden leopard sitting between ermine horns), in combat with the Duke of Bourbon, Fig. 2 (arms: Azure, semé-de-lis or, a bendlet gules; crest, on a wreath or, azure, and gules, a fleur-de-lis set with red bunches[a]), whose arms are repeated on their clothing, and on the horsecloths. The date must be from 1440 to 1450. The two figures are orginally from the Tournament Book of King René d'Anjou (see the description of Plate I. Fig. 2), reproduced by Raphael Jaqumin in his book *Iconographie générale et méthodique du Costume du iv. au xix. Siècle*.

The lower group shows two German knights, one Wolmershausen, Fig. 3 (arms: Gules, two bars argent; crest, a high hat gules, turned up silver, the upper part of the hat as the shield, and adorned with a bunch of feathers), and, as may be concluded from the formation of the crest, doubtless a knight from the Rhineland. Fig. 4 (arms: Barry of six azure and or; crest, the same shield between two azure wings). The date is 1471. Possibly this latter knight belonged to the family of Pallandt, who bore the same coat of arms in other tinctures.

"Neithardt von Wolmershausen" and "Thomann von Pallandt" were, according to Raidenbucher's Tournament Book, ardent and eager frequenters of the tournaments of that period (about 1481 in Heidelberg, 1484 in Stuttgart, &c.).

In conclusion follows an equestrian figure of the Emperor Maximilian I. (Fig. 36), in the year 1508, copied from a drawing of Hans Burgkmair. The architectural framing of the original, as here not appertaining to the subject, has been omitted to save space. According to a hand-painted print of the same time, the Emperor wears a black and gold mantling to his helmet, and the horse a black bridle, its iron head-piece, chaffron, and other armour decorated with gold buttons and pink fringe! The escutcheon on the breast of the horse shows the old Austrian armorial shield; the hindmost, the new Austrian shield, laid upon the flames of the flint, from the collar of the Order of the Golden Fleece.

FIG. 36.—The Emperor Maximilian I.

Besides the Tournament Rolls, the monumental brasses, a few of which still exist in remarkably fine preservation, furnish us with other good contemporary evidence of the manner in which armorial bearings were depicted when they were actually worn. These have been more fully dealt with in Chapters V. and VI.

Perhaps the best of all for this purpose is the brass of Sir Robert de Septvans in Chartham Church, Kent, which shows the arms upon both shield and surcoat. The accompanying illustration (Fig. 37) is from a rubbing which was taken by R. Lawrence Marsh in March 1898. A reference to the reproduction of this brass in Eve's "Decorative Heraldry" shows that it must have suffered in modern times, inasmuch as the head of the lion, upon which the feet are resting, is no longer visible.[b] The date of the brass is 1306.

The father of Sir Robert was present with King Richard I. at Acre; but Sir Robert himself does not seem to have joined the Crusade, though there is record of his being present at the siege of Caerlaverock, near Dumfries, A.D. 1300.

In Cooper's "Winchelsea" (p. 61), the author writes: "But after this, the very next ensuing year (32 Edward I.), upon an inquisition taken by Robert de Septem Vannis, Will. de Hastings, and Rob. Paulyn, whom the King had assigned to take view of the banks

---

[a] There is no equivalent English term for this if it be a heraldic detail. Possibly it is no more than illuminative decoration.

[b] Haines, writing in 1861, says, "The head and legs of the lion beneath the feet are now lost."

and ditches in this county, and to cause them to be repaired (which was returned into Chancery), it was found that the said marsh of Winchelsea could not be defended and preserved by the old wall, situated towards the east; and that if it ought to be defended, it would be necessary to have a new bank there, of the length of 350 perches, and that the said new bank could not be made by those who, according to the ancient composition before mentioned, had wont to repair the old bank, forasmuch as those who were in the soil liable to the repairs of the said bank were not able, in regard of the diminution of their lands, to bear the whole charge themselves. He therefore directed another precept unto the said Thomas Alard, requiring him to take care that such contribution should be made thereto out of his own lands and the lands of others as is above expressed. And hereupon the said King issued out a commission to the said Robert, William, and Robert to see that the contribution which the said King's bailiff was to make therein should be well and also faithfully assessed."

This brass belongs to the earliest, or "surcoat" period, during which entire suits of mail were worn, ending with the death of Edward I., 1307.

The armour may be described as follows: The hawberk, or shirt of mail, reaching nearly to the knees, slit up a short way in front for convenience in riding; the coif de mailles, or hood, which wraps round the neck and head, and fastens across the forehead with an interlaced strap; the chausses, or stockings, sometimes of two pieces, and joined at the knee by garters, encasing the thighs, legs, and feet; the long sleeves, terminating in mufflers, or gloves not divided into fingers, which are fastened round the wrist by straps; the genouillères (i.e. kneepieces), probably made of ordinary leather, or else of a prepared kind termed *cuir-bouilli*, and usually much ornamented. The surcoat was of linen or cloth, and was worn over the armour. It was a short skirt, open in front, and confined round the waist by a narrow belt or cord. The shield in this case is large and concave to the body. The spurs are single-pointed, or "pryck" spurs, and are buckled around the ankles and secured by straps, passing across the instep and under the foot. In this case ailettes are worn. These were made of leather, and tied on by silk cords; they were probably intended for

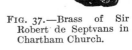

defence. The sword is large and cross-hilted, very handsome, with a highly-ornamented scabbard. It is hung in front from a broad belt fastened round the hips. The name of Setvans, or "seven fans," is derived from the ancient cognizance of the family, or, more probably, *vice versâ*, though it would seem that the shield displayed but three gold fans upon an azure field.

The rubbing of the brass in Fig. 38 was also taken by Mr. Lawrence Marsh, who writes concerning it: "One of the earliest brasses commemorative of ladies is the one in Trotton Church, Sussex, of Margaret, Lady Camoys, who died in the year 1310.

"She was the daughter and heiress of Sir John de Gatesden, and was the second wife of Sir John Camoys. This lady was granted, with her property, by a formal deed, to William Paynell, whom she married after the death of Sir John Camoys. From this brass has been abstracted a series of small shields, with which originally the robe of the lady in this most valuable memorial was semé. Their loss is to be the more regretted, not only because they were doubtless enamelled, but as a very singular specimen of costume; for this is the only sepulchral brass known to have presented this peculiar feature of ornament; and it would have been deserving of attention to ascertain whether the arms thus introduced were her own (Gatesden), those of Camoys, or those of Paynell.

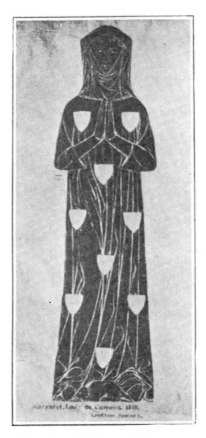

FIG. 38.—The Brass of Margaret, Lady Camoys.

"The wimple, that strange covering for the throat, chin, and the sides of the face, is here very distinctly seen. It is adjusted after a fashion prevalent in the early part of the Edwardian era, and in such a manner as to impart a triangular outline to the features. A single curl of hair appears on either side of the forehead, which is encircled by a narrow enriched fillet; and upon the head, and falling grace-

fully upon the shoulders, is a coverchef. A super-tunic envelops the entire person; it has no waist-cincture, its sleeves are loose and terminate somewhat below the elbow, thus displaying no more of the kirtle, which was worn beneath, than the tight sleeves, buttoned closely to the wrists. The clasped and uplifted hands are bare. A fine pedimental canopy, with slender side-shafts and pinnacles, eight small shields of arms, the border fillets with the letters of the legend which they enclosed, and a profusion of small stars and other ornaments with which it was semé, have been abstracted from the marble slab. The border legend, written in Longobardic capitals, originally was as follows: 'Margarete de Camoys gist ici. Dieu de sa alme eut merci. Amen.'"

Fig. 39 represents the Dauphin (afterwards Charles VI. of France) in his surcoat or "cloak of arms," from a contemporary miniature painting, together with a representation of the banner of Louis the Dauphin, from a contemporary picture of the Siege of Dieppe in 1442.

Fig. 40 shows the wearing of arms as a part of her clothing by a daughter of John, Duke of Berry (cousin of King Charles VI.), as represented in a piece of contemporary embroidery.

H. S., R. L. M., AND A. C. F-D.

CHAPTER VIII

THE COMPONENT PARTS OF AN ACHIEVEMENT

HAVING dealt with armory as actually used in warfare and tournament for the decoration of arms and armour, we now come to the science of armory and the rules governing the display of these marks of honour. We shall pass later to its application as an art to other purposes of decoration. The term "coat of arms," as we have seen, is derived from the textile garment or "surcoat" which was worn over the armour, and which bore in embroidery a duplication of the design upon the shield. There can be very little doubt that arms themselves are older than the fact of the surcoat or the term "coat of arms." The entire heraldic or armorial decoration which any one is entitled to bear may consist of many things. It must as a minimum consist of a shield of arms, for whilst there are many coats of arms in existence, and many still rightly in use at the present day, to which no crest belongs, a crest in this country cannot lawfully exist without its complementary coat of arms. For the last two certainly, and probably nearly three centuries, no grant of personal arms has ever been issued without it containing the grant of a crest except in the case of a grant to a woman, who of course cannot bear or transmit a crest; or else in the case of arms borne in right of women or descent from women, through whom naturally no right to a crest could have been transmitted. Such grants as I refer to as exceptions are those of quarterings and impalements to be borne with other arms, or else exemplifications following upon the assumption of name and arms which in fact and theory are regrants of previously existing arms, in which cases the regrant is of the original coat with or without a crest, as the case may be, and as the arms theretofor existed. Grants of *impersonal* arms also need not include a crest. As it has been impossible for the last two centuries to obtain a grant of arms without its necessarily accompanying grant of crest, a decided distinction attaches to the lawful possession of arms which have no crest belonging to them, for of necessity the arms must be at least two hundred years old. Bearing this in mind, one cannot but wonder at the actions of some ancient families like those of Astley and Pole, who, lawfully possessing arms concerning which there is and can be no doubt or question, yet nevertheless invent and use crests which have no authority.

One instance and one only do I know where a crest has had a legitimate existence without any coat of arms. This case is that of the family of Buckworth, who at the time of the Visitations exhibited arms and crest. The arms infringed upon those of another family, and no sufficient proof could be produced to compel their admission as borne of right. The arms were respited for further proof, while the crest was allowed, presumably tentatively, and whilst awaiting the further proof for the arms; no proof, however, was made. The arms and crest remained in this position until the year 1806, when Sir Buckworth Buckworth-Herne, whose father had assumed the additional name of Herne, obtained a Royal Licence to bear the name of Soame in addition to and after those of Buckworth-Herne, with the arms of Soame quarterly with the arms of Buckworth. It then became necessary to prove the right to these arms of Buckworth, and they were accordingly regranted with the trifling addition of an ermine spot upon the chevron; consequently this solitary instance has now been rectified, and I cannot learn of any other instance where these exceptional circumstances have similarly occurred; and there never has been a grant of a crest alone unless arms have been in existence previously.

Whilst arms may exist alone, and the decoration of a shield form the only armorial ensign of a person, such need not be the case; and it will usually be found that the armorial bearings of an ordinary commoner consist of shield, crest, and motto. To these must naturally be added the helmet and mantling, which become an essential to other than an abbreviated achievement when a crest has to be displayed. It should be remembered, however, that the helmet is not specifically granted, and apparently is a matter of inherent right, so that a person would not be in the wrong in placing a helmet and mantling above a shield even when no crest exists to surmount the helmet. The motto is usually to be found but is not a necessity, and there are many more coats of arms which have never been used with a motto than shields which exist without a crest. Sometimes a *cri-de-guerre* will be found instead of or in addition to a motto. The escutcheon may have supporters, or it may be displayed upon an eagle or a lymphad, &c., for which particular additions no other generic term has yet been coined save the very inclusive one of "exterior ornaments." A coronet of rank may form a part of the achievement, and the shield may be encircled by the "ribbons" or the "circles," or by the Garter of the various Orders of Knighthood, and by their collars. Below it may depend the badge of a Baronet of Nova Scotia, or of an Order of Knighthood, and added to it may possibly be what is termed a compartment, though this is a feature almost entirely peculiar to Scottish armory. There is also the crowning distinction of a badge; and of all armorial insignia this is the most cherished, for the existing badges are but few in number. Those that remain are those of persons all of whom without exception belong to the most ancient British families. The escutcheon may be placed in front of the crosiers of a bishop, the batons of the Earl Marshal, or similar ornaments. It may be displayed upon a mantle of estate, or it may be borne beneath a pavilion. With one more addition the list is complete, and that is the banner. These were anciently of quite distinct design from the arms. For these several features of armory reference must be made to the various chapters in which they are treated. Suffice it here to remark

that whilst the term "coat of arms" has through the slip-shod habits of English philology come to be used to signify a representation of any heraldic bearing, the correct term for the whole emblazonment is "achievement," most frequently employed to signify the whole, but which can correctly be used to signify anything which a man is entitled to represent of an armorial character. Had not the recent revival of interest in armory taken place, we should have found a firmly rooted and even yet more slipshod declension, for a few years ago the habit of the uneducated in styling anything stamped upon a sheet of notepaper a crest, was fast becoming stereotyped into current acceptance.

A. C. F-D.

CHAPTER IX

THE SHIELD

THE shield is the most important part of the achievement, for on it are depicted the signs and emblems of the house to which it appertains; the different marks expressive of the cadency of the members within that house; the augmentations of honour which the sovereign has conferred; the quarterings inherited from families which are represented, and the impalements of marriage; and it is with the shield principally that the laws of armory are concerned, for everything else is dependent upon the shield, and falls into comparative insignificance alongside of it. Let us first consider the shield itself, without reference to the charges it carries. A shield may be depicted in any fashion and after any shape that the imagination can suggest, which shape and fashion have been accepted at any time as the shape and fashion of a shield. There is no law upon the subject. The various shapes adopted in emblazonments in past ages, and used at the present time in imitation of past usage— for luckily the present period has evolved no special shield of its own—are purely the result of artistic design, and have been determined at the periods they have been used in heraldic art by no other consideration than the particular theory of design that has happened to dominate the decoration, and the means and ends of such decoration of that period. The lozenge certainly is reserved for and indicative of the achievements of the female sex, but, save for this one exception, the matter may be carried further, and arms be depicted upon a banner, a parallelogram, a square, a circle, or an oval; and even then one would be correct, for the purposes of armory, in describing such figures as shields when they are made the vehicles for the emblazonment of a design which properly and originally should be borne upon a shield. Let no one think that a design ceases to be a coat of arms if it is not displayed upon a shield. Many people have thought to evade the authority of the Crown as the arbiter of coat-armour, and the penalties of taxation imposed by the Revenue by using designs without depicting them upon a shield. This little deception has always been borne in mind, for we find in the Royal Warrants of Queen Elizabeth commanding the Visitations that the King of Arms to whom the warrant was addressed was to "correcte, cumptrolle and refourme all mann' of armes, crests, cognizaunces and devices unlawfull or unlawfully usurped, borne or taken by any p'son or p'sons within the same p'vince cont*ry to the due order of the laws of armes, and the

same to rev'se, put downe or otherwise deface at his discrecon as well in coote armors, helmes, standerd, pennons and hatchmets of tents and pavilions, as also in plate jewells, pap', parchement, wyndowes, gravestones and monuments, or elsewhere wheresoev' they be sett or placed, whether they be in shelde, schoocheon, lozenge, square, rundell or otherwise howsoev' cont*rie to the autentiq' and aunciant lawes, cust-tomes, rules, privileges and orders of armes."

The Act 32 & 33 Victoria, section 19, defines (for the purpose of the taxation it enforced) armorial bearings to mean and include "any armorial bearing, crest, or ensign, by whatever name the same shall be called, and whether such armorial bearing, crest, or ensign shall be registered in the College of Arms or not."

The shape of the shield throughout the rest of Europe has also varied between wide extremes, and at no time has any one particular shape been assigned to or peculiar to any country, rank, or condition, save possibly with one exception, namely, that the use of the cartouche or oval seems to have been very nearly universal with ecclesiastics in France, Spain, and Italy, though

FIG. 41.—Taken from the tomb of Geoffrey Plantagenet, Count of Anjou.

never reserved exclusively for their use. Probably this was an attempt on the part of the Church to get away from the military character of the shield. It is in keeping with the rule by which, even at the present day, a bishop or a cardinal bears neither helmet nor crest, using in place thereof his ecclesiastical mitre or tasselled hat, and by which the clergy, both abroad and in this country, seldom made use of a crest in depicting their arms. A clergyman in this country, however, has never been denied the right of using a crest (if he possesses one and chooses to display it) until he reaches episcopal rank. A grant of arms to a clergyman at the present day depicts his achievement with helmet, mantling, and crest in identical form with those adopted for any one else. But the laws of armory, official and amateur, have always denied the right to make use of a crest to bishop, archbishop, and cardinal.

At the present day, if a grant of arms is made to a bishop of the Established Church, the emblazonment at the head of his patent consists of shield and mitre only. The laws of the Church of England, however, require no vow of celibacy from its ecclesiastics, and consequently the descendants of a bishop would be placed in the position of having no crest to display if the bishop and his requirements were alone considered. So that in the case of a grant to a bishop the crest is granted for his descendants in a separate clause, being depicted by itself in the body of the patent apart from the emblazonment "in the margin hereof," which in an ordinary patent is an emblazonment of the whole achievement. A similar method is adopted in cases in which the actual patentee is a woman, and where, by the limitations attached to the patent being extended beyond herself, males are brought in who will bear the arms granted to the patentee as their pronominal arms. In these cases the arms of the patentee are depicted upon a lozenge at the head of the patent, the crest being depicted separately elsewhere. Whilst shields were actually used in warfare the utilitarian article largely governed the shape of the artistic ones, but after the fifteenth century they gradually left the beaten track of utility and passed wholly into the cognisance of art and design. The earliest shape of all is the long, narrow shape, which is now but seldom seen. This was curved to protect the body, which it nearly covered, and an interesting example of this is to be found in the monumental slab of champléve enamel, part of the tomb of Geoffrey Plantagenet, Count of Anjou (Fig. 41), the ancestor of our own Royal dynasty of Plantagenet, who died in the year 1150. This tomb was formerly in the cathedral of Le Mans, and is now in the museum there. I shall have occasion again to refer to it. The shield is blue; the lions are gold.

Other forms of the same period are found with curved tops, in the shape of an inverted pear, but the form known as the heater-shaped shield is to all intents and purposes the earliest shape which was used for armorial purposes. This is to be found on Plates LXXI. and LXXII., and on Plate VII. Fig. 1. This last mentioned plate represents the development of the heraldic shield

FIG. 42.—Shield of the Landgrave Konrad of Thuringia (died 1241).

upon the Continent. Impossible as the later variations there shown are for the purposes of war, they do not reach the depths of absurdity which have been perpetrated, and perpetrated officially, in this country, for if they were impossible in war, they were at any rate decorative. The English varieties too frequently were not.

The church of St. Elizabeth at Marburg, in Hesse, affords examples of shields which are exceedingly interesting, inasmuch as they are original and contemporary even if only pageant shields. Those which now remain are the shields of the Landgrave Konrad (d. 1241) of Thuringia and of Henry of Thuringia (d. 1298). The shield of the former (see Fig. 42) is 90 centimetres high and 74 wide. Konrad was Landgrave of Thuringia and Grand Master of the Teutonic Order of Knighthood. His arms show the lion of Thuringia barry of gules and argent on a field of azure, and between the hind feet a small shield, with the arms of the Teutonic Order of Knights. The only remains of the lion's mane are traces of the nails. The body of the lion is made of pressed leather, and the yellow claws have been supplied with a paint-brush. A precious stone probably represented the eye.

The making and decorating of the shields lay mostly in the hands of the herald painters, known in Germany as *Schilter*, who in addition to attending to the shield and crest, also had charge of all the riding paraphernalia, because those too were heraldically decorated. Many of these shield-workers' fraternities won widespread fame for themselves, and enjoyed great consideration at that time.

Thus the "History of a Celebrated Painters' Guild on the Lower Rhine" tells us of costly shields which the shield-workers of Paris had supplied, 1260, &c. Vienna, too, was the home of a not unimportant shield-workers' guild, and the town archives of Vienna contain writings of the fifteenth century treating of this subject. For instance, we learn that in an order of St. Luke's parish, June 28, 1446, with regard to the masterpiece of a member of the guild—

"Item, ein Schilter sol machen vir newe Stukeh mit sein selbs hand, ain Stechsatl, ain prustleder, ain Rosskoph und ain stechschilt das sol er tun in acht wochen und soll auch das mit sein selbs hanol malen kunnen als es Ritter und Knecht an Jn vordernt."

"Item, a shield-worker shall make four new pieces of work with his own hand, a jousting saddle, a leather apron, a horse's head-piece, and a jousting shield, that shall he do in eight weeks, and must be able to paint it with his own hand, as Knight and man-at-arms shall direct."

The shield was of wood, covered with linen or leather, the charges in relief and painted. Leather plastic was very much esteemed in the early Middle Ages. The leather was soaked in oil, and pressed or beaten into shape. Besides piecing and leather plastic, pressed linen (linen dipped in chalk and lime) was also used,

THE ART OF HERALDRY

and a kind of tempera painting on a chalk background. After the shield was decorated with the charges, it was frequently strengthened with metal clasps, or studs, particularly those parts which were more especially exposed to blows and pressure. These clasps and nails originally had no other object than to make the shield stronger and more durable, but later on their nature was misunderstood; they were treated and used as genuine heraldic charges, and stereotyped into hereditary designs. The long strips with which the edge was bound were called the "frame" (*Schildgestell*), the clasps introduced in the middle of the shield the "buckle" or "umbo" (see on Fig. 41), from which frequently circularly arranged metal snaps reached the edge of the shield. This latter method of strengthening the shield was called the "Buckelrîs," a figure which was afterwards frequently employed as a heraldic charge, and is known by the name of *Lilienhaspel* (Lily-staple) or *Glevenrad* (see Plate X. Fig. 57), or, as we term it in England, the escarbuncle.

In the second half of the fourteenth century, when the tournament provided the chief occasion for the shield, the jousting-shield, called in Germany the *Tartsche* or *Tartscher* came into use, and from this class of shield the most varied shapes were gradually developed (see Plate VII. Figs. 6–12). These *Tartschen* were decidedly smaller than the earlier Gothic shields, being only about one-fifth of a man's height. They were concave, and had on the side of the knight's right hand a circular indentation. This was the spear-rest, in which to place the tilting-spear. The later art of heraldic decoration symmetrically repeated the spear-rest on the sinister side of the shield, and, by so doing, transformed a useful fact into a matter of merely artistic design. Doubtless they argued that if indentations were correct at one point in the outline they were correct at another, and when once the actual fact was departed from the imagination of designers knew no limits. No doubt this was the beginning and source of the era of shields such as Figs. 43 to 46. But if the spear-rest as such is introduced into the outline of a shield it should be on the dexter side.

The arms which have been chosen as examples (Plate VII.) for display upon the shields, though they have no particular relation to the shape of the shield selected for their display, are as follows:—

Fig. 1. The original "heater-shaped" shield (twelfth and thirteenth centuries): Gules, a chamois argent, armed sable, langued or, environed about the loins with a collar sable, garnished and ringed or, and set with three turquoise. These are the arms of the Graf von Wilczek. The Wilczeks bore originally the Polish arms of Koziel, viz. a bouquetin (*Capra Ibex*); it was only during the course of the fifteenth century that they changed the ibex into a chamois.

Fig. 2. Shape of shield, fourteenth century. The arms are: Or, a bull's head erased and affronté sable, crowned proper, armed argent, the tongue extended gules. These are the arms of the Dukes of Mecklenburg, from a seal of Duke Albrecht II., 1349 (see *Deutsche Wappenrolle*, Fig. 65).

Fig. 3. Shape of shield, fifteenth century. The arms are: Argent, a bear rampant sable, armed gules. Arms of the Swiss canton and town of Appenzell. The rampant bear here, taken from the Legend of St. Gallus, is found for the first time on the seal of Appenzell, on a document of the year 1405. Stumpf, in his "Swiss Chronicle," speaks expressly of the red arming: "einen freyen schwartzen aufrechten Bären mit roten klawen" . . . ("a free, black, upright bear with red claws").

Fig. 4. Shape of shield, French of the fifteenth century. The arms here are: Or, on a bend gules between a gannet in chief azure and a martlet in base sable, three alerions argent. Arms of the duchy of Lorraine.

Mutilated birds are a peculiarity of West European heraldry, and frequently occur in English and French armory. The eagle without feet, and frequently also without a beak, is called an "alerion"; the mutilated ducks, "gannets"; and the swallows, "martlets." We shall have occasion to again refer to these.

Fig. 5. The shape of this shield is fifteenth-century. The arms are: Azure, a boar rampant argent, armed and crined or. Arms of the Ertzingen family in Swabia. A Friedrich von Ertzingen also appears amongst the slain at the battle of Sempach, 1386.

A boar rampant is almost unknown in British armory; in fact the only instance which has come under my notice is the coat matriculated in Lyon Register (*circa* 1672) which is blazoned "barry of six argent and gules, over all a boar rampant azure." Two boars rampant combatant, however, figure in the arms attributed to an Irish family named MacSweeney.

Fig. 6. Type of shield, German, latter half of fifteenth century. The arms are: Or, three stags' attires fesswise in pale azure. These are the arms of the county of Nellenburg. (Veringen bears the same charges, originally sable, but later gules; Würtemberg also the same, but sable). The lower antler, in a pointed shield or any kind of a shield growing narrower towards the base, is always represented with a lesser number of points (or "tines," as they are termed in Scotland) than those placed above it. On a square field this diminution would be superfluous; but it has become so customary in Germany, where this charge is more frequently met with than in England, that the omission would be regarded by heraldic pedants as a grievous mistake.

Fig. 7. This type of shield is an example of the transition towards the "Renaissance" shape of shield, and belongs to the end of the fifteenth century. The arms are: Argent, a mastiff rampant gules, gorged with a spiked collar or.

Fig. 8, which shows the spear-rest for placing the tilting-spear in, is a type belonging to the middle of the fifteenth century. The arms depicted are: Gules, a talbot passant argent, langued or.

Fig. 9, which also shows the spear-rest, belongs to the sixteenth century. The arms depicted are: Azure, a goat rampant or, armed sable, which are the arms of the Counts von Hohenembs in Vorarlberg. The old knights Von Ems, met with as early as the twelfth century, bore originally only the upper part of the body of a goat on their shield. In 1560 the Hohenembs family were raised to the rank of Counts of the Empire, but became extinct in the year 1759. The feudal "county" reverted to Austria.

Figs. 10, 11, and 12 are all sixteenth-century types of the Renaissance shield.

The arms on Fig. 10 are: Gules, on a mount in base vert, a crane argent, beaked or, holding with the dexter foot a stone proper. The crane is often made use of as the symbol of watchfulness, the old idea being that the bird held the stone in order not to fall asleep. "Wenne daz stainel vellt, so erwacht er und schreit" ("When the little stone falls, he wakes and cries out"), relates Konrad von Megenberg, about the year 1350. The crest of the Scottish Lords Cranstoun was a crane holding a stone. The pun is obvious, but the crane was always depicted asleep, with the head beneath the wing. The idea of watchfulness, however, is amply vindicated by the curious motto of the family, "Thou shalt want ere I want."

Fig. 11. Renaissance shield (sixteenth century). There are no British terms equivalent to the blazoning of the arms shown, and the literal translation of the

German blazon is: "Blue, a silver point spreading out; on the right at the top a golden lily, on the left

See Figs. 43, 44, 45, and 46, drawn by Jost Amman about 1566 and 1589.

FIG. 43.

FIG. 44.

FIG. 45.

FIG. 46.

a silver sea-leaf notched (or indented) in the form of a trefoil (a figure which was earlier erroneously described as 'beetle-horns'), and in base a rose gules, seeded or and barbed vert." One might, however, attempt the blazon by rendering it "per pile throughout, arched and reversed azure and argent in chief, on the dexter side a fleur-de-lis or, on the sinister a sea-leaf indented as a trefoil argent, and in base a rose gules, barbed and seeded proper." The French have an accepted term, *chapé-ployé*, for this peculiar division of the field.

The arms shown in Fig. 12 are: Or, a lime-tree (linden) eradicated proper. It is the coat of arms of the Bavarian town of Lindau, on Lake Constance. This device appears on a large seal of the town as early as the thirteenth century, only in that instance there is an aquatic bird of the fashion of a duck standing on each side of the roots.

In the second half of the sixteenth century, the shape of the shield becomes decoratively treated, and is then of a purely ornamental outline. The carved edges roll up, and the shield gradually becomes a cartouche.

Figs. 43–45 are taken from Amman's *Wappen-und Stammbuche* (Book of Arms and Genealogy), Fig. 46 from Rixner's *Turnier-buch* (Tournament Book).

Fig. 43. Gules, two bends or, is the coat of Hutten.

Fig. 44. Or, a harp sable, the arms of Landschaden.

Fig. 45. Per fess argent and azure, in chief a demi-wheel gules and in base a fleur-de-lis of the first, the arms of Volkamer.

Fig. 46. Argent, three helmets azure (the literal translation is "iron hat," but the charges more nearly approach the helmet than the morion).

The official types of shield adopted in England, and as a consequence almost universally imitated, were neither artistic nor particularly heraldic.

It should not be supposed that I am here condemning the officers of arms in this country. They were simply imbued with the art and ideas of their times, which they translated into their official acts. At the beginning of the seventeenth century they were still using shields as Figs. 3 and 5 on Plate VII. They, however, had made a variation which I believe was peculiar to England, inasmuch as in the

FIG. 47.—Arms of Legh of Lyme as depicted on the "Margent" of the Patent. (Photographed from the orginal Patent now in the possession of Lord Newton.)

previous century they had added a point to the bottom of the shield.

A typical instance of this style of shield is afforded by Fig. 47, which is a reproduction of the emblazonment upon the patent issued by Dugdale in 1665, in confirmation of the augmentation to the arms of the family of Legh of Lyme. The patent in itself is of considerable interest, so perhaps little excuse is needed for reproducing it in full.

To all and singular as well Nobles and Gentles as others to whom these presents shall come, be seene, heard or understood, WILLIAM DUGDALE Esquire NORROY, principall HERALD and King of Armes of the East, West, and North parts of England, from the River of Trent Northward, sendeth greeting in our Lord God everlasting WHEREAS I find that William Flower Esquire sometimes Norroy principall Herald and King of Armes of the North parts of England beyond the River of Trent hath under his hand and seale certified (as by a writeinge beareing date the Eleaventh day of June, in the yeare of our Lord God one Thousand five hundred seaventie five, and of the late Reigne of our most gratious Soveraigne Lady Queene Elizabeth, the seaventeenth yeare) that I say whereas heretofore it pleased the noble and puissant Prince Richard the second of that name sometime King of England, in consideration of the good service that PIERS LEGH Esquire the sonne of Sir Robert Legh of Adlington Knight had done, not onely unto himselfe but alsoe unto the noble Prince Edward his father (commonly called the blacke Prince) the flower of chevalry, at sundry times to remunerate and reward the said PIERS with the free gift of the Mannor of HANLEY to him and his heires for ever, as well for that hee the said PIERS did valiantly rere and advance the said princes Banner att the batâile of Cressy to the noe little encouragement of the English Army as alsoe that hee manfully tooke prisoner the Counte de Tanquervil a Norman, the King's capitall enemy in the same battaile; the memory whereof as it is most worthy of conservation to all posteritie as well for ye singular liberalitie of soe bountifull a Prince soe rigtly bestowed upon the person of one that soe well deserved as alsoe toe the dutifull endeavour of soe dutifull a subject to his prince and Soveraigne: Soe that it moved SIR PIERS LEGH, Kinght (sic) Lord of BRADLEY in the Countie of Lancaster. and of LIME and HANLEY in the Countie of Chester, whoe is lineally descended of the body of the said PIERS LEGH Esquire as being the sonne and heire of PIERS LEGH Esquire the sonne and heire of SIR PIERS LEGH Knight-Banneret the sonne and heire of PIERS LEGH Esquire the sonne and heire of Sr PIERS LEGH Knight the sonne and heire of SIR PIERS LEGH Knight Banneret the sonne and heire of the aforesaid PIERS LEGH Esquire, that tooke the said Counte de Tanquervill prisoner did move him ye said Sr Piers to require him the said NORROY King of Armes for the better preservation of the memorie thereof, to allow unto him and his posteritie some meete signification by Armory according to the auncient and laudable custome of the law of Armes heretofore used in the like cases. In consideration whereof, and at his instant request he the said Norroy King of Armes, by power and authority to him committed by Letters Patents under the greate Seale of England hath assigned, given and granted, and by those his lrs Patents did assigne give and grant unto the said SIR PIERS LEGH Knight an Escucheon or Sheilde of Augmentation sable replenished with Mollets silver therein a mans Arme bowed holdinge in the hand a Standard silver, to be by the said SIR PIERS and his posteritie and ofspring for ever hereafter borne and used as a Testimony of his Auncestours good deserts, to his and their greate worship in such place as hee caused the same among his other Coates of Armes to be in the Margent thereof depicted: which significative Sheilde or

augmentation of Armes hee the said Norroy King of Armes did by the said Lrs Patents ratify, confirme, give, and grant unto the said SIR PIERS LEGH Knight and to his Posterity and Ofspring for ever to be by him and them att all times and for everthereafter borne and used, in manner aforesaid at his and their libertie and pleasure, without the contradiction, gainesaying, inquietation, lett, trouble, molestation, vexation or disturbance of any person or persons whatsoever. In Witnesse whereof hee ye sd NORROY did sign the sd Patent with his hand and sett thereto the seale of his office the day and yeare aforsaid WHEREAS I WILLIAM DUGDALE Esqr NORROY King of Armes aforesaid doe believe this attest to bee true I doe therefore by power and authoritie to mee comitted by Letters Patents under the greate seale of England confirme, and ratifie the former grant above specified, and have assigned, and by thes prsents doe assigne unto RICHARD LEGH Esquier, Lord of BRADLEY in the County of Lancaster and of LIME and HANLEY in the County of Chester who is lineally descended of Piers Legh Esquire sonne of Sir Robert Legh of Adlington, Knight as being sonne and heire of Thomas Legh Doctor of Divinity, sonne and heire to Sir Peter Legh Knight, sonne and heire of Peter Legh Esquire, sonne and heire to the aforesaid Sir Piers Legh Knight, sonne and heire of Piers Legh Esquire, the sonne and heire of Sir Piers Legh Knight-Bannerett the sonne and heire of Piers Legh Esquire the sonne and heire of Sr Piers Legh Knight, the sonne and heire of Sir Piers Legh Knight-Bannerett the sonne and heire of the aforesaid Piers Legh Esqr that tooke the said Counte de Tanquervill prisoner ye same Escucheon or Sheilde of Augmentation Sable replenished with Molletts Silver therein a Mans Arme bowed holding in the hand a Standard Silver; to be by the said RICHARD LEGH Esquire and his posteritie for ever hereafter borne, and used, as a Testimony of his Auncestours good deserts to his and their greater worship in such place as I have caused the same amonge his other Coates of Armes to be in the Margent hereof Depicted which significative Sheilde or Augmentation of Armes I the said Norroy King of Armes doe by these presents ratifie & confirme unto the said RICHARD LEGH Esquire and to his posteritie and ofspringe for ever to be by him and them at all times and for ever hereafter borne and used in manner aforesaid att his and their libertie and pleasure without the contradiction, gainsayinge, inquietation, lett, trouble, molestation, vexation, or disturbance of any person or persons whatsoever. In Witnesse whereof I have signed these presents with my hand and sett thereto the Seale of my Office the Eight Day of April in the yeare of our Lord God One Thousand Six hundred sixtie five and of the Reigne of our most Gracious Soveraigne Lord King Charles the Second, the Seaventeenth.

WILLM DUGDALE
Norroy King of Armes.

The patent, as above quoted, is full of erasures and interlined omissions, and is surrounded by the usual border of floral decorations, &c. It will be seen that it deals only with the augmentation, the family arms having been evidently otherwise confirmed. The exact necessity of this patent seems a mystery, unless, as is probably the case, the original document, under the hand and seal of Flower, had been lost. The achievement, as depicted in the "Margent," and which is here reproduced (Fig. 47), calls for some remark. The hand and arm are depicted of silver—I take it the intention is to show the hand in a gauntlet—and it is certainly not "proper," as the still later grant of Sir Isaac Heard blazons it, and which equally wrongly blazons "estoiles" instead of mullets, as from the foregoing very plainly should have been the case. It is also worth noting that, as depicted, the "standard" displays the cross of St. George. The full blazon of the achievement is:—

PLATE II.

HERALDS IN OFFICIAL DRESS.

PLATE III.

MARCH PURSUIVANT OF ARMS.

PLATE IV.

THE ARMORIAL BEARINGS OF SIR JAMES BALFOUR PAUL,
LYON KING OF ARMS.

PLATE V.

le duc de brabant

TOURNAMENT AND OTHER EQUESTRIAN HERALDIC FIGURES.

PLATE VI.

1. 2.

3. 4.

TOURNAMENT EQUESTRIAN FIGURES.

PLATE VII.

CHRONOLOGICAL TABLE OF TYPES AND SHAPES OF SHIELDS.

PLATE VIII.

EXAMPLES OF SHIELDS, HELMETS, SUPPORTERS AND MANTLINGS FROM KNIGHT AND RUMLEY.

PLATE IX.

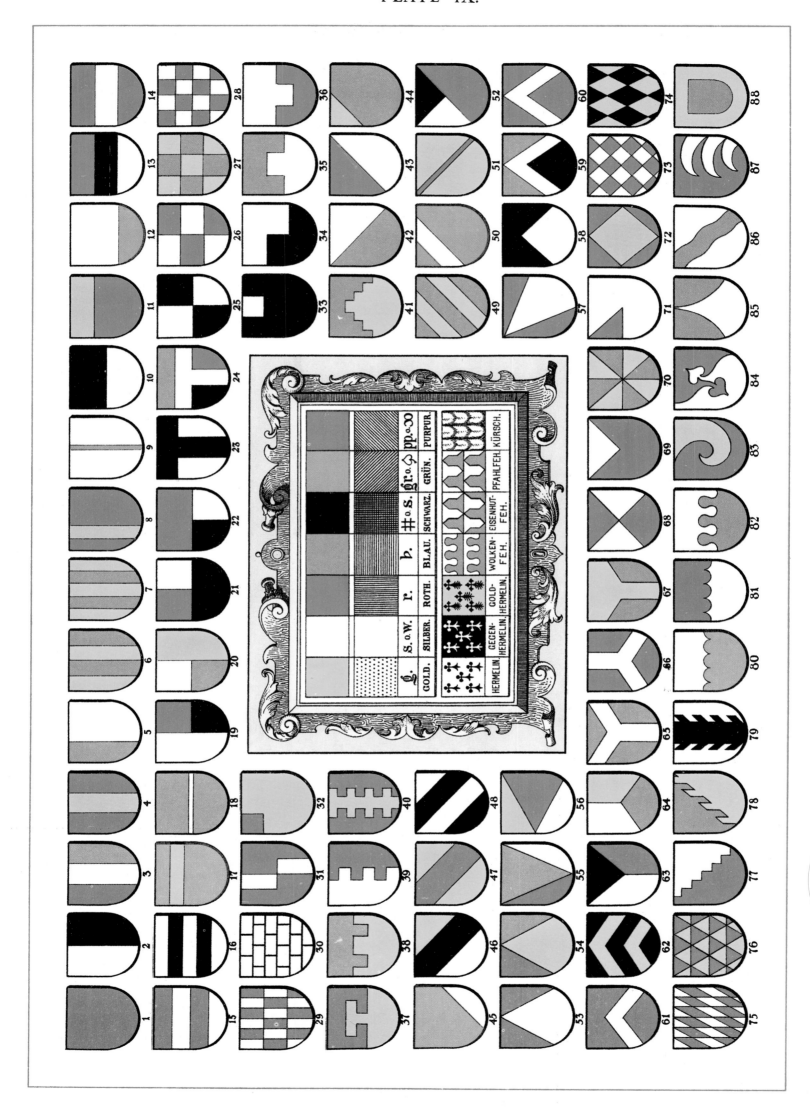

PLATE X.

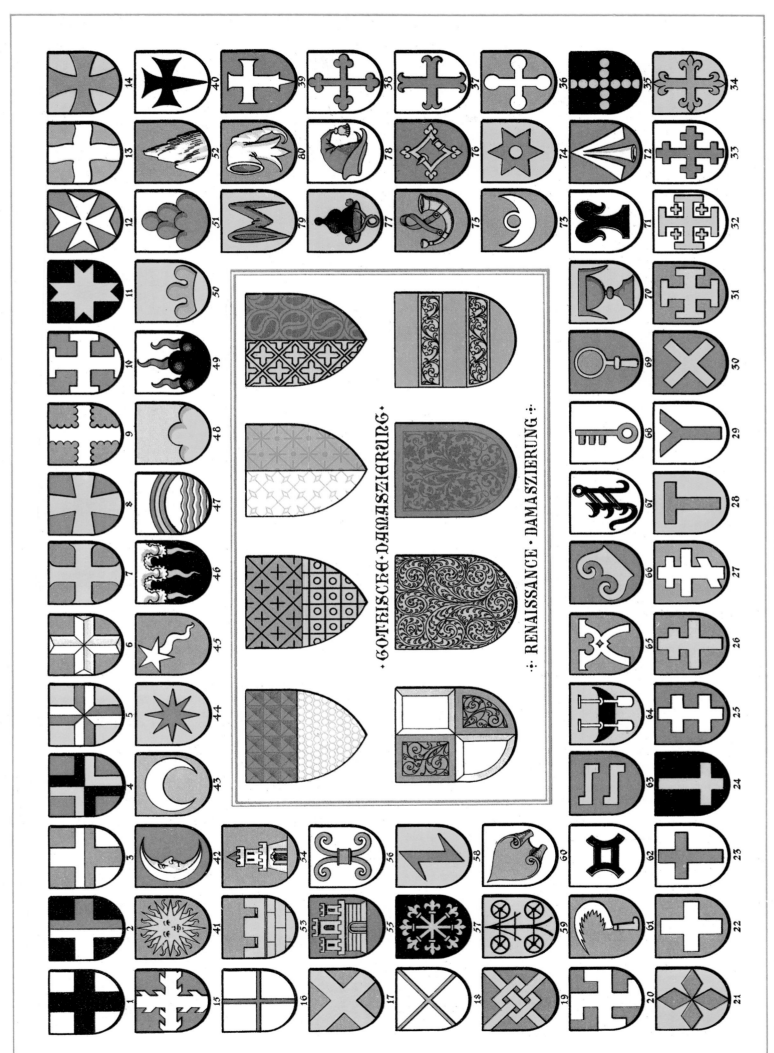

GOTHISCHE · DAMASZIERUNG ·

· RENAISSANCE · DAMASZIERUNG ·

THE ORDINARIES AND OTHER HERALDIC CHARGES.

Printed at Stuttgart.

PLATE XI.

Tryumphe·o·trespas Esse·quam·videri

THE ARMS OF CROFT OF CROFT CASTLE.

PLATE XII.

THE ARMS OF HARLEY.

Or, a bend cottised sable. *Crest*—A castle triple-towered ppr. and issuing from the centre tower a demi-lion rampant gules. *Motto*—Virtute et fide.

FROM A DESIGN BY MISS C. HELARD.

PLATE XIII.

THE ARMORIAL BEARINGS OF CUMMING-GORDON OF ALTYRE

As matriculated in Lyon Register 1795.   Quarterly 1 and 4 azure; three garbs or (for Cumming); 2 and 3 argent; three bends sable, each charged with as many roses of the field.   *Crest*—A lion rampant or, holding in the dexter paw a dagger.   *Motto*—Courage.   Over all, upon an inescutcheon, the Arms, Crest, Supporters and Motto of Gordon.

PLATE XIV.

THE ARMORIAL BEARINGS OF—

(1) Sir HENRY SEYMOUR KING, K.C.I.E.
(2) HENRY STUBBS, Esq. of Danby, Ballyshannon, Co. Donegal.
(3) ROBERT ALEXANDER GIBBONS, Esq., M.D., F.R.C.P.

(4) Lt.-Col. LLEWELLYN W. LONGSTAFF of Ridgelands, Wimbledon.
(5) STRANGMAN, of Co. Essex.

PLATE XV.

THE ARMORIAL BEARINGS OF —

(1) J. W. MELLES, Esq. of Gruline, Aros, Isle of Mull.
(2) Sir THOMAS WRIGHT, of Leicester.
(3) EDWARD THOMAS TYSON, Esq. of Wood Hall, Cockermouth.

(4) HERBERT LUSHINGTON STOREY, Esq., of Lancaster.
(5) HOWEL J. J. PRICE, Esq. of Greensted Hall, Ongar.

PLATE XVI.

THE ARMORIAL BEARINGS OF JOHN WADDINGTON, Esq. of Waddington Old Hall, Co. York, and of Ely Grange, Frant, Sussex.

PLATE XVII.

THE ARMORIAL BEARINGS OF—

(1) THOMAS WESTFALING FRESTON, Esq. of Eagle's Nest, Prestwich.

(2) ARTHUR E. H. HUTTON, Esq. of Houghton Hall, Co. Durham.

(3) WILLIAM RAE MACDONALD, Esq., Carrick Pursuivant of Arms.

(4) TREDENHAM HUGH SPRY, Esq. of Witherdon, Germansweek, Co. Devon.

(5) JOSEPH EDWARD MOORE-GWYN, Esq. of Dyffryn, Co. Glamorgan.

THE ART OF HERALDRY

Quarterly of eight: 1. azure, a plate between three ducal coronets or, a bordure argent (for Corona); 2. gules, a cross engrailed within a bordure also engrailed argent (for Legh), and in chief *superimposed over these first two quarters*, the escutcheon of augmentation, sable, semé of mullets an arm

embowed holding in the hand a standard all argent; 3. argent, on a chevron sable, three covered cups or; 4. argent, a pale lozengy sable; 5. argent, a cross, and in the first quarter a fleur-de-lis sable; 6. vert, a cross flory or; 7. vert, a chevron between three cross crosslets or; 8. argent, a mullet sable charged with an annulet of the field, in the dexter chief point a mullet of the second. A mantling of gules, double argent. Crest: out of a ducal coronet or, a ram's head argent, armed or, holding in the mouth a branch of three leaves (? hazel—they certainly are not laurel as now blazoned) vert.

The achievement prompts the following questions:—

1. Why is the *first* quarter the arms of the ancient family of Corona of Adlington?

2. When and why did the family of Legh of Lyme assume a distinct coat of arms from the paternal house of Legh of Adlington rather than the arms of the latter, differenced in some way?

3. Did not Dugdale intend that the arms of Corona and Legh should be inseparable by superimposing the augmentation over *both* and directing it to be borne in the manner depicted?

4. When and why was the first quarter subsequently discarded?

It should also be pointed out that the arms of Legh

FIG. 49.

of Lyme apparently were anciently "within a bordure engrailed argent," which bordure is not mentioned by Burke in his "Armory."

Reverting to the various shapes of shield, however,

the degeneration is explained by a remark of Mr. G. W. Eve in the able book which he has recently published under the title of "Decorative Heraldry," in which, alluding to heraldic art in general, he says (p. 235):—

"With the Restoration heraldry naturally became again conspicuous, with the worst form of the Renaissance character in full sway, the last vestiges of the Gothic having disappeared. Indeed, the contempt with which the superseded style was regarded amounted to fanaticism, and explains, in a measure, how so much of good could be relinquished in favour of so weak a successor."

Then came the era of gilded embellishments, of flowing palms, of borders decorated with grinning heads, festoons of ribbon and fruit and flowers in abundance. The accompanying examples are reproduced from a book, "Knight and Rumley's Heraldry." The book is not particularly well known to the public, inasmuch as its circulation was entirely confined to heraldic artists, coach-painters, engravers, and die-sinkers. Amongst these handicraftsmen its reputation was and is great. With the school of design it adopted, little or no

FIG. 50.

sympathy now exists, but a short time ago (how short many of those who are now vigorous advocates of the Gothic and mediæval styles would be startled to realise were they to recognise actual facts) no other style was known or considered by the public. As examples of that style the plates of Knight and Rumley were admittedly far in advance of any other book, and as specimens of copperplate engraving they are superb.

Plate VIII. shows typical examples of escutcheons from "Knight and Rumley," as are also Figs. 48, 49, and 50; and as the volume was in the hands of most of the heraldic handicraftsmen, it will be found that this type of design was constantly to be met with. The external decoration of the shield was carried to great lengths, and Fig. 48 found many admirers and users amongst the gallant "sea-dogs" of the kingdom. In fact, so far was the idea carried that a trophy of military weapons was actually granted by patent as part of the supporters of the Earl of Bantry. Fig. 49, from the same source, is the military equivalent. These plates are interesting as being some of the examples from which most of the heraldic handicraft of a recent period was adapted. The official shield eventually stereotyped itself into the

THE ART OF HERALDRY

shape shown in Fig. 50, which is still persevered with by some of the officers of arms. The official shield, however, for grants of arms has reverted to the fifteenth-century shape as shown in the accompanying reproduction from a recent patent granting arms to the town of Warrington (see Fig. 51). For paintings which are not upon patents the design of the shield rests with the individual taste of the different officers of arms, and recently some of the work for which they have been responsible has reached a high standard judged even by the strictest canons of art. In Scotland, until very recently, the actual workmanship of the emblazonments which were issued from Lyon Office was so wretchedly poor that one is hardly justified in taking them into consideration as a type. With the advent into office of the present Lyon King of Arms (Sir James Balfour Paul), a complete change has been made, and both the workmanship and design of the paintings upon the patents of grant and matriculation, and also in the Lyon Register, have been examples of everything that could be desired. Various examples taken from the Lyon Register will be found later in these pages.

A. C. F-D. and H. S.

FIG. 51.—Arms of the Borough of Warrington, co. Lancs. : Ermine, six lioncels rampant, three, two, and one gules, within a bordure azure, charged with eight covered cups or. Crest : upon a rock proper, a unicorn rampant argent, armed, maned, and unguled, supporting a flagstaff all or, thereon hoisted a flag flying to the sinister per pale argent and azure, charged with a rose gules, barbed and seeded of the first, and a garb of the second. (Granted 1897.)

THE ART OF HERALDRY

CHAPTER X

THE FIELD OF A SHIELD AND THE HERALDIC TINCTURES

THE shield itself and its importance in armory is due to its being the vehicle whereon are elaborated the pictured emblems and designs which constitute coat-armour. It should be borne in mind that theoretically all shields are of equal value, saving that a shield of more ancient date takes precedence of a more recent one, and the shield of the head of the house takes precedence of the same arms when differenced for a younger member of the family. A shield crowded with quarterings is interesting inasmuch as each quartering in the ordinary event means the representation through a female of some other family or branch thereof. But the real value of such a shield should be judged rather by the age of the single quartering which represents the strict male descent male upon male, and a simple coat of arms without quarterings may be a great deal more ancient and illustrious than a shield crowded with coat upon coat. A fictitious and far too great estimation is placed upon the right to display a long string of quarterings. In reality quarterings are no more than accidents, because they are only inherited when the wife happens to be an heiress in blood. It is quite conceivable that there may be families, in fact there are such families, who are able to begin their pedigrees at the time of the Conquest, and who have married a long succession of noble women, all of the highest birth, but yet none of whom have happened to be heiresses. Consequently the arms, though dating from the earliest period at which arms are known, would remain in their simple form without the addition of a solitary quartering. On the other hand, I have a case in mind of a marriage which recently took place. The husband is the son of an alien whose original position, if report speaks truly, was that of a pauper immigrant. His wealth and doubtless other attributes have landed him in a good position; he has no arms, and, as far as the world is aware, no ancestry whatever. Let us now consider his wife's family. Starting soon after the Conquest, they obtained high position and married heiress after heiress, and before the commencement of this century they had amassed a shield of quarterings which can readily be proved to be little short of a hundred in number. Probably the number is really much greater. A large family followed in one generation, and one of the younger sons is the ancestor of the wife. But the father of this lady never had any sons, and though there are many males of the name to carry on the family in the senior line and also in several younger branches, the wife, by the absence of brothers, happens to be a coheir; and as such she transmits to her issue the right to the quarterings she has inherited. If the husband ever obtains a grant of arms, the date of them will be subsequent to the present time; but supposing such a grant to be obtained, the children will inevitably inherit the scores of quarterings which belong to their mother. Now it would be ridiculous to suppose that such a shield is better or such a descent more enviable than the shield of a family such as I first described. Quarterings are all very well in their way, but their glorification has been carried too far.

A shield which displays an augmentation is of necessity more honourable than one without. At the same time no scale of precedence has ever been laid down below the rank of esquires; and if such precedence does really exist at all, it can only be according to the date of the grant. Here in England the possession of arms carries with it no style or title, and nothing in his designation can differentiate the position of Mr. Scrope of Danby, the male descendant of one of the oldest families in this country whose arms were upheld in the Scrope and Grosvenor controversy in 1390, or Mr. Daubeney of Cole, from a Mr. Smith, whose known history may have commenced at the Foundling Hospital twenty years ago. In this respect English usage stands apart, for whilst a German is "Von" and a Frenchman was "De," if of noble birth, there is no such apparent distinction in England, and never has been. The result has been that the technical nobility attaching to the possession of arms is overlooked in this country. On the Continent it is usual for a patent creating a title to contain a grant of the arms, because it is recognised that the two are inseparable. This is not now the case in England, where the grant of arms is one thing and the grant of the title another, and where it is possible, as in the case of Lord St. Leonards, to possess a peerage without ever having obtained the first step in rank, which is nobility or gentility.

The foregoing is in explanation of the fact that except in the matter of date all shields are equal in value.

So much being understood, it is possible to put that consideration on one side, and speaking from the artistically technical point of view, the remark one often hears becomes correct, that the simpler a coat of arms the better. The remark has added truth from the fact that a simple coat is practically invariably ancient, and a modern coat is seldom simple. The present Garter King of Arms would rather perish on the scaffold than grant a decently simple coat.

A coat of arms must consist of at least one thing, to wit, the "field." This is equivalent in ordinary words to the colour of the ground of the shield. A great many writers have asserted that every coat of arms must consist of at least the field, and a charge, though most have mentioned as a solitary exception the arms of Brittany, which were simply "ermine." A plain shield of ermine (Fig. 52) was borne by John of Brittany, Earl of Richmond (d. 1399), though some of his predecessors had relegated the arms of Brittany to a "quarter ermine" upon more elaborate escutcheons (see Plate LXXI., and Figs. 76, 181, and 635). This idea as to arms of one tincture was, however, exploded in Woodward and Burnett's "Treatise on Heraldry," where no less than forty different examples are quoted. Of these examples the following may be referred to. A plain shield of gold was borne by the Italian family of Bandinelli, of silver by the French families of Maigret or Megret, and of Bocquet or Bouquet, of azure by the French family of Fizeaux and the family of De la Barge de Ville in Loraine, of gules by the House of Dalbret borne by the Kings of Navarre, and sable by the family of Gornay. Vert is borne by the French family of Barbotte and others, and purpure by the French Auberts. The above-mentioned writer continues: "There is another use of a plain red shield which must not be omitted. In

FIG. 52.—Arms of John (de Montfort, otherwise de Bretagne), Duke of Brittany and Earl of Richmond. (From his seal.)

the full quartered coat of some high sovereign princes of Germany—Saxony (duchies), Brandenburg (Prussia), Bavaria, Anhalt—appears a plain red quartering; this is known as the *Blut Fahne* or *Regalien* quarter, and is indicative of Royal prerogatives. It usually occupies the base of the shield, and is often diapered."

But in spite of the lengthy list which is quoted in Woodward and Burnett, the fact remains that only one British instance is included. The family of Berington of Chester (on the authority of Harleian manuscript No. 1535) is said to bear a plain shield of azure. Personally I doubt this coat of arms for the Berington family of Chester, which is probably connected with the neighbouring family in Shropshire, who in later times certainly used very different arms. The plain shield of ermine is sometimes to be found as a quartering for Brittany in the achievement of those English families who have the right to quarter the Royal arms; but I know of no other British case in which, either as a quartering or as a pronominal coat, arms of one tincture exist.

But there are many coats which have no charge, the pattern consisting of the partition of the shield in some recognised heraldic method into two or more divisions of different tinctures. Amongst such coats may be mentioned the arms of Lord Waldegrave, which are simply: Party per pale argent and gules; Captain Malcolm Drummond of Megginch (Fig. 53), whose arms are simply: Party per fess wavy or and gules; and the arms of Boyle, as borne by the Earl of Cork and Orrery, which are: Per bend embattled argent and gules. The arms of Berners—which are: Quarterly or and vert—are another example (Fig. 183), as are the arms of Campbell (the first quarter in the Duke of Argyll's achievement, Fig. 54), which are: Gyronny or and sable.

The arms of Strabolgi (Fig. 55, there wrongly represented sable, three pallets or), paly of six or and sable, which are now the first quarter in the Duke of Atholl's achievement; the coat barry nebuly or and sable of

Blount of Soddington; the coat bendy argent and gules, the ancient arms of Talbot, which are still borne as a quartering by the Earl of Shrewsbury, Waterford, and Talbot; and the coat chequy or and azure, a quartering for Warren, which is still borne by the House of Howard, all come within the same category. There are hundreds of other coats which have no charge upon them. The colour of the shield is termed the field when it consists of only one colour, and when it consists of more than one colour the two together compose the field. The field is usually of one or more of the recognised metals, colours, or furs.

Plate IX. gives the necessary explanations upon the subject of heraldic tinctures, metals, and colours; but let it here be remarked that a heraldically well-composed coat of arms boasts very few tinctures.

" I mer ein schilt der varwe had
I minner der wappin werdit geacht."

("The more colours a shield has,
The less the coat of arms is esteemed,")

sings Johann Rothe in his *Ritterspiegel* ("Knight's Mirror"). In olden times only seven heraldic tinctures were known: *gold*, or *yellow*; *silver*, or *white*; *red*, *blue*, *black*, and the less frequently used *purple* and *green*.

The Austrian Herald, Peter Suchenwirt (1356 to 1395) emphasises particularly the number of *six tinctures*:—

" Der schilt der was quartieret rein
mit den pesten varben tzweyn
dy von den *sechsen* chomen sein."

("The shield, it was quartered cleanly
with the two best colours
which come from the six.")

The metals are gold and silver, these being termed "or" and "argent." The colours, which are really the "tinctures," if this word is to be used correctly, are: gules (red), azure (blue), vert (green), purpure (purple), and (in spite of the fact that it is not really a colour) black, which is known as sable.

The metal gold, otherwise "or," is often represented in emblazonments by yellow: as a matter of fact yellow has always been used for gold in the Register Books of the College of Arms, and Lyon Office has

FIG. 53.—The arms of Captain Malcolm Drummond of Megginch, namely: "Per fess wavy or and gules, and impaling the arms of Amherst, namely: quarterly 1 and 4, gules, three tilting-spears, two and one or, headed argent (for Amherst); 2. per saltire argent and or, in fess two lions rampant gules in chief and in base a dexter arm couped at the elbow, habited gules, cuffed azure, and hand proper holding a cross crosslet fitché erect also gules (for Daniel); 3. or, on a chevron azure between three marigolds slipped proper, two lions passant respecting each other or, within a bordure compony argent and azure (for Tyssen). Upon the escutcheon is placed a helmet befitting his degree, with a mantling gules and or; and upon a wreath of his liveries is set for crest, two arms proper, drawing an arrow to the head in a bow or; and in an escroll above, this motto, "Marte et arte;" and for his supporters, on the dexter side a savage wreathed head and middle with oak, holding on his dexter shoulder a club proper; and on the sinister side a knight armed at all points, the visor of his helmet up, a spear resting in his sinister arm proper."

44

THE ART OF HERALDRY

recently reverted to this practice. In ancient paintings and emblazonments the use of yellow was rather more frequent than the use of gold, but gold at all times had its use, and was never discarded. Gold seems to have been usually used upon ancient patents, whilst yellow was used in the registrations of them retained in the Offices of Arms, but I know of no instance in British armory in which the word yellow has been used in a blazon to represent any tint distinct from gold. With regard to the other metal, silver, or, as it is always termed, "argent," the same variation is found in the usage of silver and white in representing argent that we find in yellow and gold, though we find that the use of the actual metal (silver) in emblazonment does not occur to anything like the same extent as does the use of gold. Probably this is due to the practical difficulty that no one has yet discovered a silver medium which does not lose its colour. The use of aluminium was thought to have solved the difficulty, but even this loses its brilliancy, and probably its usage will never be universally adopted. This is a pity, for the use of gold in emblazonment gives a brilliancy in effect to a collection of coatarmour which it is a pity cannot be extended by an equivalent usage of silver. The use of silver upon the patents at the College of Arms has been discontinued some centuries, though aluminium is still in use in Lyon Office. Argent is therefore usually represented either by leaving the surface untouched, or by the use of Chinese white.

I believe I am the first heraldic writer to assert the existence of the heraldic colour of white in addition to the heraldic argent. Years ago I came across the statement that a white label belonged only to the Royal Family, and could be used by no one else. I am sorry to say that though I have searched high and low I cannot find the authority for the statement, nor can I learn from any officer of arms that the existence of such

a rule is asserted; but there is this curious confirmation that in the warrants by which the various labels are assigned to the different members of the Royal Family, the labels are called white labels. Now the label of the Prince of Wales is of three points and is plain. Heraldry knows nothing of the black lines which in drawing a coat of arms usually appear for the outline of a charge. In older work such lines are absent. In any case they are only mere accidents of draughtsmanship. Bearing this in mind, and bearing in mind that the sinister supporter of the Prince of Wales is a unicorn argent, how on earth is a plain label of argent to be depicted thereupon? Now it is necessary also that the label shall be placed upon the crest, which is a lion statant guardant or, crowned with the coronet of the Prince, and upon the dexter supporter which is another golden lion; to place an argent label upon either is a flat violation of the rule which requires that metal shall not be placed upon metal, nor colour upon colour; but if the unicorn is considered argent, which it is, it would if really depicted in silver be quite possible to paint a white label upon it, for the distinction between white and silver is marked, and a white label upon a gold lion is not metal upon metal. Quite recently a still further and startling confirmation has come under my notice. In the grant of a crest to Thomas Mowbray, Earl of Nottingham, of which a copy is appended, the coronet which is to encircle the neck of the leopard is distinctly blazoned argent, the label to which he is previously said to have had a just hereditary right is as distinctly blazoned white, and the whole grant is so short that inadvertence could hardly be pleaded as an explanation for the distinction in blazon. Instances of an official exemplification of coats of arms with labels are not uncommon, because the label in some number of families, for example Courtenay and Prideaux-Brune and Barrington, has become stereotyped into a charge. In none of these cases, however, is it either argent or white, but

FIG. 54—The arms of the late Duke of Argyll, K.G., K.T., d. 1900: Quarterly 1 and 4, gyronny of eight or and sable (for Campbell); 2 and 3, argent, a lymphad, her sails furled and oars in action sable, flags and pennons flying gules (for Lorne); behind the escutcheon are placed salterwise a baton powdered with thistles, on the top thereof an Imperial Crown, and thereon the Royal Crest of Scotland, and a sword proper, hilt and pommel or, as Heritable Master of the Royal Household in Scotland and Justice-General of the Shrievalty of Argyll, the Isles, and the other places thereto adjacent. Upon the escutcheon, which is surrounded by the garter, and encircled by the collars of the Most Noble Order of the Garter and the Most Noble and Most Ancient Order of the Thistle, from which depend the badges of the two respective Orders, is placed the coronet of his rank, and thereupon a helmet befitting his degree, with a mantling gules doubled ermine; and upon a wreath of his liveries is set for crest, a boar's head erased or; and upon an escroll above, the motto, "Ne obliviscaris," and below the arms, "Vix ea nostra voco;" and for his supporters, on either side of the escutcheon, a lion guardant gules.

FIG. 55.—Arms of David de · Strabolgi, Earl of Athol: "Pale dor and de sable." (From Rot. Cott., xv. 8.)

instances of the exemplification of a coat of arms bearing a label as a mark of cadency are, outside the members of the Royal Family, distinctly rare; they are necessarily so, because outside the Royal Family the label is merely the temporary mark of the eldest son or grandson during the lifetime of the head of the house, and the necessity for the exemplification of the arms of an eldest son can seldom occur. The one circumstance which might provide us with the opportunity is the exemplification consequent upon a change of name and arms by an eldest son during the lifetime of his father; but this very circumstance fails to provide it, because the exemplification only follows a change of arms, and the arms being changed, there no longer exists the necessity for a mark of cadency; so that instances of the official use of a label for cadency are rare, but of such as occur I can learn of none which has received official sanction which blazons the label white. There is, however, one coat which is said to have a label argent as a charge, this is the coat of Fitz-Simon, which is quoted in Papworth, upon the authority of one of the Harleian Manuscripts, as follows: Sable, three crescents, in chief a label of two drops and in fess another of one drop argent; and the same coat of

arms is recorded in a funeral entry in Ulster's Office. The label is not here termed white, and it is peculiar that we find it of another colour in another coat of Fitz-Simon (azure, a lion rampant ermine, a label of four point gules).

Of other colours may be mentioned purpure (purple). This in English heraldry is a perfectly well recognised colour, and though its use is extremely rare in comparison with the others, it will be found too frequently for it to be classed as an exception. The earliest instance of this tincture which I have met with is in the coat of De Lacy (Fig. 56). The Roll of Caerlaverock speaks of his

"Baniere ot de un cendall saffrin,
O un lion rampant porprin,"

whilst M.S. Cott. Calig. A. xviii. quotes the arms: "*De or, a un lion rampaund de pourpre.*" The Burton coat of the well-known Shropshire family of Lingen-Burton is: Quarterly purpure and azure, a cross engrailed or between four roses argent. The Irish baronets of the name of Burton, who claim descent from this family, bear a very similar coat, namely: Per pale azure and purpure, a cross engrailed or between four roses argent.

Two other colours will be found in nearly all textbooks of English armory. These are murrey or sanguine, and orange or tenné. The exact tint of murrey is between gules and purpure; and tenné is an orange-tawny colour. They are both "stains," and were invented by the old heralds for the perpetration of their preposterous system of abatements, which will be found set out in full in all the old heraldry books, but have yet to be found occurring in fact. The subject of abatements is one of those pleasant little insanities which have done so much to the detriment of heraldry. One, and one only, can be said to have had the slightest foundation in fact; that was the entire reversal of the escutcheon in the ceremony of degradation following upon attainder for high treason. Even this, however, was but temporary, for a man forfeited his arms entirely by attainder. They were torn down from his banner of knighthood; they were erased in the records of the College of Arms; but on that one single occa-

sion when he was drawn upon a hurdle to the place of his execution, they are said to have been painted reversed upon paper, which paper was fastened to his breast. But the arms then came to an end, and his descendants possessed none at all. They certainly had not the right to depict their shield upside down (even if they had cared to display such a monstrosity). Unless and until the attainder was reversed, arms (like a title) were void; and the proof of this is to be found in the many regrants of arms made in cases where the attainder has remained, as in the instances of the Earl of Stafford and the ancestor of the present Lord Barnard. But that any person should have been supposed to have been willing to make use of arms carrying an abatement is preposterous, and no instance of such usage is known. Rather would a man decline to bear arms at all; and that any one should have imagined the existence of a person willing to advertise himself a drunkard or an adulterer, with variations in the latter case according to the personality of his partner in guilt, is idiotic in the extreme. Consequently as no example of an abatement has ever been found, one might almost discard the "stains" of murrey and tenné were it not that they were largely made use of for the purposes of liveries, in which usage they had no such objectionable meaning. At the present day scarlet or gules being appropriated to the Royal Family for livery purposes, other people possessing a shield of gules are required to make use of a different red, and though it is now termed chocolate or claret colour by the utilitarian language of the day, it is in reality nothing more than the old sanguine or murrey. Of orange-tawny I can learn of but one livery at the present day. I refer to the orange-tawny coats used by the hunt servants of Lord Fitzhardinge, and now worn by the hunt servants of the Old Berkeley country, near London. *A propos* of this it is interesting to note the curious legend that the "pink" of the hunting field is not due to any reasons of optical advantage, but to an entirely different reason. Formerly no man might hunt even on his own estate until he had had licence of free warrant from the Crown. Consequently he merely hunted by the pleasure of the Crown, taking part in what was exclusively a Royal sport by Royal permission, and for this Royal sport he wore the King's livery of scarlet. This being the case, it is a curious anomaly that although the livery of the only Royal pack recently in existence, the Royal Buck Hounds, was scarlet and gold, the Master wore a green coat. The legend may be a fallacy, inasmuch as scarlet did not become the Royal livery until the accession of the Stuarts; but it is by no means clear to what date the scarlet hunting coat can be traced.

There is, however, one undoubted instance of the use of sanguine for the field of a coat of arms, namely, the arms of Clayhills of Invergowrie,[a] which are properly matriculated in Lyon Register.

To these colours German heraldry has added brown, blood-red (this apparently is different from the English sanguine, as a different hatching has been invented for it), earth-colour, iron-grey, water-colour, flesh-colour, ashen-grey, orange (here also a separate hatching from the one to represent tenné has been invented), and the colour of nature, *i.e.* "proper." These doubtless are not intended to be added to the list of heraldic tinctures, but are noted because various hatchings have been invented in modern times to represent them.

[a] The arms of Clayhills of Invergowrie: Parted per bend sanguine and vert, two greyhounds courant bendwise argent. Mantling gules doubled argent; and upon a wreath of the liveries is set for crest, an arm holding an Imperial crown proper; and in an escroll over the same, this motto, "Corde et animo." Matriculated in Lyon Office *circa* 1672.

THE ART OF HERALDRY

Mr. Woodward, in Woodward and Burnett's "Treatise on Heraldry," alludes to various tinctures amongst Continental arms which he has come across.

"Besides the metals, tinctures, and furs which have

FIG. 57.—The arms of Lane of King's Bromley : Party per fess or and azure, a chevron gules between three mullets counterchanged of the field, a canton of the arms of England, namely : gules, three lions passant guardant in pale or.   Mantling azure and or ; and for his crest, upon a wreath of the colours, a strawberry-roan horse salient proper, couped at the flanks, bridled sable, bitted and garnished or, supporting between the feet an Imperial crown proper.   Motto : "Garde le Roy."

been already described, other tinctures are occasionally found in the heraldry of Continental nations ; but are comparatively of such rarity as that they may be counted among the curiosities of blazon, which would require a separate volume.   That of which I have collected instances is *cendrée*, or ash colour, which is borne by (among others) the Bavarian family of Ashua, as its *armes parlantes: Cendrée, a mount of three coupeaux in base or.*

"*Brunâtre*, a brown colour, is even more rare as a tincture of the field ; the MIEROSZEWSKY in Silesia bear, '*de Brunâtre, A cross patée argent supporting a raven rising sable, and holding in its beak a horseshoe proper, its points towards the chief.*'

"*Bleu-céleste*, or *bleu du ciel*, appears occasionally, apart from what we may term 'landscape coats.'   That it differs from, and is a much lighter colour than, azure is shown by the following example.   The Florentine CINTI (now CINI) bear a coat which would be numbered among the *armes fausses*, or *à enquérir : Per pale azure and bleu-céleste, an estoile counterchanged.*

"*Amaranth* or *columbine* is the field of a coat (of which the blazon is too lengthy for

insertion in this place) which was granted to a Bohemian knight in 1701."

Carnation is the French term for the colour of naked flesh, and is often employed in the blazonry of that country.

Perhaps mention should here be made of the English term "proper."   Anything, alive or otherwise, which is depicted in its natural colours is termed "proper," and it should be depicted in its really correct tones or tints, without any attempt to assimilate these with any heraldic tincture.   It will not be found in the very ancient coats of arms, and its use is not to be encouraged.   When a natural animal is found existing in various colours it is usual to so describe it, for the term "proper" alone would leave uncertainty.   For instance, the crest of the Lane family (Fig. 57), which was granted to commemorate the ride of King Charles II. behind Mistress Jane Lane as her servant, in his perilous escape to the coast after the disastrous Battle of Worcester, is blazoned "a strawberry roan horse, couped at the flanks proper, bridled sable, and holding between the feet an Imperial crown also proper."   Lord Cowper's supporters are, on either side of the escutcheon, "a light dun horse proper, with a large blaze down the face, the mane close shorn except

FIG. 58.—Arms of Right Hon. Sir William Wallace Hozier, Lord Newlands : Vair, on a chevron gules, three bezants, a chief gyronny of eight or and sable. Upon the escutcheon, which is charged with his badge of Ulster as a Baronet, is placed the coronet of his rank, and thereupon a helmet befitting his degree. Mantling gules doubled argent ; and upon a wreath of his liveries is set for crest, a bloodhound sejant proper ; and on an escroll over the same this motto, "Aye ready."   Supporters : on either side a dapple-grey horse proper, gorged with a riband, and suspended therefrom an escutcheon gules charged with three bezants in chevron.

a tuft on the withers, a black list down the back, a bob tail, and the near fore-foot and both hind feet white." Another instance that might be quoted are the supporters of Lord Newlands (see Fig. 58), which are: "On either side a dapple-grey horse proper, gorged with a riband and suspended therefrom an escutcheon gules, charged with three bezants in chevron." The crest of the family of Bewes, of St. Neots, Cornwall, is: "On a chapeau gules, turned up ermine, a pegasus rearing on his hind legs of a bay colour, the mane and tail sable, winged or, and holding in the mouth a sprig of laurel proper" (Fig. 292).

Upon the use of these heraldic colours a few remarks may be appended:—

Gold.—Chrome-yellow may be substituted for gold, which is sometimes touched up with this colour; sepia is employed as a shading tint. If chrome-yellow be used instead of gold, white must be substituted for silver; silver is touched up with white for the high lights. In English heraldry silver is little used, white being usually introduced instead. For shading purposes neutral tint is employed.

Red is represented by vermilion, the high lights touched up with a lighter red or chrome-yellow, the shadows rendered in carmine. In arms of the style of the thirteenth and fourteenth centuries, minium (or red lead) is used instead of vermilion, and the lights are shown up in chrome-yellow.

Blue is painted with cobalt or ultramarine mixed

Upon this point Herr Ströhl in his *Heraldischer Atlas* remarks: "The system of hatching used by Marcus Vulson de la Colombière, 1639, in the course of time found acceptance everywhere, and has maintained itself in use unaltered until the present day, and these are shown on Plate IX.; only that later, hatchings have been invented for brown, grey, &c.; which, however, seems rather a superfluous enriching." None of these later creations, by the way, have ever been used in this country. For the sake of completeness, however, let them be mentioned (see Fig. 59): *a*, brown; *b*, blood-red; *c*, earth-colour; *d*, iron-grey; *e*, water-colour; *f*, flesh-colour; *g*, ashen-grey; *h*, orange; and *i*, colour of nature. In English armory "tenné" is represented by a combination of horizontal (as azure) lines with diagonal lines from sinister to dexter (as purpure), and sanguine or murrey by a combination of diagonal lines from dexter to sinister (as vert), and from sinister to dexter (as purpure).

The hatchings of the shield and its charges always accommodate themselves to the angle at which the shield is placed, those of the crest to the angle of the helmet. A curious difficulty, however, occurs when a shield, as is so often the case in this country, forms a part of the crest. Such a shield is seldom depicted quite upright upon the wreath. Are the tincture lines to follow the angle of the smaller shield in the crest or the angle of the helmet? Opinion is by no means agreed upon the point.

But though this system of representing colours by "hatching" has been adopted and extensively made use

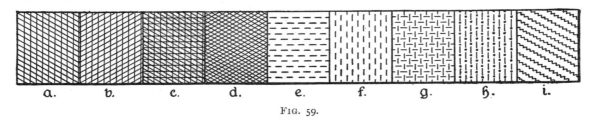

FIG. 59.

with white, which is also used for the lights, prussian blue for the shadows.

Green is represented by different artists in very different tints, formerly much darker than is now usually the case. A green a little darker than emerald green is usually adopted nowadays, the lights being indicated by white or chrome-yellow, and the shadows with sap-green.

Silver is sometimes used for the high lights of blue and black, and gold for red and green, but only in very delicate lines and in a small proportion. Most English herald-painters shade with gum, usually tinted slightly with a neutral colour, and the veinings on the outside of a mantling are almost invariably found marked in very fine gold lines.

There are and were always many occasions in which it was desired to represent armorial bearings in black and white, or where from the nature of the handicraft it was impossible to make use of actual colour. But it should always be pointedly remembered that unless the right colours of the arms could be used the tinctures were entirely ignored until the seventeeth century. Various schemes of hatchings were adopted for this purpose, the earliest being that of Francquart in Belgium, *circa* 1623. Mr. Woodward says this was succeeded by the systems of Butkens, 1626; Petra Sancta, 1638; Lobkowitz, 1639; Gelenius; and De Rouck, 1645; but all these systems differed from each other, and were for a time the cause of confusion and not of order. Eventually, however, the system of Petra Sancta (the author of *Tesseræ Gentilitia*) superseded all the others, and has remained in use up to the present time.

of, it is questionable whether it has ever received official sanction at any rate in Great Britain. It certainly has never been made use of in any *official* record or document in the College of Arms. Most of the records are in colour. The remainder are all without exception "tricked," that is, drawn in outline, the colours being added in writing in the following contracted forms: "O," or "or," for or; "A," "ar," or "arg," for argent; "G," or "gu," for gules; "Az," or "B" (for blue, owing to the likelihood of confusion between "ar" and "az," "B" being almost universally used in old trickings), for azure; "S," or "sa," for sable; "Vt" for vert, and "Purp" for purpure. It is unlikely that any change will be made in the future, for the use of tincture lines is now very rapidly being discarded by all good heraldic artists in this country. With the reversion to older and better forms and methods these hatchings become an anachronism, and save that sable is represented by solid black they will probably be unused and forgotten before very long.

The plain, simple names of colours, such as red and green, seemed so unpoetical and unostentatious to the heralds and poets of the Middle Ages, that they substituted for gold, topaz; for silver, pearl or "meergries"; for red, ruby; for blue, sapphire; for green, emerald; and for black, diamond or "zobel" (sable, the animal, whence the word "sable"). Let the following blazonment from the grant of arms to Mödling bei Wien in 1458 serve as an example of the same: "Mit namen ain Schilt gleich getailt in fasse, des ober und maister tail von Rubin auch mit ainer fasse von Berlein, der under thail von grunt des Schilts von Schmaragaden, darinnein Pantel von Silber in Rampannt"—(*lit.* "Namely, a shield equally divided in fess, the upper and greater part of ruby, also with a tess of pearl, the under part of the field of the shield of emerald, therein a panther of silver, rampant"); that is, "Per

erminites. "Ermines" is a black field with white ermine spots (the French term for this is *contre-hermin*, the German, *gegen-hermelin*). A gold back-

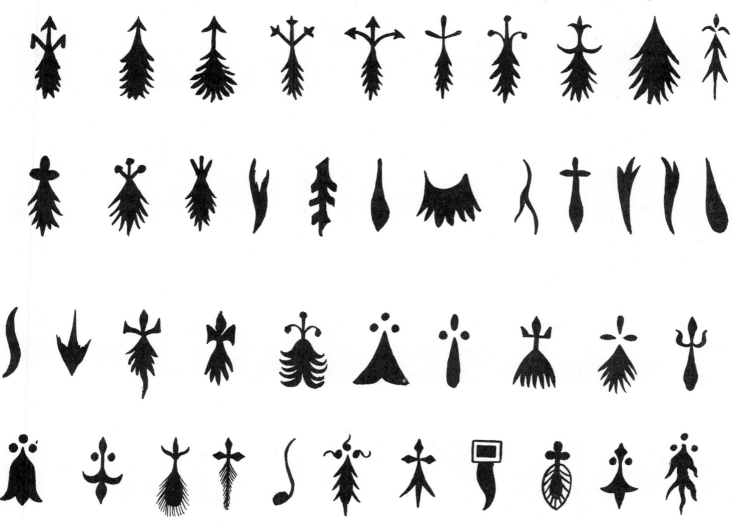

fess gules and vert, in chief a fess argent, in base a panther rampant of the last." Even the planets, and, as abbreviations, their astronomical signs, are occasionally employed: thus, the *sun* for gold, the *moon* for silver, *Mars* for red, *Jupiter* for blue, *Venus* for green, *Saturn* for black, and *Mercury* for purple.

This aberration of intellect on the part of mediæval heraldic writers, for it really amounted to little more, had very little, if indeed it had any, English official recognition. No one dreams of using such blazon at the present time, and it might have been entirely disregarded were it not that Guillim sanctions its use; and he being the high priest of English armory to so many, his example has given the system a certain currency. I am not myself aware of any instance of the use of these terms in a patent of arms.

The furs known to heraldry are now many, but originally they were only two, "ermine" and "vair." Ermine, as every one knows, is of white covered with black spots, intended to represent the tails of the animal. From ermine has been evolved the following variations, viz. ermines, erminois, pean, and

FIG. 60.

FIG. 60a.—Arms of William de Ferrers, Earl of Derby (*d.* 1247): "Scutum variatum auro & gut." (From MS. Cott. Nero, D. I.)

ground with black ermine spots is styled erminois, and pean is a black ground with gold ermine spots. Planché mentions still another, as does Parker in his "Glossary of Heraldry," namely, "erminites," which is supposed to be white, with black ermine spots and a red hair on each side of the spot. I believe there is no instance known of any such fur in British armory. It is not mentioned in Ströhl's "Heraldic Atlas," nor can I find any foreign instance, so that who invented it, or for what purpose it was invented, I cannot say; and I think it should be relegated, with abatements and the *seize quartiers* of Jesus Christ, to the category of the silly inventions of former heraldic writers, not of former heralds, for I know of no official act which has recognised the existence of erminites. The German term for erminois is *gold-hermelin*, but there are no distinctive terms either in French or German heraldry for the other varieties. Thus, erminois would be in French blazon: d'or, semé d'hermines de sable; pean would be *de sable*, semé d'hermines d'or. Though ermine is always nowadays represented upon a white background, it was sometimes depicted

49

G

with black ermine spots upon a field of silver, as in the case of some of the stall plates of the Knights of the Garter in St. George's Chapel at Windsor. Ermine spots are frequently to be found as charges. For instance, in the well-known coat of Kay, which is: "Argent, three ermine spots in bend between two bendlets sable, the whole between as many crescents azure." As charges two ermine spots figure upon the arms recently granted to Sir Francis Laking, Bart., G.C.V.O. The ermine spot has also sometimes been

divisions therefrom resulting having passed through various intermediate forms (see Fig. 62), have now been stereotyped into a fixed geometrical pattern, formed of rows of ear-shaped shields of alternate colours and alternately reversed, so depicted that each reversed shield fits into the space left by those on either side which are not reversed (see Fig. 61, *k*). The accompanying illustration will show plainly what is intended. In some of the older designs it was similar to that shown in the arms of the Earl

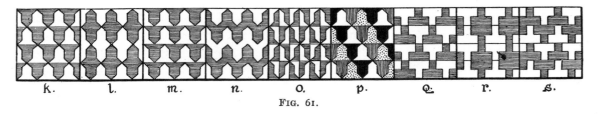

k.   l.   m.   n.   o.   p.   q.   r.   s.

FIG. 61.

used in British armory as the difference mark granted under a Royal Licence to assume name and arms when it is necessary to indicate the absence of blood relationship. Other instances of the use of an ermine spot as a charge are:—

"Or, on two bars azure, as many barrulets dancetté argent, a chief indented of the second charged with an ermine spot or (Sawbridge).

Argent, a chevron between three crows sable, in each beak an ermine spot (Lloyd, Bishop of St. Asaph, 1680; Lichfield, 1692; and Worcester, 1700–17).

Argent, a fess gules between three ermine spots sable (Kilvington).

Argent, two bars sable, spotted ermine, in chief a lion passant gules (Hill, co. Wexford).

The earliest form in which ermine was depicted shows a nearer approach to the reality of the black tail, inasmuch as the spots above the tail to which we are now accustomed are a modern variant. The forms which appear in Fig. 60 show some variety. These were very kindly collected and drawn for me by Miss Helard. Happily the art of the present day shows a tendency to revert to the older form instead of its modern evolution.

When a bend is ermine, the spots (like all other charges placed upon a bend) must be bendwise; but on a chevron, saltire, &c., they are drawn upright.

The other variety of fur is "vair." This originated from the fur of a kind of squirrel (the ver or vair, differently spelt; Latin, *varus*), which was much used for the lining of cloaks. The animal was bluey-grey upon the back and white underneath, and the whole skin was used. It will be readily seen that by sewing a number of these skins together a result is obtained of a series of cup-shaped figures, alternating bluey-grey and white, and this is well shown in Fig. 41, which shows the effigy upon the tomb of Geoffrey Plantagenet, Count of Anjou, where the lining of vair to his cloak is plainly to be seen.

The word seems to have been used independently of heraldry for fur, and the following curious error, which is pointed out in Parker's "Glossary of the Terms used in Heraldry," may be noted in passing. The familiar fairy tale of Cinderella was brought to us from the French, and the slippers made of this costly fur, written, probably, *verré* for *vairé*, were erroneously translated "glass" slippers. This was, of course, an impossible material, but the error has always been repeated in the nursery tale-books.

In the oldest records vair is represented by means of straight horizontal lines alternating with horizontal wavy or nebuly lines (see Fig. 60a), but the cup-shaped

Ferrers, Earl of Derby, 1254–65, the sketch (Fig. 62) being taken from almost contemporary stained glass in Dorchester Church, Oxon.; whilst sometimes the division lines are drawn, after the same manner, as *nebuly*. There does not seem to have been any fixed proportion for the number of rows of vair, as Fig. 63 shows the arms of the same Earl as represented upon his seal. The palpable pun upon the name which a shield vairé supplied no doubt affords the origin of the arms of Ferrers. Some families of the name at a later date adopted the horseshoes, which are to be found upon many Farrer and Ferrers shields, the popular assumption being that they are a reference to the "farrier" from whom some would derive the surname. Woodward states that a horseshoe being the badge of the Marshalls, horseshoes were assumed

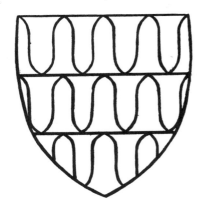

FIG. 62.—Arms of Robert de Ferrers, Earl of Derby (1254–1265). (From stained glass in Dorchester Church.)

as *armes parlantes* by their descendants the Ferrers, who appear to have borne: Sable, six horseshoes argent. As a matter of fact the only one who bore the horseshoes seems to have been William de Ferrers, Earl of Derby (*d.* 1254), as will be seen from the arms as on his seal (Fig. 64). His wife was Sybilla, daughter of William Marshall, Earl of Pembroke. His son reverted to the plain shield of vairé, or, and gules (Figs. 62 and 63). The arms of the Ferrers family at a later date are found to be: Gules, seven mascles conjoined or, in which form they are still borne by Ferrers of Baddesley Clinton; but whether the mascles are corruptions of the horseshoes, or whether (as seems infinitely more probable) they are merely a corrupted form of the vairé, or, and gules, it is difficult to say. Personally I rather doubt whether any Ferrers ever used the arms: Argent, six horseshoes sable.

The early manner of depicting vair is still occasionally met with in foreign heraldry, where it is blazoned as Vair ondé or Vair ancien. The family of MARGENS in Spain bears: Vair onde, on a bend gules three griffins or; and TARRAGONE of Spain: Vairé onde, or and gules. German heraldry seems to distinguish between *wolkenfeh* (cloud vair; see Plate IX.) and *wogenfeh* (wave

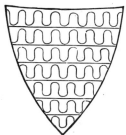

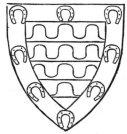

FIG. 63.—Arms of Robert de Ferrers, Earl of Derby (1254–1265). (From his seal.)

FIG. 64.—Arms of William de Ferrers, Earl of Derby: Vairé, or, and gules, a bordure argent, charged with eight horseshoes sable. (From a drawing of his seal, MS. Cott. Julius, C. vii.)

vair; see Fig. 61, *n*). The former is equivalent to vair ancient, the latter to vair en point.

The verbal blazon of vair nearly always commences with the metal, but in the arrangement of the panes there is a difference between French and English usage. In the former the white panes are generally (and one thinks more correctly) represented as forming the first, or upper, line; in British heraldry the reverse is more usually the case. It is usual to depict the white panes of ordinary vair with white rather than with silver, though the use of the latter cannot be said to be incorrect, there being precedents in favour of that form. When an ordinary is of vair or vairy, the rows of vair may be depicted either horizontally or following the direction of the ordinary. There are accepted precedents for both methods.

Vair is always blue and white, but the same subdivision of the field is frequently found in other colours; and when this is the case, it is termed vairy of such and such colours. When it is vairy, it is usually of a colour and metal, as in the case of Ferrers, Earls of Derby, above referred to; though a fur is sometimes found to take the place of one or other, as in the arms of Gresley (see Fig. 65), which are: "Vairé, gules, and ermine." I know of no instance where vairé is found of either two metals or of two colours, nor at the same time do I know of any rule against such a combination. Probably it will be time enough to discuss the contingency when an instance comes to light.

Gerard Leigh mentions vair of three or more tinctures, but instances are very rare. Parker, in his "Glossary," refers to the coat of Roger Holthouse, which he blazons: "Vairy argent, azure, gules, and or, en point."

The *Vair* of heraldry, as of commerce, was formerly of three sizes, and the distinction is continued in foreign armory. The middle or ordinary size is known as *Vair*; a smaller size as *Menu-vair* (whence our word "miniver"); the largest as *Beffroi* or *Gros vair*, a term which is used in armory when there are less than four rows. The word *Beffroi* is evidently derived from the bell-like shape of the *vair*, the word *Beffroi* being anciently used in the sense of the alarm-bell of a town. In French armory, *Beffroi* should consist of three horizontal rows; *Vair*, of four; *Menu-vair*, of six. This rule is not strictly observed, but in French blazon if the rows are more than four it is usual to specify the number; thus VARROUX bears: *de Vair de cinq traits*. *Menu-vair* is still the blazon of some families; BANVILLE DE TRU-

TEMNE bears: *de Menu-vair de six tires*; the Barons van HOUTHEM bore: *de Menu-vair, au franc quartier de gueules charge de trois maillets d'or*.

In British armory the foregoing distinctions are unknown, and *Vair* is only of one size, that being at the discretion of the artist.

When the Vair is so arranged that in two horizontal rows taken together, either the points or the bases of two panes of the same tincture are in apposition, the fur is known as COUNTER VAIR (*Contre Vair*) (see Fig. 61, *l*). Another variation, but an infrequent one, is known as VAIR IN PALE, known in German heraldry as *Pfahl-feh* (see Plate IX.), (*Vair appointé* or *Vair en pal*; but if of other colours than the usual ones, *Vairé en pal*). In this all panes of the same colour are arranged in vertical, or palar, rows. German heraldry apparently distinguishes between this and *Stürzpfahlfeh*, or reversed vair in pale (see Fig. 61, *m*). VAIR IN BEND (or in bend-sinister) is occasionally met with in foreign coats; thus MIGNIANELLI in Italy bears: *Vairé d'or et d'azur en bande*; while *Vairé en barre* (that is, in bend-sinister) *d'or et de sable* is the coat of PICHON of Geneva.

"Vair en pointe" is a term applied by Nisbet to an arrangement by which the azure shield pointing downwards has beneath it an argent shield pointing downwards, and *vice versâ*, by which method the resulting effect is as shown in Fig. 61, *n*. The German term

FIG. 65.—The arms of Sir Robert Gresley, Bart., viz.: Quarterly 1 and 4, vairé ermine and gules; 2 and 3, sable, a lion rampant argent, collared gules, impaling the arms of Spencer-Churchill, namely: quarterly 1 and 4, sable a lion rampant argent, on a canton of the last a cross gules (for Churchill); 2 and 3, quarterly argent and gules, on a bend sable between two frets or, three escallops of the first (for Spencer); and as an honourable augmentation, in chief an escutcheon argent, charged with the cross of St. George gules, and thereon an escutcheon of the arms of France, namely: azure, three fleurs-de-lis or. The escutcheon is charged with his badge of Ulster as a Baronet. Mantling gules and argent. Crest: on a wreath of the colours, a lion passant argent; with the motto, "Meliore fide quam fortuna."

for this is *Wogenfeh*, or wave vair. Fig. 61, *o* shows a purely German variety—*Wechselfeh*, or alternate vair; and Fig. 61, *p*, which is equivalent to the English vairé of four colours, is known in German armory as *Buntfeh*, i.e. gay-coloured or checked vair.

Ordinary vair in German heraldry is known as *Eisenhüt-feh*, or iron hat vair. On account of its similarity, when drawn, to the old iron hat of the fourteenth and fifteenth centuries (see Fig. 66), this skin has received the name of *Eisenhutlein* (little iron hat) from German heraldic students, a name which later gave rise to many incorrect interpretations. An old charter in the archives of the chapter-house of Lilienfield, in Lower Austria, under the seal (Fig. 67) of one Chimrad Pellifex, 1329, proves that at that time vair was so styled. The name of Pellifex (in German

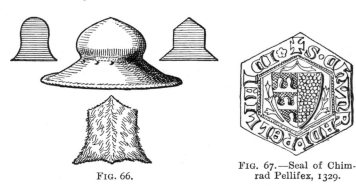

FIG. 66.

FIG. 67.—Seal of Chimrad Pellifex, 1329.

Wildwerker, a worker in skins, or furrier) is expressed in a punning or canting form on the dexter side of the shield. This Conrad the Furrier was Burgomaster of Vienna 1340–43.

A considerable number of British and foreign families bear *Vair* only; such are FERRERS and GRESLEY, above mentioned; VARANO, Dukes de CAMERINO; VAIRE and VAIRIÈRE, in France; VERET, in Switzerland; GOUVIS, FRESNAY (Brittany); DE VERA, in Spain; LOHEAC (Brittany); VARENCHON (Savoy); SOLDANIERI (Florence). *Counter vair* is borne by LOFFREDO of Naples; by BOUCHAGE, DU PLESSIS ANGERS, and BROTIN, of France. HELLEMMES of Tournay uses: *de Contre vair, à la cotice de gueules brochante sur le tout.*

Mr. Woodward, in his "Treatise on Heraldry," writes: Two curious forms of Vair occasionally met with in Italian or French coats are known as *Plumeté* and *Papelonné.*

In *Plumeté* the field is apparently covered with feathers. *Plumeté d'argent et d'azur* is the coat of Ceba (note that these are the tinctures of *Vair*); SOLDONIERI of Udine, *Plumeté au natural* (but the SOLDONIERI of Florence bore: *Vairé argent and sable* with *a bordure chequy or and azure*); TENREMONDE of Brabant: *Plumeté or and sable.* In the arms of the SCALTENIGHI of Padua, the BENZONI of Milan, the GIOLFINI, CATANEI, and NUVOLONI of Verona, each feather of the *plumeté* is said to be charged with an ermine spot sable.

The bearing of PAPELONNÉ is more frequently found; in it the field is covered with what appear to be scales; the heraldic term *papelonné* being derived from a supposed resemblance of these scales to the wings of butterflies; for example the coat of MONTI: *Gules, papelonné argent.*

DONZEL at Besançon bears: Papelonné d'or et de sable. (It is worthy of note that DONZÉ of Lorraine used: Gules, three bars wavy or. The FRANCONIS of Lausanne are said to bear: *de Gueules papelonné d'argent*, and on *a chief of the last a rose of the first*, but the coat is otherwise blazoned: *Vaire gules and or*, &c. The coat of ARQUINVILLIERS, or HARGENVILLIERS, in Picardy, of *d'Hermine papelonné de gueules* (not being understood, this has been blazoned "*semé of caltraps*"). So also the coat of CHEMILLÉ appears in French books of blazon indifferently as: *d'Or papelonné de gueules;* and *d'Or semé de chaussetrapes de gueules.* GUÉTTEVILLE DE GUÉNONVILLE is said to bear: *d'Argent semé de chaussetrapes de sable,*

but it is more probable that this is simply *d'Argent papelonné de sable.* The BARISONI of Padua bear: *Or, a bend of scales, bendwise argent, on each scale an ermine spot sable, the bend bordered sable;* this is only a roundabout way of saying: Or, a bend argent, bordered and papelonné sable.

The ALBERICI of Bologna bear: *Papelonné of seven rows, four of argent, three of or;* but the ALBERGHI of the same city: *Papelonné of six rows, three of argent, as many of gules.* The connection with *vairé* is much clearer in the latter than in the former. CAMBI (called FIGLIAMBUCHI), at Florence, carried: *d'Argent, papelonné de gueules;* MONTI of Florence and Sicily, and RONQUEROLLES of France the reverse.

No one who is familiar with the licence given to themselves by armorial painters and sculptors in Italy, who were often quite ignorant of the meaning of the blazons they depicted, will doubt for a moment the statement that Papelonné was originally a corruption from or perhaps is simply ill-drawn Vair.

POTENT, and its less common variant COUNTER POTENT, are usually ranked in British heraldic works as separate furs. This has arisen from the writers being ignorant that in early times *Vair* was frequently depicted in the form now known as *Potent* (see Plates LXXI. and LXXII. (By many heraldic writers the ordinary *Potent* is styled *Potent-counter-potent.* When drawn in the ordinary way, *Potent* alone suffices.) An example of *Vair* in the form now known as *Potent* (or, as above, *Potent-counter-potent*) is afforded by the seal of JEANNE DE FLANDRE, wife of ENGUERRAND IV. (De Courcy); here the well-known arms of COURCY, *Barry of six vair and gules,* are depicted as if the bars of *vair* were composed of a row of *potent* (VRÉE, *Généalogie des Comtes de Flandre*). In the *Roll of Arms of the time of Edward I.* the *Vair* resembles *Potent* (-counter-potent), which Dr. PERCEVAL erroneously terms an "invention of later date." The name and the differentiation may be, but not the fact. In the First Nobility Roll of the year 1297, the arms of No. 8, ROBERT DE BRUIS, Baron of Brecknock, are: Barry of six, Vaire ermine and gules, and azure. Here the vair is potent; so is it also in No. 19, where the coat of INGELRAM DE GHISNES, or GYNES, is: Gules, a chief vair. The same coat is thus drawn in the Second Nobility Roll, 1299, No. 57. POTENT, like its original *Vair*, is always of *argent* and *azure*, unless other tinctures are specified in the blazon. The name *Potent* is the old English word for a crutch or walking-staff. Chaucer, in his description of "Elde" (*i.e.* old age) writes:

> "So olde she was, that she ne went
> A fote, but it were by potent."

And though a potent is a heraldic charge, and a cross potent a well-known variety of that ordinary, "potent" is usually intended to indicate the fur of blue and white as in Fig. 61, *q.* It is not of frequent usage, but it undoubtedly has an accepted place in British armory, as also has "counter-potent," which, following the same rules as counter-vair, results in a field as Fig. 61, *r.* The German terms for Potent and counter-potent are respectively *Sturzkrückenfeh* and *gegensturzkrückenfeh.* German heraldry has evolved yet another variant of Potent, viz. *Verschobenes Gegensturzkrückenfeh* (*i.e.* displaced potent-counter-potent), as in Fig. 61, *s.* There is still yet another German heraldic fur which is quite unknown in British armory. This is the *Kursch* shown on Plate XI., otherwise "Vair bellies." This is usually shown to be hairy and represented brown. Possibly this is the same as the *Plumeté* to which Mr. Woodward refers.

Some heraldic writers also speak of *varry* as meaning the pieces of which the vair is composed; they also use the terms *vairy cuppy* and *vairy tassy* for *potent-counter-potent*, perhaps from the drawings in some instances resembling *cups;* that is a possible meaning of *tassa*. It may be said that all these variations of the ancient *vair* arise from mere accident (generally bad drawing), supplemented by over refinement on the part of the heraldic writers who have described them. This generalisation may be extended in its application from vair to many other heraldic matters. To all intents and purposes British heraldry now or hitherto has only known vair and potent.

One of the earliest rules one learns in the study of armory is that colour cannot be placed upon colour, nor metal upon metal. Now this is a definite rule which must practically always be rigidly observed. Many writers have gone so far as to say that the only case of an infraction of this rule will be found in the arms of Jerusalem: Argent, a cross potent between four crosslets or. This was a favourite windmill at which the late Dr. Woodward tilted vigorously, and in the appendix to his "Treatise on Heraldry" he enumerates some twenty-six instances of the violation of the rule. The whole of the instances he quoted, however, are taken from Continental armory, in which these exceptions—for even on the Continent such *arms fausses* are noticeable exceptions—occur much more frequently than in this country. Nevertheless such exceptions *do* occur in British armory, and the following instances of well-known coats which break the rule may be quoted.

The arms of Lloyd of Ffos-y-Bleiddied, co. Cardigan, and Danyrallt, co. Carmarthen, are: "Sable, a spearhead imbrued proper between three scaling-ladders argent, on a chief *gules* a castle of the second" (see Plate XXX.). Burke in his "General Armory" says this coat of arms was granted to Cadifor ap Dyfnwal, ninth in descent from Roderick the Great, Prince of Wales, by his cousin the great Lord Rhys, for taking the castle of Cardigan by escalade from the Earl of Clare and the Flemings in 1164. Another instance is a coat of Meredith recorded in Ulster's Office and now inherited by the Hon. Richard Edmund Meredith, a judge of the Supreme Court of Judicature of Ireland and a Judicial Commissioner of the Irish Land Commission. These arms are: "Gules, on a chevron *sable*, between three goats' heads erased, as many trefoils or." An instance of comparatively recent date will be found in the grant of the arms of Thackeray (Fig. 245). A little careful research, no doubt, would produce a large number of English instances.

Furs may be placed upon either metal or colour, as may also any charge which is termed proper. German heralds describe furs and natural colours as amphibious. It is perfectly legitimate to place fur upon fur, and though not often found, numbers of examples can be quoted; probably one will suffice. The arms of Richardson are: Sable, two hawks belled or, on a chief indented ermine, a pale ermines, and three lions' heads counterchanged. It is also correct to place ermine upon argent, as in the arms of Dundas of Arniston, which are: Argent, a lion rampant gules, a bordure ermine, and Dunscombe (see Plate XXVI.). But such coats are not very frequently found, and it is usual in designing a coat to endeavour to arrange that the fur shall be treated as metal or colour according to what may be its background. The reason for this is obvious. It is correct, though unusual, for a charge which is blazoned proper, and yet depicted in a recognised heraldic colour, to be placed upon colour; and where such cases occur, care should be taken that the charges are blazoned proper. A charge composed of more than one tincture, that is, of a metal and colour, may be placed upon a field

of either; for example the well-known coat of Stewart, which is: Or, a fess chequy azure and argent, or *vice versâ*: Per pale ermine and azure, a fess wavy gules (Broadbent); or: Azure, a lion rampant argent, debruised by a fess per pale of the second and gules (Walsh); but in such coats it will always be found that the first tincture of the composite charge should be in opposition to the field upon which it is superimposed; for instance, the arms of Stewart are: Or, a fess chequy azure and argent. To blazon or depict them with a fess chequy argent and azure would be incorrect. When an ordinary is charged upon both metal and colour, it would be quite correct for it to be of either metal, colour, or fur, and in such cases it has never been considered either exceptional or an infraction of the rule that colour must not be placed upon colour, nor metal upon metal. There is one point, however, which is one of these little points one has to learn from actual experience, and which I believe has never yet been quoted in any handbook of heraldry, and that is, that this rule must be thrown overboard with regard to crests and supporters. I cannot call to mind an instance of colour upon colour, but a gold collar around the neck of an argent crest will constantly be met with. The sinister supporter of the Royal achievement is a case in point, and this rule, which forbids colour upon colour, and metal upon metal, only holds with regard to supporters and crests when the crest or supporter itself is treated as a field and *charged with* one or more objects. The Royal labels, as already stated, appear to be a standing infraction of the rule if white and argent are to be heraldically treated as identical. The rule is also disregarded entirely as regards Scottish cadency bordures.

So long as the field is party, that is, divided into an equal number of pieces; for example, paly, barruly, or bendy, or party per bend, or per chevron; it may be composed of two metals or two colours, because the pieces all being equal, and of equal number, they all are parts of the field, none being charges.

Before leaving the subject of the field, one must not omit to mention certain exceptions which hardly fall within any of the before-mentioned categories. One of these can only be described by the word "landscape." It is not uncommon in British armory, though I know of but one instance where the actual field itself needs to be so described. This is the coat of the family of Franco, the paternal ancestors of Sir Massey Lopes, Bart., and Lord Ludlow. The name was changed from Franco to Lopes by Royal Licence dated the 4th of May 1831. Whether this coat of arms originated in an English grant, or whether the English grant of it amounts to no more than an attempt at the registration of a previously existing or greatly similar foreign coat of arms for the name of Franco, I am unaware, but the coat certainly is blazoned: "In a landscape field, a fountain, therefrom issuing a palm-tree all proper."

But landscape has very extensively been made use of in the augmentations which were granted at the end of the eighteenth and beginning of the nineteenth centuries. In these cases the augmentation very generally consisted of a chief and thereon a representation either of some fort or ship or action, and though the chief is officially blazoned argent in nearly every case, there is no doubt the artist was permitted, and perhaps intended, to depict clouds and other "atmosphere" to add to the verisimilitude of the picture. These augmentations will be more especially considered in a later chapter, but here one may perhaps be permitted to remark, that execrable as we now consider such landscape heraldry, it ought not to be condemned in the wholesale manner in which it has been, because it was typical of the over elaboration to be found in all art and all artistic ideas of the period in which we find it originating. Heraldry and heraldic art have always been a mirror of the artistic ideas prevalent at equivalent periods, and unless heraldry is to be wholly relegated to consideration as a dead subject, it is an anachronism to depict an action the date of which is well known (and which date it is desired to advertise and not conceal) in a method of art belonging to a different period. In family arms the case is different, as with those the idea apparently is always the concealment of the date of nobility.

The "landscape" variety of heraldry is more common in Germany than with us, and Herr Ströhl writes: "Of very little heraldic worth are the old house and home signs as they were used by landed proprietors, tradesmen, and artisans or workmen, as indicative of their possessions, wares, or productions. These signs, originally simply outline pictures, were later introduced into heraldic soil, inasmuch as bourgeois families raised to the nobility adopted their house signs as heraldic charges upon their shields."

There are also many coats of arms which run: "In base, a representation of water proper," and one of the best instances of this will be found in the arms of Oxford, though for the sake of preserving the pun the coat in this case is blazoned: "Argent, an ox gules passing over a ford proper." Similar instances occur in the arms of Renfrew, Queensferry, Leith, Ryde, and scores of other towns. It has always been considered permissible to represent these either by an attempt to depict natural water, or else in the ancient heraldic way of representing water, namely "barry wavy argent and azure." There are many other coats of arms which are of a similar character though specifically blazoned "barry wavy argent and azure." Now this representation of water in base can hardly be said to be a charge, but perhaps it might be dismissed as such were it not that one coat of arms exists in Scotland, the whole of the field of which is simply a representation of water. Unfortunately this coat of arms has never been matriculated in Lyon Register or received official sanction; but there is no doubt of its ancient usage, and were it to be now matriculated in conformity with the Act of 1672, there is very little doubt that the ancient characteristic would be retained. The arms are those of the town of Inverary in Argyllshire, and the blazon of the coat, according to the form it is depicted upon the Corporate seal, would be for the field: "The sea proper, therein a net suspended from the dexter chief and the sinister fess points to the base; and entangled in its meshes five herrings," which is about the most remarkable coat of arms I have ever come across.

Occasionally a "field," or portion of a field, will be found to be a representation of masonry. This may be either proper or of some metal or colour. The arms of the city of Bath are: "Party per fess embattled azure and argent, the base masonry, in chief two bars wavy of the second; over all, a sword in pale gules, hilt and pommel or." The arms of Reynell are: "Argent, masoned sable, a chief indented of the second."

SEMÉ

The use of the term "semé" must be considered before we leave the subject of the field. It simply means "powdered with" or "strewed with" any objects, the number of the latter being unlimited, the purpose being to evenly distribute them over the shield. In depicting anything semé, care is usually taken that some of the charges (with which the field is semé) shall be partly defaced by the edges of the shield, or the ordinary upon which they are charged, or by the

superior charge itself, to indicate that it is not charged with a specific number of objects.

There are certain special terms which may be noted. A field or charge semé of fleur-de-lis is termed "semé-de-lis," but if semé of bezants it is bezanté, and is termed platé if semé of plates.

A field semé of billets is billetty or billetté, and when semé of cross crosslets it is termed crusilly. A field or charge semé of drops is termed goutté or gutty.

Instances of coats of which the field is semé will be found in the arms of De la Warr (see Fig. 68), which are:

FIG. 68.—Arms of John, Lord De la Warr (d. 1398). (From MS. Ashm. 804, iv.)

FIG. 69.—Arms of John, Lord Beaumont, K.G. (d. 1396). (From his Garter Plate: 1 and 4, Beaumont; 2 and 3, azure, three garbs or (for Comyn).

FIG. 70.—Arms of Gilbert Umfraville, Earl of Kyme (d. 1421). (From Harl. MS. 6163).

Gules, crusily, and a lion rampant argent; Beaumont (see Fig. 69): Azure, semé-de-lis and a lion rampant or; and Umfraville (see Fig. 70): Gules, semé of crosses flory, and a cinquefoil or.

The goutte or drop occasionally figures (in a specified number) as a charge; but such cases are rare, its more frequent use being to show a field semé. British heraldry alone has evolved separate names for the different colours, all other nations simply using the term "goutté" or "gutté," and specifying the colour. The terms we have adopted are as follows: For drops of gold, "gutté-d'or"; silver, "gutté-d'eau" (when borne as a charge it is generally termed an icicle); for gules, "gutté-de-sang"; azure, "gutté-de-l'armes"; vert, "gutté-de-l'huile"; and sable, "gutté-de-poix."

A field semé must not be confused with diapering, for whilst the objects with which a field is semé are an integral part of the arms, diapering is a purely artistic and optional matter.

DIAPERING

The diapering of armorial emblazonments is a matter with which the *Science* of armory has no concern. It never forms any part of the blazon, and is never officially noticed, being considered, and very properly allowed to remain, a purely artistic detail. From the artistic point of view it has some importance, as in many of the earliest instances of handicraft in which armorial decoration appears very elaborate diapering is introduced. The frequency with which diapering is met with in armorial handicraft is strangely at variance with its absence in heraldic paintings of the same periods, a point which may perhaps be urged upon the attention of some of the heraldic artists of the present day, who would rather seem to have failed to grasp the true purpose and origin and perhaps also the use of diaper. In stained glass and enamel work, where the use of diaper is most frequently met with, it was introduced for the express purpose of catching and breaking up the light, the result of which was to give an enormously increased effect of brilliance to the large and otherwise flat surfaces. These tricks of their art and craft the old handicraftsmen were past masters in the use of. But no such purpose could be served in a small painting upon vellum. For this reason early heraldic emblazonments are seldom if ever found to have been diapered. With the rise of heraldic engraving amongst the "little masters" of German art, the opportunity left to their hands by the absence of colour naturally led to the renewed use of diaper to avoid the appearance of blanks in their work. The use of diaper at the present day needs to be the result of careful study and thought, and its haphazard employment is not recommended. Plate X. gives some number of typical "Gothic" and "Renaissance"

FIG. 71.—Arms of the Herren von Schonneck, from Grünenberg's *Wappenbuch*, 1483.

FIG. 72.—Arms of Richard de Beauchamp, Earl of Worcester (*d.* 1422). Gules, a fess between six cross crosslets or, a crescent sable for difference. (Note the early form of the cross crosslets.)

diaperings. A very effective example of diapering will be found in Fig. 71, which shows the arms of von Schonneck as given in the *Wappenbuch* (1483) of Grünenberg.

Another pleasing example will be found in Fig. 72, which is from a representation in stained glass of the arms of the Earl of Worcester.

If, as Woodward states (an assertion one is rather inclined to doubt), there are some cases abroad in which the constant use of diapering has been stereotyped into an integral part of the arms, these cases must be exceedingly few in number, and they certainly have no counterpart in the armory of this country. Where diapering is for artistic reasons employed, care must always be taken that the decorative form employed cannot be mistaken for a field either charged or semé.

PARTITION LINES

If there is one subject which the ordinary text-books of armory treat in the manner of classification adapted to an essay on natural history or grammar, with its attending rigidity of rule, it is the subject of partition lines; and yet the whole subject is more in the nature

of a set of explanations which must each be learned on its own merits. The usual lines of partition are themselves well enough known; and it is hardly necessary to elaborate the different variations at any great length. They may, however, be enumerated as follows: Engrailed, embattled, indented, invecked or invected, wavy or undy, nebuly, dancetté, raguly, potenté, dovetailed, and urdy. These are the lines which are recognised by most modern heraldic text-books and generally recapitulated; but we shall have occasion later to refer to others which are very well known, though apparently they have never been included in the classification of partition lines (Fig. 73). *Engrailed*, as every one knows, is formed by a continuous

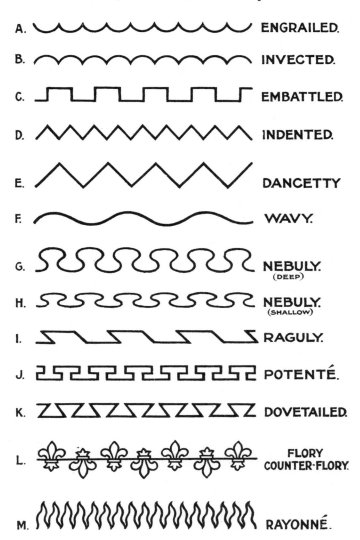

FIG. 73.—Lines of Partition.

and concurrent series of small semicircles conjoined each to each, the sharp points formed by the conjunction of the two arcs being placed outwards. This partition line may be employed for the rectilinear charges known as "ordinaries" or "sub-ordinaries." In the bend, pale, pile, cross, chief, and fess, when these are described as engrailed the enclosing lines of the ordinary, other than the edges of the shield, are all composed of these small semicircles with the points turned *outwards*, and the word "outwards" must be construed as pointing away from the centre of the ordinary when it is depicted. In the case of a chief the points are turned downwards, but it is rather difficult to describe the use of the term when used as a partition line of the field. The only instance I can call to mind where it is so employed is the case of Baird of Ury, the arms of this family being: Per pale engrailed gules and or, a boar passant counterchanged. In this instance the points are turned towards the sinister side of the shield, which would seem to be correct, as, there being no ordinary, they must be outwards from the most important position affected, which in this case undoubtedly is the dexter side of the shield. In the same way "per fess engrailed" would be presumably depicted with the points outwards from the chief line of the shield, that is, pointing downwards; and I should imagine that in "per bend engrailed" the points of the semicircles would again be placed inclined towards the dexter base of the shield. This point, however, which puzzled me much in depicting the arms of Baird of Ury, I could find explained in no text-book upon the subject.

The term *invect* or *invecked* is the precise opposite of engrailed. It is similarly composed of small semicircles, but the points are turned inwards instead of outwards, so that it is no more than the exact reverse of engrailed, and all the regulations concerning the one need to be observed concerning the other, with the proviso that they are reversed.

The partition line *embattled* has certain peculiarities of its own. When dividing the field there can be no difficulty about it, inasmuch as the crenellations are equally inwards and outwards from any point, and it should be noted that the term "crenellé" is almost as often used as "embattled." When, however, the term describes an ordinary, certain points have to be borne in mind. The fess or the bar embattled is drawn with the crenellations *on the upper side* only, the under edge being plain unless the ordinary is described both as "embattled and counter-embattled." Similarly a chevron is only crenellated on the upper edge unless it is described as both embattled and counter-embattled, but a pale or a bend embattled is crenellated on both edges as is the cross or saltire. I have never come across a pile embattled; but it would naturally be embattled on both edges.

The terms *indented* and *dancetté* need to be considered together, because they differ very little, and only in the fact that whilst indented may be drawn with any number of teeth, dancetté is drawn with a limited number, which is usually three complete teeth in the width of the field. But it should be observed that this rule is not so hard and fast that the necessity of artistic depicting may not modify it slightly. An ordinary which is indented would follow much the same rules as an ordinary which was engrailed, except that the teeth are made by small straight lines for the indentations instead of by small semicircles, and instances can doubtless be found of all the ordinaries qualified by the term indented. Dancetté, however, does not lend itself so readily to general application, and is usually to be found applied to either a fess or chief, or occasionally a bend. In the case of a fess dancetté the indentations on the top and the bottom lines are made to fit into each other, so that instead of having a straight band with the edge merely toothed, one gets an up and down zig-zag band with three complete teeth at the top and three complete teeth at the bottom. Whilst a fess, a bar, a bend, and a chief can be found dancetté, I do not see how it would be possible to draw a saltire or a cross dancetté. At any rate the resulting figure would be most ugly, and would appear ill-balanced. A pile and a chevron seem equally impossible, though there does not seem to be the like objection to a pale dancetté. An instance of a bend dancetté is found in the arms of Cuffe (Lord Desart), which are: Argent, on a bend dancetté sable, plain cotised azure, three fleurs-de-lis, and on each cotise as many bezants.

Wavy or *undy*, which is supposed to have been taken from water, and *nebuly*, which is supposed to be derived from clouds, are of course lines which are well known. They are equally applicable to any ordinary and to any partition of the field; but in both cases it should be noticed by artists that there is no one definite or accepted method of depicting these lines, and one is quite at liberty, and might be recommended to widen out the indentations, or to increase them in height as the artistic requirements of the work in hand may seem to render advisable. It is only by bearing this in mind and treating these lines with freedom that really artistic work can sometimes be produced where they occur. There is no fixed rule either as to the width which these lines may occupy or as to the number of indentations as compared with the width of the shield, and it is a pity to introduce or recognise any regulations of this character where none exist. There are writers who think it not unlikely that vairé and barry nebuly were one and the same thing. It is at any rate difficult in some old representations to draw any noticeable distinctions between the methods of depicting barry nebuly and vair.

The line *raguly* has been the subject of much discussion. It, and the two which follow, viz. potenté and dovetailed, are all comparatively modern introductions. It would be interesting if some enthusiast would go carefully through the ancient Rolls of Arms and find the earliest occurrences of these terms. My own impression is that they would all be found to be inventions of the mediæval writers on heraldry. Raguly is the same as embattled, with the crenellations put upon the slant. Some writers say they should slant one way, others give them slanting the reverse. In a pale or a bend the teeth must point upwards; but in a fess I should hesitate to say whether it were more correct for them to point to the dexter or to the sinister, and I am inclined to consider that either is perfectly correct. At any rate, whilst they are usually drawn inclined to the dexter, in "Woodward and Burnett" they are to the sinister, and Guillim gives them turned to the dexter, saying, "This form of line I never yet met with in use as a partition, though frequently in composing of ordinaries referring them like to the trunks of trees with the branches lopped off, and that (as I take it) it was intended to represent." Modern heraldry supplies an instance which in the days of Mr. Guillim, of course, did not exist to refer to. This instance occurs in the arms of the late Lord Leighton, which were: "Quarterly per fess raguly or and gules, in the second and third quarters a wyvern of the first." It is curious that Guillim, even in the edition of 1724, does not mention any of the remaining terms. Dovetailed in modern armory is even yet but seldom made use of, though I can quote two instances of coats of arms in which it is to be found, namely, the arms of Kirk, which are: "Gules, a chevron dovetailed ermine, on a chief argent, three dragons' heads couped of the field;" and Ambrose (see Plate XXX.): "Azure, two lions passant in pale argent, on a chief dovetailed, and the last a fleur-de-lis between two annulets of the first." Other instances of dovetailed used as a line of partition will be found in the case of the arms of Farmer (Fig. 396), which are: "Per chevron dovetailed gules and argent, in chief two lions' heads erased of the last, and in base a salamander in flames proper;" and in the arms of Fenton (Fig. 74), namely: "Per pale argent and sable, a cross dovetailed, in the first and fourth quarters a fleur-de-lis, and in the second and third a trefoil slipped all countercharged." There are, of course, many others. As to the term *urdy*, which is given in Woodward and Burnett and also in Berry, I can only say I personally have never come across an instance of its use as a partition line. A cross or a billet urdy one knows, but urdy as a partition line I have yet to find. It is significant that it is omitted in Parker except as a term applicable to a cross, and the instances and variations given by Berry, "urdy in point paleways" and "contrary urdy," I should be much more inclined to consider as variations of vair; and, though it is always well to settle points which can be settled, I think urdy and its use as a partition line may be well left for further consideration when examples of it come to hand. The same remarks apply to the term *potenté*.

FIG. 74.—The Arms of Fenton.

There is one term, however, which is frequently to be met with at the present time, but which I have never seen quoted in any text-book under the heading of a partition line; that is, "flory counter-flory," which is of course formed by a succession of fleurs-de-lis alternately reversed and counterchanged. They might of course be blazoned after the quotation of the field as "per bend" or "per chevron" as the case might be, simply as so many fleurs-de-lis counterchanged, and alternately reversed in a specified position; but this never appears to be the case, and consequently the fleurs-de-lis are essentially parts of the field and not charges. I have sometimes thought whether it would not be more correct to depict "per something" flory and counter-flory without completing the fleurs-de-lis, simply leaving the alternate tops of the fleurs-de-lis to show. In the cases of the illustrations which have come under my notice, however, the whole fleur-de-lis is depicted, and as an instance of the use of the term may be mentioned the arms of Dumas (Fig. 137), which are: "Per chevron flory and counter-flory or and azure, in chief two lions' gambs erased, and in base a garb counterchanged." But when the term flory and counter-flory is used in conjunction with an ordinary, *e.g.* a fess flory and counter-flory, the *half* fleurs-de-lis, only alternately reversed, are represented on the *outer* edges of the ordinary.

I think also that the word "arched" should be included as a partition line. I confess that the only form in which I know of it is that it is frequently used by York Herald in designing coats of arms with chiefs arched.

But if a chief can be arched I see no reason why a fess or a bar cannot equally be so altered, and in that case it undoubtedly becomes a recognised line of partition. Perhaps it should be stated that a chief arched is a chief with its base line one arc of a large circle (Figs. 172, 246, and 262). The diameter of the circle and the consequent acuteness of the arch do not appear to be fixed by any definite rule, and here again artistic requirements must be the controlling factor in any decision. Elvin in his "Dictionary of Heraldic Terms" gives a curious assortment of lines, the most curious of all, perhaps, being indented embowed, or hacked and hewed. Where such a term originated or in what coat of arms it is to be found I am ignorant, but the appearance is exactly what would be presented by a piece of wood hacked with an axe at regular intervals. Elvin again makes a difference between bretessed and embattled-counter-embattled, making the embattlement on either side of an ordinary identical in the former and alternated in the latter. He also makes a difference between raguly, which is the conventional form universally adopted, and raguled and trunked, where the ordinary takes the representation of the trunk of a tree with the branches lopped; but these and many others that he gives are refinements of idea which personally I should never expect to find in actual use, and of the instances of which I am unaware. I think, however, the term "rayonne," which is found in both the arms of O'Hara and the arms of Colman (Fig. 106), and which is formed by the addition of rays to the ordinary, should take a place amongst lines of partition, though I admit I know of no instance in which it is employed to divide the field.

METHODS OF PARTITION

The field of any coat of arms is the surface colour of the shield, and is supposed to include the area within the limits formed by its outline. There are, as has been already stated, but few coats of a single colour minus a charge to be found in British heraldry. But there are many which consist of a field divided by partition lines only, of which some instances were given on page 44.

A shield may be divided by partition lines running in the direction of almost any "ordinary," in which case the field will be described as "per bend" or "per chevron," &c. It may be:

Per fess . . .	Plate IX., Fig. 10	
Per bend . . .	" " 42	
Per bend sinister .	" " 43	
Per pale . . .	" " 2	
Per chevron . .	" " 58	
Per cross . . .	" " 25	
(though it should be noted that the more usual term employed for this is "quarterly")		
Per saltire . . .	Plate IX., Fig. 68	

But a field cannot be "per pile" or "per chief," because there is no other way of representing these ordinaries.

A field can be composed of any number of pieces in the form of the ordinaries filling the area of the shield, in which case the field is said to be "paly," "bendy," "chevronny," &c., but the number of pieces must be specified. As indicating at the same time the forms of the ordinaries and the methods of partitioning the shield, we cannot do better than annex the blazons of the shields on Plates IX. and X. before considering the charges themselves in detail. These will be found after the chapter on the Rules of Blazon.

Another method of partition will be found in the fields "checky" (or "chequy") and lozengy; but these divisions, as also the foregoing, will be treated more specifically under the different ordinaries. A field which is party need not necessarily have all its lines of partition the same. This peculiarity, however, seldom occurs except in the case of a field quarterly, the object in coats of this character being to prevent different quarters of one coat of arms being ranked as or taken to be quarterings representing different families. Examples of this will be found in the arms of Croft of Croft Castle[b]

[b] Arms of Croft of Croft Castle : 1. Quarterly per fess indented azure and argent, in the first quarter a lion passant guardant or (for Croft) ; 2. or, two lions passant gules ; 3. paly of six argent and gules, a lion rampant sable (for Owen ap Griffith Vychan) ; 4. gules, a bend between six lions' heads erased argent (for Skull). Crests : 1. a lion passant guardant argent ; 2. a wyvern sable, vulned in the side gules.

(see Plate XI.) and Farish (see Plate XXXII.). The latter instance consists of quarterings of Farish[c] and Garthwaite. But the design in the second and third quarterings is really one indivisible coat of arms, though (admittedly under the terms of the grant) founded upon two coats originally borne quarterly.

A. C. F-D. AND H. S.

[c] Arms of Edward Garthwaite Farish, Esq. : Quarterly, 1 and 4, argent, a chevron azure, guttée-d'eau, between two horse-shoes in chief and a bugle-horn stringed in base all of the second (for Farish) ; 2 and 3, quarterly per fess indented, i. and iv., gules, a chevron or ; ii. and iii., azure, a fret of the second (for Garthwaite). Mantling azure and argent. Crest : on a wreath of the colours, upon two horse-shoes or, a bugle-horn stringed azure. Motto : "Forward."

CHAPTER XI

THE RULES OF BLAZON

THE word "Blazon" is used with some number of meanings, but practically it may be confined to the verb "to blazon," which is to describe in words a given coat of arms, and the noun "blazon," which is such a description.

Care should be taken to differentiate between the employment of the term "blazon" and the verb "to emblazon," which means to depict in colour.

It may here be remarked, however, that to illustrate by the use of outline with written indications of colour is termed "to trick," and a picture of arms of this character is termed "a trick."

The term *trick* has of late been extended (though one almost thinks improperly) to include representations of arms in which the colours are indicated by the specified tincture lines in use.

The subject of blazon has of late acquired rather more importance than has hitherto been conceded to it, owing to an unofficial, and outside, attempt to introduce a new system of blazoning under the guise of a supposed reversion to earlier forms of description. This it is not, but even if it were what it claims to be, merely the revival of ancient forms and methods, its reintroduction cannot be said to be either expedient or permissible, because the ancient practice does not permit of extension to the limits within which more modern armory has developed, and modern armory, though less ancient, is armory equally with the more ancient and simpler examples to be found in earlier times. To ignore modern armory is simply futile and absurd.

The rules to be employed in blazon are simple, and comparatively few in number.

The commencement of any blazon is of necessity a description of the *field*, the one word signifying its colour being employed if it be a simple field; or, if it be composite, such terms as are necessary. Thus, a coat divided "per pale" or "per chevron" is so described, and whilst the Scottish field of this character is officially termed "Parted" [per pale, or per chevron], the English equivalent is "Party," though this word is more often omitted than not in the blazon which commences "per pale," or "per chevron," as the case may be.

The description of the different colours and different divisions of the field have all been detailed in earlier chapters, but it may be added that in a "party" coloured field, that colour or tincture is mentioned first which occupies the more important part of the escutcheon. Thus, in a field "per bend," "per chevron," or

"per fess," the upper portion of the field is first referred to; in a coat "per pale," the dexter side is the more important; and in a coat "quarterly," the tinctures of the 1st and 4th quarters are more important than the tinctures of the 2nd and 3rd.

The only division upon which there has seemed any uncertainty is the curious one "gyronny," but the correct method to be employed in this case can very easily be recognised by taking the first quarter of the field, and therein considering the field as if it were simply "per bend." After the field has been described, anything of which the field is semé must next be alluded to, *e.g.* gules, semé-de-lis or, &c.

The second thing to be mentioned in the blazon is the principal charge. We will consider first those cases in which it is an ordinary. Thus, one would speak of "Or, a chevron gules," or, if there be other charges as well as the ordinary, "Azure, a bend between two horses' heads or," or "Gules, a chevron between three roses argent."

The colour of the ordinary is not mentioned until after the charge, if it be the same as the latter, but if it be otherwise it must of course be specified, as in the coat: "Or, a fess gules between three crescents sable." If the ordinary is charged, the charges thereupon, being less important than the charges in the field, are mentioned subsequently, as in the coat: "Gules, on a bend argent between two fountains proper, a rose gules between two mullets sable."

The position of the charges need not be specified when they would naturally fall into a certain position with regard to the ordinaries. Thus, a chevron between three figures of necessity has two in chief and one in base. A bend between two figures of necessity has one above and one below. A fess has two above and one below. A cross between four has one in each angle. In none of these cases is it necessary to state the position. If, however, those positions or numbers do not come within the category mentioned, care must be taken to specify what the coat exactly is.

If a bend is accompanied only by one charge, the position of this charge must be stated. For example: "Gules, a bend or, in chief a crescent argent." A chevron with four figures would be described: "Argent, a chevron between three escallops in chief and one in base or," though it would be equally correct to say: "Argent, a chevron between four escallops, three in chief and one in base or." In the same way we should get: "Vert, on a cross or, and in the 1st quarter a bezant, an estoile sable;" though, to avoid confusion, this coat would more probably be blazoned: "Vert, a cross or, charged with an estoile sable, and in the 1st quarter a bezant." This example will indicate the latitude which is permissible if, for the sake of avoiding confusion and making a blazon more readily understandable, some deviation from the strict rules appears desirable.

If there be no ordinary on a shield, the charge which occupies the chief position is mentioned first. For example: "Or, a lion rampant sable between three boars' heads erased gules, two in chief and one in base." Many people, however, would omit any reference to the position of the boars' heads, taking it for granted that, as there were only three, they would be 2 and 1, which is the normal position of three charges in any coat of arms. If, however, the coat of arms had the three boars' heads all above the lion, it would then be necessary to blazon it: "Or, a lion rampant sable, in chief three boars' heads erased gules."

When a field is *semé* of anything, this is taken to be a part of the field, and not a representation of a number of charges. Consequently the arms of Long are blazoned: "Sable, semé of cross crosslets, a lion rampant argent." As a matter of fact the semé of cross crosslets is always termed *crusilly*, and a semé of fleurs-de-lis, *semé de lys*.

When charges are placed around the shield in the position they would occupy if placed upon a bordure, these charges are said to be "in orle," as in the arms of Hutchinson: "Quarterly, azure and gules, a lion rampant erminois, within four cross crosslets argent, and as many bezants alternately in orle;" though it is equally permissible to term charges in such a position "an orle of [*e.g.* cross crosslets argent and bezants alternately]," or so many charges "in orle" (see Fig. 75).

If an ordinary is engrailed, or invected, this is at once stated, the term occurring before the colour of the ordinary. Thus: "Argent, on a chevron nebuly between three crescents gules, as many roses of the field." When a charge upon an ordinary is the same colour as the field, the name of the colour is not repeated, but those charges are said to be "of the field."

It is the constant endeavour, under the recognised

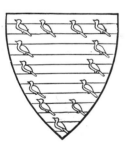

FIG. 75.—Arms of Aymer de Valence, Earl of Pembroke: "Baruly argent and azure, an orle of martlets gules." (From his seal.)

FIG. 76.—The arms of John de Bretagne, Earl of Richmond.

system of blazon, to avoid the use of the name of the same colour a second time in the blazon. Thus: "Quarterly, gules and or, a cross counterchanged between in the first quarter a sword erect proper, pommel and hilt of the second; in the second quarter a rose of the first, barbed and seeded of the third; in the third quarter a fleur-de-lis azure; and in the fourth quarter a mullet *gold*"—the use of the term "gold" being alone permissible in such a case.

Any animal which needs to be described, also needs

its position to be specified. It may be rampant, segreant, passant, statant, or trippant, as the case may be. It may also sometimes be necessary to specify its position upon the shield, but the terms peculiarly appropriated to specific animals will be given in the chapters in which these animals are dealt with.

With the exception of the chief, the quarter, the canton, the flaunch, and the bordure, an ordinary or sub-ordinary is always of greater importance, and therefore should be mentioned before any other charge, but in the cases alluded to the remainder of the shield is first blazoned, before attention is paid to these figures. Thus we should get: "Argent, a chevron between three mullets gules, on a chief of the last three crescents of the

FIG. 77.—The arms of Robert Ratcliffe, Earl of Sussex (*d.* 1542): Quarterly, 1. argent, a bend engrailed sable (Ratcliffe); 2. (Fitz Walter); 3. argent, a lion rampant sable, crowned or, within a bordure azure (Burnel); 4. argent, three bars gules (for Multon of Egremont).

FIG. 78.—Arms of John de Beaumont, Lord Beaumont (*d.* 1369): Azure, semé-de-lis and a lion rampant or, over all a bend gobony argent and gules. (From his seal.)

second;" or "Sable, a lion rampant between three fleurs-de-lis or, on a canton argent a mascle of the field;" or "Gules, two chevronels between three mullets pierced or, within a bordure engrailed argent charged with eight roses of the field." The arms in Fig. 76 are an interesting example of this point. They are those of John de Bretagne, Earl of Richmond (*d.* 1334), and would properly be blazoned: "Chequy or and azure, a bordure gules, charged with lions passant guardant or ('a bordure of England'), over all a canton (sometimes a quarter) ermine."

If two ordinaries or sub-ordinaries appear in the same field, certain discretion needs to be exercised, but the arms of Fitzwalter (see Fig. 77), for example, are as follows: "Or, a fess between two chevrons gules."

When charges are placed in a series following the direction of any ordinary they are said to be "in bend," "in chevron," or "in pale," as the case may be, and not only must their position on the shield as regards each other be specified, but their individual direction must also be noted.

A coat of arms in which three spears were placed side by side, but each erect, would be blazoned: "Gules, three tilting-spears palewise in fess;" but if the spears were placed horizontally, one above the other, they would be blazoned: "Three tilting-spears fesswise in pale," because in the latter case each spear is placed fesswise, but the three occupy in relation to each other the position of a pale. Three tilting-spears fesswise which were not *in pale* would be depicted 2 and 1.

When one charge surmounts another, the undermost one is mentioned first, as in the arms of Beaumont (see Fig. 78). Here the lion rampant is the principal charge, and the bend which debruises it is consequently mentioned afterwards.

In the cases of a cross and of a saltire, the charges when all are alike would simply be described as between four objects, though the term "cantonned by" four objects is sometimes met with. If the objects are not the same, they must be specified as being in the 1st, 2nd, or 3rd quarters, if the ordinary be a cross. If it be a saltire, it will be found that in Scotland the charges are mentioned as being in chief and base, and in the "flanks." In England they would be described as being *in pale* and *in fess* if the alternative charges are the same; if not, they would be described as *in chief*, on the dexter side, on the sinister side, and *in base*.

When a specified number of charges is immediately followed by the same number of charges elsewhere disposed, the number is not repeated, the words "as many" being substituted instead. Thus: "Argent, on a chevron between three roses gules, as many crescents of the field." When any charge, ordinary, or mark of cadency surmounts a single object, that object is termed "debruised" by that ordinary. If it surmounts *everything*, as, for instance, "a bendlet sinister," this would be termed "over all." When a coat of arms is "party" coloured in its field and the charges are alternately of the same colours transposed, the term *counterchanged* is used. For example, "Party-per pale argent and sable, three chevronels between as many mullets pierced all counterchanged." In that case the coat is divided down the middle, the dexter field being argent, and the sinister sable; the charges on the sable being argent, whilst the charges on the argent are sable. A mark of cadency is mentioned last, and is termed "for difference"; a mark of bastardy, or a mark denoting lack of blood descent, is termed "for distinction."

Certain practical hints, which, however, can hardly be termed *rules*, were suggested by the late Mr. J. Gough Nicholls in 1863, when writing in the *Herald and Genealogist*, and subsequent practice has since conformed therewith, though it may be pointed out with advantage that these suggestions are practically, and to all intents and purposes, the same rules which have been observed officially over a long period. Amongst these suggestions he advises that the blazoning of every coat or quarter should begin with a capital letter, and that, save on the occurrence of proper names, no other capitals should be employed. He also suggests that punctuation marks should be avoided as much as possible, his own practice being to limit the use of the comma to its occurrence after each tincture. He suggests also that figures should be omitted in all cases except in the numbering of quarterings. When one or more quarterings occur, each is treated separately on its own merits and blazoned entirely without reference to any other quartering.

In blazoning a coat in which some quarterings (grand quarterings) are composed of several coats placed sub-quarterly, sufficient distinction is afforded for English purposes of writing or printing if Roman numerals are employed to indicate the grand quarters, and Arabic figures the sub-quarters. But in *speaking* such a method would need to be somewhat modified in accordance with the Scottish practice, which describes grand quarterings as such, and so alludes to them.

The extensive use of bordures, charged and uncharged, in Scotland, which figure sometimes round the sub-quarters, sometimes round the grand quarters, and sometimes round the entire escutcheon, causes so much confusion that for the purposes of blazoning it is essen-tial that the difference between quarters and grand quarters should be clearly defined.

In order to simplify the blazoning of a shield, and to express the position of the charges, the *field* has been divided into *points*, of which those placed near the top, and to the dexter, are always considered the more important. In heraldry, dexter and sinister are determined, not from the point of view of the onlooker, but from that of the bearer of the shield. The following diagrams will serve to explain the plan of a shield's surface :—

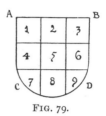

FIG. 79.

A to B, the chief; C to D, the base; A to C, dexter side; B to D, sinister side. A, dexter chief; B, sinister chief; C, dexter base; D, sinister base. 1, 2, 3, chief; 7, 8, 9, base; 2, 5, 8, pale; 4, 5, 6, fess; 5, fess point.

If a second shield be placed upon the fess point, this is called an inescutcheon (in German, the "heart-shield"). The enriching of the shield with an inescutcheon came into lively use in Germany in the course of the latter half of the fifteenth century. Later on, further points of honour were added, as the honour point (a, Fig. 80), and the nombril point (b, Fig. 80).

FIG. 80.

These extra shields laid upon the others should correspond as much as possible in shape to the chief shield. If between the inescutcheon and the chief shield still another be inserted, it is called the "middle shield," from its position, but except in Anglicised editions of Continental arms, these distinctions are quite foreign to British armory.

In conclusion, it may be stated that although the foregoing are the rules which are usually observed, and that every effort should be made to avoid unnecessary tautology, and to make the blazon as brief as possible, it is by no manner of means considered officially, or unofficially, that any one of these rules is so unchangeable that in actual practice it cannot be modified if it should seem advisable so to do. For the essential necessity of accuracy is of far greater importance than any desire to be brief, or to avoid tautology. This should be borne in mind, and also the fact that in official practice no such hide-bound character is given to these rules, as one is led to believe is the case when perusing most of the ordinary text-books of armory. They certainly are not laws, they are hardly "rules," perhaps being better described as accepted methods of blazoning.

A. C. F-D.

THE ART OF HERALDRY

CHAPTER XII

PLATES IX AND X

THE German term *Heroldsstucken* (heraldic pieces) is the nearest approach to our terms "Ordinaries" and "Sub-Ordinaries," and using it as an equivalent (though it has no such meaning of classification as our own terms possess), the figures which the term *heroldsstucken* comprises would add to the English list some number of terms and figures not met with in our own science. Probably the best method of dealing with the matter will be to append the descriptions of the shields and figures contained in Plates IX. and X. These are as follows:—

PLATE IX

1. Gules. 2. Per pale argent and sable. 3. Per pale gules and azure, a pale argent. (This is sometimes blazoned "tierced in pale" gules, argent and azure, but this is not an acceptable English version.) 4. Gules, a pale or. 5 is a figure which is never found in British armory, but in German would be blazoned : Argent, a dexter flank azure. 6. Paly of four or and azure. 7. Or, two pallets azure. The difference between these two should be noted, because whilst the one is merely paly the other has the field gold with two distinct charges or pallets upon it. The way to distinguish between these two forms will be found in the fact that whilst the one begins with a gold stripe and ends with a blue one, the other begins and ends with gold. This means that it has an uneven number of stripes, and it may be taken as a certain rule that when the number of stripes is even, 4, 6, 8, or 10, it is paly, and when they are uneven, 5, 7, or 9, it is merely a field with so many charges upon it. 8, like No. 5, is not met with in British armory. It would, however, in our terms be blazoned : Gules, in the dexter side of the shield a pallet or. 9. Argent, a pallet azure. It will be noticed that in cases 9 and 7 the width of the pallets varies, and whilst 7 is a bit too wide, 9 is a little too narrow, the width apportioned to No. 9 being really the width which would be found in the case of cottises or endorse, as to which we shall speak later. But it may be taken as a regular rule that (dealing with the ordinary of the pale) if there are more than three stripes upon the shield they are pallets if the sheet is not paly, but anything of a very narrow character is a pallet unless accompanying an ordinary. A single cottise is unknown to English armory. 10. Per fess sable and argent. 11. Gules, a chief or. 12. Argent, the base vert, though this is a form very rarely met with except in the cases where the base is meant to represent water. In English heraldry the equivalent of the base is more frequently found to be a "mount in base vert"; but this would not be represented by an absolutely horizontal line. 13. Per fess gules and argent, a fess sable. (An alternative blazon is "tierced in fess gules sable and argent.") 14. Gules, a fess argent. 15. Barry of four gules and argent. 16. Argent, two bars sable. 17. Vert, a bar in chief or. This figure will not be met with in England, the nearest approach being a chief per fess. Possibly a more correct English blazon would be a fess "enhanced." 18. Azure, a barrulet argent. This also will not be found in English heraldry, the barrulet never being depicted singly. 19. Per pale, the dexter argent, the sinister per fess gules and sable. 20. Per pale, the dexter per fess argent and azure, and the sinister or. 21. Per fess, in chief per pale gules and argent and in base sable. 22. Per fess gules, and in base per pale sable and argent. 23. Argent, a pale and a chief sable. 24. Per fess, the chief per fess azure and argent, the base per pale sable and gules, in base a pale argent. 25. Per cross argent and sable, or alternatively, quarterly argent and sable. 26. Per pale argent and gules, a fess counterchanged. 27. Or, a cross quarter-pierced azure. 28. Chequy gules and argent. (It should be noticed in blazoning anything which is chequy or lozengy that the colour is mentioned first, which is that which occurs first at the top dexter corner.) 29. Paly of six argent and gules, a fess counterchanged. 30. Masonry. 31. Gules, a pale rompu argent. 32. Or, a canton gules. 33 is a figure which is never met with in British armory; in German it is blazoned : Sable a "place" argent. 34, 35, and 36 are never met with in British armory, though 34 might be blazoned : Per fess rompu argent and sable. This would not be an *impossible* coat with us, though I have certainly never met with it. 37 is also purely German, and I should hesitate to put it into English blazon. 38. Per fess embattled azure and or. 39. Per pale embattled argent and gules.

40. Gules, a pale embattled. 41. Per chevron indented azure and or. 42. Per bend argent and azure. 43. Per bend sinister gules and argent. 44 has no British equivalent, and the same remark applies to 45. "Per bend sinister enhanced or and azure," and "per bend sinister depressed vert and argent" might respectively be permissible blazons. 46. Per bend or and argent, a bend sable. An alternative blazon would be "tierced in bend or, sable and argent." 47. Or, a bend gules. 48. Bendy of four argent and sable. 49. Azure, two bends sinister or. 50. Vert, a bend sinister enhanced argent. 51. Or, a bendlet gules. This would never be found alone in British armory, though the bendlet described as such, or as a riband, is not infrequently met with debruising some other charge. 52, though it is a form which has not been employed up to the present time, can easily be rendered into English blazon as follows : Per bend sinister, in chief per bend dexter sable and argent, in base gules. 53 is really "gules, a pile reversed throughout argent," but it will be very frequently found that the old rendering of "per chevron" approximates closely to this. It, however, introduces a well-known foreign term "the point." 54, 55, 56, and 57 are forms which, being applications of the point, are not likely to be met with in British armory, but adopting the term and figure of the point they would be blazoned : 54. Per pale gules and azure, a point or. An alternative blazon would be "tierced in point gules, or, and azure." 55. Per pale gules and argent, a point reversed azure. 56. Per fess or and argent, a point in fess to the dexter gules. 57. Gules, a point in bend argent. 58. Per chevron sable and argent. 59. Per chevron azure and sable, a chevron argent. 60 and 61 may be both blazoned : Gules, a chevron argent. In German heraldry, whilst 60 is the chevron proper, and 61 a chevron "flattened," the latter figure No. 61 is the more usually adopted form in the heraldry of the present day in this country, but the form used in 60 and also in 59 differs very little from the drawing of the chevron to be found in most of the ancient examples. 62. Sable, two chevrons or. 63 and 64 are not forms often to be met with in British armory, and strictly speaking under the English laws of blazon would be : 63. Per chevron reversed sable, and the base per pale argent and gules, or alternatively tierced in pairle. 64. Per chevron, the chief per pale argent and or and the base azure. 64, however, is a form of division which was introduced into the English Royal Arms when the arms of Hanover came to be marshalled with those of this country, and consequently the term, though foreign to our own science, should properly be included. In the case of the arms of Hanover as rendered into English blazon, the division as in 64 was described as "tierced in pairle reversed." 65 is azure, a pall throughout argent ; and 66 is gules, a pall reversed throughout. They are not of frequent occurrence, unless the representation, which is of rather a more natural form of representation of an actual pallium in the arms of the Archbishoprics of York and Canterbury, can be considered under this head. The figure, however, is not infrequent in Scottish heraldry, occurring in the arms of the Cunningham family, and in the case of themselves and allied families it is constantly to be found north of the Tweed. It is, however, known in that country as a shakefork, and the shakefork has been included in some Scottish works as one of the ordinaries. In Scotland, however, the "shakefork" is seldom represented throughout, the ends being practically always couped and pointed, or, to use the proper word, "urdy." 67 is a form which is never likely to be met with in this country, and for which there is no English equivalent. 68. Per saltire gules and argent. 69. Per chevron reversed argent and gules. Whilst having the form of the pile, it is too abbreviated in length properly to serve as a model thereof. 70. Gyronny of eight azure and or. (When this division is of eight pieces, which is the natural number, it is usually merely termed gyronny ; but if of six or twelve, it is essential that the number should be stated.) 71. Argent, a gyron or "esquire" gules. 72. Gules, a lozenge throughout or. In English armory the charge of a lozenge would never be continued as here to the edges of the shield. 73 may be blazoned in two ways. The figures are really a little too square for it to be a true example of a "lozengy" field, though I doubt not that most people would so describe it ; 74, which is more the true lozengy division, might perhaps stand for fusily if the figures were rather more acutely pointed, but taking them exactly as they are, 73 is really "bendy gules and argent, counterchanged bendy sinister," or, as it would sometimes be described, "bendy and bendy sinister counterchanged gules and argent." 74. Lozengy sable and argent. 75 is paly bendy sinister argent and gules. 76 is barry bendy and bendy sinister gules and or. 77. Per bend indented argent and gules. 78. Per bend sinister raguly azure and or. 79.

Argent, a pale raguly sable. 80. Per fess engrailed argent and vert. 81. Per fess invected gules and argent. (It is by no means with any great certainty that these last two blazons are put forward, and many might prefer to reverse Nos. 80 and 81, refer to page 56). 82. Per fess nebuly argent and azure. 83 is not an English form, nor is 84 ; but a literal translation of the German blazon of No. 83 would be "gules, a snail reversed or issuing from the sinister," and No. 84 "per bend gules and argent broken in the form of a linden leaf." 85 is really azure, a point arched argent, but it is not an English form. 86 is argent, a bend wavy azure. 87, which is purely German, is gules, three wolves' teeth argent issuing from the sinister side. 88. Azure, a bordure or.

There are many other forms of partition which can be drawn from Continental heraldry, but they do not occur in British armory, and they may well be disregarded.

PLATE X

The shields on Plate X. are as follows :—

1. Argent, a cross sable. 2. Sable, a cross per pale argent and gules. 3. Per fess azure and argent, a cross counterchanged. 4. Gules, a cross quarterly or and sable. 5. Or, a cross gyronny gules and argent. 6 is a form never met with in English armory. A translation of the German blazon is "azure, a cross facetted argent." 7 and 8 are not English forms of the cross if treated as distinct forms from others here depicted, though old representations of the cross patée throughout may be found closely akin to these two figures (see No. 14). But the translation of the German blazon is respectively "azure, a cross or, with straight arms and claws," and "gules, a pillar cross or." 9. Azure, a cross engrailed argent. 10. Gules, a cross potent throughout argent. 11. Sable, a cross couped and "fitchée of two points." (It is not found in English arms.) 12. Gules, a Maltese cross argent. 13. Vert, a cross wavy argent. 14. Or, a cross patée throughout azure. 15. Gules, a cross raguly argent. 16. This is blazoned in German as "argent, a 'thread' cross gules." It is not an English form. 17. Azure, a saltire or. 18 may be alluded to by the same remarks as No. 16. 19. Gules, a fret or. 20. Gules, a cross cramponné throughout argent. 21. Or, four lozenges conjoined in cross gules. 22. Azure, a cross couped argent. 23. Argent, a passion cross gules. 24. Sable, a passion cross reversed or (cross of St. Peter). 25. Gules, a cross of Lorraine argent. 26. Azure, a Patriarchal cross or. 27. Vert, a "Russian" cross argent. 28. Or, a "cross-tau" azure (cross of St. Anthony). 29. Argent, a "thieves'" cross gules. (This is very similar to the Scottish shakefork, except that in the latter the ends are usually pointed.) 30. Gules, a saltire couped or. 31. Azure, a cross potent or. 32. Argent, a cross of Jerusalem or. 33. Argent, a cross crosslet gules. 34. Or, a cross flory vert. 35. Sable, a cross of bezants. 36. Azure, a cross pommelled argent. 37. Argent, a cross moline gules. 38. Argent, a cross botonny gules. 39. (I know of no English term for this cross.) 40. Argent, a cross patée fitchée sable.

Though the remaining objects depicted upon Plate VII. are not included even in the German term *Heroldsstucken*, it will be better for purposes of reference that the blazons should here follow.

41. Azure, a sun in his splendour or. 42. Gules, a decrescent moon argent. 43. Vert, a crescent reversed argent. 44. Or, a mullet of eight points. 45. Azure, a comet in bend argent. 46. Sable, in chief clouds and issuant therefrom towards the base rays of the sun all proper. 47. Argent, the base barry wavy of the same and azure (alternatively "argent, in base a representation of water proper"), in chief a rainbow throughout proper. 48. "Gray" (unknown in English armory), in base a triple mound or. 49. Argent, in base a triple mound sable, from each issuant a flame of fire. 50. Or, a triple mound detached in base vert. 51. Argent, six mounds in pyramid, one, two, and three conjoined and issuing from the base gules. 52. Azure, a mountain argent. 53. Per fess azure and a battlemented wall or. 54. Azure, a base vert, thereupon a tower, towered argent, with a pointed roof gules and port ouvert. 55. Gules, a tower, triple-towered or, the port azure. 56. Argent, a cramp-iron azure. 57. Sable, an escarbuncle (the German term is a "lily-wheel"). 58. Or, a "double-hook" (an exclusively German charge) gules. 59. Or, a black carriage frame and wheel (see Fig. 80a). 60. Argent, a ploughshare in bend azure. 61. Azure, a sickle argent, the handle or, the blade serrated (used for reeds or heather). 62. Argent, a mill-rind sable (this is not a form of this charge to be met with in English heraldry). 63. Gules, two *mühlklippel* or. 64. Or, a boat sable, with two

FIG. 80a.—Carriage frame and wheels from Ulrich Reichenthal's *Concilium zu Constance* (Augsburg, 1483).

FIG. 80b.—Arms of Burckhart Zumel Wernherr von Stoffenburg (U. Reichenthal's *Concilium zu Constance*, 1483).

paddles argent. 65. Azure, a trestle (for a table) argent. 66. Gules, a fire-steel (or "furison") in bend sinister or. 67. Argent, a kettle-hook sable. 68. Argent, a key in pale wards upwards azure. (A rather different type of key is used in English armory.) 69. Gules, a mirror or. 70. Or, a *staufen* (drinking-cup) gules (Fig. 80b). 71. Argent, a chess-rook sable. (Though this form would be readily recognisable, nevertheless a rather different pattern is usually adopted in English armory.) 72. Gules, a broad-arrow point upwards argent. 73. Azure, a *wolfsangel* argent. (This is literally a "wolf-sting," and is a name applied to a German implement used in forestry.) 74. Or, a mullet of six points pierced gules. 75. Azure, a hunting-horn or, stringed gules. 76. Gules, a square buckle in bend or. 77. Or, a conical hat sable, turned up and stringed gules. 78. Argent, a long conical cap gules, turned up azure, and tasselled or. 79. Or, a maunch gules. 80. Azure, a hood argent, lined gules.

CHAPTER XIII

THE SO-CALLED ORDINARIES AND SUB-ORDINARIES

ARMS, and the charges upon arms, have been divided into many fantastical divisions. There is a type of the precise mind much evident in the scientific writing of the last and the preceding centuries which is for ever unhappy unless it can be dividing the object of its consideration into classes and divisions, into sub-classes and sub-divisions. Heraldry has suffered in this way; for, oblivious of the fact that the rules enunciated are impossible as rigid guides for general observance, and that they never have been complied with, and that they never will be, a "tabular" system exists for heraldry as for most other sciences. The "precise" mind has applied a system obviously derived from natural history classification to the principles of armory. It has selected a certain number of charges, and has been pleased to term them ordinaries. It has selected others which it has been pleased to term sub-ordinaries. The selection has been purely arbitrary, at the pleasure of the writer, and few writers have agreed in their classifications. One of the foremost rules which former heraldic writers have laid down is that an ordinary must contain the third part of the field. Now it is doubtful whether an ordinary has ever been drawn containing the third part of the field by rigid measurement, except in the solitary instance of the pale when it is drawn "per fess counterchanged," for the obvious *purpose* of dividing the shield into six equal portions, a practice which has been lately pursued very extensively owing to the ease with which, by its adoption, a new coat of arms can be designed bearing a distinct resemblance to one formerly in use without infringing the rights of the latter. Certainly, if the ordinary is the solitary charge upon the shield, it will be drawn about that specified proportion. But when an attempt is made to draw the Walpole coat (which cannot be said to be a modern one) so that it shall exhibit three ordinaries, to wit, one fess and two chevrons, which being interpreted as three-thirds of the shield, must fill it entirely and yet leave a goodly proportion of the field still visible, the absurdity is apparent. And a very large proportion of the classification and rules which occupy such a large proportion of the space in the majority of heraldic text-books are equally unnecessary, confusing, and incorrect, and what is very much more important, such rules have never been recognised by the powers that have had the control of armory from the beginning of that control down to the present day. I shall not be surprised to find that many of my critics, bearing in mind how strenuously I have pleaded elsewhere for a right and proper observance of the laws of armory, may think that the foregoing has largely the nature of a recantation. It is nothing of the kind, and I advocate as strenuously as I have ever done, the compliance with and the observance of every rule which can be shown to exist. But this is no argument whatever for the idle invention of rules which never have existed; or for the recognition of rules which have no other origin than the imagination of heraldic writers. Nor is it an argument for the deduction of unnecessary regulations from cases which can be shown to have been exceptions. Too little recognition is paid to the fact that in armory there are almost as many rules of exception as original rules. There are vastly more plain exceptions to the rules which should govern them.

On the subject of ordinaries, I cannot see wherein lies the difference between a bend and a lion rampant, save their difference in form, yet the one is said to be an ordinary, the other is merely a charge. Each has its special rules to be observed, and whilst a bend can be engrailed or invected, a lion can be guardant or regardant; and whilst the one can be placed between two objects, which objects will occupy a specified position, so can the other. Each can be charged, and each furnishes an excellent example of the futility of some of the ancient rules which have been coined concerning them. The ancient rules allow of but one lion and one bend upon a shield, requiring that two bends shall become bendlets, and two lions lioncels, whereas the instance we have already quoted—the coat of Walpole—has never been drawn in such form that either of the chevrons could have been considered chevronels, and it is rather late in the day to degrade the lions of England into unblooded whelps. To my mind the ordinaries and sub-ordinaries are no more than first charges, and though the bend, the fess, the pale, the pile, the chevron, the cross, and the saltire will always be found described as honourable ordinaries, whilst the chief seems also to be pretty universally considered as one of the honourable ordinaries, such hopeless confusion remains as to the others (scarcely any two writers giving similar classifications), that the utter absurdity of the necessity for any classification at all is amply demonstrated. Classification is only necessary or desirable when a certain set of rules can be applied identically to all the set of figures in that particular class. Even this will not hold with the ordinaries which have been quoted.

A bend embattled is embattled upon both its edges; a fess embattled is embattled only upon the upper edge; a chief is embattled necessarily only upon the lower; and the impossibility of distinguishing "per pale engrailed" from "per pale invected" shows that no rigid rules can be laid down. When we come to sub-ordinaries, the confusion is still more apparent, for as far as I can see the only reason for the classification is the tabulating of rules concerning the lines of partition. The bordure and the orle can be, and often are, engrailed or embattled; the fret, the lozenge, the fusil, the mascle, the rustre, the flanche, the roundel, the billet, the label, the pairle, it would be practically impossible to meddle with; and all these figures have at some time or another, and by some writer or other, been included amongst either the ordinaries or the sub-ordinaries. In fact there is no one quality which these charges possess in common which is not equally possessed by scores of other well-known charges, and there is no earthly reason why a certain set should be selected and dignified by the name of ordinaries; nor are there any rules relating to ordinaries which require the selection of a certain number of figures, or of any figures to be controlled by those rules, with one exception. The exception is to be found not in the rules governing the ordinaries, but in the rules of blazon. After the field has been specified, the principal charge must be mentioned first, and no charge can take precedence of a bend, fess, pale, pile, chevron, cross, or saltire, except one of themselves. If there be any reason for a subdivision those charges must stand by themselves, and might be termed the honourable ordinaries, but I can see no reason for treating the chief, the quarter, the canton, gyron, flanche, label, orle, tressure, fret, inescutcheon, chaplet, bordure, lozenge, fusil, mascle, rustre, roundel, billet, label, shakefork, and pairle, as other than ordinary charges. They certainly are purely heraldic, and each has its own special rules, but so in heraldry have the lion, griffin, and deer. Here is the complete list of the so-called ordinaries and sub-ordinaries: The bend; fess; bar; chief; pale; chevron; cross; saltire; pile; pairle, shakefork or pall; quarter; canton; gyron; bordure; orle; tressure; flanche; label; fret; inescutcheon; chaplet; lozenge; fusil; mascle; rustre; roundel; billet, together with the diminutives of such of these as are in use.

With reference to the origin of these ordinaries, by the use of which term is meant the rectilinear figures peculiar to armory, it may be worth the passing mention that the said origin is a matter of some mystery. Guillim and the old writers almost universally take them to be derived from the actual military scarf or a representation of it placed across the shield in various forms. Other writers, taking the surcoat and its decoration as the real origin of coats of arms, derive the ordinaries from the belt, scarf, and other articles of raiment. Planché, on the other hand, scouted such a derivation, putting forward upon very good and plausible grounds the simple argument that the origin of the ordinaries is to be found in the cross-pieces of wood placed across a shield for strengthening purposes. He instances cases in which shields, apparently charged with ordinaries but really strengthened with cross-pieces, can be taken back to a period long anterior to the existence of regularised armory. But then, on the other hand, shields can be found decorated with animals at an equally early or even an earlier period, and I am inclined myself to push Planché's own argument even further than he himself took it, and assert unequivocally that the ordinaries had in themselves no particular symbolism and no definable origin whatever beyond that easy method of making some pattern upon a shield which was to be gained by using straight lines. That they ever had any military meaning, I cannot see the slightest foundation to believe, their suggested and asserted symbolism I totally deny. But when we can find, as Planché did, that shields were strengthened with cross-pieces in various directions, it is quite natural to suppose that these cross-pieces afforded a ready means of decoration in colour, and this would lead a good deal of other decoration to follow similar forms, even in the absence of·cross-pieces upon the definite shield itself. The one curious point which rather seems to tell against Planché's theory is that in the earliest "rolls" of arms but a comparatively small proportion of the arms are found to consist of these rectilinear figures, and if the ordinaries really originated in strengthening cross-pieces one would have expected a larger number of such coats of arms to be found; but at the same time such arms would, in many cases, in themselves be so palpably mere meaningless decoration of cross-pieces upon plain shields, that the resulting design would not carry with it such a compulsory remembrance as would a design, for example, derived from lines which had plainly had no connection with the construction of the shield. Nor could it have any such basis of continuity. Whilst a son would naturally paint a lion upon his shield if his father had done the same, there certainly would not be a similar inducement for a son to follow his father's example where the design upon a shield were no more than different-coloured strengthening pieces, because if these were gilt, for example, the son would naturally be no more inclined to perpetuate a particular form of strengthening for his shield, which might not need it, than any particular artistic division with which it was involved, so that the absence of arms composed of ordinaries from the early rolls of arms does not amount to very much. Still further, it may well be concluded that the compilers of early rolls of arms, or the collectors of the details from which early rolls were made at a later date, may have been tempted to ignore, and may have been justified in discarding from their lists of arms, those patterns and designs which palpably were then no more than a meaningless colouring of the strengthening pieces, but which patterns and designs by subsequent continuous usage and perpetuation became accepted later by certain families as the "arms" their ancestors had worn. It is easy to see that such meaningless patterns would have less chance of survival by continuity of usage, and at the same time would require a longer continuity of usage, before attaining to fixity as a definite design.

The undoubted symbolism of the cross in so many early coats of arms has been urged strongly by those who argue either for a symbolism for all these rectilinear figures or for an origin in articles of dress. But the figure of the cross preceded Christianity and organised armory, and it had an obvious decorative value which existed before, and which exists now outside any attribute it may have of a symbolical nature. That it is an utterly fallacious argument must be admitted when it is remembered that two lines at right angles make a cross—probably the earliest of all forms of decoration—and that the cross existed before its symbolism. Herein it differs from other forms of decoration (e.g. the Masonic emblems) which cannot be traced beyond their symbolical existence. The cross, like the other heraldic rectilinear figures, came into existence, meaningless as a decoration for a shield, before armory as such existed, and probably before Christianity began. Then being in existence the Crusading instinct doubtless caused its frequent selection with an added symbolical meaning. But the argument can truthfully be pushed no farther.

THE BEND

The bend is a broad band going from the dexter chief corner to the sinister base (Plate IX. Fig. 47). According to the old theorists this should contain the third part of the field. As a matter of fact it hardly ever does,

and seldom did even in the oldest examples. Great latitude is allowed to the artist on this point, in accordance with whether the bend be plain or charged, and more particularly according to the charges which accompany it in the shield and their disposition thereupon.

"Azure, a bend or" is the well-known coat concerning which the historic controversy was waged between Scrope and Grosvenor. As every one knows, it was finally adjudged to belong to the former (see Fig. 81),

FIG. 81.—Armorial bearings of Simon Conyers Scrope, Esq., of Danby : —Azure, a bend or, with very many illustrious quarterings. Crest: out of a ducal coronet or, a plume of five ostrich feathers proper. Mottoes : "Devant si je puis ;" "En espoir je vive attendant grace."

and a right to it has also been proved by the Cornish family of Carminow.

"Or, a bend azure," is the coat of the Gloucestershire family of Trye, of Leckhampton.

A bend is, of course, subject to the usual variations of the lines of partition. Examples of a bend embattled will be found in the arms of Hornyold (Fig. 82); of a bend engrailed in the arms of Alington (Fig. 83); of a bend invecked (or invected) in the arms of Emerson[a] (see Plate XXXII.); of a bend indented in the arms of Horncastle (Fig. 84); of a bend nebuly in the arms of Marshall (Fig. 85).

A bend compony will be found in the arms of Beaumont (Fig. 86), and the difference between this and a bend barry, as in the arms of King[b] (see Plate XIV.), should be noticed.

A bend wavy is not very usual, but will be found in the arms of Wallop, De Burton, and Conder.

[a] Armorial bearings of Peter Henry Emerson, Esq., of Ailsa Lodge, Southbourne, Bournemouth : Per fess nebuly or and vert, on a bend invected azure, gutté-d'eau, a battle-axe between two lions passant argent. Mantling vert and or. Crest : on a wreath of the colours, in front of a demi-lion vert, charged on the shoulder with two barrulets dancetté or, and holding in the paws a battle-axe erect, a club fess-wise entwined by a serpent also proper. Motto : "Audacter et hilare."
[b] Armorial bearings of Sir Henry Seymour King, K.C.I.E. : Quarterly, argent and azure, in the second and third quarters a quatrefoil of the first, over all a bend barry of six of the second, charged with a quatre foil also of the first, and gules, the escutcheon being surrounded by the ribbon and badge of a K.C.I.E. Mantling azure and argent ; and for his crest, on a wreath of the colours, a lion rampant or, gorged with a collar gemel azure, and holding in the dexter forepaw a trefoil slipped vert. Motto : "Floreo in ungue leonis."

FIG. 82.—Armorial bearings of John Vincent Hornyold, Esq. (as recorded in the College of Arms in England under the Royal Licence, Feb. 1859, to him to assume the name and arms of Hornyold): Azure, on a bend embattled counter-embattled argent, a wolf passant between two escallops sable, quartering Gandolfi, &c., and impaling the arms of Langdale, namely: sable, a chevron between three estoiles argent. [*Note.*—These arms were confirmed to John Hornyold, Auditor of the Exchequer and Governor of Calais, by Thomas Benholt, Clarenceux King of Arms, at the First Visitation of co. Worcester, 1536.] Crest: on a wreath of the colours, a demi-unicorn gules, armed, crined, and unguled or. Motto: "Fidem tene."

A bend raguly appears in the arms of Strangman[c] (see Plate XIV.).

When a bend and a bordure appear upon the same arms, the bend is not continued over the bordure, as

FIG. 83.—Armorial bearings of Arthur Hildebrand Alington, Esq., of Swinhope: Sable, a bend engrailed between six billets argent. Mantling sable and argent. Crest: on a wreath of the colours, a talbot passant ermine. Motto: "Non pour haine."

[c] Armorial bearings of Strangman: Per bend sable and argent, a bend raguly counterchanged. Crest: two ragged staffs saltirewise, environed with a ducal crown or. Confirmed at the Visitations of Essex, 1558 and 1612.

FIG. 84.—Armorial bearings of William Radcliffe Horncastle, of Hackney: Argent, on a bend indented sable, between two bugle-horns of the last, stringed vert, a tower in bend of the field. Mantling sable and argent. Crest: on a wreath of the colours, upon a rock proper, the battlements of a tower sable, surmounted by a bugle-horn or, stringed vert. Motto: "Audaces fortuna juvat."

FIG. 85.—Armorial bearings of Mark Bell Marshall, Esq., J.P.: Or, on a bend nebuly, between four passion nails two and two sable, three horse-shoes of the first, a chief azure thereon three horses' heads erased argent. Upon the escutcheon is placed a helmet befitting his degree, with a mantling sable and or. Crest: on a wreath of the colours, two arrows in saltire or, flighted azure, surmounted by a passion nail in fesse proper, tied with a riband gules, pendent therefrom an escocheon of the last charged with a horse-shoe of the first. Motto: "Vi martiali, Deo adjuvante."

FIG. 86.—Arms of Henry de Beaumont, Lord Beaumont (*d.* 1340): Azure, semé-de-lis and a lion rampant or, over all a bend compony argent and gules.

will be seen from the arms of Fox (Fig. 87), and similarly it does not surmount a tressure, but stops within it.

FIG. 87.—Armorial bearings of Fox of Brislington: Azure, on a bend engrailed ermine, plain cottised or, three foxes' heads erased gules, within a bordure of the second. Mantling azure and argent. Crest: on a wreath of the colours, a fox sejant gules, collared and chained or, supporting with his sinister paw a flagstaff, thereon a banner azure, semé-de-lis or. Motto: "J'ay ma foi tenu à ma puissance."

FIG. 88.—Bookplate of William Chapman Waller, Esq.: Argent, on a bend engrailed sable, another or, charged with three walnut-leaves of the second, on a chief per pale gules and azure, a griffin's head erased between two saltires of the third. Upon the escutcheon is placed a helmet befitting his degree, with a mantling sable and argent; and for his crest, upon a wreath of the colours, a griffin's head erased sable, collared with annulets in front of a saltire or; with the motto, "Fide sed cui vide."

A bend upon a bend is by no means unusual. An example of this will be found in the arms of Waller

(Fig. 88). Cases where this happens need to be carefully scrutinised to avoid error in blazoning.

A bend lozengy will be found in the arms of Bolding (Fig. 89).

A bend flory and counterflory will be found in the arms of Fellows, a quartering of Tweedy[d] (see Plate XXVIII.).

FIG. 89.—Armorial bearings of the late George Frederick Bolding, Esq.: Per bend or and azure, a bend lozengy between two bowls all counterchanged. Mantling azure and or. Crest: upon a wreath of the colours, in front of a demi-sea-horse proper, a garb fesswise or. Motto: "Sto pro veritate."

FIG. 90.—Armorial bearings of James Haldane, Esq. Quarterly, 1 and 4, argent, a saltire engrailed sable; 2. argent, a saltire between four roses gules; 3. or, a bend chequy sable and argent, in the centre of the shield a martlet sable. Mantling gules, doubled argent. Crest: on a wreath of his liveries, an eagle's head erased or. Motto: "Suffer."

A bend chequy will be found in the third quarter of the arms of Haldane (Fig. 90), and it will be noticed that the checks run the way of the bend.

Ermine spots upon a bend are represented the way of

[d] Armorial bearings of Arthur Hearne Tweedy, Esq., of Widmore Lodge. Bromley: Quarterly, 1 and 4, argent, a saltire, engrailed between two escallops in fess gules, on a chief azure an escallop of the field (for Tweedy); 2 and 3, gules, on a bend flory and counterflory between two increscents argent, three lions' heads erased sable. Mantling gules and argent. Crest: on a wreath of the colours, on a prick-spur fesswise, a peewit rising proper, holding in the beak a trefoil slipped vert.

the bend, as will be seen in the arms of Holbrow (Fig. 91).

Occasionally two bends will be found, as in the arms of Lever : Argent, two bends sable, the upper one engrailed

FIG. 91.—Armorial bearings of Holbrow: Azure, a bend ermine, between six mullets pierced argent. Mantling azure and argent. Crest: on a wreath of the colours, a pair of wings elevated argent, including three mullets as in the arms in triangle.

(*vide* Lyon Register—escutcheon of pretence on the arms of Goldie-Scot of Craigmore, 1868); or as in the arms of James Ford, of Montrose, 1804: Gules, two bends vairé argent and sable, on a chief or, a greyhound courant sable between two towers gules. A different form appears in the arms of Zorke or Yorke (see Papworth), which are blazoned: Azure, a bend argent, im-

FIG. 92.—Armorial bearings of Lawrence William Vaile, Esq.: Ermine, on a bend between two bendlets azure, each charged with three cross crosslets fitchée or, three calves statant argent. Upon the escutcheon is placed a helmet befitting his degree, with a mantling azure and argent; and for his crest, upon a wreath of the colours, a mount vert, thereon in front of two cross crosslets fitchée in saltire gules, a wolf's head erased azure, in the mouth three ears of wheat; with the motto, "Semper paratus."

paling argent, a bend azure. A solitary instance of *three* bends (which, however, effectually proves that a

bend cannot occupy the third part of the field) occurs in the arms of Penrose, matriculated in Lyon Register in 1795 as a quartering of Cumming-Gordon of Altyre.

FIG. 93.—Arms of Tonge of Disley: Azure on a bend invected plain cottised or between six martlets of the last, a lion passant between two grappling-irons the flukes upwards of the first. Mantling azure and or. Crest: on a wreath of the colours, in front of an arm embowed in armour, the hand proper grasping a grappling-iron in bend sinister sable, a lion sejant of the last pierced in the sinister shoulder with an arrow proper. Motto, "Retineo vi leonis."

These arms of Penrose are: Argent, three bends sable, each charged with as many roses of the field (see Plate XIII.).

FIG. 94.—Armorial bearings of Charles Frederick Burnard, Esq.: Argent, three escallops in bend between two bendlets azure, in chief and in base a leopard's face jessant-de-lis of the last; and for a crest, on a wreath of the colours, on a rock proper an escallop argent, between the attires of a stag also proper; with the motto, "Bear and forbear."

A charge half the width of a bend is a bendlet, and one half the width of a bendlet is a cottise, but a cottise cannot exist alone, inasmuch as it has of itself neither direction nor position, but is only found accompanying one of the ordinaries. The arms of Harley (see Plate XII.), are a good example of a bend cottised.

FIG. 95.—Armorial bearings of Frank Debenham, Esq.: Per bend gules and sable, two bendlets indented between as many crescents each within an annulet all or. Mantling gules and or. Crest: on a wreath of the colours, a demi-lion per pale indented sable and gules, holding in the dexter paw a key in bend wards upwards and an arrow in bend sinister point downwards, and resting the sinister paw on a decrescent all or. Motto: "Laborante bona debentur."

FIG. 96.—Armorial bearings of John Eugene Clauson, Esq.: Barry of four per pale sable and or, counterchanged, three bendlets argent, within two flaunches ermine, impaling the arms of Makins, namely: argent, on a fess embattled counter-embattled gules, between in chief two falcons proper belled or and in base a lion's face of the second, an annulet or between two bezants. Above the escutcheon is placed a helmet befitting his degree, upon a mantling sable and or; and for his crest, upon a wreath of the colours, a mullet of ten points encircled by an annulet or, between two wings sable, the dexter charged with three bendlets and the sinister with as many bendlets in sinister argent; with the motto, "Spes et fides."

Bendlets will very seldom be found either in addition to a bend, or charged, but the arms of Vaile (Fig. 92) show both these peculiarities.

The arms of Tonge (Fig. 93) are another example of a bend cottised; and the arms of Brown quartered by Lees[e] show a bend with double cottises.

The arms of Burnard (Fig. 94) and Debenham (Fig. 95) are examples of coats of arms with two bendlets, either plain or subject to the variations of the lines of partition. Three bendlets occur in the arms of Clauson (Fig. 96), and four in the arms of Benson (Fig. 97).

A bend will usually be found between two charges, as in some of the above instances. Occasionally it will be found between four, but more frequently between six. In none of these cases is it necessary to specify the position of the subsidiary charge. It is presumed that the bend separates them into even numbers, but their exact position (beyond this) upon the shield is left to the judgment of the artist, and their disposition is governed by the space left available by the shape of the shield.

A further presumption is permitted in the case of a bend between *three* objects, which are presumed to be

FIG. 97.—Armorial bearings of Arthur Christopher Benson, Esq.: Argent, a quatrefoil between two trefoils slipped in bend sable between four bendlets gules. Mantling sable and argent. Crest: on a wreath of the colours, a bear's head argent, erased gules, gorged with a collar gemel, and muzzled of the second, and holding in the mouth a trefoil slipped as in the arms. Motto: "Fay bien crain rien."

two in chief and one in base. But even in the case of three the position will be usually found to be specifically stated, as would be the case with any other uneven number.

Charges on a bend are placed in the direction of the bend, as will be seen in the arms of Whewell (Fig. 98). In such cases it is not necessary to specify that the charges are bendwise.

When a charge or charges occupy the position which a bend would, they are said to be placed "in bend," as

[e] Armorial bearings of Eric Brown Lees, Esq.: Quarterly 1 and 4, argent, two bars raguly between three cross crosslets fitchée in chief and a falcon belled in base all gules (for Lees); 2. argent, on a bend invected with plain double cottises sable, gutté-d'-eau, three eagles, each with two heads displayed ermine (for Brown); 3. gules, on a bend, invected erminois between two bezants, three martlets azure, all within a bordure ermine (for Collins); and for a crest, on a wreath of the colours, in front of two cross crosslets fitchée saltirewise gules, a falcon belled argent. Motto: "Fide sed cui vide."

will be seen in the arms of Ince (Fig. 99) and Gell[†] (see Plate XXXVIII.).

This is not the same thing as a charge placed "bend-

shield, but the position of the charge upon the shield is not governed thereby. The arms of Bate (Fig. 100) are a good example of this.

FIG. 98.—Armorial bearings of Thomas Whewell, Esq.: Vairé argent and gules, on a bend cottised sable, a crescent or between two Diana's heads crined and horned of the first. Mantling gules and argent. Crest: on a wreath of the colours, a wyvern, wings elevated proper, gorged with a collar gemel or, supporting with the dexter leg a torch erect sable, fired also proper. Motto: "For faith and for fatherland."

FIG. 100.—Armorial bearings of Thomas Bate, Esq., of Kelsterton: Sable, on a fess cottised argent, between four dexter hands couped at the wrist, three in chief and one in base bendwise or, an arrow fesswise proper; and for the crest, upon a wreath of the colours, in front of a stag's head couped argent, attired or, pierced in the neck by an arrow in bend proper, a hand couped at the wrist fesswise also or; with the motto, "Live to live."

FIG. 99.—Armorial bearings of John Ince, Esq.: Argent, three torteaux in bend between two fleur-de-lis gules. Mantling gules and argent. Crest: on a wreath of the colours, a horse argent, holding in the mouth a trefoil slipped vert, resting the dexter foreleg on a caduceus erect proper. Motto: "Labore et scientia."

wise" (or bendways). In this case the charge itself is slanted into the angle at which the bend crosses the

† Armorial bearings of Philip Lyttelton Gell, Esq., of Kirk Langley, co. Derby, and Langley Lodge, Oxford: Party per bend argent and gules, a rose between two mullets of six points in bend counterchanged, impaling the arms of Brodrick, namely: argent, on a chief vert, two spear-heads of the field, the points embrued gules. Mantling gules and argent. Crest: on a wreath of the colours, a greyhound passant pean, about the neck a collar argent, charged with a rose between two mullets of six points gules. Motto, "Vocatus obedivi."

FIG. 100a.—Armorial bearings of Basil Thomas Fitz-Herbert, Esq.: Argent, a chief vairé or and gules, over all a bend sable, impaling the arms of Stafford Jerningham; and for the crest, a dexter cubit arm in armour erect, the hand appearing clenched within the gauntlet all proper; with the motto, "Ung je serviray."

When a bend and chief occur together in the same arms, the chief will usually surmount the bend, the latter issuing from the angle between the base of the chief and the side of the shield. An instance to the contrary, however, will be found in the arms of Fitz-Herbert of Swynnerton (Fig. 100a), in which the bend is continued over the chief. This instance, however (as doubtless all others of the kind), is due to the use of the bend in early times as a mark of difference. The coat of arms, therefore, had an earlier and separate existence

without the bend, which has been superimposed as a difference upon a previously existing coat. The use of the bend as a difference will be again referred to when considering more fully the marks and methods of indicating cadency.

A curious instance of the use of the sun's rays in bend will be found in the arms of Warde-Aldam.[g]

The bend sinister is very frequently stated to be the mark of illegitimacy. It certainly has been so used upon some occasions, but these occasions are very few and far between, the charge more frequently made use of being the bendlet or its derivative the baton. These will be treated more fully in the chapter on the marks of illegitimacy. The bend sinister, which is a band running from the sinister chief corner through the centre of the escutcheon to the dexter base, need not necessarily indicate bastardy. Naturally the popular idea which has originated and become stereotyped concerning it renders its appearance extremely rare, but in at least two cases it occurs without, as far as I am aware, carrying any such meaning. At any rate, in neither case are the coats "bastardised" versions of older arms. These cases are the arms of Shiffner: "Azure, a bend sinister; in chief two estoiles, in like bend or; in base the end and stock of an anchor gold, issuing from waves of the sea proper. Crest: an estoile or, between the rays six annulets azure;" and Burne-Jones: "Azure, on a bend sinister argent between seven mullets, four in chief and three in base or, three pairs of wings addorsed purpure.

Crest: in front of flames of fire proper, two wings elevated and addorsed purpure, charged with a mullet or. Motto: 'Sequar et attingnam.'"

No coat with the chief charge a single bendlet occurs in Papworth. A single case, however, is to be found in the Lyon Register in the duly matriculated arms of Porterfield of that Ilk: "Or, a bendlet between a stag's head erased in chief and a hunting-horn in base sable, garnished gules." Single bendlets, however, both dexter and sinister, occur as ancient difference marks and are then sometimes known as ribands. So described, it occurs in blazon of the arms of Abernethy: "Or, a lion rampant gules, debruised of a ribbon sable," quartered by Lindsay, Earl of Crawford and Balcarres; but here again the bendlet is a mark of cadency. In the *Gelre Armorial* (see Plate LXXVI.), in this particular coat the ribbon is made "engrailed," which is most unusual, and which does not appear to be the accepted form. In many of the Scottish matriculations of this Abernethy coat in which this riband occurs it is termed a "cost," doubtless another form of the word cottise.

When a bend or bendlets (or, in fact, any other charge) are raised above their natural position in the shield they are termed "enhanced." An instance of this occurs in the well-known coat of Byron, viz.: "Argent, three bendlets enhanced gules." and in the arms of Manchester [h] (Plate CXVI.), which were based upon this coat.

The arms of Wagstaff (Fig. 101) and of De la Ferté (Fig. 102) are rather exceptional.

When the field is composed of an even number of equal pieces divided by lines following the angle of a

bend the field is blazoned "bendy" of so many (*e.g.* Plate IX., 48 is "bendy" of four argent and sable). In most cases it will be composed of six or eight pieces, but as there is no diminutive of "bendy," the number must always be stated.

THE PALE

The pale (Plate IX. Fig. 4) is a broad perpendicular band passing from the top of the escutcheon to the bottom, as in the arms of Melles[i] (Plate XV.). Like all the other ordinaries, it is stated to contain the third part of the area of the field, and it is the only one which is at all frequently drawn in that proportion. But even with the pale, the only occasion upon which it is definitely given, this exaggerated width will be presently explained. The artistic latitude, however, permits the pale to be drawn of this proportion if this be convenient to the charges upon it.

Like the other ordinaries, the pale will be found varied by the different lines of partition, and the arms of Wright[j] (see Plate XV.), Lancaster (Fig. 103), and Pryse (Fig. 104) show the pale respectively plain, engrailed, in-

FIG. 103.—Armorial bearings of William John Lancaster, Esq. : Or, two bars sable, on a pale engrailed ermine, four cinquefoils palewise of the second. Mantling sable and or. Crest : on a wreath of the colours, two cinquefoils fesswise, that on the dexter sable, that on the sinister or, surmounted by a third cinquefoil per pale of the last and first. Motto : "Ornat fortem prudentia."

vected ; and the arms of Brain[k] (see Plate XXXII.) show the pale cottised; and the arms of Tillard (Fig. 105) and Colman (Fig. 106) are examples respectively of a pale "per pale indented point in point," and a pale "rayonnée."

The single circumstance in which the pale is regularly drawn to contain a full third of the field by measurement is when the coat is "per fess and a pale counterchanged." This, it will be noticed, divides the

[i] Armorial bearings of Joseph William Melles, Esq., of Gruline, Aros : Vert, on a pale between two cinquefoils argent, a fir-tree eradicated proper. Upon the escutcheon is placed a helmet befitting his degree, with a mantling gules, doubled argent ; and upon a wreath of his liveries is set for crest, a fir-tree erect and eradicated proper; and in an escroll over the same this motto, " Usque fidelis."

[j] Armorial bearings of Sir Thomas Wright : Or, on a pale gules, a cross botonny fitchée argent, a chief azure, thereon a pale ermine, charged with a rose gules, barbed and seeded proper, between two bezants. Mantling gules and or. Crest : upon a wreath of the colours, upon a rock, a falcon's head erased proper, holding in the beak a cross botonny fitchée in bend argent, and charged on the neck with a rose as in the arms. Motto : "Tam arte quam marte."

[k] Armorial bearings of Samuel Arthur Brain, Esq., of Roxburgh, Penarth : Per pale argent and gules, on a pale cottised, three leopards' heads couped all counterchanged. Mantling gules and argent. Crest : on a wreath of the colours, a leopard's head couped argent, charged with a pale gules and encircled by a branch of oak vert. Motto : "Ardua tendo."

shield into six equal portions. The ease with which, by the employment of these conditions, a new coat can be

FIG. 104.—Armorial bearings of Henry Louis Vanneck Pryse, Esq. : Azure, on a pale invected argent, plain cottised or, a lion rampant between two crosses botonny sable. Mantling azure and argent. Crest : upon a wreath of the colours, a lion rampant regardant or, gorged with a wreath of oak vert, holding in the dexter forepaw a cross botonny fitchée in bend sinister, and resting the dexter hind leg on two spears in saltire proper. Motto : "Duw a digon."

based upon an old one which shall leave three original charges in the same position, and upon a field of the

FIG. 105.—Armorial bearings of Philip Francis Tillard, Esq.: Argent, on a pale per pale dancetté point in point gules and azure, between two mascles in fess sable, three mullets or; and upon an escutcheon of pretence the arms of Brooks, namely : argent, three bars wavy azure, a cross fleury erminois, in chief a fountain. Mantling gules and argent. Crest : on a wreath of the colours, upon a mount vert, a dexter hand couped proper, grasping a mascle in bend sinister sable. Motto : " Audi, vide, sile."

original tincture, and yet shall produce an entirely different and distinct coat of arms, has led to this particular form being constantly repeated in modern grants. It will be found employed in the arms of "Shuttleworth" (Fig. 107).

FIG. 106.—Armorial bearings of Jeremiah Colman, Esq. : Azure, on a pale rayonnée or, gutté-de-larmes, between two fleurs-de-lis of the second, a lion rampant between two annulets palewise gules ; and for the crest, on a wreath of the colours, in front of two wings argent, each charged with an estoile azure, a rock proper, thereon a caltrap or; with the motto, "Sat cito, si sat bene."

The diminutive of the pale is the pallet, and the pale cottised is sometimes termed "endorsed."

Except when it is used as a mark of difference or distinction (then usually wavy), the pallet is not found singly ; but two pallets, as in the arms of Ebblewhite

FIG. 107.—Armorial bearings of Frank Shuttleworth, Esq. : Per fess argent and sable, a pale and three weavers' shuttles counterchanged, the latter tipped and furnished with quills of yarn or. Mantling sable and argent. Crest : issuing from a chaplet of roses gules, a cubit arm in armour, the hand in a gauntlet proper, holding a shuttle in bend sinister sable, tipped and furnished or. Motto : "Isto velocior vita."

(Fig. 108), or three, are not exceptional. Charged upon other ordinaries, particularly on the chief and the chevron, pallets are of constant occurrence. An example will be found in the arms of Walker (Fig. 109).

When the field is striped vertically it is said to be "paly" of so many, as in the arms of Wakeman (Fig. 110).

The arms shown in Fig. 111 are interesting inasmuch as they are doubtless an early form of the coat per pale indented argent and gules, which is generally described as a banner borne for the honour of Hinckley, by the Simons de Montfort, Earls of Leicester, and father and son. In a Roll *temp.* Henry III., to Simon the Younger is ascribed "Le Banner Party endentee dargent & de goules," although the arms of both father and son are known to have been as Fig. 112: "Gules, a lion rampant queue-fourchée argent." More probably the indented coat gives the original Montfort arms (see pages 195 and 196, and Plate LXXI.).

FIG. 108.—Armorial bearings of Ernest Arthur Ebblewhite, Esq. : Per fess indented argent and azure, within two pallets as many roses in pale all counterchanged, on a canton gules, a mullet of six points pierced of the first; impaling the arms of George, namely : per fess gules and sable, on a fess indented argent, between two falcons rising in pale of the third, beaked and legged or, a talbot passant of the second. Mantling azure and argent. Crest : on a wreath of the colours, a demi-wolf rampant ermine, charged on the shoulder with a mullet as in the arms, and holding between the paws a lyre or ; with the motto : "En avant."

THE FESS

The fess (Plate IX. Fig. 14) is a broad horizontal band crossing the escutcheon in the centre. It is seldom drawn to contain a full third of the area of the shield.

The arms of Waddington[1] (see Plate XVI.), Pixley[m] (see Plate XVIII.), George (Fig. 113), and West (Fig. 114) are examples respectively of the fess plain, the fess "engrailed," the fess "indented," and the fess "dancetté."

[1] Armorial bearings of John Waddington, Esq., of Ely Grange, Frant, and Waddington Old Hall, co. York : Per pale argent and gules, a fess between two fleurs-de-lis in chief, and a battle-axe fesswise in base, blade upwards, and head to the sinister all counterchanged. Mantling gules and argent. Crest : on a wreath of the colours, a dexter arm embowed, holding in the hand a tilting-spear in bend, and a battle-axe in bend sinister, all proper, the hand surmounted by a fleur-de-lis gules. Motto : "Pro recto semper."

[m] Armorial bearings of Francis William Pixley, F.S.A., of the Middle Temple : Azure, a fess engrailed or, gutté-de-larmes, between two daggers points downwards in chief and a cross crosslet fitchée in base or. Mantling azure and or. Crest : on a wreath of the colours, in front of a cross crosslet fitchèe or, a morion proper between two wings azure, each charged with a dagger as in the arms. Motto : "Per vias rectas."

PLATE XVIII.

THE ARMORIAL BEARINGS OF—

(1) COL. JOHN ALEXANDER MAN STUART, C.B., C.M.G.
(2) W. BRUCE BANNERMAN, ESQ., F.S.A., OF CROYDON.
(3) FRANCIS WILLIAM PIXLEY, ESQ., F.S.A.

(4) J. B. BROÜN-MORISON, ESQ. OF MURIE, CO. PERTH.
(5) JOHN J. JACKSON BARSTOW OF THE LODGE,
WESTON-SUPER-MARE.

PLATE XIX.

THE ARMORIAL BEARINGS OF CHARLES WILBRAHAM PERRYMAN, Esq. of Bifrons, Farnborough, Co. Southampton.

PLATE XX.

THE ARMORIAL BEARINGS OF—

(1) THE LATE JOHN PLATT, ESQ., OF LLANDUDNO.
(2) GERALD M. CONRAN, ESQ., OF SOUTH BRENT, DEVON.
(3) REV. W. H. WAYNE, OF WILLEY, CO. SALOP.

(4) ROBERT S. STONE, ESQ.
(5) CHARLES H. BARCLAY, ESQ. OF INCHDURA (a Cadet of BARCLAY OF TOWIE).

PLATE XXI.

THE ARMORIAL BEARINGS OF JOHN MAURICE COPPEN, OF ASCOT, BERKS.

PLATE XXII.

THE ARMORIAL BEARINGS OF—

(1) LT.-COL. JAMES GROVE WHITE, OF KILBYRNE, CO. CORK.
(2) MAJOR JOHN FISHWICK LEEMING OF WHALLEY RANGE.
(4) THORNTON OF YORKSHIRE.
(3) HENRY THOMAS MACDERMOTT, ESQ. OF TRINITY HOUSE, ST LEONARDS-ON-SEA.
(5) REV. DR NICHOLAS HOPKINS JAMES.

PLATE XXIII.

THE ARMORIAL BEARINGS OF—

(1) SIDNEY FLAVEL, ESQ. OF LEAMINGTON SPA.
(2) THE LATE SIR WOODBINE PARISH, K.H.
(3) JOSEPH LUCAS, ESQ. OF FOXHUNT MANOR, CO. SUSSEX.

(4) ANDREW ALEXANDER HUNTER, ESQ., BURSAR OF CHELTENHAM COLLEGE.
(5) HOWELL POWELL EDWARDS, ESQ.

PLATE XXIV.

THE ARMORIAL BEARINGS OF MAJOR HARRY NORTH, OF ELTHAM, CO. KENT.

PLATE XXV.

THE ARMORIAL BEARINGS OF—

(1) SIR WILLIAM H. QUAYLE JONES.
(2) FRANKLEN G. EVANS, ESQ., OF LLWYNARTHAN, CASTLETON,
NR. CARDIFF.
(3) R. R. MEADE-KING, ESQ., OF WEST DERBY, LIVERPOOL.
(4) THOMAS FIELDING JOHNSON, ESQ. OF BROOKFIELD, KNIGHTON,
NR. LEICESTER.
(5) SIR EDMUND T. BEWLEY.

PLATE XXVI.

THE ARMORIAL BEARINGS OF—

(1) GUSTAVUS ROCHFORT HYDE, Esq. of Lynnbury, Mullingar, Co. Westmeath.
(2) BROWN of Bonnytoun.
(3) Major H. A. CUMMINS of Devereux House, Great Malvern.

(4) CLEMENT DUNSCOMBE, Esq., of King Williamstown, Co. Cork.
(5) ALEXANDER D. O. WEDDERBURN, Esq., K.C.

PLATE XXVII.

THE ARMORIAL BEARINGS OF—

(1) Sir JOHN WATNEY, F.S.A.
(2) FRANCIS CHARLES OPPENHEIMER, Esq., of
    FRANKFORT-ON-MAINE.
(3) WILLIAM A. I'ANSON, Esq. of DENTON HALL, SCOTSWOOD.

(4) SAMUEL HYNMAN MONTGOMERIE, Esq. of SOUTHANNAN,
    FAIRLIE, N.B.
(5) JOSEPH BILLIAT, Esq. of AISTHORPE HALL, LINCOLN.

PLATE XXVIII.

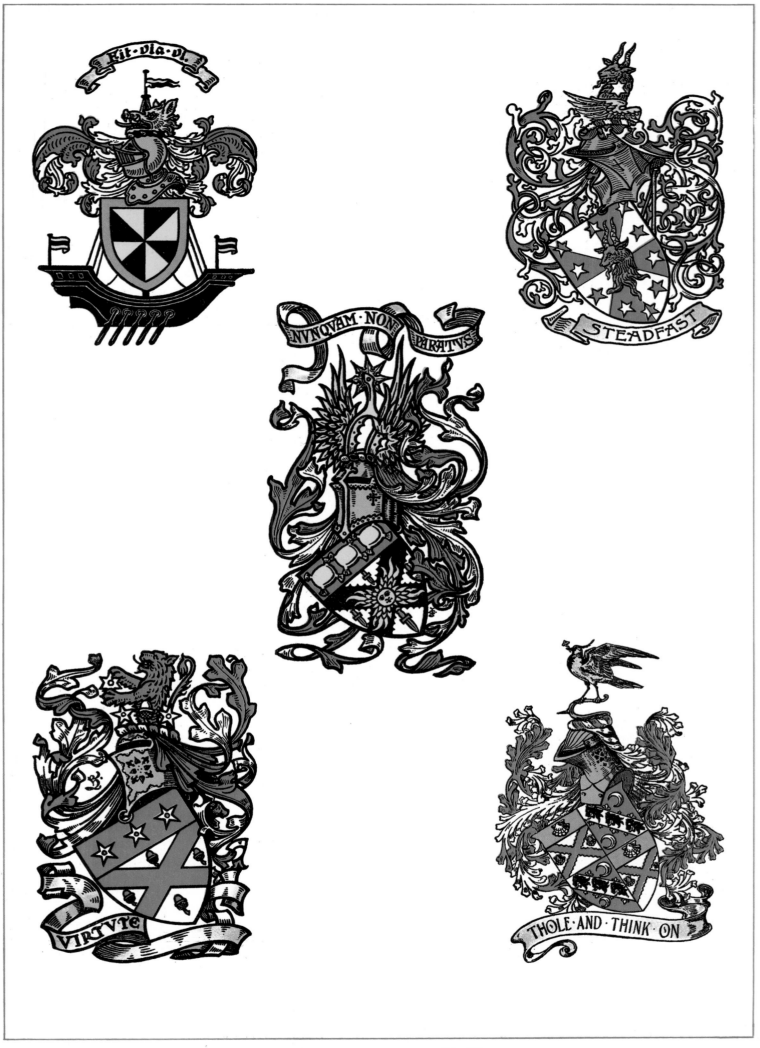

THE ARMORIAL BEARINGS OF—

(1) CAMPBELL of INVERNEIL.
(2) WILLIAM WELCHMAN, ESQ. OF BIRDBECK HOUSE, UPWELL, WISBECH.
(3) GEORGE LAWSON LAWSON-JOHNSTON, ESQ.

(4) DANIEL WINTRINGHAM STABLE, ESQ.
(5) ARTHUR HEARNE TWEEDY, ESQ. OF WIDMORE LODGE, BROMLEY, KENT.

PLATE XXIX.

THE ARMORIAL BEARINGS OF—

(1) Sir HENRY HARBEN.
(2) J. D. G. DALRYMPLE, Esq. of Woodhead, Kirkintilloch.
(3) Major ARTHUR DILLON DENNIS KELLY of Mucklon,
    Ballyforan, Co. Galway.

(4) PEARKES, of London.
(5) W. J. SANDFORD THOMPSON, Esq. of The Villa,
    Montrose.

PLATE XXX.

THE ARMORIAL BEARINGS OF—

(1) JAMES WATTS, Esq. of Abney Hall, Cheadle.
(2) HOWARD MEURIC LLOYD, Esq. of Glanyrannell, Llanwrda, South Wales.

(3) PETER DUGUID-M'COMBIE, Esq. of Easter Skene, Aberdeen.
(4) WILLIAM HENRY AMBROSE, Esq., F.R.G.S.
(5) DEWAR, of Vogrie, N.B.

PLATE XXXI.

THE ARMORIAL BEARINGS OF—

(1) JOHN THOMAS HARTHILL, ESQ., M.R.C.S., &C., OF THE MANOR HOUSE, WILLENHALL.
(2) ALFRED JOHN BOWMAN, ESQ. OF RUSTHALL LODGE, TUNBRIDGE WELLS.
(3) HENRY RIMINGTON-WILSON, ESQ. OF BROOMHEAD HALL, CO. YORK.
(4) REV. ALGERNON LINDESAY BRINE, M.A.
(5) RICHMOND R. ALLEN, ESQ., F.R.C.S.I., &C., OF WEST HILL, DARTFORD.

PLATE XXXII.

THE ARMORIAL BEARINGS OF—

(1) PETER HENRY EMERSON, ESQ., M.B., &c., OF AILSA LODGE, SOUTHBOURNE, HANTS.

(2) SAMUEL ARTHUR BRAIN, ESQ. OF ROXBURGH, PENARTH.

(3) JOHN MACRAE-GILSTRAP, ESQ OF BALLEMORE, CO. ARGYLL, AND NORTHGATE, NEWARK-ON-TRENT.

(4) EDWARD GARTHWAITE FARISH, ESQ.

(5) ROBERT GLADSTONE, ESQ. OF WOOLTON VALE, LIVERPOOL.

PLATE XXXIII.

THE ARMORIAL BEARINGS OF—

(1) Sir KENNETH JAMES MATHESON, Bart.
(2) Rev. GEORGE CANTRELL ALLEN, M.A.
(3) Dr GEORGE BAGOT FERGUSON of Altidore Villa, Pitville, Cheltenham.

(4) WILLIAM FREDERICK BUCHANAN, Esq. of Clar Innis, Sydney, New South Wales.
(5) Major-Gen. ASTLEY FELLOWES TERRY.

FIG. 109.—Bookplate of R. Crawford Walker, Esq., of Wingate Place, Newport, Fifeshire. Arms: Or, a saltire sable, on a chief ermine, a cross moline of the second between two pallets gules. Mantling gules, doubled argent. Crest: a staghound's head couped proper, collared or. Motto: "Sapere aude."

FIG. 113.—Armorial bearings of Frederic Brand George, Esq.: Per fess gules and sable, on a fess indented argent, between two falcons rising in pale of the third, beaked and legged or, a talbot passant of the second. Mantling gules and argent. Crest: on a wreath of the colours, a demi-talbot per fess indented sable and gules, charged on the shoulder with a bezant, thereon a lion's head erased of the second, and resting the sinister paw on a garb vert. Motto: "Strive to attain."

FIG. 110.—Armorial bearings of Sir Offley Wakeman, Baronet: Paly wavy of six vert and argent, a saltire engrailed ermine, impaling the arms of Rouse-Boughton, namely: quarterly, 1 and 4, sable, two bars engrailed argent (for Rouse); 2. argent, on a chevron, between three trefoils slipped sable, as many bucks' heads caboshed or, on a chief gules a goat passant of the field (for Boughton of Loughton); 3. sable, three crescents or (for Boughton). Upon the escutcheon, which is charged with his badge of Ulster as a baronet, is placed a helmet befitting his degree, with a mantling vert and argent; and for his crest, upon a wreath of the colours, between two palm branches proper, a lion's head erased argent, vomiting flames, gorged with a collar engrailed and cottised vert, and charged with three ermines spots or. Mottoes: "Nec temere nec timide," "Tout sans faillir et sans lucre."

FIG. 114.—Armorial bearings of William Cornwallis Cornwallis-West, Esq., of Ruthin Castle: Argent, a fess dancetté sable. Mantling argent and sable. Crest: out of a ducal coronet or, a griffin's head azure, beaked and eared gold. Motto: "Jour de ma vie."

A curious variety of the fess dancetté is borne by the Shropshire family Plowden of Plowden. They bear: Azure, a fess dancetté, the upper points terminating in fleurs-de-lis. A fess couped is found in the arms of Lee (Fig. 115).

The "fess embattled" is only crenellated upon the upper edge; but when both edges are embattled it is a

FIG. 111.—The arms of Amaury de Montfort, Earl of Gloucester; died before 1214. (From his seal.)

FIG. 112.—Arms of Simon de Montfort, Earl of Leicester; died 1265. (From MS. Cott., Nero, D. 1.)

fess embattled and counter - embattled. The term *bretessé* (which is said to indicate that the battlements on the upper edge are opposite the battlements on the lower edge, and the indentations likewise corresponding)

FIG. 115.—Armorial bearings of Ambrose Lee, Bluemantle : Argent, on a fess couped between three crescents sable, as many hawks' lures or, impaling the arms of Wallace, namely : gules, semé-de-lis or, a lion rampant argent within a bordure compony azure and of the third. Crest : upon a wreath of the colours, upon an eagle's leg fesswise erased at the thigh, the claws to the sinister azure, a falcon belled or, legged gules, twined round the body and neck by a hawk's lure sable ; with the motto, " Fide et constantiâ."

is a term and a distinction neither of which are regarded in British armory.

A fess wreathed (Fig. 116) is a bearing which seems to be almost peculiar to the Carmichael family, but the

FIG. 116.—Armorial bearings of James Carmichael, Esq. : Or, a fess wreathed azure and gules, between a crescent of the third in chief and a cinquefoil of the second in base. Upon the escutcheon is placed a helmet befitting his degree, with a mantling azure, doubled or ; and upon a wreath of his liveries is set for crest, an arm in armour embowed, the hand grasping a broken tilting-spear proper ; and in an escroll above this motto, " Toujours prest."

arms of Waye of Devon are an additional example, being : Sable, two bars wreathed argent and gules.

The arms of Hervey [n] (Plate XLV.) show a curious disposition of the fess over a field "per chevron," and Fig. 117, which represents the arms of Smith, exemplifies a fess flory and counterflory.

It is a fixed rule of British armory that there can be only *one* fess upon a shield. If two figures of this character are found they are termed *bars*. But it is hardly correct to speak of the bar as a diminutive of the fess, because if two bars only appear on the shield

FIG. 117.—Armorial bearings of Sir Cecil Clementi Smith, G.C.M.G. : Per fess azure and gules, a fess flory counterflory argent, between three mullets in chief or, and a rock, thereon a dove in base proper. Upon the escutcheon, which is encircled by the ribbon of the Most Distinguished Order of St. Michael and St. George, and by his collar and pendant therefrom his badge as a Knight Grand Cross of that Order, is placed a helmet befitting his degree, with a mantling azure and argent ; and for his crest, upon a wreath of the colours, in front of a lion's head erased argent, gorged with a collar flory counterflory azure, on the head of a crown vallery or, three mullets fesswise or ; with the motto, " Perseverando."

there would be little, if any, diminution made from the width of the fess when depicting the bars. As is the

FIG. 118.—Arms of Michael de la Pole, Earl of Suffolk : Azure, a fess between three leopards' faces or. (From his seal, 1384.)

case with other ordinaries, there is much latitude allowed to the artist in deciding the dimensions, it being usually permitted for these to be governed by the charges upon the fess or bars, and the charges between

[n] Armorial bearings of Matthew Wilson Hervey, Esq. : Parted per chevron gules and vert, a fess chequy argent and azure between three trefoils slipped or, a bordure of the fourth. Above the shield is placed a helmet befitting his degree, with a mantling gules, doubled or ; and upon a wreath of his liveries is set for crest, a demi-lion rampant gules, holding in his dexter paw a trefoil slipped or ; and in an escroll over the same this motto, " Delectat et ornat."

which these are placed. Figs. 118, 119, and 120 exemplify varying dimensions.

The fess and bars are of course equally subject

to the varying lines of partition, and the arms of Langhans (Fig. 121) and Perryman ⁰ (see Plate XIX.) are both instances in which bars occur.

The diminutive of the bar is the barrulet, which is half its width and double the width of the cottise. But the barrulet will *almost invariably* be found borne in *pairs*, when such a pair is usually known as a "bar gemel" and not as two barrulets. Thus a coat with four barrulets would have these placed at equal distances from each other; but a coat with two bars gemel would be depicted with two of its barrulets placed closely together

in chief and two placed closely together in base, the disposition being governed by the fact that the two barrulets comprising the "bar gemel" are only *one charge*. An exception to this is found in the arms of Moore-Gwyn ᵖ (see Plate XVII.).

There is theoretically no limit to the number of bars or bars gemel which can be placed upon the shield. In practical use, however, four will be found the maximum. Bars gemel will be found in the arms of Burlton (Fig. 122).

A field composed of four, six, eight, or ten horizontal pieces of equal width is "barry of such and such a number of pieces," the number being always specified.

A field composed of an equal number of horizontally shaped pieces, when these exceed ten in number, is termed "barruly" of such and such a number. The term barruly is also sometimes used for ten pieces. If the number is omitted it will usually be of six pieces, though sometimes of eight. On the other hand a field composed of five, seven, or nine pieces is not barry, but (*e.g.* argent) two bars, three bars, and four bars

FIG. 122.—Armorial bearings of Thomas Davies Burlton, Esq.: Argent, three bars gemel between four horse-shoes, three in chief and one in base all azure. Mantling azure and argent. Crest: on a wreath of the colours, a demi-gryphon, couped, wings elevated and addorsed argent, holding in the dexter claw a horse-shoe and resting the sinister on a fleur-de-lis, both azure. Motto: "Mens sana in corpore sano."

FIG. 121.—Armorial bearings of Johann Gottlieb Julius Langhans, Esq.: Argent, two bars wavy azure, gutté-d'eau, as many trout naiant, one in chief the other in fess gules, on a chief arched sable, two kingfishers proper. Mantling azure and argent. Crest: on a wreath of the colours, in flags on the sinister side the stump of an oak-tree in bend sinister, one branch sprouting to the dexter, thereon a kingfisher all proper. Motto: "Ich Wart Der Stund."

⁰ Armorial bearings of Charles Wilbraham Perryman, Esq., of Bifrons, Farnborough, Hants: Parted per pale ermine and azure, two bars indented, each charged with three pears slipped all counterchanged. Mantling azure and argent. Crest: on a wreath of the colours, a wolf's head ermine, erased gules, charged with a fess indented azure, surmounted by two pear branches, leaved, fructed, and slipped in saltire proper. Motto: "Per ardua stabilis."

respectively. This distinction in modern coats needs to be carefully noted, but in ancient coats it is not of equal importance. Anciently also a shield "barry" was

ᵖ Armorial bearings of Joseph Edward Moore-Gwyn, Esq., of Dyffryn, co. Glamorgan: Quarterly, 1 and 4, sable, gutté-d'or, two barrulets invected or, between as many lozenges in pale of the last, each charged with a sword erect sable (for Gwyn); 2 and 3, per pale argent and sable, a moor-cock between two greyhounds current, and as many flanches all counterchanged (for Moore). Mantling sable and or. Crests: 1. on a wreath of the colours, between two antlers sable, a cubit arm erect proper, charged with two lozenges palewise also sable, the hand grasping a sword proper, pommel and hilt or, the blade transfixing a boar's head erect and erased gules (for Gwyn); 2. on a wreath of the colours, upon a mount vert, a moor-cock sable, gorged with a collar nebuly argent, and resting the dexter leg on a greyhound's head erased at the neck also sable (for Moore). Motto: "Vim vi repellere licet."

drawn of a greater number of pieces (see Figs. 123 and 124) than would nowadays be employed. In modern armory a field so depicted would more correctly be termed "barruly."

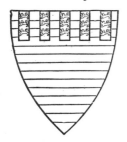

FIG. 123.—Arms of William de Valence, Earl of Pembroke (d. 1296): Barruly azure and argent, a label of five points gules, the files depending from the chief line of the shield, and each file charged with three lions passant guardant or. (From MS. Reg. 14, C. vii.)

FIG. 124.—Arms of Laurence de Hastings, Earl of Pembroke (d. 1348): Quarterly, 1 and 4, or, a maunch gules (for Hastings); 2 and 3, barruly argent and azure, an orle of martlets (for Valence). (From his seal.)

FIG. 125.—Arms of Edmund Grey, Earl of Kent (d. 1489): Quarterly, 1 and 4, barry of six, argent and azure, in chief three torteaux (for Grey); 2 and 3, Hastings and Valence sub-quarterly. (From his seal, 1442.)

Whilst a field can be and often is barry of two colours or two metals, an uneven number of pieces must of necessity be of metal and colour or fur. Consequently in a shield e.g. divided into seven equal horizontal divisions, alternately gules and sable, there must be a mistake somewhere.

Although these distinctions require to be carefully noted as regards modern arms, it should be remembered that they are distinctions evolved by the intricacies and requirements of modern armory, and ancient arms were not so trammelled.

A field divided horizontally into three equal divisions of e.g. gules, sable, and argent is theoretically blazoned by British rules "party per fess gules and argent, a fess sable" (see Plate IX. Fig. 14). This, however, gives an exaggerated width to the fess which it does not really possess with us, and the German rules, which would blazon it "tierced per fess sable, ermine, and gules," would seem preferable.

A field which is barry may also be counterchanged, as in the arms of Ballingall (Fig. 126), where it is counterchanged per pale; but it can also be counterchanged per chevron, or per bend dexter or sinister.

Such counterchanging should be carefully distinguished from fields which are "barry-bendy" or "paly-bendy." In these latter cases the field is divided first by lines horizontal (for barry) or perpendicular (for paly), and subsequently by lines bendy (dexter or sinister).

The result produced is very similar to "lozengy," and care should be taken to distinguish the two.

Barry-bendy is sometimes blazoned "fusilly in bend," whilst paly-bendy is sometimes blazoned "fusilly in bend sinister," but the other terms are the more acceptable.

"Lozengy" is made by use of lines in bend crossed by lines in bend sinister, and "fusilly" the same, only drawn at a more acute angle.

THE CHEVRON

Probably the ordinary of most frequent occurrence in British, as also in French armory, is the chevron. It is comparatively rare in German heraldry. The term is derived from the French word *chevron*, meaning a rafter, and the heraldic chevron is the same shape as a gable rafter. In early examples of heraldic art the chevron will be found depicted reaching very nearly to the top of the shield, the angle contained within the chevron being necessarily more acute. The chevron then attained very much more nearly to its full area of one-third of the field than is now given to it. As the chevron became accompanied by charges, it was naturally drawn so that it would allow of these charges being more easily represented, and its height became less whilst the angle it enclosed was increased. But now, as then, it is perfectly at the pleasure of the artist to design his chevron at the height and angle which will best allow the proper representation of the charges which accompany it.

The arms of Brown [q] (see Plate XXVI.) and Davenport (Fig. 127) are instances of the chevron drawn rather more after the ancient form, which heraldic artists nowadays seem pretty generally to follow whenever possible.

FIG. 126.—Armorial bearings of Hugh Ballingall, Esq.: Parted per pale argent and vert, three bars counterchanged. Mantling vert, doubled argent. Crest: on a wreath of his liveries, a demi-eagle displayed vert, between two lilies issuing out of the wreath proper. Motto: "Decore."

The chevron appears in the arms of Stafford (Fig. 128), Grove White [r] (see Plate XXII.), Wedderburn [s] (see

[q] The arms of Brown of Bonnytoun (matriculated in Lyon Register 1721): Or, on a chevron between three fleurs-de-lis azure, a bezant. Crest: a ship under sail proper. Motto: "Caute et sedulus."
[r] The arms of Lieutenant-Colonel James Grove-White: Quarterly, 1 and 4, argent, on a chevron gules, between three roses of the last, barbed vert, seeded gold, a cross patée or (for White); 2 and 3, ermine, on a chevron engrailed gules, three escallops argent (for Grove). Crest: upon a wreath of the colours, a dexter arm embowed in armour, holding in the hand a dagger all proper, the arm charged with a cross patée or. Motto: "Nourissez l'espérance."
[s] The arms of Alexander D. O. Wedderburn, Esq., K.C.: Argent, on a chevron, invected (for difference) between three roses gules, barbed vert, a crescent of the first (all within a bordure engrailed of the second, for difference). Mantling gules, doubled argent. Crest: on a wreath of his liveries, an eagle's head erased proper; and in an escroll over the same this motto, "Non degener," and below the arms, "Aquila non captat muscas."

FIG. 127.—Armorial bearings of Cyril James Humphreys Davenport, Esq.: Argent, a chevron between three cross crosslets fitchée sable, a canton azure for distinction. Mantling sable and argent. Crest: on a wreath of the colours, a man's head affrontée proper, around his neck a rope or, and charged upon the neck for distinction with a cross crosslet fitchée sable. Motto: "Audaces fortuna juvat."

FIG. 130.—Armorial bearings of Major Francis Ignatius Ricarde-Seaver, F.R.S.E., F.R.G.S., F.G.S., A.M.I.C.E.: Azure, a chevron embattled between two wreaths of oak in chief or and a pickaxe and sword in base proper, surmounted by a tower or. Mantling azure and or. Crest: upon a wreath of the colours, in front of a pickaxe erect, a Moor's head affrontée, couped at the shoulders proper, the turban argent, pierced through the head by a sword fesswise point to the dexter also proper. Motto: "Malo mori quam fœdari."

FIG. 128.—The arms of Stafford: Or, a chevron gules.

FIG. 129.—Armorial bearings of the late Alfred Cock, Esq., Q.C.: Azure, a chevron cottised and couped between two roses in chief and a leopard's face in base all or; and upon an escutcheon of pretence the arms of Liebreich, namely: per pale argent and vert, a stag's attire surmounted by an elephant's tusk salterwise between four eagles displayed all counterchanged. Crest: upon a wreath of the colours, in front of the stump of an oak-tree, one branch sprouting from the dexter side and fructed proper, thereon a cock or, holding in the beak a sprig of oak of the first, five mascles conjoined fesswise of the second. Motto: "Talent de bien faire."

FIG. 131.—Bookplate of George Henry Sprules, Esq. Arms: Gules, a chevron chequy argent and azure, ensigned with a fleur-de-lis of the second, between two palmer's scrips in chief and a lion rampant in base or. Mantling gules and argent; and upon a wreath of his liveries is set for his crest, a hunting-horn vert, garnished or, stringed gules. Motto: "Spe ruo."

Plate XXVI.), Coppen [t] (see Plate XXI.), Cock (Fig. 129), Ricarde-Seaver (Fig. 130), Sprules (Fig. 131), Worsley-Taylor (Fig. 132), and Athill (Fig. 17), it, of course, being subject to the usual variation of partition lines.

FIG. 132.—Armorial bearings of Henry Wilson Worsley-Taylor, K.C.: Quarterly, 1 and 4, ermine, on a chief dovetailed gules, a mallet between two escallops or; 2 and 3, azure, a chevron flory counter-flory or, between in chief two falcons and in base a wolf's head erased. Mantling gules and argent. Crests: 1. on a wreath of the colours, a demi-lion rampant sable, semé of mallets or, holding between the paws an acorn gold, slipped vert; 2. on a wreath of the colours, a wolf's head erased, encircled by a wreath of oak, and pierced by a tilting-spear fesswise. Motto: "Annoso robore quercus."

The chevron, of course, can be cottised and doubly cottised.

It is usually found between three charges, but the necessity of modern differentiation has recently introduced the disposition of four charges, three in chief and one in base, which is by no means a happy invention. An even worse disposition occurs in the arms of a certain family of Mitchell, where the four escallops which are the principal charges are arranged two in chief and two in base.

Ermine spots upon a chevron do not follow the direc-

FIG. 133.—Arms of Richard de Beauchamp, Earl of Warwick (d. 1439): Quarterly, 1 and 4, chequy or and azure, a chevron ermine (for Neuborg); 2 and 3, gules, a fess between six cross crosslets or (for Beauchamp). (From his seal.)

tion of it (see Fig. 133), but in the cases of chevrons vair, and chevrons chequy, authoritative examples can be found in which the chequers and rows of vair both do, and do not, conform to the direction of the chevron.

[t] The arms of John Maurice Coppen, of Ascot: Azure, a chevron invected argent between two boars' heads couped in chief and a demi-gryphon also couped in base or. Mantling azure and or. Crest: on a wreath of the colours, out of the battlements of a tower proper, a demi-gryphon or, holding between the claws a saltire azure. Motto: "Copia sine penuria."

A chevron quarterly is divided by a line chevronwise, apparently dividing the chevron into two chevronels, and then by a vertical line in the centre.

A chevron in point embowed will be found in the arms of Trapand quartered by Adlercron (Fig. 134).

FIG. 134.—Armorial bearings of Rodolph Ladeveze Adlercron, Esq.: Quarterly, 1 and 4, argent, an eagle displayed, wings inverted sable, langued gules, membered and ducally crowned or (for Adlercron); 2 and 3, argent, a chevron in point embowed between in chief two mullets and in base a lion rampant all gules (for Trapaud). Mantling sable and argent. Crest: on a wreath of the colours, a demi-eagle displayed sable, langued gules, ducally crowned or, the dexter wing per fess argent and azure, the sinister per fess of the last and or. Motto: "Quo fata vocant."

FIG. 135.—Armorial bearings of Thomas Irvine, Esq.: Parted per chevron argent and vert, three holly-leaves all countercharged. Mantling vert and argent. Crest: on a wreath of his liveries, a holly-wreath proper. Motto: "Sub sole sub umbra virens."

A field per chevron is often met with, as in the arms of Irvine (Fig. 135). The division line in per chevron (like the enclosing lines of a real chevron) is subject to the usual partition lines, as will be seen in the arms of Reid (Fig. 136) and Dumas (Fig. 137).

The diminutive of the chevron is the chevronel, which will be found in the arms of Mitchell-Carruthers

FIG. 138.—Arms of Gilbert de Clare, Earl of Gloucester and Hertford (*d.* 1230) (from his seal): Or, three chevrons gules.

FIG. 136.—Armorial bearings of Arthur Archibald Alexander Reid, Esq.: Party per chevron indented gules and or, in chief two eagles displayed argent, beaked and membered of the second, and in base a ship of three masts in full sail proper, flagged of the first. Mantling gules, doubled or. Crest: upon a wreath of his liveries, a demi-eagle displayed argent. Motto: "Fortitudine et labore."

FIG. 139.—Armorial bearings of Carruthers, of Howmains (matriculated in Lyon Register *c.* 1672): Gules, two chevronels engrailed between three fleurs-de-lis or. Mantling gules, doubled argent. Crest: on a wreath of the liveries, a cherub's head proper. Motto: "Promptus et fidelis."

FIG. 137.—Armorial bearings of Henry John Philip Dumas, Esq.: Per chevron flory and counterflory or and azure, in chief two lions' gambs erased, and in base a garb counterchanged. Mantling azure and or. Crest: upon a wreath of the colours, issuant from a chaplet of roses an arm embowed in armour proper, charged with a fleur-de-lis azure, and grasping a scythe in bend sinister also proper. Motto: "Adsum."

FIG. 140. Arms of Rev. H. G. Morse: Party per pale argent and sable, two chevronels between three mullets all counterchanged. Crest: upon a wreath of the colours, a demi-man in complete armour proper, garnished or, his helmet surmounted by a plume of three ostrich feathers azure, on his breast a cross-belt sable, and in his dexter hand a halberd proper. Motto: "Deo non armis fido."

(Fig. 139), Morse (Fig. 140), North [u] (Plate XXIV), and Davies (Fig. 141).

[u] Arms of Major Harry North of Eltham: Argent, two chevronels nebuly, between two mullets in chief, and a decrescent in base sable, impaling the arms of Evans, namely: or, a dragon sable, in chief three roses gules, slipped and leaved proper, and in base a fleur-de-lis also gules. Mantling sable and argent. Crest: on a wreath of the colours, a lion's head erased argent, gorged with a collar nebuly sable, and between two mullets also sable. Motto: "Animo et fide."

An example of three chevrons on one field is found in the historic arms of De Clare (Fig. 138).

The field when entirely composed of an even number of chevrons is termed "chevronny."

Chevronels interlaced or "braced" will be found in the arms of Sirr (Fig. 142). The chevronel is very seldom met with singly, but a case of this will be found in the arms of Spry [v] (see Plate XVII.).

FIG. 141.—Armorial bearings of William David Davies, Esq.: Per pale gules and azure, three chevronels nebuly between two lions passant argent. Mantling gules and argent. Crest: on a wreath of the colours, in front of two flag-staves in saltire proper, flowing from each a banner gules charged with a shepherd's crook erect or, a lion passant also propor. Motto: "Duw dy ras."

FIG. 142.—Armorial bearings of Edward Joseph Arthur Sirr, Esq.: Azure, two chevronels interlaced argent, between three estoiles or, in chief a harp of Ireland, above it the Imperial Crown both proper. Mantling azure and argent. Crest: on a wreath of the colours, an estoile or as in the arms, within two-olive branches proper; above, on an escroll, the motto, "Nautæ Fida"; and for the motto beneath the arms, "Lyræ nervos aptavi."

[v] Arms of Tredenham Hugh Spry, Esq., of Witherdon, Germanswerk, co. Devon: Quarterly, 1 and 4, azure, two bars or, in chief a chevronel of the last (for Spry); 2 and 3, sable, a plate between three towers argent, each charged with a cross crosslet gules (for Carlyon). Mantling azure and or. Crests: 1. on a wreath of the colours, a dove argent, standing on a serpent nowed proper (for Spry); 2. on a wreath

THE PILE

The pile is a triangular wedge usually (and unless otherwise specified) issuing from the chief. It occurs

FIG. 143.—Armorial bearings of Rev. William Legg, M.A.: Sable, on a pile or, between two books argent, clasped and garnished in base of the second, a leg couped at the thigh in armour of the field, spurred and garnished gold. Mantling sable and or. Crest: on a wreath of the colours, a dexter arm in armour sable, garnished gold, holding in the hand a roll of paper argent, between roses or. Motto: "Tolle, lege."

FIG. 144.—Armorial bearings of Rev. David Lamplugh, M.A.: Sable, on a pile nebuly between two roses or, barbed and seeded vert, a cross flory of the field. Mantling sable and or. Crest: on a wreath of the colours, in front of a goat's head couped argent, armed or, gorged with a collar nebuly sable, two roses gules, barbed and seeded proper. Motto: "Providentiâ Dei stabiliuntur familiæ."

in the arms of Legg (Fig. 143) and Terry [w] (see Plate XXXIII.), and will be found subject to the lines of partition in the arms of Lamplugh (Fig. 144).

of the colours, a demi-lion rampant gules, ducally crowned or, holding between the paws a bezant. Motto: "Soyez sage et simple."

[w] Arms of Major-General Astley Fellowes Terry: Argent, gutté-de-l'armes, on a pile gules a leopard's face jessant-de-lys or, within a bordure engrailed sable, charged with eight roses of the first. Mantling azure and argent. Crest: on a wreath of the colours, a lion's head erased argent, gutté-de-l'armes, between two oak branches fructed in arch proper. Motto: "Perseveranti dabitur."

The early representation of the pile (when coats of arms had no secondary charges and were nice and simple) made the point nearly reach to the base of the escutcheon, and as a consequence it naturally was not so wide. It is now usually drawn so that its upper edge occupies very nearly the whole of the top line of

FIG. 145.—Armorial bearings of William Parkin-Moore, Esq.: Quarterly, 1 and 4, ermine, on a chevron between three moorcocks sable, an escallop between two cross crosslets argent (for Moore); 2 and 3, argent, on a pile sable, between two fir-cones erect, slipped and leaved in base proper, an eagle displayed of the field, each wing charged with a cross crosslet of the second (for Parkin). Mantling sable and argent. Crests: 1. on a wreath of the colours, a Moor's head couped at the shoulders in profile proper, wreathed round the temples or and gules, and suspended from the neck by a double chain gold, an escocheon argent, charged with a cross crosslet sable (for Moore); 2. on a wreath of the colours, on a mount vert, a fir-cone as in the arms, between two wings sable. Motto: "Aut nunquam tentes aut perfice."

FIG. 147.—Armorial bearings of Alexander William Anstruther-Duncan, Esq.: Quarterly, I. and IV., argent, three piles issuing from the chief sable (for Anstruther); II. and III., quarterly, 1 and 4, gules a chevron or between two cinquefoils in chief argent and a hunting-horn in base, garnished azure, stringed of the second, a bordure of the second for difference (for Duncan); 2. argent, three Moors' heads couped sable, banded or, in the centre a saltire couped of the second, charged with a man's head of the third (for Morison); 3. counterquartered i. and iii., argent, a saltire engrailed sable; ii., argent, a saltire between four roses gules; iii., or, a bend chequy sable and argent, all within a bordure gules for difference (for Haldane). Mantling sable, doubled argent. Crest: upon a wreath of his liveries, two arms in armour, holding in the gauntlets a battle-axe proper. Motto: "Periissem ni periissem."

the escutcheon; but the angles and proportions of the pile are very much at the discretion of the artist and governed by the charges which need to be introduced in the field of the escutcheon or upon the pile. The arms of Parkin-Moore (Fig. 145) show of necessity a very wide pile.

A single pile may issue from any point of the

FIG. 148.—Arms of John le Scot, Earl of Huntingdon and Chester (from MS. Cott., Nero, D. 1): Or, three piles in point gules.

escutcheon except the base; the arms of Darbishire (Fig. 146) showing a pile issuing from the dexter chief point.

A single pile cannot issue in base if it be unaccompanied by other piles, as the field would then be blazoned per chevron.

Two piles issuing in chief will be found in the arms of Hollis, Earl of Clare, and three in the arms of Anstruther-Duncan (Fig. 147).

FIG. 146.—Armorial bearings of James Edward Darbishire: "Quarterly, 1 and 4, gules, on a pile issuant from the dexter canton argent, three leopards' faces of the field (for Darbishire); 2 and 3, argent, a cross pointed and voided sable (for Dukinfield). [The family are entitled to quarter the arms of other families appertaining to Dukinfield.] Mantling gules and argent. Crest: on a wreath of the colours, issuant from clouds, a dexter arm in armour embowed, the hand proper, grasping a cross pointed and voided sable. Motto: "Durate et vincite."

L

THE ART OF HERALDRY

When the three piles, instead of pointing directly at right angles to the line of the chief, all point to the same point, touching or nearly touching at the tips, as in the arms of the Earl of Huntingdon and Chester (Fig. 148), Isham,[x] they are described as three piles in point. This term and its differentiation probably are modern refinements, as with the early long-pointed shield any other position was impossible. The arms of Henderson (Fig. 149) show three piles issuing from the sinister side of the escutcheon.

FIG. 149.—Armorial bearings of George Henderson, Esq.: Gules, three piles issuing from the sinister or, a chief embattled ermine. Upon the escutcheon is placed a helmet befitting his degree, with a mantling gules, doubled or; and upon a wreath of the liveries is set for crest, a cubit arm erect proper, holding in the hand a star of eight points wavy argent, ensigned with a crescent of the last. Motto: "Sola virtus nobilitat."

FIG. 150.—Armorial bearings of Moses Cornwall, Esq., of Kimberley, South Africa: Or, three piles, two issuing in chief and one in base ermine, each charged with a lion rampant regardant gules, a bordure engrailed of the last, thereon four bezants and as many trefoils alternately of the field. Mantling gules and or. Crest: upon a wreath of the colours, a Cornish chough proper, holding in its beak a bezant. Motto: "La vie durante."

A disposition of three piles which will very frequently be found in modern British heraldry is two issuing in

x Armorial bearings of Isham: Gules, a fess wavy, and in chief three piles also wavy, the points meeting in fess argent.

chief and one in base, as will be seen in the arms of Cornwall (Fig. 150).

Piles terminating in fleurs-de-lis are by no means unusual, and reference may be made to the arms of Sir J. Dickson-Poynder, Bart.[y]

An unusual instance of a pile in which it issues from a chevron will be found in the arms of Wright, which are: "Sable, on a chevron argent, three spear-heads gules in chief, two unicorns' heads erased argent, armed and maned or, in base on a pile of the last, issuant from the chevron, a unicorn's head erased of the field."

THE SHAKEFORK

The pall, pairle, or shakefork, is almost unknown in English heraldry, but in Scotland its constant occurrence in the arms of the Cunninghame and allied families has given it a recognised position amongst the ordinaries.

As usually borne by the Cunninghame family the ends are couped and pointed (Fig. 150a), but in some cases it is borne throughout (Fig. 150b).

FIG 150a.—Armorial bearings of Henry Hardinge Samuel Cunninghame, Esq.: Argent, a shakefork sable, between three fleurs-de-lis azure, one in chief and two in the flanges, above a helmet with mantle gules, the doubling argent. On a wreath of his liveries is set for crest, a unicorn unguled, maned and armed or, lying on a mount vert. In an escroll above the crest this motto, "Over fork over."

The pall in its proper ecclesiastical form appears in the arms of the Archiepiscopal Sees of Canterbury, Armagh, and Dublin. Though in these cases the pall or pallium is now considered to have no other heraldic status than that of an appropriately ecclesiastical charge upon an official coat of arms, there can be very little doubt that originally the pall of itself was the heraldic symbol in this country of an archbishop, and borne for that reason by all archbishops, including the Archbishop of York, although his official archiepiscopal coat is now

y Armorial bearings of Sir J. Dickson-Poynder, Bart: Quarterly, 1 and 4 (Poynder), pily counterpily of four nails or and sable, the points ending in crosses formeé, two in chief and one in base, in the centre chief point a castle of the second, and in base two martlets of the first, a chief azure thereon a key erect, the wards upwards and to the sinister gold, between a rose on the dexter side and a fleur-de-lis on the sinister argent; 2 and 3 (Dickson), azure, an anchor erect or, encircled with an oak wreath vert, between three mullets pierced or, on a chief of the second three pallets gules, in the centre of the chief a mural crown argent.

changed to: "Gules, two keys in saltire argent, in chief a royal crown or."

The necessity of displaying this device of rank—the pallium—upon a field of some tincture has led to its corruption into a usual and stereotyped "charge."

THE CROSS

The heraldic cross, the huge preponderance of which in armory we of course owe to the Crusades, like all other armorial charges, has strangely developed. There are nearly four hundred varieties known to armory, or

possible equal. The Sacred Cross, therefore, in heraldry is now known as a "Passion Cross" (or sometimes as a "long cross"), or, if upon steps or "grieces," the number of which needs to be specified, as a "Cross Calvary."

The ordinary heraldic cross (which is always continued throughout the shield unless stated to be couped) will be found in the arms of Bigod (Fig. 151), Burke (Fig. 152), De Ufford (Fig. 153), Atkin-Roberts (Fig. 154), Douglas (Fig. 155), and Oppenheimer [z] (see Plate XXVII.).

Of the crosses more regularly in use may be men-

Fig. 150b.—Armorial bearings of John Anstruther Smith Cunninghame, Esq., of Caprington Castle: Quarterly, 1 and 4, argent, a shakefork sable, within a bordure ermine; 2 and 3, ermine, a fess azure, between two mullets in chief and a hart's head erased in base, attired with ten tynes gules. Crests: 1. a dexter hand holding a plumb-rule proper, and in an escroll over the same this motto, "Ad Amussim;" 2. a ship in distress proper, and in an escroll over this motto, "At spes infracta." Supporters: two horses at liberty argent, maned and hoofed or.

rather to heraldic text-books, and doubtless authenticated examples could be found of most if not of them all. But some dozen or twenty forms are about as many as will be found regularly or constantly occurring.

When the heraldic cross was first assumed with any reason beyond geometrical convenience, there can be no doubt that it was intended to represent the Sacred Cross itself. The symbolism of the cross is older than our present system of armory, but the cross itself is more ancient than its symbolism. A cross depicted upon the long, pointed shields of those who fought for the Cross would be of that shape, with the elongated arm in base.

But the contemporary shortening of the shield, together with the introduction of charges in its angles, led naturally to the arms of the cross being so disposed that the parts of the field left visible were as nearly as

tioned the cross bottony, as in the arms of Humphry (Fig. 156); the cross flory, as in the arms of I'Anson [a] (Plate XXVII.), which must be distinguished from the cross fleuretté as in the arms of Galpin as quartered by

[z] Armorial bearings of Francis Charles Oppenheimer, Esq., M.A., H.M.'s Consul-General at Frankfort-on-Maine: Quarterly, gules and azure, a cross invected between a lion rampant regardant, supporting a flagstaff therefrom flowing to the dexter a banner in the first and fourth quarters, and an anchor erect in the second and third all or. Mantling gules and or. Crest: upon a wreath of the colours, two branches of oak in saltire vert, fructed or, in front of a flagstaff in bend proper, therefrom flowing a banner gules, surmounting a trident in bend sinister also proper. Motto: "Nihil sine labore."

[a] Armorial bearings of William Andrew I'Anson, Esq.: Quarterly, azure and gules, a cross flory, in the first and fourth quarters an annulet or, a chief indented of the last, a crescent for difference. Mantling azure and or. Crest: upon a wreath of the colours, a cubit arm habited per pale indented azure and or, encircled by an annulet of the last, the hand proper holding a cross as in the arms. Motto: "Faire mon devoire."

Watney [b] (Plate XXVII.); the cross moline, as in the arms of Dugdale; [c] the cross potent, as in the arms of

FIG. 151.—Arms of Roger le Bigod, Earl of Norfolk (*d.* 1270): Or, a cross gules. (From MS. Cott., Nero, D. 1.)

FIG. 152.—Armorial bearings of Ulick John Burke, Esq.: Or, a cross gules, in the first and fourth quarters a lion rampant sable. Mantling gules and or; and for his crest, upon a wreath of the colours, a cat-a-mountain proper, collared and chained or, charged on the breast with a cross of the last. Motto: "Ung roy, ung foy, ung loy."

FIG. 153.—Arms of Robert de Ufford, Earl of Suffolk (*d.* 1369): Sable, a cross engrailed or. (From his seal.)

[b] Armorial bearings of Sir John Watney, F.S.A.: Quarterly, 1 and 4, azure, a cross engrailed ermine, in the first and fourth quarters a dove argent, and in the second and third a garb or (for Watney); 2 and 3, quarterly, argent and or, a cross fleurettée gules, in the first and fourth quarters a lion rampant of the last, charged with three bars of the second (for Galpin). Mantling azure and argent. Crest: upon a wreath of the colours, on a mount vert, in front of a garb erect or, a greyhound courant sable, gorged with a collar, therefrom pendent a bugle-horn of the second. Motto: "Auxilium ab alto."

[c] Armorial bearings of Adam Dugdale, Esq.: Ermine, a cross moline gules between four hurts. Upon the escutcheon is placed a helmet befitting his degree, with a mantling gules and argent; and for his crest, on a wreath of the colours, a griffin's head and wings endorsed erminois, gorged with a collar gemelle azure, and charged on the neck with a cross as in the arms; with the motto, "Perseverando."

FIG. 154.—Armorial bearings of John Roberts Atkin-Roberts, Esq.: Quarterly, 1 and 4, azure, on a chevron argent cottised or, three mullets of six points pierced sable (for Roberts); 2 and 3, argent, gutté-de-sang, a cross cottised flory, in the first and fourth quarters a trefoil slipped sable, and in the second and third quarters a mullet of six points of the last, pierced of the field (for Atkin); and for his crests, 1. upon a wreath of the colours, on a mount vert, an eagle displayed ermine, the wings argent, gorged with a chaplet of ivy proper (for Roberts); 2. upon a wreath of the colours, two greyhounds' heads addorsed and erased argent, gutté-de-sang, gorged with a collar vair, and each holding in the mouth a trefoil slipped sable (for Atkin); with the motto, "Post funera virtus."

FIG. 155.—Armorial bearings of William Charles Douglas, Esq.: Quarterly, 1 and 4, argent, a heart gules imperially crowned or, on a chief azure three mullets of the field; 2 and 3, argent, a cross embattled sable, over all dividing the quarters a cross raguly of the last, the whole within a bordure invected azure, charged with eight holly-leaves or. Mantling sable, doubled argent. Crest: on a chapeau gules, turned up ermine, a salamander in flames of fire proper. Motto: "Jamais arrière."

Leeming[d] (see Plate XXII.); the cross patée, as in the arms of Crookes (Fig. 157); the cross patonce, as in the arms of Lascelles;[e] and the cross crosslet, as in the arms of Moore (Fig. 158).

FIG. 158.—Armorial bearings of Hon. Charles Moore: Azure, a cross crosslet or, on a canton argent, a kangaroo sejant proper. Mantling azure and or. Crest: upon a wreath of the colours, out of a mural crown gules, a Moor's head in profile, couped at the shoulders proper, wreathed round the temples or and azure, and charged on the neck with a cross crosslet gold; with the motto, "Perseverando et cavendo."

Of other but much more uncommon varieties examples will be found of the cross couped in the arms

FIG. 156.—Armorial bearings of Alfred Paget Humphry, Esq.: Argent, on a cross bottony, between in the first and fourth quarters a talbot's head erased gules, a rose of the first barbed and seeded proper, between four escallops also of the first. Mantling gules and argent. Crest: on a wreath of the colours, in front of a rock, thereon a falcon close proper, belled and jessed or, holding in the beak a key argent, four escallops also or. Motto: "Persiste."

FIG. 159.—Armorial bearings of Edward Ashworth, Esq.: Quarterly, gules and argent, a cross couped and indented between two fleurs-de-lis in chief and as many quatrefoils in base all counterchanged. Mantling gules and argent. Crest: on a wreath of the colours, in front of two crosses bottonnée fitchée in saltire or, a fox passant proper, charged on the body with two fleurs-de-lis in fess, also gold. Motto: "Vincit amor patriæ."

FIG. 157.—Armorial bearings of Sir William Crookes, F.R.S.: Or, on a chevron vert, three prisms proper, between in chief two crosses pattées of the second, and in base a radiometer proper. Mantling vert and or. Crest: on a wreath of the colours, an elephant quarterly or and vert, charged with two crosses pattées counterchanged, resting the dexter forefoot on a prism proper. Motto: "Ubi crux ibi lux."

of Ashworth (Fig. 159), of the cross parted and fretty in the arms of Moresby (Fig. 160), of the cross patée

helmet befitting his degree, with a mantling gules and argent; and for his crest, upon a wreath of the colours, between two crosses potent azure, a dexter arm embowed in armour, the hand grasping a sword all proper, charged with two oak-leaves, the one above and the other below the elbow vert; with the motto: "In hoc signo vinces."

[e] Armorial bearings of Lascelles, Earls of Harewood: Sable, a cross patonce within a bordure or.

[d] Armorial bearings of Major John Fishwick Leeming: Per chevron argent and ermine, a chevron gules, in chief an oak-branch fructed and slipped proper between two roses gules, barbed and seeded also proper, and in base a cross potent azure. Upon the escutcheon is placed a

quadrate in the arms of Vickers (Fig. 161), of a cross pointed and voided in the arms of Dukinfield (quartered

patée, it is then termed "fitchée at the foot," as in the arms of Ffinden (Fig. 163).

FIG. 160.—Armorial bearings of John Moresby, Esq.: Sable, a cross parted and fretty between in dexter chief an anchor erect and in the sinister base a cinquefoil or. Mantling sable and or. Crest: upon a wreath of the colours, an heraldic antelope rampant gules, navally gorged, and with chain reflexed over the back or, supporting a tilting-spear erect sable; with the motto, "Je le feray durant ma vie."

by Darbishire, Fig. 146), and of a cross cleché voided and pommeté as in the arms of Cawston (Fig. 162).

FIG. 161.—Armorial bearings of Cuthbert Bainbridge Vickers, Esq.: Gules, on a cross patée quadrate or, five mullets of eight points of the first, on a chief arched ermine, two Cornish choughs proper. Mantling gules and or. Crest: on a wreath of the colours, in front of a demi-leopard proper, charged with three mullets of eight points palewise, and holding between the paws an increscent or, a mount vert. Motto: "Vulneror non vincor."

Whenever a cross or cross crosslet has the bottom arm elongated and pointed it is said to be "fitched," as in Plate VII. Fig. 40, or in the arms of Davenport (Fig. 127), but when a point is added at the foot e.g. of a cross

FIG. 162.—Armorial bearings of George Cawston, Esq.: Argent, on a bend sable, four crosses clechée, voided and pomettée of the first, on a chief nebuly azure a falcon, wings expanded of the field. Mantling sable and argent. Crest: on a wreath of the colours, in front of an oak-tree proper, a falcon argent, charged on the wing with a cross crosslet sable, preying on a hare azure. Motto: "Sohou, Sohou."

FIG. 163.—Armorial bearings of Rev. George Sketchley Ffinden: Azure, two chevronels engrailed argent between three escutcheons of the last, each charged with a cross patée fitchée at the foot sable, in the centre point a bull's head cabossed of the second. Crest: upon a wreath of the colours, upon a mount vert, a bull argent, pied and yoked sable, resting the dexter foot upon an escutcheon azure, charged with a cross patée fitchée at the foot argent; with the motto, "Suchet und ihr werdet finden."

FIG. 164.—Arms of Thomas Beauchamp, Earl of Warwick (d. 1401): Gules, a fess between six cross crosslets or. (From his seal.)

Of the hundreds of other varieties it may confidently be said that a large proportion originated in misunderstandings of the crude drawings of early armorists, added to the varying and alternating descriptions applied at a more pliable and fluent period of heraldic blazon. A striking illustration of this will be found in the cross botonny which is now, and has been for long, regularised with us as a distinct variety of constant occurrence. From early illustrations (Fig. 164) there is now no doubt that this was the original form of the cross crosslet. It is foolish to ignore these varieties, reducing all crosses to a few original forms, for they are now mostly stereotyped and accepted; but at the same time it is useless to attempt to learn them, for in a lifetime they will mostly be met with but once each or thereabouts.

THE SALTIRE

The saltire or saltier is more frequently to be met with in Scottish than in English heraldry. This is not surprising, inasmuch as the saltire is known as the

FIG. 165.—Armorial bearings of Laurence Currie, Esq.: Gules, a saltire couped argent, in the centre chief point a rose of the last, barbed and seeded proper; and impaling the arms of Finch, namely: argent, a chevron between three griffins passant sable, a bordure wavy ermines. Mantling gules and argent. Crest: on a wreath of the colours, a cock proper, resting its claw upon a rose argent, barbed and seeded proper.

Cross of St. Andrew, the Patron Saint of Scotland. Its form is too well known to need description. Instances of its use will be found in the arms of Stable[f] (Plate XXVIII.), Johnston[g] (Plate XXVIII.), Napier,[h] Currie

[f] Armorial bearings of Daniel Wintringham Stable, Esq.: Argent, a saltire between four acorns slipped gules, on a chief of the last three mullets pierced of the first. Mantling gules and argent. Crest: on a wreath of the colours, in front of a demi-lion gules, holding between the paws a mullet of six points pierced argent, an acorn slipped between two mullets pierced fesswise of the last. Motto: "Virtute."

[g] Armorial bearings of George L. Lawson Johnston, Esq.: Argent, on a saltire engrailed sable, between four daggers points downwards gules, the sun in his splendour or, on a chief of the third, three cushions of the fourth. Mantling sable, doubled argent. Crest: on a wreath of his liveries, a spur, between two wings or, and in an escrol over the same this motto: "Nunquam non paratus."

[h] Armorial bearings of Theodore Napier, Esq.: Gules, on a saltire, engrailed between four roses argent, a lion's head affronté of

(Fig. 165), Haldane (Fig. 90), Sir Henry Harben (see Plate XIX.), Scarisbrick (Fig. 166), Gould (Fig. 167), Beridge (Fig. 168), and Chance (Fig. 169).

FIG. 166.—Armorial bearings of Charles Scarisbrick, Esq.: Argent, a saltire engrailed parted and fretty, between two mullets of six points in pale all sable. Mantling sable and argent. Crest: on a wreath of the colours, between two trefoils slipped vert, a falcon close proper, belled and jessed, and charged on the breast with a mullet of six points or. Motto: "Patientia vincit omnia."

FIG. 167.—Armorial bearings of Hon. Albert John Gould, V.D.: Ermine, on a pale per saltire gules and or, between two saltires in fess of the second, a lion rampant gorged with a collar gemel counterchanged. Mantling gules and argent. Crest: on a wreath of the colours, a demi-lion ermine, grasping with the dexter paw a saltire argent, and resting the sinister on a bezant. Motto: "Honor virtutis premium."

When a saltire is charged the charges usually are placed conformably therewith.

the first. Mantling gules, doubled argent; and upon a wreath of his liveries is set for crest, an arm in chain armour embowed, the hand grasping a battle-axe proper; and in an escroll above this motto: "Pro rege et patria."

THE ART OF HERALDRY

The field of a coat of arms is often per saltire, as in the arms of Hickman (Fig. 170).

lines, as in the arms of Gould (Fig. 167), or by lines at right angles, as in the arms of Greenwood (Fig. 171).

FIG. 168.—Armorial bearings of Rev. Basil James Harold Beridge: Argent, a saltire nebuly between two bears' heads erased in pale and as many escallops in fess sable. Mantling sable and argent. Crest: on a wreath of the colours, in front of a bear's head erased sable, three escallops inverted or.

FIG. 170.—Armorial bearings of Sir Alfred Hickman: Party per saltire sable and or, two leopards' faces jessant-de-lis in pale, and as many fleurs-de-lis in fess, all counterchanged. Mantling sable, doubled or. Crest: on a wreath of the colours, a phœnix issuing out of flames, transfixed through the mouth by a tilting-spear palewise proper, each wing charged with two annulets erect and interlaced or. Motto: "Igne et ferro."

When one saltire couped is the principal charge it will usually be found that it is couped conformably to the outline of the shield, as in the arms of Currie (Fig.

FIG. 169.—Armorial bearings of Sir James Timmins Chance, Bart.: Gules, a saltire vair between two fleurs-de-lis in pale and as many towers in fess argent, the escutcheon being charged with his badge of Ulster as a Baronet. Mantling gules and argent. Crest: on a wreath of the colours, a demi-lion rampant gules, semé of annulets or, holding between the paws a sword erect, entwined by a wreath of oak all proper. Motto: "Deo non fortuna."

165); but if the couped saltire be one of a number or a subsidiary charge it will be found couped by horizontal

FIG. 171.—Bookplate of Hubert John Greenwood, Esq. Arms: per chevron sable and argent, a chevron ermine between three escutcheons, each charged with a saltire couped counterchanged. Mantling sable and argent. Crest: on a wreath of the colours, a leopard sejant guardant or, resting the dexter foreleg on an escutcheon sable, thereon a saltire couped argent.

88

THE CHIEF

The chief, which is a broad band across the top of the shield containing (thereotically, but not in fact) the uppermost third of the area of the field, is a very favourite ordinary. It is of course subject to the variations of the usual partition lines. It is usually drawn to contain about one-fifth of the area of the field, though in cases where it is used for a landscape augmentation it will usually be found of a rather greater area. A chief will be found, for example, in the arms of Dewar of Vogrie[i] (Plate XXX.), Bowman (Plate XXXI.),

FIG. 174.—Armorial bearings of Theodore Maxwell, Esq.: Argent, a saltire sable, a chief paly of six of the first and second, a mullet for difference. Mantling gules and argent. Crest: on a wreath of the colours, a stag's head erased proper, a mullet for difference as in the arms. Motto: "Je suis prêt."

FIG. 172.—Armorial bearings of Rev. George Preston Kelsall Winlaw: Argent, fretty sable, two salmon naiant proper, on a chief arched gules, as many crosses patée or. Mantling sable and argent. Crest: on a wreath of the colours, upon a hillock vert three javelins, one in pale and two in saltire proper, suspended therefrom by a ribbon or an escutcheon sable, charged with an acorn leaved and slipped also or. Motto: "What I win I keep."

FIG. 175.—Armorial bearings of Ross-of-Bladensburg: Per fess embattled argent and or, in chief issuant a dexter arm embowed vested gules, the cuff azure, encircled by a wreath of laurel, the hand grasping a flagstaff broken in bend sinister, therefrom flowing the colours of the United States of America proper, in base the arms of Ross of Ross-Trevor, namely: or, a chevron embattled counter-embattled between three water-bougets sable, on a canton of the third pendent from a riband a representation of the cross presented by command of His Majesty to the late Major-General Ross-of-Bladensburg, in testimony of his Royal approbation of his services; with the motto, "Bladensburg"; and impaling the arms of Foster-Skeffington, namely: quarterly, 1 and 4, argent, three bulls' heads erased sable, armed or (for Skeffington); 2 and 3, azure, a chevron between three chaplets or (for Clotworthy). Mantling sable and or; and for a crest, of honourable augmentation, out of a mural crown or, a dexter arm grasping the colours as in the arms; in addition to the crest of the family of Ross of Ross-Trevor, namely: upon a wreath of the colours, an arm vambraced and embowed, the hand grasping a dagger all proper.

FIG. 173.—Armorial bearings of Count E. de Poher de la Poer: Argent, a chief indented sable; and impaling the arms of Monsell, namely: argent, on a chevron between three mullets sable, a trefoil slipped or. Mantling sable and argent; and for his crest, upon a wreath of the colours, a stag's head caboshed proper, attired or, and between the attires a crucifix of the last; with the motto, "Per crucem ad coronam."

[i] Arms of Dewar of Vogrie: Or, a chief azure. Mantling gules and argent. Crest: on a wreath of his liveries, a dexter arm vambraced and embowed brandishing a sword proper, hilted and pommelled or. Motto: "Quid non pro patria."

M

Winlaw (Fig. 172), De la Poer (Fig. 173), Ambrose [j] (Plate XXX.), Brine [k] (Plate XXXI.), and Maxwell (Fig. 174).

FIG. 176.—Armorial bearings of Sir David Gamble, Bart., C.B.: Or, on a pile gules, between two trefoils slipped in base vert, a fleur-de-lis of the first, a chief ermine. Mantling gules and or; and for his crest, upon a wreath of the colours, on a mount between two trefoils slipped vert, a stork argent, holding in the beak a rose gules, stalked, leaved, and slipped proper. Motto: "Vix ea nostra voco."

FIG. 177.—Armorial bearings of James Maxtone-Graham, Esq.: Quarterly, 1 and 4, or, a chevron gules, between three cross crosslets fitchée azure (for Maxtone); 2 and 3, or, three piles sable, within a double tressure flory counterflory gules, on a chief of the second, a rose between two escallops of the first (for Graham). Mantling gules, doubled argent; and for his crests, 1. upon a wreath of the liveries, a bee proper (for Maxtone); 2. upon a wreath of the liveries, a dove proper (for Graham). Mottoes: "Providus esto," and "Candide ut secure."

[j] Armorial bearings of William Henry Ambrose, Esq., F.R.G.S.: Azure, two lions passant in pale argent, on a chief dovetailed of the last, a fleur-de-lis between two annulets of the first; and for his crest, on a wreath of the colours, and issuant from the battlements of a tower, a cubit arm proper, holding a billet in bend sinister or; with the motto, "J'espère en Dieu."

[k] Armorial bearings of Rev. Algernon Lindesay Brine, M.A.: Argent, an eagle displayed sable, charged with an anchor or, on a chief embattled gules, a cross moline also gold. Mantling sable and argent. Crest: on a wreath of the colours, a lion rampant argent, semé of billets and holding in the fore-paws a cross moline gules. Motto: "Confido."

The chief especially lent itself to the purposes of honourable augmentation, and is constantly found so employed. As such it will be referred to in the chapter upon augmentations, but a chief of this character may perhaps be here interposed with advantage, as this will indicate the greater area often given to it under these conditions, as in the arms of Ross-of-Bladensburg (Fig. 175).

Knights of the old Order of St. John of Jerusalem and also of the modern Order of the Hospital of St. John of Jerusalem in England display above their personal arms a chief of the order, but this will be dealt with more fully in the chapter relating to the insignia of knighthood.

Save in exceptional circumstances, the chief is never debruised or surmounted by any ordinary.

The arms of Gamble (Fig. 176), of Maxtone-Graham (Fig. 177), of Graham-Wigan (Fig. 178), and of Scott (Fig. 179), show respectively a chief and pile, a chief and bend, a chief and tressure, a chief and three piles, and a chief and bordure.

FIG. 178.—Armorial bearings of John Alfred Graham-Wigan, Esq.: Quarterly, 1 and 4, vair, on a pile or, a mount, thereon a mountain ash-tree proper (for Wigan); 2 and 3, or, three piles wavy sable, the centre one charged with a crescent of the field, within a double tressure flory and counterflory gules, on a chief engrailed sable, three escallops of the field, a canton ermine for distinction (for Graham), and upon an escutcheon of pretence these same arms of Graham without the canton. Mantling azure and or. Crests: 1. on a wreath of the colours, on a mount vert, a mountain ash-tree under a rainbow proper (for Wigan); 2. on a wreath of the colours, a flame of fire proper, charged with a cross crosslet sable, for difference (for Graham). Motto: "Recta sursum."

It will be seen from the foregoing that the chief is superimposed over the tressure and over the bordure, partly defacing them. This only happens with the bordure when it is a part of the original coat of arms. If, however, the chief was in existence at an earlier period and the bordure is added later as a mark of difference, the bordure surrounds the chief as in the arms of Kyd (see Fig. 180). On the other hand, if a bordure exists, even as a mark of difference, and a chief of augmentation is *subsequently* added, or a canton for distinction (Fig. 178), the chief or the canton in these cases would surmount the bordure.

Similarly a bend when added later as a mark of difference surmounts the chief. Such a case is very unusual, as the use of the bend for differencing has long been obsolete. It will be found, however, in the arms of Fitzherbert (Fig. 100a).

A chief is never couped or cottised, and it has no diminutive in British armory.

FIG. 179.—Armorial bearings of John Alexander Robson Scott, Esq.: Or, on a bend azure, a mullet between two crescents of the first, within a bordure of the third; on a chief gules, a stag trippant also of the first, between two boars' heads couped argent. Mantling gules, doubled argent. Crest: on a wreath of the colours, a stag trippant proper. Motto: "Patriam amo."

FIG. 180.—Armorial bearings of Alexander Kyd, Esq.: Argent, a pine-tree eradicated proper, with a bugle-horn pendent on one of the branches or, stringed gules, on a chief azure, three mullets of the third; a crescent for difference also azure, all within a bordure wavy ermine. Mantling vert and argent. Crest: on a wreath of the colours, in front of a cubit arm proper, holding three ears of wheat on one stalk, an increscent or, the whole debruised by a bendlet sinister wavy ermine. Motto: "Quem non torret hyems."

THE QUARTER

The quarter is not often met with in English armory, the best-known instance being the well-known coat of Shirley, Earl Ferrers, viz.: Paly of six or and azure, a

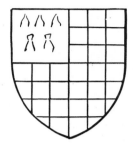

FIG. 181.—Arms of Peter de Dreux, Earl of Richmond (c. 1230): Chequy or and azure, a quarter ermine. (From his seal.)

FIG. 182.—Arms of De Vere, Earls of Oxford: Quarterly gules and or, in the first quarter a mullet argent.

quarter ermine. The arms of the Earls of Richmond (Figs. 76 and 181) supply another instance. Of course as a division of the field under the blazon of "quarterly" (e.g. or and azure) it is constantly to be met with, but a single quarter is rare.

Originally it was drawn to contain the full fourth part of the shield, but with the more modern tendency to

FIG. 183.—Armorial bearings of Berners: Quarterly or and vert. Crest: a monkey proper, environed about the loins and lined or, holding a scroll with the motto, "Del fugo I avola."

reduce the size of all charges, its area has been somewhat diminished. The diminutive of the quarter is the canton, and the diminutive of that the chequer of a chequy field. Whilst a quarter will only be found within a plain partition line, a field divided quarterly (occasionally, but I think hardly so correctly, termed "per cross") is not so limited. Examples of quarterly fields will be found in the historic shield of De Vere

FIG. 184.—Armorial bearings of Thellusson : Quarterly, wavy or and argent, in the first and fourth quarters two wings expanded barwise sable, each charged with a trefoil slipped of the first ; in the second and third quarters an oak-tree eradicated proper, charged with an escutcheon bendwise gules, thereon three guttés-d'eau. Mantling sable and or. Crest : on a wreath of the colours, a demi-greyhound salient argent, collared sable, between two wings of the last, each charged with a trefoil slipped or. Motto : "Labore et honore."

(Fig. 182), arms of Berners (Fig. 183), Croft (Plate XI.), Thellusson (Fig. 184), and Marples (Fig. 185). As has

FIG. 185.—Armorial bearings of George Jobson Marples, Esq. : Quarterly, per fess nebuly sable and ermine, in the first and fourth quarters a griffin segreant or. Mantling sable and argent. Crest : on a wreath of the colours, a griffin segreant or, resting the sinister claw on a cross crosslet fitchée sable between two wings of the latter. Motto : "Tenax justitiæ."

been done in the case of Thellusson, an irregular partition line is often introduced in a new grant to conjoin quarterings borne without authority into one single coat.

THE CANTON

The canton is supposed to occupy one-third of the chief, and that being supposed to occupy one-third of the field, a simple arithmetical sum gives us one-ninth of the field as the theoretical area of the canton. Curiously enough, the canton to a certain extent gives us a confirmation of these ancient proportions, inasmuch as all ancient drawings containing both a fess and a canton depict these conjoined. This will be seen in the Garter plate of Earl Rivers. In modern days, however, it is very seldom that the canton will be depicted of such a size, though in cases where, as in the arms of Boothby, it forms the only charge, it is even nowadays drawn to closely approximate to its theoretical area of one-ninth of the field. It may be remarked here perhaps that, owing to the fact that there are but few instances in which the quarter or the canton have been used as the sole or principal charge, a coat of arms in

FIG. 186.—Armorial bearings of Martin John Sutton, Esq. : Argent, on the trunk of a tree eradicated fesswise, a squirrel sejant cracking a nut all proper, a bordure invected azure, charged with eight fleurs-de-lis or, a canton sable, charged with a fleur-de-lis of the field. Mantling azure and argent. Crest : on a wreath of the colours, a squirrel sejant proper, resting the forepaws on an escutcheon argent; charged with a wolf's head erased proper, a canton as in the arms. Motto : "Toujours prest pour y parvenir."

which these are employed would be granted with fewer of the modern bedevilments than would a coat with a chevron for example. I know of no instance in modern times in which a quarter, when figuring as a charge, or a canton have been subject to the usual lines of partition. The canton (with the single exception of the bordure, when used as a mark of cadency or distinction) is superimposed *over* every other charge or ordinary, no matter what this may be, as will be seen in the arms of Sutton (Fig. 186) and Lowndes[1] (Plate XXXV.).

Theoretically the canton is supposed to be always a later addition to the coat, and even though a charge may be altogether hidden or "absconded" by the canton, the charge is always presumed to be there, and is mentioned in the blazon.

[1] Armorial bearings of Edward Chaddock Lowndes, Esq. : Quarterly, 1 and 4, argent, fretty azure, on a canton gules a lion's head erased or (for Lowndes) ; 2 and 3, ermine, on a pile per pale sable and azure, three pheons or (for Gorst). Mantling azure and argent. Crests : 1. upon a wreath of the colours, a lion's head erased or, gorged with a laurel wreath vert (for Lowndes) ; 2. upon a wreath of the colours, a pheon or, the shaft entwined with a serpent proper (for Gorst). Motto : "Quod adest gratum."

Both a cross and a saltire are sometimes described as "cantonned" by such-and-such charges, when they are placed in the blank spaces left by these ordinaries. In addition, the spaces left by a cross (but not by a saltire) are frequently spoken of *e.g.* as the dexter chief canton or the sinister base canton.

The canton is frequently used to carry an augmentation, and these cantons of augmentation will be referred to under that heading, though it may be here stated that a "canton of England" is a canton gules, charged with three lions passant guardant or, as in the arms of Lane (Fig. 57).

The canton, unless it is *an original charge,* need not conform to the rule forbidding colour on colour, or metal on metal; otherwise the canton of Ulster would often be an impossibility.

The canton, with rare exceptions, is always placed in the dexter chief corner. The canton of augmentation in the arms of Clerke, Bart.—"Argent, on a bend gules, between three pellets as many swans of the field; on a sinister canton azure, a demi-ram salient of the first, and in chief two fleurs-de-lis or, debruised by a baton" —is, however, a sinister one, as is the canton upon the arms of Charlton. In this latter case the sinister canton is used to signify illegitimacy. This will be more fully dealt with in the chapter upon marks of illegitimacy. The Clerke canton is an augmentation.

A curious use of the canton for the purposes of marshalling occurs in the case of a woman who, being an heiress herself, has a daughter or daughters only, whilst her husband has sons and heirs by another marriage. In such an event, the daughter being heir (or in the case of daughters these being coheirs) of the mother, but not heir of the father, cannot transmit as quarterings the arms of the father, whilst they ought to transmit the arms of the mother whom they *do* represent. The husband of the daughter, therefore, places upon an escutcheon of pretence the arms of the mother, with those of the father on a canton thereupon. The children of the marriage quarter this combined coat, the arms of the father always remaining upon a canton. This will be more fully dealt with under the subject of marshalling.

The canton has yet another use as a "mark of distinction." When, under a Royal Licence, the name and arms of a family are assumed where there is no blood descent from the family, the arms have some mark of distinction added. This is usually a plain canton. This point will be treated more fully under "Marks of Cadency."

Woodward mentions three instances in which the lower edge of the canton is "indented," one taken from the Calais Roll, viz. the arms of Sir William de la Zouche—"Gules, bezantée, a canton indented at the bottom"—and adds that the canton has been sometimes thought to indicate the square banner of a knight-baronet, and he suggests that the lower edge being indented may give some weight to the idea. As the canton does not appear to have either previously or subsequently formed any part of the arms of Zouche, it is possible that in this instance some such meaning may have been intended, but it can have no such application generally. The "Canton of Ulster"—*i.e.* "Argent, a sinister hand couped at the wrist gules"—is the badge of a baronet of England, Ireland, Great Britain, or the United Kingdom. This badge may be borne upon a canton, dexter or sinister, or upon an inescutcheon, at the pleasure of the wearer.

THE GYRON

As a charge, the gyron (sometimes termed an esquire) is very seldom found, but as a subdivision of the field, a coat "gyronny" is constantly met with, all arms for

the name of Campbell being gyronny. Save in rare cases, a field gyronny is divided quarterly and then per

FIG. 187.—Armorial bearings of Sir Archibald Spencer Lindsey Campbell, Bart., of Succoth: Quarterly, 1 and 4, gyronny of eight engrailed or and sable (for Campbell); 2 and 3, azure, a lion rampant argent, within a bordure counter-compony of the second and first (for Wallace of Ellerslie). Mantling gules, doubled argent; and upon a wreath of his liveries is set for crest, a camel's head couped proper; and for his supporters, dexter, a lion rampant guardant; sinister, a savage wreathed about the temples and loins all proper; and in an escroll over his crest this motto, "Labor omnia superat."

FIG. 188.—Armorial bearings of Louis Mortimer Lanyon, Esq.: Gules, on waves of the sea azure, a castle of two towers, on the battlements thereof a falcon rising all proper, on a chief or, a pallet between two gyrons of the field. Mantling gules and or. Crest: on a wreath of the colours, on a mount vert, a falcon rising proper, belled and jessed or. Motto: "Vive ut vivas."

saltire, making eight divisions, but it may be gyronny of six, ten, twelve, or more pieces, though such cases are seldom met with. Fig. 54 shows the arms of the late Duke of Argyll, and Fig. 187 shows the arms of Sir

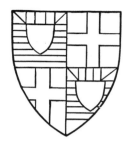

FIG. 189.—The arms of Roger Mortimer, Earl of March and Ulster (d. 1398): Quarterly, 1 and 4, azure, three bars or (sometimes but not so correctly quoted barry of six), on a chief of the first two pallets between two base esquires of the second, over all an inescutcheon argent (for Mortimer); 2 and 3, or, a cross gules (for Ulster). (From his seal.)

Archibald Campbell, Bart., of Succoth, which are gyronny of eight *engrailed*, a most unusual circumstance. A field gyronny of argent and gules occurs in the arms of Welchman[m] (Plate XXVIII.), and Fig. 188, the arms of Lanyon, affords an example of the gyron as a charge, as does also the well-known shield of Mortimer (Fig. 189).

THE INESCUTCHEON

The inescutcheon is a shield appearing as a charge upon the coat of arms. Certain writers state that it is termed an inescutcheon if only one appears as the charge, but that when more than one is present they are merely termed escutcheons. This is an unnecessary

FIG. 190.—Armorial bearings of Molesworth: Gules, an escutcheon vair, between eight cross crosslets in orle or. Mantling gules and argent. Crest: upon a wreath of the colours, a dexter arm in armour, embowed proper, holding a cross crosslet or; with the motto: "Vincit amor patriæ."

m Armorial bearings of William Welchman, Esq.: Gyronny of eight argent and gules, a goat's head erased proper, within ten mullets in orle, counterchanged. Mantling gules and argent. Crest: on a wreath of the colours, in front of a goat's head couped proper, charged on the neck with a mullet of six points argent, an eagle's wing fesswise or. Motto: "Steadfast."

refinement not officially recognised or adhered to, though one unconsciously often is led to make this

FIG. 191.—Armorial bearings of Edward Marion Chadwick, Esq.: Party per pale gules and sable, within an orle of eight martlets an inescutcheon argent, charged with a cross of the first, and in the first quarter a crescent of the second. Crest: on a wreath of the colours, a martlet argent, bearing in his bill a white lily slipped, stemmed, and leaved proper, borne fesswise, the flower to the sinister. Mottoes: (above) "In candore decus," (below) "Toujours prêt."

distinction, which seems to spring naturally to one's mind.

When one inescutcheon appears, it is sometimes difficult to tell whether to blazon the arms as charged with a bordure or an inescutcheon. Some coats of

FIG. 192.—Armorial bearings of Alfred Chadwick, Esq.: Per pale gules and sable, an inescutcheon argent, within an orle of the last, charged with eight martlets of the first. Mantling gules and argent. Crest: upon a wreath of the colours, a lily stalked and leaved proper between two quatrefoils or. Motto: "Nil desperandum."

arms, for example the arms of Molesworth (Fig. 190), will always remain more or less a matter of uncertainty.

But as a matter of fact a bordure should not be wide enough to fill up the field left by an inescutcheon, nor an inescutcheon large enough to occupy the field left

FIG. 193.—Armorial bearings of James Mitchell Mutter, Esq. : Gules, on a fess between three inescutcheons or, a boar's head couped between two mascles of the first. Mantling gules, doubled or ; and on a wreath of his liveries is set for crest, a castle triple-towered sable, masoned argent, from the centre tower a flag flying of the last, charged with a cross gules ; and in an escroll over the same this motto, " Patience and Resolution."

FIG. 194.—Armorial bearings of Sir Hector Maclean Hay, Bart. : Quarterly, 1 and 4, azure, three fraises argent (for Fraser) ; 2 and 3, gules, three bars ermine (for Gifford) ; over all, on an inescutcheon argent, three escutcheons gules, in the centre a key fesswise, pointing to the dexter, wards downwards sable for difference (for Hay) ; and pendent from the escutcheon by an orange-tawny ribbon his badge as a baronet of Nova Scotia. Mantling gules, doubled argent ; and upon a wreath of his liveries is set for crest, a goat's head erased argent, horned or. Motto : " Spare nought."

by a bordure. Examples of an inescutcheon will be found in the arms of Chadwick (Figs. 191 and 192).

Three or more inescutcheons will be found in the arms of Mutter (Fig. 193), Hay (Fig. 194), and in the arms of Portugal (see Plate CXXXI.).

The inescutcheon in German armory (or, as they term it, the heart escutcheon), when superimposed upon other quarterings, is usually the paternal or most important coat of arms. The same method of marshalling has sometimes been adopted in Scotland, and the arms of Hay here quoted are an instance. It usually in British heraldry is used to carry the arms of an heiress wife, but both these points will be dealt with later under the subject of marshalling. The inescutcheon, no matter what its position, should never be

FIG. 195.—Armorial bearings of Herbert Francis Webb Gillman, Esq. : Quarterly, 1. argent, a man's leg couped at the thigh sable, encircled below the knee by a gemel or ; 2. argent, a double-headed eagle displayed sable, beaked and membered gules, ducally gorged or ; 3. argent, three firebrands proper : 4. or, on a chevron between three martlets sable, an inescutcheon of the last charged with a cross moline between four crescents argent. Mantling sable and argent. Crest : on a wreath of the colours, an eagle's head sable, holding in the beak gules a brand sable, fired proper. Motto : " Non cantu sed actu."

termed an escutcheon of pretence if it forms a charge upon the original arms. A curious instance of the use of an inescutcheon will be found in the arms of Cumming-Gordon (Plate XIII.), and in the arms of Gillman (Fig. 195).

When an inescutcheon appears on a shield it should conform in its outline to the shape of the shield upon which it is placed.

THE BORDURE

The bordure occurs both as a charge and as a mark of difference. As may be presumed from its likeness to our word border, the bordure is simply a border round the shield. Except in modern grants in which the bordure forms a part of the original design of the arms, there can be very little doubt that the bordure has always been a mark of difference to indicate cadency or bastardy, but its stereotyped continuance without

FIG. 196.—Armorial bearings of George Edmondstone Kirk, Esq.: Gules, a crosier or, and a sword proper, pommelled and hilted gold, in saltire within a bordure indented argent, on a chief of the second, a thistle between two trefoils slipped also proper. Mantling gules and or. Crest: upon a wreath of the colours, a crosier and sword in saltire as in the arms, enfiled by a garland of thistle and trefoils proper. Motto: "Optimum quod primum."

further alteration in so many coats of arms in which it originally was introduced as a difference, and also its appearance in new grants, leave one no alternative but to treat of it in the ordinary way as a charge, leaving the consideration of it as a mark of difference to a future chapter.

There is no stereotyped or official size for the bordure,

FIG. 197.—Armorial bearings of Michael Tomkinson, Esq.: Azure, a cross flory between in the first and fourth quarters a martlet, and in the second and third quarters an heraldic tiger's head erased or, all within a bordure nebuly ermine. Mantling azure and or. Crest: upon a wreath of the colours, in front of a cross flory gules, an heraldic tiger's head erased argent, gorged with a collar flory and counterflory also gules; with the motto, "Sperans pergo."

the width of which has at all times varied, though it will almost invariably be found that a Scottish bordure is depicted rather wider than is an English one;

and naturally a bordure which is charged is a little wider than an entirely plain one.

The bordure has long since ceased to be a mark of cadency in England, but as a mark of distinction the bordure wavy is still used to indicate bastardy. The use of the bordure is, however, the recognised method of differencing in Scotland, but it is curious that with the Scots the bordure wavy is in no way a mark of illegitimacy. The Scottish bordure for indicating this fact is the bordure company which has been used occasionally for the same purpose in England, but the bordures added to indicate cadency and the various marks to indicate illegitimacy will be discussed in later chapters. Whilst the bordure as a mark of cadency or illegitimacy surrounds the whole shield, being superimposed upon even the chief and canton, a bordure when merely a charge gives way to both.

The bordure, which of course is subject to all the lines of partition, occurs as a charge in the arms of Kirk (Fig. 196), Tomkinson (Fig. 197), Buchanan [n] (Plate XXXIII.), Garnet-Orme (Fig. 198), and Graham (Fig. 199).

FIG. 198.—Armorial bearings of the late George Garnett-Orme, Esq.: Quarterly, 1 and 4, azure, an eagle displayed, and in chief three battle-axes or (for Orme); 2 and 3, gules, a lion rampant argent, a bordure invected or, over all a bend ermine, charged with three covered cups azure (for Garnett). Mantling azure and or. Crests: 1. on a wreath of the colours, in front of a battle-axe in bend surmounted by a tilting-spear in bend sinister proper, a dolphin naiant argent (for Orme); 2. on a wreath of the colours, a dexter cubit arm erect proper, grasping two sea-lions' heads erased respectant and saltirewise argent. Motto: "Deus refugium nostrum."

A certain rule regarding the bordure is the sole remaining instance in modern heraldry of the formerly recognised practice of conjoining two coats of arms (which it might be necessary to marshal together) by "dimidiation" instead of using our present-day method of impalement. To dimidiate two coats of arms, the dexter half of one shield was conjoined to the sinister half of the other. The objections to such a practice, however, soon made themselves apparent (e.g. a dimidiated chevron was scarcely distinguishable from a bend), and the "dimidiation" of arms was quickly abandoned in favour of "impalement," in which the

[n] Armorial bearings of William Frederick Buchanan, Esq., of Sydney, N.S.W.: Erminois, a lion rampant sable, charged on the shoulder with a mullet of eight points or, in chief two horses' heads couped of the second, all within a bordure invected gules. Mantling sable and or. Crest: on a wreath of the colours, in front of a dexter hand couped at the wrist proper, holding an escutcheon sable, charged with a rose argent, barbed and seeded of the first, two branches of laurel slipped and fructed in saltire of the last. Motto: "Clarior hinc honos."

entire designs of both coats of arms are depicted. But in impaling a coat of arms which is surrounded by a bordure, the bordure is not continued down the centre between the two coats, stopping short top and bottom

FIG. 199.—Armorial bearings of James Noble Graham, Esq.: Or, a bordure azure, on a chief invected ermine, three escallops of the first. Mantling azure, doubled or. Crest: on a wreath of his liveries, a falcon proper, beaked and armed or, killing a stork argent, armed gules. Motto: "Ne oublie."

at the palar line. This will be seen in Fig. 200. The same rule, by the way, applies to the tressure, but not to the orle. The curious fact, however, remains that this rule as to the dimidiation of the bordure in cases of impalement is often found to have been ignored in ancient seals and other examples (Fig. 201). The charges upon the bordure are often three, but more

FIG. 200.—Armorial bearings of William Henry Cox, Esq.: Or, a chevron azure between two spur-revels in chief and a lion's head erased in base gules, langued of the second, within a bordure of the third, impaling the arms of Kinloch of Gourdie, namely: azure, on a chevron between three mascles or, a boar's head erased of the field, a fleur-de-lis in chief of the second. Above the shield is placed a helmet befitting his degree, with a mantling azure, doubled or; and on a wreath of his liveries is set for crest, a dexter arm embowed issuing out of the sea, holding in the hand an anchor in bend sinister, cabled proper, and in an escroll over the same this motto: " Præmium virtutis honos."

usually eight in number, in the latter case being arranged three along the top of the shield, one at the base point, and two on either side. The number should, however, always be specified, unless (as in a bordure

bezantée, &c.) it is immaterial; in which case the number eight must be *exceeded* in emblazoning the shield. The rule as to colour upon colour seems often to be ignored in the cases of bordures, noticeably when these occur as marks of Scottish cadency (see Hervey, in Plate XLV.).

FIG. 201.—Armorial bearings of Thomas de Holland, Duke of Surrey (M.S. Harl. 5805, f. 392): Dexter, a coat of augmentation "azure, a cross flory between five martlets or," being the arms of St. Edward the Confessor differenced by a bordure ermine, impaling on the sinister side gules, three lions passant guardant in pale or, a bordure argent. (From a drawing of his seal, 1399.)

THE ORLE

The orle, or, as it was originally termed in ancient British rolls of arms, "un faux ecusson," is a narrow bordure following the exact outline of the shield, but within it, showing the field (for at least the width usually occupied by a bordure) between the outer edge of the orle and the edge of the escutcheon. An orle is half the width of a bordure, rather less than more. Examples of the orle will be found in the arms of Rutherfurd (Fig. 202) and Surtees (Fig. 203).

FIG. 202.—Armorial bearings of Andrew Rutherfurd: Argent, an orle, and in chief three martlets gules, all within a bordure ermine. Mantling gules, doubled argent; and upon a wreath of his liveries is set for crest, a mermaid holding in her dexter hand a mirror, and in her sinister a comb, all proper; and upon an escroll above the crest this motto, "Per mare per terras."

Though both forms are very seldom so met with, an orle may be subject to the usual lines of partition, and may also be charged. Examples of both these variations are met with in the arms of Yeatman-Biggs (Fig. 204), and the arms of Gladstone[o] (Plate XXXII.) afford an instance of an orle "flory." The arms of Knox, Earl of

FIG. 203 —Armorial bearings of Surtees: Ermine, a bordure or, on a canton gules, an orle of the second.

Ranfurly, are: Gules, a falcon volant or, within an orle wavy on the outer and engrailed on the inner edge argent.

When a series of charges are placed round the edges of the escutcheon (*theoretically* in the position occupied by the orle, but as a matter of actual fact usually more)

FIG. 204.—Armorial bearings of Yeatman-Biggs: Quarterly, 1 and 4, per pale argent and azure, a lion passant within an orle engrailed, charged with ten fleurs-de-lis all counterchanged (for Biggs); 2 and 3, per pale argent and sable, on a fesse dovetailed counter-dovetailed or, between two gates in chief and a goat's head erased in base counterchanged, three boars' heads erased gules (for Yeatman); the escutcheon being surmounted by his mitre. Crests: 1. on a wreath of the colours, in front of a javelin erect proper, a leopard's head affronté erased azure, charged with two fleur-de-lis fesswise or (for Biggs); 2. on a wreath of the colours, a goat's head erased sable, horned, bearded, and charged with a gate or (Yeatman); and the mottoes, "Propositi tenax" (for Biggs), "Those heights must be taken" (for Yeatman).

in the position occupied by the bordure, they are said to be " in orle," which is the correct term, but they will

[o] Armorial bearings of Robert Gladstone, Esq.: Argent, a savage's head affronté, distilling drops of blood, wreathed about the temples with holly proper, within an orle fleury gules, all within eight martlets in orle sable. Mantling argent and gules. Crest: on a wreath of the colours, issuant from a wreath of holly proper, a demi-griffin sable, supporting between the claws a sword, the blade enfiled by a wreath of oak also proper. Motto: " Fide et virtute."

often be found blazoned "an orle of *e.g.* martlets or mounds," as in the arms of Chadwick (Fig. 191), and Lamont (Fig. 205).

FIG. 205.—Armorial bearings of James Lamont, Esq.: Azure, a lion rampant argent, armed and langued gules, within an orle of mounds or, crossed and surmounted of a cross patée of the third. Mantling azure, doubled argent; and upon a wreath of his liveries is set for crest, a dexter hand couped at the wrist holding a dagger erect in pale proper; and in an escroll above this motto, "Ne parcas nec spernas."

THE TRESSURE

The tressure is really an orle gemel, *i.e.* an orle divided into two narrow ones set closely together, the one inside the other. It is, however, usually depicted a trifle nearer the edge of the escutcheon than the orle is generally placed.

The tressure cannot be borne singly, as it would then be an orle, but plain tressures under the name of "concentric orles" will be found mentioned in Papworth. In that Ordinary eight instances are given of arms containing more than a single orle, though the eight instances are plainly varieties of only four coats. Two concentric orles would certainly be a tressure, save that perhaps they would be drawn of rather too great a width for the term "tressure" to be properly applied to them.

If these instances be disregarded, and I am inclined to doubt them as genuine coats, there certainly is no example of a plain tressure in British heraldry, and one's attention must be directed to the tressure flory and counterflory so general in Scottish heraldry.

Originating entirely in the Royal escutcheon, one cannot do better than reproduce the remarks of Lyon King of Arms upon the subject from his work " Heraldry in relation to Scottish History and Art ":—

"William the Lion has popularly got the credit of being the first to introduce heraldic bearings into Scotland, and to have assumed the lion as his personal cognisance. The latter statement may or may not be true, but we have no trace of hereditary arms in Scotland so early as his reign (1165–1214). Certainly the lion does not appear on his seal, but it does on that of his son and successor Alexander II., with apparent remains of the double tressure flory counterflory, a device which is clearly seen on the seals of Alexander III. (1249–1285). We are unable to say what the reason was for the adoption of such a distinctive coat; of course, if you turn to the older writers you will find all sorts of fables on the subject. Even the sober and sensible Nisbet states that 'the lion has been carried on the armorial ensign of Scotland since the first founding of the monarchy by King Fergus I.'—a very mythical personage, who is said to have flourished about 300 B.C., though he is careful to say that he does not believe arms are as old as that period. He says, however, that it is 'without doubt' that Charlemagne entered into an alliance with Achaius, King of Scotland, and for the services of the Scots the French king added to the Scottish lion the double tressure fleur-de-lisée to show that the former had defended the French lilies, and that therefore the latter would surround the lion and be a defence to him."

All this is very pretty, but it is not history. Chalmers remarks in his "Caledonia" that the lion may possibly have been derived from the arms of the old Earls of Northumberland and Huntingdon, from whom some of the Scottish kings were descended; and he mentions an old roll of arms preserved by Leland,[p] which is certainly not later than 1272, in which the arms of Scotland are blazoned as: *Or, a lion gules within a bordure or fleuretté gules*, which we may reasonably interpret as an early indication of what may be considered as a foreign rendering of the double tressure. Sylvanus Morgan, one of the very maddest of the seventeenth-century heraldic writers, says that the tressure was added to the shield of Scotland, in testimony of a league between Scotland and France, by Charles V.; but that king did not ascend the throne of France till 1364, at which time we have clear proof that the tressure was a firmly established part of the Scottish arms. One of the earliest instances of anything approaching the tressure in the Scottish arms which I have met with is in an armorial of Matthew Paris, which is now in the Cottonian MSS. in the British Museum, and at one time belonged to St. Alban's Monastery. Here the arms of the King of Scotland are given as: "Or, a lion rampant flory gules in a bordure of the same." The drawing represents a lion within a bordure, the latter being pierced by ten fleurs-de-lis, their heads all looking inwards, the other end not being free, but attached to the inner margin of the shield. This, you will observe, is very like the arms I mentioned as described by Chalmers, and it may possibly be the same volume which may have been acquired by Sir Robert Cotton. In 1471 there was a curious attempt of the Scottish Parliament to displace the tressure. An Act was passed in that year, for some hitherto unexplained reason, by which it was ordained "that in tyme to cum thar suld be na double tresor about his (the king's) armys, but that he suld ber hale armys of the lyoun without ony mair." Seeing that at the time of this enactment the Scottish kings had borne the tressure for upwards of 220 years, it is difficult to understand the cause of this procedure. Like many other Acts, however, it never seems to have been carried into effect; at least I am not aware of even a solitary instance of the Scottish arms without the tressure either at or after this period.

· · · · · · · ·

There are other two representations of the Scottish arms in foreign armorials, to which I may briefly allude. One is in the *Armorial de Gelre*, a beautiful MS. in the Royal Library at Brussels, the Scottish shields in which have been figured by Mr. Stodart in his book on Scottish arms, and, more accurately, by Sir Archibald Dunbar in a paper read to the Society of Antiquaries of Scotland in 1890. The armorial is believed to be the work of Claes Heynen, Gelre Herald to the Duke of Gueldres between 1334 and 1372, with later additions by another hand. The coat assigned in it to the King of Scotland is the lion and double tressure; the lion is uncrowned, and is armed and langued azure; above the shield is a helmet argent adorned behind with a short capeline or plain mantling, on which is emblazoned the

saltire and chief of the Bruces, from which we may gather that the arms of David II. are here represented; the lining is blue, which is unusual, as mantlings are usually lined or doubled with a metal, if not with ermine. The helmet is surmounted by an Imperial crown, with a dark green bonnet spotted with red.[q] On the crown there is the crest of a lion sejant guardant gules, imperially crowned or, holding in his paw a sword upright; the tail is coué or placed between the hindlegs of the lion, but it then rises up and flourishes high above his back in a sufficiently defiant fashion. This shows that the Scottish arms were well known on the Continent of Europe nearly a hundred years before the date of the Grünenberg MS., while Virgil de Solis (c. 1555) gives a sufficiently accurate representation of the Royal shield, though the fleurs-de-lis all project outwards as in the case of Grünenberg; he gives the crest as a lion rampant holding a sword in bend over his shoulder. Another ancient representation of the Scottish arms occurs in a MS. treatise on heraldry of the sixteenth century, containing the coats of some foreign sovereigns and other personages, bound up with a Scottish armorial, probably by David Lindsay, Lyon in 1568."

The tressure, like the bordure, in the case of an impalement stops at the line of impalement, as will be seen by a reference to the arms of Queen Anne after the union of the crowns of England and Scotland.

It is now held, both in England and Scotland, that the tressure flory and counterflory is, as a part of the Royal Arms, protected, and cannot be granted to any person without the express licence of the Sovereign. This, however, does not interfere with the matriculation or exemplification of it in the case of existing arms in which it occurs.

Many Scottish families bear or claim to bear the Royal tressure by reason of female descent from the Royal House, but it would seem much more probable that in most if not in all cases where it is so borne by right its origin is due rather to a gift by way of augmentation than to any supposed right of inheritance. The apparently conflicting statements of origin are not really antagonistic, inasmuch as it will be seen from many analogous English instances (*e.g.* Mowbray, Manners, and Seymour) that near relationship is often the only reason to account for the grant of a Royal augmentation. As an ordinary augmentation of honour it has been frequently granted.

The towns of Aberdeen and Perth obtained early the right of honouring their arms with the addition of the Royal tressure. It appears on the still existing matrix of the burgh seal of Aberdeen, which was engraved in 1430.

James V. in 1542 granted a warrant to Lyon to surround the arms of John Scot, of Thirlestane, with the Royal tressure, in respect of his ready services at Soutra Edge with three score and ten lances on horseback, when other nobles refused to follow their Sovereign. The grant was put on record by the grantee's descendant, Patrick, Lord NAPIER, and is the tressured coat borne in the second and third quarters of the NAPIER arms.

When the Royal tressure is granted to the bearer of a quartered coat it is usually placed upon a bordure surrounding the quartered shield, as in the case of the arms of the Marquess of QUEENSBERRY, to whom, in 1682, the Royal tressure was granted upon a *bordure or*. A like arrangement is borne by the Earls of EGLINTON, occurring as far back as a seal of Earl HUGH, appended to a charter of 1598.

P *Collectanea*, ed. 1774, ii. 611.

q In M. Victor Bouton's edition of the *Armorial de Gelre* (Paris 1881) the bonnet is described as a mount.

99

The Royal tressure had at least twice been granted as an augmentation to the arms of foreigners. James V. granted it to NICOLAS CANIVET of Dieppe, secretary to JOHN, Duke of ALBANY (Reg. Mag. Sig.,, xxiv., 263 Oct. 24, 1529). James VI. gave it to Sir JACOB VAN EIDEN, a Dutchman on whom he conferred the honour of knighthood.

On 12th March 1762, a Royal Warrant was granted

"Scottish Arms," vol. i. pp. 262, 263, where mention is also made of an older use of the Royal tressure or, by "Sir ARCHIBALD PRIMROSE of Dalmenie, knight and baronet, be his majesty CHARLES ii. create, *Vert, three primroses within a double tressure flowered counter-flowered or.*") Another well-known Scottish instance in which the tressure occurs will be found in the arms of the Marquess of Ailsa (Fig. 206).

FIG. 206.—Armorial bearings of Sir Archibald Kennedy, Marquess of Ailsa: Argent, a chevron gules between three cross crosslets fitchée sable, all within a double tressure flory and counter-flory of the second. Mantling gules, doubled ermine. Crest: upon a wreath of his liveries, a dolphin naiant proper. Supporters: two swans proper, beaked and membered gules. Motto: "Avise la fin." (From the painting by Mr. Graham Johnston in the Lyon Register.)

directing Lyon to add a "double tressure counterflowered as in the Royal arms of Scotland" to the arms of ARCHIBALD, Viscount PRIMROSE. Here the tressure was *gules,* as in the Royal arms, although the field on which it was placed was *vert.* In a later record of the arms of ARCHIBALD, Earl of ROSEBERY, in 1823, this heraldic anomaly was brought to an end, and the blazon of the arms of Primrose is now: "Vert, three primroses within a double tressure flory counterflory or." (See Stodart,

Two instances are known in which the decoration of the tressure has differed from the usual conventional fleurs-de-lis. The tressure granted to Charles, Earl of Aboyne, has crescents without and demi-fleurs-de-lis within, and the tressure round the Gordon arms in the case of the Earls of Aberdeen [r] (see Plate LVIII.) is of thistles, roses, and fleurs-de-lis alternately.

[r] Armorial bearings of Sir John Campbell Gordon, Earl of Aberdeen, G.C.M.G.: Azure, three boars' heads couped or, armed proper and

The tressure gives way to the chief and canton, as may be seen from the arms of Graham-Wigan (Fig. 178) and Maxtone-Graham (Fig. 177), but all other ordinaries are enclosed by the tressure, as will be seen from the arms of Lord Ailsa (Fig. 206).

THE LOZENGE, THE FUSIL, THE MASCLE, AND THE RUSTRE

Why these, which are simply varying forms of one charge, should ever have been included amongst the list of ordinaries is difficult to understand, as they do not seem to be " ordinaries " any more than say the mullet or the crescent. My own opinion is that they are no more than distinctively heraldic charges. The lozenge, which is the original form, is the same shape as the " diamond " in a pack of cards, and will constantly be found as a charge. In addition to this, the arms of a lady as maid, or as widow, are always displayed upon a lozenge. Upon this point reference should be made to the chapters upon marshalling. The arms of Kyrke[s] show a single lozenge as the charge, but a single lozenge is very rarely met with. The arms of Hyde[t]

FIG. 207.—Armorial bearings of Rev. Thomas Lindsay: Gules, a fess chequy argent and azure, between three fusils in chief and one in base or. Mantling gules and argent. Crest: on a wreath of the colours, an ostrich proper holding in the beak a key or, the dexter leg supported by a fusil gules. Motto: " Endure Fort."

langued gules, within a tressure flowered and counterflowered inter-changeably with thistles, roses, and fleurs-de-lis of the second. Crest: two arms holding a bow and arrow straight upwards in a shooting posture, and at full draught all proper. Supporters: dexter, an Earl; sinister, a Doctor of Laws habited in their robes all proper. A further addition has since been made to the record of these arms in Lyon Register, a second scroll with the words " Ne nimium " having been added below the shield.

[s] Armorial bearings of Kyrke: Quarterly, party per fess or and gules, a lozenge counterchanged. Crest: upon a wreath of the colours, a boar passant sable.

[t] Armorial bearings of Gustavus Rochfort Hyde, Esq., M.A. (Camb.), J.P. (formerly Wade): Azure, ac hevron between three lozenges or. Mantling azure and or. Crest: on a wreath of the colours, an eagle with wings expanded sable, beaked and membered or. Motto: " Soyez Ferme.'

(Plate XXVI.) and Lindsay (Fig. 207) afford examples of the lozenge as a charge. The arms of Guise show seven lozenges conjoined. The arms of Barnes (Fig. 208) show four lozenges conjoined in cross, and the

FIG. 208.—Armorial bearings of Robert Barnes, Esq.: Gules, four lozenges conjoined in cross between as many trefoils slipped all argent. Crest: upon a wreath of the colours, upon a rock a bear proper, muzzled or, and resting the dexter forepaw on a trefoil slipped vert. Motto: " For-bear."

arms of Bartlett[u] (Plate XXXVIII.) show five lozenges conjoined in fess. Although the lozenge is very seldom found in English armory as a single charge, nevertheless as a lozenge throughout (that is, with its four points touching the borders of the escutcheon) it will be found in some number of instances in Continental heraldry, for instance in the family of Eubing of Bavaria. An indefinite number of lozenges conjoined as a bend or a pale are known as a bend lozengy, or a pale lozengy, but care should be taken in using this term, as it is possible for these ordinaries to be plain ordinaries tinctured "lozengy of two colours." The arms of Bolding (see Fig. 89) are an example of a bend lozengy.

The *fusil* is supposed to be, and is generally depicted of a greater height and less width than a lozenge, being an altogether narrower figure. Though this distinction is generally observed, it is not always easy to decide which it is intended to represent, unless the blazon of the arms in question is known. In many cases the variations of different coats of arms to suit, or to fit the varying shapes of shields, have resulted in the use of lozenges and fusils indifferently. Fusils occur in the historic arms of Daubeney (Fig. 210), and the same coat (Plate XXXVI.) belongs to the family of Daubeny[v] of Cote, near Bristol, one of the few families who have an undoubted male descent from a companion of William the Conqueror. In the ordinary way five or more lozenges in fess would be fusils, as in the arms of Percy, Duke of Northumberland, who bears in the first quarter: Azure, five fusils conjoined in fess or. The charges in the arms of Montagu, though only three in

[u] Armorial bearings of Bartlett, of Liverpool: Quarterly, argent and gules, five lozenges conjoined in fess, between four crescents all counterchanged. Mantling gules and argent. Crest: upon a wreath of the colours, on a mount vert, a moor-cock sable, combed and wattled gules, in the beak an ear of wheat leaved and slipped proper, resting the dexter claw on a crescent gules. Motto: " Deo favente cresco."

[v] Armorial bearings of Daubeney, of Cote: Gules, four fusils conjoined in fess argent. Mantling gules and argent. Crest: on a wreath of the colours, a holly tree proper.

number, are always termed fusils (Figs. 211, 212, 213). The canting crest of Fussell [w] is also termed a Fusil.

The *mascle* is a lozenge voided, *i.e.* only the outer framework is left, the inner portion being removed.

FIG. 210. — Arms of Henry Daubeney, Earl of Bridgwater (d.1548): Gules, four fusils conjoined in fess argent.

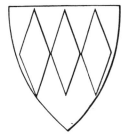

FIG. 211.—Arms of William de Montagu, Earl of Salisbury (d. 1344): Argent, three fusils conjoined in fess gules. (From his seal.)

FIG. 212. — Arms of Thomas de Montagu, Earl of Salisbury (d. 1428): Quarterly, 1 and 4,the arms of Montagu; 2 and 3, or, an eagle displayed vert, armed and beaked gules (for Monthermer). (From his seal.)

FIG. 213.—Arms of Richard Nevill, Earl of Salisbury and Warwick, "The King-maker" (d. 1471): Quarterly, i. and iiii., quarterly, 1 and 4, Montagu; 2 and 3, Monthermer; quarterly, ii. and iii., gules, a saltire argent, a label compony argent and azure (for Nevill). (From his seal

FIG. 215.—Armorial bearings of Henry Ferrers, Esq., of Baddesley Clinton: Quarterly, 1 and 4, gules, seven mascles conjoined or, three, three, and one, a canton ermine (for Ferrers); 2 and 3, or, a fess nebuly between three cross crosslets fitchée in chief azure, and a tun in base proper (for Croxton). Mantling gules and or. Crests: 1. on a wreath of the colours, a unicorn passant ermine (for Ferrers); 2. on a wreath of the colours, a dexter cubit arm vested azure, cuffed argent, encircled by a wreath of oak, the hand supporting a cross botony fitchée or, on the dexter side of the wreath (for Croxton). Motto: "Splendeo tritus."

FIG. 216.—Armorial bearings of Rev. David Avenel Vipont: Quarterly, 1 and 4, argent, a saltire engrailed sable between a lion rampant in chief and two crescents in flanks gules (for Anderson); 2 and 3, gules, three mascles interlaced between as many quatrefoils or (for Whyte). Mantlings sable, doubled argent, and gules, doubled or. Crests: 1. on a wreath of his liveries, on the dexter side, a thistle slipped proper, with the motto, in an escroll above, "Per aspera ad alta"; 2. on a wreath of his liveries, on the sinister side, a demi-eagle displayed gules, charged on the breast with a mascle or (for Whyte), with the motto on the escroll, "Vinculis fortior."

FIG. 214.—Armorial bearings of James Munro Coats, Esq.: Or, a stag's head erased gules, charged on the neck with a mullet of the first, between the attires a pheon azure, all between three mascles sable. Mantling gules, doubled or. Crest: on a wreath of his liveries, an anchor gules; and in an escroll over the same this motto, "Be firm."

Mascles have no particular or special meaning, but are frequently to be met with, as in the arms of Coats

[w] Armorial bearings of James Cecil Coldham Fussell, Esq.: Sable, a fess engrailed between four fusils or, on a chief of the last three

crosses flory of the first. Mantling sable and or. Crest: on a wreath of the colours, between two laurel branches proper, a fusil or, charged with a cross flory sable. Motto: "ΔΙΑ."

(Fig. 214), Whittaker (sable, three mascles argent), Ferrers (Fig. 215), Vipont (Fig. 216), De Quincy (Fig. 217), and Mitchell.

The blazon of the arms of De Quincy in Charles's Roll is : "De goules poudré à fause losengez dor," and in another Roll (MS. Brit. Mus. 29,796) the arms are described : "De gules a set fauses lozenges de or." The

FIG. 217.—Arms of Roger de Quincy, Earl of Winchester (d. 1264): Gules, seven mascles conjoined, three, three and one or. (From his seal.)

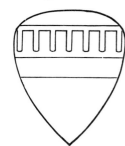

FIG. 218.—Arms of Seiher de Quincy, Earl of Winchester (d. 1219) : Or, a fess gules, a label of seven points azure. (From his seal.)

great Seiher de Quincy, Earl of Winchester, father of Roger, bore quite different arms (Fig. 218). In 1472 Louis de Bruges, Lord of Gruthuyse, was created Earl of Winchester, having no relation to the De Quincy line. The arms of De Bruges, or rather of Gruthuyse, were very different, yet, nevertheless, we find upon the Patent Roll (12 Edward IV. pt. 1, m. 11) a grant of the following arms : "Azure, dix mascles d'Or, enormé d'une canton de nostre propre Armes de Angleterre ; cest a savoir de Gules a une Lipard passant d'Or, armée d'Azure," to Louis, Earl of Winchester (Fig. 219). The recurrence of the mascles in the arms of the successive Earls of Winchester, whilst each had other family arms, and in the arms of Ferrers, whilst not being the original Ferrers coat, suggests the thought that there may be hidden some reference to a common saintly patronage which all enjoyed, or some territorial honour common to the three of which the knowledge no longer remains with us.

There are some number of coats which are said to have a field masculy. Of course this is quite possible,

FIG. 219.—Arms of Louis de Bruges, Earl of Winchester (d. 1492.)

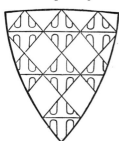

FIG. 220 —Arms of Hubert de Burgh, Earl of Kent (d. 1243). (From his seal.)

and the difference between a field masculy and a field fretty is that in the latter the separate pieces of which it is composed interlace each other ; but when the field is masculy it is all one fretwork surface, the field being visible through the voided apertures. Nevertheless it seems by no means certain that in every case in which the field masculy is found it may not be found in other, and possibly earlier, examples as fretty. At any rate, very few such coats of arms are even supposed to exist. The arms of De Burgh (Fig. 220) are blazoned in the Grimaldi Roll : "Masclee de vêre and de goules," but whether the inference is that this blazon is wrong or

that lozenge and mascle were identical terms I am not aware.

The *rustre* is comparatively rare. It is a lozenge pierced in the centre with a circular hole. It occurs in the arms of J. D. G. Dalrymple, Esq., F.S.A. (Plate XXIX.). Some few coats of arms are mentioned in Papworth in which the rustre appears; for example the arms of Pery, which are : "Or, three rustres sable;" and Goodchief, which are : "Per fess or and sable, three rustres counterchanged ;" but so seldom is the figure met·with that it may be almost dropped out of consideration. How it ever reached the position of being considered one of the ordinaries has always been to me a profound mystery.

THE FRET

The fret, which is very frequently found occurring in British armory, is no doubt derived from earlier coats of arms, the whole field of which was covered by an interlacing of alternate bendlets and bendlets sinister, because many of the families who now bear a simple fret are found in earlier representations and in the early rolls of arms bearing coats which were fretty. Instances of this kind will be found in the arms of Maltravers, Verdon, Tollemache, and other families.

"Sable fretty or" was the original form of the arms of the ancient and historic family of Maltravers. At a later

FIG. 221.—Arms of John Fitz Alan, Earl of Arundel (d. 1435): Quarterly, 1 and 4, gules, a lion rampant or (for Fitz Alan) ; 2 and 3, sable, fretty or (for Maltravers). (From his seal, c. 1432.)

date the arms of Maltravers are found simply "sable, a fret or," but, like the arms of so many other families which we now find blazoned simply as charged with a fret, their original form was undoubtedly "fretty." They appear fretty as late as the year 1421, which is the date at which the Garter plate of Sir William Arundel, K.G. (1395–1400), was set up in St. George's Chapel at Windsor. His arms as there displayed are in the first and fourth quarters, "gules, a lion rampant or," and in the second and third, "purpure fretty or" for Maltravers. Probably the seal of John Fitz Alan, Earl of Arundel (d. 1435), roughly marks the period, and shows the source of the confusion (Fig. 221). But it should be noted that Sir Richard Arundel, Lord Maltravers, bore at the siege of Rouen, in the year 1418, gules a lion rampant or, quarterly with "sable a fret or" (for Maltravers). This would seem to indicate that those who treat the fret and fretty as interchangeable have good grounds for so doing. A Sir John Maltravers bore "sable fretty or" at the siege of Calais, and another Sir John Maltravers, a knight banneret, bore at the first Dunstable tournament "sable fretty or, a label of three points argent." As he is there described as Le Fitz, the label was probably a purely temporary mark of difference. In a roll of arms, which is believed to belong to the latter part of the reign of Henry III., a Sir William Maltravers is credited with "sable fretty or, on a quarter argent, three lions passant in pale gules." The palpable origin of the fret or fretty in the case of the arms of Maltravers is simply the canting similarity between a traverse and the name Maltravers. Another case, which starting

FIG. 222.—Armorial bearings of Sir Henry Blake, G.C.M.G.: Quarterly, I and 4, argent, a fret gules (for Blake); 2 and 3, sable, three lions passant between four bendlets argent, in chief a fleur-de-lis of the last for difference (for Browne). Mantling gules and argent. Crest: on a wreath of the colours, a cat-a-mountain passant guardant proper, charged with a crescent gules for difference. Motto: "Virtus sola nobilitat."

fretty has ended in a fret, occurs in the arms of the family of Harington. Sir John de Haverington, or Sir

FIG. 223.—Armorial bearings of Denys Alexander Lawlor-Huddleston, Esq.: Quarterly I and 4, gules, a fret argent (for Huddleston); 2 and 3, argent, a lion rampant gules, between four trefoils vert (for Lawlor). Mantling gules and argent. Crests: I. on a wreath of the colours, two arms embowed dexter and sinister, vested and cuffed argent, the hands proper holding a stone sable (for Huddleston); 2. on a wreath of the colours, upon a mount vert, a stag lodged in front of a spear-head in pale point upwards all proper (for Lawlor). Mottoes: over the Lawlor crest, "Mea culpa fides," and under the arms, "Soli Deo honor et gloria."

John de Harington, is found at the first Dunstable tournament in 1308 bearing "sable fretty argent," and

this coat of arms variously differenced appears in some number of the other early rolls of arms. The Harington family, as may be seen from the current baronetages, now bear "sable a fret argent," but there can be little doubt that in this case the origin of the fretty is to be found in a representation of a herring-net.

The fret is usually depicted *throughout* when borne singly, and is then composed of a bendlet dexter and a bendlet sinister, interlaced in the centre by a mascle. Occasionally it will be found couped, but it is then, as a rule, only occupying the position of a subsidiary charge. A coat which is *fretty* is entirely covered by the interlacing bendlets and bendlets sinister, no mascles being introduced. Instances in which the fret occurs will be found in the arms of Blake (Fig. 222), Lawlor-Huddlestone (Fig. 223), Howard (Fig. 224), and Farish [x] (Plate XXXII.); whilst the arms of Lowndes (Plate XXXV.) afford an example of fretty.

FIG. 224.—The bookplate of the late Joseph Jackson Howard, Esq., Maltravers Herald: Gules, on a bend or, between a fret couped in chief and a cross crosslet in base, both of the last, three annulets vert, the escutcheon being surmounted by his collar of SS. Mantling gules and or. Crest: upon a wreath of the colours, a lion rampant proper, charged on the body with two annulets in pale vert, holding between the paws a fret as in the arms, and resting the dexter hind paw on two S's as linked in a herald's collar argent. Motto: "Credo Christi cruce." (From an etched plate by Mr. G. W. Eve, R.E.)

THE FLAUNCH

The flaunch, which is never borne singly, and for which the additional names of "flasks" and "voiders" are sometimes found, is the segment of a circle of large diameter projecting from either side of the escutcheon, of a different colour to the field. It is by no means an

[x] Armorial bearings of Edward Garthwaite Farish, Esq.: Quarterly, I and 4, argent, a chevron azure, gutée-d'eau, between two horse-shoes in chief and a bugle-horn stringed in base, all of the second (for Farish); 2 and 3, quarterly per fess indented i. and iiii., gules, a chevron or; ii. and iii., azure, a fret of the second (for Garthwaite). Mantling azure and argent. Crest: on a wreath of the colours, upon two horse-shoes or, a bugle-horn stringed azure. Motto: "Forward."

unusual charge to be met with, and, like the majority of other ordinaries, is subject to the usual lines of

FIG. 225.—Armorial bearings of Godfrey Fitzhugh, Esq.: Ermine, two flaunches sable, on a chief gules, four martlets or. Mantling sable and argent. Crest: on a wreath of the colours, a quatrefoil sable, thereon a martlet erminois. Motto: "Moderation is my glory."

FIG. 226.—Armorial bearings of (Edward Charles) Robson Roose, Esq.: Gules, three water-bougets in pale between two flaunches invected argent. Mantling gules and argent. Crest: on a wreath of the colours, a peacock in his pride proper, gorged with a collar and pendent therefrom a four-leaved shamrock or. Motto: "Je ne change qu'en mourant."

partition, but so subject is, however, rather rare. Examples of flaunches will be found in the arms of Allen [y] (Plate XXXIII.) and Pickering [z] (Plate XXXVI.), Fitz-

[y] Armorial bearings of Rev. George Cantrell Allen, M.A.: Per fess indented sable and gules, a garb or, between two flaunches of the last, each charged with two bars raguly of the first. Mantling sable and or. Crest: upon a wreath of the colours, on a mount vert, a wheatear rising and regardant, holding in the beak an ear of wheat, stalked and bladed between four similar ears of wheat, two on either side or. Motto: "God giveth the increase."

[z] Armorial bearings of Benjamin Pickering, Esq., J.P., of Bellefield, Hull: Argent, guttée-de-poix, a lion rampant azure, between two flaunches of the last, each charged with a bear's paw erect and erased

hugh (Fig. 225), and Roose (Fig. 226), the latter being an example of flaunches invected.

Planché, in his "Pursuivant of Arms," mentions the old idea, which is repeated by Woodward, "that the base son of a noble woman, if he doe gev armes, must give upon the same a surcoat, but unless you do well mark such coat you may take it for a coat flanchette." The surcoat is much the same figure that would remain after flaunches had been taken from the field of a shield, with this exception, that the flaunches would be wider and the intervening space necessarily much narrower. In spite of the fact that this is supposed to be one of the recognised rules of armory, one instance only appears to be known of its employment, which, however, considering the circumstances, is not very much to be wondered at.

THE ROUNDLE

The roundle is a generic name which comprises all charges which are plain circular figures of colour or metal (Plate LXVII.). Foreign heraldry merely terms them roundles of such and such a colour, but in England we have special terms for each tincture.

When the roundle is gold it is termed a "bezant" (a), when silver a "plate" (b), when gules a "torteau" (c), when azure a "hurt" (i), when sable an "ogress," "pellet," or "gunstone" (f), when vert a "pomeis" (h), when purpure a "golpes" (e), when tenné an "orange" (g), when sanguine a "guze" (d). The golpes, oranges, and guzes are seldom, if ever, met with, but the others are of constant occurrence, and roundles of fur are by no means unknown. A roundle of more than one colour is described as a roundle "per pale," for example of gules and azure, or whatever it may be. The plates and bezants are naturally flat and must be so represented. They should

FIG. 227.—The Arms of Stourton.

never be shaded up into a globular form. The torteau is sometimes found shaded, but is more correctly flat, but probably the pellet or ogress and the pomeis are intended to be globular. Roundles of fur are always flat. One curious roundle is a very common charge in British armory, that is the "fountain" (k), which is a roundle barry wavy argent and azure. This is the conventional heraldic representation of water, of course. A fountain will be found termed a "syke" when occurring in the arms of any family of the name of Sykes. It typifies naturally anything in the nature of a well, in which meaning it occurs on the arms of Stourton (Fig. 227). These arms as an instance, the meaning of which can be clearly shown, are of some interest, as will be seen from the following remarks.

The arms of Stourton are one of the few really ancient coats concerning which a genuine explanation exists. The blazon of them is: Sable a bend or, between six fountains proper.

argent. Mantling azure and argent. Crest: on a wreath of the colours, in front of a bear's paw erect and erased argent, encircled with a wreath of oak vert, a demi-catherine-wheel azure. Motto: "Je garde bien."

Concerning this coat of arms Aubrey says: "I believe anciently 'twas only Sable a bend or." With all deference to Aubrey, I personally neither think he was right,

FIG. 228.—Arms of Hugh Courtenay, Earl of Devon (*d.* 1422): Or, three torteaux, a label azure. (From his seal.)

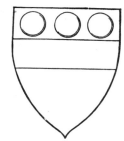

FIG. 229.—Arms of Devereux, Viscounts Hereford: Argent, a fess gules, and in chief three torteaux. (From the cloisters at Hereford.)

FIG. 230.—Arms of George Hastings, Earl of Huntingdon (MS. Add., 22,306): Quarterly, 1. argent, a maunch sable (for Hastings); 2. sable, two bars argent, and in chief three plates (for Hungerford); 3. argent, a griffin segreant gules, armed azure (for Botreaux); 4. paly wavy of four or and gules (for Moleyns).

nor do I pay much attention to his *opinions*, particularly in this case, inasmuch as every known record of the Stourton arms introduces the six fountains.

The name Stourton, originally "de Stourton," is emphatically a territorial name, and there is little opportunity for this being gainsaid, inasmuch as the lordship and manor of Stourton, in the counties of Wilts and Somerset, remained in the possession of the Lords Stourton until the year 1714. The present Lord Mowbray and Stourton still owns land within the parish. Consequently there is no doubt whatever that the Lords Stourton derived their surname from this manor of Stourton.

Equally is it certain that the manor of Stourton obtained its name from the river Stour, which rises within the manor. The sources of the river Stour are six wells, which exist in a tiny valley in Stourton Park, which to this day is known by the name of "The Six Wells Bottom." In the present year of grace only one of the six wells remains visible. When Sir Richard Colt Hoare wrote, there were four visible. Of these four, three were outside and one inside the park wall. The other two within the park had been then closed up. When Leland wrote in 1540 to 1542, the six wells were in existence and visible; for he wrote: "The ryver of Stoure risith ther of six fountaynes or springes, wherof 3 be on the northe side of the Parke, harde withyn the Pale, the other 3 be north also, but withoute the Parke. The Lorde Stourton giveth these 6 fountaynes yn his Armes."

Guillim says the same thing: "These six Fountains are borne in signification of six Springs, whereof the River of Sture in Wiltshire hath his beginning, and passeth along to Sturton, the seat of that Barony." Here, then, is the origin of the six fountains upon the coat of arms; but Aubrey remarks that three of the six springs in the park are in the county of Wilts, whereas Mr. Camden has put them all in Somersetshire. However, the fact is that three of the springs were inside the park and three outside, and that three were in Wiltshire and three in Somersetshire. Here, then, is to be found the division upon the coat of arms of the six fountains in the two sets of three each, and it is by no means an improbable suggestion that the bend which separates the three from the three is typical of, or was suggested by, either the park wall or pale, or by the line of division between the two counties, and the more probable of the two seems to be the park wall. The coat of arms is just a map of the property. Now, with regard to the arms, as far as is known there has not been at any time the slightest deviation by the family of the Lords Stourton from the coat quoted and illustrated. But before leaving the subject it may be well to point out that in the few

FIG. 231.—Armorial bearings of James Fitzalan Hope, Esq.: Azure, on a chevron or, between three bezants, a bay-leaf slipped vert, a bordure ermine for difference. Mantling azure, doubled or; and upon a wreath of his liveries is set for crest, a broken globe surmounted of a rainbow proper; and in a scroll above, this motto, "At spes infracta."

cases in which an ancient coat of arms carries with it an explanation, such explanation is usually to be found either in some such manner as that in which these arms of Stourton have been explained, or else in some palpable pun, and not in the mythical accounts and legends of supernatural occurrences which have been handed down, and seldom indeed in any explanation of personal nobility which the tinctures or charges are sometimes said to represent.

Amongst the arms in which roundles of various colour are to be found are the arms of Courtenay (Fig. 228), Devereux (Fig. 229), Hungerford (Fig. 230), and Hope (Fig. 231).

What is now considered quite a different charge from the fountain is the whirlpool or gurges, which is likewise intended to represent water, and is borne by a family of the name of Gorges, the design occupying the whole of the field. This is represented by a spiral line of azure commencing in the centre of an argent field, continuing round and round until the edges of the shield are reached; but there can be very little doubt that this was an early form of representing the watery

FIG. 232.—Armorial bearings of Frederick Platt, Esq.: Sable, semé of plates, a fret couped or, between four roses in cross argent. Crest: upon a wreath of the colours, in front of a demi-lion proper, semé of plates, holding between the paws a rose argent, an escallop or. Motto: "Virtute et labore."

roundle which happens to have been perpetuated in the instance of that one coat. The fountains upon the seal of the first Lord Stourton are represented in this manner.

Examples of a field semé of roundles are very usual, these being termed bezanté or platé if semé of bezants or plates; but in the cases of roundles of other colours the words "semé of" need to be used. Examples of this will be found in the arms of Platt (Fig. 232).

THE ANNULET

Closely akin to the roundel is the annulet, and though, as far as I am aware, no text-book has as yet included this in its list of ordinaries and sub-ordinaries, one can see no reason, as the annulet is a regularly used heraldic figure, why the lozenge should have been included and the annulet excluded, when the annulet is of quite as frequent occurrence. It is, as its name implies, simply a plain ring of metal or colour, as will be found in the

arms of De Plessis (Fig. 233), Lowther, Hutton (Fig. 234), and many other families. Annulets appear anciently to have been termed false roundles.

Annulets will frequently be found interlaced, as in the crest of Athill (Fig. 17).

A curious instance of the annulet will be found in the arms of Gossett (Fig. 235).

Care should be taken to distinguish them from gem-rings, which are always drawn in a very natural manner with stones, which, however, in real life would approach an impossible size.

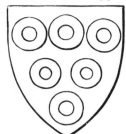

FIG. 233.—Arms of John de Plessis, Earl of Warwick (d. 1263): Argent, six annulets gules. Glover's Roll terms the charges, "six faux rondelettes de gules."

Dat Deus incrementum

FIG. 234.—Armorial bearings of Rev. Charles Frederick Hutton, M.A.: Per chevron nebuly or and gules, in chief two annulets, and in base a crescent all counterchanged. Mantling gules and or. Crest: on a wreath of the colours, on two annulets in fess gules, a crescent or. Motto: "Dat Deus incrementum."

FIG. 235.—Armorial bearings of Gosset: "D'Azure, à un annulet d'or, et trois gousses de fives, fruillés et tigés manorantes de l'annulet, et rangées en pairles de même, au chef d'argent, chargé d'une aiglette de sable." Crest: a greyhound's head erased proper, collared gules. Motto: "Probitas verus honos."

THE ART OF HERALDRY

THE LABEL

The label as a charge must be distinguished from the label as a mark of difference for the eldest son, though there is no doubt that in those cases in which it now exists as a charge its use as a difference must have been the origin. Concerning its use as a difference it will be treated further in the chapter upon marks of difference and cadency, but as a charge it will seldom be found in any position except in chief, and not often of other than three points, and it will always be found drawn throughout, that is, with the upper line extended to the size of the field. It consists of a narrow band straight across the shield, from which depend at right angles three short bands. These shorter arms have each of late years been drawn more in the shape of a dovetail, but this was not the case until a comparatively recent period, and nowadays we are more inclined to revert to the old forms than to perpetuate this modern variety. Other names for the label are the "lambel" and the "file." The label is the only mark of difference now borne by the Royal Family. Every member of the Royal Family has the Royal arms assigned to him for use presumably during life, and in these warrants, which are separate and personal for each individual, both the coronet and the difference marks which are to be borne upon the label are quoted and assigned. This use of the label as its more usual use for the purpose of differencing will be found fully dealt with later. As a charge, the label occurs in the arms of Barrington: "Argent, three chevronels gules, a label azure;" and Babington: "Argent, ten torteaux, four, three, two, and one, in chief a label of three points azure;" also in the earlier form of the arms of De Quincy (Fig. 218) and Courtenay (Fig. 228). Various curious coats of arms in which the label appears are given in Papworth as follows :—

". . . a label of four points in bend sinister . . . Wm. de Curli, 20th Hen. III. (Cotton, Julius F., vii. 175.)

"Argent, a label of five points azure. Henlington, co. Gloucester. (Harl. MS. 1404, fo. 109.)

"Or a file gules, with three bells pendent azure, clappers saltire. (Belfile.)

"Sable, three crescents, in chief a label of two drops and in fess another of one drop argent. Fitz-Simons. (Harl. MS. 1441 and 5866.)

"Or, three files borne barways gules, the first having five points, the second four, and the last three. Liskirke, Holland. (Gwillim)."

A curious label will have been noticed in the arms of De Valence (Fig. 123).

THE BILLET

The billet, though not often met with as a charge, does sometimes occur, for example, as in the arms of Alington (Fig. 83).

Another instance is in the case of the crest of Ambrose (Plate XXX.). Its more frequent appearance is as an object with which a field or superior charge is semé, in which case these are termed billetté. The best known instance of this is probably the coat borne on an inescutcheon over the arms of England during the joint reign of William and Mary. The arms of Gasceline afford another example of a field billetté. These are "or, billetté azure, and a label gules." Though not many instances are given under each subdivision, Papworth affords examples of coats with every number of billets from 1 to 20, but many of them, particularly some of those from 10 to 20 in number, are merely mistaken renderings of fields which should have been termed billetté. The billet, slightly widened, is sometimes known as a block, and as such will be found in the arms of Paynter (Fig. 236). Other instances are to be found where the billets

are termed delves or gads. The billet will sometimes be found pointed at the bottom, in which case it is termed "urdy at the foot." But neither as a form of semé, nor as a charge, is the billet of sufficiently frequent use to warrant its inclusion as one of the ordinaries or sub-ordinaries.

FIG. 236.—Armorial bearings of Paynter: Quarterly, 1. azure, three blocks argent, on each of them an annulet sable (for Paynter); 2. azure, three faggots argent (for Antron); 3. argent, three bends gules (for Bodrugan); 4. argent, two chevronels nebuly gules, between three sheaves of as many arrows sable, banded of the second (for Best). Mantling gules and argent. Crest: upon a wreath of the colours, three broken broad-arrows gold, knit with a lace gules (for Paynter). Motto: "Carpe diem."

THE CHAPLET

Why the chaplet was ever included amongst the ordinaries and sub-ordinaries passes my comprehension. It is not of frequent occurrence, and I have yet to ascertain in which form it has acquired this status. The chaplet which is usually meant when the term is employed is the garland of oak, laurel, or other leaves or flowers which is found more frequently as part of a crest. There is also the chaplet, which it is difficult to describe, save as a large broad annulet such as the one which figures in the arms of Nairn, and which is charged at four regular intervals with roses, mullets, or some other objects. Examples of chaplets will be found in the shield of Berry (see Fig. 237), in which these arms of Nairn are quartered, and in the arms of Yerburgh (see Fig. 238).

The chaplet of oak and acorns is sometimes known as a civic crown, but the term chaplet will more frequently be found giving place to the use of the word wreath, and a chaplet of laurel or roses, unless completely conjoined and figuring as a charge upon the shield, will be far more likely to be termed a wreath or garland of laurel or roses than a chaplet.

There are many other charges which have no great distinction from some of these which have been enumerated, but as nobody hitherto has classed them as ordinaries we suppose there could be no excuse for

THE ART OF HERALDRY

so introducing them, but the division of any heraldic charges into ordinaries and sub-ordinaries, and their

FIG. 237.—Armorial bearings of Robert Berry, Esq.: Quarterly, 1 and 4, vert, a cross crosslet argent (for Berry); 2 and 3, parted per pale argent and sable, on a chaplet four mullets counterchanged (for Nairne), in the centre of the quarters a crescent or, for difference. Mantling vert, doubled argent. Crest: upon a wreath of the colours, a demi-lion rampant gules, armed and langued, holding in his dexter paw a cross crosslet fitchée azure; and in an escroll over the same this motto, "In hoc signo vinces," and in another under the shield, "L'esperance me comforte."

FIG. 238.—Armorial bearings of R. E. Yerburgh, Esq.: Per pale argent and azure, on a chevron between three chaplets all counterchanged, an annulet for difference. Mantling azure and argent. Crest: on a wreath of the colours, a falcon close or, belled of the last, preying upon a mallard proper.

separation from other figures, seems to a certain extent incomprehensible and very unnecessary.

A. C. F-D.

CHAPTER XIV

THE HUMAN FIGURE IN HERALDRY

IF we include the many instances of the human head and the human figure which exist as crests, and also the human figure as a supporter, probably it or its parts will be nearly as frequently met with in armory as the lion; but if crests and supporters be disregarded, and the human figure be simply considered as a charge upon the shield, it is by no means often to be met with.

English official heraldry now and for a long time past has set its face against the representation of any specific saint or other person in armorial bearings. In many cases, however, particularly in the arms of ecclesiastical sees and towns, the armorial bearings registered are simply the conventionalised heraldic representation of seal designs dating from a very much earlier period.

Seal engravers laboured under no such limitations, and their representations were usually of some specific saint or person readily recognisable from accompanying objects. Consequently, if it be desirable, the identity of a figure in a coat of arms can often be traced in such cases by reference to a seal of early date, whilst all the time the official coat of arms goes no further than to term the figure that of a saint.

The only representation which will be found in British heraldry of the Deity is in the arms of the See of Chichester, which certainly originally represented our Lord seated in glory. Whether by intention or carelessness, this, however, is now represented and blazoned as: "Azure, a Prester [Presbyter] John sitting on a tombstone, in his left hand a mound, his right hand extended all or, with a linen mitre on his head, and in his mouth a sword proper." Possibly it is a corruption, but I am rather inclined to think it is an intentional alteration to avoid the necessity of any attempt to pictorially represent the Deity.

Christ upon the Cross, however, will be found represented in the arms of Inverness (Fig. 239), and in the arms used by the town of Halifax. The latter shield has the canting "Holy Face" upon a chequy field. This coat, however, is without authority, though it is sufficiently remarkable to quote the blazon in full: "Chequy or and azure, a man's face with long hair and bearded and dropping blood, and surmounted by a halo, all proper; in chief the letters HALEZ, and in base the letters FAX."

No other instance is known, but, on the other hand, representations of the Virgin Mary with her babe are not uncommon. She will be found so described in the arms of the Royal Burgh of Banff.

The Virgin Mary and Child appear also in the arms of the town of Leith, viz.: "Argent, in a sea proper, an ancient galley with two masts, sails furled sable, flagged gules, seated therein the Virgin Mary with the Infant Saviour in her arms, and a cloud resting over their heads, all also proper."

The Virgin and Child appear in the crest of Marylebone (Fig. 240), but in this case, in accordance with the modern English practice, the identity is not alluded to. The true derivation of the name from "St. Mary le Bourne" (and not "le bon") is perpetuated in the design of the arms.

A demi-figure of the Virgin is the crest of Ruther-

FIG. 239.—Armorial bearings of the Royal Burgh of Inverness: Gules, our Lord upon the Cross proper. Mantling gules, doubled or. Crest: upon a wreath of the proper liveries a cornucopia proper. Supporters: dexter, a dromedary; sinister, an elephant both proper. (From a painting by Mr. Graham Johnston in Lyon Register.)

arms, and amongst them will be found the following:—

St. Andrew, in the arms of the National Bank of Scotland, granted in 1826 ["Or, the image of St. Andrew with vesture vert and surcoat purpure bearing before him the cross of his martyrdom argent, all resting on a base of the second, in the dexter flank a garb gules, in the sinister a ship in full sail sable, the shield surrounded with two thistles proper, disposed in orle"]; St. Britius, in the arms of the Royal Burgh of Kirkcaldy ["Azur, ane abbay of three pyramids argent, each ensigned with a cross patée or. And on the reverse of the seal is insculped in a field azure the figure of St. Bryse with long garments, on his head a mytre, in the dexter a fleur-de-lis, the sinister laid upon his breast all proper. Standing in ye porch of the church or abbay. Ensigned on the top as before all betwixt a decrescent and a star in fess or. The motto is 'Vigilando Munio.' And round the escutcheon of both sydes these words—'Sigillum civitatus

glen; [a] and the Virgin and Child figure, amongst other ecclesiastical arms, on the shields of the Sees of Lincoln ["Gules, two lions passant-guardant or; on a chief azure, the Holy Virgin and Child, sitting crowned, and bearing a sceptre of the second"], Salisbury ["Azure, the Holy Virgin and Child, with sceptre in her left hand all or"], Sodor and Man ["Argent, upon three ascents the Holy Virgin standing with her arms extended between two pillars, on the dexter whereof is a church; in base the ancient arms of Man upon an inescutcheon"], Southwell ["Sable, three fountains proper, a chief paly of three, on the first or, a stag couchant proper, on the second gules, the Virgin holding in her arms the infant Jesus, on the third also or, two staves raguly couped in cross vert"], and Tuam ["Azure, three figures erect under as many canopies or stalls of Gothic work or, their faces, hands, and legs proper; the first representing an archbishop in his pontificals; the second the Holy Virgin Mary, a circle of glory over her head, holding in her left arm the infant Jesus; and the third an angel having his dexter arm elevated, and under the sinister arm a lamb, all of the second"].

Various saints figure in different Scottish coats of

[a] Arms of Rutherglen: Argent, in a sea proper an ancient galley sable, flagged gules, therein two men proper, one rowing, the other furling the sail. Above the shield is placed a suitable helmet, with a mantling gules, doubled argent; and on a wreath of the proper liveries is set for crest, a demi-figure of the Virgin Mary with the Infant Saviour in her arms proper; and on a compartment below the shield, on which is an escroll confaining this motto, "Ex fumo fama," are placed for supporters, two angels proper, winged or.

FIG. 240.—Arms of Marylebone: Per chevron sable and barry wavy of six, argent and azure in chief, in the dexter a fleur-de-lis, and in the sinister a rose, both or. Crest: on a wreath of the colours, upon two bars wavy argent and azure, between as many lilies of the first, stalked and leaved vert, a female figure affronté proper, vested of the first, mantled of the second, on the left arm a child also proper, vested or, around the head of each a halo of the last. Motto: "Fiat secundum verbum tuum."

THE ART OF HERALDRY

Kirkaldie'"]; St. Columba, in the arms of the College of the Holy Spirit at Cumbrae ["Quarterly, 1 and 4 grand quarters, azure, St. Columba in a boat at sea, in his sinister hand a dove, and in the dexter chief a blazing star all proper; 2 and 3 grand quarters, quarterly, i. and iv., argent, an eagle displayed with two heads gules; ii. and iii., parted per bend embattled gules and argent; over the second and third grand quarters an escutcheon of the arms of Boyle of Kelburne, viz. or, three stags' horns gules"]; St. Duthacus, in the arms of the Royal Burgh of Tain ["Gules, St. Duthacus in long garments argent, holding in his dexter hand a staff garnished with ivy, in the sinister laid on his breast a book expanded proper"]; St. Ægidius (St. Giles), in the arms of the Royal Burgh of Elgin ["Argent, Sanctus Ægidius habited in his robes and mitred, holding in his dexter hand a pastoral staff, and in his left hand a clasped book, all proper. Supporters: two angels proper, winged or volant upwards. Motto: 'Sicitur ad astra,' upon ane compartment suitabill to a Burgh Royal, and for their colours red and white"]; St. Ninian, in the arms of the Episcopal See of Galloway ["Argent, St. Ninian standing and full-faced proper, clothed with a pontifical robe purple, on his head a mitre, and in his dexter hand a crosier or"]; and St. Adrian, in the arms of the town of Pittenweem ["Azur, in the sea a gallie with her oars in action argent, and therein standing the figure of St. Adrian, with long garments close girt, and a mytre on his head proper, holding in his sinister hand a crosier or. On the stern a flag developed argent, charged with the Royall Armes of Scotland, with this word, 'Deo Duce'"].

Biblical characters of the Old Testament have found favour upon the Continent, and the instances quoted by Woodward are too amusing to omit:—

"The families who bear the names of saints, such as ST. ANDREW, ST. GEORGE, ST. MICHAEL, have (perhaps not unnaturally) included in their arms representations of their family patrons.

"The Bavarian family of REIDER include in their shield the mounted effigy of the good knight ST. MARTIN dividing his cloak with a beggar (date of diploma 1760). The figure of the great Apostle of the Gentiles appears in the arms of VON PAULI JOERG, and JORGER, of Austria, similarly make use of St. George.

"Continental Heraldry affords not a few examples of the use of the personages of Holy Writ. The ADAMOLI of Lombardy bear: "Azure, the Tree of Life entwined with the Serpent, and accosted with our first parents, all proper" (i.e. in a state of nature). The addition of a chief of the Empire to this coat makes it somewhat incongruous.

"The family of ADAM in Bavaria improve on Sacred History by eliminating EVE, and by representing ADAM as holding the apple in one hand, and the serpent wriggling in the other. On the other hand, the Spanish family of EVA apparently consider there is a sufficiently transparent allusion to their own name, and to the mother of mankind, in the simple bearings: "Or, on a mount in base an apple-tree vert, fruited of the field, and encircled by a serpent of the second."

"The family of ABEL in Bavaria make the patriarch in the attitude of prayer to serve as their crest; while the coat itself is: "Sable, on a square altar argent, a lamb lying surrounded by fire and smoke proper."

"SAMSON slaying the lion is the subject of the arms of the VESENTINA family of Verona. The field is gules, and on a terrace in base vert the strong man naked bestrides a golden lion and forces its jaws apart. The Polish family of SAMSON naturally use the same device, but the field is azure and the patriarch is decently habited. The STARCKENS of the Island of OESEL also use the like as *armes parlantes*; the field in this case is or. After

these we are hardly surprised to find that Daniel in the lions' den is the subject of the arms of the Rhenish family of DANIELS, granted late in the eighteenth century; the field is azure. The Bolognese DANIELS are content to make a less evident allusion to the prophet; their arms are: "Per fess azure and vert, in chief 'the lion of the tribe of Judah' naissant or, holding an open book with the words 'LIBRI APERTI SUNT'" (DANIEL vii. 10).

"The Archangel ST. MICHAEL in full armour, as conventionally represented, treading beneath his feet the great adversary, sable, is the charge on an azure field of the VAN SCHOREL of Antwerp."

Other instances will be found, as St. Kentigern (who is sometimes said to be the same as St. Mungo), and who occurs as the crest of Glasgow: "The half-length figure of St. Kentigern affronté, vested and mitred, his right hand raised in the act of benediction, and having in his left hand a crosier, all proper" (Plate CXVII.); St. Michael, in the arms of Linlithgow: "Azure, the figure of the Archangel Michael, with wings expanded, treading on the belly of a serpent lying with its tail nowed fesswise in base, all argent, the head of which he is piercing through with a spear in his dexter hand, and grasping with his sinister an escutcheon charged with the Royal

FIG. 241.—Arms of Dover: A man on horseback (St. Martin) and the beggar within a bordure semé of lions.

Arms of Scotland. The same saint also figures in the arms of the city of Brussels (see Plate CXVIII.); while the family of MITCHELL-CARRUTHERS bears as a crest: "St. Michael in armour, holding a spear in his dexter hand, the face, neck, arms and legs bare, all proper, the wings argent, and hair auburn."

St. Martin occurs in the arms of Dover (Fig. 241), and he also figures, as has been already stated, on the shield of the Bavarian family of REIDER, whilst St. Paul occurs as a charge in the arms of the Dutch family of VON PAULI.

The arms of the See of Clogher are: "A Bishop in pontifical robes seated on his chair of state, and leaning towards the sinister, his left hand supporting a crosier, his right pointing to the dexter chief, all or, the feet upon a cushion gules, tasselled or."

A curious crest will be found belonging to the arms of Stewart (Fig. 242), which is: "A king in his robes, crowned." The arms of the Episcopal See of Ross afford another instance of a bishop, together with St. Boniface.

The arms of the town of Queensferry, in Scotland, show an instance of a queen. "A king in his robes, and crowned," will be found in the arms of Dartmouth ["Gules, the base barry wavy, argent and azure, thereon the hulk of a ship, in the centre of which is a king robed and crowned, and holding in his sinister hand a sceptre, at each end of the ship a lion sejant guardant all or]."

Allegorical figures, though numerous as supporters, are comparatively rare as charges upon a shield; but the arms of the University of Melbourne show a representation of the figure of Victory, which also appears in other coats of arms ["Azure, a figure intended to represent Victory, robed and attired proper, the dexter hand

FIG. 242.—Armorial bearings of Charles Balfour Stewart, M.A., B.C. (Cantab), M.R.: Quarterly, 1 and 4 grand quarters, quarterly i. and iiii., or, a lion rampant within a double tressure flory and counterflory gules, debruised by a ribbon sable; ii. and iii., azure, a ship with her sails trussed up or (for Orkney), the whole within a bordure compony argent and azure (for Stewart); 2 and 3 grand quarters, argent, a chevron sable, charged with an otter's head erased of the field (for Balfour of Pharay). Mantling gules, doubled or. Crest: on a wreath of his liveries, a king enthroned, holding in his dexter hand a sword, and in his sinister a falcon all proper. Motto: "Sic fuit est et erit."

extended holding a wreath of laurel or, between four stars of eight points, two in pale and two in fess argent."]

The figure of Truth will be found in the coats of arms for various members of the family of Sandeman.[b]

The bust of Queen Elizabeth was granted by that Queen, as a special mark of her Royal favour, to Sir Anthony Weldon, her Clerk of the Spicery.

Apollo is represented in the arms of the Apothecaries' Company: "Azure, Apollo, the inventor of physic, proper, with his head radiant, holding in his left hand a bow and in his right hand an arrow or, supplanting a serpent argent." The figure of Justice appears in the arms of Wiergman [or Wergman].

[b] Armorial bearings of John Glas Sandeman, Esq., F.S.A.: Argent, the emblem of Truth, a naked woman standing on a terrestrial globe, issuing out of the base in her dexter hand an open book, in her sinister, which is elevated above her head, a branch of palm, on her breast the sun in his splendour all proper, and a veil across her middle of the first, within a bordure engrailed gules, charged with three fleurs-de-lis, and as many trefoils alternately also of the first. Mantling gules, doubled argent; and upon a wreath of his liveries is set for crest, a rock proper; and in an escroll over the same this motto, "Stat veritas," and under the arms, "Olim cruore nunc candore."

Neptune appears in the arms granted to Sir Isaac Heard, Lancaster Herald, afterwards Garter King of Arms, and is again to be found in the crest of the arms of Monneypenny ["On a dolphin embowed, a bridled Neptune astride, holding with his sinister hand a trident over his shoulder"].

The figure of Temperance occurs in the crest of Goodfellow (Fig. 243).

The head of St. John the Baptist in a charger figures in the crest (Plate CXX.) of the Tallow Chandlers' Livery Company and in the arms of Ayr, whilst the head of St. Denis is the charge upon the arms of a family of that name.

Angels, though very frequently met with as supporters, are far from being usual, either as a charge upon a shield or as a crest. The crest of Leslie (Fig. 244), however, is an angel.

The crest of Lord Kintore is an angel praying [Arms: "Quarterly, 1 and 4, azure, a falcon displayed argent, charged on the breast with a man's heart gules, between three mullets of the second (for Falconer); 2 and 3, argent, on a chief gules, three pallets or (for Keith), on an escutcheon gules, a sword in bend sinister, surmounted by a sceptre in bend dexter; in chief an imperial crown, the whole within an orle of eight thistles or, as a coat of augmentation for preserving the regalia of Scotland. Crest: an angel in a praying posture or, within an orle of laurel proper. Supporters: two men in complete armour, each holding a pike or spear in a sentinel's posture proper. Motto: 'Quæ amissa salva'"].

Cherubs are far more frequently to be met with.

FIG. 243.—Armorial bearings of General William West Goodfellow, C.B.: Argent, a chevron gules, between two gabions in chief proper, and in base on a mount, vert an elephant sable, a chief embattled azure, thereon on the dexter, pendent from a riband of the second, a representation of the silver medal presented to Samuel Goodfellow by the Honourable East India Company, in commemoration of his services at the taking of Seringapatam; and on the sinister, pendent from a riband also of the second, a representation of the gold medal presented to the said Samuel Goodfellow by the Grand Seignor, for his services in Egypt. Crest: upon a wreath of the colours, a demi-female figure representing Temperance, vested argent, mantle azure, in the dexter hand a palmbranch, and in the sinister a bridle proper. Motto: "Temperance."

They are represented in various forms, and will be found in the arms of Thackeray (Fig. 245), Maddocks (Fig. 246), and in the crest of Carruthers (Fig. 139).

FIG. 244.—Armorial bearings of Robert Charles Leslie, Esq.: Quarterly, 1 and 4, argent, on a bend azure, three buckles or (for Leslie); 2 and 3, argent, a lion rampant sable (for Abernethy). Upon the escutcheon is placed a helmet befitting his degree. Mantling azure and argent. Crest: on a wreath of the colours, an angel affronté proper. Motto: "Grip fast."

FIG. 245.—Armorial bearings of Rev. Arthur Thomas James Thackeray, M.A.: Vert, two garbs or, in base an arrow argent, on a chief purpure, a cherub's head proper, between the like number of estoiles of the third. Mantling vert and or. Crest: on a wreath of the colours, an eagle, the wings elevated proper, charged on the breast with a like cherub's head, and holding in the beak an arrow as in the arms. Motto: "Nobilitas sola virtus."

The nude figure is perhaps the most usual form in which the human being is made use of as a charge,

and examples will be found in the arms of Wood (Lord Halifax), as shown upon Plate LXII., and in the arms of Oswald (Fig. 247).

The arms of Dalziell show an example—practically unique in British heraldry—of a naked man, the earliest entry (1685) of the arms of Dalziell of Binns

FIG. 246.—Armorial bearings of John Maddocks, Esq.: Argent, on a pale indented azure, a flaming sword erect proper, pommel and hilt or, on a chief arched sable, a cherub's head of the fourth between two roses of the field. Mantling azure and argent. Crest: on a wreath of the colours, in front of a passion cross gules, a cherub's head or, each wing charged with a rose also gules. Motto: "Justice and gratitude."

(a cadet of the family) in the Lyon Register, having them then blazoned: "Sable, a naked man with his arms extended *au naturel*, on a canton argent, a sword and pistol disposed in saltire proper."

This curious coat of arms has been the subject of much speculation. The fact that in some early ex-

FIG. 247.—Armorial bearings of John Oswald, Esq.: Azure, ane savage proper wreathed with bay leaves, and bearing in the sinister ane batton erected on his shoulder vert, and in the dexter a cross-staff pointing to a star placed in the dexter chief or. Above the shield ane helmet befitting his degree, with a mantle gules, doubled argent; with this motto, "Monstrant astra viam."

amples the body is swinging from a gibbet has led some to suppose the arms to be an allusion to the fact, or legend, that one of the family recovered the body of Kenneth III., who had suffered death by hanging at the hands of the Picts. But it seems more likely that if the gibbet is found in any authoritative versions of

P

the arms possibly the coat may owe its origin to a similar reason to that which is said, and probably correctly, to account for the curious crest of the Davenport family (Fig. 127), viz.: "A man's head in profile couped at the shoulders proper, about the neck a rope or," or as it is sometimes termed, "a felon's head proper, about

FIG. 248.—Armorial bearings of Sir Bryan O'Loghlen, Bart.: Gules, a man in armour shooting an arrow from a cross-bow proper; the escutcheon charged with his badge of Ulster as a Baronet. Mantling gules and argent. Crest: on a ducal coronet or, an anchor erect, entwined with a cable proper. Motto: "Anchora salutis."

the neck a halter or." There is now in the possession of the Capesthorne branch of the Davenport family a

FIG. 249.—Armorial bearings of Julian Marshall, Esq.: Barry of six sable and argent, on a pale ermine, three horse-shoes palewise or. Mantling sable and argent. Crest: on a wreath of the colours, a man affronté in armour proper, holding in his dexter hand a javelin in bend or, and supporting with his sinister hand a flagstaff proper, therefrom flowing to the sinister a banner sable, charged with two horse-shoes fesswise also or. Motto: "Nec citò nec tardè."

long and very ancient roll, containing the names of the master robbers captured and beheaded in the times of Koran, Roger, and Thomas de Davenport, and probably the Davenport family held some office or Royal Commission which empowered them to deal in a summary

way with the outlaws which infested the Peak country. It is more than probable that the crest should be traced to some such source as this.

As a crest the savage and demi-savage are constantly met with.

Men in armour are sometimes met with. The arms of O'Loghlen (Fig. 248) are an instance in point, as are the crests of Marshall (Fig. 249), Morse (Fig. 140), Bannerman (Plate XVIII.), and Seton of Mounie (Fig. 250).

Figures of all nationalities and in all costumes will be found in the form of supporters, and are occasionally met with as crests, but it is difficult to classify them, and it must suffice to mention a few curious examples. The human figure as a supporter is fully dealt with in the chapter devoted to that subject.

The arms of Jedburgh have a mounted warrior, and

FIG. 250.—Armorial bearings of Alexander David Seton of Mounie: Quarterly, 1 and 4, or, three crescents, and in the fess point a man's heart distilling drops of blood, within a Royal double tressure flowered and counterflowered of fleurs-de-lis gules (for Seton); 2 and 3, argent, issuing out of a bar wavy sable, a demi-otter of the last crowned with an antique crown or (for Meldrum). Mantling gules, doubled argent; and issuing from a wreath of the liveries or and gules, is set for crest, a demi-man in armour, bearing up in his dexter hand the Royal banner of Scotland, namely: gules, on a canton azure, a saltire argent bendwise, and displayed all proper, scarf over dexter shoulder, plume and waistbelt argent; and in an escroll over the same this motto: "Sustento sanguine signo."

the same device occurs in the crest of the Duke of Fife (Fig. 251), and in the arms of Lanigan-O'Keefe (Fig. 252).

The arms of Londonderry afford an instance of a skeleton.

The emblematical figure of Fortune is a very favourite charge in foreign heraldry, and the blazon of the crest of Langer[c] will indicate the form in which it is usually represented.

A family of the name of Rodd use the Colossus of Rhodes as a crest: and the arms of Sir William Dunn,

[c] Crest of Langer and others: Upon a globe or, winged sable, a maiden balancing herself proper, the hair or, her eyes covered with a bandage argent, the dexter arm embowed and extended grasping the end of a veil sable, passing in an arch above her head and held around the loins by her sinister hand. Motto: "Ora et labora."

Bart., are worth the passing mention ["Azure, on a mount in base a bale of wool proper, thereon seated a female figure representing Commerce, vested argent,

tween a thistle slipped proper on the dexter and a fleur-de-lis azure on the sinister. Crest: a cornucopia fesswise, surmounted by a dexter hand couped proper,

ermine; and upon a wreath of his liveries is set for crest, a horse in full gallop argent, covered with a mantling gules, bestrewed with escutcheons or, each charged with a lion rampant of the second, on his back a knight in complete armour, with his sword drawn proper, on his sinister arm a shield, charged as the escutcheons, on the helmet a wreath of the colours, thereon a demi-lion rampant gules. Supporters: two savages wreathed about the head and waist with laurel, and holding in their exterior hands branches of trees over their shoulders all proper. Mottoes: "Deo juvante", under the shield, "Virtute et opera;" and upon the sinister side of his achievement, upon a lozenge surmounted by the coronet of her rank, being composed of crosses patée, fleurs-de-lis, and strawberry leaves, are placed the arms of Her Royal Highness as upon the second escutcheon, the lozenge being supported on the dexter side by a lion guardant or, crowned with a like coronet and charged with a like label; and on the sinister side a unicorn argent, armed, crined, and unguled or, gorged with a like coronet, therefrom a chain passing between the forelegs and reflexed over the back or, and charged with a label as the dexter. (From a drawing by Mr. G. W. Eve, R.E.).

FIG. 251.—Armorial bearings of the Duke and Her Royal Highness the Duchess of Fife (Duff): Quarterly, 1 and 4, or, a lion rampant gules (for Macduff); 2 and 3, vert, a fess dancetté ermine between a hart's head caboshed in chief and two escallops in base or (for Duff); the escutcheon being surrounded by the ribbon and the collar, and pendent therefrom the badge of the Most Ancient and Most Noble Order of the Thistle, and upon a second escutcheon the arms of his wife, namely: quarterly, 1 and 4, gules, three lions passant guardant in pale or (for England); 2. or, a lion rampant within a double tressure flory and counterflory gules (for Scotland); 3. azure, a harp or, stringed argent (for Ireland); and upon an escutcheon of pretence the arms of Saxony, namely: barry of ten or and sable, a crown of rue in bend vert. In chief is the distinctive label of Her Royal Highness Princess Louise Duchess of Wales, Duchess of Fife, being of five points argent, charged in the centre and outer points with the cross of St. George gules, and in the two others with a thistle proper. Above the escutcheon is placed the coronet of his rank, and thereupon a helmet befitting his degree, with a mantling gules, doubled

resting the dexter hand on a stock of an anchor, and in the sinister a caduceus, both or, on the chief of the last a tree eradicated, thereon hanging a hunting-horn be-

holding a key in bend sinister or. Motto: 'Vigilans et audax'"].

The crest of Lord Vivian ["A demi-hussar of the

18th Regiment, holding in his right hand a sabre, and

FIG. 252.—Armorial bearings of Stephen Martin Lanigan-O'Keefe, Esq.: Quarterly, 1. azure, a lion rampant argent; 2. gules, a knight in armour on horseback at full speed proper, the horse argent; 3. or, a peacock in his pride proper; 4. vert, three lizards in pale or. Mantling azure and argent; and for his crest, upon an antique crown a gryphon segreant or, holding in the dexter claw a sword erect argent, pommelled gold. Motto: "Forti et fideli nihil difficile."

FIG. 253.—Armorial bearings of Robert Mure M'Kerrell, Esq.: Azure, on a fess or, three lozenges gules, within a bordure engrailed argent. Mantling gules, doubled argent; and upon a wreath of his liveries is set for crest, a Roman soldier on his march, with standard and utensils all proper; and upon an escroll above the same this motto, "Dulcis pro patria labor."

in his left a pennon flying to the sinister gules, and

inscribed in gold letters, 'Croix d'Orade,' issuant from a bridge of one arch, embattled, and at each end a tower"], and Macgregor ["two brass guns in saltire in front of a demi-Highlander armed with his broadsword, pistols, and with a target, thereon the family arms of Macgregor," viz.: "Argent: a sword in bend dexter azure, and an oak-tree eradicated in bend sinister proper, in the dexter chief an antique crown gules, and upon an escroll surmounting the crest the motto, 'E'en do and spare not'"] are typical of many crests of augmentation granted in the early part of the nineteenth century.

The crest of the Devonshire family of Arscot ["A demi-man affronté in a Turkish habit, brandishing in his dexter hand a scimitar, and his sinister hand resting on a tiger's head issuing from the wreath"] is curious, as is the crest granted by Sir William Le Neve in 1642 to Sir Robert Minshull, viz.: "A Turk kneeling on one knee, habited gules, legs and arms in mail proper, at the side a scymitar sable, hilted or, on the head a turban

FIG. 254.—Armorial bearings of William John Home Mylne, Esq., M.A., F.R.S.: Or, a cross, moline azure, quartered-pierced of the field, between three mullets of the second within a bordure gules for difference. Mantling azure, doubled or; and on a wreath of his liveries is set for crest, a Pallas's head couped at the shoulders proper, vested about the neck vert, on the head a helmet azure, beaver turned up, and on the top a plumaish gules; and in an escroll over this motto, "Tam arte quam marte."

with a crescent and feather argent, holding in the dexter hand a crescent of the last."

The crests of M'Kerrel (Fig. 253) and Mylne (Fig. 254) are rather uncommon, as are also those of Pilkington ["a mower with his scythe in front habited as follows: a high-crowned hat with flap, the crown party per pale, flap the same, counterchanged; coat buttoned to the middle, with his scythe in bend proper, habited through quarterly and counterchanged argent and gules"], and De Trafford (Fig. 255).

The crest of Clerk of Pennycuick[d] (Plate XXXIV.) refers to the curious tenure by which the Pennycuick estate is supposed to be held, namely, that whenever the sovereign sets foot thereupon, the proprietor must blow a

[d] Armorial bearings of Robert Mildmay Clerk, Esq., of Westholme: Or, a fess chequy azure and argent, between two crescents in chief gules and in base a boar's head couped sable, all within a bordure invected of the second, charged with three cross crosslets fitchèe of the first. Mantling azure and or. Crest: on a wreath of the colours, a demi-huntsman winding a horn all proper. Mottoes (over the crest): "Free for a blast;" (under the arms), "Amat victoria curam."

FIG. 255.—Armorial bearings of Sir Humphrey Francis de Trafford, Bart. : Quarterly of twenty, 1. argent, a griffin segreant gules (for Trafford) ; 2. argent, two bears, and in chief two mullets pierced azure (for Venables) ; 3. argent, on a bend azure, three garbs proper (for Tritten) ; 4. quarterly, gules and or, in the first quarter a lion passant argent (for Massey) ; 5. paly of six argent and gules, a chief vairé (for Whitney) ; 6. argent, on a bend gules, three escarbuncles sable (for Thornton) ; 7. vert, a cross engrailed ermine (for Kingsley) ; 8. or, a saltire sable (for Hellesby) ; 9. azure, a chevron argent, between three garbs proper (for Hatton) ; 10. bendy barry gules and argent (for Crispen) ; 11. argent, a chevron gules, between three chaplets (for Ashton) ; 12. argent, three bars sable (for Legh) ; 13. gules, two lions passant guardant in pale argent (for De la Mere) ; 14. argent, on a chevron quarterly gules and sable, between three birds of the second as many bezants (for Kitchen) ; 15. argent, three garbs proper, banded or (for Aughton) ; 16. argent, a fess sable, in chief three torteaux (for Mason) ; 17. argent on a child proper, wrapped in swaddling clothes gules, and banded or, an eagle sable (for Culcheth) ; 18. argent, a griffin segreant azure (for Culcheth) ; 19. argent, a griffin segreant sable, ducally crowned or (for Risseley) ; 20. azure, a hind trippant argent (for Hindley), and impaling the arms of Franklin, namely : azure, on a bend invected between two martlets or, a dolphin naiant between two lions' heads erased of the field. Mantling gules and argent. Crest : upon a wreath of the colours, a thrasher proper, his hat and coat per pale argent and gules, his breeches and stockings of the third and second, holding in both hands a flail or, uplifted over a garb on the dexter side ; and over the crest upon an escroll the motto, "Now thus," and below the arms the motto, "Gripe griffin" ("hold fast").

117

horn from a certain rocky point. The motto, "Free tor a blast," has reference to the same.

The arms of the College of Surgeons in Edinburgh afford the only instance of what is presumably a corpse, the blazon being: "Azure, a man (human body) fesswise between a dexter hand having an eye on the palm issuing out of a cloud downward and a castle situate on a rock proper, within a bordure or charged with several instruments peculiar to the art (sic); on a canton of the first a saltire argent surmounted of a thistle vert, crowned of the third."

When we come to parts of the human body instances of heads, arms, and legs are legion.

There are certain well-known heraldic heads, and though many instances occur where the blazon is simply a "man's head," it will be most frequently found that it is more specifically described.

Sloane Evans in his " Grammar of Heraldry " specifies eight different varieties, namely: 1. The wild man's; 2. The Moor's; 3. The Saracen's; 4. The Saxon's; 5. The Englishman's; 6. The old man's; 7. The woman's; 8. The child's.

The wild man's or savage's head is usually represented with a wreath of leaves about the temples, but not necessarily so.

The head of the Moor, or "blackamoor," as it is more usually described, is almost always in profile, and nearly always adorned with a twisted wreath (torse) about the temples.

The head of the Saracen is also usually found with wreaths about the temples.

The head of the Saxon is borne by several Welsh families, and is supposed to be known by the absence of a beard.

The Englishman's head, which is borne by the Welsh family of Lloyd of Plymog, has no very distinctive features, except that whilst the hair and beard of the savage are generally represented brown, they are black in the case of the Moor and Saracen, and fair for the Saxon and Englishman.

The old man's head, which, like that of the Saxon and Englishman, is seldom met with, is bald and grey haired and bearded.

But for all practical purposes these varieties may be all disregarded except the savage's, the blackamoor's, and the Saracen's. Examples of the savage's head will be found in the arms of Eddington of Balbartan [" Azure, three savages' heads couped argent "], in the arms of Gladstone (Plate XXXII.), and in the canting coat of Rochead of Whitsonhill [" Argent, a savage's head erased, distilling drops of blood proper, between three combs azure "]. Moir of Otterburn bears the Moors' heads [" Argent, three negroes' heads couped proper within a bordure counter-indented sable and or "], and Moir of Stonniwood matriculated a somewhat similar coat in which the heads are termed Mauritanian [" Argent, three Mauritanian negroes' heads couped and distilling guttés-de-sang "]. The crest of Broün-Morison [e] (Plate XVIII.) is curious. Alderson of Homerton, Middlesex, bears Saracens' heads [" Argent, three Saracens' heads affronté, couped at the shoulders proper, wreathed about the temples of the first and sable "].

The woman's head in heraldry is always represented

young and beautiful (that is, if the artist is capable of so drawing it), and it is almost invariably found with golden hair. The colour, however, should be blazoned, the term "crined" being used. Five maidens' heads appear upon the arms of the town of Reading and the crest of Thornhill shows the same figure. The arms of the Mercers' Livery Company [" Gules, a demi-virgin couped below the shoulders, issuing from clouds all proper, vested or, crowned with an Eastern crown of the last, her hair dishevelled, and wreathed round the temples with roses of the second, all within an orle of clouds proper "] (see Plate CXXI.) and of the Master of the Revels in Scotland [" Argent, a lady rising out of a cloud in the nombril point, richly apparelled, on her head a garland of ivy, holding in her right hand a poinziard crowned, in her left a vizard all proper, standing under a veil or canopy azure, garnished or, in base a thistle vert "] are worthy of quotation.

The boy's head will seldom be found except in Welsh coats, of which the arms of Vaughan and Price [f] (Plate XV.) are examples.

Another case in which the heads of children appear are the arms of Fauntleroy [" Gules, three infants' heads couped at the shoulders proper, crined or "], which are a very telling instance of a canting device upon the original form of the name, which was " Enfantleroy."

Children, it may be here noted, are seldom met with in armory, but instances will be found in the arms of Davies, of Marsh, county Salop [" Sable, a goat argent, attired or, standing on a child proper swaddled gules, and feeding on a tree vert "], of the Foundling Hospital [" Per fesse azure and vert, in chief a crescent argent, between two mullets of six points or, in base an infant exposed, stretching out its arms for help proper "], and in the familiar " bird and bantling " crest of Stanley, Earls of Derby. Arms and hands are constantly met with, and have certain terms of their own. A hand should be stated to be either dexter or sinister, and is usually blazoned and always understood to be couped at the wrist. If the hand is open and the palm visible it is " apaumé," but this being by far the most usual position in which the hand is met with, unless represented to be holding anything, the term "apaumé" is not often used in blazon, that position being presumed unless anything contrary is stated. The arms of Bate (Fig. 100) and Maynard (Fig. 256) are instances.

The hand is occasionally represented " clenched," as in the arms and crest of Fraser-Mackintosh (Fig. 257). When the thumb and first two fingers are raised, they are said to be " raised in benediction."

The cubit arm should be carefully distinguished from the arm. couped at the elbow. The former includes only about two-thirds of the entire arm from the elbow.

The arm " couped at the elbow " is not so frequently met with.

When the whole arm from the shoulder is used, it is always bent at the elbow, and this is signified by the term "embowed" and an "arm embowed" necessarily includes the whole arm. Fig. 116 shows the usual position of an arm embowed, but it is sometimes placed upon the point of the elbow, and also, but still more infrequently, on the upper arm. Either of the latter positions must be specified in the blazon. An example of the last mentioned occurs in the crest of Pretor-

---

[e] Armorial bearings of John Broün Broün-Morison, Esq., J.P., D.L., F.S.A. : Quarterly, 1 and 4, argent, a fess sable between three Moors' heads couped proper, banded or (for Morison); 2 and 3, gules, a chevron between three fleurs-de-lis argent (for Broün). Mantling gules, doubled argent. Crests : on the dexter side, on a wreath of the liveries, three Moors' heads conjoined in one neck proper, banded or, one looking upwards, the others to the dexter and sinister (for Morison); and on the sinister side, on a wreath of the liveries, a lion rampant proper, holding in the dexter fore-paw a fleur-de-lis argent (for Broün); and in escrolls above the crests these mottoes, " Prudentia præstat," and " Floreat majestas."

[f] Armorial bearings of Howel John James Price, Esq. : Party per fess sable and or, a pale counterchanged, three boys' heads affronté, couped at the shoulders two and one proper, and as many serpents nowed one and two vert. Crest: on a wreath of the colours, in front of a boys' head affronté, couped at the shoulders proper, two serpents saltirewise, heads upward vert, and a spear-head fessewise; with the motto, " Innocentes sicut pueri sagaces sicut serpentes."

Pinney (Fig. 258). The crest of Longstaff[g] (Plate XIV.) shows two arms "counter-embowed."

When the arm is bare it is termed "proper." When

FIG. 256.—Armorial bearings of Edmund Anthony Jefferson Maynard: Quarterly, 1 and 4, argent, on a chevron vert, between three sinister hands couped at the wrist gules, five ermine spots or (for Maynard); 2 and 3, barry of six erminois and gules, on a chief azure three catherine-wheels or (for Lax). Crest: upon a wreath of the colours, a stag trippant or. gorged with a collar invected argent fimbriated sable. Motto: "Manus justa nardus."

FIG. 258.—Armorial bearings of Frederick Wake Pretor-Pinney, Esq.: Quarterly, 1 and 4, gules, three crescents or, issuing from each a cross crosslet fitchée argent (for Pinney); 2 and 3, or, an eagle displayed with two heads vert, beaked and membered gules, standing on a fasces proper, and holding in each beak a trefoil slipped of the second, and impaling the arms of Smith, namely: or, a chevron cottised between three demi-griffins, the two in chief respecting each other sable. Mantling gules and or. Crests: 1. upon a wreath of the colours, an arm in armour embowed, the part above the elbow in fess proper, the hand holding a cross crosslet fitchée argent (for Pinney); 2. upon a wreath of the colours, a demi-eagle couped or, wings endorsed sable, semé of trefoils slipped of the first, and holding in the beak a trefoil slipped vert (for Pretor). Motto: "Amor patriæ."

FIG. 257.—Armorial bearings of Charles Fraser-Mackintosh, Esq.: Quarterly, 1 and 4, per pale or and argent, a lion rampant between three dexter hands fesswise, couped at the wrist and clenched gules (for Mackintosh); 2 and 3, per chevron argent and azure, three escutcheons, each charged with a cinquefoil all counterchanged (for Fraser). Mantling gules and or. Crests: 1. upon a wreath of the colours, a cat proper, collared gules, resting the dexter paw upon an escutcheon or, charged with a dexter hand as in the arms (for Mackintosh); 2. upon a wreath of the colours, a stag's head erased argent, attired and collared gules, in the mouth a sprig of fern proper, and pendent from the collar an escutcheon azure, charged with a cinquefoil argent (for Fraser). Motto: "Onwards."

g Armorial bearings of Lieutenant-Colonel Llewellyn Wood Longstaff, of Ridgelands, Wimbledon: Quarterly, argent and sable, on a bend indented gules, between two pheons of the first a quarterstaff or; and for a crest, upon a wreath of the colours, two arms embowed, vested sable, semé-de-lis, and cuffed argent, the hands proper, grasping a quarterstaff fesswise or; with the motto, "Vigilate."

FIG 259.—Armorial bearings of Briane Barttelot Barttelot, Esq.: Quarterly of 8, 1. sable, three sinister gloves pendent argent, tasselled or (for Barttelot); 2. quarterly per fesse indented argent and gules, four crescents counterchanged (for Stopham); 3. azure, three chevronels argent, in the sinister chief a martlet for difference (for Lewknor); 4. gules, three bucks' heads caboshed argent (for Doyley); 5. azure, two bars gemel, in chief a lion passant guardant or (for Tregoz); 6. or, on a chief gules, three bezants (for Camoys); 7. argent, three hawks' heads erased sable (for Walton); 8. argent, an eagle with two heads displayed sable (for Sykeston); and for his crest, upon a wreath of the colours, a swan couchant with wings endorsed argent; and the motto, "Matura."

clothed it is termed either "vested" or "habited." The cuff is very frequently of a different colour, and the crest is then also termed "cuffed." The hand is nearly always bare, but if not represented of flesh colour it will be presumed and termed to be "gloved" of such and such a tincture. When it is represented in armour it is termed "in armour" or "vambraced." Even when in armour the hand is usually bare, but if in a gauntlet this must be specifically so stated.

The armour is always represented as rivetted *plate* armour unless it is specifically stated to be *chain armour*, as in the crest of Bathurst (see Plate LXII.), or *scale armour*.

The armour is sometimes decorated with gold, when the usual term employed will be "garnished or," though occasionally the word "purfled" is used.

Gloves are occasionally met with as charges, *e.g.* in the arms of Barttelot (Fig. 259).

Gauntlets will be found in the arms of Wayne [h] (Plate XX.).

Legs are not so frequently met with as arms. They will be found in the arms of Gillman (Fig. 195), Bower (Fig. 260), Legg (Fig. 143), and as the crest of Eyre.

Boots will be found in the crest of Hussey (Fig. 261).

Bones occur in the arms of Scott-Gatty (Fig. 262), and Baines (Fig. 263).

A skull occurs in the crest of Græme ["Two arms issuing from a cloud erected and lighting up a man's skull encircled with two branches of palm, over the head a marquess's coronet, all proper"].

FIG. 260.—Armorial bearings of Edmund Thomas Chivers Bower, Esq.: Azure, a human leg couped at the thigh and pierced bendwise by a broken tilting-spear or, a chief argent, thereon between two castles sable a pale of the first charged with a rose of the second, impaling the arms of Trollope, namely: vert, three stags courant within a bordure argent. Mantling azure and or. Crest: on a wreath of the colours, on a mount vert a quiver azure, garnished or, and filled with arrows proper in saltire, with a bow unstrung also proper. Motto: "Veritas prævalebit."

A woman's breast occurs in the arms of Dodge ["Barry of six or and sable, on a pale gules, a woman's

breast distilling drops of milk proper. Crest: upon a wreath of the colours, a demi sea-dog azure, collared, maned, and finned or"].

An eye occurs in the crest of Blount of Maple-Durham

FIG. 261.—Arms of Thomas Hussey, Esq.: Quarterly of twenty-five, namely, 1. barry of six ermine and gules, on a canton of the second a cross patonce argent (for Hussey); 2. azure, a pale lozengy or, between two flaunches of the last (for Daniel); 3. azure, an eagle displayed argent (for Cotton, otherwise Redware); 4. argent, a bend sable between three pellets (for Cotton, ancient); 5. azure, an eagle displayed argent; 6. sable, three swords, two and one palewise proper, pommels and hilts or (for Waldechef); 7. or, six eagles displayed sable, a canton ermine (for Basing); 8. argent, three falcons gules, belled or (for Falconer); 9. sable, three owls or (for Thurcaston); 10. azure, two bars argent (for Venables); 11. or, a fesse azure (for Vernon); 12. sable, a fesse dancetté between three mullets argent (for Wesenham); 13. azure, a saltire and chief or (for Bruce of Connington); 14. or, a saltire and chief gules (for Bruce of Annandale); 15. or, three piles in point issuing from the chief gules (for David, Earl of Huntingdon); 16. or, a lion rampant within a double tressure flory and counterflory gules (for Scotland); 17. azure, a cross flory between four martlets or (for the Saxon kings of England); 18. azure, a lion rampant argent, a chief gules (for Waltheof, Earl of Northumberland); 19. gules, a saltire argent (for Aldred, Earl of Northumberland); 20. azure, six garbs, three, two and one or (for Kevelioc, Earl of Chester); 21. gules, a lion rampant argent (for Gernons, Earl of Chester); 22. or, a lion rampant gules (for Meschines, Earl of Chester); 23. azure, a wolf's head erased argent (for Lupus, Earl of Chester); 24. sable, a double-headed eagle displayed or (for Algar, Earl of Leicester); 25. or, a chevron between three leopards' faces gules (for Harvey). Upon the escutcheon is placed a helmet befitting his degree, with a mantling gules and argent; and for his crest, upon a wreath of the colours, a boot sable, spurred or, and turned over ermine, surmounted by a heart proper, supported by two arms embowed in armour, the hands gauntleted also proper; with the motto: "Cor immobyle."

["On a wreath of the colours, the sun in splendour charged in the centre with an eye all proper"].

The man-lion, the merman, mermaid, melusine, satyr, satyral, harpy, sphinx, centaur, saggitarius, and weir-

PLATE XXXIV.

THE ARMORIAL BEARINGS OF—

(1) Lt.-Col. ROBERT MILDMAY, CLERK OF WESTHOLME, CO.
   SOMERSET.
(2) REV. JOHN ARCHIBALD DUNBAR-DUNBAR OF SEA PARK,
   FORRES.

(3) MAJOR E. UVEDALE PRICE.
(4) EYTON.
(5) T. A. CARLYON, ESQ. OF BOSCOMBE PARK, BOURNEMOUTH.

PLATE XXXV.

THE ARMORIAL BEARINGS OF EDWARD CHADDOCK LOWNDES, Esq. of Castle Combe, Chippenham.

PLATE XXXVI.

THE ARMORIAL BEARINGS OF—

(1) DAUBENEY of Cote.
(2) HENRY WILLIAM DAUGLISH, Esq.
(3) Rt. Hon. VISCOUNT DILLON.

(4) WILLIAM HENRY CLELAND, Esq. of Rook's Nest, Banstead, Surrey.
(5) BENJAMIN PICKERING, Esq. of Bellefield, Sutton, Hull.

PLATE XXXVII.

THE ARMORIAL BEARINGS OF—

(1) E. R. FISHER-ROWE, ESQ. OF THORNCOMBE, NR. GUILDFORD.
(2) ALEXANDER JOHN FORBES-LEITH, ESQ. OF FYVIE CASTLE, ABERDEEN.
(3) SIR JONATHAN E. BACKHOUSE, BART.

(4) CAPT. JOHN GEORGE EDMUND TEMPLER OF LINDRIDGE, TEIGNMOUTH, CO. DEVON.
(5) CLIFFORD JOHN CORY, ESQ. OF LLANTARNAM ABBEY, MONMOUTHSHIRE.

PLATE XXXVIII.

THE ARMORIAL BEARINGS OF—

(1) JAMES BINNEY, Esq. of Pampisford Hall, Cambs.
(2) BARTLETT, of Liverpool.
(3) JOHN WILLIAM MACFIE, Esq., of Dreghorn and Colinton, N.B.

(4) PHILIP LYTTELTON GELL, Esq. of Kirk Langley, Co. Derby.
(5) WILLIAM KID MACDONALD, Esq. of Windmill House, Arbroath.

PLATE XXXIX.

THE ARMORIAL BEARINGS OF—

(1) SIR HUMPHREY DE TRAFFORD, BART.
(2) WM. SPEKE, ESQ. OF JORDANS, CO. SOMERSET.
(3) DR A. ABERCROMBY, OF CAPE TOWN.
(4) SIR REGINALD WINGATE, K.C.B., K.C.M.G.

(5) THOMAS BONAR, CO. KENT—MATRICULATED 1812.
(6) ARTHUR FITZ HERBERT WRIGHT, ESQ. OF ALDECAR HALL.
(7) THEODORE NAPIER, ESQ. OF BALMANNO, EDINBURGH.
(8) LIND, OF CROYDON AND OPORTO.

PLATE XI.

VARIOUS EXAMPLES OF HERALDIC LIONS.

PLATE XLI.

HIS TRUTH SHALL BE THY SHIELD

THE ARMORIAL BEARINGS OF HANNEN, OF LONDON.

PLATE XLII.

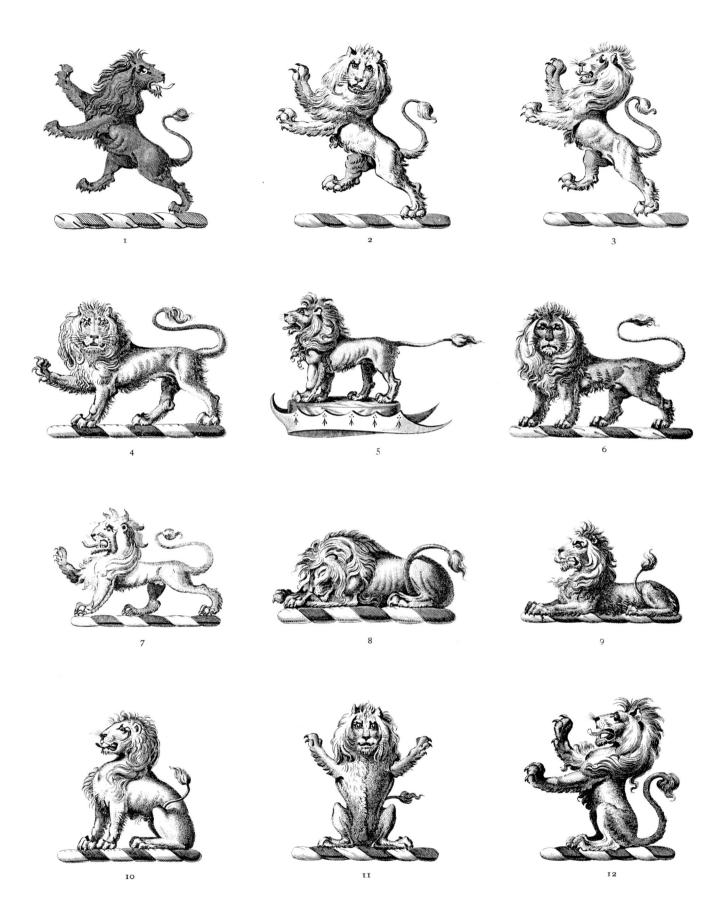

THE VARIOUS POSITIONS OF THE HERALDIC LION.
REPRODUCED FROM FAIRBAIRN'S BOOK OF CRESTS.

(1) Rampant regardant.	(3) Rampant.	(5) Statant with tail extended.	(7) Passant.	(9) Couchant.	(11) Sejant affronté erect.
(2) Rampant guardant.	(4) Passant guardant.	(6) Statant guardant.	(8) Dormant.	(10) Sejant.	(12) Sejant erect.

PLATE XLIII.

Ut · vinclo · vir · verbo · ligitur ·

THE ARMORIAL BEARINGS OF GEORGE ROBERT CLOVER, Esq. of Ramlé, Birkenhead.

PLATE XLIV.

THE ARMORIAL BEARINGS OF
COL. ALBERT CANTRELL CANTRELL-HUBBERSTY, ESQ. OF TOLLERTON HALL, NOTTS.

PLATE XLV.

THE ARMORIAL BEARINGS OF—

(1) JOHN ALEXANDER GALBRAITH, Esq.
(2) MATTHEW WILSON HERVEY, Esq.
(3) FRANCIS JAMES GRANT, Esq., Rothesay Herald and Lyon Clerk.

(4) ALBEMARLE O'BEIRNE WILLOUGHBY DEWAR, Esq. of "Doles" Hants.
(5) REGINALD HENRY TUDOR DRUMMOND, Esq. of Balquhandy.

PLATE XLVI.

HERALDIC MONSTERS.

PLATE XLVII.

THE HERALDIC EAGLE.

PLATE XLVIII.

THE ARMS OF CULLEN.
Or, an eagle displayed sable, beaked and membered gules.
DESIGNED BY MISS C. HELARD.

PLATE XLIX.

THE ARMORIAL BEARINGS OF GEORGE ANDREW HOBSON, Esq. of Coverdale Lodge, Richmond, Surrey.

wolf are included in the chapter upon mythical animals.

FIG. 262.—Arms of Alfred Scott Scott-Gatty, Esq., York Herald: Quarterly, 1 and 4, per fess sable and azure, in chief a demi-cat issuant guardant argent, and in base a shin-bone in bend surmounted by another in bend sinister, between four fleurs-de-lis or (for Gatty); 2 and 3, argent, gutté-de-poix, on a bend cottised azure, a mullet of six points pierced between two crescents of the first (for Scott); the escutcheon being encircled by his collar of SS); and impaling the arms of Foster, namely: ermine, a buglehorn vert, garnished and stringed or, on a chief arched gules two roses argent. Mantling sable and argent; and for his crests, 1. upon a wreath of the colours, a fern-brake, rising therefrom a cock pheasant all proper (for Gatty); 2. upon a wreath of the colours, on a mount vert, a stag trippant proper, gorged with a collar gemelle argent, and supporting with the sinister foreleg a trident in bend sinister or (for Scott); with the motto, "Cate at caute."

FIG. 263.—Armorial bearings of Rev. Montague Charles Alexander Baines, M.A.: Quarterly, 1. sable, a thigh-bone in pale surmounted by another in fess argent, between two crosses patée in bend or (for Baines); 2, argent, a bend sable, on a chief of the last three cushions of the first (for Johnson); 3. argent, a fess sable, a demi-lion rampant issuant gules, in base three mullets of six points azure (for Oeils); 4. argent, on a fess gules, a cross patée between two cross crosslets fitchée or (for Cuthbert). Mantling sable and argent. Crest: on a wreath of the colours, a dexter arm embowed, vested azure, cuff argent, the hand grasping a jaw-bone proper, on the arm a cross patée or. Motto: "Furor arma ministrat."

CHAPTER XV

THE HERALDIC LION

HERALDIC art without the lion would not amount to very much, for no figure plays such an important or such an extensive part in armory as the lion, in one or other of its many positions. These nowadays manifold positions are the results of modern differentiations, arising from the necessity of a larger number of varying coats of arms; but there can be little doubt that in early times the majority of these positions did not exist, having been gradually evolved, and that originally the heraldic animal was just "a lion." The shape of the shield was largely a governing factor in the manner in which we find it depicted; the old artists, with a keener artistic sense than is evidenced in so many later examples of heraldic design, endeavoured to fill up as large a proportion of the space available as was possible, and consequently when only one lion was to be depicted upon the shield they very naturally drew the animal in an upright position, this being the one most convenient and adaptable for their purpose. Probably their knowledge of natural history was very limited, and this upright position would seem to them the most natural, and probably was the only one they knew; at any rate, at first it is almost the only position to be found. A curious commentary upon this may be deduced from the head-covering of Geoffrey of Anjou (Fig. 41), which shows a lion. This lion is identically of the form and shape of the lions rampant upon the shield, but from the nature of the space it occupies, is what would now be termed statant; but there is at the same time no such alteration in the relative position of the limbs as would now be required. This would seem to indicate very clearly that there was but the one stereotyped pattern of a lion, which answered all their purposes, and that they applied that one pattern to the spaces they desired to decorate.

Early heraldry, however, when the various positions came into recognised use, soon sought to impose this definite distinction, that the *lion* could only be depicted erect in the *rampant* position, and that an animal represented to be walking must therefore be a *leopard* from the very position which it occupied. This, however, was a distinction known only to the more pedantic heralds, and found greatest favour amongst the French; but we find in Glover's Roll, which is a copy of a roll originally drawn up about the year 1250, that whilst he gives lions to six of the English earls, he commences with "le Roy d'Angleterre porte, Goules, trois lupards d'or." On the other hand, the monkish chronicler John of Harmoustier in Touraine (a contemporary writer) relates that when Henry I. chose Geoffrey, son of Foulk, Earl of Anjou, Tourain, and Main, to be his son-in-law, by marrying him to his only daughter and heir, Maud the Empress, and made him knight, after the bathing and other solemnities (pedes ejus solutaribus in superficie Leonculos aureos habentibus muniuntur), boots embroidered with golden lions were drawn on his legs, and also that (Clypeus Leonculos aureos imaginarios habens collo ejus suspenditur) a shield with lions of gold therein was hung about his neck.

It is, therefore, evident that the refinement of distinction between a lion and a leopard was not of the beginning; it is a later addition to the earlier simple term of lion. This distinction having been invented by French heralds, and we, taking so much of our heraldry, our language, and our customs from France, adopted, and to a certain extent used, this description

121   Q

of lions passant as "leopards." There can be no doubt, however, that the lions passant guardant upon the English shield have always been represented as *lions*,

FIG. 264.—Shield, helmet, and crest of Edward the Black Prince, suspended over his tomb in Canterbury Cathedral.

no matter what they may have been called, and the use of the term leopard in heraldry to signify a certain position for the lion never received any extensive sanction, and has long since become obsolete in British armory. In French blazon, however, the old distinction is still observed. The French lion is our lion rampant, the French leopard is our lion passant guardant, whilst they term our lion passant a *léopard-lionné*, and our lion rampant guardant is their *lion-léopardé*.

A lion rampant and any other beast of prey is usually represented in heraldry with the tongue and claws of a different colour from the animal. If it is not itself gules, its tongue and claws are usually represented as of that colour, unless the lion be on a field of gules. They are then represented azure, the term being "armed and langued" of such and such a colour. It is not necessary to mention that a lion is "armed and langued" in the blazon when they are emblazoned in gules, but whenever any other colour is introduced for the purpose it is better that it should be specified. Outside British heraldry a lion is always supposed to be rampant unless otherwise specifically described. The earliest appearance of the lions in the arms of any member of the Royal Family in England would appear to be the seal of King John when he was Prince and before he ascended the throne. This seal shows his arms to be two lions passant. The English Royal crest, which originated with Richard I., is now always depicted as a lion statant guardant. There can be no doubt, however, that this guardant attitude is a subsequent derivation from the position of the lions on the shield, when heraldry was ceasing to be actual and becoming solely pictorial. We find in the case of the crest of Edward the Black Prince, now suspended over his tomb in Canterbury Cathedral, that the lion upon the chapeau looks straight forward over the front of the helm (see Fig. 264).

Another ancient rule belonging to the same period as the controversy between leopards and lions was that there cannot be more than *one lion* upon a shield, and this was one of the great arguments used to determine that the charges on the Royal Arms of England must be leopards and not lions. It was admitted as a rule of British armory to a limited extent, viz. that when two or more lions rampant appear upon the same shield, unless they are combatant, they were always formerly described as lioncels. Thus the arms of Bohun are: "Azure, a bend argent, cottised between six lioncels rampant or" (Fig. 265). British heraldry has, however, long since disregarded any such rule (if any definite rule ever really existed upon the point), though curiously enough in the recent grant of arms to the town of Warrington (Fig. 51) the animals are there blazoned six "lioncels."

The artistic evolution of the lion rampant can be readily traced in the examples and explanations which follow, but, as will be understood, the employment in the case of some of these models cannot strictly be said to be confined within a certain number of years, though the details and periods given are roughly accurate, and sufficiently so to typify the changes which have occurred.

Until perhaps the second half of the thirteenth century the body of the lion appears straight upright ("*zum Grimmen geschickt* [set into a fury] rampant"), so that the head, the trunk, and the left hind-paw fall into the angle of the shield. The left fore-paw is horizontal, the right fore- and the right hind-paw are placed diagonally (or obliquely) upwards (Fig. 266). The paws each end in three knobs, similar to a clover leaf, out of which the claws come forth. The fourth or inferior toes appeared in heraldry somewhat later. The jaws are closed or only very slightly opened, without the tongue being visible. The tail is thickened in the middle with a bunch of longer hair and is turned down towards the body.

In the course of the period lasting from the second half of the thirteenth to the second half of the fourteenth centuries, the right hind-paw sinks lower until it forms a right angle with the left. The mouth grows pointed, and in the second half of the period the tongue becomes visible. The tail also shows a knot near its root (Fig. 267).

In examples taken from the second half of the fourteenth century and the fifteenth century the lion's body is no longer placed like a pillar, but lays its head back to the left so that the right fore-paw falls into an oblique upward line with the trunk. The toes are lengthened, appearing almost as fingers, and spread out from one another; the tail, adorned with flame-like bunches of hair, strikes outwards and loses the before-mentioned knot, which only remains visible in a forked

FIG. 265.—Arms of Humphrey de Bohun, Earl of Hereford (d. 1275): Azure, a bend argent, cottised or, between six lioncels of the last. (From MS. Reg. 14, C. vii.)

tail (queue-fourché). The jaws grow deep and are widely opened, and the breast rises and expands under the lower jaw (Fig. 268).

The actual evolution may perhaps be more readily grasped from the instances collected on Plate XL. by Herr Ströhl, which to the heraldic artist are distinctly instructive.

The notes relating to the figures upon Plate XL., it

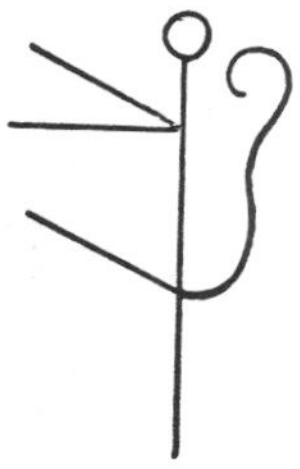

FIG. 266. 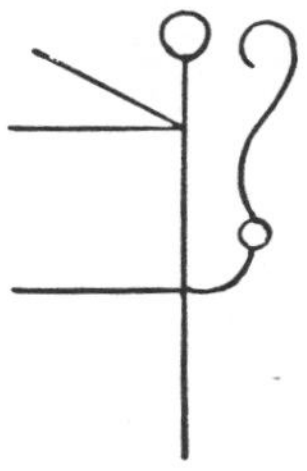   FIG. 267.   FIG. 268.

should be remarked, are not given here in the order in which they occur on the plate, but are arranged chronologically.

Fig. 1 (Plate XL.). Shield from the convent of Seedorf in the canton of Uri, from the first half of the thirteenth century. The shield shows: Azure, a lion rampant argent. The lion is so modelled that it is partially raised from the chalk background. In the base of the

FIG. 269.—Arms of Ulrich der Schenke von Hauspach.

shield appears a silver rectangle. The shield is one centimetre thick and made of firwood, is covered in front with parchment and at the back with leather. The nails visible in front served for the attaching of the shield-chain and arm-frames. Seedorf, originally a monastery, was founded in 1184 by Arnold v. Briens, and it is always possible that this shield belonged to some member of this family.

Fig. 2 (Plate XL.). Lion from the seal of "Karvlvs De. Gvtrat" in the year 1231.

Fig. 9 (Plate XL.). Lion from the seal of Heinrich von Silberberg (Kärnten), 1249. The legend runs: "Sigillvm Heinrici De Silberberch." The arms are probably: Gules, a lion rampant or, surmounting a bend argent.

Fig. 10 (Plate XL.). Lion from the shield of "Tancredi De Rosciano."

Fig. 3 (Plate XL.). Lion from the seal of a Schenk von Hausbach (Lower Austria), of the year 1250. The seal legend runs: "S. Heinrici De Havspach Pincerne." The arms are: Argent, a lion rampant sable, crowned gules. The Vienna Minoriten Necrologium (Index or Register of the patrons of the order buried in the Monastery of the Minoriten), drawn up at the turn of the fourteenth century, also contains, amongst many other coats of arms, that of a Schenken von Hausbach (Fig. 269), with an exquisitely conventionalised lion.

Fig. 4 (Plate XL.). Lion from the seal of Ezelinus von Egna (Enn, near Neumarkt, in S. Tyrol), on a document dated May 28, 1276. The seal legend runs: "Sigillvm Ecerini De Egna," and the arms are: Azure, a lion rampant argent, armed or. The gravestone of Wilhelmus de Enna, died 1335, is of great heraldic

FIG. 270.—Arms of Strange and Talbot. (From a design for a banner.)

interest, inasmuch as there are on the shield two pail-helmet rests facing one another. It is probably the oldest example of such a position.

Fig. 12 (Plate XL.). Arms of the kingdom of Bohemia, from the monument of Przemisl Ottokar I. in St Veit's Cathedral at Prague, fourteenth century. The lion is there represented in low relief, and is crowned. The lion rampant argent crowned or on a field gules has been the territorial arms of Bohemia since the second half of the thirteenth century.

Fig. 6 (Plate XL.). Armorial shield of "Lewppolt von Ekchartsaw" (beginning of fifteenth century). The arms are: Sable, a lion rampant argent, crowned and chained, the chain hanging down the back or. The shield is taken from the Sti Christophori Bruderschaftsbuche von Arlberg (the "Book of the Brotherhood of St. Christopher of Arlberg"). Further examples of arms from this source will be found in the latter part of the volume.

Fig. 7 (Plate XL.). Armorial shield from Conrad Grünenberg's Wappenbuch, 1483, the arms being there ascribed to "Das Land von Rusen" (Reuss). The narrow white border of the shield there shown has here been omitted as superfluous. The arms on the shield are: Sable, a lion rampant, armed and eyed gules. This lion is magnificently drawn.

THE ART OF HERALDRY

Fig. 5 (Plate XL.). Armorial shield of Paulus Hector Mair (Augsburg, 1550) by an unknown artist. As a charge appears a lion brandishing a club (or Pusikan).

Fig. 13 (Plate XL.). Armorial shield of the Dukes of Swabia: Or, three lions passant guardant in pale sable. The two last drawings are from Jost Amman's hand

FIG. 271.

FIG. 273.—Lion rampant.
(By Mr. G. Scruby.)

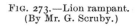

FIG. 274.—Lion passant guardant.
(By Mr. G. Scruby.)

FIG. 272.—Lions. (Drawn by Mr. J. Forbes Nixon.)

FIG. 275.—Lion rampant.
(By Mr. G. Scruby.)

FIG. 276.—Lion rampant and lion statant guardant, by Mr. G. W. Eve. (From "Decorative Heraldry.")

FIG. 277.—Lion statant, lion passant guardant, and lion passant regardant, by Mr. G. W. Eve. (From "Decorative Heraldry.")

Fig. 11 (Plate XL.). Armorial shield of the Counts Palatine of the Rhine: Sable, a lion rampant, crowned gules.

and are taken from the Tournament Book of the Count Palatine's Herald George Rixner, surnamed "Jerusalem," 1566.

Lions of peculiar virility and beauty appear upon a fourteenth-century banner which shows the arms of the family of Talbot, Earls of Shrewsbury: Gules, a lion rampant within a bordure engrailed or, quartered with the arms of *Strange*: Argent, two lions passant in pale gules, armed and langued azure. Fig. 270 gives the lower half of the banner which was published in colours in the Catalogue of the Heraldic Exhibition in London, 1894. Other examples from the series will be found on Plates LXXXII. and LXXXIII.

Fig. 8 (Plate XL.) shows the arms of St. Gimignano, in the province of Siena. The shield is: Per fess gules and or, a lion rampant argent. This shield, with the conventionalised lion of a genuinely Italian type, is taken from the work on the arms of Tuscan towns, *Le Armi dei Municipj Toscani*, Florence, 1864, by L. Passerini.

Fig. 271 is an Italian coat of arms of the fourteenth century, and shows a lion of almost exactly the same design, except the paws are here rendered somewhat

passant crowned. A lion passant. A lion rampant. A lion rampant to the sinister. A lion passant guardant, ducally gorged. A lion statant guardant, ducally

FIG. 279.—Armorial bearings of Alexander Charles Richards Maitland, Esq.: Or, a lion rampant gules, couped in all his joints of the field, within a double tressure flory and counterflory azure, a bordure engrailed ermine. Mantling gules and or. Crest: upon a wreath of his liveries, a lion sejant erect and affronté gules, holding in his dexter paw a sword proper, hilted and pommelled gold, and in his sinister a fleur-de-lis argent. Motto: "Consilio et animis."

FIG. 278.—Armorial bearings of Arthur Lazenby Liberty, Esq., of The Lee Manor, Great Missenden, Bucks: Per fess azure and gules, a tower between two fleurs-de-lis in chief and a lion passant in base, all or. Mantling azure and or. Crest: on a wreath of the colours, in front of a tower gules, a lion passant, holding in the dexter forepaw a fleur-de-lis, both or. Motto: "Libertas." (Reproduced from a painting by Mr. G. W. Eve, R.E.)

more heraldically. The painting (azure, a lion rampant argent) served as an "Ex libris," and bears the inscription "Libe accusacionum mey p. he . . ." (The remainder has been cut away.) It is reproduced from Warnecke's "German Bookplates," 1890.

When we come to modern examples of lions, it is evident that the artists of the present day very largely copy lions which are really the creations of, or adaptations from, the work of their predecessors. The lions of Mr. Forbes Nixon, as shown in Fig. 272, which were specially drawn by him at my request as typical of his style, are respectively as follows:—

A winged lion passant coward. A lion rampant regardant. A lion rampant queue-fourché. A lion

FIG. 280.—Armorial bearings of Capt. Michael James Hughes, of Sherdley Hall: Gules, two lions passant in pale, and in chief a rose argent, in the dexter chief point a mullet for difference. Mantling gules and argent. Crest: out of a coronet or, a demi-lion rampant argent, holding in the paws a rose gules, slipped vert. Motto: "Heb Dduw heb ddim, Duw a digon."

crowned. A lion rampant. A lion statant guardant. A lion sejant guardant erect. The lions on the cover of this volume, however, are far better examples of Mr. Forbes Nixon's artistic power. Lions drawn by Mr. Scruby will be found in Figs. 273, 274, and 275, which are respectively: "Argent, a lion rampant sable," "Sable, a lion passant guardant argent," and "Sable, a lion rampant argent." These again were specially drawn by Mr. Scruby as typical of his style.

The lions of Mr. Eve would seem to be entirely original. Their singularly graceful form and proportions are perhaps best shown by Figs. 276 and 277, which are taken from his book "Decorative Heraldry." His lions upon the Windsor Castle bookplates, which will be figured later, are worthy of notice, as are the lions in the arms of Liberty (see Fig. 278).

The lions of Mr. Graham Johnston can be appreciated from the examples of the arms of Eyton[a] (Plate XXXIV.), Hervey[b] (Plate XLV.), Maitland (Fig. 279), and Hughes (Fig. 280).

Examples of lions drawn by Miss Helard will be found in Figs. 281, 282, 283.

FIG. 281.—Bookplate of Rev. F. B. Dickinson. (Designed by Miss C. Helard.)

Good examples of lions drawn after the old-fashioned naturalistic type will be found on Plate XLII. These are from "Knight and Rumley" and Fairbairn's "Book of Crests." They are all represented as crests, and are respectively: (1) Rampant regardant; (2) rampant guardant; (3) rampant; (4) passant guardant; (5) statant tail extended; (6) statant guardant; (7) passant; (8) dormant; (9) couchant; (10) sejant; (11) sejant affronté erect; and (12) sejant erect.

To revert to rather more ancient examples of lions, it will be noticed that although closely following upon the German lines which Herr Ströhl has traced, the development in England has not been quite identical.

[a] Armorial bearings of Eyton. Arms: ermine, a lion rampant gules. Crest: a demi-lion rampant, holding between the paws a ducal coronet all or. Motto: "Fy nûw fy ngwlad a'i gwyrthiau."

[b] Armorial bearings of Matthew Wilson Hervey, Esq., M.I.C.E.: Parted per chevron gules and vert, a fess chequy argent and azure between three trefoils slipped or, all within a bordure of the fourth. Mantling gules, doubled or. Crest: upon a wreath of his liveries, a demi-lion rampant gules, holding in his dexter paw a trefoil slipped or. Motto: "Delectat et ornat."

Some of the earliest known English examples will be found on Plates LXXI. and LXXII., and those in Prince Arthur's Book (Plates XCIX. and C.), and the extravagant creatures on Plates LXXXV. and LXXXVI. may be taken as typical of their period. Other examples which will be appreciated are given in Figs. 284–291.

Some number of lions as supporters, from various

FIG. 282.—A lion rampant. (By Miss Helard.)

sources and by different artists, will be found in the chapter devoted to Supporters.

The various positions which modern heraldry has evolved for the lions, together with the terms of blazon used to describe these positions, are as follows:—

Lion rampant.—The animal is here depicted in profile, and erect, resting upon its sinister hind paw (see Figs. 273 and 275). Amongst the many families which bear the lion rampant may be mentioned the family of Price (Barts.) who bear: Gules, a lion rampant argent (see Plate XXXIV.).

Lion rampant guardant.—In this case the head

FIG. 283.—A lion rampant. (By Miss Helard.)

of the lion is turned to face the spectator (Plate XLII. Fig. 2).

Lion rampant regardant.—In this case the head is turned completely round, looking backwards (Plate XLII. Fig. 1).

Lion rampant double-queued.—In this case the lion is represented as having two tails. These must both be apparent from the base of the tail, otherwise confusion will arise with the next example.

Lion rampant queue-fourché.—In this case one tail

springs from the base, which is divided or "forked" in the centre. There is no doubt that whilst in modern

FIG. 284.—Arms of Hugh de Albini, Earl of Arundel (d. 1243): Gules, a lion rampant or. (MS. Cott., Nero, D. I.)

FIG. 285.—Arms of William Marshall, Earl of Pembroke (d. 1234): Per pale vert and or, a lion rampant gules. (MS. Cott., Nero, D. I.)

FIG. 286.—Arms of Edmund, Earl of Cornwall: Argent, a lion rampant gules, crowned or, within a bordure sable, bezanté. (From his seal, 1275.)

FIG. 287.—Arms of Richard Fitz Alan, Earl of Arundel (d. 1302): Gules, a lion rampant or. (From his seal.)

FIG. 288.—Arms of Lyon de Welles, Baron de Welles: Or, a lion rampant sable, queue-fourché, armed gules. (From his seal, 1447.)

FIG. 289.—Arms of Mowbray (d. 1461): Gules, a lion rampant or. He more usually used the arms of England with a label argent. (From a seal of John Mowbray.)

FIG. 290.—Arms of William Herbert, Earl of Pembroke (d. 1469): Per pale gules and azure, three lions rampant argent. (From MS. Reg. 18, D. ii.)

FIG. 291.—Arms of John de Mowbray, Earl of Nottingham. (From MS. Ashmole, 804, iv.)

times and with regard to modern arms this distinction must be adhered to, anciently queue-fourché and double-queued were interchangeable terms.

Lion rampant tail nowed.—The tail is here tied in a knot. It is not a term very frequently met with, but an example will be found in the arms of Bewes (Fig. 292).

Lion rampant tail elevated and turned over its head.—The only instances of the existence of this curious variation which have come under my own notice occur in the coats of two families of the name of Buxton, the one being obviously a modern grant founded upon the other.

Lion rampant with two heads.—This occurs in the coat of arms, probably founded on an earlier instance, granted in 1739 to Mason of Greenwich, the arms being: "Per fess ermine and azure, a lion rampant with two heads counterchanged." This curious charge had been adopted by Mason's College in Birmingham, and on the foundation of Birmingham University it was incorporated in its arms (Fig. 293).

Lion rampant guardant bicorporated.—In this case the lion has one head and two bodies. An instance of

FIG. 292.—Armorial bearings of Cecil Edward Bewes, Esq.: Argent, a lion rampant tail nowed gules, gorged with an Eastern crown or, in chief three falcons proper, belled of the third. Mantling gules and argent. Crest: on a chapeau gules, turned up ermine, a Pegasus rearing on his hind legs, of a bright bay colour, mane and tail sable, wings displayed or, holding in the mouth a laurel branch proper. Motto: "Major ab adversis."

this curious creature will be seen in the arms of Attewater (Plate XCIX.).

Lion rampant tricorporate.—In this case three bodies are united in one head. Both this and the preceding variety are most unusual, but the tricorporate lion occurs in a coat of arms (*temp.* Car. II.) registered in Ulster's Office: "Or, a tricorporate lion rampant, the bodies disposed in the dexter and sinister chief points and in base, all meeting in one head guardant in the fess point sable."

Lion coward.—In this case the tail of the lion is depressed, passing between its hind legs. The exactitude of this term is to some extent modern. Though a lion cowarded was known in ancient days, there can be no doubt that formerly an artist felt himself quite at liberty to put the tail between the legs if this seemed artistically desirable, without necessarily having interfered with the arms by so doing.

Lion couped in all its joints is a charge which seems

FIG. 293.—The Seal of the University of Birmingham. (Actual size. Designed by Mr. G. W. Eve, R.E.). The Arms are : Per chevron, the chief per pale gules and azure, in dexter a lion rampant with two heads, in sinister a mermaid holding in the dexter hand a mirror, and in the sinister a comb or, the base sable charged with an open book proper with two buckles and straps and edges of the third, inscribed "Per ardua ad alta" of the fourth. (Granted August 27, 1900.)

peculiar to the family of Maitland, and it would be interesting to learn to what source its origin can be traced. It is represented with each of its four paws, its head and its tail severed from the body, and removed slightly away therefrom. A Maitland coat of arms exhibiting this peculiarity will be found in Fig. 279.

Lions rampant combatant are so termed when two are depicted in one shield facing each other in the attitude of fighting.

A very curious and unique instance of a lion rampant occurs in the arms of Williams (matriculated in Lyon Register in 1862, as the second and third quarterings of the arms of Sir James Williams Drummond of Hawthornden), the coat in question being : "Argent, a lion rampant, the body sable, the head, paws, and tuft of the tail of the field."

Lion passant.—A lion in this position is represented in the act of walking, the dexter forepaw being raised, but all three others being upon the ground. An example of lions passant occurs in the case of the arms of Ambrose (see Plate XXX.) and Strangways (see Plate XCIX.). These same arms of Strangeways are now borne within a bordure by Mr. L. R. Strangways (Fig. 294).

Lion passant guardant.—This is the same as the previous position, except that the head is turned to face the spectator (Plate XLII. Fig. 4). The lions in the quartering for England in the Royal coat of arms are "three lions passant guardant in pale." Examples of the Royal lions will be found in Fig. 295, which at the same time strikingly illustrates the greater freedom and virility of the work of the older artists.

Lion of England.—This is "a lion passant guardant or," and the term is only employed for a lion of this description when it occurs as or in an honourable augmentation then being usually represented on a field of gules. Lions passant guardant or, are now never granted to any applicant except under a specific Royal

Warrant to that effect. It occurs in many augmentations, *e.g.* Wolfe, Camperdown, and many others ; and when three lions passant guardant or upon a canton gules are granted, as in the arms of Lane (Fig. 57), the augmentation is termed a "canton of England."

Lion passant regardant is as the lion passant, but with the head turned right round looking behind. A lion is not often met with in this position.

Lions passant dimidiated.—A curious survival of the ancient but now obsolete practice of dimidiation is found in the arms of several English seaport towns. Doubtless all can be traced to the "so-called" arms of the "Cinque Ports,"[c] which show three lions passant guardant dimidiated with the hulls of three ships. There can be no doubt whatever that this originally came from the dimidiation of two separate coats, viz. the Royal Arms of England (the three lions passant guardant), and the other "azure, three ships argent," typical of the Cinque Ports, referring perhaps to the protection of the coasts for which they were liable, or possibly merely to their seaboard position. Whilst Sandwich[d] uses the two separate coats simply dimidiated upon one shield, the arms of Hastings[e] vary slightly, being : "Party per pale gules and azure, a lion passant guardant or, between in chief and in base a lion passant guardant of the last dimidiated with the hull a ship argent." From long usage we have grown acccustomed to consider these two conjoined and dimidiated figures as one figure, and in the recent grant of arms to Ramsgate[3] a figure of this kind was granted as a simple charge.

FIG. 294.—Armorial bearings of Leonard Richard Fleming Strangways, Esq., of Merton, Cullenswood, co. Dublin : Sable, two lions passant paly of six argent and gules, within a bordure engrailed or. Mantling sable and or. Crest : on a wreath of the colours, a lion as in the arms, gorged with a ducal coronet or. Motto : "Soys joyeux et ne doubte point."

[c] Arms of Sandwich : Party per pale gules and azure, three demi-lions passant guardant or, conjoined to the hulks of as many ships argent.

[d] Arms of Hastings : Party per pale gules and azure, a lion passant guardant or, between in chief and in base a lion passant guardant or, dimidiated with the hull of a ship argent.

[e] Arms of Ramsgate : Quarterly gules and azure, a cross parted and fretty argent between a horse rampant of the last in the first quarter, a demi-lion passant guardant of the third conjoined to the hulk of a ship or in the second, a dolphin naiant proper in the third, and a lymphad also or in the fourth. Crest : a naval crown or, a pier-head, thereon a lighthouse, both proper. Motto : "Salus naufragis salus ægris."

128

The arms of Yarmouth [f] afford another instance of a resulting figure of this class, the three lions passant guardant of England being here dimidiated with as many herrings naiant.

Lion statant.—The distinction between a lion passant and a lion statant is that the lion statant (Plate XLII. Fig. 6) has all four paws resting upon the ground. The two forepaws are sometimes placed together. Whilst

Lion statant guardant.—This (crowned) is of course the Royal crest of England, and examples of it will be found in the arms of the Sovereign and other descendants, legitimate and illegitimate, of Sovereigns of this country. An exceptionally fine rendering of it occurs in the Windsor Castle Bookplates, which are reproduced in a later chapter.

Lion salient.—This, which is a very rare position

FIG. 295.—The Arms of Edward III. (From his tomb in Westminster Abbey.)

but seldom met with as a charge upon a shield, it is by no means rare as a crest.

Lion statant tail extended.—This term is a curious and, seemingly, a purposeless refinement, resulting from the perpetuation in certain cases of one particular method of depicting the crest—originally when a crest a lion was always so drawn—but it cannot be overlooked, because in the crests of both Talbot, Earl of Shrewsbury, and Percy, Duke of Northumberland, the crest is now stereotyped as a lion in this form upon a chapeau (see Plate XLII. Fig. 5).

f Arms of Yarmouth : Party per pale gules and azure, three demi-lions passant guardant or, conjoined to the bodies of as many herrings argent. Motto : " Rex et nostra jura."

for a lion, represents it in the act of springing, the *two* hind legs being on the ground, the others in the air. An instance of a lion salient will be found in the arms of Keegan (Fig. 296).

Lion salient guardant.—There is no reason why the lion salient may not be guardant or regardant, though an instance of the use of either does not come to mind.

Lion sejant.—Very great laxity is found in the terms applied to lions sejant, consequently care is necessary to distinguish the various forms. The true lion sejant is as in Plate XLII. Fig. 10, *i.e.* represented in profile, seated on its haunches, with the forepaws resting on the ground.

Lion sejant guardant.—This is as the foregoing, but with the face (only) turned to the spectator, as in the crest of Sir James Balfour Paul, Lyon King of Arms (Plate IV.).

Lion sejant regardant.—In this the head is turned right back to gaze behind.

Lion sejant erect (or, as it is sometimes not very happily termed, sejant-rampant).—In this position the lion is sitting upon its haunches, but the body is erect, and it has its forepaws raised in the air (Plate XLII. Fig. 12).

FIG. 296.—Armorial bearings of Edward Wells Keegan, Esq.: Gules, a lion salient, crowned, and holding in the dexter paw a crescent all or, a chief nebuly of the last. Mantling gules and or. Crest: on a wreath of the colours, a dexter hand holding a sheaf of five arrows all proper, charged on the wrist with a harp or, stringed argent. Motto: "Nunquam non paratus."

In this form it occurs in a crest of Goodwin ["A lion sejant guardant erect sable, holding between the paws a lozenge vair"].

Lion sejant guardant erect is as the last figure, but the head faces the spectator.

Lion sejant regardant erect is as the foregoing, but with the head turned right round to look backwards.

Lion sejant affronté.—In this case the lion is seated on its haunches, but *the whole body* is turned to face the spectator, the forepaws resting upon the ground in front of its body. Ugly as this position is, and impossible as it might seem, it certainly is to be found in some of the early rolls.

Lion sejant erect affronté (Fig. 279).—This position is by no means unusual in Scotland. A lion sejant erect and affronté, &c., is the Royal crest of Scotland, and it will also be found in the arms of Lyon Office (see Plate IV.).

A good representation of the lion sejant affronté and erect is shown in Fig. 297, which is taken from Jost Amman's *Wappen und Stammbuch* (1589). It represents the arms of the celebrated Lansquenet Captain Sebastian Schärtlin (Schertel) von Burtenbach

FIG. 297.—Arms of Sebastian Schärtlin von Burtenbach.

["Gules, a lion sejant affronté erect, double-queued, holding in its dexter paw a key argent, and in its sinister a fleur-de-lis 'eradicated'"]. His victorious assault on Rome in 1527, and his striking successes against France in 1532, are strikingly typified in these arms, which were granted in 1534.

Lion couchant (Plate XLII. Fig. 9).—In this position the lion is represented lying down, but the head is erect and alert. An instance will be found in the arms of Sir Lawrence Jones, Bart. ["Azure, on a fess or, three grenades fired proper, in chief a castle and over it the word 'Netherlands' in letters of gold, and in base a lion couchant argent. Crest: in front of a castle argent, a lion couchant or, gorged with a wreath of laurel and pendent therefrom an escutcheon

gules charged with a representation of the Badajoz medal as in the arms. Motto: 'Marte et arte'"].

Lion dormant (Plate XLII. Fig. 8).—A lion dormant is in much the same position as a lion couchant, except that the eyes are closed, and the head rests on the extended forepaws. Lions dormant are seldom met with, but they occur in the arms of Lloyd, of Stockton Hall, near York ["Argent, three lions dormant in pale sable between two flaunches of the last, each charged with three mullets palewise of the first. Mantling sable and argent. Crest: on a wreath of the colours, in front of a cubit arm vested azure, cuff argent, the hand grasping a lizard fesswise proper, a lion dormant sable"].

Lion morné.—This is a lion without teeth and claws, but no instance of the use of the term would appear to exist in British armory. Woodward mentions amongst other Continental examples the arms of the old French family of De Mornay ["Fascé d'argent et de gueules au lion morné de sable, couronné d'or brochant sur le tout"].

Lions as supporters.—Refer to the chapter on Supporters.

Winged lion (Fig. 298).—The winged lion—usually known as the lion of St. Mark—is not infrequently met

FIG. 298.—The Arms of Markham.

with. It will be found both passant and sejant, but more frequently the latter, in which position it will be found in the arms and crest of Sir John Mark. These are: "Azure, on a rock in base proper, a lion of St. Mark sejant, with wings addorsed or, resting the dexter paw upon an escutcheon of the last charged with a bee volant of the second, on a chief also or, a terrestrial globe also proper between two saltires couped gules. Mantling azure and or. Crest: upon a wreath of the colours, a lion as in the arms, semé of bees volant proper, and resting the dexter paw upon a rose gules; with the motto, 'Manu et corde.'" It also occurs in the crest of Markham ["the lion of St. Mark sejant guardant supporting a harp"] (Fig. 298) and Domenichetti. The true lion of St. Mark (that is, when used as a badge for sacred purposes to typify St. Mark) is illustrated later. Winged lions are the supporters of Lord Braye.

Sea lion (or, to use another name for it, a *morse*) is the head, forepaws, and upper part of a lion conjoined to the tail of a fish. The most frequent form in which sea lions appear are as supporters, but they are also met with as crests and charges. When placed horizontally they are termed naiant. Sea lions, however, will also be found "sejant" and "sejant-erect." When issuing from waves of the sea they are termed "assurgeant." A sea lion's head appears in the arms of Pollard (Fig. 299).

Lion-dragon.—One hesitates to believe this creature has any existence outside heraldry books, where it is stated to be of similar form and construction to the sea lion, the difference being that the lower half is the body and tail of a wyvern. I know of no arms in which it figures.

Man-lion or *man-tiger.*—This is as a lion but with a human face. Two of these are the supporters of Lord Huntingdon, and one was granted to the late Lord Donington as a supporter (Fig. 300), whilst as charges they also occur in the arms of Radford (Fig. 301).

FIG. 299.—Armorial bearings of Rear-Admiral E. J. Pollard, of Haynford Hall, co. Norfolk: Azure, a chevron ermine between two crosses fleury in chief and a sea lion's head erased in base or, impaling the arms of Hawkins-Whitshed, namely: quarterly, 1 and 4, party per pale indented argent and vert, three demi-lions rampant, those in chief respectively gules and or, and the one in base party per pale indented of the third and fourth (for Whitshed); 2 and 3, party per chevron argent and vert, three hinds trippant (for Hawkins). Mantling azure and argent. Crest: upon a wreath of the colours, a stag trippant proper, holding in the mouth two wheat ears or, gorged with a collar and therefrom pendent a cross fleury of the last; with the motto, "Fortiter Deo juvante."

This semi-human animal is sometimes termed a "lympago."

Other terms relating to lions occur in many heraldic works—both old and new—but their use is very limited, if indeed of some, any example at all could be found in British armory. In addition to this, whilst the fact may sometimes exist, the *term* has never been adopted or officially recognised. Personally I believe most of the terms which follow may for all practical purposes be entirely disregarded. Amongst such terms are *contourné*, applied to a lion passant or rampant to the sinister. It would, however, be found blazoned in these words and not as contourné. "Dismembered," "Demembré," "Dechaussée," and "Trononnée" are all "heraldry-book" terms specified to mean the same as "couped in all its joints," but the uselessness and uncertainty concerning these terms is exemplified by the

fact that the same books state "dismembered" or "demembré" to mean (when applied to a lion) that

FIG. 300.—Arms of the late Lord Donington, showing a man-lion as the dexter supporter.

the animal is shown without legs or tail. The term "embrued" is sometimes applied to a lion to signify that its mouth is bloody and dropping blood; and "vulned" signifies wounded, heraldically represented by a blotch of gules, from which drops of blood are falling. A lion "disarmed" is without teeth, tongue, or claws.

A term often found in relation to lions rampant, but by no means peculiar thereto, is "debruised." This is

FIG. 301.—Armorial bearings of Radford: Per pale sable and argent, three lions passant in pale counterchanged, with human faces proper, between two flanches also counterchanged, a chief arched ermine (a mullet for difference). Mantling sable and argent. Crest: on a wreath of the colours, a lion salient guardant argent, guttée-de-sang, with a human face proper, holding in the dexter forepaw a rose argent, slipped and leaved, and resting the sinister on the point of a sword erect also proper, pommel and hilt or.

used when it is partly defaced by another charge (usually an ordinary) being placed over it. Instances of this will be found in the arms of Beaumont (Fig. 86).

Another of these guide-book terms is "decollated," which is said to be employed in the case of a lion which has its head cut off. A lion "defamed" or "diffamed" is supposed to be rampant to the sinister but looking backwards, the supposition being that the animal is being (against his will) chased off the field with infamy. A lion "evire" is supposed to be emasculated and without signs of sex. In this respect it is interesting to note that in earlier days, before mock modesty and prudery had become such prominent features of our national life, the genital organ was always represented of a pronounced size in a prominent position, and it was as much a matter of course to paint it gules as it now is to depict the tongue of that colour.

Lions placed back to back are termed "endorsed" or "addorsed," but when two lions passant in pale are represented, one passing to the dexter and one to the sinister, they are termed "counter-passant." This term is, however, also used sometimes when they are merely passant towards each other, as in the arms of Lafone (Fig. 302) or Lord Gardner ["Or, on a chevron gules

FIG. 302.—Bookplate of Alfred Lafone, Esq. Arms: azure, within two chevronels or, two lions passant counter-passant of the last, supporting a fleur-de-lis argent, the whole between three mullets argent, pierced of the field. Upon the escutcheon is placed a helmet befitting his degree, with a mantling azure and or; and for his crest, upon a wreath of the colours, a lion sable, charged on the body with a fleur-de-lis argent, gorged with a collar nebuly and ducally crowned or, resting the dexter forepaw on a mullet as in the arms. Motto: "Fidus ut olim."

between three griffins' heads erased azure, an anchor erect, between two lions guardant counter-passant chevronwise of the field. Crest: A demi-griffin azure, collared and lined, and supporting in the claws an anchor or. Motto: 'Valet anchora virtus.' Supporters: two griffins, wings elevated azure, beaked, membered, and gorged with a naval coronet or, each resting the interior hind foot on an anchor, with cable sable"]. A more correct description in either of these cases would be passant "respecting" or "regarding" each other.

The term *lionné* is one stated to be used with animals other than lions when placed in a rampant position. Whilst doubtless of regular acceptation in French heraldry as applied to a leopard, it is unknown in English, and the term rampant is indifferently applied; e.g. in the case of a leopard, wolf, or tiger when in the rampant position.

Lionced is a term seldom met with, but it is said to be applied (for example to a cross) when the arms end in lions' heads. I have yet to find an authentic example of the use of such a cross.

When a bend or other ordinary issues from the mouths of lions (or other animals), the heads issuing from the edges or angles of the escutcheon, the ordinary is said to be "engouled."

A curious term, of the use of which I know only one example, is "fleshed" or "flayed." This, as doubtless will be readily surmised, means that the skin is removed, leaving the flesh gules. This was the method

by which the supporters of Wurtemburg were "differenced" for the Duke of Teck, the forepaws being "fleshed."

Woodward gives the following very curious instances of the lion in heraldry :—

"Only a single example of the use of the lioness as a heraldic charge is known to me. The family of COING, in Lorraine, bears: d'Azure, à une lionne arrêtée d'or.

"The following fourteenth-century examples of the use of the lion as a heraldic charge are taken from the oft-quoted *Wappenrolle von Zurich*, and should be of interest to the student of early armory :—

.   .   .   .

"51. END: Azure, a lion rampant-guardant argent, its feet or.

"305. WILDENVELS: Per pale argent and sable, in the first a demi-lion statant-guardant issuant from the dividing line.

"408. TANNENVELS: Azure, a lion rampant or, queué argent.

"489. RINACH: Or, a lion rampant gules, headed azure.

"A curious use of the lion as a charge occurs in several ancient coats of the Low Countries, e.g. in that of TRASEGNIES, whose arms are: Bandé d'or et d'azur, à l'ombre du lion brochant sur le tout, à la bordure engrêlée d'or. Here the ombre du lion is properly represented by a darker shade of the tincture (either of or or of azure), but often the artist contents himself with simply drawing the outline of the animal in a neutral tint.

"Among other curiosities of the use of the lion are the following foreign coats :—

"BOISSIAU, in France, bears : De gueules, semé de lions d'argent.

"MINUTOLI, of Naples : Gules, a lion rampant vair, the head and feet or.

"LOEN, of Holland : Azure, a decapitated lion rampant argent, three jets of blood spurting from the neck proper.

"PAPACODA, of Naples : Sable, a lion rampant or, its tail turned over its head and held by its teeth.

"The Counts REINACH, of Franconia : Or, a lion rampant gules, hooded and masked azure (see above)."

To these instances the arms of Westbury may well be added, these being : Quarterly, or and azure, a cross patonce, on a bordure twenty lions rampant all counterchanged. No doubt the origin of such a curious bordure is to be found in the "bordure of England," which, either as a mark of cadency or as an indication of affinity or augmentation, can be found in some number of instances. Probably one will suffice as an example. This is forthcoming in Fig. 76, which shows the arms of John de Bretagne, Earl of Richmond. Of a similar nature is the bordure of Spain (indicative of his maternal descent) borne by Richard of Conisburgh, Earl of Cambridge, who bore: Quarterly France and England, a label of three points argent, each charged with as many torteaux, on a bordure of the same twelve lions rampant purpure (Fig. 303). Before leaving the lion, the hint may perhaps be usefully conveyed that the temptation to over-elaborate the lion when depicting it heraldically should be carefully avoided. The only result is confusion—the very contrary of the essence of heraldic emblazonment, which was, is, and should be, the method of clear advertisement of identity. Examples of over-elaboration can, however, be found in the past, as will be seen from Fig. 304. This example belongs to the latter half of the fifteenth century, and represents the arms of Bohemia. It is taken from a shield on the "Pulver Turme" at Prague.

Parts of lions are very frequently to be met with,

particularly as crests. In fact the most common crest is the *demi-lion rampant*. This is the upper half of a lion rampant. It is comparatively seldom found other than rampant and couped, so that the term "a demi-lion," unless otherwise qualified, may always be assumed to be a demi-lion rampant couped. As charges upon the shield three will be found in the arms of Bennet, Earl of Tankerville ["Gules, a bezant between three demi-lions rampant argent. Crests: 1. out of a

mural coronet or, a lion's head gules, charged on the neck with a bezant. Supporters: two lions argent, ducally crowned or, each charged on the shoulder with a torteau"], and it appears as the crest of Hannen [g] (Plate XLI.).

The demi-lion may be both guardant and regardant.

Demi-lions rampant and erased are more common as charges than as crests. They are to be found in many Harrison coats of arms.

Demi-lions passant are rather unusual, but in addition to the seeming cases in which they occur by dimidiation they are sometimes found, as in the arms of Newman (Fig. 305).

Demi-lion affronté.—The only case which has come

FIG. 304.—Arms of Bohemia, from the "Pulver Turme" at Prague. (Latter half of the fifteenth century.)

under notice would appear to be the crest of Campbell of Aberuchill.

Demi-lion issuant.—This term is applied to a demi-lion when it issues from an ordinary, *e.g.* from the base line of the chief, as in the arms of Dormer, Markham, and Abney; or from behind a fess, as in the arms of Chalmers.

[g] Armorial bearings of the late Hon. James Chitty Hannen, B.A.; Sable, a demi-lion between three portcullises or, within a bordure of the last. Mantling sable and or. Crest: on a wreath of the colours, a demi-lion sable, gorged with a collar, and therefrom pendent from a chain an escutcheon or, charged with a portcullis sable. Motto: "His truth shall be thy shield."

Demi-lion naissant issues from the centre of an ordinary, and not from behind it.

Lions' heads, both couped and erased, are very fre-

FIG. 305.—Armorial bearings of John Robert Branston Newman, Esq. Argent, a chief azure, a chevron between three demi-lions passant gules, impaling the arms of Plunket. Mantling gules and argent. Crest: an eagle's head erased azure, charged with a scollop or. Motto: "Fidelitatis vis Magna."

FIG. 306.—Bookplate of Francis Alexander Newdigate, Esq. Arms: Gules, three lions' gambs erased argent, impaling the arms of Bagot, namely: ermine, two chevronels azure. Mantling gules and argent. Crest: on a wreath of the colours, a fleur-de-lis argent. Motto: "Foyall loyall."

quently met with both as charges on the shield and as crests.

Lion's gamb.—Many writers make a distinction between the *gamb* (which is stated to be the lower part only, couped or erased half-way up the leg) and the *paw*, but this distinction cannot be said to be always rigidly observed. In fact some authorities quote the exact reverse as the definition of the terms. As charges the gamb or paw will be found to occur in the arms of Lord Lilford [" Or, a lion's gamb erased in bend dexter between two crosslets fitchée in bend sinister gules "], and in the arms of Newdigate (Fig. 306). This last is a curious example, inasmuch as, without being so specified in the blazon, the gambs are represented in the curious position there shown. The almost invariable position in which they will be found is as they appear in the arms of Dumas (Fig. 137).

The crest upon the Garter Plate of Edward Cherleton, Lord Cherleton of Powis, must surely be unique. It consists of two lions' paws embowed, the outer edge of each being adorned with fleurs-de-lis issuant therefrom.

A *lion's tail* will sometimes be found as a crest and it also occurs as a charge, in the arms of Corke, viz. : " Sable, three lions' tails erect and erased argent."

A *lion's face* should be carefully distinguished from a lion's head. In the latter case the neck, either couped or erased, must be shown ; but a lion's face is affronté and cut off closely behind the ears. The distinction between the head and the face can be more appropriately considered in the case of the leopard.

CHAPTER XVI

BEASTS

NEXT after the lion should be considered the tiger, but it should be distinctly borne in mind that heraldry knows two kinds of tigers—the heraldic tiger and the Bengal tiger. Doubtless the heraldic tiger, which was the only one found in British armory until a comparatively recent date, is the attempt of artists to depict their idea of a tiger. The animal was unknown to them, except by repute, and consequently the creature they depicted bears little relation to the animal in real life ; but there can be no doubt that their intention was to depict an animal which they knew to exist. The heraldic tiger had a body much like the natural tiger, it had a lion's tufted tail and mane, and the curious head which it is so difficult to describe, but which appears to be more like the wolf than any other animal we know. This, however, will be again dealt with in the chapter on fictitious animals, and is here only introduced to demonstrate the difference which heraldry makes between the heraldic tiger and the real animal.

A curious conceit is that the heraldic tiger will anciently be often found spelt " tyger," but this peculiar spelling does not seem ever to have been applied to the tiger of nature. When it became desirable to introduce the real tiger into British armory as typical of India and our Eastern Empire, something of course was necessary to distinguish it from the tiger which had previously usurped the name in armory, and for this reason the natural tiger is always heraldically known as the Bengal tiger. This armorial variety appears towards the end of the eighteenth century in this country, though in foreign heraldry it appears to have been recognised somewhat earlier. Fig. 307 represents the arms showing a tiger thereupon, which are the arms of Barberino di Valdesa.

There are, however, few cases in which the Bengal tiger has appeared in armory, and in the majority of these cases as a supporter, as in the supporters of Outram, which are two tigers rampant guardant gorged with wreaths of laurel and crowned with Eastern crowns all proper.

Another instance of the tiger as a supporter will be found in the arms of Bombay (see Plate CXVIII.). An instance in which it appears as a charge upon a shield will be found in the arms granted to the University of Madras (Fig. 308).

FIG. 307.—Arms of Barberino di Valdesa.

Another coat is that granted in 1874 to Augustus Beaty Bradbury of Edinburgh, which was : " Argent, on a mount in base vert, a Bengal tiger passant proper, on a chief of the second two other tigers dormant also proper."

FIG. 308.—Arms of the University of Madras : Argent, on a mount issuing from the base vert, a tiger passant proper, on a chief sable, a pale or, thereon between two elephants' heads couped of the field, a lotus-flower, leaved and slipped of the third. Motto : " Doctrina vim promovet insitam."

A *tigress* is said to be occasionally met with, and when so, is sometimes represented with a mirror, in relation to the legend that ascribes to her such personal vanity that her young ones might be taken from under her charge if she had the counter attraction of a hand-glass!

The leopard has to a certain extent been referred to already. Doubtless it is the peculiar cat-like and stealthy walk which is so characteristic of the leopard which led to any animal in that position being considered a leopard; but the leopard in its natural state was of course known to Europeans in the early days of heraldry, and appears amongst the lists of heraldic animals apart from its existence as "a lion passant."

visible, and this should be borne in mind, because this constitutes the difference between the leopard's head and the leopard's face. The leopard's face is by far the most usual form in which the leopard will be found in armory, and can be traced back to quite an early period in heraldry. The leopard's face shows no neck at all, the head being removed close behind the ears. It is then represented affronté. It will be found in the arms of Freston[a] (Plate XVII.), and in the arms of the town of Shrewsbury ["Azure, three

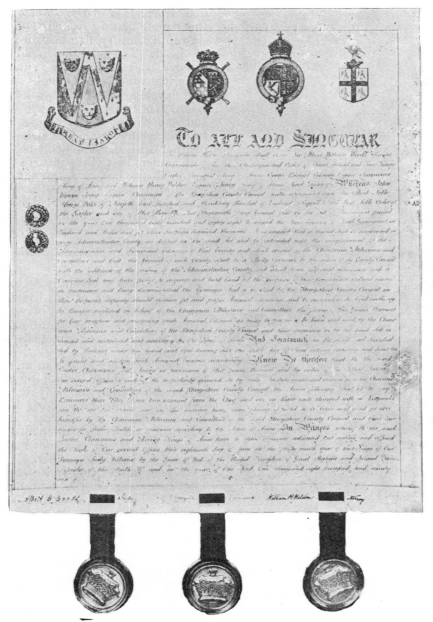

FIG. 309.—Facsimile of the Grant of Arms to Shropshire.

The animal, however, except as a supporter or crest, is by no means common in English heraldry. It will be found, however, in the crests of some number of families; for example in the crest of Taylor and in the crests of Potts.

A very similar animal is the ounce, which for heraldic purposes is in no way altered from the leopard. Parts of the latter will be found in use as of the lion. As a crest the demi-leopard, the leopard's head, and the leopard's head affronté are often to be met with. In all these cases it should be noticed that *the neck is*

leopards' faces. Motto: 'Floreat Salopia'"]. For some unfathomable reason these charges are locally usually referred to as "loggerheads." They were perpetuated in the arms of the county in its recent grant (Fig. 309). As a crest a leopard's face will be found in the arms of Griggs, Du Moulin-Browne, and Bunbury. A curious development or use of the leopard's face occurs when

[a] Armorial bearings of Thomas Westfaling Freston, Esq., of Prestwich, Lancs.: Azure, on a fess or, three leopards' faces gules. Mantling azure and or. Crest: on a wreath of the colours, a demi-greyhound sable, collared or, charged with three torteaux,

it is jessant-de-lis. This will be found referred to at greater length under the heading of the Fleur-de-lis.

The *panther* is an animal which in its relation to heraldry it is difficult to know whether to place amongst the mythical or actual animals. No instance occurs to me in which the panther figures as a charge in British heraldry, and the panther as a supporter, in the few cases in which it is met with, is certainly not the actual animal, inasmuch as it is invariably found flammant, *i.e.* with flames issuing from the mouth and ears. In this character it will be found as a supporter of the Duke of Beaufort, and derived therefrom as a supporter of Lord Raglan.

Foreign heraldry carries the panther to a most curious

FIG. 310.—Arms of Styria. (Drawn by Hans Burgkmair, 1523.)

result. It is frequently represented with the tail of a lion, horns, and for its forelegs the claws of an eagle. It is always represented vomiting flames, but the usual method of depicting it on the Continent (see Plate XLVI. Fig. 3) is greatly at variance with our own. This is from a bas-relief in stone above the porch of the doorway of St. Stephen's Cathedral in Vienna; flames issue from the jaws, nose, and ears. Fig. 310 represents the same arms of Styria—Vert, a panther argent, armed close, vomiting flames of fire—from the title-page of the *Land-bond* of Styria in the year 1523, drawn by Hans Burgkmair. Plate XLVI. Fig. 4 is yet another illustration of the arms of Styria, drawn in the manner in which the animal is now represented. In *Physiologus*, a Greek writing of early Christian times of about the date 140, which in the course of time has been translated into every tongue; mention is made of the

panther, to which is there ascribed the gaily spotted coat and the pleasant, sweet-smelling breath which induces all other animals to approach it; the dragon alone retreats into its hole from the smell, and consequently the panther appears to have sometimes been used as a symbol of Christ. The earliest armorial representations of this animal show the form not greatly dissimilar to nature; but very soon the similarity disappears in Continental representations, and the fancy of the artist transferred the animal into the fabulous creature which is now represented. The sweet-smelling breath, *suozzon-stanch* as it is called in the early German translation of the *Physiologus*, was expressed by the flames issuing from the mouth, but later in the sixteenth century, flames issued from every opening in the head. The head was in old times similar to that of a horse, occasionally horned (as in the seal of Count Heinrich von Lechsgemünd, 1197); the forefeet were well developed. In the second half of the fourteenth century the forefeet assume the character of eagle's claws, and the horns of the animal were a settled matter. In the neighbourhood of Lake Constance we find the panther with divided hoofs on his hind feet; perhaps with a reference to the panther's "cleanness." According to the Mosaic law, of course, a four-footed animal, to be considered clean, must not have paws, and a ruminant must not have an undivided hoof. Italian heraldry is likewise acquainted with the panther, but under another name (*La Dolce*, the sweet one) and another form. The dolce has a head like a hare, and is unhorned. (See A. Anthony v. Siegenfeld. "The Territorial Arms of Styria," Graz, 1898.)

The panther as given by Segar, Garter King of Arms 1603–1633, as one of the badges of King Henry VI., where it is silver, spotted of various colours, and with flames issuing from its mouth and ears. No doubt this Royal badge is the origin of the supporter of the Duke of Beaufort.

English armory knows an animal which it terms the male griffin, which has no wings, but which has gold rays issuing from its body in all directions. Ströhl terms the badge of the Earls of Ormonde, which from his description are plainly male griffins, *keythongs*, which he classes with the panther; and probably he is correct in looking upon our male griffin as merely one form of the heraldic panther.

The *cat*, under the name of the cat, the wild cat, the cat-a-mountain, or the cat-a-mount, is by no means infrequently found in British armory, though it will usually be found in Scottish examples, as the crest of Macpherson (Fig. 311) and Duguid M'Combie[b] (Plate XXX.). It is constantly met with in Scotland, and it will be found for example in the arms of Keates (Fig. 312), and Scott-Gatty (Fig. 262).

The wolf is a very frequent charge in English armory. Apart from its use as a supporter, in which condition it is found in conjunction with the shields of Lord Welby ["On either side a wolf regardant sable, semé of fleurs-de-lis argent"], Lord Rendell (Plate LXII.) and Viscount Wolseley ["Two wolves proper, each charged on the shoulder with a laurel and palmbranch in saltire or, gorged with a mural crown also or, and holding in the paw a sword erect proper, pommel and hilted gold"], it will be found in the arms

[b] Armorial bearings of Peter Duguid - M'Combie, Esq., of Easter Skene, Aberdeen: Quarterly, 1 and 4, or, a lion rampant gules, armed and langued azure, a chief of the second (for M'Combie); 2 and 3, azure, a fess between three crosses patée argent, a bordure parted per pale of the second and or (for Duguid). Mantling gules, doubled argent. Crests: 1. upon a wreath of the liveries, a wild cat sejant proper; 2. upon a wreath of the liveries, a dove holding a laurel branch in her beak proper. Mottoes: "Touch not the cat but a glove"; "Patientia et spe."

THE ART OF HERALDRY

of Lovett[c]; and in by far the larger proportion of the coats for the name of Wilson[d] (Plate XXXI. and Fig. 313) and in the arms of Low (Fig. 314).

The wolf, however, in earlier representations has a less distinctly wolf-like character, it being sometimes difficult to distinguish the wolf from other heraldic animals. This is one of these cases in which, owing to insufficient knowledge and crude draftsmanship, ancient

Wolfe. The latter crest is worthy of remark, inasmuch as the Royal crown which is held within its paws typifies the assistance given to King Charles II., after the battle of Worcester, by Mr. Francis Wolfe of Madeley, to whom the crest was granted. King Charles, it may be noted, also gave to Mr. Wolfe a silver tankard, upon the lid of which was a representation of this crest.

Wolves' heads are particularly common, especially in

FIG. 311.—Armorial bearings of "Cluny" Macpherson: Per fess or and azure, a lymphad of the first, with her sails furled, oars in action, mast and tackling all proper, flags flying gules, in the dexter chief point a hand couped grasping a dagger point upwards gules, in the sinister chief a cross crosslet fitchée of the last. Upon the escutcheon is placed a helmet befitting his degree, with a mantling gules, doubled argent; and upon a wreath of his liveries is set for crest, a cat sejant proper. Supporters: two Highlanders in short tartan jackets and hose, with steel helmets on their heads, thighs bare, their shirts tied between them, and round targets on their arms. Motto: "Touch not the cat bot a glove."

heraldry is not to be preferred to more realistic treatment. Examples of well-drawn wolves will be found in the chapter dealing with supporters, a notable instance being the arms of Lord Rendel, as shown on Plate LXII.

The demi-wolf is a very frequent crest, occurring not only in the arms and crests of members of the Wilson and many other families, but also as the crest of

Scottish heraldry. An example of them will be found in the arms of "Struan" Robertson, and in the coats used by all other members of the Robertson Clan having or claiming descent from, or relationship with, the house of Struan.

The wolf's head also appears in the arms of Skeen (Fig. 315), which affords a good representation of the usual form adopted for a wolf's head. Woodward states that the wolf is the most common of all heraldic animals in Spanish heraldry, where it is frequently represented as *ravissant*, *i.e.* carrying the

[c] Armorial bearings of Lovett: Argent, three wolves passant in pale sable. Crest: a wolf passant proper.
[d] Armorial bearings of Reginald H. R. Rimington-Wilson, Esq.: Sable, a wolf salient, in chief three estoiles or.

S

body of a lamb in its mouth or across its back. A curious, but unusual, and not officially recognised method of representing a wolf's head will be found in the arms of Paton (Fig. 316).

FIG. 312.—Armorial bearings of Joseph Andrew Keates, Esq.: Argent, on a pale sable, three cats-a-mountain of the field, on a canton of the second a cake of copper proper. Upon the escutcheon is placed a helmet befitting his degree, with a mantling sable and argent; and for his crest, upon a wreath of the colours, a tiger proper, charged with three bezants fesswise resting the dexter paw upon an escutcheon sable, thereon a cake of copper proper. Motto: "Esto memor."

Much akin to the wolf is the *Lynx ;* in fact the heraldic representation of the two animals is not greatly different. The lynx does not often occur in heraldry except as a supporter, but it will be found as the crest of the family of Lynch. The lynx is nearly always

FIG. 313.—Armorial bearings of Rev. Joseph Bowstead Wilson: Vert, on a cross argent, between in the first and fourth quarters a wolf salient of the last, and in the second and third a mullet of six points or, a rose gules, barbed and seeded proper, between four quatrefoils also gules, in the dexter chief a crescent or for difference. Mantling vert and argent. Crest: on a wreath of the colours, in front of a demi-lion sable, holding between the paws a quatrefoil gules, a pommée charged with a mullet of six points or; with the motto, "Semper vigilans."

depicted and blazoned "coward," *i.e.* with its tail between its legs. Another instance of this particular animal is the crest of Comber (Fig. 317).

A *Fox,* which from the similarity of its representation is often confused with a wolf, is said by Woodward to be very seldom met with in British heraldry. This is

FIG. 314.—Armorial bearings of Sir James Low, of Kincraig House, Arbroath.

hardly a correct statement, inasmuch as countless instances can be produced in which a fox figures as a charge, a crest, or a supporter. The fox as a supporter is found with the arms of Lord Ilchester, and instances of its appearance will be found amongst others in the arms or crests, for example, of Fox (Fig. 318), Colfox (Fig. 319), Ashworth (Fig. 159). Sir Joseph Renals, Bart., bears as crest: "Upon a rock a fox sejant regardant proper, charged on the shoulder with a

FIG. 315.—Armorial bearings of Skene.

lozenge or; and supporting with the dexter foreleg a fasces also proper." Probably the most curious example of the heraldic fox will be found in the arms of Sir Watkin Williams Wynn, who for the arms of Williams quarters: "Argent, two foxes counter-salient gules, the dexter surmounted of the sinister." The representation of this coat of arms in Foster's Baronetage is strikingly good.

The Bear is constantly met with figuring largely in coats of arms for the names of Barnard, Baring, Barnes, and Bearsley, and for other names which can be considered to bear canting relation to the charge. In fact the arms, crest, and motto of Barnard together form such an excellent example of the little jokes which characterise early heraldry that I quote it in full. The

FIG. 316.—Armorial bearings of the late Sir Noel Paton : Azure, a wolf's head erased argent, between two crescents in chief and a fleur-de-lis in base or. Mantling azure, doubled argent ; and upon a wreath of his liveries is set for crest, between two doves' wings expanded proper, a cubit arm erect also proper, charged on the palm with a passion cross gules ; and in an escroll above, this motto, " Do richt and fear nocht."

coat is "argent, a bear rampant sable," the crest is a demi-bear sable, and the motto, "Bear and forbear." Other examples of the use of the bear will be found in the

FIG. 317.—Armorial bearings of John Comber, Esq. : Quarterly, 1 and 4, or, a fess dancetté gules, between three estoiles sable (for Comber) ; 2 and 3, argent, a chevron sable, between three thorn-trees proper (for Thornton). Mantling gules and argent. Crest : on a wreath or and sable, a lynx's head couped or, pelleté.

arms of Layland-Barratt (Fig. 320) and in the crest of Christie (Fig. 321). The representation of a bear on Plate LXXI. in the arms of FitzUrse is most curious.

The bear is generally found muzzled, but this must

not be presumed unless mentioned in the blazon. Bears' paws are often found both in crests and as charges upon

FIG. 318.—Armorial bearings of Fox, of Grovehill, co. Cornwall : Ermine, on a chevron azure, three foxes' heads erased or, within a bordure flory of the second, and on a canton of the same, a drinking-cup of the third, surmounted by three fleurs-de-lis argent. Upon the escutcheon is placed a helmet befitting his degree, with a mantling azure and argent ; and for his crest, upon a wreath of the colours, a fox sejant or, collared flory azure, the paw resting on a fleur-de-lis of the last ; with the motto, " Faire sans dire."

shields (see Pickering, Plate XXXVI.), but as they differ little if anything in appearance from the lion's gamb, they need not be further particularised. To the bear's head, however, considerable attention should be paid, inasmuch as the manner of depicting it in England and Scotland differs. The bears' head, according to English ideas of heraldry, would be depicted down to the shoulders, and would show the neck couped or erased. In Scottish heraldry, bears' heads are almost invariably found couped close behind the ears without any of the neck being visible ; they are not, however, repre-

FIG. 319.—Armorial bearings of William Colfox, Esq., J.P., D.L., of Allington, Dorset : Sable, three spinning-cogs erect and in fess or, on a chief argent as many foxes' heads couped at the neck gules. Mantling sable and or. Crest : on a wreath of the colours, a fox proper, charged on the body with two fleurs-de-lis in fess sable, and resting the sinister paw on a fleur-de-lis gules. Motto : " Lux, lex, libertas."

sented as caboshed or affronté, and the form can best be seen from the illustration in the *arms* of Forbes-Leith (Plate XXXVII.), though singularly enough the crest in this case has the boar's head depicted in the English style.

FIG. 320.—Armorial bearings of Francis Layland-Barratt, Esq.: Quarterly, 1 and 4, argent, on a chevron indented between three bears statant sable, muzzled or, as many pallets of the last, each charged with a cross crosslet fitchée of the second (for Barratt); 2. per pale argent and or, a greyhound courant between in chief two Cornish choughs and in base as many crosses patée all sable (for Williams); 3. per fess gules and sable, in chief two demi-lions rampant, and in base as many bezants (for Bennetts); impaling the arms of Layland, namely: argent, on a fess raguly gules, between six ears of wheat, three and three vert, banded or, in chief and two escallops in base of the third, a lion passant of the first. Mantling sable and argent. Crest: on a wreath of the colours, a bear sable, muzzled, semé of escallops, and resting the dexter forepaw on an escallop all or. Motto: "Cui debeo fidus."

FIG. 321.—Armorial bearings of William Langham Christie, Esq: Azure, a lamb passant, the dexter leg supporting in bend sinister a banner argent, staff or, on a chief of the last a tower with two turrets between as many gabions proper, and upon an escutcheon of pretence the arms of Cleveland, namely: azure, a hare salient or, collared gules, to the collar a bugle-horn pendent sable. Mantling azure and argent. Crest: upon a wreath of the colours, a brown bear passant muzzled, the chain reflexed over the shoulder or, on the back a bezant charged with a cross sable, the dexter paw resting on an escutcheon per pale of the last and gules. Motto: "Integer vitæ."

The Boar is an animal which, with its parts, will constantly be met with in British armory. Theoretically there is a difference between the boar, which is the male of the domestic animal, and the wild boar, which is the untamed creature of the woods. Whilst the latter is usually blazoned as a wild boar or sanglier, the latter is just a boar; but for all practical purposes no difference whatever is made in heraldic representations of these varieties, though it may be noted that the crest of Swinton (Plate LXIII.) is often described as a sanglier, as is also the crest of Douglas, Lord Penrhyn ["A sanglier sticking between the cleft of an oak-tree fructed, with a lock holding the clefts together all proper"]. The boar, like the lion, is usually described as armed and langued, but this is not necessary when the tusks are represented in their own colour and when the tongue is gules. It will, however, be very frequently found that the tusks are or. The "armed," however, does not include the hoofs, and if these are to be of any colour different from that of the animal, it must be blazoned "unguled" of such and such a tincture.

Precisely the same distinction occurs in the heads of

FIG. 322.—Armorial bearings of Joseph Robert Heaven, Esq., of Forest of Birse: Azure, semé of cross crosslets argent, three boars' heads couped or, armed and langued gules, a chief of the third. Mantling azure, doubled or. Crest: on a wreath of his liveries, a boar's head couped or, semé of cross crosslets azure; and in an escroll over the same this motto, "Non omnis moriar."

boars that was referred to in bears. The real difference is this, that whilst the English boar's head has the neck attached to the head and is couped or erased at the shoulders, the Scottish boar's head is separated close behind the ears. No one ever troubled to draw any distinction between the two, because the English boars' heads were more usually drawn with the neck, and the boars' heads in Scotland were drawn couped close. Matters of coats of arms, however, are now cosmopolitan, and one can no longer ascertain that the crest of Campbell must be Scottish, or that the crest of any other family must be English; and consequently, though the terms will not be found employed officially, it is just as well to distinguish them, because armory provides means of such distinction—the true term for an English boar's head being couped or erased "at the neck," and the Scottish term being a boar's head couped or erased "close." Examples of a boar's head of the English type will be found in the arms of McDermot[e] (Plate XXII.), and of a Scottish type in the arms of

[e] Armorial bearings of Henry Thomas McDermott, Esq.: Party per pale chevron argent and or, on a chevron gules, between in chief three boars' heads erased at the neck and in base a cross crosslet azure, three trefoils slipped of the second; and for his crest, on a wreath of the colours, a demi-lion rampant or, holding between the paws a boar's head erased as in the arms; with the motto, "Honor virtutis præmium."

Gooden-Chisholm (Plate LVII.), Abercromby [f] (Plate XXXIX.), Sandford-Thompson (Plate XXIX.), Bannerman (Plate XVIII.), Heaven (Fig. 322), and Wyatt

FIG. 323.—Armorial bearings of Hugh Richard Penfold Wyatt, Esq.: Gules, on a fess or, between three boars' heads couped ermine, a lion passant, enclosed by two pheons azure. Mantling gules and or. Crest: on a wreath of the colours, a demi-lion rampant erased azure, holding in his dexter paw an arrow proper, headed with a pheon argent.

(Fig. 323). Occasionally a boar's head will be stated to be borne erect; this is then shown with the mouth pointing upwards. A curious example of this is found in the crest of Tyrrell: "A boar's head erect argent, in the mouth a peacock's tail proper."

Woodward mentions three very strange coats of arms in which the charge, whilst not being a boar, bears very close connection with it. He states that among the curiosities of heraldry we may place the canting arms of Ham, of Holland: "Gules, five hams proper, 2, 1, 2." The Verhammes also bear: "Or, three hams sable." These commonplace charges assume almost a poetical savour when placed beside the matter-of-fact coat of the family of Bacquere: "d'Azur, à un ecusson d'or en abîme, accompagné de trois groins de porc d'argent," and that of the Wursters of Switzerland: "Or, two sausages gules on a gridiron sable, the handle in chief."

HORSES

It is not a matter of surprise that the horse is frequently met with in armory. It will be found, as in the arms of Jedburgh, carrying a mounted warrior, and

[f] Armorial bearings of Alexander Abercromby, Esq.: Parted per pale argent and gules, a chevron between two boars' heads erased in chief, and a bee volant en arrière in base all counterchanged. Above the shield is placed a helmet befitting his degree, with a mantling gules, doubled argent; and upon a wreath of his liveries is set for crest, a bee volant or, and upon an escroll above, this motto, "Vive ut vivas."

the same combination appears as the crest of the Duke of Fife (Fig. 251).

The horse will be found · rampant (or forcene, or salient), as in the arms of Bewes (Fig. 292), and will be found courant in the crest of Stone (Plate XX.), and trotting in the arms of Trotter (Fig. 324).

When it is "comparisoned" or "furnished" it is shown with saddle and bridle and all appurtenances; but if the saddle is not present it would only be blazoned "bridled."

"Gules, a horse argent," really the arms of Westphalia, is popularly known in this country as the coat of Hanover, inasmuch as it was the most prominent charge upon the inescutcheon or quartering of Hanover formerly borne with the Royal Arms. Every one in this country is familiar with the expression "the white horse of Hanover."

Horses will also be found in many cases as supporters, and these will be referred to in the chapter upon that subject, but reference should be particularly made here to the crest of the family of Lane, of King's Bromley (Fig. 57), which is a strawberry roan horse, couped at the flanks, bridled, saddled, and holding in its feet the Imperial crown proper. This commemorates the heroic action of Mistress Jane Lane, afterwards Lady Fisher, and the sister of Sir Thomas Lane, of King's Bromley, who, after the battle of Worcester and when King Charles was in hiding, rode from Staffordshire to the south coast upon a strawberry roan horse, with King Charles as her serving-man. For this the Lane family were first of all granted the canton of England as an augmentation to their arms, and shortly afterwards this crest of the demi-horse.

The arms of Trevelyan afford an interesting example of a horse, being: "Gules, issuant out of water in base proper, a demi-horse argent, hoofed and maned or."

FIG. 324.—Armorial bearings of William Trotter, Esq.: Quarterly, 1 and 4, argent, a crescent gules, on a chief indented azure, three mullets pierced of the field (for Trotter); 2 and 3, gules, a lion rampant argent, crowned or, armed and langued azure, charged on the shoulder with a crescent of the first (for Mowbray), all within a bordure engrailed or. Mantling gules and argent. Crest: on a wreath of his liveries, a horse trotting proper. Motto: "Festina lente."

The heads of horses are either so described or (and more usually) termed "nags' heads," though what the difference may be is beyond the comprehension of most people; at any rate heraldry knows none. These will be found, amongst other coats, in the arms of Lloyd (Fig. 325) and Barstow (Plate XVIII.). As a crest its use is even more frequent.

The crest of the family of Duncombe is curious, and is as follows: "Out of a ducal coronet or, a horse's hind

FIG. 325.—Armorial bearings of Henry Crampton Lloyd, Esq., of Stockton, co. Salop: Quarterly of five, viz.: 1. Lloyd of Stockton: Sable, three nags' heads erased argent; 2. Sir Griffith Vaughan, Knight Banneret of Agincourt: quarterly 1 and 4, sable, three nags' heads erased argent; 2 and 3, argent, a " castle " triple-towered sable, port overt chained transverse or (Sir John Oldcastle, Lord Cobham); 3. Griffith ap Beli, de la Garth, Lord of Guilsfield: Per pale or and gules, two lions rampant addorsed counterchanged; 4. Sable, three escutcheons or, each charged with a lion rampant gules; 5. Beli Mawr, or Belinus the Great, King of Britain: Azure, three ducal crowns in pale or.

tar from being an uncommon charge. It will be found in various arms for the name of Ferrar, Ferrers (Figs. 64 and 215), and Farrer; and Marshall (Figs. 249 and 326), and, in the arms of Smith, three horse-shoes interlaced together form rather a curious charge (Fig. 327).

Other instances in which it occurs will be found in the

FIG. 327.—Armorial bearings of William Smith, Esq., of Binn Cottage, Dundee: Argent, a bend azure, between three horse-shoes interlaced sable in chief and an eagle displayed of the third in base, beaked and membered gules. Mantling azure, doubled argent. Crest: upon a wreath of the liveries, a fleur-de-lis argent, interlaced with a horse-shoe sable; and on an escroll over same this motto, " Ready and fit."

arms of Burlton (Fig. 122), and in the arms used by the town of Oakham. In the latter case it doubtless has

FIG. 326.—Armorial bearings of Dr. G. W. Marshall, Rouge Croix Pursuivant of Arms: Barry of six ermine and azure, a horse-shoe or between three bezants. Mantling azure and or. Crest: upon a wreath of the colours, a bezant charged with a horse-shoe azure, between two wings barry of six ermine and azure; with the motto, " Vi martiali."

leg sable, the shoe argent." Founded upon this, doubtless, was the confirmation of arms and crest to the family of Dunscombe (Plate XXVI.). Though they can hardly be termed animate charges, perhaps one may be justified in here mentioning the horse-shoe, which is

FIG. 328.—Armorial bearings of Pirrie of Belfast: Argent, a saltire gules, between in chief and in base a bugle-horn stringed sable, and in fess two sea-horses respecting one another proper. Crest: on a wreath of the colours, a falcon's head erased per saltire argent and gules. Motto : " Deeds, not words."

reference to the toll of a horse-shoe, which the town collects from every peer or member of the Royal Family who passes through its limits. The collection of these, which are usually of silver, and are carefully preserved, is one of the features of the town.

The sea-horse, the unicorn, and the pegasus may perhaps be more properly considered as mythical

FIG. 329.—Bookplate of Walter Edwin Carson M'Cammond, Esq. Arms: or, a fess vair between three sea-horses proper. Mantling azure and or. Crest: out of a mural crown a lion's head gules, charged on the neck with a bell argent. Motto: "Justus ac tenax." (Designed by J. Vinycomb, Esq., M.R.I.A.)

FIG. 330.—Armorial bearings of John Maunsell Richardson, Esq.: Per pale sable and or, a pegasus rampant between three lions' heads erased all counterchanged, impaling the arms of Hare, namely: gules, two bars or, and a chief indented of the last. Mantling sable and or. Crest: on a wreath of the colours, a pegasus sejant sable, resting the dexter foot on a pheon or. Motto: "Honorantes me honorabo."

animals, and the unicorn will, of course, be treated under that heading; but the sea-horse and the pegasus are so closely allied in form to the natural animal that

perhaps it will be simpler to treat of them in this chapter. The sea-horse is composed of the head and neck of a horse and the tail of a fish, but in place of the forefeet, legs and webbed paws are usually substituted.

FIG. 331.—Armorial bearings of Tankerville James Chamberlayne, Esq.: Quarterly, 1 and 4, gules, a chevron engrailed argent, between three escallops or (for Chamberlayne); 2 and 3, argent, a hand gloved, couped at the wrist, and grasping a thistle between three holly-leaves all proper (for Irwin of Tanragoe); impaling the arms of Ruspoli, "d'azur, à un mont de six coupeaux d'or, sommé de deux ceps devigne passés en double sautoir et fruités de deux grappes de raisins à dextre et à sinestre le tout au naturel" (*vide* Reitstap). Mantling gules and argent. Crest: upon a wreath of the colours, a pegasus argent. Motto: "Nemo me impune lacessit."

Two sea-horses respecting each other will be found in the coat of arms of Pirrie (Fig. 328); and sea-horses

FIG. 332.—Arms of Herr von Frouberg.

naiant will be found in the arms of M'Cammond (Fig. 329). It is a matter largely left to the discretion of the artist, but the sea-horse will be found as often as not depicted with a fin at the back of its neck in place of a mane. A sea-horse as a crest will be found in the case of Belfast and in the crests of Clippingdale and Jenkinson. The sea-horse is sometimes represented winged, but I know of no officially sanctioned example. When represented rising from the sea the animal is said to be "assurgeant."

The pegasus, though often met with as a crest or found in use as a supporter, is very unusual as a charge upon an escutcheon. It will be found, however, in the arms of the Society of the Inner Temple and in the arms of Richardson (Fig. 330), which affords an example of a pegasus rampant and also an example of a pegasus sejant, which at present is the only one which exists in British heraldry. Another example of the pegasus will be found in the crest of Chamberlayne (Fig. 331).

Fig. 332 gives a solitary instance of a mare. The arms, which are from Grünenberg's *Wappenbuch* (1483), are attributed to "Herr von Frouberg from the Forest in Bavaria," and are: Gules, a mare rampant argent, bridled sable.

DOGS

Dogs will be found of various kinds in many English and Scottish coats of arms, though more frequently in the former than in the latter. The original English dog, the hound of early days, is, of course, the talbot. Under the heading of supporters certain instances will be quoted in which dogs of various kinds and breeds figure in heraldry, but the talbot as a charge will be found in the arms of the old Staffordshire family, Wolseley of Wolseley, a cadet of which house is the present Field-Marshal, Viscount Wolseley. Their arms are: "Argent, a talbot passant gules" (Fig. 333).

Other instances of the talbot will be found in the arms or crests of the families of Grosvenor, Gooch, Smith-Ryland, and Allen (see Plate XXXI.). The arms "Azure, three talbots statant or" were granted by Cooke to Edward Peke of Heldchurchgate, Kent. A sleuth-hound treading gingerly upon the points of a coronet ["On a ducal coronet, a sleuthhound proper, collared

FIG. 333.—Armorial bearings of Lieutenant-General Sir George Benjamin Wolseley, K.C.B.: Argent, a talbot passant gules, a crescent for difference. Upon the escutcheon, which is surrounded by the ribbon of the Most Honourable Order of the Bath, and pendent therefrom his badge as a Knight Commander thereof, is placed a helmet befitting his degree, with a mantling gules and argent; and for his crest, out of a ducal coronet or, a wolf's head proper; with the motto, "Homo homini lupus."

and leashed gules"] was the crest of the Earl of Perth and Melfort, and one wonders whether the motto, "Gang warily," may not really have as much relation to the perambulations of the crest as to the dangerous foot-

hold amongst the galtraps which is provided for the supporters.

FIG. 334.—Armorial bearings of Charles Hunter, Esq., J.P., D.L., F.R.S., F.S.A., of Plas Coch, Anglesey: Vert, three greyhounds courant at full speed in pale argent, collared gules, within a bordure or, on a chief engrailed of the second a fleur-de-lis azure between two bugles of the field, stringed and veruled of the third. Mantling vert and argent. Crest: upon a wreath of the liveries, a greyhound's head and neck couped argent, collared gules. Motto: "Dum spiro spero."

Greyhounds are, of course, very frequently met with, amongst the instances which can be mentioned being the arms of Clayhills (see page 46), and in the arms of Hunter of Plas Coch (Fig. 334), and Hunter of Hunterston (Fig. 800). A very artistic representation of a greyhound will be found in the arms of Blackwall (Fig. 345), and a curious coat of arms will be found under the name of Udney of that Ilk, registered in the Lyon Office, namely: "Gules, two greyhounds counter-salient argent, collared of the field, in the inner point a stag's head couped, and attired with ten tynes, all between the three fleurs-de-lis, two in chief and one in base, or." Another very curious coat of arms is registered as the design of the reverse of the seal of the Royal Burgh of Linlithgow, and is: "Or, a greyhound bitch sable, chained to an oak-tree within a loch proper." This curious coat of arms, however, being the reverse of the seal, is seldom if ever made use of. Two bloodhounds are the supporters to the arms of Campbell of Aberuchill.

The dog, as far as I am aware, is not found rampant, but may be salient, that is, springing, its hind feet on the ground; passant, when it is sometimes known as trippant, otherwise walking; and courant when it is at full speed. It will be found occasionally couchant or lying down, but if depicted chasing another animal it is described as "in full chase."

A mastiff will be found in the arms of Crawshay (Fig. 346), and there is a well-known crest of a family named Phillips which has for its crest "a dog sejant regardant surmounted by a bezant charged with a representation of a dog saving a man from drowning." Whether this crest has any official authority or not I do not know, but I should imagine it is highly doubtful.

Foxhounds appear as the supporters of Lord Hindlip;

FIG. 345.—Armorial bearings of Blackwall: Argent, a greyhound courant sable, collared chequy or and gules, on a chief indented sable three bezants. Crest: two arms embowed in chain mail, holding in the hands proper a greyhound's head couped sable, collared chequy or and gules. Motto: "Fidelitas."

FIG. 346.—Armorial bearings of Codrington Fraser Crawshay, Esq.: Argent, on a mount in base vert, a plough proper, on a chief azure a pale or, charged with the chemical sign of Mars ♂ sable, between two lions' heads erased gold. Mantling vert and argent. Crest: on a mount vert, a dog standing over a heap of cannon-balls proper. Motto: "Perseverance."

and when depicted with its nose to the ground a dog is termed a hound on scent.

A winged greyhound is stated to be the crest of a family of Benwell. A greyhound in full course or "courant" will be found in the crest of Daly and Watney (see Plate XXVII.); and a curious crest is that of Biscoe, which is a greyhound seizing a hare. The crest of Anderson, now borne by the Earl of Yarborough, is a water spaniel.

The sea-dog (Fig. 347) is a most curious animal. It is represented much as the talbot, but with scales, webbed

FIG. 347.—The Sea-dog.

feet, and a broad scaly tail like a beaver. In my mind there is very little doubt that the sea-dog is really the early heraldic attempt to represent a beaver, and I am confirmed in that opinion by the arms of the city of Oxford. There has been considerable uncertainty as to what the sinister supporter was intended to represent. A reference to the original record shows that a beaver is the real supporter, but the representation of the animal, which in form has varied little, is very similar to that of a sea-dog. The only instances I am aware of in British heraldry in which it occurs under the name of a sea-dog are the Stourton supporters and the crest of Dodge.[g]

BULLS

The bull, and also the calf, and very occasionally the cow and the buffalo, have their allotted place in heraldry. They are amongst the few animals which can never be represented proper, inasmuch as in its natural state the bull is of very various colours. And yet there is an exception to even this apparently obvious fact, for the bulls connected with or used either as crests, badges, or supporters by the various branches of the Nevill family are all pied bulls ["Arms of the Marquis of Abergavenny: Gules, on a saltire argent, a rose of the field, barbed and seeded proper. Crest: a bull statant argent, pied sable, collared and chain reflexed over the back or. Supporters: two bulls argent, pied sable, armed, unguled, collared and chained, and at the end of the chain two staples or. Badges: on the dexter a rose gules, seeded or, barbed vert; on the sinister a portcullis or. Motto: 'Ne vile velis.'"] The bull in the arms of the town of Abergavenny, which are obviously based upon the arms and crest of the Marquess of Abergavenny, is the same (Fig. 348).

Examples of the bull will be found in the arms of Verelst (Fig. 349), Blyth (Fig. 350), and Ffinden (Fig. 163). In the arms of Oxford (Plate CXVIII.) the animal naturally would be blazoned an ox. A bull salient occurs in the arms of De Hasting ["Per pale vert and or, a bull salient counterchanged"]. The

g Armorial bearings of Dodge: Barry of six or and sable, on a pale gules, a woman's breast distilling drops of milk proper. Crest: upon a wreath of the colours, a demi sea-dog azure, collared, maned, and finned or. Motto: "Leni perfruar otio."

arms of the Earl of Shaftesbury show three bulls, which happen to be the quartering for Ashley. This coat of arms affords an instance, and a striking one, of the manner in which arms have been assumed in England. The surname of the Earl of Shaftesbury is Ashley-Cooper. It may be mentioned here in passing, though the subject is properly dealt with elsewhere in the volume, that in an English sub-quarterly coat for a

FIG. 349.—Armorial bearings of Harry William Verelst, Esq.: Argent, on a mount in front of an oak-tree fructed proper, a bull passant sable, in chief two estoiles of the last. Mantling sable and argent. Crest: on a wreath of the colours, on a mount a rudder with tiller proper, between two elephants' trunks or.

lordship) are: "Gules, a bend engrailed between six lions rampant or." The ludicrous result has been that

FIG. 348.—Arms of Abergavenny: Gules, a saltire argent, between a rose in chief and two fleurs-de-lis in fess and a portcullis chained in base or. Crest: on a wreath of the colours, upon the trunk of a tree fesswise, eradicated and sprouting to the dexter proper, a bull passant argent, pied and unguled sable, gorged with a collar and chain reflexed over the back and charged on the body with two fleurs-de-lis all or. Motto: "Hostes nunc amici."

double name the arms for the last and most important name are the first and fourth quarterings. But Lord Shaftesbury himself is the only person who bears the name of Cooper, all other members of the family except his lordship being known by the name of Ashley only. Possibly this may be the reason which accounts for the fact that by a rare exception Lord Shaftesbury bears the arms of Ashley in the first and fourth quarters, and Cooper in the second and third. But by a very general mistake these arms of Ashley ["Argent, three bulls passant sable, armed and unguled or"] were until recently almost invariably described as the arms of Cooper. The result has been that during the last century they were "jumped" right and left by people of the name of Cooper, entirely in ignorance of the fact that the arms of Cooper (if it were, as one can only presume, the popular desire to indicate a false relationship to his

to those who know the arms have stood self-condemned, and in the course of time, as it has become necessary for these Messrs. Cooper to legalise these usurped in-

FIG. 350.—Armorial bearings of Sir James Blyth, 1st baronet: Azure, on a mount vert, a bull statant argent, ringed and chained or, on a chief arched of the fourth, a stag's head erased proper between two annulets gules, the escutcheon being charged with his badge of Ulster as a baronet. Mantling azure and argent, Crest: on a wreath of the colours, in front of a mount vert thereon a bull as in the arms, three roses gules. Motto: "Spero meliora."

signia, the new grants, differentiated versions of arms previously in use, have nearly all been founded upon this Ashley coat. At any rate there must be a score or more Cooper grants with bulls as the principal charges, and innumerable others are still using without authority the old Ashley coat pure and simple.

The bull as a crest is not uncommon, belonging amongst other families to Ridley, Sykes, and De Hoghton; and the demi-bull, and more frequently the bull's head, are often met with. A bull's leg is the crest of De la Vache, and as such appears upon two of the early Garter plates. Winged bulls are the supporters of the Butchers' Livery Company.

A bull's scalp occurs upon a canton over the arms of Cheney, a coat quartered by Johnston and Cure.

The ox seldom occurs, except that, in order sometimes to preserve a pun, a bovine animal is sometimes so blazoned. Cows also are equally rare, but occur in the arms of Cowell ["Ermine, a cow statant gules, within a bordure sable, bezantée"] and in the recent grants to the towns of Rawtenstall and Cowbridge. Cows' heads appear on the arms of Veitch ["Argent, three cows' heads erased sable"], and these were transferred to the cadency bordure of the Haig arms when these were rematriculated for Mr. H. Veitch Haig (Plate LXV.).

Calves are of much more frequent occurrence than cows, appearing in many coats of arms in which they are a pun upon the name. They will be found in the arms of Vaile (Fig. 92) and Metcalfe (Fig. 351). Special

FIG. 351.—Armorial bearings of John Henry Metcalfe, Esq.: Argent, three calves passant sable, a canton gules.

attention may well be drawn to the last-mentioned illustration, inasmuch as it is by Mr. J. H. Metcalfe, whose heraldic work has obtained a well-deserved reputation. A bull or cow is termed "armed" if the horns are of a different tincture from the head. The term "unguled" applies to the hoofs, and "ringed" is used when, as is sometimes the case, a ring passes through the nostrils. A bull's head is sometimes found caboshed, as in the crest of Macleod, or as in the arms of Walrond. The position of the tail is one of those matters which are left to the artist, and unless the blazon contains any statement to the contrary, it may be placed in any convenient position.

STAGS

The stag, using the term in its generic sense, under the various names of stag, deer, buck, hart, hind, doe, reindeer, springbok, roebuck, and other varieties, is constantly met with in British armory, as well as in that of other countries.

In the specialised varieties, such as the springbok and the reindeer, naturally an attempt is made to follow the natural animal in its salient peculiarities, but as to the remainder, heraldry knows little if any distinction after the following has been properly observed. The stag, which is really the male red deer, has horns which are branched with pointed branches from the bottom to the top; but a buck, which is the fallow deer, has broad and flat palmated horns. Anything in the

nature of a stag must be subject to the following terms. If lying down it is termed lodged, if walking it is termed trippant, if running it is termed courant or at speed or at full chase. It is termed salient when springing,

FIG. 352.—Armorial bearings of Sir Thomas Richardson: Per fess azure and barry wavy of six argent and of the first, a stag statant at gaze or, on a chief arched of the last, two lions' heads erased sable. Mantling azure and argent. Crest: on a wreath of the colours, a mount vert, thereon, in front of the battlements of a tower, a lion's head erased sable, gorged with a collar vair. Motto: "Virtute acquiritur honos."

though the term springing is sometimes employed, and it is said to be "at gaze" when statant with the head turned to face the spectator; but it should be noted that a stag may also be statant; and it is not "at gaze"

FIG. 353.—Armorial bearings of George Walter Charles Rothe, Esq.: Or, on a mount in base vert, a stag trippant argent, under an oak-tree of the second. Mantling vert and or; and for his crest, upon a wreath of the colours, on a mount vert, a stag lodged argent, attired or; with the motto, "Solo salus servire Deo."

unless the head is turned round. When it is necessary owing to a difference of tincture or for other reasons to refer to the horns, a stag or buck is described as attired of such and such a colour, whereas bulls, rams, and goats are said to be armed.

When the stag is said to be attired ot ten or any other number of tynes, it means that there are so many points to its horns. Like other cloven-footed animals, the stag can be unguled of a different colour.

The animal will be found in the arms of Harthill [h] (Plate XXXI.), Richardson (Fig. 352), Rothe (Fig. 353), and Greene (Fig. 354).

The stag's head is very frequently met with, as in the arms of Rodger (Fig. 355), but it will be more frequently found as a stag's head caboshed, as in the arms of Wakely (Fig. 356), and Barton (Fig. 357). In these cases the head is represented affronté and removed close behind the ears, so that no part of the neck is visible.

the crest of Hatton [i] whilst a hind's head is the crest of Conran [j] (Plate XX.).

The reindeer is less usual, but reindeer heads will be

FIG. 355.—Armorial bearings of Edward Rodger, Esq., of Glasgow: Sable, a stag's head erased argent, holding in his mouth a mullet or, within a bordure party per pale of the last and ermine, charged with three escallops of the first. Mantling sable, doubled argent; and upon a wreath of his liveries is set for crest, on a mount a stag courant between two laurel branches, all proper; and in an escroll over the same this motto, "Nos nostraque Deo."

found in the arms of Fellows.[k] It, however, appears as a supporter for several English peers. The stag's head caboshed occurs in the arms of Cavendish and Stanley (Fig. 359), and also in the arms of Legge, Earl of Dartmouth.

☞ Much akin to the stag is the antelope, which, unless specified to be an heraldic antelope, or found in a very

FIG. 354.—Armorial bearings of Richard Greene, Esq.: Vert, three bucks trippant or, each gorged with a ducal coronet gules. Mantling vert and or. Crest: issuant from a ducal coronet gules, a buck's head or. Motto: "Nec timeo nec sperno."

FIG. 356.—Armorial bearings of Wakely: Gules, a chevron between three cross crosslets argent, on a chief of the second, a stag's head caboshed of the first.

A roebuck feeding is the crest of Bell.

The attires of a stag are sometimes met with, either singly or in the form of a pair attached to the scalp. The crest of Jeune (Fig. 358) shows an instance of a scalp. The hind or doe is sometimes met with, as in

[h] Armorial bearings of John Thomas Harthill, Esq., J.P., M.R.C.S., of Manor House, Willenhall: Argent, on a mount in base vert, a hart lodged and regardant gules, a chief of the last, thereon an arrow in pale point downwards between two hearts of the first. Mantling gules and argent; and for the crest, on a wreath of the colours, upon a mount vert, a hart lodged and regardant gules, holding in the mouth an arrow in bend sinister argent, and resting the dexter fore-leg on a heart also gules. Motto: "Diligentes Deus ipse juvat."

[i] Armorial bearings of Villiers Hatton, Esq.: Azure, on a chevron between three garbs or, an annulet gules. Mantling azure and or. Crest: upon a wreath of the colours, a hind statant or, charged on the body with an annulet as in the arms. Motto: "Virtus tutissima cassis."

[j] Armorial bearings of Captain Gerald Marcell Conran, of South Brent: Vert, on a chevron argent, three martlets of the field between as many hinds' heads erased of the second. Mantling vert and argent. Crest: upon a wreath of the colours, a hind's head erased argent. Motto: "In Deo spes mea."

[k] Armorial bearings of Frederick Burnington Fellows, Esq.: Per fess or and azure, in chief two reindeer heads erased proper, and in base, on the base thereof barry wavy of four argent and of the second, an ancient ship of three masts, sails furled also proper. Mantling azure and or. Crest: on a wreath of the colours, in front of a lion's head erased proper, crowned with a crown vallery of the first, holding in the mouth an antler of a reindeer also proper. Motto: "Fac et spera."

old coat, is usually represented in the natural form of the animal, and subject to the foregoing rules.

FIG. 357.—Armorial bearings of Everard William Barton, Esq., F.S.A.: Party per fess argent and azure, four stags' heads caboshed two and two within a bordure charged with eight crescents, the whole counterchanged; and for his crest, upon a wreath of the colours, on a mount vert, an owl argent between two acorns slipped and leaved proper; with the motto, "I byde my time."

FIG. 358.—Armorial bearings of the Rt. Hon. Sir Francis Henry Jeune, K.C.B.: Sable, a stag trippant between four estoiles argent, impaling the arms of Stewart-Mackenzie, namely: quarterly, 1 and 4, azure, a stag's head caboshed or (for Mackenzie); 2 and 3, or, a double tressure flory counterflory of the last (for Stewart). Upon the escutcheon is placed a helmet befitting his degree. Mantling sable and argent. Crest: upon a wreath of the colours, between the attires of a stag affixed to the scalp, an estoile all argent; with the motto, "Faire sans dire."

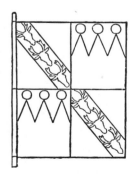

FIG. 359.—Armorial bearings of Thomas Stanley, Earl of Derby (d. 1504): Quarterly, 1 and 4, argent, on a bend azure, three bucks' heads cabossed or (for Stanley); 2 and 3, or, on a chief indented azure, three bezants (for Latham). (From a drawing of his seal, MS. Cott., Julius, C. vii.)

Antelope (heraldic).—This animal is found in English heraldry more frequently as a supporter than as a charge. As an instance, however, of the latter form may be mentioned the family of Dighton (Lincolnshire): "Per pale argent and gules, an antelope passant counter-

FIG. 360.—The Heraldic Antelope.

changed." It bears little if any relation to the real animal, though there can be but small doubt that the earliest forms originated in an attempt to represent an antelope or an ibex. Since, however, heraldry has found a use for the antelope, it has been necessary to distinguish it from the creations of the early armorists, which are now known as heraldic antelopes. Examples will be found in the supporters of Lord Carew, in the crest of Moresby, and of Bagnall.

The difference chiefly consists in the curious head and horns and in the tail, the heraldic antelope being an heraldic tiger, with the feet and legs similar to those of a deer, and with two straight serrated horns.

Ibex.—This is another form of the antelope, but with two saw-edged horns projecting from the forehead.

FIG. 361.—Armorial bearings of Marindin.

A curious animal, namely, the sea-stag, is often met with in German heraldry. This is the head, antlers, forelegs, and the upper part of the body of a stag conjoined to the fish-tail end of a mermaid. The only instance which occurs in British armory is in the case of the arms of Marindin, which were recently matriculated in Lyon Register (Fig. 361). This, coat, however, it should be observed, is really of German or perhaps of Swiss origin.

THE RAM

The ram, the consideration of which must of necessity include the sheep, the paschal lamb, and the fleece, plays no unimportant part in armory. The chief

FIG. 362.—Armorial bearings of William Francis Marwood, Esq.: Gules, a chevron ermine, between three goats' heads erased argent. Mantling gules and argent. Crest: on a wreath of the colours, on a mount vert, a ram couchant argent, horned and hoofed or.

FIG. 363.—Armorial bearings of Alexander MacMorran, Esq., K.C.: Azure, a sword in bend proper, pommelled and hilted or, in the sinister chief a dexter hand couped, and in the dexter base a paschal lamb or, carrying a banner argent charged with a cross gules. Mantling azure, doubled or; and upon a wreath of his liveries is set for crest, a dexter hand couped gules; and in an escroll over the same this motto, " Virtus virtutis præmium."

heraldic difference between the ram and the sheep, to some extent, in opposition to the agricultural distinctions, lies in the fact that the ram is always represented with horns and the sheep without. The lamb

and the ram are always represented with the natural tail, but the sheep is deprived of it. A ram can of course be "armed" (i.e. with the horns of a different colour) and "unguled," but the latter will seldom be found to be the case. The ram, the sheep, and the lamb will nearly always be found either passant or statant, but a demi-ram is naturally represented in a rampant posture, though in such a case the word " rampant " is not necessary in the blazon. Occasionally, as in the crest of Marwood (Fig. 362), the ram will be found couchant. As a charge upon a shield the ram will be found in the arms of Sydenham [" Argent, three rams passant sable"], and a ram couchant occurs in the arms of Pujolas (granted 1762) [" Per fess wavy azure and argent, in base on a mount vert, a ram couchant sable, armed and unguled or, in chief three doves proper "].

The arms of Ramsey [" Azure, a chevron between three rams passant or "] and the arms of Harman [" Sable, a chevron between six rams counter-passant two and two argent, armed and unguled or "] are other instances in which rams occur. A sheep occurs in the arms of

FIG. 364.—Armorial bearings of Lees Knowles, Esq.: Gules, on a chevron cottised between two crescents in chief and a cross crosslet in base argent, three roses of the field. Upon the escutcheon is placed a helmet befitting his degree, with a mantling gules and argent; and for his crest, upon a wreath of the colours, in front of a ram's head couped argent, attired or, three roses gules. Motto: "Nec diu nec frustra."

Sheepshanks [" Azure, a chevron erminois between in chief three roses and in base a sheep passant argent. Crest: on a mount vert, a sheep passant argent "].

The lamb, which is by no means an unusual charge in Welsh coats of arms, is most usually found in the form of a "paschal lamb," or some variation evidently founded thereupon. The lamb will be found in the arms or crests of MacMorran (Fig. 363), Platt[1] (Plate XX.), Fisher-Rowe[m] (Plate XXXVII.), and also in the arms of the city of Perth and the town of Preston.

[1] Armorial bearings of the late John Platt, Esq., of Llandudno: Azure, on a chevron or, between two fleurs-de-lis in chief and a lamb statant in base of the last, a fleur-de-lis between two cinquefoils of the first; and for the crest, on a wreath of the colours, a lamb or, resting the dexter foreleg on a fleur-de-lis azure, holding in the mouth three cinquefoils slipped vert: with the motto, " Neminem metue innocens."

[m] Armorial bearings of Edward Rowe Fisher-Rowe, Esq.: Quarterly, 1 and 4, party per pale sable and gules, three crosses patée in fess or, between as many lambs passant proper, each supporting with the dexter foreleg a pennon argent, charged with the Cross of St. George (for Rowe): 2 and 3, ermine, on a fess wavy vert, between three kingfishers, as many fountains proper, and impaling the arms of Liddell, namely: argent, fretty gules, on a chief of the last three leopards' faces or. Upon the escutcheon is placed a helmet befitting his degree, with a mantling sable and or, and for his crests, 1. upon a wreath of the colours, a lamb resting the dexter foreleg on a bee-hive proper, and charged on the body with a cross patée or (for Rowe); 2. upon a wreath of the colours, on a fountain between six bulrushes, a kingfisher all proper (for Fisher); with the motto, " Favente Deo."

The fleece—of course originally of great repute as the badge of the Order of the Golden Fleece—has in recent years been frequently employed in the grants of arms to towns or individuals connected with the woollen industry. In this connection it will be found in the arms of Johnson (Plate XXV.), the city of Leeds (Plate CXVII.), and the town of Nelson.

The demi-ram and the demi-lamb are to be found as

FIG. 365.—Armorial bearings of James Ritchie, Esq. : Vert, a chevron engrailed between two lions' heads erased in chief or, and a ram's head caboshed in base proper, horned of the second. Upon the escutcheon is placed a helmet befitting his degree, with a mantling vert, doubled or ; and on a wreath of his liveries is set for crest, a cubit arm and hand proper, holding a cross fleury or ; and in an escroll over the same this motto, " Ostendo non ostento."

FIG. 367.—Armorial bearings of Wilson Lloyd, Esq. : Azure, a chevron between three cocks argent, armed, crested, and wattled or. Mantling azure and argent. Crest : on a wreath of the colours, in front of a fern-brake proper, a goat salient argent, armed and unguled or, gorged with a collar flory counterflory sable. Motto : " Esto vigilans."

FIG. 366.—Armorial bearings of Alexander Fowler Roberts, Esq. : Gules, a hawk's lure argent, between two cushions or, in chief and in base a ram's head proper, horned gold, all within a bordure of the second. Mantling gules, doubled argent. Crest, on a wreath of his liveries, a demi-lion rampant azure, holding in the dexter paw a fleur-de-lis or. Motto : " Industria et probitate."

FIG. 368.—Armorial bearings of John Fleming, Esq. : Argent, a chevron charged with three towers triple-towered of the field, a chevron gules, between two fir-trees eradicated in chief and a lymphad with sails furled sable in base, flagged of the second. Mantling gules, doubled argent. Crest : on a wreath of his liveries, a goat's head erased argent, armed or. Motto : " Let the deed shaw."

crests, but far more usual are the rams' heads, which figure in the arms of Ramsden, and Knowles (Fig. 364), and in the arms of the towns of Huddersfield, and Barrow-in-Furness. The ram's head will sometimes be found caboshed, as in the arms of Ritchie (Fig. 365) and Roberts (Fig. 366).

Perhaps here reference may fittingly be made to the arms granted by Lyon Office in 1812 to Thomas Bonar, co. Kent ["Argent, a saltire and chief azure, the last charged with a dexter hand proper, vested with a shirtsleeve argent, issuing from the dexter chief point, holding a shoulder of mutton proper to a lion passant or, all within a bordure gules"].

The Goat is very frequently met with in armory. Its positions are passant, statant, rampant, and salient. When the horns are of a different colour it is said to be "armed."

Examples of the goat will be found in the arms of Lloyd (Fig. 367), and Fleming (Fig. 368).

The Elephant is by no means unusual in heraldry, appearing as a crest, as a charge, and also as a supporter. Nor, strange to say, is its appearance modern. It will be found in the arms or crest of Goodfellow (Fig. 243), Butcher (Fig. 369), Crookes (Fig. 157), and Concanon. The elephant's head, however, is much more frequently met with than the entire animal, and an example will be found in the arms of Saunders (Fig. 370).

Heraldry generally finds some way of stereotyping one of its creations as peculiarly its own, and in regard to the elephant, the curious "elephant and castle" is an example, this latter object being, of course, simply a derivative of the howdah of Indian life. Few early examples of the elephant omit the castle. The elephant and castle is seen in the arms of Dumbarton and in the crest of Corbet.

FIG. 369.—Armorial bearings of Samuel Butcher, Esq., F.R.G.S.: Vert, an elephant argent. Mantling vert and argent. Crest: on a wreath of the colours, a branch of a cotton-tree fructed proper. Motto: "Be steady."

A curious practice, the result of pure ignorance, has manifested itself in British armory. As will be explained in the chapter upon crests, a large proportion of German crests are derivatives of the stock basis of two bull's horns, which formed a recognised ornament for a hel-

met in Viking and other pre-heraldic days. As heraldry found its footing it did not in Germany displace those horns which in many cases continued alone as the crest or remained as a part of it in the form of additions to other objects. The craze for decoration at an early

FIG. 370.—Armorial bearings of William Henry Radcliffe Saunders, Esq.: Per chevron azure and argent, a chevron per chevron between two elephants' heads erased in chief and a lion sejant in base all counterchanged. Mantling azure and argent. Crest: on a wreath of the colours, an elephant's head argent, erased gules, charged on the neck with an annulet azure, between two palmbranches slipped vert. Motto: "Fide sed cui vide."

period seized upon the horns, which carried repetitions of the arms or their tinctures. As time went on the decoration was carried further, and the horns were made with bell-shaped open ends to receive other objects, usually bunches of feathers or flowers. So universal did this custom become that even when nothing was inserted the horns came to be always depicted with these open mouths at their points. But German heraldry now, as has always been the case, simply terms the figures "horns."

In course of time German immigrants made application for grants of arms in this country, which, doubtless, were based upon other German arms previously in use, but which, evidence of right not being forthcoming, could not be recorded as borne of right and needed to be granted with alteration as a new coat. The curious result has been that these horns have been incorporated in some number of English grants, but they have universally been described as elephants' proboscides, and are now always so represented in this country. A case in point is the crest of Verelst (Fig. 349).

Elephants' tusks have also been introduced into grants, as in the arms of Liebreich, borne in pretence by Cock (Fig. 129) and Randles ["Or a chevron wavy azure between three pairs of elephants' tusks in saltire proper"].

The Hare is but rarely met with in British armory. It appears in the arms of Cleland[n] (Plate XXXVI.), and also

[n] Armorial bearings of William Henry Cleland, Esq.: Azure, a hare salient argent, holding between the forelegs a bugle-horn stringed or, within two flaunches of the second, each charged with a bugle-horn stringed of the first, and impaling the arms of Chichester, namely: chequy or and gules, a chief vair. Mantling azure and argent. Crest: on a wreath of the colours, on a mount vert a falcon proper, belled and jessed or, between two dexter hands couped at the wrist also proper. Motto: "Je pense a qui pense plus."

in the crest of Shakerley, Bart. ["A hare proper resting her forefeet on a garb or"].

A very curious coat ["Argent, three hares playing

FIG. 371.—Armorial bearings of the Rev. Edward John Cumming Whittington-Ince: Quarterly, 1 and 4, argent, three torteaux, each charged with a cross or, between two bendlets engrailed sable, the whole between as many crosses patée fitchée gules (for Ince); 2 and 3, gules, a lion's head erased argent, collared sable, between three annulets or, a chief invected chequy of the last and azure (for Whittington). Mantling gules and argent. Crests: 1. on a wreath of the colours, upon a rock proper, a rabbit sejant argent, gorged with a collar gemel gules, resting the dexter foreleg on a cross patée fitchée sable (for Ince); 2. on a wreath of the colours, on a mount vert, a lion's head erased sable, semé of mullets or, gorged with a collar invected argent, and holding in the mouth an annulet gold (for Whittington). Motto: "Garde la foi."

bagpipes gules"] belongs to an ancient Derbyshire family FitzErcald, now represented (through the Sacheverell family) by Coke of Trussley who quarter the FitzErcald shield.

The Rabbit, or, as it is more frequently termed heraldically, the *Coney,* appears more frequently in heraldry

FIG. 372.—Armorial bearings of Arthur Warren Samuels, Esq.: Argent, two squirrels sejant and addorsed gules, between two crosses formée fitchée in pale sable. Mantling gules and argent. Crest: on a wreath of the colours, on the stump of a tree couped proper, sprouting on each side vert, a squirrel sejant gules, cracking a nut or, stalked and leaved also proper, charged on the shoulder with a cross formée fitchée gold. Motto: "Licet ex multo parvum."

than the hare, being the canting charge on the arms of Cunliffe ["Sable, three conies courant argent"], and

FIG. 373.—Armorial bearings of William John Atkinson Baldwin, Esq. Or, a chevron ermines, between two sprigs of oak in chief vert and an acorn in base azure. Mantling sable and or. Crest: on a wreath of the colours, a squirrel sejant or, charged with a fess azure, holding in his paws a feather argent. Motto: "Vim vi repello."

figuring also as the supporters of Montgomery-Cunningham ["Two conies proper"]. It will also be found as one of the crests of Whittington-Ince (Fig. 371).

The Squirrel occurs in many English coats of arms. It is always sejant, and very frequently cracking a nut. It occurs in the arms of Samuels (Fig. 372) and

FIG. 374.—Armorial bearings of William Blackstone Lee, Esq., of Seend, Melksham: Quarterly, 1 and 4, gules, a fess chequy or and azure, between ten billets, four in chief, and three, two and one in base argent (for Lee); 2 and 3, azure, a cinquefoil pierced ermine within a bordure engrailed of the last (for Astley). Mantling gules and argent. Crest: on a wreath of the colours, on a staff raguly lying fesswise, a squirrel sejant proper cracking a nut, from the dexter end of the staff an oak-branch vert, fructed or. Motto: "Ne incautus futuri."

Chambers and as the crest of De Cartaret, Pearkes (Plate XXIX.), Baldwin (Fig. 373), and Lee (Fig. 374). Fouquet, the celebrated Finance Minister of Louis XIV., bore: "Argent, a squirrel gules, a bordure of the last, semé-de-lis." The family of Fouquet, who has been sometimes identified with the Man in the Iron Mask, is now represented by an English family of the name of Sutton, to whom the arms borne by Fouquet in a slightly modified form have been granted (Fig. 186).

The Ape is not often met with, except in the cases of the different families of the great Fitzgerald clan. It is usually the crest, though the Duke of Leinster also has apes as supporters. One family of Fitzgerald, however, bear it as a charge upon the shield ["Gules, a saltire invected per pale argent and or, between four monkeys statant of the second, environed with a plain collar and chained of the second. Mantling gules and argent. Crest: on a wreath of the colours, a monkey as in the arms, charged on the body with two roses, and resting the dexter foreleg on a saltire gules. Motto: 'Crom-a-boo'"], and the family of Yorke bear an ape's head for a crest.

The ape is usually met with "collared and chained," though, unlike any other animal, the collar of an ape environs its loins and not its neck. A winged ape is included in Elvin's "Dictionary of Heraldry" as a heraldic animal, but I am not aware to whom it is assigned. Other examples will be found in the arms of Berners (Fig. 183) and Carter.

The Brock or *Badger* figures in some number of English arms. It is most frequently met with as the crest of Brooke, but will be also found in the arms or crests of Brocklebank and Motion (Fig. 375).

FIG. 375.—Armorial bearings of Andrew Richard Motion, Esq.: Gules, on a pale argent, between two lions rampant of the last, a lion rampant of the first, a chief or, thereon a badger statant proper between two roses of the field, barbed and seeded, also proper. Mantling gules and argent. Crest: upon a wreath of the colours, a millrind fesswise or, thereon a badger as in the arms; with the motto, "Suscipere et finire."

The Otter is not often met with except in Scottish coats, but an English example is that of Sir George Newnes, and a demi-otter issuant from a fess wavy will be found quartered by Seton of Mounie (Fig. 250).

An otter's head, sometimes called a seal's head, for it is impossible to distinguish the heraldic representations of the one or the other, appears in many coats of arms of different families of the name of Balfour, and two otters are the supporters belonging to the head of the Scottish house of Balfour.

The Ermine, the Stoat, and *the Weasel,* &c., are not very often met with, but the ermine appears as the crest of Crawford and the marten as the crest of a family of that name.

The Hedgehog, or, as it is usually heraldically termed, the *Urcheon,* occurs in some number of coats. For example, in the arms of Maxwell ["Argent, an eagle with two heads displayed sable, beaked and membered gules,

on the breast an escutcheon of the first, charged with a saltire of the second, surcharged in the centre with a

FIG. 376.—Armorial bearings of Walter Henry Harris, Esq., C.M.G.: Per bend gules and sable, on a bend or between two crescents fesswise in chief of the last and a sword erect in base proper, pommel and hilt gold, three hedgehogs of the second, and pendent below the escutcheon his badge as a C.M.G. Mantling gules and or. Crest: on a wreath of the colours, upon a rock proper, a hedgehog azure between on the dexter side a decrescent and on the sinister side an increscent or. Motto: "Ubique patriam reminisci."

hurcheon (hedgehog) or, all within a bordure gules"], Harris (Fig. 376), and as the crest of Money-Kyrle (Fig. 935).

The Beaver has been introduced into very many coats of late years for those connected in any way with Canada. It figures in the arms of Lord Strathcona and Mount Royal, and in the arms of Christopher (Fig. 377) and Evans[o] (Plate XXV.).

FIG. 377.—Armorial bearings of Captain Alfred Charles Seton Christopher: Per chevron wavy azure and erminois, a chart of Chesterfield's Inlet, between two estoiles in chief argent and on a mount in base vert a beaver passant proper, impaling the arms of Chenevix-Trench, namely: argent, a lion passant gules, between three fleurs-de lis azure, on a chief of the last, the sun in his splendour or. Mantling azure and or. Crest: on a wreath of the colours, two arms embowed, vested azure, the hands proper, supporting an anchor erect sable, cable argent. Motto: "Arte conservatus."

The beaver is one of the supporters of the city of Oxford, and is the sole charge in the arms of the town of Biberach (Fig. 378). Originally the arms were:

[o] Armorial bearings of Franklen George Evans, Esq.: Azure, on a chevron invected or, between two beavers statant in chief proper and a mullet in base of six points of the second, three crosses couped gules. Mantling azure and or. Crest: on a wreath of the colours, between two crosses as in the arms, a tower proper, thereon a flagstaff of the last with a pennant flying to the sinister gules, charged with two mullets of six points argent. Motto: "Nisi Dominus frustra."

"Argent, a beaver azure, crowned and armed gules," but the arms authorised by the Emperor Frederick IV., 18th July 1848, were: "Azure, a beaver or."

It is quite impossible, or at any rate very unnecessary, to turn a work on armory into an Illustrated Guide to Natural History, which would be the result if under the description of heraldic charges the attempt were made to deal with all the various animals which have

bibrach

FIG. 378.—Arms of the town of Biberach. (From Ulrich Reichenthal's *Concilium von Constanz*, Augsburg, 1483.)

by now been brought to the armorial fold, owing to their inclusion for special and sufficient reasons in one or two isolated grants.

Far be it from me, however, to make any remark which should seem to indicate the raising of any objection to such use. In my opinion it is highly admirable, providing there is some definite reason in each case for the introduction of these strange animals other than mere caprice. They add to the interest of heraldry, and they give to modern arms and armory a definite status and meaning, which is a relief from the endless monotony of meaningless lions, bends, chevrons, mullets, and martlets.

But at the same time the isolated use in a modern

FIG. 379.—Armorial bearings of John Cole Kemsley, Gentleman: Or, on a mount in base vert, a man in armour holding over his dexter shoulder a battle-axe, head downwards proper, a chief arched per pale sable and gules, thereon two lions passant counter-passant argent. Mantling vert and or. Crest: upon a wreath of the colours, on a mount vert, a demi-zebra proper, gorged with a collar gemel or, resting the sinister foreleg on an Esquire's helmet also proper. Motto : " Semper paratus."

grant of such an animal as the kangaroo does not make it one of the peculiarly heraldic menagerie, and con-

sequently many such instances must be dismissed herein with brief mention, particularly as many of these creatures heraldically exist only as supporters, in which chapter some are more fully discussed. Save as a supporter, the only instance I know of the *Kangaroo* is in the coat of Moore (Fig. 158) and in the arms of Arthur, Bart.

The Zebra will be found as the crest of Kemsley (Fig. 379).

The Camel, which will be dealt with later as a supporter, in which form it appears in the arms of Viscount

FIG. 380.—Armorial bearings of George Henry Cammel, Esq. : Sable, on a chevron argent, cottised or, between three camels statant of the second, as many trefoils slipped of the first. Mantling sable and argent; and for his crest, upon a wreath of the colours, a camel's head erased argent, gorged with a collar gemel sable, holding in the mouth a trefoil as in the arms. Motto : "Perseverando."

Kitchener, the town of Inverness (Fig. 239), and some of the Livery Companies, also figures in the reputed but unrecorded arms of Camelford, and in the arms of Cammell of Sheffield (Fig. 380), Clover [p] (Plate XLIII.), and various other families of a similar name.

The fretful *Porcupine* was borne [" Gules, a porcupine erect argent, tusked, collared, and chained or "] by Simon Eyre, Lord Mayor of London in 1445 : and the creature also figures as one of the supporters and the crest of Sidney, Lord De Lisle and Dudley.

The Bat will be found in the arms of Heyworth and as the crest of a Dublin family named Wakefield.

The Tortoise occurs in the arms of a Norfolk family named Gandy, and is also stated by Papworth to occur in the arms of a Scottish family named Goldie. This coat, however, is not matriculated. It also occurs in the crests of Deane and Hayne.

The Springbok, which is one of the supporters of Cape Colony (Plate LXI.), and two of which are the supporters of Viscount Milner, is also the crest of Randles ["On a wreath of the colours, a springbok or South African antelope statant in front of an assegai erect all proper "].

The Rhinoceros occurs as one of the supporters of Viscount Colville of Culross, and also as the crest of Wade.

[p] Armorial bearings of George Robert Clover, Esq.: Sable, a camel with two humps between three trefoils slipped all or. Mantling sable and or. Crest: on a wreath of the colours, a camel's head erased or, charged with three trefoils slipped in pale sable, and holding in the mouth a like trefoil. Motto : " Ut vinclo vir verbo ligitur."

The Alpaca, and also two *Angora Goats'* heads figure in the arms of Benn (Fig. 381).

FIG. 381.—Armorial bearings of William Henry Benn, Esq.: Party per chevron or and azure, on a mount in base an alpaca statant, and two angora goats' heads affronté in chief all proper. Mantling azure and or. Crest: on a wreath of the colours, an alpaca's head couped at the neck between two sprigs of oak fructed all proper. Motto: "Curâ atque industria."

The Rat occurs in the arms of Ratton,[q] which is a peculiarly good example of a canting coat.

The Mole occurs in the arms of Mitford ["Argent, a fess sable between three moles displayed sable"] and Cantrell-Hubbersty (Plate XLIV.).

The Crocodile, which is the crest and one of the supporters of Speke (Plate XXXIX.), is also the crest of Westcar ["A crocodile proper, collared and chained or"].

CHAPTER XVII

MONSTERS

THE heraldic catalogue of beasts runs riot when we reach those mythical or legendary creatures which can only be summarised under the generic term of monsters. Most mythical animals, however, can be traced back to some comparable counterpart in natural history.

The fauna of the New World was of course unknown to those early heraldic artists with whose knowledge and imagination, no less than with their skill (or lack of it) in draughtsmanship, lay the nativity of so much of our heraldry. They certainly thought they were representing animals in existence in most if not in all cases, though one gathers that they considered many of the animals they used to be misbegotten hybrids. Doubtless, working on the assumption of the mule as the hybrid of the horse and the ass, they jumped to the conclusion that animals which contained salient characteristics of two other animals which they knew were likewise hybrids.

[q] Armorial bearings of James Joseph Louis Ratton, Esq.: Azure, in base the sea argent, and thereon a tunny sable, on a chief of the second a rat passant of the third. Upon the escutcheon is placed a helmet befitting his degree, with a mantling azure and argent; and for his crest, upon a wreath of the colours, an ibex statant guardant proper, charged on the body with two fleurs-de-lis fesswise azure, and resting the dexter foreleg on a shield argent charged with a passion cross sable. Motto: "In Deo spero."

A striking example of their theories is to be found in the heraldic *Camelopard*, which was anciently devoutly believed to be begotten by the leopard upon the camel. A leopard they would be familiar with, also the camel, for both belong to that corner of the world where the north-east of the African Continent, the south-east of Europe, and the west of Asia join, where were fought out the wars of the Cross, and where heraldry took on itself a definite being. There the known civilisations of the world met, taking one from the other knowledge, more or less distorted, ideas and wild imaginings. A stray giraffe was probably seen by some journeyer up the Nile, who, unable to otherwise account for it, considered and stated the animal to be the hybrid offspring of the leopard and camel. Another point needs to be borne in mind. Earlier artists were in no way fettered by any supposed necessity for making their pictures realistic representations. Realism is a modernity. Their pictures were decoration, and they thought far more of making their subject fit the space to be decorated than of making it a "speaking likeness."

Nevertheless, their work was not all imagination. In the *Crocodile* we get the basis of the dragon, if indeed the heraldic dragon be not a perpetuation of ancient legends, or even perhaps of then existing representations of those winged antediluvian animals, the fossilised remains of which are now available. Wings, however, need never be considered a difficulty. It has ever been the custom (from the angels of Christianity to the personalities of Mercury and Pegasus) to add wings to any figure held in veneration. Why, it would be difficult to say, but nevertheless the fact remains.

The Unicorn, however, it is not easy to resolve into an original basis, because until the seventeenth century

FIG. 382.—Armorial bearings of Hamon Le Strange, Esq.: Quarterly, 1. quarterly, i. and iiii., gules, two lions passant in pale argent (for Le Strange); ii. and iii., sable, a unicorn statant or, on a chief of the last, three billets of the first (for Styleman); 2. the same arms of Styleman; 3. the same arms of Le Strange; 4. or, a maunch gules (for Hastings). Mantling gules and argent. Crests: 1. on a wreath of the colours, a lion statant, tail extended or (for Le Strange); 2. on a wreath of the colours, a bear's head erased azure, bezantée, collared and chained or (for Styleman). Motto: "Mihi parta tueri." Supporters (dexter, a stag argent, with a lion's forepaws and tail, collared, and sinister, a lion gules) are used, but they are not of official authority.

every one fondly believed in the existence of the animal. Mr. Beckles Wilson appears to have paid considerable attention to the subject, and was responsible for the article "The Rise of the Unicorn" which recently appeared in *Cassell's Magazine*. That writer traces the matter to a certain extent from non-heraldic sources, and the following remarks, which are taken from the above article, are of considerable interest :—

"The real genesis of the unicorn was probably this : at a time when armorial bearings were becoming an indispensable part of a noble's equipment, the attention of those knights who were fighting under the banner of the Cross was attracted to the wild antelopes of Syria and Palestine. These animals are armed with long, straight, spiral horns set close together, so that at a side view they appeared to be but a single horn. To confirm this, there are some old illuminations and drawings extant which endow the early unicorn with many of the attributes of the deer and goat kind. The sort of horn supposed to be carried by these Eastern antelopes had long been a curiosity, and was occasionally brought back as a trophy by travellers from the remote parts of the earth. There is a fine one to be seen to-day at the abbey of St. Denis, and others in various collections in Europe. We now know these so-called unicorn's horns, usually carved, to belong to that marine monster the narwhal, or sea-unicorn. But the fable of a breed of horned horses is at least as old as Pliny [Had the 'gnu' anything to do with this?], and centuries later the Crusaders, or the monkish artists who accompanied them, attempted to delineate the marvel. From their first rude sketches other artists copied ; and so each presentment was passed along, until at length the present form of the unicorn was attained. There was a time—not so long ago— when the existence of the unicorn was as implicitly believed in as the camel or any other animal not seen in these latitudes ; and the translators of the Bible set their seal upon the legend by translating the Hebrew word *reem* (which probably meant a rhinoceros) as 'unicorn.' Thus the worthy Thomas Fuller came to consider the existence of the unicorn clearly proved by the mention of it in Scripture ! Describing the horn of the animal, he writes, 'Some are plain, as that of St. Mark's in Venice ; others wreathed about it, which probably is the effect of age, those wreaths being but the wrinkles of most vivacious unicorns. The same may be said of the colour : white when newly taken from the head ; yellow, like that lately in the Tower, of some hundred years' seniority ; but whether or no it will soon turn black, as that of Plinie's description, let others decide.'

"All the books on natural history so late as the seventeenth century describe at length the unicorn ; several of them carefully depict him as though the artist had drawn straight from the life.

"If art had stopped here, the wonder of the unicorn would have remained but a paltry thing after all. His finer qualities would have been unrecorded, and all his virtues hidden. But, happily, instead of this, about the animal first conceived in the brain of a Greek (as Pegasus also was), and embodied through the fertile fancy of the Crusader, the monks and heraldists of the Middle Ages devised a host of spiritual legends. They told of his pride, his purity, his endurance, his matchless spirit.

"'The greatnesse of his mynde is such that he chooseth rather to dye than be taken alive.' Indeed, he was only conquerable by a beautiful maiden. One fifteenth-century writer gives a recipe for catching a unicorn. 'A maid is set where he hunteth ; and she openeth her lap, to whom the unicorn, as seeking rescue from the force of the hunter, yieldeth his head and leaveth all his fierceness, and resteth himself under her protection, sleepeth until he is taken and slain.' But although many were reported to be thus enticed to their destruction, only their horns, strange to say, ever reached Europe. There is one in King Edward's collection at Buckingham Palace.

"Naturally, the horn of such an animal was held a sovereign specific against poison, and 'ground unicorn's horn' often figures in mediæval books of medicine.

"There was in Shakespeare's time at Windsor Castle the 'horn of a unicorn of above eight spans and a half in length, valued at above £10,000.' This may have been the one now at Buckingham Palace. One writer, describing it, says :—

"'I doe also know that horn the King of England possesseth to be wreathed in spires, even as that is accounted in the Church of St Dennis, than which they suppose none greater in the world, and I never saw anything in any creature more worthy praise than this horne. It is of soe great a length that the tallest man can scarcely touch the top thereof, for it doth fully equal seven great feet. It weigheth thirteen pounds, with their assize, being only weighed by the gesse of the hands it seemeth much heavier.'

CHARLES THOMAS-STANFORD

Fig. 383.—Bookplate of Charles Thomas-Stanford, Esq. Arms : Quarterly, 1 and 4, per pale or and sable, on a chevron nebuly between three bugles stringed, as many martlets all counterchanged, and (for distinction) in the centre chief point a cross crosslet also counterchanged (for Stanford) ; 2 and 3, gules, two chevronels argent between in chief as many plates, each charged with a fleur-de-lis of the field, and in base a wolf's head erased of the second (for Thomas). Mantling sable and or. Crests : 1. on a wreath of the colours, a buffalo's head caboshed sable within a chain in arch or, the head charged, for distinction, with a cross crosslet also or (for Stanford) ; 2. on a wreath of the colours, a demi-unicorn gules, charged on the body with two chevronels as in the arms, and supporting with the sinister forepaw a plate charged with a fleur-de-lis of the first. Motto : "Æquus in arduis." (From an engraved plate by C. W. Sherborne, R.E.)

"Spenser, in the 'Faerie Queen,' thus describes a contest between the unicorn and the lion :—

' Like as the lyon, whose imperial powre
A proud rebellious unicorn defyes,
T'avoide the rash assault and wrathfull stowre
Of his fiers foe, him to a tree applies.
And when him running in full course he spyes
He slips aside ; the whiles that furious beast
His precious horne, sought of his enimyes,
Strikes in the stroke, ne thence can be released,
But to the victor yields a bounteous feast.'

"'It hath,' remarked Guillim, in 1600, 'been much questioned among naturalists which it is that is properly called the unicorn; and some have made doubt whether there be such a beast or no. But the great esteem of his horn in many places to be seen may take away that needless scruple.'

"Another old writer, Topsell, says:—

"'These beasts are very swift, and their legs have not articles. They keep for the most part in the deserts, and live solitary in the tops of the mountaines. There was nothing more horrible than the voice or braying of it, for the voice is strained above measure. It fighteth both with the mouth and with the heeles, with the mouth biting like a lyon, and with the heeles kicking like a horse.'

"Nor is belief in the unicorn confined to Europe. By Chinese writers it is characterised as a 'spiritual beast.' The existence of the unicorn is firmly credited by the most intelligent natives and by not a few Europeans. A very trustworthy observer, the Abbé Huc, speaks very positively on the subject: 'The unicorn really exists in Tibet. . . . We had for a long time a small Mongol treatise on Natural History, for the use of children, in which a unicorn formed one of the pictorial illustrations.'"

The unicorn, however, as it has heraldically developed, is drawn with the body of a horse, the tail of the heraldic lion, the legs and feet of the deer, the head and mane of a horse, to which is added the long twisted horn from which the animal is named and a beard. Good representations of the unicorn will be found in the various figures of the Royal Arms which appear herein, and in Fig. 384, which is as fine a piece of heraldic design as could be wished.

The crest of Yonge of Colbrooke, Devonshire, is "a demi-sea-unicorn argent, armed gules, finned or," and the crest of Tynte (Kemeys-Tynte of Cefn Mably and

FIG. 385.—Armorial bearings of the Rev. Thomas Erskine Swanzy: Gules, a fess argent between two unicorns counter-courant or. Mantling gules and argent. Crest: on a wreath of the colours, a unicorn's head or, collared with a bar gemel gules. Motto: "Per Deum et ferrum obtinui."

Halswell) is "on a mount vert, a unicorn sejant argent, armed and crined or."

The unicorn will be found in the arms of Styleman, quartered by Le Strange (Fig. 382), Thomas-Stanford (Fig. 383), and Swanzy (Fig. 385).

The Griffin or *Gryphon.*—Though in the popular mind any heraldic monster is generically termed a griffin, the griffin has, nevertheless, very marked and distinct peculiarities. It is one of the hybrid monstrosities which heraldry is so fond of, and is formed by the body, hind legs, and tail of a lion conjoined to the head and claws of an eagle, the latter acting as its forepaws. It has the wings of the eagle, which are never represented close, but it also has ears, and this, by the way, should be noted, because herein is the only distinction between a griffin's head and an eagle's head when the rest of the body is not represented. Though but very seldom so met with, it is occasionally found proper, by which description is meant that the plumage is of the brown colour of the eagle, the rest of the body being the natural colour of the lion. The griffin is frequently found with its beak and forelegs of a different colour from its body, and is then termed "armed," though another term, "beaked and forelegged," is almost as frequently used. A very popular idea is that the origin of the griffin was the dimidiation of two coats of arms, one having an eagle and the other a lion as charges, but taking the origin of armory to belong to about the end of the eleventh century, or thereabouts, the griffin can be found as a distinct creation, not necessarily heraldic, at a very much earlier date. An exceedingly good and an early representation of the griffin will be found in Fig. 386. It is a representation of the great seal of the town of Schweidnitz in the jurisdiction of Breslau, and belongs to the year 1315. The inscription is "+S universitatis civium de Swidnitz." In the grant of arms to the town in the year 1452, the griffin is gules on a field

FIG. 384.—A unicorn rampant. (Designed by Miss Helard.)

of argent. Fig. 5 on Plate XLVI. is taken from Conrad Grünenberg's *Wappenbuch*, 1483, and is the imaginary coat of arms ascribed by that writer to Judas Maccabæus, who assigns him: "Azure, a griffin segreant or, armed gules." Plate XLVI. Fig. 6 represents a coat of arms showing a griffin with the label of three points which exists at the Palazzi Guadagni in Florence. It belongs to the second half of the fifteenth century. Fig. 7 on the same plate is a carving in relief belonging to the end of the thirteenth century, and shows the arms of Fornbach, a Bavarian dynastic family which became extinct so long ago as 1158. The monastery at Fornbach, now Vornbach, between Neuburg and Scharding on the Inn, made use of the same arms, which are: "Argent, a griffin segreant gules, holding in its claws a hare or." The griffin will be found in all sorts of positions, and the terms applied to it are the same as would be applied to a lion, except in the single instance of the rampant position. A griffin is then termed "segreant." The wings are usually represented as endorsed and erect, but this is not compulsory, as will be seen by a reference to the supporters of the Earl of Mar and Kellie. There is a certain curiosity in

the world), and more gret and stronger than an 100 egles such as we han amonges us . . . ," and other

FIG. 387.—Armorial bearings of Thomas Myles Sandys, Esq.: Or, a fess dancetté between three cross crosslets fitché gules. Mantling gules and or. Crest: on a wreath of the colours, a griffin segreant per fess or and gules. Motto: "Probum non pœnitet."

FIG. 386.—Seal of the Town of Schweidnitz.

English heraldry wholly peculiar to it which may be here referred to. A griffin in the ordinary way is merely so termed, but a male griffin by some curious reasoning has no wings, but is adorned with spikes showing at some number of points on its body. I have, under remarks upon the panther, hazarded the supposition that the male griffin of English heraldry is nothing more than a British development and form of the Continental heraldic panther which is unknown to us. The origin of the clusters and spikes, unless they are to be found in the flames of fire associated with the panther, must remain a mystery. The male griffin is very seldom met with, but two of these creatures are the supporters of Sir George John Egerton Dashwood, Bart. Whilst we consider the griffin a purely mythical animal, there is no doubt whatever that earlier writers devoutly believed that such animals existed. Sir John Maundeville tells us in his "Travels" that they abound in Bacharia. "Sum men seyn that thei han the body upward as an egle, and benethe as a lyoun; and treuly thei seyn sothe that thei ben of that schapp. But a Griffoun hathe the body more gret and more strong than eight lyouns of such lyouns as ben o' this half (of

FIG. 388.—Bookplate of William Swaine Chisenhale-Marsh, Esq.: Sable, a horse's head erased between two pheons in pale argent, two flaunches of the last, each charged with a cross crosslet fitché gules. Mantling sable and argent. Crest: on a wreath of the colours, in front of a cross crosslet fitché gules, a griffin argent, resting the dexter claw on a pheon in bend and erect sable. Motto: "In hoc signo vinces." (Designed and etched by G. W. Eve, R.E.)

writers, whilst not considering them an original type of

animal, undoubtedly believed in their existence as hybrid of the eagle and the lion. It is of course a well-known fact that the mule, the most popular hybrid, does not breed. This fact would be accepted as accounting for the rarity of animals which were considered to be hybrids.

Though there are examples of griffins in some of the earliest rolls of arms, the animal cannot be said to have come into general use until a somewhat later period. Nowadays, however, it is next in popularity possibly to the lion. It will be found in the coats of arms of Marples (Fig. 184), De Trafford (Plate XXXIX.), and Sandys (Fig. 387), in all of which cases it is segreant. It is salient in the arms of Murray-Stewart, and passant in the crest of Chisenhale-Marsh (Fig. 388), and the arms of Rylands (Fig. 389). It is not often found sejant, but it so occurs in the crest of Sir John Wolfe-Barry ["A gryphon sejant gules, wings elevated and addorsed, barry of six or and azure, in its mouth a rose argent, leaved and slipped proper, resting the dexter claw on a portcullis as in the arms"], and in the achievements of Benyon, Forsaith, and Thomas.

The demi-griffin is very frequently found as a crest,

FIG. 389.—Armorial bearings of John Paul Rylands: Quarterly, 1 and 4, per fess dancetté or and gules; 2 and 3, ermine; over all on a fess azure a griffin passant regardant between two fleurs-de-lis of the first, impaling the arms of Glazebrook, namely: ermine, an eagle displayed gules, beaked, legged, and holding in the beak a fleur-de-lis or, on a chief sable two bezants, each charged with a fleur-de-lis azure; and for his crest, upon a wreath of the colours, a demi-lion azure, charged on the shoulder with a bezant, thereon a fleur-de-lis also azure, and supporting a flagstaff entwined with a branch of oak proper, therefrom flowing to the sinister a banner gules, charged with a lion passant and fringed gold; with the motto, "Dum spiro spero."

as in the arms of Burlton (Fig. 122), Watts[a] (Plate XXX.), Johnson[b] (Plate XXV.).

A griffin's head is still yet more frequently met with,

[a] Armorial bearings of James Watts, Esq.: Ermine, on a chief sable, a garb between two bees or. Upon the escutcheon is placed a helmet befitting his degree, with a mantling sable and argent; and for his crest, upon a wreath of the colours, a demi-griffin sable, with wings extended chequy or and sable, the sinister claw resting on a garb or; with the motto, "Fide sed cui vide."

[b] Armorial bearings of Thomas Fielding Johnson, Esq.: Argent, three chevronels between two griffins' heads erased in chief and a fleece in base gules. Mantling gules and argent. Crest: on a wreath of the colours, a demi-griffin gules holding a pheon in the dexter claw and resting the sinister on a lozenge or. Motto: "Labore et honore."

and as a charge upon the shields it will be found in the arms of Raikes (Fig. 390), Kay, and many other families.

FIG. 390.—Armorial bearings of Lieut.-Col. Frederick Duncan Raikes, C.I.E.: Argent, a chevron engrailed pean between three griffins' heads erased sable, each charged with an ermine spot gules, and pendent below the escutcheon his badge as C.I.E. Mantling sable and argent. Crest: upon a wreath of the colours, a griffin's head as in the arms. Motto: "Honestum præferre utili."

A variety of the griffin is found in the gryphon-marine, or sea-griffin. In it the fore part of the creature is that of the eagle, but the wings are sometimes omitted; and the lower half of the animal is that of a fish, or rather of a mermaid. Such a creature is the charge in the arms of the Silesian family of Mestich: "Argent, a sea-griffin proper" (Siebmacher, *Wappenbuch*, i. 69). "Azure, a (winged) sea-griffin per fess gules and argent crowned or," is the coat of the Barons von Puttkammer. One or two other Pomeranian families have the like charge without wings.

The Dragon.—Much akin to the griffin is the dragon, but the similarity of appearance is more superficial than real, inasmuch as in all details it differs, except in the broad similarity that it has four legs, a pair of wings, and is a terrible creature. The much referred to "griffin" opposite the Law Courts in the Strand is really a dragon. The head of a dragon is like nothing else in heraldry, and

FIG. 391.—The Dragon.

from what source it originated or what basis existed for ancient heraldic artists to imagine it from must remain a mystery, unless it has developed from the crocodile or some antediluvian animal much akin. It is like nothing else in heaven or on earth. Its neck is covered with

THE ART OF HERALDRY

scales not unlike those of a fish. All four legs are scaled and have claws, the back is scaled, the tongue is barbed, and the under part of the body is likewise scaled, but here, in rolls of a much larger size. Great differences will be found in the shape of the ears, but the wings of the dragon are always represented as the wings of a bat, with the long ribs or bones carried to the base. The dragon is one of the most artistic of heraldic creations, and lends itself very readily to the genius of any artist. In nearly all modern representations the tail, like the tongue, will be found ending in a barb, but it should be observed that this is a comparatively recent addition. All dragons of the Tudor period were invariably represented without any such additions to their tails. The tail was long and smooth, ending in a blunt point. A good example of the Tudor dragon will be found in the chapter herein on "Prince Arthur's Book."

Whilst we have separate and distinct names for many varieties of dragonian creatures, other countries in their use of the word "dragon" include the wyvern, basilisk, cockatrice, and other similar creatures, but the distinct name in German heraldry for our four-footed dragon is the *Lindwurm*, and Fig. 391 is a representation of the dragon according to German ideas, which nevertheless might form an example for English artists to copy, except that we very seldom represent ours as coward. Fig. 392 is a clever design of

FIG. 392.—Example of a dragon. (Designed by Miss C. Helard.)

a dragon by Miss Helard, the wings in this case being expanded.

The red dragon upon a mount vert, which forms a part of the Royal achievement as the badge of Wales, is known as the red dragon of Cadwaller, and in deference to a loudly expressed sentiment on the subject, His Majesty the King has just added the Welsh dragon differenced by a label of three points as an additional badge to the achievement of His Royal Highness the Prince of Wales. The red dragon was one of the supporters of the Tudor kings, being used by Henry VII., Henry VIII., and Edward VI. Queen Elizabeth, however, whose liking for gold is evidenced by her changing the Royal mantle from gules and ermine to gold and ermine, also changed the colour of the dragon as her supporter to gold. There is some room for doubt whether the dragon in the Royal Arms was really of Welsh origin. The point was discussed at some length by the present writer in the *Genealogical Magazine* (October 1902). It was certainly in use by King Henry III.

A dragon may be statant, rampant, or passant, and the crests of Bicknell and of Sir Charles Young, Garter King of Arms, are examples of dragons couchant.

Dragons are not so frequently met with as griffins, but they occur in the arms of Evans impaled by North (see Plate XXIV.), Sloggett (Fig. 393), and Lowdell, and the favourite Welsh device of the dragon's head

FIG. 393.—Armorial bearings of William Henry Sloggett, Esq.: Or, on a bend sable between two pellets, a bezant within a bordure of the second, charged with annulets of the field and bezants alternately, on a canton argent, gutté-de-poix, a dragon passant sable. Upon the escutcheon is placed a helmet befitting his degree, with a mantling sable and or; and for his crest, upon a wreath of the colours, a dragon sable, semé of annulets or, and resting the dexter claw on a bezant; with the motto, "Bethon dur."

holding a human hand will be met with, for example, in the arms of Edwards (Plate XXIII.), and a sea-dragon, whatever that creature may be, occurs in one of the crests of Mr. Mainwaring-Ellerker-Onslow (Fig. 686). A curious crest is that of Langton, namely: "On a wreath of the colours, an eagle or and a wyvern vert, interwoven and erect on their tails," and an equally curious one is the crest of Maule, *i.e.* "A wyvern vert, with two heads vomiting fire at both ends proper, charged with a crescent argent."

Variations such as that attributed to the family of Raynor ["Argent, a dragon volant in bend sable"] and the sinister supporter of the arms of Viscount Gough ["The dragon (or) of China gorged with a mural crown and chained sable"] may be noted. The Chinese dragon, which is also the dexter supporter of Sir Robert Hart, Bart., follows closely the Chinese model, and is without wings.

The Wyvern.—There is no difference whatever between a wyvern's head and a dragon's, but there is considerable difference between a wyvern and a dragon, at any rate in English heraldry, though the wyvern appears to be the form more frequently met with under the name of a dragon in other countries. The wyvern has only two legs, the body curling away into the tail, and is usually represented as resting upon its legs and tail. On the other hand, it will occasionally be found sitting erect upon its tail with its claws in the air, and the supporters of the Duke of Marlborough are generally so represented. As a charge or crest, however, probably the only instance of a wyvern sejant erect is the crest of Mansergh (Fig. 394).

Plate XLVI. Fig. 10 is another of those mythical coats taken from Conrad Grünenberg's *Wappenbuch* of 1483.

In this he assigns "argent a wyvern sable vomiting flames of fire" to the "First Emperor Julius," and the arms as represented give one some notion of the German idea of what this creature should be.

Occasionally the wyvern is represented without wings and with the tail nowed. Both these peculiarities occur in the case of the crest of a Lancashire family named Ffarington.

The wyvern will also be found in the arms of Maclulich and in the crest of Whewell (Fig. 98).

FIG. 394.—Armorial bearings of James Mansergh, Esq.: Barry wavy of eight argent and azure, gutté-d'eau, on a bend between six arrows barbed and flighted gules, three fountains proper. Mantling azure and argent. Crest: on a wreath of the colours, a wyvern sejant and erect gules, gorged with a collar wavy argent, and supporting with the claws an arrow erect gules, barbed and flighted argent. Motto: "Tout jour prêt."

The Cockatrice.—The next variety is the cockatrice, which is, however, comparatively rare. Two cockatrices are the supporters to the arms of the Earl of Westmeath, and also to the arms of Sir Edmund Charles Nugent, Bart. But the animal is not common as a charge. The difference between a wyvern and a cockatrice is that the latter has the head of a cock substituted for the dragon's head with which the wyvern is decorated. Like the cock, the beak, comb, and wattles are often of another tincture, and the animal is then termed armed, combed, and wattled.

The cockatrice is sometimes termed a basilisk, and according to ancient writers the basilisk is produced from an egg laid by a nine-year-old cock and hatched by a toad on a dunghill. Probably this is merely the expression of the intensified loathing which it was desired to typify. But the heraldic basilisk is stated to have its tail terminating in a dragon's head. In English heraldry, at any rate, I know of no such example.

The Hydra, or *Seven-headed Dragon*, as the crest, is ascribed to the families of Barret, Crespine, and Lownes.

The Camelopard, which is nothing more or less than an ordinary giraffe, must be properly included amongst mythical animals, because the form and semblance of the giraffe was used to represent a mythical hybrid creation which the ancients believed to be begotten between a leopard and a camel. Possibly they represented the real giraffe (which they may have known), taking that to be a hybrid between the two animals stated. It occurs as the crest of several coats of arms for the name of Crisp, one of which will be seen in Fig. 395.

FIG. 395.—Armorial bearings of Fred Crisp, Esq.: Sable, on a chevron argent, surmounted by a pale engrailed of the last, pierced of the field, five horse-shoes counterchanged. Mantling sable and argent. Crest: on a wreath of the colours, in front of a camelopard statant argent, semé of pellets, gorged with a collar with line reflexed over the back gules, three horse-shoes sable. Motto: "Mens conscia recti."

The Camelopardel, which is another mythical animal fathered upon armory, is stated to be the same as the camelopard, but with the addition of two long horns curved backwards. I know of no instance in which it occurs.

The human face or figure conjoined to some other animal's body gives us a number of heraldic creatures, some of which play no inconsiderable part in armory.

The human figure (male) conjoined to the tail of a fish is known as the *Triton* or *Merman*. Though there are some number of instances in which it occurs as a supporter (Plate CXVI.), it is seldom met with as a charge upon a shield. It is, however, assigned as a crest to the family of Tregent, and a family of Robertson, of London.

The Mermaid is much more frequently met with. It is generally represented with the traditional mirror and comb in the hands. It will be found appearing, for example, in the arms of Ellis, of Glasfryn, co. Monmouth. The crest of Mason, used without authority by the founder of Mason's College, led to its inclusion in the arms of the University of Birmingham (Fig. 293). It will also be found as the crest of Rutherford (Fig. 202).

The Melusine, i.e. a mermaid with two tails, though not unknown in British heraldry, is more frequent in German. It is represented on Plate LVI.

The Sphinx, of course originally derived from the Egyptian figure, has the body, legs, and tail of a lion conjoined to the breasts, head, and face of a woman (Fig. 1). As a charge it occurs in the arms of Cochrane (Plate LXVIII.) and Cameron of Fassiefern. This last-mentioned coat affords a striking example of the over-elaboration to be found in so many of the grants which owe their origin to the Peninsular War and the other "fightings" in which England was engaged at the period.

THE ART OF HERALDRY

A winged sphinx is the crest of a family of the name of Asgile.

The Centaur—the familiar fabulous animal, half man, half horse—is sometimes represented carrying a bow and arrow, when it is called a "sagittarius." It is not infrequently met with in heraldry, though it is to be found more often in Continental than in English blazonry. In its "sagittarius" form it is sculptured on a column in the Romanesque cloister of St. Aubin at Angers. It will be found as the crest of most families named Lambert, and it is one of the supporters of Lord Hood of Avelon. It is also the crest of a family of Fletcher. A very curious crest was borne by a family of Lambert, and is to be seen on their monuments. They could establish no official authority for their arms as used, and consequently obtained official authorisation in the early part of the eighteenth century, when the crest then granted was a regulation sagittarius (Fig. 495). Up to that time, however, they had always used a "female centaur."

Chimera.—This legendary animal happily does not figure in English heraldry, and but rarely abroad. Instances where it occurs depict it as having the head and breast of a woman, the forepaws of a lion, the body of a goat, the hind legs of a griffin, and the tail of a dragon. It is about as ugly and misbegotten a creature as can readily be imagined.

The Man-Lion will be found under the heading of lions, and Elvin mentions in addition the *Weir-Wolf*, *i.e.* the wolf with a human face and horns. Probably this creature has strayed into heraldic company by mistake. I know of no armorial use of it.

The Satyr, which has a well-established existence in other than heraldic sources of imagination, is composed of a demi-savage united to the hind legs of a goat.

The Satyral is a hybrid animal having the body of a lion and the face of an old man, with the horns of an antelope.

The Harpy—which is a curious creature consisting of the head, neck, and breasts of a woman conjoined to the wings and body of a vulture—is peculiarly German, though it does exist in the heraldry of this country. The German name for it is the *Jungfraunadler*. The German method of depicting this will be seen on Plate XLVI. Fig. 11, which represents the arms, or more correctly speaking the seal-device, of the town of Nürnberg, where it occurs as early as 1243. The arms are: "Azure, a jungfraunadler crowned or," and the example here given is from *Jost Amman* (Rixner's "Tournament Book," 1566).

The shield of the Rietbergs, Princes of Ost-Friesland, is: "Sable, a harpy crowned, and with wings displayed all proper; between four stars, two in chief as many in base, or."

The harpy will be found as a crest in this country.

The Devil is not, as may be imagined, a favourite heraldic charge. The arms of Sissinks of Groningen, for instance, are: "Or, a horned devil having six paws, the body terminating in the tail of a fish all gules." The family of Bawde have for a crest: "A satyr's head in profile sable, with wings to the side of the head or, the tongue hanging out of his mouth gules." Though so blazoned, I feel sure it is really intended to represent a fiend. On the Garter Hall-plate of John de Grailly, Captal de Buch, the crest is a man's head with ass's ears. This is, however, usually termed a Midas' head. A certain coat of arms which is given in the "General Armory" under the name of Dannecourt, and also under the name of Morfyn or Murfyn, has crest: "A blackamoor's head couped at the shoulders, habited paly of six ermine and ermines, pendents in

his ears or, wreathed about the forehead, with bat's wings to the head sable, expanded on each side."

Many mythical animals can be more conveniently considered under their natural counterparts. Of these the notes upon the heraldic antelope and the heraldic ibex accompany those upon the natural antelope, and the heraldic panther is included with the real animal. The heraldic tiger, likewise, is referred to concurrently with the Bengal or natural tiger. The pegasus, the sea-horse, and the winged sea-horse are mentioned with other examples of the horse, and the sea-dog is included with other breeds and varieties of that useful animal. The winged bull, of which only one instance is known to me, occurs as the supporters of the Butchers' Livery Company, and has been already alluded to, as also the winged stag. The sea-stag is referred to under the sub-heading of stags. The two-headed lion, the double-queued lion, the lion queue-fourché, the sea-lion (which is sometimes found winged) are all included in the chapter upon lions, as are also the winged lion and the lion-dragon. The winged ape is mentioned when considering the natural animal, and perhaps it may be as well to allude to the asserted heraldic existence of the sea-monkey, though I am not aware of any instance in which it is borne.

The arms of Challoner afford an instance of the *Sea-Wolf*, the crest of that family being: "A demi-sea-wolf rampant or." Guillim, however (p. 271), in quoting the arms of Fennor, would seem to assert the sea-wolf and sea-dog to be one and the same.

The Phœnix and the *Double-headed Eagle* will naturally be more conveniently dealt with in the chapter upon the eagle.

The Salamander has been represented in various ways, and is usually described as a dragon in flames of fire. It is sometimes so represented, but without

FIG. 396.—Armorial bearings of Sir William Farmer: Per chevron dovetailed gules and argent, in chief two lions' heads erased of the last, and in base a salamander in flames proper, and impaling the arms of Perkins, namely: erminois, an eagle displayed, in chief, an escallop between two fleurs-de-lis, and in base a fleur-de-lis between two escallops all azure. Mantling gules and argent. Crest: on a wreath of the colours, upon a mount vert, an antelope argent, semé of estoiles sable, armed and unguled or resting the dexter forefoot upon a fountain proper; with the motto, "Agendo honeste."

163

THE ART OF HERALDRY

wings, but the more usual form in which it is seen is as in Fig. 155, which represents the arms and crest of Douglas. It also occurs in the arms of Farmer (Fig. 396).

The salamander is, however, best known as the personal device of Francis I., King of France. It is doubtless from this origin that the arms of the city of Paris (Plate CXVIII.) are taken.

The remainder of the list of heraldic monsters can be very briefly dismissed. In many cases a good deal of research has failed to discover an instance of their use, and one is almost inclined to believe that they were invented by those mediæval writers of prolific imagination for their treatises, without ever having been borne or emblazoned upon helmet or shield.

The Allocamelus is supposed to have the head of an ass conjoined to the body of a camel. I cannot call to mind any British instance of its use.

The Amphiptère is the term applied to a "winged serpent," a charge of but rare occurrence in either English or foreign heraldry. It is found in the arms of the French family of Potier, viz.: "Azure, a bendlet purpure between two amphiptères or," while they figure as supporters also in that family, and in those of the Ducs de Tresmes and De Gevres.

The Apres is an animal with the body similar to that of a bull, but with a bear's tail. It is seldom met with outside heraldic text-books.

The Amphisbene is usually described as a winged serpent (with two legs) having a head at each end of its body, but in the crest of Gwilt ["On a saltire or, interlaced by two amphisbænæ azure, langued gules, a rose of the last, barbed and seeded proper"] the creatures certainly do not answer to the foregoing description.

The Cockfish is a very unusual charge, but it is to be met with in the arms of the family of Geyss, in Bavaria, *i.e.*: "Or, a cock sable, beaked of the first, crested and armed gules, its body ending in that of a fish curved upwards, proper."

The Enfield is a purely fanciful animal, having the head of a fox, chest of a greyhound, talons of an eagle, body of a lion, and hind legs and tail of a wolf. It occurs as the crest of most Irish families of the name of Kelly[c] (Plate XXIX.).

The Bagwyn is an imaginary animal with the head of and much like the heraldic antelope, but with the body and tail of a horse, and the horns long and curved backwards. It is difficult to say what it is intended to represent, or to give any instance in which it occurs.

The Musimon is a fabulous animal with the body and feet of a goat and the head of a ram, with four horns. It is supposed to be the hybrid between the ram and the goat, the four horns being the two straight ones of the goat and the two curled ones of the ram. Though no heraldic instance is known to me, one cannot definitely say such an animal never existed. Another name for it is the tityron.

The Opinicus is another monster seldom met with in armory. When it does occur it is represented as a winged gryphon, with a lion's legs and short tail. Another description of it gives it the body and forelegs of a lion, the head, neck, and wings of an eagle, and the tail of a camel. It is the crest of the Livery Company

c Armorial bearings of Arthur Dillon Denis Kelly, Esq.: Quarterly, 1 and 4, azure, a tower triple-towered, supported by two lions rampant argent, as many chains descending from the battlements between their legs or (for Kelly); 2 and 3, argent, a lion rampant between three crescents gules, issuant from each a star with six points of the field, over all a fess azure (for Dillon), and impaling the arms of Skeffington, namely: quarterly, 1 and 4, argent, three bulls' heads erased sable; 2 and 3, azure, a chevron between three chaplets or. Mantling azure and argent. Crest: on a wreath of the colours, an enfield statant vert with a bushy tail turned over the back. Motto: "Turris fortis mihi Deus."

of Barbers in London, which doubtless gives us the origin of it in the recent grant of arms to Sir Frederick Treves, Bart. Sometimes the wings are omitted.

The Manticora, Mantegre, or *Man-Tiger* is the same as the man-lion, but has horns attached to its forehead.

The Hippogriff has the head, wings, and foreclaws of the griffin united to the hinder part of the body of a horse.

The Calopus or *Chatloup* is a curious horned animal difficult to describe, but which appears to have been at one time the badge of the Foljambe family. No doubt, as the name would seem to indicate, it is a variant of the wolf.

Many of the foregoing animals, particularly those which are or are supposed to be hybrids, are, however well they may be depicted, ugly, inartistic, and unnecessary. Their representation leaves one with a disappointed feeling of crudity of draughtsmanship. No such objection applies to the pegasus, the griffin, the sea-horse, the dragon, or the unicorn, and in these modern days, when the differentiation of well-worn animals is producing singularly inept results, one would urge that the sea-griffin, the sea-stag, the winged bull, the winged stag, the winged lion, and the winged heraldic antelope might produce (if the necessity of differentiation continue) very much happier results.

A. C. F-D.

CHAPTER XVIII

BIRDS

BIRDS of course play a large and prominent part in heraldry. Those which have been impressed into the service of heraldic emblazonment comprise almost every species known to the zoological world.

Though the earliest rolls of arms give us instances of various other birds, the bird which first makes the most prominent appearance is the *Eagle*, and in all early representations this will invariably be found "displayed." A double-headed eagle displayed, from a Byzantine silk of the tenth century, is illustrated by Mr. Eve in his "Decorative Heraldry," so that it is evident that neither the eagle displayed nor the double-headed eagle originated with the science of armory, which appropriated them ready-made, together with their symbolism. An eagle displayed as a symbolical device was certainly in use by Charlemagne.

It may perhaps here be advantageous to treat of the artistic development of the eagle displayed. Of this, of course, the earliest prototype is the Roman eagle of the Cæsars, and it will be to English eyes, accustomed to our conventional spread-eagle, doubtless rather startling to observe that the German type of the eagle which follows the Roman disposition of the wings (which so many of our heraldic artists at the present day appear inclined to adopt either in the accepted German or in a slightly modified form as an eagle displayed) is certainly not a true displayed eagle according to our English ideas and requirements, inasmuch as the wings are inverted. It should be observed that in German heraldry it is simply termed an eagle, and not an eagle displayed. Considering, however, its very close resemblance to our eagle displayed, and also its very artistic appearance, there is every excuse for its employment in this country, and I for one should be sorry to observe its slowly increasing favour checked in this country. It is quite possible, however, to transfer the salient and striking points of beauty to the more orthodox position of the wings, and this has been adopted with singular success by Miss Helard in Plate XLVIII., and in the bookplate (Fig. 397) which she designed for

164

THE ART OF HERALDRY

Mr. J. G. Crozier. Fig. 398 is another example of the application of the German model to English require-

FIG. 397.—Bookplate of Mr. John George Crozier.
(Designed by C. Helard.)

ments. The eagle (compared with the lion and the ordinaries) had no such predominance in early British heraldry that it enjoyed in Continental armory, and

FIG. 398.—Arms of the poet Milton (d. 1764):
Argent, a double-headed eagle displayed
gules, armed sable.

therefore it may be better to trace the artistic development of the German eagle.

In the twelfth and thirteenth centuries the eagle appears with the head raised and the beak closed. The *sachsen* (bones of the wings) are rolled up at the ends like a snail, and the pinions (like the talons) take a

FIG. 399.   FIG. 400.   FIG. 401.

vertical downward direction. The tail, composed of a number of stiff feathers, frequently issues from a knob or ball, as is shown in the *Züricherrolle* (Plate LXXV. Figs. 2 and 6) and in Fig. 11 of Plate XLVII. Compare also Fig. 399 herewith.

With the end of the fourteenth century the head straightens itself, the beak opens and the tongue becomes visible. The rolling up of the wing-bones gradually disappears, and the claws form an acute angle

with the direction of the body; and at this period the claws occasionally receive the "hose" covering the upper part of the leg. The feathers of the tail spread out sicklewise (Fig. 400).

The fifteenth century shows the eagle with *sachsen* forming a half circle, the pinions spread out and radiating therefrom, and the claws more at a right angle (Fig. 401). The sixteenth century draws the eagle in a more ferocious aspect and depicts it in as ornamental and ornate a manner as possible. Plate XLVII. gives some specimens of eagles illustrative of the development of the bird. The notes in explanation are arranged in chronological sequence, and not according to the order of their numbers on the Plate.

Fig. 4 (Plate XLVII.). Eagle from the seal of Heinrich von Mödling (1158–1223), the son of Heinrich Jasomirgott, brother of Duke Leopold the Virtuous, as on a document of the year 1203, now remaining in the Archives of the monastery of Heiligenkreuz in Lower Austria. Inscription: "✠ Hainricvs."

Fig. 3 (Plate XLVII.). Eagle from the oldest seal of the city of Vienna, on a document of the year 1239. Legend: "✠ Sigillvm Civivm VVinnensivm."

Fig. 11 (Plate XLVII.). Eagle from the counter-seal of Duke Bolco II. of Silesia, on a document of the year 1334. Legend: "✠ Sigillvm Dvcis Bolconis." The eagle has a crescent placed over it, the head being hidden in a "pot" helmet carrying the Silesian crest, viz.: "Two peacock's feathers with the ends crossed in saltire," which has been customary in the family of the Silesian Piasten since the year 1290, and which took the place of the former displayed plume of a peacock's tail.

Fig. 5 (Plate XLVII.). This figure represents an arched, three-cornered pageant-shield belonging to the middle of the fourteenth century, discovered in the church of Notre Dame de Valère, near Sitten (Sion), in the canton of Valais (Switzerland), (80 cm. high). It shows a coat of arms which unfortunately cannot be identified, viz.: "Azure, an eagle argent." The beak is broken off. The method of the manufacture of this shield is the same as that of the Seedorf shield depicted on Plate XL., and described on page 123.

Fig. 10 (Plate XLVII.). Armorial shield of the kingdom of Bohemia. A bas-relief on the monument of Ottokar I. in the Sternberg Chapel of St. Veit's Cathedral at Prague, fourteenth century. The flaming eagle sable, on a field of argent, was the old armorial device of Bohemia, which, however, about the middle of the thirteenth century, under Przemisl Ottokar II., gave way to the double-queued lion. The coat of arms with the eagle thus unappropriated was later (1339), at the request of Bishop Nicolaus of Trient, assigned to that bishopric by King John of Bohemia, and is borne as the coat of the bishopric at the present day.

Fig. 1 (Plate XLVII.). Eagle from an Italian seal of the fourteenth century. Inscription: "✠ S. Gottifredi Amatoris D' Preotis."

Fig. 2 (Plate XLVII.). Crowned eagle, from a heart-shaped seal of Bartholomäus Ermanni von Perugio, end of the fourteenth century. The seal shows three armorial devices, (i.) the keys of the Pope, (ii.) the eagle of the German Emperor (as in Fig. 2), and (iii.) the family arms of the Ermanni. The legend runs: "S. Btholomei Ermanni De Perusio Militis Et Legvm Doctoris Palatni Comitis Apostolici Et Imperialis." (An impression of this peculiarly shaped seal is now in the Imperial and Royal House, Court and State Archives of Vienna.)

Fig. 6 (Plate XLVII.). Armorial shield of the Dukedom of Silesia, from Konrad Grünenberg's *Wappenbuch*, Constance, 1483. The eagle in this shield is one of the most successful figures of this period of late Gothic heraldic work. From the same Register is repro-

165

duced the shield (Fig. 402) with the boldly sketched *Adlerflügel mit Schwerthand* (eagle's wing with the sword hand), the supposed arms of the Duke of Calabria.

FIG. 402.—Arms of Duke of Calabria.

Fig. 9 (Plate XLVII.). Eagle from the arms of the town of Schongau in Bavaria, viz.: "Or, an eagle sable, charged on the breast with the arms of Bavaria, a chief gules." This example is from a shield in the Bavarian National Museum at Munich, and belongs to the last quarter of the fifteenth century.

Fig. 12 (Plate XLVII.). Armorial shield of Johannes Stabius (compare Plate XXXV. Fig. 2), from a drawing by Albrecht Dürer (1471-1528).

Quite in the same style is the eagle of Tyrol on a corporate flag of the Society of the Schwazer Bergbute (Fig. 403), which belongs to the last quarter of the

FIG. 403.—Eagle of Tyrol.

fifteenth century. This is reproduced from the impression in the Bavarian National Museum given in Hefner-Alteneck's "Book of Costumes."

Fig. 7 (Plate XLVII.). German Imperial (or State) eagle, from a drawing by Hans Burgkmair (1473-1531). This shows the initials of the artist. The breast of the eagle is charged with a shield containing the arms of Austria, Hungary, Burgundy, Tyrol, Limburg, and Flanders.

Fig. 8 (Plate XLVII.) is an eagle drawn by Jost Amman, and is reproduced from the *Wappen und Stammbuch*, Frankfort-on-Maine, 1589.

Fig. 404.—A modern German eagle drawn by H. G. Ströhl. The illustration is of the arms of the Prussian province of Brandenburg.

FIG. 404.—Arms of the Prussian Province of Brandenburg.
(From Ströhl's *Deutsche Wappenrolle.*)

The double eagle has, of course, undergone a somewhat similar development. Plate XLVI. Fig. 1 shows the Imperial arms of the Roman-German Empire as they appear in a vignette on the title-page of the Imperial County Court Order for Swabia. This representation belongs to the second half of the sixteenth century. The artist is unknown. On the shield with which the breast of the eagle is charged (the shield being crowned and surrounded by the Collar of the Golden Fleece) are shown the arms of Old Hungary, Bohemia, Austria, and Old Burgundy, as also the sub-quarterly quartering of Castile and Leon. Over the nimbussed heads of the eagle is placed the Imperial crown.

Fig. 2 (Plate XLVI.). Double eagle. Arms of the city of Vienna from the grant thereof dated 26th September 1461, at Leoben, by the Emperor Friedrich III. (IV.): "Sable, a double eagle or, langued gules, with a nimbus, and surmounted by the Imperial crown or, the labels gules." In 1463, after he had deprived the city of these arms as a punishment to the rebellious Viennese, the Emperor bestowed the shield on the sister towns of Krems and Stein, which had remained faithful to him and which still bear it at the present day. In 1465, after a successful reconciliation between the Kaiser and the Viennese, these latter again bore the Imperial eagle, but it was then charged on the breast with a shield, "Gules, a cross argent." This addition, it may be stated, was an older emblem of the Viennese than the double eagle, and can be pointed out as early as 1346 on the breast of the then oneheaded Viennese eagle (Plate IX. Fig. 3).

The annexed illustration (Fig. 405) shows the Russian double eagle on the gold seal depending, from the Treaty of

![Russian Double Eagle](FIG. 405.—Russian Double Eagle (1574).)

FIG. 405.—Russian Double Eagle (1574).

Alliance between the Grand Duke and Gospodar Wassilij Iwanowitsch (1505-1533), and the Emperor

FIG. 406.—Bookplate of Thomas Greer, Esq.: Azure, a lion rampant or, armed and langued gules, between three antique crowns of the second, on a canton argent, an oak-tree eradicated surmounted by a sword in bend sinister, ensigned on the point with a royal crown all proper; and for the crest, upon a wreath of the colours, an eagle displayed proper, charged on the breast with a quadrangular lock argent. Motto: "Memor Esto."

FIG. 407.—Armorial bearings of the Earl of Southesk. K.T.: Argent, an eagle displayed azure, armed, beaked, and membered gules, on its breast an antique covered cup or; the escutcheon being surrounded by the ribbon and by the collar, and pendent therefrom the badge of the Most Ancient and Most Noble Order of the Thistle, and by an orange-tawny ribbon his badge as a Baronet of Nova Scotia. Mantling gules, doubled ermine; and upon a wreath of his liveries is set for crest, a thunderbolt proper, winged or; and in an escroll above, the motto, "Dred God." Supporters: two talbots argent, collared gules.

FIG. 408.—Armorial bearings of William Joseph Kelson Millard, M.D.: Sable, a lion rampant or, charged on the shoulder with a fer-de-moline of the first within an orle of five fers-de-moline of the second and as many bezants alternately. Mantling sable and or. Crest: upon a wreath of the colours, an eagle displayed sable, entwined round the body and neck by a serpent and holding in each claw a fer-de-moline or. Motto: "Beware, ye Myllwarde."

FIG. 409.—Armorial bearings of Robert George Gentleman, Esq.: Ermine, two eagles displayed, each with two heads in chief sable, and an esquire's helmet in base proper, a chief indented gules. Mantling sable and argent; and for his crest, upon a wreath of the colours, a demi-eagle displayed with two heads sable, on each wing a trefoil or. Motto: "Truth, honour, and courtesy."

Max I. (1514). The original is in the Imperial and Royal House, Court and State Archives of Vienna. The double eagle occurs in the East as well as in the

FIG. 410.—Armorial bearings of Robert Swan Aitchison, M.D., F.R.C.P.E.: Or, a double-headed eagle displayed sable, beaked and membered gules, on a chief engrailed vert, a pheon between two spur-revels of the first; in the centre of the shield an escutcheon of pretence gules, on a chevron between three demi-lions rampant, and in chief a cross crosslet fitché or, a trefoil between two anchors sable (for Pepper-Staveley). Mantling sable, doubled or; and for his crest, upon a wreath of his liveries, an eagle's head erased sable; and on an escroll over the same this motto, "Vigilantibus."

West in very early times. Since about 1335 the double eagle has appeared sporadically as a symbol of the Roman-German Empire, and under the Emperor Sigismund (d. 1447) became the settled armorial device of the Roman Empire. King Sigismund, before his coronation as Emperor, bore the single-headed eagle.

An example of an eagle displayed, by Mr. G. W. Eve,

FIG. 411.—Armorial bearings of Iain Ramsay, Esq., of Kildalton, Islay, co. Argyll: Parted per fess argent and sable, an eagle displayed, beaked gules, charged on the breast with a galley, sails furled, all countercharged. Mantling sable and argent. Crest: on a wreath of his liveries, a unicorn's head couped argent, armed and crined or. Motto: "Nunquam sine spe."

will be found in Fig. 406, which is a reproduction of a bookplate by him of T. Greer, Esq. Another is given in Fig. 407, which is a reproduction of the arms of the Earl of Southesk. Many incorrect versions of the arms of this

family were in currency, so a few years ago Lord Southesk rematriculated his arms in Lyon Office, and Fig. 407 correctly depicts them. Other examples of eagles

FIG. 412.—Armorial bearings of Captain John Howard Cartland: Or, a demi-eagle rising, couped proper, on a chief nebuly sable, three garbs argent. Mantling sable and or. Crest: on a wreath of the colours, in front of a demi-eagle as in the arms, holding in the beak an ear of wheat leaved and slipped, a garb fesswise or. Motto: "Loyal à devoir."

displayed will be found in the arms of Millard (Fig. 408), Parkin-Moore (Fig. 145), and Gentleman (Fig. 409), these being from designs by Mr. Scruby. Mr. Graham Johnston has been responsible for the eagles displayed in the arms of Aitchison (Fig. 410), Adlercron (Fig. 134), Ramsay (Fig. 411), and Reid (Fig. 136).

FIG. 413.—Bookplate of Tertius Joynson, Esq.: Azure, an eagle's head erased or, between four roses saltirewise argent, impaling the arms of Glazebrook, namely: ermine, an eagle displayed gules, beaked, legged, and holding in the beak a fleur-de-lis or, on a chief sable, two bezants, each charged with a fleur-de-lis azure. Crest: on a wreath of the colours, upon a mount vert, an eagle with two heads displayed azure, semé of roses argent. Motto: "Ad honorem industria ducit." (Engraved by C. W. Sherborne, R.E.)

PLATE L.

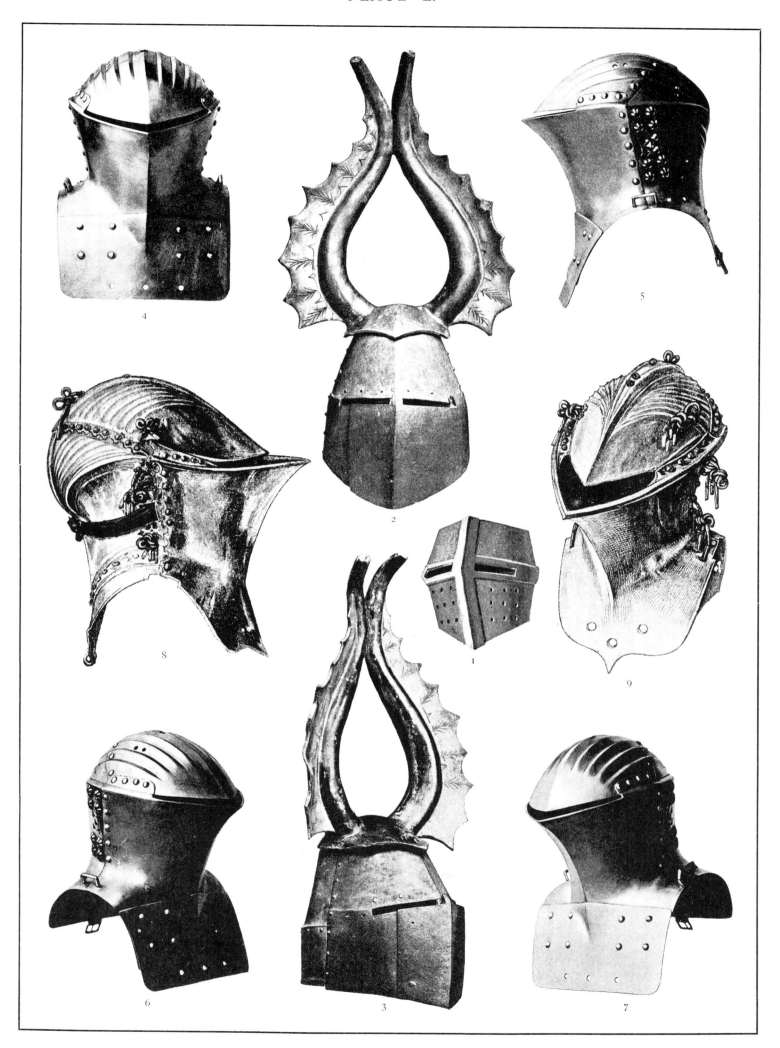

EXAMPLES OF HELMETS.

PLATE LI.

THE IMPERIAL STATE CROWN OF KING EDWARD VII.
This Plate is very kindly Presented to the Present Work by Messrs Garrard of The Haymarket, London, S.W.

PLATE LII.

IMPERIAL AND ROYAL CROWNS OF EUROPE.

PLATE LIII.

CORONETS OF RANK IN GREAT BRITAIN.

THIS PLATE HAS BEEN PRESENTED BY THE GOLDSMITHS AND SILVERSMITHS COMPANY, LTD., OF 112, REGENT STREET, LONDON, W., BY WHOM THE ACTUAL CORONETS WERE MADE FOR USE ON THE OCCASION OF THE CORONATION OF KING EDWARD VII.

PLATE LIV.

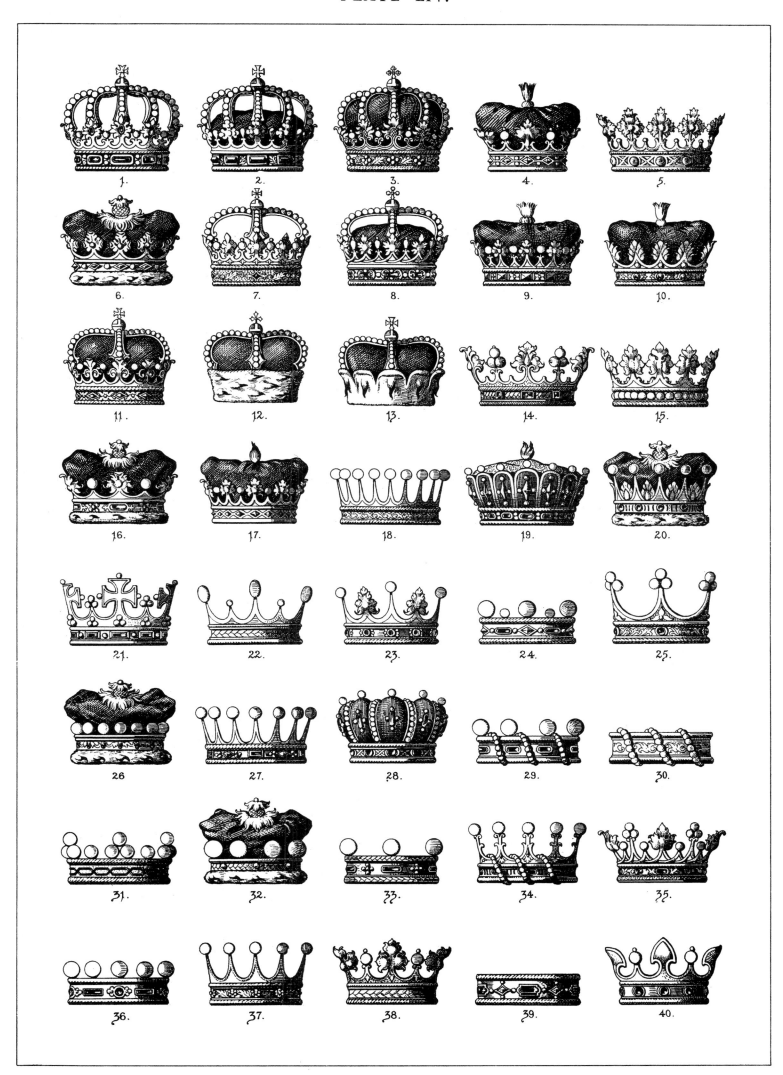

CORONETS OF RANK.

PLATE LV.

EXAMPLES OF SUPPORTERS.

PLATE LVI.

HUMAN FIGURES AS SUPPORTERS.

PLATE LVII.

THE ARMORIAL BEARINGS OF CHISHOLM GOODEN-CHISHOLM—"THE CHISHOLM."

PLATE LVIII.

THE ARMORIAL BEARINGS OF THE EARL OF ABERDEEN, G.C.M.G.

REPRODUCED IN FACSIMILE FROM THE PAINTING BY MR GRAHAM JOHNSTON IN LYON REGISTER.

PLATE LIX.

THE ARMORIAL BEARINGS OF JOHN ALLAN MACONOCHIE-WELLWOOD, Esq. of Meadowbank, Midlothian.

PLATE LX.

THE ARMORIAL BEARINGS OF SIR WILLIAM OGILVY DALGLEISH, Bart. of Errol Park, Perthshire.

PLATE LXI.

RES EST INVICTA VERITAS.

DICKIVS AB HILIPRANTSECK CÆS MAIESTA CONS SACRIQVE PAL COMES

LEOPOLDVS V.I. DOCTOR

DEI DON

VIRIBUS UNITIS

SPES BONA

PLATE LXII.

THE ARMORIAL BEARINGS OF—

(1) THE MARQUESS OF ELY. (2) EARL BATHURST. (3) VISCOUNT HALIFAX. (4) LORD RENDEL.

PLATE LXIII.

THE ARMORIAL BEARINGS OF SWINTON OF THAT ILK.

PLATE LXIV.

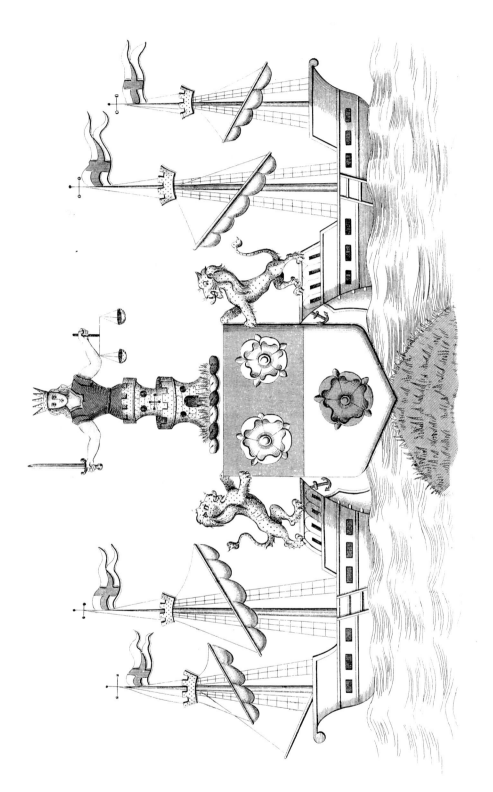

THE ARMS OF THE TOWN OF SOUTHAMPTON.

PLATE LXV.

THE ARMS OF HAIG OF BEMERSYDE,
AS BORNE BY THE HEAD OF THAT HOUSE, AND AS DIFFERENCED FOR VARIOUS CADETS.

Reference may also be made to the arms of Brine (Plate XXXI.).

Eagles in other positions will be found in the arms or crests of Cartland (Fig. 412), Joynson (Fig. 413), Pretor-Pinney (Fig. 258), M'Donald [a] (Plate XXXVIII.), and Goldthorpe (Fig. 414).

FIG. 414.—Armorial bearings of William Goldthorpe, Esq.: Per pale argent and or, in base a mount vert, issuant therefrom six oak-trees, three on either side proper, a chief nebuly azure, thereon three bezants. Mantling vert and argent. Crest: upon a wreath of the colours, a rock, and volant above an eagle proper, in the beak a billet or, surmounted by a rainbow, also proper. Motto: "Endeavour."

FIG. 415.—Examples of eagles. (Drawn by Mr. Forbes Nixon.)

Fig. 415, specially drawn for me by Mr. Forbes Nixon as typical of his style, shows the following: An eagle rising with wings addorsed; an eagle displayed with wings inverted; an eagle rising with wings addorsed and inverted; a double-headed eagle displayed; an eagle displayed with wings inverted; an eagle rising with wings displayed and inverted; an eagle displayed with wings inverted; as the previous one; an eagle rising with wings addorsed and inverted; an eagle displayed; an eagle close preying on an eagle's leg erased à la quise.

It may perhaps be as well to point out, with the exception of the two positions "displayed" and "close," very little if any agreement at all exists amongst authorities either as to the terms to be employed or as to the position intended for the wings when a given term is used in a blazon.

Practically every other single position is simply blazoned "rising," this term being employed without any additional distinctive terms of variation in official blazons and emblazonments. Nor can one obtain any certain information from a reference to the real eagle,

for the result of careful observation would seem to show that in the first stroke of the wings, when rising from the ground, the wings pass through every position from the wide outstretched form, which I term with wings displayed, to a position practically "close." As a consequence, therefore, no one form can be said to be more correct than any other, either from the point of view of nature or from the point of view of ancient precedent. This state of affairs is eminently unsatisfactory, because in these days of necessary differentiation no heraldic artist of any appreciable knowledge or ability has claimed the liberty (which certainly has not been officially conceded) to depict an eagle rising with wings displayed, when it has been granted with the wings in the position addorsed and inverted. Such a liberty when the wings happen to be charged, as they so frequently are in English crests, must clearly be an impossibility.

Until some agreement has been arrived at, I can only recommend my readers to follow the same plan which I have long adopted in blazoning arms of which the official blazon has not been available to me. That is, to use the term "rising," followed by the necessary description of the position of the wings. This obviates both mistake and uncertainty. Originally with us, as still in Germany, an eagle was always displayed, and in the days when coats of arms were few in number and simple in character the artist may well have been permitted to draw an eagle as he chose, providing it was an eagle. But

[a] Armorial bearings of William Kid Macdonald, Esq.: Party per bend indented or and ermine, a double-headed eagle displayed proper, beaked and membered gules, surmounted of a galley sable flagged of the third, and in the sinister chief point a pine-tree eradicated proper. Mantling sable, doubled or; and upon a wreath of his liveries is set for crest, a raven proper on a rock azure. Motto: "Nec tempore nec fato."

arms and their elaboration in the last four hundred years have made this impossible. It is foolish to overlook this, and idle in the face of existing facts to attempt to revert to former ways. Although now the English eagle displayed has the tip of its wings pointed upwards, and the contrary needs now to be mentioned in the blazon, this even with us was not so in the beginning. A reference to Plate LXXI., and Figs. 416, 417, and 418 will show how the eagle was formerly depicted.

FIG. 416.—Arms of Ralph de Monthermer, Earl of Gloucester and Hereford: Or, an eagle vert. See also Figs. 212 and 213. (From his seal, 1301.)

FIG. 417.—Crest of Ralph de Monthermer, Earl of Gloucester and Hereford. (From his seal, 1301.)

FIG. 418.—Arms of Piers de Gaveston, Earl of Cornwall (d. 1312): Vert, six eagles or.

The earliest instance of the eagle as a definitely heraldic charge upon a shield would appear to be its appearance upon the Great Seal of the Markgrave Leopold of Austria in 1136, where the equestrian figure of the Markgrave carries a shield so charged. More or less regularly, subsequently to the reign of Frederick Barbarossa, elected King of the Romans in 1152, and crowned as Emperor in 1155, the eagle with one or two heads (there seems originally to have been little unanimity upon the point) seems to have become the recognised heraldic symbol of the Holy Roman Empire; and the seal of Richard, Earl of Cornwall, elected King of the Romans in 1257, shows his arms ["Argent, a lion rampant gules, within a bordure sable, bezanté"] displayed upon the breast of an eagle, but no properly authenticated contemporary instance of the use of this eagle by the Earl of Cornwall is found in this country. The origin of the double-headed eagle has been the subject of endless controversy, the tale one is usually taught to believe being that it originated in the dimidiation upon one shield of two separate coats of arms. Nisbet states that the Imperial eagle was "not one eagle with two heads, but two eagles, the one laid upon the other, and their heads separate, looking different ways, which represent the two heads of the Empire after it was divided into East and West." The whole discussion is an apt example of the habit of earlier writers to find or provide hidden meanings and symbolisms when no such meanings existed. The real truth undoubtedly is that the double-headed eagle was an accepted figure long before heraldry came into existence, and that when the displayed eagle was usurped by armory as one of its peculiarly heraldic figures, the single-headed and double-headed varieties were used indifferently, until the double-headed eagle became stereotyped as the Imperial emblem. Napoleon, however, reverted to the single-headed eagle, and the present German Imperial eagle has likewise only one head.

The Imperial eagle of Napoleon had little in keeping with then existing armorial types of the bird. There can be little doubt that the model upon which it was based was the Roman eagle of the Cæsars as it figured upon the head of the Roman standards. In English terms of blazon the Napoleonic eagle would be: "An eagle displayed with wings inverted, the head to the sinister, standing upon a thunderbolt or."

The then existing double-headed eagles of Austria and Russia probably supply the reason which explains why, when the German Empire was created, the Prussian eagle in a modified form was preferred to the resuscitation of the older double-headed eagle, which had theretofore been more usually accepted as the symbol of Empire.

By the same curious idea which was noticed in the earlier chapter upon lions, which ruled that the appearance of two or more lions rampant in the same coat of arms *ipse facto* made them into lioncels, more than one eagle upon a shield resulted sometimes in the birds becoming eaglets. Such a rule has never had official recognition, and no artistic difference is made between the eagle and the eaglet. The charges on the arms of Piers Gaveston, Earl of Cornwall, are blazoned as eagles (Fig. 418). In the blazon of a few coats of arms, the term eaglet, however, still survives, *e.g.* in the arms of Child ["Gules, a chevron ermine, between three eaglets close argent"], and in the arms of Smitheman ["Vert, three eaglets statant with wings displayed argent, collared or"].

When an eagle has its beak of another colour, it is termed "armed" of that colour, and when the legs differ it is termed "membered."

An eagle volant occurs in the crest of Jessel ["On a wreath of the colours, a torch fesswise, fired proper, surmounted by an eagle volant argent, holding in the beak a pearl also argent. Motto: 'Persevere'"]. Parts of an eagle are almost as frequently met with as the entire bird. Eagles' heads abound as crests (they can be distinguished from the head of a griffin by the fact that the latter has always upstanding ears). As a charge upon the shield the eagle's head occurs in the arms of Joynson (Fig. 413). Unless otherwise specified (*e.g.* the crest of the late Sir Noel Paton was between the two wings of a dove), wings occurring in armory are always presumed to be the wings of an eagle. This, however, in English heraldry has little effect upon their design, for probably any well-conducted eagle (as any other bird) would disown the English heraldic wing, as it certainly would never recognise the German heraldic variety. A pair of wings when displayed and conjoined at the base is termed "conjoined in leure," from the palpable similarity of the figure in its appearance to the lure with which, thrown into the air, the falconer brought back his hawk to hand. The best known, and most frequently quoted instance, is the well-known coat of Seymour or St. Maur ["Gules, two wings conjoined in leure the tips downwards or"]. It should always be stated if the wings (as in the arms of Seymour) are inverted. Otherwise the tips are naturally presumed to be in chief. Other instances in which wings conjoined in leure occur will be found in the arms of Cloete (Fig. 419), Willans (Fig. 420), and Wingfield (Fig. 421).

Pairs of wings not conjoined can be met with in the arms and crest of Burne-Jones ["Azure, on a bend sinister

FIG. 419.—Armorial bearings of William Brodrick Cloete, Esq.: Per pale argent and or, two wings conjoined in leure gules, on a chief engrailed of the last two javelins in saltire of the first. Mantling gules and argent. Crest: on a wreath of the colours, two javelins in pale points upwards interlaced by as many saltirewise, banded gules, between two wings per fess argent and gules. Motto: "Ubi cras."

FIG. 420.—Armorial bearings of John Bancroft Willans, Gentleman: Per chevron gules and or, two chevronels between as many catherine-wheels in chief and in base a pair of wings conjoined in leure, tips downwards, all counterchanged. Mantling gules and or. Crest: on a wreath of the colours, a demi-man affronté proper, supporting with his dexter hand a rod of Esculapius proper, and resting his sinister on a catherine-wheel or. Motto: "Hold on."

FIG. 421.—Arms of Michael de la Pole, Earl of Suffolk (d. 1415): Quarterly, 1 and 4, azure, a fess between three leopards' faces or (for De la Pole); 2 and 3, argent, on a bend gules, three pairs of wings conjoined in leure of the field (for Wingfield).

argent between seven mullets, four in chief and three in base or, three pairs of wings addorsed purpure, charged

with a mullet or. Crest: in front of fire proper two wings elevated and addorsed purpure, charged with a

FIG. 422.—Armorial bearings of Robert Nicholl Byass, Esq.: Argent, three wings bendwise azure, in chief two escutcheons of the last, each charged with a fleur-de-lis of the first. Mantling azure and argent; and for his crest, upon a wreath of the colours, between two wings azure, a wing argent, charged with an escutcheon as in the arms. Motto: "By assiduity."

mullet or"]; but two wings, unless conjoined or addorsed, will not usually be described as a pair. Occasionally, however, a pair of wings will be found in saltire, but such a disposition is most unusual. Single wings, unless

FIG. 423.—Armorial bearings of the Rev. Charles Eccles Edmond Williams, Clerk in Holy Orders, D.D. (Oxon.): Argent, three piles, two in chief and one in base azure, each charged with a wing of the first. Mantling azure and argent. Crest: on a wreath of the colours, three arrows, one in pale and two in saltire or, barbed and flighted proper, between two wings argent, each charged with an annulet azure. Motto: "Fidus in finem."

specified to be the contrary, are presumed to be dexter wings. Examples of single wings as a charge occur in the arms of Byass (Fig. 422) and Williams (Fig. 423).

THE ART OF HERALDRY

A single wing, or two wings, as crests, or a crest between two wings, is a form so very frequently to be met with that one need hardly detail examples as such, though possibly it may be well to add the conceptions of wings according to the ideas of different artists. For this purpose reference may perhaps be made to the arms of Hallen (Fig. 424) and Johnston [b] (Plate XXVIII.).

Care needs to be exercised in some crests to observe the difference between a bird's head *between two wings*, a bird's head winged (a form not often met with, but in which rather more of the neck is shown, and the wings are conjoined thereto), and a bird's head between two wings addorsed. The latter form, which of course is really no more than a representation of a crest between two wings turned to be represented upon a profile helmet, is one of the painful results of our absurd position rules for the helmet.

A pair of wings conjoined is sometimes termed a vol, and one wing a demi-vol. Though doubtless it is desirable to know these terms, they are but seldom found in use, and are really entirely French.

Eagles' legs are by no means an infrequent charge.

FIG. 424.—Armorial bearings of Arthur Erskine Herbert Cornelius Hallen, Gentleman, M.D. (Edin.): Gules, a lion rampant or, crowned, armed, and langued azure, charged on the shoulder with a hammer of the last for difference. Upon the escutcheon is placed a helmet befitting his degree, with a mantling gules and or. Crest: a demi-lion rampant or, crowned, armed, and langued, and charged on the shoulder with a hammer azure, between two antique wings sable. Motto: "Sine Deo nil."

They will usually be found erased at the thigh, for which there is a recognised term "erased à la quise," which, however, is by no means a compulsory one. The eagle's leg will sometimes be found couped below the feathers. The eagle's leg erased at the thigh will be found in the crest of Lee (Fig. 115), and in the arms of Willis-Bund (Fig. 425).

A curious form of the eagle is found in the alerion, which is represented without beak or legs. It is diffi-

[b] Armorial bearings of George Lawson Johnson, Esq.: Argent, on a saltire sable, between four daggers points downwards gules, the sun in his splendour or, on a chief of the third, three cushions of the fourth. Mantling sable and argent. Crest: on a wreath of his liveries, a spur between two wings or; and upon an escrol over the same this motto, "Nunquam non paratus."

cult to conjecture what may have been the origin of the bird in this debased form, unless its first beginnings

FIG. 425.—Armorial bearings of John William Willis-Bund, Esq.: Ermine, three piles gules, two issuing from the chief and one in base, each charged with an eagle's leg erased at the thigh or; and impaling the arms of Temple, namely: quarterly, 1 and 4, or, an eagle displayed sable; 2 and 3, argent, two bars sable, each charged with three martlets or. Mantling gules and argent. Crest: upon a wreath of the colours, two lions' gambs erased and erect or, holding a griffin's head erased. Motto: "Optivo floreo nomine."

may be taken to be found in the unthinking perpetuation of some crudely drawn example. Its best-known appearance is, of course, in the arms of Loraine;

FIG. 426.—Armorial bearings of Sir Robert Pullar, Knight Bachelor: Or, three alerions sable, on a chief gules, a Holy Lamb passant regardant, staff and cross argent, with the banner of St. Andrew proper. Mantling sable and or. Crest: on a wreath of his liveries, a demi-eagle displayed or, beaked and membered gules. Motto: "Perseverantia et industria."

and as Planché has pointed out, this is as perfect an example of a canting anagram as can be met with in armory. Another example of the use of alerions will be found in the arms of Pullar (Fig. 426).

THE ART OF HERALDRY

The Phœnix, one of the few mythical birds which heraldry has familiarised us with is another, and perhaps the most patent example of all, of the appropriation by heraldic art of an ancient symbol, and its symbolism ready made. It belongs to the period of Grecian mythology. As a charge upon a shield it is comparatively rare, though it so occurs in the arms of Samuelson. On the other hand, it is frequently to be found as a crest. It is always represented as a demi-eagle issuing from flames of fire, and though the flames of fire will generally be found mentioned in the verbal blazon, this is not essential. Without its fiery surroundings it would cease to be a phœnix. On the other hand, though it is always depicted as a *demi*-bird (no instance to the contrary exists), it is never considered necessary to so specify it. It occurs as the crest of the Seymour family ["Out of a ducal coronet a phœnix issuant from flames of fire"]. Amongst the many other families who bear it as a crest may be mentioned Mitchell, of Newcastle-on-Tyne.

The Osprey may perhaps be here mentioned, because its heraldic representation always shows it as a white eagle. It is however seldom met with, though it figures in the crests of Roche (Lord Fermoy) and Trist. The osprey is sometimes known as the sea-eagle, and heraldically so termed.

The Vulture (probably from its repulsive appearance in nature and its equally repulsive habits) is not a heraldic favourite. Two of these birds occur, however, as the supporters of Lord Graves.

The Falcon naturally falls next to the eagle for consideration. Considering the very important part this

Fig. 427.—Armorial bearings of Sir Arthur Nicolson, Bart., K.C.I.E., &c. &c.: Or, a lion's head between three falcons' heads erased gules, a bordure azure. Mantling gules, doubled or. Crest: on a wreath of his liveries, a lion's head erased gules. Motto: "Nil sistere contra."

bird played in the social life of earlier centuries, this cannot be a matter of any surprise. Heraldry, in its emblazonment, makes no distinction between the appearance of the hawk and the falcon, but for canting and other reasons the bird will be found described by all its different names, *e.g.* in the arms of Hobson[c]

[c] Armorial bearings of Hobson, Gentleman: Quarterly, 1 and 4, per pale azure and sable, two hobbies close in chief proper, and a sun in

(Plate XLIX.); to preserve the obvious pun, the two birds are blazoned as hobbie-hawks. The falcon is frequently (more often than not) found belled.

With the slovenliness (or some may exalt it into the virtue of freedom from irritating restriction) characteristic of many matters in heraldic blazon, the simple term

Fig. 428.—Bookplate of William Ridley Richardson : Sable, two hawks belled or, on a chief indented ermine, a pale ermine and three lions' heads erased counterchanged, impaling the arms of Tweedy, namely: quarterly, 1 and 4, argent, a saltire engrailed between two escallops in fess gules, on a chief azure an escallop of the field (for Tweedy); 2 and 3, gules, on a bend flory and counterflory between two increscents argent, three lions' heads erased sable. Crest : on a wreath of the colours, upon a mount vert and in front of a tilting-spear fesswise, a dexter arm embowed in armour proper, encircled by an annulet or, the hand grasping a sword by the blade in bend sinister also proper, pommel and hilt gold, pendent from the wrist by a riband gules an escutcheon argent, charged with a hawk likewise proper ; with the motto, " Ben ti voglio."

"belled" is found used indiscriminately to signify that the falcon is belled on one leg or belled on both, and if it is belled the bell must of necessity be on a jess. Others state that every falcon must of necessity (whether so blazoned or not) be belled upon at least one leg, and that when the term " belled " is used it signifies that it is belled upon both legs. There is still yet another alternative, viz. that when " belled " it has the bell on only one leg, but that when " jessed and belled " it is belled on both legs.

The jess is the leather thong with which the bells are attached to the leg, and it is generally considered, and this may be accepted, that when the term "jessed" is included in the wording of the blazon the jesses are represented with the ends flying loose, unless the use of the term is necessitated by the jesses being of a different colour. When the term "vervelled" is also employed it signifies that the jesses have small rings

splendour in base or (for Hobson); 2 and 3, azure, a chevron between two fleurs-de-lis in chief and a battle-axe in base argent (for Falshaw). Mantling azure and or. Crest: on a wreath of the colours, a cubit arm erect proper, holding a rose argent, barbed, seeded, and slipped of the first, and two lilies in saltire of the second. Motto: "Vive ut vivas."

attached to the floating ends. In actual practice, however, it should be remembered that if the bells and jesses are of a different colour, the use of the terms

FIG. 429.—Armorial bearings of John Falconer, Esq. : Parted per fess argent and azure, in chief a falcon's head issuing out of a heart proper between two mullets of the second, and in base two claymores in saltire points downwards proper, entwined at the point of intersection by a serpent embowed biting his tail, head to the sinister or. Mantling azure, doubled argent ; and upon a wreath of his liveries is set for crest, a falcon rising proper ; and in an escroll above this motto, "Ad æthera."

FIG. 430.—Armorial bearings of Utrick Alexander Ritson, Esq. : Sable, a falcon close and belled, and in chief two lions' heads erased all argent. Mantling sable and argent. Crest : on a wreath of the colours, issuant from the battlements of a tower or, a lion's head sable, in front thereof a hawk's lure fesswise also or. Motto : "Virtute acquiritur honos."

"jessed" and "belled" is essential. A falcon is seldom drawn without at least one bell, and when it is found described as "belled," in most cases it will be found that the intention is that it shall have two bells. Like all

other birds of prey the falcon may be "armed," a technical term which theoretically should include the beak and legs, but in actual practice a falcon will be far more usually found described as "beaked and legged" when these differ in tincture from its plumage.

When a falcon is blindfolded it is termed "hooded." It was always so carried on the wrist until it was flown. The position of the wings and the confusion in the terms applied thereto is even more marked in the case of the falcon than the eagle.

Demi-falcons are not very frequently met with, but an example occurs in the crest of Jerningham.

A falcon's head is constantly met with as a crest, and will also be found in the arms of Nicolson (Fig. 427).

Examples of arms in which falcons occur will be found in the cases of Richardson (Fig. 428), Falconer (Fig. 429), Ritson (Fig. 430), Sandford Thompson (Plate XXIX), and George (Fig. 113).

When a falcon is represented preying upon anything it is termed "trussing" its prey, though sometimes the description "preying upon" is (perhaps less accurately) employed. Examples of this will be found in the arms of Madden ["Sable, a hawk or, trussing a mallard proper,

FIG. 431.—Armorial bearings of "Joscelin" of the "Libertie of St. Bartholomew the Greate" given at p. 22 of vol. ii. of Harl. Vis. London (pub. 1883), and the quarterings of the shield are there given as: 1. Joscelin ; 2. Joscelin ; 3. Chaselin ; 4. Battaile ; 5. Enfeild ; 6. Hide ; 7. Patmer ; 8. Baude.

on a chief of the second a cross botonny gules "], and in the crests of Graham (Fig. 199), Cawston (Fig. 162), and Yerburgh (Fig. 238).

A falcon's leg appears in the crest of Joscelin (Fig. 431).

The Pelican, with its curious heraldic representation and its strange terms, may almost be considered an instance of the application of the existing name of a bird to an entirely fanciful creation.

Mr. G. W. Eve, in his "Decorative Heraldry," states that in early representations of the bird it was depicted in a more naturalistic form, but I confess I have not myself met with it in such a character.

Heraldically, it has been practically always depicted with the head and body of an eagle, with wings elevated and with the neck embowed, pecking with its beak at its breast. The term for this is "vulning" itself, and although it appears to be necessary always to describe it in the blazon as "vulning itself," it will never be met with save in this position; a pelican's head even, when erased at the neck, being always so represented. It is supposed to be pecking at its breast to provide drops of blood as nourish-

FIG. 432.—Armorial bearings of Henry John Wastell Coulson, Esq., Barrister-at-Law: Quarterly, 1 and 4, per pale argent and ermine, on a bend sable, three fleurs-de-lis or (for Coulson); 2 and 3, argent, a fess between three garbs banded sable (for Blenkinsopp). Mantling sable and argent. Crest: on a wreath of the colours, between two spears, a pelican in her piety all proper. Motto: "Je mourrai, pour ceux que j'aime."

ment for its young, and it is termed "in its piety" when depicted standing in its nest and with its brood of young. It is difficult to imagine how the pelican came to be always considered in this position, because there is nothing in the nature of a natural habit from which this could be derived. There are, however, other birds which, during the brooding season, lose their feathers upon the breast,

FIG. 433.—Armorial bearings of Edmund Frost, Esq., M.B.: Argent, a pelican vulning itself, between three trefoils slipped azure. Mantling azure and argent. Crest: on a wreath of the colours, upon a rock proper, between two wings azure, each charged with a quatrefoil argent, a trefoil as in the arms. Motto: "Terra ad cœlum."

and some which grow red feathers there, and it is doubtless from this that the idea originated.

In heraldic and ecclesiastical symbolism the pelican

has acquired a somewhat sacred character as typical of maternal solicitude. It will never be found "close," or in any other positions than with the wings endorsed and either elevated or inverted.

When blazoned "proper," it is always given the colour and plumage of the eagle, and not its natural colour of white. In recent years, however, the tendency has rather made itself manifest to give the pelican its natural and more ungainly appearance, and its curious pouched beak.

Pelicans will be found in the arms and crest of Coulson (Fig. 432) and Frost (Fig. 433), whilst the arms of Gibson (Fig. 434) afford an instance of pelicans' heads.

PANDITE · CŒLESTES · PORTÆ

FIG. 434.—Armorial bearings of William Gibson, Esq.: Per pale gules and or, three pelicans' heads erased in fess between two keys fesswise, wards downwards, all counterchanged. Mantling gules and or. Crest: on a wreath of the colours, upon the trunk of a tree fesswise eradicated and sprouting to the dexter all proper, a pelican, wings elevated and addorsed argent, vulned and charged on the wings with a key erect, wards to the sinister gules. Motto: "Pandite cœlestes portæ."

The Ostrich is doubtless the bird which is most frequently met with after the falcon, unless it be the dove. The former bird is heraldically emblazoned in a very natural manner, and it is difficult to understand why in the case of such a bird heraldic artists of earlier days should have remained so true to the natural form of the bird, whilst in other cases, in which they could have had no less intimate acquaintance with the bird, greater variation is to be found.

As a charge it is not common, although instances are to be found in the arms of MacMahon ["Argent, an ostrich sable, in its beak a horse-shoe or"], and in the arms of Mahon ["Per fess sable and argent, an ostrich counterchanged, holding in its beak a horse-shoe or"].

It is curious that, until quite recent times, the ostrich is never met with heraldically, unless holding a horse-shoe, a key, or some other piece of old iron in its beak.

The digestive capacity of the ostrich, though somewhat exaggerated, is by no means fabulous, and in the earliest forms of its representation in all the old natural history books it is depicted feeding upon this unnatural food. If this were the popular idea of the bird, small wonder is it that heraldic artists perpetuated the idea, and even now the ostrich is seldom met with without a key or a horse-shoe in its beak.

The ostrich's head alone is sometimes met with, as in the crest of the Earl of Carysfort.

The wing of an ostrich charged with a bend sable is the crest of a family of Gulston (Fig. 435), but an ostrich wing is by no means a general heraldic charge.

FIG. 435—Bookplate of Alan Stepney Gulston : Argent, two bars nebuly gules, over all a bend sable charged with three plates. Crest : an ostrich wing of five feathers alternately argent and gules, over all a bend sable charged with three plates. Motto (over crest) : "Crescent sub pondere virtus."

Ostrich feathers, of course, play a large part in armory, but the consideration of these may be postponed for the moment until the feathers of cocks and peacocks can be added thereto.

The Dove—at least the heraldic bird—has one curious peculiarity. It is always represented with a slight tuft on its head. Mr. Eve considers this to be merely the perpetuation of some case in which the crude draughts-man has added a tuft to its head. Possibly he is correct, but I think it may be an attempt to distinguish between the domestic dove and the wood-pigeon—both of which varieties would be known to the early heraldic artists.

The dove with an olive branch in its beak is constantly and continually met with. When blazoned "proper" it is quite correct to make the legs and feet of the natural pinky colour, but it will be more usually found that a dove is specifically described as "legged gules." It is usually met with close, but it is also referred to as volant, and instances are known in which the wings are raised. These are, however, infrequent.

The ordinary heraldic dove will be found most frequently holding a branch of laurel in its beak, but it also occurs volant and with outstretched wings. It is then frequently termed a "dove rising." It will be found in the arms of Tweedy (Fig. 436), and Smith-Shand (Fig. 437).

The doves in the arms of the College of Arms (Plate

II.) are always represented with the sinister wing close, and the dexter wing extended and inverted. This has

FIG. 436.—Armorial bearings of Henry Colpoys Tweedy : Quarterly, 1 and 4, argent, a saltire engrailed gules, on a chief azure, three fleams or (for Tweedy) ; 2. argent, on a saltire sable, five trefoils slipped or, on a chief gules, three cushions of the third (for Johnston) ; 3. argent, a maunch ermine (for Colpoys), and upon an escutcheon of pretence the arms of Meredith, namely : azure, a lion rampant per pale argent and or. Mantling gules and argent. Crest : on a wreath of the colours, a dove volant argent. Motto : "Fais ce que doit advienne que pourra."

given rise to much curious speculation ; but whatever may be the reason of the curious position of the wings, there can be very little doubt that the coat of arms itself is based upon the coat of St. Edward the Confessor.

FIG. 437.—Armorial bearings of Alexander Kenneth Smith-Shand : Azure, a boar's head couped argent, on a chief of the second, a mullet between two chess-rooks sable. Mantling gules, doubled argent. Crest : on a wreath of his liveries, a dove volant over the waters with an olive branch in its beak proper. Motto : "Virtute duce comite fortuna."

The so-called coat of St. Edward the Confessor (refer to Fig. 201) is a cross patonce between five martlets, but it is pretty generally agreed that these martlets are a corruption of the doves which figure upon his coins, and one of which surmounts the sceptre which is known as St. Edward's staff, or "the sceptre with the dove."

The Wood-Pigeon is not often met with, but it does occur, as in the crest of the arms of Bradbury ["On a wreath of the colours, in front of a demi-wood-pigeon, wings displayed and elevated argent, each wing charged with a round buckle tongue pendent sable, and holding in the beak a sprig of barberry, the trunk of a tree fess-wise eradicated, and sprouting to the dexter, both proper"].

The Martlet is another example of the curious perpetuation in heraldry of popular errors in natural history. Even at the present day, in many parts of the country, it is popularly believed that a swallow has no feet, or, at any rate, cannot perch upon the ground, or raise itself therefrom. The fact that one never does see a swallow upon the ground supports the foundation of

FIG. 438.—Armorial bearings of Ronald Bailey, Gentleman : Gules, on a fess nebuly between four martlets, three in chief and one in base argent, two roses of the first, barbed and seeded proper. Mantling gules and argent. Crest : on a wreath of the colours, in front of an anchor in bend sinister proper, a female figure vested vert, supporting with the right hand an escocheon gules, charged with a martlet argent, and resting the left on the stock of the anchor. Motto : "Vallum æneum esto."

the idea. At any rate the heraldic swallow, which is known as the martlet, is never represented with feet, the legs terminating in the feathers which cover the upper parts of the leg. It is curious that the same idea is perpetuated in the little legend of the explanation, which may or may not be wholly untrue, that the reason the martlet has been adopted as the mark of cadency for the fourth son is to typify the fact that whilst the eldest son succeeds to his father's lands, and whilst the second son may succeed, perhaps, to the mother's, there can be very little doubt that by the time the fourth son is reached, there is no land remaining upon which he can settle, and that he must, perforce, fly away from the homestead to gather him means elsewhere. At any rate, whether this be true or false, the martlet certainly is never represented in heraldry with feet.

Most heraldry books state also that the martlet has no beak. How such an idea originated I am at a loss to understand, because I have never yet come across an official instance in which the martlet is so depicted. The martlet, however, is frequently met with, but a few

FIG. 439.—Armorial bearings of Bertram C. A. Windle, Esq., D.Sc., M.D., F.S.A., &c., Professor of Anatomy in Birmingham University : Gules, on a pile between two crosses patée in base or, three martlets of the field. Mantling gules and or. Crest : on a wreath of the colours, a stag's head caboshed proper, between two crosses patée or. Motto : "Non omnis moriar."

FIG. 440.—Armorial bearings of John Moels Pyke-Nott, Esq., of By-down : Quarterly, 1 and 4, gules, on a bend engrailed or, between four leopards' faces, two and two argent, an estoile of eight points between two martlets of the field (for Nott) ; 2 and 3, quarterly or and gules, on a chevron barry wavy of four argent and azure, between two trefoils in chief and another in base counterchanged, a pike naiant proper (for Pyke). Mantling gules and or. Crests : 1. upon a wreath of the colours, two mascles fesswise, interlaced or, thereon a martlet gules, ducally gorged gold, in the beak a sprig of laurel proper (for Nott) ; 2. upon a wreath of the colours, on a mount vert, a demi-pike haurient proper, between two wings gules, each charged with a trefoil or (for Pyke). Motto : "Res es spes."

instances must be sufficient as examples. The arms of the County Council of West Sussex show six martlets, and other instances occur in the arms of Bailey (Fig. 438), and as a crest it will be found in the cases of Hartley ["Upon a mount vert, a martlet sable, holding in the beak a cross patée fitchée or"] and Pyke-Nott (Fig. 440).

It is very seldom that the martlet occurs except close, and consequently it is never specified as such. An instance, however, in which it occurs "rising" will be found in the crest of Smith (Fig. 441).

FIG. 441.—Armorial bearings of Francis Patrick Smith, Gentleman: Erminois, a chevron gules, on a chief engrailed of the last a rose argent, barbed and seeded proper, between two martlets or, quartering Green and McKenzie, a crescent for difference, and impaling the arms of Gatty, namely: party per fess sable and azure, in chief a demi-cat issuant guardant argent, and in base a shin bone in bend, surmounted by another in bend sinister between four fleurs-de-lis or. Mantling gules and or. Crest: issuant from a chaplet of roses argent, a rock proper, thereon a martlet rising or, holding in the beak a rose as in the arms, leaved and slipped proper. Motto: "Suaviter sed fortiter."

The Swallow, as distinct from the martlet, is sometimes met with, as in the case of the arms of the family of Arundell, which are: "Sable, six martlets, three, two and one or." The pun upon "l'hirondelle" was too good for ancient heralds to pass by.

A swallow "volant" appears upon the arms usually ascribed to the town of Arundel. These, however, are not recorded as arms in the Visitation books, the design being merely noted as a seal device, and one hesitates to assert definitely what the status of the design in question may be.

Perhaps the confusion between the foreign merlette—which is drawn like a duck without the wings, feet, or forked tail—and the martlet may account for the idea that the martlet should be depicted without a beak.

The Swan is a very favourite charge, and will be found both as a crest and as a charge upon a shield, and in all varieties of position. It is usually, however, when appearing as a charge, to be found "close," and as such occurs in the arms of Brodribb (Fig. 442). A swan couchant appears as the crest of Barttelot (Fig. 259), a swan regardant as the crest of Swaby, and a swan "rising" will be found as a crest of Guise and as a charge upon the arms of Muntz (Fig. 443). Swimming in water it occurs in the crest of Stilwell, and a swan to which the unusual term of "rousant" is sometimes applied figures as the crest of Stafford: "Out of a ducal coronet per pale gules and sable, a demi-swan rousant,

wings elevated and displayed argent, beaked gules." It is, however, more usually blazoned as: "A demi-swan issuant (from the coronet, per pale gules and sable")."

FIG. 442.—Armorial bearings of Brodribb, of Victoria, Australia: Party per chevron gules and argent, in chief two swans ermine, beaked of the first, legged sable, and in base a mount vert, therefrom springing three roses gules, stalked and leaved proper. Crest: on a wreath of the colours, a mount vert, therefrom springing three roses gules, stalked and leaved proper, interlaced by as many mascles also interlaced fesswise or; with the motto, "Prudentia tutus."

Swans' heads and necks are not often met with as a charge, though they occur in the arms of Baker. As a

FIG. 443.—Armorial bearings of Muntz: Pean, on a mount in base proper, a swan rising argent, charged on each wing with a trefoil slipped vert, in chief a staff raguly erect between two estoiles or. Mantling sable and argent. Crest: on a wreath of the colours, in front of a demi-swan wings expanded argent, semé of trefoils slipped vert, a staff raguly fesswise or. Motto: "Fortiter sed suaviter."

crest they are very common, and will be found in the cases of Lindsay and Bates.

The Duck—with its varieties of the moorhen and eider-duck—is sometimes met with, and appears in the arms of Duckworth (Fig. 444) and Billiat[d] (Plate XXVII.). Few better canting examples can be found than the latter coat, in which the duck is holding the billet in its bill.

The other domestic bird—the *Cock*—is often met with, though it more often figures as a crest than upon

a shield. A cock "proper" is generally represented of the kind which in farmyard phraseology is known as a gamecock. Nevertheless the gamecock—as such—does occur; though in these cases, when so blazoned, it is usually depicted in the artificial form—deprived of its comb and wattles. Birds of this class are usually met with, with a comb and wattles, &c. of a different colour, and it is then termed "combed, wattled, and jelopped" —if it is desired to be strictly accurate—though it will be generally found that the term is dropped to "combed and jelopped." If it is termed "armed," the beak and spurs are thereby referred to. It occurs in the arms of Handcock (Lord Castlemaine) ["Ermine, on a chief sable, a dexter hand between two cocks argent"] and in the arms of Cokayne ["Argent, three cocks gules, armed, crested, and jelopped sable"], and also in that of Law. It likewise occurs in the arms of Aitken (Fig. 445).

The Sheldrake appears occasionally under another name, *i.e.* that of the *Shoveller*, and as such will be found in the arms of Jackson,[e] of Doncaster.

The gorgeous plumage of the *Peacock* has of course resulted in its frequent employment. It has a special term of its own, being stated to be "in his pride" when shown affronté, and with the tail displayed. It is seldom met with except in this position, though the well-known crest of Harcourt is an example to the contrary, as is the crest of Sir Jamsetjee Jejeebhoy, Bart.: "A mount vert, thereon a peacock amidst wheat, and in the beak an ear of wheat all proper."

With the tail closed it also figures as one of the supporters of Sir Robert Hart, Bart. ["Sinister, a peacock close proper"]: its only appearance in such a position that I am aware of.

As a charge upon a shield it is rather uncommon, its most frequent appearance being in the form of a crest, but it occurs in the arms of Lanigan-O'Keefe (Fig. 252).

A peacock's tail is not a familiar figure in British armory, though the exact contrary is the case in German practices. "Issuant from the mouth of a boar's head erect" it occurs as the crest of Tyrell, and "A plume of peacock's feathers"—which perhaps is the same thing—"issuant from the side of a chapeau" is the crest of Lord Sefton.

Another bird for which heraldry has created a term of its own is the *Crane*. It is seldom met with except holding a stone in its claw, the term for which stone is its "vigilance," a curious old fable, which explains the whole matter, being that the crane held the stone in its foot so that if by any chance it fell asleep, the stone, by dropping, would awaken it, and thus act as its "vigilance." It is a pity that the truth of such a charming example of the old world should be dissipated by the fact that the crest of Cranstoun is the crane *asleep*—or rather dormant—with its head under its wing, and nevertheless holding its "vigilance" in its foot! The crane is not often met with, but it occurs in the arms of Cranstoun, with the curious and rather perplexing motto, "Thou shalt want ere I want." Before leaving the crane, it may be of interest to observe that the derivation of the word "pedigree" is from *pied de grue*, the appearance of a crane's foot and the branching lines indicative of issue being similar in shape.

Heraldic representation makes little if any difference when depicting a crane, a stork, or a heron, except that the tuft on the head of the latter is never omitted when a heron is intended.

Instances of the *Stork* will be found in the arms of Gibson (Fig. 446), the usual heraldic method of depicting the bird, however, being with the wings close.

FIG. 446.—Armorial bearings of Thomas George Gibson, Esq.: Per pale azure and argent, three acorns slipped and leaved in fess, between as many storks rising all counterchanged. Mantling azure and argent. Crest: on a wreath of the colours, a stork rising argent, between two acorns slipped and leaved, and holding in the beak an acorn slipped proper. Motto: "Per ardua ad alta." (Reproduced from a painting by Mr. G. W. Eve, R.E.)

More often than not the stork is met with a snake in its beak; and the fact that a heron is generally provided with an eel to play with adds to the confusion.

The Heron—or, as it is more frequently termed heraldically, *Herne*—will naturally be found in the arms of Hearne and some number of other coats and crests.

The Raven occurs almost as early as any other heraldic bird. It is said to have been a Danish de-

vice. The powerful Norman family of Corbet, one of the few remaining families which can show an unbroken male descent from the time of the Conquest to the present day, have always remained faithful to the raven, though they have added to it sometimes a *bordure* or additional numbers of its kind. "Or, a raven sable," the well-known Corbet coat, is, of course, a canting allusion to their Norman name, or nickname, "Le Corbeau." Their name, like their pedigree, is unique, inasmuch as it is one of the few names of undoubted Norman origin which are not territorial, and possibly the fact that their lands of Moreton Corbett, one of their chief seats, were known by their name has assisted in the perpetuation of what was, originally, undoubtedly a nickname.

FIG. 448.

The raven will also be found in the arms of Jones[f] (Plate XXV.) and Craster (Fig. 447).

Fig. 448 is a striking example of the virility which can be imparted to the raven. It is reproduced from Grünenberg's "Book of Arms" (1483). Herr Ströhl suggests it may be of "Corbie" in Picardy, but the identity of the arms leads one to fancy the name attached may be a misdescription of the English family of Corbet.

Heraldically, no difference is made in depicting the raven, the rook, and the crow; and examples of the *Crow* will be found in the arms of Crawhall (Fig. 449), and of the *Rook* in the crest of Abraham.

FIG. 449.—Bookplate of George Crawhall, Esq.: Argent, three battle-axes chevronwise sable, between two chevronels engrailed gules, the whole between three crows, also sable, impaling the arms of Synnott, namely: argent, three swans in pale sable, ducally gorged or; on a canton gules a sword in pale proper. Mantling sable and argent. Crest: on a wreath of the colours, upon a mount vert, a crow sable, holding in the dexter claw a battle-axe in bend proper. Motto: "Præsto et persto."

FIG. 447.—Armorial bearings of Thomas Williams Craster, Esq., of Craster: Quarterly, or and gules, in the first quarter a raven proper, impaling the arms of Osborn, namely: argent, a bend between two lions rampant sable. Mantling gules and or. Crest: on a wreath of the colours, a raven proper, charged on the breast with an escallop or. Motto: "Hodie felix cras ter."

[f] Armorial bearings of the Sir William Quayle Jones: Quarterly, 1 and 4, argent, a chevon ermines between three ravens sable, on a chief engrailed of the second a heart or (for Jones); 2 and 3, argent, on a chevron sable, gutté-d'eau, between three quails proper, in the centre chief point a pellet, two swords points upward of the first (for Quayle), and for his crest, on a wreath of the colours, on a heart or, a raven sable, gorged with a collar gemel argent; with the motto, "Deus pascit corvos."

The arms of the Yorkshire family of Creyke are always blazoned as rooks, but I am inclined to think they may possibly have been originally *creykes*, or corn-crakes.

The Cornish Chough is very much more frequently met with than either the crow, rook, or raven, and it occurs in the arms of Bewley [g] (Plate XXV.), the town of Canterbury, and (as a crest) Cornwall (Fig. 150).

It can be distinguished from the raven by the fact that the Cornish chough is always depicted and frequently blazoned as "beaked and legged gules," as it is found in its natural state.

The Owl, too, is a very favourite bird. It is always

FIG. 450.—Armorial bearings of Oldham: Sable, a chevron invected plain cottised or, between three owls argent, on a chief engrailed of the second, a rose gules, barbed and seeded proper, between two annulets, also gules. Crest: on a wreath of the colours, in front of a rock thereon an owl argent, three roses fesswise gules, barbed and seeded proper. The motto is "Sapere Aude." [Granted Nov. 7, 1894.]

[g] Armorial bearings of Sir Edmund Thomas Bewley: Argent, a chevron sable, between three Cornish choughs' heads erased proper, in chief an ermine spot. Mantling sable and argent. Crest: on a wreath of the colours (argent and sable), an ibex's head or, issuant from the centre of a rose gules, stalked and leaved proper. Motto: "Virtutis gloria merces."

depicted with the face affronté, though the body is not usually so placed. It occurs in the arms of Leeds (Plate CXVII.)—which, by the way, are an example of colour upon colour—Oldham (Fig. 450), Dewsbury, and in the arms of the family of Howatson (Fig. 451).

FIG. 451.—Armorial bearings of Charles Howatson, Esq.: Sable, two chevronels between as many owls in chief and a wolf's head erased argent in base. Mantling sable and argent. Crest: on a wreath of his liveries, a dexter hand couped at the wrist apaumé proper. Motto: "Hinc orior."

The Lark will be found in many cases of arms or crests for families of the name of Clarke, and also in the arms of Mylchreest (Fig. 452).

FIG. 452.—Armorial bearings of Thomas George Mylchreest, Esq.: Azure, a cross crosslet argent, in chief two larks with wings elevated and addorsed proper. Mantling azure and argent. Crest: on a wreath of the colours, upon a rock proper, two cross crosslets or, thereon a lark as in the arms. Motto: "My shegin dy ve bee eh."

The Parrot, or, as it is more frequently termed heraldically, the *Popinjay*, will be found in the arms of Saville, *i.e.* as a charge upon supporters: "Two talbots ermine, each gorged with a collar wavy sable; pendent therefrom an escutcheon or, charged with a popinjay vert, collared gules." It also occurs in the arms of Curzon: "Argent, on a bend sable three popinjays or, collared gules."

There is nothing about the bird, or its representations, which needs special remark, and its usual heraldic form follows nature pretty closely.

The Moorcock or *Heathcock* is curious, inasmuch as there are two distinct forms in which it is depicted. Neither of them are correct from the natural point of view, and they seem to be pretty well interchangeable from the heraldic point of view. The bird is always represented with the head and body of an ordinary cock, but sometimes it is given the wide flat tail of black game, and sometimes a curious tail of two or more erect feathers at right angles to its body.

Examples of the latter kind will be found in the arms of Highmore and Middlemore, and of the former kind in Bartlett, of Liverpool (Plate XXXVIII.).

Though usually represented close, it is sometimes with open wings, as in the crest of a certain family of Moore.

Many other birds are to be met with in heraldry, but they have nothing at all especial in their bearing, and no special rules govern them.

The Lapwing, under its alternative names of *Peewhit*,

FIG. 453.—Bookplate of Charles Villiers S. Downes, Esq.: Per pale sable and gules, a stag lodged argent, holding in the mouth an ear of wheat leaved and slipped or, between four garbs saltirewise of the third (for Downes). Mantling sable and argent. Crest: on a wreath of the colours, upon two ears of wheat leaved and slipped or, a lapwing with wings addorsed proper. Motto: "Soies content."

Plover, and *Tyrwhitt*, will be found in the arms of Downes (Fig. 453), Tyrwhitt, and Tweedy (see Plate XXVIII.).

The Pheasant will be found in the crest of Scott-Gatty (Fig. 262), and the *Kingfisher* in many cases of arms of the name of Fisher (Plate XXXVII.).

The Magpie occurs in the arms of Dusgate (Fig. 454), and in those of Finch.[h]

FIG. 454.—Armorial bearings of Richard Dusgate Dusgate, Gentleman: Argent, three magpies proper. Mantling sable and argent; and for his crest, upon a wreath of the colours, a lion's head erased sable.

Woodward mentions an instance in which the *Bird of Paradise* occurs (p. 267): "Argent, on a terrace vert, a cannon mounted or, supporting a Bird of Paradise proper" [Rjevski and Yeropkin], and the arms of Thornton show upon a canton the Swedish bird *tjader*: "Ermine, a chevron sable between three hawthorn trees eradicated proper, a canton or, thereon the Swedish bird tjader, or cock of the wood, also proper." Two similar birds were granted to the late Sir Edward Thornton, G.C.B., the father of the present Sir Edward Thornton, G.C.B., as supporters, he being a Knight Grand Cross.

Single feathers as charges upon a shield are sometimes met with, as in the "shield of peace" of Edward the

FIG. 455.—The "Shield of Peace" of Edward the Black Prince (d. 1376): Sable, three ostrich feathers with scrolls argent. (From his tomb in Canterbury Cathedral.)

Black Prince (Fig. 455), and in the arms of Clarendon (Plate LXVII.). These two examples are, however, derivatives from the historic ostrich-feather badges of the English Royal Family, and will be more conveniently dealt with later when considering the subject of badges. The single feather enfiled by the circlet of crosses patée and fleurs-de-lis, which is borne upon a canton of augmentation upon the arms of Gull, Bart., is likewise a derivative, but feathers as a charge occur in the arms of Jervis: "Argent, six ostrich feathers, three, two, and one sable." A modern coat founded upon this, in which the ostrich feathers are placed upon a pile, between two bombshells fracted in base, belongs to a family of the same name, and the crest granted therewith is a single

[h] Armorial bearings of Henry Finch, Gentleman: Azure, on a chevron engrailed ermine, between three gryphons passant, with wings elevated or, a lion's head erased sable, between two magpies proper; and for a crest, upon a wreath of the colours, a gryphon segreant azure, bezanté, the wings elevated or, holding between the paws an escocheon ermine, charged with a lion's head erased as in the arms; with the motto, "Carpe diem."

ostrich feather between two bombs fired. Cock's feathers occur as charges in the arms of Galpin (Fig. 456).

FIG. 456.—Armorial bearings of the Rev. Arthur John Galpin, M.A.: Per chevron gules and or, two cock's feathers in chief of the last, and a bear's head erased in base sable. Mantling gules and or. Crest: upon a wreath of the colours, a cock's head erased sable, combed and wattled gules, charged with a galtrap between two cock's feathers or. Motto: "Vigilat validus."

In relation to the crest, feathers are constantly to be found, which is not to be wondered at, inasmuch as fighting and tournament helmets, when actually in use, frequently did not carry the actual crests of the owners, but were simply adorned with the plume of ostrich feathers. A curious instance of this will be found in the case of the family of Dymoke of Scrivelsby, the Honourable the King's Champion. The crest is really: "Upon a wreath of the colours, the two ears of an ass sable," though other crests [" 1. a sword erect proper; 2. a lion as in the arms"] are sometimes made use of. When the Champion performs his service at a Coronation the shield which is carried by his esquire is not that of his sovereign, but is emblazoned with his personal arms of Dymoke: "Sable, two lions passant in pale argent, ducally crowned or." The helmet of the champion is decorated with a triple plume of ostrich feathers and not with the Dymoke crest. In old representations of tournaments and warfare the helmet will far oftener be found simply adorned with a plume of ostrich feathers than with a heritable crest, and consequently such a plume has remained in use as the crest of a very large number of families. This point is, however, more fully dealt with in the chapter upon crests.

The plume of ostrich feathers is, moreover, attributed as a crest to a far greater number of families than it really belongs to, because if a family possessed no crest the helmet was generally ornamented with a plume of ostrich feathers, which later generations have accepted and adopted as their heritable crest, when it never possessed such a character. A notable instance of this will be found in the crest of Astley, as given in the Peerage Books.

The number of feathers in a plume requires to be stated; it will usually be found to be three, five, or seven, though sometimes a larger number are met with. When it is termed a double plume they are arranged in two rows, the one issuing above the other, and a triple plume is arranged in three rows; and though it is correct

to speak of any number of feathers as a plume, it will usually be found that the word is reserved for five or more. A plume of three feathers would simply be termed three ostrich feathers. Whilst they are usually white they are also found of varied colours, and there is even an instance to be met with of ostrich feathers of ermine. When the feathers are of different colours they need to be carefully blazoned; if alternately, it is enough to use the word "alternately," the feather at the extreme dexter side being depicted of the colour first mentioned. In a plume which is of three colours, care must be used in noting the arrangement of the colours, the colours first mentioned being that of the dexter feather; the others then follow from dexter to sinister, the fourth feather commencing the series of colours again. If any other arrangement of the colours occurs it must be specifically detailed. The rainbow-hued plume from which the crest of Sir Reginald Barnewall[i] issues is the most variegated instance I have met with.

Two peacock's feathers in saltire will be found in the crest of a family of Gatehouse, and also occur in the crest of Crisp-Molineux-Montgomerie (Fig. 684). The pen in heraldry is always of course of the quill variety, and consequently should not be mistaken for a single feather. Ostrich and other feathers are very frequently found on either side of a crest, both in British and Continental armory; but though often met with in this position, there is nothing peculiar about this use in such character. German heraldry has evolved one use of the peacock's feather, or rather for the eye from the peacock's feather, which happily has not yet reached this country. It will be found adorning the outer edges of every kind of object, and it even occurs as a kind of dorsal fin down the back of animals as on Plates LXXIII. and LXXIV. Bunches of cock's feathers are also frequently made use of for the same purpose. There has been considerable diversity in the method of depicting the ostrich feather. In its earliest form it was stiff and erect as if cut from a piece of board (Fig. 455), but gradually, as the realistic type of heraldic art came into vogue, it was represented more naturally and with flowing and drooping curves. Of later years, however, we have followed the example of His Majesty when Prince of Wales and reverted to the earlier form, and it is now very general to give to the ostrich feather the stiff and straight appearance which it originally possessed when heraldically depicted. Occasionally a plume of ostrich feathers is found enclosed in a "case," that is, wrapped about the lower part similar to a bouquet, and this form is the more usual in Germany.

In German heraldry these plumes are constantly met with in the colours of the arms, or charged with the whole or a part of the device upon the shield. This is not a common practice in this country, but an instance of it will be found in the arms of Lord Waldegrave: "Per pale argent and gules. Crest: out of a ducal coronet or a plume of five ostrich feathers, the first two argent, the third per pale argent and gules, and the last two gules."

A. C. F.-D.

CHAPTER XIX

FISH

HERALDRY has a system of "natural" history all its very own, and included in the comprehensive heraldic term of fish are dolphins, whales, and other creatures. There are certain terms which apply to

---

[i] Upon a wreath of the colours, from a plume of five ostrich feathers or, gules, azure, vert, and argent, a falcon rising of the last; with the motto, "Malo mori quam foedari."

heraldic fish which should be noted. A fish in a horizontal position is termed "naiant," whether it is in or upon water or merely depicted as a charge upon a shield. A fish is termed "hauriant" if it is in a perpendicular position, but though it will usually be represented with the head upwards in default of any specific direction to the contrary, it by no means follows that this is always the case, and it is more correct to state whether the head is upwards or downwards, a practice which it is usually found will be conformed to. When the charges upon a shield are simply blazoned as "fish," no particular care need be taken to represent any particular variety, but on the other hand it is not in such cases usual to add any distinctive signs by which a charge which is merely a fish might become identified as any particular kind of fish.

The heraldic representations of the *Dolphin* are strangely dissimilar from the real creature, and also show amongst themselves a wide variety and latitude. It is early found in heraldry, and no doubt its great importance in that science is derived from its use by the Dauphins of France. Concerning its use by these Princes there are all sorts of curious legends told, the most usual being that recited by Berry.

Woodward refers to this legend, but states that "in 1343 King Philip of France *purchased* the domains of Humbert III., Dauphin de Viennois," and further remarks that the legend in question "seems to be without solid foundation." But neither Woodward nor any other writer seems to have previously suggested what is doubtless the true explanation, that the title of Dauphin and the province of Viennois were a separate dignity of a sovereign character, to which were attached certain territorial and sovereign arms ["Or, a dolphin embowed azure, finned and langued gules"]. The assumption of these sovereign arms with the sovereignty and territory to which they belonged, was as much a matter of course as the use of separate arms for the Duchy of Lancaster by his present Majesty King Edward VII., or the use of separate arms for his Duchy of Cornwall by H.R.H. the Prince of Wales.

The arms of the Dauphin of France will be found in Fig. 39 and upon Plate CXXVIII.

Berry is wrong in asserting that no other family were permitted to display the dolphin in France, because a very similar coat (but with the dolphin lifeless) to that of the Dauphin was quartered by the family of La Tour du Pin, who claimed descent from the Dauphins d'Auvergne, another ancient House which originally

FIG. 457.—Arms of the Grauff von Dälffin lett och in Dalffinat (Count von Dälffin), which also lies in Dauphiné (from Grünenberg's " Book of Arms "): Argent, a dolphin azure within a bordure compony of the first and second.

bore the sovereign title of Dauphin. A dolphin was the charge upon the arms of the Grauff von Dälffin (Fig. 457).

The dolphin upon the coat of the Dauphin, it will be noticed, is neither naiant nor hauriant, but is " embowed," that is, with the tail curved towards the head.

But the term "embowed" really signifies nothing further than "bent" in some way, and as a dolphin is never heraldically depicted straight, it is always understood to be and usually is termed "embowed," though it will generally be "naiant embowed" or "hauriant embowed." The dolphin occurs in the arms of many British families, *e.g.* in the arms of Ellis (Fig. 461), Monypenny, Loder-Symonds, Symonds-Taylor, Fletcher, and Stuart-French.

Woodward states that the dolphin is used as a supporter by the Trevelyans, Burnabys, &c. In this statement he is clearly incorrect, for neither of those families are entitled to or use supporters. But his statement probably originates in the practice which, in accordance with the debased ideas of artistic decoration at one period added all sorts of fantastic objects to the edges of a shield for purely decorative (!) purposes. The only instance within my knowledge in which a dolphin figures as a supporter will be found in the case of the arms of Waterford.

The Whale is seldom met with in British armory, one of its few appearances being in the arms of Whalley, viz.: "Argent, three whales' heads erased sable."

The crest of an Irish family named Yeates is said to be: "A shark issuant regardant swallowing a man all proper," and the same device is also attributed to some number of other families.

Another curious piscine coat of arms is that borne, but still unmatriculated, by Inveraray, namely: "The field is the sea proper, a net argent suspended to the base from the dexter chief and the sinister fess points, and in chief two and in base three herrings entangled in the net."

Salmon are not infrequently met with, but they need

FIG. 458.—Armorial bearings of James David Lumsden, Esq.: Azure, a ship under sail between two wolves' heads couped in chief and an escallop in base, all within a bordure argent. Mantling azure, doubled argent; and upon a wreath of his liveries is set for crest, an eagle preying on a salmon proper; and in an escroll above this motto, "Fide et perseverantia."

no specific description. They occur in the arms of Peebles,[a] a coat of arms which introduces to one's notice the term "contra-naiant." The explanation of the quaint and happy conceit of these arms and motto is that for every fish which goes up the river to spawn two return to the sea. A salmon on its back

[a] Armorial bearings of Peebles: Gules, three salmon naiant in pale, the centre towards the dexter, the others towards the sinister. Motto: "Contra nando incrementum."

figures in the arms of the city of Glasgow (Plate CXVII.), and also in the arms of Lumsden (Fig. 458) and Finlay

FIG. 459.—Armorial bearings of Major John Finlay: Argent, on a chevron between two roses in chief gules, and in base a salmon on its back proper, with a signet ring in its mouth or, two swords chevronwise, points downwards of the first, hilted and pommelled gold, all within a bordure of the second. Mantling gules and argent. Crest: on a wreath of the colours, a dexter hand couped at the wrist holding a sword in bend all proper. Motto: "I'll be wary."

(Fig. 459), whilst other instances of salmon occur in the arms of Blackett-Ord, Sprot, and Winlaw (Fig. 172).

The Herring occurs in the arms of Maconochie (Fig. 460), the *Roach* in the arms of Roche ["Gules, three

FIG. 460.—Armorial bearings of Archibald White Maconochie, M.P.: Parted per fess gules and gyronny of eight or and sable, in chief two herrings hauriant argent, and in base a lymphad, sails furled, oars in saltire all proper, flagged gules. Mantling gules and or. Crest: on a wreath of his liveries, a demi-highlander habited proper, holding in his dexter hand a sheaf of arrows also proper; and in an escroll above, this motto, "Nitimur et munitur."

roaches naiant within a bordure engrailed argent. Crest: a rock, thereon a stork close, charged on the breast with a torteau, and holding in his dexter claw a roach proper"], and *Trout* in the arms of Troutbeck ["Azure, three trout fretted tête à la queue argent"]. The same arrangement of three fish occurs upon the seal of Anstruther-Wester, but this design unfortunately has never been matriculated as a coat of arms.

The arms of Iceland present a curious charge, which is included upon the Royal shield of Denmark. The coat in question is: "Gules, a stockfish argent, crowned with an open crown or." The stockfish is a dried and cured cod, split open and with the head removed.

A *Pike* or *Jack* is more often termed a "lucy" in English heraldry and a "ged" in Scottish. Under its various names it occurs in the arms of Lucas [b] (Plate XXIII.) and Pyke.

The Eel is sometimes met with, as in the arms of Ellis (Fig. 461), and though, as Woodward states, it is always

FIG. 461.—Armorial bearings of Richard Adam Ellis, Esq.: Per pale argent and azure, a dolphin naiant embowed between two eels also naiant all counterchanged. Mantling azure and argent. Crest: on a wreath of the colours, in front of a sun in splendour, a dolphin naiant proper, charged on the body with a cross couped sable. Motto: "Obsta."

given a wavy form, the term "ondoyant," which he uses to express this, has no place in an English armorist's dictionary.

The Lobster and *Crab* are not unknown to English armory, being respectively the crests of the families of Dykes and Bridger. The arms of Bridger are: "Argent, a chevron engrailed sable, between three crabs gules." Lobster claws are a charge upon the arms of Platt-Higgins.

The arms of Birt are given in Papworth as: "Azure, a birthfish proper," and of Bersich as: "Argent, a perch azure." The arms of Cobbe (Bart., extinct) are: "Per chevron gules and sable, in chief two swans respecting and in base a herring cob naiant proper." The arms of Bishop Robinson of Carlisle were: "Azure, a flying fish in bend argent, on a chief of the second, a rose gules between two torteaux," and the crest of Sir Philip Oakley Fysh is: "On a wreath of the colours, issuant

[b] Armorial bearings of Joseph Lucas, Esq., of Foxhunt Manor, Sussex; Per chevron vert and or, in chief a crescent ermine, between two lucies hauriant of the second, and in base a catherine-wheel of the first. Mantling vert and or. Crest: on a wreath of the colours, in front of three caltraps or, on a mount vert, a fox passant in front of three oak trees proper. Motto: "Respice finem."

from a wreath of red coral, a cubit arm vested azure, cuffed argent, holding in the hand a flying fish proper." The coat of arms of Colston of Essex is: "Azure, two barbels hauriant respecting each other argent," and a barbel occurs in the crest of Binney[c] (Plate XXXVIII.), and "Vert, three sea-breams or hakes hauriant argent" is the coat of arms attributed to a family of Dox or Doxey. "Or, three chabots gules" is the crest of a French family of the name of Chabot. "Barry wavy of six argent and gules, three crevices (crayfish) two and one or" is the coat of Atwater. They also occur in another coat for the same name illustrated herein. Codfish occur in the arms of Beck, dogfish in the arms of Dodds, flounders or flukes in the arms of Arbutt, garvinfishes in the arms of Garvey, and gudgeon in the arms of Gobion. Papworth also includes instances of mackerel, prawns, shrimps, soles, sparlings, sturgeon, sea-urchins, turbots, whales, and whelks. The whelk shell appears in the arms of Storey (Plate XV.). A. C. F-D.

CHAPTER XX

REPTILES

IF armorial zoology is "shaky" in its classification of and dealings with fish, it is most wonderful when its laws and selections are considered under the heading of reptiles. But with the exception of serpents (of various kinds), the remainder must have no more than a passing mention.

The usual heraldic *Serpent* is most frequently found "nowed," that is interlaced in a knot. There is a certain well-understood form for the interlacing which is always officially adhered to, but of late there has manifested itself amongst heraldic artists a desire to break loose to a certain extent from the stereotyped form. A serpent will sometimes be found "erect" and occasionally gliding or "glissant," and sometimes it will be met with in a circle with its tail in its mouth—the

FIG. 462.—Armorial bearings of Thomas Chaplin, Gentleman: Or, on a fess sable, between two serpents nowed vert, a Maltese cross between as many crosses potent argent. Mantling sable and or. Crest: upon a wreath of the colours, in front of a cross potent or, a caduceus fesswise proper. Motto: "Labore et fide."

ancient symbol of eternity. Its constant appearance in British armory is due to the fact that it is what is

[c] Armorial bearings of James Binney, Esq., M.A., of Pampisford Hall, Cambs.: Per saltire or and azure, four horses' heads couped at the neck, counterchanged. Mantling azure and or. Crest: upon a wreath of the colours, a barbel in front of two bullrushes in saltire proper.

constantly accepted as the sign of medicine, and many grants of arms made to doctors and physicians introduce in some way either the serpent or the rod of Æscu-

FIG. 463.—Armorial bearings of Sir William Bartlett Dalby: Barry wavy of six gules and or, on a pale of the last, between two doves rising, a rod erect entwined by a serpent proper. Upon the escutcheon is placed a helmet befitting his degree, with a mantling gules and or; and for his crest, upon a wreath of the colours, in front of a dexter arm embowed to the sinister, holding in the hand an ancient lamp, a serpent nowed all proper. Motto: "Probitas verus honos."

lapius, or a serpent entwined round a staff. Serpents nowed will be found in the arms of Chaplin (Fig. 462), and Price (see Plate XV.). A serpent embowed biting its tail occurs in the arms of Falconer (Fig. 429), and in the crest of Walker. A serpent entwined round a staff will be found in the arms of Dalby (Fig. 463), and other coats of arms in which the serpent occurs are those of Sutton, borne in pretence by Wall (Fig. 464) and Duignan (Fig. 465). A serpent on its back is to be seen in the arms of Backhouse (Plate XXXVII.). Save for the matter of position, the serpent of British armory

FIG. 464.—Armorial bearings of Arthur Wall, Esq.: Party per fess indented vert and or, in chief a lymphad sail furled of the last, and in base a bugle-horn stringed gules, and upon an escutcheon of pretence the arms of Sutton, namely: argent, a chaplet of oak vert, fructed or, on a chief azure, a serpent nowed or and a dove argent respecting each other. Mantling vert and or. Crest: on a wreath of the colours, in front of a demi-boy affronté resting his dexter hand on a human heart, two torches in saltire fired all proper. Motto: "Tute celeriter et jucunde."

THE ART OF HERALDRY

is always drawn in a very naturalistic manner. It is otherwise, however, in Continental armory, where the serpent with them takes up a position closely allied to that of our dragon. It is even sometimes found winged, and the arms of the family of Visconti, which subsequently came into use as the arms of the Duchy of Milan (Fig. 466), have familiarised us as far as Continental armory is concerned with a form of serpent which is very different from the real animal or from our own heraldic variety. Another instance of a serpent will be found in the arms of the Irish family of Cotter, which are: "Argent, a chevron gules between three serpents proper," and the family of Lanigan O'Keefe (Fig. 252) bear in one quarter of their shield: "Vert,

FIG. 465.—Armorial bearings of William Henry Duignan, Gentleman: Argent, on a mount in base vert, an oak-tree, the stem entwined with two serpents interwoven and respecting each other all proper; and for a crest, upon a wreath of the colours, an owl at gaze proper; with the motto, "Historia magistra vitæ."

three lizards in pale or." The family of Cole bear: "Argent, a chevron gules between three scorpions reversed sable," a coat of arms which is sometimes quoted with the chevron and the scorpions both gules or both sable. The family of Preed of Shropshire bear: "Azure, three horse-leeches;" and the family of Whitby bear: "Gules, three snakes coiled or; on a chief of the second, as many pheons sable." A family of Sutton bears: "Or, a newt vert, in chief a lion rampant gules, all within a bordure of the last," and Papworth mentions a coat of arms for the name of Ory: "Azure, a chameleon on a shady ground proper, in chief a sun or." Another coat mentioned by Papworth is the arms of Bume: "Gules, a stellion serpent proper," though what the creature may be it is impossible to imagine. Unfortunately, when one comes to examine so many of these curious coats of arms, one finds no evidence that such families existed, and that there is no official authority or record of the arms to which reference can be made. There can be no doubt that they largely consist of misreadings or misinterpretations of both names and charges, and I am sorely afraid this remark is the true explanation of what otherwise would be most strange and interesting curiosities of arms. Sir Walter Scott's little story in "Quentin Durward" of Toison d'Or, who depicted the "cat looking through the dairy window" as the arms of Childebert, and bla-

zoned it "sable a musion passant or, oppressed with a trellis gules, cloué of the second," gives in very truth the real origin of many quaint coats of arms and heraldic terms. Ancient heraldic writers seem to have amused themselves by inventing "appropriate" arms for mythological or historical personages, and I verily believe that when so doing they never intended these arms to stand for more than examples of their own wit. Their credulous successors incorporated these little witticisms in the rolls of arms they collected, and one can only hope that in the distant future the charming drawings of Mr. E. T. Reed which have appeared in *Punch* may not be used in like manner.

There are but few instances in English armory in which the *Toad* or *Frog* are met with. In fact, the only instance which one can recollect is the coat of arms attributed to a family of Botreaux, who are said to have borne: "Argent, three toads erect sable." I am confident, however, that this coat of arms, if it ever existed, and if it could be traced to its earliest sources, would be found to be really three buckets of water, a canting allusion to the name. Toads of course are the charges on the mythical arms of Pharamond (see Plate LXXXVI.). The only instance I have come across of a snail in

FIG. 466.—Arms of the Visconti, Dukes of Milan: Argent, a serpent azure, devouring a child gules. (A wood-carving from the castle of Passau at the turn of the fifteenth century.)

187

British armory is the coat attributed by Papworth to the family of Bartan or Bertane mentioned by Papworth, as bearing, "Gules, three snails argent in their shells or." This coat, however, is not matriculated in Scotland, so that one cannot be certain that it was ever borne. It occurs, however, as the crest of a family named Billers, and is attributed also to several other families as a crest.

Lizards appear occasionally in heraldry, though more frequently in Irish than English or Scottish coats of arms. A lizard forms part of the crest of Sillifant (Fig. 466), and a hand grasping a lizard is the crest of M'Carthy, and "Azure, three lizards or" the first quarter of the arms of an Irish family of the name of Cotter, who, however, blazon these charges upon their shield as evetts. The family of Enys, who bear : "Argent, three wyverns volant in pale vert," probably derive their arms from some such source. A. C. F-D.

FIG. 467.—Armorial bearings of Arthur Onslow Sillifant, Esq., of Coombe, N. Devon : Per pale sable and argent, on a fess between two boars passant, the one in chief towards the dexter, the other in base towards the sinister, two cross crosslets all counterchanged. Mantling sable and argent. Crest : on a wreath of the colours, at the foot of a cross calvary or, a lizard proper. Motto : "Mens conscia recti."

CHAPTER XXI

INSECTS

THE insect which is most usually met with in heraldry is undoubtedly the *Bee*. Being considered, as it is, the symbol of industry, small wonder that it has been so frequently adopted. It is usually represented as if displayed upon the shield, and it is then termed volant, though of course the real term which will sometimes be found used is "volant *en arrière*." It occurs in the arms of Dorée, Beatson, Abercromby (Plate XXXIX.), Samuel (Fig. 468), and Sewell (Fig. 469), either as a charge or as a crest. Its use, however, as a crest is slightly more varied, inasmuch as it is found walking in profile, and with its wings elevated, and also perched upon a thistle as in the arms of Ferguson (Plate XXXIII.). A bee-hive "with bees diversely volant" occurs in the arms of Rowe, and the popularity of the bee in British armory is doubtless due to the frequent desire to perpetuate the fact that the foundation of a house has been laid by business industry. The fact that the bee was adopted as a badge by the Emperor Napoleon gave it considerable importance in French armory, inasmuch as he assumed it for his own badge, and the mantle and pavilion around the armorial bearings of the Empire were semé of these insects. They also appeared upon his own coronation mantle. He adopted them under the impression, which may or may not be correct, that they had at one time been the badge of Childeric, father of Clovis. The whole story connected with their assumption by Napoleon has been a matter of much controversy, and little purpose would be served by going into the matter here, but it may be added that Napoleon

changed the fleur-de-lis upon the chief in the arms of Paris to golden bees upon a chief of gules, and a chief

FIG. 468.—Armorial bearings of Stuart Montagu Samuel, Esq. : Vert, two bars between seven bees volant, four in chief and three in base or, on a chief nebuly of the last, three roses sable. Mantling vert and or. Crest : on a wreath of the colours, upon a mount vert, a rose argent, barbed, seeded, stalked and leaved proper, between two bees volant also proper. Motto : "Excel."

azure, semé of bees or, was added as indicative of their rank to the arms of "Princes-Grands-Dignitaries of the Empire." A bee-hive occurs as the crest of a family

FIG. 469.—Armorial bearings of Col. Thomas Davies Sewell, Esq., F.R.A.S., F.R.S.L,: Gules, a pale argent surmounted by a chevron invected counterchanged between two escutcheons in chief of the second and one in base of the first, each charged with a bee volant proper. Mantling gules and argent. Crest : upon a wreath of the colours, a pomme charged with a bee as in the arms, encircled by a wreath of oak fructed proper ; with the motto, "Non nobis nascimus."

named Gwatkin, and also upon the arms of the family of Kettle of Wolverhampton.

The Grasshopper is most familiar as the crest of the family of Gresham, and this is the origin of the golden grasshoppers which are so constantly met with in the city of London. "Argent, a chevron sable between three grasshoppers vert" is the coat of arms of Woodward of Kent. Two of them figure in the arms of Treacher, which are now quartered by Bowles.

Ants are but seldom met with. "Argent, six ants, three, two, and one sable," is a coat given by Papworth to a family of the name of Tregent; "Vert, an ant argent," to Kendiffe; and "Argent, a chevron vert between three beetles proper" are the arms attributed by the same authority to a family named Muschamp. There can be little doubt, however, that these "beetles" should be described as flies.

Butterflies figure in the arms of Papillon ["Azure, a chevron between three butterflies volant argent"] and in the arms of Penhellicke ["Sable, three butterflies volant argent"].

Gadflies are to be found in a coat of arms for the name of Adams ["Per pale argent and gules, a chevron between three gadflies counterchanged"]. "Sable, a hornet argent" is one blazon for the arms of Bollord or Bolloure, but elsewhere the same coat is blazoned: "Sable, a harvest-fly in pale volant *en arrière* argent." Harvest flies were the charges on the arms of the late Sir Edward Watkin, Bart.

The arms of Bassano (really of foreign origin and not an English coat) are: "Per chevron vert and argent, in chief three silkworm flies palewise *en arrière*, and in base a mulberry branch all counterchanged." "Per pale gules and azure, three stag-beetles, wings extended or," is assigned by Papworth to the Cornish family of Dore, but elsewhere these charges (under the same name) appear both as bees, gadflies, and flies. "Or, three spiders azure" is quoted as a coat for Chettle. A spider also figures as a charge on the arms of Macara (Fig. 470). The crest of Thorndike of Great Carleton, Lincolnshire, is: "On a wreath of the colours a damask

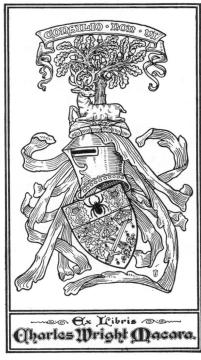

FIG. 470.—The Bookplate of Chas. W. Macara. (From a design by Mr. Graham Johnston.)

rose proper, leaves and thorns vert, at the bottom of the shield a beetle or scarabæus proper."

Woodward, in concluding his chapter upon insects, quotes the arms of the family of Pullici of Verona, viz.: "Or, semé of fleas sable, two bends gules, surmounted by two bends sinister of the same."

A. C. F-D.

CHAPTER XXII

TREES, LEAVES, FRUITS, AND FLOWERS

THE vegetable kingdom plays an important part in heraldry. Trees will be found of all varieties and in all numbers, and though little difference is made in the appearance of many varieties when they are heraldically depicted, for canting purposes the various names are carefully preserved. When, however, no name is specified, they are generally drawn after the fashion of oak-trees.

A Hurst of Trees figures both on the shield and in the crest of France-Hayhurst (Fig. 471), and in the arms

FIG. 471.—Armorial bearings of Charles Hosken France-Hayhurst, Esq.: Quarterly, 1 and 4, per chevron sable and or, in chief two crosses patée fitchée, and in base a pair of wings conjoined and elevated counterchanged (for Hayhurst); 2 and 3, argent, on a mount in base a hurst proper, on a chief wavy azure, three fleurs-de-lis or (for France). Upon the escutcheon is placed a helmet befitting his degree, with a mantling sable and or; and for his crests, 1. upon a wreath of the colours, a cubit arm proper, holding in the hand a cross patée fitchée or, between two wings sable, each charged with an annulet gold (for Hayhurst); 2. upon a wreath of the colours, a mount, thereon a hurst as in the arms, from the centre tree pendent by a strap azure a shield gules, charged with a fleur-de-lis or (for France). Motto: "Virtus semper viridis."

of Lord Lismore ["Argent, in base a mount vert, on the dexter side a hurst of oak-trees, therefrom issuing a wolf passant towards the sinister, all proper"].

A hurst of elm-trees very properly is the crest of the family of Elmhurst.

Under the description of a forest, trees figure in the arms of Forrest.[a]

The arms of Walkinshaw of that Ilk are: "Argent, a grove of fir-trees proper," and Walkinshaw of Barrowfield and Walkinshaw of London have matriculated more or less similar arms.

The Oak-Tree is of course the tree most frequently met with. Perhaps the most famous coat in which it occurs will be found in the arms granted to Colonel Carlos, to commemorate his risky sojourn with King Charles in the oak-tree at Boscobel, after the King's flight subsequent to the ill-fated battle of Worcester.

[a] Armorial bearings of Forrest (Australia): Argent, on a mount, a forest of trees proper, on a chief azure, three stars of eight points of the first. Upon the escutcheon is placed a helmet befitting his degree, with a mantling gules, doubled argent; and upon a wreath of his liveries is set for crest, a cubit arm erect, vested azure, the cuff argent, holding in the hand proper a cross botonny fitchée in bend sinister of the second, and in an escroll over the same this motto, "Vivunt dum virent."

The coat was: "Or, on a mount in base vert, an oak-tree proper, fructed or, surmounted by a fess gules, charged with three imperial crowns of the third." Other instances of the oak-tree will be found in the arms of Rothe (Fig. 353), Daugleish [b] (Plate XXXVI.), Macara (Fig. 470), and in the crest of Swinton (Plate LXIII.).

When a tree issues from the ground it will usually be blazoned "issuant from a mount vert," but when the roots are shown it is termed "eradicated."

Fir-Trees will be found in the arms of Greg, Melles

FIG. 472.—Armorial bearings of George Farquharson: Quarterly, 1 and 4, argent, a lion rampant gules; 2 and 3, or, a fir-tree growing out of a mount in base proper, on a chief gules, the banner of Scotland displayed, a canton ermine, charged with a dagger proper point downwards. Mantling gules, doubled argent; and upon a wreath of his liveries is set for crest, a demi-lion rampant gules, holding in his dexter paw a sword erect proper, hilted and pommelled or; and in an escroll above this motto, "Fide et fortitudine;" and below the shield, "I force nae frien; I fear nae fae."

(Plate XV.), De la Ferte (Fig. 102), and Farquharson (Fig. 472).

A *Cedar-Tree* occurs in the arms of Montefiore

FIG. 473.—Armorial bearings of Arthur MacMurrogh-Murphy, Esq., "The O'Morchoe": Argent, a hawthorn-tree eradicated vert, fructed gules, on a chief of the last, a lion passant guardant or.

["Argent, a cedar-tree, between two mounts of flowers proper, on a chief azure, a dagger erect proper, pommel and hilt or, between two mullets of six points gold"], and a hawthorn-tree in the arms of MacMurrogh-Murphy (Fig. 473), Thornton [c] (Plate XXII.), and the crest of Kynnersley.

A *Maple-Tree* figures in the arms of Lord Mount-Stephen ["Or, on a mount vert, a maple-tree proper, in chief two fleurs-de-lis azure"], and in the crest of Lord Strathcona ["On a mount vert, a maple-tree, at the base thereof a beaver gnawing the trunk all proper"].

A *Cocoanut-Tree* is the principal charge in the arms of Glasgow (now Robertson-Glasgow) of Montgrennan, matriculated in 1807 ["Argent, a cocoanut-tree fructed proper, growing out of a mount in base vert, on a chief azure, a shakefork between a martlet on the dexter and a salmon on the sinister argent, the last holding in the mouth a ring or"].

The arms of Clifford (Fig. 474) afford an instance of a *Coffee-Tree*, and the coat of Chambers [d] has a negro cutting down a *Sugar-Cane*.

NEC·SINE·LABORE·FRUCTÛS

FIG. 474.—Armorial bearings of Frederick Clifford, Esq., K.C.: Or, on a mount in base vert, a coffee-tree proper within a bordure engrailed compony sable and gules, charged with eight bezants. Mantling vert and or. Crest: on a wreath of the colours, in front of a demi-infant affronté (representing the infant Hercules) grasping in each hand elevated a serpent entwined around the arm, and respecting each other, a serpent nowed all proper. Motto: "Nec sine labore fructus."

A *Palm-Tree* occurs in the arms of Besant and in the armorials of many other families. The crest of Grimké-Drayton affords an instance of the use of palmetto-

[c] Armorial bearings of Thornton (Yorkshire): Argent, a chevron sable between three thorn trees proper. Crest: on a wreath argent and vert, a lion's head erased purpure, gorged with a ducal coronet or.

[d] Armorial bearings of George Frederick Chambers, Esq.: Argent, on a mount in base, a negro cutting with a bill a sugar-cane all proper, on a chief azure two pine-apples or, leaved and crowned of the last. Mantling azure and argent. Crest: on a wreath of the colours, an arm in armour embowed proper, charged with a cross couped gules, holding in the hand proper a scimitar argent, hilt and pommel or. Motto: "Vi et virtute."

[b] Armorial bearings of Henry William Daugleish, Esq.: Argent, an oak-tree eradicated and lying fesswise proper between two crescents in chief gules and a pheon in base azure. Upon the escutcheon is placed a helmet befitting his degree, with a mantling gules, doubled argent; and upon a wreath of his liveries is set for crest, a camel's head and neck couped proper; with the motto, "Be hardy."

trees. An *Olive-Tree* is the crest of Tancred, and a *Laurel-Tree* occurs in the crest of Somers (Fig. 475).

A *Mountain-Ash* figures in the shield and crest of Wigan (Fig. 476), and a *Walnut-Tree* is the crest of

FIG. 476.—Armorial bearings of Wigan: Vair, on a pile or a mount in base vert, thereon a mountain ash-tree proper. Mantling azure and argent. Crest: on a wreath of the colours, upon a mount a mountain ash-tree surmounted by a rainbow all proper; with the motto, "Carpe Diem."

Waller, of Groombridge ["On a mount vert, a walnut-tree proper, on the sinister side an escutcheon pendent, charged with the arms of France, and thereupon a label of three points argent."]

The arms of Arkwright (Fig. 477) afford an example of a *Cotton-Tree*.

FIG. 475.—Armorial bearings of Benjamin Edward Somers, Esq.: Quarterly of fifteen, 1 and 15, partly per fess vert and sable, a fess dancetté ermine, cotised argent, between a wolf's head erased in chief, and an escallop in base of the fourth; 2. vert, gutté-d'eau, three chevronels between as many wolves' heads erased ermine; 3. or, a chevron between three eagles displayed vert; 4. azure, three bendlets within a bordure argent; 5. argent, a chevron sable, in chief a label of three points gules; 6. argent, a chevron between in chief two crosses patée, and in base a saltire sable; 7. argent, three moor-cocks sable; 8. or, on a chevron gules, three martlets argent; 9. azure, two bars between eight martlets, three, two and three or; 10. azure, a chevron between three chess-rooks or; 11. argent, two bars gules, on a canton of the last, a lion passant guardant or; 12. or, a fleur-de-lis azure; 13. azure, a chevron argent, between three pears or; 14. argent, a chevron engrailed between three roses gules, seeded or. Mantling vert and argent. Crest: on a wreath of the colours, a laurel-tree suspended therefrom a cuirass with tasses proper, on either side of the tree an escallop or, and in front thereof a tilting-spear fess-wise also proper; with the motto, "Prodesse quam conspici."

FIG. 477.—Armorial bearings of Arthur William Arkwright, Esq.: Argent, on a mount vert, a cotton-tree fructed proper; on a chief azure, between two bezants, an escutcheon of the field charged with a bee volant proper. Mantling vert and argent. Crest: on a wreath of the colours, an eagle rising or, in its beak an escutcheon pendent by a ribbon gules, thereon a hank of cotton argent. Motto: "Multa tuli fecique."

Cypress-Trees are quoted by Papworth in the arms of Birkin, probably an error for birch-trees, but the cypress does occur in the arms of Tardy, Comte de Montravel ["Argent, three cypress-trees eradicated vert, on a chief gules, as many bezants"] and "Or, a willow (salix) proper" is the coat of the Counts de Salis (now Fane-de-Salis).

The arms of Sweetland, granted in 1808, are: "Argent, on a mount vert, an orange-tree fructed proper, on a chief embattled gules, three roses of the field, barbed and seeded also proper."

The curious crest of Sir John Leman, Lord Mayor of London, affords an instance of a *Lemon-Tree* ["In a lemon-tree proper, a pelican in her piety proper"].

The arms of a family whose name appears to have been variously spelled Estwere, Estwrey, Estewer, Esto-wer, and Esture, have: "Upon an argent field a tree proper," variously described as an apple-tree, an ash-tree, and a cherry-tree. The probabilities largely point to its being an ash-tree. "Or, on a mount in base vert, a pear-tree fructed proper" is the coat of arms of Pyrton or Peryton, and the arms granted in 1591 to Dr. Lopus, a physician to Queen Elizabeth, were: "Or, a pomegranate-tree eradicated vert, fructed gold, supported by a hart rampant proper, crowned and attired of the first."

A Poplar-Tree occurs in the arms of Gandolfi (Fig. 82), but probably the prime curiosity must be the coat of Abank, which Papworth gives as: "Argent, a China-cokar tree vert." Its botanical identity remains a mystery.

Trunks of Trees for some curious reason play a prominent part in heraldry. The arms of Borough, of Chetwynd Park, granted in 1702, are: "Argent, on a mount in base, in base the trunk of an oak-tree sprouting out two branches proper, with the shield of Pallas hanging thereon or, fastened by a belt gules," and the arms of Houldsworth (1868) of Gonaldston, co. Notts, are: "Ermine, the trunk of a tree in bend raguly eradicated at the base proper, between three foxes' heads, two in chief and one in base erased gules." But it is as a crest that this figure of the withered trunk sprouting again is most often met with, it being assigned to no less than forty-three families.

In England again, by one of those curious fads by which certain objects are repeated over and over again in spite of their unsuitability, tree-trunks fesswise eradicated and sprouting are constantly met with either as the basis of the crest or placed "in front of it" to help in providing necessary differences and distinctions in a new grant. An example of such use of it will be found in the arms of the town of Abergavenny (Fig. 348).

Stocks of Trees "couped and eradicated" are by no

They also occur in the arms of Grove, of Shenston Park, co. Stafford, and in the arms of Stubbs[e] (Plate XIV.).

The arms matriculated in Lyon Register by Capt. Peter Winchester (c. 1672-7) are: "Argent, a vine growing out of the base, leaved and fructed, between two papingoes endorsed feeding upon the clusters all proper." The vine also appears in the arms of Ruspoli (impaled by Chamberlayne) (Fig. 331), and the family of Archer-Houblon bear for the latter name: "Argent, on a mount in base, three hop-poles erect with hop-vines all proper."

The town of St. Ives (Cornwall) has no authorised arms, but those usually attributed to the town are: "Argent, an ivy branch overspreading the whole field vert."

"Gules, a flaming bush on the top of a mount proper, between three lions rampant argent, in the flanks two roses of the last" is the coat of Brander (now Dunbar-Brander) of Pitgaveny. Holly-bushes are also met with, as in the crest of Daubeney (Plate XXXVI.), Crackanthorpe, and a rose-bush as the crest of Inverarity (Fig. 478).

The arms of Owen, co. Pembroke, are: "Gules, a boar argent, armed, bristled, collared, and chained or to a holly-bush on a mount in base both proper."

A Fern-Brake is another stock object used in designing modern crests, and will be seen in the cases of Harter (Fig. 479), Scott-Gatty (Fig. 262), and Lloyd (Fig. 367).

FIG. 479.—Armorial bearings of George Loyd Foster Harter, Esq.: Argent, a lion rampant double-queued between three mullets of six points azure, pierced of the field. Mantling azure and argent. Crest: on a wreath of the colours, a stag springing from a fern-brake proper, and gorged with a collar azure. Motto: "Deo omnia."

FIG. 478.—Armorial bearings of John Duncan Inverarity: Gules, on a chevron or, between six arrows in chief, three and three, the points upwards, two saltirewise and one in pale, plumed and banded argent, and in base a hunting-horn stringed of the third, an elephant's head couped sable. Mantling gules and or. Crest: on a wreath of his liveries, a rose-bush proper. Motto: "Semper floreat."

means uncommon. They figure in the arms of the Borough of Woodstock: "Gules, the stump of a tree couped and eradicated argent, and in chief three stags' heads caboshed of the same, all within a bordure of the last charged with eight oak-leaves vert."

Branches are constantly occurring, but they are usually oak, laurel, palm, or holly. They need to be distinguished from "slips," which are much smaller and with fewer leaves. Definite rules of distinction between *e.g.* an acorn "slipped," a slip of oak, and

[e] Armorial bearings of Henry Stubbs, Esq., J.P., D.L., of Danby, co. Donegal: Sable, on a bend between three pheons or, as many round buckles gules, on a chief of the second three stumps of trees eradicated proper. Crest: upon a wreath of the colours, a stump of a tree eradicated proper, thereon a demi-eagle displayed or, collared sable, holding in the beak an oak branch also proper; with the motto, "Dominus exaltatio mea."

an oak-branch have been laid down by purists, but no such minute detail is officially observed, and it

FIG. 480.—Armorial bearings of Lloyd, of Dolobran: Azure, a chevron between three cocks argent, wattled, crested, and armed or. Mantling azure and argent. Crest: upon a wreath of the colours, in front of a fern-brake proper, a goat salient argent, armed and unguled or, gorged with a collar flory counterflory sable. Motto: "Esto vigilans."

seems better to leave the point to general artistic discretion ; the colloquial difference between a slip and a branch being quite a sufficient guide upon the point.

An example of an *Oak-Branch* occurs in the arms of

FIG. 481.—Armorial bearings of Thomas Stokes George Hugh Robertson Aikman, Esq.: Argent, a sinister hand holding a branch of oak palewise proper, surmounted of a bend engrailed gules. Mantling gules, doubled argent. Crest: on a wreath of his liveries, an oak-tree proper; and in an escroll over the same this motto, "Sub Robore Virtus."

Aikman (Fig. 481), and another, which is rather curious, in the crest of Accrington.[f]

Oak-Slips, on the other hand, occur in the arms of Baldwin (Fig. 373).

A *Palm-Branch* occurs in the crests of Innes, Chafy, and Corfield.

Laurel-Branches occur in the arms of Cooper (Fig. 482), and sprigs of laurel in the arms of Meeking.

FIG. 482.—Armorial bearings of George Alexander Cooper, Esq.: Argent, a chevron gules, between two laurel-branches in chief vert and a wolf's head erased of the second in base. Mantling gules, doubled argent. Crest: on a wreath of his liveries, a dexter hand grasping a wolf's head erased all proper. Motto: "Virtute et fortitudine."

Holly-Branches are chiefly found in the arms of families named Irvine or Irwin, but they are invariably blazoned as "sheaves" of holly or as holly-branches of three leaves. To a certain extent this is a misnomer, because the so-called "branch" is merely three holly-leaves tied together.

"Argent, an almond-slip proper" is the coat of arms attributed to a family of Almond, and Papworth assigns "Argent, a barberry-branch fructed proper" to Berry.

"Argent, three sprigs of balm flowered proper" is stated to be the coat of a family named Balme, and "Argent, three teasels slipped proper" the coat of Bowden. A teasle on a canton figures in the arms of Chichester-Constable.

The Company of Tobacco-Pipe Makers in London, incorporated in the year 1663, bore : "Argent, on a mount in base vert, three plants of tobacco growing and flowering all proper." The crest recently granted to Sir Thomas Lipton, Bart. ["On a wreath of the colours, two arms in saltire, the dexter surmounted by the sinister holding a sprig of the tea-plant erect, and the other a like sprig of the coffee-plant both slipped and leaved proper, vested above the elbow argent"], affords an example of both the coffee-plant and the tea-plant, which have both assisted him so materially in piling up his immense fortune. "Or, three birch-twigs sable" is the coat of Birches, and "Or, a bunch of nettles vert" is the coat of Mallerby of Devonshire. The pun in the last case is apparent.

The Cotton-Plant figures in the arms of the towns of

f Arms of Accrington: Gules, on a fess argent, a shuttle fesswise proper, in base two printing cylinders, issuant therefrom a piece of calico (parsley pattern) also proper, on a chief per pale or and vert, a lion rampant purpure and a stag current or ; and for the crest, an oak-branch bent chevronwise, sprouting and leaved proper, fructed or. Motto: "Industry and prudence conquer."

2 B

Darwen, Rochdale, and Nelson, and two culms of the papyrus plant occur in the arms of Bury.

The Coffee-Plant also figures in the arms of Yockney: "Azure, a chevron or, between a ship under sail in chief proper, and a sprig of the coffee-plant slipped in base of the second. Mantling azure and or. Crest: on a wreath of the colours, in front of a dexter arm embowed in armour, the hand in a gauntlet grasping a roll of paper all proper, a pair of compasses extended or. Motto: 'Labore et scientia.'"

A branch, slip, bush, or tree is termed "fructed" when the fruit is shown, though the term is usually disregarded unless "fructed" of a different colour. When represented as "fructed," the fruit is usually drawn out of all proportion to its relative size.

Leaves are not infrequent in their appearance. Holly-leaves occur in the various coats for most people of the name of Irwin and Irvine (Fig. 135), as already men-

FIG. 483.—Armorial bearings of Elise Josephine Foulds are, upon a lozenge: Per chevron azure and argent, a rose between two fleurs-de-lis in chief of the last, and three bay-leaves erect and slipped in base vert.

tioned. Laurel-leaves occur in the arms of Leveson-Gower, Foulis, and Foulds (Fig. 483).

Oak-Leaves occur in the arms of Trelawney ["Argent, a chevron sable, between three oak-leaves slipped proper"]; and hazel-leaves in the arms of Hesilrige or Hazlerigg ["Argent, a chevron, between three hazel-leaves vert. Crest: on a chapeau gules turned up ermine, a man's head proper"].

Linden-Leaves are constantly met with in German heraldry, and many instances of these will be found in this volume. "Argent, three edock (dock or burdock) leaves vert" is the coat of Hepburn. Papworth assigns "Argent, an aspen leaf proper" to Aspinal, and "Or, a betony-leaf proper" to Betty. "Argent, three aspen-leaves" is an unauthorised coat used by Espin, and the same coat with varying tinctures is assigned to Cogan. Killach is stated to bear: "Azure, three bay-leaves argent," and to Woodward, of Little Walsingham, Norfolk, was granted in 1806: "Vert, three mulberry-leaves or."

The Maple-Leaf has been generally adopted as a Canadian emblem, and consequently figures upon the arms of that dominion, and in the arms of many who have had Canadian associations.

A curious leaf—usually called the "sea-leaf," which is properly the "nenuphar-leaf," is often met with in German heraldry, and is referred to on page 39.

"Vert, three vine-leaves or" is assigned by Papworth to Wortford, and the same authority mentions coats in which woodbine-leaves occur for Browne, Theme, and Gamboa. Rose-leaves occur in the arms of Utermarck

FIG. 484.—Armorial bearings of Reginald John Guthrie Utermarck: Per fess or and azure, in chief a sprig of three rose-leaves slipped vert, and in base a mullet of six points of the first, pierced of the field. Mantling azure and or. Crest: on a wreath of the colours, a sprig of three rose-leaves slipped vert, between two buffalo-horns per fess or and azure. Motto: "Va outre marque."

(Fig. 484), and walnut-leaves figure in the arms of Waller (Fig. 88).

Although theoretically leaves, the trefoil, quatrefoil, and cinquefoil are a class by themselves, having a recognised heraldic status as exclusively heraldic charges, and the quatrefoil and cinquefoil, in spite of the derivation of their names, are as likely to have been originally flowers as leaves.

The heraldic Trefoil, though frequently specifically described as "slipped," is nevertheless always so depicted, and it is not necessary to so describe it. Of late a tendency has been noticeable in paintings from Ulster's Office to represent the trefoil in a way more nearly approaching the Irish shamrock, from which it has undoubtedly been derived. Instances of the trefoil

FIG. 485.—Armorial bearings of Rodd: Argent, two trefoils slipped sable, a chief of the last.

occur in the arms of Rodd (Fig. 485), Dobrée, MacDermott (Plate XXII.), and Gilmour (Fig. 486).

The crowned trefoil is one of the national badges of Ireland.

FIG. 486.—Armorial bearings of Sir John Gilmour, 1st Baronet: Argent, on a chevron between three trefoils slipped vert, as many hunting-horns of the first, the escutcheon being charged with his badge as a baronet. Mantling vert, doubled argent. Crest: upon a wreath of his liveries, a dexter hand fesswise couped, holding a writing-pen proper, and on an escroll over the same this motto, "Nil penna sed usus."

A four-leaved "lucky" shamrock has been introduced into the arms of Sir Robert Hart, Bart.

The Quatrefoil is not often met with, but it occurs

FIG. 487.—Armorial bearings of Frederic James Eyre, Gentleman: Argent, on a chevron sable, three quatrefoils or, in chief a mullet gules (for cadency), and (for distinction) the whole within a bordure wavy vert. Mantling sable and argent; and for his crest, upon a wreath of the colours, a leg in armour couped at the thigh proper, garnished and spurred gold, charged with a mullet as in the arms (for cadency), and debruised (for distinction) with a baton sinister sable. Motto: "Pro Rege sæpe, pro patria semper."

in the arms of Eyre (Fig. 487), King (Plate XIV.), and Dreyer (Fig. 488).

FIG. 488.—Armorial bearings of John Louis Emil Dreyer, Esq.: Per fess argent and gules, chaperonné azure, in chief a trefoil slipped and inverted vert, and in base three roundels, each charged with a quatrefoil argent. Mantling gules and argent. Crest: on a wreath of the colours, an arm vambraced, the hand gauntleted, grasping a trident bend sinisterwise argent, the shaft proper. Motto: "Uden arbeide ingen lykke."

The Cinquefoil is constantly met with, but, save in exceedingly rare instances, neither the quatrefoil nor the cinquefoil will be met with "slipped." The constant occurrence of the cinquefoil in early rolls of arms is out of all proportion to its distinctiveness or artistic beauty, and the frequency with which it is met with in conjunction with the cross crosslet points clearly to the fact that there is some allusion behind, if this could only be fathomed. Many a man might adopt a lion through independent choice, but one would not expect independent choice to lead so many to pitch upon a combination of cross crosslets and cinquefoils. The cross crosslets, I am confident, are a later addition in many cases, for the original arms of D'Arcy were simply: "Argent, three cinquefoils gules." The arms of the town of Leicester are: "Gules, a cinquefoil ermine," and this is the coat attributed to the family of the De Beaumonts or De Bellomonts, Earls of Leicester. Simon de Montfort, the great Earl of Leicester, was the son or grandson of Amicia, a coheir of the former Earls, and as such entitled to quarter the arms of the De Bellomonts. As stated on page 72 (*vide* Figs. 111 and 112), there are two coats attributed to De Montfort. His only status in this country depended solely upon the De Bellomont inheritance, and, conformably with the custom of the period, we are far more likely to find him using arms of De Bellomont or De Beaumont than of Montfort. From the similarity of the charge to the better-known Beaumont arms (Fig. 489), I am inclined

FIG. 489.—Arms of William Beaumont, Viscount Beaumont (*d.* 1507), from his brass at Wivenhoe: Quarterly, 1. azure, semé-de-lis and a lion rampant or (for Beaumont); 2. azure, three garbs or (for Comyn); 3. quarterly gules and or, in the first quarter an eagle displayed argent (for Phelipp); 4. azure, three cinquefoils pierced argent (for Bardolph).

to think the lion rampant to be the real De Bellomont coat. The origin of the cinquefoil has yet to be accounted for. The earliest De Bellomont for whom I can find proof of user thereof is Robert "Fitz-Pernell," otherwise De Bellomont, who died in 1206, and whose seal (Fig. 490) shows it. Be it noted it is not on a shield, and though of course this is not proof in any way, it is in accord with my suggestion that it is nothing more than a pimpernel flower adopted as a device or badge to typify his own name and his mother's name, she being Pernelle or Petronilla, the heiress of Grantmesnil. The cinquefoil was not the coat of Grantmesnil but a quaint little conceit, and is not therefore likely to have been used as a coat of arms by the De Bellomonts, though no doubt they used it as a badge and device, as

FIG. 490.—From the seal of Robert Fitz-Pernell, Earl of Leicester, d. 1206. (Probably gules, a cinquefoil ermine.)

FIG. 491.—Arms of Earl of Angus (d. 1308): Gules, crusilly fitchée and a cinquefoil or.

no doubt did Simon de Montfort. Simon de Montfort split England into two parties. Men were for Montfort or the king, and those that were for De Montfort very probably took and used his badge of a cinquefoil as a party badge.

The cinquefoil in its ordinary heraldic form also occurs in the arms of Umfraville (Fig. 491), Bardolph, quartered by Beaumont (Fig. 489), and in the arms of Hamilton, Saltmarshe (Fig. 492), Cory (Plate XXXVII.),

FIG. 492.—Armorial bearings of Philip Saltmarshe, Esq.: Argent, crusily, and three cinquefoils gules. Upon the escutcheon is placed a helmet befitting his degree, with a mantling gules and argent; and for his crest, upon a wreath of the colours, a rudder or; with the motto, "Ad astra virtus."

and D'Arcy (Fig. 493), and sprigs of cinquefoil will be found in the arms of Hill, and in the crest of Kersey. The cinquefoil is sometimes found pierced. The five-

foiled flower being the blossom of so many plants, what are to all intents and purposes cinquefoils occur in

FIG. 493.—Armorial bearings of D'Arcy: Azure, semé of cross crosslets and three cinquefoils argent. Mantling azure and argent. Crest: on a wreath of the colours, on a chapeau gules, turned up ermine, a bull passant sable, armed or. Motto: "Un Dieu un roy."

FIG. 494.—Armorial bearings of Alexander Edmund Fraser, Esq.: Quarterly, 1 and 4, azure, on a chevron between three fraisiers argent, as many fleurs-de-lis gules; 2 and 3, argent, three ancient Scots crowns gules; all within a bordure of the last (for difference); and (as a Knight of St. John), on a chief gules, a cross argent embellished alternately in each of the principal angles with a lion guardant and a unicorn, both passant, or. Upon the escutcheon is placed a helmet befitting his degree, with a mantling azure, doubled argent; and for his crest, upon a wreath of his liveries, a buck's head attired and couped proper, gorged with an ancient Scots crown or; for mottoes, in an escroll above the crest, "Je suis prest," and in an escroll beneath the escutcheon, "Tout bien ou rien."

the arms of Fraser, where they are termed "fraises" (Fig. 494), of Primrose, where they are blazoned "primroses," and of Lambert (Fig. 495), where they are called "narcissus flowers."

FIG. 495.—Armorial bearings of Frederick Arthur Heygate Lambert, Esq. : Gules, three narcissuses argent, and a canton or. Mantling gules and argent; and for his crest, upon a wreath of the colours, on a mount vert, a centaur passant regardant, the human part proper, and the hind part ermine, girt with a laurel wreath vert, holding a bow and arrow gules. Motto : "Nosce Teipsum."

The double Quatrefoil is cited as the English difference mark for the ninth son, but as these difference marks are but seldom used, and as ninth sons are somewhat of a rarity, it is seldom indeed that this particular mark is seen in use. Personally I have never seen it.

The Turnip makes an early appearance in armory, being found on Plate LXXV., and it also occurs in the coat of Dammant ["Sable, a turnip leaved proper, a chief or, gutté-de-poix"].

The curious crest of Lingen, which is "Seven leeks root upwards issuing from a ducal coronet all proper," is worthy of especial mention.

In considering flowers as a charge, a start must naturally be made with the rose, which figures so prominently in the heraldry of England.

The heraldic Rose until a much later date than its first appearance in armory—it occurs, however, at the earliest period—was always represented in what we now term the "conventional" form, with five displayed petals. Accustomed as we are to the more ornate form of the cultivated rose of the garden, those who speak of the "conventional" heraldic rose rather seem to overlook that it is an exact reproduction of the wild rose of the hedgerow, which, moreover, has a tendency to show itself "displayed" and not in the more profile attitude we are perhaps accustomed to. It should also be observed that the earliest representations of the heraldic rose depict the intervening spaces between the petals which are noticeable in the wild rose. Under the Tudor sovereigns, the heraldic rose often shows a double row of petals, a fact which is doubtless accounted for by the then increasing familiarity with the cultivated variety, and also by the attempt to conjoin the rival emblems of the warring factions of York and Lancaster.

Though the heraldic rose is seldom, if ever, otherwise depicted, it should be described as "barbed vert" and "seeded or" (or "barbed and seeded proper") when the centre seeds and the small intervening green leaves (the calyx) between the petals are represented in their natural colours. In the reign of the later Tudor sovereigns the conventionality of earlier heraldic art was slowly giving way to the pure naturalism into which heraldic art thereafter steadily degenerated, and we find that the rose then begins (both as a Royal badge and elsewhere) to be met with "slipped." The Royal fleurs-de-lis are turned into natural lilies in the grant to Eton College (Plate CXXII.), and in the grant to William Cope, Cofferer to Henry VII., the roses are slipped ["Argent, on a chevron azure, between three roses gules, slipped and leaved vert, as many fleurs-de-lis or. Crest : out of a fleur-de-lis or, a dragon's head gules"]. A rose when "slipped" theoretically has only a stalk added, in practice it will always have at least one leaf added to the slip, and a rose "slipped and leaved" would have a leaf on either side. A rose "stalked and leaved" is not so limited and will usually be found with a slightly longer stalk and several leaves, but these technical refinements of blazon, which are really unnecessary, are not greatly observed or taken into account. The arms of the Burgh of Montrose afford an example of a single rose as the only charge, although other instances will be met with in the arms of Boscawen, Viscount Falmouth ["Ermine, a rose gules, barbed and seeded proper"], and of Sir Henry Dickinson Nightingale, Bart. ["Per pale ermine and gules, a rose counterchanged"].

Amongst the scores of English arms in which the rose figures, it will be found in the original heraldic form in the cases of the arms of Leech (Fig. 496),

FIG. 496.—Armorial bearings of Stephen Leech, Esq.: Ermine, a rose gules, on a chief indented of the last, three ducal coronets or. Mantling gules and argent. Crest: on a wreath of the colours, an arm erect proper, grasping a snake vert. Motto : "Virtus est venerabilis."

Southampton (Plate CXV.), and Eshelby (Fig. 497); and either stalked or slipped in the arms of Brodribb (Fig. 442) and White-Thomson (Fig. 498). A curious instance of the use of the rose will be found in the crest of Bewley (Plate XXV.), and the "cultivated" rose was depicted in the emblazonment of the crest of Inverarity (Fig. 478), which is a rose-bush proper.

THE ART OF HERALDRY

Heraldry, with its roses, has accomplished what horticulture has not. There is an old legend that when Henry VII. succeeded to the English throne some

FIG. 498.—Armorial bearings of Sir Robert Thomas White-Thomson, K.C.B.: Quarterly, 1 and 4, argent, a stag's head caboshed and attired with ten tines proper, on a chief azure, a cross crosslet fitchée between two roses slipped of the field (for Thomson); 2 and 3, party per fess raguly or and gules, three roses counterchanged, all barbed and seeded, and slipped proper, on a chief of the last three sand-glasses proper (for White), the escutcheon being surrounded by the ribbon and pendent the badge of a K.C.B.; and impaling the arms of Ferguson-Davie, namely: quarterly, 1 and 4, argent, a chevron sable between three mullets pierced gules (for Davie); 2 and 3, azure, three cinquefoils two and one or, on a chief of the last, a lion passant gules (for Ferguson); and for his crests, 1. upon a wreath of the colours, a dexter cubit arm in armour fesswise, holding a cross crosslet fitché erect argent (for Thomson); 2. upon a wreath of the colours, a stork resting the dexter claw upon a sand-glass, and holding in the beak a bulrush leaved all proper (for White); with the motto, "Deus providebit."

enterprising individual produced a natural parti-coloured rose which answered to the conjoined heraldic rose of gules and argent. Our roses "or" may really find their natural counterpart in the primrose, but the arms of Rochefort ["Quarterly or and azure, four roses counterchanged"] give us the *blue* rose, the arms of Berendon ["Argent, three roses sable"] give us the *black* rose, and the coat of Smallshaw ["Argent, a rose vert, between three shakeforks sable"] is the long-desired *green* rose.

The Thistle ranks next to the rose in British heraldic importance. Like the rose, the reason of its assumption as a national badge remains largely a matter of mystery, though it is of nothing like so ancient an origin. Of course one knows the time-honoured and wholly impossible legend that its adoption as a national symbol dates from the battle of Largs, when one of the Danish invaders gave away an attempted surprise by his cry of agony caused by stepping barefooted upon a thistle.

The fact, however, remains that its earliest appearance is on the silver coinage of 1474, in the reign of James III., but during that reign there can be no doubt

FIG. 499.—Armorial bearings of Thomas Robert Dewar, Esq.: Per saltire or and azure, a seax erect proper, surmounted by a saltire engrailed per saltire of the first and second, between two cinquefoils in fess also of the first. Mantling azure and or. Crest: on a wreath of the colours, between two thistles leaved and slipped proper, a cock gules, armed and spurred argent, charged on the breast with a cinquefoil or. Motto: "Gloria Patri."

that it was accepted either as a national badge or else as the personal badge of the sovereign. The period in question was that in which badges were so largely used, and it is not unlikely that desiring to vie with his brother of England, and fired by the example of the broom badge and the rose badge, the Scottish king, remembering the ancient legend, chose the thistle as his badge. In 1540, when the thistle had become recognised as one of the national emblems of the kingdom, the foundation of the Order of the Thistle stereotyped the fact for all future time. The conventional heraldic representation of the thistle is as it appears upon the star of that Order, that is, the flowered head upon a short stalk with a leaf on either side. Though sometimes represented of gold, it is nearly always proper. It has frequently been granted as an augmentation, though in such a meaning it will usually be found crowned. The coat of augmentation carried in the first quarter of his arms by Lord Torphichen is: "Argent, a thistle vert, flowered gules (really a thistle proper), on a chief azure an imperial crown or." The thistle also occurs in the arms of Aikenhead, Dewar (Fig. 499), Gibbons[g] (Plate XIV.), and Ferguson (Plate XXXIII.). "Sable, a thistle or, between three pheons argent" is the coat of Teesdale, and "Gules, three thistles or" is attributed in Papworth to Hawkey. A curious use of the thistle occurs in the arms of the National Bank of Scotland (granted 1826), which are: "Or, the image of St. Andrew with vesture vert, and surcoat purpure, bearing before him the cross of his martyrdom argent, all resting on a base of the second, in the dexter flank a garb gules, in the sinister a ship in full sail sable, *the shield surrounded with two thistles proper disposed in orle.*

The Lily in its natural form sometimes occurs, though of course it generally figures as the fleur-de-lis, which will presently be considered. The natural lily will be found in the arms of Aberdeen University, of Dundee, and in the crests of various families of the name of Chadwick (Figs. 191 and 192). They also occur in the arms of the College of St. Mary the Virgin, at Eton ["Sable, three lilies argent, on a chief per pale azure and gules a fleur-de-lis on the dexter side, and a lion passant guardant or on the sinister"] (Plate CXXII.). Here they doubtless typify the Virgin, to whom they have reference; as also in the case of Marylebone (Fig. 240).

The arms of Lilly, of Stoke Prior, are : "Gules, three lilies slipped argent;" and the arms of J. E. Lilley, Esq., of Harrow, are: "Azure, on a pile between two fleurs-de-lis argent, a lily of the valley eradicated proper. Crest: on a wreath of the colours, a cubit arm erect proper, charged with a fleur-de-lis argent and holding in the hand two lilies of the valley, leaved and slipped in saltire, also proper."

Columbine Flowers occur in the arms of Cadman (Fig. 500), and *Gillyflowers* in the arms of Livingstone.

FIG. 500.—Armorial bearings of the Rev. William Snape Cadman, M.A.: Per fess or and gules, a pale counterchanged, three columbines, two and one vert. Mantling gules and or. Crest: on a wreath of the colours, in front of a rock, a stork's head, both proper, ducally crowned or. Motto: "Deus et patria."

Fraises—really the flowers of the strawberry-plant—occur, as has been already mentioned, in the arms of Fraser, and *Narcissus Flowers* in the arms of Lambeth. "Gules, three poppy bolles on their stalks in fess or" are the arms of Boller.

g Armorial bearings of Robert Alexander Gibbons, Esq.: Paly of six argent and gules, on a bend engrailed cottised also engrailed sable, a thistle slipped and leaved proper between two escallops or. Mantling gules and argent. Crest: on a wreath of the colours, upon a mount vert, a demi-lion sable, holding in the dexter paw a thistle as in the arms, and resting the sinister on an escallop or. Motto: "Nitor donec supero."

The Lotus-Flower, which is now very generally becoming the recognised emblem of India, is constantly met with in the arms granted to those who have won fortune or reputation in that country. Instances in which it occurs are the arms of Sir Roper Lethbridge, K.C.I.E.,[h] Sir Thomas Seccombe, G.C.I.E. (Fig. 955), and the University of Madras (Fig. 308).

The *Sylphium-Plant* occurs in the arms of Smyth (Fig. 501).

FIG. 501.—Armorial bearings of General Sir Henry Augustus Smyth, K.C.M.G.: Vert, a chevron erminois, charged with a chevron gules, between three Saracen's heads habited in profile couped at the neck proper, and for augmentation a chief argent, thereon a mount vert inscribed with the Greek letters K Y P A gold and issuant therefrom a representation of the plant Silphium proper. Crests: 1. (of augmentation) on a wreath of the colours, a mount vert inscribed with the aforesaid Greek letters and issuant therefrom the Silphium as in the arms; 2. on a wreath of the colours, an anchor fesswise sable, thereon an ostrich erminois holding in the beak a horse-shoe or. Motto: "Vincere est vivere."

The arms granted to Sir Richard Quain were: "Argent, a chevron engrailed azure, in chief two fers-de-moline gules, and issuant from the base a rock covered with daisies proper."

Primroses occur (as was only to be expected) in the arms of the Earl of Rosebery ["Vert, three primroses within a double tressure flory counterflory or"].

The Sunflower or *Marigold* occurs in the crest of Buchan ["A sunflower in full bloom towards the sun in the dexter chief"], and also in the arms granted in 1614 to Florio. Here, however, the flower is termed a heliotrope. The arms in question are: "Azure, a heliotrope or, issuing from a stalk sprouting from two leaves vert, in chief the sun in splendour proper."

Tulips occur in the arms of Raphael, and the *Cornflower* or *Bluebottle* occurs in the arms of Chorley of Chorley, Lancs. ["Argent, a chevron gules between three bluebottles slipped proper"], and also in the arms of the town.

The arms granted to Sir Edgar Boehm, Bart., were:

h Armorial bearings of Sir Roper Lethbridge, K.C.I.E., M.A.: Azure, over water a bridge of three arches embattled proper, on a chief argent, an eagle displayed sable, between two roses gules, barbed and seeded proper, the escutcheon being surrounded by the ribbon of the Most Eminent Order of the Indian Empire, and pendent his badge as a Knight Commander. Upon the escutcheon is placed a helmet befitting his degree. Mantling azure and argent. Crest: on a wreath of the colours, in front of a demi-tower proper, issuant therefrom a demi-eagle displayed sable, each wing charged with a rose argent, a lotus-flower leaved and slipped proper. Motto: "Spes mea in Deo."

"Azure, in the sinister canton a sun, issuing therefrom eleven rays, over all a clover-plant eradicated proper."

The Fleur-de-Lis.—Few figures have puzzled the antiquary so much as the fleur-de-lis. Countless origins have been suggested for it; we have even lately had the height of absurdity urged in a suggested phallic origin, which only rivals in ridiculousness the long since exploded legend that the fleurs-de-lis in the arms of France were a corrupted form of an earlier coat, "Azure, three toads or," the reputed coat of arms of Pharamond!

To France and the arms of France one must turn for the origin of the fleur-de-lis. To begin with, the heraldic form of the fleur-de-lis as a mere presumably meaningless form of decoration is found long before the days of armory, in fact from the earliest period of decoration. It is such an essentially natural development of decoration that it may be accepted as such without any attempt to give it a meaning or symbolism. Its earliest heraldic appearances as the finial of a sceptre or the decoration of a coronet need not have had any symbolical character.

We then find the "lily" accepted as having some symbolical reference to France, and it should be remembered that the iris was known by the name of a lily until comparatively modern times.

It is curious—though possibly in this case it may be only a coincidence—that, on a coin of the Emperor Hadrian, Gaul is typified by a female figure holding in the hand a lily, the legend being, "Restutori Galliæ." The fleur-de-lis as the finial of a sceptre and as an ornament of a crown can be taken back to the fifth century. Fleurs-de-lis upon crowns and coronets in France are at least as old as the reign of King Robert (son of Hugh Capet), whose seal represents him crowned in this manner.

We have, moreover, the ancient legendary tradition that at the baptism of Clovis, King of the Franks, the Virgin (whose emblem the lily has always been) sent a lily by an angel as a mark of her special favour. It is difficult to determine the exact date at which this tradition was invented, but its accepted character may be judged from the fact that it was solemnly advanced by the French bishops at the Council of Trent in a dispute as to the precedence of their sovereign. The old legend as to Clovis would naturally identify the flower with him, and it should be noted that the names Clovis, Lois, Loys, and Louis are identical. "Loys" was the signature of the kings of France until the time of Louis XIII. It is worth the passing conjecture that what are sometimes termed "Cleves lilies" may be a corrupted form of Clovis lilies. There can be little doubt that the term "fleur-de-lis" is quite as likely to be a corruption of "fleur-de-lois" as flower of the lily. The chief point is that the desire was to represent a *flower* in allusion to the old legend, without perhaps any very definite certainty of the flower intended to be represented. Philip I. on his seal (A.D. 1060) holds a short staff terminating in a fleur-de-lis. The same object occurs in the great seal of Louis VII. In the seal of his wife, Queen Constance, we find her represented as holding in either hand a similar object, though in these last cases it is by no means certain that figures are not attempts to represent the natural flower. A signet of Louis VII. bears a single fleur-de-lis "florencée" (or flowered), and in his reign the heraldic fleur-de-lis undoubtedly became stereotyped as a symbolical device, for we find that when in the lifetime of Louis VII. his son Philip was crowned, the king prescribed that the prince should wear "ses chausses appelées sandales ou bottines de soye, couleur bleu azuré sémée en moult endroits de fleurs-de-lys or, puis aussi sa dalmatique de même

couleur et œuvre." On the oval counterseal of Philip II. (*d.* 1223) appears a heraldic fleur-de-lis. His great seal, as also that of Louis VIII., shows a seated figure crowned with an open crown of "fleurons," and holding in his right hand a flower, and in his left a sceptre surmounted by a heraldic fleur-de-lis enclosed within a lozenge-shaped frame. On the seal of Louis VIII. the conjunction of the essentially heraldic fleur-de-lis (within the lozenge-shaped head of the sceptre), and the more natural flower held in the hand, should leave little if any doubt of the intention to represent flowers in the French fleur-de-lis. The figure held in the hand represents a flower of five petals. The upper pair turned inwards to touch the centre one, and the lower pair curved downwards, leave the figure with a marked resemblance both to the iris and to the conventional fleur-de-lis. The counter-seal of Louis VIII. shows a Norman-shaped shield semé of fleurs-de-lis of the conventional heraldic pattern. By then, of course, "Azure, semé-de-lis or" had become the fixed and determined arms of France. By an edict dated 1376, Charles V. reduced the number of fleurs-de-lis in his shield to three: "Pour symboliser la Sainte-Trinité."

The claim of Edward III. to the throne of France was made on the death of Charles IV. of France in 1328, but the decision being against him, he apparently acquiesced, and did homage to Philip of Valois (Philip VI.) for Guienne. Philip, however, lent assistance to David II. of Scotland against King Edward, who immediately renewed his claim to France, assumed the arms and the title of king of that country, and prepared for war. He commenced hostilities in 1339, and upon his new Great Seal (made in the early part of 1340) we find his arms represented upon shield, surcoat, and housings as: "Quarterly, 1 and 4, azure, semé-de-lis or (for France); 2 and 3, gules, three lions passant guardant in pale or (for England)" (Fig. 295). The Royal Arms thus remained until 1411, when upon the second Great Seal of Henry IV. the fleurs-de-lis in England (as in France) were reduced to three in number, and so remained as part of the Royal Arms of this country until the latter part of the reign of George III.

Fleurs-de-lis (probably intended as badges only) had figured upon all the Great Seals of Edward III. On the first seal (which with slight alterations had also served for both Edward I. and II.), a small fleur-de-lis appears over each of the castles which had previously figured on either side of the throne. In the second Great Seal, fleurs-de-lis took the places of the castles.

The similarity of the Montgomery arms to the Royal Arms of France has led to all kinds of wild genealogical conjectures, but at a time when the arms of France were hardly determinate, the seal of John de Mundegumbri is met with, bearing a single fleur-de-lis, the original from which the arms of Montgomery were developed. Other instances in which fleurs-de-lis occur will be found in the arms of Brown (Fig. 502), Bonython,[i] Balfour (Fig. 503), Lloyd-Owen (Fig. 504), MacMicking,[j] and Chance (Fig. 169). Letters of nobility and the name of Du Lis were granted by Charles VII. in December 1429 to the brothers of Joan of Arc, and the following arms were then assigned to them: "Azure, a sword in pale proper, hilted and supporting on its point an open crown or, between two fleurs-de-lis of the last."

[i] Armorial bearings of Sir John Langdon Bonython: Argent, a chevron between three fleurs-de-lis sable. [These arms were granted to the Bonythons of Bonython, in Cornwall, prior to the general use of crests.] Motto: "In Deo spes mea."

[j] Armorial bearings of Robert MacMicking: Azure, four fleurs-de-lis in cross, the tops to the exterior of the shield or. Crest: a demi-savage bearing in his dexter hand an arrow, at his back a quiver full proper. Mottoes: "Res non verba," and "We hae dune."

The fleur-de-lis "florencée," or the "fleur-de-lis flowered," as it is termed in England, is officially considered a distinct charge from the simple fleur-de-lis. Eve employs the term "seeded," and remarks of it: "This being one of the numerous instances of pedantic, because unnecessary distinction, which showed marks of decadence; for both forms occur at the same period, and adorn the same object, evidently with the same intention."

The difference between these forms really is that the fleur-de-lis is "seeded" when a stalk having seeds at the end issues in the upper interstices. In a fleur-de-lis "florencée," the natural flower of a lily issues instead of the seeded stalk. This figure formed the arms of Florence, and will be seen on Plate CXXX.

FIG. 502.—Armorial bearings of James Millar Brown, B.L. : Parted per fess or and gules, three fleurs-de-lis and in the fess point a mullet, all counterchanged. Mantling gules, doubled or; and upon a wreath of his liveries is set for crest, a demi-lion rampant vert, holding in his dexter paw a fleur-de-lis gold; with the motto, "Floreat majestas."

FIG. 504.—Armorial bearings of Einion ap Seisyllt, now borne by his descendant David Charles Lloyd Owen, F.R.C.S.: Argent, a lion passant sable between three fleurs-de-lis gules.

Some of the many varied artistic forms of the fleur-de-lis will be seen in Fig. 505, from a drawing by Miss Helard, who has very kindly collected for me the different examples there shown. Fleurs-de-lis, like all other Royal emblems, are frequently to be met with in the arms of towns, e.g. in the arms of Lancaster, Maryborough, Wakefield, and Great Torrington. Fleurs-de-lis of rather elegant form occur in Fig. 506, which is reproduced from Grünenberg's "Book of Arms." The arms of Wareham afford an instance of fleurs-de-lis reversed, and the Corporate Seals of Liskeard and Tamworth merit reproduction, did space permit, from the designs of the fleurs-de-lis which there appear. One cannot leave the fleur-de-lis without referring to one curious development of it, viz. the leopard's face jessant-de-lis, a curious charge which undoubtedly originated in the arms of the family of Cantilupe. This charge is not uncommon, though by no means so usual as the leopard's face (see the arms of Terry, Plate XXXIII.). Planché considers that it was originally derived from the fleur-de-lis, the circular boss which in early representations so often figures as the centre of the fleur-de-lis being merely *decorated* with the leopard's face. One can follow Planché a bit further by imagining that this face need not necessarily be that of a leopard, for at a certain period all decorative art was crowded with grotesque marks whenever opportunity offered. The leopard's face jessant-de-lis is now represented as a leopard's face with the lower part of a fleur-de-lis issuing from the mouth, and the upper part rising from behind the head. Instances of this charge occur as early as the thirteenth century as the arms of the Cantilupe family, and Thomas de Cantilupe having been Bishop of Hereford 1275 to 1282, the arms of that See have since been three leopards' faces jessant-de-lis, the distinction being that in the arms of the See of Hereford the leopards' faces are reversed.

FIG. 503.—Armorial bearings of Balfour of Dawyck : Parted per pale argent and sable on a chevron between three fleurs-de-lis, all counterchanged, an otter's head erased proper. Mantling sable, doubled argent; and upon a wreath of his liveries is set for crest, a mermaid, holding in her dexter hand an otter's head erased, and in her sinister a comb all proper; with the motto, "Nil temere."

FIG. 505.—Examples of varying forms of fleurs-de-lis collected by Miss C. Helard.

202

The origin may perhaps make itself apparent when we remember that the earliest form of the name was

FIG. 506.

Cantelowe. Is it not probable that "lions'" faces (*i.e.* head *de leo*) may have been suggested by the name? Possibly, however, wolf-heads may have been meant, suggested by *lupus*, or by the same analogy which gives us wolf-heads or wolves upon the arms of Low

FIG. 507.—Armorial bearings of Joseph Horace Noble, M.A.: Ermine, two chevronels gules, between three leopards' faces jessant-de-lis sable. Mantling gules and argent. Crest: on a wreath of the colours, a leopard passant regardant sable, semé of annulets or, holding in the dexter forepaw a battle-axe erect proper.

and Lowe. The arms of Noble (Fig. 507) are an instance in which this charge occurs.

Fruit—the remaining division of those charges which can be classed as belonging to the vegetable kingdom—must of necessity be but briefly dealt with.

Grapes perhaps cannot be easily distinguished from vines (to which refer, page 192), but the arms of Bradway of Potsclif, co. Gloucester ["Argent, a chevron gules between three bunches of grapes proper"] and of Viscountess Beaconsfield, the daughter of Captain John Viney Evans ["Argent, a bunch of grapes stalked and leaved proper, between two flaunches sable, each charged with a boar's head argent"] are instances in point.

Apples occur in the arms of Robert Applegarth (Edward III. Roll) ["Argent, three apples slipped gules"] and "Or, a chevron between three apples gules" is the coat of a family named Southbey.

Pears occur in the arms of Allcroft, of Stokesay Castle, Perryman (Plate XIX.), and Pirie (Fig. 508).

FIG. 508.—Armorial bearings of Gordon Pirie, Esq.: Or, a boar's head erased sable, between three pears slipped vert, within a bordure of the last. Mantling sable, doubled or; and on a wreath of his liveries is set for crest a fawn's head, with the sprig of a pear-tree in its mouth proper; and in an escroll over the same this motto, "Virtute non astutia."

Oranges are but seldom met with in British heraldry, but an instance occurs in the arms of Lord Polwarth, who bears over the Hepburn quarterings an inescutcheon azure, an orange slipped and surmounted by an imperial crown all proper. This was an augmentation conferred by King William III., and a very similar augmentation (in the 1st and 4th quarters, azure, three oranges slipped proper within an orle of thistles or) was granted to Livingstone, Viscount Teviot.

The Pomegranate, which dimidiated with a rose was one of the badges of Queen Mary (Fig. 827), is not infrequently met with. It occurs in the arms of Perrins (Fig. 509) and in the coat used by the town of Tregony.

The Pineapple in heraldry is nearly always the fir-

FIG. 509.—Bookplate of Charles William Dyson Perrins, Esq.: Gules, three piles, two in chief and one in base or, each charged with a pomegranate slipped proper, on a chief ermine three leopards' faces of the first. Mantling gules and or. Crest: on a wreath of the colours, a demi-talbot gorged with a collar nebuly gules, charged on the shoulder with two annulets interlaced fesswise of the last, holding between the paws a pomegranate as in the arms. Motto: "Perenne sub sole nihil."

cone. In the arms of Pering, Bart. ["Argent, on a chevron engrailed sable between three pineapples (fir-cones) pendent vert, as many leopards' faces of the first. Crest: on a mount a pineapple (fir-cone) vert"], and in the crest of Parkyns, Bart. ["Out of a ducal coronet or, a pineapple proper"], and also in the arms of Pyne ["Gules, a chevron ermine between three pineapples or"] and Parkin-Moore (Fig. 145), the fruit is the fir or pine cone. Latterly the likelihood of confusion has led to the general use of the term "pine-cone" in such cases, but the ancient description was certainly "pineapple." The arms of John Apperley, as given in the Edward III. Roll, are: "Argent, a chevron gules between three pineapples (fir-cones) vert, slipped or."

The real pineapple of the present day does, however, occur, e.g. in the arms of Benson, of Lutwyche, Shropshire ["Argent, on waves of the sea, an old English galley all proper, on a chief wavy azure a hand couped at the wrist, supporting on a dagger the scales of Justice between two pineapples erect or, leaved vert. Mantling azure and argent. Crest: upon a wreath of the colours, a horse caparisoned, passant, proper, on the breast a shield argent, charged with a pineapple proper. Motto: 'Leges arma tenent sanctas'"]. Another instance is in the arms of Chambers (see page 190).

Bean-Pods occur in the arms of Rise of Trewardreva, co. Cornwall ["Argent, a chevron gules between three bean-pods vert"], and Papworth mentions in the arms of Messarney an instance of cherries ["Or, a chevron per pale gules and vert between three cherries of the second slipped of the third"]. Elsewhere, however, the charges on the shield of this family are termed apples. Strawberries occur in the arms and crest of Hollist (Fig. 510), and the arms of Duffield are: "Sable, a chevron between three cloves or." The arms of the Grocers' Livery Company, granted in 1531–1532,

are: "Argent, a chevron gules between nine cloves, three, three and three." The arms of Garwynton are stated to be: "Sable, a chevron between three heads of garlick pendent argent," but another version gives the charges as pomegranates. "Azure, a chevron between three gourds pendent, slipped or" is a coat attributed to Stukele, but here again there is uncertainty, as the charges are sometimes quoted as pears. The arms of Bonefeld are: "Azure, a chevron between three quinces or." The arms of Alderberry are naturally: "Argent, three branches of alder-berries proper." The arms of Haseley of Suffolk are: "Argent, a fess gules, between three hazel-nuts or, stalks and leaves vert." Papworth also mentions the arms of Tarsell, viz.: "Or, a chevron sable, between three hazel-nuts erect, slipped gules."

The fruit of the oak—the *Acorn*—has already been incidentally referred to, but other instances occur in the arms of Baldwin (Fig. 373), Stable (Plate XXVIII.), and Huth (Fig. 511).

FIG. 511.—Armorial bearings of Edward Huth, Esq., of Wykehurst Park, Sussex: Argent, two chevronels gules, in chief a human heart of the last, and in base a hat sable with an ostrich feather proper; and for crest, on a wreath of the colours, three sprigs of oak erect proper, each bearing an acorn or; with the motto, "Animus non res."

Wheat and other grain is constantly met with in

FIG. 510.—Armorial bearings of Edward Ommanney Hollist, Esq.: Sable, on a bend between a greyhound courant bendwise in chief and a dolphin hauriant in base argent, three torteaux, on a chief of the second, three sprigs of strawberry fructed proper. Mantling sable and argent. Crest: on a wreath of the colours, between two sprigs of strawberry as in the arms, a dexter arm embowed in armour, the hand within a gauntlet holding a sprig of holly all proper. Mottoes: "Currendo," and over the crest, "Gardez le Capron."

FIG. 512.—Armorial bearings of George Clerk Cheape, Esq.: Argent, three ears of wheat slipped in fess vert, and on an escutcheon of pretence in right of his wife the arms of Hemming, namely: argent, on a chevron engrailed azure, between three lions' heads erased gules, an ostrich with wings endorsed of the first, holding in the beak a key between two pheons or; and for his crest, upon a wreath of the colours, a garb or, banded vert; with the motto, "Ditat virtus."

British armory. The arms of Bigland ["Azure, two ears of big wheat erect in fess and bladed or. Mantling azure and or. Crest: on a wreath of the colours, a lion passant regardant gules, holding in his fore-paw an ear of big wheat as in the arms"] and of Cheape (Fig. 512) are examples, and others occur in the arms of Layland-Barratt (Fig. 320), Cross (Fig. 513), and Rye ["Gules, on a

FIG. 513.—Armorial bearings of Alexander Cross, Esq.: Argent, an ear of wheat proper, between four cross crosslets fitché sable, one, two, and one, within a bordure parted per pale of the second and or. Mantling gules, doubled argent. Crest: upon a wreath of his liveries, a griffin segreant sable, armed, beaked, and winged or. Motto: "Sub cruce copia."

bend argent, between two ears of rye, stalked, leaved, and slipped or, three crosses cramponné sable"].

Garbs, as they are invariably termed heraldically, are sheaves, and are of very frequent occurrence. The earliest appearance of the garb in English heraldry is on the seal of Ranulph, Earl of Chester, who died in 1232. Garbs therefrom became identified with the Earldom of Chester, and subsequently "Azure, three garbs or" became and still remain the territorial or possibly the sovereign coat of that Earldom (Fig. 514). Garbs

FIG. 514.—Arms of the Earldom of Chester: Azure, three garbs or.

naturally figure, therefore, in the arms of many families who originally held land by feudal tenure under the Earls of Chester, *e.g.* the families of Cholmondeley ["Gules, in chief two helmets in profile argent, and in base a garb vert"] and Kevilioc ["Azure, six garbs, three, two, and one or"]. Grosvenor ["Azure, a garb or"] is usually quoted as another example, and possibly correctly, but a very interesting origin has been sug-

gested by Mr. W. G. Taunton in his work "The Tauntons of Oxford, by One of Them":—

"I merely wish to make a few remarks of my own that seem to have escaped other writers on genealogical matters.

"In the first place, Sir Gilbert le Grosvenor, who is stated to have come over with William of Normandy at the Conquest, is described as nephew to Hugh Lupus, Earl of Chester; but Hugh Lupus was himself nephew to King William. Now, William could not have been very old when he overthrew Harold at Hastings. It seems, therefore, rather improbable that Sir Gilbert le Grosvenor, who was his nephew's nephew, could actually have fought with him at Hastings, especially when William lived to reign for twenty-one years after, and was not very old when he died.

"The name Grosvenor does not occur in any of the versions of the Roll of Battle Abbey. Not that any of these versions of this celebrated Roll are considered authentic by modern critics, who say that many names were subsequently added by the monks to please ambitious parvenus. The name Venour is on the Roll, however, and it is just possible that this Venour was the Grosvenor of our quest. The addition of 'Gros' would then be subsequent to his fattening on the spoils of the Saxon and cultivating a corporation. 'Venour' means hunter, and 'Gros' means fat. Gilbert's uncle, Hugh Lupus, was, we know, a fat man; in fact, he was nick-named 'Hugh the Fat.' The Grosvenors of that period probably inherited obesity from their relative, Hugh Lupus, therefore, and the fable that they were called Grosvenor on account of their office of 'Great Huntsman' to the Dukes of Normandy is not to be relied on.

"We are further on told by the old family historians that when Sir Robert Grosvenor lost the day in that ever-memorable controversy with Sir Richard le Scrope, Baron of Bolton, concerning the coat of arms—'Azure, a bend or'—borne by both families, Sir Robert Grosvenor took for his arms one of the garbs of his kinsman, the Earl of Chester.

"It did not seem to occur to these worthies that the Earl of Chester, who was their ancestor's uncle, never bore the garbs in his arms, but a wolf's head.

"It is true that one or two subsequent Earls of Chester bore garbs, but these Earls were far too distantly connected with the Grosvenors to render it likely that the latter would borrow their new arms from this source.

"It is curious that there should have been in this same county of Chester a family of almost identical name also bearing a garb in their arms, though their garb was surrounded by three bezants.

"The name of this family was Grasvenor, or Gravenor, and, moreover, the tinctures of their arms were identical with those of Grosvenor. It is far more likely, therefore, that the coat assumed by Sir Robert after the adverse decision of the Court of Chivalry was taken from that of Grasvenor, or Gravenor, and that the two families were known at that time to be of common origin, although their connection with each other has subsequently been lost.

"In French both *gros* and *gras* mean fat, and we have both forms in Grosvenor and Grasvenor.

"A chief huntsman to Royalty would have been Grandvenor, not Grosvenor or Grasvenor.

"All these criticisms of mine, however, only affect the origin of the arms, and not the ancient and almost Royal descent of this illustrious race. Hugh Lupus, Earl of Chester, was a son of the Duke of Brittany, as is plainly stated in his epitaph.

"This connection of uncle and nephew, then, between 'Hugh the Fat' and Gilbert Grosvenor implies a mater-

THE ART OF HERALDRY

"In virtue of their descent from an heiress of the house of Grosvenor, it is only necessary to add the Tauntons of Oxford are Grosvenors, heraldically speaking, and that quartering so many ancient coats through

nal descent from the Dukes of Brittany for the first ancestor of the Grosvenor family.

somewhat erratic. So I think there is some point in my arguments regarding the coat assumed by Sir Robert Grosvenor of Hulme."

Though a garb, unless quoted otherwise, is presumed

FIG. 515.—Armorial bearings of Lieut.-Colonel Johnston Shearer: Gules, in chief two reaping-hooks proper, and in base a tower triple-towered argent, masoned sable. Mantling gules, doubled argent. Crest : on a wreath of his liveries, a garb or, banded with a serpent proper. Motto : "Vive ut postea vivas."

FIG. 517.—Armorial bearings of the late John Polson : Azure, a chevron or between two bears' heads couped close argent, muzzled gules, in chief and a cross moline of the third in base. Mantling azure and or. Crest : upon a wreath of his liveries, a garb proper. Motto : "In ardua tendit."

FIG. 516.—Armorial bearings of James Dunsmure, Gentleman, M.D. : Vert, three garbs or, banded sable, within a bordure argent. Mantling gules, doubled argent. Crest : upon a wreath of his liveries, an anchor or. Motto : "Spes anchora tuta."

FIG. 518.—Bookplate of Archibald Kelso, Esq.

the Tanners and the Grosvenors with our brand-new grant is like putting old wine into new bottles.

"Hugh Lupus left no son to succeed him, and the subsequent descent of the Earldom of Chester was

to be a sheaf of wheat, the term is not so confined. The arms of Comyn, which figure as a quartering in so many

Scottish coats, are really of cummin, as presumably are the garbs in the arms of Cummins[k] (Plate XXVI.). When a garb is "banded" of a different colour this should be stated, and Elvin states that it may be "eared" of a different colour, though I confess I am aware of no such in tance. Garbs will be found in the arms of Shearer (Fig. 515), Dunsmure (Fig. 516), Polson (Fig. 517), and Kelso (Fig. 518).

"Argent, two bundles of reeds in fess vert" is the coat of Janssen of Wimbledon, Surrey (Bart., extinct), and a bundle of rods occurs in the arms of Evans,[l]

FIG. 519.—Armorial bearings of Alfred Harris, Esq. : Azure, on a chevron ermine, between three hedgehogs or, as many wheatstalks bladed vert, in the centre chief a faggot of the third banded of the fourth. Mantling azure and argent ; and for his crest, upon a wreath of the colours, in front of a demi-pelican displayed argent, collared gemmel azure, and charged on the breast with three gouttés-de-sang, a faggot fesswise proper, banded vert.

and the crest of Harris (Fig. 519), though in this case it is termed a faggot.

Reeds also occur in the crest of Reade,[m] and the crest of Middlemore ["On a wreath of the colours, a moorcock amidst grass and reeds proper "] furnishes another example.

Bulrushes occur in the crest of Billiat (Plate XXVII.), and in the arms of Scott ["Argent, on a mount of bulrushes in base proper, a bull passant sable, a chief pean, billetté or "].

Grass is naturally presumed on the mounts vert which are so constantly met with, but more definite instances

can be found in the arms of Sykes (Fig. 520), Hulley, and Hill (Fig. 521).

FIG. 520.—Armorial bearings of Arthur Henry Sykes, Esq. : Argent, on a chevron sable, gutté-d'eau, between three tufts of grass vert, as many fountains proper. Mantling sable and argent. Crest : on a wreath of the colours, upon the trunk of a tree eradicted fesswise and sprouting to the dexter, a swan, wings elevated argent, beaked and legged sable, charged on the breast with a fountain proper. Motto : " Puritas fons honoris."

FIG. 521.—Armorial bearings of John Hill, Esq., of Saltburn : Ermine, on a fess nebuly per pale sable and azure, between three hillocks vert, a castle triple-towered or, impaling the arms of Kirk, namely : gules, a chevron dovetailed ermine, on a chief or, three dragons' heads erased of the field. Mantling sable and argent. Crest : on a wreath of the colours, a castle triple-towered or, charged with an escutcheon azure, thereon a rose argent, all between four ears of wheat bladed and slipped or, two on either side. Motto : " Avancez."

A. C. F-D.

[k] Armorial bearings of Major Henry Alfred Cummins, C.M.G. : Azure, a chevron ermine, cotised argent, between three garbs or, banded gules, on a canton of the third, a ship in full sail proper. Mantling azure and or. Crest : on a wreath of the colours, two arms embowed, vambraced, the hands proper, holding a garb as in the arms. Motto : " Hinc garbae nostrae."

[l] Armorial bearings of Patrick Fleming Evans, Esq. : Per pale argent and gules, a lion passant regardant between two fleurs-de-lis in chief and in base a bundle of rods banded, all counterchanged. Mantling gules and argent. Crest : on a wreath of the colours, a lion regardant argent, the body charged with three crosses moline gules, and resting the dexter paw upon a bundle of rods banded also gules. Motto : " Libertas."

[m] Armorial bearings of Charles Darby Reade : Quarterly, 1 and 4, argent, a saltire vairé, azure, and or, between four Cornish choughs proper (for Reade) ; 2 and 3, erminois, on a chevron embattled gules, three estoiles or, all within a bordure engrailed sable (for Revell). Mantling sable and argent. Crest : on a wreath of the colours, a mount vert, thereon between two reeds proper a Cornish chough wings elevated also proper. Motto : " Cedant arma togæ."

CHAPTER XXIII

INANIMATE OBJECTS

IN dealing with those charges which may be classed under the above description, mention may, at the outset, be made of those which are comprised of certain letters of the *alphabet*. Instances of these are scarcely common, but the family of Kekitmore may be adduced as bearing "Gules, three S's or," while Bridlington Priory had for arms: "Per pale, sable and argent, three B's counterchanged." Sir C. B. Rashleigh bears: "Sable, a cross or, between in the first quarter a Cornish chough argent, beaked and legged gules; in the second a text 𝔗; in the third and fourth a crescent all argent."

FIG. 522.—Bermondsey Arms.

Corporate arms (in England) afford an instance of alphabetical letters in the case of the B's on the shield of Bermondsey (Fig. 522).

The Anchor.—This charge figures very largely in English armory, as may, perhaps, be looked for when it is remembered that maritime devices occur more frequently in sea-board lands than in continents. Anchors occur in the arms of Oppenheimer (Plate XXVII.), and a family of Chappell bears: "Or, an anchor sable." The arms of the town of Musselburgh are: "Azure, three anchors in pale, one in the chief and two in the flanks or, accompanied with as many mussels, two in the dexter and two in the sinister chief points, and the third in base proper." The Comtes de St. Cricq, with

"Argent, two anchors in saltire sable, on a chief three mullets or," will be an instance in point as to France.

Annulets are of common occurrence both in English and other armories. The family of Hutton (Fig. 234) may be mentioned as an example, while for annulets *interlaced* reference can be made to the crests of Athill (Fig. 17) and Burton: "In front of two arms embowed in armour, the hands proper, holding a fleur-de-lis argent, six annulets interlaced fesswise, also argent."

A further case of annulets gemmed may be seen in the family of Eglinton, which has: "Gules, three gem-rings (two and one) or," and in that of Montgomerie[a] (Plate XXVII.).

Anvils.—These are occasionally met with, as in the case of the Walkers of Yorkshire, who bear: "Argent, on a chevron gules, between two anvils in chief and an anchor in base sable, a bee between two crescents or. Mantling gules and argent. Crest: upon a wreath of the colours, on a mount within a wreathed serpent a dove all statant proper.

FIG. 523.—Armorial bearings of Sir Wroth Acland Lethbridge, 4th Baronet: Argent, over water proper, a bridge of five arches embattled, on the centre arch a turret gules, in chief an eagle displayed sable, charged with a bezant. Upon the escutcheon, which is charged with his badge of Ulster as a Baronet, is placed a helmet befitting his degree, with a mantling gules and argent; and for his crest, upon a wreath of the colours, issuant from an embattled arch gules, a demi-eagle displayed sable, the wings erminois, charged on the breast with a leopard's face or. Mottoes: "Spes mea in Deo," and above the crest, "Truth."

[a] Armorial bearings of Samuel Hynman Montgomerie, Esq.: Quarterly, 1 and 4, quarterly i. and iiii., azure, three fleurs-de-lis or; ii. and iii., gules, three annulets or, stoned azure, all within a bordure or, charged with a double tressure flory and counterflory gules, a canton ermine for difference (for Montgomerie); 2 and 3, argent, on a chevron engrailed azure, between three horses' heads erased gules, as many crescents argent, a bordure of the second (for Allenby), and upon an escutcheon of pretence the arms of Montgomerie, Earls of Eglinton and Winton, namely: quarterly, 1 and 4, quarterly i. and iiii., azure, three fleurs-de-lis or; ii. and iii., gules, three annulets or, stoned azure, all within a bordure or charged with a double tressure flory and counterflory gules; 2 and 3, quarterly i. and iiii., azure, three fleurs-de-lis or; ii. and iii., gules, three annulets or, stoned azure, over all a sword in pale point upwards proper. Upon the escutcheon is placed a helmet befitting his degree, with a mantling azure and or; and for his crest, upon a wreath of the colours, a female figure (representing Hope) proper, vested azure, holding in the dexter hand an anchor or, and in her sinister by the hair a human head also proper, charged upon the breast with a cross crosslet for difference. Motto: "Garde bien." [Owing to the detail the escutcheon of pretence is omitted in the plate.]

Arches, castles, towers, and turrets may be exemplified, amongst others, by the following.

The family of Lethbridge (Fig. 523) bears a *Bridge*.

Instances of *Castles* and *Towers* will be found in Plate VII. Figs. 57 and 55, and in the arms of Carlyon [b] (Plate XXXIV.), and Kelly (Fig. 524), and of the for-

FIG. 524.—Armorial bearings of Edward Festus Kelly, Esq., of Northerwood Park, Lyndhurst, Hants: Azure, two lions rampant combatant argent, chained or, supporting a tower with three turrets of the second, in the centre chief point a mullet of the third. Mantling azure and argent. Crest: upon a wreath of the colours, an enfield vert, charged on the shoulder with a mullet as in the arms. Motto: "Turris fortis mihi Deus."

mer fractured castles will be found in the shield of Willoughby quartered by Bertie; while an example of a quadrangular castle may be seen in the arms of Rawson (Fig. 525).

FIG. 525.—Armorial bearings of Thomas Luke Plunkett, Esq.: Sable, a bend argent, in chief a tower triple-towered of the last, a bordure gules.

An instance of a *Fortification* as a charge occurs in the shield of Sconce: "Azure, a fortification (sconce) argent, masoned sable, in the dexter chief point a mullet of six points of the second."

Gabions were hampers filled with earth to form part of fortifications and earthworks. They are of occasional occurrence in English armory at any rate, and may be seen in the shields of Christie (Fig. 321) and of Goodfellow (Fig. 243).

The family of Liberty (Fig. 278) uses a *Tower*, both as a charge and as a crest, while the arms of Banks (Fig. 527) supply an instance of *Arches*. Mention may here perhaps be made of William Arches, who bore at the siege of Rouen: "Gules, three double arches argent."

FIG. 527.—Armorial bearings of Herbert Delamark Banks, Esq.: Sable, on a cross between four fleurs-de-lis or, five arches of the field, within the centre arch a fleur-de-lis of the last. Mantling sable and or. Crest: on a wreath of the colours, upon a mount vert, a stone column of the Tuscan order fesswise thereon a stork proper, the dexter claw resting on a fleur-de-lis or. Motto: "Perseverando."

The family of Plunkett (Fig. 526) supplies an instance of a tower triple-towered.

FIG. 525.—Armorial bearings of Arthur Pelham Rawson, Esq.: Per fess wavy sable and azure, gutté-d'or, a quadrangular castle with four towers argent, on a chief or, three ravens' heads erased of the first. Mantling sable and argent. Crest: on a wreath of the colours, issuant from an annulet or, a raven's head erased sable, gutté-d'or, holding in the beak an annulet gold. Motto: "Laus virtutis actio."

---

[b] Armorial bearings of Carlyon: Sable, a plate between three castles argent, each charged with a cross crosslet gules. Mantling sable and argent. Crest: on a wreath of the colours, a demi-lion rampant gules, ducally crowned or, collared argent, holding between the paws a bezant. Motto: "Turris tutissima virtus."

An Abbey occurs in the arms of Maitland of Dundrennan ["Argent, the ruins of an old abbey on a piece of ground all proper"], and a monastery in that of McLarty ["Azure, the front of an ancient monastery argent"].

A somewhat curious instance of a *Temple* may be seen in the shield of Templer [c] (Plate XXXVII.).

A curious canting grant of arms may be seen in that to the town of Eccles (Fig. 528), in which the charge is an *Ecclesiastical Building*, and similar though somewhat unusual charges figure also in the quartering for Chappel ["Per chevron or and azure, in chief a mullet of six points between two crosses patée of the last, and in base the front elevation of a chapel argent"], borne by Brown-Westhead, and in the arms of Wilson.[d]

FIG. 528.—Arms of Eccles : Or, on a mount vert, an ecclesiastical building masoned proper, a chief azure, thereon between two sprigs of the cotton-tree slipped and fructed of the third, a pale argent, charged with a representation of a Nasmyth steam-hammer sable. Crest : on a wreath of the colours, in front of a rock surmounted by a lighthouse a ship under sail to the sinister all proper. Motto : "Labore omnia florent."

[c] Armorial bearings of John George Edmund Templer, Esq. : Quarterly, azure and gules, the perspective of an antique temple argent, on the pinnacle and exterior battlements a cross or ; in the first quarter an eagle displayed ; in the second a stag trippant regardant of the last. Mantling azure and argent. Crest : on a wreath of the colours, a mount vert, thereon a holy lamb argent, in the dexter foot a pennon of the second, charged with a cross of St. George, the streamers wavy azure and gules, the staff or, under an oak tree proper, fructed or. Motto : "Nihil sine labore."

[d] Armorial bearings of Gordon Chesney Wilson, Esq., M.V.O. : Per pale sable and gules, a wolf rampant or, charged on the shoulder with

Arrows, Pheons, &c.—Instances of these charges are very frequent, and an example of three of the former may be seen in the arms of Hutchison (Fig. 529), while

FIG. 529.—Armorial bearings of John William Hutchison, Esq. : Argent, a fess azure, over all three arrows in point, points to the base counterchanged, between a boar's head erased close in chief sable, and two escallops in base ermines. Mantling gules, doubled argent. Crest : A stag's head erased gules, attired or. Motto : "Memor esto."

FIG. 530.—Armorial bearings of Captain Eli George Hales : Gules, a fess embattled or, between three arrows erect, points downwards, in chief of the last, flighted argent, and a spade palewise in base proper. Mantling gules and or. Crest : on a wreath of the colours, a dexter arm embowed in armour grasping a sword in bend, a spade in bend sinister and an arrow in pale point upwards all proper. Motto : "Vis unita fortior."

an estoile gules, between four mullets in cross of the third, on a chief of the last, a representation of the end elevation of the Wilson Hall of the Melbourne University between two salmon naiant proper. Mantling sable and or ; and for his crest, upon a wreath of the colours, a demi-lion or, charged on the shoulder with an estoile gules, and resting the sinister paw on an escutcheon per pale sable and gules, thereon a wolf's head erased also or ; with the motto, "Semper vigilans."

the shield of Inverarity (Fig. 478) also affords an instance of their use.

The family of Hales (Fig. 530) supplies another example of this charge, while a bow—without the arrows—may be instanced in the shield of Bowes: "Ermine, three bows bent and stringed palewise in fess sable," and in the arms of Bowman (Plate XXXI.).

Arrow-Heads, too—or pheons—are of common usage, and occur in the arms of Foster. Pheons, it may be noticed in passing, are arrow-heads with an inner engrailed edge, while when depicted without this peculiarity they are termed "broad arrows." This is not a distinction very stringently adhered to.

Instances of these may be seen in the arms of Lowndes (Plate XXXV.) and of Smith (Fig. 531).

FIG. 531.—Armorial bearings of Sidney Smith, Esq.: Gyronny of eight gules and sable, four pheons in saltire points to the centre. Crest: upon a wreath of the colours on a Roman fasces, a pheon point upwards or, between two laurel-branches fructed proper. Motto: "Concedat laurea linguæ."

Charges associated with warfare and military defences are frequently to be found both in English and foreign heraldry.

Battle-Axes, for example, may be seen in the shield of Firth and in that of Renty in Artois, which has: "Argent, three doloires, or broad-axes, gules, those in chief addorsed."

The somewhat infrequent device of a *Battering-Ram* is seen in the arms of Bertie, who bore: "Argent, three battering-rams fesswise in pale proper, armed and garnished or (azure ?)"

An instrument of military defence consisting of an iron frame of four points, and called a *Caltrap* or *Galtrap* (and sometimes a Cheval trap, from its use of impeding the approach of cavalry), is found in the arms of Trappe ["Argent, three caltraps sable"], Gilstrap[e] (Plate XXXII.); while French armory supplies us with another example in the case of the family of Guetteville de Guénonville, who bore for arms: "D'argent, semée de chausse-trapes de sable."

As the well-known badge of the Royal House of Tudor, the *Portcullis* is well known to any one conversant with Henry VII.'s Chapel at Westminster Abbey,

[e] Armorial bearings of John MacRae-Gilstrap, Esq., of Ballimore, co. Argyll: Quarterly, 1 and 4 (Gilstrap), argent, a chevron engrailed vert between in chief two escutcheons gules, each charged with a galtrap of the field, and in base a talbot's head erased of the third, and for distinction, in the centre chief point a cross crosslet gules; 2 and 3 (MacRae), argent, a fess azure between two mullets in chief and a lion rampant in base gules, in chief point a crescent of the second for difference. Mantling vert and argent. Crests: 1. on a wreath of the colours, upon a rock, a cubit arm erect in armour all proper grasping an escutcheon gules, charged with a galtrap argent for distinction, the arm charged with a cross crosslet gules (for Gilstrap); 2, on a wreath of his liveries, an arm in armour embowed, holding a scimitar proper; and over the crest the mottoes, "Candide secure" (for Gilstrap); "Fortitudine" (for MacRae); under the shield, "Nec curo nec care" (for MacRae).

but it also appears as a charge in the arms of the family of Wingate ["Gules, a portcullis and a chief embattled or"] (Plate XXXIX.), where it forms an obvious pun on the earliest form of the name, viz. Windygate, and in that of Langman (Fig. 532), while it figures as the crest of the

FIG. 532.—Armorial bearings of John Lawrence Langman, Esq., Knight of Grace of the Order of the Hospital of St. John of Jerusalem in England: Argent, on a pile engrailed sable, a water-bouget of the first between two flaunches of the second, each charged with a water-bouget also of the first. Mantling sable and argent; and for the crest, on a wreath of the colours, in front of a mount vert, thereon a portcullis with chains sable, three water-bougets fesswise of the last. Motto: "Justus esto et non metue."

Dukes of Beaufort ["A portcullis or, nailed azure, chained of the first"], and also as the crest in the achievement of Porter (Fig. 533). A few other charges,

FIG. 533.—Armorial bearings of Henry Robert Mansel Porter, Esq.: Quarterly, 1 and 4, per fess nebuly sable and ermine, a pale counterchanged and three bells argent (for Porter); 2 and 3, or, on a fess dancetté gules, between two escallops sable, a ducal coronet of the first between two roses argent, barbed and seeded proper (for Taylor). Mantling sable and argent. Crests: 1. upon a wreath of the colours, upon a mount vert, in front of a portcullis with chains or, a tilting-spear fesswise proper (for Porter); 2. upon a wreath of the colours, a demi-lion sable, gorged with a collar and pendent therefrom an escutcheon or, charged with two escallops palewise sable, and holding between the paws a ducal coronet or (for Taylor). Motto: "Quod vult valde vult."

directly or indirectly connected with military affairs, may fitly, perhaps, find a place in this connection.

Beacons, for example—used, as is well known, as a signal to call to arms, on the approach of a foe—occur occasionally. In England examples are furnished by the families of Buddicom, Compton, and in the arms of Wolverhampton (Fig. 533*a*).

Bombs, Grenades, &c., figure in the shields of Vavasseur (Fig. 534) and Slade.[f]

FIG. 534.—Armorial bearings of Josiah Vavasseur, Esq.: Party per chevron and in chief two grenades, and in base, upon a mount vert, a machine-gun upon a Vavasseur mounting, and below the escutcheon his badge as a C.B. Crest: upon a wreath of the colours, in front of a dexter cubit arm holding in the hand a——, two swords in saltire proper. Motto: "Tout par faveur divine."

Among the more recent grants *Cannon* have figured, as in the case of the Pilter arms (Fig. 535) and in those of the burgh of Portobello; while its earlier counterpart, in the form of a culverin, forms the charge of the Leigh family: "Argent, a culverin in fess sable."

FIG. 533*a*.—Arms of Wolverhampton: Gules, a cross formée or, between a pillar in the first quarter, a woolpack in the second, an open book in the third all argent, and in the fourth a padlock of the second. Crest: on a wreath of the colours, in front of a beacon sable, fired proper, two keys in saltire, wards upwards or. Motto: "Out of darkness cometh light." [Granted December 31, 1898.]

Chains, though forming part of the collection of objects which are rightly classed as pertaining to war, are singularly scarce in armory, and indeed nearly wholly absent as *charges*, usually occurring where they do as part of the crest.

The English shield of Anderton, it is true, bears: "Sable, three chains argent;" while another one (Duppa de Uphaugh) has: "Quarterly, 1 and 4, a lion's paw couped in fess between two chains or, a chief nebuly of the last, thereon two roses of the first, barbed and seeded proper (for Duppa); 2 and 3, party fess azure and sable, a trident fesswise or, between three turbots argent (for Turbutt)."

Used as a part of a crest, the family of Slade affords a case in point.

In Continental heraldry, however, chains are more frequently met with. Principal amongst these cases may be cited the arms of Navarre ["Gules, a cross saltire and double orle of chains, linked together or"], while many other instances are found in the armories of Southern France and of Spain.

FIG. 535.—Armorial bearings of William Frederick Pilter, Esq., C.B.: Per chevron argent and sable, two pelts (or hides) in chief of the last, and a cannon mounted on its carriage in base proper. Mantling sable and argent. Crest: on a wreath of the colours, in front of a fleur-de-lis or, a dolphin naiant proper. Motto: "Fide patiente labore."

---

[f] Armorial bearings of Slade: Party per fess argent and sable, a pale counterchanged and three horses' heads erased of the second, on a chief ermine, two bombs fired proper. Mantling sable and argent. Crest: on a wreath of the colours, on a mount vert, a horse's head erased sable, within a chain in arch gold.

THE ART OF HERALDRY

The *Column* appears as a crest in the arms of Coles.[g] Between two cross crosslets it occurs in the arms of Adam of Maryburgh ["Vert, a Corinthian column with capital and base in pale proper, between two cross crosslets fitchée in fess or"], and also as forming part of the crest of the family of Willey (Fig. 536); while

FIG. 536.—Armorial bearings of Henry Alfred Willey: Sable, gutté-d'eau, two antique lamps fired in chief all argent, and a sun in splendour in base or. Mantling sable and argent. Crest: on a wreath of the colours, upon a column fesswise, the top to the sinister sable, an antique lamp or, fired proper. Motto: "Lucet et lucebit."

the arms of the See of Sodor and Man are blazoned: "Argent, upon a pedestal the Virgin Mary with her arms extended between two pillars, in the dexter hand a church proper, in base the arms of Man in an escutcheon."

As a charge, the Majors, of Suffolk, bear: "Azure,

three Corinthian columns, each surmounted by a ball, two and one argent."

As perhaps may be looked for in this connection, *Helmets* figure frequently as charges, and an example is afforded by the Salvesen arms (Fig. 537).

Scaling-Ladders (viz. ordinary shaped ladders with grapnels affixed to the tops) are to be seen in the English coats of D'Urban (Fig. 538) and Lloyd (Plate XXX.), while the Veronese Princes della Scala bore the

FIG. 538.—Armorial bearings of William Stewart Mitchell D'Urban, Esq.: Or, on a chevron between three mullets of six points sable, a bombshell or, between two scaling-ladders, and as an honourable augmentation, granted in 1817 to Lt.-Gen. Sir Benjamin D'Urban, G.C.B., K.C.H., K.C.T.S., on a canton gules, a representation of the Military Gold Cross inscribed with the words Busaco, Albu-hera, Badajos, and Salamanca, pendent from a riband of the first, fimbriated azure, with five gold clasps inscribed with the words Vittoria, Pyrenees, Nivelle, Nive, and Toulouse. Mantling sable and or. Crest: on a wreath of the colours, in front of a palm-tree, a sphinx couchant. Motto: "Firme."

FIG. 537.—Armorial bearings of Edward Theodore Salvesen, Esq.: Or, on a fess vert, between two esquires' helmets in chief and a water-bouget in base gules, two battle-axes in saltire of the first. Mantling vert, doubled or; and upon a wreath of the liveries is set for crest, a dragon ship vert, mast and tackling proper, flagged gules. Motto: "Inveni portum."

FIG. 539.—Armorial bearings of Amherst: Gules, three tilting-spears two and one or, headed argent. Mantling gules and or. Crest: on a wreath of the colours, on a mount vert, three like spears, one erect and two in saltire, girt with a wreath of laurel proper. Motto: "Constantia et virtute."

---

[g] Armorial bearings of Ernest Harry Coles, Gentleman: Gules, three bezants chevronwise within two chevronels or, between three lions' heads erased erminiois. Mantling gules and or. Crest: on a wreath of the colours, upon a mount vert, a column erect entwined by a serpent holding in the mouth a branch of olive all proper. Motto: "Perseverez."

ordinary ladder: "Gules, a ladder of four steps in pale argent." A further instance of this form of the charge occurs in the Swiss shield of Laiterberg: "Argent, two ladders in saltire gules."

Spears and *Spear-Heads* are to be found in the arms of many families both in England and abroad; at home in the arms of Amherst (Fig. 539) and Lind (Plate XXXIX.), while spear-heads are seen in the arms of Edwards [h] (Plate XXIII.).

The Shakespeare arms (Fig. 540), too, are: "Or, on a

FIG. 540.—Arms of William Shakespeare (*d.* 1616): Or, on a bend sable, a tilting-spear of the field.

bend sable a spear of the first steeled (or pointed) argent," while "Azure, a lance or enfiled at its point by an annulet argent" represents the French family of Danby.

Spurs occur in coat armour as such in the arms of Harben (Plate XXIX.), and also occasionally "winged," as in the arms of Johnston (Plate XXVIII.).

An example of a spur-rowel is seen in the crest of Jardine (Fig. 541).

FIG. 541.—Armorial bearings of David Jardine Jardine, Esq.: Parted per pale argent and or, a saltire gules, on a chief of the third, three mullets of the first. Mantling gules, doubled argent; and upon a wreath of the colours is set for crest, a spur-rowel gules. Motto: "Cave adsum."

Examples of *Stirrups* are but infrequent, and the best-known one (as regards English armory) is that of Scuda-

[h] Armorial bearings of Howell Powell Edwards, Esq., M.A., of Novington Manor, Sussex: Sable, a chevron vair, in base a spear-head or, embrued proper, on a chief of the third, three spear-heads of the first also embrued proper. Mantling sable and argent. Crest: on a wreath of the colours, a dragon's head erased vert, gorged with a collar vair and charged with two quatrefoils in pale or, holding in the mouth a dexter hand couped at the wrist distilling drops of blood proper, between two spear-heads erect argent.

more (Fig. 542), while the Polish Counts Brzostowski bore: "Gules, a stirrup argent, within a bordure or."

FIG. 542.—Armorial bearings of Edward Scudamore Lucas-Scudamore, Esq.: Quarterly, 1 and 4, gules, three stirrups leathered and buckled or (for Scudamore); 2 and 3, argent, a fess between six annulets gules (for Lucas). Mantling gules and or. Crest: 1. out of a ducal coronet or, a bear's paw sable (for Scudamore); 2. upon a wreath of the colours, a demi-griffin argent, beaked and membered or.

Stones are even more rare, though a solitary example is to be seen in the arms of Staniland ["Quarterly, 1 and 4 [per pale or and vert, a pale counterchanged, three eagles displayed two and one, and as many], flint-stones one and two all proper (for Staniland); 2 and 3, azure, an estoile or between four bezants in saltire, in each corner of the field a castle argent (for Stainbank)"]. The "vigilance" of the crane has been already alluded to on page 179.

The mention of stones brings one to the kindred subject of *Catapults*. These engines of war, needless to say on a very much larger scale than the object which is nowadays associated with the term, were also known by the mame *balistæ*, and also by that of *swepe*. Their occurrence is very infrequent, but for that very reason one may, perhaps, draw attention to the arms of the (English) family of Magnall: "Argent, a swepe azure charged with a stone or."

Swords, differing in number, position, and kind are, perhaps, of this class of charges the most numerous.

A single sword as a charge may be seen in the shield of Dick of Wicklow,[i] and Macfie [j] (Plate XXXVIII.), and a sword entwined by a serpent in that of Mackesy. Used in the crest it appears in the case of Brooke (Fig. 543), and broken off in that of Colby (Fig. 544). A flaming sword occurs in the arms of Maddocks (Fig. 246). A scimitar figures in the crest of Drummond (Plate XLV.).

Swords frequently figure, too, in the hands or paws of supporters, accordingly as the latter are human figures or animals, whilst they figure as the "supporters" themselves in the unique case of the family of Bastard (in Breton), whose shield is cottised by "two swords, point in base."

[i] Armorial bearings of Captain Quintin Dick Dick: Quarterly, 1 and 4, gules, a sword in pale point upwards proper, hilted and pommelled or, between two mullets in chief of the last (for Dick); 2 and 3, vert, a lion rampant argent (for Hume). Mantling gules and argent. Crest: on a wreath of the colours, a leopard sejant proper. Motto: "Semper fidelis."

[j] Armorial bearings of John William Macfie, of Dreghorn and Colinton, Esq., J.P.: Parted per fess nebuly azure and or, in chief a sword argent, point downwards, hilted and pommelled of the second, and in base a lymphad sable under sail of the third, flags and pennons flying gules. Mantling gules, doubled argent; and on a wreath of his liveries is set for crest, a demi-lion rampant proper; and on an escroll over the same this motto, "Pro Rege."

A "seax" is the term employed to denote a curved scimitar, or falchion, having a notch at the back of the

owing to this origin were included in the grant of arms to the town of Ealing (Fig. 545).

FIG. 543.—Armorial bearings of Sir Thomas Brooke, Bart., F.S.A. : Argent, a cross nebuly per pale gules and sable, in the first and fourth quarters a boar's head erased of the last ; and for the crest, upon a wreath of the colours, in front of a sword erect, the blade entwined by two serpents respecting each other proper, a boar's head erased sable ; with the motto, " Est nec astu."

blade. In heraldry their use occurs fairly frequently, though generally, it must be added, in shields of arms

FIG. 544.—Armorial bearings of the Rev. Samuel Reynolds Colby, A.K.C., Clerk in Holy Orders : Azure, two chevronels between two escallops in chief and as many palmers' staves saltirewise in base or, a crescent for difference. Mantling azure and or. Crest : on a wreath of the colours, between two palm-branches, a dexter arm embowed in armour, the hand in a gauntlet grasping a broken sword proper, suspended from the hand a palmer's scrip or. Motto : " Non omnis frangar."

of doubtful authority. As such they are to be seen, amongst others, in the reputed arms of Middlesex, and

FIG. 545.—Arms of Ealing : Party per chevron gules and argent, in chief on the dexter side two swords in saltire proper, pommels and hilts gold, and on the sinister side three seaxes barwise in pale of the third, pommels and hilts to the dexter of the fourth, in base an oak-tree fructed and eradicated also of the third.

Torches or *Firebrands* are depicted in the arms and crest of Gillman (Fig. 195) and Tyson (Plate XV.).

Trumpets are not of frequent occurrence either in English or Continental armory. As forming part of the crest one occurs in the arms of Blackburne and rather as a bugle-horn or hunting-horn in the arms of Hunter [k] (Plate XXIII.), and in the impaled shield of Scott-Gatty (Fig. 262).

Barnacles (or *Breys*)—horse curbs—occur in some of the earlier coats, as in the arms of Wyatt ["Gules, a barnacle argent"], while another family of the same name (or, possibly, Wyot) bore: " Per fess gules and azure (one or) three barnacles argent"].

Bells are well instanced in the shield of Porter (Fig. 533), and the poet Wordsworth bore: " Argent, three bells azure." It may be noted in passing that in Continental armory the clapper is frequently of a different tincture to that of the bell. As, for instance, " D'Azur, à la cloche d'argent, bataillé [viz. with the clapper] de sable"—the arms of the Comtes de Bellegarse.

Bridle-Bits are of very infrequent use, though they may be seen in the achievement of the family of Milner.

Blocks, too, are of about as rare occurrence as any charge. They occur in the arms of Paynter (Fig. 236).

[k] Armorial bearings of Andrew Alexander Hunter, Esq., Bursar of Cheltenham College : Argent, on a chevron azure, between three hunting-horns vert, garnished and stringed gules, a crescent of the first. Mantling gules, doubled argent ; and on a wreath of his liveries is set for crest, a stag's head caboshed or ; and in an escroll over the same this motto, " Vigilantia, robur, voluptas."

The unusual device of a block of granite is to be seen in the Farren shield (Fig. 546).

(Fig. 431), and Joslin (Fig. 547), and also appears as part of the crest of the Lumb family (Fig. 548).

FIG. 546.—Armorial bearings of George Farren, Esq.: Argent, on a pile gules, between two blocks of dressed red granite proper, a lion passant regardant of the first. Mantling gules and argent. Crest: on a wreath of the colours, upon a block of dressed grey granite proper, a lion passant regardant gules, resting the dexter forepaw on a saltire or. Motto: "Perseverantia vincit."

FIG. 548.—Armorial bearings of James Lumb, Esq.: Or, three escutcheons sable, each charged with a mullet pierced of the first, a martlet for difference. Mantling or and sable. Crest: on a wreath of the colours, a blackamoor's head in profile couped at the shoulders proper, wreathed about the temples or and sable, and charged on the neck with a mullet of six points gold, within a wreath in arch or and sable. Motto: "Respice finem."

Chaplets, Coronets, and even the *Torse* (or wreath surmounting the helm) occasionally figure as charges, though in most cases they are themselves charged.

FIG. 547.—Armorial bearings of Walter Joslin, Esq.: Per chevron azure and or, two fleurs-de-lis in chief of the last, and in base a circular wreath sable and of the first, with four hawks' bells conjoined thereto proper. Mantling azure and or. Crest: upon a wreath of the colours, between two hawks' bells, a rock thereon a falcon's leg erased at the thigh and belled, all proper. Motto: "Faire mon devoir."

Such an instance may be seen in the shield of Berry (Fig. 237).

The torse figures as a charge in the arms of Jocelyn

Bowls may be seen in the Bolding arms (Fig. 89).

The Buckle.—This is a charge which is of much more general use than those which we have recently been surveying. It appears very frequently both in English and foreign heraldry—sometimes oval-shaped, but more generally lozengewise: especially is this the case in Continental arms. In a *circular* form they appear in the arms of Stubbs (Plate XIV.), while a single buckle (lozenge-shaped) appears on the shield of Ferguson [1] (Plate XXXIII.).

A somewhat curious variation occurs in the arms of the Prussian Counts Wallenrodt, which are: "Gules, a lozenge-shaped buckle argent, the tongue broken in the middle."

In the form of a *Badge* the buckle is used by the Pelhams, Earls of Chichester and Earls of Yarborough.

The University of Aberdeen affords an instance of a *Pot of Lilies.*

Though blazoned as a *Cauldron,* the device occurring in the crest of De la Rue may be perhaps as fittingly described as an open bowl, and as such may find a place in this classification: "Between two olive-branches vert a cauldron gules, fired and issuant therefrom a snake nowed proper."

The use of a *Pitcher* occurs in the arms of Bertrand de Monbocher, who bore at the siege of Carlaverock: "Argent, three pitchers sable (sometimes found gules) within a bordure sable bezanté."

[1] Armorial bearings of George Bagot Ferguson, Esq., M.A., M.D.: Azure, a buckle or, between three boars' heads erased argent, a bordure of the second, semé of trefoils slipped vert. Mantling azure and or. Crest: upon a wreath of the colours, on a thistle proper, passing through a buckle or, a bee alighting of the last, winged azure, and on an escroll above, "Dulcis ex asperis." Motto below the arms: "Ut prosim aliis."

The somewhat singular charge of a *Chart* appears in the arms of Christopher (Fig. 377), and also as the crest of the family of Cook (Fig. 549).

FIG. 549.—Armorial bearings of Henry Cook, Esq.: Gules, on a bend or, two cinquefoils azure, on a sinister canton argent, a cross crosslet fitché issuing out of a crescent of the first, all within a bordure of the second. Mantling gules, doubled argent. Crest: on a wreath of his liveries, a sea-chart proper. Motto: "Tutum monstrat iter."

Clifton College also affords a case of the use of *Books*

FIG. 550.—Arms of the Corporation of Clifton College: Argent, a chevron between two trefoils slipped in chief and a garb in base azure, a chief gules, thereon a ducal coronet or, between two books argent clasped and garnished gold. Motto: "Spiritus intus alit." [Granted April 8, 1895.]

(Fig. 550), while an open book forms part of the crest of the Hutton family (Plate XVII.).

Chess-Rooks are somewhat favourite heraldic devices, and are to be met with in the shield of Smith (Fig. 551).

FIG. 551.—Armorial bearings of William Macadam Smith, Esq.: Azure, in chief a drinking-cup and in base a chess-rook or, on a chief engrailed of the last, a chess-rook of the first. Mantling azure and or. Crest: on a wreath of the colours, in front of a dolphin hauriant or, three chess-rooks azure. Motto: "Generosity with Justice."

Cups (covered) appear in the Butler arms, and derived therefrom in the arms of the town of Warrington (Fig. 51). This charge is familiar to both Scottish and also foreign heraldry, the Lauries of Maxwelltown, for example, using: "Sable, a cup argent, issuing therefrom a garland between two laurel-branches all proper," and the Veronese Bicchieri: "Argent, a fess gules between three drinking-glasses half filled with red wine proper." The arms of the Neapolitan Princess Pignatelli are: "Or, three pots with handles sable (those in chief affrontés)." Another curious form of the German heraldic cup occurs on Plate VII.

Uncovered cups occur in the arms of Fox (Fig. 318), and also in those of Smith (Fig 551). In this connection we may note in passing the rare use of the device of a *Vase*, which forms a charge in the coat of the town of Burslem, whilst it is also to be met with in the crest of the family of Doulton: "On a wreath of the colours, a demi-lion sable, holding in the dexter paw a cross crosslet or, and resting the sinister upon an escutcheon charged with a vase proper." The motto is perhaps well worth recording: "Le beau est la splendour de vrai."

Both the *Crescent* and the *Mullet* figure largely in all armories, both as charges and (in English heraldry) as difference marks.

In the more usual form the crescent may be seen in the arms of Hutton (Fig. 234).

Variations, too, of the form of the crescent occur, such as when the horns are turned to the dexter, when it is termed "a crescent increscent," or when they are turned to the sinister—when it is styled "decrescent." An example of the latter will be found in the arms of North (Plate XXIV.).

An instance of the crescent "reversed" may be seen in the shield of the Austrian family of Puckberg, whose blazon was: "Azure, three crescents, those in chief addorsed, that in base reversed."

In English "difference marks" the crescent is used to denote the second son, but under this character it will be discussed later.

Mullets (three) occur in the chief of the shield of Wilson (Fig. 552), and pierced in that of the Lafone family (Fig. 302).

FIG. 552.—Armorial bearings of Walter Henry Wilson, Esq. : Argent, a chevron between three mullets gules. Mantling gules, doubled argent. Crest: upon a wreath of his liveries, a demi-lion rampant gules. Motto: "Semper vigilans."

In "differencing" the mullet is the mark of the third son, and that also will be again referred to. The mullet must be distinguished from the estoile (see pages 219 and 228). It may have any number of points, but unless the number is specified it must be represented with five.

Independent of its use in conjunction with ecclesiastical armory, the *Crosier* is not widely used in ordinary achievements.

It does occur, however, as the principal charge, as in the arms of Benoit (in Dauphiny) ["Gules, a pastoral staff argent"], while as forming part of the crest it occurs in the achievement of Alford.

The term "crosier" is synonymous with the pastoral or episcopal staff, and is independent of the cross which is borne *before* (and not *by*) Archbishops and Metropolitans.

The use of pastoral staves as charges is to be seen in the shield of Were,[m] while MacLaurin of Dreghorn bears: "Argent, a shepherd's crook sable."

The palmer's staff has been introduced into many coats of arms for families having the surname of Palmer, as have also the palmer's wallet, whilst purses occur in the arms of James[n] (Plate XXII.).

Cushions, somewhat strangely, form the charges in many British shields, occurring, for example, in the

FIG. 553.—Armorial bearings of Charles Thomas Brisbane, Esq. : Sable, a chevron chequy or and gules between three cushions pendent by the corners of the second, a chief of honourable augmentation embattled argent, thereon on waves of the sea a ship of war under sail between two forts, the guns firing and on the battlements the Dutch flag all proper. Above the shield is placed a helmet befitting his degree, with a mantling gules, doubled argent; and next the same are set the two following crests, namely : upon the dexter side the crest of honourable augmentation, that is to say, out of a naval crown or, a dexter arm embowed in the uniform of a captain of the Royal Navy, the hand grasping a cutlass proper, hilted and pommelled or, and from the hand pendent by a ribbon argent, fimbriated azure, a gold medal representing that given by His Majesty to Sir Charles Brisbane ; and in an escroll over the same this motto, "Curaçoa" ; and upon the sinister side, on a wreath of his liveries, the family crest, namely : a stork's head erased holding in the beak a serpent writhing proper ; and in an escroll over the same this motto, "Certamine summo" ; and on a compartment below the shield are placed for supporters two talbots proper.

arms of the Brisbane (Fig. 553), and on the shield in the Johnstone family (Fig. 554). In Scottish heraldry, indeed, cushions appear to have been of very ancient (and general) use, and are frequently to be met with. The Earls of Moray bore: "Argent, three cushions lozengewise within a double tressure flory-counterflory gules," and the charge also occurs in the arms of Macdonald [o]

---

[m] Armorial bearings of Were : Argent, on a bend vert, between six crosses crosslet fitché gules, three sheep-hooks or. Crest : a demi-lion rampant proper, holding a cross crosslet fitché gules.

[n] Armorial bearings of Rev. Nicholas Hopkins James, D.D.: Party per pale gules and azure, on a chevron engrailed between three lions passant guardant or, as many purses sable. Mantling gules and or ; and for his crest, upon a wreath of the colours, a hart's head erased proper, charged on the neck with a fleur-de-lis azure. Motto: "J'aime jamais."

[o] Armorial bearings of Wm. Rae Macdonald, Esq., Carrick Pursuivant : Quarterly argent and or, in the first quarter a lion rampant gules, armed and langued azure ; in the second a dexter hand proper, couped fesswise, holding a cross crosslet fitchée gules ; in the third a lymphad, sails furled, and oars in saltire sable ; in the fourth a salmon naiant proper ; over all, on a fess of the third, a cushion of the second. Upon the escutcheon is placed a helmet befitting his degree, with a mantling gules, doubled argent. Crest : a dexter hand holding a dirk erect proper. Motto: "Nec tempore nec fato."

(Plate XVII.), but an English example occurs in the arms of Hutton [p] (Plate XVII.).

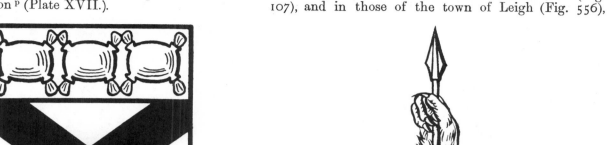

FIG. 554.—Armorial bearings of Johnstone: Argent, a saltire sable, in base a man's heart regally crowned all proper, on a chief gules, three cushions or.

The Distaff, which is supposed to be the origin of the lozenge upon which a lady bears her arms, is seldom seen in heraldry, but occasionally in English armory it does occur. The family of Body, for instance, bear one in chief, and three occur in the arms of a family of Lees (Fig. 555). Abroad this charge is not

PERGE · SED · CAUTE

FIG. 555.—Armorial bearings of Joseph Lees, Esq.: Per chevron or and gules, a chevron counterchanged between two roses in chief of the second, barbed and seeded proper, and three distaffs, one in pale and two saltirewise in base of the first. Mantling gules and or. Crest: on a wreath of the colours, in front of a cotton-hank fesswise or, thereon an owl close, holding in the beak a branch of cotton-tree, a distaff fesswise also proper. Motto: "Perge sed caute."

to be met with, and it is somewhat surprising that in German armory this domestic figure has no place.

[p] Armorial bearings of Arthur Edward Hill Hutton, Esq., of Houghton Hall, co. Durham: Gules, on a fess between three cushions argent, fringed or tasselled or, as many fleurs-de-lis of the field, Mantling gules and argent. Crest: on a wreath of the colours, on a cushion gules placed lozengewise an open book, the edges gilt, with the words "Odor vitæ" inscribed. Motto: "Spiritus gladius."

The *Shuttle* occurs in the arms of Shuttleworth (Fig. 107), and in those of the town of Leigh (Fig. 556),

FIG. 556.—Arms of Leigh: Quarterly gules and argent, a cross quarterly counterchanged between a spear-head of the last in the first quarter, a mullet sable in the second, a shuttle fesswise the thread pendent of the last in the third, and a sparrow-hawk close proper in the fourth; and for the crest, on a wreath of the colours, the battlements of a tower proper issuant therefrom a bear's paw gules, holding a javelin erect or.

while the town of Pudsey (Fig. 557) affords an illustration of shuttles in conjunction with a woolpack.

The Escarbuncle (an illustration of which occurs on Plate X. Fig. 57) is an instance of a charge having become such as the evolution of an integral part of the shield itself. In ancient warfare *Shields* were sometimes strengthened by being bound with iron bands radiating from the centre, and these bands, from the shape they assumed, became in course of time a charge in themselves under the term escarbuncle. An example may be seen in the three escarbuncles which form the arms of the family of Boyce (Fig. 558).

The Estoile.—This charge, although so similar in general design to the "star" proper, is yet not to be confused with it.

Most frequently the estoile has five (and occasionally six) straight rays, and is not pierced, though usually the rays are wavy.

Sometimes, too, more points than even six are de-

FIG. 558.—Armorial bearings of Robert Henry Boyce, Esq., C.B.: Per chevron embattled or and azure, three escarbuncles counterchanged. Mantling azure and or. Crest: on a wreath of the colours, out of a tower proper, a demi-lion rampant gules, holding between the paws an escarbuncle or. Motto: "Semper fidelis."

picted, in which case the number of them should be specified, as an estoile of . . . points.

The Princes of Waldeck bear: "Or, an estoile of eight points sable," while the Counts of Erpach show a shield of "Per fess gules and argent, three estoiles of six points counterchanged." The family of Ingleby bears as arms: "Sable, an estoile argent," and three estoiles occur in the arms of Langdale (Fig. 559). Reference should be made to page 228.

FIG. 559.—Armorial bearings of Henry Joseph Grattan Langdale, Esq.: Sable, a chevron between three estoiles argent. Mantling sable and argent. Crest: on a wreath of the colours, an estoile argent. Motto: "Post tenebras lucem."

The Fanmakers' Company's crest is: "A hand couped proper holding a *fan* displayed," while the chief charge in the arms is ". . . a fan displayed . . . the sticks gules . . ." This, however, appears to be the only case I can cite of this object.

The Fasces.—This charge, emblematic of the Roman magisterial symbol, is very frequently introduced in grants of arms to Mayors and Lord Mayors, which no doubt accounts for its appearance in the arms of Durning-Lawrence,[q] and Spokes (Fig. 560).

An instance of *Fetterlocks* occurs in the arms of Kirkwood, and also in the coat of Lockhart.

Flames of Fire are not frequently met with, but they are to be found in the arms of Baikie (Fig. 561), and as crests they figure in the achievements of Graham-Wigan (Fig. 178), and also in conjunction with keys

[q] Armorial bearings of Sir Edward Durning-Lawrence, Bart.: Ermine, on a cross raguly gules between in the first and fourth quarters a fasces erect, encircled by a wreath of oak proper, a pair of compasses extended or. Mantling gules and argent. Crest: on a wreath of the colours, a wolf's head erased argent, crusily, and charged with a pair of compasses extended sable. Motto: "Per ardua stabilis."

in that of Flavel[r] (Plate XXIII.). In connection with certain other objects flames are common enough.

FIG. 560.—Bookplate of Russell Spokes, Esq.: Azure, on a pile between two fasces erect or, three catherine-wheels, two and one gules, in chief a martlet for difference. Upon the escutcheon is placed a helmet befitting his degree, with a mantling azure and or; and for his crest, upon a wreath of the colours, a fasces erect between two ostrich feathers; with the motto: "Fiat justitia ruat cœlum."

The phœnix always issues from flames, and a salamander is always in the midst of flames (Fig. 155). The flaming sword, a device, by the way, included in the recent grant to Sir George Lewis, Bart., has been already alluded to, as has also the flaming brand. A notable example of the torch occurs in the crest of Sir William Gull, Bart., no doubt an allusion (as is his augmentation) to the skill by which he kept

FIG. 561.—Armorial bearings of Alfred Baikie, Esq., of Tankerness, Orkney.

the torch of life burning in the then Prince of Wales during his serious illness in 1871. The same charge

occurs in the arms of Edward T. Tyson, Esq., of Wood Hall, Cockermouth (Plate XV.), the blazon of which is: "Vert, gutté-d'eau, three lions rampant argent, each holding in the dexter paw a torch erect, fired proper. Crest: on a wreath of the colours, a demi-lion rampant vert, guttě-d'eau, holding in the dexter paw a torch as in the arms, and resting the sinister upon a rose gules, barbed and seeded proper. Motto: 'Fortiter et vigilanter.'" A flaming mountain occurs as the crest of several families of the name of Grant.

A curious instrument now known nearly exclusively in connection with its use by farriers, and termed a *Fleam*, occurs on the chief of the shield of Moore. A fleam, however, is the ancient form and name of a surgeon's lancet, and some connection with surgery may be presumed when it occurs. It is one of the charges on the arms recently granted to Sir Frederick Treves, Bart.

Furisons.—Two of these singular charges are depicted in the shield of Black (Fig. 562), and also in

FIG. 562.—Armorial bearings of William George Black: Argent, a saltire sable, on a chief of the last, a wolf's head erased of the first, in the flanks two furisons azure. Mantling gules, doubled argent. Crest: on a wreath of his liveries, a demi-lion gules, armed and langued azure, and in an escroll over the same, this motto, "Non crux sed lux."

that of Steel.[s] They were apparently the instruments by which fire was struck by flint stones. The German form of this charge will be found on Plate X. Fig. 66.

Charges in connection with music and musical instruments do not occur very frequently, though the heraldic use of the *Clarion* and the *Harp* may, perhaps, be mentioned.

The Human Heart, which should perhaps have been more correctly referred to in an earlier chapter, is a charge which is well known in heraldry, both English and foreign. A family of Adams bears this device as a

---

[r] Armorial bearings of Sidney Flavell, Esq., J.P., of Leamington: Argent, a maunch gules, bezantée, between three keys wards upwards, over all, a chevron azure. Crest: on a wreath of the colours, two keys in saltire, wards upwards, in front of flames of fire proper. Motto: "Tu Deus ale flammam."

[s] Armorial bearings of the late John James Steel: Or, on a bend sable, between two furisons azure, a book expanded argent. Mantling sable, doubled or; and upon a wreath of his liveries is set for crest, a lion's head erased gules; and in an escroll above this motto: "Ferro non furto."

charge, while it also figures in the arms and crest of Corfield (Fig. 563).

SERVA · FIDEM

FIG. 563.—Armorial bearings of Frederick Channer Corfield, Esq. : Per chevron gules and argent, in chief two escutcheons of the second, and in base an escutcheon ermine, each charged with a heart of the first, and impaling the arms of Alleyne, namely : per chevron gules and ermine, in chief two lions' heads erased or. Mantling gules and argent. Crest : on a wreath of the colours, in front of a cubit arm erect, the hand grasping two palm-branches in orle all proper, a heart as in the arms. Motto : "Serva fidem."

LABORARE · ET · TEMPUS · AUCUPARI

FIG. 564.—Armorial bearings of Benjamin Minors Woollan, Gentleman : Per chevron per pale azure and gules and argent, gutté-de-poix, two ingots of gold fesswise in chief and a fleece in base proper. Mantling azure and argent. Crest : upon a wreath of the colours, in front of a palm-tree on a rock proper, a lion couchant regardant per pale indented azure and gules, supporting with the dexter fore-paw an ingot of gold erect. Motto : "Laborare et tempus aucupari."

A further, and perhaps the best known, example of the heart ensigned with a crown is seen in the shield of Johnstone (Fig. 554). The legend which accounts for the appearance of this charge in the arms of Douglas is too well known to need repetition.

Money, Coins, &c., deserve a passing notice, although the instances of devices connected therewith are but few. This usually takes the form of the Bezant.

The well-known heraldic term "bezanté" is, of course, a field covered with bezants, or metal discs—representing coins—and probably taking their origin from the size, &c., of the coins current in Byzantium.

Bezants themselves frequently figure as charges, as in

FIG. 565.—Armorial bearings of John Gibsone, Esq., of Pentland : Gules, three keys fesswise in pale, wards downwards, or. Mantling gules, doubled argent. Crest : on a wreath of his liveries, a pelican vulning herself and feeding her young proper. Supporters : two angels with wings expanded proper. Motto : "Pandite cœlestes portæ."

the family of Murray, who bore : "Azure, a bezant between three mullets argent (another for difference)." "Azure, a chevron or between three bezants" is the shield of Hope (Fig. 231).

Impersonal arms in this connection afford an instance of ingots of silver, as seen in the shield of St. Helen's, whilst the family of Woollan (Fig. 564) go one better by bearing ingots of gold.

Keys may be seen in many coats of Gibson (Fig. 565), and they also — naturally — figure largely in ecclesiastical armory. York, Exeter, and Winchester, among Home Dioceses, bear this charge on the shield, while abroad it is unnecessary to add that two keys, in conjunction with the tiara, form the charges of Papal arms, and "Gules, the papal tiara proper" is the canting coat of the Dutch family of Pabst.

A Maunch, which is a well-known heraldic term for

FIG. 566.—Arms of William de Hastings, Lord Hastings (d. 1483) : Argent, a maunch sable. (From his seal, 1468.)

the sleeve, is, as it is drawn, scarcely recognisable as such. Nevertheless its evolution can be clearly traced. Figs. 40 and 1023 show the sleeve worn, and it again appears distinctly as a sleeve on Plate LXXXII. In a less recognisable form it will be seen in Figs. 124, 125, and 230. The maunch—which, of course, as a heraldic charge, originated in the knightly "favour" of a lady's sleeve—was borne from the earliest periods in different tinctures by the three historic families of Conyers, Hastings (Fig. 566), and Wharton (Fig. 567). Another

FIG. 567.—Armorial bearings of William Henry Anthony Wharton, Esq.: Sable, a maunch argent. Upon the escutcheon is placed a helmet befitting his degree, with a mantling sable and argent; and for his crest, upon a wreath of the colours, a bull's head erased argent, armed or, crined sable.

instance of its use will be found in the arms of Flavel (Plate XXIII.). Other garments have been used as heraldic charges; gloves in the arms of Fletcher and Barttelot (Fig. 259); stockings in the arms of Hose (Plate LXXXV.); a boot in the crest of Hussey (Fig. 261), and a hat in the arms of Huth (Fig. 798). Armour is frequently met with, a cuirass appearing in the crest of Somers (Fig. 475), helmets in the arms of Salvesen (Fig. 537), Trayner, Roberton, and many other families, and a morion in the crest of Pixley (Plate XVIII.). The

Garter is, of course, due to that Order of knighthood; and the Blue Mantle of the same Order, besides giving his title to one of the Pursuivants of Arms, who uses it as his badge, has also been used as a charge.

The *Mill-rind* or *Fer-de-moline* is, of course, as its name implies, the iron from the centre of a grindstone. It is depicted in varying forms, the most usual being shown in the arms of Milne (Fig. 568) and Elgood (Fig. 569).

FIG. 569.—Armorial bearings of Edgar J. Elgood, Esq., J.P., of The Manor House, Sidcup, Kent: Or, on a rock in base proper, a greyhound current sable, a chief azure, thereon a key wards upwards between two fers-de-moline erect of the first. Mantling sable and or. Crest: on a wreath of the colours, in front of a mount vert, thereon a greyhound current sable, holding in the mouth a key in bend, wards upwards or, a pile of six pellets, one, two, and three; with the motto, " Tenax propositi."

Mirrors occur almost exclusively in crests and in connection with mermaids who, as a general rule, are represented as holding one in the dexter hand with

FIG. 568.—Armorial bearings of Samuel Milne Milne, Gentleman: Argent, a millrind gules within an orle of eight millrinds sable. Mantling gules and argent. Crest: upon a wreath of the colours, a millrind fesswise sable, thereon a lion rampant argent, holding between the paws a millrind gules. Motto: " Quærito sapientiam."

FIG. 570.—Armorial bearings of Robert Edward Bredon, Esq.: Gules, a lion rampant or, within a bordure invected of the last, charged with ten passion-nails proper. Mantling gules and or. Crest: upon a wreath of the colours, a demi-lion rampant argent, holding in the dexter paw a cross patée fitchée gules, the sinister paw resting on a passion-nail or. Motto: " Vincit veritas."

a comb in the sinister. The crest of Rutherford (Fig. 202) will give an illustration of this.

Very occasionally, however, mirrors appear as charges, an example being that of the Counts Spiegel zum Desenberg, who bore: "Gules, three round mirrors argent in square frames or."

Symbols connected with the Sacred Passion—other than the cross itself—are not of very general use in armory, though there are instances of the *Passion-Nails* being used, as, for example, in the shield of Bredon (Fig. 570). Nails are also to be found in the arms of Proctor, viz.: "Or, three passion-nails sable."

Pelts, or *Hides*, may be seen in the shield of Pilter

Two *Plummets* (or *Sinkers* used by masons) form the charges in the arms of Jennings,[t] quartered by Lingard-Monk.

A solitary instance, too, of *Reed-Pipes* occurs in the accompanying shield of Stainer (Fig. 572).

FIG. 573.—Arms of Todmorden: Or, on a fess wavy azure, between a rose gules in chief and a rose argent in base, both barbed, seeded, and slipped proper, a shuttle in bend sinister of the first, and a spindle in bend of the fourth. Crest: on a wreath of the colours, upon a mount vert, an obelisk proper. Motto: "By industry we prosper."

FIG. 571.—Armorial bearings of Sir John Joseph Grinlinton: Azure, a sword in bend proper, pommel and hilt or, surmounting a pen in bend sinister argent, in fess two spurs of the last. Mantling azure and argent. Crest: on a wreath of the colours, a sword erect proper, pommel and hilt gold, surmounting a pen fesswise argent, interlaced by a spur or. Motto: "Fide et fortitudine."

(Fig. 535); and the Fleece has been mentioned under the division of Rams and Sheep. A *Pen* in that of Billiat (Plate XXVII.), and also in the crest of Gilmour (Fig. 486); while the shield of Grinlinton (Fig. 571) shows a use of a pen saltirewise with a sword.

An instance of a *Pyramid* is met with in the crest of Malcolm, Bart., and an *Obelisk* in that of the town of Todmorden (Fig. 573).

The shield of Crookes (Fig. 157) affords an example of two devices of very rare occurrence, viz. a *Prism* and a *Radiometer*.

Water, lakes, ships, &c., are constantly met with in armory, but a few instances must suffice. The various methods of heraldically depicting water have been already referred to (page 54).

FIG. 572.—Armorial bearings of the late Sir John Stainer: Per chevron gules and or, in base a stork proper, a chief of the second, thereon two branches of laurel saltirewise and slipped between two reed-pipes proper. Crest: on a wreath of the colours, in front of a cubit arm erect, the hand holding a reed-pipe in bend sinister, a wreath of laurel all proper. Motto: "Onerari est honorari."

[t] Or, a chevron azure between two plummets in chief of the last, and a saltire couped gules in base (for Jennings).

Three Wells figure in the arms of Hodsoll (Fig. 574), and a masoned well in that of Camberwell (Fig. 575).

FIG. 574.—Armorial bearings of Hodsoll: Azure, a fess wavy between three stone fountains argent. Mantling azure and argent. Crest: on a wreath of the colours, a fountain argent. Motto: " Maintien le droit."

The shields of Stourton (Fig. 227) and Mansergh (Fig. 394) supply instances of *Fountains*.

A *Tarn*, or *Loch*, occurs in the shield of the family of

FIG. 576.—Armorial bearings of Harry Holmes-Tarn: Parted per saltire or and gules, two terns naiant in tarns or lochs undy proper, one in chief and one in base. Mantling gules, doubled or. Crest: on a wreath of his liveries, on a garb fesswise, a raven all proper ; and on an escroll over the same this motto, " Viret in æternum."

Tarn (Fig. 576), while Lord Loch bears: " Or, a saltire engrailed sable, between in fess two swans in water proper, all within a bordure vert."

FIG. 575 —Arms of Camberwell: Quarterly, gules and argent, a cross quarterly between a well in the first and fourth quarters, a chevron couped between three cinquefoils in the second, and a lion rampant in the third, all counterchanged. Crest: in front of a crosier erect gules, a hind lodged argent, gutté-de-sang and pierced through the neck with an arrow fesswise sable. Motto: " All's well."

FIG. 577.—Armorial bearings of Frederick Burnington Fellows, Gentleman : Per fess or and azure, in chief two reindeer heads erased proper, and in base, on the base thereof barry wavy of four argent and of the second, an ancient ship of three masts, sails furled also proper. Mantling azure and or. Crest: on a wreath of the colours, in front of a lion's head erased proper, crowned with a crown vallery of the first, holding in the mouth an antler of a reindeer also proper. Motto: " Fac et spera."

In this connection we may note that *Drops* [of water] are of very frequent occurrence in all armories. They have been already alluded to (page 54), as has also

FIG. 578.—Arms of Sir Arthur Macpherson, K.C.I.E.: Azure, a lymphad or, sail furled and oars in action, mast and tackling all proper, flags flying of the field, each charged with a saltire argent, on a chief indented of the last a hand fesswise, couped, grasping a dagger point upwards on the dexter, and on the sinister a cross crosslet fitchée of the first, the escutcheon being surrounded by the ribbon and pendent the badge of a K.C.I.E. Above the shield is placed a helmet befitting his degree; with a mantling azure, doubled argent; and upon a wreath of his liveries is set for crest, a cat rampant guardant proper; and in an escroll over the same this motto, "Touch not the cat but a glove."

FIG. 579.—Armorial bearings of Conder, of Terry Bank, co. Westmorland: Argent, on a bend wavy azure, between two lymphads sable, sails furled, flags flying, and oars in motion, also sable, an anchor entwined with a cable or. Crest: on a wreath of the colours, in front of a lymphad as in the arms, an anchor fesswise, the flukes to the dexter or; with the motto, "Je conduis."

the isolated case of a *Whirlpool* in the shield of Gorges (or Gurges), which is: "Argent, a whirlpool azure." This, as also the heraldic "fountain," will be found to be dealt with more fully under the term Roundel. The fountain in the form in which this word is now used occurs in the arms of Lopes and in the crest of Brunner.

The term "gutté" implies being sprinkled with drops of any liquid, and the nature of that liquid is affixed to the word "gutté," such as: "gutté-de-l'armes," sprinkled with tears [which are depicted azure]; "gutté-de-l'eau," sprinkled with water [argent]; and "gutté-de-sang," sprinkled with blood [gules]. Gutté *reversed* is, of course, with the drops "upside down."

The use of *Ships* may be instanced by the shield of

FIG. 580.—Arms of Oban: In the waves of the sea proper, a lymphad sable, oars in action, with a beacon on the top of the mast proper; in base a salmon naiant argent; on a chief parted per pale dexter, azure, a lion rampant argent, sinister gyronny of eight or and sable; and on an escroll below this motto, "Air aghart."

Fellows (Fig. 577), Brown, of Bonnytoun (Plate XXVI.), and of Reid (Fig. 136), while a *Galley* or *Lymphad* occurs in that of Macpherson (Fig. 578), and in the arms of Conder (Fig. 579), Campbell (Figs. 54 and 187), Macdonald (Plate XXXVIII.), Galbraith (Plate XLV.), Dewar (Plate XLV.), Macfie (Plate XXXVIII.), and also in the arms of Oban (Fig. 580).

Another instance of a coat of arms in which a galley appears will be found in the arms recently granted to the burgh of Alloa (Fig. 581), while Wandsworth (Fig. 582) and Lerwick each afford instances of a *Dragon Ship*.

A modern form of ship in the shape of a *Yacht* may

THE ART OF HERALDRY

be seen in the arms of Ryde; while two Scottish families afford instances of the use of the *Ark.* " Argent, an ark on the waters proper, surmounted of a dove azure, bearing in her beak an olive-branch vert,"

of Chorleywood. Lastly, we may note the appropriate use of a *Steamer* in the arms of Barrow-in-Furness. The curious figure of the lion dimidiated with the hulk of a ship which is met with in the arms of several of the

FIG. 581.—Arms of Alloa: Argent, on the waves of the sea an ancient galley sable, in full sail, the sail charged with the arms of the Earls of Mar and Kellie, pennon gules, flag of the field, charged with a pale of the second, on a chief vert, in the dexter a garland, the dexter half hops, the sinister barley all or, and in the sinister a golden fleece. Above the shield is placed a helmet befitting their degree, with a mantling sable, doubled argent; and on a wreath of their liveries is set for crest, a griffin gules, winged armed and beaked or, langued azure, and on an escroll over the same this motto, " In the forefront." (From the painting by Mr. Graham Johnston in Lyon Register.)

are the arms borne by Gellie of Blackford; and " Argent, an ark in the sea proper, in chief a dove azure, in her beak a branch of olive of the second, within a bordure of the third " are quoted as the arms of Primrose Gailliez

towns of the Cinque Ports has been referred to on page 128.

The *Prow of a Galley* appears in the arms of Pitcher (Fig. 583).

227

Astronomical charges likewise take many different forms.

An heraldic representation of a *Comet* occurs in Plate X. Fig. 45.

FIG. 582.—Arms of Wandsworth : Per fess nebuly chequy azure and or, each of the last charged with a goutte of the first, and sable, in base five estoiles, four and one of the second, all within a bordure argent charged with eight crosses couped gules. Crest : an ancient ship having a dragon-head at the prow sable, five oars in action, the like number of shields resting against the bulwarks, and suspended from the stem and stern an anchor, all or, mast and rigging proper, with a flag flying to the dexter gules, the sail azure, charged with a wyvern, wings elevated, within eight gouttes in orle argent. Motto : "We serve."

Clouds (Plate VII. Fig. 46) form part of the arms of Lord Milltown, the second quarter (for Leeson) being :

"Gules, a chief nebuly argent, the rays of the sun issuing therefrom or."

The *Rainbow* (Plate X. Fig. 47), though not in itself a distinctly modern charge, for it occurs in the crest of Hope (Fig. 231), has been of late very frequently granted as part of a crest. Instances occur in the crest of the family of Pontifex, and again in that of Thurston, and of Wigan (Fig. 476). It use as a part of a crest is to be deprecated, but in these days of complicated armory it might very advantageously be introduced as a charge upon a shield.

An unusual device, the *Thunderbolt*, is that of the crest of Carnegy (Fig. 407).

The arms of the German family of Donnersperg very appropriately are : "Sable, three thunderbolts or issuing

FIG. 583.—Armorial bearings of Colonel Duncan George Pitcher, Indian Staff Corps : Per chevron ermine and azure, in chief two acorns slipped proper, in base the prow of an antique galley argent. Mantling azure and argent. Crest : on a wreath of the colours, a griffin's head couped, gorged with a wreath of oak proper between two wings each charged with a bezant. Motto : "Perseverentia et labore."

from a chief nebuly argent, in base a mount of three coupeaux of the second."

Blackpool furnishes an instance of a thunderbolt in dangerous conjunction with windmill sails (Fig. 584).

Stars, a very common charge, may be instanced by the Scottish shield of Alston (Fig. 585).

There has, owing to their similarity, been much confusion between stars, estoiles, and mullets. The difficulty is increased by the fact that no very definite lines have ever been followed officially. In England stars under that name are practically unknown. When the rays are wavy the charge is termed an estoile, but when they are straight the term mullet is used. That being so, these rules follow : that the estoile is never pierced (and from the accepted method of depicting the estoile this would hardly seem very feasible), and that unless the number of points is specified there will be six (see Fig. 559). Other numbers are quite permissible, but the number of points (more usually in an estoile termed "rays") must be stated. The arms of Hobart, for example, are : "Sable, an estoile of eight rays or, between two flaunches ermine." An estoile of sixteen

FIG. 584.—Arms of Blackpool : Barry wavy of eight sable and or, a seagull volant proper, on a chief argent, a thunderbolt also proper, between a fleur-de-lis and a lion rampant both gules. Crest : upon a wreath of the colours, on the battlements of a tower or, the sails of a windmill saltirewise proper, surmounted in the centre by a rose gules, barbed and seeded also proper. Motto : "Progress."

rays is used by the town of Ilchester, but the arms are not of any authority. Everything with straight points

being in England a mullet, it naturally follows that the English practice permits a mullet to be plain or pierced. They are occasionally met with pierced of a colour other than the field they are charged upon. According to the English practice, therefore, the mullet is not represented as pierced unless it is expressly stated to be so. The mullet both in England and Scotland is of five points unless a greater number are specified. But mullets pierced and unpierced of six or eight points are frequent enough in English armory.

The Scottish practice differs, and it must be admitted that it is more correct than the English, though, strange to say, more complicated. In Scottish armory

FIG. 585.—Armorial bearings of Charles Henry Alston, Esq. : Azure, ten stars of six points or, four, three, two, and one, within a bordure wavy of the last, charged with three fleurs-de-lis gules. Mantling gules, doubled argent. Crest : upon a wreath of the liveries, a demi-eagle rising proper, on each wing a crescent reversed gules. Motto : "In altum."

they have the estoile, the star, and the mullet. As to the estoile, of course, their practice is similar to the English. But in Scotland a straight-pointed charge is a mullet if it be pierced, and a star if it be not. As a mullet is really the "molette" or rowel of a spur, it certainly could not exist as a fact unpierced, so that the Scottish practice is doubtless the more correct. Nevertheless it is by no means stringently adhered to in that country, and they make confusion worse confounded by the frequent use of the additional name of "spur-rowel," or "spur-revel" for the pierced mullet. The mullet in the arms of Vere, which was also their badge, is seen in Figs. 586 and 587. The part this badge once played in history is well known. Had the De Veres worn another badge on that fatal day the course of "English History" might have been changed.

FIG. 586.—Arms of Aubrey de Vere, Earl of Oxford: Quarterly gules and or, in the first quarter a mullet argent. (From his seal, 1378.)

FIG. 587.—Arms of John de Vere, Earl of Oxford (d. 1513): Quarterly, 1 and 4, De Vere; 2 and 3, gules, a bend between six cross crosslets fitched argent. (From his seal, 1509.)

The six-pointed mullet pierced occurs in the arms of De Clinton (Fig. 588).

FIG. 588.—Arms of William de Clinton, Earl of Huntingdon (d. 1354): Argent, six cross crosslets fitched sable, on a chief azure, two (sometimes three) mullets or. (From his seal, 1340.)

The *Sun in Splendour* is depicted in Plate X. Fig. 41, and occurs in the arms of Hurst, and many other families, while the family of Warde-Aldham affords an example of the *Rays* of the sun alone.

The town of Porto-Rico (Fig. 589) instances the somewhat infrequent variation of the *Rising Sun*.

A *Crescent Moon* is shown in Plate X. Fig. 42, and a *Moon reversed* in Fig. 43. A Scottish coat, that of Baillie of Walstoun, has "Azure, the moon in her complement, between nine mullets argent, three, two, three and one." The term "in her complement" signifies that the moon is full, but with the moon no rays are shown, in this of course differing from the sun in splendour. The face is usually represented in the full moon, and sometimes in the crescent moon, but the crescent moon must not be confused with the ordinary heraldic crescent as in the arms of Bartlett (Plate XXXVIII.) and Kilpin (Fig. 590).

In concluding this class of charges, we may fitly do so by subjoining the shield of Sir William Herschel (Fig. 591), with its appropriate though clumsy device of a *Telescope*.

As may be naturally expected, the insignia of sovereignty are of very frequent occurrence in all armories, both English and foreign. Long before the days of heraldry, some form of decoration for the head to indicate rank and power had been in vogue amongst, it is hardly too much to say, all nations on the earth. As in most things, Western nations have borrowed both ideas,

and added developments of those ideas, from the East, and in traversing the range of armory where crowns and

FIG. 589.—Arms of Porto Rico.

FIG. 590.—Armorial bearings of Ernest Fuller Kilpin, Esq., C.M.G.: Per fess argent and or, three crescents fesswise azure, between two oak-trees eradicated in pale proper. Crest: upon a wreath of the colours, in front of an oak proper, charged with a pheon or, a mount vert, thereon a saltire azure. Motto: "Firmus in firmus."

THE ART OF HERALDRY

coronets appear in modern Western heraldry, we find a large proportion of these devices are studiously and of purpose delineated as being *Eastern*.

FIG. 591.—Armorial bearings of Sir William James Herschel, Baronet: Argent, on a mount vert, a representation of the forty-feet reflecting telescope with its apparatus proper, a chief azure, thereon the astronomical symbol of Uranus, or the Georgium Sidus irradiated or; the escutcheon charged with his badge of Ulster as a Baronet. Mantling vert and argent. Crest: on a wreath of the colours, a demi-terrestrial sphere proper, thereon an eagle, wings elevated or. Motto: "Cœlis exploratis."

With crowns and coronets as symbols of rank I am not now, of course, concerned, but only with those cases which may be cited as supplying examples where the different kinds of crowns appear either as charges on shields, or as forming parts of crests.

Crowns, in heraldry, may be differentiated under the Royal or the Imperial, the Eastern or antique, the Naval, the Mural, and with the Crowns Vallery and Palisado are all known to heralds. Some modern grants of crowns of Eastern character are seen in connection with valuable service performed in the East by the recipient of the grant (*e.g.* the Eastern Crown in the grant to Sir Abraham Roberts, G.C.B., the father of Field-Marshal Earl Roberts, K.G.), while other cases are those of local tradition, or of legendary connection.

In order of antiquity one may best perhaps at the outset allude to the arms borne by the seaport towns of Boston, and of Kingston-on-Hull [or "Hull"], inasmuch as a tradition has it that the three crowns which figure on the shield of both these towns originate from a recognised device of merchantmen who, travelling beyond and likening themselves to the Magi, in the Bethlehem visit, adopted these crowns as the device or badge of their business. The same remarks apply to the arms of Cologne: "Argent, on a chief gules, three crowns or" (Plate CXXIV.).

From this fact (if it be one) to the development of the towns with which they traded adopting the same device is not a far step.

One may notice in passing that unlike what, from the legend itself, one would expect, these crowns are not of Eastern design, but of a class wholly connected with heraldry itself. The legend and device, however, are both much older than these modern minutiæ of detail.

Ecclesiastical Sees figure to some extent as possessing *Royal Crowns* as part of their armorial bearings.

The Archbishopric of York has the well-known coat: "Gules, two keys in saltire argent, in chief a regal crown proper."

The reputed arms of St. Etheldreda, who was both Queen, and also Abbess of Ely, find their perpetuation in the arms of that See, which are: "Gules, three ducal (an early form of the Royal) crowns or;" while the recently-created See of St. Alban's affords an example of a celestial crown: "Azure, a saltire or, a sword in pale proper; in chief a celestial crown of the second." The *Celestial Crown* is to be observed in the arms of the Borough of Kensington (Fig. 593) and as a part of the crest of Dunbar (Plate XXXIV.). The See of Bristol bears: "Sable, three open crowns in pale or." The Royal or Imperial Crown occurs in the crest of Eye, while an *Imperial Crown* is seen in the crest surmounting the shield of Lane (Fig. 57).

The family of Douglass (Fig. 155 and 592) affords an instance of a crown ensigning a human heart. Abroad the Royal Arms of Toledo afford a case in this connection, *i.e.*: 'Azure, a Royal Crown or" (the cap being gules).

Here one may, perhaps, draw attention to what is not generally known, *i.e.* that the crimson velvet cap inside

FIG. 592.—Armorial bearings of John William Edward James Douglass, Esq.: Quarterly, 1 and 4, argent, a heart imperially crowned proper, on a chief azure, three mullets of the field; 2. argent, three piles gules, on a chief of the last two mullets of the first; 3. argent, three mascles sable, on a chief of the last, as many lions passant guardant of the first. Mantling gules and argent. Crest: on a wreath of the colours, a dexter hand issuing from clouds holding a sword erect proper. Motto (over the crest): "God for us." Supporters: two savages wreathed head and middle with a garland of oak-leaves, each with a club in his exterior hand resting on his shoulder proper.

state crowns is in reality the "cap of maintenance," the ermine border of the crown being, strictly speaking, the turned-up ermine edge of the cap itself.

Antique Crowns—as such—appear in the arms of

Fraser (Fig. 494), and also in the arms of Grant [u] (Plate XLV.).

Eastern Crowns, which are of the identical form of Antique Crowns, figure in the shields of Benyon and Seccombe, while the crest of Sir Richard Wellesley Barlow is: "Out of an Eastern crown a demi-lion argent, the paws supporting a cross crosslet fitchée azure, issuing from the crown on the dexter side of the lion a branch of olive, and on the sinister another of palm, both proper."

The crest of the Marquess of Ripon supplies an unusual variation, inasmuch as it issues from a coronet composed of fleurs-de-lis.

The other chief emblem of sovereignty—*the Sceptre*—is occasionally met with, as in the Whitgreave crest of augmentation (Fig. 594).

The Marquises of Mun bear the Imperial orb: "Azure, an orb argent, banded, and surmounted by the cross or." The reason for the selection of this particular charge in the grant of arms to Mr. H. E. Moss (Fig. 595), of the Empire Theatre in Edinburgh

FIG. 593.—Arms of Kensington: Quarterly, gules and or, a celestial crown in chief and a fleur-de-lis in base of the last; in the dexter canton a mullet argent in the first quarter; a cross flory between four martlets sable in the second; a cross botony gules between four roses of the last, stalked and leaved proper, in the third; a mitre of the second in the fourth; all within a bordure quarterly. also or and sable. Motto: "Quid nobis ardui."

FIG. 595.—Armorial bearings of Horace Edward Moss, Esq.: Azure, on a fess or, a horse courant gules, between three orbs gold, banded of the third. Mantling azure and or. Crest: on a wreath of his liveries, a dove holding in its beak a sprig of olive proper. Motto: "Peace with Power."

and the London Hippodrome, will be readily guessed, though I am puzzled to account for it in the arms of Lamont (Fig. 205).

Under the classification of tools and implements the *Pick* may be noted, this being depicted in the arms of Mawdsley (Fig. 596), and a pick and shovel in the arms of Hales (Fig. 530).

The arms of Crawshay (Fig. 346) supply an instance of a *Plough*—a charge which also occurs in the arms of Waterlow, but is otherwise of very infrequent occurrence.

Scythes, or, as they are sometimes termed, *Sneds*, will rightly be placed in this connection, though Polish wars have seen them used by the peasantry with great execution, and on that account they may be reckoned as weapons of war. In English armory their use is but occasional, though, as was only to be expected, this

FIG. 594.—Armorial bearings of Robert Whitgreave, Gentleman: Azure, on a cross quarterly pierced or, four chevrons gules, with an honourable augmentation, a chief argent, thereon a rose gules, irradiated gold, within a wreath of oak proper. Mantling azure and or. Crests: out of a ducal coronet gules, a demi-antelope or; and another of augmentation, namely: out of a ducal coronet a sceptre in pale or, surmounted by a branch of oak proper, and a rose gules, slipped in saltire also proper. Motto: "Regem defendere victum."

[u] Armorial bearings of Francis James Grant, Esq., Lyon Clerk: Gules, three antique crowns or, within a bordure of the second and first, charged with three crescents azure. Mantling gules, doubled or. Crest: on a wreath of his liveries, a demi-savage proper; and on an escroll above this motto, "I'll stand sure."

232

PLATE LXVI.

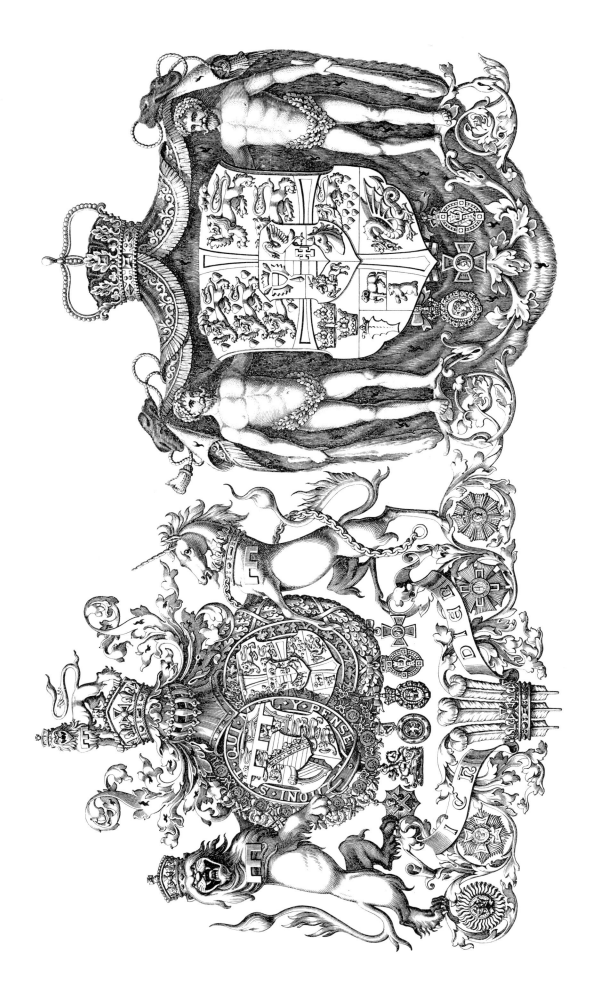

THE ARMS OF KING EDWARD VII. AND QUEEN ALEXANDRA, AS BORNE WHEN PRINCE AND PRINCESS OF WALES.

PLATE LXVII.

EXAMPLES OF "DIFFERENCED" COATS OF ARMS, &c.

PLATE LXVIII.

De l' honorable Chevalier ALEXANDRE FORRESTER COCHRANE Vice-Amiral de l' Escadre blanche de la flote de sa Majesté Gouverneur de l'Isle de la Guadaloupe et Chevalier du très honorable Ordre du BAIN. Installé le Ier jour de Juin MDCCCXII.

THE STALL-PLATE OF ADMIRAL SIR ALEXANDER COCHRANE, K.B.

FROM THE PLATE IN HENRY VII.'S CHAPEL IN WESTMINSTER ABBEY.

PLATE LXIX

STAR, COLLAR, AND BADGE OF THE MOST NOBLE
ORDER OF THE GARTER.

STAR, COLLAR, AND BADGE OF THE KNIGHTS GRAND COMMANDER
OF THE MOST EMINENT ORDER OF THE INDIAN EMPIRE.

STAR, COLLAR, AND BADGE OF THE MOST ANCIENT
AND MOST NOBLE ORDER OF THE THISTLE.

STAR, COLLAR, AND BADGE OF THE MILITARY
KNIGHTS GRAND CROSS OF THE MOST
HONOURABLE ORDER OF THE
BATH.

STAR, COLLAR, AND BADGE OF THE CIVIL
KNIGHTS GRAND CROSS OF THE MOST
HONOURABLE ORDER OF THE
BATH.

STAR OF THE KNIGHTS COMMANDERS OF THE
BATH.—*Military Division.*

STAR, COLLAR, AND BADGE OF THE KNIGHTS GRAND
CROSS OF THE MOST DISTINGUISHED ORDER
OF SAINT MICHAEL AND SAINT
GEORGE.

STAR OF THE KNIGHTS COMMANDERS OF
THE BATH.—*Civil Division.*

PLATE LXX.

STAR, COLLAR, AND BADGE OF THE KNIGHTS GRAND
COMMANDER OF THE MOST EXALTED ORDER
OF THE STAR OF INDIA.

BADGE OF THE IMPERIAL SERVICE
ORDER.

Instituted 1902.

BADGE OF THE BARONETS OF NOVA SCOTIA.

BADGE OF THE ROYAL ORDER OF
VICTORIA AND ALBERT.

BADGE OF THE IMPERIAL ORDER
OF THE CROWN OF INDIA.

THE DISTINGUISHED SERVICE ORDER.

ORDER OF MERIT.

Military Division.

Civil Division.

THE VOLUNTEER OFFICERS'
DECORATION (V.D.).

ROYAL VICTORIAN ORDER.

STARS.

KNIGHTS GRAND CROSS.

KNIGHTS COMMANDERS.

STAR, COLLAR, AND BADGE OF THE MOST
ILLUSTRIOUS ORDER OF ST. PATRICK.

BADGE OF THE ORDER OF THE
HOSPITAL OF ST. JOHN OF
JERUSALEM IN ENGLAND.

BADGE OF ALL CLASSES.

PLATE LXXI.

AN EARLY ENGLISH ROLL OF ARMS.

PLATE LXXII.

Sentu Impatorif Rom. San Reg Francoy. Sent Reg Scocie. Sent Nichol de mole. Sant. H. de kevetz

1. 2. 3. 4. 5.

Willi longa spata. Iohn de bello cuw. Comitis Rič Comitis de legr. Rič de agulichet

6. 7. 8. 9. 10.

Hugonis de nouill Ioh. de vaufigefne Rač fič Hicholai Comitis Ceftrie. Comitis chololie

11. 12. 13. 14. 15.

Wať de rey Ion de Bruton Ion de Hepondi Sile Huffhman Henr' de mortui

16. 17. 18. 19. 20.

Ioh la fitz mayman Witt sorbet Witt de eftoker Ioh de kereshale Witt de stephelbe

21. 22. 23. 24. 25.

ARMS.
Drawn by Matthew Paris, &c.

PLATE LXXIII.

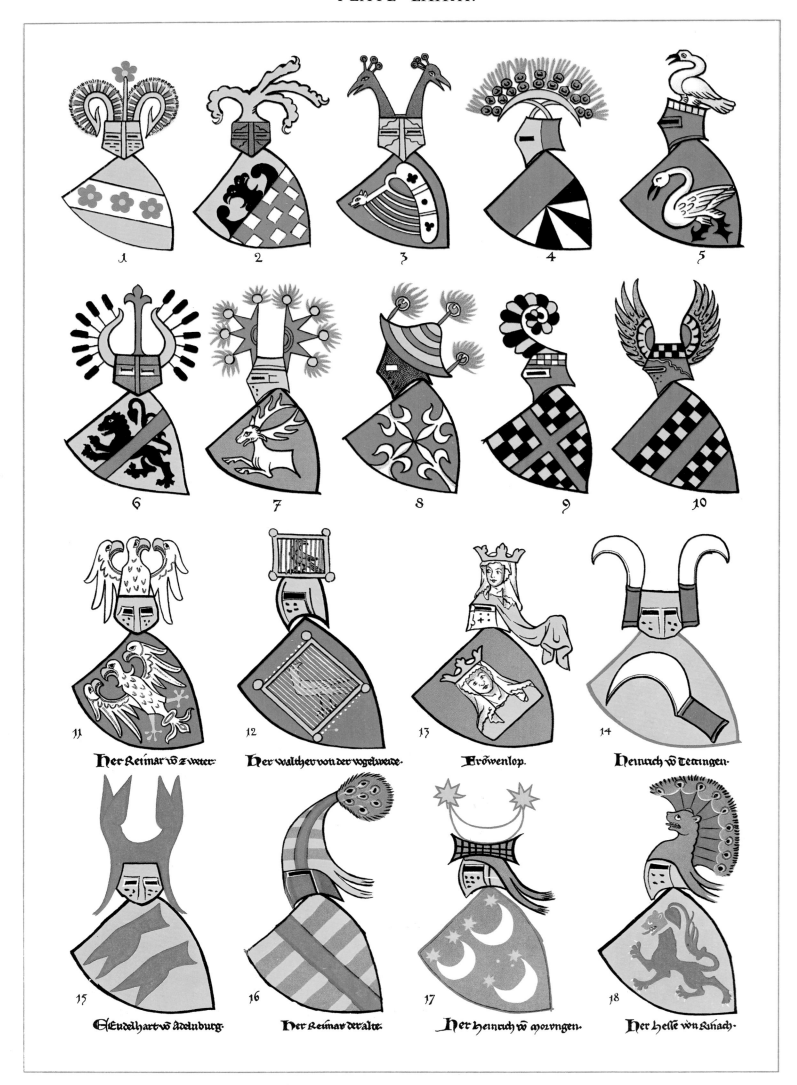

Her Reimar vō z̄weter.

Her walther von der vogelweide.

Frowenlop.

Heinrich vō Tettingen.

GEudelhart vō Adelnburg.

Her Reimar deralte.

Her heinrich vō morungen.

Her helle von Rhach.

ARMS FROM THE WEINGARTNER AND HEIDELBERG SONG BOOKS.

PLATE LXXIV.

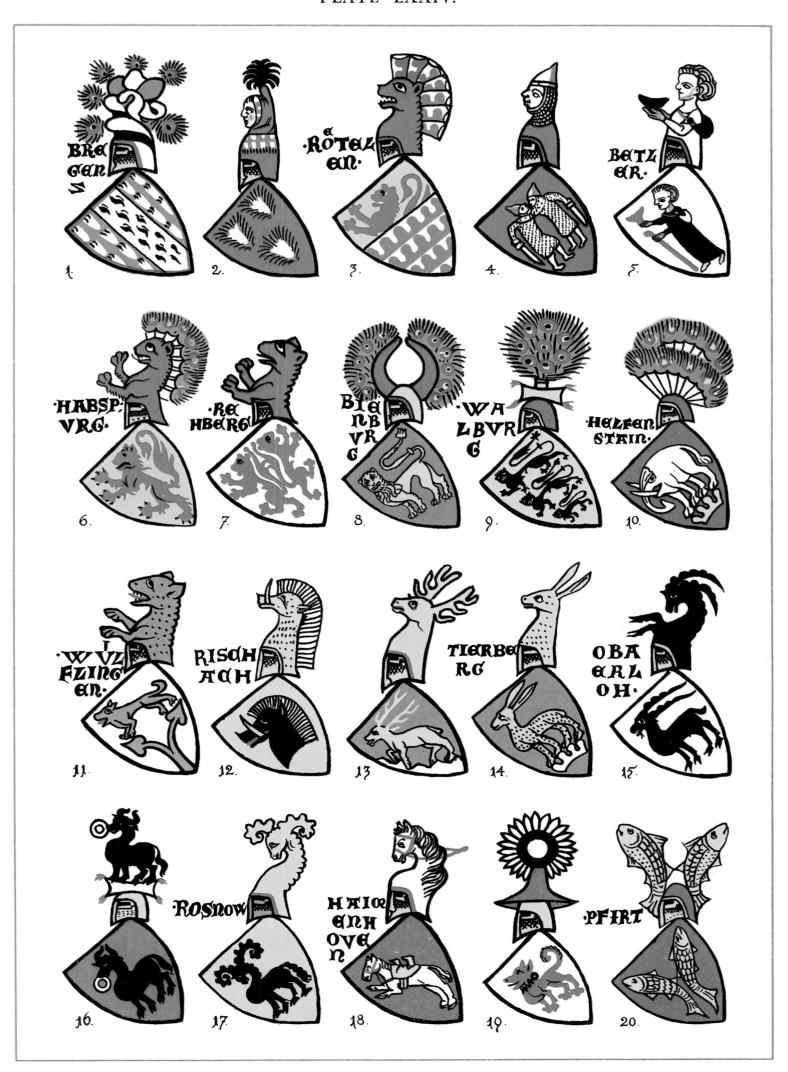

PLATE LXXV.

1. HVN
2. ARBON·
3.
4. HVNR HVSAN
5.
6. ·SLAT
7. OLTING ER·
8. TENG EN·
9.
10. KILCH AIN·
11. OBRAHOV EN
12. ·GVTIN GEN·
13. ROSCH ACH
14. OTA·bER RANO
15. OLING EN·
16. BLATTE NBERG·
17. AEM TVR N
18. HEL OIS HOV EN
19. PHLEG ELBER G
20. GRASO WER·

EXAMPLES FROM THE ZURICH "WAPPENROLLE."

PLATE LXXVI.

ARMS FROM GELRE'S "WAPENBOECK."

PLATE LXXVII.

ARMS FROM THE ST CHRISTOPHER AM ARLBERG REGISTER.

PLATE LXXVIII.

ARMS FROM THE ST CHRISTOPHER AM ARLBERG REGISTER.

PLATE LXXIX.

ARMS FROM THE ST CHRISTOPHER AM ARLBERG REGISTER.

PLATE LXXX.

ARMS FROM THE ST CHRISTOPHER AM ARLBERG REGISTER.

PLATE LXXXI.

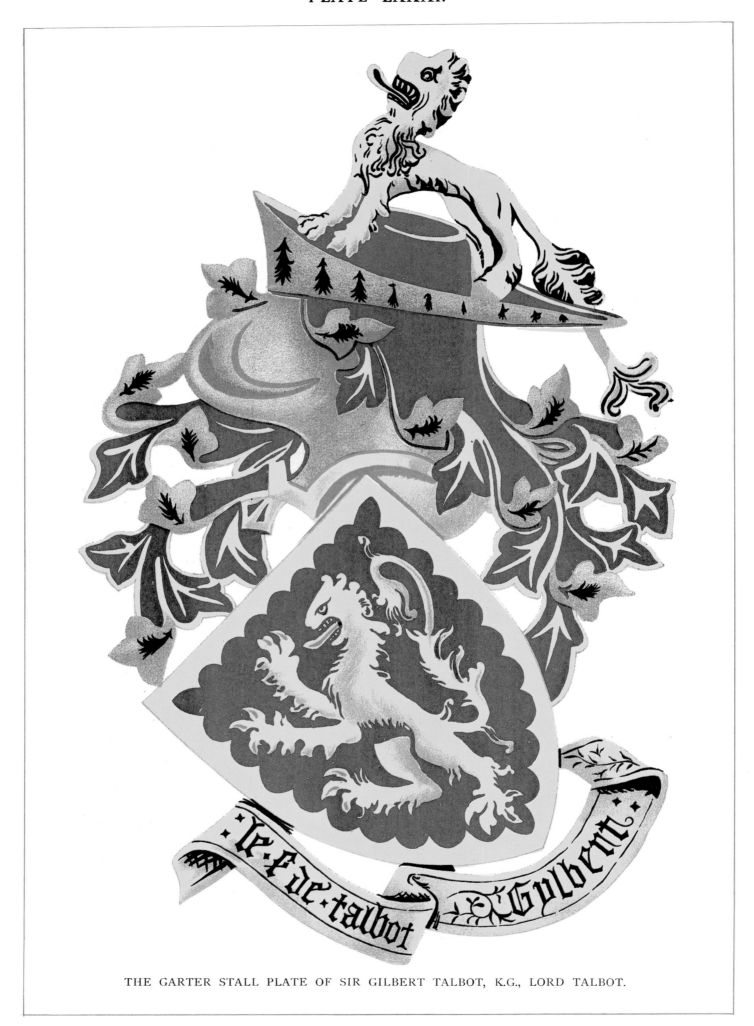

THE GARTER STALL PLATE OF SIR GILBERT TALBOT, K.G., LORD TALBOT.

device appears in the Sneyd coat, as follows: "Argent, a scythe, the blade in chief, the sned in bend sinister sable, in the fess point a fleur-de-lis of the second." In Poland, where their use is not frequent, the Counts Jezierski bore: "Gules, two scythe-blades in oval, the points crossing each other argent, and the ends in base tied together or, the whole surmounted in chief

in some cases the arms are far from being of assured authority.

FIG. 597.—Armorial bearings of Mrs. Enriqueta Augustina Rylands of Longford Hall: Azure, a cross patonce or, on a chief of the last, an open book proper, and impaling the arms of Tennant, namely: argent, gutté-de-poix, two bars invected per pale sable and gules, each bar charged with three bezants.

Buckets and *Water-bougets* can claim a wider use. In English armory Pemberton has three buckets (Fig. 598), and water-bougets appear in the well-known

FIG. 598.—Armorial bearings of the Rev. Thomas Percy Pemberton, M.A.: Quarterly, 1 and 4, argent, a chevron between three buckets sable, with hoops and handles or; 2 and 3, argent, three dragons' heads erect sable, couped and langued gules, and (for distinction) in the centre of the quarters a cross patée gules. Mantling sable and argent. Crest: on a wreath of the colours, a dragon's head erect sable, couped and langued gules, and (for distinction) charged with a cross patée argent. Motto: "Nec temere nec timide."

FIG. 599.—Arms of Henry Bourchier, Earl of Essex, K.G.: Quarterly, 1 and 4, argent, a cross engrailed gules, between four water-bougets sable (for Bourchier); 2 and 3 gules, billetté or, a fess argent (for Louvain). (From his seal.)

FIG. 596.—Armorial bearings of James Platt Mawdsley, Gentleman: Sable, two chevronels argent between as many hammers in chief and a fleur-de-lis in base of the last; and for his crest, on a wreath of the colours, an eagle displayed sable, semé of annulets argent, and holding in the beak a hammer as in the arms; with the motto, "Conatu."

by a cross-patriarchal-patée, of which the lower arm on the sinister side is wanting."

Two sickles appear in the arms of Shearer (Fig. 515), while the Hungerford crest in the case of the Holdich-Hungerford family is blazoned: "Out of a ducal coronet or, a pepper garb of the first between two sickles erect proper."

A *Balance* forms one of the charges of the Scottish Corporation of the Dean and Faculty of Advocates: "Gules, a balance or, and a sword argent in saltire, surmounted of an escutcheon of the second, charged with a lion rampant within a double tressure flory counterflory of the first," but it is a charge of infrequent appearance. It also figures in the arms of the Institute of Chartered Accountants (Plate CXXI.).

Bannerman of Elsick bears a *Banner* for arms: "Gules, a banner displayed argent and thereon on a canton azure a saltire argent as the badge of Scotland." A variation of this blazon may be seen in the arms of Bruce Bannerman [v] (Plate XVIII.).

A *Book* or *Books* are, however, of more frequent use. The family of Rylands, to whose generosity Manchester owes the Rylands Library (Fig. 597), affords a case in point, and such charges occur in many university and collegiate achievements, though

[v] Arms of William Bruce Bannerman, F.S.A., and F.S.A. Scot.: Gules, a fess between two boars' heads erased or in chief, and a banner displayed bendwise in base argent, thereon a canton azure, charged with a saltire of the third. Mantling gules, doubled or. Crest: on a wreath of his liveries, a demi-man in armour affronté, his dexter hand grasping a sword all proper, and his sinister hand holding a banner displayed as in the arms. Motto: "Pro patria."

arms of Bourchier (Fig. 599) and in the coat of Heard (Fig. 600).

FIG. 600.—Armorial bearings of Samuel Thomas Heard, Esq.: Argent on a chevron gules, between three water-bougets sable, as many crescents or. Mantling gules and argent. Crest: on a wreath of the colours, a demi-antelope proper, ducally gorged or, and charged on the shoulder with a water-bouget as in the arms. Motto: "Audior."

Water-bougets, which are really the old form of water-bucket, were leather bags or bottles, two of which were carried on a stick over the shoulder. The heraldic water-bouget represents the pair. The shield of Fairlie (Fig. 601), and of Islington (Fig 602), will afford illustration of the shape of these charges.

FIG. 601.—Arms of James Ogilvy Fairlie, Esq., of Mynes Castle, Fifeshire: A chevron between three water-bougets sable, within a bordure engrailed ermines, charged with as many lions' heads affronté gules, imperially crowned proper. Upon the escutcheon is placed a helmet befitting his degree, with a mantling sable, doubled argent; and upon a wreath of his liveries is set for crest, a lion's head couped gules; and in an escroll over the same this motto, "Tak' thocht."

The use of *Combs* is infrequent, though as regards English arms the instance of Ponsonby, Earls of Bessborough, may be cited. They also figure in the delightfully punning Scottish coat for Rocheid.

Generally when they do occur in heraldry they represent combs for carding wool, as in the shield of Tun-

stall: "Sable, three wool-combs argent," while the Russian Counts Anrep-Elmpt use: "Or, a comb in bend azure, the teeth downwards."

As a charge an *Ermine Spot* or *Spots* do not figure very frequently, though cases are to be found instancing their occasional use. The family of Bury (Fig. 603) affords a case of a single ermine spot. Charged upon another charge they appear in the shield of Stone[w] (Plate XX.), but instances of such use are very rare.

FIG. 602.—Arms of Islington: Per fess gules and argent, a cross counterchanged between a cross potent or in the first quarter, a lion rampant argent in the second quarter, an eagle displayed in the third, and a water-bouget in the fourth, both sable. Crest: in front of a water-bouget sable, a long bow stringed fesswise, and an arrow erect proper.

Coloured ermine spots occur in the arms of Maynard (Fig. 256).

Escallops may perhaps be allowed to rank as one of the most widely used heraldic charges both in English and other armories. They figured in early days outside the limits of heraldry as the badge of pilgrims going to the Holy Land, and may be seen on the shields of many families at the period of the Crusades. Many other families have adopted them in the hope of a similar

[w] Armorial bearings of Robert Sidney Stone, Esq., Barrister-at-Law: Gules, a chevron ermine between three lozenges or, each charged with an ermine spot sable. Upon the escutcheon is placed a helmet befitting his degree. Mantling gules and argent. Crest: on a wreath of the colours, a horse courant sable, bridled, crined, and hoofed or. Motto: "Quid merui meum est."

interpretation being applied to the appearance of them in the arms of their own families. Indeed, so numerous are the cases in which they occur that

The Scottish family of Pringle, of Greenknowe, supplies an instance in: "Azure, three escallops or within a bordure engrailed of the last;" while the Irish Earls

FIG. 603.—Armorial bearings of William Pennefather Arthur Forbes Phineas Bury: Vert, a cross crosslet or, on a canton argent, an ermine spot sable. Mantling vert and or. Crest: on a wreath of the colours, a boar's head or, couped at the shoulder, pierced at the neck with a spear embrued proper. Motto: "Virtus sub cruce crescit."

a few representative ones must suffice, e.g. the arms of Fletcher (Fig. 604), Foster (Fig. 605), and the shield of the University Extension College at Reading (Fig. 606).

FIG. 605.—Armorial bearings of William Henry Foster, Esq., M.P.: Party per pale argent and sable, on a chevron a pheon between two escallops, in chief as many pheons and in pale two escallops, all counterchanged, and impaling the arms of Pakenham-Mahon, namely: quarterly, 1 and 4, or, a lion rampant azure, armed and langued gules; 2 and 3, quarterly, or and gules, in the first quarter an eagle displayed vert. Mantling sable and argent. Crest: on a wreath of the colours, in front of an antelope's head erased proper, gorged with a collar vair, ringed and lined or, an escallop between two pheons fesswise of the last. Motto: "Excitari non hebescere."

FIG. 604.—Armorial bearings of the Rev. William Dudley Saul Fletcher, Clerk in Holy Orders, B.D.: Per bend sable and gules, a cross flory quarter-pierced argent, between four escallops or. Mantling sable and argent. Crest: upon a wreath of the colours, a demi-talbot rampant gules, ducally gorged and charged with an escallop or. Motto: "Dieu pour nous."

FIG. 606.—Arms of the University Extension College at Reading: Per fess gules and sable, in chief three escallops fesswise or, and in base on a cross engrailed argent, a rose of the first, barbed and seeded proper.

They also occurred in the arms of the Lords Dacre, who bore: "Gules, three escallops argent;" and an escallop argent was used by the same family as a badge.

of Bandon bore: "Argent, on a bend azure three escallops of the field."

In this connection we may notice the appearance of

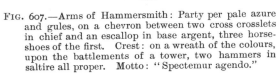

FIG. 607.—Arms of Hammersmith: Party per pale azure and gules, on a chevron between two cross crosslets in chief and an escallop in base argent, three horse-shoes of the first. Crest: on a wreath of the colours, upon the battlements of a tower, two hammers in saltire all proper. Motto: "Spectemur agendo."

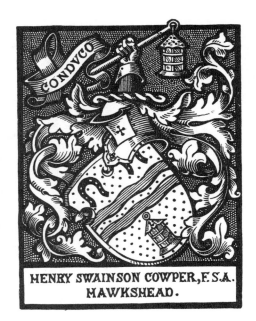

FIG. 609.—Bookplate of Henry Swainson Cowper, Esq., F.S.A.: Or, two barrulets wavy azure, between two horse-shoes in chief sable and a lantern in base proper, a crescent for distinction. Mantling azure and or. Crest: on a wreath of the colours, a cubit arm erect, vested gules, cuff argent, holding in the hand a lantern suspended to a staff proper. Motto: "Conduco."

FIG. 608.—Arms of Swindon: Quarterly per fess nebuly azure and gules, a pile argent, thereon three crescents of the second in the first quarter; three castles, one and two, of the third in the second; a mitre or in the third; a winged wheel of the last in the fourth; and a chief also of the third, thereon a locomotive engine proper. Crest: on a wreath of the colours, a dexter arm embowed proper, grasping two hammers in saltire or. Motto: "Salubritas et industria."

Whelk-Shells in the arms of Storey [x] (Plate XV.); while Whitby affords a variety of a shell bearing some resemblance to a cornucopia. This coat, however, has no authority.

Hammers figure in the arms of Hammersmith (Fig. 607) and of Swindon (Fig. 608).

(Fig. 609), and the arms of the town of Hove (Fig. 610) affords the absolutely unique instance of the use of *Leg-Irons.*

Three towns—Eccles (Fig. 528), Bootle, and Ramsgate—supply cases in which *Lighthouses* are depicted, and these would appear, so far as can be ascertained, not

FIG. 610.—Arms of Hove: Per chevron, the chief per pale or and gules, on the dexter a saltire azure surmounted by another argent, and on the sinister two pairs of leg-irons, one chevronwise, the other reversed and interlaced of the first; the base chequy azure and or, three martlets one and two of the last, all within a bordure ermine charged with six martlets also or. Crest: upon a wreath of the colours, on a mount of shingle, an ancient ship proper, with the sail displayed azure, semé of cross crosslets or, and on a banner gules, flying from the masthead to the dexter, a martlet as in the arms. Motto: "Floreat Hova."

A *Lantern* is depicted in the shield of Cowper

[x] Armorial bearings of Herbert Lushington Storey, Esq.: Per fess indented argent and gules, a pale with three whelk-shells, two and one, and as many storks, one and two, all counterchanged. Mantling gules and argent. Crest: on a wreath of the colours, upon a rock proper, a whelk-shell fesswise gules, thereon a stork argent. Motto: "Deficiam aut efficiam."

only to be restricted to English armory, but to the three towns now named.

Locomotives appear in the arms of Swindon (Fig. 608) and the Great Central Railway (Fig. 611).

Of a similar industrial character is the curious coat of arms granted at his express wish to Mr. Samson Fox, which contains a representation of the *Corrugated*

Boiler-Flue which formed the basis of his fortune (Fig. 612).

FIG. 611.—Arms of the Great Central Railway: Argent, on a cross gules, voided of the field, between two wings in chief sable and as many daggers erect in base of the second, in the fess point a morion winged of the third, on a chief also of the second a pale of the first, thereon eight arrows saltirewise banded also of the third, between on the dexter side three bendlets enhanced and on the sinister a fleur-de-lis or. Crest: on a wreath of the colours, a representation of the front of a locomotive engine proper, between two wings or. [The grant is dated February 25, 1898.]

FIG. 612.—Armorial bearings of the late Samson Fox, Esq.: Argent, a representation of a corrugated boiler-flue fesswise proper, between two foxes courant gules, each holding in its mouth a trefoil slipped vert. Crest: upon a wreath of the colours, a representation of a corrugated boiler-flue as in the arms and thereupon a fox gules, resting the dexter paw upon a trefoil slipped vert; with the motto, "Forti nihil difficile."

An instance of the use of a *Sand-Glass* occurs in the arms of the Scottish family of Joass of Collinwort, which

are thus blazoned: "Vert, a sand-glass running argent, and in chief the Holy Bible expanded proper." This charge is also met with in the arms of White-Thomson (Fig. 498).

FIG. 613.—Armorial bearings of Henry Hargreaves Bolton, Esq.: Per [pale] argent and gules, two bird-bolts in saltire, surmounted in the centre by a tun between three roses all counterchanged. Mantling gules and argent. Crest: on a wreath of the colours, three bird-bolts, two in saltire and one in fess proper, thereon a falcon close, belled and jessed or. Motto: "Sursum corda."

A Scottish corporation, too, supplies a somewhat unusual charge, that of *Scissors*: "Azure, a pair of scissors or" (Incorporation of Tailors of Aberdeen); though a Swabian family (by name Jungingen) has for its arms: "Azure, a pair of scissors open, blades upwards argent."

FIG. 614.—Armorial bearings of John Robert Carter, Esq.: Per chevron or and purpure, two taus in chief and a cartwheel of eight spokes in base all counterchanged. Mantling purpure and or. Crest: on a wreath of the colours, in front of a tau purpure, a demi-cartwheel or. Motto: "In hoc signo vinces."

Barrels and *Casks*, which in heraldry are always known as "tuns," naturally figure in many shields where the name lends itself to a pun, as in the arms of Bolton (Fig. 613).

Viols are depicted in the shield of Suttie ["Azure,

three viols argent, stringed sable "], though these should more accurately have been classified with the musical instruments which have been already alluded to.

Wheels occur in the shield of Oldfield and Turner [" Argent, gutté-de-sang, a wheel of eight spokes sable, on a chief wavy azure, a dolphin naiant of the first "] and Carter (Fig. 614), and also in the arms of Gooch.

The list of heraldic charges is very far from being exhausted. The foregoing must, however, suffice, as there does not appear to be any good purpose served by turning a heraldic work into a general encyclopædia or a trade catalogue. Those who are curious to pursue the subject further should examine the arms, both ancient and modern, of towns and trade companies.

A. C. F-D.

CHAPTER XXIV

THE HERALDIC HELMET

SINCE one's earliest lessons in the rules of heraldry, we have been taught, as one of the fundamental laws of the achievement, that the helmet by its shape and position is indicative of rank; and we early learnt by rote that the esquire's helmet was of steel, and was placed in profile, with the visor closed; the helmet of the knight and baronet was to be open and affronté; that the helmet of the peer must be of silver, guarded by grills and placed in profile; and that the royal helmet was of gold, with grills, and affronté. Until recent years certain stereotyped forms of the helmet for these varying circumstances were in use, hideous alike both in the regularity of their usage and the atrocious shapes into which they had been evolved. These regulations, like some other adjuncts of heraldic art, are comparatively speaking of modern origin. Heraldry in its earlier and better days knew them not, and they came into vogue about the Stuart times, when heraldic art was distinctly on the wane. It is puzzling to conceive a desire to stereotype these particular forms, and we take it that the fact, which is undoubted, arose from the lack of heraldic knowledge on the part of the artists, who, having one form before them, which they were assured was correct, under the circumstances simply reproduced this particular form in facsimile time after time, not knowing how far they might deviate from the lines they copied and still remain correct. The knowledge of heraldry by the heraldic artist was the real point underlying the excellence of mediæval heraldic art, and underlying the excellence of much of the heraldic art in the revival of the last few years. As it has been often pointed out, in olden times they " played " with heraldry, and therein lay the excellence of that period. The old men knew the lines within which they could " play," and knew the laws which they could not transgress. Their successors, ignorant of the laws of arms, and afraid of the hidden meanings of armory, had none but the stereotyped lines to follow. The result was bad. Still later followers, ignorant alike of the laws and the meaning of heraldry, made hash of both arts and laws. Let us first consider the development of the actual helmet, and then its application to heraldic purposes will be more readily followed.

To the modern mind, which grumbles at the weight of present-day head coverings, it is often a matter of great wonder how the knights of ancient days managed to put up with the heavy weight of the great iron helmet, with its wooden or leather crest. A careful study of ancient descriptions of tournaments and battle will supply the clue to the explanation, which is simply that the helmet was very seldom worn. In ceremonial purposes and occasions it was carried by a page, and in actual use it was carried slung at the saddle-bow until the last moment, when it was donned for action as blows and close contact became imminent. Then, by

the nature of its construction, the weight was carried by the shoulders, the head and neck moving freely within necessary limits inside. All this will be more readily apparent when the helmet itself is considered. Our present-day ideas of helmets—their shape, their size, and their proportions—are largely taken from the specimens manufactured (not necessarily in modern times) for ceremonial purposes; *e.g.* for exhibition as insignia of knighthood. By far the larger proportion of the helmets now to be seen were purposely made (certainly at remote dates) not for actual use in battle or tournament, but for ceremonial use, chiefly at funerals. Few, indeed, are the examples still existing of helmets which have been actually used in battle or tournament. Why there are so few remaining to us, when every person of position must necessarily have possessed one throughout the Plantagenet period, and probably at any rate to the end of the reign of Henry VII., is a mystery which has puzzled many people—for helmets are not, like glass and china, subject to the vicissitudes of breakage. The reason is doubtless to be found in the fact that at that period they were so general, and so little out of the common, that they possessed no greater value than any other article of clothing; and whilst the real helmet, lacking a ceremonial value, was not preserved, the sham ceremonial helmet of a later period, possessing none but a ceremonial value, was preserved from ceremonial to ceremonial, and has been passed on to the present day. But a glance at so many of these helmets which exist will plainly show that it is quite impossible for any man's head to have gone inside them, and the sculptured helmets of what may seem to us uncouth shape and exaggerated size, which are occasionally to be found as part of a monumental effigy, are the size and shape of the helmets that were worn in battle. This accounts for the much larger-sized helmets in proportion to the size of shield which will be found in heraldic emblazonments of the Plantagenet and Tudor periods. The artists of those periods were accustomed to the sight of real helmets, and knew and drew the real proportion which existed between the fighting helmet and the fighting shield. Artists of Stuart and Georgian days knew only the ceremonial helmet, and consequently adopted and stereotyped its impossible shape, and equally impossible size. Victorian heraldic artists, ignorant alike of the actual and the ceremonial, reduced the size even further, and until the recent revulsion in heraldic art, with its reversion to older types, and its copying of older examples, the helmets of heraldry had reached the uttermost limits of absurdity.

The recent revival of heraldry is due to men with accurate and extensive knowledge, and many recent examples of heraldic art well compare with ancient types. One happy result of this revival is a return to older and better types of the helmet. But it is little use discarding the "heraldic" helmet of the stationer's shop unless a better and more accurate result can be shown, so that it will be well to trace in detail the progress of the real helmet from earliest times.

In the Anglo-Saxon period the common helmet was merely a cap of leather, often four-cornered, and with a serrated comb (Figs. 615 and 616), but men of rank had

FIG. 615.

FIG. 616.

a conical one of metal (Fig. 617), which was frequently richly gilt. About the time of Edward the Confessor a small piece, of varying breadth, called a "nasal," was added (Fig. 618), which, with a quilted or gamboised

FIG. 617.

FIG. 618.

hood, or one of mail, well protected the face, leaving little more than the eyes exposed; and in this form the helmet continued in general use until towards the end of the twelfth century, when we find it merged into or

FIG. 619.

supplanted by the "chapelle-de-fer," which is first mentioned in documents at this period, and was shaped like a flat-topped, cylindrical cap. This, however, was soon enlarged so as to cover the whole head (Fig. 619), an

FIG. 620.

FIG. 621.

opening being left for the features, which were sometimes protected by a movable "aventaille," or visor, instead of the "nasal." This helmet (which was adopted by Richard I., who is also sometimes represented with

a conical one) was the earliest form of the large war and tilting "heaume" (or helm), which was of great weight and strength, and often had only small openings or slits for the eyes (Figs. 620 and 621). These eyepieces were either one wide slit or two, one on either side. The former was, however, sometimes divided into two by an ornamental bar or buckle placed across. It was afterwards pointed at the top, and otherwise slightly varied in shape, but its general form appears to have been the

FIG. 622.

FIG. 623.

same until the end of the fourteenth century (Figs. 622, 623, and 642 to 645).

Plate L. Fig. 1 is a representation of a helmet of this character from a carving in the St. Maurice Chapel in the Cathedral at Constance, and the date of it is 1218. This type of helmet is usually known as the "pot-shaped." The helmets themselves were sometimes painted, and Fig. 624 represents an instance which is

FIG. 624.—Painted "Pot-Helmet," c. 1241.

painted in green and white diagonal stripes. The illustration is from a parchment MS. of about 1241 now in the Town Library of Leipzic. Fig. 625 shows another

FIG. 625.—"Pot-Helmet," from the *Eneit* of Heinrich von Veldeke.

German example of this type, being taken from the *Eneit* of Heinrich von Veldeke, a MS. now in the Royal Library in Berlin, belonging to the end of the twelfth century. The crest depicted in this case, a red lion, must be one of the earliest instances of a crest. These are the helmets which we find on early seals and effigies, as will be seen from Figs. 626 to 635.

FIG. 626.—Helmet of Hamelin, Earl of Surrey and Warenne (d. 1202). (From MS. Cott., Julius, C. vii.)

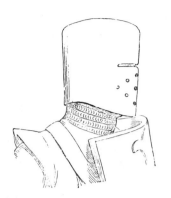

FIG. 627.—From the seal of William de Fortis, Earl of Albemarle (d. 1242).

FIG. 628.—From the seal of Richard de Clare, Earl of Gloucester and Hertford (d. 1262).

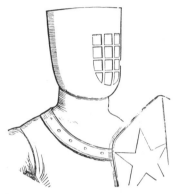

FIG. 629.—From the seal of Hugh de Vere, Earl of Oxford (d. 1263).

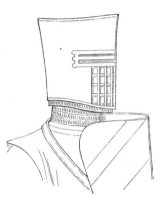

FIG. 630.—From the seal of Gilbert de Clare, Earl of Gloucester and Hertford (d. 1295).

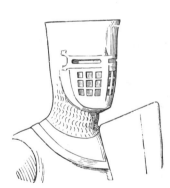

FIG. 631.—From the seal (1231–1240) of Roger le Bigod, Earl of Norfolk.

FIG. 632.—From the seal of Richard Plantagenet, Earl of Cornwall, King of the Romans (d. 1272).

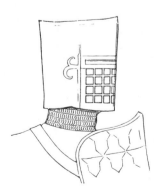

FIG. 633.—From the seal of Robert de Ferrars, Earl of Derby (d. before 1279).

FIG. 634.—From the seal of John de Warenne, Earl of Surrey (d. 1305).

FIG. 635.—From the seal (1315) of John de Bretagne, Earl of Richmond.

2 H

The cylindrical or "pot-shaped" helmet of the Plantagenets, however, disappears in the latter part of the thirteenth century, when we first find mention of the "bascinet" (from Old French for a basin), Figs. 636 to 641. This was at first merely a hemispherical steel

FIG. 636.   FIG. 637.   FIG. 638.

cap, put over the coif of mail to protect the top of the head, when the knight wished to be relieved from the weight of his large helm (which he then slung at his back or carried on his saddlebow), but still did not consider the mail coif sufficient protection. It soon became pointed at the top, and gradually lower at the back, though not so much as to protect the neck. In the fourteenth century the mail, instead of being

FIG. 639.   FIG. 640.   FIG. 641.

carried over the top of the head, was hung to the bottom rim of the helmet, and spread out over the shoulders, overlapping the cuirass (Figs. 636 to 641). This was called the "camail," or "curtain of mail." It is shown in Figs. 637 to 639 fastened to the bascinet by a lace or thong passing through staples.

The large helm, which throughout the fourteenth century was still worn over the bascinet, did not fit down

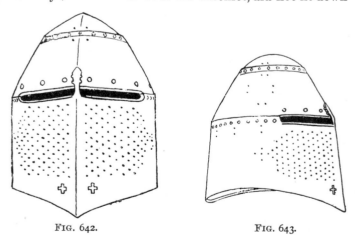

FIG. 642.   FIG. 643.

closely to the cuirass (though it may have been fastened to it with a leather strap), its bottom curve not being sufficiently arched for that purpose; nor did it wholly

rest on the shoulders, but was probably wadded inside so as to fit closely to the bascinet.

It is doubtful if any actual helm previous to the fourteenth century exists, and there are very few of that period remaining. In that of the Black Prince at Canterbury (Fig. 264) the lower, or cylindrical, portion is composed of a front and back piece, riveted together at the sides, and this was most likely the usual form of construction; but in the helm of Sir Richard Pembridge (Figs. 642 and 643) the three pieces (cylinder, conical piece, and top piece) of which it is formed are fixed with nails, and are so welded together that no trace of a join is visible. The edges of the metal,

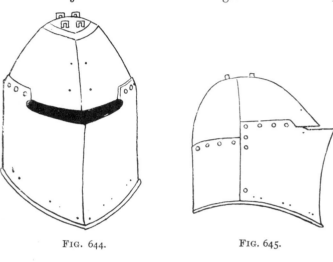

FIG. 644.   FIG. 645.

turned outwards round the ocularium, are very thick, and the bottom edge is rolled inwards over a thick wire, so as not to cut the surcoat. There are many twin holes in the helmet for the aiglets, by which the crest and lambrequin were attached, and in front, near the bottom, are two + shaped holes for the T bolt, which was fixed by a chain to the cuirass.

The helm of Sir Richard Hawberk (Figs. 644 and 645),

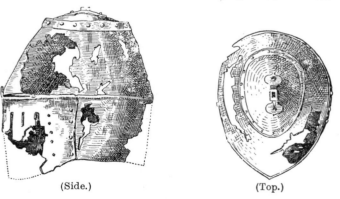

(Side.)   (Top.)

FIGS. 646 and 647.—The "Linz" Pot-Helmet.

who died in 1417, is made of five pieces, and is very thick and heavy. It is much more like the later form adapted for jousting, and was probably only for use in the tilt-yard; but, although more firmly fixed to the cuirass than the earlier helm, it did not fit closely down to it, as all later helms did.

Singularly few examples of the pot-helmet actually exist. The "Linz" example (Figs. 646 and 647), which is now in the Francisco-Carolinum Museum at Linz, was dredged out of the Traun, and is unfortunately very much corroded by rust. The fastening-place for the crest, however, is well preserved. The example belongs to the first half of the fourteenth century.

The so-called "Pránker-Helm" (Plate L. Fig. 2, and

Plate L. Fig. 3, see also Fig. 648), from the chapter of Seckau, now in the collection of armour in the Historical Court Museum at Vienna, and belonging to the middle of the fourteenth century, could only have been used for tournaments. It is made of four strong hammered

FIG. 648.—Pranker-Helm.

sheets of iron 1–2 millimetres thick, with other strengthening plates laid on. The helmet by itself weighs 5 kilogrammes 357 grammes. The crest depicted upon the helmet in Plate L., viz. two golden horns with silver combs, which is made, as were most crests, of stiffened leather, certainly belongs to the same family (Prank of Styria), but not to the same helmet; for whilst the latter belongs to the middle of the fourteenth century, the crest only originated at the beginning of the fifteenth century. The crest itself weighs 1 kilogramme 409 grammes.

The custom of wearing the large helm over the bascinet being clumsy and troublesome, many kinds of visor were invented, so as to dispense with the large helm, except for jousting, three of which are represented in Figs. 636, 640, and 641. In the first a plate shaped somewhat to the nose was attached to the part of the camail which covered the mouth. This plate, and the mail mouth-guard, when not in use, hung downwards towards the breast: but when in use it was drawn up and attached to a staple or locket on the front of the bascinet. This fashion, however, does not appear to have been adopted in England, but was peculiar to Germany, Austria, &c. None of these contrivances seem to have been very satisfactory, but towards the end of the fourteenth century the large and salient

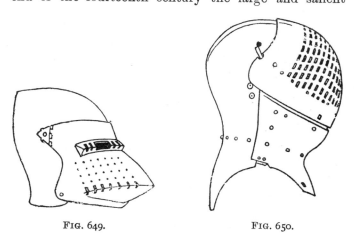

FIG. 649.   FIG. 650.

beaked visor was invented (Fig. 649). It was fixed to hinges at the sides of the bascinet with pins, and was removable at will. A high collar of steel was next added as a substitute for the camail. This form of helmet remained in use during the first half of the

fifteenth century, and the large helm, which was only used for jousting, took a different form, or rather several different forms, which may be divided into three kinds. In this connection it should be remembered that the heavy jousting helmet to which the crest had relation was probably never used in actual warfare. The first was called a bascinet, and was used for combats on foot. It had an almost spherical crown-piece, and came right down to the cuirass, to which it was firmly fixed, and was, like all large helms of the fifteenth century, large enough for the wearer to move his head about freely inside. The helm of Sir Giles Capel (Fig. 650) is a good specimen of this class; it has a visor of great thickness, in which are a great number of holes, thus enabling the wearer to see in every direction. The "barbute," or ovoid bascinet, with a chin-piece riveted to it, was somewhat like this helm, and is often seen on the brasses of 1430–1450; the chin-piece retaining the name of "barbute," after the bascinet had gone out of fashion.

The second kind of large helm used in the fifteenth century was the "jousting-helm," which was of great strength, and firmly fixed to the cuirass. One from the Brocas Collection (Figs. 651 and 652, date about 1500)

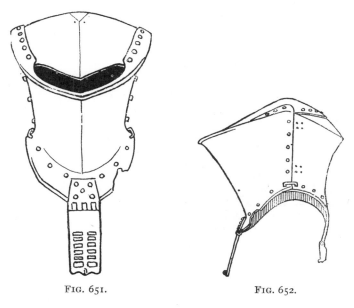

FIG. 651.   FIG. 652.

is perhaps the grandest helm in existence. It is formed of three pieces of different thicknesses (the front piece being the thickest), which are fixed together with strong iron rivets with salient heads and thin brass caps soldered to them. The arrangements for fixing it in front and behind are very complete and curious.

Figs. 4, 5, 6, 7, on Plate L. are four different views of the jousting or tilting helmet, and are reproduced from a model specially made for this purpose from a good original. The shape and style correspond to the second half of the fifteenth century. The manner in which the helmet was connected with the rest of the armour is shown in Fig. 653, which is a representation of a German suit of tilting armour of the period about 1480, now in the collection of armour at the Royal Museum in Vienna. The illustration was made and is reproduced by the courtesy of Herr Director Boheim.

A custom, peculiar apparently to Germany, was the wearing of the "monile," sometimes termed a neck crest. This, suspended by a chain round the neck, was usually the badge of a tournament association or league of knights, occasionally a personal "favour" or badge of high service. These have sometimes been introduced into heraldic achievements, and are doubtless the origin of collars and badges of knighthood.

FIG. 653.—German Tilting Armour, 1480, from the Collection in the Museum at Vienna.

The Emperor Maximilian commissioned Albrecht Dürer about the year 1514 to design and prepare sketches of armour, in which the Gothic design of the armour of the period should be brought into harmony with the artistic taste of the Renaissance. Figs. 8 and 9 on Plate L. are representations of two helmets according to his designs. The sheet from which these two figures are taken is to be found in the collection of Léon Bonnat in Paris (compare the two figures, Figs. 1 and 2, on Plate XCIII.).

Of the same character but of a somewhat different shape is the helmet (Fig. 654) of Sir John Gostwick,

FIG. 654.—Tilting-Helmet of Sir John Gostwick, 1541.

who died in 1541, which is now in Willington Church, Bedfordshire. The illustration here given is taken from

"The Portfolio," No. 33. The visor opening on the right side of the helmet is evidently taken from an Italian model.

The third and last kind of helm was the "tournament helm," and was similar to the first kind, and also called a "bascinet"; but the visor was generally barred, or, instead of a movable visor, the bars were riveted on the helm, and sometimes the face was only protected by a sort of wire-work, like a fencing-mask. It was only used for the tourney or mêlée, when the weapons were the sword and mace.

The "chapelle-de-fer," which was in use in the thirteenth, fourteenth, and fifteenth centuries, was a light iron head-piece, with a broad, flat brim, somewhat turned down. Fig. 655 represents one belonging to the end of the fifteenth century, which

FIG. 655.

is one of the few remaining, and is delicately forged in one piece of thin, hard steel.

During the fourteenth century a new kind of helmet arose, called in England the "sallad," or "sallet." The word appears to have two derivations, each of which was applied to a different form of head-piece. First, the Italian "celata" (Fig. 656), which seems originally to have been a modification of the bascinet. Second, the German "schallern," the form of which was probably suggested by the chapelle-de-fer. Both of these were called by the French "salade," whence our English

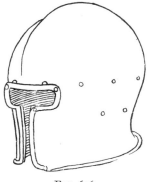 

FIG. 656. FIG. 657.

"sallad." The celata came lower down than the bascinet, protected the back and sides of the neck, and, closing round the cheeks, often left only the eyes, nose, and mouth exposed. A standard of mail protected the neck if required. In the fifteenth century the celata ceased to be pointed at the summit, and was curved outwards at the nape of the neck, as in Fig. 657.

The "schallern" (from *shale*, a shell, or bowl) was

 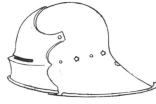

FIG. 658. FIG. 659.

really a helmet and visor in one piece; it had a slit for the eyes, a projecting brim, and a long tail, and was completed by a chin-piece, or "bavier" (Eng. "beaver"), which was strapped round the neck. Fig. 658 shows a German sallad and a Spanish beaver. The sallad was much used in the fifteenth century, during the latter half of which it often had a visor, as in one from Rhodes (Fig. 659), which has a spring catch on the right side to hold the visor in place when down. The rivets for its lining-cap have large, hollow, twisted heads, which are seldom found on existing sallads, though often seen in sculpture.

The schale, schallern (sehélern), or sallad, either with

FIG. 660.—Schallern, with Crest of Bavaria (Duke Ludwig of Bavaria, 1449).

or without a visor, is very seldom seen in heraldic use. An instance, however, in which it has been made use of heraldically will be found in Fig. 660, which is from a pen and ink drawing in the *Fest-Buch* of Paulus Kel, a MS. now in the Royal Library at Munich. This shows the schallern with the slit for seeing through, and the fixed neck-guard. The " bart," " bavière," or beaver, for the protection of the under part of the face,

FIG. 661.—Schallern (end of fifteenth century).

is also visible. It is not joined to the helmet. The helmet bears the crest of Bavaria, the red-crowned golden lion of the Palatinate within the wings of the curiously disposed Bavarian tinctures. Fig. 661 is a very good representation of a schallern dating from the latter part of the fifteenth century, with a sliding neck-guard. It is reproduced from the *Deutscher Herold*, 1892, No. 2.

Until almost the middle of the fifteenth century all helmets fitted on the top of the head, or were put right over ; but about 1440 the Italians made a great improvement by inventing the " armet," the lower part of which opened out with hinges, so that when put on it enclosed the head, fitting closely round the lower part of it, while its weight was borne by the steel collar, or " gorget." The Italian armet had a roundel or disc to protect the opening at the back of the neck, and a bavier strapped on in front to cover the joining of the two cheek-pieces, The earlier armets, like the beaked bascinet, had a camail attached by a row of staples (Fig. 662), which was continued later, but then fixed either to a metal band or leather strap and riveted to the base of the armet. This form of helmet was not in common use in England until about 1500.

Fig. 662 shows the earliest form of Italian armet, with

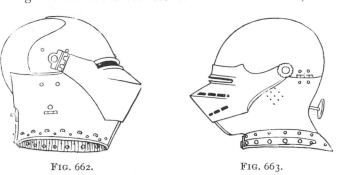

FIG. 662.   FIG. 663.

a reinforcing-piece on the forehead, and a removable visor. Date 1450–1480. Fig. 663 represents an armet of very fine form (probably Italian), which is a nearer approach to the close-helmet of the sixteenth century, as the visor cannot be removed, and the eye-slit is *in* the visor instead of being formed by the space between it and the crown-piece, and there is also no reinforcing-piece in the crown. Date 1480–1500. Fig. 664 is still more like the sixteenth-century helmet, for it opens down the sides instead of down the chin and back, and the same pivot which secures the visor also serves as a hinge for the crown and chin-piece. The small men-

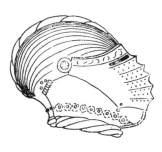

FIG. 664.   FIG. 665.

tonnière, or bavier, is equal on both sides, but it was often of less extent on the right. Date about 1500.

Fig. 665 shows a German fluted helmet, of magnificent form and workmanship, which is partly engraved and gilded. Date 1510–1525. It opens down the chin, like the early armets, but the tail-piece of the crown is much broader. The skill shown in the forging of the crown and the fluting of the twisted comb is most remarkable, and each rivet for the lining-strap of the cheek-pieces forms the centre of an engraved six-leaved rose. A grooved rim round the bottom of the helmet fitted closely on a salient rim at the top of the steel gorget, or hause-col, so that when placed on its gorget and closed, it could not be wrenched off, but could yet be moved round freely in a horizontal direction. The gorget being articulated, the head could also be raised or lowered a little, but not enough to make this form of joint very desirable, and a looser kind was soon substituted. Fig. 666 gives a front view of a German helmet much like the last, except as regards the visor. Date about 1520. Fig 667 is

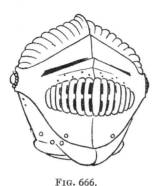

FIG. 666.   FIG. 667.

a very small, but prettily-shaped, Italian helmet. Date 1520–1540.

Fig. 668 shows what is perhaps the most perfect type of close helmet. The comb is much larger than was the custom at an earlier date, and much resembles those of the morions of this period. The visor is formed of two separate parts; the upper fits inside the lower, and could be raised to facilitate seeing without unfixing

FIG. 668.   FIG. 669.

the lower portion. It is engraved with arabesques, and is probably Italian. Date 1550–1570. Fig. 669 is an English helmet, half-way between a close helmet and a "burgonet." It is really a "casque," with cheek-pieces to meet in front. The crown-piece is joined down the middle of the comb. This helmet was probably made for the Earl of Leicester. Date about 1590.

The word "burgonet" first appeared about the be-

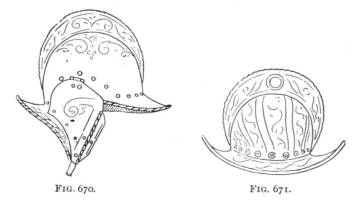

FIG. 670.   FIG. 671.

ginning of the fifteenth century, and described a form of helmet like the "celata," and called by that name in Italy. It was completed by a "buffe," or chin-piece, similar to the bavier. Fig. 670 is an Italian example,

the form of which is particularly graceful and classic. Date 1530–1540.

During this century the "morion" (Fig. 671), really an improved "chapelle-de-fer," was much in use. It had a curved top, surmounted by a comb and a broad, turned-up brim, and was often elaborately engraved and gilt. The "cabasset" (Fig. 672) was a similar head-piece, but had a peaked top, surmounted by a small spike turned backwards, and generally a flatter, narrower brim than the morion. These three forms of helmet were all called casques. Early in the seventeenth century the pikeman's helmet (Fig. 673) shows a revival of almost the exact shape of the chapelle-de-fer of the fifteenth (Fig. 655), but the workmanship is very inferior.

Fig. 674 shows a close helmet (probably French) with a wide gorget. It has strong reinforcing-pieces on the

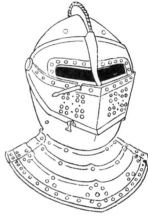

FIG. 672.

FIG. 673.   FIG. 674.

crown, which is very thick, the visor being thin. It is very heavy, the total weight being 10 lbs., and was probably meant for siege operations. It is of inferior workmanship. Date 1600–1610. In the latter part of the sixteenth century and later the tilting-helm was no longer used, but a heavy plate of metal was fixed in front of the helmet, which must have made it impossible for the wearer to move his head.

The barred or grilled helmet owed its introduction to

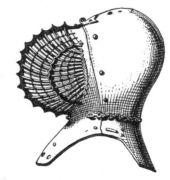

FIG. 675.—"Grid-iron" Helmet (fifteenth century).

tournaments with swords and clubs, which necessitated better opportunities of vision than the earlier tilting-helm afforded, sufficient though that was for encounters with the tilting-spear. The earliest form of this type of helmet will be seen in Fig. 675, which is termed a "grid-iron" helmet, developing shortly afterwards into the form of Fig. 676, which has a lattice-work visor. The former figure, the "grid-iron" helmet, is a representation taken from an original now in the possession of Count

Hans Wilczek, of Vienna. Fig. 676, the helmet with the latticed visor, is from an example in the German

FIG. 676.—Helmet, with Latticed Visor (end of fifteenth century).

FIG. 676.—Helmet, with Latticed Visor (end of fifteenth century).

National Museum at Nürnberg. Neither of these types of helmet appears to have been regularly adopted into heraldic art. Indeed they are seldom, if ever, to be found in heraldic emblazonment. For pictorial and artistic purposes they seem to be entirely supplanted in paintings, in seals, and in sculpture by the "grilled" helmet or "buckler." Whether this helmet, as we find it depicted in paintings or on seals, was ever really worn in battle or tournament seems very doubtful, and no actual instance appears to have been preserved. On the other hand, the so-called "Prunkhelme" (pageant helmet) bucklers, frequently made of gilded leather and other materials, are extant in some number. It is evident from their nature, however, that they can only have been used for ceremonial or decorative purposes.

Fig 677 shows one of these buckled "pageant" helmets

with many others of the same character, in the pageant of the funeral procession of the Emperor Frederick III. (IV.) in 1493. The helmets were made of leather, and

FIG. 678.—Pageant Helmet, with the Crest of Austria (ancient) or Tyrol.

gilded, the two crests being carved out of boards and painted. The Burgau wings, which are inclined very far forward, are: "Bendy of six argent and gules, charged with a pale or." In their normal position the wings are borne upright. The second crest, which is 86 cm. in height, is black, and adorned on the outside with eared pegs 4 cm. long, from which gold linden-leaves hang. These helmets and crests, which were formerly in St. Stephen's Cathedral, are now in the Vienna Historical Museum.

Fig. 679 is another, and a rather interesting

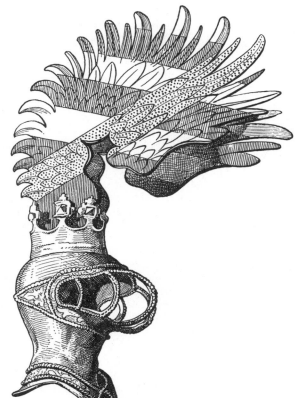

FIG. 677.—Pageant Helmet with the Crest of Burgau.

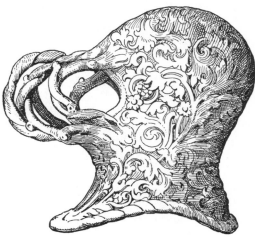

FIG. 679.—Pageant Helm, second half of the fifteenth century (Sigmaringen).

surmounted by the crest of the Margraviate of Burgau. Fig. 678 shows another of these pageant helmets, with the crest of Austria (ancient) or of Tyrol. These were borne,

example, of these ceremonial helmets, and is constructed of leather and linen, covered with a gilded design. The twig-shaped grills can surely never have had a counterpart in actual armour. The height is about 38 cm.

During the seventeenth century the close helmet often had a barred visor, and the face was gradually more and more exposed.

The helmet of the Emperor Charles V. (Figs. 680 and 681) is a most magnificent example of this type.

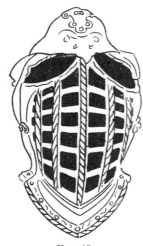

FIG. 680.   FIG. 681.

At the beginning of the seventeenth century the workmanship became inferior, and beauty of line was no longer sought after. Shortly afterwards helmets ceased to be worn outside the regular army, and with the subsequent evolution of military head coverings heraldry has no concern. As a part of a heraldic achievement the helmet is not so old as the shield. It was not until the introduction of the crest that any one thought of depicting a helmet with a shield. They then bore no further relation to one another than did the cuirass and the shield.

A careful and attentive examination of the early "Rolls of Arms," and of seals and other ancient examples of heraldic art and handicraft, will at once make it plainly apparent that the helmets heraldically depicted were in close keeping and of the style then actually in use for warfare or tournament at the period. This is particularly noticeable in the helmets shown upon the stall plates of the Knights of the Garter in St. George's Chapel at Windsor. The helms on the early stall plates, though far from being identical in shape, all appear to be of the same class or type of tilting-helm drawn in profile. Amongst the early plates only one instance (Richard, Duke of Gloucester, elected 1475) can be found of the barred helmet. This is the period when helmets actually existed in fact, and were actually used, but at the end of the sixteenth and the beginning of the seventeenth centuries, when the helmet was being fast relegated to ceremonial usage and pictorial emblazonment, ingenious heralds began to evolve the system by which rank and degree were indicated by the helmet.

Before proceeding to consider British rules concerning the heraldic helmet, it may be well to note those which have been accepted abroad. In Germany heraldry has known but two classes of helmet, the open helmet guarded by bars (otherwise buckles or grills), and the closed or "visored" helmet. The latter were the helmets used by the newly ennobled, the former by the older families of higher position, it being originally held that only those families whose birth qualified them to tilt were permitted to use this buckled helmet. Tournaments were of course always conducted on very strict lines. Woodward reprints in his "Treatise on Heraldry" the "Tourney Regulations for the Exposure of Arms

and Crest, drawn up by René, Duke of Anjou, King of Sicily and Jerusalem," from Menêtrier's *L'Origin des Armoiries*. The rules to be complied with are there set out. Fig. 13 herein is a representation of a "Helmschau," where this examination is being carried on. It is interesting to notice therein that the whole of the helmets without exception have the grilles. Germany was perhaps the earliest country to fall from grace in the matter, for towards the end of the fifteenth century the buckled helmet is found with the arms of the lower Briefadels (those ennobled by patent), and the practice continued despite the violent protests of the tournament families, who considered their prerogative had been infringed. The closed helmet consequently sank gradually in Germany to the grade of a mere burgess's helmet, and as such became of little account, although in former times it had been borne by the proudest houses.

Similarly in France the "buckled" helmet was considered to be reserved for the military noblesse, and newly ennobled families were denied its use until the third generation, when they became *bons gentilhommes*. Woodward states that when "in 1372 Charles V. conferred on the bourgeoisie of Paris the right to use armorial bearings, it was strenuously denied that they could use the timbred helm. In 1568 an edict of Charles IX. prohibited the use of *armoiries timbrées* to any who were not noble by birth." The grilles of the helmet produced with the old French heralds the opportunity of a minutiæ of rule which, considering the multitude of rules fathered, rightly or wrongly, upon British heraldry, we may be devoutly happy never reached our shores. They assigned different numbers of grilles to different ranks, but as the writers differ as to the varying numbers, it is probable that such rules were never officially accepted even in that country. In France the rule was, much as in this country, a gold helmet for the Sovereign, silver for princes and great nobles, steel for the remainder. It is curious that though the timbred helm was of course known in England whilst the controversy as to its heraldic use was raging in France and Germany, no heraldic use of it whatever occurs till the beginning of the seventeenth century. From Royalty to the humblest gentleman, all used for heraldic purposes the closed or visored helms.

The present rules concerning helmets which hold in Great Britain are that the helmet of the Sovereign and the Royal princes of this country shall be of gold, placed in an affronté position, and shall have grilles. The helmet of a peer shall be of silver, shall be placed in profile, and shall have golden grilles, frequently stated to be five in number, a detail not stringently adhered to. The helmet of a knight or baronet shall be of steel, placed full faced, and shall be open, whilst the helmet of an esquire or gentleman shall be of steel and in profile, with the visor closed. Within these limits considerable latitude is allowed, and even in official grants of arms, which, as far as emblazonment goes, are very much of a stereotyped style, actual unvarying adherence to a particular pattern is not insisted upon.

There is not much latitude in the helmet of a peer, but the arms of the Marquess of Ailsa, as shown in Fig. 206, and the helmet of the Duke of Fife (Fig. 251), are both good renderings of the heraldic helmet of a peer as ordinarily depicted.

From the artistic point of view, surely nothing could be uglier than the helmet assigned to the peer and baronet. Fig. 1, which represents the arms of Sir Edward Malet, G.C.B., and Fig. 65, which gives the arms of Sir Robert Gresley, Bart., afford two good examples of the open and full-faced helmet. Other artists have expressed their ideas of the definition somewhat differently, as will be seen from Figs. 117, 157, 169, 170, 187, 222, 255, 298, 316, and 333.

The methods of rendering the closed profile helmet of an esquire or gentleman are legion. The helmets in the illustrations of the arms of Mr. W. G. Taunton (Fig. 680), Burnard (Fig. 94), and Warrington (Fig. 51) are examples of the present official types. But other accep-

table and accurate examples will be found in Figs. 84, 91, 92, 93, 98, 100, 114, 127, 132, and 165.

Typically weak and impossible helmets of the regulation style adopted by heraldic stationers will be found in the reproductions of the bookplates in Figs. 89, 126, and in Fig. 50.

The earliest instance amongst the Garter plates in which a helmet with grilles is used to denote the rank

FIG. 680.—Armorial bearings of William Garnett Taunton, Esq.: Quarterly of twenty-five, namely: 1 and 25, or, on a chevron cottised gules, between three Cornish choughs proper, five lozenges of the field (for Taunton); 2. argent, on a chief sable, three Moors' heads or, wreathed gules (for Tanner); 3. argent, a chevron between three escallops sable (for Tregarthyn); 4. azure, a lion rampant within an orle of eight escallops or (for Hender); 5. argent, a lion rampant gules, within a bordure engrailed sable, charged with eight bezants (for Cornwall); 6. argent, on a bend sable, five bezants (for Chamberlayne); 7. argent, on a chevron gules, three fleurs-de-lis or (for Pever); 8. azure, a garb or, between three bezants (for Grosvenor); 9. azure, a garb or (for Grosvenor); 10. azure, a bend or (for Grosvenor); 11. argent, two chevronels gules, on a canton of the last a cross crosslet fitchée or (for Moberley); 12. azure, a stag lodged argent (for Downes); 13. sable, a cross patonce argent (for Pulford); 14. azure, three pheasants or (for Fesant); 15. argent, a cross patée flory sable, on a canton gules, a wolf's head erased of the field (for Pershall); 16. argent, a cross patée flory charged with an escutcheon sable (for Pershall); 17. vert, two lions passant in pale or (for Knighton); 18. azure, fretty argent, a fess gules (for Caverswell); 19. azure, a chevron between three mullets or (for Chetwynd); 20. gules, three pheons argent (for Malpas); 21. gules, a scythe, the blade in chief and the handle in bend sinister within a bordure argent (for Praers); 22. argent, a Moor's head in profile couped at the neck proper (for Blackenhall); 23. gules, two scythes in saltire, the blades in chief argent (for Prayers); 24. gules, two lions rampant combatant argent (for Winstanton); and for his crest, upon a wreath of the colours, five lozenges conjoined fesswise or, thereon a Cornish chough proper; with the motto, "Virtus non stemma."

of a peer is the stall plate of Lord Knollys in 1615. In the Visitations but few instances can be found in which the arms of peers are included. Peers were not compelled to attend and enter their arms and pedigrees at Visitations, doubtless owing to the fact that no Garter King of Arms ever made a Visitation, whilst it has been the long-asserted prerogative of Garter to deal with peers and their arms by himself. At the same time, however, there are some number of instances of peers' arms and pedigrees in the Visitation Books, several occurring in the 1587 Visitation of Yorkshire. In these cases the arms of peers are set out with supporters and mottoes, but there is no difference between their helmets and what we should now term the helmet of an esquire or gentleman. This is all the more curious because neither helmet nor motto is found in the tricks given of the arms of commoners. Consequently one may with certainty date the introduction of the helmet with grilles as the distinguishing mark of a peer in this country between the years 1587 and 1615. The introduction of the open full-faced helmet as indicative of knight or baronet is known to date from about the period of the Restoration.

Whilst these fixed rules as to helmets are still scrupulously adhered to by English heralds, Lyon King of Arms would seem to be inclined to let them quietly lapse into desuetude, and the illustration of the arms of Sir George Duff-Sutherland-Dunbar, Bart., which will be found in the chapter on supporters (Fig. 812), and which was reproduced by photography from the painting made in the Lyon Register at the recent rematriculation of the arms, affords an instance in which the rules have been ignored.

Some of the objections one hears raised to official heraldry will not hold water when all facts are known; but one certainly thinks that those who object to the present helmet and its methods of usage have ample reason for such remarks as one frequently sees in print upon the subject. To put it mildly, it is absolutely ridiculous to see a helmet placed affronté, and a lion passant looking out over the side of it; or to see a helmet in profile with the crest of a man's head affronté placed above it, and as a consequence also peeping over the side. The necessity for providing a resting-place for the crest other than unoccupied space has also led to the ridiculous practice of depicting the wreath or torse in the form of a straight bar balanced upon the apex of the helmet. The rule itself as to the positions of helmets for the varying ranks is officially recognised, and the elaboration of the rule with regard to the differing metals of the Royal helmet and the helmets of peers and knights and baronets is officially followed; though the supposed regulation, which requires that the helmet of an esquire or gentleman shall be of steel alone is not, inasmuch as the helmet painted upon a grant is *always* ornamented with gold.

These rules in England only date from the times of the Stuarts, and they cannot be said to be advantageous from any point of view; they are certainly distinctly harmful from the artistic standpoint. It is plainly utterly impossible to depict some crests upon a profile helmet, and equally impossible to display others upon an affronté helmet. In Scotland the crests do not afford quite such a regular succession of glaring examples for ridicule as is the case in England. No need is recognised in Scotland for necessarily distinguishing the crest of one family from that of another, though proper differences are rigidly adhered to with regard to the coats of arms. Nevertheless, Scotland provides us with many crests which it is utterly impossible to actually carry on an actual helmet, and examples of this kind can be found in the rainbow which floats above the broken globe of

the Hopes (Fig. 231), and the coronets in space to which the hand points in the crest of the family of Dunbar of Boath, with many other similar absurdities.

In England an equal necessity for difference is insisted upon in the crest as is everywhere insisted upon with regard to the coat of arms; and it is now rapidly becoming almost impossible to obtain a new crest which has not got a row of small objects in front of it, or else two somethings, one on either side. If a crest is to be depicted between two ostrich feathers, for example, it stands to reason that the central object should be placed upon the centre of the helmet, whilst the ostrich feathers would be one on either side—that is, placed in a position slightly above the ears. Yet, if a helmet is to be rigidly depicted in profile, with such a crest, it is by no means inconceivable that the one ostrich feather at the one side would hide both the other ostrich feather and the central object, leaving the crest to appear when properly depicted (for example if photographed from a profile view of an actual helmet) as a single ostrich feather. Take, for instance, the Sievier crest, which is an estoile between two ostrich feathers. If that crest were properly depicted upon a profile helmet, the one ostrich feather would undoubtedly hide everything else, for it is hardly likely that the estoile would be placed edge-forwards upon an actual helmet; and to properly display it, it ought to take its place upon an affronté helmet. Under the present rules it would be officially depicted with the estoile facing the side, one ostrich feather in front over the nose, and the other at the back of the head, which of course reduces it to an absurdity. To take another example, one might instance the crest of Sir William Crookes (Fig. 157). It is hardly to be supposed that a helmet would ever have been borne into a tournament surmounted by an elephant looking out over the side; it would most certainly have had its head placed to the front; and yet, because Sir William Crookes is a knight, he is required to use an affronté helmet, with a crest which most palpably was designed for use in profile. The absurd position which has resulted is chiefly due to the position rules and largely a consequence of the hideous British practice (for no other nation has ever adopted it) of depicting, as is so often done, a coat of arms and crest without the intervening helmet and mantling; though perhaps another cause may have had its influence. I allude to the fact that an animal's head, for example, in profile, is considered quite a different crest to the same animal's head when placed affronté; and so long as this idea holds, and so long as the rules concerning the position of the helmet exist, for so long shall we have these glaring and ridiculous anomalies. And whilst one generation of a family has an affronté helmet and another using the same crest may have a profile one, it is useless to design crests specifically to fit the one or the other.

Mr. G. W. Eve, who is certainly one of the most accomplished heraldic artists of the present time, has adopted a plan in his work which, whilst conforming with the rules to which I have referred, has reduced the peculiarities resulting from their observance to a minimum. His plan is simple, inasmuch as, with a crest which is plainly affronté, and has to be depicted upon a profile helmet, he slightly alters the perspective of each, twisting round the helmet, which, whilst remaining slightly in profile, more nearly approaches the affronté position, and bringing the crest slightly round to meet it. In this way he has obtained some very good results from awkward predicaments. Mr. Joseph Foster, in his "Peerage and Baronetage," absolutely discarded all rules affecting the position of the helmet; and though

THE ART OF HERALDRY

the artistic results may be excellent, his plan cannot be commended, because whilst rules exist they ought to be adhered to. At the same time, it must be frankly admitted that the laws of position seem utterly unnecessary. No other country has them—they are, as has been shown, impracticable from the artistic standpoint; and there can be very little doubt that it is highly desirable that they should be wholly abolished.

It is quite proper that there should be some means of distinction, and it would seem well that the helmet with grilles should be reserved for peers. In this we should be following or closely approximating to the rules observed formerly upon the Continent, and if all questions of position are waived the only difficulty which remains is the helmet of baronets and knights. The full-faced open helmet is ugly in the extreme—anything would be preferable except an open helmet in profile, and probably it would be better to wipe out the rule on this point as well. Knights of any Order have the circle of that order within which to place their shields, and baronets have the augmentations of their rank and degree. The knight bachelor would be the only one to suffer. The gift of a plain circlet around the shield or (following the precedent of a baronet), a spur upon a canton or inescutcheon, could easily remove any cause of complaint.

But whilst one may think it well to urge strongly the alteration of existing rules, it should not be considered permissible to ignore rules which undoubtedly do exist whilst those rules remain in force.

The helmets of knights and baronets and of esquires and gentlemen, in accordance with present official practice, are usually ornamented with gold, though this would not appear to be a fixed and unalterable rule.

When two or more crests need to be depicted, various

FIG. 681.—Armorial bearings of James Andrew Colville Wedderburn-Maxwell, Esq.: Quarterly, 1 and 4, argent, a saltire sable, in chief a mullet gules, within a bordure azure (for Maxwell); 2 and 3, argent, a chevron between three roses gules, barbed vert (for Wedderburn). Mantling gules and argent. Crests: 1. on a wreath of his liveries, a stag lodged in front of a holly-tree proper (for Maxwell); 2. on a wreath of his liveries, an eagle's head erased proper (for Wedderburn). Mottoes: "Reviresco" (for Maxwell); "Non degener" (for Wedderburn).

expedients are adopted. The English official practice is to paint one helmet only, and Fig. 553, which represents the arms of Brisbane of that Ilk, or Fig. 300, will show the official English method of depicting two crests. The same plan was adopted in Scotland, and Fig. 681, the arms of J. A. C. Wedderburn-Maxwell, Esq., is a reproduction from an official Scottish emblazonment. The

dexter crest is naturally the more important and the principal one in each case. By using one helmet only the necessity of turning the dexter crest to face the sinister was obviated.

The present official method adopted in England of depicting three crests is to use one helmet only, and all three crests face to the dexter. The centre one, which is placed on the helmet, is the principal or first crest, that on the dexter side the second, and the one on the sinister the third.

In Germany, the land of many crests (no less than thirteen were borne above the shield of the Markgraves of Brandenburg-Anspach), there has from the earliest times been a fixed invariable practice of never dissociating a crest from the helmet which supported it, and consequently one helmet to every crest has long been the only recognised procedure. In this country and all others duplication of crests is quite a modern practice. Amongst the Plantagenet Garter plates there is not a single example to be found of a coat of arms with more than a single crest, and there is no ancient British example of more than one helmet which can be referred to for guidance. The custom originated in the sixteenth and seventeenth centuries in Germany. This point is more fully dealt with in the chapter devoted to the consideration of crests, but it may be here noted that in Austria a knight may place two and a baron three helmets over his shield. The Continental practice is as follows: "When the number of the helms is even, they are arranged so that all look inwards towards the centre line of the escutcheon, half being turned to the dexter, half to the sinister. If the number be uneven, the principal helm is placed in the centre affronté, the others with their crests being turned towards it; thus, some face to the dexter, some to the sinister. The crests are always turned with the helmets. In Scandinavia the centre helm is affronté; the others, with their crests, are often turned outwards.

English officialism, whilst confining its own emblazonments to one helmet only, has never sought to assert that the use of two or more was either incorrect or faulty heraldry, and particularly in these later days of the revival of heraldic art in this country, all heraldic artists of the present day, following the German example, are inclined to give each crest its own helmet. This practice has been adopted during the last few years by Lyon King of Arms, and now all paintings of arms in Lyon Register which have two crests have the same number of helmets. Some of the Bath Stall plates in Henry VII.'s chapel in Westminster Abbey also display two helmets (see Plate LXVIII.).

When two helmets are used, it has been customary, still following the German model, to turn them to face each other, except in the cases of the full-faced helmets of a knight or baronet, and (with the same exception) when three helmets have been employed the outer ones have been placed to face the centre, whilst the centre one has been placed in profile, as would be the case were it standing alone. But the multiplication of English crests in number, all of which as granted are required to differ, has naturally resulted in the stereotyping of points of difference in attitude, &c., and the inevitable consequence is unfortunately that without sacrificing this character of differentiation it is impossible to allow the English heraldic artist the same latitude and freedom of disposition with regard to crests that his German confrère enjoys. These remarks apply solely to English and Irish crests, for Scottish practices, requiring no differentiation in the crests, have left Scottish crests simple and unspoiled. In England the result is that to "play" with the position of a crest frequently results in an entire alteration of its character, and consequently, as there is nothing whatever in the nature of a law or of a rule to the contrary, it is quite as usual to now find that two profile helmets are both placed to face the dexter as placed to face each other. Another point seems also in England to have been lost sight of in borrowing our methods from Germany. They hold themselves at liberty to, and usually *do*, make all their *charges on the shield* face to the centre. This is never done in England, where all face to the dexter. It seems therefore to me an anomaly to apply one rule to the shield and another to the helmet, and personally I prefer that both helmets and all charges should face the dexter.

As instances of the use of two or more helmets, the following representations of armorial bearings are included: Atkin-Roberts (Fig. 154); Parkin-Moore (Fig. 145); Graham-Wigan (Fig. 178); Vipont (Fig. 216); Lawlor-Huddleston (Fig. 223); Ross - of - Bladensburg (Fig. 175); Meade-King (Plate XXV.); Chaworth-Musters (Fig. 682); Baron de Hochepied (Fig. 683);

FIG. 682.—Armorial bearings of John Patricius Chaworth-Musters, Esq.: Quarterly, 1 and 4, argent, on a bend gules, a lion passant guardant or, within a bordure engrailed of the second (for Musters); 2 and 3, barry of ten argent and gules, three martlets two and one sable, within a bordure engrailed ermines (for Chaworth). Mantling gules and argent. Crests: 1. upon a wreath of the colours, a lion sejant guardant or, supporting with the forepaws a shield of the arms (for Musters); 2. upon a wreath of the colours, a tower argent, charged with a bendlet wavy gules, thereon a lion passant or, issuant from the battlements an ostrich feather sable between four others of the first (for Chaworth).

Crisp-Molineux-Montgomerie (Fig. 684); Shaw-Lefevre-St.-John-Mildmay (Fig. 685); and Mainwaring-Ellerker-Onslow (Fig. 686).

In British heraldry (and in fact the rule is universal) no woman other than a reigning Sovereign is permitted to surmount her arms by a helmet.

"Many writers have denied the right of ecclesiastics (and, of course, of women) to the use of helmet and crest. Spener, the great German herald, defends their use by ecclesiastics, and says that, in Germany at any rate, universal custom is opposed to the restriction. There the prelates, abbots, and abbesses, who held princely fiefs by military tenure, naturally retained the full knightly insignia."

In official English heraldry, there is a certain amount of confirmation and a certain amount of contradiction of this supposed rule which denies a helmet to an ecclesiastic. A grant of arms to a clergyman at the

present day, and at all times previously, after the granting of crests had become usual, contains the grant of the crest and the emblazonment shows the helmet.

FIG. 683—Armorial bearings of John Melvill de Hochepied-Larpent, 9th Baron De Hochepied (1704), a Baron and Magnate of Hungary: Per pale argent and azure, on the dexter a chevron gules between three crescents sable, and on the sinister a dexter hand expanded issuant from the sinister in bend, and beneath a pair of manacles, the chains broken proper. Crests: 1. out of a ducal coronet or, a crescent sable; 2. out of a ducal coronet or, a dexter hand issuant proper. Motto: "Optivo cognomine crescit."

FIG. 684.—Armorial bearings of Cecil Thomas Crisp-Molineux-Montgomerie, Esq.: Quarterly, 1 and 4, quarterly i. and iiii., azure, a branch of palm-tree in bend sinister between three fleurs-de-lis or; ii. and iii., gules, three rings or, each enriched with a sapphire (for Montgomerie); 2. quarterly, azure and or, a cross moline counterchanged (for Molineux); 3. per pale argent and sable, on a chevron five horse-shoes all counterchanged (for Crisp), impaling the arms of Lascelles, namely: sable, a cross patonce within a bordure or. Mantling azure and or. Crests: 1. on a wreath of the colours, a palm-branch proper (for Montgomerie); 2. upon a wreath of the colours, in front of two peacock's feathers in saltire, a cross moline or (for Molineux); 3. upon a wreath of the colours, a mount vert, thereon a camelopard argent, armed and unguled or, semé of pellets and hurts alternately, collared and line reflexed over the back gules (for Crisp). Motto: "Procedamus in pace."

But the grant of arms to a bishop is different. The emblazonment of the arms is surmounted by a mitre, and the crest is depicted in the body of the patent away from and distinct from the emblazonment proper in the margin. But the fact that a crest is granted proves that there is not any disability inherent in the ecclesiastic which debars him from the possession of the helmet and crest, and the rule which must be deduced, and which really is the definite and accepted rule, is that a mitre cannot be displayed together with a helmet or crest. It must be one or other, and as the mitre is indicative of the higher rank, it is the crest and helmet which are discarded.

There are few rules in heraldry to which exceptions cannot be found, and there is a painting now preserved in the College of Arms, which depicts the arms of the Bishop of Durham surmounted by a helmet, that in its turn being surmounted by the mitre of episcopal rank. But the Bishopric of Durham was, in addition to

a knight or baronet (Fig. 581). But in the grant of arms to a county where it includes a crest, the helmet is that of an esquire, which is certainly curious.

In Ireland no helmet at all was painted upon the patent granting arms to the city of Belfast, in spite of the fact that a crest was included in the grant, and the present Ulster King of Arms informs me he would not allow a helmet to any impersonal arms.

Care should be taken to avoid errors of anachronism when depicting helmet and shield. The shapes of these should bear some approximate relation to each other in point of date. It is preferable that the helmet should be so placed that its lower extremity reaches somewhat over the edge of the shield. The inclined position of the shield in emblazonment is borrowed from the natural order of things, because the shield hanging by its chain

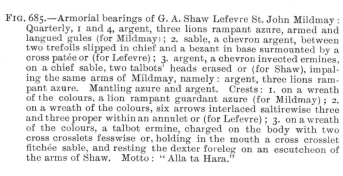

FIG. 685.—Armorial bearings of G. A. Shaw Lefevre St. John Mildmay : Quarterly, 1 and 4, argent, three lions rampant azure, armed and langued gules (for Mildmay); 2. sable, a chevron argent, between two trefoils slipped in chief and a bezant in base surmounted by a cross patée or (for Lefevre); 3. argent, a chevron invected ermines, on a chief sable, two talbots' heads erased or (for Shaw), impaling the same arms of Mildmay, namely : argent, three lions rampant azure. Mantling azure and argent. Crests: 1. on a wreath of the colours, a lion rampant guardant azure (for Mildmay); 2. on a wreath of the colours, six arrows interlaced saltirewise three and three proper within an annulet or (for Lefevre); 3. on a wreath of the colours, a talbot ermine, charged on the body with two cross crosslets fesswise or, holding in the mouth a cross crosslet fitchée sable, and resting the dexter foreleg on an escutcheon of the arms of Shaw. Motto : "Alla ta Hara."

its episcopal character, a temporal Palatinate, and the arms of the Bishops of that See therefore logically present many differences and exceptions from established heraldic rules.

The rules with regard to the use of helmets for the coats of arms of corporate bodies are somewhat vague and vary considerably. All cities and towns, and all corporate bodies to whom crests have been granted in England, have the ordinary closed profile helmet of an esquire or gentleman. No grant of a crest has as yet been made to an English county or university, so that it is impossible to say that no helmet would be allowed, or if it were allowed what it would be. For some reason the arms of the City of London are always depicted with the helmet of a peer, but as the crest is not officially recorded, the privilege necessarily has no official sanction or authority.

In Scotland the helmet painted upon a grant of arms to town or city is always the open full-faced helmet of

FIG. 686.—Armorial bearings of Charles Vere Townshend Mainwaring-Ellerker-Onslow, Esq. : Quarterly of 8, quarterly, i. and iiii., argent, a fess gules between six Cornish choughs proper (for Onslow); ii., azure, a fret and chief argent, a canton of the first for distinction (for Ellerker); iii., argent, two bars gules (for Mainwaring); 2. gules, seven mascles conjoined, three, three and one or, a canton ermine (for Ferrers of Groby); 3. azure, a chevron ermine between three escallops argent (for Townshend); 4. sable, a lion passant guardant or, between three esquires' helmets argent (for Compton); 5. paly of six or and azure, a canton ermine (for Shirley); 6. argent, a fess gules, in chief three torteaux (for Devereux); 7. argent, a cross engrailed gules, between four water-bougets sable (for Bourchier); 8. quarterly, i. and iiii., azure, three fleurs-de-lis or (for France); ii. and iii., gules, three lions passant guardant in pale or (for England), all within a bordure argent (for Thomas Plantagenet of Woodstock, Duke of Gloucester, son of King Edward III.). Mantling gules and argent. Crests: 1. upon a wreath of the colours, an eagle sable, preying on a partridge or (for Onslow); 2. (on the dexter side) a dolphin hauriant and a sea-dragon or, emitting flames of fire proper, embowed and addorsed, and enfiled by a ducal coronet, charged (for distinction) with a roundel counterchanged (for Ellerker); 3. (on the sinister side) out of a ducal coronet or, an ass's head proper (for Mainwaring). Motto : "Festina lente."

or shield-strap (the guige), which was so balanced that the shield should most readily fall into a convenient position when slung on the rider's shoulders, would naturally retain its equilibrium only in a slanting direction. Figs. 687 and 688 are good examples of the

correct proportions of helmets (of those particular shapes) and shields, and of the angle at which the shield may be tilted.

FIG. 687.—Arms of the Herren von Stein (Swabia): Or, the "wolf-claws" (a German implement used in forestry) inverted sable. Mantling sable and or. Crest: a "wolf-claw" sable, the points adorned with peacock feathers.

FIG. 688.—Arms of the Freiherren von Münsterol (Montreux): Or, a lion rampant sable, within a bordure engrailed gules. Mantling sable and or. Crest: a lion statant sable. The striking disposition of the lion in the crest merits attention.

[*The basis of the foregoing chapter is an article by Mr. F. R. Earles published in the " Genealogical Magazine."*]

CHAPTER XXV

THE CREST

IF uncertainty exists as to the origin of arms, it is as nothing to the huge uncertainty that exists concerning the beginnings of the crest. Most wonderful stories are told concerning it; that it meant this and meant the other, that the right to bear a crest was confined to this person or the other person. But practically the whole of the stories of this kind are either wild imagination or conjecture founded upon insufficient facts.

The real facts—which one may as well state first as a basis to work upon—are very few and singularly unconvincing, and are useless as original data from which to draw conclusions.

First of all we have the definite, assured, and certain fact that the earliest known instance of a crest is in 1198, and we find evidence of the use of arms before that date.

The next fact is that we find infinitely more variation in the crests used by given families than in the arms, and that whilst the variations in the arms are as a rule trivial, and not affecting the general design of the shield, the changes in the crest are frequently radical, the crest borne by a family at one period having no earthly relation to that borne by the same family at another.

Again, we find that though the occasional use of a crest can (by isolated instances) be taken back, as already stated, to a fairly early period, the use of crests did not become general until very much later.

Another fact is that, except perhaps in the persons of sovereigns, there is no official instance, nor any other authentic instance of importance, in which a crest appears ever to have been used by a woman until these recent and unfortunate days when unofficial examples can be found of the wildest ignorance of all armorial rules.

The foregoing may be taken as general principles which no authentic instance known can be said to refute.

Bearing these in mind, let us now see what other results can be obtained by deduction from specific instances.

The earliest form in which anything can be found in the nature of a crest is the lion upon the head-dress of Geoffrey, Count of Anjou (Fig. 41). This has been already referred to.

The helmet of Philippe D'Alsace, Count of Flanders (c. 1181), has painted upon the side the same figure of a lion which appears upon his shield.

What is usually accepted as the earliest authenticated instance of a regular crest is that afforded by the Great Seal of King Richard I. of England, which shows over the helmet a lion passant painted upon the fan-shaped ornament which surmounts the helmet.

If one accepts—as most people nowadays are inclined to do—the Darwinian theory of evolution, the presumption is that the development of the human being, through various intermediate links including the ape, can be traced back to those cell-like formations which are the most "original" types of life which are known to us. At the same time one is hardly disposed to assert that some antediluvian jellyfish away back in past ages was the first human being. By a similar, but naturally more restricted argument, one cannot accept these paintings upon helmets, nor possibly can one accept paintings upon the fan-like ornaments which surmounted the helmet, as examples of crests. The rudiments and origin of crests doubtless they were. Crests they were not.

We must go back, once again, to the bed-rock of the peacock-popinjay vanity ingrained in human nature. The same impulse which nowadays leads to the decoration of the helmets of the Life Guards with horsehair plumes and regimental badges, the cocked hats of field-marshals and other officers with waving plumes, the képis of commissionaires, and the smasher hats of Colonial irregulars with cock's feathers, the hat of the poacher and gamekeeper with a pheasant's feather, led unquestionably to the "decoration" of the helmets of the armoured knights of old. The matter was just a combination of decoration and vanity. At first (Fig. 624) they frequently painted their helmets, and as with the gradual evolution and crystallisation of armory a certain form of decoration (the device upon his shield) became identified with a certain person, that particular device was used for the decoration of the helmet and painted thereupon.

Then it was found that a fan-shaped erection upon the helmet improved its appearance, and, without adding greatly to its weight, advantaged it as a head protection by attracting the blow of an opponent's sword, and lessening or nullifying its force ere the blow reached the actual crown-plates of the helmet. Possibly in this we see the true origin (as in the case of the scalloped edges of the mantling) of the serrated border which always appears upon these fan-shaped erections. But this last suggestion is no more than a conjecture of my own, and may not be correct, for human nature has always had a weakness for decoration, and ever has been agreeable to pay the extra penny in the "tuppence" for the coloured or decorated variety. The many instances which can be found of these fan-shaped ornaments upon helmets in a perfectly undecorated form leads me to unhesitatingly assert that they originated *not* as crests, nor as a vehicle for the display of crests, but as an integral and protective part of the *helmet* itself. The origin of the crest is due to the decoration of the fan. The derivation of the word "crest," from the Latin *crista*, a cock's comb, should put the supposition beyond any doubt.

Disregarding crests of later grant or assumption, one can assert with confidence that a large proportion of those—particularly in German armory, where they are so frequent—which we now find blazoned or depicted as wings or plumes, carrying a device, are nothing more than developments of or derivatives from these fan-shaped ornaments.

These fans being (from other reasons) in existence, of course, and very naturally, were painted and decorated, and equally of course such decoration took the form of the particular decoration associated with the owner, namely, the device upon the shield. It seems to me, and for long has so seemed, essentially strange that no specialist authority, writing upon armory, has noticed that these "fans" (as I will call them) are really a part, though possibly only a decorative part, of the helmet itself. There has always in these matters been far too great a tendency on the part of writers to accept conclusions of earlier authorities ready made, and to simply treat these fans as selected and chosen crests. Figs. 689–693 are instances of helmets having these fans. All are taken from seals, and it is quite possible that the actual fans upon the seal helmets had some device painted upon them which it was impossible by reason of the size to represent upon the seal. As has been already stated, the great seal of Richard I. does show a lion painted on the fan.

There are many examples of the heraldic development of these fans,—for their use obtained even in this country long after the real heraldic crest had an assured footing—and a typical example occurs in Fig. 701, but probably the best-known instance, one which has been often illustrated, is that from the effigy of Sir Geoffrey de Luttrell (*c.* 1340), which shows a fan of this character upon which the entire Luttrell arms are depicted.

A much later instance in this country will be found in the seal (dated 1539) of the City of London, which

shows upon the helmet one of these fan-shaped ornaments, charged with the cross of the City arms (Fig. 694).

FIG. 689.—From the seal (1301) of Henry de Lacy, Earl of Lincoln.

FIG. 690.—From the seal (1301) of Richard FitzAlan, Earl of Arundel.

FIG. 691.—From the seal (1301) of Humphrey de Bohm, Earl of Hereford.

FIG. 692.—From the seal (1305) of Edward of Carnarvon, Prince of Wales.

FIG. 693.—From the seal (1322) of Henry de Beaumont, Earl of Buchan.

The arms of the City of London are recorded in the College of Arms (Vincent) without a crest (and by the way without supporters), and this seal affords a curious but a very striking and authentic instance of the extreme accuracy of the records of the College of Arms. There being no crest for the City of London at the time of the preparation of this seal, recourse was had to the ancient practice of depicting the whole or a part (in this case a part) of the device of the shield upon a fan surmounting the helmet. In course of time this fan, in the case of London, as in so many other cases, has through ignorance been converted or developed into a wing, but the "rays" of the fan in this instance are preserved in the "rays" of the dragon's wing (charged with a cross) which the crest is now supposed to be.

Whilst dealing with the arms of London, one of the favourite "flaring" examples of ancient but unrecorded arms often mentioned as an instance in which the Records of the College of Arms are at fault, perhaps I may be pardoned for adding that the shield *is* recorded. The crest and supporters are not. The seeming omission as to the crest is explained above. The real supporters

FIG. 694.—Modern reverse of the Common Seal of the City of London (1539).

of the City of London, to which a claim by user *could* (even now) be established (they are two lions, not dragons), had, with the single exception of their use upon the Mayor's seal, which use is continued to the present day, been practically discarded. Consequently the lions as supporters remained unclaimed, and therefore are not recorded.

The supporters now used (two dragons) are *raw new* adornments, of which no example can be found before the seventeenth century. Those naturally, being "assumed" without authority at so recent a date, are not recorded, which is yet another testimony to the impartial accuracy of the Heralds' College Records.

The use of the fan-crest has long been obsolete in British armory, in which it can hardly ever be said to have had a very great footing, unless such use was prevalent in the thirteenth century; but it still survives in Germany at the present day, where, in spite of the fact that many of these fans have now degenerated into reduplications of the arms upon wings or plumes of feathers, other crests to a considerable number are still displayed upon "fans."

Many of the current practices in British armory are the culmination of long-continued ignorance. Some, mayhap, can be allowed to pass without comment, but others deserve at any rate their share of criticism and remark. Amongst such may be included the objectionable practice, in the grants of so many modern crests, of making the crest itself a *shield* carrying a repetition of the arms or some other device, or of introducing in the crest an escutcheon. To the resuscitation of these "fan" repetitions of the shield device there is not, and cannot be, any objection. One would even, in these days of the multiplication of differentiated crests, recommend this as a relief from the abominable rows of

assorted objects nowadays placed (for the purposes of differentiation) in front of so many modern crests. One would gladly see a reversion to the German development (from this source) of wings charged with the arms or a part of the armorial device; but one of the things a new grantee should pray to be absolved from is an escutcheon of any sort, shape, or form in the crest assigned to him.

To return, however, to the "fans" upon the early helmets. Many of the examples which have come down to us show the fan of a rather diminutive height but (in the form of an arc of a much enlarged circle) projected far forward beyond the front of the helmet, and carried far back, apparently as a safeguard from blows which would otherwise descend upon the neck. (A survival of the fan, by the way, will be found in the dragoon helmets of the time of the Peninsular War, in the firemen's helmets of to-day, and in the helmets now worn by different regiments in the Italian army.) The very shape of these fans should prove they were originally a protective part of the helmet. The long low shape, however, did not, as a general circumstance, lend itself to its decoration by a duplication thereupon of the whole of the arms. Consequently these fans will nearly always be found simply adorned with one figure from the shield. It should not be forgotten that we are now dealing with a period in armory when the charges were very much, as far as number and position are concerned, of an indeterminate character. If they were indeterminate for the shield, it evidences that there cannot have been any idea of a necessity to repeat the whole of the device upon the fan. As there was seldom room or opportunity for the display of the whole device, we invariably find that these fan decorations were a duplication of a distinctive part, but not necessarily the whole of the device; and this device was disposed in the most suitable position which the shape of the fan would accommodate. Herein is the explanation of the fact that whilst the arms of Percy, Talbot, and Mowbray were all, in varying tinctures, a lion rampant, the crest in each case was a lion passant or statant. In short, the fan did not lend itself to the representation of a lion rampant, and consequently there is no early instance of such a crest. Perhaps the insecurity of a large and heavy crest balanced upon one leg may be an added reason.

The next step in the evolution of the crest, there can be little doubt, was the cutting of the fan into the outline of the crest, and though I know of no instance of such a crest on any effigy, there can be no reasonable doubt on the point, if a little thought is given to the matter. Until a very much later period, we never find in any heraldic representation that the helmet or crest are represented in an affronté position. Why? Simply because crests at that period were merely profile representations.

In later days, when tournament crests were made of leather, the weight even of these was very considerable, but for tournament purposes that weight could be endured. Half-a-dozen courses down the *barrière* would be a vastly different matter to a whole day under arms in actual battle. Now a crest cut out from a thin plate of metal set on edge would weigh but little. But perhaps the strongest proof of all is to be found in the construction of so many German crests, which are adorned down the back with a fan.

Now it is hardly likely, if the demi-lion in relief had been the earliest form, that the fan would have been subsequently added to it. The fan is nothing more than the remains of the original fan-shaped ornament left when the crest, or most likely only the front outline of it, had been cut out in profile from the fan. We

THE ART OF HERALDRY

have no instance until a very much later period of a crest which could not be depicted in profile, and in the representations of crests upon seals we have no means of forming a certain judgment that these representations are not of profile crests, for the very nature of the craft of seal-engraving would lead the engraver to add a certain amount of relief, even if this did not actually exist. It is out of the question to suppose, by reason of their weight, that crests were made in metal. But if made of leather, as were the tournament crests, what protection did the crest add to the helmet? The fact that wreaths and coronets did not come into use at the earliest advent of crests is confirmatory evidence of the fact that modelled crests did not exist, inasmuch as the fan prolonged in front and prolonged behind was narrowed at its point of contact with the helmet into such a diminished length that it was comparatively easy to slip the mantling by means of a slit over the fan, or even drape it round it.

Many of the old illustrations of tournaments and battles which have come down to us show no crests on the helmets, but merely plumes of feathers or some fan-shaped erection. Consequently it is a fairly safe conclusion that for the actual purposes of warfare modelled crests never had any real existence, or, if they had any such existence, that it was most limited. Modelled crests were tournament crests. The crests that were used in battle must have been merely cut out in profile from the fan. Then came the era, in Plantagenet times, of the tournament. We talk glibly about tournaments, but few indeed really know much about them. Trial by combat and the real tournament à l'outrance seldom occurred, and though trial by combat remained upon the statute books until the 59 Geo. III., it was seldom invoked. Tournaments were chiefly in the nature of athletic displays, taking the place of our games and sports, and inasmuch as they contributed to the training of the soldier, were held in the high repute that polo, for example, now enjoys amongst the upper and military classes. Added to this, the tournament was the essential climax of ceremony and ceremonial, and in all its details was ordered by such strict regulations, rules, and supervision that its importance and its position in the public and official estimate was far in advance of its present-day equivalents.

The joust was fought with tilting-spears, the "tourney" with swords. The rules and regulations for jousts and tournaments drawn up by the High Constable of England in the reign of Edward IV. show clearly that in neither was contemplated any risk of life.

In the tourney the swords were blunted and without points, but the principal item was always the joust, which was fought with tilting-spears and shields. Many representations of the tourney show the participants without shields. The general ignorance as to the manner in which the tilt was run is very widespread. A strong barrier was erected straight down the centre of the lists, and the knights were placed one on either side, so that by no possible chance could the two horses come into contact Those who will read Mallory's "Morte d'Arthur" carefully—bearing in mind that Mallory described legendary events of an earlier period clothed in the manners and customs of his own day (time of Edward IV.), and made no attempt to reproduce the manners and customs and real atmosphere of the Arthurian times, which could have had no relation to the manners and proceedings which Sir Thomas Mallory employs in telling his legends—will notice that, when it came to jousting, some half-dozen courses would be all that were run between contending knights. In fact the tournament rules above referred to say, for the

tourney, that two blows at passage and ten at the joining ought to suffice.

The time which this would occupy would not exceed the period for which any man could easily sustain the weight of a modelled crest. Another point needs to be borne in mind. The result of a joust depended upon the points scored, the highest number being gained for the absolute unhorsing of an opponent. This, however, happened comparatively seldom, and points or "spears" were scored for the lances broken upon an opponent's helmet, shield, or body, and the points so scored were subject to deduction if the opponent's horse were touched, and under other circumstances. The head of the tilting-spear which was used was a kind of rosette, and heraldic representations are really incorrect in adding a point when the weapon is described as a tilting-spear. Whilst a fine point meeting a wooden shield or metal armour would stick in the one or glance off the other, and neither result in the breaking of the lance nor in the unhorsing of the opponent, a broad rosette would convey a heavy shock. But to effect the desired object the tilting-spear would need to meet resistance, and little would be gained by knocking off an opponent's ornamental crest. Certainly no prize appears to have been allotted for the performance of this feat (which always attracts the imagination of the novelist), whilst there was for striking the "sight" of the helmet. Consequently there was nothing to be gained from the protection to the helmet which the fan of earlier date afforded, and the tendency of ceremonial led to the use in tournaments of helmets and elaborate crests which were not those used in battle. The result is that we find these tournament or ceremonial crests were of large and prominent size, and were carved in wood, or built up of leather. But I firmly believe that these crests were used only for ceremonial and tournament purposes, and were never actually worn in battle. That these modelled crests in relief are the ones that we find upon effigies is only natural, and what one would expect, inasmuch as a man's effigy displayed his garments and accoutrements in the most ornate and honourable form. The same idea exists at the present day. The subjects of modern effigies and modern portraits are represented in robes, and with insignia which are seldom if ever worn, and which sometimes even have no existence in fact. In the same way the ancient effigies are the representations of the ceremonial dress and not the everyday garb of those for whom they stand. But even allowing all the foregoing, it must be admitted that it is from these ceremonial or tournament helmets and crests that the heraldic crest has obtained its importance, and herein lies the reason of the exaggerated size of early heraldic crests, and also the unsuitability of some few for actual use. Tournaments were flourishing in the Plantagenet, Yorkist, and Lancastrian periods, and ended with the days of the Tudor dynasty; and the Plantagenet period witnessed the rise of the ceremonial and heraldic crest. But in the days when crests had any actual existence they were made to fit the helmet, and the crests in Figs. 695 to 699 show crests very much more naturally disposed than those of later periods. Crests appear to have come into wider and more general use in Germany at an earlier period than is the case in this country, for in the early part of the thirteenth century seals are there to be met with having only the device of helmet and crest thereupon, a proof that the "oberwappen" (helmet and crest) was then considered of equal or greater value than the shield.

The actual tournament crests were made of light material, pasteboard, cloth, or a leather shell over a wood or wire framework filled with tow, sponge, or sawdust. Fig. 264, which shows the shield, helmet,

2 K

and crest of the Black Prince undoubtedly contemporary, dating from 1376, and now remaining in Canterbury Cathedral, is made of leather and is a good example of an actual crest, but even this, there can be little doubt, was never carried in battle or tournament, and is no more than a ceremonial crest made for the funeral pageant.

FIG. 695.—Crest of Roger de Quincey, Earl of Winchester (d. 1264). (From his seal.)

FIG. 696.—Crest of Thomas, Earl of Lancaster. (From his seal, 1301.)

FIG. 697.—Crest of John de Warenne, Earl of Surrey. (From his seal, 1329.)

FIG. 698.—Crest of William de Montagu, Earl of Salisbury (d. 1344). (From his seal.)

Actual crests were fastened to the helmets they surmounted by means of ribbons, straps, laces (which developed later into the fillet and torse), or rivets, and in Germany they were ornamented with hanging and tinkling metal leaves, tiny bells, buffalo horns, feathers, and projecting pieces of wood, which formed vehicles for still further decorative appendages.

The heraldic wings which are so frequently met with in crests are not the natural wings of a bird, but are

a development from the fan, and in actual crests were made of wooden or basket-work strips, and probably at an earlier date were not intended to represent wings, but were mere pieces of wood painted and existing for the display of a certain device. Their shape and position led to their transition into "wings," and then they were covered with dyed or natural-coloured feathers. It was the art of heraldic emblazonment which ignored the practical details, that first copied the wing from nature.

Then comes the question, what did the crest signify? Many have asserted that no one below the rank of a knight had the right to use a crest; in fact some writers have asserted, and doubtless correctly as regards a certain period, that only those who were of tournament

FIG. 699.—Crest of Thomas de Mowbray, Earl of Nottingham, and Earl Marshal. (From a drawing of his seal, 1389: MS. Cott., Julius, C. vii.

rank might assume the distinction, and herein lies another confirmation of the supposition that crests had a closer relation to the tournament than to the battle-field.

Doubts as to a man's social position might disqualify him from participation in a tournament—hence the "helme-schau" previously referred to—but they certainly never relieved him from the obligations of warfare imposed by the tenure under which he held his lands. There is no doubt, however, that whatever the regulation may have been—and there seems little chance of our ever obtaining any real knowledge upon the point— the right to display a crest was an additional privilege and honour, something extra and beyond the right to a shield of arms. For how long any such supposition held good it is difficult to say, for whilst we find in the latter part of the fourteenth century that all the great nobles had assumed and were using crests, and whilst there is but one amongst the Plantagenet Garter plates without a crest where a helmet has been represented above the shield, we also find that the great bulk of the lesser landed gentry bore arms, but made no pretension to a crest. The lesser gentry were bound to fight in war, but not necessarily in the tournament. Arms were a necessity of warfare, crests were not. This continued to be the case till the end of the sixteenth century, for we find that at one of the Visitations no crests whatever are inserted with the arms and pedigrees of the families set out in the Visitation Book, and one is probably justified in assuming that whilst this state of feeling and this idea existed, the crest was highly thought of, and valued possibly beyond the shield of arms, for with those of that rank of life which aspired to the display of a crest the right to arms would be a matter of course. In the latter part of the reign of Queen Elizabeth and in Stuart days the granting of crests to ancient arms became a widespread practice. Scores upon scores of such grants can be referred to, and I have myself been led to the irresistible conclusion

THE ART OF HERALDRY

that the opportunity afforded by the grant of a crest was urged by the heralds and officers of arms, in order to give them the opportunity of confirming and recording arms which they knew needed such confirmation to be rendered legal, without giving offence to those who had borne these arms merely by strength of user for some prolonged but at the same time insufficient period to confer an unquestioned right. That has always seemed to me the obvious reason which accounts for these numberless grants of crests to apparently existing arms, which arms are recited and emblazoned in the patents, because there are other grants of crests which can be referred to, though these are singularly few in number, in which the arms are entirely ignored. But as none of these grants, which are of a crest only, appear to have been made to families whose right to arms was not absolutely beyond question or dispute, the conclusion above recited appears to be irresistible. The result of these numerous grants of crests, which I look upon as carrying greater importance in the sense that they were also confirmations of the arms, resulted in the fact that the value and dignity of the crest slowly but steadily declined, and the cessation of tournaments and, shortly afterwards, the marked decline in funereal pageantry no doubt contributed largely to the same result. Throughout the Stuart period instances can be found, though not very frequently, of grants of arms without the grant of a crest being included in the patent; but the practice was soon to entirely cease, and roughly speaking one may assert that since the beginning of the Hanoverian dynasty no person has ever been granted arms without the corresponding grant of a crest, if a crest could be properly borne with the arms. Now no crest has ever been granted where the right to arms has not existed or been simultaneously conferred, and therefore, whilst there are still many coats of arms legally in existence without a crest, a crest cannot exist without a coat of arms, so that those people, and they are many, who vehemently assert a right to the "*crest* of their family," whilst admitting they have no right to arms, stand self-convicted heraldically both of having spoken unutterable rubbish, and of using a crest to which they can have no possible right. One exception, and one only, have I ever come across to the contrary, and very careful inquiry can bring me knowledge of no other. That crest is the crest of a family of Buckworth, now represented by Sir Charles Buckworth-Herne-Soame, Bart. This family at the time of the Visitations exhibited a certain coat of arms and crest. The coat of arms, which doubtless interfered with the rights of some other family, was respited for further proof; but the crest, which did not, appears to have been allowed, and as nothing further was done with regard to the arms, the crest stood, whilst the arms were bad. But even this one exception has long since been rectified, for when the additional name and arms of Soame were assumed by Royal License the arms which had been exhibited and respited were (with the addition of an ermine spot as a charge upon the chevron) granted as the arms of Buckworth to be borne quarterly with the arms of Soame.

With the cessation of tournaments, we get to the period which some writers have stigmatised as that of "paper" heraldry. That is a reference to the fact that arms and crests ceased to be painted upon shields or erected upon helmets that enjoyed actual use in battle and tournament. Those who are so ready to decry modern heraldry forget that from its very earliest existence heraldry has always had the *same* significance as a symbol of rank and social position which it now enjoys and which remains undiminished in extent, though doubtless less potent in effect. They forget

also that from the very earliest period armory had three uses—viz. its martial use, its decorative use, and its use as a symbol of ownership. The two latter uses still remain in their entirety, and whilst that is the case, armory cannot be treated as a dead science.

But with the cessation of tournaments the decorative became the chief use of arms, and the crest soon ceased to have that distinctive adaptability to the purpose of a helmet ornament. Up to the end of the Tudor period crests had retained their original simplicity. Animals' heads and animals passant, human heads and demi-animals, comprised the large majority of the early crests. Scottish heraldry in a marked degree has retained the early simplicity of crests, though at the expense of lack of distinction between the crests of different families. German heraldry has to a large extent retained the same character as has Scottish armory, and though many of the crests are decidedly elaborated, it is noticeable that this elaboration is never such as to render the crest unsuitable for its true position upon a helmet.

In England this aspect of the crest has been almost entirely lost sight of, and the large proportion of the crests in modern English grants are utterly unsuitable for use in relief upon an actual helmet. Our present rules of position for a helmet, and our unfortunate stereotyped form of wreath, are largely to blame, but the chief reason is the definite English rule that the crests of separate English families must be differentiated as are the arms. No such rule holds good in Scotland, hence their simple crests.

Whether the rule is good or bad it is difficult to say. When all the pros and cons have been taken into consideration, the whole discussion remains a matter of opinion, and whilst one dislikes the Scottish idea under which the same identical crest can be and regularly is granted to half-a-dozen people of as many different surnames, one objects very considerably to the typical present-day crest of an English grant of arms. Whilst a collar can be put round an animal's neck, and whilst it can hold objects in its mouth or paws, it does seem ridiculous to put a string of varied and selected objects "in front" of it, when these plainly would only be visible from one side, or to put a crest "between" objects if these are to be represented "fore and aft," one toppling over the brow of the wearer of the helmet and the other hanging down behind.

The crests of the present day are the crying grievance of modern English heraldry, and though a large proportion are far greater abortions than they need be, and though careful thought and research even yet will sometimes result in the grant of at any rate a quite unobjectionable crest (see Figs. 330 and 394, both of which are quite modern grants), nevertheless we shall not obtain a real reform, or attain to any appreciable improvement, until the "position" rule as to helmets is abolished, or until the extreme differentiation insisted upon between crests is somewhat modified. Some of the crests mentioned hereunder are typical and awful examples of modern crests.

Crest of Bellasis of Marton, Westmoreland: A mount vert, thereon a lion couchant guardant azure, in front of a tent proper, lined gules.

Crest of Hermon of Preston, Lancashire, and Wyfold Court, Checkendon, Oxon.: In front of two palm-trees proper, a lion couchant guardant erminois, resting the dexter claw upon a bale of cotton proper. Motto: "Fido non timeo."

Crest of James Harrison, Esq., M.A., Barrister-at-Law: In front of a demi-lion rampant erased or, gorged with a collar gemelle azure, and holding between the paws a wreath of oak proper, three mascles interlaced also azure. Motto: "Pro rege et patria."

Crest of Colonel John Davis, F.S.A., of Bifrons, Hants: A lion's head erased sable, charged with a caltrap or, upon two swords in saltire proper, hilted and pommelled also or. Motto: "Ne tentes, aut perfice."

259

Crest of the late Sir Saul Samuel, Bart., K.C.M.G.: Upon a rock in front of three spears, one in pale and two in saltire, a wolf current sable, pierced in the breast by an arrow argent, flighted or. Motto: " A pledge of better times."

Crest of Johnson of Kennal Manor, Chislehurst, Kent: In front of a dexter arm embowed in armour proper, the hand also proper, grasping a javelin in bend sinister, pheoned or, and enfiled with a chaplet of roses gules, two branches of oak in saltire vert.

Crest of C. E. Lamplugh, Esq.: In front of a cubit arm erect proper, encircled about the wrist with a wreath of oak and holding in the hand a sword also proper, pommel and hilt or, an escutcheon argent, charged with a goat's head couped sable. Mottoes: " Through," and " Providentia Dei stabiliuntur familiæ."

Crest of Glasford, Scotland: Issuing from clouds two hands conjoined grasping a caduceus ensigned with a cap of liberty, all between two cornucopiæ all proper. Motto: " Prisca fides."

We now come to the subject of the inheritance of crests, concerning which there has been much difference of opinion.

It is very usually asserted that until a comparatively recent date crests were not hereditary, but were assumed, discarded, and changed at pleasure. Like many other incorrect statements, there is a certain modicum of truth in the statement, for no doubt whilst arms themselves had a more or less shifting character, crests were certainly not "fixed" to any greater extent.

But I think no one has as yet discovered, or at anyrate brought into notice, the true facts of the case, or the real position of the matter, and I think I am the first to put into print what actually were the rules which governed the matter. The rules, I believe, were undoubtedly these:—

Crests were, save in the remote beginning of things heraldic, definitely hereditary. They were hereditary even to the extent (and herein lies the point which has not hitherto been observed) that they were transmitted by an heiress. Perhaps this heritability was limited to those cases in which the heiress transmitted the *de facto* headship of her house. We, judging by present laws, look upon the crest as a part of the *one* heraldic achievement inseparable from the shield. What proof have we that in early times any necessary connection between arms and crest existed? We have none. The shield of arms was one inheritance, descending by known rules. The crest was another, but a separate inheritance, descending equally through an heir or coheir-general. The crest was, as an inheritance, as separate from the shield as were the estates then. The social conditions of life prevented the possibility of the existence or inheritance of a crest where arms did not exist. But a man inheriting several coats of arms from different heiress ancestresses could marshal them all upon one shield, and though we find the heir often made selection at his pleasure, and marshalled the arms in various orders, the determination of which was a mere matter of arbitrary choice, he could, if he wished, use them all upon one shield. But he had but one helmet, and could use and display but one crest. So that, if he had inherited two, he was forced to choose which he would use, though he sometimes tried to combine two into one device. It is questionable if an instance can be found in England of the regular display of two helmets and crests together, surmounting one shield, before the eighteenth century, but there are countless instances of the contemporary but separate display of two different crests, and the Visitation Records afford us some number of instances of this tacit acknowledgment of the inheritance of more than one crest.

The patent altering or granting the Mowbray crest seems to me clear recognition of the right of inheritance of a crest passing through an heir female. This, however, it must be admitted, may be really no more than a grant, and is not in itself actual evidence that any

crest had been previously borne. Fig. 699 would seem, however, to decide the point. My own opinion, however, is that it is fair presumptive evidence upon the point, and conveys an alteration and not a grant.

The grant or confirmation in question (Patent Roll 339, 17 Ric. II. pt. 1, memb. 2) is as follows: " P' Thoma Comite Marescallo 't Notyngh'. " R' Om'ibz ad quos 'tc' sal't'm. Sciatis q'd cum dil'c'us 't fidelis Consanguineus n'r Thomas Comes marescallus 't Notyngh' h'eat iustu' titulu' hereditatiuu' ad portand' p' cresta sua vnu' leopardum de auro cum vno labello albo qui de iure esset cresta filii n'ri primogeniti si quem procreassem'. Nos ea considerac'o'e concessim' p' nob' 't heredibz n'ris eidem Thome 't heredibz suis q'd ip'i p' differencia in ea p'te deferre possint 't deferant vnu leopardum 't in loco labelli vna' coronam de argento absqz impedimento n'ri vel heredu' n'ror sup'd'c'or'. In cuius 'tc. T. R. apud Westm. xii die Januar [17 Ric. II.]. P' br'e de priuato sigillo."

The translation of the foregoing is as follows: " The King to all to whom, &c., Greeting, Know that whereas our well-beloved and faithful kinsman, Thomas, Earl-Marshal and Earl of Nottingham, has a just hereditary title to bear for his crest a leopard or with a white label, which should be of right the crest of our eldest son if we had begotten a son. We, for this consideration, have granted for us and our heirs to the said Thomas and his heirs that for a difference in this crest they shall and may bear a leopard, and in place of a label a crown argent, without hindrance from us or our heirs aforesaid. —In witness, &c. Witness the King at Westminster, the 12th day of January [17 Ric. II.]. By writ of Privy Seal."

Cases will constantly be found in which the crests have been changed. I necessarily totally exclude from consideration crests which have been changed owing to specific grants, and also changes due to the discarding of crests which can be shown to have been borne without right. Changes in crests must also be disregarded where the differences in emblazonment are merely differences in varying designs of the same crest. Necessarily from none of these instances can a law of inheritance be deduced. But if other changes in the crests of important families be considered, I think it will be very evident that practically the whole of these are due to the inheritance through heiresses or ancestresses of an alternative crest. It can be readily shown that selection played an important part in the marshalling of quarterings upon an escutcheon, and where important quarterings were inherited they are as often as not found depicted in the first quarter. Thus the Howards have borne at different periods the wings of Howard; the horse of Fitzalan; and the Royal crest granted to the Mowbrays with remainder to the heir general; and these crests have been borne, as will be seen from the Garter plates, quite irrespective of what the surname in use may have been. Consequently it is very evident the crests were considered to be inherited with the representation of the different families. The Stourton crest was originally a stag's head, and is to be seen recorded in one of the Visitations, and upon the earliest seal in existence of any member of the family. But after the inheritance through the heiress of Le Moyne, the Le Moyne crest of the demi-monk was adopted. The Stanleys, Earls of Derby, whatever their original crest may have been, inherited the well-known bird and bantling of the family of Lathom. The Talbot crest was originally a talbot, and this is still so borne by Lord Talbot of Malahide: it was recorded at the Visitation of Dublin; but the crest at present borne by the Earls of Shrewsbury is derived from the arms inherited by descent from Gwendolin, daughter of Rhys ap Griffith.

THE ART OF HERALDRY

The Nevill crest was a bull's head as it is now borne by the Marquess of Abergavenny, and as it will be seen on the Garter plate of William Nevill, Lord Fauconberg. An elder brother of Lord Fauconberg had married the heiress of the Earl of Salisbury, and was summoned to Parliament in her earldom. He quartered her arms, which appear upon his Garter plate and seal, in the first and fourth quarters of his shield, and adopted her crest. A younger son of Sir Richard Nevill, Earl of Salisbury, bore the same crest differenced by two annulets conjoined, which was the difference mark added to the shield. The crest of Bourchier was a soldan's head crowned, and with a pointed cap issuing from the crown, but when the barony of Bourchier passed to the family of Robsart, as will be seen from the Garter plate of Sir Lewis Robsart, Lord Bourchier, the crest of Bourchier was adopted with the inheritance of the arms and Barony of Bourchier.

I am aware of no important case in English heraldry where the change has been due to mere caprice, and it would seem therefore an almost incontrovertible assertion that changes were due to inheritance, and if that can be established it follows even more strongly that until the days when armory was brought under rigid and official control, and even until a much later date, say up to the beginning of the Stuart period, crests were heritable through heiresses equally with quarterings. The fact that we find comparatively few changes considering the number of crests in existence is by no means a refutation of this theory, because a man had but one helmet, and was forced therefore to make a selection. Unless, therefore, he had a very strong inclination it would be more likely that he would select the crest he was used to than a fresh one. I am by no means certain that to a limited extent the German idea did not hold in England. This was, and is, that the crest had not the same personal character that was the case with the arms, but was rather attached to or an appanage of the territorial fief or lordship. By the time of the Restoration any idea of the transmission of crests through heiresses had been abandoned. We then find a Royal License necessary for the assumption of arms and crests. Since that date and at the present time it is stringently held, and is the official rule, that no woman can bear or inherit a crest, and that no woman can transmit a right to one. Whilst that is the official and accepted interpretation of heraldic law upon the point, and whilst it cannot now be gainsaid, it cannot, however, be stated that the one assertion is the logical deduction of the other, for whilst a woman cannot inherit a lordship of Parliament, she undoubtedly can transmit one, together with the titular honours, the enjoyment of which is not denied to her.

In Scotland crests have always had a very much less important position than in England. There has been little if any continuity with regard to them, and instances of changes for which caprice would appear to be the only reason are met with in the cases of a large proportion of the chief families in that kingdom. To such a widespread extent has the permissive character been allowed to the crest, that many cases will be found in which each successive matriculation for the head of the house, or for a cadet, has produced a change in the crest, and instances are to be found where the different crests are the only existing differences in the achievements of a number of cadets of the same family. At the present time, little if any objection is ever made to an entire and radical change in the crest—if this is wished at the time of a rematriculation—and as far as I can gather such changes appear to have always been permitted. Perhaps it may be well here to point out that this is not equivalent to

permission to change the crest at pleasure, because the patent of matriculation until it is superseded by another is the authority, and the compulsory authority, for the crest which is to be borne. In Germany the crest has an infinitely greater importance than is the case with ourselves, but it is there considered in a large degree a territorial appanage, and it is by no means unusual in a German achievement to see several crests surmounting a single coat of arms. In England the Royal coat of arms has three crests, which, it may be noted, are all in a manner territorial; but the difference of idea with which crests are regarded in Germany may be gathered from the fact that the King of Saxony has five, the Grand Duke of Mecklenburg-Schwerin five, the Grand Duke of Saxe-Meiningen six, the Grand Duke of Saxe-Altenburg seven, the Duke of Anhalt seven, the Duke of Saxe-Coburg and Gotha six, the Prince of Schwartzburg-Sondershausen six, the Prince of Schwartzburg-Rudolstadt six, the Prince of Waldeck-Pyrmont five, the Prince of Lippe five, the Duke of Brunswick five, and instances can be quoted of sixteen and seventeen. Probably Woodward is correct when he says that each crest formerly denoted a noble fief, for which the proprietor had a right to vote in the "circles" of the Empire, and he instances the Margraves of Bradenburg-Anspach, who were entitled to no less than thirteen crests. In France the use of crests is not nearly so general as in England or Germany. In Spain and Portugal it is less frequent still, and in Italy the use of the crest is the exception.

The German practice of using horns on either side of the crest, which the ignorance of English heralds has transformed into the proboscides of elephants, is dealt with at some length on page 152. The horns, which are termed buffalo's or bull's horns until the middle of the thirteenth century, were short and thick-set. It is difficult to say at what date these figures came to be considered as heraldic *crests*, for as mere helmet ornaments they probably can be traced back very far beyond any proof of the existence of armory. In the fourteenth century we find the horns curved inwards like a sickle

Fig. 700.—From the back of the mint seal of King Christopher II. of Denmark, 1321.

(Fig. 700), but later the horns are found more erect, the points turning outwards, slimmer in shape, and finally they exhibit a decidedly marked double curve. Then the ends of the horns are met with open, like a trumpet, the fact which gave rise to the erroneous idea that they represented elephant's tusks. The horns became ornamented with feathers, banners, branches of leaves, balls, &c., and the orifices garnished with similar adornments.

In England, crests are theoretically subject to marks of cadency and difference. This is not the case, however, in any other country. In Germany, in cases where the crests reproduce the arms, any mark of cadency with which the arms are distinguished will of

261

course be repeated; but in German heraldry, doubtless owing to the territorial nature of the crest, a change in the crest itself is often the only mark of distinction

FIG. 701.—Arms of the family of Schaler (Basle): Gules, a bend of lozenges argent. (From the Zürich Roll of Arms.)

between different branches of the same family, and in Siebmacher's *Wappenbuch* thirty-one different branches of the Zorn family have different crests, which are the sole marks of difference in the achievements.

But though British crests are presumed to be subject to the recognised marks of cadency, as a matter of fact it is very seldom indeed that they are ever so marked, with the exception that the mark used (usually a cross crosslet) to signify the lack of blood relationship, when arms are assumed under a Royal License, is compulsory. Marks of distinction added to signify illegitimacy are also compulsory and perpetual. What these marks are will be dealt with in a subsequent chapter upon the subject. How very seldom a mark of difference is added to a crest may be gathered from the fact that with the exception of labels, chiefly upon the Royal crest, one crest only amongst the Plantagenet Garter plates is differenced, that one being the crest of John Neville, Lord Montague. Several crests, however, which are not Royal, are differenced by similar labels to those which appear upon the shields; but when we find that the difference marks have very much of a permissive character, even upon the shield, it is not likely that they are perpetuated upon the crest, where they are even less desirable. The arms of Cokayne, as given in the funeral certificate of Sir William Cokayne, Lord Mayor of London, show upon the shield three crescents, sable, or, and gules, charged one upon the other, the Lord Mayor being the second son of a second son of Cokayne of Sturston, descending from William, second son of Sir John Cokayne of Ashborne. But, in spite of the fact that three difference marks are charged upon the shield (one of the quarterings of which, by the way, has an additional mark), the crest itself is only differenced by one crescent. These difference marks, as applied to arms, are in England (the rules in Scotland are utterly distinct) practically permissive, and are never enforced against the wish of the bearer except in one circumstance. If, owing to the grant of a crest or supporters, or a Royal License, or any similar opportunity, a formal exemplification of the arms is entered on the books of the College of Arms, the opportunity is generally taken to add such mark of cadency as may be necessary; and no certificate would be officially issued to any one claiming arms through that exemplification except subject to the mark of cadency therein depicted. In such cases as these the crest is usually differenced, because the necessity for an exemplification does not often occur, except owing to

the establishment of an important branch of the family, which is likely to continue as a separate house in the future, and possibly to rival the importance of the chief of the name. Two examples will show my meaning. The crest of the Duke of Bedford is a goat statant argent, armed or. When Earl Russell, the third son of the sixth Duke of Bedford, was so created, the arms, crest, and supporters were charged with a mullet argent. When the first Lord Ampthill, who was the third son of the father of the ninth Duke of Bedford, was so created, the arms of Russell, with the crest and supporters, were charged with mullets, these being of different tinctures from those granted to Earl Russell. The crest of the Duke of Westminster is a talbot statant or. The first Lord Stalbridge was the second son of the Marquess of Westminster. His arms, crest, and supporters were charged with a crescent. Lord Ebury was the third son of the first Marquess of Westminster. His arms, crest, and supporters were charged with a mullet. In cases of this kind the mark of difference upon the crest would be considered permanent; but for ordinary purposes, and in ordinary circumstances, the rule may be taken to be that it is not necessary to add the mark of cadency to a crest, even when it is added to the shield, but that, at the same time, it is not incorrect to do so.

Crests must nowadays always be depicted upon either a wreath, coronet, or chapeau; but these, and the rules concerning them, will be considered in a more definite and detailed manner in the separate chapters in which those objects are discussed.

Crests are nowadays very frequently used upon livery buttons. Such a usage is discussed at some length in the chapter on badges.

When two or more crests are depicted together, and when, as is often the case in England, the wreaths are depicted in space, and without the intervening helmets, the crests always all face to the dexter side, and the stereotyped character of English crests, perhaps more than any other reason, has led of late to the depicting of English helmets all placed to face in the same direction to the dexter side. But if, as will often be found, the two helmets are turned to face each other, the crests also must be turned.

Where there are two crests, the one on the dexter side is the first, and the one on the sinister side is the second. When there are three, the centre one comes first, then the one on the dexter side, then the one on the sinister. When there are four crests, the first one is the dexter of the two inner ones; the second is the sinister inner one; the third is the dexter outer, and the fourth the sinister outer. When there are five (and I know of no greater number in this country), they run as follows: (1) centre, (2) dexter inner, (3) sinister inner, (4) dexter outer, (5) sinister outer.

A very usual practice in official emblazonments in cases of three crests is to paint the centre one of a larger size, and at a slightly lower level, than the others. In the case of four, Nos. 1 and 2 would be of the same size, Nos. 3 and 4 slightly smaller, and slightly raised.

It is a very usual circumstance to see two or more crests displayed in England, but this practice is of comparatively recent date. How recent may be gathered from the fact that in Scotland no single instance can be found before the year 1809 in which two crests are placed above the same shield. Scottish heraldry, however, has always been purer than English, and the practice in England is much more ancient, though I question if in England any authentic official exemplification can be found before 1700. There are, however, many cases in the Visitation Books in which two crests are allowed to the same family, but this fact does not prove the point, because a Visitation record is merely an official record of inheritance and possession, and not necessarily evidence of a regulation permitting the simultaneous display of more than one. It is of course impossible to use two sets of supporters with a single shield, but there are many peers who are entitled to two sets; Lord Ancaster, I believe, is entitled to three sets. But an official record in such a case would probably emblazon both sets as evidence of right, by painting the shield twice over.

During the eighteenth century we find many instances of the grant of additional crests of augmentation, and many exemplifications under Royal License for the use of two and three crests. Since that day the correctness of duplicate crests has never been questioned, where the right of inheritance to them has been established. The right of inheritance to two or more crests at the present time is only officially allowed in the following cases.

If a family at the time of the Visitations had two crests recorded to them, these would be now allowed. If descent can be proved from a family to whom a certain crest was allowed, and also from ancestors at an earlier date who are recorded as entitled to bear a different crest, the two would be allowed unless it was evident that the later crest had been granted, assigned, or exemplified *in lieu* of the earlier one. Two crests are allowed in the few cases which exist where a family has obtained a grant of arms in ignorance of the fact that they were then entitled to bear arms and crest of an earlier date to which the right has been subsequently proved, but on this point it should be remarked that if a right to arms is known to exist a second grant in England is point-blank refused unless the petition asks for it to be borne instead of, and in lieu of, the earlier one: it is then granted in those terms.

To those who think that the Heralds' College is a mere fee-grabbing institution, the following experience of an intimate friend of mine may be of interest. In placing his pedigree upon record it became evident that his descent was not legitimate, and he therefore petitioned for and obtained a Royal License to bear the name and arms of the family from which he had sprung. But the illegitimacy was not modern, and no one would have questioned his right to the name which all the other members of the family bear, if he had not himself raised the point in order to obtain the ancient arms in the necessarily differenced form. The arms had always been borne with some four or five quarterings and with two crests, and he was rather annoyed that he had to go back to a simple coat of arms and single crest. He obtained a grant for his wife, who was an heiress, and then, with the idea of obtaining an additional quartering and a second crest, he conceived the brilliant idea—for money was of no object to him—of putting his brother forward as a petitioner for arms to be granted to him and his descendants and to the other descendants of his father, a grant which would of course have brought in my friend. He moved heaven and earth to bring this about, but he was met with the direct statement that two grants of arms could not be made to the same man to be borne simultaneously, and that if he persisted in the grant of arms to his brother, his own name, as being then entitled to bear arms, would be specifically exempted from the later grant, and the result was that this second grant was never made.

In Scotland, where re-matriculation is constantly going on, two separate matriculations *to the same line* would not confer the right to two crests, inasmuch as the last matriculation supersedes everything which has preceded it. But if a cadet matriculates a different crest, *and subsequently* succeeds to the representation under an earlier matriculation, he legally succeeds to both crests,

and incidentally to both coats of arms. As a matter of ordinary practice, the cadet matriculation is discarded. A curious case, however, occurs when after matriculation by a cadet there is a *later* matriculation behind it, by some one nearer the head of the house to which the first-mentioned cadet succeeds; in such an event selection must be brought into play, when succession to both occurs. But the selection lies only between the two patents, and not from varied constituent parts.

Where as an augmentation an additional crest is granted, as has been the case in many instances, of course a right to the double crest is thereby conferred, and a crest of augmentation is not granted in lieu, but in addition.

A large number of these additional crests have been granted under specific warrants from the Crown, and in the case of Lord Gough, two additional crests were granted as separate augmentations and under separate patents. Lord Kitchener recently received a grant of an additional crest of augmentation.

The other cases in which double and treble crests occur are the results of exemplifications following upon Royal Licences to assume name and arms. As a rule, when an additional surname is adopted by Royal License, the rule is that the arms adopted are to be borne in addition to those previously in existence; and where a name is adopted instead of another the warrant very frequently permits this, and at the same time permits or requires the new arms to be borne quarterly with those previously possessed, and gives the right to two crests. But in cases where names and arms are assumed by Royal License the arms and crest or crests are in accordance with the patent of exemplification, which, no matter what its terms (for some do not expressly exclude any prior rights), is always presumed to super-

Fig. 702.—Arms of the late Rev. Andrew Wallis Milroy, M.A.: Per fess, in chief chequy or and vert, in base gules, the latter charged with a lion rampant argent, on a canton of the fourth a rose of the third, barbed of the second, and on an escutcheon of pretence the arms of Rosher, namely: quarterly, 1 and 4, per chevron engrailed ermine and erminois, three crosses patée azure, each charged with an estoile or (for Rosher); 2 and 3, per pale gules and azure, a fess ermine between two fleurs-de-lis in chief argent and a serpent erect in base or (for Burch); and for his crests, 1. upon a wreath of the liveries, an ostrich proper, with the motto, "Espérance" (for Milroy); 2. upon a wreath of the liveries, an elephant's head couped ermine, between two elephants' probosces or, with the motto, "Consider the end" (for Rosher).

sede everything which has gone before, and to be the authority by which the subsequent bearing of arms is regularised and controlled. Roughly speaking, under a Royal License one generally gets the right to one crest for every surname, and if the original surname be discarded in addition a crest for every previous surname. Thus Mainwaring-Ellerker-Onslow (Fig. 686) has three crests, Wyndham-Campbell-Pleydell-Bouverie has four, and the last Duke of Buckingham and Chandos, who held the record, had one for each of his surnames, namely, Temple-Nugent-Brydges-Chandos-Grenville. In addition to the foregoing, there are one or two exceptions which it is difficult to explain. The Marquess of Bute for some reason or other obtained a grant, in the year 1822, of the crest of Herbert. The late Lord Liverpool obtained a grant of an additional crest, possibly an augmentation, and his present representative, Lord Hawkesbury, for some reason or other which I am quite at a loss to understand, obtained a grant of a crest very similar to that of Lord Liverpool to commemorate the representation which had devolved upon him. Sir

Charles Young, Garter King of Arms, obtained the grant of a second crest, and a former Marquess of Camden did the same thing; Lord Swansea is another recent case, and though the right of any person to obtain the grant of a second crest is not officially admitted, and is in fact strenuously denied, I cannot for the life of me see how in the face of the foregoing precedents any such privilege can be denied. Sir William Woods also obtained the grant of a second crest when he was Garter, oblivious of the fact that he had not really established a right to arms. Those he used were certainly granted in Lyon Office to a relative, but no matriculation of them in his own name was ever registered. Another instance of the possession of two crests is the case of Milroy (Fig. 700), but this is a result of a Scottish matriculation. A. C. F-D.

CHAPTER XXVI

CROWNS AND CORONETS

THE origin of the crown or coronet is, of course, to be met with in the diadem and fillet. In one of the Cantor Lectures delivered by Mr. Cyril Davenport, F.S.A., in February 1902, on "The History of Personal Jewellery from Prehistoric Times," he devoted considerable attention to the development of the diadem, and the following extracts are from the printed report of his lecture :—

"The bandeau or fillet tied round the head was probably first used to keep long hair from getting into the eyes of primitive man. Presently it became specialised, priests wearing one pattern and fighting men another.

"The soft band which can be seen figured on the heads of kings in early coins, is no doubt a mark of chieftainship. This use of a band, of special colour, to indicate authority, probably originated in the East. It was adopted by Alexander the Great, who also used the diadem of the King of Persia. Justinian says that Alexander's predecessors did not wear any diadem. Justinian also tells us that the diadems then worn were of some soft material, as in describing the accidental wounding of Lysimachus by Alexander, he says that the hurt was bound up by Alexander *with his own diadem.* This was considered a lucky omen for Lysimachus, who actually did shortly afterwards become King of Thrace.

"In Egypt diadems of particular shape are of very ancient use. There were crowns for Upper and Lower Egypt, and a combination of both for the whole country. They were also distinguished by colour. The Uraeus or snake worn in the crowns and head-dresses of the Pharaohs was a symbol of royalty. Representations of the Egyptian gods always show them as wearing crowns.

"In Assyrian sculptures deities and kings are shown wearing diadems, apparently bands of stuff or leather studded with discs of *repoussé* work. Some of these discs, detached, have actually been found. Similar discs were plentifully found at Mycenæ, which were very likely used in a similar way. Some of the larger ornamental head-dresses worn by Assyrian kings appear to have been conical-shaped helmets, or perhaps crowns; it is now difficult to say which, because the material of which they were made cannot be ascertained. If they were of gold, they were probably crowns, like the

wonderful openwork golden Scythian headdress found at Kertch, but if of an inferior metal they may have been only helmets.

"At St. Petersburg there is a beautiful ancient Greek diadem representing a crown of olive. An Etruscan ivy wreath of thin gold still encircling a bronze helmet, is in the British Museum.

"Justinian says that Morimus tried to hang himself with the diadem, evidently a ribbon-like bandeau, sent to him by Mithridates. The Roman royal diadem was originally a white ribbon, a wreath of laurel was the reward of distinguished citizens, while a circlet of golden leaves was given to successful generals.

"Cæsar consistently refused the royal white diadem which Antony offered him, preferring to remain perpetual dictator. One of his partisans ventured to crown Cæsar's bust with a coronet of laurel tied with royal white ribbon, but the tribunes quickly removed it and heavily punished the perpetrator of the offence.

"During the Roman Empire the prejudice against the white bandeau remained strong. The emperors dared not wear it. Caligula wished to do so, but was dissuaded on being told that such proceeding might cost his life. Eliogabalus used to wear a diadem studded with precious stones, but it is not supposed to have indicated rank, but only to have been a rich lady's parure, this emperor being fond of dressing himself up as a woman. Caracalla, who took Alexandra the Great as his model as far as possible, is shown on some of his coins wearing a diadem of a double row of pearls, a similar design to which was used by the kings of Parthia. On coins of Diocletian, there shows a double row of pearls, sewn on a double band and tied in a knot at the back.

"Diadems gradually closed in and became crowns, and on Byzantine coins highly ornate diadems can be recognised, and there are many beautiful representations of them in enamels and mosaics, as well as a few actual specimens. At Ravenna, in mosaic work in the church of San Vitale, are crowned portraits of Justinian and his Empress Theodosia; in the enamel portrait of the Empress Irene in the Pal d'Oro at Venice, can be seen a beautiful jewelled crown with hinged plaques, and the same construction is used on the iron crown of Lombardy; the sacred crown of Hungary, and the crown of

Charlemagne, all most beautiul specimens of jewellers' work.

"On the plaques of the crown of Constantine Monomachos are also fine enamel portraits of himself and his queen Zoë, wearing similar crowns. The cataseistas, or jewelled chains, one over each ear and one at the back, which occur on all these crowns, may be the survival of the loose ends of the tie of the original fillet.

"In later times of Greece and Rome, owing to the growth of republican feeling the diadem lost its political significance, and was relegated to the ladies.

"In the middle ages the diadem regained much of its earlier significance, and ceased to be only the simple head ornament it had become. Now it became specialised in form, reserved as an emblem of rank. The forms of royal crowns and diadems is a large and fascinating study, and where original examples do not now exist, the development can often be followed in sculpture, coins, or seals. Heraldry now plays an important part. Diadems or circlets gradually give way to closed crowns, in the case of sovereigns possessing independent authority."

But to pass to the crown proper, there is no doubt that from the earliest times of recorded history crowns have been a sign and emblem of sovereignty. It equally admits of no doubt that the use of a crown or coronet was by no means exclusive to a sovereign, but whilst our knowledge is somewhat curtailed as to the exact relation in which great overlords and nobles stood to their sovereign, it is difficult to draw with any certainty or exactitude definitive conclusions of the symbolism a crown or coronet conveyed. Throughout Europe in the eleventh, twelfth, and thirteenth, and well into the fourteenth centuries, the great territorial lords enjoyed and exercised many—in fact most—of the attributes of sovereignty, and in England especially, where the king was no more than the first amongst his peers, the territorial earls were in much the position of petty sovereigns. It is only natural, therefore, that we should find them using this emblem of sovereignty. But what we do find in England is that a coronet or fillet was used, apparently without let or hindrance, by even knights. It is, however, a matter for thought as to whether many of these fillets were not simply the turban or "puggaree" folded into the shape of a fillet, but capable of being unrolled if desired. What the object of the wholesale wearing of crowns and coronets was, it is difficult to conjecture.

The development of the crown of the English sovereigns has been best told by Mr. Cyril Davenport in his valuable work on "The English Regalia" (Kegan Paul, Trench, Trübner & Co.). Mr. Davenport, whose knowledge on these matters is probably unequalled, may best be allowed to tell the story in his own words, he and his publishers having very kindly permitted this course to be taken:—

THE CROWN OF GREAT BRITAIN

By Cyril Davenport, F.S.A.

"Crowns appear to have been at an early period worn by kings in battle, in order that they might be easily recognised; and although it is quite possible that this outward sign of sovereignty may have marked the wearer as being entitled to special protection by his own men, it is also likely that it was often a dangerous sign of importance. Upon the authority of their coins, the heads of the early British kings were adorned with variously formed fillets and ornamental wreaths. Helmets are also evidently intended to be shown, and on some of the coins of Athelstan the helmet bears

upon it a crown of three raised points, with a single pearl at the top of each (Fig. 703). Other coins bear the crown with the three raised points without the helmet (Fig. 704). This crown of three points, bearing sometimes one and sometimes three pearls at the top of each, continued to be used by all the sole monarchs until Canute, on whose head a crown is shown in which the three points develop into three clearly-marked trefoils (Fig. 705). On the great seal of Edward the

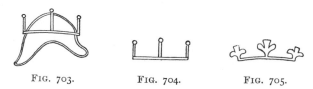

FIG. 703.   FIG. 704.   FIG. 705.

Confessor the king is wearing an ornamental cap, which is described by Mr. Wyon in his book about the Great Seals as bearing a crown with three points trefoiled; but the impressions of this Great Seal that I have been able to see are so indistinct in this particular that I do not feel justified in corroborating his opinion. On some of the coins, however, of Edward the Confessor, an arched crown is very clearly shown, and this crown has depending from it, on each side, tassels with ornamental ends (Fig. 706).

"In the list of the English regalia which were destroyed under the Commonwealth in 1649 is found an item of great interest, viz. "a gold wyer work crown with little bells," which is there stated to have belonged to King Alfred, who appears to have been the

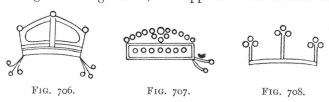

FIG. 706.   FIG. 707.   FIG. 708.

first English king for whom the ceremony of coronation was used; and it is remarkable that on several of the crowns on coins and seals, from the time of Edward the Confessor until Henry I., little tassels or tags are shown which may indeed represent little bells suspended by a ribbon.

"On King Alfred's own coins there is unfortunately nothing which can be recognised as a crown.

"On the coins of Henry II. a crown is shown with arches, apparently intended to be jewelled, as is also the rim. There are also tassels with ornamental ends at the back of the crown (Fig. 707).

"William I. on his Great Seal wears a crown with three points, at the top of each of which are three pearls (Fig. 708), and on some of his coins a more ornamental form

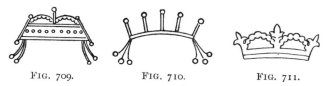

FIG. 709.   FIG. 710.   FIG. 711.

of crown occurs having a broad jewelled rim and two arches, also apparently jewelled, and at each side are two pendants with pearl ends (Fig. 709). William II. on his Great Seal has a crown with five points (Fig. 710), the centre one being slightly bigger than the others, and at the top of each a single pearl. At each side of the crown are pendants having three pearls at the ends.

"On some of the coins of Stephen a pretty form of crown is seen. It has three fleurs-de-lis and two jewelled arches (Fig. 711). The arches disappear from this time until the reign of Edward IV. On the Great Seal of Henry I. the king wears a simple crown with three fleurs-de-lis points, and two pendants each with three pearls at the ends (Fig. 712), and after this the pendants seem to have been discontinued.

"On the first Great Seal of Henry III. a crown with three fleurs-de-lis is shown surmounting a barred helmet (Fig. 713), and Edward I. wore a similar crown with three fleurs-de-lis, but having supplementary pearls between each (Fig. 714), and this form lasted for a long time, as

FIG. 712.   FIG. 713.   FIG. 714.

modifications of it are found on the coins of all the kings till Henry VII. On the third Great Seal of Edward IV. the king wears a crown with five fleurs-de-lis, the centre one being larger than the others, and the crown is arched and has at the top an orb and cross (Fig. 715). Henry VI. on his first seal for foreign affairs, on which occurs the English shield, uses above it a crown with three crosses-patée and between each a pearl (Fig. 716), this being the first distinct use of the cross-patée on the English crown; and it probably was used here in place of the fleurs-de-lis hitherto worn in order to make a clear distinction between it and the French crown, which has the fleurs-de-lis only and surmounts the coat of arms of that country. The king

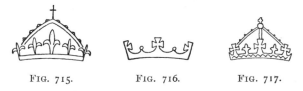

FIG. 715.   FIG. 716.   FIG. 717.

himself wears an arched crown, but the impressions are so bad that the details of it cannot be followed.

"Henry VII. on his Great Seal uses, as ornaments for the crown, crosses-patée alternately with fleurs-de-lis, and also arches with an orb and cross at the top (Fig. 717), and, on some of his coins, he reverts to the three fleurs-de-lis with points between them, arches being still used, with the orb and cross at the top (Fig. 718). An ornamental form of crown bearing five ornamental leaves alternately large and small, with arches, orb, and cross at the top (Fig. 719), occurs on the shillings of Henry VII. On the crowns of Henry VIII., as well as upon his Great Seals, the alternate crosses-patée and

FIG. 718.   FIG. 719.

fleurs-de-lis are found on the rim of the crown, which is arched, and has an orb and cross at the top, and this is the form that has remained ever since (Fig. 720). So we may consider that the growth of the ornament on the rim of the crown has followed a regular sequence from the points with one pearl at the top, of Æthelstan, to the trefoil of Canute; the arches began with Edward the Confessor, and the centre trefoil turned into the cross-patée of Henry VI. The fact that the remaining trefoils turned eventually into fleurs-de-lis is only, I

think, a natural expansion of form, and does not appear to have had anything to do with the French fleur-de-lis, which was adopted as an heraldic bearing for an entirely different reason. The Royal coat of arms of England did bear for a long time in one of its quarterings the actual fleurs-de-lis of France, and this, no doubt, has given some reason to the idea that the fleurs-de-lis on the crown had also something to do with France; but as a matter of fact they had existed on the crown of England long anterior to our use of them on the coat of arms, as well as remaining there subsequently to their discontinuance on our Royal escutcheon.

"The cross-patée itself may possibly have been evolved in a somewhat similar way from the three pearls of William I., as we often find the centre trefoil, into which, as we have seen, these three points eventually turned, has a tendency to become larger than the others, and this difference has been easily made more apparent by squaring the ends of the triple leaf. At the same time it must not be forgotten that the cross-patée was actually used on the sceptre of Edward the

FIG. 720.   FIG. 721.   FIG. 722.

Confessor, so it is just possible it may have had some specially English significance.

"I have already mentioned that as well as the official crown of England, which alone I have just been describing, there has often been a second or State crown, and this, although it has in general design followed the pattern of the official crown, has been much more elaborately ornamented, and in it has been set and reset the few historic gems possessed by our nation. The fact that these State crowns have in turn been denuded of their jewels accounts for the fact that the old settings of some of them still exist.

"Charles II.'s State Crown is figured in Sir Edward Walker's account of his coronation, but the illustration

FIG. 723.   FIG. 724.

of it is of such an elementary character that little reliance can be placed on it; the actual setting of this crown, however—which was the one stolen by Colonel Blood on May 13, 1671—is now the property of Lord Amherst of Hackney, and the spaces from which the great ruby and the large sapphire—both of which are now in King Edward's State Crown—have been taken are clearly seen (Fig. 721). James II.'s State Crown, which is very accurately figured in Sandford's account of his coronation, and pieces of which are still in the Tower, also had this great ruby as its centre ornament (Fig. 722). In Sir George Nayler's account of the coronation of George IV. there is a figure of his so-called "new crown," the arches of which are composed of oak-leaf sprays with acorns, and the rim adorned with laurel sprays (Fig. 723). The setting of this crown also belongs to Lord Amherst of Hackney, and so does another setting of a small State queen's crown, the ownership of which is doubtful. William IV. appears to have had a very beautiful State crown, with arches of laurel sprays and a cross at the top with large diamonds. It is figured in Robson's 'British Herald,' published in 1830 (Fig. 724).

"There is one other crown of great interest, which, since the time of James Sixth of Scotland and First of England, forms part of our regalia. This is the crown of Scotland, and is the most ancient piece of State jewellery of which we can boast.

"Edward I., after his defeat of John Baliol in 1296, carried off the crown of Scotland to England, and Robert Bruce had another made for himself. This in its turn, after Bruce's defeat at Methven, fell into Edward's hands. Another crown seems to have been made for Bruce in 1314, when he was established in the sovereignty of Scotland after Bannockburn, and the present crown probably consists largely of the material of the old one, and most likely follows its general design. It has, however, much French work about it, as well as the rougher gold work made by Scottish jewellers, and it seems probable that the crown, as it now is, is a reconstruction by French workmen, made under the care and by order of James V. about 1540. It was with this crown that Queen Mary was crowned when she was nine months old.

"In 1661 the Scottish regalia were considered to be in danger from the English, and were sent to Dunottar Castle for safety. From 1707 until 1818 they were locked up in a strong chest in the Crown-Room of Edinburgh Castle, and Sir Walter Scott, in whose presence the box was opened, wrote an account of them in 1810. The crown consists of a fillet of gold bordered with flat wire. Upon it are twenty-two large stones set at equal distances, i.e. nine carbuncles, four jacinths, four amethysts, two white topazes, two crystals with green foil behind them, and one topaz with yellow foil. Behind each of these gems is a gold plate, with bands above and below of white enamel with black spots, and between each stone is a pearl. Above the band are ten jewelled rosettes and ten fleurs-de-lis alternately, and between each a pearl. Under the rosettes and fleurs-de-lis are jewels of blue enamel and pearls alternately.

FIG. 725.

The arches have enamelled leaves of French work in red and gold upon them, and the mount at the top is of blue enamel studded with gold stars. The cross at the top is black enamel with gold arabesque patterns; in the centre is an amethyst, and in this cross and in the corners are Oriental pearls set in gold. At the back of the cross are the letters I. R. V. in enamel-work. On the velvet cap are four large pearls in settings of gold and enamel (Fig. 725).

"Generally, the Scottish work in gold is cast solid and chased, the foreign work being thinner and repoussé. Several of the diamonds are undoubtedly old, and are cut in the ancient Oriental fashion; and many of the pearls are Scottish. It is kept in Edinburgh Castle with the rest of the Scottish regalia. None of the other pieces at all equal it in interest, as with the exception of the coronation ring of Charles I. they are of foreign workmanship, or, at all events, have been so altered that there is little or no original work left upon them."

Very few people are aware, when they speak of the crown of England, that there are two crowns. The one is the official crown, the sign and symbol of the sovereigns of England. This is known by the name of St. Edward's Crown, and is never altered or changed. As to this Mr. Cyril Davenport writes:—

"St. Edward's Crown was made for the coronation of

Charles II. in 1662, by Sir Robert Vyner. It was ordered to be made as nearly as possible after the old pattern, and the designs of it that have been already mentioned as existing in the works of Sir Edward Walker and Francis Sandford show that in a sensual form it was the same as now; indeed, the existing crown is in all probability mainly composed of the same materials as that made by Sir Robert. The crown consists of a rim or circlet of gold, adorned with rosettes of precious stones surrounded with diamonds, and set upon enamel arabesques of white and red. The centre gems of these rosettes are rubies, emeralds, and sapphires. Rows of large pearls mark the upper and lower edges of the rim, from which rise the four crosses-patée and four fleurs-de-lis alternately, adorned with diamonds and other gems. The gem clusters upon the crosses are set upon enamel arabesques in white and red, of similar workmanship to that upon the rim. From the tops of the crosses rise two complete arches of gold crossing each other, and curving deeply downwards at the point of intersection. The arches are considered to be the mark of independent sovereignty. They are edged with rows of large pearls, and have gems and clusters of gems upon them set in arabesques of red and white, like those upon the crosses. From the intersection of the arches springs a mound of gold, encircled by a fillet from which rises a single arch, both of which are ornamented with pearls and gems. On the top of the arch is a cross-patée of gold, set in which are coloured gems and diamonds. At the top of the cross is a large spheroidal pearl, and from each of the side arms, depending from a little gold bracelet, is a beautifully formed pear-shaped pearl. The crown is shown in the Tower with the crimson velvet cap, turned up with miniver, which would be worn with it.

"This crown is very large, but whether it is actually worn or not it would always be present at the coronation, as it is the 'official' crown of England."

St. Edward's Crown will be found represented on Plate XV. Fig. 10, but it should be noticed that this illustration does not show the pearl which surmounts the orb upon the cross, nor the two smaller pearls which depend from the arms of the cross.

St. Edward's Crown is the crown supposed to be heraldically represented when for State or official purposes the crown is represented over the Royal Arms or other insignia. In this, it will be noticed, the fleurs-de-lis upon the rim are only half fleurs-de-lis. This detail is scrupulously adhered to, but during the reign of Queen Victoria many of the other details were very much "at the mercy" of the artist. Soon after the accession of King Edward VII. the matter was brought under consideration, and the opportunity afforded by the issue of a War Office Sealed Pattern of the Royal Crown and Cypher for use in the army was taken advantage of to notify his Majesty's pleasure, that for official purposes the Royal Crown should be as shown in Fig. 726, which is a reproduction of the War Office Sealed Pattern already mentioned. It should be noted that whilst the cap of the real crown is of purple velvet, the cap of the heraldic crown is always represented as of crimson.

The second Crown is what is known as the "Imperial State Crown." This is the one which is actually worn, and which the Sovereign after the ceremony of his coronation wears in the procession from the Abbey. It is also carried before the Sovereign at the opening of Parliament. Whilst the gems which are set in it are national property, the crown is usually remade for each successive sovereign. The following is Mr. Davenport's description of Queen Victoria's State Crown, which is illustrated on Plate LII. Fig. 11:—

THE ART OF HERALDRY

"This beautiful piece of jewellery was made by Roundell & Bridge in 1838. Many of the gems in it are old ones reset, and many of them are new. The entire weight of the crown is 39 ozs. 5 dwts. It consists of a circlet of open work in silver, bearing in the front the great sapphire from the crown of Charles II. which was bequeathed to George III. by Cardinal York, with other Stuart treasure. At one end this gem is partly pierced. It is not a thick stone, but it is a fine colour.

points of emeralds encircled with diamonds, and a large pearl above each. On these festoons are set alternately eight crosses-patée, and eight fleurs-de-lis of silver set with gems. The crosses-patée are thickly set with brilliants, and have each an emerald in the centre, except that in front of the crown, which contains the most remarkable jewel belonging to the regalia. This is a large spinal ruby of irregular drop-like form, measuring about 2 ins. in length, and is highly polished

FIG. 726.—The New Royal Cypher. (From a War Office sealed pattern.)

Opposite to the large sapphire is one of smaller size. The remainder of the rim is filled in with rich jewel clusters having alternately sapphires and emeralds in their centres, enclosed in ornamental borders thickly set with diamonds. These clusters are separated from each other by trefoil designs also thickly set with diamonds. The rim is bordered above and below with bands of large pearls, 129 in the lower row, and 112 in the upper. [The crown as remade for King Edward VII. now has 139 pearls in the lower row, and 122 in the upper.] Above the rim are shallow festoons of diamonds caught up between the larger ornaments by

on what is probably its natural surface, or nearly so. Its irregular outline makes it possible to recognise the place that it has formerly occupied in the older State crowns, and it seems always to have been given the place of honour. It is pierced after an Oriental fashion, and the top of the piercing is filled with a supplementary ruby set in gold. Don Pedro, King of Castille in 1367, murdered the King of Granada for the sake of his jewels, one of which was this stone, and Don Pedro is said to have given it to Edward the Black Prince after the battle of Najera, near Vittoria, in the same year. After this, it is said to have been worn by Henry V.

in his crown at Agincourt in 1415, when it is recorded that the King's life was saved from the attack of the Duc D'Alençon, because of the protection afforded him by his crown, a portion of which, however, was broken off. It may be confidently predicted that such a risk of destruction is not very likely to happen again to the great ruby.

"In the centre of each of the very ornamental fleurs-de-lis is a ruby, and all the rest of the ornamentation on them is composed of rose diamonds, large and small. From each of the crosses-patée, the upper corners of which have each a large pearl upon them, rises an arch of silver worked into a design of oak-leaves and acorn-cups. These leaves and cups are all closely encrusted with a mass of large and small diamonds, rose brilliant, and table cut; the acorns themselves formed of beautiful drop-shaped pearls of large size. From the four points of intersection of the arches at the top of the crown depend large egg-shaped pearls. From the centre of the arches, which slope slightly downwards, springs a mound with a cross-patée above it. The mound is ornamented all over with close lines of brilliant diamonds, and the fillet which encircles it, and the arch which crosses over it, are both ornamented with one line of large rose-cut diamonds set closely together. The cross-patée at the top has in the centre a large sapphire of magnificent colour set openly. The outer lines of the arms of the cross are marked by a row of small diamonds close together and in the centre of each arm is a large diamond, the remaining spaces being filled with more small diamonds. The large sapphire in the centre of this cross is said to have come out of the ring of Edward the Confessor, which was buried with him in his shrine at Westminster, and the possession of it is supposed to give to the owner the power of curing the cramp. If this be indeed the stone which belonged to St. Edward, it was probably recut in its present form of a 'rose' for Charles II., even if not since his time.

"Not counting the large ruby or the large sapphire, this crown contains: Four rubies, eleven emeralds, sixteen sapphires, two hundred and seventy-seven pearls, two thousand seven hundred and eighty-three diamonds. [As remade for King Edward VII. the crown now has 297 pearls and 2818 diamonds.]

"The large ruby has been valued at £110,000.

"When this crown has to take a journey it is provided with a little casket, lined with white velvet, and having a sliding drawer at the bottom, with a boss on which the crown fits closely, so that it is safe from slipping. The velvet cap turned up with miniver, with which it is worn, is kept with it."

This crown has been recently remade for King Edward VII., but has not been altered in any essential details. The illustration of it in Plate LI. is reproduced from a photograph taken after its alteration for King Edward. This plate has been very kindly presented to the present work by Messrs. R. & S. Garrard & Co., of the Haymarket, S.W. The cap of the *real* crown is of purple velvet as shown in the plate.

Fig. 727 represents the crown of the Queen Consort with which Queen Alexandra was crowned on August 9, 1902. It will be noticed that, unlike the King's crowns, this has eight arches. The circlet which forms the base is 1½ inches in height. The crown is entirely composed of diamonds, of which there are 3972, and these are placed so closely together that no metal remains visible. The large diamond visible in the illustration is the famous Koh-i-noor. Resting upon the rim are four crosses patée, and as many fleurs-de-lis, from each of which springs an arch.

There is yet another crown, probably the one with which we are most familiar. This is a small crown entirely composed of diamonds: and the earliest heraldic use which can be found of it is in the design by Sir Edgar Boehm for the 1887 Jubilee coinage. Though effective enough when worn, it does not, from its small size, lend itself effectively to pictorial representation, and as will be remembered, the design of the 1887 coinage was soon abandoned. This crown was made at the personal expense of Queen Victoria, and under her instructions, owing to the fact that her late Majesty found her "State" Crown uncomfortable to wear, and too heavy for prolonged or general use. It is understood, also, that the Queen found the regulations concerning its custody both inconvenient and irritating. During the later part of her reign this smaller crown was the only one Queen Victoria ever wore. By her will the crown was settled as an heirloom upon Queen Alexandra, to devolve

FIG. 727.

upon future Queens Consort for the time being. This being the case, it is not unlikely that in the future this crown may come to be regarded as a part of the national regalia, and it is as well, therefore, to reiterate the remark, that it was made at the personal expense of her late Majesty, and is to no extent and in no way the property of the nation.

OTHER EUROPEAN CROWNS

The crowns used by other ruling European sovereigns will be found on Plate LII. In order to facilitate reference thereto, they are here referred to and arranged according to the countries to which they belong, and not in the order in which they stand upon the plate.

AUSTRIA-HUNGARY

Fig. 1. *Austrian Imperial Crown.*—The Emperor Rudolph II. had this admirable piece of the goldsmith's art made in the year 1602. The crown was probably made by the Augsburg goldsmith David Attemstetter, who was appointed goldsmith to the Crown. It is supposed to have cost 700,000 thalers. (A thaler is a little less than 3s.) On the point or summit of the cross upon the crown is an uncut sapphire, and the golden, dome-like, upper pieces show coronation pictures in embossed work. The Imperial crown of Frederick III., on his monument in St. Stephen's Cathedral, Vienna, probably served as a model (Fig. 728). In the year 1804, on the raising of Austria into an Empire,

FIG. 728.—Imperial Crown of Frederick III. (IV.), (d. 1493).

this crown was declared the Imperial crown of Austria. The gold-fringed, blue crown-ribbons which appear in the representation of the crown in the arms of Austria are not present in the real crown.

Fig. 6 (Plate LII.). *Bohemian Royal Crown*, also called *Wenzels-crown*.—In the year 1347, Blanche of Valois, wife of the Emperor Charles IV., had a Bohemian Royal Crown made after the pattern of the old French Royal Crown, using the materials of the Bohemian Ducal Crown of the time of St. Wenzel (St. Wenceslaus). It consists of four parts, fastened together by hinges. In the cross, a relic, a thorn from the crown of Christ, is introduced. The cap inside was not added until later. The crown remains amongst the Crown treasures at St. Veit's, Prague.

Fig. 13 (Plate LII.). *Austrian Archducal Crown* (or *Cap*).—A cherry-red velvet cap, turned up with ermine, scalloped into rounded pieces, is the foundation for a clasp, or buckle crown, and is so arranged that the spikes of the circlet are visible between the rounded points of the ermine. The arches of the crown are four-sided, and set with pearls and rubies. A lentiform or ball-shaped sapphire serves

FIG. 729.—Styrian Ducal Hat.

as the Imperial orb. The Archducal Crown was deposited for safe keeping with the Monastery of Klosterneuberg on November 27, 1616, by the Archduke Maximilian III., Grand Master of the Teutonic Order of Knightood, where it still remains, in the treasure-chamber. A much older Austrian Ducal Crown is to be found in the Landhause (the house where the States of a country meet) at Graz, and is called the Styrian Ducal Hat (Fig. 729). It is the crown of Duke Ernest der Eiserne (Ernest the Iron), died 1424, in which he appears crowned on his monument in the Monastery of Reun, near Graz. In the time of Maria

Theresa the frame-work of the crown was readjusted, the tips of the crown points set with pearls, and the inner cap bordered with ermine, but unfortunately incorrectly placed. The original in the proper shape is shown in the crown of Duke Max, the son of Frederic III. (Fig. 730), in the *Wappenbuch für die österreichischen Herzoge* ("Book of Arms for the Austrian Dukes"), 1445. (See Plate XXVIII.) It is to be met with in precisely the same shape over the five-eagle shield on the monument of the Emperor Frederick III. in St. Stephen's Cathedral, Vienna.

FIG. 730.—Maximilian's Ducal Hat, 1445.

Fig. 4 (Plate LII.). *Hungarian Crown of St. Stephen.*—This national relic of the Magyars is made out of two different crowns. The two hoops crossing one another and the cap itself, consisting of thin sheet-gold, belong to the Latin crown which King Stephen I. is said to have received from Pope Sylvester II. on his conversion to Christianity in the year 1000. The second Byzantine or Greek crown consists of a circlet which is adorned in front with nine ornamental pediments. At the back the circlet is set with pearls. This second crown was a gift of the East Roman Emperor, Michael Dukas, who sent it to Duke Geysa in 1705. The cross is a later addition, and is fastened on without regard for the enamelled pictures on the hoops or rings of the crown. In course of time the sheets of gold, to which the new ornament had been somewhat carelessly attached, got loose, and the cross lost its stability.

Very similarly composed to the Byzantine part of

FIG. 731.—Crown sent by the Emperor Monomachos to King Andreas of Hungary.

St. Stephen's crown is the crown which King Andreas of Hungary received about the middle of the eleventh century from the Emperor Constantine Monomachos as a present. In 1860 and 1861 the plates of this crown (Fig. 731) were turned up by the plough near Nyitra Jvanka (Neutraer Comitat).

Transylvania (Siebenbürgern), united to Hungary in 1688, was raised to a Grand Duchy by Diploma, by Maria Theresa on November 2, 1765, and received a new crown invented for the purpose (Fig. 732). This Grand

FIG. 732.—Crown of Transylvania.

Ducal Crown of Transylvania shows two hoops, spanning from front to back, and a purple cap, covered with a golden network.

GERMAN EMPIRE

Fig. 2 (Plate LII.). *German Imperial Crown.*—This crown, which has no actual existence apart from heraldry, is that of the New German Empire, and shows four larger and four smaller plates or medallions of gold placed octagonally side by side; these medallions are rounded at the top and bordered with diamonds. The larger medallions each show a large cross that has two smaller crosses in the corners below it; the small medallions each contain an eagle, with an eight-rayed star suspended over its head. On the large medallions rest richly ornamented golden hoops or arches, which at the summit of the crown spread out into a leaf-shaped ornament which supports a blue Imperial orb adorned with precious stones. The crown is lined with gold, and encloses a low cap of gold brocade which is diapered with Imperial eagles and crowns. If the crown is represented suspended, gold crown-ribbons are added.

The crown of the *Roman-German Empire*, wrongly but universally called "the crown of Charlemagne" (Fig. 733), served as model for the one which has just

FIG. 733.—Crown of the Roman-German Empire, wrongly known as the crown of Charlemagne.

been described. It was a Southern Italian piece of work of the eleventh century, and until the year 1796 was preserved with the other Imperial jewels in the Church of the Holy Ghost at Nürnberg; at the present time, however, it is in the Imperial treasure-chamber at Vienna. This crown, as a crown of sovereignty, has played but a small heraldic rôle with the exception of a short interval from 1804 to 1806, when it appeared suspended over the newly-formed Austrian coat of arms. But as the charge upon the smaller inescutcheon

superimposed upon the quartering or inescutcheon of Hanover on the arms of Great Britain, it figured as the emblem of the office of Treasurer of the Holy Roman Empire from the accession of George I. to the close of the reign of George IV.

Fig. 5 (Plate LII.). *Crown of the German Empress.*—The same is adorned with rubies and diamonds, lined with gold, and provided with a cap of gold brocade.

Fig. 8 (Plate LII.). *Crown of the German Crown Prince.*—The circlet bears, alternately, four crosses and four eagles, composed of brilliants. Under the hoops appears a red velvet cap with lining of the same colour.

Fig. 7 (Plate LII.). *Prussian Royal Crown.*—This is composed of a gold circlet adorned with diamonds. The eight lower ends of the four intersecting arches, each of which is adorned with ten brilliants, are covered by fleurons, each of four diamonds, between which rise up spikes, each surmounted by a pearl. A large sapphire appears on the top as the Imperial orb.

Fig. 9 (Plate LII.). *Royal Crown of Bavaria.*—This crown is of the usual shape of a Royal crown, only the golden hoops are not adorned with pearls, but with precious stones. The crown of Bavaria, through the means of the court jeweller Borgnis, at Frankfort-on-the-Main, was in the beginning of this century designed and made in the same Parisian workshop as the crown and insignia of Napoleon I. It is preserved in the treasure-chamber of the Royal residence at Münich.

In the arms of the Grand Duchy of Mecklenburg-Schwerin there has appeared, since 1884, the so-called "Wendische Krone" (Fig. 734), a green-enamelled

FIG. 734.—" Wendische Krone " of Mecklenburg-Schwerin.

hinged ring, adorned with an emerald, the shape of which was copied from a bronze ring dug up near Treehow. This is believed to belong to the later period of the Bronze Age.

RUSSIA

Fig. 3 (Plate LII.). *Russian Emperor's Crown.*—This is entirely made of diamonds (5012), and is surmounted by a large (399 carat) ruby. The crown was made in the time of the Empress Catherine II., by the celebrated Genoese jeweller Panzié. When heraldically represented, blue crown ribbons are added.

FIG. 735.—Crown of the Empress of Russia.

The *Crown of the Empress* is similarly shaped (Fig. 735). Both crowns are imposing, more from their colossal value than from their artistic composition.

Far more interesting are the really national crown-caps of the kingdom of Kasan (Fig. 736) and Astrachan (Fig. 737), which are erected in the shape of the old

FIG. 736.—Crown of Kasan.

FIG. 737.—Crown of Astrachan.

Knjasen caps, while the crown of the Tsarina Anna, borne for the kingdom of Poland (Fig. 738), is of the West European type. Of national make again are the crowns of the kingdom of *Siberia* (Fig. 739) and of the *Taurian*

FIG. 738.—Crown of Poland.

FIG. 739.—Crown of Siberia (1684).

Chersonesus (Fig. 740). The crown of the kingdom of Georgia or Grusinien, on the contrary, is an ordinary Royal crown of well-known pattern.

FIG. 740.—Crown of Taurien.

FIG. 741.—Crown of Kiew.

The united *Grand Duchies of Kiew, Vladimar,* and *Novgorod* received under Peter the Great a crown (Fig. 741) copied from the Taurian crown-cap. Uniquely made is the crown of the *Grand Duchy of Finland,*

FIG. 742.—Crown of Finland.

which was united by personal union to Russia (Fig. 742); this crown is borne in the great coat of arms of Russia.

ITALY

Fig. 12 (Plate LII.). *Italian Royal Crown.*—The crown is an eight-hooped crown with a low purple cap. The circlet, which is decorated with the corde-

lière of the Order of the Annunciation, bears alternately leaves set with precious stones, and Savoy crosses. The *Crown Prince's Crown* is similar to that of the

FIG. 743.—Crown of the Italian Crown Prince.

king, but it only possesses half the number of hoops (Fig. 743).

The new State coat of arms of Italy, of the year 1890, shows on the Royal helmet the *Iron Crown* (Fig. 744), a broad band in six pieces, which, enamelled green, shows twenty-two stones. The circlet bears on the inner side a narrow iron ring, which is supposed to have originally

FIG. 744.—The Iron Crown of Lombardy.

been a nail from the cross of Christ, hence its name. The Iron Crown was considered the old crown of the kingdom of Lombardy, and Napoleon I. had himself crowned King of Italy with this crown at Milan in 1805.

FIG. 745.—The Crown of Tuscany.

The crown is preserved in the Cathedral treasures at Monza.

The Crown of the Grand Duchy of Tuscany also be-

FIG. 746.—The Cap of the Doge of Venice.

FIG. 747.—The Crown of the Republic of San Marino.

longs to the Italian crowns (Fig. 745), and was worn by the Medicis, Dukes of Florence. It is a crown with points, adorned in the middle of the front with the figure of the Florentine coat of arms, the "florenced" fleur-de-lis. In old representations, the leaves on the sides are not to be met with.

Fig. 746 shows the *Venetian Doge's Cap,* which, it is

true, disappeared from history with the last Doge of Venice, Ludovico Manin, 12th May 1797, but was borne later by a few noble Venetian families (Giustiniani, Manin Sagredo, Vendrami, and others) in their arms. It is of the shape of a fisherman's cap, with a circlet richly set with pearls and precious stones, which is occasionally made like a foliage crown. Here belongs finally, also, the crown of the little Italian Free State of *San Marino* (Fig. 747). It is a spiked crown (David's crown) with four hoops, and a low purple cap.

SWEDEN

Fig. 14 (Plate LII.). *Crown of the Crown Prince of Sweden*, Duke of Vermland.—The circlet bears eight high points with pearls on the tips, between them similar but lower ones are visible. On the front, in place of the lower points, the armorial charge of the House of Wasa, a sheaf or fascine (Wasar), is introduced. The blue cap is diapered with gold crowns, the armorial bearings of the kingdom of Sweden. The Dukes (of Vestergötland, Nerike, von Schoonen, Södermanland, and Vestmanland) bear a similar crown, only, instead of the lower points, the black sheaves continue all the way round (Fig. 748). Of the King's crown, a Dutch

FIG. 748.—Crown of the Dukes of Sweden.

piece of work of the time of King Erich IV., which is very richly elaborated, it was unfortunately not possible to obtain any sufficiently clear description or representation.

ROUMANIA

Fig. 15 (Plate LII.). *Plevna Crown.*—The Royal crown of Roumania was made by the officers of the Artillery of the Arsenal at Bucharest, after the Royal Proclamation of March 26, 1881, from the material of an iron cannon captured by the Roumanians at Plevna. It is independent of any gilding or any jewelled ornaments.

BULGARIA

The Crown of Prince Ferdinand of Bulgaria (elected July 7, 1887, by the Sobranie) was designed in 1891 by Huyer von Rosenfeld, and shows a circlet with lily-

FIG. 749.—Crown of Prince Ferdinand of Bulgaria.

shaped points, behind which eight hoops arch over a low purple cap (Fig. 749). The gold-fringed white-crown

ribbons are edged with red and green. (White, green, and red are the national colours of Bulgaria.)

FRANCE

The different French dynasties (Bourbon, Orleans, Napoleonic) likewise bore crowns of their own, but the representation of them seems unnecessary.

The closed crown is said to have been assumed by Charles VIII. in 1495, but it does not appear upon the Great Seal of any of the French sovereigns until it is found on that of Henry II. in 1547. The Royal Crown of France was a circlet of gold surmounted by eight demi-fleurs-de-lis and closed by *eight* pearled bands uniting and terminating in a fleur-de-lis. The Imperial Crown of France, first adopted by the Emperor Napoleon, was a golden circlet adorned with gems, supporting (see Woodward, p. 621) " and completely closed in by eight Imperial eagles whose elevated wings were united with alternate conventional palm-branches rising from Greek honeysuckle floriations, to support the orb and the cross."

EXOTIC CROWNS

Amongst other crowns which will have interest may be mentioned the *Crown of the Khedive of Egypt* (Fig. 750). It is a hooped crown, lined with purple, the Imperial orb being replaced by a crescent and star.

FIG. 750.—Crown of the Khedive of Egypt.

FIG. 751.—Crown of the Shah of Persia.

The Crown of the Shah of Persia (Fig. 751), and the *Chulah Crown of Siam* (Fig. 752), which is the crown of the King of Cambodia (Kambodscha), show quite an Oriental type, whereas the *Crown of the*

FIG. 752.—Crown of Siam.

FIG. 753.—Crown of the Sultan of Johore.

Sultan of Johore (Fig. 753) seems to be an imitation of the European shape of crown.

CORONETS OF RANK

In spite of various Continental edicts, the heraldic use of coronets of rank, as also their actual use, seems elsewhere than in Great Britain to be governed by no such strict regulations as are laid down and conformed to in this country. For this reason, no less than for the greater interest these must necessarily possess for readers in this country, English coronets will first claim our attention. It has been already observed that coronets or jewelled fillets are to be found upon the helmets even of simple knights from the earliest periods. They probably served no more than decorative purposes, unless these fillets be merely turbans, or

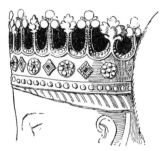

FIG. 754.—Coronet of Thomas FitzAlan, Earl of Arundel. (From his monument in Arundel Church, 1415.)

suggestions thereof. As late as the fifteenth century there appears to have been no regularised form, as will be seen from Fig. 754, which represents the coronet as shown upon the effigy of Thomas FitzAlan, Earl of Arundel, in Arundel Church (1415). A very similar coronet surmounts the head-dress of the effigy of Beatrice, Countess of Arundel, at the same period. In his will, Lionel, Duke of Clarence (1368), bequeaths "two golden circles," with one of which he was created duke. It is of interest to compare this with Fig. 755,

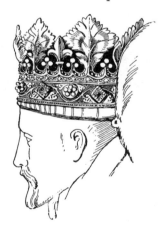

FIG. 755.—Crown of King Henry IV. (1399–1413). (From his monument in Trinity Chapel, Canterbury Cathedral.)

which represents the Crown of King Henry IV. as represented on his effigy. Richard, Earl of Arundel, in his will (December 5, 1375) leaves his " melieure coronne " to his eldest son Richard, his " second melieure coronne " to his daughter Joan, and his " tierce coronne " to his daughter Alice. Though not definite proof of the point, the fact that the earl distributes his coronets amongst his family irrespective of the fact that the earldom (of which one would presume the coronets to be a sign) would pass to his son, would seem to show that the wearing of a coronet even at that date was merely indicative of high nobility of birth, and not of the possession of a substantive Parliamentary peerage. In spite of the variations in form, coronets were, however, a necessity. When both dukes and earls were created they were invested with a coronet in open Parliament. As time went on the coronet, however, gradually came to be considered the sign of the possession of a peerage, and was so borne;

but it was not until the reign of Charles II. that coronets were definitely assigned by Royal Warrant (February 19, 1660) to peers not of the Blood Royal. Before this date a coronet had not (as has been already stated) been used heraldically or in fact by barons, who, both in armorial paintings and in Parliament, had used a plain crimson cap turned up with white fur.

The coronet of the Prince of Wales is exactly like the official (St. Edward's) crown, except that instead of two intersecting arches it has only one. An illustration of this is given in Fig. 756 (this being the usual form in which it is heraldically depicted), and it also appears on Plate LIII. Fig. 1 and on Plate LVI., which represents the armorial bearings of King Edward VII. and Queen Alexandra as Prince and Princess of Wales. It should be noticed, however, that this coronet belongs to the Prince as eldest son of the Sovereign and heir-apparent to the Throne, and not as Prince of Wales. It was assigned by Royal Warrant 9th February, 13 Charles II. The coronet of the Princess of Wales, as such, is heraldically the same as that of her husband,

FIG. 756.—Coronet of the Prince of Wales.

FIG. 757.—Coronet of the younger children of the Sovereign.

but in Plate LVI. the coronet shown over the personal shield of her present Majesty (to which she was entitled in her own right, and not by marriage), is her coronet as a Princess of Denmark.

The coronets of the sons and daughters or brothers and sisters of a sovereign of Great Britain (other than a Prince of Wales) is as in Fig. 757 and Plate LIII. Fig. 2, that is, the circlet being identical with that of the Royal Crown, and of the Prince of Wales' coronet, but without the arch. This was also assigned in the warrant of 9th February, 13 Charles II. Officially this coronet is described as being composed of crosses-patée and fleurs-de-lis alternately.

The grandchildren of a sovereign being sons and daughters of the Prince of Wales, or of other sons of the sovereign, have a coronet in which strawberry leaves are substituted for the two outer crosses-patée appearing at the edges of the coronet, which is officially described as composed of crosses-patée, fleurs-de-lis, and strawberry leaves (Plate LIII. Fig. 3).

Princes of the English Royal Family being sons of younger sons of a sovereign, or else nephews of a sovereign being sons of brothers of a sovereign, and having the rank and title of a duke of the United Kingdom, have a coronet composed alternately of crosses-patée and strawberry leaves, the latter taking the place of the fleurs-de-lis upon the circlet of the Royal Crown. This coronet was also assigned in the warrant of 9th February, 13 Charles II. (Plate LIII. Fig. 4).

It will be observed by those who compare one heraldic book with another that I have quoted these rules differently from any other work upon the subject. A moment's thought, however, must convince any one of the accuracy of my version. It is a cardinal rule of armory that save for the single circumstance of attainder no man's armorial insignia shall be degraded. Whilst any man's status may be increased, it cannot be lessened. Most heraldic books quote the coronet of crosses-patée, fleurs-de-lis, and strawberry leaves, as the coronet of the "grandsons" of the sovereign, whilst the coronet of crosses patée and strawberry leaves is stated to be the coronet of "nephews" or cousins of the sovereign. Such a state of affairs would be intolerable, because it would mean the liability at any moment to be degraded to the use of a less honourable coronet. Take, for example, the case of Prince Arthur of Connaught. During the lifetime of Queen Victoria, as a grandson of the sovereign he would be entitled to the former, whereas as soon as King Edward ascended the throne he would have been forced to relinquish it in favour of the more remote form. Take the case of the Duke of Cambridge. He was certainly the nephew of the sovereign for the time being when the coronet of crosses-patée and strawberry leaves was assigned to him by Royal Warrant in the reign of King William IV., but he is also the grandson of George III., and he has ceased to be the nephew of the sovereign for the time being to a no greater extent than he has ceased to be the grandson of the sovereign for the time being.

The real truth is that the members of the Royal Family do not inherit these coronets *ipso facto* or as a matter of course. They technically and in fact have no coronets until these have been assigned by Royal Warrant with the arms. When such warrants are issued, the coronets assigned have up to the present time conformed to the above rules. I am not sure that the "rules" now exist in any more potent form than that up to the present time those particular patterns happen to have been assigned in the circumstances stated. But the warrants (though they contain no hereditary limitation) certainly contain no clause limiting their operation to the lifetime of the then sovereign, which they certainly would do if the coronet only existed whilst the particular relationship continued.

The terms "grandson of the sovereign" and "nephew of the sovereign," which are usually employed, are not correct. The coronets only apply to the children of *princes*. The children of princesses, who are undoubtedly included in the terms "grandson" and "nephew," are not technically members of the Royal Family, nor do they inherit either rank or coronet from their mothers.

By a curious fatality there has never, since these Royal coronets were differentiated, been any male descendant of an English sovereign more remotely related than a nephew, with the exception of the Dukes of Cumberland. Their succession to the throne of Hanover renders them useless as a precedent, inasmuch as their right to arms and coronet must be derived from Hanover and its laws, and not from this country. The Princess Frederica of Hanover, however, uses an English coronet and the Royal Arms of England, presumably preferring her status as a princess of this country to whatever *de jure* Hanoverian status might be claimed. It is much to be wished that a Royal Warrant should be issued to her which would decide the point—at present in doubt—as to what degree of relationship the coronet of the crosses-patée and strawberry leaves is available for, or failing that coronet what the coronet of prince or princess of this country might be, he or she not being child, grandchild, or nephew or niece of a sovereign.

The unique use of actual coronets in England at the occasion of each coronation ceremony has prevented them becoming (as in so many other countries) mere pictured heraldic details. Consequently the instructions concerning them which are issued prior to each coronation will be of interest. The following is from the *London Gazette* of October 1, 1901:—

"EARL MARSHAL'S OFFICE,
NORFOLK HOUSE, ST. JAMES'S SQUARE, S.W.,
October 1, 1901.

"The Earl Marshal's Order concerning the Robes, Coronets, &c., which are to be worn by the Peers at the Coronation of Their Most Sacred Majesties King Edward the Seventh and Queen Alexandra.

"These are to give notice to all Peers who attend at the Coronation of Their Majesties, that the robe or mantle of the Peers be of crimson velvet, edged with miniver, the cape furred with miniver pure, and powdered with bars or rows of ermine (*i.e.*, narrow pieces of black fur), according to their degree, viz.:

"Barons, two rows.

"Viscounts, two rows and a half.

"Earls, three rows.

"Marquesses, three rows and a half.

"Dukes, four rows.

"The said mantles or robes to be worn over full Court dress, uniform, or regimentals.

"The coronets to be of silver-gilt; the caps of crimson velvet turned up with ermine, with a gold tassel on the top; and no jewels or precious stones are to be set or used in the coronets, or counterfeit pearls instead of silver balls.

"The coronet of a Baron to have, on the circle or rim, six silver balls at equal distances.

"The coronet of a Viscount to have, on the circle, sixteen silver balls.

"The coronet of an Earl to have, on the circle, eight silver balls, raised upon points, with gold strawberry leaves between the points.

"The coronet of a Marquess to have, on the circle, four gold strawberry leaves and four silver balls alternately, the latter a little raised on points above the rim.

"The coronet of a Duke to have, on the circle, eight gold strawberry leaves.

"By His Majesty's Command,

"NORFOLK, *Earl Marshal.*"

"EARL MARSHAL'S OFFICE,
NORFOLK HOUSE, ST. JAMES'S SQUARE, S.W.,
October 1, 1901.

"The Earl Marshal's Order concerning the Robes, Coronets, &c., which are to be worn by the Peeresses at the Coronation of Their Most Sacred Majesties King Edward the Seventh and Queen Alexandra.

"These are to give notice to all Peeresses who attend at the Coronation of Their Majesties, that the robes or mantles appertaining to their respective ranks are to be worn over the usual full Court dress.

"That the robe or mantle of a Baroness be of crimson velvet, the cape whereof to be furred with miniver pure, and powdered with two bars or rows of ermine (*i.e.* narrow pieces of black fur); the said mantle to be edged round with miniver pure 2 inches in breadth, and the train to be 3 feet on the ground; the coronet to be according to her degree—viz. a rim or circle with six pearls (represented by silver balls) upon the same, not raised upon points.

"That the robe or mantle of a Vicountess be like that of a Baroness, only the cape powdered with two rows and a half of ermine, the edging of the mantle 2 inches as before, and the train 1¼ yards; the coronet to be according to her degree—viz. a rim or circle with pearls (represented by silver balls) thereon, sixteen in number, and not raised upon points.

"That the robe or mantle of a Countess be as before, only the cape powdered with three rows of ermine, the edging 3 inches in breadth, and the train 1½ yards; the coronet to be composed of eight pearls (represented by silver balls) raised upon points or rays, with small strawberry leaves between, above the rim.

THE ART OF HERALDRY

"That the robe or mantle of a Marchioness be as before, only the cape powdered with three rows and a half of ermine, the edging 4 inches in breadth, the train 1¾ yards; the coronet to be composed of four strawberry leaves and four pearls (represented by silver balls) raised upon points of the same height as the leaves, alternately, above the rim.

"That the robe or mantle of a Duchess be as before, only the cape powdered with four rows of ermine, the edging 5 inches broad, the train 2 yards; the coronet to be composed of eight strawberry leaves, all of equal height, above the rim.

"And that the caps of all the said coronets be of crimson velvet, turned up with ermine, with a tassel of gold on the top.
"By His Majesty's Command,
"Norfolk, *Earl Marshal.*"

The Coronation Robe of a peer is not identical with his Parliamentary Robe of Estate. This is of fine scarlet cloth, lined with taffeta. The distinction between the degrees of rank is effected by the guards or bands of fur. The robe of a duke has four guards of *ermine* at equal distances, with gold lace above each guard and tied up to the left shoulder by a white riband. The robe of a marquess has four guards of *ermine* on the right side, and three on the left, with gold lace above each guard and tied up to the left shoulder by a white riband. An earl's robe has three guards of ermine and gold lace. The robes of a viscount and baron are identical, each having two *guards* of plain *white* fur.

By virtue of various warrants of Earls Marshal, duly recorded in the College of Arms, the use or display of a coronet of rank by any person other than a peer is stringently forbidden. This rule, unfortunately, is too often ignored by many eldest sons of peers, who use peerage titles by courtesy.

The heraldic representations of these coronets of rank are as follows:—

The coronet of a duke shows five strawberry leaves (see Plate LIII. Fig. 5). This coronet should not be confused with the ducal *crest* coronet.

The coronet of a marquess shows two balls of silver technically known as "pearls," and three strawberry leaves (Plate LIII. Fig. 6).

The coronet of an earl shows five "pearls" raised on tall spikes, alternating with four strawberry leaves (Plate LIII. Fig. 7).

The coronet of a viscount shows nine "pearls," all set closely together, directly upon the circlet (Plate LIII. Fig. 8).

The coronet of a baron shows four "pearls" upon the circlet (Plate LIII. Fig. 9). This coronet was assigned by Royal Warrant, dated 7th August, 12 Charles II., to Barons of England and to Barons of Ireland by warrant 16th May, 5 James II.

All coronets of degree actually, and are usually represented to, enclose a cap of crimson velvet, turned up with ermine. None of them are permitted to be jewelled, but the coronet of a duke, marquess, earl, or viscount is chased in the form of jewels. In recent times, however, it has become very usual for peers to use, heraldically, for more informal purposes a representation of the circlet only, omitting the cap and the ermine edging.

The crown or coronet of a king of arms is of silver-gilt formed of a circlet, upon which is inscribed part of the first verse of the 51st Psalm, viz.: "Miserere mei Deus secundum magnam misericordiam tuam." The rim is surmounted with sixteen leaves, in shape resembling the oak-leaf, every alternate one being somewhat higher than the rest, nine of which appear in the profile view of it or in heraldic representations. The cap is of crimson satin, closed at the top by a gold tassel and turned up with

ermine. This can be seen in Figs. 19, 20, 21, and in Fig. 758.

Fig. 758.—Sir Arthur Vicars, K.C.V.O., Ulster King of Arms.
(From a photograph by Chancellor, Dublin.)

Anciently, the crown of Lyon King of Arms was, in shape, an exact replica of the crown of the King of Scotland, the only difference being that it was not jewelled.

Coronets of rank are used very indiscriminately on the Continent, particularly in France and the Low Countries. Their use by no means implies the same as with us, and frequently indicates little if anything beyond mere "noble" birth.

The remaining coronets of which illustrations are given are those of other countries.

The *Krönenführung* (List or Guide of the Crowns) proposed for Germany by Count Rudolf von Stillfried-Rattonitz and Aléantara, President of the Royal Prussian Heraldic Office in Berlin, in spite of its recognised suitability and opportuneness, has not been consistently adopted in those cases indicated by the use of square brackets. The majority of these coronets having no actual existence, and being merely heraldic representations, in the counting of the points of the coronets and the pearls, only those visible in a drawing are specified, and not the presumed number in the whole circumference of the circlet. The following, Nos. 1 to 40, relate exclusively to Plate LIV.

Fig. 1. *Royal Crown.*—A crown with five arches, This crown is borne over their shields by the Austrian Archdukes, the Royal Princes of Prussia, Bavaria, Saxony, and Würtemberg, the Princes of Baden, Hesse, Mecklenburg, Saxe-Weimar, and Saxe-Altenburg. The State coats of arms of Baden, Greece, Hesse, Mecklenburg, the Netherlands, Oldenburg, Roumania, Saxony, Saxe-Altenburg, Saxe-Weimar, Servia, Spain, and Würtemberg show the same crown. Originally, a Royal or king's crown only consisted of a circlet with leaf and pearl points (Fig. 755). With few exceptions, the crowns "enclosed" at the top by arches are only occasionally to be found in the course of the fifteenth century. There are instances, however, of the use of the closed crown in England at a much earlier date, as has been noted in the previous chapter.

Fig. 2. *Grand Ducal Crown* [Crown Prince's Crown]. —A coronet with eight arches and a low purple cap. This crown is borne by many states—Belgium, Denmark, Portugal, Sweden, and Norway—and also as a Royal crown. We find it, besides, in the State coats of arms of Anhalt, Brunswick, Bulgaria, Luxembourg, Monaco, Reuss ä. u. j. Linie (Reuss älterer und jüngerer Linie), Saxe-Meiningen, and Saxe-Coburg and Gotha.

Fig. 3. *Ducal Crown* [Crown of the Princes of Royal Houses and of Hereditary Grand Dukes].—This shows the same formation as the last, only the space under the buckles is entirely filled up by the cap. Of equal authority, but older, is the *Ducal Hat* (Fig. 759). The

FIG. 759.—Ducal Cap.

circlet is here replaced by an ermine brim, scalloped out in circular form. This hat was formerly also worn as an "Electoral Hat." An older shape of Elector's hat is shown in Fig. 760, the very old shape in Fig. 761. The

FIG. 760.—Elector's Bonnet.

FIG. 761.—Ancient form of the Electoral Hat.

ducal crown is nowadays only used in a State coat of arms by Schaumburg-Lippe, but it may also be observed on a seal of the Prince von Waldeck-Pyrmont. The electoral "bonnet," as it is termed in England, was borne upon the Royal Arms, over the inescutcheon of Hanover for a short time during the reign of George III., viz. from 1801 until Hanover was erected into a kingdom. A crown was then substituted.

Fig. 4. *Ducal Coronet in Belgium and the Netherlands.*—The purple cap, ornamented with a golden tassel on the top, is enclosed in a circlet on which stand three leaves and two pearl-points.

Fig. 5. *Ducal Coronet in France, Italy, Spain, and Portugal.*—A simple circlet with five leaf-points, small

FIG. 762.—Old Spanish Ducal Coronet.

points being inserted between. The *old Spanish Ducal Coronet* is shown in Fig. 762.

Fig. 6. *Coronet of an English Duke.*

Fig. 7. *Landgrave's Crown* [Crown of the Princes of Grand-Ducal Houses, of Dukes, of the Dukes of Bavaria and Würtemberg].—Circlet with five leaf and four pearl points, surmounted by four arches.

Fig. 8. [Crown of the Hereditary Princes of Ducal

Houses].—The same crown as in Fig. 7, but provided with a low purple cap.

Fig. 9. *Coronet of Princes in Italy and Principes in Spain.*—This is very like Fig. 4, only here there are five leaf and four pearl points on the circlet. Spanish "principes" sometimes bear the circlet alone.

Fig. 10. *Coronet of a Prince* [Fürst—this word should be distinguished from "Prinz." The latter is applied to a Prince of Royal birth, the former is a rank created] *in Belgium and the Netherlands.*—This shows the same cap as the last figure, but the circlet bears five leaves only. Instead of the tassel, occasionally an imperial globe and cross appear.

Fig. 11. *Prince's Crown* [Crown of the Princes of Ducal Houses].—It is shaped the same as crowns 7 and 8, but in this case there is a high purple cap, which entirely fills the space under the four arches. Besides Germany and Denmark, it is used in Russia, even by the Princes with the title of "Highness" or "Serene Highness." It may be seen in the State coat of arms of Schwarzburg-Rudolstadt and in the "Privy-Seal" of the Prince von Schwarzburg-Sondershausen.

Fig. 12. *Crown of the Russian Princes with the title of "Highness."*—It is similar to the last, but the circlet is replaced by a turned-up brim of ermine.

Fig. 13. *Prince's Hat* [worn by the Sovereigns and Princes of Sovereign Princely Houses, the mediatised Dukes and Princes, as also their Princes].—It is distinguished from the Prince's Crown (No. 11) by the scalloped ermine brim, which replaces the circlet. It is borne in Austria, Germany, France, and Belgium. It may be seen on the State coat of arms of Lichtenstein, Lippe, Montenegro, Schwarzburg-Sondershausen, and Waldeck-Pyrmont.

Fig. 14. *Coronet of a Marquis.*—The circlet of this crown consists of three leaf and two pearl points, the latter bearing three pearls each. This shape of coronet is used in Denmark, Italy, France, and Spain. The *old French Marquis's Coronet* shows three plain pearl-points between each leaf. The latter form, therefore, has these three points united in one.

Fig. 15. *Coronet of a Marquis in Belgium and the Netherlands* [Crown of the younger sons of mediatised countly families, formerly ruling States of the Empire]. —The circlet has five leaf-points. It is known in Germany, Austria, Sweden, and Norway as the *old Count's Crown.*

Fig. 16. *Coronet of an English Marquess.*

Fig. 17. *Highness' Crown* [Crown of the heads of mediatised countly families, formerly ruling States of the Empire, with the title of "Erlaucht" (Highness)].— The circlet boasts five leaf and four pearl points; the purple cap is adorned on the top with a little ermine tail.

Fig. 18. *Count's Coronet.*—Circlet with nine pearl-points. This shape is borne in Germany, Austria, France, Spain, Belgium, Russia (high and low points alternately), and in Italy (low points). Occasionally the pearls appear without points, placed directly upon the circlet, as in the coronet of a viscount in England.

FIG. 763.—Spanish Count's Coronet.

Fig. 763 shows a *Spanish Count's Coronet.*—It is seldom borne, it is true, and it, moreover, as "Erlaucht-krone" (Highness' crown), was formerly used in Germany. In France and Belgium, in earlier times, three pearls were placed on the middle and the two side points (Fig. 764).

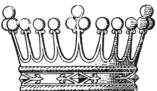

Fig. 19. *Count's Coronet in Belgium.*—The circlet bears seven red-velvet plates or shields, set with precious stones, rounded off at the top, each with a pearl on the upper edge, and with the edges bound with gold; these surround a cap of gold brocade. This peculiarly-shaped coronet is no longer in use.

Fig. 20. *Coronet of an English Earl.*

Fig. 21. *Vidame's Coronet in France.* — On the circlet are placed three crosses, between which rise pearl-points. The term *Vidames* is used for those counts to whom was entrusted the protectorate over the bishoprics.

Fig. 22. *Viscount's Coronet.*—The circlet bears three large and two small pearl-points. This coronet is in use in France and Spain. The *Viconde* crown in Portugal is of the same shape, only the low points have no pearls.

Fig. 23. *Viscount's [or Burggrave's] Coronet in the Netherlands.*—The circlet is adorned with three pearl and two leaf points.

Fig. 24. *Viscount's Coronet in Italy.* — The circlet bears three large and two small pearls, without points.

Fig. 25. *Viscount's Coronet in Belgium.*—This shows three points, each adorned with three pearls.

Fig. 26. *English Viscount's Coronet.*

Fig. 27. *Freiherr's Coronet.*—The circlet is set with seven pearl-points. Occasionally the pearls are placed directly on the circlet. This coronet is used in Germany, Austria, Russia, Belgium, and in the Netherlands. An old form of this coronet is shown in Fig. 765.

Fig. 765.—Old Freiherr's (Baron's) Coronet.

The circlet is set with five pearls, and wound round by a string of pearls.

Fig. 28. *Baron's Coronet [Freiherr's] in Belgium.*—The circlet encloses a red velvet cap, which is spanned by four rows or arches of pearls. The portions of the cap thus partitioned are adorned with precious stones and each bears a pearl on its summit.

Fig. 29. *Baron's Coronet in Spain and Portugal.*—The circlet, wound round with a string of pearls, bears four pearls without points. The *old Spanish Baron's Coronet* was likewise a circlet wound round with a pearl string, but had seven plain points (Fig. 766).

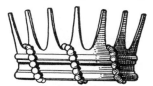

Fig. 766.—Old Spanish Baron's Coronet.

Fig. 30. *Baron's Coronet in France and Italy.*—A plain circlet, three times wound round with a string of

pearls. In Italy the string of pearls is generally placed diagonally, but to the left.

Fig. 31. *Baron's Coronet in Sweden and Norway, Finland and the Baltic Provinces.*—The circlet bears three groups of pearls, three in each, and between each of these groups is a solitary pearl.

Fig. 32. *Coronet of an English Baron.*

Fig. 33. *Hereditary Knights in Italy.*—The coronet of hereditary knights (*Chevalier héréditaire*) consists of a circlet on which are set three unmounted pearls.

Fig. 34. *Chevalier's Coronet in Belgium.*—The circlet, wound round with a pearl-string, bears five pearl-points.

The "*Ritter's*" [Knight's] *Coronets in the Netherlands* is exactly the same. The distinguishing mark of the chevalier in France consists, on the contrary, of a wreath (tortillon) of two colours, with fluttering ribbons (Fig. 767).

Fig. 767.—The Wreath of a French Chevalier.

Fig. 35. *Caballero's Coronet in Spain and Portugal.*—The circlet is adorned with three leaves and two points, each with three pearls, between which four small pearl-points emerge.

Fig. 36. *Coronet of "Noble" Persons in Italy.*—The circlet bears five unmounted pearls.

Figs. 37 and 38. *Coronets of "Noble" Persons in Germany and Austria.*—In Belgium and the Netherlands, in Denmark, France, and Russia, as also in Sweden and Norway, the coronet Fig. 38, which is identical with the crest coronet, is borne as a coronet of "nobility" or rank.

For the lower nobility [or gentry—knights and edeleute—people with the prefix *von* and no other title] coronets are not officially recognised, at any rate in Germany and Austria as officially belonging; as, according to the patent, only shield and helmet are granted them. However, as can be understood, no other prohibition or protest is raised against the use of them, and Figs. 37 and 38 are the patterns usually adopted.

Fig. 39. *Coronet of a "Banneret" in France.*—This consisted of a simple circlet, without pearls or points.

Fig. 40. "*Patrician*" *Coronet in Italy.*—The circlet bears three spade-shaped points, between each of which a pearl-point appears.

The cap introduced by Napoleon I., in the place of the coronet of rank, and which had variously-coloured brims or turned-up borders and feathers, had fortunately, as indeed the whole of the heraldic regulation invented by him, so short a lifetime that we can certainly spare ourselves an enumeration and description of them.

In conclusion, a few crowns follow which certainly cannot be regarded as coronets of rank, and have no existence in fact, but yet must be mentioned here, because they, and especially the "Mauerkrone" [mural crown] are used in heraldry.

Fig. 768.—Antique Crown.

The *Zacken Crown* [notched, scalloped, sharply-pointed] (Fig. 768), also called the antique or heathen crown, or David's crown, shows a circlet with twelve sharp points round it, of which seven are visible. The twelve sharp points have a symbolic significance, and relate to the twelve rays [months] of the sun.

In the medium-sized coat of arms of Austria [these states all seem to possess a big, little, and an intermediate coat of arms] this crown rests upon the shield of the kingdom of Illyria. In the arms of San Marino a "Zacken" crown appears as circlet of the arched crown. (See Plate LII. Fig. 38.)

The *Mauerkrone* [mural crown] (Fig. 769) is used in

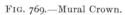

FIG. 769.—Mural Crown.

FIG. 770.—Naval Crown.

Germany principally as an adornment to the arms of towns. It is borne with three, four, or five battlemented towers. The tincture, likewise, is not always the same: gold, silver, red, or the natural colour of a wall being variously employed. Residential [*i.e.* having a *royal* residence] and capital towns usually bear a Mauerkrone with five towers, large towns one with four towers, smaller towns one with three. Strict regulations in the matter do not yet exist. It should be carefully noted

that this practice is peculiar to Germany and is quite incorrect in Great Britain.

The *Naval Crown* [Schiffskrone] (Fig. 770), on the circlet of which sails and sterns of ships are alternately introduced, is very rarely used on the Continent. With us it appears as a charge in the arms of the towns of Chatham, Ramsgate, Devonport, &c. The Naval Coronet, however, is more properly a crest coronet, and as such will be more fully considered in the next chapter. It had, however, a limited use as a coronet of rank at one time, inasmuch as the admirals of the United Provinces of the Netherlands placed a crown composed of prows of ships above their escutcheons, as may be seen from various monuments.

The crown of the Dauphin of France was a gemmed circlet of gold supporting eight demi-fleurs-de-lis, and arched in by four dolphins, heads downwards, the tails uniting to support the fleurs-de-lis in which the coronet terminated. The coronets used by the princes and princesses of France, sons and daughters of the sovereign or the Dauphin, was a circlet supporting eight demi-fleurs-de-lis, whilst other Royal princes and princesses placed upon the circlet four demi-fleurs-de-lis and as many "strawberry leaves" alternately.

The Chancellor of France and the Premiers-Presidents used, in lieu of a coronet, a "mortier," or cap edged with gold. The various caps, or chapeaux, which occur in heraldry have a chapter to themselves later, and the Papal tiara, and the various forms of the ecclesiastical hat, will be found dealt with subsequently.

A. C. F-D. AND H. S.

CHAPTER XXVII

CREST CORONETS AND CHAPEAUX

THE present official rules are that crests must be upon, or must issue from, a wreath (or torse), a coronet, or a chapeau. It is not at the pleasure of the wearer to choose which he will, one or other being specified and included in the terms of the grant. If the crest have a lawful existence, one or other of them will unchangeably belong to the crest, of which it now is considered to be an integral part.

In Scotland and Ireland, Lyon King of Arms and Ulster King of Arms have always been considered to have, and still retain, the right to grant crests upon a chapeau or issuing from a crest. But the power is (very properly) exceedingly sparingly used; and, except in the cases of arms and crests matriculated in Lyon Register as of ancient origin and in use before 1672, or "confirmed" on the strength of user by Ulster King of Arms, the ordinary ducal crest coronet and the chapeau are not now considered proper to be granted in ordinary cases.

Since about the beginning of the nineteenth century the rules which follow have been very definite, and have been very rigidly adhered to in the English College of Arms.

Crests issuing from the ordinary "ducal crest coronet" are not now granted under any circumstances. The chapeau is only granted in the case of a grant of arms to a peer, a mural coronet is only granted to officers in the army of the rank of general or above, and the naval coronet is only granted to officers in his Majesty's Royal Navy of the rank of admiral and above. An Eastern coronet is now only granted in the case

of those of high position in one or other of the Imperial Services, who have served in India and the East.

The granting of the other forms of crest coronets, the "crown-vallary" and the "crown palisado," is always discouraged, but no rule exists denying them to applicants, and they are to be obtained if the expectant grantee is sufficiently patient and pertinacious. Neither form is, however, particularly ornamental, and both are of modern origin.

There is still yet another coronet, the "celestial coronet." This is not unusual as a charge (see Fig. 593), but as a coronet from which a crest issues I know of no instance, nor am I aware of what rules, if any, govern the granting of it.

Definite rank coronets have been in times past granted for use as crest coronets, but this practice, the propriety of which cannot be considered as other than highly questionable, has only been pursued, even in the more lax days which are past, on rare and very exceptional occasions, and has long since been definitely abandoned as improper.

In considering the question of crest coronets, the presumption that they originated from coronets of rank at once jumps to the mind. This is by no means a foregone conclusion. It is difficult to say what is the earliest instance of the use of a coronet in this country as a coronet of rank. When it is remembered that the coronet of a baron had no existence whatever until it was called into being by a warrant of Charles II. after the Restoration, and that differentiated coronets for the several ranks in the Peerage are not greatly anterior in date, the question becomes distinctly complicated. From certainly the reign of Edward the Confessor the kings of England had

FIG. 771.—Various Crest Coronets taken from ancient examples.

worn crowns, and the great territorial earls, who it must be remembered occupied a position akin to that of a petty sovereign

(far beyond the mere high dignity of a great noble at the present day), from an early period wore crowns or coronets not greatly differing in appearance from the crown of the king. But the Peerage as such certainly neither had nor claimed the technical right to a coronet as a mark of their rank, in the thirteenth and fourteenth centuries. But coronets of a kind were used, as can be seen from early effigies, long before the use of crests became general. But these coronets were merely in the nature of a species of decoration for the helmet, many of them far more closely resembling a jewelled torse than a coronet. Parker in his "Glossary of Terms used in Heraldry" probably correctly represents the case when he states: "From the reign of Edward III. coronets of various forms were worn (as it seems indiscriminately) by princes, dukes, earls, and even knights, but apparently rather by way of ornament than distinction, or if for distinction, only (like the collar of SS) as a mark of gentility. The helmet of Edward the Black Prince, upon his effigy at Canterbury, is surrounded with a coronet totally different from that subsequently assigned to his rank."

The instance quoted by Parker might be amplified by countless others, but it may here with advantage be pointed out that the great helmet (or as this probably is the ceremonial representation of it) suspended above the Prince's tomb (Fig. 264) has no coronet, and the crest is upon a chapeau. Of the fourteen instances in the Plantagenet Garter plates in which the *torse* appears, twelve were peers of England, one was a foreign count, and one only a commoner. On the other hand, of twenty-nine whose Garter plates show crests issuing from coronets, four are foreigners, seven are commoners, and eighteen were peers. The coronets show very great variations in form and design, but such variations appear quite capricious and to carry no meaning, nor does it seem probable that a coronet of gules or of azure, of which there are ten, could represent a coronet of rank. The Garter plate of Sir William De la Pole, Earl of (afterwards Duke of) Suffolk, shows his crest upon a narrow black fillet. Consequently, whatever may be the conclusion as to the wearing of coronets alone, it would seem to be a very certain conclusion that the heraldic crest coronet bore no relation to any coronet of rank or to the right to wear one. Its adoption must have been in the original instance, and probably even in subsequent generations, a matter of pure fancy and inclination. This is borne out by the fact that whilst the Garter plate of Sir Henry Bourchier, Earl of Essex, shows his crest upon a torse, his effigy represents it issuing from a coronet.

Until the reign of Henry VIII., the Royal crest, both in the case of the sovereign and all the other members of the Royal Family, is always represented upon a chapeau or cap of dignity. The Great Seal of Edward VI. shows the crest upon a coronet, though the present form of crown and crest were originated by Queen Elizabeth. In depicting the Royal Arms, it is usual to omit one of the crowns, and this is always done in the official warrants

PLATE LXXXII.

DESIGN FOR A TALBOT BANNER.

PLATE LXXXIII.

DESIGN FOR A TALBOT BANNER.

PLATE LXXXIV.

ARMS FROM THE "SCHEIBLERSCHEN WAPPENBUCHE."

ARMS FROM A MANUSCRIPT AT THE COLLEGE OF ARMS.
TEMP. HENRY VI.

PLATE LXXXVI.

Elam

pharamont

Wandeycs

Wesnau

Eyrle Genewyle

Sr Gawayne y good knyght

Sr thomas holland of thepwator

Ser Emond Darell

Wyllm de Slyne

ARMS FROM A MANUSCRIPT AT THE COLLEGE OF ARMS.
TEMP. HENRY VI.

PLATE LXXXVII.

PLATE LXXXVIII.

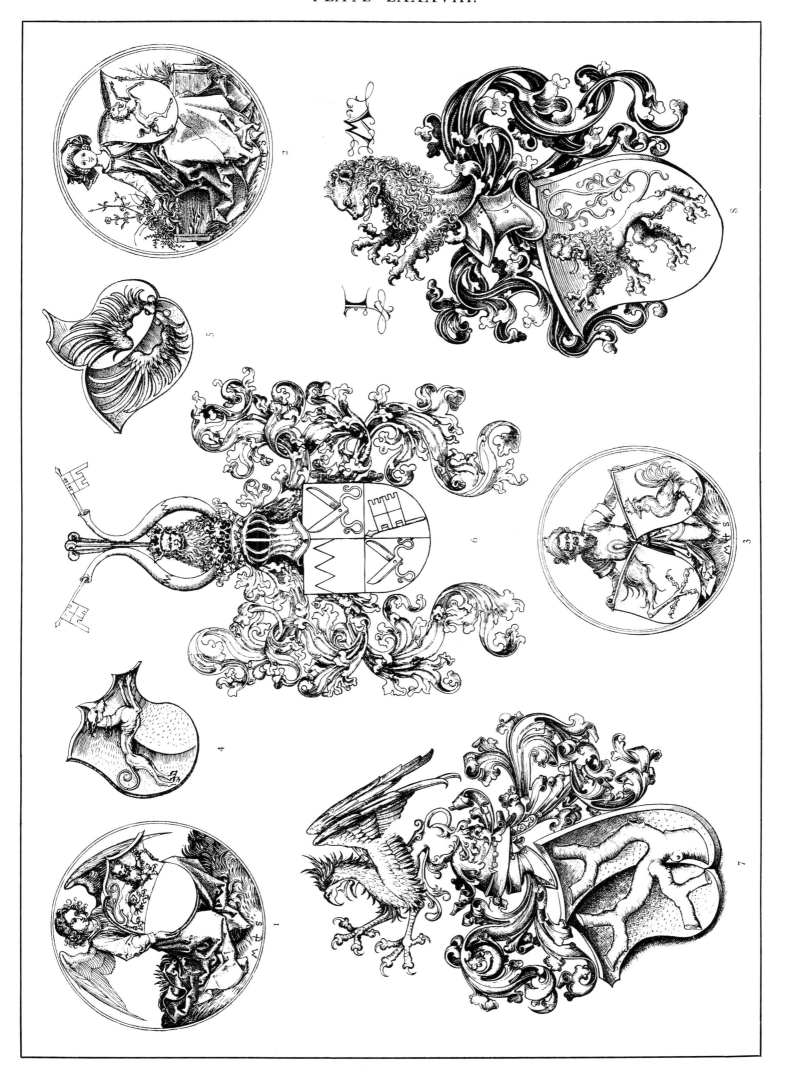

PLATE LXXXIX.

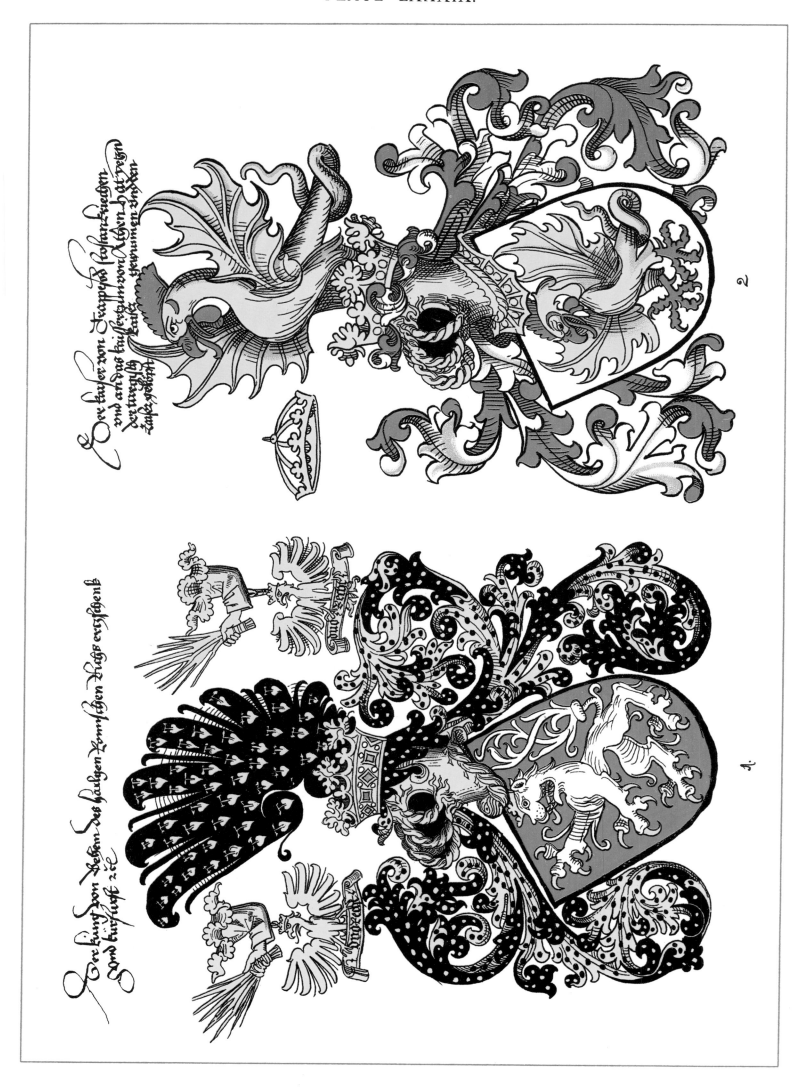

PLATE XC

EXAMPLES FROM CONRAD GRUNENBERG'S WAPPENBUCH.

PLATE XCI.

EXAMPLES FROM CONRAD GRUNENBERG'S WAPPENBUCH.

PLATE XCII.

EXAMPLES FROM CONRAD GRUNENBERG'S "OESTERREICHISCHER CHRONIK."

PLATE XCIII.

1

2

3

4

THE WORK OF ALBRECHT DURER.

PLATE XCIV.

לטהורים כל טהור
ΠΆΝΤΑ ΚΑΘΑΡΆ ΤΟΪΣ ΚΑΘΑΡΟΪΣ⸱
OMNIA MVNDA MVNDIS
D. HECTOR POMER PRÆPOS. S. LAVR⸱

1

FLAMMEVS ECCE VOLAT CLVPEO IOVIS ARMIGER AVREO

ioANN   STABIVS

2

STEPHANVS ROSINVS CANONICVS PATAVIEN.

3

4

THE WORK OF ALBRECHT DURER AND HIS SCHOOL.

PLATE XCV.

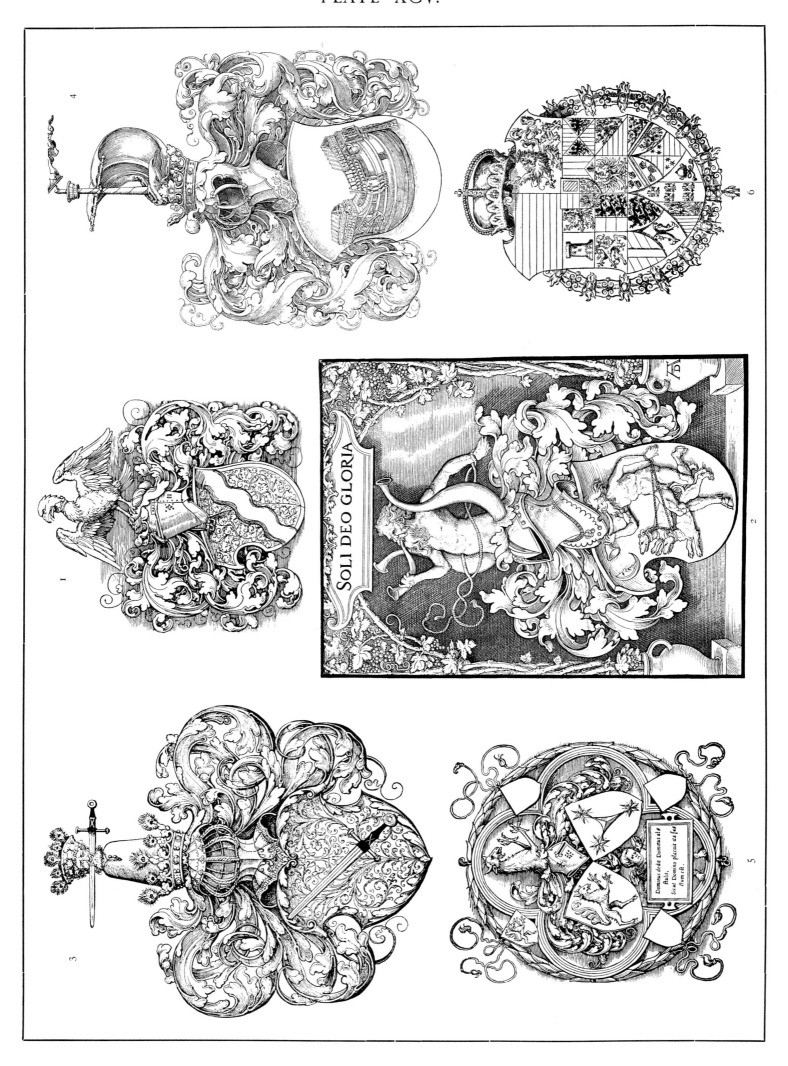

SOLI DEO GLORIA

PLATE XCVI.

ARMS BY GERMAN ARTISTS, FIRST HALF OF XVI. CENTURY.

PLATE XCVII.

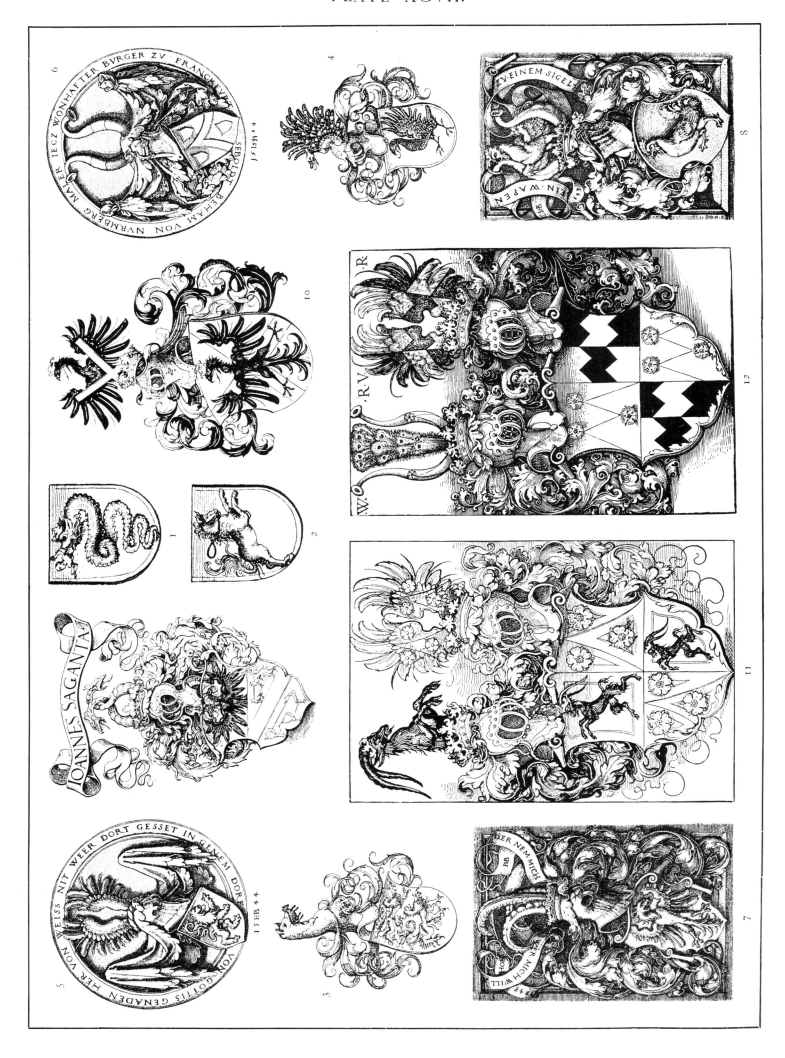

controlling the arms. One crown is placed upon the helmet, and upon this crown is placed the crest (Plate CXIV.), but theoretically the Royal achievement has two crowns, inasmuch as one of the crowns is an inseparable part of the crest. Plate CXIV. above referred to shows the usual form of depicting the Royal crest. This plate is by Mr. G. W. Eve, but probably the finest representation of the Royal crest which has ever been done is the design for one of the smaller bookplates for the Windsor Castle Library. This also is by Mr. Eve, and a reproduction will be found herein in a later chapter. It would be impossible to imagine anything finer. Like the rest of the Royal achievement, the Royal crest is of course not hereditary, and consequently it is assigned by a *separate* Royal Warrant to each male member of the Royal Family, and the opportunity is then taken to substitute for the Royal crown, which is a part of the sovereign's crest, a coronet identical with whatever may be assigned in that particular instance as the coronet of rank. In the case of Royal bastards the crest has always been assigned upon a chapeau.

The only case which comes to one's mind in which the Royal crown has (outside the sovereign) been allowed as a crest coronet is the case of the town of Eye.

The Royal crown of Scotland is the crest coronet of the sovereign's crest for the kingdom of Scotland. This crest, together with the crest of Ireland, is never assigned to any member of the Royal Family except the sovereign. The crest of Ireland (which is on a wreath or and azure) is by the way confirmatory evidence that the crowns in the crests of Scotland and England have a duplicate and separate existence apart from the crown denoting the sovereignty of the realm.

The ordinary crest coronet or, as it is usually termed in British heraldry, the " ducal coronet " (Ulster, however, describes it officially as " a ducal crest coronet "), is quite a separate matter from a duke's coronet of rank. Whilst the coronet of a duke has upon the rim five strawberry leaves visible when depicted, a ducal coronet has only three. The " ducal coronet " is the conventional " regularised " development of the crest coronets employed in early times. Fig. 771 shows different variations of ancient examples of the crest coronet, but it is now always officially depicted as in Figs. 81 and 550.

Unfortunately it has in many instances been depicted of a much greater and very unnecessary width, the result being inartistic and allowing unnecessary space between the leaves, and at the same time leaving the crest and coronet with little circumferential relation. It should be noted that it is quite incorrect for the rim of the coronet to be jewelled in colour though the outline of jewelling is indicated.

Though ducal crest coronets are no longer granted (of course they are still exemplified and their use permitted where they have been previously granted), they are of very frequent occurrence in older grants and confirmations.

It is quite incorrect to depict a cap (as in a coronet of rank) in a crest coronet, which is never more than the metal circlet, and consequently it is equally incorrect to add the band of ermine below it which will sometimes be seen.

The coronet of a duke has in one or two isolated cases been granted as a crest coronet. In such a case it is not described as a duke's coronet, but as a " ducal coronet of five leaves." It so occurs in the case of Ormsby-Hamilton.

The colour of the crest coronet must be stated in the blazon. Crest coronets are of all colours, and will be sometimes found bearing charges upon the rim (parti-

cularly in the cases of mural and naval coronets). An instance of this will be seen in the case of Sir John W. Moore, and of Mansergh (Fig. 772), the label in this case

FIG. 772.—Armorial bearings of Richard Southcote Mansergh, Esq.: Argent, a bend raguly gules, between three arrows points downwards of the last, flighted and barbed or (for Mansergh). Mantling gules, doubled argent. Crest: out of a ducal crest coronet proper, charged with a label of three points gules, a demi-lion rampant argent, gorged with a collar raguly of the second, and holding in the dexter paw an arrow point downwards of the last, flighted and barbed or. Motto: "Tout jour prêt."

being an unalterable charge and not the difference mark of an eldest son. Though the tincture of the coronet ought to appear in the blazon, nevertheless it is always a fair presumption (when it is not specified) that it is of gold, coronets of colour being very much less frequently met with. On this point it is interesting to note that in some of the cases where the crest coronet is figured upon an early Garter plate as of colour, it is now borne by the present descendants of the family gold. For example on the Garter plate of Sir Walter Hungerford, Lord Hungerford, the crest ["A garb or, between two silver sickles"] issues from a coronet azure. The various Hungerford families now bear it or. The crest upon the Garter plate of Sir Humphrey Stafford, Duke of Buckingham ["A demi-swan argent, beaked gules"], issues from a coronet gules. This crest is now borne (by the present Lord Stafford): "Out of a ducal coronet per pale gules and sable," &c.

Another instance of coloured coronets will be found in the crest of Nicholson now borne by Shaw.[a]

Probably, however, the most curious instance of all will be found in the case of one of the coats of arms reproduced from Gelre's "Armorial." Here the crest coronet is of *ermine* (see Plate LXXVI.).

A very general misconception—which will be found stated in practically every text-book of armory—is that when a crest issues from a coronet the wreath must be

[a] Armorial bearings of William Otho Nicholson Shaw, Esq.: Quarterly, 1 and 4, argent, two chevronels between three lozenges ermines (for Shaw); 2 and 3, azure, two bars ermine, in chief three suns proper (for Nicholson); and for his crests, 1. upon a wreath of the colours, a dove bendy sinister of six argent and sable, holding in the beak an olive-branch proper, the dexter leg resting on a lozenge as in the arms (for Shaw); 2. out of a ducal coronet gules, a lion's head ermine (for Nicholson); with the motto, " Per castra ad astra."

omitted. There is not and never has been any such rule. The rule is rather to the contrary. Instances where both occur are certainly now uncommon, and the presence of a wreath is not in present-day practice considered to be essential if a coronet occurs, but the use or absence of a wreath when the crest issues

placed upon a torse argent and sable. Another instance will be found in the case of the grant of the crest of Hanbury (Fig. 773).

A quite recent case was the grant by Sir Bernard Burke, Ulster King of Arms, of a crest to Sir Richard Quain, Bart., the blazon of which was: "On a wreath

FIG. 773.—Facsimile of a certificate by William Camden, Clarenceux King of Arms, of the arms and crest of Hanbury.

from a coronet really depends entirely upon the original grant. If no wreath is specified with the coronet, none will be used or needed, but if both are granted both should be used. An instance of the use of both will be found on the Garter Hall plate of Sir Walter Devereux, Lord Ferrers. The crest (a talbot's head silver) issues from a coronet or, which is

argent and azure, and out of a mural coronet proper a demi-lion rampant or, charged on the shoulder with a trefoil slipped vert, and holding between the paws a battle-axe also proper, the blade gold."

Other instances are the crests of Hamilton of Sunningdale (Fig. 774) and Tarleton (Fig. 775).

Another instance will be found in the grant to Ross-of-Bladensburg, a facsimile of which document appears

FIG. 774.—Armorial bearings of John Hamilton, Esq.: Gules, a spurrowel of six points or, between three cinquefoils argent, all within a bordure engrailed erminois; and impaling the arms of Crutchley, namely: argent, a chevron gules, cottised azure, between three torteaux, each encircled by two branches of oak proper. Mantling gules, doubled argent. Crest: an oak-tree issuing from a ducal coronet, having a saw across it all proper, the last having the word "Through" upon the iron part of it as motto.

FIG. 775.—Armorial bearings of Alfred Henry Tarleton, Esq.: Quarterly, 1 and 4, gules, a chevron erminois between three cinquefoils or (for Tarleton); 2 and 3, argent, on a fess dancetté, between three mullets azure, as many bezants (for Dimsdale), and impaling the arms of Tennyson-D'Eyncourt, namely: quarterly, 1 and 4, azure, a fess dancetté between ten billets or, four in chief and six in base, three, two, and one (for D'Eyncourt); 2 and 3, gules, three leopards' faces or, jessant-de-lis azure, over all a bend of the last (for Tennyson). Crest: on a wreath of the colours, a mural crown, thereon a leopard's face, all between two ostrich feathers proper. Motto: "Post nubila phœbus."

in Fig. 776. Possibly this blazon may be a clerical error in the engrossment, because it will be noticed that the wreath does not appear in the emblazonment.

I wonder how many of the officers of arms are aware of the existence of a warrant, dated in 1682, issued by the Deputy Earl-Marshal to the Companies of Painters, Stainers, and Coachmakers, forbidding them to paint crests which issue out of ducal coronets without putting them upon "wreaths of their collours." The wording of the warrant very plainly shows that at that date a wreath was always painted below a crest coronet. The warrant, however, is not so worded that it can be accepted as determining the point for the future, or that it would override a subsequent grant of a crest in contrary form. But it is evidence of what the law then was.

No crest is now granted without either wreath, coronet, or chapeau.

An instance of the use of the coronet of a marquess as a crest coronet will be found in the case of the Bentinck crest.[b]

There are some number of instances of the use of an earl's coronet as a crest coronet. Amongst these may be mentioned the crests of Sir Alan Seton Steuart, Bart. ["Out of an earl's coronet a dexter hand grasping a thistle all proper"], that granted to Cassan of Sheffield House, Ireland ["Issuant from an earl's coronet proper, a boar's head and neck erased or, langued gules"], James Christopher Fitzgerald Kenney, Esq., Dublin ["Out of an earl's coronet or, the pearls argent, a cubit arm erect vested gules, cuffed also argent, the hand grasping a roll of parchment proper"], and Davidson ["Out of an earl's coronet or, a dove rising argent, holding in the beak a wheat-stalk bladed and eared all proper"].

I know of no crest which issues from the coronet of viscount, but a baron's coronet occurs in the case of Forbes of Pitsligo and the cadets of that branch of the family: "Issuing out of a baron's coronet a dexter hand holding a scimitar all proper."

Foreign coronets of rank have sometimes been granted as crest coronets in this country, as in the cases of Sir Francis George Manningham Boileau, Bart., Norfolk ["In a nest or, a pelican in her piety proper, charged on the breast with a saltire couped gules, the nest resting in a foreign coronet"], Henry Chamier, Esq., Dublin ["Out of a French noble coronet proper, a cubit arm in bend vested azure, charged with five fleurs-de-lis in saltire or, cuffed ermine, holding in the hand a scroll, and thereon an open book proper, garnished gold"], John Francis Charles Fane De Salis, Count of the Holy Roman Empire ["1. Out of a marquis' coronet or, a demi-woman proper, crowned or, hair flowing down the back, winged in place of arms and from the armpits azure; 2. out of a ducal coronet or, an eagle displayed sable, ducally crowned also or; 3. out of a ducal coronet a demi-lion rampant double-queued and crowned with a like coronet all or, brandishing a sword proper, hilt and pommel of the first, the lion cottised by two tilting-spears of the same, from each a banner paly of six argent and gules, fringed also or"], and Mahony, Ireland ["Out of the coronet of a Count of France a dexter arm in armour embowed, grasping in the hand a sword all proper, hilt and pommel or, the blade piercing a fleur-de-lis of the last"].

A curious crest coronet will be found with the Sackville crest. This is composed of fleurs-de-lis only, the blazon of the crest being: "Out of a coronet composed of eight fleurs-de-lis or, an estoile of eight points argent."

A curious use of coronets in a crest will be found in the crest of Sir Archibald Dunbar, Bart. ["A dexter hand apaumée reaching at an astral crown proper"] (compare the arms of Dunbar on Plate XXXIV.),

[b] Crest of Bentinck: Out of a marquess's coronet proper, two arms counter-embowed, vested gules, on the hands gloves or, and in each hand an ostrich feather argent.

THE ART OF HERALDRY

and Sir Alexander James Dunbar, Bart. ["A dexter hand apaumée proper reaching to two earls' coronets tied together"].

Next after the ordinary "ducal coronet" the one most usually employed is the mural coronet, which is composed of masonry. Though it may be and often is of an ordinary heraldic tincture, it will usually be found "proper." In the crest of Every-Halstead ["Out of a mural coronet chequy or and azure, a demi-eagle ermine beaked or"] it is chequy. Instances of

it is becoming somewhat difficult to introduce differences in a stock pattern kind of crest, led to its very frequent use in grants during the last hundred years. Instances of its use will be found in the crests of Horncastle (Fig. 84), Ritson (Fig. 430), Leigh (Fig. 556), and Blackpool (Fig. 584).

Care should also be taken to distinguish between the "battlements of a tower" and a crest issuing from "a castle," as in the arms of Harley (Plate XII.); "a tower," as in the arms of Boyce (Fig. 558); and upon

FIG. 776.

crests issuing from mural coronets will be found in the crests of Tarleton (Fig. 775), Moore (Fig. 158), and M'Cammond (Fig. 329).

Care should be taken to distinguish the mural crown from the "battlements of a tower." This originated as a modern "fakement" often granted to those who have been using a mural coronet, and desire to continue within its halo, but are not qualified to obtain in their own persons a grant of it. It should be noticed that the battlements of a tower must always be represented upon a wreath. Its facility for adding a noticeable distinction to a crest has, however, in these days when

the "capital of a column," as in the arms of Cowper-Essex (Fig 777).

Abroad, e.g. in the arms of Paris, it is very usual to place a mural crown over the shield of a town, and some remarks upon the point will be found on page 279. This at first sight may seem an appropriate practice to pursue, and several heraldic artists have followed it and advocate it in this country. But the correctness of such a practice is, for British purposes, strongly and emphatically denied officially, and whilst we reserve this privilege for army officers, it does not seem proper that it should be available for casual and haphazard assump-

284

THE ART OF HERALDRY

CONDUCO

Fig. 777.—Armorial bearings of Thomas Christopher Cowper-Essex, Esq.: Quarterly, 1 and 4, azure, within two chevronels or, a quatrefoil of the last, between two griffins' heads couped ermine, the whole between three eagles displayed of the second (for Essex); 2 and 3 or, two barrulets wavy azure between two horse-shoes in chief sable, and a lantern in base proper (for Cowper). Crests: 1. on a wreath of the colours, on the capital of an Ionic column a griffin's head couped sable, charged with two quatrefoils or (for Essex): 2. on a wreath of the colours, a cubit arm erect vested gules, the cuff argent, holding in the hand a lantern suspended from a staff proper (for Cowper); with the motto, "Conduco."

Fig. 778.—Patent of Augmentation to Sir Philip Bowes Vere Broke.

285

tion by a town or city. That being the case, it should be borne in mind that the practice is not permissible in British armory.

The naval coronet (Fig. 770), though but seldom granted now, was very popular at one time. In the latter part of the eighteenth and the early part of the nineteenth centuries, naval actions were constantly being fought, and in a large number of cases where the action of the officer in command was worthy of high praise and reward, part of such reward was usually an augmentation of arms. Very frequently it is found that the crest of augmentation issued from a naval coronet (Fig. 778). This is, as will be seen, a curious figure composed of the sail and stern of a ship repeated and alternating on the rim of a circlet. Sometimes it is entirely gold, but usually the sails are argent. An instance of such a grant of augmentation will be found in the crest of augmentation for Brisbane (Fig. 553) and in Fig. 778, which is a reproduction of the patent granting a crest of augmentation to Sir Philip Bowes Broke to commemorate his glorious victory in the *Shannon* over the American ship *Chesapeake*.

Any future naval grant of a crest of augmentation would probably mean, that it would be granted issuing out of a naval coronet, but otherwise it is now confined to those grants of arms in which the patentee is of the rank of admiral. Instances of its use will be found in

FIG. 779.—Armorial bearings of Sir Arthur Farquhar, K.C.B.: Supporting a sword erect proper, the blade encircled by a wreath of laurel also proper, between three sinister hands couped gules, a chief wavy azure, thereon out of waves of the sea a representation of a fortified town of the third, and above the word "Gluckstadt" in letters of gold, the escutcheon being surrounded by the ribbon of the Most Honourable Order of the Bath, and pendent his badge as a Knight Commander. Upon the escutcheon is placed a helmet befitting his degree, with a mantling sable and or; and for his crest, out of a naval crown or, a sword as in the arms, and a flag flowing towards the sinister in saltire azure, inscribed with the word "Acheron" in letters of gold, surmounted by a dexter hand issuant gules; with the motto, "Sto cado fide et armis."

the crests of Schomberg and Farquhar (Fig. 779), and in the crest of Dakyns of Derbyshire: "Out of a naval

coronet or, a dexter arm embowed proper, holding in the hand a battle-axe argent, round the wrist a ribbon azure."

The crest of Dakyns is chiefly memorable for the

FIG. 780.—Armorial bearings of Robert Townley Caldwell, Esq.: Or, three piles sable, each charged with a fountain; in base four barrulets wavy alternately gules and vert. Mantling sable and or. Crest: out of an Eastern crown argent, the rim inscribed "Gooty" in letters sable, a demi-lion rampant holding in its dexter paw a falchion proper, and supporting in its sinister paw an escutcheon azure charged with a representation of the medal conferred upon Sir Alexander Caldwell in commemoration of his services at the siege of Seringapatam pendent from a riband tenné. Motto: "Virtus et spes."

curious motto which accompanies it: "Strike, Dakyns, the devil's in the hempe," of which no one knows the explanation.

The crest of Lord St. Vincent ["Out of a naval coronet or, encircled by a wreath of oak proper, a demi-pegasus argent, maned and hoofed of the first, winged azure, charged on the wing with a fleur-de-lis gold"] is worthy of notice owing to the encircling of the coronet, and in some number of cases the circlet of the coronet has been made use of to carry the name of a captured ship or of a naval engagement.

The Eastern Coronet is a plain rim heightened with spikes. Formerly it was granted without restriction, but now, as has been already stated, it is reserved for those of high rank who have served in India or the East. Instances of its occurrence will be found in the arms of Lord Roberts, which were granted to his father, Sir Abraham Roberts, G.C.B., and of Rawlinson, Bart. ["Sable, three swords in pale proper, pommels and hilts or, two erect, points upwards, between them one, point downwards, on a chief embattled of the third an antique crown gules. Crest: out of an Eastern crown or, a cubit arm erect in armour, the hand grasping a sword in bend sinister, and the wrist encircled by a laurel wreath proper"], and in the crest of Caldwell (Fig. 780).

Of *identically* the same shape is what is known as the "Antique Coronet." It has no particular meaning, and though no objection is made to granting it in Scotland and Ireland, it is not granted in England. Instances in which it occurs under such a description will be found in the cases of Lanigan O'Keefe (Fig. 252) and Matheson [c] (Plate XXXIII.).

The Crown Vallary or Vallary Coronet and the Palisado Coronet were undoubtedly originally the same, but now the two forms in which it has been depicted are considered to be different coronets. Each has the rim, but the vallary coronet is now heightened only by pieces of the shape of vair, whilst the palisado coronet is formed by high "palisadoes" affixed to the rim. These two are the only forms of coronets granted to ordinary and undistinguished applicants in England. An example of the former will be found in the crests of Seale (Fig. 781) and Bethell (Lord Westbury).

A recent instance of the grant of a palisado coronet will be found in the case of the town of Dukinfield (Fig. 782).

The form of the Celestial Crown will be seen in the arms of Dunbar-Dunbar [d] (Plate XXXIV.) and in the arms of Kensington (Fig. 593), but though one of the regularly recognised heraldic crowns, I know of no instance in which a crest issues from one.

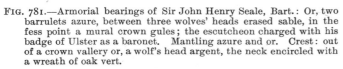

FIG. 781.—Armorial bearings of Sir John Henry Seale, Bart.: Or, two barrulets azure, between three wolves' heads erased sable, in the fess point a mural crown gules; the escutcheon charged with his badge of Ulster as a baronet. Mantling azure and or. Crest: out of a crown vallery or, a wolf's head argent, the neck encircled with a wreath of oak vert.

FIG. 782.—Arms of Dukinfield: Quarterly, azure and argent, a cross pointed and voided quarterly of the last and sable, between in the first quarter a raven close and in the fourth a garb, both or. Crest: out of a crown palisado or, a cubit arm vested azure, cuffed argent, the hand proper, holding an escutcheon of the second, charged with the sun in his splendour of the first between two ostrich-feathers of the third. Motto: "Integrity."

The circlet from the crown of a king of arms has once at least been granted as a crest coronet, this being in the case of Rogers Harrison.[e]

[c] Armorial bearings of Sir Kenneth Matheson, Bart.: Argent, three dexter hands couped two and one gules, within a bordure of the second. Mantling gules, doubled argent; and for crest, issuing out of an Eastern crown or, a dexter hand holding a scimitar in fess all proper. Motto: "Fac et spera."

[d] Armorial bearings of Rev. John Archibald Dunbar-Dunbar: Quarterly, 1 and 4, gules, a lion rampant argent, within a bordure of the last, charged with eight roses of the first; 2 and 3, or, three cushions within a double tressure flory counterflory gules, the whole within a bordure invected and quartered azure and of the last; in the centre of the quarters a deer's head cabossed proper. Crest: on a wreath of his liveries, a dexter hand apaumée reaching to an astral crown proper.

[e] Armorial bearings of George Harrison Rogers Harrison, Esq., Windsor Herald: Quarterly, 1 and 4, azure, three demi-lions rampant erased or, each crowned with an Eastern crown argent (for Harrison); 2 and 3, or, three stags trippant proper (for Rogers), in the centre chief point on an inescutcheon gules a lion rampant argent (in allusion to his office of Blanche Lion Pursuivant). Crests: 1. out of a mural coronet azure, a demi-lion issuant or, crowned as in the arms, and holding between the paws a chaplet of roses proper; 2. on a ducal coronet or, a lion rampant argent; 3. on a chapeau gules, turned up

THE CHAPEAU

Some number of crests will be found to have been granted to be borne upon a "chapeau" in lieu of wreath or coronet. Other names for the chapeau, under which it is equally well known, are the "cap of maintenance" or "cap of dignity."

There can be very little doubt that the heraldic chapeau combines two distinct origins or earlier prototypes. The one is the real cap of dignity, and the other is the hat or "capelot" which covered the top of the helm before the mantling was introduced, but from which the lambrequin developed. The curious evolu-

ermine, a stag trippant proper gorged with a coronet of a king of arms, therefrom a chain passing between the forelegs or; 4. out of a coronet composed of trefoils gold, a plume of five ostrich-feathers alternately argent and or.

tion of the chapeau from the "capelot," which is so marked and usual in Germany, is the tall conical hat, often surmounted by a tuft or larger plume of feathers, and usually employed in German heraldry as an opportunity for the repetition of the livery colours, or a part of, and often the whole design of, the arms. But it should at the same time be noticed that this tall conical hat is much more closely allied to the real cap of maintenance than our present crest "chapeau."

Exactly what purpose the real cap of maintenance served, or of what it was a symbol, remains to a certain extent a matter of mystery. The "Cap of Maintenance" —a part of the regalia borne before the sovereign at the State opening of Parliament (but *not* at a coronation) by the Marquesses of Winchester, the hereditary bearers of the cap of maintenance—bears, in its shape, no relation to the heraldic chapeau. The only similarity is its crimson colour and its lining of ermine. It is a tall conical cap, and is carried on a short staff. Whilst crest-coronets in early days appear to have had little or no relation to titular rank, there is no doubt whatever that caps of dignity had. Long before, a coronet was assigned to the rank of baron; in the reign of Charles II. all barons had their caps of dignity, of scarlet lined with white fur; and in the old pedigrees a scarlet cap with a gold tuft or tassel on top and a lining of fur will be found painted above the arms of a baron. This fact, the fact that until after Stuart days the chapeau does not appear to have been allowed or granted to others than peers, the fact that it is now reserved for the crests granted to peers, the fact that the velvet cap is a later addition both to the sovereign's crown and to the coronet of a peer, and finally the fact that the cap of maintenance is borne before the sovereign only in the precincts of Parliament, would seem to indubitably indicate that the cap of maintenance was inseparably connected with the lordship and overlordship of Parliament vested in peers and in the sovereign. In the crumpled and tasselled top of the velvet cap, and in the ermine border visible below the rim, the high conical form of the cap of maintenance proper can be still traced in the cap of a peer's coronet, and that the velvet cap contained in the crown of the sovereign and in the coronet of a peer is the survival of the old cap of dignity there can be no doubt. This is perhaps even more apparent in Fig. 783, which shows the crown of

FIG. 783.—The Crown of King Charles II.

King Charles II., than in the representations of the Royal crown which we are more accustomed to see. The present form of a peer's coronet is undoubtedly the conjoining of two separate emblems of his rank. The cap of maintenance or dignity, however, as repre-

sented above the arms of a baron, as above referred to, was not of this high conical shape. It was flatter and more like that represented in Fig. 761.

The high conical original shape is, however, preserved in many of the early heraldic representations of the chapeau, as will be noticed from an examination of the ancient Garter plates or from a reference to Fig. 264, which shows the helmet with its chapeau-borne crest of Edward the Black Prince.

Of the chapeaux upon which crests are represented in the early Garter plates the following facts may be observed. They are twenty in number of the eighty-six plates reproduced in Mr. St. John Hope's book. It should be noticed that until the end of the reign of Henry VIII. the Royal crest of the sovereign was always depicted upon a chapeau gules, lined with ermine. Of the twenty instances in which the chapeau appears, no less than twelve are representations of the Royal crest, borne by closely allied relatives of the sovereign, so that we have only eight examples from which to draw deductions. But of the twenty it should be pointed out that nineteen are peers, and the only remaining instance (Sir John Grey, K.G.) is that of the eldest son and heir apparent of a peer, both shield and crest being in this case boldly marked with the "label" of an eldest son. Consequently it is a safe deduction that whatever may have been the regulations and custom concerning the use of coronets, there can be no doubt that down to the end of the fifteenth century the use of a chapeau marked a crest as that of a peer. Of the eight non-Royal examples one has been repainted and is valueless as a contemporary record. Of the remaining seven, four are of the conventional gules and ermine. One only has not the ermine lining, that being the crest of Lord Fanhope. It is plainly the Royal crest "differenced" (he being of Royal but illegitimate descent), and probably the argent in lieu of ermine lining is one of the intentional marks of distinction. The chapeau of Lord Beaumont is azure, semé-de-lis, lined ermine, and that of the Earl of Douglas is azure lined ermine, this being in each case in conformity with the mantling. Whilst the Beaumont family still use this curiously coloured chapeau with their crest, the Douglas crest is now borne (by the Duke of Hamilton) upon one of ordinary tinctures. Chapeaux, other than of gules lined ermine, are but rarely met with, and unless specifically blazoned to the contrary a cap of maintenance is always presumed to be gules and ermine.

About the Stuart period the granting of crests upon chapeaux to others than peers became far from unusual, and the practice appears to have been frequently adopted prior to the beginning of this century. Some of these crest chapeaux, however, were not of gules. An instance of this kind will be found in the grant in 1667 to Sir Thomas Davies, then one of the sheriffs of the City of London, but afterwards (in 1677) Lord Mayor. The crest granted was: "On a chapeau sable, turned up or, a demi-lion rampant of the last." The reason for the grant at that date of such a simple crest and the even more astonishingly simple coat of arms ["Or, a chevron between three mullets pierced sable"] has always been a mystery to me.

The arms of Lord Lurgan (granted 1840) afford another instance of a chapeau of unusual colour, his crest being: "Upon a chapeau azure turned up ermine, a greyhound statant gules, collared or."

There are some number of cases in which peers whose ancestors originally bore their crests upon a wreath have subsequently placed them upon a chapeau. The Stanleys, Earls of Derby, are a case in point, as are also the Marquesses of Exeter. The latter case is curious, because although they have for long enough so depicted their crest, they only comparatively recently (within the last few years) obtained the necessary authorisation by the Crown. Their arms and crest (for Cecil) are as the first and fourth quarters, with the dexter crest as in the accompanying illustration of the arms and crest of Lord John Pakenham Joicey-Cecil (Fig. 784).

FIG. 784.—Armorial bearings of Lord John Pakenham Joicey-Cecil: Quarterly, 1 and 4, barry of ten argent and azure, over all six escutcheons sable, three, two and one, each charged with a lion rampant of the first (for Cecil); 2 and 3, argent, three torteaux each charged with a lozenge in bend of the first between two bendlets gules (for Joicey). Mantling azure and argent. Crests: 1. upon a cap of maintenance, a garb or, supported by two lions, the dexter argent, the sinister azure (for Cecil); 2. upon a wreath of the colours, a demi-man affronté in armour proper, the helmet adorned with three feathers gules, argent and azure, resting the dexter hand on an escutcheon of the arms of Joicey, and supporting with the sinister a spiked mace also proper. Motto: "Cor unum via una."

At the present time the official form of the chapeau is as in Fig. 785 with the turn up split at the back into

FIG. 785.—The Chapeau.

two tails. No such form can be found in any early representation, and most heraldic artists have now reverted to the earlier type as in Fig. 786, which represents the arms of Sir Claude Champion-de Crespigny, Bart.

Before leaving the subject of the cap of maintenance, reference should be made to another instance of a curious heraldic headgear often, but *quite incorrectly*, styled a "cap-of-maintenance." This is the fur cap invariably used over the shields of the cities of London, Dublin, and Norwich. There is no English official authority whatever for such an addition to the arms, but there does appear to be some little official recognition of it in Ulster's Office in the case of the city of Dublin. Ulster King of Arms states that he would, in the case of Dublin, have no hesitation whatever in certifying the right of the city arms to be so displayed (Fig. 787).

In the utter absence of anything in the nature of a precedent, it is quite unlikely that the practice will be

sanctioned in England. The hat used is a flat-topped brown fur hat of the shape depicted in Fig. 787. It is merely (in London) a part of the official uniform or livery of the City sword-bearer. It does not even appear to have been a part of the costume of the Lord Mayor, and it must always remain a mystery why it was

FIG. 786.—Armorial bearings of Major Sir Claude Champion-de Crespigny, Bart.: Quarterly, 1 and 4, argent, a lion rampant sable, armed and langued gules, in the dexter base a fer-de-moulin pierced of the second (for Champion-de Crespigny); 2 and 3, azure, three bars argent (for Vierville de Vierville). Mantling sable, lined with argent. Crest: on a chapeau gules, turned up ermine, a cubit arm in armour holding in the hand a broadsword proper; with the motto, "Mens sibi conscia recti."

ever adopted for heraldic use. But then the chain of the Lord Mayor of London is generally called a Collar of SS. London uses a Peer's helmet, a bogus modern

FIG. 787.—Arms of the City of Dublin.

crest, and even more modern bogus supporters, so a few other eccentricities need not in that instance cause surprise. A. C. F-D.

THE ART OF HERALDRY

CHAPTER XXVIII

THE MANTLING OR LAMBREQUIN

THE mantling is the ornamental design which in a representation of an armorial achievement depends from the helmet, falling away on either side of the escutcheon. Many authorities have considered it to have been no more than a fantastic series of flourishes, devised by artistic minds for the purpose of assisting design and affording an artistic opportunity of filling up unoccupied spaces in a heraldic design. There is no doubt that its readily apparent advantages in that character have greatly led to the importance now attached to the mantling in heraldic art. But equally is it certain that its real origin is to be traced elsewhere.

The genesis of the heraldry of to-day was in the East during the period of the Crusades, and the burning heat of the Eastern sun upon the metal helmet led to the introduction and adoption of a textile covering, which would act in some way as a barrier between the two. It was simply in fact and effect a primeval prototype of the "puggaree" of Margate and Hindustan. It is plain from all early representations that originally it was short, simply hanging from the apex of the helmet to the level of the shoulders, overlapping the textile tunic or "coat of arms," but probably enveloping a greater part of the helmet, neck, and shoulders than we are at present (judging from pictorial representations) inclined to believe.

Adopted first as a protection against the heat, and perhaps also the rust which would follow damp, the lambrequin soon made evident another of its advantages, an advantage to which we doubtless owe its perpetuation outside Eastern warfare in the more temperate climates of Northern Europe and England. Textile fabrics are peculiarly and remarkably deadening to a sword-cut, to which fact must be added the facility with which such a weapon would become entangled in the hanging folds of cloth. The hacking and hewing of battle would show itself plainly upon the lambrequin of one accustomed to a prominent position in the fore-front of a fight, and the honourable record implied by a ragged and slashed lambrequin accounts for the fact that we find at an early period after their introduction into heraldic art, that they are depicted cut and "torn to ribbons." This opportunity was quickly seized by the heraldic artist, who has always, from those very earliest times of absolute armorial freedom down to the point of greatest and most regularised control, been allowed an entire and absolute freedom in the design to be adopted for the mantling. Hence it is that we find so much importance is given to it by heraldic artists, for it is in the design of the mantling, and almost entirely in that opportunity, that the personal character and abilities of the artist have their greatest scope. Some authorities have derived the mantling from the robe of estate, and there certainly has been a period in British armory when most lambrequins found in heraldic art are represented by an unmutilated cloth, suspended from and displayed behind the armorial bearings and tied at the upper corners (Fig. 47). In all probability the robes of estate of the higher nobility, no less than the then existing and peremptorily enforced sumptuary laws, may have led to the desire and to the attempt, at a period when the actual lambrequin was fast disappearing from general knowledge, to display arms upon something which should represent either the parliamentary robes of estate of a peer, or the garments of rich fabric which the sumptuary laws forbade to those of humble degree. To this period undoubtedly belongs the term "mantling," which is so much more frequently employed than the word lambrequin, which is really—from the armorial point of view—the older term.

The heraldic mantling was, of course, originally the representation of the actual "capeline" or textile covering worn upon the helmet, but many early heraldic representations are of mantlings which are of skin, fur, or feathers, being in such cases invariably a continuation of the crest drawn out and represented as the lambrequin. The plates in this book taken from early rolls of arms afford numberless examples, and when the crest was a part of the human figure, the habit in which that figure was arrayed is almost invariably found to have been so employed. The Garter plate of Sir Ralph Bassett, one of the Founder Knights, shows the crest as a black boar's head, the skin being continued as the sable mantling.

Some Sclavonic families have mantlings of fur only, that of the Hungarian family of Chorinski is a bear skin, and by a study of the present volume countless other instances can be found of the use by German families of a continuation of the crest for a mantling. This affords instances of many curious mantlings, this in one case in the Zurich *Wappenrolle* being the scaly skin of a salmon. The mane of the lion, the crest of Mertz, and the hair and beard of the crests of Bohn and Landschaden, are similarly continued to do duty for the mantling. This practice has never found great favour in England, the cases amongst the early Garter plates where it has been followed standing almost alone. In a manuscript (M. 3, 67*b*) of the reign of Henry VII., now in the College of Arms, probably dating from about 1506, an instance of this character can be found. It is a representation of the crest of Stourton (Fig. 788) as it was

FIG. 788.—The Crest of Stourton.

borne at that date, and was a black Benedictine demi-monk proper holding erect in his dexter hand a scourge. Here the proper black Benedictine habit (it has of later years been corrupted into the russet habit of a friar) is continued to form the mantling.

By what rules the colours of the mantlings were decided in early times it is impossible to say. No rules have been handed down to us—the old heraldic books are silent on the point—and it seems equally hopeless to attempt to deduce any from ancient armorial examples. The one fact that can be stated with certainty is that the rules of early days, if there were any, were not the rules presently observed. Some hold that the colours of the mantling were decided by the colours of the actual livery in use as distinct from the "livery colours" of the arms. It is difficult to check this rule, because our knowledge of the liveries in use in early days is so meagre and limited; but in the few instances of which we now have knowledge we look in vain for a repetition of the colours worn by the retainers as liveries in the mantlings used. The fact that the livery colours are represented in the background of some of the early Garter plates, and that in such instances in no single case do they agree with the colours of the mantling, must certainly dissipate once and for all any such supposition as far as it relates to that period.

A careful study and analysis of early heraldic emblazonment, however, reveals one point as a dominating characteristic. That is, that where the crest, by its nature, lent itself to a continuation into the mantling it generally was so continued. This practice, which was almost universal upon the Continent, and is particularly to be met with in German heraldry, though seldom adopted in England, certainly had some weight in English heraldry. In the recently published reproductions of the Plantagenet Garter plates eighty-seven armorial achievements are included. Of these, in ten instances the mantlings are plainly continuations of the crests, being "feathered" or in unison. Fifteen of the mantlings have both the outside and the inside of the principal colour and of the principal metal of the arms they accompany, though in a few cases, contrary to the present practice, the metal is outside, the lining being of the colour. Nineteen more of the mantlings are of the principal colour of the arms, the majority (eighteen) of these being lined with ermine. No less than forty-nine are of some colour lined with ermine, but thirty-four of these are of gules lined ermine, and in the large majority of cases in these thirty-four instances neither the gules nor the ermine are in conformity with the principal colour and metal (what we now term the "livery colours") of the arms. In some cases the colours of the mantling agree with the colours of the crest, a rule which will usually be found to hold good in German heraldry. The constant occurrence of gules and ermine incline one much to believe that the colours of the mantling were not decided by haphazard fancy, but that there was some law—possibly in some way connected with the sumptuary laws of the period—which governed the matter, or, at any rate, which greatly limited the range of selection. Of the eighty-seven mantlings, excluding those which are gules lined ermine, there are four only the colours of which apparently bear no relation whatever to the colours of the arms or the crests appearing upon the same Stall plate. In some number of the plates the colours certainly are taken from a quartering other than the first one, and in one at least of the four exceptions the mantling (one of the most curious examples) is plainly derived from a quartering inherited by the knight in question though not shown upon the Stall plate. Probably a closer examination of the remaining three instances would reveal a similar reason in each case. That any law concerning the colours of their mantlings was enforced upon those concerned would be an unwarrantable deduction not justified by the instances

under examination, but one is clearly justified in drawing from these cases some deductions as to the practice pursued. It is evident that unless one was authorised by the rule or reason governing the matter—whatever such rule or reason may have been—in using a mantling of gules and ermine, the dominating *colour* (not as a rule the metal) of the coat of arms (or of one of the quarterings), or sometimes of the crest if the tinctures of arms and crest were not in unison, decided the colour of the mantling. That there was some meaning behind the mantlings of gules lined with ermine there can be little doubt, for it is noticeable that in a case in which the colours of the arms themselves are gules and ermine, the mantling is of gules and argent, as by the way in this particular case is the chapeau upon which the crest is placed. But probably the reason which governed these mantlings of gules lined with ermine, as also the ermine linings of other mantlings, must be sought outside the strict limits of armory. That the colours of mantlings are repeated in different generations, and in the plates of members of the same family, clearly demonstrates that selection was not haphazard.

Certain of these early Garter plates exhibit interesting curiosities in the mantlings:—

1. Sir William Latimer, Lord Latimer, K.G., c. 1361–1381. Arms: gules a cross patonce or. Crest: a plume of feathers sable, the tips or. Mantling gules with silver vertical stripes, lined with ermine.

2. Sir Bermond Arnaud de Presac, Soudan de la Tran, K.G., 1380–*post* 1384. Arms: or, a lion rampant double-queued gules. Crest: a Midas' head argent. Mantling sable, lined gules, the latter veined or.

3. Sir Simon Felbrigge, K.G., 1397–1442. Arms: or, a lion rampant gules. Crest: out of a coronet gules, a plume of feathers ermine. Mantling ermine, lined gules (evidently a continuation of the crest).

4. Sir Reginald Cobham, Lord Cobham, K.G., 1352–1361. Arms: gules, on a chevron or, three estoiles sable. Crest: a soldan's head sable, the brow encircled by a torse or. Mantling sable (evidently a continuation of the crest), lined gules.

5. Sir Edward Cherleton, Lord Cherleton of Powis, K.G., 1406–7 to 1420–1. Arms: or, a lion rampant gules. Crest: on a wreath gules and sable, two lions' gambs also gules, each adorned on the exterior side with three demi-fleurs-de-lis issuing argent, the centres thereof or. Mantling: on the dexter side, sable; on the sinister side, gules; both lined ermine.

6. Sir Hertong von Clux, K.G., 1421–1445 or 6. Arms: argent, a vine branch couped at either end in bend sable. Crest: out of a coronet or, a plume of feathers sable and argent. Mantling: on the dexter side, azure; on the sinister, gules; both lined ermine.

7. Sir Miles Stapleton, K.G. (Founder Knight, died 1364). Arms: argent, a lion rampant sable. Crest: a soldan's head sable, around the temples a torse azure, tied in a knot, the ends flowing. Mantling sable (probably a continuation of the crest), lined gules.

8. Sir Walter Hungerford, Lord Hungerford and Heytesbury, K.G., 1421–1449. Arms: sable, two bars argent, and in chief three plates. Crest: out of a coronet azure a garb or, enclosed by two sickles argent. Mantling (within and without): dexter, barry of six ermine and gules; sinister, barry of six gules and ermine. (The reason of this is plain. The mother of Lord Hungerford was a daughter and coheir of Hussey. The arms of Hussey are variously given: "Barry of six ermine and gules," or "Ermine, three bars gules.")

9. Sir Humphrey Stafford, Earl of Stafford, 1429–1460. Arms: or, a chevron gules. Crest: out of a coronet gules, a swan's head and neck proper, beaked gules, between two wings also proper. Mantling: the

dexter side, sable; the sinister side, gules; both lined ermine. Black and gules, it may be noted, were the livery colours of Buckingham, an earldom which had devolved upon the Earls of Stafford.

10. Sir John Grey of Ruthin, K.G., 1436–1439. Arms: quarterly, 1 and 4, barry of six argent and azure, in chief three torteaux; 2 and 3, quarterly i. and iiii., or, a maunch gules; ii. and iii., barry of eight argent and azure, an orle of ten martlets gules; over all a label of three points argent. Crest: on a chapeau gules, turned up ermine, a wyvern or, gorged with a label argent. Mantling or, lined ermine.

11. Sir Richard Nevill, Earl of Salisbury, K.G., 1436–1460. Arms: quarterly, 1 and 4, quarterly i. and iiii., argent, three lozenges conjoined in fess gules; ii. and iii., or, an eagle displayed vert; 2 and 3, gules, a saltire argent, a label of three points company argent and (? sable or azure). Crest: on a coronet, a griffin sejant, with wings displayed or. Mantling: dexter side, gules; the sinister, sable; both lined ermine.

12. Sir Gaston de Foix, Count de Longueville, &c., K.G., 1438–1458. Arms: quarterly, 1 and 4, or, three pallets gules; 2 and 3, or, two cows passant in pale gules, over all a label of three points, each point or, on a cross sable five escallops argent. Crest: on a wreath or and gules, a blackamoor's bust with ass's ears sable, vested paly or and gules, all between two wings, each of the arms as in the first quarter. Mantling paly of or and gules, lined vert.

13. Sir Walter Blount, Lord Mountjoye, K.G., 1472–1474. Arms: quarterly, 1. argent, two wolves passant in pale sable, on a bordure also argent eight saltires couped gules (for Ayala); 2. or, a tower (? gules) (for Mountjoy); 3. barry nebuly or and sable (for Blount); 4. vairé argent and gules (for Gresley). Crest: out of a coronet two ibex horns or. Mantling sable, lined on the dexter side with argent, and on the sinister with or.

14. Frederick, Duke of Urbino. Mantling or, lined ermine.

In Continental heraldry it is by no means uncommon to find the device of the arms repeated either wholly or in part upon the mantling. In reference to this the "Tournament Rules" of René, Duke of Anjou, throw some light on the point. These it may be of interest to quote:—

"Vous tous Princes, Seigneurs, Barons, Cheualiers, et Escuyers, qui auez intention de tournoyer, vous estes tenus vous rendre és heberges le quartrième jour deuan le jour du Tournoy, pour faire de vos Blasons fenestres, sur payne de non estre receus audit Tournoy. Les armes seront celles-cy. Le tymbre doit estre sur vne piece de cuir boüilly, la quelle doit estre bien faultrée d'vn doigt d'espez, ou plus, par le dedans: et doit contenir la dite piece de cuir tout le sommet du heaulme, et sera couuerte la dite piece du lambrequin armoyé des armes de celuy qui le portera, et sur le dit lambrequin au plus haut du sommet, sera assis le dit Tymbre, et autour d'iceluy aura vn tortil des couleurs que voudra le Tournoyeur.

"Item, et quand tous les heaulmes seront ainsi mis et ordonnez pour les departir, viendront toutes Dames et Damoiselles et tous Seigneurs, Cheualiers, et Escuyers, en les visitant d'vn bout à autre, la present les Juges, qui meneront trois ou quatre tours les Dames pour bien voir et visiter les Tymbres, et y aura vu Herault ou poursuivant, qui dira aux Dames selon l'endroit où elles seront, le nom de ceux à qui sont les Tymbres, afin que s'il en a qui ait des Dames médit, et elles touchent son Tymbre, qu'il soit le lendemain pour recommandé." (Menêtrier, *L'Origine des Armoiries*, pp. 79–81.)

Whilst one can call to mind no instance of importance of ancient date where this practice has been followed in this country, there are one or two instances in the Garter plates which approximate closely to it. The mantling of John, Lord Beaumont, is azure, semé-de-lis (as the field of his arms), lined ermine. Those of Sir John Bourchier, Lord Berners, and of Sir Henry Bourchier, Earl of Essex, are of gules, billetté or, evidently derived from the quar-

tering for Louvaine upon the arms, this quartering being: "Gules, billetté and a fess or."

According to a MS. of Vincent, in the College of Arms, the Warrens used a mantling chequy of azure and or with their arms.

A somewhat similar result is obtained by the mantling, "Gules, semé of lozenges or," upon the small plate of Sir Sanchet Dabrichecourt. The mantling of Sir Lewis Robessart, Lord Bourchier, is: "Azure, bezanté, lined argent."

"The azure mantling on the Garter plate of Henry V., as Prince of Wales, is 'semé of the French golden fleurs-de-lis.' . . . The Daubeny mantling is 'semé of mullets.' On the brass of Sir John Wylcote, at Tew, the lambrequins are chequy. . . . On the seals of Sir John Bussy, in 1391 and 1407, the mantlings are barry, the coat being 'argent, three bars sable.'"

There are a few cases amongst the Garter plates in which badges are plainly and unmistakably depicted upon the mantlings. Thus, on the lining of the mantling on the plate of Sir Henry Bourchier (elected 1452) will be found water-bougets, which are repeated on a fillet round the head of the crest. The Stall plate of Sir John Bourchier, Lord Berners, above referred to (elected 1459), is lined with silver on the dexter side, semé in the upper part with water-bougets, and in the lower part with Bourchier knots. On the opposite side of the mantling the knots are in the upper part, and the water-bougets below. That these badges upon the mantling are not haphazard artistic decoration is proved by a reference to the monumental effigy of the Earl of Essex, in Little Easton Church, Essex. The differing shapes of the helmet, and of the coronet and the mantling, and the different representation of the crest, show that, although depicted in his Garter robes, upon his effigy the helmet, crest, and mantling upon which the earl's head there rests, and the representations of the same upon the Garter plate, are not slavish copies of the same original model. Nevertheless upon the effigy, as on the Garter plate, we find the outside of the mantling "semé of billets," and the inside "semé of water-bougets." Another instance amongst the Garter plates will be found in the case of Viscount Lovell, whose mantling is strewn with gold padlocks.

Nearly all the mantlings on the Garter Stall plates are more or less heavily "veined" with gold, and many are heavily diapered and decorated with floral devices. So prominent is some of this floral diapering that one is inclined to think that in a few cases it may possibly be a diapering with floral badges. In other cases it is equally evidently no more than a mere accessory of design, though between these two classes of diapering it would be by no means easy to draw a line of distinction. The veining and "heightening" of a mantling with gold is at the present day nearly always to be seen in elaborate heraldic painting.

From the Garter plates of the fourteenth century it has been shown that the colours of a large proportion of the mantlings approximated in early days to the colours of the arms. The popularity of gules, however, was then fast encroaching upon the frequency of appearance which other colours should have enjoyed; and in the sixteenth century, in grants and other paintings of arms, the use of a mantling of gules had become practically universal. In most cases the mantling of "gules, doubled argent" forms an integral part of the terms of the grant itself, as sometimes do the "gold tassels" which are so frequently found terminating the mantlings of that and an earlier period. This custom continued through the Stuart period, and though dropped officially in England during the eighteenth century (when the mantling reverted to the livery colours of the arms, and became in this form a matter of course and so understood, not being expressed in the wording of the patent), it continued in force in Lyon Office in Scotland until the year 1890, when the present Lyon King of Arms (Sir James Balfour Paul) altered the practice, and, as had earlier been done in England, ordered that all future Scottish mantlings should be depicted in the livery colours of the arms, but in Scotland the mantlings, though now following the livery colours, are still included in the terms of the grant, and thereby stereotyped. In England, in an official "exemplification" at the present day of an ancient coat of arms (*e.g.* in an exemplification following the assumption of name and arms by Royal License), the mantling is painted in the livery colours, irrespective of any ancient patent in which "gules and argent" may have been *granted* as the colour of the mantling. Though probably most people will agree as to the expediency of such a practice, it is at any rate open to criticism on the score of propriety, unless the new mantling is expressed in terms in the new patent. This would of course amount to a grant overriding the earlier one, and would do all that was necessary; but failing this, there appears to be a distinct hiatus in the continuity of authority.

Ermine linings to the mantling were soon denied to the undistinguished commoner, and with the exception of the early Garter plates, it would be difficult to point to an instance of their use. The mantlings of peers, however, continued to be lined with ermine, and English instances under official sanction can be found in the Visitation Books and in the Garter plates until a comparatively recent period. In fact the relegation of peers to the ordinary livery colours for their mantlings is, in England, quite a modern practice. In Scotland, however, the mantlings of peers have always been lined with ermine, and the present Lyon continues this whilst usually making the colours of the outside of the mantlings agree with the principal colour of the arms. This, as regards the outer colour of the mantling is not a fixed or stereotyped rule, and in some cases Lyon has preferred to adopt a mantling of gules lined with ermine as more comfortable to a peer's Parliamentary Robe of Estate (see Plate LVIII.).

In the Deputy Earl-Marshal's warrant referred to on page 283 are some interesting points as to the mantling. It is recited that "some persons under yᵉ degree of yᵉ Nobilitie of this Realme doe cause Ermins to be Depicted upon ye Lineings of those Mantles which are used with their Armes, and also that there are some that have lately caused the Mantles of their Armes to be painted like Oistrich feathers as tho' they were of some peculiar and superior degree of Honor," and the warrant commands that these points are to be rectified.

The Royal mantling is of cloth of gold. In the case of the sovereign and the Prince of Wales it is lined with ermine, and for other members of the Royal Family it is lined with argent. Queen Elizabeth was the first sovereign to adopt the golden mantling, the Royal tinctures before that date (for the mantling) being gules lined ermine. The mantling of or and ermine has, of course, since that date been rigidly denied to all outside the Royal Family. Two instances, however, occur amongst the early Garter plates, viz. Sir John Grey de Ruthyn and Frederick, Duke of Urbino. It is sometimes stated that a mantling of or and ermine is a sign of sovereignty, but our own sovereign is really the only case in which it is presently so used.

In Sweden, as in Scotland, the colours of the mantling are specified in the patent, and, unlike our own, are often curiously varied.

The present rules for the colour of a mantling are as follows in England and Ireland:—

1. That with ancient arms of which the grant specified the colour, where this has not been altered by a subsequent exemplification, the colours must be as stated in the grant, *i.e.* usually gules, lined argent.
2. That the mantling of the sovereign and Prince of Wales is of cloth of gold, lined with ermine.
3. That the mantling of other members of the Royal Family is of cloth of gold lined with argent.
4. That the mantlings of all other people shall be of the livery colours.

The rules in Scotland are now as follows:—

1. That in the cases of peers whose arms were matriculated before 1890 the mantling is of gules lined with ermine (the Scottish term for "lined" is "doubled").
2. That the mantlings of all other arms matriculated before 1890 shall be of gules and argent.
3. That the mantlings of peers whose arms have been matriculated since 1890 shall be either of the principal colour of the arms, lined with ermine, or of gules lined ermine (conformably to the Parliamentary Robe of Estate of a peer) as may happen to have been matriculated.
4. That the mantlings of all other persons whose arms have been matriculated since 1890 shall be of the livery colours, unless other colours are, as is occasionally the case, specified in the patent of matriculation.

Whether in Scotland a person is entitled to assume of his own motion an ermine lining to his mantling upon his elevation to the peerage, without a rematriculation in cases where the arms and mantling have been otherwise matriculated at an earlier date, or whether in England any peer may still line his mantling with ermine, one hesitates to express an opinion.

When the mantling is of the livery colours the following rules must be observed. The outside must be of some colour and the lining of some metal. The colour must be the principal colour of the arms, *i.e.* the colour of the field if it be of colour, or if it is of metal, then the colour of the principal ordinary or charge upon the shield. The metal will be as the field, if the field is of metal, or if not, it will be as the metal of the principal ordinary or charge. In other words, it should be the same tinctures as the wreath.

If the field is party of colour and metal (*i.e.* per pale, barry, quarterly, &c.), then that colour and that metal are "the livery colours." If the field is party of two *colours* the principal colour (*i.e.* the one first mentioned in the blazon) is taken as the colour, and the other is ignored. The mantling is *not* made party to agree with the field in British heraldry, as would be the case in Germany. If the field is of a fur, then the dominant metal or colour of the fur is taken as one component part of the "livery colours," the other metal or colour required being taken from the next most important tincture of the field. For example, "ermine, a fess gules" has a mantling of gules and argent, whilst "or, a chevron ermines" would need a mantling of sable and or. The mantling for "azure, a lion rampant erminois" would be azure and or. A field of vair has a mantling argent and azure, but if the charge be vair the field will supply the one, *i.e.* either colour or metal, whilst the vair supplies whichever is lacking. Except in the cases of Scotsmen who are peers and of the Sovereign and Prince of Wales, no fur is ever used nowadays in Great Britain for a mantling.

In cases where the principal charge is "proper," a certain discretion must be used. Usually the heraldic

THE ART OF HERALDRY

colour to which the charge approximates is used. For example, "argent, issuing from a mount in base a tree proper," &c., would have a mantling vert and argent. The arms "or, three Cornish choughs proper," or "argent, three negroes' heads couped proper," would have mantlings respectively sable and or and sable and argent. Occasionally one comes across a coat which supplies an "impossible" mantling, or which does not supply one at all. Such a coat would be "per bend sinister ermine and erminois, a lion rampant counterchanged." Here there is no colour at all, so the mantling would be gules and argent. "Or, three stags trippant proper" would have a mantling gules and argent. A coat of arms with a landscape field would also probably be supplied (in default of a chief, e.g. supplying other colours and tinctures) with a mantling gules and argent. It is quite permissible to "vein" a mantling with gold lines, this being always done in official paintings.

In English official heraldry, where, no matter how great the number of crests, one helmet only is painted, it naturally follows that one mantling only can be depicted. This is always taken from the livery colours of the chief (i.e. the first) quartering or sub-quartering. In Scottish patents at the present day in which a helmet is painted for each crest the mantlings frequently vary, being in each case in accordance with the livery colours of the quartering to which the crest belongs. Consequently this must be accepted as the rule in cases where more than one helmet is shown.

In considering the fashionings of mantlings it must be remembered that styles and fashions much overlap, and there has always been the tendency in armory to repeat earlier styles. Whilst one willingly concedes the immense gain in beauty by the present reversion in heraldic art to older and better, and certainly more artistic types, there is distinctly another side to the question which is strangely overlooked by those who would have the present-day heraldic art slavishly copied in all minutiæ of detail (and even according to some), in all the crudity of draughtsmanship from examples of the earliest periods.

Hitherto each period of heraldic art has had its own peculiar style and type, each within limits readily recognisable. Whether that style and type can be considered when judged by the canons of art to be good or bad, there can be no doubt that each style in its turn has approximated to, and has been in keeping with, the concurrent decorative art outside and beyond heraldry, though it has always exhibited a tendency to lag behind. When all has been said and done that can be, heraldry, in spite of its symbolism and its many other meanings, remains but a form of decorative art; and therefore it is natural that it should be influenced by other artistic ideas and other manifestations of art and accepted forms of design current at the period to which it belongs. For, from the artistic point of view, the part played in art by heraldry is so limited in extent compared with the part occupied by other forms of decoration, that one would naturally expect heraldry to show the influence of outside decorative art to a greater extent than decorative art as a whole would be likely to show the influence of heraldry. In our present revulsion of mind in favour of older heraldic types, we are apt to speak of "good" or "bad" heraldic art. But art itself cannot so be divided, for after all allowances have been made for crude workmanship, and when bad or imperfect examples have been eliminated from consideration (and given always necessarily the essential basis of the relation of line to curve and such technical details of art), who on earth is to judge, or who is competent to say, whether any particular style of art is good or bad? No

one from preference executes speculative art which he knows whilst executing it to be bad. Most manifestations of art, and peculiarly of decorative art, are commercial matters executed with the frank idea of subsequent sale, and consequently with the subconscious idea, true though but seldom acknowledged, of pleasing that public which will have to buy. Consequently the ultimate appeal is to the taste of the public, for art, if it be not the desire to give pleasure by the representation of beauty, is nothing. Beauty, of course, must not necessarily be confounded with prettiness; it may be beauty of character. The result is, therefore, that the decorative art of any period is an indication of that which gives pleasure at the moment, and an absolute reflex of the artistic wishes, desires, and tastes of the cultivated classes to whom executive art must appeal. At every period it has been found that this taste is constantly changing, and as a consequence the examples of decorative art of any period are a reflex only of the artistic ideas current at the time the work was done.

At all periods, therefore, even during the early Victorian period, which we are now taught and believe to be the most ghastly period through which English art has passed, the art in vogue has been what the public have admired, and have been ready to pay for, and most emphatically what they have been taught and brought up to consider good art. In early Victorian days there was no lack of educated people, and because they liked the particular form of decoration associated with their period, who is justified in saying that, because that peculiar style of decoration is not acceptable now to ourselves, their art was bad, and worse than our own? If throughout the ages there had been one dominating style of decoration equally accepted at all periods and by all authorities as the highest type of decorative art, then we should have some standard to judge by. Such is not the case, and we have no such standard, and any attempt to arbitrarily create and control ideas between given parallel lines of arbitrary thought, when the ideas are constantly changing, is impossible and undesirable. Who dreams of questioning the art of Benvenuto Cellini, or of describing his craftsmanship as other than one of the most vivid examples of his period, and yet what had it in keeping with the art of the Louis XVI. period, or of the later art of William Morris and his followers? Widely divergent as are these types, they are nevertheless all accepted as the highest expressions of three separate types of decorative art. Any one attempting to compare them, or to rank these schools of artistic thought in order of superiority, would simply be laying themselves open to ridicule unspeakable, for they would be ranked by the highest authorities of different periods in different orders, and it is as impossible to create a permanent standard of art as it is impossible to ensure a permanence of any particular public taste. The fact that taste changes, and as a consequence that artistic styles and types vary, is simply due to the everlasting desire on the part of the public for some new thing, and their equally permanent appreciation of novelty of idea or sensation. That master-minds have arisen to teach, and that they have taught with some success their own particular brand of art to the public, would seem rather to argue against the foregoing ideas were it not that, when the master-mind and the dominating influence are gone, the public, desiring as always change and novelty, are ready to fly to any new teacher and master who can again afford them artistic pleasure. The influence of William Morris in household decoration is possibly the most far-reaching modern example of the influence of a single man upon the art of his period; but master-mind as was his, and master-craftsman as he was, it has needed but a few years since his death to initiate the undoing of much that he taught. After the movement initiated by Morris and carried further by the Arts and Crafts Society, which made for simplicity in structural design as well as in the decoration of furniture, we have now fallen back upon the flowery patterns of the early Victorian period, and there is hardly a drawing-room in fashionable London where the chairs and settees are not covered with early Victorian chintzes.

Artistic authorities may shout themselves hoarse, but the fashion having been set in Mayfair will be inevitably followed in Suburbia, and we are doubtless again at the beginning of the cycle of that curious manifestation of domestic decorative art which was current in the early part of the nineteenth century. It is, therefore, evident that it is futile to describe varying types of art of varying periods as good or bad, or to differentiate between them, unless some such permanent basis of comparison or standard of excellence be conceded. The differing types must be accepted as no more than the expression of the artistic period to which they belong. That being so, one cannot help thinking that the abuse which has been heaped of late (by unthinking votaries of Plantagenet and Tudor heraldry) upon heraldic art in the seventeenth, eighteenth, and nineteenth centuries has very greatly overstepped the true proportion of the matter. Much that has been said is true, but what has been said too often lacks proportion. There is consequently much to be said in favour of allowing each period to create its own style and type of heraldic design, in conformity with the ideas concerning decorative art which are current outside heraldic thought. This is precisely what is not happening at the present time, even with all our boasted revival of armory and armorial art. The tendency at the present time is to slavishly copy examples of other periods. One much-advertised heraldic artist at the moment is working by the aid of tracing-paper and the craftsmanship of clever heraldic artists who have predeceased him in the far distant past, appearing to especially favour those whose work exhibits that strange tendency to bad execution which of necessity one must expect at the period when they worked. There is another point which is usually overlooked by the most blatant followers of this school of thought. What are the ancient models which remain to us? The early Rolls of Arms of which we hear so much are not, and were never intended to be, examples of artistic execution. They are merely memoranda of *fact*. It is absurd to suppose that an actual shield was painted with the crudity to be met with in the Rolls of Arms. It is equally absurd to accept as unimpeachable models, Garter plates, seals, or architectural examples unless the purpose and medium—wax, enamel, or stone—in which they are executed is borne in mind, and the knowledge used with due discrimination. Mr. Eve, without slavishly copying, originally appears to have modelled his work upon the admirable designs and ideas of the "little masters" of German art in the sixteenth and seventeenth centuries. He has since progressed therefrom to a distinctive and very excellent style of his own. Mr. Forbes Nixon and Mr. Graham Johnson model themselves—or rather their work—upon Plantagenet and Tudor examples. The work of Père Anselm, and of Pugin, the first start towards the present ideas of heraldic art, embodying as it did so much of the beauty of the older work whilst possessing a character of its own, and developing ancient ideals by increased beauty of execution, has placed their reputation far above that of others, who, following in their footsteps, have not possessed their abilities. Of the artists of the present day, Mr. Eve affords the greatest promise, inasmuch as he has

added to the strength and virility of ancient examples a most marvellous executive craftsmanship, and an originality of design and character which place him high in the scale. He has probably not yet reached the highest point to which his work will attain, and his further progress will be watched with deep interest by many. But with regard to most of the heraldic design of the present day as a whole it is very evident that we are simply picking and choosing tit-bits from the work of bygone craftsmen, and copying, more or less slavishly, examples of other periods. This makes for no advance in design either in its character or execution, nor will it result in any peculiarity of style which it will be possible in the future to identify with the present period. Our heraldry, like our architecture, though it may be dated in the twentieth century, will be a heterogeneous collection of isolated specimens of Gothic, Tudor, or Queen Anne style and type which surely is as anachronistic as we consider to be those Dutch paintings which represent Christ and the Apostles in modern clothes.

Roughly the periods into which the types of mantlings can be divided, when considered from the standpoint of their fashioning, are somewhat as follows. There is the earliest period of all, when the mantling depicted approximated closely if it was not an actual representation of the capelote really worn in battle. Examples of this will be found in the *Armorial de Gelre* and the Zurich *Wappenrolle*. This style has been reproduced in the illustration of the arms of Mr. W. Rae Macdonald, Carrick Pursuivant of Arms (see Plate XVII). As the mantling worn lengthened and evolved itself into the lambrequin, the mantling depicted in heraldic art was similarly increased in size, terminating in the long mantle drawn in profile but tasselled and with the scalloped edges, a type which is found surviving in some of the early Garter plates. This is the transition stage. The next definite period is when we find the mantling depicted on both sides of the helmet and the scalloped edges developed, in accordance with the romantic ideas of the period, into the slashes and cuts of the bold and artistic mantlings of Plantagenet armorial art.

Slowly decreasing in strength, but at the same time increasing in elaboration, this mantling and type continued until it had reached its highest pitch of exuberant elaboration in Stuart and early Georgian times. Of this the arms of Scroop (Fig. 800) are a good example. Side by side with this over-elaboration came the revulsion to a Puritan simplicity of taste which is to be found in other manifestations of art at the same time, and which made itself evident in heraldic decoration by the use as mantling of the plain uncut cloth suspended behind the shield (Fig. 47). Originating in Elizabethan days, this plain cloth was much made use of, but towards the end of the Stuart period came that curious evolution of British heraldry which is peculiar to these countries alone. That is the entire omission of both helmet and mantling. How it originated it is difficult to understand, unless it be due to the fact that a large number, in fact a large proportion, of English families possessed a shield only and neither claimed nor used a crest, and that consequently a large number of heraldic representations give the shield only. It is rare indeed to find a shield surmounted by helmet and mantling when the former is not required to support a crest. At the same time we find, amongst the official records of the period, that the documents of chief importance were the Visitation Books. In these, probably from motives of economy or to save needless draughtsmanship, the trouble of depicting the helmet and mantling was dispensed with, and the crest is almost universally found depicted on the wreath, which is made to rest upon the shield, the helmet being omitted. That being an accepted official way of representing an achievement, small wonder that the public followed, and we find as a consequence that a large proportion of the bookplates during the seventeenth and eighteenth centuries had no helmet or mantling at all, the elaboration of the edges of the shield, together with the addition of decorative and needless accessories bearing no relation to the arms, fulfilling all purposes of decorative design. It should also be remembered that from towards the close of the Stuart period onward, England was taking her art and decoration almost entirely from Continental sources, chiefly French and Italian. In both the countries the use of crests was very limited indeed in extent, and the elimination of the helmet and mantling, and the elaboration in their stead of the edges of the shield, we probably owe to the effort to assimilate French and Italian forms of decoration to English arms. So obsolete had become the use of helmet and mantling that it is difficult to come across sufficient examples that one can put forward as mantlings typical of the period. Figs. 789 and 790

are examples of the style of heraldic decoration then in vogue.

Helmets and mantlings were of course painted upon grants and upon the Stall plates of the knights of the various orders, but whilst the helmets became weak, of a pattern impossible to wear, and small in size, the mantlings became of a stereotyped pattern, and of a design poor and wooden according to our present ideas. Fig. 90, which represents the arms of Haldane, shows what had become the accepted official pattern in Scotland prior to 1890. Plate LXVIII., which represents the Stall plate of Sir Alexander Cochrane, K.B., will show an English example. A stereotyped pattern is still adhered to in England for official purposes, and will be found in Fig. 51, which is from a photograph of the recent patent granting arms to the town of Warrington.

Another variety of the official pattern will be found in the arms of Burnard (Fig. 94).

Unofficial heraldry had sunk to an even lower style

FIG. 791.—Armorial bearings of Ralph Bagnall Bagnall-Wild, Esq.: Quarterly, 1 and 4, ermine, a fess engrailed between in chief two stags' heads erased, and in base an escallop all sable (for Wild); 2 and 3, or, two bars ermine, a lion rampant azure between two flaunches of the last (for Bagnall); and for his crests: 1. upon a wreath of the colours, a demi-stag sable, gutté-d'or, attired and resting the sinister foot on an escallop or (for Wild); 2. upon a wreath of the colours, upon the trunk of a tree fesswise eradicated and sprouting proper, an heraldic antelope sejant azure, bezanté, gorged with a collar gemel and horned or (for Bagnall); with the motto, "Sûr et loyal."

FIG. 789.—Armorial bearings of Hugh Aldersey, Esq.: Gules, on a bend argent, between two cinquefoils or, three leopards' faces vert, with many quarterings. Crest: on a wreath of the colours, a demi-griffin segreant gules, beaked and armed, and issuing from a plume of five ostrich feathers or. Motto: "Alnus semper floreat."

of art, and the regulation heraldic stationer's type of shield, mantling, and helmet are awe-inspiring in their ugliness, and are as represented in Figs. 791 and 792.

The term "mantle" is sometimes employed, but it would seem hardly quite correctly, to the parliamentary robe of estate upon which the arms of a peer of the realm were so frequently depicted at the end of the eighteenth and in the early part of the nineteenth centuries. Its popularity is an indication of the ever-constant predilection for something which is denied to others and the possession of which is a matter of privilege. Woodward, in his "Treatise on Heraldry," treats of and dismisses the matter in one short sentence: "In England the suggestion that the arms of peers should be mantled with their Parliament robes was never generally adopted." In this statement he is quite incorrect, for as the accepted type in one particular opportunity of armorial display its use was absolutely universal. The opportunity in question was

FIG. 790.—Armorial bearings of Ettrick of High Barnes, co. Durham: Quarterly, 1 and 4, argent, a lion rampant and a chief gules (for Ettrick); 2 and 3, quarterly i. and iiii., paly of six argent and vert; ii. and iii., argent, a cockatrice with wings raised sable, beaked and membered gules (for Langley of Higham Gobion). Crest: on a wreath of the colours, a demi-lion rampant gules, holding in the dexter paw a marshal's staff sable, tipped at each end or.

the emblazonment of arms upon carriage panels. In the early part of the nineteenth and at the end of the

FIG. 792.—Armorial bearings of Francis Augustus Bevan, Esq.: Ermine, a bull passant, between three annulets gules. Mantling gules and argent. Crest: on a wreath of the colours, a griffin passant or, semé of annulets gules, holding in his dexter claw two annulets interlaced also gules. Motto: "Deus præsidium."

eighteenth centuries armorial bearings were painted of some size upon carriages, and there were few such paintings executed for the carriages, chariots, and state coaches of peers that did not appear upon a background of the robe of estate. With the modern craze for ostentatious unostentation (the result, there can be little doubt, in this respect of the wholesale appropriation of arms by those without a right to bear these ornaments), the decoration of a peer's carriage nowadays seldom shows more than a simple coronet, or a coronetted crest, initial, or monogram; but the State chariots of those who still possess them almost all, without exception, show the arms emblazoned upon the robe of estate. The Royal and many other State chariots made or refurbished for the recent coronation ceremonies show that, when an

FIG. 793.—Carriage Panel of Georgiana, Marchioness of Cholmondeley.

opportunity of the fullest display properly arises, the robe of estate is not yet a thing of the past. Fig. 793 is from a photograph of a carriage panel, and shows the arms of

a former Marchioness of Cholmondeley displayed in this manner. Incidentally it also shows a practice frequently resorted to, but quite unauthorised, of taking one supporter from the husband's shield and the other (when the wife was an heiress) from the arms of her family. The arms are those of Georgiana Charlotte, widow of George James, first Marquess of Cholmondeley, and younger daughter and coheir of Peregrine, third Duke of Ancaster. She became a widow in 1827 and died in 1838, so the panel must have been painted between those dates. The arms shown are: "Quarterly, 1 and 4, gules, in chief two esquires' helmets proper, and in base a garb or (for Cholmondeley); 2. gules, a chevron between three eagles' heads erased argent; 3. or, on a fess between two chevrons sable, three cross crosslets or (for Walpole), and on an escutcheon of pretence the arms of Bertie, namely: argent, three battering-rams fesswise in pale proper, headed and garnished azure." The supporters shown are: "Dexter, a griffin sable, armed, winged, and membered or (from the Cholmondeley achievement); sinister, a friar vested in russet with staff and rosary or" (one of the supporters belonging to the Barony of Willoughby D'Eresby, to which the Marchioness of Cholmondeley in her own right was a coheir until the abeyance in the Barony was determined in favour of her elder sister).

Another example of the use of a robe of estate as an armorial accessory will be found in Plate LXVI., which shows the arms of their Majesties King Edward VII. and Queen Alexandra when Prince and Princess of Wales. The arms of her Majesty are there depicted in accordance with an official certificate transmitted from Denmark to me as the editor of "Armorial Families" through the Danish Minister. The robe of estate was also not infrequently to be met with in this country upon hatchments. Its employment abroad is, and has always been, more general than has been the case in this country.

"In later times the arms of sovereigns—the German Electors, &c.—were mantled, usually with crimson velvet fringed with gold, lined with ermine, and crowned; but the mantling armoyé was one of the marks of dignity used by the Pairs de France, and by cardinals resident in France; it was also employed by some great nobles in other countries. The mantling of the Princes and Dukes of Mirandola was chequy argent and azure, lined with ermine. In France the mantling of the Chancelier was of cloth of gold; that of Présidents, of scarlet, lined with alternate strips of ermine and *petit gris.* In France, Napoleon I., who used a mantling of purple semé of golden bees, decreed that the princes and grand dignitaries should use an azure mantling thus semé; those of dukes were to be plain, and lined with vair instead of ermine. In 1817 a mantling of azure, fringed with gold and lined with ermine, was appropriated to the dignity of Pair de France."

The pavilion is a feature of heraldic art which is quite unknown to British heraldry, and one can call to mind no single instance of its use in this country; but as its use is very prominent in Germany and other countries, it cannot be overlooked. It is confined to the arms of sovereigns, and the pavilion is the tent-like erection within which the heraldic achievement is displayed. The pavilion seems to have originated in France, where it can be traced back upon the Great Seals of the kings to its earliest form and appearance upon the seal of Louis XI. In the case of the Kings of France, it was of azure semé-de-lis or. The pavilion used with the arms of the German Emperor is of gold semé alternately of Imperial crowns and eagles displayed sable, and is lined with ermine. The motto is carried on a crimson band, and it is surmounted by the

THE ART OF HERALDRY

Imperial crown, and a banner of the German colours gules, argent, and sable. The pavilion used by the German Emperor as King of Prussia is of crimson, semé of black eagles and gold crowns, and the band which carries the motto is blue. The pavilions of the King of Bavaria and the Duke of Baden, the King of Saxony, the Duke of Hesse, the Duke of Mecklenburg-Schwerin, the Duke of Saxe-Weimar-Eisenach, the Duke of Saxe-Meiningen-Hildburghausen, the Duke of Saxe-Altenburg, and the Duke of Anhalt are all of crimson.

In German heraldry a rather more noticeable distinction is drawn than with ourselves between the lambrequin (*Helmdecke*) and the mantle (*Helmmantel*). This more closely approximates to the robe

of estate, though the *helmmantel* has not in Germany the rigid significance of peerage degree that the robe of estate has in this country. The German *helmmantel* with few exceptions is always of purple lined with ermine, and whilst the mantle always falls directly from the coronet or cap, the pavilion is arranged in a dome-like form which bears the crown upon its summit. The pavilion is supposed to be the invention of the Frenchman Philip Moreau (1680), and found its way from France to Germany, where both in the Greater and Lesser Courts it was enthusiastically adopted. Great Britain, Austria-Hungary, Spain, Portugal, and Würtemberg are the only Royal Arms in which the pavilion does not figure.   A. C. F-D.

CHAPTER XXIX

THE TORSE, OR WREATH

THE actual helmet, from the very *earliest* heraldic representations which have come down to us, would appear not to have had any mantling, the crest being affixed direct to the (then) flat top of the helmet in use. But crests appear very early in the existence of "ordered" armory, and at much about the same time we find the "textile" covering of the helmet coming into heraldic use. In the earliest times we find that frequently the crest itself was continued into the mantling. But where this was not possible, the attaching of the crest to the helmet when the mantling intervened left an unsightly joining. The unsightliness very soon called forth a remedy. At first this remedy took the form of a coronet or a plain fillet or ribbon round the point of juncture, sometimes with and sometimes without the ends being visible. If the ends were shown they were represented as floating behind, sometimes with and sometimes without a representation of the bow or knot in which they were tied. The plain fillet still continued to be used long after the torse had come into recognised use. The consideration of crest coronets has been already included, but with regard to the wreath an analysis of the Plantagenet Garter plates will afford some definite basis from which to start deduction.

Of the eighty-six achievements reproduced in Mr. St. John Hope's book, five have no crest. Consequently we have eighty-one examples to analyse. Of these there are ten in which the crest is not attached to the lambrequin and helmet by anything perceptible, eight are attached with fillets of varying widths, twenty-one crests are upon chapeaux, and twenty-nine issue from coronets. But at no period governed by the series is it possible that either fillet, torse, chapeau, or coronet was in use to the exclusion of another form. This remark applies more particularly to the fillet and torse (the latter of which undoubtedly at a later date superseded the former), for both at the beginning and at the end of the series referred to we find the fillet and the wreath or torse, and at both periods we find crests without either coronet, torse, chapeau, or fillet. The fillet must soon afterwards (in the fifteenth century) have completely fallen into desuetude. The torse was so small and unimportant a matter that upon seals it would probably equally escape the attention of the engraver and the observer, and probably there would be little to be gained by a systematic hunt through early seals to discover the date of its introduction, but it will be noticed that no wreaths

appear in some of the early Rolls. Gerard Leigh says, "In the time of Henry the Fifth, and long after, no man had his badge set on a wreath under the degree of a knight. But that order is worn away." It probably belongs to the end of the fourteenth century. There can be little doubt that its twisted shape was an evolution from the plain fillet suggested by the turban of the East. We read in the old romances, in Mallory's "Morte d'Arthur" and elsewhere, of valiant knights who in battle or tournament wore the favour of some lady, or even the lady's sleeve upon their helmets. It always used to be a puzzle to me how the sleeve could have been worn upon the helmet, and I wonder how many of the present-day novelists, who so glibly make their knightly heroes of olden time wear the "favours" of their lady-lovers, know how it was done? The favour did not take the place of the crest. A knight did not lightly discard an honoured, inherited, and known crest for the sake of wearing a favour only too frequently the mere result of a temporary flirtation; nor to wear her colours could he at short notice discard or renew his lambrequin, surcoat, or the housings and trappings of his horse. He simply took the favour—the colours, a ribbon, or a handkerchief of the lady, as the case might be—and twisted it in and out or over and over the fillet which surrounded the joining-place of crest and helmet. To put her favour on his helmet was the work of a moment. The wearing of a lady's sleeve, which must have been an honour greatly prized, is of course the origin of the well-known "maunch," the solitary charge in the arms of both Conyers and Hastings. Doubtless the sleeve twined with the fillet would be made to encircle the base of the crest, and it is not unlikely that the wide hanging mouth of the sleeve might have been used for the lambrequin. The dresses of ladies at that period were decorated with the arms of their families, so in each case would be of the "colours" of the lady, so that the sleeve and its colours would be quickly identified, as it was no doubt usually intended they should be. The accidental result of twining a favour in the fillet, in conjunction with the pattern obviously suggested by the turban of the East, produced the conventional torse or wreath. As the conventional slashings of the lambrequin hinted at past hard fighting in battle, so did the conventional torse hint at past service to and favour of ladies, love and war being the occupations of the perfect knight of romance. How far short of the ideal knight of romance the knight of fact fell, perhaps the frequent bordures and batons of heraldry are the best indication. At first, as is evident from the Garter plates, the colours of the torse seem to have had little or no compulsory relation to the "livery colours" of the arms. The instances to be gleaned from the Plantagenet Garter plates which have been reproduced are as follows :—

Sir John Bourchier, Lord Bourchier. Torse: sable and vert. Arms: argent and gules.

Sir John Grey, Earl of Tankerville. Torse: vert, gules, and argent. Arms: gules and argent.

Sir Lewis Robsart, Lord Bourchier. Torse: azure, or, and sable. Arms: vert and or. [The crest, derived from his wife (who was a daughter of Lord Bourchier) is practically the same as the one first quoted. It will be noticed that the torse differs.]

Sir Edward Cherleton, Lord Cherleton of Powis. Torse: gules and sable. Arms: or and gules.

Sir Gaston de Foix, Count de Longueville. Torse: or and gules. Arms: or and gules.

Sir William Nevill, Lord Fauconberg. Torse: argent and gules. Arms: gules and argent.

Sir Richard Wydville, Lord Rivers. Torse: vert. Arms: argent and gules.

Sir Henry Bourchier, Earl of Essex. Torse: sable and vert. Arms: argent and gules. [This is the same crest above alluded to.]

Sir Thomas Stanley, Lord Stanley. Torse: or and azure. Arms: or and azure.

Sir John Bourchier, Lord Berners. Torse: gules and argent. Arms: argent and gules. [This is the same crest above alluded to.]

Sir Walter Devereux, Lord Ferrers. Torse: argent and sable. Arms: argent and gules. [The crest really issues from a coronet upon a torse in a previous case, this crest issues from a torse only.]

Sir Francis Lovel, Viscount Lovel. Torse: azure and or. Arms: or and gules.

Sir Thomas Burgh, Lord Burgh. Torse: azure and sable. Arms: azure and ermine.

Sir Richard Tunstall, K.G. Torse: argent and sable. Arms: sable and argent.

I can suggest no explanation of these differences unless it be, which is not unlikely, that they perpetuate "favours" worn, or perhaps a more likely supposition is that the wreath or torse was of the "family colours," as these were actually worn by the servants or retainers of each person. If this be not the case, why are the colours of the wreath termed the livery colours? At the present time in an English or Irish grant of arms the colours are not specified, but the crest is stated to be "on a wreath of the colours." In Scotland, however, the crest is granted in the following words: "and upon a wreath of his liveries is set for crest." Consequently, I have very little doubt, the true state of the case is that originally the wreath was depicted of the colours of the livery which was worn. Then new families came into prominence and eminence, and had no liveries to inherit. They were granted arms and chose the tinctures of their arms as their "colours," and used these colours for their personal liveries. The natural consequence would be in such a case that the torse, being in unison with the livery, was also in unison with the arms. The consequence is that it has become a fixed, unalterable rule in British heraldry that the torse shall be of the principal metal and of the principal colour of the arms. I know of no recent exception to this rule, the latest, as far as I am aware, being a grant in the early years of the eighteenth century. This, it is stated in the patent, was the regranting of a coat of foreign origin. Doubtless the formality of a grant was substituted for the usual registration in this case, owing to a lack of

formal proof of a right to the arms, but there is no doubt that the peculiarities of the foreign arms, as they had been previously borne, were preserved in the grant. The peculiarity in this case consisted of a torse of three tinctures. The late Lyon Clerk once pointed out to me, in Lyon Register, an instance of a coat there matriculated with a torse of three colours, but I unfortunately made no note of it at the time. Woodward alludes to the curious chequy wreath on the seals of Robert Stewart, Duke of Albany, in 1389. This appears to have been repeated in the seals of his son Murdoch.

The wreath of Patrick Hepburn appears to be of roses in the Gelre "Armorial," and a careful examination of the plates in this volume will show many curious Continental instances of substitutes for the conventional torse. Though by no means peculiar to British heraldry, there can be no manner of doubt that the wreath in the United Kingdom has obtained a position of legalised necessity and constant usage and importance which exists in no other country.

As has been already explained, the torse should fit closely to the crest, its object and purpose being merely to hide the joining of crest and helmet. Unfortunately in British heraldry this purpose has been ignored. Doubtless resulting first from the common practice of depicting a crest upon a wreath and without a helmet, and secondly from the fact that many English crests are quite unsuitable to place on a helmet, in fact impossible to affix by the aid of a wreath to a helmet, and thirdly from our ridiculous rules of position for a helmet, which result in the crest being depicted (in conjunction with the representation of the helmet) in a position many such crests never could have occupied on any helmet, the effect has been to cause the wreath to lose its real form (which is as Fig. 767), which approximated it to the *helmet*, and to become considered a straight support for and relating only to the crest. When, therefore, the crest and its supporting basis is transferred from indefinite space to the helmet, the support, which is the torse, is still represented as a flat resting-place for the crest, and it is consequently depicted as a straight and rigid bar, balanced upon the apex of the helmet. This is now and for long has been the only accepted official way of depicting a wreath in England. Certainly this is an ungraceful and inartistic rendering, and a rendering far removed from any actual helmet wreath that can ever have been actually borne. Whilst one has no wish to defend the "rigid bar," which has nothing to recommend it, it is at the same time worth while to point out that the heraldic day of actual helmets and actual usage is long since over, never to be revived, and that our heraldry of to-day is merely decorative and pictorial. The rigid bar is none other than a conventionalised form of the actual torse, and is perhaps little more at variance with the reality than is our conventionalised method of depicting a lambrequin. Whilst this conventional torse remains the official pattern, it is hopeless to attempt to banish such a method of representation: but Lyon King of Arms, happily, will have none of it in his official register or on his patents, and few heraldic artists of any repute now care to so design or represent it. As always officially painted it must consist of six links alternately of metal and colour (the "livery colours" of the arms), of which the metal must be the first to be shown to the dexter side. The torse is now supposed to be and represented as a skein of coloured silk interwined with a gold or silver cord.

Figs. 51, 65, 94, and 104 show the conventional rigid bar. Figs. 74, 91, 93, and 100 represent wreaths of the better sort. A. C. F-D.

THE ART OF HERALDRY

CHAPTER XXX

SUPPORTERS

IN this country a somewhat fictitious importance has become attached to supporters owing to their almost exclusive reservation to the highest rank. The rules which hold at the moment will be recited presently, but there can be no doubt that originally they were in this country little more than mere decorative and artistic appendages, being devised and altered from time to time by different artists according as the artistic necessaries of the moment demanded. The subject of the origin of supporters has been very ably dealt with in "A Treatise on Heraldry" by Woodward and Burnett, and with all due acknowledgment I take from that work the subjoined extract:—

"Supporters are figures of living creatures placed at the side or sides of an armorial shield, and appearing to support it. French writers make a distinction, giving the name of *Supports* to animals, real or imaginary, thus employed; while human figures or angels similarly used are called *Tenants*. Trees, and other inanimate objects which are sometimes used, are called *Soutiens*.

"Menêtrier and other old writers trace the origin of supporters to the usages of the tournaments, where the shields of the combatants were exposed for inspection, and guarded by their servants or pages disguised in fanciful attire: 'C'est des Tournois qu'est venu cet usage parce que les chevaliers y faisoient porter leurs lances, et leurs écus, par des pages, et des valets de pied, deguisez en ours, en lions, en mores, et en sauvages' (*Usage des Armoiries*, p. 119).

"The old romances give us evidence that this custom prevailed; but I think only after the use of supporters had already arisen from another source.

"There is really little doubt now that Anstis was quite correct when, in his *Aspilogia*, he attributed the origin of supporters to the invention of the engraver, who filled up the spaces at the top and sides of the triangular shield upon a circular seal with foliage, or with fanciful animals. Any good collection of mediæval seals will strengthen this conviction. For instance, the two volumes of Laing's "Scottish Seals" afford numerous examples in which the shields used in the thirteenth and fourteenth centuries were placed between two creatures resembling lizards or dragons. (See the seal of ALEXANDER DE BALLIOL, 1295.—LAING, ii. 74.)

.   .   .   .

"The seal of John, Duke of Normandy, eldest son of the King of FRANCE, before 1316 bears his arms (FRANCE-ANCIENT, *a bordure gules*) between two lions rampant away from the shield, and an eagle with expanded wings standing above it. The *secretum* of Isabelle de FLANDRES (*c.* 1308) has her shield placed between three lions, each charged with a bend (Vrée, *Gen. Com. Flanr.*, Plates XLIII., XLIV., XCII.). In 1332 AYMON OF SAVOY places his arms (SAVOY, *with a label*) between a winged lion in chief and a lion without wings at either side. Later, on the seal of AMADEUS VI., a lion's head between wings became the crest of SAVOY. In 1332 AMADEUS bears SAVOY on a lozenge (*vide* p. 58) between in chief two eagles, in base two lions. (CIBRARIO, Nos. 61, 64; and GUICHENON, tome i. No. 130.) In Scotland the shield of REGINALD CRAWFORD in 1292 is placed between two dogs, and surmounted by a fox; in the same year the paly shield of REGINALD, Earl of ATHOLE, appears between two lions in chief and as many griffins in flanks.—LAING, i. 210, 761.

"The seal of HUMBERT II., Dauphin de Viennois in 1349, is an excellent example of the fashion. The shield of DAUPHINY is in the centre of a quatrefoil. Two savages mounted on griffins support its flanks; on the upper edge an armed knight sits on a couchant lion, and the space in base is filled by a human face between two wingless dragons. The spaces are sometimes filled with the Evangelistic symbols, as on the seal of YOLANTE DE FLANDRES, Countess of BAR (*c.* 1340). The seal of JEANNE, Dame de PLASNES, in 1376 bears her arms *en bannière* (p. 57) a quatrefoil supported by two kneeling angels, a demi-angel in chief, and a lion couchant guardant in base."

Corporate and other seals afford countless examples of the interstices in the design being filled with the figures similar to those from which in later days the supporters of a family have been deduced. Before passing to supporters proper, it may be well to briefly allude to various figures which are to be found in a position analogous to that of supporters. The single human figure entire, or in the form of a demi-figure appearing above the shield, is very frequently to be met with, but the addition of such figures *was and remains purely artistic*, and I know of no single instance in British armory where one figure, animate or inanimate, has ever existed alone in the character of a single supporter, and as an integral part of the heritable armorial achievement. Of course I except those figures upon which the arms of certain families are properly displayed. These will be presently alluded to, but though they are certainly exterior ornaments, I do not think they can be properly classed as supporters unless to this term is given some elasticity or has added to it some qualifying remarks of reservation. There are, however, many instances of armorial ensigns depicted, and presumably correctly, in the form of banners supported by a single animal, but it will always be found that the single animal is but one of the pair of duly allocated supporters. Many instances of arms depicted in this manner will be found in "Prince Arthur's Book," from which Plate C. is reproduced. The same method of display was adopted in some number of cases, and with some measure of success, in Foster's "Peerage." Single figures are very frequently to be met with in German and Continental heraldry, but on these occasions, as with ourselves, the position they occupy is merely that of an artistic accessory, and bears no inseparable relation to the heraldic achievement. The single exception to the foregoing statement of which I am aware is to be found in the arms of the Swiss Cantons. These thirteen coats are sometimes quartered upon one shield, but when displayed separately each is accompanied by a single supporter. Zurich, Lucerne, Uri, Unter-Walden, Glarus, and Basle all bear the supporter on the dexter side; Bern, Schweig, Zug, Freiburg, and Soluthurn on the sinister. Schathausen (a ram) and Appenzell (a bear) place their supporters in full aspect behind the shield.

On the corbels of Gothic architecture, shields of arms are frequently supported by *Angels*, which, however, cannot generally be regarded as heraldic appendages—being merely supposed to indicate that the owners have contributed to the erection of the fabric. Examples of this practice will be found on various ecclesiastical edifices in Scotland, and among others at Melrose Abbey, St. Giles', Edinburgh, and the church of Seton in East

Lothian. An interesting instance of an angel supporting a shield occurs on the beautiful seal of Mary of Gueldres, Queen of James II. (1459); and the Privy Seal of David II., a hundred years earlier, exhibits a pretty design of an escutcheon charged with the ensigns of Scotland, and borne by two arms issuing from clouds above, indicative of Divine support.[a]

Of instances of single objects from which shields are found depending or supported the "Treatise on Heraldry" states:—

"Allusion has been made to the usage by which on vesica-shaped shields ladies of high rank are represented as supporting with either hand shields of arms. From this probably arose the use of a single supporter. MARGUERITE DE COURCELLES in 1284, and ALIX DE VERDUN in 1311, bear in one hand a shield of the husband's arms, in the other one of their own. The curious seal of MURIEL, Countess of STRATH-ERNE, in 1284, may be considered akin to these. In it the shield is supported partly by a falcon, and partly by a human arm issuing from the sinister side of the *vesica*, and holding the falcon by the jesses (LAING, i. 764). The early seal of BOLESLAS III., King of POLAND, in 1255, bears a knight holding a shield charged with the Polish eagle (VOSSBERG, *Die Siegel des Mittelalters*). In 1283 the seal of FLORENT of HAINAULT bears a warrior in chain mail supporting a shield charged with a lion impaling an eagle dimidiated.

"On the seal of HUMPHREY DE BOHUN in 1322 the *guige* is held by a swan, the badge of the Earls of HEREFORD; and in 1356 the shield of the first Earl of DOUGLAS is supported by a lion whose head is covered by the crested helm, a fashion of which there are many examples. A helmed lion holds the shield of MAGNUS I., Duke of BRUNSWICK, in 1326.

"On the seal of JEAN, Duc de BERRI, in 1393 the supporter is a helmed swan (compare the armorial slab of HENRY of LANCASTER, in BOUTELL, Plate LXXIX.). Jean IV., Comte d'ALENÇON (1408), has a helmed lion sejant as supporter. In 1359 a signet of LOUIS VAN MALE, Count of FLANDERS, bears a lion sejant, helmed and crested, and mantled with the arms of FLANDERS between two small escutcheons of NEVERS, or the county of Burgundy ["Azure, billetty, a lion rampant or"], and RETHEL ["Gules, two heads of rakes fesswise in pale or"].

"A single lion sejant, helmed and crested, bearing on its breast the quartered arms of BURGUNDY between two or three other escutcheons, was used by the Dukes up to the death of CHARLES THE BOLD in 1475. In LITTA'S splendid work, *Famiglie celebri Italiane*, the BUON-AROTTI arms are supported by a brown dog sejant, helmed, and crested with a pair of dragon's wings issuing from a crest-coronet. On the seal of THOMAS HOLLAND, Earl of KENT, in 1380 the shield is buckled round the neck of the white hind lodged, the badge of his half-brother RICHARD II. Single supporters were very much in favour in the thirteenth and fourteenth centuries, and the examples are numerous. CHARLES, Dauphin de VIENNOIS (c. 1355), has his shield held by a single dolphin. In 1294 the seal of the Dauphin JEAN, son of HUMBERT I., bears the arms of DAUPHINÉ pendent from the neck of a griffon. The shields of arms of BERTRAND DE BRICQUEBEC, in 1325; PIERRE DE TOURNEBU, in 1339; of CHARLES, Count of ALENÇON, in

[a] Plate XI. Fig. 10, Laing's "Catalogue," No. 29. At each side of the King's seated figure on the counter-seal of Robert II. (1386) the arms of Scotland are supported from behind by a skeleton within an embattled buttress ("Catalogue," No. 34).

1356; and of OLIVER DE CLISSON, in 1397, are all supported by a warrior who stands behind the shield. In England the seal of HENRY PERCY, first Earl, in 1346, and another in 1345, have similar representations.

"On several of our more ancient seals only one supporter is represented, and probably the earliest example of this arrangement occurs on the curious seal of William, first Earl of Douglas (c. 1356), where the shield is supported from behind by a lion "sejant," *with his head in the helmet*, which is surmounted by the crest.

"On the seal of Archibald, fourth Earl of Douglas (c. 1418), the shield is held, along with a club, in the right hand of a savage *erect*, who bears a helmet in his left; while on that of William, eighth Earl (1446), a *kneeling* savage holds a club in his right hand, and supports a couché shield on his left arm."

Some number of examples will be found on Plate LV. in which human figures, single or double, appear to have been introduced in the nature of supporters in armorial designs. In practically all these instances the human figures which appear are in the nature of artistic accessories, and form no official part of the hereditary insignia of those individuals to whom the arms appertain. The examples selected are all chosen from the work of the old masters.

Fig. 1 on Plate LV. (the Nos. 1 to 9 which follow relate exclusively to the figures on that plate), which shows a single youth standing behind the shield, is the publishing mark of the "Fratelli Bernardini" of Venice (1498), known as "The Albane-sotti."

Fig. 2, which shows two angels as supporters, and behind the shield the mitred figure of a bishop, is probably a design by Albrecht Glockenton. The shield has the arms of the cathedral chapter of "Wurzburg," viz.: "Argent, a chief dancetté gules." These arms are taken from those of the Duchy of Franconia. The design dates from 1484.

Fig. 3 shows the single figure of a lady as a supporter. In this design she holds the helmet and crest, from the former of which the shield is suspended by a strap.

Fig. 4 is a design very similar in its detail and arrangement to the preceding one, both of which are attributed to Egidius Stecher of Cologne, 1466.

Fig. 5, the date of which is 1486, is from the Erfurt University Register. The shield is that of Count Friedrich *v.* Beichlingen, namely: "Barry of four argent and gules." The mantling is of argent and gules. The crest is a cap barry as the arms, and thereupon five plumes of peacock feathers.

Fig. 6, which shows the arms of Ludovico Diedo, the Venetian prætor of Zara, has on either side a child, which supports the shield with one hand and a wand with the other. These wands carry the two crested helmets.

Fig. 7 is an example of the use of the demi-figure of an angel, of which many instances can be found, particularly, as has been already stated, in ecclesiastical buildings. The design here reproduced shows the arms of Sir Richard Nanfant, 1507. As here depicted they are: "Quarterly, 1 and 4, sable, a chevron argent (properly ermine) between three wings inverted also argent; 2. argent, three wolves azure; 4. chequy argent and sable, a chief of the first, gutté-de-sang, a crescent for difference; impaling on the sinister side, argent, a chevron sable between three stag-beetles volant."

Fig. 8, which is a printer's mark, shows the arms of Loys M. Cruse of Geneva, 1480. In this case the two negresses which figure as supporters partake of the character of the arms, and very probably are intended as part of the fixed heraldic achievement.

In Fig. 9 the single female figure is employed to support both the shield and a banner. The achievement is that of Gebhard II., "Truchsess" of Waldburg,

THE ART OF HERALDRY

Elector and Archbishop of Cologne. He died May 21, 1601. The banner and the inescutcheon both show the arms of the Waldburgs, namely: "Or, three lions passant in pale sable." The principal escutcheon is quarterly, namely: "1. a cross sable (for the Archbishopric of Cologne); 2. gules, a horse springing argent (for the titular duchy of Westphalia); 3. gules, three sea-leaves or (for the titular duchy of Eugern); 4. azure, an eagle displayed argent (for the Countship of Arnsberg)." This design is reproduced from Jost Amman's *Wappen und Stammbuch*, published at Frankfurt, 1589.

FIG. 794.—Arms of Sigmund Hagelshaimer.

Another example by the same artist will be found in Fig. 794. In this the figure partakes more of the char-

FIG. 795.—Arms of Vöhlin of Augsberg.

acter of a shield guardian than a shield supporter. The arms are those of "Herr Sigmund Hagelshaimer,"

otherwise "Helt," living at Nürnberg. This design has been appropriated by the publisher of Sigmund Teyerabend's "Book of Arms." The arms are "Sable, on a bend argent, an arrow gules." The crest is the head and neck of a hound sable, continued into a mantling sable, lined argent. The crest is charged with a pale argent, and thereupon an arrow as in the arms, the arrow-head piercing the ear of the hound.

Seated figures as supporters are rare, but one occurs in Fig. 795, which shows the arms of the Augsberg family (both merchant and patrician) of Vöhlin. They bear: "Argent, on a fess sable, three 'P's' argent." The wings which form the crest are charged with the same device. This curious charge of the three letters is explained in the following saying:—

> "Piper Peperit Pecuniam,
> Pecunia Peperit Pompam,
> Pompa Peperit Pauperiem,
> Pauperies Peperit Pietatem."

Another pleasing example of the use of a single figure as an "artistic accessory" will be found in Fig. 796. This is a reproduction of a bookplate designed by Herr Ströhl for Alexander Freiherr von Dachenhausen. As these arms are a rather interesting example of a

FIG. 796.—Bookplate of Alexander von Dachenhausen.

"canting" coat, the blazon is appended. The name "Dachenhausen" is derived from *dach* (roof), and *haus* (house). The arms are: "Chequy argent and sable (to typify the wall of the house), a chief gules (to typify the roof)." The crest is a pair of wings, each charged with the arms. To the dexter and sinister appear the arms of the parents, viz. Dachenhausen and Plathner, namely: "Argent, a bunch of grapes azure, leaved vert."

Fig. 797 is a reproduction of the bookplate of Charles Louis de Bourbon, designed by Acry of Paris. In this case the supporting figure must be intended as a heraldic supporter.

FIG. 797.—Bookplate of Charles Louis de Bourbon, Count of Villafranca.

Fig. 1 on Plate LVI. is an example of the use of a "melusine" (or double-tailed mermaid), but in this case, as also in Fig. 4 on the same plate, the figures are merely artistic enrichment, and no part of the heritable armorial bearings. At the present time one scarcely ever sees such figures made use of in British armorial design, doubtless owing to the customary more rigid adherence to law and precedent in the matter of heraldic supporters and their meaning, but an isolated example may be found in the case of the bookplate of Frederick Henry Huth, Esq. (Fig. 798).

FIG. 798.—Armorial bearings of Frederick Henry Huth, Esq.: Argent, two chevronels gules, in chief a human heart of the last, and in base a hat sable with an ostrich feather proper; and for a crest, three sprigs of oak erect proper, each bearing an acorn or. Motto: "This too will pass."

There are, however, certain exceptions to the British rule that there can be no single supporters, if the objects upon which shields of arms are displayed are accepted as supporters. It was always customary to display the arms of the Lord High Admiral on the sail of the ship. In the person of King William IV., before he succeeded to the throne, the office of Lord High Admiral was vested for a short time, but it had really fallen into desuetude at an earlier date and has not been revived again, so that to all intents and purposes it is now extinct, and this recognised method of depicting arms is consequently also extinct. But there is one other case which forms a unique instance which can be classified with no others. The arms of Campbell of Craignish are always represented in a curious manner, the gyronny coat of Campbell appearing on a shield displayed in front of a lymphad. What the origin of this practice is it would be difficult to say; probably it merely originated in the imaginative ideas of an artist when making a seal for that family, artistic reasons suggesting the display of the gyronny arms of Campbell in front of the lymphad of Lorne. The family, however, seem to have universally adopted this method of using their arms, and in the year 1875, when Campbell of Inverneil matriculated in Lyon Register, the arms were matriculated in that form with the bordure azure of a cadet (see Plate XXVIII.). In 1886 the head (James Campbell of Blackerton, co. Devon) of that branch of the Campbell family, technically Campbell of Craignish, matriculated the undifferenced coat also displayed in front of a lymphad. I know of no other instance of any such coat of arms, and this branch of the Ducal House of Campbell possesses armorial bearings which, from the official standpoint, are absolutely unique from one end of Europe to the other.

In Germany the use of arms depicted in front of the eagle displayed, either single-headed or double-headed, is very far from being unusual. Whatever may have been its meaning originally in that country, there is no doubt that now and for some centuries past it has been accepted as meaning, or as indicative of, princely rank or other honours of the Holy Roman Empire. With this meaning the use of the eagle has been frequently employed in England, being found in the case of Richard of Cornwall, who was elected King of the Romans in 1256, and again in the case of his son Edmund. About the same date the Earl of Menteith placed his shield on the breast of an eagle, as did Alexander, Earl of Ross, in 1338; and in 1394 we find the same ornamentation in the seal of Euphemia, Countess of Ross. The shield of Ross is borne in her case on the breast of an eagle, while the arms of Leslie and Comyn appear on its displayed wings.

On several other Scottish seals of the same era, the shield is placed on the breast of a displayed eagle, as on those of Alexander Abernethy and Alexander Cumin of Buchan (1292), and Sir David Lindsay, Lord of Crawford. English heraldry supplies several similar examples, of which we may mention the armorial insignia of Richard, Earl of Cromwell, brother of Henry III. above mentioned, and of the ancient family of Latham, in the fourteenth century. A curious instance of a shield placed on the breast of a *hawk* is noticed by Hone in his "Table Book," viz. the arms of the Lord of the Manor of Stoke-Lyne, in the county of Oxford. It appears therefrom that when Charles I. held his Parliament at Oxford, the offer of knighthood was gratefully declined by the then Lord of Stoke-Lyne, who merely requested, and obtained, the Royal permission to place the arms of his family upon the breast of a hawk, which has ever since been employed in the capacity of single supporter. What authority exists for this statement it is impossible to ascertain, and one must doubt its accuracy, because in England at any rate no arms, allocated to any particular *territorial estate*, have ever received official recognition.

THE ART OF HERALDRY

In later years, as indicative of rank in the Holy Roman Empire, the eagle has been rightly borne by the first Duke of Marlborough and by Henrietta his daughter, Duchess of Marlborough, but the use of the eagle by the later Dukes of Marlborough would appear to be entirely without authority, inasmuch as the princedom, created in the person of the first duke, became extinct on his death. His daughters, though entitled of right to the courtesy rank of princess and its accompanying privilege of the right to use the eagle displayed behind their arms, could not transmit it to their descendants upon whom the title of Duke of Marlborough was specially entailed by English Act of Parliament.

The Earl of Denbigh and several members of the Fielding family have often made use of it with their arms, in token of their supposed descent from the Counts of Hapsburg, which, if correct, would apparently confer the right upon them. This descent, however, has been much questioned, and in late years the claim thereto would seem to have been practically dropped. Earl Cowper, the only remaining Prince of the Holy Roman Empire in the British Peerage, is entitled to use the double eagle behind his shield, being the descendant and representative of George Nassau Clavering Cowper, third Earl Cowper, created a Prince of the Holy Roman Empire by the Emperor Joseph II., the patent being dated at Vienna, 31st January 1778, and this being followed by a Royal Licence from King George III. to accept and bear the title in this country.

There are some others who have the right by reason of honours of lesser rank of the Holy Roman Empire, and amongst these may be mentioned Lord Methuen, who bears the eagle by Royal Warrant dated 4th April 1775. Sir Thomas Arundel, who served in the Imperial army of Hungary, having in an engagement with the Turks near Strignum taken their standard with his own hands, was by Rodolph II. created Count of the Empire to hold for him and the heirs of his body for ever, dated at Prague 14th December 1595, Count of the Holy Roman Empire. This patent, of course, means that every one of his descendants in the male line is a Count of the Empire, and that every daughter of any such male descendant is a Countess, but this does not confer the rank of count or countess upon descendants of the daughters. It was this particular patent of creation that called forth the remark from Queen Elizabeth that she would not have her sheep branded by any foreign shepherd, and we believe that this patent was the origin of the rule in later times (*temp.* George IV.), translated into a definite Royal Warrant, requiring that no English subject shall, without the express Royal Licence of the Sovereign conveyed in writing, accept or wear any foreign title or decoration. No Royal Licence was subsequently obtained by the Arundel family, who therefore, according to British law, are denied the use of the privileged Imperial eagle. Outside those cases in which the double eagle is used in this country to denote rank of the Holy Roman Empire, the usage of the eagle displayed behind the arms or any analogous figure is in British heraldry most limited.

One solitary authoritative instance of the use of the displayed eagle is found in British armory, this being the coat of arms of the city of Perth. These arms are recorded in Lyon Register, having been matriculated for that Royal Burgh about the year 1672. The official blazon of the arms is as follows: "Gules ane holy lambe passant regardant staff and cross argent, with the banner of St. Andrew proper, all within a double tressure counter-flowered of the second, the escutcheon being surmounted on the breast of ane eagle with two necks displayed or. The motto in ane Escroll, 'Pro Rege Lege et Grege.'"

Another instance of usage, though purely devoid of authority, occurs in the case of a coat of arms set up on one of the panels in the Banqueting-Hall of Lincoln's Inn. In this case the achievement is displayed on the breast of a single-headed eagle. What reason led to its usage in this manner I am quite unaware, and I have not the slightest reason for supposing it to be authentic. The family of Stuart-Menteith also place their arms upon a single-headed eagle displayed gules, as was formerly to be seen in Debrett's Peerage, but though arms are matriculated to them in Lyon Register, this particular adornment forms no part thereof, and it has now disappeared from the printed Peerage books. Occasionally batons or wands or other insignia of office are to be found in conjunction with armorial bearings, but these will be more fully dealt with under the heading of Insignia of Office. Before dealing with the usual supporters, one perhaps may briefly allude to "inanimate" supporters.

Probably the most curious instance of all will be found in the achievement of the Earls of Errol as it appears in the MS. of Sir David Lindsay. In this two ox-yokes take the place of the supporters (Fig. 799).

FIG. 799.—The Arms of the Earl of Erroll. (From a MS. of Sir David Lindsay of The Mount.)

The curious tradition which has been attached to the Hay arms is quoted as follows by Sir James Balfour Paul, Lyon King of Arms, in his "Heraldry in relation to Scottish History and Art," who writes: "Take the case of the well-known coat of the Hays, and hear the description of its origin as given by Nisbet: 'In the reign of Kenneth

THE ART OF HERALDRY

III., about the year 980, when the Danes invaded Scotland, and prevailing in the battle of Luncarty, a country Scotsman with his two sons, of great strength and courage, having rural weapons, as the yokes of their plough, and such plough furniture, stopped the Scots in their flight in a certain defile, and upbraiding them with cowardice, obliged them to rally, who with them renewed the battle, and gave a total overthrow to the victorious Danes; and it is said by some, after the victory was obtained, the old man lying on the ground, wounded and fatigued, cried, "Hay, Hay," which word became a surname to his posterity. He and his sons being nobilitate, the King gave him the aforesaid arms (argent, three escutcheons gules) to intimate that the father and the two sons had been luckily the three shields of Scotland, and gave them as much land in the Carse of Gowrie as a falcon did fly over without lighting, which having flown a great way, she lighted on a stone there called the Falcon Stone to this day. The circumstances of which story is not only perpetuated by the three escutcheons, but by the exterior ornaments of the achievement of the family of Errol; having for crest, on a wreath, a falcon proper; for supporters two men in country habits, holding the oxen-yokes of a plough over their shoulders; and for motto, "Serva jugum."'

"Unfortunately for the truth of this picturesque tale there are several reasons which render it utterly incredible, not the least being that at the period of the supposed battle armorial bearings were quite unknown, and could not have formed the subject of a royal gift. Hill Burton, indeed, strongly doubts the occurrence of the battle itself, and says that Hector Boece, who relates the occurrence, must be under strong suspicion of having entirely invented it. As for the origin of the name itself, it is, as Mr. Cosmo Innes points out in his work on 'Scottish Surnames,' derived from a place in Normandy, and neither it nor any other surname occurred in Scotland till long after the battle of Luncarty. I have mentioned this story in some detail, as it is a very typical specimen of its class; but there are others like unto it, often traceable to the same incorrigible old liar, Hector Boece."

It is not unlikely that the ox-yoke was a badge of the Hays, Earls of Errol, and a reference to the variations of the original arms, crest, and supporters of Hay will show how the changes have been rung on the shields, falcon, ox-yokes, and countrymen of the legend.

Another instance is to be found in the arms of the Mowbray family as they were at one time depicted with an ostrich feather on either side of the shield (Fig. 823), and at first one might be inclined to class these amongst the inanimate supporters. The Garter plate, however, of John Beaufort, Duke of Somerset (Plate CXXXII.), probably supplies the key to the whole matter, for this shows not only the ostrich feathers but also supporters of the ordinary character in their usual position. From the last-mentioned instance, it is evident the ostrich feathers can be only representations of the badge, their character doubtless being peculiarly adaptable to the curious position they occupy. They are of course the same in the case of the Mowbray arms, and doubtless the ox-yoke of the Earl of Errol is similarly no more than a badge.

A most curious instance of supporters is to be found in the case of the arms of Viscount Montgomery. This occurs in a record of them in Ulster's Office, where the arms appear without the usual kind of supporters, but represented with an arm in armour on either side issuing from clouds in base, the hands supporting the shield.

When supporters are inanimate objects, the escut-cheon is said to be cottised—a term derived from the French word *côté* (a side)—in contradistinction to supported. An old Scottish term for supporters was "bearers."

Amongst other cases where the shield is cottised by inanimate objects may be mentioned the following. The Breton family of "Bastard" depict their shield cottised by two swords, with the points in base. The Marquises Alberti similarly use two lighted flambeaux, and the Dalzells (of Binns) the extraordinary device of a pair of tent-poles. Whether this last has been officially sanctioned I am unaware. The "Pillars of Hercules" used by Charles V. are, perhaps, the best known of this group of supporters. In many cases (notably foreign) the supporters appear to have gradually receded to the back of the shield, as in the case of the Comte d'Erps, Chancellor of Brabant, where two maces (or) are represented saltirewise *behind* the shield. Generally, however, this variation is found in conjunction with purely official or corporate achievements.

A curious example of inanimate supporters occurs on the English seal of William, Lord Botreaux (1426), where, on each side of a couché shield exhibiting a griffin "segreant" and surmounted by a helmet and crest, a buttress is quaintly introduced, in evident allusion to the owner's name. A somewhat similar arrangement appears on the Scottish seal of William Ruthven (1396), where a tree growing from a mount is placed on each side of the escutcheon. Another instance is to be found in the seal of John de Segrave, where a garb is placed on either side of the shield. Perhaps mention should here be made of the arms (granted in 1826) of the National Bank of Scotland, the shield of which is "surrounded with two thistles proper disposed in orle."

Heraldic supporters as such and not merely as artistic accessories in England date from about the beginning of the fourteenth century. Very restricted in use at first, they later rapidly became popular, and there were few peers who did not display them upon their seals. For some reason, however, very few indeed appear on the early Garter plates. It is a striking fact that by far the larger number of the ancient standards display as the chief device not the arms but one of the supporters, and I am inclined to think that it is quite possible the device for the standard is the older, that being transferred to the seal, and not *vice versâ*.

Even after the use of two supporters had become general, a third figure is often found placed behind the shield, and forms a connecting link with the old practice of filling the void spaces on seals, to which we have already referred. On the seal of WILLIAM STERLING, in 1292, two lions rampant support the shield in front of a tree. The shield on the seal of OLIVER ROUILLON, in 1376, is supported by an angel, and by two demi-lions couchant-guardant in base. That of PIERRE AVOIR, in 1378, is held by a demi-eagle above the shield, and by two mermaids. On many ancient seals the supporters are disposed so that they hold the crested helm above a couché shield.

The counter-seals of RUDOLF IV., Archduke of AUSTRIA, in 1359 and 1362, afford instances in which a second set of supporters is used to hold up the crested helm. The shield of AUSTRIA is supported by two lions, on whose volets are the arms of HAPSBURG and PFIRT; the crested helm (coroneted, and having a panache of ostrich feathers) is also held by two lions, whose volets are charged with the arms of STIRIA, and of CARINTHIA (HUEBER, *Austria Illustrata*, tab. xviii.).

In 1372 the seal of EDMUND MORTIMER represents his shield hanging from a rose-tree, and supported by two lions couchant (of MARCH), whose heads are covered by coroneted helmets with a panache (azure) as crest.

305   2 Q

THE ART OF HERALDRY

BOUTELL directs attention to the fact that the shield of EDMUND DE ARUNDEL (1301–1326) is placed between similar helms and panaches, without the supporting beasts ("Heraldry: Historical and Popular," pp. 271–418).

Crested supporters have sometimes been misunderstood, and quoted as instances of double supporters—for instance, by LOWER, "Curiosities of Heraldry," who gives (p. 144) a cut from the achievement of the French D'ALBRETS as "the most singular supporters, perhaps, in the whole circle of heraldry." These supporters are two lions couchant (or), each helmed, and crested with an eagle au vol leve. These eagles certainly assist in holding the shield, but the lions are its true supporters; nor is this arrangement by any means unique. The swans which were used as supporters by JEAN, DUC DE BERRI, in 1386, are each mounted upon a bear. Two wild men, each à cheval on a lion, support the escutcheons of GERARD D'HARCHIES (1476) and of NICOLE DE GIRESME (1464). Two lions sejant, helmed and crested (the crest is a human head with the ears of an ass) were the supporters of ARNAUD D'ALBREY in 1368.

Scotland, which is the home of curiosities of heraldry, gives us at least two instances of the use of supporters which must be absolutely unique—that is, the surcharging of an escutcheon with an inescutcheon, to the latter of which supporters are attached. The first instance occurs in the cases of Baronets of Nova Scotia, a clause appearing in all the earlier patents which ordained "that the Baronets, and their heirs-male, should, as an *additament of honour* to their armorial ensigns, bear, either on a canton or inescutcheon, in their option, the ensign of Nova Scotia, being *argent*, a cross of St. Andrew *azure* (the badge of Scotland counterchanged), charged with an inescutcheon of the Royal Arms of Scotland, supported on the dexter by the Royal unicorn, and on the sinister by a savage, or wild man, proper; and for crest, a branch of laurel and a thistle issuing from two hands conjoined, the one being armed, the other naked; with the motto, "Munit hæc et altera vincit." The incongruity of these exterior ornaments within a shield of arms is noticed by Nisbet, who informs us, however, that they are very soon removed. In the year 1629, after Nova Scotia was sold to the French, the Baronets of Scotland, and their heirs-male, were authorised by Charles I. "to wear and carry about their necks, in all time coming, an orange-tawny silk ribbon, whereon shall be pendent, in a scutcheon *argent*, a saltire *azure*, thereon an inescutcheon of the arms of Scotland, with an Imperial crown above the scutcheon, and encircled with this motto: 'Fax mentis honestæ gloria.'" According to the same authority, this badge was never much used "about their necks," but was carried, by way of canton or inescutcheon, in their armorial bearings, without the motto, and, of course, since then the superimposed supporters have been dropped.

The same peculiarity of supporters being surcharged upon a shield will be found, however, in the matriculation (1795) to Cumming-Gordon of Altyre. These arms are depicted on Plate XIII. In this the entire achievement (arms, crest, motto, and supporters) of Gordon of Gordon is placed upon an inescutcheon superimposed over the arms of Cumming.

In Scotland the arms, and the arms only, constitute the mark of a given family, and whilst due difference is made in the respective shields, no attempt is made as regards crest or supporters to impose any distinction between the figures granted to different families even where no blood relationship exists. The result is that whilst the same crests and supporters are duplicated over and over again, they at any rate remain in Scotland simple, graceful, and truly heraldic, even when judged by the most rigid mediæval types. They are, of course,

necessarily of no value whatever for identification. In England the simplicity is relinquished for the sake of distinction, and it is held that due distinction must be made, both in regard to the crests and the supporters, as is made between the shields of different families. The result as to modern crests is truly appalling, and with supporters it is almost equally so, for by their very nature it is impossible to design adequate differences for crests and supporters, as can readily be done in the charges upon a shield, without creating monstrosities. With regret one has to admit that the dangling shields, the diapered chintz-like bodies, and the fasces and other footstools so frequently provided for modern supporters in England would seem to be pedantic, unnecessary, and inartistic strivings after a useless ideal.

In England the right to bear supporters is confined to those to whom they have been granted or recorded, but such grant or record is very rigidly confined to peers, to Knights of the Garter, Thistle, and St. Patrick, and to Knights Grand Cross, or Knights Grand Commanders (as the case may be) of other Orders. Before the Order of the Bath was divided into classes, Knights of the Bath had supporters. As by an unwritten but nowadays invariably accepted law, the Orders of the Garter, Thistle, and St. Patrick are confined to members of the peerage, those entitled to claim (upon their petitioning) a grant of supporters in England are in practice limited to peers and Knights Grand Cross. In the cases of peers, the grant is always attached to a particular peerage, the "remainder" in the limitations of the grant being to "those of his descendants upon whom the peerage may devolve," or some other words to this effect. In the cases of life peers and Knights Grand Cross the grant has no hereditary limitation, and the right to the supporters is personal to the grantee. There is nothing to distinguish the supporters of a peer from those of a Knight Grand Cross. Baronets of England, Ireland, Great Britain, and the United Kingdom as such are not entitled to claim grants of supporters, but there are some number of cases in which, by special favour of the sovereign, specific Royal Warrants have been issued—either as marks of favour or as augmentations of honour—conveying the pleasure of the sovereign to the kings of arms, and directing the latter to grant supporters —to descend with the baronetcy. Of the cases of this nature the following may be quoted: Guise (Royal Warrant, dated July 12, 1863), Prevost (Royal Warrant, October 1816), Guinness, now Lord Ardilaun (Royal Warrant, dated April 15, 1867), Halford (Royal Warrant, May 19, 1827), and Otway (Royal Warrant, June 10, 1845). These, of course, are exceptional marks of favour from the sovereign, and this favour in at least two instances has been extended to untitled families. In 1815 Mr. George Watson-Taylor, an especial intimate of the then Prince Regent, by Royal Warrant dated September 28, 1815, was granted the following supporters: "On either side a leopard proper, armed and langued gules, collared and chained or." A more recent instance, and the only other one within the knowledge of the writer, is the case of the Speke [b] arms (Plate XXXIX.).

[b] Armorial bearings of William Speke, Esq.: Argent, two bars azure, over all an eagle displayed with two heads gules, and as an honourable augmentation (granted by Royal Licence, dated July 26, 1867, to commemorate the discoveries of the said John Hanning Speke), a chief azure, thereon a representation of flowing water proper, superinscribed with the word "Nile" in letters gold. Upon the escutcheon is placed a helmet befitting his degree, with a mantling azure and argent; and for his crests: 1. (of honourable augmentation) upon a wreath of the colours, a crocodile proper; 2. upon a wreath of the colours, a porcupine proper; and as a further augmentation for supporters (granted by Royal Licence as above to the said William Speke, Esq., for and during his life)—on the dexter side, a crocodile; and on the sinister side, a hippopotamus, both proper; with the motto, "Super æthera virtus."

306

THE ART OF HERALDRY

It is recited in the Royal Warrant, dated July 26, 1867, that Captain John Hanning Speke "was by a deplorable accident suddenly deprived of his life before he had received any mark of our Royal favour" in connection with the discovery of the sources of the Nile. The Warrant goes on to recite the grant to his father, William Speke, of Jordans, co. Somerset, of the following augmentations to his original arms (argent, two bars azure) namely: on a chief a representation of flowing water superinscribed with the word "Nile," and for a crest of honourable augmentation a "crocodile," also the supporters following—that is to say, on the dexter side a crocodile, and on the sinister side a hippopotamus. Some number of English baronets have gone to the trouble and expense of obtaining grants of supporters in Lyon Office; for example Sir Christopher Baynes, by grant dated June 10, 1805, obtained two savages, wreathed about the temples and loins, each holding a club over the exterior shoulder. It is very doubtful to what extent such grants in Scotland to domiciled Englishmen can be upheld. Many other baronets have at one time or another assumed supporters without any official warrant or authority in consequence of certain action taken by an earlier committee of the baronetage, but cases of this kind are slowly dropping out of the Peerage books, and this, combined with the less ostentatious taste of the present day in the depicting of armorial bearings upon carriages and elsewhere, is slowly but steadily reducing the use of supporters to those who possess official authority for their display.

Another fruitful origin of the use of unauthorised supporters at the present day lies in the fact that grants of supporters personal to the grantee for his life only have been made to Knights Grand Cross or to life peers in cases where a hereditary title has been subsequently conferred. The limitations of the grant of supporters having never been extended, the grant has naturally expired with the death of the life honour to which the supporters were attached.

In addition to these cases there is a very limited number of families which have always claimed supporters by prescriptive right, amongst whom may be mentioned Tichborne of Tichborne (two lions guardant gules), De Hoghton of Hoghton (two bulls argent), Scroope of Danby (two choughs) (Fig. 800), and Stapylton. Concerning such cases it can only be said that in England no official sanction has ever been given to such use, and no case exists of any official recognition of the right of an untitled family to bear supporters to their arms save those few exceptional cases governed by specific Royal Warrants. In many cases, notably Scroope, Luttrell, Hilton, and Stapylton, the supporters have probably originated in their legitimate adoption at an early period in connection with peerage or other titular distinction, and have continued inadvertently in use when the titular distinctions to which they belonged have ceased to exist or have devolved upon other families. Possibly their use in some cases has been the result of a *claim* to *de jure* honours. The cases where supporters are claimed "by prescriptive right" are few indeed in England, and need not be further considered.

Whilst the official laws in Ireland are, and have apparently always been, the same as in England, there is no doubt that the heads of the different septs assert their claim to the right to use supporters. On this point Sir Bernard Burke, Ulster King of Arms, wrote: "No registry of supporters to an Irish chieftain appears

in Ulster's Office, in right of his chieftaincy only, and without the honour of peerage, nor does any authority to bear them exist." But nevertheless "The O'Donovan" uses, dexter, a lion guardant, and sinister a griffin; "The O'Gorman" uses, dexter, a lion, and sinister, a horse; "The O'Reilly" uses two lions or. "The O'Connor Don," however, is in the unique position of bearing supporters by unquestionable right, inasmuch as the late Queen Victoria, on the occasion of her last visit to Dublin, issued her Royal Warrant conferring the right upon him. The supporters granted to him were "two lions rampant gules, each gorged with an antique crown, and charged on the shoulder with an Irish harp or."

The right to bear supporters in Scotland is on a widely different basis from that in any other country. As in England and Ireland, peers and Knights Grand

FIG. 800.—The arms and quarterings of Simon Scroope of Danby.

Cross are permitted to obtain grants of these distinctions. But outside and beyond these there are many other families who bear them by right. At the official inquiry concerning the Lyon Office, the Lyon Depute, Mr. George Tait, put in a Note of Persons whom he considered might lawfully bear supporters under Scottish Heraldic Law. The following is the text of the note in question:—

"NOTE OF PERSONS who are considered by GEORGE TAIT, Esq., Lyon-Depute, to be entitled to supporters, furnished to the Commissioners of Inquiry by their desire, intimated to him at his examination this day, June 27, 1821.

"1. *Peers.*—By immemorial usage, Peers have right to supporters, and supporters are commonly inserted in modern patents of Peerage. This includes Peeresses in their own right.

" 2. *Ancient Usage.*—Those private gentlemen, and the lawful heirs male of their bodies, who can prove immemorial usage of carrying supporters, or a usage very ancient, and long prior to the Act 1672, are entitled to have their supporters recognised, it being presumed that they received them from lawful authority, on account of feats of valour in battle or in tournaments, or as marks of the Royal favour (see *Murray of Touchadam's Case,* June 24, 1778).

" 3. *Barons.*—Lawful heirs male of the bodies of the smaller Barons, who had the full right of free barony (not mere freeholders) prior to 1587, when representation of the minor Barons was fully established, upon the ground that those persons were Barons, and sat in Parliament as such, and were of the same as the titled Barons. Their right is recognised by the writers on heraldry and antiquities. Persons having right on this ground, will almost always have established it by ancient usage, and the want of usage is a strong presumption against the right.

" 4. *Chiefs.*—Lawful heirs-male of Chiefs of tribes or clans which had attained power, and extensive territories and numerous members at a distant period, or at least of tribes consisting of numerous families of some degree of rank and consideration. Such persons will in general have right to supporters, either as Barons (great or small) or by ancient usage. When any new claim is set up on such a ground, it may be viewed with suspicion, and it will be extremely difficult to establish it chiefly from the present state of society, by which the traces of clanship, or the patriarchal state, are in most parts of the country almost obliterated; and indeed it is very difficult to conceive a case in which a new claim of that kind could be admitted. Mr. Tait has had some such claims, and has rejected them.

" 5. *Royal Commissions.*—Knights of the Garter and Bath, and any others to whom the King may think proper to concede the honour of supporters.

" These are the only descriptions of persons who appear to Mr. Tait to be entitled to supporters.

" An idea has gone abroad, that Scots Baronets are entitled to supporters; but there is no authority for this in their patents, or any good authority for it elsewhere. And for many years subsequent to 1672, a very small portion indeed of their arms which are matriculated in the Lyon Register, are matriculated with supporters; so small as necessarily to lead to this inference, that those whose arms are entered with supporters had right to them on other grounds, *e.g.* ancient usage, chieftainship, or being heirs of Barons. The arms of few Scots Baronets are matriculated during the last fifty or sixty years; but the practice of assigning supporters gradually gained ground during that time, or rather the practice of assigning supporters to them, merely as such, seems to have arisen during that period; and it appears to Mr. Tait to be an erroneous practice, which he would not be warranted in following.

" British Baronets have also, by recent practice, had supporters assigned to them, but Mr. Tait considers the practice to be unwarranted; and accordingly, in a recent case, a gentleman, upon being created a Baronet, applied for supporters to the King—having applied to Mr. Tait, and been informed by him that he did not conceive the Lord Lyon entitled to give supporters to British Baronets.

" No females (except Peeresses in their own right) are entitled to supporters, as the representation of families is only in the male line. But the widows of Peers, by courtesy, carry their arms and supporters; and the sons of Peers, using the lower titles of the

peerage by courtesy, also carry the supporters by courtesy.

" Mr. Tait does not know of any authority for the Lord Lyon having a discretionary power of granting supporters, and understands that only the King has such a power.

" Humbly submitted by

(Signed)   " G. Tait."

Though this statement would give a good general idea of the Scottish practice, its publication entails the addition of certain qualifying remarks. Supporters are most certainly not " commonly inserted in modern patents of peerage." Supporters appertaining to peerages are granted by special and separate patents. These are now under the hand and seal of Garter alone. In the event of a grant following upon the creation of an Irish peerage, the patent of supporters would be issued by Ulster King of Arms. But it is competent to Lyon King of Arms to matriculate the arms of Scottish peers with supporters, or to grant these to such as may still be without them. Garter claims the right to grant supporters in all cases of Peerages of England, Great Britain, or the United Kingdom, no matter what the domicile of the grantee may be. In this I totally disagree with him, though I do not flatter myself that my opinion will have any effect upon his contention. But I consider it little short of an official scandal that a Scotsman, bearing properly recorded supporters by Scottish law, should have their validity questioned in England. With regard to the second paragraph of Mr. Tait's memorandum, there will be few families within its range who will not be included within the range of the paragraph which follows, and the presumption would rather be that the use of supporters by an untitled family originated in the right of barony than in any mythical grant following upon mythical feats of valour.

Mr. Tait, however, is clearly wrong in his statement that " no females (except peeresses in their own right) are entitled to supporters." They have constantly been allowed to the heir of line, and their devolution through female heirs must of necessity presuppose the right thereto of the female heir through whom the inheritance is claimed. A recent case in point occurs with regard to the arms of Hunter-Weston (Fig. 800a), matriculated in 1880, Mrs. Hunter-Weston being the heir of line of Hunter of Hunterston. Widows of peers, providing they have arms of their own to impale with those of their husbands, cannot be said to only bear the supporters of their deceased husbands by courtesy. With them it is a matter of right. The eldest sons of peers bearing courtesy titles most certainly do not bear the supporters of the peerage to which they are heirs. Even the far more generally accepted " courtesy " practice of bearing coronets is expressly forbidden by an Earl-Marshal's Warrant.

Consequently it may be asserted that the laws concerning the use of supporters in Scotland are as follows: In the first place, no supporters can be borne of right unless they have been the subject of formal grant or matriculation. The following classes are entitled to obtain, upon payment of the necessary fees, the grant or matriculation of supporters to themselves, or to themselves and their descendants according as the case may be : (1) Peers of Scotland, and probably other peers who are domiciled Scotsmen. (This, however, raises a point concerning which there is a conflict of authority, and with the subject of jurisdiction as between the various offices of arms I prefer not to deal.) (2) Knights of the Garter, Knights of the Thistle, and Knights of St. Patrick, being Scotsmen, are entitled as such to obtain grants of supporters to themselves for use during life, but as these three orders are now confined to members of the peerage, the supporters used would be probably those appertaining to their peerages, and it is unlikely that any further grants for life will be made under these circumstances. (3) Knights of the Bath until the revision of the order were entitled to obtain grants of supporters to themselves for use during their lifetimes, and there are many instances in the Lyon Register where such grants have been made. (4) Knights Grand Cross of the Bath, of St. Michael and St. George, and of the Royal Victorian Order, and Knights Grand Commanders of the Orders of the Star of India, and of the Indian Empire, are entitled to obtain grants of supporters for use during their lifetimes. (5) The lawful heirs of the minor barons who had the

And the result was the growth and acceptance of the fixed idea that it was within the power of Lyon King of Arms to grant supporters to any one whom he might choose to so favour. Consequently many grants of supporters were placed upon the records, and many untitled families of Scotland apparently have the right under these patents of grant to add supporters to their arms. Though it is an arguable matter whether the Lord Lyon was justified in making these grants, there can be no doubt that, so long as they remain upon the official register, and no official steps are taken to cancel the patents, they must be accepted as existing by legal right. Probably the most egregious instance of such a grant is to be found in the case of the grant to the first baronet of the family of Antrobus, who on purchasing the estate of Rutherford, the seat of the extinct Lords

FIG. 800a.—Arms of Hunter-Weston.

full right of free barony prior to 1587 may matriculate supporters if they can show their ancestors used them, or may now obtain grants. (Though practically the whole of these have been at some time or other matriculated in Lyon Register, there still remain a few whose claims have never been officially adjudicated upon. For example, it is only within the last few months that the ancient Swinton supporters (Plate LXIII.) have been formally enrolled on the official records.) (6) There are certain others, being chiefs of clans and the heirs of those to whom grants have been made in times past, who also have the right, but as no *new* claim is likely to be so recognised in the future, it may be taken that these are confined to those cases which have been already entered in the Lyon Register.

During the latter part of the eighteenth century, the executive of Lyon Office had fallen into great disrepute. The office of Lyon King of Arms had been granted to the Earls of Kinnoul, who had contented themselves with appointing deputies and drawing fees. The whole subject of armorial jurisdiction in Scotland had become lax to the last degree, and very many irregularities had crept in. One, and probably the worst result, had been the granting of supporters in many cases where no valid reason other than the payment of fees could be put forward to warrant the obtaining of such a privilege.

Rutherford, obtained from the then Lyon King of Arms a grant of the peerage supporters carried by the previous owners of the property.

With regard to the devolution of Scottish supporters, the large proportion of those registered in Lyon Office are recorded in the terms of some patent which specifies the limitations of their descent, so that there are a comparatively small number only concerning which there can be any uncertainty as to whom the supporters will descend to. The difficulty can only arise in those cases in which the arms are matriculated with supporters as borne by ancient usage in the early years of the Lyon Register, or in the cases of supporters still to be matriculated on the same grounds by those families who have so far failed to comply with the Act of 1672. Whilst Mr. Tait, in a memorandum which has been previously quoted, would deny the right of inheritance to female heirs, there can be no doubt whatever that in many cases such heirs have been allowed to succeed to the supporters of their families. Taking supporters as an appanage of right of barony (either greater or lesser), there can be no doubt that the greater baronies, and consequently the supporters attached to them, devolved upon heirs female, and upon the heir of line inheriting through a female ancestor; and, presumably, the same considerations must of necessity hold good with regard

THE ART OF HERALDRY

to those supporters which are borne by right of lesser barony, for the greater and the lesser were the same thing, differing only in degree, until in the year 1587 the lesser barons were relieved of compulsory attendance in Parliament. At the same time there can be no doubt that the headship of a family must rest with the heir male, and consequently it would seem that in those cases in which the supporters are borne by right of being head of a clan or chief of a name, the right of inheritance would devolve upon the heir male. There must of necessity be some cases in which it is impossible to determine whether the supporters were originally called into being by right of barony or because of chieftainship, and the consequence has been that concerning the descent of the supporters of the older untitled families there has been no uniformity in the practice of Lyon Office, and it is impossible from the precedents which exist to deduce any certain and unalterable rule upon the point. Precedents exist in each case, and the well-known case of Smith-Cunningham and Dick-Cunningham, which is often referred to as settling the point, did nothing of the kind, inasmuch as that judgment depended upon the interpretation of a specific Act of Parliament, and was not the determination of a point of heraldic law. The case, however, afforded the opportunity to Lord Jeffrey to make the following remarks upon the point (see p. 355, Seton):—

"If I may be permitted to take a common-sense view, I should say that there is neither an inflexible rule nor a uniform practice in the matter. There may be cases where the heir of line will exclude the heir male, and there may be cases where the converse will be held. In my opinion the common-sense rule is, that the chief armorial dignities should follow the more substantial rights and dignities of the family. *If the heir male succeed to the title and estates, I think it reasonable that he should also succeed to the armorial bearings of the head of the house.* I would think it a very difficult proposition to establish that the heir of line, when denuded of everything else, was still entitled to retain the barren honours of heraldry. But I give no opinion upon that point."

Mr. Seton, in his "Law and Practice of Heraldry in Scotland," sums up the matter of inheritance in these words (see p. 357): "As already indicated, however, by one of the learned Lords in his opinion on the case of Cuninghame, the practice in the matter in question has been far from uniform; and accordingly we are very much disposed to go along with his relative suggestion, that 'the chief armorial dignities should follow the more substantial rights and dignities of the family'; and that when the latter are enjoyed by the female heir of line, such heir should also be regarded as fairly entitled to claim the principal heraldic honours."

The result has been in practice that the supporters of a family have usually been matriculated to whoever has carried on the name and line of the house, unless the supporters in question have been governed by a specific grant, the limitations of which exist to be referred to; but in cases where both the heir of line and the heir male have been left in a prominent position, the difficulty of decision has in many cases been got over by allowing supporters to both of them. The most curious instance of this within our knowledge occurs with regard to the family of Chisholm.

Chisholm of Erchless Castle appears undoubtedly to have succeeded as head and chief of his name—"The Chisholm"—about the end of the seventeenth century. As such supporters were carried, namely: "On either side a savage wreathed about the head and middle with laurel, and holding a club over his exterior shoulder."

At the death of Alexander Chisholm—"The Chisholm"—7th February 1793, the chieftainship and the estates passed to his half-brother William, but his heir of line was his only child Mary, who married James Gooden of London. Mrs. Mary Chisholm or Gooden in 1827 matriculated the *undifferenced* arms of Chisholm ["Gules, a boar's head couped or"], without supporters, but in 1831 the heir male *also* matriculated the same *undifferenced* arms, in this case with supporters.

The chieftainship of the Chisholm family then continued with the male line until the death of Duncan Macdonell Chisholm—"The Chisholm"—in 1859, when his only sister and heir became heir of line of the later chiefs. She was then Jemima Batten, and by Royal Licence in that year she and her husband assumed the additional surname of Chisholm, becoming Chisholm-Batten, and, contrary to the English practice in such cases, the arms of Chisholm *alone* were matriculated in 1860 to Mrs. Chisholm-Batten and her descendants. These once again were the *undifferenced* coat of Chisholm, viz.: "Gules, a boar's head couped or." Arms for Batten have since been granted in England, the domicile of the family being English, and the illustration of the arms of the present Mr. Chisholm-Batten (Fig. 801), though including the quartering for Chis-

FIG. 801.—Armorial bearings of James Forbes Chisholm Chisholm-Batten, Esq.: Quarterly, 1 and 4, azure, a chevron nebuly ermine between three anchors erect, entwined by a cable or, a chief in arch of the last (for Batten); 2 and 3, gules, a boar's head couped or, langued azure (for Chisholm), impaling the arms of Utermarck, namely: per fess or and azure, in chief a sprig of three rose-leaves slipped vert, and in base a mullet of six points of the first, pierced of the second. Crest (for Batten): in front of the stump of an oak-tree sprouting on either side proper, three roses argent, barbed and seeded proper. [Under the Scottish matriculation for Chisholm. Mantling gules, doubled argent; and for crest, on a wreath of his liveries, a dexter hand erect holding a dagger proper, on its point a boar's head erased or; and on an escroll over the same this motto, "Feros ferio."] Badge (for Chisholm): a fern-leaf.

holm, is marshalled as allowed in the College of Arms by English rules.

Though there does not appear to have been any subsequent rematriculation in favour of the heir male who succeeded as "The Chisholm," the undifferenced arms were also considered to have devolved upon him together with the supporters. On the death of the last known male heir of the family, Roderick Donald

Matheson Chisholm, The Chisholm in 1887, Mr. James Chisholm Gooden-Chisholm [c] claimed the chieftainship as heir of line, and in that year the Gooden-Chisholm arms were again rematriculated. In this case supporters were added to the again undifferenced arms of Chisholm, but a slight alteration in the supporters was made, the clubs being reversed and placed to rest on the ground, as shown in Plate LVII.

Amongst the many other untitled Scottish families who rightly bear supporters, may be mentioned Gibsone of Pentland (Fig 565), Barclay of Urie, Barclay of Towie (Fig. 802), Drummond of Megginch (Fig. 53), Maclachlan

FIG. 802.—Armorial bearings of Barclay of Towie (Charles A. Barclay, Esq., of Aberdour House, Fraserburgh): Azure, a chevron or, between three crosses patée argent. Mantling azure and or. Crest: on a wreath of his liveries, a hand holding a dagger proper. Motto: "Aut agere aut mori." Supporters: two hounds argent, collared gules.

of that ilk, "Cluny" Macpherson (Fig. 311), Cunninghame (Fig. 150b), and Brisbane of that Ilk (Fig. 553).

Armorial matters in the Channel Islands present a very unsatisfactory state of affairs. There never appears to have been any Visitation, and the arms of Channel Island families which officially pass muster must be confined to those of the very few families (for example, De Carteret, Dobrée, and Tupper) who have found it necessary or advisable on their own initiative to register their arms in the official English sources. In none of these instances have supporters been allowed, nor I believe did any of these families claim to use them, but some (Lemprière, De Saumerez, and other families) assert the possession of such a distinction by prescriptive right. If the right to supporters be a privilege of peerage, or if, as in Scotland, it anciently depended upon the right of free barony, the position of these Channel Island families in former days as seigniorial lords was much akin. But it is highly improbable that the right to bear supporters in such cases will ever be officially recognised, and the case of De Saumerez, in which the supporters were bedevilled and regranted to descend with the peerage, will probably operate as a decisive

[c] Armorial bearings of Chisholm Gooden-Chisholm, Esq: Gules, a boar's head erased or, langued azure. Mantling gules, doubled argent. Crest: on a wreath of his liveries, a dexter hand couped at the wrist, holding a dagger erect on which is transfixed a boar's head couped. Motto: "Feros ferio." Supporters: two savages wreathed about the head and loins with laurel, their clubs reversed and resting on the ground.

precedent upon the point and against such a right. There are some number of families of foreign origin who bear supporters or claim them by the assertion of foreign right. Where this right can be established their use has been confirmed by Royal Licence in this country in some number of cases; for example, the cases of Rothschild and De Salis. In other cases (for example, the case of Chamier) no official record of the supporters exists with the record of the arms, and presumably the foreign right to the supporters could not have been established at the time of registration.

With regard to impersonal arms, the right to supporters in England is not easy to define. In the case of counties, one can only say that no supporters have as yet been granted to any county; but county grants have been so very few in number that it is hardly safe to draw the conclusion that they are not eligible to obtain them if they choose to pay the necessary fees. No English county has as yet obtained the grant of a crest, but this has been due to the fact that those responsible for the petitions have considered it an anomaly that a crest should be granted to such a body, and it has yet to be seen whether a crest would be refused if it were asked for and insisted upon. It is to be hoped that the next few grants to counties which may be issued will be minus both crest and supporters, and that a precedent will thereby become stereotyped that a shield only shall be granted.

In the case of towns, the rule in England is that an ordinary town may not have supporters but that a city may, and instances are numerous where supporters have been granted upon the elevation of a town to the dignity of a city. Birmingham, Sheffield, and Nottingham are all recent instances in point. This rule, however, is not absolutely rigid, and an exception may be pointed to in the case of Liverpool, the supporters being granted in 1797, and the town not being created a city until a subsequent date. In Scotland, where, of course, until quite recently supporters were granted practically to anybody who chose to pay for them, a grant will be found for the county of Perth dated in 1800, in which supporters were included. But as to towns and cities it is no more than a matter of fees, any town in Scotland eligible for arms being at liberty to obtain supporters also if they are desired. In grants of arms to corporate bodies it is difficult to draw the line or to deduce any actual rule. In 23rd of Henry VIII. the Grocers' Livery Company were granted "two griffins per fess gules and or," and many other of the Livery Companies have supporters to their arms. Others, for no apparent reason, are without them. The "Merchant Adventurers' Company or Hamburg Merchants" have supporters, as had both the old and the new East India Companies. The arms of Jamaica and Cape Colony and of the British North Borneo Company have supporters, but on the other hand no supporters were assigned to Canada or to any of its provinces. In Ireland the matter appears to be much upon the same footing as in England, and as far as impersonal arms are concerned it is very difficult to say what the exact rule is, if this is to be deduced from known cases and past precedents.

Probably the freedom—amounting in many cases to great laxity—with which in English heraldic art the positions and attitudes of supporters are changed, is the one point in which English heraldic art has entirely ignored the trammels of conventionalised officialism. There must be in this country scores of entrance gates where each pillar of the gateway is surmounted by a shield held in the paws of a single supporter, and the Governmental use of the Royal supporters in an amazing variety of attitudes, some of which are grossly un-

THE ART OF HERALDRY

heraldic, has not helped towards a true understanding. The reposeful attitude of watchful slumber in which the Royal lion and unicorn are so often depicted, may perhaps be in the nature of submission to the biblical teaching of Isaiah that the lion shall lie down with the lamb (and possibly therefore also with the unicorn), in these times of peace which have succeeded those earlier days when "the lion beat the unicorn round and round the town."

In official minds, however, the sole attitude for the supporters is the rampant, or as near an approach to it as the nature of the animal will allow. A human being, a bird, or a fish naturally can hardly adopt the attitude.

FIG. 803.—The Arms used by Kilmarnock, Ayrshire: Azure, a fess chequy gules and argent. Crest: a dexter hand raised in benediction. Supporters: on either side a squirrel sejant proper.

In Scotland, the land of heraldic freedom, various exceptions to this can be found. Of these one can call to mind the arms of Kilmarnock (Fig. 803), in which the supporters, "squirrels proper," are depicted always as sejant. These particular creatures, however, would look strange to us in any other form. These arms unfortunately have never been matriculated as the arms of the town (being really the arms of the Boyd family, the attainted Earls of Kilmarnock), and consequently can hardly as yet be referred to as a definite precedent, because official matriculation might result in a similar "happening" to the change which was made in the case of the arms of Inverness. In all representations of the arms of earlier date than the matriculation, the supporters, (dexter) a camel and (sinister) an elephant, are depicted statant on either side of the shield, no actual contact being made between the escutcheon and the supporters. But in 1900, when in a belated compliance with the Act of 1672 the armorial bearings of the Royal Burgh of Inverness were matriculated, the position had been altered to that more usually employed for supporters, as will be seen from Fig. 239.

The supporters always used by Sir John Maxwell Stirling-Maxwell of Pollok are two lions sejant guardant. These, as appears from an old seal, were in use as far back as the commencement of the fifteenth century, but the supporters officially recorded for the family are two apes. In English armory one or two exceptional cases may be noticed; for example, the supporters of the city of Bristol, which are: "On either side, on a mount vert, a unicorn sejant or, armed, maned, and unguled sable." Another instance will be found in the supporters of Lord Rosmead, which are: "On the dexter side an ostrich and on the sinister side a kangaroo, both regardant proper." From the nature of the animal, the kangaroo is depicted sejant.

Supporters in Germany date from the same period as with ourselves, being to be met with on seals as far back

as 1276. At first they were similarly purely artistic adjuncts, but they have retained much of this character and much of the purely permissive nature in Germany to the present day. It was not until about the middle of the seventeenth century that supporters were granted or became hereditary in that country. Grants of supporters can be found in England at an earlier date, but such grants were isolated in number. Nevertheless supporters had become hereditary very soon after they obtained a regularly heraldic (as opposed to a decorative) footing. Their use, however, was governed at that period by a greater freedom as to alteration and change than was customary with armory in general. Supporters were an adjunct of the peerage, and peers were not subject to the Visitations. With his freedom from arrest, his high social position, and his many other privileges of peerage, a peer was "too big" a person formerly to accept the dictatorial armorial control of the Crown enforced upon lesser people. Short of treason, a peer in any part of Great Britain for most practical purposes of social life was above the ordinary law. In actual fact it was only the rights of one peer as opposed to the rights of another peer that kept a Lord of Parliament under any semblance of control. When the great lords of past centuries could and did raise armies to fight the King he was hardly likely to, nor did he, brook much control, Of the development of supporters in Germany Herr Ströhl writes:—

"Only very late, about the middle of the seventeenth century, were supporters granted as hereditary, but they appear in the arms of burghers in the first half of the fifteenth century, and the arms of many towns also possess them as decorative adjuncts.

"The first supporters were human figures, generally portraits of the arms-bearers themselves; then women, young men, and boys, so-called Schildbuben. In the second half of the fourteenth century animals appear: lions, bears, stags, dogs, griffins, &c. In the fifteenth century one frequently encounters angels with richly curling hair, saints (patrons of the bearer or of the town), then later, nude wild men and women (Waldmenschen) thickly covered with hair, with garlands round their loins and on their heads (Fig. 803a; see also Plate

FIG. 803a.—Arms of Holzhausen (Frankfort): Sable, three roses argent, seeded gules. (From Jost Amman's "Book of Arms and Genealogy," 1589.

PLATE XCVIII.

EXAMPLES FROM THE "KATZE" ROLL IN CONSTANCE.

PLATE XCIX.

Monsz̃ water ffauconberge

Le seigneuz de Welles

Monsz̃ Richard de Shirbnrne

Sir James Strangweys

le sr̃ de Shasta de halghton

le sr̃ de Anerleton

Comes de Sepne

Sir John Xyseley

attewater

frier an Roy

Jonkot

Robert thorne

The emperour

Coche

Indde

dautrey

ARMS FROM "PRINCE ARTHUR'S BOOK."

PLATE C.

The armes of the Realme of france

Duc de yorke

the lord tho mas wuley cardinal legat de latere archebisshop of yorke and chancelor of Jngland

Dockwra

DESIGNS FROM "PRINCE ARTHUR'S BOOK."

PLATE CI.

BADGES FROM "PRINCE ARTHUR'S BOOK."

PLATE CII.

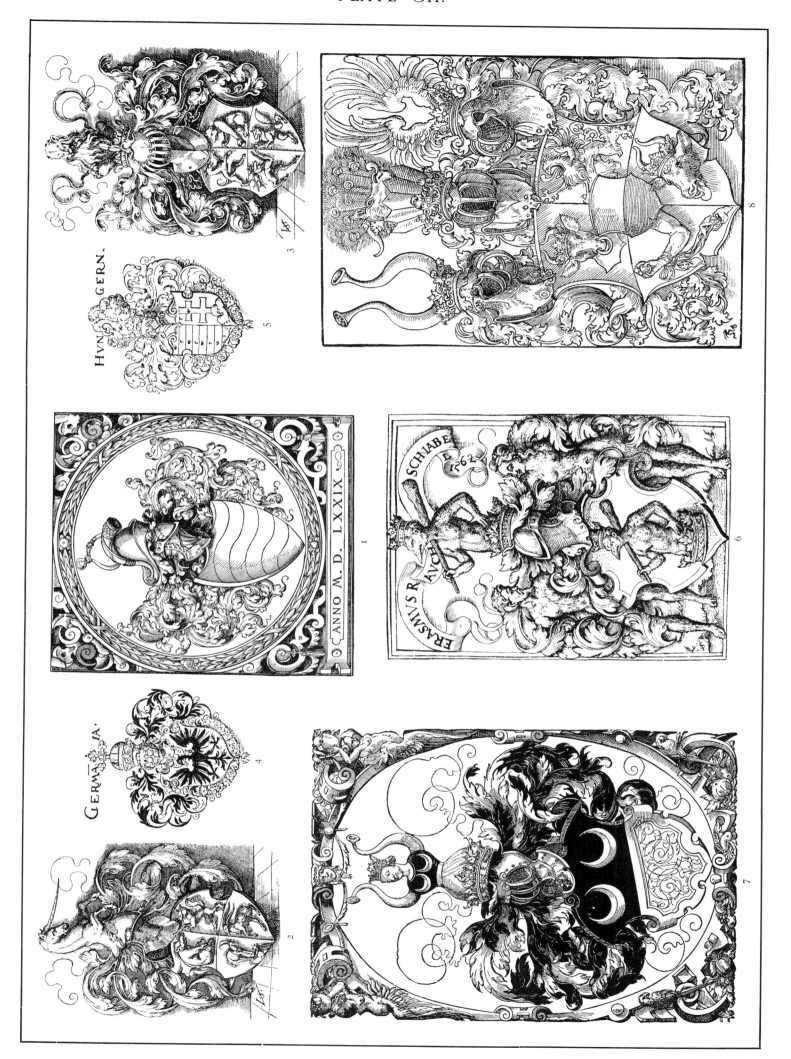

HERALDIC DESIGNS BY GERMAN ARTISTS, SECOND HALF OF XVI. CENTURY.

PLATE CIII.

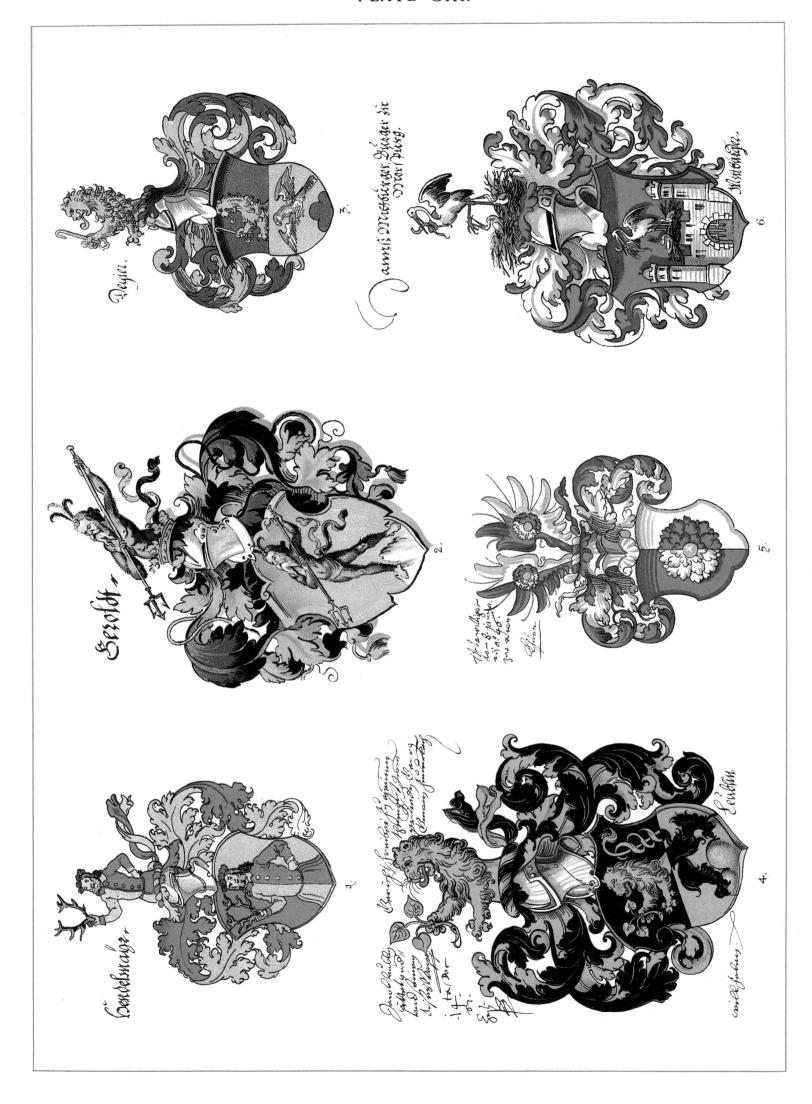

PLATE CIV.

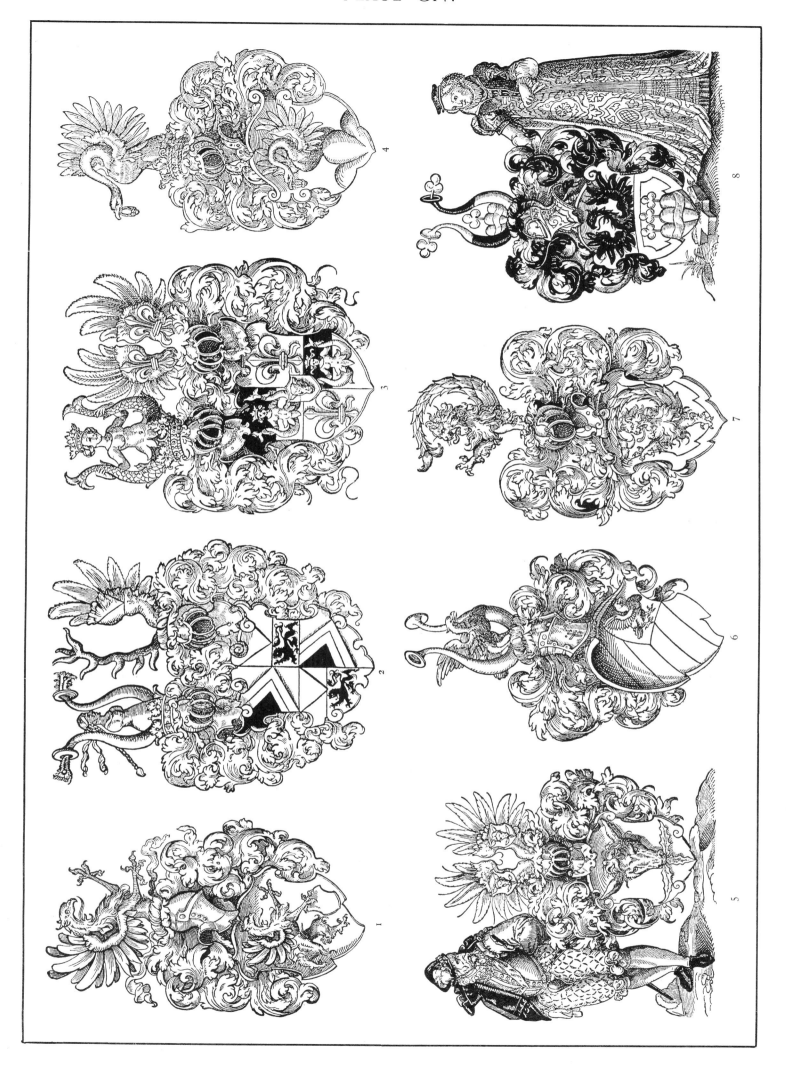

EXAMPLES FROM JOST AMMAN'S WAPPEN UND STAMMBUCH.

PLATE CV.

PLATE CVI.

1

2

3

4

EXAMPLES FROM THE "ARCHITECTVRA" OF WENDEL DIETTERLIN.

PLATE CVII.

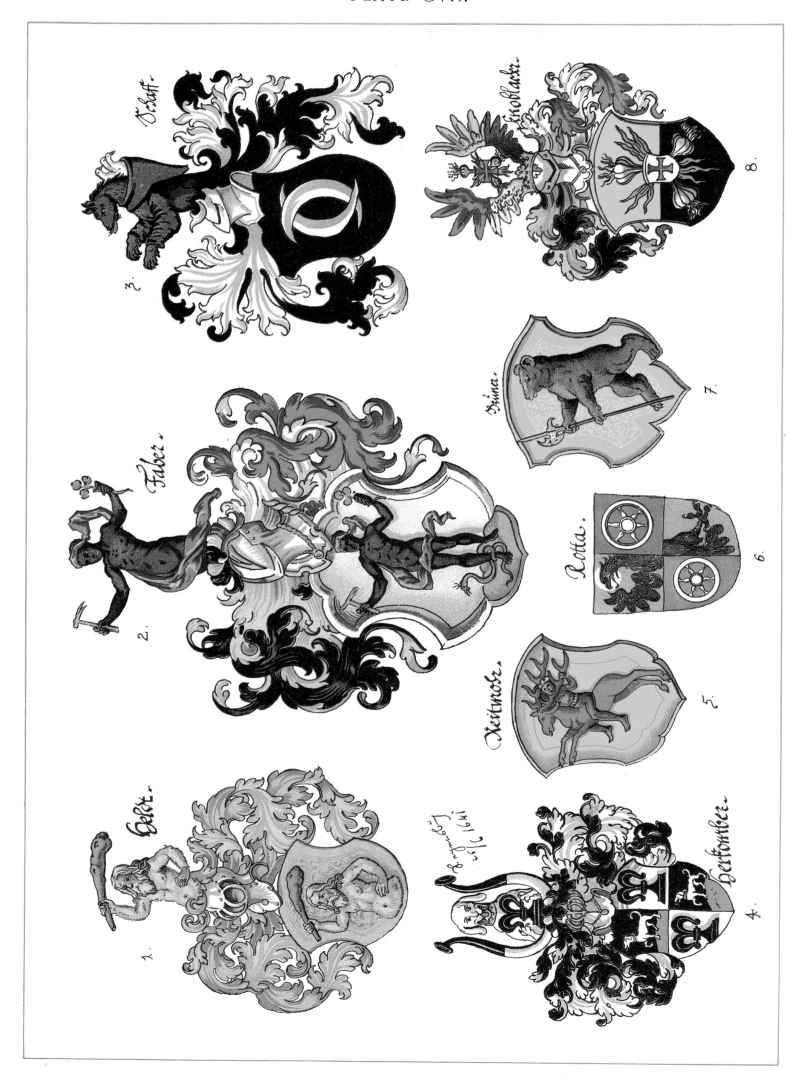

PLATE CVIII.

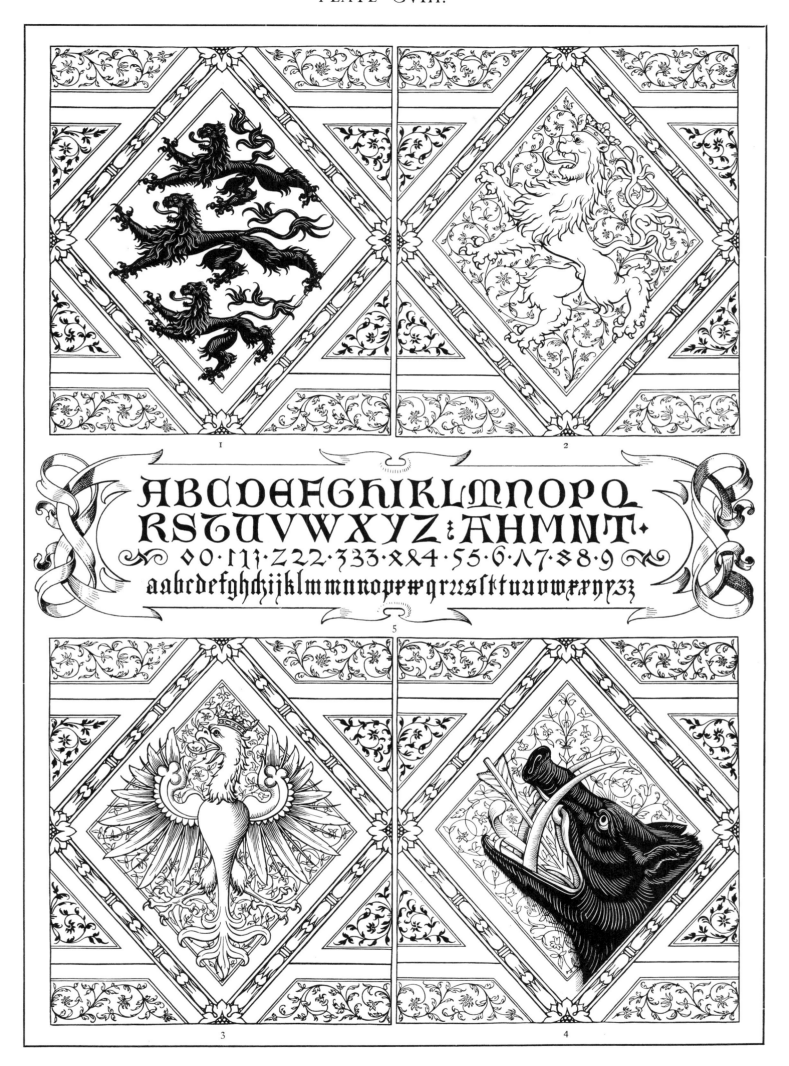

HERALDIC WOOD-CARVINGS IN THE POSSESSION OF THE AUSTRIAN IMPERIAL FAMILY.

PLATE CIX.

MANTLINGS OF THE XVI. AND XVII. CENTURIES.

PLATE CX.

EXAMPLES OF HERALDIC DESIGNS OF THE XVII. AND XVIII. CENTURIES.

PLATE CXI.

PLATE CXII.

THE ARMORIAL BEARINGS OF THE RT. REV. ÆNEAS CHISHOLM (Roman Catholic), Bishop of Aberdeen.
Reproduced from the Painting in Lyon Register by Mr Graham Johnston.

PLATE CXIII.

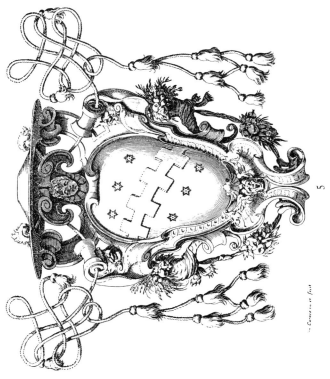

ALEXANDRO VII·P·M·

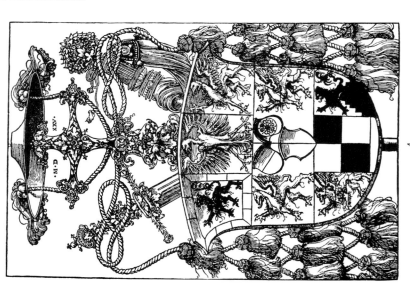

EXAMPLES OF ECCLESIASTICAL HERALDRY.

XIII. Figs. 2 and 3). The thick hairy covering of the body in the case of women is only to be met with in the very beginning. Later the endeavour was to approach the feminine ideal as nearly as possible, and only the garlands were retained to point out the origin and the home of these figures.

"At the end of the fifteenth and in the sixteenth century, there came into fashion lansquenets (Fig. 466), huntsmen, pretty women and girls, both clothed and unclothed." Speaking of the present day, and from the executive standpoint, he adds :—

"Supporters, with the exception of flying angels, should have a footing on which they can stand in a natural manner, whether it be grass, a pedestal, a tree, or line of ornament, and to place them upon a ribbon of a motto is less suitable because a thin ribbon can hardly give the impression of a sufficiently strong support for the invariably heavy-looking figures of the men or animals. The supporters of the shield may at the same time be employed as bearers of the helmets. They bear the helmets either over the head (see Plate LXI. Fig. 6) or hold them in their hands (see Plate LV.). Figures standing near the shield, but not holding or supporting it in any way, cannot in the strict sense of the word be designated supporters ; such figures are called *Schildwächter* (shield-watchers or guardians)."

HUMAN FIGURES AS SUPPORTERS

Of all figures employed as supporters probably human beings are of most frequent occurrence, even when those single and double figures referred to on an earlier page, which are not a real part of the heraldic achieve-

FIG. 804.—Armorial bearings of Hugh Robert Wallace, Esq. : Quarterly, 1 and 4, grand quarters, gules, a lion rampant argent within a bordure company of the last and azure (for Wallace of Ellerslie) ; 2. grand quarter, quarterly i. and iiii., gules, a lion rampant argent ; ii. and iii., gules, a fess chequy argent and azure (for Wallace of Craigie) ; 3. grand quarter, quarterly i. and iiii., argent, on a chief gules, three lions' heads erased of the first ; ii. and iii., azure, a crescent or between three cross crosslets argent (for Ritchie of Craigton) ; over all an escutcheon of pretence gyronny of eight or and sable, on a chief azure, a galley, oars in action, pennons flying, between two mullets of the first (for Campbell of Cammo). Mantling gules, doubled argent. Crests : dexter, on a wreath of the liveries, a dexter arm vambraced, the hand brandishing a sword all proper ; and in an escroll over same this motto, " Pro libertate " (for Wallace of Ellerslie) ; sinister, on a wreath of the liveries, an ostrich head and neck couped, holding a horse-shoe in his beak all proper. Motto (over) : " Sperandum est." Supporters : two savages wreathed about the head and middle with laurel, each carrying over his exterior shoulder a club all proper.

ment, are excluded from consideration. The endless variety of different figures perhaps gives some clue to the reason of their frequent occurrence.

Though the human figure *in nudas veritas* appears (male) upon the shield of Dalziel and (female) in the crest of Ellis (Agar-Ellis, formerly Viscount Clifden),

FIG. 805.—Armorial bearings of Lord Moncrieff : Quarterly, 1 and 4, argent, a lion rampant gules, armed and langued azure, a chief ermine ; 2 and 3, argent, an oak-tree growing out of a well in base both proper. Above the escutcheon, which is charged with his badge of Ulster as a Baronet of the United Kingdom, and from which is pendent by an orange-tawny ribbon his badge as a Baronet of Nova Scotia, is placed the coronet of his rank, and thereupon a helmet befitting his degree, with a mantling gules, doubled ermine ; and upon a wreath of the liveries is set for crest, a demi-lion rampant gules, armed and langued azure. Supporters : on either side a man in armour, holding in the exterior hand a spear resting on his shoulder all proper, the breastplate charged with a crescent gules. Motto : " Sur esperance."

one cannot call to mind any instance of such an occurrence in the form of supporters, though possibly the supporters of the Glaziers' Livery Company [" Two naked boys proper, each holding a long torch inflamed of the last "] and of the Joiners' Livery Company [" Two naked boys proper, the dexter holding in his hand an emblematical female figure, crowned with a mural coronet sable, the sinister holding in his hand a square "] might be classed in such a character. Nude figures in armory are practically always termed " savages," or occasionally " woodmen " or " wildmen," and garlanded about the loins with foliage. Figs. 2, 3, 5, and 6 on Plate LVI. are excellent illustrations of such figures. These were specially drawn for the present work by Professor Emil Döpler.

With various adjuncts—clubs, banners, trees, branches, &c.—*Savages* will be found as the supporters of the arms of the German Emperor, and in the sovereign arms of Prussia, Brunswick, Denmark, Schwarzburg-Sondershausen, and Rudolstadt, as well as in the arms of the province of Prussia. They also appear in the arms of the kingdom of Greece, though in this case they should perhaps be more properly described as figures of Hercules.

In British armory—amongst many other families—two savages are the supporters of the Marquess of Ailesbury, Lord Calthorpe, Viscount de Vesci, Lord Elphinstone, the Earl of Elgin and Kincardine, the Duke of Fife (Fig. 251), Earl Fitzwilliam (each holding in the exterior hand a tree eradicated), Lord Kinnaird, the Earl of Morton; and amongst the baronets who possess supporters, Menzies, Douglas of Carr, and Williams-Drummond have on either side of their escutcheons a "savage." Earl Poulett alone has both man and woman, his supporters being: "Dexter, a savage man; sinister, a savage woman, both wreathed with oak, all proper." As some one remarked on seeing a representation of this coat of arms by Catton, R.A., the blazon might more appropriately have concluded "all improper."

Fig. 251 represents the achievement of the Duke and Her Royal Highness the Duchess of Fife. This illus-

of a savage which I have seen, perhaps the finest heraldic design he has produced, and probably one of the best and freest examples of recent heraldic draughtsmanship.

Next after savages, the most favourite variety of the human being adopted as a supporter is the *Man in Armour*. If so described without any additional particularisation, the official type is usually in the form of the supporters of Lord Moncrieff, as will be seen in Fig. 805. This illustration is from a drawing by Mr. Eve. Another representation of knights in armour as supporters will be found in Fig. 806, which is a representation of the arms of Count Lubienski.

Even as heraldic and heritable supporters angels are not uncommon, and are to be met with amongst other cases in the arms of the Marquess of Waterford, the Earl of Dudley, and Viscount Dillon (Plate XXXVI.).

It is rare to find supporters definitely stated to represent any specific person, but in the case of the arms of Arbroath (Fig. 807) the supporters are "Dexter: 'St.

FIG. 806.—Armorial bearings of Count Louis Pomian Bodenham Lubienski: Quarterly of four, within a bordure or, 1. gules, a wounded ram passant proper (for Bielinski); 2. or, a bison's head regardant transfixed with a sword all proper (for Lubienski); 3. gules, an armed knight on a white horse (for Sanguszko); 4. tierced in bend azure or and gules, on first and third a stag courant proper, on second two roses of the third (for Szembek). Over all an inescutcheon, Lubienski repeated. Crest: hand and arm armed, grasping a falchion rising from a count's coronet.

tration is from a design by Mr. G. W. Eve, R.E., and probably is the best possible example of savages depicted "sans freedom" in the style adopted officially in England.

The arms of Gooden-Chisholm (Plate LVII.) are savages from the pencil of Mr. Graham Johnston.

The arms upon the patent of the matriculation which Mr. Forbes Nixon emblazoned in 1898, when the arms of Wallace of Ellerslie were rematriculated in Lyon Register for Mr. Hugh Robert Wallace of Busbie, are an example of that artist's work. His design was fac-similed into the Lyon Register, from which Fig. 804 was reproduced. This is the finest example of his idea

Thomas à Becket,' and sinister, a Baron of Scotland." Another instance, again from Scotland, appears in a most extraordinary grant by the Lyon in 1816 to Sir Jonathan Wathen Waller, Bart., of Braywick Lodge, co. Berks, and of Twickenham, co. Middlesex. In this case the supporters were two elaborately "harnessed" ancient warriors, "to commemorate the surrender of Charles, Duke of Orleans, at the memorable battle of Agincourt (that word being the motto over the crest) in the year 1415, to Richard Waller of Groombridge in Kent, Esq., from which Richard the said Sir Jonathan Wathen Waller is, according to the tradition of his family, descended." This pedigree is set out in Burke's

THE ART OF HERALDRY

Peerage, which assigns as arms to this family the old coat of Waller of Groombridge, with the augmented crest, viz.: "On a mount vert, a walnut-tree proper, and pendent therefrom an escutcheon of the arms of France with a label of three points argent." Considerable doubt, however, is thrown upon the descent by the fact that in 1814, when Sir Jonathan (then Mr. Phipps) obtained a Royal Licence to assume the name and arms of Waller, a very different and much bedevilled edition of the arms and not the real coat of Waller of Groombridge was ex-

Highlanders in modern costume figure as supporters to the arms of Maconochie-Wellwood (Plate LIX.), and in more ancient garb in the case of Cluny Macpherson (Fig. 311), and soldiers in the uniforms of every regiment, and savages from every clime, have at some time or other been pressed into heraldic service as supporters; but a work on Armory is not a handbook on costume, military and civil, nor is it an ethnographical directory, which it would certainly become if any attempt were to be made to enumerate the different varieties of men

FIG. 807.—Arms of Arbroath: Gules, a portcullis with chains pendent or. Motto: "Propter Libertatem." Supporters: dexter, St. Thomas à Becket in his archiepiscopal robes all proper; sinister, a Baron of Scotland armed cap-à-pie, holding in his exterior hand the letter from the Convention of the Scottish Estates, held at Arbroath in the year 1320, addressed to Pope John XXII., all proper.

emplified to him. These supporters (the grant was quite *ultra vires*, Sir Jonathan being a domiciled Englishman) do not appear in any of the Peerage books, and it is not clear to what extent they were ever made use of, but in a painting which came under my notice the Duke of Orleans, in his surcoat of France, could be observed handing his sword across the front of the escutcheon to Mr. (or Sir) Richard Waller. The supporters of the Needlemakers' Company are commonly known as Adam and Eve, and the motto of the Company ["They sewed fig-leaves together and made themselves aprons"] bears this supposition out. The blazon, however, is: "Dexter, a man; sinister, a woman, both proper, each wreathed round the waist with leaves of the last, in the woman's dexter hand a needle or." The supporters of the Earl of Aberdeen, "dexter an Earl and sinister a Doctor of Laws, both in their robes all proper," are illustrated on Plate LVIII., which is a facsimile of the painting in Lyon Register. A scroll below the arms, carrying the words "Ne nimium," has, however, been since added to the arms in the Register. These additional words, however, are always regarded as a part of the other motto, and not as a second motto.

and women, clothed and unclothed, which have been used for the purposes of supporters.

ANIMALS AS SUPPORTERS

When we turn to animals as supporters, we at once get to a much wider range, but little can be said concerning them beyond stating that though usually rampant, they are sometimes sejant, and may be guardant or regardant. One may, however, append examples of the work of different artists, which will doubtless serve as models, or possibly may develop ideas in other artists. The *Lion* naturally first claims one's attention. Fig. 808 shows an interesting and curious instance of the use of a single lion as a supporter. This is taken from a drawing in the possession of the town library at Breslau (*Herold*, 1888, No. 1), and represents the arms of Dr. Heinrich Rubische, Physician to the King of Hungary and Bohemia. The arms are, "per fesse," the chief argent, a "point" throughout sable, charged with a lion's face, holding in the jaws an annulet, and the base also argent charged with two bars sable. The mantling is sable and argent. Upon the helmet as crest are two buffalo's horns of the

FIG. 808.—Arms of Dr. Heinrich Rubische.

colours of the shield, and between them appears (apparently as a part of the heritable crest) a lion's face holding an annulet as in the arms. This, however, is the face of the lion, which, standing behind the escutcheon, is employed as the supporter, though possibly it is intended that it should do double duty. This employment of one animal to serve a double armorial purpose is practically unknown in British armory, except possibly in a few early examples of seals, but in German heraldry it is very far from being uncommon. Another instance of it will be found on Plate LXI. Fig. 6. This represents the arms of the Count Palatine Wolfgang bei Rhein, Duke in Bavaria (born 1526, died 1569), of the House of Zweibrücken, ancestor of all the later Counts Palatine. The design is by Virgil Solis, 1559. The arms are: "Quarterly, 1 and 4, sable, a lion rampant or, armed and crowned gules (for the County Palatine on the Rhine); 2 and 3, bendy lozengy argent and azure (for the Duchy of Bavaria)." On an inescutcheon are the arms of the Countship of Veldeny, namely: "Argent, a lion rampant azure, crowned." The supporters are two lions rampant or, but these are depicted as wearing the two helmets upon which the crests are displayed, the faces of the lions being visible through the visors of the helmets. Each crest issues from a coronet, and is a lion sejant or, armed and crowned gules, the dexter being between two buffalo's horns, and the sinister between two wings, both horns and wings being of azure and argent as the second quarter.

Two typical lions as supporters, drawn by Mr. J. Forbes Nixon, will be found in Fig. 54, which represents the arms of his Grace the late Duke of Argyll, K.G., K.T., and others by the same artist appear in Plate LX., which shows the arms of Sir William Ogilvy Dalgleish,[1] Bart.

[1] Armorial bearings of Sir William Ogilvy-Dalgleish: Quarterly, 1 and 4, argent, a tree eradicated fesswise vert, between three pheons points downwards azure (for Dalgleish); 2 and 3, quarterly, i. and iiii., argent, a lion passant guardant gules (for Ogilvy); ii. and iii., or, three crescents gules (for Edmonstone); over all dividing the coats a cross engrailed sable (for Sinclair), all for Ogilvy of Boyne; over all on an escutcheon of pretence in right of his wife the arms of Mollinson, namely: or, two cross crosslets fitché in chief and in base the attires of a hart affixed to the scalp gules, a chief chequy of the second and argent, in the fess point a crescent sable for difference. Above the shield, which is charged with his badge of Ulster as a baronet, is placed a helmet befitting his degree, mantled vert, doubled argent; and upon a wreath of his liveries is set for crest, the stump of an oak-tree sprouting out branches and leaves proper; and upon an escroll above the crest this motto, "Revirescam"; and for his supporters, upon either side of the escutcheon a lion rampant or, charged upon the shoulder with a pheon point downwards azure, such being personal to the above-mentioned William Ogilvy-Dalgleish.

The arms of the Duke of Norfolk (Fig. 809) show a good example of a lion as a supporter, from a drawing by Mr. G. W. Eve.

Probably, however, the most characteristic and the

FIG. 809.—Arms of the Duke of Norfolk, K.G., E.M.: Quarterly, 1. gules, on a bend between six cross crosslets fitchée argent, an escutcheon or, charged with a demi-lion rampant pierced through the mouth by an arrow within a double tressure flory counterflory of the first (for Howard); 2. gules, three lions passant guardant in pale or, in chief a label of three points argent (for Brotherton); 3. chequy or and azure (for Warren); 4. gules, a lion rampant or (for Fitzalan), behind the shield two gold batons in saltire, enamelled at the ends sable (the insignia of his office of Earl-Marshal). Mantling gules and argent. Crests: 1. on a chapeau gules, turned up ermine, a lion statant with tail extended or, gorged with a ducal coronet argent; 2. issuant from a ducal coronet or, a pair of wings gules, each charged with a bend between six cross crosslets fitchée argent; 3. on a mount vert, a horse passant argent, holding in the mouth a slip of oak fructed proper. Supporters: Dexter, a lion; sinister, a horse, both argent, the latter holding in his mouth a slip of oak vert, fructed proper. Motto: "Sola virtus invicta."

PER · VIAS · RECTAS

FIG. 811.—Armorial bearings of Marquess of Dufferin and Ava (Hamilton-Temple-Blackwood): Quarterly, 1 and 4, azure, a fess or, in chief a crescent argent, between two mullets of the second, and in base a mascle of the third (for Blackwood); 2. quarterly, i. and iiii., or, an eagle displayed sable; ii. and iii., argent, two bars sable, each charged with three martlets or (for Temple); 3. gules, three cinquefoils pierced ermine, on a chief or a lion passant of the field (for Hamilton); and impaling the arms of Hamilton, namely: gules, three cinquefoils ermine, on a chief argent, a man's heart proper. Crests: 1. on a cap of maintenance gules, turned up ermine, a crescent argent; 2. on a ducal coronet or, a martlet gold; 3. on a wreath of the colours, a demi-antelope affronté ermine, attired and unguled or, holding between his hoofs a heart gules. Supporters: dexter, a lion gules, gorged with a collar flory counterflory or, supporting a staff proper, therefrom flowing to the sinister a flag or, charged with a peacock in its pride also proper; sinister, an heraldic tiger ermine, gorged with a collar flory counterflory gules, and supporting a staff proper, therefrom a flag flying to, and charged as that of the dexter. Motto: "Per vias rectas."

FIG. 810.—Armorial bearings of Sir Thomas North Dick-Lauder, 9th Bart.: Gules, a gryphon salient within a bordure argent (for Lauder); and pendent from an orange-tawny ribbon his badge as a baronet of Nova Scotia. Mantling gules, doubled argent. Crest: on a wreath of his liveries, a tower with portcullis down and the head and shoulders of a sentinel appearing above the battlements in a watching posture proper. Supporters: two lions rampant argent. Mottoes (over the crest): "Turris prudentia custos;" (below the arms) "Ut migraturus habita."

best lion supporters which Mr. Eve has ever drawn are in the largest of the Royal bookplates which he designed for use in the Windsor Castle Library (Fig. 1098).

Fig. 810 is a reproduction of a bookplate by Mr. Sherborn, and shows the arms as used by Sir Thomas Dick-Lauder, Bart.

Fig. 811, which shows the achievement of the late Marquess of Dufferin and Ava, and Fig. 812, which shows the arms of Sir George Duff-Sutherland-Dunbar,

collared or." Two lions rampant double-queued, the dexter or, the sinister sable, are the supporters of the Duke of Portland, and the supporters of both the Earl of Feversham and the Earl of Dartmouth afford instances of lions crowned with a coronet, and issuing therefrom a plume of ostrich feathers.

Sea-lions will be found as supporters to the arms of Viscount Falmouth ["Two sea-lions erect on their tails argent, gutté-de-l'armes"], and the Earl of Howth

FIG. 812.—Armorial bearings of Sir George Duff-Sutherland-Dunbar, 6th Bart. : Quarterly, 1. gules, a lion rampant within a bordure argent, charged with eight roses of the field (for Dunbar) ; 2. gules, three mullets or, a crescent of the last for difference (for Sutherland) ; 3. vert, on a fess dancetté ermine, between a buck's head caboshed in chief and two escallops in base or, a mullet of the first for difference (for Duff) ; 4. or, three cushions within a double tressure flory and counterflory gules (for Randolph) ; the whole within a bordure vairy or and gules. Mantling gules, doubled argent. Crest : on a wreath of his liveries, a sword and key in saltire proper. Supporters : dexter, a lion rampant argent ; sinister, a savage man holding a club over his shoulder proper. Motto (over the crest) : " Sub spe."

afford examples of lion supporters from designs by Mr. Graham Johnston.

Winged lions are not very usual, but they occur as the supporters of Lord Braye : " On either side a lion guardant or, winged vair." A winged lion is also one of the supporters (the dexter) of Lord Leconfield, but this, owing to the position of the wings, is quite unique. The blazon is : " A lion with wings inverted azure,

bears : " Dexter, a sea-lion as in the crest ; sinister, a mermaid proper, holding in her exterior hand a mirror."

The Heraldic Tiger is occasionally found as a supporter, and an instance occurs in Fig. 811, just referred to, in the arms of the Marquess of Dufferin and Ava. It also occurs as the sinister supporter of the Duke of Leeds, and of the Baroness Darcy de Knayth, and was the dexter supporter of the Earls of Holderness. Two heraldic tigers are the supporters both of Sir Andrew Noel Agnew, Bart., and of the Marquess of Anglesey. Of recent years the natural tiger has taken its place in the heraldic menagerie, and instances of its appearance will be found in the arms of Sir Mortimer Durand, and will be seen on Plate CXVIII., where it appears as one of the supporters of the arms of the city of Bombay.

When occurring in heraldic surroundings it is always termed for distinction a "Bengal tiger," and two Royal Bengal tigers are the supporters of Sir Francis Outram, Bart.: "On either side a Royal Bengal tiger guardant proper, gorged with a wreath of laurel vert, and on the head an Eastern crown or."

The Griffin is perhaps the next most favourite supporter, and a good example of the official type of this

Mr. Eve. Male griffins are the supporters of Sir George John Egerton Dashwood: "On either side a male gryphon argent, gorged with a collar flory counter-flory gules."

Fig. 814, also by Mr. Eve, shows the arms of the Earl of Mar.

Continental artists assume even a greater freedom than our own in depicting their supporters. Plate LXI. Fig. 1 represents the arms of his Apostolic Majesty the Emperor Franz Joseph, King of Hungary. The griffin supporters are from a drawing by Herr Ströhl (Ströhl's "Austro-Hungarian Roll of Arms," Vienna, 1895). The shield shows the arms of Austria, the Collar of the Golden Fleece, &c., but it is here introduced to show the supporters, which are griffins per fess sable and

FIG. 813.—Armorial bearings of the Earl of Mar and Kellie (Erskine): Quarterly, 1 and 4, argent, a pale sable (for Erskine); 2 and 3, azure, a bend between six cross crosslets fitché or (for Mar). Over all, on an escutcheon gules, the Imperial crown of Scotland proper, within a double tressure flory counterflory or, ensigned with an Earl's coronet (for the Earldom of Kellie), impaling the arms of Ashley-Cooper, namely: argent, three bulls passant sable, armed and unguled or (for Ashley); 2 and 3, gules, a bend engrailed between six lions rampant or (for Cooper). Above the escutcheon is placed the coronet of his rank, and thereupon a helmet befitting his degree, with a mantling sable, doubled ermine; and upon wreaths of the proper liveries are set the two following crests: upon the dexter side, a dexter hand holding a skene in pale argent, hilted and pommelled or; and on an escroll over the same this motto, "Je pense plus" (for Erskine); and upon the sinister side, a demi-lion rampant guardant gules, armed argent, and on an escroll over the same this motto, "Decori decus addit avito" (for Kellie). Supporters: two griffins gules, armed, beaked, and winged or; underneath this motto, "Unione fortior."

animal occurs on Plate LXII., which shows the arms of Viscount Halifax.[d] Fig. 813, which represents the arms of the Earl of Mar and Kellie, is from a design by

or. The motto, "Viribus unitis," is the personal motto of the Emperor.

A very curious supporter is borne by Mr. Styleman Le Strange. Of course, as a domiciled English commoner, having no Royal Licence to bear supporters, his

[d] Armorial bearings of Viscount Halifax (Wood): Azure, three naked savages ambulant in fess proper, in the dexter hand of each a shield argent charged with a cross gules, in the sinister a club resting on the shoulder also proper, on a canton ermine, three lozenges conjoined in fess sable, and upon an escutcheon of pretence the arms of Courtenay, namely; quarterly, 1 and 4, or, three torteaux surmounted by a label of three points azure (for Courtenay); 2 and 3, or, a lion rampant azure (for Redvers). Above the escutcheon, which is charged with his badge

of Ulster as a baronet, is placed the coronet of his rank, and thereupon a helmet befitting his degree, with a mantling azure and argent; and for his crest, upon a wreath of the colours, a savage as in the arms, the shield sable, charged with a griffin's head erased argent. Supporters: on either side a griffin sable, gorged with a collar and pendent therefrom a portcullis or. Motto: "I like my choice."

claim to these additions would not be recognised, but their use no doubt originated in the fact that he represents the lines of several coheirships to different baronies by writ, to some one of which, no doubt, the supporters may have at some time belonged. The dexter supporter in question is " a stag argent with a lion's forepaws and tail, collared."

The supporters recently granted to Lord Milner are two "springbok," and the same animal (an "oryx" or "springbok") is the sinister supporter of the arms of Cape Colony (Plate LXI.).

Goats are the supporters of the Earl of Portsmouth (who styles his "chamois or wild goats"), of Lord Bagot and Lord Cranworth, and they occur in the achievements of the Barony of Ruthven and the Marquess of Nor-

of Mowbray, but the sinister supporter still remained a " sea-dog."

The *Horse* and the *Pegasus* are constantly met with supporting the arms of peers and others in this country. In Fig. 920 a bay horse regardant appears as the dexter supporter of the Earl of Yarborough, and the horses which support the shield of Earl Cowper are very specifically detailed in the official blazon : "Two dun horses close cropped (except a tuft upon the withers) and docked, a large blaze down the face, a black list down the back, and three white feet, viz. the hind-feet and near fore-foot."

Fig. 809 represents the official type, and Fig. 58, which is the coat of arms of Lord Newlands, is a characteristic piece of work by Mr. Graham Johnston.

FIG. 814.—Armorial bearings of the Earl of Mar (Goodeve-Erskine): Quarterly, 1 and 4, azure, a bend between six cross crosslets fitché or (for Mar) ; 2 and 3, argent, a pale sable (for Erskine). Above the escutcheon is placed the coronet of his rank, and thereupon a helmet befitting his degree, with a mantling gules, doubled ermine ; and upon a wreath of his liveries is set for crest, a dexter hand proper, holding a cutlass argent, hilted and pommelled or. Supporters : two griffins argent, armed, beaked, and winged or. Motto : "Je pense plus."

manby. The supporters of Viscount Southwell are two "Indian" goats.

Rams are the supporters of Lord De Ramsey and Lord Sherard. A ram is also one of the supporters attached to the Barony of Ruthven, and one of the supporters used by the town of New Galloway. These arms, however, have never been matriculated, which on account of the curious charge upon the shield is very much to be regretted.

The supporters of Lord Mowbray and Stourton afford an example of a most curious and interesting animal. Originally the Lords Stourton used two antelopes azure, but before the seventeenth century these had been changed to two "sea-dogs." When the abeyance of the Barony of Mowbray was determined in favour of Lord Stourton the dexter supporter was changed to the lion

The arms of the City of London[e] are always used with *Dragons* for supporters (Plate CXVI.), but these supporters are not officially recorded. The arms of the city of London are referred to at greater length elsewhere in these pages. The town of Appleby uses dragons with wings expanded (most fearsome creatures), but these are not official, nor are the "dragons sejant addorsed gules, each holding an ostrich feather argent affixed to a scroll" which some enterprising artist designed for Cheshire. Dragons will be found as supporters to the arms of the Earl of Enniskillen, Lord St.

[e] Arms of the City of London: Argent, a cross gules in the first quarter, a sword in pale point upwards of the last. Crest: a dragon's sinister wing argent, charged with a cross gules. Supporters: on either side a dragon with wings elevated and endorsed argent, and charged on the wing with a cross gules. Motto: "Domine dirige nos."

Oswald, the Earl of Castlestuart, and Viscount Arbuthnott.

The heraldic dragon is not the only form of the creature now known to armory. The Chinese dragon was granted to Lord Gough as one of his supporters, and it has since also been granted as a supporter to Sir Robert Hart, Bart.

Wyverns are the supporters of the Earl of Meath and Lord Burghclere, and the sinister supporter of both Lord Raglan and Lord Lyveden.

The arms of the Royal Burgh of Dundee are quite unique. The official blazon runs: " Azure, a pott of growing lillies argent, the escutcheon being supported by two dragons, their tails nowed together underneath vert, with this word in an escroll above a lilie growing out of the top of the shield as the former, ' Dei Donum.' " Though blazoned as dragons, the creatures are undoubtedly wyverns, and a representation of this coat of arms will be found on Plate LXI.

Wyverns when figuring as supporters are usually represented standing on the one claw and supporting the shield with the other, but in the case of the Duke of Marlborough, whose supporters are two wyverns, these are generally represented sejant erect, supporting the shield with both claws. This position is also adopted for the wyvern supporters of Sir Robert Arbuthnot, Bart., and the Earl of Eglinton.

Two Cockatrices are the supporters of Lord Donoughmore, the Earl of Westmeath, and Sir Edmund Nugent, Bart., and the dexter supporter of Lord Lanesborough is also a cockatrice.

The Basilisk is the same creature as the cockatrice, and Plate LXI., Fig. 4, which shows the arms of the town of Basle (German Basel), is an example of a supporter blazoned as a basilisk. The arms are: " Argent, a crosier sable." The supporter is a basilisk vert, armed and jelloped gules. The design, which is signed " D. S.," and which, as will be seen, is dated 1511, is really a printer's mark. In a second design by the same artist, and used for the same purpose, the basilisk is holding the shield strap in its beak.

The peculiar shape of the Basle crosier, it may be here noticed, is to be found on the Great Seal of the Council of the town as early as the fifteenth century with the legend: " ✠ S' Consvlvm Civitatis Basiliensis." The figure is borrowed from the arms of the Bishopric of Basle, which shows: " Argent, a crosier gules." The crosier gules is also borne by the Province of Basle (Basel-Landschaft). The canton since 1833 has been composed of the town of Basle (Basel-Stadt) and Basel-Landschaft, and the arms of the canton show both on the one shield, but the red crosier has the addition of a knob on the top, as it will be found on a fourteenth-century seal of the little town of Liestal, now the principal town of Basle-Province.

The supporters of the Plasterers' Company, which were granted with the arms (January 15, 1556), are: " Two opimaci (figures very similar to griffins) vert pursted (? purfled) or, beaked sable, the wings gules." The dexter supporter of the arms of Cape Colony is a " gnu " (Plate LXI.).

The zebra, the giraffe, and the okapi are as yet unclaimed as supporters, though the giraffe, under the name of the camelopard, figures in some number of cases as a crest, and there is at least one instance (Kemsley) of a zebra as a crest. The ass, though there are some number of cases in which it appears as a crest or a charge, does not yet figure anywhere as a supporter, nor does the mule. The hyena, the sacred cow of India, the bison, the giant-sloth, and the armadillo are all distinctive animals which still remain to be withdrawn from the heraldic " lucky bag " of Garter. The

mythical human-faced winged bull of Egyptian mythology, the harpy, and the female centaur would lend themselves well to the character of supporters.

Robertson of Struan has no supporters matriculated with his arms, and it is difficult to say for what length of time the supporters now in use have been adopted. But he is chief of his name, and the representative of one of the minor barons, so that there is no doubt that supporters would be matriculated to him if he cared to apply. Those supporters in use, viz. " Dexter, a serpent; sinister, a dove, the heads of each encircled with rays," must surely be no less unique than is the strange compartment, " a wild man lying in chains," which is borne below the arms of Robertson, and which was granted to his ancestor in 1451 for arresting the murderers of King James I.

The supporters belonging to the city of Glasgow [f] are also unique, being two salmon, each holding a signet-ring in the mouth (Plate CXVII.).

The supporters of the city of Waterford, though not recorded in Ulster's Office, have been long enough in use to ensure their official " confirmation " if a request to this effect were to be properly put forward. They are, on the dexter side a lion, and on the sinister side a dolphin. Two dolphins azure, finned or, are the supporters of the Watermen and Lightermen's Livery Company, and were granted 1655.

BIRDS AS SUPPORTERS

Whilst eagles are plentiful as supporters, nevertheless if eagles are eliminated the proportion of supporters which are birds is not great.

A certain variety and differentiation is obtained by altering the position of the wings, noticeably in regard to eagles, but these differences do not appear to be by any means closely adhered to by artists in pictorial representations of armorial bearings.

The arms of Nicolson (Fig. 815) afford a good example of eagles " close." These are from a design by Mr. G. W. Eve. The arms of the Bishop of Argyll and the Isles (Fig. 816) afford examples of eagles with wings inverted, from designs by Mr. J. Forbes Nixon.

Fig. 817 ought perhaps more properly to have been placed amongst those eagles which, appearing as single figures, carry shields charged upon the breast, but in the present case, in addition to the shield charged upon it in the usual manner, it so palpably supports the two other escutcheons, that we are tempted to include it amongst definite supporters. The figure represents the arms of the free city of Nürnberg, and the design is reproduced from the title-page of the German edition of Andreas Vesili's *Anatomia*, printed at Nürnberg in 1537. The eagle is that of the German Empire, carrying on its breast the impaled arms of Castile and Austria. The shields it supports may now be said both to belong to Nürnberg. The dexter shield, which is the coloured seal device of the old Imperial city, is: " Azure, a harpy (in German *frauenadler* or maiden eagle) displayed and crowned or." The sinister shield

[f] Arms of Glasgow: Argent, on a mount in base vert an oak-tree proper, the stem at the base thereof surmounted by a salmon on its back also proper, with a signet-ring in its mouth or, on the top of the tree a redbreast, and in the sinister fess point an ancient hand-bell, both also proper. Above the shield is placed a suitable helmet, with a mantling gules, doubled argent; and issuing from a wreath of the proper liveries is set for crest, the half-length figure of St. Kentigern affronté, vested and mitred, his right hand raised in the act of benediction, and having in his left hand a crosier, all proper. On a compartment below the shield are placed for supporters, two salmon proper, each holding in its mouth a signet-ring or, and in an escroll entwined with the compartment this motto, " Let Glasgow flourish."

FIG. 816.—Armorial bearings of the Bishop of Argyll and the Isles (Chinnery-Haldane): Quarterly, 1 and 4, argent, a saltire engrailed sable (for Haldane); 2. argent, a saltire between four roses gules (for Lennox); 3. or, a bend chequy sable and argent (for Menteith); and on an escutcheon of pretence the arms of Chinnery, namely: azure, a chevron ermine between three lions rampant or, on a canton vert a harp of the third, stringed argent. Upon the escutcheon is placed a helmet befitting his degree, with a mantling gules, doubled argent; and for his crests, I. on the dexter side, on a wreath of the liveries, an eagle's head erased or, and in an escroll above the motto, "Suffer" (for Haldane); 2. on the sinister side, upon a wreath of the liveries, on a globe or, an eagle rising proper, collared of the first, and in an escroll over the motto, "Nec temere nec timide" (for Chinnery); and for his supporters, on either side an eagle proper.

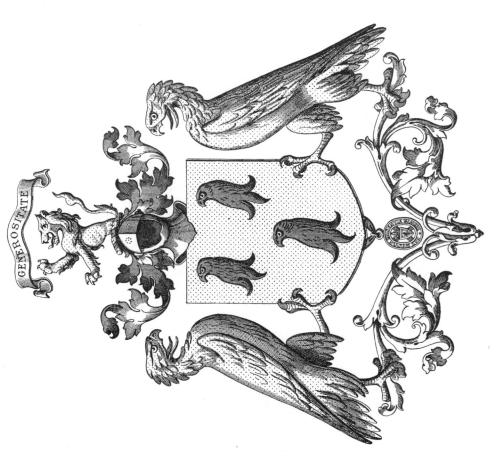

FIG. 815.—Armorial bearings of Nicolson: Or, three falcons heads erased gules. Crest: a demi-lion or, armed and langued gules. Supporters: two eagles or, armed gules. Motto: "Generositate."

(which may more properly be considered the real arms of Nürnberg) is: "Per pale or, a double-headed Imperial

Herons: "On either side a heron proper, collared or."

FIG. 818.—Arms of Calcutta: Per chevron or and sable, a lion passant guardant gules, between two palm-trees eradicated in chief vert, and a ship under sail in base argent. Crest: issuant out of an Eastern crown, a sea-lion holding in the dexter paw a lotus-flower leaved and slipped proper. Motto: "Per ardua stabilis esto." Supporters: on either side a representation of an adjutant bird holding in the beak a serpent proper, charged on the shoulder with an Eastern crown or.

FIG. 817.—The Arms of Nürnberg.

eagle displayed, dimidiated with bendy of six gules and argent."

The supporters of Lord Amherst of Hackney are two

The city of Calcutta, to which arms and supporters were granted in 1896, has for its supporters *Adjutant Birds* (Fig. 818), which closely approximate to storks.

A. C. F-D. AND H. S.

THE ART OF HERALDRY

CHAPTER XXXI

THE COMPARTMENT

A COMPARTMENT is anything depicted below the shield as a foothold or resting-place for the supporters, or indeed for the shield itself. Sometimes it is a fixed part of the blazon and a constituent part of the heritable heraldic bearings. At other times it is a matter of mere artistic fancy, and no fixed rules exist to regulate or control nor even to check the imagination of the heraldic artist. The fact remains that supporters must have something to stand upon, and if the blazon supplies nothing, the discretion of the artist is allowed considerable laxity.

On the subject of compartments a great deal of diversity of opinion exists. There is no doubt that in early days and early examples supporters were placed to stand upon some secure footing, but with the decadence of heraldic art in the seventeenth century came the introduction of the gilded "freehand copy" scroll with which we are so painfully familiar, which one writer has aptly termed the heraldic gas-bracket. Arising doubtless from and following upon the earlier habit of balancing the supporters upon the unstable footing afforded by the edge of the motto scroll, the "gas-bracket" was probably accepted as less open to objection. It certainly was not out of keeping with the heraldic art of the period to which it owed its evolution, or with the style of armorial design of which it formed a part. It still remains the accepted and "official" style and type in England, but Scotland and Ireland have discarded it, and "compartments" in those countries are now depicted of a nature requiring less gymnastic ability on the part of the animals to which they afford a foothold. The style of compartment is practically always a matter of artistic taste and design. With a few exceptions it is always entirely disregarded in the blazon of the patent, and the necessity of something for the supporters to stand upon is as much an understood thing as is the existence of a shield whereon the arms are to be displayed. But as the shape of the shield is left to the fancy of the artist, so is the character of the compartment, and the Lyon Register nowadays affords examples of achievements where the supporters stand on rocks and flowery mounds or issue from a watery abiding-place. The example set by the Lyon Register has been eagerly followed by most heraldic artists.

It is a curious commentary upon the heraldic art of the close of the eighteenth and the early part of the nineteenth centuries that whilst the gymnastic capabilities of animals were admitted to be equal to "tight-rope" exhibitions of balancing upon the ordinary scroll, these feats were not considered practicable in the case of human beings, for whom little square platforms were always provided. Fig. 813, which gives the arms of the Earl of Mar and Kellie, is a good example of the official "gas-bracket," and Fig. 819, which represents the sinister supporter of Lord Scarsdale (viz. the figure of Liberality represented by a woman habited argent, mantled purpure, holding a cornucopia proper) shows the method by which platform accommodation was provided for human figures when acting as supporters. Fig. 812, which represents the achievement of Sir George Duff-Sutherland-Dunbar, is reproduced direct from the painting in the Lyon Register, and is a good example of the more rational treatment supporters now receive.

At the same time this greater freedom of design may occasionally lead to mistakes in relation to English supporters and their compartments. Following upon the English practice already referred to of differentiating the supporters of different families, it has apparently been found necessary in some cases to place the supporters to stand upon a definite object, which object

FIG. 819.

is recited in the blazon and becomes an integral and unchangeable portion of the supporter. Thus Lord Torrington's supporters are each placed upon dismounted ships' guns ["Dexter, an heraldic antelope ermine, horned, tusked, maned and hoofed or, standing on a ship gun proper; sinister, a sea-horse proper, on a like gun"], Lord Hawke's[a] dexter supporter rests his sinister foot upon a dolphin, and Lord Herschell's supporters each stand upon a fasces ["Supporters: on either side a stag proper, collared azure, standing on a fasces or"]. The supporters of Lord Iveagh each rest a hind foot upon an escutcheon ["Supporters: on either side a stag gules, attired and collared gemel or, resting the inner hoof on an escutcheon vert charged with a lion rampant of the second"], whilst the inner hind foot of each of Lord Burton's supporters rests upon a stag's head caboshed proper. Probably absurdity could go no further. But in the case of the supporters granted to Cape Town (Fig. 820), the official blazon runs as follows: "On the dexter side, standing on a rock, a female figure proper, vested argent, mantle and sandals azure, on her head an estoile radiated or, and supporting with her exterior hand an anchor also proper; and on the sinister side, standing on a like rock, a lion rampant guardant gules." In this case it will be seen that the rocks form

[a] Supporters of Lord Hawke: Dexter, Neptune, his mantle of a sea-green colour, edged argent, crowned with an Eastern coronet or, his dexter arm erect, darting downwards his trident sable, resting his sinister foot on a dolphin, also sable; sinister, a sea-horse or, sustaining in his forefins a banner argent, the staff broken proper.

an integral part of the supporters, and are not merely an artistic rendering of the compartment. The illustration, which was made from an official drawing supplied from the Heralds' College, shows the curious way in which the motto scroll is made to answer the purpose of the compartment.

Occasionally the compartment itself—as a thing apart from the supporters—receives attention in the blazon, e.g. in the case of the arms of Baron de Worms, which are of foreign origin, recorded in this country by

having the right to supporters, and doubtless those in use have originated in the old artistic custom, previously referred to, of putting escutcheons of arms under the guardianship of angels. They may be so deciphered upon an old stone carving upon one of the municipal buildings in that city. The result has been that two angels have been regularly adopted as the heraldic supporters of the city arms. The point that renders them worthy of notice is that they are invariably represented each standing upon its own little pile of clouds.

Fig. 820.—Arms of Cape Town: Or, an anchor erect sable, stock proper, from the ring a riband flowing azure, and suspended therefrom an escocheon gules charged with three annulets of the field; and for the crest, on a wreath of the colours, upon the battlements of a tower proper, a trident in bend dexter or, surmounted by an anchor and cable in bend sinister sable.

Royal Warrant. His supporters are: "On a bronze compartment, on either side a lion gold, collared and chained or, and pendent from the compartment a golden scroll, thereon in letters gules the motto, 'Vinctus non victus.'"

In the Royal Arms of the United Kingdom the motto "Dieu et mon Droit" is required to be on the compartment below the shield, and thereon the Union Badge of the Rose, Thistle, and Shamrock engrafted on the same stem.

The city of Norwich is not officially recognised as

The arms of the Royal Burgh of Montrose (Forfarshire) afford an official instance of another variety in the way of a compartment, which is a fixed matter of blazon and not depending upon artistic fancy. The entry in Lyon Register is as follows:—

"The Royal Burgh of Montrose gives for Ensignes Armoriall, Argent, a rose gules. The shield adorned with helmet, mantling, and wreath suteable thereto. And for a crest, a hand issuing from a cloud and reaching down a garland of roses proper, supported by two mermaids aryseing from the sea proper. The motto, 'Mare

THE ART OF HERALDRY

ditat Rosa decorat.' And for a revers, Gules, St. Peter on the cross proper, with the keyes hanging at his girdle or. Which Arms, &c., Ext. December 16, 1694."

An English example may be found in the case of the arms of Boston,[b] which are depicted with the supporters (again two mermaids) rising from the sea, though to what extent the sea is a fixed and unchangeable part of the achievement in this case is less a matter of certainty.

Probably of all the curious "supporters" to be found in British armory, those of the city of Southampton (Plate LXIV.) must be admitted to be the most unusual. As far as the actual usage of the arms by the corporation is concerned, one seldom if ever sees more than the simple shield employed. This bears the arms: "Per fess gules and argent, three roses counterchanged." But in the official record of the arms in one of the Visitation books a crest is added, namely: "Upon a mount vert, a double tower or, and issuing from the upper battlements thereof a demi-female affronté proper, vested purpure, crined and crowned with an Eastern coronet also or, holding in her dexter hand a sword erect point upwards argent, pommel and hilt of the second, and in her sinister hand a balance sable, the pans gold. The shield in the Visitation book rests upon a mount vert, issuing from waves of the sea, and thereupon placed on either side of the escutcheon a ship of two masts at anchor, the sails furled all proper, the round top or, and from each masthead flying a banner of St. George, and upon the stern of each vessel a lion rampant or, supporting the escutcheon.

From the fact that in England the compartment is so much a matter of course, it is scarcely ever alluded to, and the *term* "Compartment" is practically one peculiar to Scottish heraldry. It does not appear to be a very ancient heraldic appendage, and was probably found to be a convenient arrangement when shields were depicted erect instead of couché, so as to supply a resting-place (or standpoint) for the supporters. In a few instances the compartment appears on seals with couché shields, on which, however, the supporters are usually represented as resting *on the sides of the escutcheon,* and bearing up the helmet and crest, as already mentioned. Sir George Mackenzie conjectures that the compartment "represents the bearer's land and territories, though sometimes (he adds) it is bestowed in recompense of some honourable action." Thus the Earls of Douglas are said to have obtained the privilege of placing their supporters with a pale of wood wreathed, because the doughty lord, in the reign of King Robert the Bruce, defeated the English in Jedburgh Forest, and "caused wreathe and impale," during the night, that part of the wood by which he conjectured they might make their escape. Such a fenced compartment appears on the seal of James Douglas, second Earl of Angus, "Dominus de Abernethie et Jedworth Forest" (1434), on that of George Douglas, fourth Earl (1459), and also on those of several of his successors in the earldom (1511-1617). A still earlier example, however, of a compartment "representing a park with trees, &c., enclosed by a wattled fence," occurs on the seal of Walter Stewart, Earl of Atholl (c. 1430), where the escutcheon is placed in the entrance to the park between two trees. Nisbet refers to a seal of William, first Earl of Douglas (1377), exhibiting a single supporter (a lion) "sitting on a compartment like to a rising ground, with a tree growing out of it, and semé of hearts, mullets, and cross crosslets," these being the charges of Douglas and Mar in the escutcheon.

According to Sir George Mackenzie, these compartments were usually allowed only to sovereign princes; and he further informs us that, besides the Douglases, he knows of no other subject in Britain, except the Earl of Perth, whose arms stand upon a compartment. In the case of the Perth family, the compartment consists of a green hill or mount, semé of caltraps[c] (or cheval-traps), with the relative motto, "Gang warily," above the achievement. "Albeit of late," says Mackenzie, "compartments are become more common, and some families in Scotland have some creatures upon which their achievement stand, as the Laird of Dundas, whose achievement has for many hundreds of years stood upon a salamander in flames proper (a device of the kings of France), and Robertson of Struan has a monstrous man lying under the escutcheon chained, which was given him for his taking the murderer of James I. . . ." Such figures, however, as Nisbet remarks, cannot properly be called compartments, having rather the character of devices; while, in the case of the Struan achievement, the chained man would be more accurately described as "an honourable supporter." Sir George Mackenzie engraves "the coat of Denham of ould," viz. a stag's head "caboshed," below a shield couché charged with three lozenges, or fusils, conjoined in bend. In like manner, Nisbet represents the crest and motto of the Scotts of Thirlstane, "by way of compartment," below the escutcheon of Lord Napier, and a blazing star, with the legend, "Luceo boreale," under that of Captain Robert Seton, of the family of Meldrum; while in the case of the illumination which accompanies the latest entry in the first volume of the Lyon Register (1804), relative to the arms of John Hepburn Belshes of Invermay, the trunk of an oak-tree sprouting forth anew is placed on a compartment under the shield, with the motto, "Revirescit."

Two other instances of regular compartments are mentioned by Nisbet, viz. those carried by the Macfarlanes of that Ilk and the Ogilvies of Innerquharity. The former consists of a wavy representation of Loch Sloy, the gathering-place of the clan, which word is also inscribed on the compartment as their *cri de guerre* or slogan; while the latter is a "green hill or rising terrace," on which are placed two serpents, "nowed," spouting fire, and the motto, "Terrena pericula sperno." For some of the foregoing instances I am indebted to Seton's well-known "Law and Practice of Heraldry in Scotland."

A. C. F-D.

---

[b] Arms of Boston: Sable, three coronets composed of crosses patté and fleurs-de-lis in pale or. Crest: A woolpack charged with a ram couchant all proper, ducally crowned azure.

[c] The caltrap was an instrument thrown on the ground to injure the feet of horses, and consisted of four iron spikes, of which one always pointed upwards.

THE ART OF HERALDRY

CHAPTER XXXII

MOTTOES

TO the uninitiated, the subject of the motto of a family has a far greater importance than is conceded to it by those who have spent any time in the study of armory. Perhaps it may clear the ground if the rules presently in force are first recited. It should be carefully observed that the status of the motto is vastly different in England and in other countries. Except in the cases of impersonal arms (and not always then), the motto is never mentioned or alluded to in the terms of the patent in a grant of arms in England; consequently they are not a part of the "estate" created by the Letters Patent, though if it be desired a motto will always be painted below the emblazonment in the margin of the patent. Briefly speaking, the position in England with regard to personal armorial bearings is that mottoes are *not hereditary* nor are they made the subject of grant. No one is compelled to bear one, nor is any authority needed for the adoption of a motto, the matter is left purely to the personal pleasure of every person; but if that person elects to use a motto, the officers of arms are perfectly willing to paint any motto he may chose upon his grant, and to add it to the record of his arms in their books. There is no necessity expressed or implied to use a motto at all, nor is the slightest control exercised over the selection or change of mottoes, though, as would naturally be expected, the officers of arms would decline to record to any private person any motto which might have been appropriated to the sovereign or to any of the orders of knighthood. In the same way no control is exercised over the position in which the motto is to be carried or the manner in which it is to be displayed. In Scotland, however, the matter is on an entirely different footing. The motto is included within the terms of the patent, and is consequently made the subject of grant. It therefore becomes inalienable and unchangeable without a rematriculation, and a Scottish patent moreover always specifies the position in which the motto is to be carried. This is usually "in an escroll over the same" (*i.e.* over the crest), though occasionally it is stated to be borne on "a compartment below the arms." The matter in Ireland is not quite the same as in either Scotland or England. Sometimes the motto is expressed in the patent—in fact this is the most usual alternative—but it is not a universal rule, and to a certain extent the English permissiveness is recognised. Possibly the subject can be summed up in the remark that if any motto has been granted or is recorded with a particular coat of arms in Ireland, it is expected that that shall be the motto to be made use of therewith. As a general practice the use of mottoes in England did not become general until the eighteenth century—in fact there are very few, if any, grants of an earlier date on which a motto appears. The majority, well on towards the latter part of the eighteenth century, had no motto added, and many patents are still issued without such an addition. With rare exceptions, no mottoes are to be met with in the Visitation books, and it does not appear that at the time of the Visitations the motto was considered to be essentially a part of the armorial bearings. The one or two exceptions which I have met with where mottoes are to be found on Visitation pedigrees are in every case the arms of a peer. There are at least two

such in the Yorkshire Visitation of 1587, and probably it may be taken for granted that the majority of peers at that period had begun to make use of these additions to their arms. Unfortunately we have no exact means of deciding the point, because peers were not compelled to attend a Visitation, and there are but few cases in which the arms or pedigree of a peer figure in the Visitation books. In isolated cases the use of a motto can, however, be traced back to an even earlier period. There are several instances to be met with upon the early Garter plates.

Many writers have traced the origin of mottoes to the "slogan" or war-cry of battle, and there is no doubt whatever that instances can be found in which an ancient war-cry has become a family motto. For example, one can refer to the Fitzgerald "Crom-a-boo": other instances can be found amongst some of the Highland families, but the fact that many well-known war-cries of ancient days never became perpetuated as mottoes, and also the fact that by far the greater majority of mottoes, even at a much earlier period than the present day, cannot by any possibility have ever been used for or have originated with the purposes of battle-cries, inclines me to believe that such a suggested origin for the motto in general is without adequate foundation. There can be little if any connection between the war-cry as such and the motto as such. The real origin would appear to be more correctly traced back to the badge. As will be found explained elsewhere, the badge was some simple device used for personal and household purposes and seldom for war, except by persons who used the badge of the leader they followed. No man wore his own badge in battle. It generally partook of the nature of what ancient writers would term "a quaint conceit," and much ingenuity seems to have been expended in devising badges and mottoes which should at the same time be distinctive and should equally be or convey an index or suggestion of the name and family of the owner. Many of these badges are found in conjunction with words, mottoes, and phrases, and as the distinction between the badge in general and the crest in general slowly became less apparent, they eventually in practice became interchangeable devices, if the same device did not happen to be used for both purposes. Consequently the motto from the badge became attached to the crest, and was thence transferred to its present connection with the coat of arms. Just as at the present time a man may and often does adopt a maxim upon which he will model his life, some pithy proverb, or some trite observation, without any question or reference to armorial bearings —so, in the old days, when learning was less diffuse and when proverbs and sayings had a wider acceptance and vogue than at present, did many families and many men adopt for their use some form of words. We find these words carved on furniture, set up on a cornice, cut in stone, and embroidered upon standards and banners, and it is to this custom that we should look for the beginning of the use of mottoes. But because such words were afterwards in later generations given an armorial status, it is not justifiable to presume such status for them from their beginnings. The fact that a man put his badges on the standard that he carried into battle, and with his badges placed the mottoes that

THE ART OF HERALDRY

thereto belonged, has led many people mistakenly to believe that these mottoes were *designed for* war-cries and for use in battle. That was not the case.

With regard to the mottoes in use at the moment, some of course can be traced to a remote period, and many of the later ones have interesting legends connected therewith. Of mottoes of this character may be instanced the "Jour de ma vie" of West, which was formerly the motto of the La Warr family, adopted to commemorate the capture of the King of France at the battle of Poictiers. There are many other mottoes of this character, amongst which may be mentioned the "Grip fast" of the Leslies, the origin of which is well known. But though many mottoes relate to incidents in the remote past, true or mythical, the motto and the incident are seldom contemporary. Nothing would be gained by a recital of a long list of mottoes, but I cannot forbear from quoting certain curious examples which by their very weirdness must excite curiosity as to their origin. A family of Martin used the singular words, "He who looks at Martin's ape, Martin's ape shall look at him," whilst the Curzons use, "Let Curzon hold what Curzon helde." The Cranston motto is still more grasping, being, "Thou shalt want ere I want;" but probably the motto of Dakyns is the most mysterious of all, "Strike Dakyns, the devil's in the hempe." The motto of Corbet, "Deus pascit corvos," evidently alludes to the raven or ravens (corby crows) upon the shield. The mottoes of Trafford, "Now thus," and "Gripe griffin, hold fast;" the curious Pilkington motto, "Pilkington Pailedown, the master mows the meadows;" and the "Serva jugum" of Hay have been the foundation of many legends. The "Fuimus" of the Bruce family is a pathetic allusion to the fact that they were once kings, but the majority of ancient mottoes partake rather of the nature of a pun upon the name, which fact is but an additional argument towards the supposition that the motto has more relation to the badge than to any other part of the armorial bearings. Of mottoes which have a punning character may be mentioned "Mon Dieu est ma roche," which is the motto of Roche, Lord Fermoy; "Cavendo tutus," which is the motto of Cavendish; "Forte scutum salus ducum," which is the motto of Fortescue; "Set on," which is the motto of Seton; and "Ver non semper veret," the well-known pun of the Vernons. Another is the apocryphal "Quid rides" which Theodore Hook suggested for the wealthy and retired tobacconist. This punning character has of late obtained much favour, and wherever a name lends itself to a pun the effort seems nowadays to be made that the motto shall be of this nature. Perhaps the best pun which exists is to be found in the motto of the Barnard family, who, with arms "Argent, a bear rampant sable, muzzled or," and crest "A demi-bear as in the arms," use for the motto, "Bear and Forbear," or in Latin, as it is sometimes used, "Fer et perfer." Others that may be alluded to are the "What I win I keep" of Winlaw; the "Libertas" of Liberty; the "Ubi crux ibi lux" of Sir William Crookes; the "Bear thee well" of Bardwell; the "Gare le pied fort" of Bedford; the

"Gare la bête" of Garbett; and the "Cave Deus videt" of Cave. Other mottoes—and they are a large proportion—are of some saintly and religious tendency. However desirable and acceptable they may be, and however accurately they may apply to the first possessor, they sometimes are sadly inappropriate to later and more degenerate successors.

In Germany, a distinction appears to be drawn between their "Wahlsprüche" (*i.e.* those which are merely dictated by personal choice) and the "armorial mottoes" which remained constantly and heritably attached to the armorial bearings, such as the "Gott mit uns" ("God with us") of Prussia and the "Nihil sine Deus" of Hohenzollern.

The Initial or Riddle Mottoes appear to be peculiar to Germany. Well-known examples of these curiosities are the "W. G. W." (*i.e.* "Wie Gott will"—"As God wills"), or "W. D. W." (*i.e.* "Wie du willst"—"As thou wilt"), which are both frequently to be met with. The strange but well-known alphabet or vowel-motto "A. E. I. O. V" of the Emperor Frederick III. has been variously translated, "Aquila Electa Juste Omnia Vincit" ("The chosen eagle vanquishes all by right"), "Aller Ehren Ist Oesterrich Voll" ("Austria is full of every honour"), or perhaps with more likelihood, "Austria Est Imperare Orbe Universo" ("All the earth is subject to Austria").

The *cri-de-guerre* both as a heraldic fact and as an armorial term, is peculiar, and exclusively so, to British and French heraldry. The national *cri-de-guerre* of France, "Montjoye Saint Denis," appeared above the pavilion in the old Royal Arms of France, and probably the English Royal motto, "Dieu et mon Droit," is correctly traced to a similar origin. A distinction is still made in modern heraldry between the *cri-de-guerre* and the motto, inasmuch as it is considered that the former should always of necessity surmount the crest. This is very generally adhered to in Scotland in the cases where both a motto and a *cri-de-guerre* (or, as it is frequently termed in that country, a "slogan") exist the motto, contrary to the usual Scottish practice, being then placed below the shield. It is to be hoped that a general knowledge of this fact will not, however, result in the description of every motto found above a crest as a *cri-de-guerre*, and certainly the concentrated piety now so much in favour in England for the purposes of a motto can be quite fitly left below the shield.

Artists do not look kindly on the motto for decorative purposes. It is usually depicted in heraldic emblazonment in black letters upon a white scroll, tinted and shaded with pink, but with the present revival of heraldic art, it has become more general to paint the motto ribbon in conformity with the colour of the field, the letters being often shown thereon in gold. The colour and shape of the motto ribbon, however, are governed by no heraldic laws, and except in Scottish examples should be left as they are purely unimportant accessories of the achievement, wholly at the discretion of the artist.

A. C. F-D. AND H. S.

THE ART OF HERALDRY

CHAPTER XXXIII

BADGES

THE exact status of the badge in this country, to which it is peculiar, has been very much misunderstood. This is probably due to the fact that the evolution of the badge was gradual, and that its importance increased unconsciously. Badges do not appear to have ever been made the subjects of grants, and the instances which can be referred to showing their control, or attempted control, by the Crown are *very rare indeed*. As a matter of fact, the Crown seems to have perhaps purposely ignored them. They are not, as we know them, found in the earliest times of heraldry, unless we are to presume their existence from early seals, many of which show isolated charges taken from the arms; for if in the cases where such charges appear upon the seals we are to accept those seals as proofs of the contemporary existence of those devices as heraldic badges, we should often be led into strange conclusions.

There is no doubt that these isolated devices which are met with were not only a part of the arms, but in many cases the *origin* of the arms. Devices possessing a more or less personal possessive character occur in many cases before record of the arms they later developed into can be traced. This will be noticed in relation to the arms of Swinton, to which reference is made elsewhere. If these are badges, then badges go back to an earlier date than arms. Such devices occur many centuries before such a thing as a shield of arms existed.

The *Heraldic Badge, as we know it*, came into general use about the reign of Edward III., that is, the heraldic badge as a separate matter having a distinct existence in addition to concurrent arms, and having at the same time a distinctly heraldic character. But long before that date, badges are found with an allied reference to a particular person, which very possibly are rightly included in any enumeration of badges. Of such a character is the badge of the broom plant, which is found upon the tomb of Geoffrey, Count of Anjou, from which badge the name of the Plantagenet dynasty originated (Plantagenet, by the way, was never a personal surname, but was the name of the dynasty).

It is doubtful, however, if at that early period there existed the opportunity for the use of heraldic badges. At the same time, as far back as the reign of Richard I.—and some writers would take examples of a still more remote period—these badges were depicted upon banners, for Richard I. appears to have had a dragon upon one of his banners.

These banner decorations, which at a later date have been often accepted as badges, can hardly be quite properly so described, for there are many cases where no other proof of usage can be found, and there is no doubt that many such are instances of no more than banners prepared for specific purposes; and the record of such and such a banner cannot necessarily carry proof that the owner of the banner claimed or used the objects depicted thereupon as personal badges. If they are to be so included some individuals must have revelled in a multitude of badges.

But the difficulty in deciding the point very greatly depends upon the definition of the badge; and if we are to take the definition according to the manner of acceptance and usage at the period when the use of badges was greatest, then many of the earliest cannot be taken as coming within the limits.

In later Plantagenet days, badges were of considerable importance, and certain characteristics are plainly marked. They were never worn by the owner—in the sense in which he carried his shield, or bore his crest; they were his sign-mark indicative of ownership; they were stamped upon his belongings in the same way in which Government property is marked with the broad arrow, and they were worn by his servants. They were worn by his retainers and very probably worn more or less temporarily by adherents of his party if he were big enough to lead a party in the State. At all times badges had very extensive decorative use.

There was never any fixed form for the badge; there was never any fixed manner of usage. I can find no fixed laws of inheritance, no common method of assumption. In fact the use of a badge, in the days when everybody who was anybody possessed arms, was quite subsidiary to the arms, and very much akin to the manner in which nowadays monograms are made use of. At the same time care must be taken to distinguish the "badge" from the "rebus," and also from the temporary devices which we read about as having been so often adopted for the purpose of the tournament when the combatant desired his identity to be concealed. Modern novelists and poets give us plenty of illustrations of the latter kind, but proof of the fact even that they were ever adopted in that form is by no means easy to find, though their professedly temporary nature of course militates against the likelihood of contemporary *record*. The rebus had never an heraldic status, and it had seldom more than a temporary existence. A fanciful device adopted (we hear of many such instances) for the temporary purpose of a tournament could generally be so classed, but the rebus proper has some device, usually a pictorial rendering of the name of the person for whom it stood. In such form would be included printers' and masons' marks, but probably the definition of Dr. Johnson of the word rebus, as a word represented by a picture, is as good a definition and description as can be given. The rebus in its nature is a different thing, and may best be described as a pictorial signature, the most frequent occasion for its use being in architectural surroundings, where it was frequently introduced as a pun upon some name which it was desired to perpetuate. The best-known and perhaps the most typical and characteristic rebus is that of Islip, the builder of part of Westminster Abbey. Here the pictured punning representation of his name had nothing to do with his armorial bearings or personal badge; but the great difficulty, in dealing with both badges and rebuses, is the difficulty of knowing which is which, for very frequently the same or a similar device was used for both purposes. Parker, in his glossary of heraldic terms, gives several typical examples of rebuses which very aptly illustrate their status and meaning. At Lincoln College at Oxford, and on other buildings connected with Thomas Beckynton, Bishop of Bath and Wells, will be found carved the rebus of a beacon issuing from a tun. This is found in conjunction with the letter T for his Christian name, Thomas, but this design was not his coat of arms, and was not his crest, nor was it his badge. Another rebus which is found at Canterbury shows an ox and the letters N, E, as the rebus of John Oxney. A rebus which indicates Thomas Conyston,

Abbot of Cirencester, which can be found in Gloucester Cathedral, is a comb and a tun, and the printer's mark of Richard Grifton, which is a good example of a rebus and its use, was a tree, or graft, growing on a tun. In none of these cases are the designs mentioned on any part of the arms, crest, or badge of the persons mentioned. Rebuses of this character abound on all our ancient buildings, and their use has lately come very prominently into favour in connection with the many allusive bookplates, the design of which originates in some play upon the name. The words "device," "ensign," and "cognisance" have no definite heraldic meaning, and are used impartially to apply to the crest, the badge, and sometimes to the arms upon the shield, so that they may be eliminated from consideration. There remains therefore the crest and the badge between which to draw distinctions. The crest was the ornament upon the helmet, seldom if ever actually used, and never used except by the person to whom it belonged. The badge, on the other hand, was worn by the servants and retainers, and was used right and left on his belongings as a sign of ownership. So great and extensive was the use of these badges, that they were far more generally employed than either arms or crest, and whilst the knowledge of a man's badges would be every-day knowledge and common repute throughout the kingdom, few people would know a man's crest, fewer still would ever have seen it worn.

It is merely an exaggeration of the difficulty that we are always in uncertainty whether any given device is merely a piece of decoration borrowed from the arms or crest, or whether it had continued usage as a badge. In the same way many families who had never used crests, but who had used badges, took the opportunity of the Visitations to record their badges as crests. A notable example of the subsequent record of a badge as a crest is met with in the Stourton family. Their crest, originally a buck's head, but after the marriage with the heiress of Le Moigne, a demi-monk, can be readily substantiated, as can their badge of the drag or sledge. At one of the Visitations, however, a cadet of the Stourton family recorded the sledge as a crest. Uncertainty also arises from the lack of precision in the diction employed at all periods, the words badge, device, and crest having so often been used interchangeably.

Another difficulty which is met with in regard to badges is that, with the exception of the extensive records of the Royal badges and some other more or less informal lists of badges of the principal personages at different periods, badges were never a subject of official record, and whilst it is difficult to determine the initial point as to whether any particular device is a badge or not, the difficulty of deducing rules concerning them becomes practically impossible, and after most careful consideration I have come to the conclusion that there were never any rules relating to badges, that they were originally and were allowed to remain matters of personal fancy, and that although well-known cases can be found where the same badge has been used generation after generation, those cases are perhaps the exception rather than the rule. Badges should be considered and accepted in the general run as not being matters of permanence, and as of little importance except during the time from about the reign of Edward III. to about the reign of Henry VIII. Their principal use upon the clothes of the retainers came to an end by the creation of the standing army in the reign of Henry VIII., and as badges never had any ceremonial use to perpetuate their status, they practically ceased altogether at that period except as regards the Royal family.

Speaking broadly, regularised and *recorded* heraldic control as a matter of operative fact dates little if any further back than the end of the reign of Henry VIII., consequently badges do not appear to have been taken much cognisance of by the Heralds. Their use from that period onwards rapidly declined, and now to all intents and purposes is, and for the last two hundred years has been, at an end.

Though the use of badges has become almost obsolete, there are still one or two occasions on which badges are used as badges, in the style formerly in vogue. Perhaps the one which is most familiar is the broad arrow which is used to mark Government stores. It is a curious commentary upon heraldic officialdom and its ways that though this is the only badge which has really any extensive use, it is not a Crown badge in any degree. It originated in the fact that one of the Sydney family, when Master of the Ordnance, to prevent disputes as to the stores for which he was responsible, marked everything with his private badge of the broad arrow, and this private badge has since remained in constant use. One wonders at what date the officers of His Majesty will observe that this has become one of His Majesty's recognised badges, and will include it with the other Royal badges in the warrants in which they are recited. Already more than two centuries have passed since it first came into use, and either they should represent to the Government that the pheon is not a Crown mark, and that some recognised Royal badge should be used in its place, or else they should place its status upon a definite footing.

Another instance of a badge used at the present day in the ancient manner is the conjoined rose, thistle, and shamrock which is embroidered front and back upon the tunics of the Beef-eaters. The crowned harps which are worn by the Royal Irish Constabulary are another instance of the kind, but though a certain number of badges are recited in the warrant each time any alteration or confirmation of the Royal Arms occurs, their use has now become limited to the last degree. Present badges are the crowned rose for England, the crowned thistle for Scotland, and the crowned trefoil and the crowned harp for Ireland; for the union there is the conjoined rose, thistle, and shamrock under the crown, and the crowned shield which carries the device of the Union Jack. The badge of Wales, which has existed for long enough, is the uncrowned dragon upon a mount vert, and the crowned cyphers, one within and one without the Garter, are also depicted upon the warrant. These badges, which appear on the Sovereign's warrant, are never assigned to any other member of the Royal Family, of whom the Prince of Wales is the only one who rejoices in the possession of officially assigned badges. The badge of the eldest son of the Sovereign, as such, and not as Prince of Wales, is the plume of three ostrich feathers, enfiled with the circlet from his coronet (Plate LXVII. Fig. 34). Recently an additional badge (on a mount vert, a dragon passant gules, charged with a label of three points argent) has been assigned to His Royal Highness. This action was taken with the desire to in some way gratify the forcibly expressed wishes of Wales, and it is probable that, the precedent having been set, it will be assigned to all those who may bear the title of Prince of Wales in future.

The only instances I am personally aware of in which a real badge of ancient origin is still worn by the servants are the cases of the state liveries of the Earl of Yarborough, whose servants wear an embroidered buckle, and Lord Mowbray and Stourton, whose servants wear an embroidered sledge. I believe the servants of Lord Braye still wear the badge of the hemp-brake, and doubtless there are a few other instances. When the old families were becoming greatly reduced in number, and the nobility and the upper classes were being recruited from families of later origin, the wearing of badges, like so much else connected with heraldry, became lax in its practice, and the custom to all intents and purposes has been at an end for the last two centuries.

The uniform of the Beef-eaters and Yeomen of the Guard at the Tower of London is the best and, as far as I know, the only instance of the use of a badge at the present date in the style and manner in which badges were originally worn. An examination of this old-world uniform shows the rose, thistle, and shamrock conjoined below the Royal crown, and embroidered of some considerable size on the breast and on the back. The servants of all the great nobles appear to have worn the badges of their masters in such a manner, although sometimes they were embroidered upon the sleeve; and the wearing of the badge by the retainers is the chief and principal use to which badges were anciently put. Nisbet alludes on this point to a paragraph from the Act for the Order of the Riding of Parliament in 1681, which says that "the noblemen's lacqueys may have over their liveries velvet coats with their badges, *i.e.* their crests and mottoes done on plate, or embroidered on the back and breast conform to ancient custom." A curious survival of these plates is to be found in the large silver plaques worn by so many bank messengers. Badges appear, however, to have been frequently depicted semé upon the lambrequins, as will be seen from many of the old Garter plates; but here, again, it is not always easy to distinguish between definite badges and artistic decoration, nor between actual badges in use and mere appropriately selected charges from the shield.

The water-bougets of Lord Berners, the knot of Lord Stafford, popularly known as "the Stafford knot"; the Harrington fret; the ragged staff or the bear and the ragged staff of Lord Warwick (this being really a conjunction of two separate devices); the Rose of England, the Thistle of Scotland, and the sledge of Stourton, the hemp-brake of Lord Braye wherever met with are readily recognised as badges, but there are many badges which it is difficult to distinguish from crests, and even some which in all respects would appear to be more correctly regarded as coats of arms.

It is a point worthy of consideration whether or not a badge needs a background; here, again, it is a matter most difficult to determine, but it is singular that in any matter of *record* the badge is almost invariably depicted upon a background, either of a banner or a mantling, or upon the "field" of a roundel, and it may well be that their use in such circumstances as the two cases first mentioned may have only been considered correct when the colour of the mantling or the banner happened to be the colour of the background of the badge.

Badges are most usually met with in stained glass upon roundels of some colour, and though one would hesitate to assert it as an actual fact, there are many instances which would lead one to suppose that the background of a badge was usually the livery colour or colours of its then owner, or of the family from which it was originally inherited. Certain is it that there are very few contemporary instances of badges which, when emblazoned, are not upon the livery colours; and if this fact be accepted, we get at once a ready explanation on several points which have puzzled antiquaries. The name of Edward "the Black Prince" has often been a matter of discussion, and the children's history books tell us that the nickname originated from the colour of his armour. This may be true enough, but as most armour would be black when it was unpolished, and as all armour was either polished or dull, the probabilities are not very greatly in its favour. No one painted his armour red or green. It seems to me far more probable that black was the livery colour of the Black Prince,

and that his own retainers and followers wore the livery of black. If that were the case, one understands at once how he would obtain the nickname. Even if his armour were enamelled black, it would be so usually hidden by his surcoat that he is hardly likely to have been nicknamed from it. The nickname is doubtless contemporary. A curious confirmation of my supposition is met with in the fact that his shield for peace was: "Sable, three ostrich feathers two and one, the quill of each passing through a scroll argent." There we get the undoubted badge of the three ostrich feathers depicted upon his livery colour—black (Fig. 455). The badges depicted in Prince Arthur's Book in the College of Arms, an important source of our knowledge upon the subject, are all upon backgrounds (see pages 429 and 430); and the curious divisions of the colours on the backgrounds would seem to show that each badge had its own background, several badges being only met with upon the same ground when that happens to be the true background belonging to them. But in attempting to deduce rules, it should be remembered that in all and every armorial matter there was greater laxity of rule at the period of the actual use of arms than it was possible to permit when the multiplication of arms made regulation necessary and more restrictive; so that an occasional variation from any deduction need not necessarily vitiate the conclusion, even in a matter exclusively relating to the shield. How much more, then, must we remain in doubt when dealing with badges which appear to have been so entirely a matter of personal caprice.

It is a striking comment that of all the badges presently to be referred to of the Stafford family, each single one is depicted upon a background. It is a striking fact that of the eighteen "badges" exemplified as belonging to the family of Stafford, nine are upon partycoloured fields, and whilst this is not an unreasonable proportion if the fields are considered to be the livery colours of the families from whom the badges were originally derived, it is altogether out of proportion to the number of shields in any roll of arms which would have the field party per pale, or party in any other form of division. With the exception of the second badge, which is on a striped background of green and white, all the party backgrounds are party per pale, which was the most usual way of depicting a livery in the few records which have come down to us of the heraldic use of livery colours, and of the eighteen badges, no less than eight are upon a party-coloured field of which the dexter is sable and the sinister gules. Scarlet and black are known to have been the livery colours of Edward Stafford, Duke of Buckingham, who was beheaded in 1521. The arms of the town of Buckingham are on a field per pale sable and gules.

With regard to the descent of badges and the laws which govern their descent still less is known. The answer to the question, "How did badges descend?" is simple: "Nobody knows." One can only hazard opinions more or less pious, of more or less value. It is distinctly a point upon which it is risky to be dogmatic. Whilst the secrecy of the records of the College of Arms is so jealously preserved it is impossible to speak definitely, for an exact and comprehensive knowledge of exact and authoritative instances of fact is necessary before a decision can be definitely put forward. Unless some officer of arms will carefully collate the information which can be gleaned from the records in the College of Arms which are relevant to the subject, it does not seem likely that our knowledge will advance greatly.

In recently reading through the evidence of the Stafford Peerage Case, a certain document which was then put in evidence excited my curiosity, and I have been at pains to procure a copy of the grant or exemplification of the Stafford badges to the Earl of Stafford, paternally and by male descent Howard, but who was known by the name of Stafford-Howard, and who was the heir-general of the Stafford family. To make the matter complete, perhaps it will be well to first reprint a certain clause in the Act of Restoration, 1 Edward VI., upon which was based the necessity for action by the Crown: "And that the said Henry and theirs Males of his Bodye shall and may by Aucthoritie of this Acte be restored and inhabled from hensfurthe to beare and give all and singuler suche the Armes of the Barons of Stafforde as the same Barons and Ancestoʳˢ to yoʳ saide Subgecte have doon and used to doo in the tyme of your noble Progenitʳˢ before theie or anny of them were called or created Earles or Dukes without chalenging bearing or giving any other Armes that were of the said late Dukes his Father."

The Stafford Descent and Attainders with the Restorations will be found detailed in the pages of the *Genealogical Magazine*, September and October 1900. Here it will be sufficient to point out that by restricting the Act to the arms of the Barons Stafford, any claim to the Royal Arms inherited after they became Earls of Stafford was prevented. It is curious that, whilst the heir-general was held to be debarred from succession to the barony which *was* restored to the heir male, the former was not debarred from succession to the Royal quarterings which *were* specifically *withheld* from the heir male. The "opinion" referred to subsequently might throw some light upon the point were it available.

Suffice it to say that the following is a verbatim extract from the Stafford Minutes of Evidence:

"Mr. Adam, the Counsel for the Petitioner, stated, they would next produce a Register in the College of Arms of a Petitionary Letter dated the 26th April 1720 from William Stafford to Henry Bowes Howard Earl of Berkshire, Deputy Earl Marshall, desiring to have assigned to him such Supporters as his Grandfather William the last Viscount Stafford used in his Life Time, and that the Arms of Woodstock and Stafford might be quartered with his Paternal Arms, and depicted in the Margin of the Grant with the Badges of the Family of Stafford.

"Also the Register in the College of Arms of a Warrant dated the 3rd of May 1720 from the Earl of Berkshire to John Anstis Esquire Garter Principal King of Arms, ordering him to grant Supporters and Arms to the said Earl of Stafford; also the Register in the College of Arms to the opinion of Nathaniel Pigot Esquire, dated the 20th January 1719, that the Heirs general of the restored Henry Lord Stafford were not affected by the Restriction in the Act of the 1st of Edward the 6th on the Heirs Male of the said restored Henry Lord Stafford to the bearing of Arms; and the Register in the College of Arms dated the 1st of August 1720 of a grant of Supporters to William Stafford Howard Earl of Stafford expressing that the Arms of Thomas of Woodstock Duke of Gloucester were depicted in the Margin and quartered as the same were borne by the Staffords, Dukes of Buckingham, with 18 Badges belonging to the Family of Stafford.

"Whereupon FRANCIS TOWNSEND Esquire was again called in, and producing a Book, was examined as follows:—

"'What is that you have before you?'

"'It is a Book containing Entries of Grants of Coats of Arms and Supporters; it is the Seventh Volume of a Series.'

"'From whence do you bring it?'

"'From the Heralds' College.'

"'Is that an official copy of the grant?'

"'It is an official record of the whole process relating to it.'

"'Turn to April 26, 1720, and read the entry.'

"'Read the following entries in the same:'—

"My LORD,

"Whereas his late Majesty King James the Second was pleased by Letters Patents under the Great Seal to create my late Uncle Henry Earl of Stafford with remainder for want of Issue Male of him to John and Francis his brothers and the heirs Male of their Bodies respectively by means whereof the said Title is now vested in me the Son and heir of the said John: And it being an indisputable right belonging to the Peers to have Supporters to their Arms and my said Uncle having omitted to take any Grant thereof (as I am informed is usually practised on such Occasions) I desire yʳ Loᵖ would please to issue proper directions for the assigning to me such Supporters as my Grandfather the late Viscount Stafford used in his life time, to be born by me and such on whom the said Honor is settled.

"And whereas by my Descent from my Grandmother, Mary late Countess of Stafford, I am intitled (as I am advised by Council) to the Arms and Quarterings of her Family, I desire the Arms of Woodstock and Stafford may be quartered with my Paternal Arms and depicted in the Margin of the said Grant, together with the Badges which have been born and used by the Family of Stafford: This will extremely oblige

"Yoʳ Lordsᵖˢ

"most affectionate Kinsman

"and humble Servant

"STAFFORD.

"Ap. 26, 1720."

"Whereas the Rᵗ Honᵇˡᵉ William Stafford Howard Earl of Stafford hath by Letter represented unto me that his late Majesty King James the Second was pleased by Letters Patent under the Great Seal to create his late Uncle Henry Earl of Stafford with remainder for want of Issue Male of him to John and Francis his Brothers, and the Heirs Male of their Bodies respectively by means whereof the said Title is now vested in him, the Son and Heir of the said John; and it being an indisputable Right belonging to the Peers of the Realm to have Supporters added to their Arms, and his said Uncle having omitted to take any Grant as (he is informed) is usually practiced on such occasions, has therefore desired my Warrant for the assigning to him such Supporters as his Grandfather the late Viscount Stafford used in his life time to be born and used by him and such on whom the said Honour is settled: And whereas he hath further represented to me that by his Descent from his Grandmother Mary late Countess of Stafford he is entituled (as he is advised by Council) to the Arms and Quarterings of her Family and has further desired that the Arms of Woodstock and Stafford may be quartered with his Paternal Arms and depicted in the Margin of the said Grant together with the Badges which have been born and used by the Family of Stafford, I, Henry Bowes Howard Earl of Berkshire Deputy (with the Royal Approbation) to the Most Noble Thomas Duke of Norfolk Earl Marshal and Hereditary Marshall of England, considering the Request of the said Henry Stafford Howard Earl of Stafford, and also the Opinion of Council learned in the Law hereunto annexed, do hereby Order and Direct you to grant and assign to him the same Supporters as his Grandfather the late Viscount Stafford used in his life time; To be born and used by him and such, on whom the said Honour is setled; and that you cause to be depicted in the Margin of the said Grant the Arms of Thomas of Woodstock Duke of Gloucester, and Stafford Quartered with his Lordships Arms together with the Badges which have been born and used by the said Family of Stafford; Requiring you to take care that the said Letter, these Presents, the said Opinion of Council and yor Grant be duely entered by the Register in the College of Arms: For all which Purposes this shall be your sufficient Warrant.

"Given under my Hand Seal this third day of May Anno Dñi 1720.

"BERKSHIRE.

"To John Anstis Esqr Garter
"Principal King of Arms.

"Then the Witness being about to read the Registry of the Opinion of Counsel, as stated by Mr. Adam;

"Mr. Attorney General objected to the same.

"Mr. Adam, Counsel for the Petitioner, waived the Production of it.

"Read from the same Book the following Entry:

"To all and singular to whom these Presents shall come, John Anstis Esqr Garter principal King of Arms, sends greeting, Whereas his late Majesty King James the Second by Letters Patents under the Great Seal, did create Henry Stafford Howard to be Earl of Stafford, to have and hold the same to him and the heirs males of his body; and for default thereof to John and Francis his Brothers and the heirs males of their bodies respectively, whereby the said Earldom is now legally vested in the right Honble William Stafford Howard Son and Heir of the said John; And in regard that ye said Henry late Earl of Stafford omitted to take any Grant of Supporters, which the Peers of this Realm have an indisputable Right to use and bear, the right Honble Henry Bowes Howard Earl of Berkshire Deputy (with the Royal Approbation) of his Grace Thomas Howard Duke of Norfolk Earl Marshall and Hereditary Marshall of England hath been pleased to direct me to grant to the said right Honble William Stafford Howard Earl of Stafford the Supporters formerly granted to ye late Viscount Stafford, Grandfather to the said Earl; as also to order me to cause to be depicted in the Margin of my said Grant ye Arms of Thomas of Woodstock Duke of Gloucester quartered with the Arms of the said Earl of Stafford, together with the Badges of the said Noble Family of Stafford: Now these presents Witness that according to the consent of the said Earl of Berkshire signified under his Lordship's hand and seal I do by the Authority and power annexed to my Office hereby grant and assign to ye said Right Honourable William Stafford Howard Earl of Stafford, the following Supporters which were heretofore borne by the late Lord Viscount Stafford, that is to say, on the Dexter side a Lion Argent, and on the Sinister Side a Swan surgiant Argent Gorged with a Ducal Coronet per Pale Gules and Sable beaked and membered of the Second; to be used and borne at all times and upon all occasions by the said Earl of Stafford and the heirs males of his body, and such persons to whom the said Earldom shall descend according to the Law and Practice of Arms without the let or interruption of any Person or Persons whatsoever. And in pursuance of the Warrant of the said Earl of Berkshire, The Arms of Thomas of Woodstock Duke of Gloucester, as the same are on a Plate remaining in the Chapel of St George within ye Castle of Windsor, set up there for his Descendant the Duke of Buckingham are depicted in the Margin, and quartered in such place and manner as the same were formerly borne by the Staffords Dukes of Buckingham, together with Eighteen badges belong-

ing to the said most ancient and illustrious Family of Stafford, as the same are represented in a Manuscript remaining in the College of Arms. In Witness whereof I the said Garter have hereto subscribed my Name and affixed the Seal of my Office this First Day of August Anno Domini 1720.

"JOHN ANSTIS Garter
"Principal King of Arms.

"The Witness was directed to withdraw."

It may be of interest to call attention to the fact that the Royal Arms are displayed before those of Stafford (Fig. 821). On the face of it, the document—as far as it relates to the badges—is no more than a certificate or exemplification, in which case it is undoubted evidence

FIG 821.—The Stafford Arms and Supporters as exemplified in 1720 to William Stafford Howard, Earl of Stafford.

that badges descend to the heir-general as do quarterings; but there is the possibility that the document is a re-grant in the nature of an exemplification following a Royal Licence, or a re-grant to remove uncertainty as to the attainder. And if the document—as far as its relation to the badges goes—has any of the character of a grant, it can have but little value as evidence of the descent of badges. It is remarkable that it is absolutely silent as to the future destination of the badges. The real fact is that the whole subject of the descent and devolution of badges is shrouded in mystery. Each of the badges (Fig. 822) is depicted within a circle adorned with a succession of Stafford knots, as is shown in the one instance at the head. Five of these badges appear upon a well-known portrait of Edward, Duke of Buckingham. The fact that some of these *badges* are really crests depicted upon wreaths goes far as an authority for the use of a crest upon livery buttons for the purposes of a badge.

In ancient days all records seemed to point to the fact that badges were personal, and that though they were worn by the retainers, they were the property of *the head* of the family, rather than (as the arms) of the whole family, and though the information available is meagre to the last degree, it would appear probable that in all cases where their use by other members of the family than the head of the house can be proved, the likelihood is that the cadets would render feudal service and would wear the badge as retainers of the man whose banner they followed into battle, so that we should expect to find the badge following the same descent as the peerage, together with the lands and liabilities which accompanied it. This undoubtedly makes for the inheritance of a badge upon the same line of descent as a barony by writ, and such a method of inheritance accounts for the known descent of most of the badges heraldically familiar to us. Probably we shall be right in so accepting it. This then gives us the badge, the property in and of which would descend to the heir-general, whilst it would be used in token of allegiance

FIG. 822.—The Stafford Badges as exemplified in 1720 to William Stafford Howard, Earl of Stafford.

or service, actual, quasi-actual, or sentimental, by the cadets of the house and their servants; for whilst the use of the cockade is a survival of the right to be waited on and served by a soldier servant, the use of a badge by a cadet is a survival and reminder of the day when (until they married heiresses and continued or found other families) the cadets of a house owed and gave military service to the head of their own family, and in return were supported by him.

The use of badges at the present day is singularly limited, though perhaps this is not a matter of surprise when we remember how few indeed are the families belonging to the days when badges were in use, of whom there are now direct representatives. The absence of rule and regulation leaves it very much a matter of personal taste how badges, where they now exist, shall be depicted, and perhaps it is better to leave their

manner of display to artistic requirements. The most usual place is on either side of the crest, and they may well be depicted in that position. Where they exist, however, they ought undoubtedly to be continued in use upon the liveries of the servants, and the present practice is for them to be placed on the livery buttons, and embroidered upon the epaulettes or on the sleeves of state liveries. Undoubtedly the former practice of placing the badge upon the servants' livery is the precursor of the present vogue of placing crests upon livery buttons, and many heraldic writers complain of the impropriety of placing the crest in such a position. I am not sure that I myself may not have been guilty in this way, but when one bears in mind the number of cases in which the badge and the crest are identical, and when, as in the above instance, devices which are undoubtedly crests are exemplified as and termed badges, even as such being represented upon wreaths, whilst in other cases the action has been the reverse, it leaves one under the necessity of being careful in making dogmatic assertions. Now that the wearing of crests upon helmets is entirely at an end, and now that it is impossible to obtain a grant of a badge, it is difficult to say why it should not be correct to give to the crest the *additional* character and usage of a badge, and use the same device as a badge and term it both badge and crest. If for the purposes of a badge the wreath be omitted there can be no objection at all, and my advice is that this should be done. The pity of such a suggestion is that so many of the modern crests artistically prove quite unsuitable for the purpose when this suggestion is brought under consideration.

Having dealt with the laws (if there ever were any) and the practice concerning the use and display of badges, it will be of interest to notice some of those which were formerly in use.

I have already referred to the badge of the ostrich feathers. The old legend that the Black Prince won the badge at the battle of Crecy by the capture of John, King of Bohemia, together with the motto "Ich dien," has been long since exploded. Sir Harris Nicolas brought to notice the fact that among certain pieces of plate belonging to Queen Philippa of Hainault was a large silver-gilt dish enamelled with a black escutcheon with ostrich feathers, "vuo scuch nigro cum pennis de ostrich," and upon the strength of that, suggested that the ostrich feather was probably originally a badge of the Counts of Hainault derived from the County of Ostrevaus, a title which was held by their eldest sons. The suggestion in itself seems probable enough and may be correct, but it would not account for the use of the ostrich feathers by the Mowbray family, who did not descend from the marriage of Edward III. and Philippa of Hainault. Contemporary proof of the use of badges is often difficult to find. The Mowbrays had many badges, and certainly do not appear to have made any very extensive use of the ostrich feathers. But there seems to be very definite authority for the existence of the badge. There is in one of the records of the College of Arms (R. 22, 67), which is itself a copy of another record, the following statement:—

"The discent of Mowbray written at length in lattin from the Abby booke of newborough wherein Rich 2 gaue to Thomas Duke of norff. & Erle Marshall the armes of Saint Edward Confessor in theis words:

"Et dedit eidem Thome ad pertandum in sigillo et vexillo quo arma S^ti Edwardi. Idcirco arma bipartata

THE ART OF HERALDRY

portavit scil' 't Sci Edwardi et domini marcialis angliæ cum duabus pennis strutionis erectis et super crestam leonem et duo parva scuta cum leonibus et utraq' parto predictorum armorum."

Accompanying this is a rough-tricked sketch of the arms upon which the illustration (Fig. 823) has been

FIG. 823.—The arms granted by King Richard II. to Thomas de Mowbray, Duke of Norfolk, and showing the ostrich feather badges.

based. Below this extract in the College Records is written in an another hand: "I find this then in ye chancell window of Effingham by Bungay in the top of the cot window with Mowbraye & Segrave on the side in glass there."

Who the writer was I am unaware. He appends a further sketch to his note, which slightly differs. No helmet or crest is shown, and the central shield has only the arms of Brotherton. The feathers which flank it are both enfiled below the shield by one coronet. Of the smaller shields at the side, the dexter bears the arms of Mowbray and the sinister those of Segrave.

An ostrich feather piercing a scroll was certainly the favourite badge of the Black Prince and so appears on several of his seals, and triplicated it occurs on his "shield of peace" (Fig. 455; the illustration of this shield, Plate LXVII. Fig. 30, unfortunately wrongly depicts the feathers and scrolls gold instead of silver). The arms of Sir Roger de Clarendon, the illegitimate son of the Black Prince (Plate LXVII. Fig. 31), were derived from this "shield of peace," which I take it was not a coat of arms but merely the badge of the Prince depicted upon his livery colour, and which might equally have been displayed upon a roundle. In the form of a shield bearing three feathers the badge occurs on the obverse of the second seal of Henry IV. in 1411. A single ostrich feather with the motto "Ich dien" upon the scroll is to be seen on the seal of Edward, Duke of York, who was killed at the battle of Agincourt in 1415. Henry IV. as Duke of Lancaster placed on either side of his escutcheon an ostrich feather with a garter or belt carrying the motto "Sovereygne" *twined around* the feather, John of Gaunt used the badge with a chain laid along the quill, and Thomas, Duke of Gloucester, used it with a garter and

buckle instead of the chain; whilst John Beaufort, Duke of Somerset, placed an ostrich feather on each side of his shield, the quills in his case being compony argent and azure, like the bordure round his arms (see Plate CXXXII. Fig. 1).

There is a note in Harl. MS. 304, folio 12, which, if it be strictly accurate, is of some importance. It is to the effect that the "feather silver with the pen gold is the King's, the ostrich feather pen and all silver is the Prince's (*i.e.* the Prince of Wales), and the ostrich feather gold the pen ermine is the Duke of Lancaster's." That statement evidently relates to a time when the three were in existence contemporaneously, *i.e.* before the accession of Henry IV. In the reign of Richard II. there was no Prince of Wales. During the reign of Edward III. from 1376 onwards, Richard, afterwards Richard II., was Prince of Wales, and John of Gaunt was Duke of Lancaster (so cr. 1362). But John of Gaunt used the feather in the form above stated, and to find a Duke of Lancaster *before* John of Gaunt we must go back to before 1360, when we have Edward III. as King, the Black Prince as Prince, and Henry of Lancaster (father-in-law of John of Gaunt) as Duke of Lancaster. He derived from Henry III., and like the Mowbrays had no blood descent from Philippa of Hainault. A curious confirmation of my suggestion that black was the livery colour of the Black Prince is found in the fact that there was in a window in St. Dunstan's Church, London, within a wreath of roses a roundle per pale sanguine and azure, a plume of ostrich feathers argent, quilled or, enfiled by a scroll bearing the words "Ich dien." Above was the Prince's coronet and the letters E. & P., one on each side of the plume. This was intended for Edward VI., doubtless being erected in the reign of Henry VIII. The badge in the form in which we know it, *i.e.* enfiled by the princely coronet (Plate LXVII. Fig. 34), dates from about the beginning of the Stuart dynasty, since when it appears to have been exclusively reserved for the eldest son and heir-apparent to the throne. At the same time the right to the display of the badge would appear to have been reserved by the Sovereign, and Woodward remarks:—

"On the Privy Seals of our Sovereigns the ostrich feather is still employed as a badge. The shield of arms is usually placed between two lions sejant guardant addorsed, each holding the feather. On the Privy Seal of Henry VIII. the feathers are used without the lions, and this was the case on the majority of the seals of the Duchy of Lancaster. On the reverse of the present seal of the Duchy the feathers appear to be ermine."

Fig. 824 shows the seal of James II. for the Duchy of Lancaster. The seal of the Lancashire County Council shows a shield supported by two talbots sejant addorsed, each supporting in the exterior paw an ostrich feather semé-de-lis. It is possible that the talbots may be intended for lions and the fleurs-de-lis for ermine spots. On Plate LXVII. Fig. 32 will be seen the silver swan, one of the badges of King Henry V., and used also by Henry IV. It was derived from the De Bohuns, Mary de Bohun being the wife of Henry IV. From the De Bohuns it has been traced to the Mandevilles, Earls of Essex, who may have adopted it to typify their descent from Adam Fitz Swanne, *temp.* Conquest. Fig. 33 on the same plate is the white hart of Richard II. Although some have traced this badge from the white hind used as a badge by Joan, the Fair Maid of Kent, the mother of Richard II., it is probably a device punning upon his name, "Rich-hart." Richard II. was not the heir of his mother. The heir was his half-brother, Thomas Holland, Earl of Kent, who *did* use the badge of the hind, and perhaps the real truth is that the Earl of Kent having the better claim to the hind, Richard was under the necessity of making an alteration which the obvious pun upon his name suggested. There is no doubt that the crest of Ireland (Plate CXV.) originated therefrom. The stag in this case was undoubtedly "lodged" in the earliest versions, and I have been much interested in tracing the steps by which the springing attitude has developed owing to the copying of badly drawn examples.

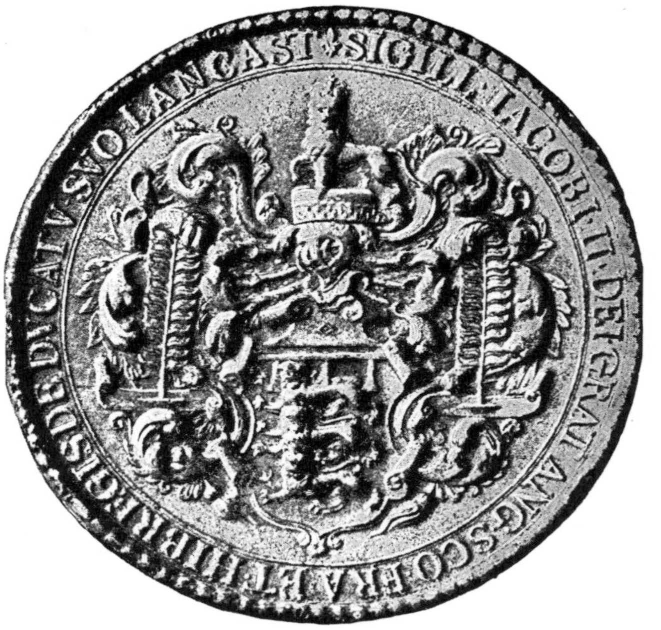

FIG. 824.—Seal of King James II. for the Duchy of Lancaster.

Figs. 32 and 33 are taken from "Prince Arthur's Book," other examples therefrom being reproduced elsewhere in the present volume. Amongst the many Royal and other badges in this country there are some of considerable interest. Fig. 825 represents the famous badge of the "broom-cod" or "planta genista," from which the name of the dynasty was derived. It appears to have been first used by King Henry II., though it figures in the decoration of the tomb of Geoffrey, Count of Anjou. "Peascod" Street in Windsor of course derives its name therefrom. The well-known badges of the white and red roses of York and Lancaster have been already referred to, and Fig. 826, the well-known device of the

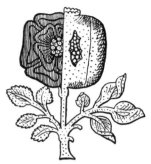

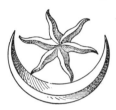

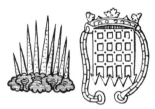

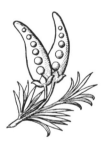

FIG. 825.—Badge of King Henry II.

FIG. 826.—Badge of Edward IV.

"rose-en-soleil" used by King Edward IV., was really a combination of two distinct badges, viz. "the blazing sun of York" and the "white rose of York." The rose again appears in Fig. 827, here dimidiated with the pomegranate of Catharine of Aragon. This is taken from the famous Tournament Roll (now in the College of Arms), which relates to the Tournament, 13th and 14th of February 1510, to celebrate the birth of Prince Henry. For the forms in which the rose still exists as a Royal badge reference should be made to Plate CXIV. Richard I., John, and Henry III. are all said to have used the device

FIG. 827.—Compound Badge of Henry VIII. and Catharine of Aragon. (From the Westminster Tournament Roll.)

of the crescent and star (Fig. 828). Henry VII. is best known by his two badges of the crowned portcullis and the "sun-burst" (Fig. 829). The suggested origin of

FIG. 828.—Badge of Richard I.

FIG. 829.—Two badges of Henry VII., viz. the "sun-burst" and the crowned portcullis.

the former, that it was a pun on the name Tudor (*i.e.* two-door) is confirmed by the motto "Altera securitas" which was used with it, but at the same time is rather vitiated by the fact that it was also used by the Beauforts, who had no Tudor descent. Save a very tentative remark hazarded by Woodward, no explanation has as yet been suggested for the sun-burst. My own strong conviction, based on the fact that this particular badge was principally used by Henry VII., who was always known as Henry of Windsor, is that it is nothing more than an attempt to pictorially represent the name "Windsor" by depicting "winds" of "or." The badge is also attributed to Edward III., and he, like Henry VII., made his principal residence at Windsor. Edward IV. also used the white lion of March (whence is derived the shield of Ludlow: "Azure, a lion couchant guardant, between three roses argent," Ludlow being one of the fortified towns in the Welsh Marches), and the black bull which, though often termed "of Clarence," is generally associated with the Duchy of Cornwall. Richard III., as Duke of Gloucester, used a white boar.

The Earl of Northumberland used a silver crescent; the Earl of Douglas, a red heart; the Earl of Pembroke, a golden pack-horse with collar and traces; Lord Hastings bore as badge a black bull's head erased, gorged with a coronet; Lord Stanley, a golden griffin's leg, erased; Lord Howard, a white lion charged on the shoulder with a blue crescent; Sir Richard Dunstable adopted a white cock as a badge; Sir John Savage, a silver unicorn's head erased; Sir Simon Montford, a golden lily; Sir William Gresham, a green grasshopper.

Two curious badges are to be seen in Figs. 830 and 831. The former is an ape's clog argent, chained or, and was used by William de la Pole, Duke of Suffolk (*d.* 1450). Fig. 831, "a salet silver" (MS. Coll. of Arms, 2nd M. 16), is the badge of Thomas Howard, Duke of Norfolk (*d.* 1524). Various families used knots of different design, of which the best known is the Stafford knot (Fig. 832). The wholesale and improper appropriation of this badge with a territorial application has unfortunately caused it to be very generally referred to as a "Staffordshire" knot, and that it was the personal badge of the Lords Stafford is too often overlooked. Other badge knots are

FIG. 830.—Badge of the Duke of Suffolk.

FIG. 831.—Badge of Thomas Howard, Duke of Norfolk.

FIG. 832.—Stafford Knot.

FIG. 833.—Wake or Ormond Knot.

FIG. 834.—Bourchier Knot.

FIG. 835.—Heneage Knot.

but from that time forward the Royal badges obtained a territorial character: the rose of England, the thistle of Scotland, and the shamrock of Ireland. To these popular consent has added the lotus-flower for India, the

the Wake or Ormonde knot (Fig. 833), the Bourchier knot (Fig. 834), and the Heneage knot (Fig. 835).

The personal badges of the members of the Royal Family continued in use until the reign of Queen Anne,

maple for Canada, and in a lesser degree the wattle or mimosa for Australia; but at present these lack any official confirmation. The two first named, nevertheless, figured on the Coronation Invitation Cards.

A. C. F-D.

CHAPTER XXXIV

HERALDIC FLAGS AND BANNERS

WHEN it comes to the display of flags, the British-born individual usually makes a hash of the whole business, and flies either the Sovereign's personal coat of arms, which really should only be made use of over a residence of the Sovereign when the Sovereign is actually there, or flown at sea when the Sovereign is on board; or else he uses the national flag, colloquially termed the "Union Jack," which ought never to be made use of on land except over the residence of the Sovereign in his absence, or on a fortress or other Government building. The banner of St. George, which is a white flag with a plain red cross of St. George throughout, is now appropriated to the Order of the Garter, of which St. George is the patron saint, though I am by no means inclined to assert that it would be incorrect to make use of it upon a church which happened to be specifically placed under the patronage of St. George.

The white ensign, which is a white flag bearing the cross of St. George and in the upper quarter next to the staff a reproduction of the Union device, belongs to the Royal Navy, and certain privileged individuals to whom the right has been given by a specific warrant. The blue ensign, which is a plain blue flag with the Union device on a canton in the upper corner next the staff, belongs to the Royal Naval Reserve; and the red ensign, which is the same as the former, except that a red flag is substituted for the blue one, belongs to the ships of the merchant service. These three flags have been specifically called into being by specific warrants for certain purposes which are stated in these warrants, and these purposes being wholly connected with the sea, neither the blue, the red, nor the white ensign ought to be hoisted on land by anybody. Of course there is no penalty for doing so on land, though very drastic penalties can be enforced for misuse of these ensigns on the water, a step which is taken frequently enough. For a private person to use any one of these three flags on land for a private purpose, the only analogy which I can suggest to bring home to people the absurdity of such action would be to instance a private person for his own private pleasure

adopting the exact uniform of some regiment whenever he might feel inclined to go bathing in the sea. If he were to do so, he would find under the recent Act that he had incurred the penalty, which would be promptly enforced, for bringing His Majesty's uniform into disrepute. It is much to be wished that the penalties exacted for the wrongful display of these flags at sea should be extended to their abuse on shore.

The development of the Union Jack and the warrants relating to it are dealt with herein by the Rev. J. R. Crawford, M.A., in a subsequent chapter, and I do not propose to further deal with the point, except to draw attention to a proposal, which is very often mooted, that some change or addition to the Union Jack should be made to typify the inclusion of the colonies.

But to begin with, what is the Union Jack? Probably most would be inclined to answer, "The flag of the Empire." It is nothing of the kind. It is in a way stretching the definition to describe it as the King's flag. Certainly the design of interlaced crosses is a badge of the King's, but that badge is of a later origin than the flag.

The flag itself is the fighting emblem of the Sovereign, which the Sovereign has declared shall be used by his soldiers or sailors for fighting purposes under certain specified circumstances. That it is used, even officially, in all sorts of circumstances with which the King's warrants are not concerned is beside the matter, for it is to the Royal Warrants that one must refer for the theory of the thing.

Now let us go further back, and trace the "argent, a cross gules," the part which is England's contribution to the Union Jack, which itself is a combination of the "crosses" of St. George, St. Andrew, and St. Patrick. The theory of one is the theory of the three, separately or conjoined.

"Argent, a cross gules" was never the coat of arms of England (except under the Commonwealth, when its use for armorial purposes may certainly be disregarded), and the reason it came to be regarded as the flag of England is simply and solely because fighting was always done under the supposed patronage of some saint, and England

THE ART OF HERALDRY

fought, *not* under the arms of England, but under the flag of St. George, the patron saint of England and of the Order of the Garter. The battle-cry "St. George for Merrie England!" is too well known to need more than the passing mention. Scotland fought under St. Andrew; Ireland, by a similar analogy, had for its patron saint St. Patrick (if indeed there was a Cross of St. Patrick before one was needed for the Union flag, which is a very doubtful point), and the Union Jack was not the combination of three territorial flags, but the combination of the recognised emblems of the three recognised saints, and though England claimed the sovereignty of France, and for that reason quartered the arms of France, no Englishman bothered about the patronage of St. Denis, and the emblem of St. Denis was never flown in this country. The fact that no change was ever made in the flag to typify Hanover, whilst Hanover duly had its place upon the arms, proves that the flag was recognised to be, and allowed to remain, the emblem of the three patron saints under whose patronage the British fought, and not the badge of any sovereignty or territorial area. If the colonies had already any saint of their own under whose patronage they had fought in bygone days, or in whose name they wished to fight in the future, there might be reason *for including the emblem of that saint* upon the fighting flag of the Empire; but they have no recognised saintly patrons, and they may just as well fight for our saints as choose others for themselves at so late a day; but having a flag which is a *combination* of the emblems of three saints, and which contains nothing that is not a part of those emblems to make any addition heraldic or otherwise to it now, would in my opinion be best expressed by the following illustration. Imagine three soldiers in full and complete uniform, one English, one Scottish, and one Irish, it being desired to evolve a uniform that should be taken from all three for use by a Union regiment. A tunic from one, trousers from another, and a helmet from a third, might be blended into a very effective and harmonious composite uniform. Following the analogy of putting a bordure, which is not the emblem of a saint, round the recognised emblems of the three recognised saints, and considering it to be in keeping because the bordure was heraldic and the emblems heraldic, one might argue, that because a uniform was clothing as was also a ballet-dancer's skirt, therefore a ballet-dancer's skirt outside the whole would be in keeping with the rest of the uniform. For myself I should dislike any addition to the Union device, as much as we should deride the donning of tulle skirts outside their tunics and trousers by the brigade of Guards.

The flag which should float from a church tower should have no more on it than the recognised ecclesiastical emblems of the saint to whom it is dedicated: the keys of St. Peter, the wheel of St. Catherine, the sword of St. Paul, the cross and martlets of St. Edmund, the lily of St. Mary, the emblem of the Holy Trinity, or whatever the emblem may be of the saint in question. The flags upon public buildings should bear the arms of the corporate bodies to whom those buildings belong. The flag to be flown by a private person, as the law now stands, should bear that person's private arms, if he has any, and if he has not he should be content to forego the pleasures arising from the use of bunting. A private flag should be double its height in length. The entire surface should be occupied by the coat of arms.

These flags of arms are *banners*, and it is quite a misnomer to term the banner of the Royal Arms the Royal Standard. The flags of arms hung over the stalls of the Knights of the Garter, St. Patrick, and the former Knights of the Bath are properly, and are always termed *banners*. A *standard* one never meets with nowadays. The term properly refers to the long tapering flag used

in battle, and under which an overlord mustered his retainers in battle. This did *not* display his armorial bearings. Next to the staff came the cross of St. George, which was depicted, of course, on a white field. This occupied rather less than one-third of the standard. The remainder of the standard was of the colour or colours of the livery, and thereupon was represented all sorts of devices, usually the badges and sometimes the crest; but almost invariably the largest and most prominent object on a standard was *one of the supporters*. The motto was usually on transverse bands, which frequently divided the standard into compartments for the different badges. These mottoes from their nature are *not* war-cries, but undoubtedly relate and belong to the badges with which they appear in conjunction. The whole banner was usually fringed with the livery colours, giving the effect of a bordure compony. These standards do not seem, except for the ceremonial purposes of funerals, to have survived the Tudor period, this doubtless being the result of the creation of the standing army in the reign of Henry VIII. The few exotic standards, *e.g.*, remaining from the Jacobite rebellion, seldom conform to the old

FIG. 836.—"Middle" arms of the Duchy of Saxe-Altenburg. (From Ströhl's *Deutsche Wappenrolle*.)

patterns, but although the shape is altered, the artistic character largely remains in the regimental colours of the present day with their assorted regimental badges and scrolls with the names of battle honours.

The armorial use of the banner in connection with the display of heraldic achievements is very limited in this country. In the cases of Cochrane (Plate LXVIII.) and the Marquess of Dufferin and Ava (Fig. 811) the banner or flag is an integral and unchangeable part of the heraldic supporters, and in Ross-of-Bladensburg, *e.g.*, it is similarly an integral part of the crest. Other cases where arms have been depicted on banners are generally no more than matters of artistic design, but in the arms of Scotland as matriculated in Lyon Register for King Charles II. the supporters are accompanied by banners, the dexter being of the arms of Scotland, and the sinister the banner of St. Andrew. These banners possess rather a different character, and approach very closely to the German use. The same practice has been followed in the seals of the Duchy of Lancaster, inasmuch as on the obverse of the seal of George IV. and the seal of Queen Victoria the Royal supporters hold banners of the arms of England and of the Duchy (*i.e.* England, a label for difference). James I. on his Great Seal had the banners of Cadwallader (azure, a cross patté fitché or) and King Edgar (azure, a cross patonce between four martlets or), and on the Great Seal of Charles I. the dexter supporter holds a banner of St. George, and the sinister a banner of St. Andrew.

Of the heraldic use of the banner in Germany Herr Ströhl writes :—

"The banner appears in a coat of arms, either in the hands or paws of the supporters (Fig. 836), also set up behind the shield (see Plate CXVIII. Fig. 3), or the pavilion, as, for instance, in the larger achievement of his Majesty the German Emperor, in the large achievement of the kingdom of Prussia, of the dukedom of Saxe-Altenburg, and further in the Arms of State of Italy, Russia, Roumania, &c.

"Banners on the shield as charges, or on the helmet as a crest (Plate LXXXVIII. Fig. 6), are here, of course, not in question, but only those banners which serve as *Prachtstücke* (appendages of magnificence).

"The banners of the twelfth and thirteenth centuries are long and narrow, and frequently run in stripes, like

FIG. 837.—Arms of Tetnang: Argent, an ecclesiastical banner gules. (From the Zurich *Wappenrolle*.)

FIG. 838.—Arms of the town of Tangermünde : Argent, the eagle of Brandenburg displayed gules armed or, each wing charged with a rose of the field.

battlements (Plate CXXXVI. Fig. 3). However, in the second half of the thirteenth century flags were also to be met with, with the longer side attached to the stick (Plates V Fig. 1, and CXXXVI. Fig. 1). Later on the banners became more square, and show on the top a long strip, generally of another colour, the *Schwenkel* (*i.e.* something that flourishes, waves to and fro), Fig. 1002 ; Plates CXXXVI. Fig. 5 ; CXXXVII. Fig. 3. To bear a red *schwenkel* was a special privilege, similar to the right of sealing with red wax.

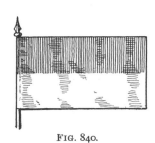

FIG. 839.

FIG. 840.

"The ecclesiastical banner has three points, and is provided with rings on the top in order that it may be fastened to the stick by them, in an oblique position (Fig. 837 ; see also Plate CXXXIX. Fig. 18).

"The banner always represents the field of the shield, and assumes accordingly its tincture. The charges of the shield should be placed upon the banner without the outline of a shield, and the edge against the flag-staff is considered the dexter ; it follows from this that the figure must be turned towards it (see Fig. 1002 and Plate CXVIII. Fig. 3).

"For instance, if the shield bear the following arms, argent an eagle gules (Fig. 838), the same figure, suited to

the size of the flag, appears on the banner, with its head turned towards the staff (Fig. 839). If it be wished to represent only the *colours* of the arms upon the flag, that of the charge is placed above, and that of the field below (Fig. 840). Thus, for example, the Prussian

FIG. 841.

FIG. 842.

flag is black and white, corresponding to the black eagle on the silver field ; the flag of Hohenzollern is white and black, corresponding to their coat of arms, quartered silver and black, because in the latter case, so soon as a heraldic representation is available, from the position of the coloured fields, the correct order of the tinctures is determined.

"Where flags are used for purely decorative purposes, one is no longer strictly tied down to the simple square or rectangular shape ; some scope for fancy may be

FIG. 843.

accorded, but the cut of the flag must not interfere with its clearness, and the heraldic character of the charge must not be disturbed. A few examples of such different shapes (Figs. 841, 842, and 843) will bring more nearly before the eyes what has been mentioned."

H. S. AND A. C. F-D.

THE ART OF HERALDRY

CHAPTER XXXV

MARKS OF CADENCY

THE manner in which cadency is indicated in heraldic emblazonment forms one of the most important parts of British armory, but our own intricate and minutely detailed systems are a purely British development of armory. I do not intend by the foregoing remark to assert that the occasional use, or even, as in some cases, the constant use of altered arms for purposes of indicating cadency is unknown on the Continent, because different branches of one family are constantly found using, for the purposes of distinction, variations of the arms appertaining to the head of the family; in France especially the bordure has been extensively used, but the fact nevertheless remains that in no other countries is there found an organised system or set of rules for the purpose.

The obligation of cadet lines to difference their arms was recognised practically universally in the fourteenth century; and when, later, the systematic use of differencing seemed in danger of being ignored, it was made the subject of specific legislation. In the treatise of ZYPŒUS, *de Notitia juris Belgici*, lib. xii., quoted also in MENETRIER, *Recherches du Blazon*, p. 218, we find the following:—

"Ut secundo et ulterius geniti, quinimo primogeniti vivo patre, integra insignia non gerant, sed aliqua nota distincta, ut perpetuo linæ dignosci possint, et ex qua quique descendant, donec anteriores defecerint. Exceptis Luxenburgis et Gueldris, quibus non sunt ii mores." (The exception is curious.)

The choice of these *brisures*, as marks of difference are often termed, was, however, left to the persons concerned; and there is, consequently, a great variety of differences or differentiation which seem to have been used for the purpose. The term "brisure" is really French, whilst the German term for these marks is "Beizeichen."

British heraldry, on the contrary, is remarkable for its use of two distinct sets of rules—the English and the Scottish—the Irish system being identical with the former. Nor is this idea of the indication of cadency wholly a modern development, though some, in fact most, of the rules presently in force are no doubt a result of modern requirements, and do not date back to the earliest periods of heraldry in this country.

To understand the question of cadency it is necessary to revert to the status of a coat of arms in early periods. In the first chapter we dealt with the origin of armory; and in a subsequent chapter with the status of a coat of arms in Great Britain, and it will therefrom have been apparent that arms, and a right to them, developed in this country as an adjunct of, or contemporaneously with, the extension of the feudal system. Every landowner was at one time required to have his seal—presumably, of arms—and as a result arms were naturally then considered to possess something of a territorial character. I do not by this mean to say that the arms belonged to the land and were transferable with the sale and purchase thereof. There never was in this country a period at which such an idea held; nor were arms originally purely personal. They belonged rather to a position half-way between the two. They were the arms of a given family, originating because that family held land and accepted the consequent responsibilities thereto belonging, but the arms appertained for the time being to the member of that family who owned the land, and that this is the true idea of the former status of a coat of arms is perhaps best evidenced by the Grey and Hastings controversy, which engaged the attention of the Court of Chivalry for several years prior to 1410. The decision and judgment in the case gave the undifferenced arms of Hastings to the heir-general (Grey de Ruthyn), the heir-male (Sir Edward Hastings) being found only capable of bearing the arms of Hastings subject to some mark of difference.

This case, and the case of Scrope and Grosvenor, in which the king's award was that the bordure was not sufficient difference for a stranger in blood, being only the mark of a cadet, show clearly that the status of a coat of arms in early times was that it belonged to one person only for the time being, and that person the head of the family, though it should be noted that the term "Head of the Family" seems to have been interpreted into the one who held the lands of the family—whether he were heir-male or heir-general being apparently immaterial.

Thus much being recognised, it follows that some means were needed to be devised to differentiate the armorial bearings of the younger members of the family. Of course the earliest definite instances of any attempt at a systematic "differencing" for cadency which can be referred to are undoubtedly those cases presented by the arms of the younger members of the Royal Family in England. These cases, however, it is impossible to take as precedents. Royal Arms have always, from the very earliest times, been a law unto themselves, subject only to the will of the Sovereign, and it is neither safe nor correct to deduce precedents to be applied to the arms of subjects from proved instances concerning the Royal Arms.

Probably, apart from these, the earliest mark of cadency which is to be met with in heraldry is the label (Fig. 844) used to indicate the eldest son, and

FIG. 844.—The label.

this mark of difference dates back far beyond any other regularised methods applicable to "younger" sons. The German name for the label is "Turnierkragen," *i.e.* Tournament Collar, which may indicate the origin of this curious figure. Probably the use of the label can be taken back to the middle or early part of the thirteenth century, but the opportunity and necessity of marking the arms of the heir-apparent temporarily, he having the expectation of eventually succeeding to the undifferenced arms, is a very different matter to the other opportunities for the use of marks of cadency. The lord and his heir were the two most important members of the family, and all others sunk their identity in their position in the household of their chief unless they were established by marriage, or otherwise, in lordships of their own, in which cases they are usually found to have preferred the arms of the family from whom they inherited the lordships they enjoyed; and their identities being to such a large extent overlooked, the necessity for any system of marking the arms of a younger son was not so early apparent as the necessity for marking the arms of the heir.

The label does not appear to have been originally confined exclusively to the heir. It was at first the only method of differencing known, and it is not therefore to be wondered at that we find that it was fre-

FIG. 845.—Arms of John de Lacy, Earl of Lincoln (d. 1240): Quarterly, or and gules, a bend sable, and a label argent.

FIG. 846.—Arms of John de la Pole, Earl of Lincoln (son of John, Duke of Suffolk), d. 1487: Quarterly, 1 and 4, azure, a fess between three leopards' faces or; 2 and 3, per fess gules and argent, a lion rampant queue fourché or, armed and langued azure, over all a label argent. (From his seal.)

FIG. 847.—Arms of William Le Scrope, Earl of Wiltes (d. 1399): Quarterly, 1 and 4, the arms of the Isle of Man, a label argent; 2 and 3, azure, a bend or, a label gules. (From Willement's Roll, sixteenth century.)

quently used by other cadets, who used it with no other meaning than to indicate that they were not the Head of the House. It has, consequently, in some few cases [for example, in the arms of Courtenay (Fig. 228), Babington, and Barrington] become stereotyped as a charge, and is continuously and unchangeably used as such, whereas doubtless it may have been no more originally than a mere mark of cadency. The label was originally drawn with its upper edge identical with the top of the shield (Fig. 123 and Plate LXVII. Fig. 26), but later its position on the shield was lowered. The number of points on the label was at first without meaning, a five-pointed label occurring in Fig. 123 and a seven-pointed one in Fig. 218.

In the Roll of Caerlaverock the label is repeatedly referred to. Of Sir MAURICE DE BERKELEY it is expressly declared that

"... un label de asur avoit,
Porce qe ces peres vivoit."

Sir PATRICK DUNBAR, son of the Earl of LOTHIAN (i.e. of MARCH), then bore arms similar to his father, with the addition of a label "azure." On the other hand, Sir JOHN DE SEGRAVE is said to bear his deceased father's arms undifferenced, while his younger brother NICHOLAS carries them with a label "gules"; and in the case of EDMUND DE HASTINGS the label is also assigned to a younger brother. Further proof of its being thus borne by cadets is furnished by the evidence in the GRAY and HASTINGS controversy in the reign of HENRY IV., from which it appeared that the younger line of the HASTINGS family had for generations differenced the paternal coat by a label of three points; and,

as various knights and esquires had deposed to this label being the cognisance of the nearest heir, it was argued that the defendant's ancestors would not have borne their arms in this way had they not been the reputed next heirs of the family of the Earl of PEMBROKE. The label will be seen in Figs. 845, 846, and 847.

WILLIAM RUTHVEN, Provost of PERTH, eldest son of the Master of RUTHVEN, bore a label of four points in 1503. Two instances occur of a label borne by a powerful younger brother. One is WALTER STEWART, Earl of MENTEITH, the fourth High Steward, in 1292; and we find the label again on the seal of his son ALEXANDER STEWART, Earl of MENTEITH.

At Caerlaverock, HENRY of Lancaster, brother and successor of THOMAS, Earl of LANCASTER—

"Portait les armes son frère
Au beau bastoun sans label,"

i.e. he bore the Royal Arms, differenced by a bendlet "azure."

JANE FENTOUN, daughter and heir-apparent of WALTER FENTOUN of Baikie, bore a label in 1448, and dropped it after her father's death. This is apparently an instance quite unique. I know of no other case where the label has been used by a woman as a mark of difference.

In FRANCE the label was the chief recognised mode of difference, though the bend and the bordure are frequently to be met with.

In GERMANY, SPENER tells us that the use of the label, though occasional, was not infrequent: "Sicuti in Gallia vix alius discerniculorum modus frequentior est, ita rariora exempla reperimus in Germania," and he gives a few examples, though he is unable to assign the reason for its assumption as a hereditary bearing. The most usual method of differencing in Germany was by the alteration of the tinctures or by the alteration of the charges. As an example of the former method, the arms of the Bavarian family of Parteneck may be instanced (Figs. 848 to 852), all representing the arms of

FIG. 848.—Parteneck.   FIG. 849.—Cammer.   FIG. 850.—Cammerberg.

FIG. 851.—Hilgertshauser.   FIG. 852.—Massenhauser.

different branches of the same family. The arms of the family of Freiberg are an instance of the change of charges. The original family, who were settled in Swabia, bore: "Per fesse argent and azure, three

FIG. 853.—Arms of Freiberg (Swabia).   FIG. 854.—Arms of Freiberg (Bavaria).

bezants" (Fig. 853); the bezants in this case being intended to represent the yolks of eggs. A cadet branch which settled in Bavaria changed the bezants to stars (Fig. 854).

THE ART OF HERALDRY

Next to the use of the label in British heraldry came the use of the bordure, and the latter as a mark of cadency can at any rate be traced back *as a well-established matter of rule* and precedent as far as the Scrope and Grosvenor controversy in the closing years of the fourteenth century.

At the period when the bordure as a difference is to be found most frequently met with in English heraldry, it never had any more definite status or meaning than a sign that the bearer was *not* the head of the house, as in the case of Humphrey Stafford, Earl of Devonshire (Fig. 855), though one cannot but think that in many cases

FIG. 855.—Arms of Humphrey Stafford, Earl of Devonshire (*d.* 1469): Or, a chevron gules, a bordure engrailed sable. (From MS. Harl. 6129.)

in which it occurs its significance is a doubt as to legitimate descent, or a doubt of the probability of an asserted descent. In modern *English* practice the bordure as a difference for cadets only continues to be used by those whose ancestors bore it in ancient times. Its other use as a modern mark of illegitimacy is dealt with in the chapter upon marks of illegitimacy, and the curious and unique Scottish system of cadency bordures will be presently referred to. In Germany of old the use of the bordure as a difference does not appear to have been very frequent, but it is now used to distinguish the arms of the Crown Prince. In Italian heraldry, although differences are known, there is no system whatever.

In Spain and Portugal marks of cadency, in our sense of the word, are almost unknown, but nevertheless the bordure, especially as indicating descent from a maternal ancestor, is very largely employed. The most familiar instance is afforded by the Royal Arms of Portugal, in which the arms of PORTUGAL are surrounded by a "bordure" of CASTILE.

Differencing, however, had become a necessity at an earlier period than the period at which we find an approach to the systematic usage of the label, bordure, and bend, but it should be noticed that those who wished, and needed, to difference were those younger members of the family who by settlement, or marriage, had themselves become lords of other estates, and heads of distinct houses. For a man must be taken as a "Head of a House" for all intents and purposes as soon as by his possession of lands "held in chief" he became *himself* liable to the Crown to provide stated military service, and as a consequence found the necessity for a banner of arms, under which his men could be mustered. Now having these positions as overlords, the inducement was rather to set up arms for themselves than to pose merely as cadets of other families, and there can be no doubt whatever that at the earliest period differencing, for the above reason, took the form of and was meant as a *change in the arms*. It was something quite beyond and apart from the mere condition of a right to recognised arms, with an indication thereupon that the bearer was not the person chiefly entitled to the display of that particular coat. We therefore find cadets bearing the arms of

their house with the tincture changed, with subsidiary charges introduced, or with some similar radical alteration made. Such coats should properly be considered essentially *different* coats, merely *indicating* in their design a given relationship rather than as the *same* coat differenced to indicate cadency. For instance, the three original branches of the Conyers family bear: "Azure, a maunch ermine; azure, a maunch or; azure, a maunch ermine debruised by a bendlet gules." The coat differenced by the bend, of course, stands self-confessed as a differenced coat, but it is by no means certain, nor is it known whether "azure, a maunch ermine," or "azure, a maunch or" indicates the original Conyers arms, for the very simple reason that it is now impossible to definitely prove which branch supplies the true head of the family. It is known that a wicked uncle intervened, and usurped the estates to the detriment of the nephew and heir, but whether the uncle usurped the arms with the estates, or whether the heir changed his arms when settled on the other lands to which he migrated, there is now no means of ascertaining.

Similarly we find the Darcy arms ["Argent, three cinquefoils gules," which is probably the oldest form], "Argent, crusuly and three cinquefoils gules," and "Azure, crusuly and three cinquefoils argent," and countless instances can be referred to where, for the purpose of indicating cadency, the arms of a family were changed in this manner. This reason, of which there can be no doubt, supplies the origin and the excuse for the custom of assigning *similar* arms when the descent is but doubtful. Similarity originally, though it *may* indicate consanguinity, was never intended to be proof thereof.

The principal ancient methods of alteration in arms, which nowadays are apparently accepted as former modes of differencing merely to indicate cadency, may perhaps be classified into: (*a*) Change of tincture; (*b*) the addition of small charges to the field, or to an ordinary; (*c*) the addition of a label or (*d*) of a canton or quarter; (*e*) the addition of an inescutcheon; (*f*) the addition (or change) of an ordinary; (*g*) the changing of the lines of partition enclosing an ordinary, and perhaps also (*h*) diminishing the number of charges; (*i*) a change of some or all of the minor charges. At a later date came (*j*) the systematic use of the label, the bordure, and the bend; and subsequently (*k*) the use of the modern systems of "marks of cadency." Perhaps, also, one should include (*l*) the addition of quarters, the use of (*m*) augmentations and official arms, and (*n*) the escutcheon *en surtout*, indicating a territorial and titular lordship, but the three last-mentioned, though useful for distinction and frequently obviating the necessity of other marks of cadency, did not originate with the theory or necessities of differencing, and are not properly marks of cadency. At the same time, the warning should be given that it is not safe always to presume cadency when a change of tincture or other slight deviation from an earlier form of the arms is met with. Many families when they exhibited their arms at the Visitations could not substantiate them, and the heralds, in confirming arms, frequently deliberately changed the tinctures of many coats they met with, to introduce distinction from other authorised arms.

Practically contemporarily with the use of the bordure came the use of the bend, then employed for the same purpose. In the *Armorial de Gelre*, one of the earliest armorials now in existence which can be referred to, the well-known coat of Abernethy is there differenced by the bendlet engrailed, and the arms of the King of Navarre bear his quartering of France differenced by a bendlet compony. These two instances will be seen on Plate LXXVI., and amongst other instances in which the bend or bendlet appears originally as a mark of cadency, but now as a charge, may be mentioned the arms of Fitzherbert, Fulton, Stewart (Earl of Galloway), and others. It is a safe presumption with regard to ancient coats of arms that any coat in which the field is semé is in nine cases out of ten a differenced coat for a junior cadet, as is also any coat in which a charge or ordinary is debruised by another. Of course in more modern times no such presumption is permissible. An instance of a semé field for cadency will be found in the case of the D'Arcy arms already mentioned. Little would be gained by a long list of instances of such differences, because the most careful and systematic investigations clearly show that in early times no definite rules whatever existed as to the assumption of differences, which largely depended upon the pleasure of the bearer, and no system can be deduced which can be used to decide that the appearance of any given difference or kind of difference meant a given set of circumstances. Nor can any system be deduced which has any value for the purposes of precedents.

Certain instances are appended which will indicate the style of differencing which was in vogue, but it should be distinctly remembered that the object was not to allocate the bearer of any particular coat of arms to any specific place in the family pedigree, but merely to show that he was not the head of the house, entitled to bear the undifferenced arms, if indeed it would not be more accurate to describe these instances as simply examples of different coats of arms used by members of the same family. For it should be remembered that anciently, before the days of "black and white" illustration, prominent change of tincture was admittedly a sufficient distinction between strangers in blood. Beyond the use of the label and the bordure there does not seem to have been any recognised system of differencing until at the earliest the fifteenth century—probably any regulated system does not date much beyond the commencement of the series of Visitations.

Of the four sons of GILLES DE MAILLY, who bore, "Or, three mallets vert," the second, third, and fourth sons respectively made the charges "gules," "azure," and "sable." The "argent" field of the DOUGLAS coat was in some branches converted into "ermine" as early as 1373; and the descendants of the DOUGLASES of Dalkeith made the chief "gules" instead of "azure." A similar mode of differencing occurs in the Lyon Register in many other families. The MURRAYS of Culbin in the North bore a "sable" field for their arms in lieu of the more usual "azure," and there seems reason to believe that the Southern Frasers originally bore their field "sable," the change to

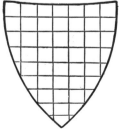

FIG. 856.—Arms of Warenne: Chequy or and azure.

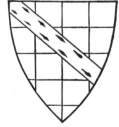

FIG. 857.—Arms of Henry, Earl of Warwick (d. 1229): Chequy or and azure, a bend ermine. (After Matthew Paris, MS. Reg. 14, C. vii. folio 134.)

"azure" being an alteration made by those branches who migrated northwards. An interesting series of arms is met with in the case of the differences employed

by the Earls of Warwick. Waleran, Earl of Warwick (d. 1204), appears to have added to the arms of Warenne (his mother's family) (Fig. 856) "a chevron ermine." His son Henry, Earl of Warwick (d. 1229), changed the chevron to a bend (Fig. 857), but Thomas, Earl of Warwick (d. 1242), reverted to the chevron (Fig. 858), a

FIG. 858.—Arms of Thomas, Earl of Warwick (d. 1242): Chequy or and azure, a chevron ermine. (From MS. L. 14, Coll. Arms.)

FIG. 859.—Arms of William de Bohun, Earl of Northampton (d. 1360): Azure, on a bend argent, cottised, and between six lioncels rampant or, three mullets gules, pierced vert. (MS. Otho, D. IV. folio 93.)

form which was perpetuated after the earldom had passed to the house of Beauchamp (Fig. 133). An instance of the addition of mullets to the bend in the arms of Bohun (Fig. 265) is met with in the cadet line created Earls of Northampton (Fig. 859).

The shield of WILLIAM DE ROUMARE, Earl of LINCOLN, who died in 1198, is adduced by Mr. PLANCHÉ as an early example of differencing by crosses crosslet; the principal charges being seven mascles conjoined, three, three, and one. We find in the Rolls of Arms of the thirteenth and early part of the fourteenth century many instances of coats crusily, billetty, bezanty, and "pleyn d'escallops," fleurette, and "a les trefoilles d'or." With these last Sir EDMOND DACRE of Westmoreland powdered the shield borne by the head of his family: "Gules, three escallops or" (Roll of Edward II.). The coat borne by the ACTONS of Aldenham, "Gules, crusily or, two lions passant argent," is sometimes quoted as a gerated coat of LESTRANGE; for EDWARD DE ACTON married the coheiress of LESTRANGE (living 1387), who bore simply: "Gules, two lions passant argent." That the arms of Acton are derived from Lestrange cannot be questioned, but the probability is that they were *a new invention* as a distinct coat, the charges suggested by Lestrange. The original coat of the House of Berkeley in England (Barclay in Scotland) appears to have been: "Gules, a chevron or" (or "argent"). The seals of ROBERT DE BERKELEY, who died 4 Henry III., and MAURICE DE BERKELEY, who died 1281, all show the shield charged with a chevron only. MORIS DE BARKELE, in the Roll *temp.* Henry III., bears: "Goules, a cheveron argent."

But THOMAS, son of MAURICE, who died 15 EDWARD II., has the present coat: "Gules, a chevron between ten crosses patée argent" (Fig. 860); while in the Roll of Edward II., "De goules od les rosettes de argent et un chevron de argent" is attributed to Sir THOMAS DE BERKELEY. In Leicestershire the BERKELEYS gerated with cinquefoils, an ancient and favourite bearing in that county, derived of course from the arms or badge of the Earl of Leicester. In Scotland the BARCLAYS differenced by change of tincture, and bore: "Azure, a chevron argent between (or in chief) three crosses patée of the same" (Fig. 802). The same coat differenced for a cadet (Mr. Charles Herbert Barclay) will be seen on Plate XX. An interesting series of differences is met with upon the arms of NEVILLE of Raby, which are: "Gules, a saltire argent," and which were differenced by a crescent "sable"; a martlet "gules"; a mullet "sable" and a mullet azure (Fig. 861); a

FIG. 860.—Arms of Thomas, Lord Berkeley of Berkeley (d. 1321): Gules, a chevron between ten crosses patée argent. (From his seal, 1301.)

FIG. 861. — Arms of William Nevill, Lord Fauconberg and Earl of Kent : Quarterly, 1 and 4, gules, a saltire argent, a mullet of the field for difference (Nevill) ; 2 and 3, argent, a lion rampant azure (for Fauconberg, this being however really the coat of Bruce). (From MS. Harl. 6163.)

"fleur-de-lis"; a rose "gules" (Fig. 862 and Plate LXVII. Fig. 29); a pellet, or annulet, "sable" (Plate LXVII. Fig. 28), this being the difference of Lord Latimer; and two interlaced annulets "azure," all

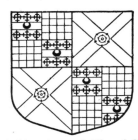

FIG. 862.—Arms of Edward Nevill, Baron Bergavenny (d. 1476): Quarterly, i. and iiii., quarterly 1 and 4, gules, a fess between six cross crosslets or, a crescent sable for difference ; 2 and 3, chequy or and azure, ii. and iii., gules, on a saltire argent, a rose of the field for difference. (From his seal.)

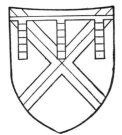

FIG. 863.—Arms of Richard Nevill, Earl of Salisbury: Gules, a saltire argent, a label compony argent and azure. (From his seal, 1428.)

borne on the centre point of the saltire. The interlaced annulets were borne by Lord Montagu, as a *second* difference on the arms of his father, Richard Nevill, Earl of Salisbury (Fig. 863), he and his brother the King Maker (Fig. 213) *both* using the curious compony label of azure and argent borne by their father, which indicated their descent from John of Gaunt. One of the best known English examples of differencing by a change of charges is that of the coat of the COB-HAMS, "Gules, a chevron or," in which the ordinary was charged by various cadets with three pierced estoiles, three lions, three crossed crosslets, three "fleur-de-lis," three crescents, and three martlets, all of "sable."

The original GREY coat ["Barry of six argent and azure"] is differenced in the Roll of Edward I. by a bend gules for JOHN DE GREY, at Caerlaverock this is engrailed.

The SEGRAVE coat ["Sable, a lion rampant argent"] is differenced by the addition of "a bendlet or"; or "a bendlet gules"; and the last is again differenced by engrailing it.

The LESLIES of Balquhain differenced the chief coat of their family ["Argent, on a bend azure three buckles or"] by turning the bend into a fess. A very early cadet of the GRAHAM family, GRAHAM of Morphie, adopted an unusually pronounced difference, substituting a chevron for the chief, and at the same time changing the tinctures. The principal GRAHAM coat is : "Or, on

a chief sable three escallops of the field"; that of Morphie: "Sable, a chevron between three escallops argent."

In the Calais Roll the arms of WILLIAM DE WARREN [" Chequy or and azure "] are differenced by the addition of a canton said to be that of FITZALAN (but really that of NERFORD).

Whilst no regular system of differencing has survived in France, and whilst outside the Royal Family arms in that country show comparatively few examples of difference marks, the system as regards the French Royal Arms was well observed and approximated closely to our own. The Dauphin of France bore the Royal Arms undifferenced but never alone, they being always quartered with the sovereign arms of his personal sovereignty of Dauphiné: " Or, a dolphin embowed azure, finned gules" (Plate LXVII. Fig. 1). This has been more fully referred to on page 184. It is much to be regretted that the arms of H.R.H. the Prince of Wales do not include the arms of his sovereignty of the Duchy of Cornwall, nor any allusion to his dignities of Prince of Wales or Earl of Chester.

The arms of the Dukes of Orleans (Plate LXVII. Fig. 2) show the arms of France differenced by a label argent. This is to be observed, for example, upon the seal (Fig. 864) of the Duchess Charlotte Elizabeth of Orleans, widow of Philip of Orleans, brother of King Louis XIV. of France. She was a daughter of the Elector Charles Louis. The arms of the old Dukes of Anjou were the ancient coat of France (azure, semé-de-lis or) differenced by a label of five points gules, but the younger house of Anjou bore the modern arms of France differenced by a bordure gules (Plate LXVII. Fig. 3). The Dukes d'Alencon also used the bordure gules, but charged this with eight plates (Plate LXVII. Fig. 4), whilst the Dukes de Berri used a bordure *engrailed* gules.

FIG. 864.—Seal of Elizabeth, widow of Philip, Duke of Orleans.

The Counts d'Angoulême used the arms of the Dukes of Orleans, adding a crescent gules on each point of the label (Plate LXVII. Fig. 13), whilst the Counts d'Artois used France (ancient) differenced by a label gules, each point charged with three castles (towers) or.

Plate LXVII. Fig. 17 shows the shield of Pier de Luxembourg, Count de St. Paul (d. 1433): "Argent, a lion rampant double-queued gules, crowned or, differenced by a label of three points argent."

The rules which govern the marks of cadency at present in England are as follows, and it should be carefully borne in mind that the Scottish system bears no relation whatever to the English system. The eldest son during the lifetime of his father differences his arms by a label of three points couped at the ends. This is placed in the centre chief point of the escutcheon. There is no rule as to its colour, which is left to the pleasure of the bearer; but it is usually decided as follows : (1) That it shall not be metal on metal, or colour on colour; (2)

that it shall not be argent or white; and, if possible, that it shall differ from any colour or metal in which any component part of the shield is depicted. Though anciently the label was drawn throughout the shield, this does not now seem to be a method officially adopted. At any rate drawn throughout it apparently obtains no official countenance for the arms of subjects. The eldest son bears this label during his father's lifetime, succeeding to the undifferenced shield on the death of his father. His children—being the grandchildren of the then head of the house—difference upon the label, but such difference marks are, like their father's, but contemporary with the life of the grandfather, and, immediately upon the succession of their father, the children remove the label, and difference upon the original arms. The use of arms by a junior grandson is so restricted in ordinary life that to all intents and purposes this may be ignored, except in the case of the heir apparent of the heir apparent, i.e. of the grandson in the lifetimes of his father and grandfather. In his case a label of *five* points is used, and to place a label upon a label is not correct when both are marks of cadency, and not charges. But the grandson on the death of his father, during the lifetime of the grandfather, and when the grandson succeeds as heir apparent of the grandfather, succeeds also to the label of three points, which may therefore more properly be described as the difference mark of the heir apparent than the difference mark of the eldest son. It is necessary, perhaps, having said this, to add the remark that heraldry knows no such thing as disinheritance, and heirship is an inalienable matter of blood descent, and not of worldly inheritance. Though now the number of points on a label is a matter of rule, this is far from having been always the case, and prior to the Stuart period no deductions can be drawn with certainty from the number of the points in use. It seems a very great pity that no warrants were issued for the children of the then Duke of York during the lifetime of Queen Victoria, as labels for *great*-grandchildren would have been quite unique.

If the eldest son succeeds through the death of his mother to her arms and quarterings during his father's lifetime, he must be careful that the label which he bears as heir apparent to his father's arms does not cross the quartering of his mother's arms.

If his father bears a quarterly shield, the label is so placed that it shall apparently debruise all his father's quarterings, i.e. in a shield quarterly of four the label would be placed in the centre chief point, the centre file of the label being upon the palar line, and the other files in the first and second quarters respectively, whilst the colour would usually depend, as has been above indicated, upon the tinctures of the pronominal arms. Due regard, however, must be had that a label of gules, for example, is not placed on a field of gules. A particoloured label is not nowadays permissible, though instances of its use can occasionally be met with in early examples. Supposing the field of the first quarter is argent, and that of the second azure, in all probability the best colour for the label would be gules, and indeed gules is the colour most frequently met with for use in this purpose.

If the father possess the quarterly coat of, say, four quarterings, which are debruised by a label by the heir apparent, and the mother die, and the heir apparent succeed to her arms, he would of course, after his father's death, arrange his mother's quarterings with these, placing his father's pronominal arms 1 and 4, the father's quartering in the second quarter, and the mother's arms in the third quarter. This arrangement, however, is not permissible during his father's lifetime, because otherwise his label in chief would be held to

debruise all the four coats, and the only method in which such a combination could be properly displayed in the lifetime of the father but after the death of his mother is to place the father's arms in the grand quartering in the first and fourth quarters, each being debruised by the label, and the mother's in the grand quartering in the second and third quarters without any interference by the label.

The other marks of difference are: For the second son a crescent; for the third son a mullet; for the fourth son a martlet; for the fifth son an annulet; for the sixth son a fleur-de-lis; for the seventh son a rose;

FIG. 865.—The English marks of cadency.

for the eighth son a cross moline; for the ninth son a double quatrefoil (Fig. 865).

Of these the first six are given in BOSSEWELL'S "Workes of Armorie" (1572), and the author adds: "If there be any more than six brethren the devise or assignment of further difference only appertaineth to the kingis of armes especially when they visite their severall provinces; and not to the father of the children to give them what difference he list, as some without authoritie doe allege."

The position of a mark of difference is in the centre chief point, though it is not incorrect (and many such instances will be found) for it to be charged on a chevron or fess, on the centre point (Fig. 72). This, however, is not a very desirable position for it in a simple coat of arms. The second son of the second son places a crescent upon a crescent, the third son a mullet on a crescent, the fourth son a martlet on a crescent, and so on; and there is an instance in the Visitation of London in which the arms of Cokayne appear with *three* crescents one upon another: this instance has been already referred to on p. 262. Of course, when the English system is carried to these lengths it becomes absurd, because the crescents charged one upon each other become so small as to be practically indistinguishable. There are, however, very few cases in which such a display would be correct—as will be presently explained. This difficulty, which looms large in theory, is very little in practical use, but it nevertheless is the one outstanding objection to the English system of difference marks. It is constantly held up to derision by those people who are unaware of the next rule upon the subject, which is, that as soon as a quartering comes into the possession of a cadet branch—which quartering is not enjoyed by the head of the house—all necessity for any marks of difference at all is considered to be ended, provided that that quartering is always displayed—and that cadet branch then begins afresh from that generation to redifference.

Now there are few English families in whose pedigree during three or four generations one marriage is not with an heiress in blood, so that this theoretical difficulty very quickly disappears.

No doubt there is always an inducement to retain the quarterings of an historical or illustrious house which may have been brought in the past, but if the honours and lands brought in with that quartering are wholly enjoyed by the head of the house, it becomes, from a practical point of view, mere affectation to prefer that quartering to another (brought in subsequently) of a family, the entire representation of which belongs to the junior branch and not to the senior. If the old idea of confining a shield to four quarters be borne in mind, concurrently with the necessity—for purposes of distinction—of introducing new quarterings, the new quarterings take the place of the old, the use of which is left to the senior branch. Under such circumstances, and the regular practice of them, the English system is seldom wanting, and it at once wipes out the difficulty which is made much of—that under the English system there is no way of indicating the difference between the arms of uncle and nephew. If the use of impalements is also adhered to, the difficulty practically vanishes.

To difference a *single* coat the mark of difference is placed in the centre chief point; to difference a *quarterly* coat of four quarters the same position on the shield is most generally used, the mark being placed over the palar line, though occasionally the difference mark is placed, and not incorrectly, in the centre of the quarterings. A coat of six quarters, however, is always differenced on the fess line of partition, the mark being placed in the fess point, because if placed in the centre chief point it would only appear as a difference upon the second quartering, so that on all shields of six or more quarterings the difference mark must be placed on some line of partition at the nearest possible point to the true centre fess point of the escutcheon. It is then understood to difference the whole of the quarterings over which it is displayed, but directly a quartering is introduced which has been inherited subsequently to the cadency which produced the difference mark, that difference mark must be either discarded or transferred to the first quartering only.

The use of these difference marks is optional. Neither officially nor unofficially is any attempt made to enforce their use in England—they are left to the pleasure and discretion of the bearers, though it is a well-understood and well-accepted position that, unless differenced by quarterings or impalement, it is neither courteous nor proper for a cadet to display the arms of the head of his house: beyond this, the matter is usually left to good taste.

There is, however, one position in which the use of difference marks is compulsory. If under a Royal Licence, or other exemplification—for instance, the creation of a peerage—a difference mark is painted upon the arms, or even if an exemplification of the arms differenced is placed at the head of an official record of pedigree, those arms would not subsequently be exemplified, or their use officially admitted, without the difference mark that has been recorded with them.

The differencing of crests for cadency is very rare. Theoretically, these should be marked equally with the shield, and when arms are exemplified officially under the circumstances above referred to, crest, supporters, and shield are all equally differenced, but the difficulty of adding difference mark on difference mark when no marriage or heiress can ever bring in any alteration to the crest is very generally recognised and admitted, even officially, and it is rare indeed to come across a crest carrying more than a single difference mark.

The grant of an augmentation to any cadet obviates the slightest necessity for any further use of difference marks inherited before the grant.

There are no difference marks whatever for daughters, there being in the English law no seniority between the different daughters of one man. They succeed equally, whether heiresses or not, to the arms of their father for use during their lifetimes, and they must bear them on their own lozenges or impaled on the shields of their husbands, with the difference marks which their father needed to use. It would be permissible, however, to discard these difference marks of their fathers if subsequently to his death his issue succeeded to the position of head of the family. For instance, suppose the daughters of the younger son of an earl are under consideration. They would bear upon lozenges the

arms of their father, which would be those of the earl, charged with the mullet or crescent which he had used as a younger son. If by the extinction of issue the brother of these daughters succeed to the earldom, they would no longer be compelled to bear their father's difference mark.

There are no marks of difference between illegitimate children. In the eye of the law an illegitimate person has no relatives, and stands alone. Supposing it be subsequently found that a marriage ceremony had been illegal, the whole issue of that marriage becomes of course illegitimate. As such, no one of them is entitled to bear arms. A Royal Licence, and exemplification following thereupon, is necessary for each single one. Of these exemplifications there is one case on record in which I think nine follow each other on successive pages of one of the Grant Books: all differ in some way—usually in the colour of the bordure; but the fact that there are illegitimate brothers of the same parentage does not prevent the descendants of any daughter quartering the differenced coat exemplified to her. As far as heraldic law is concerned, she is the heiress of herself, representing only herself, and consequently her heir quarters her arms.

Marks of difference are never added to an exemplification following upon a Royal Licence *after illegitimacy*. Marks of difference are to indicate cadency, and there is no cadency vested in a person of illegitimate birth—their right to the arms proceeding only from the regrant of them in the exemplification. What is added in lieu is the *mark of distinction* to indicate the bastardy.

The method of differencing the English Royal Arms is quite unique, and has no relation to the method ordinarily in use in this country for the arms of subjects. The Royal Arms are not personal. They are the sovereign arms of dominion, indicating the sovereignty enjoyed by the person upon the throne. Consequently they are in no degree hereditary, and from the earliest times, certainly since the reign of Edward I., the right to bear the undifferenced arms has been confined exclusively to the sovereign upon the throne. In early times there were two methods employed, namely, the use of the bordure and of varieties of the label, the label of the heir apparent to the English throne being originally of azure. The arms of Thomas of Woodstock, the youngest son of Edward I., were differenced by a bordure argent; his elder brother, Thomas de Brotherton, having had a label of three points argent; whilst the eldest son, Edward II., as Prince of Wales used a label of three points azure. From that period to the end of the Tudor period the use of labels and bordures seems to have continued concurrently, some members of the Royal Family using one, some the other, though there does not appear to have been any precise rules governing a choice between the two. When Edward III. claimed the throne of France and quartered the arms of that country with those of England, of course a portion of the field then became azure, and a blue label upon a blue field was no longer possible. The heir apparent therefore differenced his shield by the plain label of three points argent, and this has ever since, down to the present day, continued to be the "difference" used by the heir apparent to the English throne. A label of gules upon the gules quartering of England was equally impossible, and consequently from that period all labels used by any member of the Royal Family have been argent, charged with different objects, these being frequently taken from the arms of some female ancestor. Figs. 866 to 897 are a somewhat extensive collection of variations of the Royal Arms, and reference may perhaps be also made to Figs. 76, 123, 181, 189, 201, 251, 264, 295, 303, 455, 635.

FIG. 866.—William FitzRobert, Earl of Gloucester, d. 1183 (son of Robert de Caen, natural son of Henry I.). (From a drawing of his seal, MS. Cott., Julius, C. vii., f. 233.)

FIG. 867.—King John, before his accession to the throne. (From MS. Cott., Julius, C. vii.)

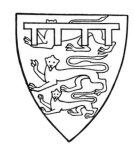

FIG. 868.--Edmund "Crouchback," Earl of Lancaster, second son of Henry III. (From his tomb.) His arms are elsewhere given: De goules ove trois leopardes passantz dor, et lambel dazure florete d'or.

FIG. 869.—Thomas, Earl of Lancaster, d. 1322 (son of preceding): England with a label azure, each point charged with three fleurs-de-lis. (From his seal, 1301.)

FIG. 870.—Henry of Lancaster, 1295-1324 (brother of preceding, before he succeeded his brother as Earl of Lancaster): England with a bend azure. (From his seal, 1301.) After 1324 he bore England with a label as his brother.

FIG. 871.—Henry, Duke of Lancaster, son of preceding. (From his seal, 1358.)

FIG. 872.—Edward of Carnarvon, Prince of Wales (afterwards Edward II.), bore before 1307: England with a label azure. (From his seal, 1305.)

FIG. 873.—John of Eltham (second son of Edward II.): England with a bordure of the arms of France. (From his tomb.)

FIG. 874.—Arms of Edmund of Woodstock, Earl of Kent, 3rd son of Edward I.: England within a bordure argent. The same arms were borne by his descendant, Thomas de Holand, Earl of Kent.

FIG. 875.—Arms of John de Holand, Duke of Exeter (d. 1400): England, a bordure of France. (From his seal, 1381.)

FIG. 876.—John de Holand, Duke of Exeter, son of preceding. Arms as preceding. (From his seal.)

FIG. 877.—Henry de Holand, Duke of Exeter, son of preceding. Arms as preceding. (From his seal, 1455.)

FIG. 878.—Thomas of Brotherton, Earl of Norfolk, second son of Edward I.: Arms of England, a label of three points argent.

FIG. 879.—Thomas de Mowbray, Duke of Norfolk (d. 1400). (From a drawing of his seal, MS. Cott., Julius, C. vii., f. 166.) Arms, see page 335.

FIG. 880.—John de Mowbray, Duke of Norfolk (d. 1432): Arms as Fig. 878. (From his Garter plate.)

FIG. 881.—John de Mowbray, Duke of Norfolk (d. 1461): Arms as Fig. 878. (From his seal).

FIG. 882.—Edward the Black Prince: Quarterly, 1 and 4 France (ancient); 2 and 3 England, and a label of three points argent. (From his tomb.)

FIG. 883. — Richard, Prince of Wales (afterwards Richard II.), son of preceding: Arms as preceding. (From his seal, 1377.)

FIG. 884.—Edmund of Langley, Duke of York, fifth son of King Edward III.: France (ancient) and England quarterly, a label of three points argent, each point charged with three torteaux. (From his seal, 1391).

FIG. 885. — Richard, Duke of York (son of Edward, Earl of Cambridge and Duke of York): Arms as preceding. (From his seal, 1436).

His son, Edward, Earl of Cambridge, until he succeeded his father, i.e. before 1462, bore the same with an additional difference of a bordure of Spain (Fig. 303). Vincent attributes to him, however, a label as Fig. 886, which possibly he bore after his father's death.

FIG. 886.—Referred to under Fig. 884.

FIG. 887.—Thomas of Woodstock, Earl of Buckingham, seventh son of Edward III.: France (ancient) and England quarterly, a bordure argent. (From a drawing of his seal, 1391, MS. Cott., Julius, C. vii.).

FIG. 888.—Henry of Monmouth, afterwards Henry V.: France (modern) and England quarterly, a label of three points argent. (From his seal.)

FIG. 889.—Richard, Duke of Gloucester (afterwards Richard III.): A label of three points ermine, on each point a canton gules.

FIG. 890.—Humphrey of Lancaster, Duke of Gloucester, fourth son of Henry IV.: France (modern) and England quarterly, a bordure argent. (From his seal.)

FIG. 891.—John de Beaufort, Earl and Marquis of Somerset, son of John of Gaunt. Arms subsequent to his legitimation: France and England quarterly, within a bordure gobony azure and argent. Prior to his legitimation he bore: Per pale argent and azure (the livery colours of Lancaster), a bend of England (i.e. a bend gules charged with three lions passant guardant or) with a label of France.

FIG. 892.—Thomas, Duke of Clarence, second son of Henry IV. France and England quarterly, a label of three points ermine. (From his seal, 1413.)

FIG. 893.—George Plantagenet, Duke of Clarence, brother of Edward IV.: France and England quarterly, a label of three points argent, each charged with a canton gules. (From MS. Harl. 521.)

FIG. 894.—John, Duke of Bedford, third son of Henry IV.: France and England quarterly, a label of five points, the two dexter ermine, the three sinister azure, charged with three fleurs-de-lis or. (From MS. Add. 18,850.)

FIG. 895.—Jasper Tudor, Duke of Bedford: France and England quarterly, a bordure azure, charged with martlets or. (From his seal.) Although uncle of Henry VII., Jasper Tudor had no blood descent whatever which would entitle him to bear these arms. His use of them is very remarkable.

FIG. 896.—Thomas de Beaufort, Earl of Dorset, brother of John, Earl of Somerset (Fig. 891): France and England quarterly, a bordure compony ermine and azure. (From his Garter plate.)

FIG. 897.—John of Gaunt, Duke of Lancaster, bore: France (ancient) and England quarterly, a label of three points ermine (i.e. each point charged with three ermine spots).

Lionel of Antwerp, Duke of Clarence, third son of Edward III., bore: France (ancient) and England quarterly, a label of three points argent, and on each point a canton gules.

The use of the bordure as a legitimate difference upon the Royal Arms ceased about the Tudor period, and differencing between members of the Royal Family is now exclusively done by means of these labels. A few cases of bordures to denote illegitimacy can, however, be found. The method of deciding these labels is for separate warrants under the hand and seal of the sovereign to be issued to the different members of the Royal Family, assigning to each a certain coronet, and the label to be borne over the Royal Arms, crest, and supporters. These warrants are personal to those for whom they are issued, and are *not* hereditary. Of late their use, or perhaps may be their issue, has not been quite so particularly conformed to as is desirable, and at the present time the official records show the arms of their Royal Highnesses the Duchess of Fife, the Princess Victoria, and the Princess Charles of Denmark, still bearing the label of five points indicative of their position as grandchildren of the sovereign, which of course they were when the warrants were issued in the lifetime of the late Queen Victoria. In spite of the fact that the warrants have no hereditary limitation, I am only aware of two modern instances in which a warrant has been issued to the son of a cadet of the Royal House who had previously received a warrant. One of these is the present Duke of Cambridge. The warrant was issued to him in his father's lifetime, and to the label previously assigned to his father a second label of three points gules, to be borne directly below the other, was added. The label of the eldest son of the heir apparent to the English throne is not, as might be imagined, a plain label of five points, but the plain label of three points, the centre point only being charged. The other case was that of his cousin, afterwards Duke of Cumberland and King of Hanover.

The late Duke of Clarence charged his centre point with a cross couped gules. After his death the Duke of York relinquished the label of five points which he had previously borne, receiving one of three, the centre point charged with an anchor. In every other case all of the points are charged. The following examples of the labels in use at the moment will show how the system now exists:—

Prince of Wales.—A label of three points argent (see Plate LXVI.).

Princess Royal (Louise, Duchess of Fife).—A label of five points argent, charged on the centre and outer points with a cross of St. George gules, and on the two others with a thistle proper.

Princess Victoria.—A label of five points argent, charged with three roses and two crosses gules.

Princess Maud (Princess Charles of Denmark).—A label of five points argent, charged with three hearts and two crosses gules.

The Duke of Edinburgh (Duke of Saxe-Coburg and Gotha).—A label of three points argent, the centre point charged with a cross gules, and on each of the others an anchor azure. His son, the hereditary Prince of Saxe-Coburg and Gotha, who predeceased his father, bore a label of five points, the first, third, and fifth each charged with a cross gules, and the second and fourth each with an anchor azure (Fig. 898).

FIG. 898.—Label of the late Hereditary Prince of Saxe-Coburg and Gotha.

The Duke of Connaught.—A label of three points argent, the centre point charged with St. George's cross, and each of the other points with a fleur-de-lis azure.

The late Princess Royal (German Empress). — A label of three points argent, the centre point charged with a rose gules, and each of the others with a cross gules.

The late Grand Duchess of Hesse.—A label of three points argent, the centre point charged with a rose gules, and each of the others with an ermine spot sable.

Princess Christian of Schleswig-Holstein.—A label of three points, the centre point charged with St. George's cross, and each of the other points with a rose gules.

Princess Louise (Duchess of Argyll).—A label of three points, the centre point charged with a rose, and each of the other two with a canton gules.

Princess Henry of Battenberg.—A label of three points, the centre point charged with a heart, and each of the other two with a rose gules.

The late Duke of Albany.—A label of three points, the centre point charged with a St. George's cross, and each of the other two with a heart gules.

The late Duke of Cambridge.—A label of three points argent. The centre point charged with a St. George's cross, and each of the other two with *two* hearts in pale gules. The warrant to the present Duke assigned him the same label with the addition of a second label, plain, of three points gules, to be borne below the former label.

The first Duke of Cumberland.—A label of three points argent, the centre point charged with a fleur-de-lis azure, and each of the other two points with a cross of St. George gules.

Of the foregoing recently assigned labels all are borne over the plain English arms (1 and 4 England, 2 Scotland, 3 Ireland), charged with the escutcheon of Saxony, except those of the Dukes of Saxe-Coburg and Gotha, Cambridge, and Cumberland. In the two latter cases the labels are borne over the *latest* version of the arms of King George III., *i.e.* with the inescutcheon of Hanover, but, of course, neither the electoral bonnet nor the later crown which surmounted the inescutcheon of Hanover was made use of, and the smaller inescutcheon bearing the crown of Charlemagne was also omitted for the children of George III., except in the case of the Prince of Wales, who bore the plain inescutcheon of gules, but without the crown of Charlemagne thereupon.

The labels for the other sons and daughters of King George III. were as follows:—

The Duke of York.—A label of three points argent, the centre point charged with a cross gules. The Duke of York bore upon an inescutcheon argent (in the place occupied in the Royal Arms by the inescutcheon charged with the crown of Charlemagne) charged with a wheel of six spokes gules, for the Bishopric of Osnaburgh, which he possessed.

The Duke of Clarence (afterwards William IV.).—A label of three points argent, the centre point charged with a cross gules, and each of the others with an anchor erect azure.

The Duke of Kent had his label charged with a cross gules between two fleurs-de-lis azure.

The Duke of Sussex.—The label argent charged with two hearts in pale gules in the centre point between two crosses gules.

The Princess Royal (Queen of Würtemberg).—A rose between two crosses gules.

The Princess Augusta.—A like label, charged with a rose gules between two ermine spots.

The Princess Elizabeth (Princess of Hesse-Homburg). —A like label charged with a cross between two roses gules.

The Princess Mary (Duchess of Gloucester).—A like label, charged with a rose between two cantons gules.

The Princess Sophia.—A like label, charged with a heart between two roses gules,

The Princess Amelia.—A like label, charged with a rose between two hearts gules.

The Duke of Gloucester (brother of George III.).—A label of *five* points argent, charged with a fleur-de-lis azure between four crosses gules. His son (afterwards Duke of Gloucester) bore an additional plain label of three points during the lifetime of his father.

The foregoing labels are placed across the shield, on the crest, and on each of the supporters. The crest stands upon and is crowned with a coronet identical with the circlet of any coronet of rank assigned in the same patent; the lion supporter is crowned and the

which the Royal Arms were quartered, were again the arms of Saxony, these appearing in the second and third quarters.

Abroad there is now no equivalent whatever to our methods of differencing the Royal Arms. An official certificate was issued to me recently from Denmark of the undifferenced Royal Arms of Denmark certified as correct for the "Princes and Princesses" of that country. But the German Crown Prince bears his shield within a bordure gules, and anciently in France (from which country the English system was very probably originally derived) the differencing of the Royal French Arms for the younger branches seems to have been carefully attended to, as has been already specified.

Differencing in Scotland is carried out on an entirely different basis from differencing in England. In Scotland the idea is still rigidly preserved and adhered to that the coat of arms of a family belongs only to the head of the family for the time being, and the terms of a Scot-

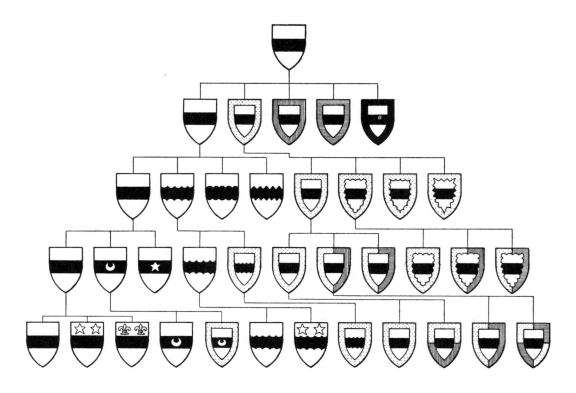

FIG. 899.—The scheme of Cadency Bordures devised by Mr. Stodart.

unicorn supporter is gorged with a similar coronet. It may perhaps be of interest to note that no badges and no motto are ever assigned in these Royal Warrants except in the case of the Prince of Wales.

F.-M. H.S.H. Prince Leopold of Saxe-Coburg, the Consort of H.R.H. the Princess Charlotte (only child of George IV.), received by warrant dated April 7, 1818, the right "to use and bear the Royal Arms (without the inescocheon of Charlemagne's crown, and without the Hanoverian Royal crown) differenced with a label of five points argent, the centre point charged with a rose gules, quarterly with the arms of his illustrious House ['Barry of ten sable and or, a crown of rue in bend vert'], the Royal Arms in the first and fourth quarters."

By Queen Victoria's desire this precedent was followed in the case of the late Prince Consort, the label in his case being of three points argent, the centre point charged with a cross gules, and, by a curious coincidence, the arms of his illustrious House, with

tish grant are as follows: "Know ye therefore that we have devised and do by these presents assign ratify and confirm to the said —— —— and his descendants *with such congruent differences as may hereafter be matriculated for them the following ensigns armorial.*" Under the accepted interpretation of Scottish armorial law, whilst the inherent gentility conferred by a patent of arms is not denied to cadets, no right to make use of arms is conceded to them until such time as they shall elect to matriculate the arms of their ancestors in their own names. This point has led to a much purer system of heraldry in Scotland than in England, and there is far less heraldic abuse in that country as a result, because the differences are decided not haphazardly by the user himself, as is the case in England, but by a competent officer of arms. Moreover the constant occasions of matriculation bring the arms frequently under official review. There is no fixed rule which decides *ipse facto* what difference shall be borne, and consequently this decision has retained in the hands of the heraldic executive an amount of control which they still possess far exceeding that of the executive in England, and perhaps the best way in which to state the rules which hold good will be to reprint a portion of one of Sir James Balfour Paul's Rhind Lectures, which is devoted to the point:—

"I have said that in Scotland the principle which limited the number of paternal coats led to a careful differencing of these coats as borne by the junior branches of the family. Though the English system was sometimes used, it has never obtained to any great extent in Scotland, the practice here being generally to difference by means of a bordure, in which way many more generations are capable of being distinguished than is possible by the English method. The weak point of the Scottish system is that, whilst the general idea is good, there is no definite rule whereby it can be carried out on unchanging lines; much is left to the discretion of the authorities.

"As a general rule, it may be stated that the second son bears a plain bordure of the tincture of the principal charge in the shield, and his younger brothers also bear plain bordures of varying tinctures. In the next generation the eldest son of the second son would bear his father's coat and bordure without change; the second son would have the bordure engrailed; the third, invected; the fourth, indented, and so on, the other sons of the younger sons in this generation differencing their father's bordures in the same way. The junior members of the next generation might have their bordures parted per pale, the following generations having their bordures parted per fess and per saltire, per cross or quarterly, gyronny or compony, that is, divided into alternate spaces of metal or colour in a single trace—this, however, being often in Scotland a mark of illegitimacy—counter-compone or a similar pattern in two tracts, or chequy with three or more tracts.

"You will see that these modifications of the simple bordure afford a great variety of differences, and when they are exhausted the expedient can then be resorted to of placing on the bordures charges taken from other coats, often from those of a maternal ancestor; or they may be arbitrarily assigned to denote some personal characteristic of the bearer, as in the case of James Maitland, Major in the Scots regiment of Foot Guards, who carries the dismembered lion of his family within a bordure wavy azure charged with eight hand grenades or, significant, I presume, of his military profession.

"You will observe that, with all these varieties of differencing we have mentioned, the younger branches descending from the original eldest son of the parent house are still left unprovided with marks of cadency. These, however, can be arranged for by taking the ordinary which appears in their father's arms and modifying its boundary lines. Say the original coat was 'argent a chevron gules,' the second son of the eldest son would have the chevron engrailed, but without any bordure; the third, invected, and so on; and the next generations the systems of bordures accompanying the modified chevron would go on as before. And when all these methods are exhausted, differences can still be made in a variety of ways, e.g. by charging the ordinary with similar charges in a similar manner to the bordure as Erskine of Shielfield, a cadet of Balgownie, who bore: 'Argent, on a pale sable, a cross crosslet fitchée or within a bordure azure'; or by the introduction of an ordinary into a coat which had not one previously, a bend or the ribbon (which is a small bend) being a favourite ordinary to use for this purpose. Again, we occasionally find a change of tincture of the field of the shield used to denote cadency.

"There are other modes of differencing which need not be alluded to in detail, but I may say that on analysing the earlier arms in the Lyon Register, I find that the bordure is by far the most common method of indicating cadency, being used in no less than 1080 cases. The next most popular way is by changing the boundary lines of an ordinary, which is done in 563 shields; 233 cadets difference their arms by the insertion of a smaller charge on the ordinary and 195 on the shield. A change of tincture, including counterchanging, is carried out in 155 coats, and a canton is added in 70 cases, while there are 350 coats in which two or more of the above methods are used. From these figures, which are approximately correct, you will see the relative frequency of the various modes of differencing. You will also note that the original coat of a family can be differenced in a great many ways so as to show the connection of cadets with the parent house. The drawback to the system is that heralds have never arrived at a uniform treatment so as to render it possible to calculate the exact relationship of the cadets. Much is left, as I said, to the discretion of the officer granting the arms; but still it gives considerable assistance in determining the descent of a family."

The late Mr. Stodart, Lyon Clerk Depute, who was an able herald, particularly in matters relating to Scotland,

FIG. 900.—Arms of Lieut.-Col. Arthur Balfour Haig, C.M.G., M.V.O., of Bemersyde: Azure, a saltire between two mullets in chief and base, and a decrescent and an increscent in the flanks argent, a bordure engrailed party per pale or and argent, charged with three hedgehogs sable. Mantling azure, doubled argent; and upon a wreath of his liveries is set for crest, a rock proper; and in an escroll over the same this motto, "Tyde what may."

had elaborated a definite system of these bordures for differencing which would have done much to simplify Scottish cadency. Its weak point was obviously this, that it could only be applied to new matriculations of arms by cadets; and so, if adopted as a definite and unchangeable matter of rule, it might have occasioned doubt and misunderstanding in future times with regard to many important Scottish coats now existing, without reference to Mr. Stodart's system. But the scheme elaborated by Mr. Stodart is now accepted as the broad basis of the Scottish system for matriculations (Fig. 899).

THE ART OF HERALDRY

In early Scottish seals the bordures are to so large an extent engrailed as to make it appear that the later and present rule, which gives the plain bordure to immediate cadets, was not fully recognised or adopted. Bordures charged appear at a comparatively early date in Scotland. The bordure company in Scotland and the bordure wavy in England, which are now used to signify illegitimacy, will be further considered in a subsequent chapter, but neither one nor the other originally carried any such meaning. The doubtful legitimacy of the Avondale and Ochiltree Stewarts, who bore the bordure company in Scotland, along with its

during the first twenty years of the Lyon Register were unquestionably legitimate, whilst others, as Scott of Gorrenberry and Patrick Sinclair of Ulbester, were illegitimate, or at best only legitimated. The light in which the bordure company had come to be regarded is shown by a Royal Warrant granted in 1679 to John Lundin of that Ilk, allowing him to drop the coat which his family had hitherto carried, and, as descended of a natural son of William the Lion, to bear the arms of Scotland within a bordure company argent and azure.

The bordure counter-compony is assigned to fifteen persons, none of them, it is believed, of illegitimate

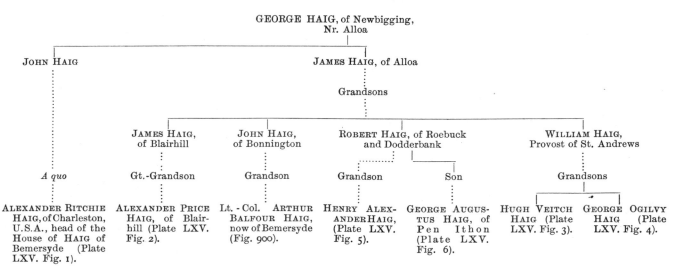

HAIG OF BEMERSYDE

Arms: Azure, a saltire between two mullets in chief and base, and a decrescent and an increscent in the flanks argent. Crest: a rock proper. Motto: "Tyde what may."

"Tyde what may betyde
Haig shall be Haig of Bemersyde."

GEORGE HAIG, of Newbigging, Nr. Alloa

| JOHN HAIG | | | JAMES HAIG, of Alloa | | | |

Grandsons

	JAMES HAIG, of Blairhill	JOHN HAIG, of Bonnington	ROBERT HAIG, of Roebuck and Dodderbank		WILLIAM HAIG, Provost of St. Andrews	
A quo	Gt.-Grandson	Grandson	Grandson	Son	Grandsons	
ALEXANDER RITCHIE HAIG, of Charleston, U.S.A., head of the House of HAIG of Bemersyde (Plate LXV. Fig. 1).	ALEXANDER PRICE HAIG, of Blairhill (Plate LXV. Fig. 2).	Lt.-Col. ARTHUR BALFOUR HAIG, now of Bemersyde (Fig. 900).	HENRY ALEXANDER HAIG, (Plate LXV. Fig. 5).	GEORGE AUGUSTUS HAIG, of Pen Ithon (Plate LXV. Fig. 6).	HUGH VEITCH HAIG (Plate LXV. Fig. 3).	GEORGE OGILVY HAIG (Plate LXV. Fig. 4).

use by the Beauforts in England, has tended latterly to bring that difference into disrepute in the cadency of lawful sons—yet some of the bearers of that bordure

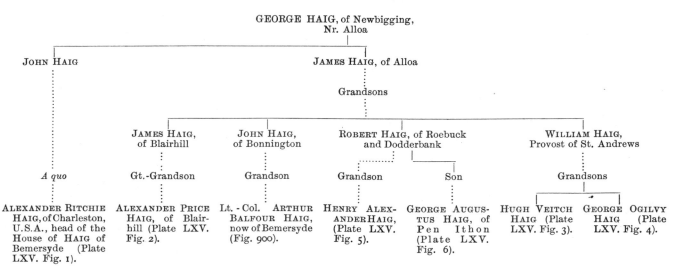

FIG. 901.—Arms of Arthur Samuel Haigh, Esq., of Cat Cay, Bahamas: Azure, on a saltire invected ermine, between two rocks in pale proper and a decrescent and an increscent in fess argent, an estoile of the first. Mantling azure and argent. Crest: upon a wreath of the colours, in front of a demi-man affrontée proper holding in the dexter hand a crescent or, a rock also proper. Motto: "Tyde what may."

descent, and some expressly said to be "lineallie and lawfulie descended" from the ancestor whose arms they bore thus differenced. The idea of this bordure having been at any time a mark of bastardy is a very modern error, arising from a confusion with the bordure company.

A very instructive series of bordures will be found upon Plate LXV., which shows, with Fig. 900, some number of variations upon the Haig coat of arms, and above is a key pedigree showing the relationship of the owners of the varying differences.

Fig. 901 is also instructive, as it is an example of an English grant of arms founded upon the old Scottish coat for a family who, though they had long used the same arms, could prove no descent from the Bemersyde stock.

In conclusion, attention needs to be pointedly drawn to the fact that all changes in arms are not due to cadency, nor is it safe always to presume cadency from proved instances of change. Instead of merely detailing isolated instances of variation in a number of different families, the matter may be better illustrated by closely following the successive variations in the same family, and an instructive instance is met with in the case of the arms of the family of Swinton of that Ilk. This is peculiarly instructive, because at no point in the descent covered by the arms referred to is there any doubt or question as to the fact of descent.

Claiming as they do a male descent and inheritance from Liulf the son of Edulf, Vicecomes of Northumbria, whose possession before 1100 of the lands of Swinton is the earliest contemporary evidence which has come down to us of landowning by a Scottish subject, it is unfortunate that we cannot with authority date their armorial ensigns before the later half of the thirteenth century. Charters there are in plenty. Out of the twenty-three earliest Scottish writings given in the National MSS. of Scotland, nine, taken from the Coldingham documents preserved at Durham, refer to the village and lands of Swinton. Among these are two confirmations by David I., i.e. before 1153, of Swinton "in hereditate sibi et heredibus" to "meo militi Hernulfo" or "Arnolto isti meo Militi," the first of the family to follow the Norman fashion, and adopt the territorial designation of de Swinton; while at Durham and elsewhere, Cospatric de Swinton and his son Alan and grandson Alan appear more than eighty times in charters before 1250. But it is not till we come to c. 1271 that we find a Swinton seal still attached to a charter.

This is a grant by a third Alan of the Kirk croft of Lower Swinton to God and the blessed Cuthbert and the blessed Ebba and the Prior and Monks of Coldingham. The seal is of a very early form (Fig. 902), and

FIG. 902.—Seal of Alan de Swinton, c. 1271.

FIG. 903.—Seal of Henry de Swinton, 1378.

may perhaps have belonged to the father and grandfather of the particular Alan who uses it.

Of the Henry de Swinton who came next, and who swore fealty to Edward the First of England at Berwick in 1296, and of yet a fourth Alan, no seals are known. These were turbulent days throughout Scotland: but then we find a distinct advance; a shield upon a diapered ground, and upon it the single boar has given place to the three boars' heads which afterwards became so common in Scotland. Nisbet lends his authority to the tradition that all the families of Border birth who carried them—Gordon, Nisbet, Swinton, Redpath, Dunse, he mentions, and he might have added others—were originally of one stock, and if so, the probability must be that the breed sprung from Swinton.

This seal (Fig. 903) was put by a second Henry de Swynton to one of the family charters, probably of the date of 1378, which have lately been placed for safe keeping in the Register House in Edinburgh.

His successor, Sir John, the hero of Noyon in Picardy, of Otterburn, and Homildon, was apparently the first of the race to use supporters. His seal (Fig. 904) belongs to the second earliest of the Douglas charters preserved at Drumlanrig. Its date is 1389, and Sir John de Swyntoun is described as Dominus de Mar, a title he bore by right of his marriage with Margaret, Countess of Douglas and Mar. This probably also accounts for his coronet, and it is interesting to note that the helmet, coronet, and crest are the exact counterpart of those on the Garter plate of Ralph, Lord Basset, in St. George's Chapel at Windsor. It is possibly more than a coincidence, for Froissart mentions them both as fighting in France ten to twenty years earlier.

Of his son, the second Sir John, "Lord of that Ilk," we have no seal. His lance it was that overthrew Thomas, Duke of Clarence, the brother of Henry V., at Beaugé in 1421, and he fell, a young man, three years later with the flower of the Scottish army at

FIG. 904.—Seal of Sir John de Swinton, 1389.

Verneuil; but in 1475 his son, a third Sir John, uses the identical crest and shield which his descendants carry to this day (Fig. 905). John had become a common name in the family, and the same or a similar seal did duty for the next three generations; but in 1598 we find the great-great-grandson, Robert Swinton of that Ilk, who represented Berwickshire in the first regularly constituted Parliament of Scotland,

FIG. 905.—Seal of Sir John de Swinton, 1475.

FIG. 906.—Seal of Robert Swinton, of that Ilk, 1598.

altering the character of the boars' heads (Fig. 906). He would also appear to have placed upon the chevron something which is difficult to decipher, but is probably the rose so borne by the Hepburns, his second wife having been a daughter of Sir Patrick Hepburn of Whitecastle.

Whatever the charge was, it disappeared from the shield (Fig. 907) erected on the outer wall of Swinton

FIG. 907.—Arms of Swinton. (From Swinton Church, 163–.)

Church by his second son and eventual heir, Sir Alexander, also member for his native county; but the boars' heads are turned the other way, perhaps in imitation of those above the very ancient effigy of the first Sir Alan inside the church.

Sir Alexander's son, John Swinton, "Laird Swinton" Carlyle calls him, wrecked the family fortunes. According to Bishop Burnet he was "the man of all Scotland most trusted and employed by Cromwell," and

THE ART OF HERALDRY

he died a Quaker, excommunicated and forfeited. To the circumstance that when, in 1672, the order went out that all arms were to be officially recorded, he was a broken man under sentence that his arms should be "laceret and delete out of the Heralds' Books," we probably owe it that until of late years no Swinton arms appeared on the Lyon Register.

Then to come to less stirring times, and turn to book-

FIG. 908.—Bookplate of Sir John Swinton of that Ilk, 1707.

plates. His son, yet another Sir John of that Ilk, in whose favour the forfeiture was rescinded, sat for Berwickshire in the last Parliament of Scotland and the first of Great Britain. His bookplate (Fig. 908) is one of the earliest Scottish dated plates.

FIG. 909.—Bookplate of Archibald Swinton of Kimmerghame.

His grandson, Captain Archibald Swinton of Kimmerghame, county Berwick (Fig. 909), was an ardent book collector up to his death in 1804, and Archibald's great-grandson, Captain George C. Swinton (Fig. 910), walked as March Pursuivant in the procession in Westminster Abbey at the coronation of King Edward the Seventh of England in 1902, and smote on the gate

when that same Edward as First of Scotland claimed admission to his castle of Edinburgh in 1903.

The arms as borne to-day by the head of the family, John Edulf Blagrave Swinton of Swinton Bank, a lieutenant in the Lothians and Berwickshire Imperial Yeomanry, are as given on Plate LXIII.

The heraldic use of party badges is unknown in British armory. Elsewhere we have suggested that perhaps the cinquefoil where it occurs in early coats may be a perpetuation of the party badge of Simon de Montfort, the great Earl of Leicester. Many of the red roses and the white roses which survive in our armory are doubtless due to the party badges of York and Lancaster. The red rose for Lancashire grantees

FIG. 910.—Bookplate of Captain George S. Swinton, March Pursuivant of Arms.

and the white rose for Yorkshire grantees, the thistle for Scotsmen and the shamrock for Irishmen, all in a way may approach the category, but the party badge proper we have never known. It is really a peculiarity of Italian heraldry, the result of the curious party strife of the "Ghibellines" and the "Guelphs." The former party bore on a chief the Imperial eagle, the latter a chief of Anjou. On Plate LXVII. Fig. 23 will be seen the Ghibelline badge over the arms of the Counts of Gambara, Pralboina, and Verola-Nuova. These are: "Or, a lobster erect gules, on a chief of the field the crowned Imperial eagle displayed sable." The alternate badge is represented in Fig. 24 on the same plate over the arms of the Manfredi family, Papal Vicars, and Lords of Faenza, Imola, Cesena, and Forli, their arms being quarterly argent and azure, and the Guelph badge being the azure chief charged with the three fleurs-de-lis or of France and the label gules of Anjou.

A. C. F-D.

THE ART OF HERALDRY

CHAPTER XXXVI

MARKS OF BASTARDY

IT has been remarked that the knowledge of "the man in the street" is least incorrect when he knows nothing. Probably the only heraldic knowledge that a large number possess is summed up in the assertion that the heraldic sign of illegitimacy is the "bar sinister."

No doubt it is to the novelists—who, seeking to touch lightly upon an unpleasant subject, have ignorantly adopted a French colloquialism—that we must attribute a great deal of the misconception which exists concerning illegitimacy and its heraldic marks of indication. I assert most unhesitatingly that there are not now and never have been any unalterable laws as to what these marks should be, and the colloquialism which insists upon the "bar sinister" is a curiously amusing example of an utter misnomer. To any one with the most rudimentary knowledge of heraldry it must plainly be seen to be radically impossible to depict a bar sinister, for the simple reason that the bar is neither dexter nor sinister. It is utterly impossible to draw a bar sinister—such a thing does not exist. But the assertion of many writers with a knowledge of armory that "bar sinister" is a mistake for "bend sinister" is also somewhat misleading, because the real mistake lies in the spelling of the term. The "barre sinistre" is merely the French translation of bend sinister, the French word "barre" meaning a *bend*. The French "barre" is not the English bar.

In order to properly understand the true significance of the marks of illegitimacy, it is necessary that the attempt should be made to transplant oneself into the environment when the laws and rules of heraldry were in the making. At that period illegitimacy was of little if any account. It has not debarred the succession of some of our own sovereigns, although, from the earliest times, the English have always been more prudish upon the point than other nations. In Ireland, even so late as the reign of Queen Elizabeth, it is a striking genealogical difficulty to decide in many noble pedigrees which if any of the given sons of any person were legitimate, and which of the ladies of his household, if any, might be legally termed his wife. In Scotland we find the same thing, though perhaps it is not quite so blatant to so late a date, but considering what are and have been the Scottish laws of marriage, it is the *fact* or otherwise of marriage which has to be ascertained; and though in England the legal status was recognised from an earlier period, the social status of the offspring of a given man depended little upon the legal legitimacy of birth, but rather upon the amount of recognition the bastard received from his father. If a man had an unquestionably legitimate son, that son undoubtedly succeeded; but if he had not, any technical stain upon the birth of the others had little effect in preventing their succession. A study of the succession to the Barony of Meinill clearly shows that the illegitimate son of the second Lord Meinill succeeded to the estates and peerage of his father in preference to his legitimate uncle. There are many other analogous cases. And when the Church juggled at its pleasure with the sacrament of marriage—dispensing and annulling or recognising marriages for reasons which we nowadays can only term whimsical—

small wonder is it that the legal fact, though then admitted, had little of the importance which we now give to it. When the actual fact was so little more than a matter at the personal pleasure of the person most concerned, it would be ridiculous to suppose that any perpetuation of a mere advertisement of the fact would be considered necessary, whilst the fact itself was so often ignored; so that until comparatively recent times the Crown certainly never attempted to enforce any heraldic marks of illegitimacy. Rather were these enforced by the legitimate descendants if and when such descendants existed.

The point must have first arisen when there were both legitimate and illegitimate descendants of a given person, and it was desired to make record of the true line in which land or honours should descend. To effect this purpose, the arms of the illegitimate son were made to carry some charge or alteration to show that there was some reason which debarred inheritance by their users, whilst there remained those entitled to bear the arms without the mark of distinction. But be it noted that this obligation existed equally on the legitimate cadets of a family, and in the earliest periods of heraldry there is little or no distinction either in the marks employed or in the character of the marks, which can be drawn between mere marks of cadency and marks of illegitimacy. Until a comparatively recent period it is absolutely unsafe to use these marks as signifying or proving either legitimate cadency or illegitimacy. The same mark stood for both, the only object which any distinctive change accomplished, being the distinction which it was necessary to draw between those who owned the right to the undifferenced arms, and owned the land, and those who did not. The object was to safeguard the right of the real possessors, and not to penalise the others. There was no particular mark either for cadency or for illegitimacy, the distinctions made being dictated by what seemed the most suitable and distinctive mark applicable to the arms under consideration.

When that much has been thoroughly grasped, one gets a more accurate understanding of the subject. One other point has to be borne in mind (and to the present generation, which knows so well how extensively arms have been improperly assumed, the statement may seem startling), and that is, that the use of arms was formerly evidence of pedigree. As late as the beginning of the nineteenth century evidence of this character was submitted to the Committee of Privileges at the hearing of a Peerage case. The evidence was *admitted* for that purpose, though doubt (in that case very properly) was thrown upon its value.

Therefore, in view of the two foregoing facts, there can be very little doubt that the use of armorial marks of bastardy *was not invented or instituted, nor were they enforced, as punishment or as a disgrace.*

It is a curious instance how a careful study of words and terms employed will often afford either a clue or confirmation, when the true meaning of the term has long been overlooked.

The official term for a mark of cadency is a "difference" mark, *i.e.* it was a mark to show the difference between one member of a family and another. The mark used to signify a lack of blood relationship, and a mark used to signify illegitimacy are each termed a mark of distinction, *i.e.* a mark that shall make something plainly "distinct." What is that something? The fact that the use of the arms is not evidence of descent through which heirship can be claimed or proved. This, by the way, is a patent example of the advantage of adherence to precedent.

The inevitable conclusion is that a bastard was originally only required to mark his shield sufficiently to be distinctly apparent that heirship would never accrue. The arms had to be distinct from those borne by those members of the family upon whom heirship might devolve. The social position of a bastard as "belonging" to a family was pretty generally conceded, therefore he carried their arms, sufficiently marked to show he was not in the line of succession.

This being accepted, one at once understands the great variety of the marks which have been employed. These answered the purpose of distinction, and nothing more was demanded or necessary. Consequently a recapitulation of marks, of which examples can be quoted, are largely lists of isolated instances, and as such are useless for the purposes of deduction in any attempt to arrive at a correct conclusion as to what the ancient rules were. In brief, there were no rules until the eighteenth, or perhaps even until the nineteenth century. The only rule was that the arms must be sufficiently marked in *some* way. This is borne out by the dictum of Menêstrier.

Except the label, which has been elsewhere referred to, the earliest marks of either cadency or illegitimacy for which accepted use can be found are the bend and the bordure; but the bend for the purpose of illegitimacy seems to be the earlier, and a bend superimposed over a shield remained a mark of illegitimate cadency until a comparatively late period. This bend as a difference naturally was originally depicted as a bend dexter, and as a mark of legitimate cadency is found in the arms of the *younger* son of Edmund Crouchback, Earl of Lancaster, before he succeeded his elder brother.

There are scores of other similar instances which a little research will show. Whether the term "left-handed marriage" is the older, and the sinister bend is derived therefrom, or whether the slang term is derived from the sinister bend, it is perhaps not necessary to inquire. But there is no doubt that from an early period the bend of cadency, when such cadency was illegitimate, is frequently met with in the sinister form. But concurrently with such usage instances are found in which the dexter bend was used for the same purpose, and it is very plainly evident that it was never at that date looked upon as a penalty, but was used merely as a *distinction*, or for the purpose of showing that the wearer was not the head of his house or in possession of the lordship. The territorial idea of the nature of arms, which has been alluded to in the chapter upon marks of cadency, should be borne in mind in coming to a conclusion.

Soon after the recognition of the bend as a mark of illegitimacy we come across the bordure; but there is some confusion with this, bordures of all kinds being used indiscriminately to denote both legitimate and illegitimate cadency. There are countless other forms of marking illegitimacy, and it is impossible to attempt to summarise them, and absolutely impossible to draw conclusions as to any family from marks upon its arms when this point is under discussion. To give a list of these instances would rather seem an attempt to deduce a rule or rules upon the point, so I say at once that there was no recognised mark, and any plain distinction seems to have been accepted as sufficient; and no distinction whatever was made when the illegitimate son, either from failure of legitimate issue or other reason,

succeeded to the lands and honours of his father. Out of the multitude of marks, the bend, and subsequently the bend sinister, emerge as most frequently in use, and finally the bend sinister exclusively; so that it has come to be considered, and perhaps correctly at one period, that its use was equivalent to a mark of illegitimacy in England.

But there has always remained to the person of bastard descent the right of discarding the bastardised coat, and adopting a new coat of arms, the only requirement as to the new coat being that it shall be so distinct from the old one as not to be liable to confusion therewith. And it is a moot point whether or not a large proportion of the instances which are tabulated in most heraldic works as examples of marks of bastardy are anything whatever of the kind. My own opinion is that many are not, and that it is a mistake to so consider them, the true explanation undoubtedly in some—and outside the Royal Family probably in most—being that they are new coats of arms adopted *as* new coats of arms doubtless bearing relation to the old family coat, but sufficiently distinguished therefrom to rank as new arms, and were never intended to be taken as, and never were bastardised examples of formerly existing coats. It is for this reason that I have refrained from giving any extensive list such as is to be found in most other treatises on heraldry, for all that can be said for such lists is that they are lists of the specific arms of specific bastards, which is a very different matter from a list of heraldic marks of illegitimacy.

Another objection to the long lists which most heraldic works give of early instances of marks of bastardy as data for deduction lies in the fact that most are instances of the illegitimate children of Royal personages. It is singularly unsafe to draw deductions, to be applied to the arms of others, from the Royal Arms, for these generally have laws unto themselves. The bend sinister in its bare simplicity was seldom used, the more frequent form being the sinister bendlet, or even the diminutive of that, the cottise. There is no doubt, of course, that when a sinister bend or bendlet debruises another coat that that is a bastardised version of an older coat, but examples can be found of the sinister bend as a charge which has no reference whatever to illegitimacy. Two instances that come to mind, which can be found by reference to any current peerage, are the arms of Shiffner and Burne-Jones. Certainly in these cases I know of no illegitimacy, and neither coat is a bastardised version of an older existing coat. Anciently the bendlet was drawn across arms and quarterings, and an example of a coat of arms of some number of quarterings debruised for an illegitimate family is found in the registration of a Talbot pedigree in one of the Visitation Books. As a mark of distinction upon arms the bend sinister for long past has fallen out of use, though for the purpose of differencing crests a bendlet wavy sinister is still made use of, and will be again presently referred to.

Next to the bend comes the bordure. Bordures of all kinds were used for the purposes of cadency from practically the earliest periods of heraldic differencing. But they were used indiscriminately, as has been already stated, both for legitimate and illegitimate cadency. John of Gaunt, as is well known, was the father of Henry IV. and the ancestor of Henry VII., the former being the issue of his legitimate wife, the latter coming from a son who, as one of the old chroniclers puts it, "was of double advowtrie begotten." But, as every one knows, John of Gaunt's children by Catherine Roet or Swynford were legitimated by Act of Parliament, the Act of Parliament not excepting the succession to the Throne, a disability later introduced in Letters Patent of the Crown when giving a subsequent confirmation of the Act, but which, nevertheless, they could not overrule. But taking the sons of the latter family as legitimate, which (whatever may have been the moral aspect of the case) they were undoubtedly in the eyes of the common law after the passing of the Act referred to, they existed concurrently with the undoubtedly senior descendants of the first marriage of John of Gaunt with Blanche of Lancaster, and it was necessary—whether they were legitimate or not—to distinguish the arms of the junior from the senior branch. The result was that as legitimate cadets, and not as bastards, the arms of John of Gaunt were differenced for the line of the Dukes of Somerset by the addition of the bordure compony argent and azure—the livery colours of Lancaster.

The fight as to whether these children were legitimate or illegitimate was, of course, notorious, and a matter of history; but from the fact that they bore a bordure compony, an idea grew up both in this country and in Scotland from the similarity of the cases of the doubtful legitimacy of the Avondale and Ochiltree Stewarts, who both used the bordure compony, that the bordure compony was a sign of illegitimacy, whereas in both countries at an earlier period it undoubtedly was accepted as a mark of legitimate cadency.

As a mark of bastardy it had subsequently some extensive use in both countries, and it still remains the only mark now used for the purpose in Scottish heraldry. Whether it was that it was not considered as of a fixed nature, or whether it was that it had become notorious and unacceptable, it is difficult to say, though the officers of arms have been blamed for making a change on the assumption that it was the latter.

Some writers who clamour strongly for the *penalising* of bastard arms, and for the plain and recognisable marking of them as such (a position adopted rather vehemently by Woodward, a singularly erudite heraldic writer), are rather uncharitable, and at the same time rather lacking in due observation and careful consideration of ancient ideas and ancient precedents. That the recognised mark has been changed at different periods, and as a consequence that to a certain extent the advertisement it conveys has been less patent is, of course, put down to the "venality" of mediæval heralds (happily their backs are broad) by those who are too short-sighted to observe that the one thing an official herald moves heaven and earth to escape from is the making of a new precedent; and that, on the score of signs of illegitimacy, the official heralds, when the control of arms passed into their hands, found no established rule. So far from having been guilty of venality, as Woodward suggests, they have erred on the other side, and by having worked only on the limited number of precedents they found they have stereotyped the advertisement, and thereby made the situation more stringent than they found it.

We have it from biblical sources that the sins of the fathers shall be visited upon the children unto the third and fourth generations, and this spirit has undoubtedly crept into the views of many writers, but to get into the true perspective of the matter one needs to consider the subject from the point of view of less prudish days than our own.

I have no wish to be misunderstood. In these days much heraldic reviewing of the blatant and baser sort depends not upon the value of the work performed, a point of view which is never given a thought, but entirely upon the identity of the writer whose work is under review, and is largely composed of misquotation and misrepresentation. It may perhaps be as well, therefore, to state that I am not seeking to condone illegitimacy or to combat present opinions upon the point. I merely state that our present opinions are a modern growth, and that in the thirteenth, fourteenth, fifteenth, and sixteenth centuries, when the

fundamental principles of heraldry were in the making, it was not considered a disgrace to have an illegitimate son, nor to be of illegitimate birth.

At any rate, the fact remains that a new mark was called into being in England about the year 1780 when in a grant to Zachary to quarter the arms of Sacheverell, from which family he was in the female line illegitimately descended, the bordure wavy was first met with as a sufficient and proper mark of illegitimacy. The curious point is that before that date in Scotland and in England the bordure wavy possessed nothing of this character, and to the present day the bordure wavy in Scotland is undoubtedly nothing more than a legitimate mark of legitimate cadency, for which mark Mr. Stodart provides a place in the scheme of differencing which he tabulated as the basis of cadency marks in Scotland (Fig. 899). Since that date the bordure wavy has remained the mark which has been used for the purpose in England, as the bordure compony has remained the mark in Scotland.

Bearing in mind that the only necessity was some mark which should carry sufficient *distinction* from the arms of the family, it follows, as a natural consequence of human nature, that as soon as any particular mark became identified with illegitimacy (after that was considered to be a stigma), that mark was quietly dropped and some other substituted, and no one would be surprised to find the bordures wavy and compony quietly displaced by something else. If any change is to be made it is to be hoped that no existing mark will be adopted, and that the marks in England and Scotland shall not conflict even if they do not coincide.

The bendlet sinister, however, survives in the form of the baton sinister, which is a bendlet couped placed across the centre of the shield. The baton sinister, however, is a privilege which is preserved, such as it is, for Royal bastards. The latest instance of this was in the exemplification of arms to the Earl of Munster and his brothers and sisters early in the nineteenth century. Other surviving instances are met with in the arms of the Duke of St. Albans and the Duke of Grafton. Another privilege of Royal bastards is that they may have the baton of *metal*, a privilege which is, according to Berry, denied to those of humbler origin. According to present law the position of an illegitimate person heraldically is based upon the common law of the country, which practically declares that an illegitimate child has no name, no parentage, and no relations. The illegitimacy of birth is an insuperable bar to inheritance, and a person of illegitimate birth inherits no arms at all, the popular idea that he inherits a right to the arms subject to a mark of distinction being quite incorrect. He has none at all. There has never been any mark which, as a matter of course and of mere motion, could attach itself automatically to a shield, as is the case with the English marks of difference, *e.g.* the crescent of the second son or the mullet of the third. This is a point upon which I have found mistaken ideas very frequently held, even by those who have made some study of heraldry.

But a very little thought should make it plain that by the very nature of the fact there cannot be either a recognised mark, compulsory use, or an *ipse facto* sign.

Illegitimacy is negative, not positive—a fact which many writers hardly give sufficient weight to. If any one of illegitimate birth desires to obtain a right to arms he has two courses open to him. He can either (not disclosing the fact of his illegitimacy, and not attempting to prove that he is a descendant of any kind from any one else) apply for and obtain a new grant of arms on his own basis, and worry through the College the grant of a coat as closely following in design that of the old family as he can get, which means that he would be treated and penalised with such *alterations* (not "marks of distinction") as

THE ART OF HERALDRY

would be imposed upon a stranger in blood endeavouring to obtain arms founded upon a coat to which he had no right. The cost of such a proceeding in England is £76, 10s., the usual fees upon an ordinary grant.

The alternative course is simple. He must avow himself a bastard, and must prove his paternity or maternity, as the case may be (for in the eye of the law—common and heraldic—he bears the same relation, which is nil, and the same right to the name and arms, which is nil, of both his father and his mother).

Illegitimacy under English law affords one of the many instances in which anomalies exist, for, strange as the statement is, a bastard comes into the world without any name at all.

Legally, at birth a bastard child has then no name at all, and no arms. It must subsequently acquire such right to a name (whatever right that may amount to) as user of and reputation therein may give him. He inherits no arms at all, no name, and no property, save by specific devise or bequest. The lack of parents operates as a *chasm* which it is impossible to bridge. It is not a case of a peculiar bridge or a faulty bridge; there is no bridge at all.

Names, in so far as they are matters of law, are subject to canon law; at any rate, the law upon the subject, such as it is, originated in canon law, and not in statute or civil law. Canon law was made, and has never since been altered, at a time when surnames were not in existence. A bastard no more inherits the surname of the mother than it does the surname of its father; and the spirit of petty officialism, so rampant amongst the clergy, which seeks to impose upon a bastard *nolens volens* the surname of its mother, has no justification in law or fact. A bastard has precisely as little right to the surname of its mother as it has to the surname of its father. Obviously, however, under the customs of our present social life, every person must have a surname of one kind or another; and it is here that the anomaly in the British law exists, inasmuch as neither statute nor canon law provide any means for conferring a surname. That the King has the prerogative, and exercises it, of conferring or confirming surnames is, of course, unquestioned, but it is hardly to be supposed that the King will trouble himself to provide a surname for every illegitimate child which may be born; and outside this prerogative, which probably is exercised about once a year, there is no method provided or definitely recognised by the law to meet this necessity. To obviate the difficulty, the surname has to be that which is conferred upon the child by general custom; and as an illegitimate child is in ninety-nine cases out of a hundred brought up by its mother, it is usually by the same custom which confers the surname of its owner upon a dog in so many parts of the country that a bastard child gets known by its mother's surname, and consequently has that surname conferred upon it by general custom. The only names that an illegitimate child has inalienable right to are the names by which it is baptized; and if two names are given, and the child or its guardians elect that it should be known only by those baptismal names, and if common repute and general custom, as would be probable, uses the last of those names as a surname, there is no legal power on earth which can force upon the child any other name; and if the last of the baptismal names happens to be its father's surname, the child will have an absolute right to be known only by its Christian names, which to all intents and purposes will mean that it will be known by its father's surname.

In the same way that an illegitimate child inherits no surname at all, it equally inherits no arms. Consequently it has no shield upon which to carry a mark of bastardy, if such a mark happened to be in existence. But if under a will or deed of settlement an illegitimate child is required to assume the name and arms of its father *or of*

its mother, a Royal Licence to assume such name and arms is considered to be necessary. It may be here noted that voluntary applications to assume a name and arms in the case of an illegitimate child are not entertained unless it can be clearly shown (which is not always an easy matter) what the parentage really was.

It will be noticed that I have said he will be required to prove his paternity. This is vigorously insisted upon, inasmuch as it is not fair to penalise the reputation of a dead man by inflicting upon him a record of bastard descendants whilst his own life might have been stainless. An illegitimate birth is generally recorded under the name of the mother only, and even when it is given, the truth of any statement as to paternity is always open to grave suspicion. There is nothing, therefore, to prevent a person asserting that he is the son of a duke, whereas his real father may have been in a very plebeian walk in life; and to put the arms of the duke's family at the mercy of any fatherless person who chose to fancy a differenced version of them would be manifestly unjust, so that without proof in a legal action of the actual paternity, or some recognition under a will or settlement, it is impossible to adopt the alternative in question. But if such recognition or proof is forthcoming, the procedure is to petition the Sovereign for a Royal Licence to use (or continue to use) the name desired and to bear the arms of the family. Such a petition is always granted, on proper proof of the facts, if made in due form through the proper channels. The Royal Licence to that effect is then issued. But the document contains two conditions, the first being that the arms shall be exemplified according to the laws of arms "with due and proper marks of distinction," and that the Royal Licence shall be recorded in the College of Arms, otherwise "to be void and of none effect." The invariable insertion of this clause puts into the hands of the College one of the strongest weapons the officers of arms possess.

Under the present regime the due and proper marks of distinction are, for the arms, a bordure wavy round the shield of the most suitable colour, according to what the arms may be, but if possible of some colour or metal different from any of the tinctures in the arms. The crest is usually differenced by a bendlet wavy sinister, but a pallet wavy is sometimes used, and sometimes a saltire wavy, couped or otherwise. The choice between these marks generally depends upon the nature of the crest. But even with this choice, the anomaly is frequently found of blank space being carefully debruised. Seeing that the mark of the debruising is not a tangible object or thing, but a mark painted upon another object, such a result seems singularly ridiculous, and ought to be avoided. Whilst the ancient practice certainly appears to have been to make some slight change in the crest, it does not seem to have been debruised in the present manner. There are some number of more recent cases where, whilst the existing arms have been charged with the necessary marks of distinction, entirely new, or very much altered crests have been granted without any recognisable "marks of distinction." There can be no doubt that the bendlet wavy sinister upon the crest is a palpable penalising of the bearer, and I think the whole subject of the marks of bastardy in the three kingdoms might with advantage be brought under official consideration, with a view to new regulations being adopted. A bendlet wavy sinister is such an absolute defacement of a crest that few can care to make use of a crest so marked. It carries an effect far beyond what was originally the intention of marks of distinction.

The last few bastardised exemplifications which have issued from Ulster's Office have had the crest charged with a baton couped sinister. The baton couped sinister has always hitherto been confined to the arms of Royal bastards, but there was no exclusive reservation of it to

358

THE ART OF HERALDRY

such circumstances. Of course no circumstances can be conceived in which it is necessary to debruise supporters, as under no circumstances can these be the subject of a Royal Licence of this character. They signify some definite honour which cannot ordinarily survive illegitimacy.

The bordure wavy is placed round the pronominal arms only, and no right to any quarterings the family may have enjoyed previously is conferred, except such right to a quarterly coat as might ensue through the assumption of a double name. Quartering is held to signify representation which cannot be given by a Royal Licence, but a quartering of augmentation or a duplicate coat for the pronominal name which had been so regularly used with the alternative coat as to constitute the two something in the nature of a compound coat, would be exemplified " all within a bordure wavy." Each illegitimate coat stands on its own basis, and there is a well-known instance in which a marriage was subsequently found to be illegal, or to have never taken place, after which, I believe, some number of brothers and sisters obtained Royal Licences and exemplifications. The descendants of one of the brothers will be found in the current Peerage Books, and those who know their peerage history well will recognise the case I allude to. All the brothers and sisters had the same arms exemplified, each with a bordure wavy *of a different colour*. If there were descendants of any of the sisters, those descendants would have been entitled to quarter the arms, because the illegitimacy made each sister an heiress for heraldic purposes. This is a curious anomaly, for had they been legitimate the descendants would have enjoyed no such right.

In Scotland the mark of illegitimacy for the arms is the bordure compony, which is usually but not always indicative of the same. The bordure counter-compony has been occasionally stated to have the same character. This is hardly correct, though it may be so in a few isolated cases, but the bordure chequy has nothing whatever of an illegitimate character. It will be noticed that whilst the bordure compony and the bordure counter-compony have their chequers or "panes," to use the heraldic term, following the outline of the shield, by lines parallel to those which mark its contour, the bordure chequy is drawn by lines parallel to and at right angles to the palar line of the shield, irrespective of the outline. A bordure chequy must, of course, at one point or another show three rows of checks.

The bastardising of crests even in England is a comparatively modern practice. I know of no single instance ancient or modern of the kind in Scottish heraldry, though I could mention scores of achievements in which the shields carry marks of distinction. This is valuable evidence, for no matter how lax the official practice of Scottish armory may have been at one period, the theory of Scottish armory far more nearly approaches the ancient practices and rules of heraldry than does the armory of any other country. That theory is much nearer the ideal theory than the English one, but unfortunately for the practical purposes of modern heraldic needs, it does not answer so well. At the present day, therefore, a Scottish crest is not marked in any way.

Most handbooks refer to a certain rule which is supposed to exist for the differencing of a coat to denote illegitimacy when the coat is that of the mother and not the father, the supposed method being to depict the arms under a surcoat, the result being much the same as if the whole of the arms appeared in exaggerated flaunches, the remainder of the shield being left vacant. As a matter of fact only one instance is known, and consequently we must consider it as a new coat devised to bear reference to the old one, and not as a regularised method of differencing for a particular set of circumstances.

In Ireland the rules are to all intents and purposes the same as in England, with the exception of the occasional use of a sinister baton instead of a bendlet wavy sinister upon the crest. In Scotland, where Royal Licences are unknown, it is merely necessary to prove paternity, and rematriculate the arms with due and proper marks of distinction.

It was a very general idea during a former period, but subsequently to the time when the bendlet sinister and the bordure were recognised as in the nature of the accepted marks of bastardy, and when their penal nature was admitted, that whatever mark was adopted for the purpose of indicating illegitimacy need only be borne for three generations. Some of the older authorities tell us that after that length of time had elapsed it might be discarded, and some other and less objectionable mark be taken in its place. The older writers were striving, consciously or unconsciously, to reconcile the disgrace of illegitimacy which they knew with heraldic facts which they also knew, and to reconcile in certain prominent families undoubted illegitimacy with unmarked arms, the probability being that their sense of justice and regard for heraldry prompted them to the remark that some other mark of distinction *ought* to be added, whilst all the time they knew it never was. The arms of Byron, Somerset, Meinill, and Herbert are all cases where the marks of illegitimacy have been quietly dropped, entire reversion being had to the undifferenced original coat. At a time when marks of illegitimacy, both in fact and in theory, were nothing more than marks of cadency and difference from the arms of the head of the house, it was no venality of the heralds, but merely the acceptance of current ideas, that permitted them to recognise the undifferenced arms for the illegitimate descendants when there were no legitimate owners from whose claim the arms of the others needed to be differentiated, and when lordships and lands had lapsed to a bastard branch. To this fact must be added another. The armorial control of the heralds after the days of tournaments was exercised through the Visitations and the Earl Marshal's Court. Peers were never subject to the Visitations, and so were not under control unless their arms were challenged in the Earl Marshal's Court by the rightful owner. The cases that are notorious are cases of the arms of peers.

The Visitations gave the officers of arms greater control over the arms of Commoners than they had had theretofore, and the growing social opinions upon legitimacy and marriage brought social observances more into conformity with the technical law, and made that technical law of no inheritance and no paternity an operative fact. The result is that the hard legal fact is now rigidly and rightly insisted upon, and the claim and right to arms of one of illegitimate descent depends and is made to depend solely upon the instruments creating that right, and the conditions of "due and proper marks of distinction" subject to which the right is called into being. Nowadays there is no release from the penalty of the bordures wavy and compony save through the avenue of a new and totally different grant and the full fees payable therefor. But, as the bearer of a bordure wavy once remarked to me, " I had rather descend illegitimately from a good family and bear their arms marked than descend from a lot of nobodies and use a new grant." But until the common law is altered, if it ever is, the game must be played fairly and the conditions of a Royal Licence observed, for the sins of the fathers are visited upon the children.

Although I have refrained from giving any extended list of bastardised coats as examples of the rules for indicating illegitimacy, reference may nevertheless be made to various curious examples.

The canton has occasionally been used. Sir John de Warren, a natural son of John, Earl of Surrey, Sussex, and Warenne (*d.* 1347), bore a canton of the arms of his mother, Alice de Nerford ["Gules, a lion rampant ermine"], over the chequy shield of Warren. A similar instance can be found in modern times, the arms of Charlton of Apley Castle, co. Salop, being bastardised by a sinister canton which bears two coats quarterly, these coats having formerly been quarterings borne in the usual manner.

The custom of placing the paternal arms upon a bend has been occasionally adopted, but this of course is the creation of a *new* coat. It was followed by the Beauforts (see page 356) before their legitimation, and by Sir Roger de Clarendon, the illegitimate son of the Black Prince (see page 182 and Plate LXVII. Fig. 31). The Somerset family, who derived illegitimately from the Beauforts, Dukes of Somerset, first debruised the Beaufort arms by a bendlet sinister, but in the next generation the arms were placed upon a wide fess, this on a plain field of or. Although the Somersets, Dukes of Beaufort, have discarded all signs of bastardy from their shield, the version upon the fess was continued as one of the quarterings upon the arms of the old Shropshire family of Somerset Fox. One of the most curious bastardised coats is that of Henry Fitz-Roy, Duke of Richmond and Somerset, illegitimate son of Henry VIII. (Fig. 911). This shows the Royal Arms within a bordure quarterly ermine and counter-compony or and azure, debruised by a baton sinister argent, an inescutcheon quarterly gules and vairé [doubtless hinting at the Blount arms of his mother, barry nebuly or and sable], or and vert, over all a lion rampant argent, on a chief azure a tower between two stags' heads caboshed argent, attired or. The ownership of the arms depicted on Plate XCIX. Fig. 10, described as the arms of

FIG. 911.—Arms of Henry FitzRoy,
Duke of Richmond.

the King's brother, and showing England debruised by an escarbuncle azure, is an absolute mystery to me. The escarbuncle is attributed as a badge to Henry II., and there is good reason to suppose he derived it from Anjou. It is not unlikely it is intended for one of his sons, or for one of the illegitimate sons of King John. It will be seen (Fig. 41) on the shield of Geoffrey, Count of Anjou, and appears as the sole charge on the arms of his natural son Hamelin, Earl of Surrey and Warenne (Fig. 626), and elsewhere herein as the crest of his descendant, John de Warenne, Earl of Surrey.

Some Continental examples of arms, differenced either for bastardy or cadency, are to be seen on Plate LXVII. It will be seen therefrom that in France it is not always possible to decide from the arms alone whether the line be legitimate or illegitimate. Fig. 6 thereupon shows the shield of the old Dukes of Bourbon, viz. France (ancient) debruised by a bendlet gules. At a later date these Bourbons (Condé Bourbons) shortened the bendlet to a

baton (see Fig. 7 on the same Plate), and it should be noticed that the baton in France was depicted very much smaller than was ever the case in this country. The Princes of Bourbon Conti (cadets of the House of Condé) added the bordure gules as in Fig. 8. All these were legitimate.

The Counts of Toulouse, whose line was illegitimate, bore the same arms but with a sinister baton. How insignificant was such a mark can be seen from Fig. 912, which represents the seal of Louis Alexandre de Bourbon,

FIG. 912.—Seal of Louis Alexandre de Bourbon,
Count of Toulouse.

Comte of Toulouse, Duke of Damville, Penthièvre Château-villain and Rambouillet, Peer of France, the natural son of Louis XIV. and the Marquise de Montespan. The arms of France, differenced as stated above, are surrounded by the collars of the Orders of St. Michael and of the Holy Ghost. The anchor upon which the shield is displayed is the badge of his office of Lord High Admiral of France.

Fig. 10 on Plate LXVII. shows the coat of the Dukes of Montpensier, viz. the arms of France debruised by a bend dexter gules, the upper part being charged with the arms of Dauphiné. The following shield (Fig. 11) is that of the Duc de Vendome, son of Henry IV. by Gabrielle d'Estrées, and Fig. 12 on the same plate is the shield of the Counts d'Evreux, who were legitimate, as were also the Counts d'Etámpes, who differenced (Fig. 15) by a bordure compony ermine and gules. The Dukes of Touraine bore a bordure engrailed compony gules and argent (Fig. 16). Fig. 18, also on Plate LXVII., shows the arms of John, the Bastard "de Luxembourg," Seigneur de Haubourdin (1457). Here a bendlet sinister azure is the mark. The next shield is that of Joseph Zabeltitz (natural son of Prince Xavier of Saxony). Here the shield of Saxony is debruised by a fess sable. Fig. 20 shows the arms of Francis Louis, Count of Holnstein, illegitimate son of the Elector Charles Albert of Bavaria. Here the curious coat of Bavaria is debruised by a baton sinister gules. Plate LXVII. Fig. 21 depicts the coat of John George, Count von Sontheim (1807), the natural son of Duke Ludwig of Würtemberg, the arms of that country being charged with a bendlet sinister gules. The last example on that Plate (Fig. 22) shows the arms of James Welser, natural son of James Welser of Nürnberg, legitimated by the Emperor Charles in 1545. Here a sinister bendlet azure is employed.

A. C. F-D. AND H. S.

PLATE CXIV.

THE ROYAL ARMS OF GREAT BRITAIN, AS DETERMINED BY THE WARRANT,
IN THE REIGN OF QUEEN VICTORIA.

PLATE CXV.

ARMS OF SOVEREIGNTY, DOMINION, &c.

PLATE CXVI.

BIRMINGHAM.

MANCHESTER.

LONDON.

LIVERPOOL.

NEWCASTLE-ON-TYNE.

COATS OF ARMS OF TOWNS.

PLATE CXVII.

GLASGOW.

LEEDS.

EDINBURGH.

SHEFFIELD.

BRISTOL.

COATS OF ARMS OF TOWNS.

PLATE CXVIII.

COATS OF ARMS OF TOWNS.

PLATE CXIX.

ARMS GRANTED TO THE CARPENTERS COMPANY.
OF LONDON. 6TH EDWARD VI, 1466.

ARMS GRANTED TO THE MASONS COMPANY.
OF LONDON. 12TH EDWARD IV. 1472-3.

ARMS OF THE SCULPTURES OR MARBLERS,
FROM THE GATESHEAD CHARTER, 1671.

ARMS OF THE FREE MASONS,
FROM THE GATESHEAD CHARTER, 1671.

ARMS OF CORPORATE BODIES.

PLATE CXX.

THE GRANT OF SUPPORTERS TO THE TALLOW CHANDLERS' COMPANY.

PLATE CXXI.

DRAPERS' COMPANY.

INSTITUTE OF CHARTERED ACCOUNTANTS.

BANK OF SCOTLAND.

MERCERS' COMPANY.

GOLDSMITHS' COMPANY.

COATS OF ARMS OF TRADE CORPORATIONS.

PLATE CXXII.

ARMS OF SOCIETIES AND CORPORATIONS.

PLATE CXXIII.

THE TRINITY HOUSE.

STATIONERS' COMPANY.

GREAT CENTRAL RAILWAY COMPANY.

FISHMONGERS' COMPANY.

NORTH BORNEO COMPANY.

CARPENTERS' COMPANY.

CUTLERS' COMPANY OF SHEFFIELD

COATS OF ARMS OF TRADE CORPORATIONS.

PLATE CXXIV.

PAINTED PANEL IN THE POSSESSION OF
W. HY RYLANDS, *circa 1680.*

HOLINESS TO THE LORD

BANNER IN THE POSSESSION OF THE LODGE
OF YORK. *circa 1779.*

Arms of the
CITY OF COLOGNE.

STONE MASONS OF STRASBURG.
from seal circa 1725.

STONE MASONS OF NURENBURG.
from seal circa 1725.

The arms borne by
GRAND LODGE OF ALL ENGLAND.
circa 1725.

IN GOD IS AL OVR TRVST

BRICKLAYERS AND TILERS.
from Gateshead charter 1671.

MASONS OF COLOGNE.
from seal 1396 (colours restored)

ARMS OF MASONIC AND KINDRED BODIES.

PLATE CXXV.

TILERS *OF TOURS*

TILERS *LA ROCHELLE*

MASONS *SAUMUR*

MASONS *TOURS*

TILERS *PARIS*

CARPENTERS *VILLEFRANCHE*

JOINERS *METZ*

CARPENTERS *BAYONNE*

MASONS *BEAULIEU*

MS. ROLL DATED 1686 *MUSEUM 33 GOLDEN SQUARE*

MS. ROLL DATED 1686 *LODGE OF ANTIQUITY Nº 2*

ARMS OF THE MASONS *GERMAN from an old drawing A.D. 1515 (Heideloff.)*

CARPENTERS *ANGERS*

JOINERS *PERONNE*

JOINERS *AMIENS*

JOINERS *LONDON Stow 1633*

MARBLERS *LONDON Stow 1633*

MASON'S COMPANY *LONDON Stow 1633*

CARPENTERS *LONDON Stow 1633*

MASON'S COMPANY *EDINBURGH Burke (description)*

ARMS OF MASONS, CARPENTERS, &c.

PLATE CXXVI.

PLATE CXXVII.

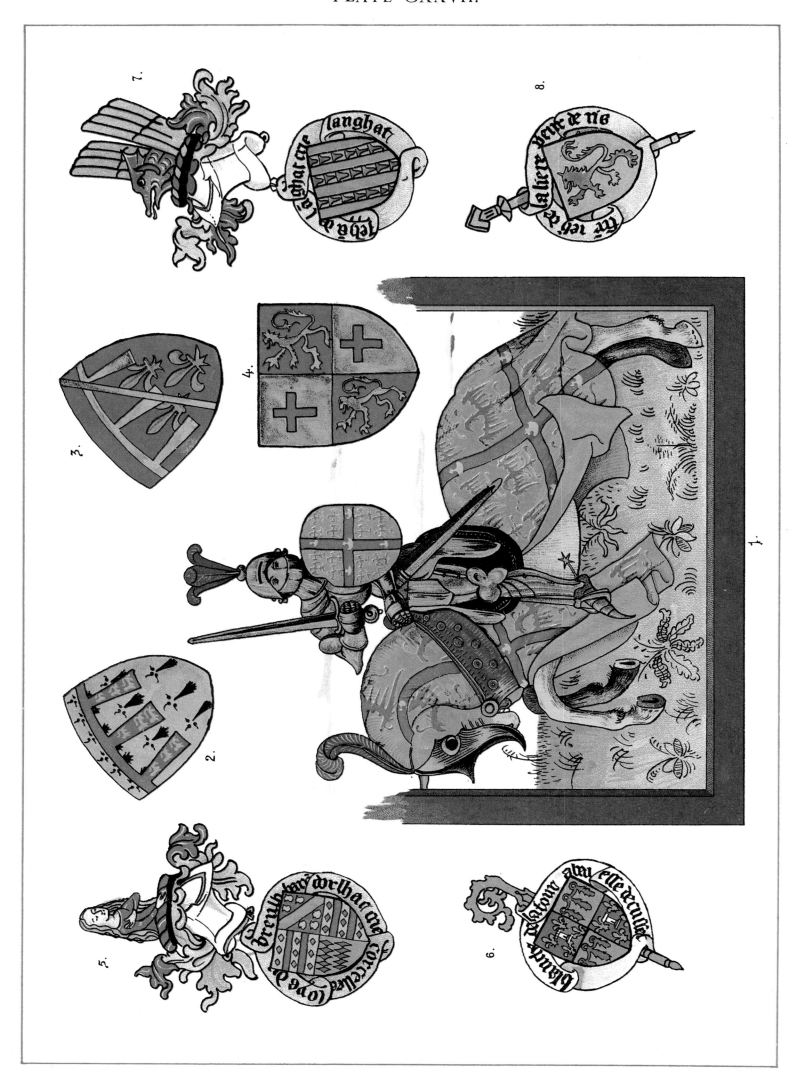

EXAMPLES OF FRENCH HERALDRY.

PLATE CXXVIII.

PLATE CXXIX.

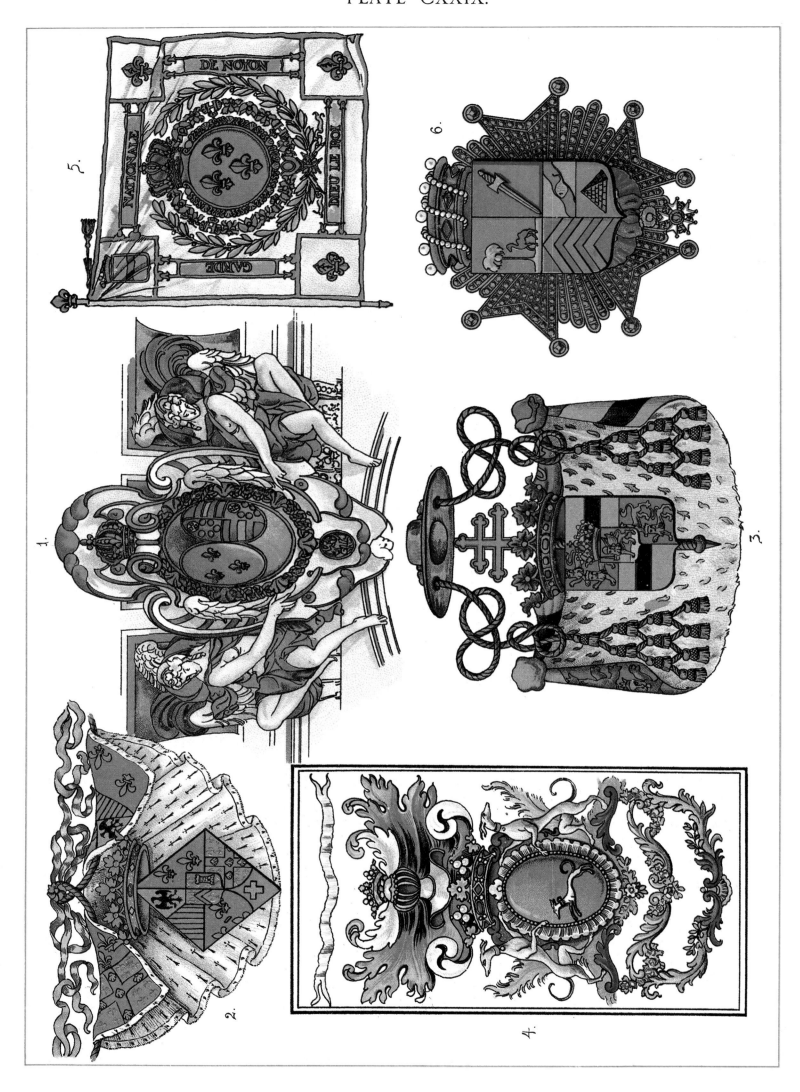

EXAMPLES OF FRENCH HERALDRY.

THE ART OF HERALDRY

CHAPTER XXXVII

THE MARSHALLING OF ARMS

THE science of marshalling is the conjoining of two or more coats of arms upon one shield for the purpose of indicating sovereignty, dominion, alliance, descent, or pretension, according to recognised rules and regulations, by the employment of which the story of any given achievement shall be readily translatable.

The methods of marshalling are (1) dimidiation, (2) impalement, (3) quartering, (4) superimposition.

Instances of quartered shields are to be met with possibly before impalements or dimidiation. The earliest attempt at anything like a regularised method of procedure to signify marriage was that usually males *quartered* the arms of their wives or ancestresses from whom they acquired their lands; whilst impaled coats were to all intents and purposes the armorial bearings of married women, or more frequently of widows who took an immediate interest in their husbands' property. This ancient usage brings home very forcibly the former territorial connection of arms and land. The practice of the husband impaling the wife's arms, whether heiress or not, probably arose near the close of the fifteenth century. Even now it is laid down that the arms of a wife should not in general be borne upon the husband's banner, surcoat, or official seal. But impalement as we now know it was preceded by dimidiation.

Dimidiation, which was but a short-lived method, was effected by the division of the shield down the centre. On the dexter side was placed the dexter half of the husband's arms, and on the sinister side was placed the sinister half of the wife's arms. With some coats of arms no objection could be urged against the employment of this method. But it was liable to result (*e.g.* with two coats of arms having the same ordinary) in the creation of a design which looked far more like one simple coat than a conjunction of two. The dimidiation of "argent, a bend gules" and "argent, a chevron sable" would simply result in a single coat "argent, a bend per pale gules and sable." This fault of the system must have made itself manifest at an early period, for we soon find it became customary to introduce about two-thirds of the design of each coat for the sake of demonstrating their separate character. It must soon thereafter have become apparent that if two-thirds of the design of a coat of arms could be squeezed into half of the shield, there was no valid reason why the whole of the design could not be employed. This therefore became customary under the name of impalement, and the practice has ever since remained with us. Few examples indeed of dimidiation are to be met with, and as a practical method of conjunction, the practice was chiefly in vogue during the earlier part of the fourteenth century.

Occasionally quartered coats were dimidiated, in which case the first and third quarters of the husband's coat were conjoined with the second and fourth of the wife's. As far as outward appearance went, this practice resulted in the fact that no distinction existed from a plain quartered coat. Thus the seal of Margaret of Bavaria, Countess of Holland, and wife of John, Count de Nevers, in 1385 (afterwards Duke of Burgundy), bears a shield on which is apparently a simple instance of quartering, but really a dimidiated coat. The two coats to the dexter side of the palar line are: In chief Burgundy-Modern ("France-Ancient, a bordure compony argent and gules"), and in base Burgundy-Ancient. On the sinister side the coat in chief is Bavaria ("Bendy-lozengy argent and azure"); and the one in base

contains the quartered arms of Flanders ("Or, a lion rampant sable"); and Holland ("Or, a lion rampant gules"); the pourfilar lines dividing these latter quarters being omitted, as is usually found to be the case with this particular shield.

Certain examples can be found amongst the Royal Arms in England which show much earlier instances of dimidiation. The arms of Margaret of France, who died in 1319, the second queen of Edward I., remain on her tomb in Westminster Abbey as an example of this method of conjunction. The arms of England appear on the dexter side of the escocheon; and this coat undergoes a certain amount of curtailment, though the dimidiation is not complete, portions only of the hindmost parts of the lions being cut off by the palar line. The coat of France, on the sinister side, of course does not readily indicate the dimidiation.

Boutell, in his chapter on marshalling in "Heraldry, Historical and Popular," gives several early examples of dimidiation. The seal of Edmond Plantagenet, Earl of Cornwall (*d.* 1300), bears his arms (those of Richard, Earl of Cornwall, and King of the Romans) dimidiating those of his wife, Margaret de Clare. Here only the sinister half of his bordure is removed, while the Clare coat ("Or, three chevrons gules") is entirely dimidiated, and the chevrons are little distinguishable from bends. Both coats are dimidiated in other examples mentioned by Boutell, viz. William de Valence and his wife, and Alianore Montendre and her husband Guy Ferre. On the seal of Margaret Campbell, wife of Alexander Napier, in 1531, the shield shows upon the dexter side the arms of Lennox, and on the sinister the dimidiated coat (the sinister half of the quartered arms) of Campbell and Lorn. This results in the galley of Lorn being in chief, and the Campbell gyrons in base.

An early and interesting Irish example of this kind of marshalling is afforded by a dimidated coat of Clare and Fitzgerald, which now figures on the official seal of the Provosts of Youghal (Clare: "Or, three chevrons gules." Fitzgerald: "Argent, a saltire gules, with a label of five points in chief.") Both these coats are halved. They result from the marriage of Richard Clare, Earl of Hereford, with Juliana, daughter and heir of Maurice Fitz-Gerald, feudal lord of Inchiquin and Youghal.

An even more curious case of dimidiation comes to light in the arms formerly used by the Abbey of St. Etienne at Caen, in which the arms of England and those attributed to the Duchy of Normandy ("Gules, two lions passant guardant or") were dimidiated, so that in the former half three of the fore-quarters of the lions appear, while in the sinister half only two of the hind-quarters are represented.

Dimidiation was not always effected by conjunction down the palar line, other partition lines of the shield being occasionally, though very rarely, employed in this manner.

Certain curious (now indivisible) coats of arms remain which undoubtedly originated in the dimidiation of two separate coats, *e.g.* the arms of Yarmouth, Sandwich, Hastings, Rye, and Chester. In all cases some Royal connection can be traced which has caused the Royal Arms of England to be conjoined with the earlier devices of fish, ships, or garbs which had been employed by the towns in question. It is worth the passing thought, however, whether the conjoined lions and hulks used by the Cinque Ports may not originally have been a device of the Sovereign for naval purposes, or possibly the naval version of the Royal Arms (see pages 128 and 129).

One other remainder from the practice of dimidiation still survives amongst the presently existing rules of heraldry. It is a rule to which no modern authoritative exception can be mentioned. When a coat within a bordure is impaled with another coat, the bordure is not continued down the centre of the shield, but stops short at top and bottom when the palar line is reached (Figs. 165, 200, 260). This rule is undoubtedly a result of the ancient method of conjunction by dimidiation, but the curious point is that, at the period when dimidiation was employed and during the period which followed, some number of examples can be found where the bordure is continued round the whole coat which is within it (Fig. 201).

The arms of man and wife are now conjoined according to the following rules :—If the wife is not an heiress the two coats are impaled (Figs. 53, 65, 82, 96, 100a, 108, 110, 255, 258, 262, 299, 305). If the wife be an heraldic heir or coheir, in lieu of impalement the arms of her family are placed on an inescutcheon superimposed on the centre of her husband's arms, the inescutcheon being termed an escutcheon of pretence, because *jure uxoris* she being an heiress of her house, the husband "pretends" to the representation of her family (Figs. 105, 129, 321, 436, 464, and 512).

For heraldic purposes it therefore becomes necessary to define the terms heir and heiress. It is very essential that the point should be thoroughly understood, because quarterings other than those of augmentation can only be inherited from or through female ancestors who are in themselves heirs or coheirs (this is the true term, or, rather, the ancient term, though they are now usually referred to colloquially as heiresses or coheiresses) in blood, or whose issue subsequently become in a later generation the representatives of any ancestor in the male line of that female ancestor. A woman is an "heir" or "heiress" (1) if she is an only child; (2) if all her brothers die without leaving any issue to survive, either male or female; (3) she becomes an heiress "in her issue," as it is termed, if she die leaving issue herself if and when all the descendants male and female of her brothers become absolutely extinct. The term "coheir" or "coheiress" is employed in cases similar to the foregoing when, instead of one daughter, there are two or more. The table on page 363 may make things a little clearer.

No person can be "heir or "coheir" of another person until the latter is dead, though he or she may be heir-apparent or heir-presumptive. Though the word "heir" is frequently used with regard to material matters, such usage is really there incorrect, except in cases of intestacy. A person benefiting under a will is a legatee of money, or a devisee of land, and not an heir to either. In this article intestacy is ignored, and the explanations apply solely to *heirship of blood*.

Charles in the accompanying pedigree is, after 1800, *heir* of David. Thomas is *heir-apparent* of Charles, being a son and the eldest born. He dies *v.p.* (*vita patris, i.e.* in the lifetime of his father) and never becomes heir. A daughter can never become an heir-apparent, as there is always, during the lifetime of her father, the possibility of a son being born. Mary, Ellen, and Blanche are coheirs of Thomas their father, whom they survive, and they are also coheirs of their grandfather Charles, to whom they succeed, and they would properly in a pedigree be described as both. They are heirs-general of Thomas, Charles, and David, and, being the heirs of the senior line, they are heirs-general or coheirs-general of their house. David being possessed of the barony " by

writ " of Cilfowyr, it would " fall into abeyance " at the death of Charles between the three daughters equally.

In Scotland Mary, Ellen, and Blanche would be termed " heirs portioners," and Mary, being an heiress and the eldest born in the direct and senior line, would be termed the " heir of line." David being possessed of an ancient Scottish peerage not limited to males (the Earldom of Edinburgh), Mary, the heir of line, would at once succeed in her own right as Countess of Edinburgh on the death of her grandfather Charles. If the family were an untitled Scottish family entitled to supporters, these would descend to Mary unless they had been specifically granted with some other limitation.

At the death of Thomas in 1830 Edmond becomes heir male apparent, and at the death of his father in 1840 Edmond becomes heir male of his house until his death. David having been created a peer (Duke of London) with remainder to the heirs male of his body, Edmond succeeded as Duke of London at the death of Charles in 1840. Grace and Muriel are coheirs of Edmond after his death. They are *not* either coheirs or heirs-general of Charles, in spite of the fact that their father was his heir male. At the death of Charles in 1840, when Edmond succeeded as heir male, John succeeded as heir male presumptive to Edmond. He was not heir-apparent, because a son might at any moment have been born to Edmond. An heir-apparent and an heir-presumptive cannot exist at the same time, for whilst there is an heir-apparent there cannot be an heir-presumptive. John succeeded as heir male of his house, and therefore as Duke of London, in 1850, at the death of his elder brother Edmond; but, though John was the " heir male " of his said elder brother, he was *not* his " heir " (Grace and Muriel being the coheirs of Edmond), nor was he the " heir male of the body " of Edmond, not being descended from him. John, however, was "heir male of the body " of Charles. George is heir-apparent of John until his death in 1870, when George succeeds as " heir " of his father and heir male of his house, and consequently Duke of London. At his death in 1880 Dorothy becomes the " sole heir," or, more properly, the " sole heir-general," of her father George; but his kinsman Robert becomes his " heir male," and therefore Duke of London, in spite of the fact that there was a much nearer male relative, viz. a nephew, Arthur, the son of his sister. Robert also becomes the heir male of the body of Owen and heir male of his house, and as such Duke of London. He would also be generally described as the heir male of the body of David.

At the death of Dorothy in 1885 her coheirs were her aunt Alice and her cousin Arthur equally, and though these really were the coheirs of *Dorothy* (the claims of Alice and Annie being equal, and the rights of Annie having devolved upon Arthur), they would more usually be found described as the coheirs of George or of John. Annie was never *herself* really a coheir, because she died before her brother, but "in her issue " she became the coheir of Dorothy, though she would, after 1885, be usually described as "in her issue " a coheir of George, or possibly even of John, though this would be an inexact description. Arthur was heir of his mother after 1870, heir of his father after 1872, and heir-apparent of his father before that date; after 1885 he is a coheir of Dorothy, and after 1887 sole heir of Dorothy and sole heir of Alice. He would also be usually described as heir-general of George, and heir-general of John. Let us suppose that John had married Edith Torkington, an English baroness (*suo jure*) by writ (Baroness Neville), who had died in 1862. At that date the barony would have descended to her eldest son George until his death in 1880, when Dorothy, *suo jure*, would have succeeded. At her death in 1885 the barony would have fallen into abeyance between Alice and Arthur. At the death of Alice in

DAVID CILFOWYR, created Duke of London in the Peerage of the United Kingdom, remainder to him and the heirs male of his body, was Earl of Edinburgh in the Peerage of Scotland (with remainder to his heirs), and Lord Cilfowyr by writ in the Peerage of England (with remainder to his heirs general). Died 1800.

CHARLES CILFOWYR, elder son and heir; head of his house, Duke of London, Earl of Edinburgh, and Lord Cilfowyr. Died 1840.

OWEN CILFOWYR, Esq., commonly called Lord Owen Cilfowyr by courtesy. Died 1870.

THOMAS CILFOWYR, Esq., eldest son and heir-apparent, styled Earl of Edinburgh by courtesy. Died *v.p.* 1830, so never succeeds.

ROBERT CILFOWYR, Esq., eldest son, becomes heir male of his house in 1880 at the death of George, and as such succeeds as Duke of London. Died 1896.

PHILIP CILFOWYR, Esq., second son. Died 1879.

ADA, only child, has no courtesy title. Living 1900.

CECIL CILFOWYR, Esq., third son. When his brother succeeds in 1880 as Duke of London he petitions the Queen for that style and precedence which he would have enjoyed had his father lived to inherit the Dukedom. His petition being granted, he becomes by courtesy Lord Cecil Cilfowyr, until he succeeds in 1896, at the death of his brother, to the Dukedom of London.

HARRIET CILFOWYR, only child, by courtesy after 1880 Lady Harriet Cilfowyr. Died 1897.

MARY CILFOWYR, Countess of Edinburgh. Living 1900. *Heir of Line.*

EDMOND CILFOWYR, Esq., second son, styled by courtesy Lord Edmond Cilfowyr until 1840, when he succeeds as Duke of London. Died 1850.

ELLEN CILFOWYR, styled by courtesy Lady Ellen Cilfowyr. Living 1900.

BLANCHE CILFOWYR, styled by courtesy Lady Blanche Cilfowyr. Living 1900.

GRACE CILFOWYR, styled by courtesy Lady Grace Cilfowyr, elder dau. Living 1900.

MURIEL CILFOWYR, styled by courtesy Lady Muriel Cilfowyr. Living 1900.

The Barony of Cilfowyr falls into abeyance between these three equally. In Scottish phraseology they are termed heirs portioners.

363

JOHN CILFOWYR, Esq., third son, styled by courtesy Lord John Cilfowyr until 1850, when he succeeds as Duke of London. Died 1870. = EDITH TORKINGTON, succeeds in 1861 as *suo jure* Baroness Neville by writ in England, and Countess of Torkington (to herself and her heirs) in Scotland). Died 1862.

GEORGE CILFOWYR, Esq., only son, and so styled until 1850, when his father succeeds as Duke of London. As son of a Duke he then becomes by courtesy Lord George Cilfowyr, and this is his proper description, because his father has no minor title which he could assume. But by a quite modern custom which has sprung up of late years he would very probably call himself "Lord Cilfowyr." In 1861 his mother succeeds in her own right to two titles, and by courtesy he would thenceforward be styled by her minor title as Lord Neville until her death in 1862, when he becomes Earl of Torkington in his own right and also Lord Neville. At his father's death in 1870 he becomes Duke of London. Died 1880.

ALICE CILFOWYR, styled by courtesy Lady Alice Cilfowyr until 1885, when she succeeds as Countess of Torkington. Died 1887, *s.p.*

DOROTHY CILFOWYR, styled Lady Dorothy Cilfowyr until 1880, when she becomes *suo jure* Countess of Torkington and Baroness Neville. Died *s.p.* 1885.

IRENE CILFOWYR, styled by courtesy as Lady Irene Cilfowyr. Living 1900.

ISABEL CILFOWYR, styled by courtesy as Lady Isobel Cilfowyr. Living 1900.

ANNIE CILFOWYR, styled by courtesy Lady Annie Cilfowyr and Lady Annie Sherwin. Died 1870. = REGINALD SHERWIN. Died 1872.

ARTHUR SHERWIN, only son and heir, succeeds as Earl of Torkington and Lord Neville in 1887, at the death of his aunt. Died 1888.

LILIAN SHERWIN, daughter, known as Lady Lilian Sherwin until 1896, when she succeeds as Countess of Torkington and Baroness Neville. Living 1900.

MARIA SHERWIN, called by courtesy Lady Maria Sherwin, succeeds in 1888 as Countess of Torkington and senior coheir to the barony of Neville, which falls into abeyance between herself and her sisters. The Queen determines the abeyance in her favour, and she consequently becomes also Baroness Neville. Died *s.p.* 1889.

JANE SHERWIN, by courtesy Lady Jane Sherwin, succeeds as Countess of Torkington in 1889, but the Barony of Neville again falls into abeyance between herself and her younger sister. Died *s.p.* 1890.

HANNAH SHERWIN, called by courtesy Lady Hannah Sherwin. She succeeds in 1890 as sole heir of her father, and consequently the abeyance determines of itself, and she becomes both Countess of Torkington and Baroness Neville. Died *s.p.* 1896.

1887 the abeyance would be at an end, and the barony in its entirety would have devolved upon Arthur, who would have enjoyed it until at his death in 1888 the barony would have again fallen into abeyance between Maria, Jane, and Hannah equally. It is not unlikely that Her Majesty might have "determined the abeyance," or "called the barony out of abeyance" (the meanings of the terms are identical) in favour of Maria, who would consequently have enjoyed the barony in its entirety. At her death in 1889 it would again fall into abeyance between Jane and Hannah. At Jane's death in 1890 Hannah became sole heir, and the abeyance came to an end when Hannah succeeded to the barony. At her death it would pass to her aunt Lilian. Hannah would usually be described as "coheir and subsequently sole heir of" Arthur. If the Baroness Neville had been possessed of an ancient Scottish Peerage (the Earldom of Torkington) it would have passed undividedly and in full enjoyment to the heir of line, i.e. in 1862 to George, 1880 to Dorothy, 1885 to Alice, 1887 to Arthur, 1888 to Maria, 1889 to Jane, 1890 to Hannah, and 1896 to Lilian, the last (shown on the pedigree) in remainder. Lilian does not become an heiress until 1896, when the whole issue of her brother becomes extinct. Irene and Isabel never become heirs at all.

Robert, as we have seen, became heir male of his house and Duke of London in 1880. At his death (1896) Harriet becomes sole heir of Robert, but at her death in 1897 his niece Ada, the only child of his younger brother Philip, who had predeceased him, would be usually referred to as heir of Robert, whilst Cecil is heir male of his house.

When the term "of the body" is employed, *actual descent* from that person is signified, *e.g.* Arthur after 1885 is "collateral" heir-general of Dorothy, but heir-general of the body of Edith Torkington.

An "heir of entail," or, to use the Scottish term, the "heir of tailzie," is merely the person succeeding to *property* under a specific remainder contained in a deed of entail. This has no relation to heirship in blood, and the term, from an armorial point of view, might be entirely disregarded, were it not that some number of Scottish coats of arms, and a greater number of Scottish supporters, are specifically granted and limited to the heir of entail. There are a few similar English grants following upon Royal Licences for change of name and arms.

The term "heir in expectancy" is sometimes heard, but it is not really a proper term, and has no exact or legal meaning. When George was alive his daughter Dorothy was his heir-presumptive, but supposing that Dorothy were a Catholic nun and Alice a lunatic, in each of which cases there would be very little likelihood of any marriage ever taking place, Arthur would very generally be described as the "heir in expectancy," for though he was neither heir-apparent nor heir-presumptive, all probability pointed to the eventual succession of himself or his issue.

Anybody is said to be "in remainder" to entailed property or a peerage if he is included within the recited limits of the entail or peerage. The "heir in remainder" is the person next entitled to succeed after the death of the existing holder.

Thus (excluding heirs in expectancy and women who are heirs-presumptive) a marriage with any woman who is an heir or coheir results in her arms being placed upon an escutcheon of pretence over the arms of the husband. In the cases of all other women the arms are "impaled" only. To "impale two coats" the shield is divided by a straight line down the centre, the whole design of the arms of the husband being placed on the dexter side of the escutcheon, and the whole design of the wife's arms being placed on the sinister side.

It may perhaps be as well to here exemplify the different methods of the conjunction of the arms of man and wife, arranging the same two coats in the different methods in which they might be marshalled before reverting to ancient practices.

An ordinary commoner impales his wife's arms as in Fig. 913. If she be an heiress, he places them on an

FIG. 913.   FIG. 914.

escutcheon of pretence as in Fig. 914. If the husband is a companion of any order, this does not give him the right to use the circle of his order round his arms, and his badge is simply hung below the escutcheon, the arms of the wife being impaled or placed on an escutcheon of pretence thereupon as the case may necessitate. The wife of a Knight Bachelor shares the state and rank with her husband, and the only difference is in the helmet (Figs. 396 and 915). But if the husband be a knight of any

FIG. 915.

order, the ensigns of that order are personal to himself, and cannot be shared with his wife, and consequently two shields are employed. On the dexter shield are the arms of the husband with the circle of his order of knighthood, and on the sinister shield are the arms of the husband impaling the arms of the wife. Some meaningless decoration, usually a wreath of oak-leaves, is placed round the sinister shield to "balance" from the artistic point the ribbon, or the ribbon and collar, as the case may be, of the order of knighthood of the husband (Figs. 358, 498, and 916). A Knight Grand Cross, of course, adds his collar to the dexter shield, and if he has supporters, these are placed outside the *two* shields (Fig. 1).

A peer impales the arms of his wife as in the case of a commoner, the arms of the wife being, of course, under the protection of the supporters, coronet, and helmet of the peer (Fig. 917). If, in addition to being a peer, he is also a knight of an order, he follows the rules which prescribe the use of two shields as already described (Figs. 251 and 407).

Supposing the wife to be a peeress in her own right, she cannot nowadays confer any

FIG. 916.

rank whatever upon her husband; consequently, if she marry a commoner, the husband places her arms upon an escutcheon of pretence surmounted by a coronet of her rank, but the supporters belonging to her peerage cannot be added to his shield. The arms of the wife are consequently repeated alone, but in this case upon a lozenge on the sinister side of the husband's shield. Above this lozenge is placed the coronet of her rank, and the supporters belonging to her peerage are placed on either side of the lozenge (Fig. 918). In the case of a peeress in her own right marrying a peer, the arms of the peeress are placed upon an escutcheon of pretence in the centre of the husband's shield, the only difference being that this escutcheon of

FIG. 917.

pretence is surmounted by the coronet belonging to the peerage of the wife; and on the sinister side the arms of the wife are repeated upon a lozenge with the supporters and coronet belonging to her own peerage. It is purely

an artistic detail, but it is a happy conceit in such an instance to join together the compartments upon which

FIG. 918.

the two pairs of supporters stand to emphasise the fact that the whole is in reality but one achievement (Figs.

FIG. 919.

919 and 920). The former is imaginary, the latter is the achievement of the Earl of Yarborough and his wife, who is in her own right Baroness Fauconberg and Conyers.

Now, it is not uncommon to see an achievement displayed in this manner, for there have been several instances in recent years of peeresses in their own right who have married peers. Every woman who *inherits* a peerage must of necessity be an heir or coheir, and, as will have been seen, the laws of armory provide for this circumstance; but supposing that the peeress were a peeress by creation and were not an heiress, how would her arms be displayed? Apparently it would not be permissible to place them on an escutcheon of pretence, and consequently there is no way upon the husband's shield of showing that his wife is a peeress in her own right. Such an instance did arise in the case of the late Baroness Stratheden, who was created a peeress whilst not being an heiress. Her husband was subsequently created Baron Campbell. Now, how were the arms of Lord Campbell and Lady Stratheden and Campbell displayed? I think I am correct in saying that not a single textbook on armory recites the method which should be employed, and I candidly confess that I myself am quite ignorant upon the point.

All the foregoing are simply instances of how to display the arms of man and wife, or, to speak more correctly, they are instances of the methods *in which a man should bear arms for himself and his wife when he is married;*

for the helmet and mantling clearly indicate that it is the man's coat of arms, and not the woman's. In olden days, when the husband possessed everything, this might have

borne by her father (Fig. 922), or with the latter upon an escutcheon of pretence if the widow be herself an heiress (Fig. 923). The widow of a knight has no way

FIG. 920.—Armorial bearings of the Earl of Yarborough as borne for himself and for his wife, *suo jure* Baroness Fauconberg and Conyers: Quarterly, 1 and 4, the two coats of Pelham, namely : quarterly i. and iiii., azure three Pelicans vulning themselves argent ; ii. and iii. (of augmentation), gules, two pieces of belts with buckles erect in pale, the buckles argent (for Pelham) ; 2 and 3, argent, a chevron between three crosses flory sable (for Anderson), and for and in right of his wife, upon an escutcheon of pretence surmounted by the coronet of her rank, the arms of Fox, namely : argent, a chevron between three foxes' heads erased gules, with many quarterings. Above the escutcheon is placed the coronet of his rank, and there-upon two helmets befitting his degree, the dexter with a mant-ling azure and argent, the sinister with a mantling sable and argent ; and for his crests, 1. upon a wreath of the colours, a peacock in his pride proper (for Pelham) ; 2. upon a wreath of the colours, a water-spaniel dog passant or (for Anderson). Sup-porters : dexter, a bay horse regardant, charged on the body with three ancient buckles gold ; sinister, a water-spaniel dog regardant or, charged on the body with three crosses flory sable ; with the motto, "Vincit amor patriæ ;" and also for and in right of his wife, upon the sinister side of his achievement, upon a lozenge, which is surmounted by the coronet of her rank, the same arms of Fox, with the supporters appertaining to her barony of Conyers, viz. : on either side a lion azure.

been enough for all the circumstances which were likely to occur.

A lady whilst unmarried bears arms on a lozenge (Fig. 921), and upon becoming a widow, bears again upon a lozenge the arms of her husband impaled with the arms

whatever of indicating that her husband was of higher rank than an ordinary untitled gentleman. The widow of a baronet, however, places the inescutcheon with the hand of Ulster upon her husband's arms (Fig. 924). I have often heard this disputed, but a reference to the

Grant Books at the College of Arms (*vide* a grant of arms some years ago to Lady Pearce) will provide the

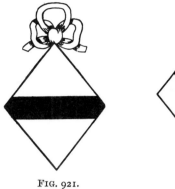

FIG. 921.

FIG. 922.

necessary precedent. If, however, the baronetcy is of Nova Scotia, this means of indicating the rank cannot be

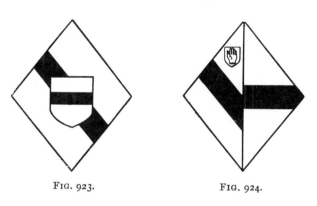

FIG. 923.

FIG. 924.

employed. The widow of a peer (not being a peeress in her own right) uses a lozenge of her husband's and her own arms, with his supporters and his coronet (Fig. 925).

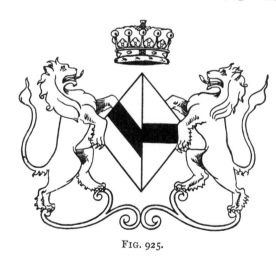

FIG. 925.

If a peeress, after marriage with a commoner, becomes a widow she bears on the dexter side a lozenge of her late husband's arms and superimposed thereupon her own on an escutcheon of pretence surmounted by a coronet. (The coronet, it should be noted, is over the escutcheon of pretence and not above the lozenge.) On the sinister side she bears a lozenge of her own arms alone with her supporters and with her coronet above the lozenge. Fig. 926, which represents the arms of the Baroness Kinloss, shows an example of such an arrangement, of two lozenges, but as Lady Kinloss does not possess supporters these additions could not be introduced.

Impalement is used occasionally in other circumstances than marriage, *i.e.* to effect conjunction of official and personal arms.

FIG. 926.—Armorial bearings of Baroness Kinloss: Upon two lozenges, the dexter being the arms of Morgan-Grenville, namely: quarterly 1 and 4, vert, on a cross argent five torteaux, and for distinction a canton or (for Grenville): 2 and 3, paly of six argent and or, a lion rampant regardant sable, charged on the shoulder with a cross crosslet of the second, between four quatrefoils saltirewise of the third (for Morgan) and upon an escutcheon of pretence, surmounted by the coronet of a Baroness, the arms of Temple-Nugent-Brydges-Chandos-Grenville, namely: quarterly 1 and 6, vert, on a cross argent, five torteaux (for Grenville); 2. quarterly i. and iiii., or, an eagle displayed sable; ii. and iii., argent, two bars sable, each charged with three martlets or (for Temple); 3. ermine, two bars gules (for Nugent); 4. argent, on a cross sable, a leopard's face or (for Brydges); 5. or, a pile gules (for Chandos), and upon the sinister lozenge, which is surmounted by the coronet of a Baroness, the arms and quarterings of Temple-Nugent-Brydges-Chandos-Grenville, namely: quarterly 1 and 8, the arms of Temple-Nugent-Brydges-Chandos-Grenville as previously; 2. argent, on a cross sable, a leopard's face or (for Brydges, Dukes of Chandos); 3. or, a saltire and a chief gules, on a canton argent, a lion rampant azure (for Bruce, Earls of Elgin and Ailesbury); 4. quarterly i. and iiii., or, on a pile gules, between six fleurs-de-lis azure, three lions of England (being the coat of augmentation granted by King Henry VIII. on his marriage with Lady Jane Seymour); ii. and iii., gules, two wings conjoined in leure, points downwards or (for Seymour, Dukes of Somerset); 5. barry of six argent and azure, in chief three torteaux, a label of three points ermine (for Grey, Duke of Suffolk and Marquess of Dorset); 6. barry of ten argent and gules, a lion rampant or, ducally crowned per pale of the first and second (for Brandon, Duke of Suffolk); 7. quarterly i. and iiii., azure, three fleurs-de-lis or (for France); ii. and iii., gules, three lions passant guardant in pale or (for England), being the arms of the Princess Mary (Tudor), younger dau. and co-heir of King Henry VII.; pendent from the lozenges is the Badge of the Order of the Crown of India.

With rare exceptions, the official arms which exist are those of Archiepiscopal and Episcopal Sees, of the Kings of Arms (Figs. 19 and 21), and for the Regius Professors at Cambridge. Here certainly, in the ecclesiastical cases, the theory of marriage remains, the official arms being placed on the dexter side and the personal arms on the sinister, inasmuch as the laws of armory for ecclesiastics were made at a time when the clergy were celibate. The personal helmet and crest are placed above the impaled coat, except in the cases of bishops and archbishops, who, of course, use a mitre in place thereof. It is not correct to impale the arms of a wife upon the same shield which carries the impalement of an official coat of arms, because the wife does not share the office. In such a case it is necessary to make use of two shields placed side by side, as is done in conjoining the arms of a knight of any order with those of his wife.

In impaling the arms of a wife, it is not correct to impale more than her pronominal coat. This is a definite rule in England, somewhat modified in Scotland, as will be presently explained. Though it has never been considered good form to impale a quartered shield, it is only recently that the real fact that such a proceeding is definitely incorrect has come to light. It appears from the State Papers, Domestic Series, Eliz. xxvi. 31, 1561 :—

"At a Chapitre holden by the Office of Armes at the Embroyderers' Hall in London, anno 4° Reginæ Elizabethæ it was agreed that no inhiritrix eyther mayde wife or widow should bear or cause to be borne any Creast or cognizance of her Ancestors otherwise than as followeth. If she be unmarried to bear in her ringe, cognizaunce or otherwise, the first coate of her ancestors in a Lozenge. And during her widdowhood to set the first coate of her husbande in pale with the first coate of her Auncestors. And if she mary on who is noe gentleman, then she to be clearly exempted from the former conclusion."

Whilst this rule holds in England, it must, to a certain extent, be modified in relation to the arms of a Scottish wife. Whilst the inalienable right *to quarter arms derived* from an heiress cannot be said to be non-existent in Scotland, it should be noted that the custom of indiscriminately quartering is much less frequent than in England, and comparatively seldom adopted, unless estates, or chief representation in an important or appreciable degree, follow the technical heraldic representation. In England the claim is always preferred to quarter the arms of an ancestress who had no brothers whether she transmitted estates or not. Of course, technically and theoretically the claim is perfectly correct, and cannot, and should not, be denied. But in practice in England it has in some cases reached a rather absurd extent, when a man on marrying an only daughter of the youngest son of the youngest branch of a family consequently acquires the right to display with his own ensigns the full arms and quarterings of the head of a house from which he has inherited no lands, and which is still thriving in the senior male line. In Scottish practice such an event would be ignored, and in that country it is not usual to add quarterings to a shield, *nor are these officially recognised* without a rematriculation of the arms. In England it is merely a question of recording the pedigree and proving heirship, and many quarterings are proved and recorded that there is not the slightest intention to use regularly. Rematriculation has a more permanent character than mere registration, inasmuch as the coat with its quarterings upon matriculation as far as usage be concerned becomes indivisible, and, consequently, for a Scottish wife the impalement should be of the indivisible arms and quarterings matriculated to her father in Lyon Register, with his bordure and other "difference" marks.

All the old armorists provide ways of impaling at one and the same time the arms of several wives, and consequently the idea has grown up that it is permissible and correct to bear and use the arms of two wives at the same time. This is a mistake, because, strictly and technically speaking, the right to impale the arms of a wife ceases at her death. Impalement means marriage, and when the marriage is dissolved the impalement becomes meaningless, and should be discontinued. A man cannot be married to two people at one time, nor can he as a consequence impale two coats of arms at the same time.

The matter is more clearly apparent if the question of an escutcheon of pretence be considered in place of an impalement. The escutcheon of pretence means that the husband *pretends* to represent the family of his wife. This *jure uxoris* he undoubtedly does whilst she is alive, but the moment she dies the *actual* representation of her family passes to her son and heir, and it is ridiculous for her husband to *pretend* to represent when there is an undoubted representative in existence, and when the representation, such as it was when vested in himself, has come to an end, and passed elsewhere. If his heiress-wife had been a peeress, he would have borne her escutcheon of pretence surmounted by her coronet; but it is ridiculous for him to continue to do so when the right to the coronet and to the peerage has passed to his wife's heir. The same argument holds good with regard to impalement. That, of course, raises the point that in every authority (particularly in those of an earlier period) will be found details of the methods to be adopted for impaling the arms of several wives. People have quite failed to appreciate the object of these rules. Armory from its earliest introduction has had great memorial use, and when a monument or hatchment is put up to a man it has been usual, prior to these utilitarian days of funeral reform, to memorialise *all* the wives he has been possessed of. In the same way, in a pedigree it is necessary to enumerate the names and arms of all the wives of a man. Consequently for tombs and pedigrees—when all being dead, there is no reason to indicate any particular woman as the present *wife*—plans have been devised for the combination of several coats into one memorial achievement, plans necessitated by the circumstances of the cases, and plans to which no objection can be taken. Tombs, pedigrees, and other memorials are the usual form in which the records of arms have chiefly come down to us, and from the frequency in which cases of achievements with double impalements have been preserved, a mistaken idea has arisen that it is correct to bear, and actually use and carry, two impalements at one and the same time. Outside memorial instances, I have utterly failed to find any instance in former days of a man himself using in his own lifetime two impalements, and I believe and state it to be absolutely incorrect for a man to use, say on a carriage, a bookplate, or a seal, the arms of a deceased wife. You may *have been* married to a presently deceased woman, therefore impale her arms in a record or memorial; but no one *is* married to a deceased woman, therefore is it wrong to advertise that you are married to her by impaling her arms; and as you cannot be married to two people at the same time, it is illogical and wrong to *use* or carry two impalements. I know of no instance of a grant to a man of arms to bear in right of a deceased wife. It is for these occasions of memorial and record that methods have been devised to show a man's marriage with several wives. They certainly were not devised for the purpose of enabling him to bear and use for contemporary purposes the arms of a series of dead women, the representation of whom is no longer vested in himself.

Whilst admitting that for purposes of record or memorial rules *do* exist, it should at the same time be pointed out that even for such occasions it is much more usual to see two shields displayed, each carrying its separate impalement, than to find two impalements on one shield. The use of a separate shield for each marriage is the method that I would strongly advocate, but as a knowledge of past observances must be had fully, if one is to read aright the records of the tombs, I recite what the rules are :—

(1) *To impale the arms of two wives.*—Either the husband's arms are placed in the centre, with the first wife on the dexter and the second wife on the sinister, or else the husband's arms are placed on the dexter side, and the sinister side is divided in fess, the arms of the first wife being placed in chief and those of the second in base. The former method is the one more generally employed of the two.

(2) *Three wives.*—Husband's arms in centre, first wife's on dexter side, second wife's on sinister side in chief, and third wife in base.

(3) *Four wives.*—Husband's in centre, first and second wives' in chief and base respectively on the dexter side, and third and fourth similarly on the sinister.

THE ART OF HERALDRY

If one of two wives be an heiress her arms might be found in pretence and the other coat or coats impaled, but it is impossible in such a case to place a number to the wife, and it is impossible to display an escutcheon of pretence for more than one wife, as if the escutcheon of pretence is removed from the exact centre it at once ceases to be an escutcheon of pretence. Consequently, if more than one wife be an heiress, separate escutcheons should be used for each marriage. Plans have been drawn up and apparently accepted providing for wives up to nearly twenty in number, but no useful purpose will be served by repeating them. A man with more than four wives is unusual in this country.

Divorce nullifies marriage, and both husband and wife must at once revert to bachelor and maiden achievements respectively.

It is difficult to deduce any certain conclusions as to the ancient rules connected with impalement, for a simple reason which becomes very noticeable on an examination of ancient *seals* and other armorial records. In early times there can be no doubt whatever that men did not impale, or bother about the arms of wives who were not great heiresses. A man bore his own arms, and he left his father-in-law, or his brother-in-law, to bear those of the family with which he had matched. Of course, we find many cases in which the arms of a wife figure upon the husband's shield, but a careful examination of them shows that in practically every case the reason is to be found in the fact that the wife was an heiress. Husbands were called to Parliament in virtue of the peerages vested in their wives, and we cannot but come to the conclusion that whenever one finds use in early times of the arms of a wife, it is due to the fact that the husband was bearing them not because of his mere marriage, but because he was enjoying the estates, or peerage, of his wife.

For that reason we find in many cases the arms of the wife borne in preference to the paternal arms of descent, or meet with them quartered with the arms of the husband frequently being given precedence over his own; and on the analogy of the coats of arms of wives at present borne with the wife's surname by the husband under Royal Licence, there can be little doubt that at a period when Royal Licences had not come into regular vogue the same idea was dominant, and the appearance of a wife's coat of arms meant the assumption of those arms by the husband as his own, with or without the surname of the wife.

The connection between name and arms was not then so stereotyped as it is at present; rather was it a connection between arms and land, and perhaps more pointedly of arms and a peerage title where this existed, for there are many points and many facts which conclusively show that at an early period a coat of arms was often considered to have a territorial character; or perhaps it should be said that, whilst admittedly personal, arms have territorial attributes or connection.

This is borne out by the pleadings and details remaining to us concerning the Grey and Hastings controversy, and if this territorial character of a coat of arms is admitted, together with another characteristic no less important—and certainly equally accepted—that a coat of arms could belong to but one person at the same time, it must be recognised that the appearance of a wife's arms on a husband's shield is not an instance of a sign of mere marriage or anything analogous thereto. But when we turn to the arms of women, the condition of affairs is wholly reversed. A woman, who of course retained her identity, drew her position from her marriage and from her husband's position, and from the very earliest period we find that whilst a man simply bore his own arms, the wife upon her seal displayed both the arms of her own family and the arms of her husband's. Until a much later period it cannot be said to have been customary for the husband to bear the arms of his wife unless she were an heiress, but from almost the beginning of armory the wife conjoined the arms of her husband and herself. But the instances which have come down to us from an early period of dimidiated or impaled coats are chiefly instances of the display of arms by a widow.

The methods of conjunction which can be classed as above, however, at first seem to have been rather varied. Originally separate shields were employed for the different coats of arms, then dimidiated examples occur; at a later period we find the arms impaled upon one shield, and at a subsequent date the escutcheon of pretence comes into use as a means of indicating that the wife was an heiress.

The origin of this escutcheon is easy to understand. Taking arms to have a territorial character—a point which still finds a certain amount of acceptance in Scottish heraldry—there was no doubt that a man, in succeeding to a lordship in right of his wife, would wish to bear the arms associated therewith. He placed them, therefore, upon his own, and arms exclusively of a territorial character have certainly very frequently been placed "in pretence." His own arms he would look upon as arms of descent; they consequently occupied the field of his shield. The lordship of his wife he did not enjoy through descent, and consequently he would naturally incline to place it "in pretence," and from the constant occasions in which such a proceeding would seem to be the natural course of events (all of which occasions would be associated with an heiress-wife), one would be led to the conclusion that such a form of display indicated an heiress-wife; and consequently the rule deduced, as are all heraldic rules, from past precedents became established.

In the next generation, the son and heir would have descent from his mother equally with his father, and the arms of her family would be equally arms of descent to him, and no longer the mere territorial emblem of a lordship. Consequently they became on the same footing as the arms of his father. The son would naturally, therefore, quarter the arms. The escutcheon of pretence being removed, and therefore having enjoyed but a temporary existence, the association thereof with the heiress-wife becomes emphasised in a much greater degree.

This is now accepted as a definite rule of armory, but in reciting it as a rule it should be pointed out, first, that no man may place the arms of his wife upon an escutcheon of pretence during the lifetime of her father, because whilst her father is alive there is always the opportunity of a re-marriage, and of the consequent birth of a son and heir. No man is compelled to bear arms on an escutcheon of pretence, it being quite correct to impale them merely to indicate the marriage—if he so desires. There are many cases of arms which would appear meaningless and undecipherable when surmounted by an escutcheon of pretence.

"Sometimes, also (says Guillim), he who marries an heretrix may carry her arms in an inescutcheon upon his own, because the husband pretends that his heirs shall one day inherit an estate by her; it is therefore called an escutcheon of pretence; but this way of bearing is not known abroad upon that occasion."

A man on marrying an heiress-wife has no great space at his disposal for the display of her arms, and though it is now considered perfectly correct to place any number of quarterings upon an escutcheon of pretence, the opportunity does not in fact exist for more than the display of a limited number. In practice, three or four are as many as will usually be found, but theoretically it is correct to place the whole of the quarterings to which the wife is entitled upon the escutcheon of pretence.

3 A

Two early English instances may be pointed out in the fifteenth century, in which a husband placed his wife's arms *en surtout*. These are taken from the Garter Plates of Sir John Neville, Lord Montagu, afterwards Marquess of Montagu (elected K.G. *circa* 1463), and of Richard Beauchamp, fifth Earl of Warwick and Albemarle (elected K.G. *circa* 1400); but it was not until about the beginning of the seventeenth century that the regular practice arose by which the husband of an heiress places his wife's arms in an escutcheon *en surtout* upon his personal arms, whether his coat be a quartered one or not. Another early instance is to be found in Fig. 927, which is in-

FIG. 927.—Arms of John Talbot, Earl of Shrewsbury, K.G.: Quarterly, 1 and 4, gules, a lion rampant within a bordure engrailed or (Talbot); 2 and 3, argent, two lions passant in pale gules (Strange); impaling the arms of his first wife whose Peerage he enjoyed, viz.: quarterly, 1 and 4, argent, a bend between six martlets gules (Furnival); 2 and 3, or, a fret gules (Verdon); and upon an escutcheon of pretence the arms of the mother of his second wife (to whom she was coheir, conveying her mother's Peerage to her son), viz.: 1 and 4, gules, a lion passant guardant argent, crowned or (Lisle); 2 and 3, argent, a chevron gules (Tyes). (From MS. Reg. 15, E. vi.)

teresting as showing the arms of both wives of the first Earl of Shrewsbury. His first was *suo jure* Baroness Furnivall. Her arms are, however, impaled. His second wife was the daughter (but not the heir) of Richard Beauchamp, Earl of Warwick, but she was coheir of her mother, the Baroness Lisle.

It should be borne in mind that even in England an inescutcheon *en surtout* does not always mean an heiress-wife. The Earl of Mar and Kellie bears (Fig. 813) an inescutcheon surmounted by an earl's coronet for his Earldom of Kellie, and other instances are to be found in the arms of Cumming-Gordon (see Plate XIII.), and Sir Hector Maclean Hay, Bart., thus bears his pronominal arms (Fig. 194). Inescutcheons of augmentation occur in the arms of the Dukes of Marlborough and Wellington, Lord Newton, and on the shields of Newman, Wolfe, and others.

Under the Commonwealth the Great Seals of Oliver Cromwell and his son Richard, as Protectors, bear a shield of arms: "Quarterly, 1 and 4, argent, a cross gules (for England); 2. azure, a saltire argent (for Scotland); 3. azure, a harp or, stringed argent (for Ireland);" and upon these quarterings *en surtout* an escutcheon of the personal arms of Cromwell: "Sable, a lion rampant argent."

In the heraldry of the Continent of Europe it has long been the custom for an elected sovereign to place his hereditary arms in an escutcheon *en surtout* above those of his dominions. As having obtained the crown by popular election, the Kings of the Hellenes also place *en surtout* upon the arms of the Greek kingdom ("Azure, a Greek cross couped argent") an escutcheon of their personal arms. Another instance is to be found in the arms of the Dukes of Saxe-Coburg and Gotha. Whilst all the descendants of the late Prince Consort (other than his Majesty King Edward VII.) bear in England the Royal Arms of this country, differenced by their respective labels with an

escutcheon of Saxony *en surtout* as Dukes and Duchesses of Saxony, the late Duke of Saxe-Coburg and Gotha bore the arms of Saxony, placing the differenced Royal shield of this country *en surtout*.

We now come to the subject of quartering. Considering the fact that every single text-book on armory gives the ordinary rules for the marshalling of quarterings, it is strange how many mistakes are made, and how extremely funny are the ideas of some people upon the subject of quartering. As has already been stated, the rules of quartering are governed by the simple, but essential and important fact, that every quartering exhibited means the representation in blood of some particular person. Quarterings, other than those of augmentation, can only be inherited from or through those female ancestors who are in themselves heirs or coheirs in blood, or whose issue subsequently become in a later generation the representatives of any ancestor in the male line of that said female ancestor. Briefly speaking, a woman is an heiress, first, if she is only child; second, if all her brothers die without issue in her own lifetime; and third, if the entire issue, male and female, of her brothers, becomes extinct in her own lifetime. A woman becomes an "heiress in her issue," as it is termed, if she die before her brothers, if and when all the descendants of her brothers become absolutely extinct. The following pedigrees may help to explain :—

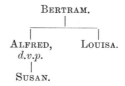

BERTRAM.

ALFRED,   LOUISA.
d.v.p.

SUSAN.

In this case Susan is the heir, *not* Louisa.

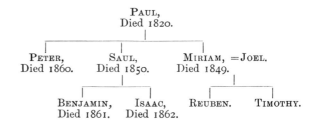

PAUL,
Died 1820.

PETER,   SAUL,   MIRIAM, =JOEL.
Died 1860.   Died 1850.   Died 1849.

BENJAMIN,   ISAAC,   REUBEN.   TIMOTHY.
Died 1861.   Died 1862.

In this case Miriam becomes "in her issue" heir of Paul at the death of Isaac in 1862, and Reuben and Timothy would both quarter the arms of Paul.

If the wife be either an heir or coheir, she transmits after her death to *all* her children the arms and quarterings—*as quarterings to add to their paternal arms, and as such only*—which she was entitled to place upon her own lozenge.

The origin and theory of quartering is as follows: If the daughter be an heiress or coheiress she represents either wholly or in part her father and his branch of the family, even if "his branch" only commenced with himself. Now in the days when the science of armory was slowly evolving itself there was no Married Women's Property Act, and the husband *ipso facto* became to all intents and purposes possessed of and enjoyed the rights of his wife. But it was at the same time only a possession and enjoyment by courtesy, and not an actual possession in fee, for the reversion remained with the wife's heirs, and did not pass to the heirs of the husband; for in cases where the husband or wife had been previously married, or where there was no issue of their marriage, their heirs would not be identical. Of course during the lifetime of his wife he could not actually *represent* his wife's family, and consequently could not quarter the arms, but in right of his wife he "pretended" to the representation of her house, and consequently the inescutcheon of her arms is termed an "escutcheon of pretence."

After the death of a wife her children immediately and actually become the representatives of their mother, and are as such *entitled* of right to quarter the arms of their mother's family.

The earliest example which has been discovered at the present time of the use of a quartered coat of arms is afforded by the seal of Joanna of Ponthieu, second wife of Ferdinand III., King of Castile and Leon, in 1272. This seal bears on its reverse in a vesica the triple-towered castles of Castile, and the rampant lion of Leon, repeated as in the modern quarterings of Spain. There is, however, no separation of the quarters by a line of partition. This peculiarity will be also noticed as existing in the early quartered coats of Hainault a quarter of a century later. The quartered coat of Castile and Leon remains upon the monument in Westminster Abbey erected in memory of Eleanor of Castile, who died in 1290, the first wife of Edward I.

Providing the wife be an heiress—and for the remainder of this chapter, which deals only with quarterings, this will be assumed—the son of a marriage *after the death* of his mother quarters her arms with those of his father, that is, he divides his shield into four quarters, and places the arms of his father in the first and fourth quarters, and the arms of his mother in the second and third. That is the root, basis, and original rule of all the rules of quartering, but it may be here remarked, that no man is entitled to quarter the arms of his mother whilst she is

FIG. 928.—Arms of John de Welles, Viscount de Welles, son of Lionel, Lord Welles, by his wife Margaret, daughter of Sir John Beauchamp, Lord Beauchamp : Quarterly, 1 and 4, or, a lion rampant queue-fourché sable (for Welles); 2 and 3, gules, a fess dancetté between six cross crosslets or (for Beauchamp). (From MS. Harl. 6163.)

alive, inasmuch as she is alive to represent herself and her family, and her issue cannot assume the representation whilst she is alive. An example of such a simple quartered coat occurs in Fig. 928.

But it should not be imagined that the definite rules which exist at the moment had any such unalterable character in early times. Husbands quartered the arms of their wives if they were heiresses, and if important lordships devolved through the marriage. Territorial arms of dominion were quartered with personal arms as in Figs. 189 and 929, quarterings of augmentation were granted, and the present system is the endeavour to reconcile all the varying circumstances and precedents which exist. One point, however, stands out clearly from all ancient examples, viz. that quartering meant quartering, and a shield was supposed to have but four quarters upon it. Consequently we find that instead of the elaborate schemes now in vogue showing 10, 20, 50, or 100 quarterings, the shield had but four; and this being admitted and recognised, it became essential that the four most important should be shown, and consequently we find that quarterings were selected in a manner which would seem to us haphazard. Paternal quarterings were dropped, and the result has been that many coats of arms are now known as the arms of a family with quite a different surname from that of the

family with which they originated. The matter was of little consequence in the days when the "upper-class" and arms-bearing families were few in number. Every one

FIG. 929.—Arms of Thomas Stanley, Earl of Derby, (d. 1572); Quarterly, 1. quarterly, i. and iiii., argent, on a bend azure, three bucks' heads caboshed or (Stanley); ii. and iii., or, on a chief indented azure, three bezants (Lathom); 2 and 3, gules, three legs in armour conjoined at the thigh and flexed at the knee proper, garnished and spurred or (for the Lordship of Man); 4. quarterly, i. and iiii., gules, two lions passant in pale argent (for Strange); ii. and iii., argent, a fess and a canton gules (for Wydeville). The arms on the escutcheon of pretence are not those of his wife (Anne Hastings), who was not an heiress, and they seem difficult to account for unless they are a coat for Rivers or some other territorial lordship inherited from the Wydeville family. The full identification of the quarterings borne by Anthony, Lord Rivers, would probably help in determining the point.

knew how Stafford derived his Royal descent, and that it was not male upon male, so that no confusion resulted from the Earls of Buckingham giving the Royal coat precedence before their paternal quartering of Stafford (see Fig. 930), or from their using only the arms of Woodstock; but as time went on the upper classes became more numerous, arms-bearing ancestors by the succession of generations increased in number, and while in the thirteenth and fourteenth centuries it would be a physical impossibility for any man to have represented one hundred different heiresses of arms-bearing families, in later days such became the case. The result has been the necessity to formulate those strict and rigid rules which for modern purposes must be conformed to, and it is futile and childish to deduce a set of rules from ancient examples originating in and suitable for the simpler genealogical circumstances of an earlier day, and assert that it is equally permissible to

FIG. 930.—Arms of Edward Stafford, Duke of Buckingham (d. 1521): Quarterly, 1 and 4, quarterly, i. and iiii., France; ii. and iii., England, within the bordure argent of Thomas of Woodstock; 2 and 3, or, a chevron gules (for Stafford). (From MS. Add. 22,306.)

adopt them at the moment, or to marshal a modern shield accordingly.

The first attempt to break away from the four quarters of a shield was the initiation of the system of grand quarters (see Figs. 213, 926, 929, 931, and 932). By this means the relative importance could roughly be shown. Supposing a man had inherited a shield of four quarters and then married a wife in whom was vested a peerage, he naturally wished to display the arms connected with that peerage, for these were of greater importance than his own four quarterings. The problem was how to introduce the fifth. In some cases we find it borne in pretence, but in other cases,

FIG. 931.—Arms of Charles Brandon, Duke of Suffolk: Quarterly, 1 and 4, barry of ten argent and gules, a lion rampant queue-fourché or, crowned per pale of the second and first; 2 and 3, quarterly, i. and iiii., azure, a cross moline or (Bruyn); ii. and iii., lozengy gules and ermine (Rokeley).

particularly in a later generation, we find that important quarter given the whole of a quarter of the shield to itself, the other four being conjoined together and displayed so as to occupy a similar space. These, therefore, became sub-quarters. The system also had advantages, because it permitted coats which by constant quartering had become indivisible to be perpetuated in this form. So definite was this rule, that in only one of the series of Garter plates anterior to the Tudor period is any shield found containing more than four quarters, though many of these are grand quarters containing other coats borne sub-quarterly. The one instance which I refer to as an exception is the shield of the Duke D'Urbino, and it is quite possible that this should not be quoted as an instance in point. He appears to have borne in the ordinary way four quarters, but he subsequently added thereto two quarterings which may or may not have been one and the same coat of arms by way of augmentation. These he placed in pale in the centre of the others, thus making the shield apparently one of six quarters.

But one is safe in the assertion that during the Plantagenet period no more than four quarters were usually placed upon a shield. Then we come to the brief period of "squeezed-in" quarterings (Figs. 932

FIG. 932.—Arms of Henry Algernon Percy, Earl of Northumberland (d. 1527): Quarterly, 1. quarterly, i. and iiii., or, a lion rampant azure (Percy); ii. and iii., gules, three lucies haurient argent (Lucy); 2. azure, five fusils conjoined in fess or (for Percy); 3. barry of six or and vert, a bendlet gules (Poynings); 4. gules, three lions passant in pale argent, a bendlet azure (FitzPayne), or three piles azure (Brian).

and 933). In the early Visitations we get instances of six, eight, and even a larger number, and the start once being made, and the number of four relinquished, there was of course no reason why it should not be extended indefinitely. This appears to have rapidly become the case, and we find that schemes of quarterings are now proved and recorded officially in England and Ireland some of which exceed 200 in number. The record number of officially proved and recorded quarterings is at present held by Mr. Lloyd, of Stockton in Chirbury, co. Salop (Fig. 934), but many of these quarterings are mere repetition owing to constant inter-

marriages, and to the fact that a single Welsh line of male descent often results in a number of different shields. Welsh arms did not originally have the hereditay unchangeability we are accustomed to in English heraldry, and moreover a large proportion are later inventions borne to denote descent and are not arms actually used by those they stand for, so that the quarterings of Mr. Money-Kyrle (Fig. 935), or of the sister Countesses of Yarborough and Powis, respectively Baroness Fauconberg and Conyers and Baroness Darcy de Knayth (Fig. 936), are decidedly more enviable. Nobody of course attempts to bear such a number. In Scotland, however, even to the present day, the system of four quarterings is still adhered to. The result is that in Scotland the system of grand quarterings is still pursued, whilst in England it is almost unknown, except in cases where coats of arms have for some reason or another become indivisible. This is a very patent difficulty when it becomes necessary to marshal indivisible Scottish coats with English ones, and the system of cadency adopted in Scotland, which has its chief characteristic in the employment of bordures, makes the matter sometimes very far from simple. The system adopted at the present time in the case of a Royal Licence, for example, to bear a Scottish name and arms in cases where the latter is a coat of many quarterings within a bordure, is to treat such coat as made indivisible by and according

FIG. 933.—Arms of George Nevill, Baron Abergavenny (d. 1535): Quarterly, 1. gules, on a saltire argent, a rose of the field (Nevill); 2. chequy or and azure (Warenne); 3. or, three chevrons gules (Clare); 4. quarterly argent and gules, in the second and third quarters a fret or, over all a bend sable (Le Despencer); 4. gules, on a fess between six cross crosslets or, a crescent sable (for (Beauchamp). (Add. MS. 22,306.)

to the most recent matriculation. That coat is then treated as a grand quartering of an equivalent value to the pronominal coat in England.

But reverting to the earlier chart, by the aid of which heirship was demonstrated, the following were entitled to transmit the Cilfowyr arms as quarterings. Mary, Ellen, Blanche, Grace, Muriel, and Dorothy all had the right to transmit. By the death of Dorothy v.p. Alice and Annie both became entitled. Maria Jane and Hannah would have been entitled to transmit Sherwin and Cilfowyr, but not Cilfowyr alone, if there had been no arms for Sherwin, though they could have transmitted Sherwin alone if there had been arms for Sherwin and none for Cilfowyr. Harriet would have transmitted the arms of Cilfowyr if she had survived, and Ada would, each subject to the differences as has been previously explained.

As has been already explained, every woman is entitled to bear upon a lozenge in her own lifetime the arms, quarterings, and difference marks which belonged to her father. If her mother were an heiress she adds her mother's arms to her father's, and her mother's quarterings also, marshalling the whole into a correct sequence, and placing the said sequence of quarterings upon a lozenge. Such are the armorial bearings of a daughter. If the said daughter be not an heraldic heiress in blood she *cannot* transmit either arms or quarterings to her descendants. Needless to say, no woman, heiress or non-heiress, can now transmit a crest, and no woman can bear either crest, helmet, mantling, or motto. A daughter not being an heiress simply confers the right upon her husband to *impale* upon his shield such arms and differ-

until arms are established for their father's line, inasmuch as they can only inherit armorially from their mother *through* their father. In England it is always optional

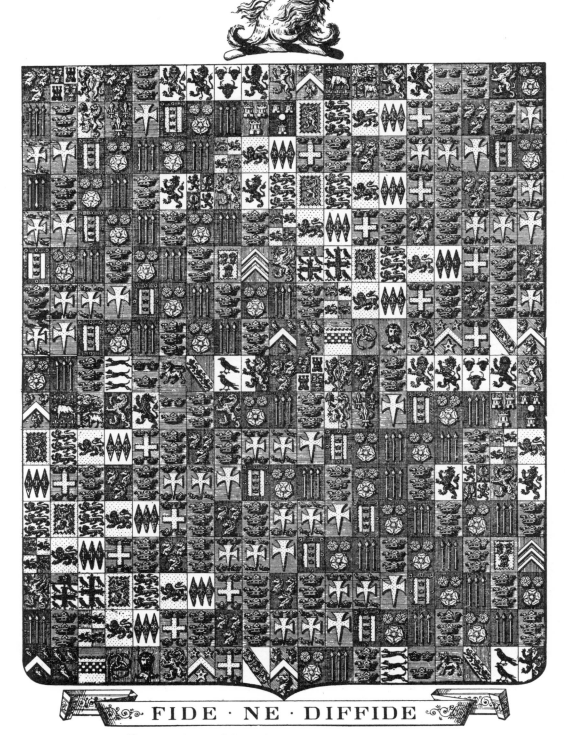

FIDE · NE · DIFFIDE

FIG. 934.—Arms and Quarterings of Henry Crampton Lloyd, Esq., of Stockton in Chirbury, co. Salop.

ence marks as her father bore in his own right. If an heiress possessing arms marry a man with illegal arms, or a man making no pretensions to arms, her children have no arms at all, and really inherit nothing; and the rights, such as they are, to the arms of the mother as a quartering remain, and must remain, *dormant* unless and

for a man to have arms assigned to him to fill in any blanks which would otherwise mar his scheme of quarterings.

Let us now see how various coats of arms are marshalled as quarterings into one achievement.

The original theory of quartering upon which all rules are based is that after a marriage with an heiress, necessi-

373

tating for the children the combination of the two coats, the shield is divided into four quarters. These four are numbered from the top left-hand (the dexter) corner (No. 1) across towards the sinister (No. 2) side of the shield; then the next row is numbered in the same way

to) that places the arms of the father in the first and fourth quarters, and the arms of the mother in the second and third; such, of course, being on the assumption that the father possessed only a simple coat without quarterings, and that the mother was in the same position. The

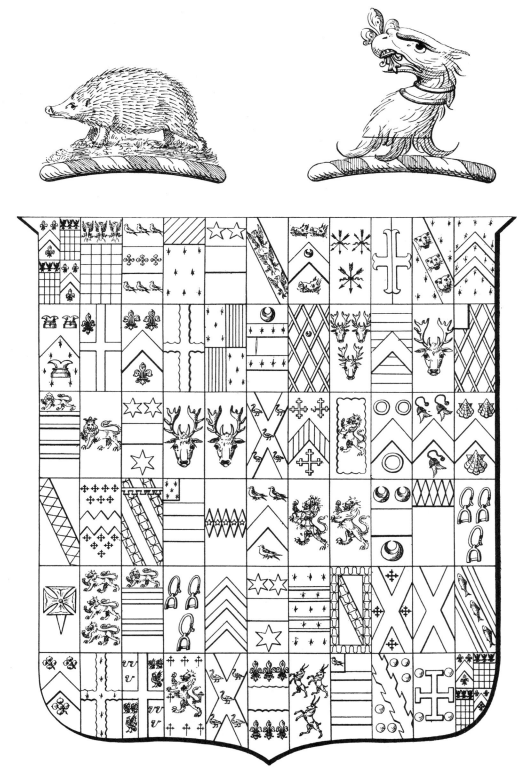

FIG. 935.—Arms and Quarterings of Audley Waller Washbourne Money-Kyrle, of Homme House, Dymock, Gloucs.

(Nos. 3 and 4). This rule as to the method of numbering holds good for any number of quarterings.

In allocating the position of the different coats to their places in the scheme of quarterings, the pronominal coat must *always* be in the first quartering.

In a simple case (the exceptions will presently be referred

children therefore possess a coat of four quarters (Figs. 937 and 938). Suppose a son of theirs in his turn marries another heiress, also possessing only a simple coat without quarterings, the grandchildren descending from the aforesaid marriage put that last-mentioned coat in the third quarter, and the coat, though still of only four quarters, is : 1 and 4, the pronominal coat; 2. the first heiress; 3. the second.

If another single quartering is brought in, in a later generation, that takes the place of No. 4 (Fig. 939). So far it is all plain sailing, but very few text-books carry one beyond this point. Another single quartering inherited gives five quarterings to be displayed on one shield. The usual plan is to repeat the first quartering, when this gives you six, which are then arranged in two rows of three.

they devolve (according to the *pedigree* and *not* necessarily according to the *date* order in which they are inherited) must be rigidly adhered to; but a person is perfectly at liberty (1) to repeat the *first* quartering at the end to make an even number or not at his pleasure, but no more than the first quartering must be repeated in such cases; (2) to arrange the quarters in any number of rows he may find most convenient according to the shape of the space the quarterings will occupy.

FIG. 936.—Arms and Quarterings of the late Sackville George Lane-Fox, Lord Darcy de Knayth and Conyers (*d.* 1888), which have now devolved upon his daughters and coheirs, Marcia, Countess of Yarborough, Baroness Fauconberg and Conyers, and Violet, Countess of Powis, Baroness Darcy de Knayth.

If the shield be an impaled shield one sometimes sees them arranged in three rows of two, but this is unusual though not incorrect. But five quarterings are sometimes arranged in two rows, three in the upper and two in the lower, as in the illustration of the arms of Lloyd (Fig. 325). and with a shield of this long pointed variety this plan may be adopted with advantage. Subsequent quarterings, as they are introduced by subsequent marriages, take their places, Nos. 6, 7, 8, 9, 10, and so on *ad infinitum*.

In arranging them on one shield, the order in which

Upon the Continent it is usual to specify the number and position of the lines by which the shield is divided. Thus, while an English herald would say simply, *Quarterly of six*, and leave it to the painter's or engraver's taste to arrange the quarterings in three rows of two, or in two rows of three, a French or German herald would ordinarily specify the arrangement to be used in distinct terms.

If a man possessing only a simple coat of arms without quarterings marry an heiress with a number (*e.g.* say twenty) of quarterings, he places the arms and quarterings of his wife in pretence. Their children eventually, as a consequence, inherit twenty-one quarterings. The first is

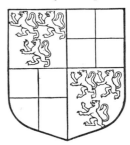

FIG. 937.—Arms of Fiennes, Lord Saye de Sele: Quarterly, 1 and 4, azure, three lions rampant or (Fiennes); 2 and 3, quarterly or and gules (Saye).

the coat of their father, the second is the first coat of the mother, and the remaining nineteen follow in a regular sequence, according to their position upon their mother's achievement.

To sum the rule up, it is necessary first to take *all* the quarterings inherited from the father and arrange them

FIG. 938.—Arms of Richard Fitz Alan, Earl of Arundel, son of Edmund Fitz Alan and Alice de Warenne: Quarterly, 1 and 4, gules, a lion rampant or (Fitz-Alan); 2 and 3, chequy or and azure (Warenne).

in a proper sequence, and then follow on *in the same sequence* with the arms and quarterings inherited from the mother.

The foregoing explanations should show how generation by generation quarterings are added to a paternal shield, but I have found that many of those who possess a know-

FIG. 939.—Arms of Edward Courtenay, Earl of Devonshire (*d.* 1509): Quarterly, 1. or, three torteaux (Courtenay); 2. or, a lion rampant azure, armed and langued gules (Réviers); 3. gules, a cross patonce vair (De Fortis); 4. per pale dexter chequy or and azure, sinister vert, over all two bars argent (stated to be for the Barony of Okehampton, which is highly improbable).

ledge of the laws to this extent are yet at a loss, given a pedigree, to marshal the resulting quarterings in their right order.

Given your pedigree—the first quartering *must* be *the pronominal coat* (I am here presuming no change of name or arms has occurred), which is the coat of the strict male line of descent. Then follow this male line back as far as it is known. The second quartering is the coat of the *first* heiress who married your earliest ancestor in the male line who is known to have married an heiress.

Then after her coat will follow all the quarterings which she was entitled to and which she has "brought in" to your family. Having exhausted these, you then follow your male line *down* to the next heiress, adding her arms as a quartering to those already arranged, and following it by her quarterings. The same plan must be pursued until you arrive at your own name upon the pedigree. Unless some exceptional circumstance has arisen (and such exceptions will presently be found detailed at length), all the quarterings are of equal heraldic value, and must be the same size when displayed.

If after having worked out your quarterings you find that you have more than you care to use, you are quite at liberty to make a selection, omitting any number, *but* it is entirely *wrong* to display quarterings without those quarterings which brought them into the paternal line. Supposing your name to be Brown, you *must* put the Brown arms in the first quarter, but at your pleasure you can quarter the arms of each single heiress who married an ancestor of yours in the male line (*i.e.* who herself became Mrs. Brown), or you can omit the whole or a part. But supposing one of these, Mrs. Brown (*née* Smith), was entitled to quarter the arms of Jones, which arms of Jones had brought in the arms of Robinson, you are not at liberty to quarter the arms of Jones without quartering Smith, and if you wish to display the arms of Robinson you *must* also quarter the arms of Jones to bring in Robinson and the arms of Smith to bring in Robinson and Jones to your own Brown achievement. You can use Brown only: or quarterly, 1 and 4, Brown; 2 and 3, Smith: or 1 and 4, Brown; 2. Smith; 3. Jones: or quarterly, 1. Brown; 2. Smith; 3. Jones; 4. Robinson; but you are *not* entitled to quarter: 1 and 4. Brown; 2. Jones; 3. Robinson, because Smith, which brought in Jones and Robinson, has been omitted, and there was never a match between Brown and Jones.

Quarterings are not compulsory, and their use or disuse is quite optional.

So much for the general rules of quartering. Let us now consider certain cases which require rules to themselves.

It is possible for a daughter to be the sole heir or co-heir of her mother whilst not being the heir of her father, as in the following imaginary pedigree:—

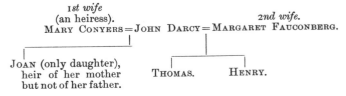

In this case Joan is not the heir of her father, inasmuch as he has sons Thomas and Henry, but she is the heir of her mother and the only issue capable of inheriting and transmitting the Conyers arms and quarterings. Joan is heir of her mother but not of her father.

The husband of Joan can either impale the arms of Darcy as having married a daughter of John Darcy, or he can place upon an escutcheon of pretence arms to indicate that he has married the heiress of Conyers. But it would be quite incorrect for him to simply place Conyers in pretence, because he has not married a Miss Conyers. What he must do is to charge the arms of Conyers with a dexter canton of the arms of Darcy and place this upon his escutcheon of pretence.[1] The children will quarter the arms of Conyers with the canton of Darcy and inherit likewise all the quarterings to which Mary Conyers succeeded, but the Conyers arms must be always thereafter charged with the arms of Darcy on a canton.

---

[1] Arms borne on a sinister canton suggest illegitimacy.

The following curious, but quite genuine case, which was pointed out to me by Ulster King of Arms, presents a set of circumstances absolutely unique, and it still remains to be decided what is the correct method to adopt :—

1st wife.		2nd wife.
Lady MARY, dau. and coheir of Thomas Bermingham, Earl of Louth. Married 1777, died 1793.	= WILLIAM ST. LAWRENCE, 2nd Earl of Howth. =	MARGARET, dau. of William Burke.

Three other daughters and coheirs of their mother.	THOMAS ST. LAWRENCE. 3rd Earl of Howth.	Other issue.

Lady ISABELLA ST. LAWRENCE, 2nd dau. and coheir of her mother, but not heir of her father, therefore entitled to transmit the arms of Bermingham with those of St. Lawrence on a canton. First wife of Earl Annesley. Married 1803, died 1827.	= WILLIAM RICHARD ANNESLEY, 3rd Earl of Annesley.	= PRISCILLA, 2nd dau. of Hugh Moore.

WILLIAM, 4th Earl Annesley.	HUGH, 5th Earl Annesley.

Lady MARY ANNESLEY, only child and sole heir of her mother and sole heir of her grandmother, but not heir of her father or of her grandfather. She is therefore entitled to transmit the arms of Bermingham with St. Lawrence on a canton plus Annesley on a canton. Married 1828. = WILLIAM JOHN M'GUIRE of Rostrevor.

How the arms of Bermingham are to be charged with both St. Lawrence and Annesley remains to be seen. I believe Ulster favours two separate cantons, dexter and sinister respectively, but the point has not yet come before him officially, and I know of no official decision which affords a precedent.

The reverse of the foregoing affords another curious point when a woman is the heir of her father but not the heir of her mother :—

JOHN SMITH = MARY JONES.

1st husband.		2nd husband.
JOHN WILLIAMS =	ETHEL SMITH, only child and heir.	= HENRY ROBERTS.

ALICE WILLIAMS, only child and heir of John Williams.	= ARTHUR ELLIS.	EDWARD ROBERTS, heir of his mother.
		Issue.

THEODORE ELLIS,
who claims to quarter :
1 and 4, Ellis ; 2. Williams ; 3. Smith.

It is officially admitted (see the introduction to Burke's "General Armory") that the claim is accurately made. The process of reasoning is probably thus. John Williams places upon an escutcheon of pretence the arms of Smith, and Alice Williams succeeds in her own right to the arms of her mother because the latter was an heiress, and for herself is entitled to bear, as would a son, the arms of the two parents quarterly ; and having so inherited, Alice Williams being herself an heiress, is entitled to transmit. At any rate Arthur Ellis is entitled to impale or place upon his escutcheon of pretence Williams and Smith quarterly. To admit the right for the descendants to quarter the arms Arthur Ellis so bore is no more than a logical progression, but the eventual result appears faulty, because we find Theodore Ellis quartering the arms of Smith, whilst the representation of Smith is in the line

of Edward Roberts. This curious set of circumstances, however, is rare in the extreme.

It frequently happens, in devising a scheme of quarterings, that a person may represent heiresses of several families entitled to bear arms, but to whom the pedigree must be traced through an heiress of another family which did not possess arms. Consequently any claim to quarterings inherited through the non-armorial heiress is dormant, and the quarterings must not be used or inserted in any scheme drawn up. It is always permissible, however, to petition for arms to be granted to be borne for that non-armorial family for the purpose of introducing the quarterings in question, and such a grant having been made, the dormant claim then becomes operative and the new coat is introduced, followed by the dormant quartering in precisely the same manner as would have been the case if the arms granted had always existed. Grants of this character are constantly being obtained.

When a Royal Licence to assume or change name and arms is granted it very considerably affects the question of quartering, and many varying circumstances attending these Royal Licences make the matter somewhat intricate. If the Royal Licence is to assume a name and arms in lieu of those previously used, this means that for everyday use the arms are *changed*, the right to the old arms lapsing except for the purpose of a scheme of quarterings. The new coat of arms under the terms of the Royal Licence, which requires it first "to be exemplified in our Royal College of Arms, otherwise this our Royal Licence to be void and of none effect," is always exemplified, this exemplification being from the legal point of view equivalent to a new grant of the arms to the person assuming them. The terms of the Royal Licence have always carefully to be borne in mind, particularly in the matter of remainder, because frequently these exemplifications are for a limited period or intended to devolve with specified property, and a Royal Licence only nullifies a prior right to arms to the extent of the terms recited in the Letters Patent of exemplification. In the ordinary way, however, such an exemplification is equivalent to a new grant affecting all the descendants. When it is assumed in lieu, for the ordinary purpose of use the new coat of arms takes the place of the old one, but the right to the old one remains in theory to a certain extent, inasmuch as its existence *is necessary* in any scheme of quartering *to bring in* any quarterings previously inherited, and these cannot be displayed with the new coat unless they are preceded by the old one. Quarterings, however, which are brought into the family through a marriage in the generation in which the Royal Licence is obtained, or in a subsequent generation, can be displayed with the new coat without the interposition of the old one.

If the Royal Licence be to bear the name of a certain family in lieu of a present name, and to bear the arms of that family quarterly with the arms previously borne, the quarterly coat is then exemplified. In an English or Irish Royal Licence the coat of arms for the name assumed is placed in the first and the fourth quarters, and the old paternal arms figure in the second and third. This is an invariable rule. The quarterly coat thus exemplified becomes an indivisible coat for the new name, and it is not permissible to subsequently divide these quarterings. They become as much one coat of arms as "azure, a bend or" is the coat of arms of Scrope. If this quarterly coat is to be introduced in any scheme of quarterings it will only occupy the same space as any other single quartering and counts only as one, though it of course is in reality a grand quartering. In devising a scheme of quarterings for which a sub-quarterly coat of this character exemplified under a Royal Licence is the pronominal coat, that sub-quarterly coat is placed in the first quarter (Fig. 935). Next to it is placed the original coat of arms borne as the pronominal coat before the Royal Licence and exemplified in the second and third sub-quarters of the first quarter. When here repeated it occupies an entire quarter. Next to it are placed the whole of the quarterings belonging to the family in the order in which they occur. If the family whose name has been assumed is represented through an heiress that coat of arms is also repeated in its proper position and in that place in which it would have appeared if unaffected by the Royal Licence. But if it be the coat of arms of a family from whom there is no descent, or of whom there is no representation, the fact of the Royal Licence does not give any further right to quarter it beyond its appearance in the pronominal grand quartering. The exact state of the case is perhaps best illustrated by the arms of Reid-Cuddon. The name of the family was originally Reid, and representing an heiress of the Cuddons of Shaddingfield Hall they obtained a Royal Licence to take the name and arms of Cuddon in addition to the name and arms of Reid, becoming thereafter Reid-Cuddon. The arms were exemplified in due course, and the achievement then became: Quarterly, 1 and 4, Reid-Cuddon sub-quarterly, 2. the arms of Reed, 3. the arms of Cuddon. In Scotland no such thing as a Royal Licence exists, the matter being determined merely by a rematriculation following upon a voluntary change of name. There is no specified order or position for the arms of the different names, and the arrangement of the various quarterings is left to be determined by the circumstances of the case. Thus in the arms of Anstruther-Duncan the arms of Anstruther are in the first quarter (Fig. 147), and the matter is always largely governed by the importance of the respective estates and the respective families. In England this is not the case, because it is an unalterable rule that the arms of the last or principal surname if there be two, or the arms of the one surname if that be the case when the arms of two families are quartered, must always go in the 1st and 4th quarters. If three names are assumed by Royal Licence, the arms of the last name go in the 1st and 4th quarters, and the last name but one in the second quarter, and of the first name in the third (Figs. 684 and 686). These cases are, however, rare. But no matter how many names are assumed, and no matter how many original coats of arms the shield as exemplified consists of, it thereafter becomes an indivisible coat.

When a Royal Licence is issued to an illegitimate person to bear the name and arms of another family, no right is conferred to bear the quarterings of that family even subject to difference marks. The Royal Licence is only applicable to whatever arms were the pronominal coat used with the name assumed. Though instances certainly can be found in some of the Visitation Books and other ancient records of a coat with quarterings, the whole debruised by a bendlet sinister, notably in the case of a family of Talbot, where eight quarters are so marked, the fact remains that this practice has long been definitely considered incorrect, and is now never permitted. If a Royal Licence is issued to an illegitimate woman the exemplification is to herself personally, for in the eyes of the law she has no relatives; and though she may be one of a large family, her descendants are entitled to quarter the arms with the marks of distinction exemplified to her because such quartering merely indicates the representation of that one woman, who in the eyes of the law stands alone and without relatives. In the case of a Royal Licence to take a name and arms subject to these marks of distinction for illegitimacy, and in cases where the arms to be assumed are a sub-quarterly coat, the mark of distinction, which in England is now invariably a bordure wavy, will surround both quarterings, which remain an indivisible coat. If an augmentation is granted to a person whose pronominal coat is sub-quarterly, that augmentation, whatever form it may assume, is superimposed upon all quarterings. Thus a chief of augmenta-

tion would go across the top of the shield, the four quarters being displayed below, and the whole of this shield would be only one quartering in any scheme of quartering. An inescutcheon is superimposed over all. If the augmentation take the form of a quartering, then the pronominal coat is a grand quartering, equivalent in size to the augmentation. If a person entitled to a sub-quarterly coat and a double name obtains a Royal Licence to bear another name and arms, and to bear the arms he has previously borne quarterly with those he has assumed, the result would be: Quarterly, 1 and 4, the new coat assumed, quarterly 2 and 3, the arms he has previously borne sub-quarterly. But it should be noticed that the arrangements of coats of arms under a Royal Licence largely depends upon the wording of the document by which authority is given by the Sovereign. The wording of the document in its terms is based upon the wording of the petition, and within reasonable limits any arrangement which is desired is usually permitted, so that care should be taken as to the wording of the petition.

A quartering of augmentation is always placed in the first quarter of a shield, but it becomes indivisible from and is depicted sub-quarterly with the paternal arms; for instance, the Duke of Westminster bears as an augmentation the arms of the city of Westminster in the 1st and 4th quarters of his shield, and the arms of Grosvenor in the 2nd and 3rd, but this coat of Westminster and Grosvenor is an indivisible sub-quarterly coat which together would only occupy the first quarter in a shield of quarterings. Then the second one would be the arms of Grosvenor alone, which would be followed by the quarterings previously inherited.

If under a Royal Licence a name is assumed and the Royal Licence makes no reference to the arms of the family, the arms for all purposes remain unchanged and as if no Royal Licence had ever been issued. If the Royal Licence issued to a family simply exemplifies a single coat of arms, it is quite wrong to introduce any other coat of arms to convert this single coat into a sub-quarterly one.

To all intents and purposes it may be stated that in Scotland there are only four quarters in a shield, and if more than four coats are introduced grand quarterings are employed. Grand quarterings are very frequent in Scottish armory. The Scottish rules of quartering follow no fixed principle, and the constant rematriculations make it impossible to deduce exact rules; and though roughly approximating to the English ones, no greater generalisation can be laid down than the assertion that the most recent matriculation of an ancestor governs the arms and quartering to be displayed.

A royal quartering is never subdivided.

In combining Scottish and English coats of arms into one scheme of quartering, it is usual if possible to treat the coat of arms as matriculated in Scotland as a grand quartering equivalent in value to any other of the English quarterings (Fig. 684). This, however, is not always possible in cases where the matriculation itself creates grand quarterings and sub-quarterings; and for a scheme of quarterings in such a case it is more usual for the Scottish matriculation to be divided up into its component parts, and for these to be used as simple quarterings in succession to the English ones, regardless of any bordure which may exist in the Scottish matriculation. It cannot, of course, be said that such a practice is beyond criticism, though it frequently remains the only practical way of solving the difficulty.

Until comparatively recent times, if amongst quarterings inherited the Royal Arms were included, it was considered a fixed, unalterable rule that these should be placed in the first quarter, taking precedence of the pronominal coat, irrespective of their real position according to the date or pedigree place of introduction. This rule, however, has long since been superseded, and Royal quarterings now take their position on the same footing as the others. It very probably arose from the misconception of the facts concerning an important case which doubtless was considered a precedent. The family of Mowbray, after their marriage with the heiress of Thomas de Brotherton, used either the arms of Brotherton alone (Figs. 878, 879, 880, and 881), these being England differenced by a label, or else placed them in the first quarter of their shield. Consequently from this precedent a rule was deduced that it was permissible and correct to give a Royal quartering precedence over all others. The position of the Mowbrays, Dukes of Norfolk, as Earls Marshal no doubt led to their own achievement being considered an exemplary model. But it appears to have been overlooked that the Mowbrays bore these Royal Arms of Brotherton not as an inherited quartering but as a grant to themselves. Richard II. apparently granted them permission to bear the arms of Edward the Confessor impaled with the arms of Brotherton, the whole between the two Royal ostrich feathers (Fig. 823), and consequently, the grant having been made, the Mowbrays were under no necessity to display the Mowbray or the Segrave arms to bring in the arms of Brotherton. A little later a similar case occurred with the Stafford family, who became sole heirs-general of Thomas of Woodstock, and consequently entitled to bear his arms as a quartering. The matter appears to have been settled at a chapter of the College of Arms, and the decision arrived at was as follows :—

Cott. MS., Titus, C. i. fol. 404, in handwriting of end of sixteenth century.

[An order made for Henry Duke of Buckingham to beare the Armes of Thomas of Woodstock alone without any other Armes to bee quartered therewith. Anno 13 E 4.]

Memorandum that in the yeare of the Reigne of our Soveraign Lord King Edward the iiij[th], the Thurtein in the xviij[tin] day of ffeverir, it was concluded in a Chapitre of the office of Armes that where a nobleman is descended lenyalle Ineritable to iij. or iiij. Cotes and afterward is ascended to a Cotte neir to the King and of his royall bloud, may for his most onneur bere the same Cootte alone, and none lower Coottes of Dignite to be quartered therewith. As my Lord Henry Duke of Buckingham, Eirll of Harford, Northamton, and Stafford, Lord of Breknoke and of Holdernes, is assended to the Coottes and ayer to Thomas of Woodstoke, Duke of Glocestre and Sonne to King Edward the third, hee may beire his Coottte alone. And it was so Concluded by [Claurancieulx King of Armes, Marche King of Armes, Gyen King of Armes, Windesor Herauld, Fawcon Herauld, Harfford Herald].

But I imagine that this decision was in all probability founded upon the case of the Mowbrays, which was not in itself an exact precedent, because with the Staffords there appears to have been no such Royal grant as existed with the Mowbrays. Other instances at about this period can be alluded to, but though it must be admitted that the rule existed at one time, it has long since been officially over-ridden.

A territorial coat or a coat of arms borne to indicate the possession of a specific title is either placed in the first quarter or borne in pretence ; see the arms of the Earl of Mar and Kellie (Fig. 813). A singular instance of a very exceptional method of marshalling occurs in the case of the arms of the Earl of Caithness. He bears four coats of arms, some being stated to be territorial coats, quarterly, dividing them by the cross engrailed sable from his paternal arms of Sinclair. The arms of the Earls of Caithness are thus marshalled : "Quarterly,

1. azure, within a Royal tressure a ship with furled sails all or." Orkney : " 2 and 3, or, a lion rampant gules." Spar (a family in possession of the Earldom of Caithness before the Sinclairs): " 4. Azure, a ship in sail or, Caithness"; and over all, dividing the quarters, a cross engrailed "sable," for Sinclair. The Barons Sinclair of Sweden (so created 1766, but extinct ten years later) bore the above quartered coats as cadets of Caithness, but separated the quarters, not by the engrailed cross sable of Sinclair, but by a cross patée throughout ermine. In an escutcheon *en surtout* they placed the Sinclair arms : " Argent, a cross engrailed sable "; and, as a mark of cadency, they surrounded the main escutcheon with " a bordure chequy or and gules." This arrangement was doubtless suggested by the Royal Arms of Denmark, the quarterings of which have been for many centuries separated by the cross of the Order of the Dannebrog : " Argent, a cross patée throughout fimbriated gules." In imitation of this a considerable number of the principal Scandinavian families use a cross patée throughout to separate the quarters of their frequently complicated coats. The quarterings in these are often not indicative of descent, but were all included in the original grant of armorial bearings. On the centre of the cross thus used, an escutcheon, either of augmentation or of the family arms, is placed *en surtout*.

The main difference between British and foreign usage with regard to quartering is this, that in England quarterings are usually employed to denote simply descent from an heiress, or representation in blood ; in Scotland they also implied the possession of lordships. In foreign coats the quarterings are often employed to denote the possession of fiefs acquired in other ways than by marriage (*e.g.* by bequest or purchase), or the *jus expectationis*, the right of succession to such fiefs in accordance with certain agreements.

In foreign heraldry the base of the quartered shield is not unfrequently cut off by a horizontal line, forming what is known as a *Champagne*, and the space thus made is occupied by one or more coats. At other times a pile with curved sides runs from the base some distance into the quartered shield, which is then said to be *enté en point*, and this space is devoted to the display of one or more quarterings. The definite and precise British regulations which have grown up on the subject of the marshalling of arms have no equivalent in the armorial laws of other countries.

Very rarely quartering is affected *per saltire*, as in the arms of Sicily and in a few other coats of Spanish origin, but even as regards foreign armory the practice is so rare that it may be disregarded.

The laws of marshalling upon the Continent, and particularly in Germany, are very far from being identical with British heraldic practices.

The British method of impaling two coats of arms upon one shield to signify marriage is now wholly discarded, and two shields are invariably made use of. These shields are placed side by side, the dexter shield being used to display the man's arms and the sinister those of the woman's family. The shields are tilted towards each other (the position is not quite identical with that which we term accollé). But—and this is a peculiarity practically unknown in England—the German practice invariably reverses the charges upon the dexter shield, so that the charges upon the two shields "respect" each other. This perhaps can be most readily understood by reference to Figs. 940 and 941. The former shows the simple arms of Von Bibelspurg, the latter the same coat allied with another. Other examples of this practice will be seen on Plate CXLIX. But it should be noted that letters or words, if they appear as charges upon the shield, are not reversed. This reversing of the charges is by no means an uncommon practice in Germany for other purposes. For instance, if the arms of a State are

FIG. 940.—Arms of Hans Wolf von Bibelspurg.

FIG. 941.—Arms of Hans Wolf von Bibelspurg and his wife Catherina Waraus, married in 1507 at Augsburg.

depicted surrounded by the arms of provinces, or if the arms of a reigning Sovereign are grouped within a bordure of the shields of other people, the charges on the shields to the dexter are almost invariably shown in reflection regarding the shield in the centre. This practice, resting only on what may be termed "heraldic courtesy," dates back to very early times, and is met with even in Rolls of Arms where the shields are all turned to face the centre. Such a system was adopted in Siebmacher's "Book of Arms." But what the true position of the charges should be when represented upon a simple shield should be determined by the position of the helmet. It may be of interest to state that in St. George's Chapel at Windsor the early Stall plates as originally set up were all disposed so that helmets and charges alike faced the High Altar.

The conjunction of three coats of arms in Germany is effected as shown in Fig. 942. Although matrimonial alliance does not in Germany entail the conjunction of different coats of arms on one shield, such conjunction does occur in German heraldry, but it is comparable (in its meaning) with our rules of quartering and not with our rules of impalement. No such exact and definite rules exist in that country as are to be met with in our own to determine the choice of a method of conjunction, nor to indicate the significance to be presumed from whatever method may be found in use. Personal selection and the adaptability to any particular method of the tinctures and the charges themselves of the coats to be conjoined seem to be the determining factors, and the existing territorial attributes of German armory have a greater weight in

some of the various modes of conjunction which have been or are still practised. These include impalement per pale or per fess (Fig. 943) and dimidiation (Fig. 944), which is more usual on the Continent than in these kingdoms. The subdivision of the field, as with ourselves, is most frequently adopted; though we are usually confined to quartering, German armory knows no such restrictions. The most usual subdivisions are as given in Fig. 945. The ordinary quartered shield is met with in Fig. 946,

FIG. 946.—Arms of the Elector and Archbishop of Treves.

which represents the arms of James III., Von Eltz, Elector and Archbishop of Treves (1567–1581), in which his personal arms of Eltz ("Per fess gules and argent, in chief a demi-lion issuing or") are quartered with the impersonal arms of his archbishopric, "Argent, a cross gules." Another method of conjunction is superimposition, by which the design of the one shield takes the form of an ordinary imposed upon the other (Fig. 947). A curious method of conjoining three coats is by engrafting the third in base (Fig. 948). The constant use of the inescutcheon has been already referred to, and even early English armory (Figs. 76 and 303) has examples of the widespread Continental practice (which obtains largely in Spanish and Portuguese heraldry) of surrounding one coat with a bordure of another.

The German method of conjunction by incorporation has been frequently pleaded in British heraldry, in efforts to account for ancient arms, but with us (save for occasional use for cadency differencing at an early and for a limited period) such incorporation only results in and signifies an originally *new* coat, and not an authorised marshalling of existing arms of prior origin and authority. The German method can best be explained by two ex-

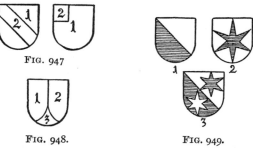

FIG. 947

FIG. 948.

FIG. 949.

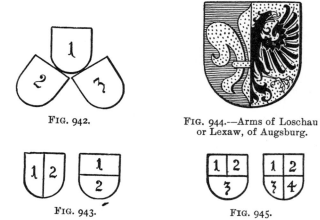

FIG. 942.

FIG. 944.—Arms of Loschau or Lexaw, of Augsburg.

FIG. 943.

FIG. 945.

marshalling than the principle of heirship which is practically the sole governing factor in British heraldry. One must therefore content oneself with a brief recital of

amples. Let us suppose a coat "per fess argent and gules," with which another coat "gules, a fleur-de-lis argent," is to be marshalled. The result would be "per fess argent and gules, a fleur-de-lis counterchanged." With smaller objects a more usual method would duplicate the charges, thus "per bend argent and azure," and "argent, a star of six points azure" would result in "per bend argent and azure, two stars of six points counterchanged" (Fig. 949).

A. C. F-D. AND H. S.

THE ART OF HERALDRY

CHAPTER XXXVIII

THE ARMORIAL INSIGNIA OF KNIGHTHOOD

IT hardly falls within the scope of the present work to detail or discuss the various points concerning the history or statutes of the different British Orders of Knighthood, and still less so of the Foreign Orders. The history of the English Orders alone would make a bulky volume. But it is necessary to treat of the matter to some limited extent, inasmuch as in modern heraldry in every country in Europe additions are made to the armorial achievement whenever it is desired to signify rank in any of the orders of knighthood.

Though a large number of the early Plantagenet Garter Stall-plates date as far back as the year 1420, it is evident that nothing in the armorial bearings with which they are emblazoned bears any relation to the order of knighthood to which they belonged until the year 1469 or thereabouts, when Charles the Bold, Duke of Burgundy, was elected a Knight of the Garter. His Stall plate, which is of a very exceptional style and character, is the first to bear the garter encircling the shield. It is curious to notice, by the way, that upon the privy seal of the Duke of Burgundy, which shows the same arms depicted upon his Garter plate, the shield is surrounded by the collar, from which depends the badge of the Order of the Golden Fleece, so that it is highly probable that the custom of adding marks of knighthood to a shield came to us from the Continent. The next Garter plate which shows the garter around the shield, is that of Viscount Lovel, who was elected in 1483; and the shield of the Earl of Derby, who was elected in the same year, also is encircled by the garter. The Garter itself encircling the shields of knights of that order remained the only mark of knighthood used armorially in this country for a considerable period, though we find that the example was copied in Scotland soon afterwards with regard to the Order of the Thistle. At the commencement of the present Lyon Register, which dates from the year 1672, the arms of the King of Scotland, which are given as such and not as the King of England and Scotland, are described as encircled by the collar of the Order of the Thistle. This probably was used as the equivalent of the garter in England, for we do not find the collar of the Garter, together with the garter itself or the ribbon circle of the Thistle, together with the collar of that order, until a much later period. The use of collars of knighthood upon the Continent to encircle coats of arms has been from the fifteenth century very general and extensive; examples are to be found at an earlier date; but the encircling of arms with the garter carrying the motto of the order, or with the ribbon (which is termed the circle) and motto of any other order is an entirely English practice, which does not appear to have been copied in any other country. It, of course, arose from the fact that the actual garter as worn by the knight of the order carried the motto, and that by representing the garter round the shield, the motto of the order was of necessity also added. The Lyon Register, however, in the entry of record (dated 1672), states that the shield is "encircled with the Order of Scotland, the same being composed of rue and thistles having the image of St. Andrew with his crosse on his brest y'unto pendent," and it is by no means improbable that occasional instances of the heraldic use of the collar of the garter might be discovered at the same period. But it is not until the later part of the eighteenth century that it obtained anything like a regular use.

During the Hanoverian period it became customary to encircle the shield first with the garter, and that in its turn with the collar of the order whenever it was desired to display the achievement in its most complete style; and though even then and at the present day for less elaborate representations the garter only was used without the collar, it still remains correct to display both in a full emblazonment of the arms. An impetus to the practice was doubtless given by the subdivision of the Order of the Bath, which will be presently referred to. An example of this will be found in Figs. 809 and 54, which respectively represent the arms of the Duke of Norfolk, K.G., and the late Duke of Argyll, K.G., K.T. Pendent from the collar, it will be noticed, hangs the badge of the order which is known as the Greater George. In speaking of the garter, the opportunity should be taken to protest strongly against the objectionable practice which has arisen of using a garter to encircle a crest or shield and to carry the family motto. No matter what motto is placed upon the garter, it is both bad form and absolutely incorrect for any one who is not a Knight of the Garter to use a garter in any heraldic display.

But to tabulate the existing practice the present rules as to the display of the arms of knights of the different orders are as follows :—

A Knight of the Garter encircles his escutcheon by a representation of the garter he wears. This is a belt of dark blue velvet edged with gold and ornamented with a heavy gold buckle and ornament at the end. It carries the motto of the Order, "Honi soit qui mal y pense," in gold letters of plain Roman character. Anciently the motto was spelled "Hony soit qy mal y pense," as may be noticed from some of the early Garter plates, and the style of the letter was what is now known as "Old English." The garter is worn buckled, with the end tucked under and looped in a specified manner, which is the method also adopted in heraldic representations (Fig. 809). It is quite permissible to use the garter alone, but a Knight of the Order is allowed to add outside the garter the representation of the collar of the order, as represented in Fig. 809. This is of gold, consisting of twenty-six buckled garters enamelled in the correct colour, each surrounding a rose, the garter alternated with gold knots all joined up by chain links of gold. From the collar depends the "George," or figure of St. George on horseback encountering the dragon, enamelled in colours. In heraldic representations it is usual to ignore the specified number of links in the collar. A Knight of the Garter as such is entitled to claim the privilege of a grant of supporters, but as nowadays the order is reserved for those of the rank of earl and upwards, supporters will always have a prior existence in connection with the peerage.

Knights of the Thistle are entitled to surround their arms with a plain circle of green edged with gold and bearing the motto in gold letters, "Nemo me impune lacessit." They are also entitled to surround their arms with the collar of the order, which is of gold, and composed of sprigs of thistle and rue (Andrew) enamelled in their proper colours. From the collar the badge (the figure of St. Andrew) depends (Figs. 251 and 407).

Knights of St. Patrick are entitled to surround their arms by a plain circle of sky-blue, edged with gold bearing the motto, " Quis Separabit. M.D.C.C.LXXXIII," as enamelled on the star of the order. This is encircled by the collar of the order, which is of gold, composed of roses and harps alternately, tied together with knots of gold, the said roses enamelled alternately, white leaves within red and red leaves within white ; and in the centre of the said collar shall be an Imperial crown surmounting a harp of gold, from which shall hang the badge (Fig. 950).

people now imagine. There is nobody at the present time who is entitled to use these letters. Upon those of the Bath plates which now remain in the chapel of Henry VII. in Westminster Abbey, one of which is represented on plate LXVIII., no instance will be found in which the collar is represented outside the circle, which is pretty good evidence that although isolated examples may possibly be found at an earlier date, it was not the usual custom up to the end of the eighteenth century to encircle a shield with a collar of knighthood.

FIG. 950.—Arms of Viscount Powerscourt, K.P. : Argent, on a bend gules, three pairs of wings conjoined in lure of the field. The escutcheon is surrounded by the ribbon of St. Patrick, and by the collar and pendent therefrom the badge of that Order ; and impaling upon a second escutcheon the arms of Coke, namely : per pale gules and azure, three eagles displayed argent. Mantling gules and argent. Crest : upon a wreath of the colours, a demi-eagle rising, wings expanded argent, looking at the sun in its glory. Supporters : two pegasi argent, winged, maned, and hoofed or. Motto : "Fidélité est de Dieu."

Knights of the Thistle and St. Patrick are entitled as such to claim a grant of supporters on payment of the fees, but these orders are nowadays confined to peers.

The Order of the Bath.—Knights of the Bath who have existed from a remote period do not appear as such to have made any additions to their arms prior to the revival of the order in 1725. At that time, similarly to the Orders of the Garter and the Thistle, the order was of one class only and composed of a limited number of knights. Knights of that order were then distinguished by the letters K.B., which, it should be noted, mean Knight of the Bath, and not Knight Bachelor, as so many

These Knights of the Bath (K.B.), as they were termed, surrounded their escutcheons with circlets of crimson edged with gold, and bearing thereupon the motto of the order, " Tria juncta in uno," in gold letters. Plate LXVIII. is a reproduction of a Stall plate now remaining in the chapel of Henry VII. in Westminster Abbey, and represents that of Admiral Sir Alexander Cockburn, K.B., and shows the arms: " Argent, a chevron gules between three boars' heads erased azure, and as an honourable augmentation, on a chief wavy azure, a sphinx couchant argent. Crests: 1. (of honourable augmentation) out of a naval coronet or, a dexter arm embowed, vested azure, cuffed argent, holding in the hand proper a flag-staff in bend sinister of the last, therefrom floating to the sinister a banner argent, charged with a cross gules, and thereon in letters of gold the words 'St. Domingo'; 2. on a wreath of the colours, a horse passant argent. Supporters: on either side a greyhound argent, collared and lined or, each supporting a flagstaff and banner as in the crest. Motto: 'Virtute et labore.'"

Although at that time it does not appear that the collar of the order was ever employed for armorial purposes, instances are to be found in which the laurel wreath surrounded the circlet with the motto of the order. The collar at any rate does not appear upon any Stall plates. In the year 1815, owing to the large number of officers who had merited reward in the Peninsular Campaign, it was considered necessary to largely increase the extent

FIG. 951.—Arms of General Sir Charles H. Brownlow, G.C.B.: Party per pale or and argent, an inescutcheon within an orle of martlets sable. Upon the escutcheon, which is encircled by the ribbon of the Order of the Bath, by a wreath of laurel, and by the collar and pendent therefrom the badge of a G.C.B., is placed a helmet befitting his degree, with a mantling sable and or; and for his crest, upon a chapeau azure, turned up ermine, a greyhound gules, collared or.

and scope of the order. For this purpose it was divided into two divisions—the Military Division and the Civil Division—and each of these were divided into three classes, namely, Knights Grand Cross (G.C.B.), Knights Commanders (K.C.B.), and Companions (C.B.) The then existing Knights of the Bath became Knights Grand Cross. The existing collar served for all Knights Grand Cross, but the old badge and star were assigned for the civil division of the order, a new pattern being designed for the military division. The number of stalls in Henry VII.'s Chapel being limited, the erection of Stall plates and the display of banners ceased; those then in position were allowed to remain, and still remain at the present moment. Consequently there are no Stall plates to refer to in the matter as precedents since that period, and the rules need to be obtained from other sources. They are now as follows: A Knight Grand Cross of the Order of the Bath surrounds his arms with the circlet as was theretofore the case, and in addition he surrounds the circlet by his collar, from which depends the badge (either military or civil) of the division to which he belongs. The collar is really for practical purposes the distinguishing mark of a Knight Grand Cross, because although as such he is entitled upon payment of the fees to claim a grant

of supporters, he is under no compulsion to do so, and comparatively but few avail themselves of the privilege. All Knights of the Bath, before the enlargement of the order, had supporters. A Knight Grand Cross of the *military* division encircles his arms with the laurel wreath in addition, this being placed outside the circlet and within the collar of the order. The collar is composed of gold having nine Imperial crowns and eight devices of the rose, the thistle, and shamrock issuing from a sceptre placed alternately and enamelled in their proper colours, the links being connected with seventeen knots enamelled white. The badges of the military and civil divisions differ considerably, as may be seen from Figs. 951 and I respectively.

Knights Commanders of the Bath have no collar and cannot claim a grant of supporters, but they encircle their shields with the circlet of the order, suspending their badge below the shield by the ribbon from which it is worn (Figs. 333 and 358). Knights Commanders of the military division use the laurel wreath as do Knights Grand Cross (Figs. 951, 333, and 779), but no members of any class of the civil division are entitled to display it.

Companions of the Order (C.B.) do not use the helmet of a knight as does a G.C.B. or a K.C.B.; in fact, the only difference which is permissible in their arms is that they are allowed to suspend the badge of a C.B. from a ribbon below their shields (Figs. 243, 534, and 535). They do not use the circlet of the order. Certain cases have come under my notice in which a military C.B. has added a laurel wreath to his armorial bearings, but whether such a practice is correct I am unaware, but I think it is not officially recognised.

The Most Exalted Order of the Star of India (like the Order of the Bath as at present constituted) is divided into three classes, Knights Grand Commanders, Knights Commanders, and Companions. Knights Grand Commanders place the circlet of the order around their shields (Fig. 953). This is of light blue inscribed with the motto, "Heaven's light our guide." This in its turn is surrounded by the collar of the order, which is composed of alternate links of the Indian lotus flower, crossed palm-branches, and the united red and white rose of England. In the centre of the collar is an Imperial crown from which depends the badge of the order, this being an onyx cameo of the effigy of her late Majesty Queen Victoria within the motto of the order, and surmounted by a star, the whole being richly jewelled. The surrounding of the shield by the circlet of the order doubtless is a consequence and follows upon the original custom of the armorial use of the garter, but this being admitted, it is yet permissible to state that that practice came from the Continent, and there is little reason to doubt that the real meaning and origin of the custom of using the circlet is derived from the Continental practice which has for long been usual of displaying the shield of arms upon the star of an order of knighthood. The star of every British order—the Garter included—contains the circlet and motto of the order, and it is easy to see how, after depicting the shield of arms upon the star of the order, the result will be that the circlet of the order surrounds the shield. No armorial warrant upon the point is ever issued at the creation of an order; the thing follows as a matter of course, the circlet being taken from the star to surround the shield without further authorisation. Upon this point there can be no doubt, inasmuch as the garter which surrounds the shield of a K.G. is in *all* authoritative heraldic paintings buckled in the peculiar manner in which it is worn and in which it is depicted upon the star. The Star of the Thistle shows the plain circlet, the Star of St. Patrick the same, and the arms of a Knight of St. Patrick afford a curious confirmation of my contention, because whilst the motto of the order is specified to be,

"Quis separabit," the circlet used for armorial purposes includes the date (MDCCLXXXIII.) as shown upon the star. The Order of the Bath, again, has a plain circlet upon the star, and the badges and stars of the military knights have the laurel wreath represented in heraldic drawings, the laurel wreath being absent from the stars and the shields of those who are members of the civil division. Now with regard to the Order of the Star of India the motto on the star is carried upon a representation of a ribbon which is tied in a curious manner, and my own

FIG. 953.—Arms of Lieut.-Gen. Sir Richard Strachey, G.C.S.I.: Quarterly, 1 and 4, argent, a cross between four eagles displayed gules (Strachey); 2 and 3, or, three crescents sable, on a canton of the East, a ducal coronet of the first, and impaling the arms of Grant, namely: quarterly 1 and 4, gules three antique crowns or (for Grant); 2. or, a fess chequy azure and argent between three wolves' heads couped sable (for Stewart of Atholl); 3. azure, a dexter arm vambraced, grasping a sword erected in pale argent, between three boars' heads couped or, langued gules (for Gordon), all within a bordure wavy or. Upon the escutcheon, which is surrounded by the ribbon and the collar of the Star of India, from which is pendent his badge as a G.C.S.I., is placed a helmet befitting his degree, with a mantling gules and argent: and for his crest, upon a wreath of the colours, an eagle displayed gules, charged on the breast with a cross patée fitchée argent.

opinion is that the circlet used to surround the shield of a G.C.S.I. or K.C.S.I. should (as in the case of the garter) be represented not as a simple circlet like the Bath or Thistle, but as a ribbon tied in the curious manner represented upon the star. This tying is not, however, duplicated upon the badge, and possibly I may be told that the circlet and its use are taken from the badge and not from the star. The reply to such a statement is, first, that there is no garter upon the badge of that order, there is no circlet on the badge of the Thistle, and the circlet on the badge of St. Patrick is surrounded by a wreath of trefoils which in that case ought to appear round the shield of a K.P. This wreath of trefoils is absent from the K.P. star. Further, no Companion of an Order is permitted to use the Circlet of the Order, whilst every Companion has his badge. No Companion has a star. Though I hold strongly that the circlet of the Star of India should be a ribbon tied as represented on the star of the order, I must admit I have never yet come across an official instance of it being so represented. This, however, is a point upon which there is no definite warrant of instruction, and is not the conclusion justifiable that on this matter the officers of arms have been led into a mistake in their general practice by an oversight and possible unfamiliarity with the actual star? A Knight Grand Commander is entitled to claim a grant of supporters on payment of the fees. A Knight Commander

encircles his shield with the circlet of the order and hangs his badge from a ribbon below (Fig. 963), a Companion of the Order simply hangs the badge he wears below his shield.

The Most Distinguished Order of St. Michael and St. George.—This order again is divided into three classes—Knights Grand Cross, Knights Commanders, and Companions. Knights Grand Cross place the circlet of the order and the collar with the badge around their shields, and, like other Knights Grand Cross, they are entitled to claim a grant of supporters (Figs. 117 and 222). The circlet of the order is of blue edged with gold, and bearing in gold letters the motto of the order, "Auspicium melioris ævi." The collar is composed alternately of lions of England, of Maltese crosses, and of the ciphers S.M. and S.G., and having in the centre an Imperial crown over two lions passant guardant, each holding a bunch of seven arrows. At the opposite point of the collar are two similar lions. The whole is of gold except the crosses, which are of white enamel, and the various devices are linked together by small gold chains. Knights Commanders of the Order encircle their shields with a similar circlet of the order, and hang their badges below (Fig. 501). A Companion simply suspends his badge from a ribbon below his shield (Fig. 954).

FIG. 954.—Arms of John Roberts, Esq., C.M.G., of Littlebairn House, Dunedin, New Zealand: Gules, a hawk's lure argent, between two cushions or in chief, in base a ram's head proper, horned gold, all within a bordure azure, and below the escutcheon his badge as a C.M.G. Mantling gules, doubled argent. Crest: on a wreath of his liveries, a demi-lion rampant azure, holding in the dexter paw a fleur-de-lis or. Motto: "Industria et probitate."

The Most Eminent Order of the Indian Empire.—This order is divided into three classes—Knights Grand Commanders, Knights Commanders, and Companions. Knights Grand Commanders and Knights Commanders encircle their shields with the circlet of the order, which is of purple inscribed in letters of gold, with the motto of the order, "Imperatricis auspiciis." The collar of the order, which is used by the Knights Grand Commanders, in addition to the circle, is composed of elephants, lotus flowers, peacocks in their pride, and Indian roses, and in the centre is an Imperial crown, the whole being linked together by chains of gold (Fig. 955). Knights Com-

FIG. 955.—Arms of Sir Thomas Lawrence Seccombe, G.C.I.E., K.C.S.I., C.B.: Argent, on a fess gules, between three lions rampant sable, a lotus-flower slipped and leaved proper, in the centre chief point an Eastern crown of the second, a bordure invected of the third. Upon the escutcheon, which is surrounded by the ribbon of the Order of the Indian Empire, and by the collar and pendent therefrom the star of a G.C.I.E., of a K.C.S.I., and the badge of a C.B. (Civ. Div.), is placed a helmet befitting his degree, with a mantling gules and argent; and for his crest, upon a wreath of the colours, a lion rampant sable between two elephants' proboscides proper: with the motto, "Paratus et fidelis."

manders suspend their badges from their shields (Figs. 427 and 578). Companions are only permitted to suspend their badges from a ribbon, and, as in the cases of the other orders, are not allowed to make use of the circlet of the order (Fig. 390).

The Royal Victorian Order is divided into five classes, and is the only British order of which this can be said. There is no collar belonging to the order, so a G.C.V.O. cannot put one round his shield. Knights Grand Cross surround their shields with the circlet of the order, which is of dark blue carrying in letters of gold the motto, "Victoria." Knights Commanders also use the circlet, with the badge suspended from the ribbon. Commanders and members of the fourth and fifth classes of the Order suspend the badge which they are entitled to wear below their shields. The "Victorian Chain" is quite apart from the Victorian Order, and up to the present time has only been conferred upon the late Archbishop of Canterbury and Lord Curzon of Kedleston. It apparently exists by the pleasure of His Majesty, no statutes having been ordained.

The Distinguished Service Order (Fig. 964), the Imperial Service Order, and the Order of Merit are each of but one class only, none of them conferring the dignity of knighthood. They rank heraldically with the Companions of the other Orders, and for heraldic purposes merely confer upon those people entitled to the decorations the right to suspend the badges they wear below their shields or lozenges as the case may be, following the rules observed by other Companions. The Victoria Cross (Fig. 956), the Albert Medal, the Conspicuous Service Cross, the Kaisar-i-

Hind Medal, the Royal Red Cross, the Volunteer Officers' Decoration (Fig. 127), and the Decoration of the League of Mercy all rank as decorations. Though none confer any style or precedence of knighthood, those entitled to them are permitted to suspend representations of such decorations as are enjoyed below their shields.

The members of the Orders of Victoria and Albert and of the Crown of India are permitted to display the badges they wear below their lozenges.

Some people, notably in the early part of the nineteenth century, adopted the practice of placing war medals below the escutcheons amongst other decorations. It is doubtful, however, how far this practice is correct, inasmuch as a medal does not technically rank as a decoration or as a matter of honour. That medals are "decorations" is not officially recognised, with the exception, perhaps, of the Jubilee medal, the Diamond Jubilee medal, and the Coronation medal, which have been given

FIG. 956.—Arms of Admiral Charles Davis Lucas, V.C.: Argent, a fess between six annulets gules. Mantling gules and argent. Crest: on a wreath of the colours, a demi-griffin argent, beaked and membered or; with the motto, "Stat religione parentum."

a status more of the character of a decoration than of simple medals.

Plate XXIII. Fig. 2 represents the arms of Sir Woodbine Parish, K.H., and illustrates the method of displaying the arms of a Knight of the Royal Hanoverian Order.

The Order of the Hospital of St. John of Jerusalem in England does not rank with other orders or decorations, inasmuch as it was initiated without Royal intervention, and carries no precedence or titular rank. In 1888, however, a Royal charter of incorporation was obtained, and the distribution of the highest offices of the order in the persons of the Sovereign, the Prince of Wales, and other members of the Royal Family has of late years very much increased its social status. The Crown is gradually acquiring a right of veto, which will probably eventually result in the order becoming a recognised honour, of which the gift lies with the Crown. In the charter of incorporation, Knights of Justice and Ladies of Justice were permitted to place as a chief over their arms the augmentation anciently used by knights of the English language of the original Roman Catholic Celibate Order.

THE ART OF HERALDRY

The chief used is: "Gules, charged with a cross throughout argent, the cross embellished in its angles with lions passant guardant and unicorns passant alternately both or," as in the cross of the order. The omission, which is all the more inexplicable owing to the fact that the present Garter King of Arms is the officer for the order, that the heraldic provisions of this charter have never been conveyed, as should have been the case, in a Royal Warrant to the Earl Marshal, has caused some confusion, for the officers of the College of Arms, when speaking officially, decline to admit the insignia of the order in any official emblazonment of arms. Lyon King of Arms has been less punctilious, and Fig. 494, which represents the arms of Mr. A. E. Fraser, a Knight of Justice of the Order, shows his shield as now registered in Lyon Office with the chief.

Knights of Justice, Knights of Grace, and Esquires of the Orders all suspend the badges they wear from a black watered-silk ribbon below their shields (Fig. 334), and Ladies of Justice and Ladies of Grace do the same below their lozenges. By the Statutes of the Order Knights of Justice are required to show that all their four grandparents were legally entitled to bear arms, but so many provisions for the exercise of discretion in dispensing with this requirement were at the same time created that to all intents and purposes such a regulation might never have been included. Some of the Knights of Justice even yet have no arms at all, others are themselves grantees, and still others would be unable to show what is required of them if the claims of their grandparents were properly investigated. Figs. 957 and 958,

FIG. 958.—Arms from the tomb of Sir Thomas Tresham.

added to a shield, as does the coat of Colonel John Alexander Man Stuart, C.B., C.M.G. (Plate XVIII. Fig. 1).

It should perhaps be stated that the supporters issued to Knights Grand Cross are personal to themselves, and in the patents by which they are granted the grant is made for life only, no hereditary limitation being added.

Any person in this country holding a Royal Licence to wear the insignia of any foreign order is permitted to adopt any heraldic form, decoration, or display which that order confers in the country of origin. Official recognition exists for this, and many precedents can be quoted.

The rules which exist in foreign countries concerning heraldic privileges of the knights of different orders are very varied, and it is impossible to briefly summarise them. It may, however, be stated that the most usual practice is to display the shield alone in the centre of the star (Fig. 959). As with us, the collars of the orders are placed around the shields, and the badges depend below, but the use of the circlet carrying the motto of the order is exclusively a British practice. In the case of some of the Orders, however, the official coat of arms of the order is quartered, impaled, or borne in pretence with the personal arms, and the cross patée of the Order of the

FIG. 959.—" Bailli profès " of the Catholic Order of the Knights Hospitallers or the Order of Malta.

Dannebrog is to be met with placed in front of a shield of quarterings, the charges thereupon appearing in the angles of the cross. I am not sure, however, that the cases which have come under my notice should not be rather considered definite and hereditary grants of augmentation, this being perhaps a more probable explanation than that such a method of display followed as a matter of course on promotion to the order. The Grand Masters of the Teutonic Order quarter the arms of that order with those of their family. The Knights of the Order of St. Stephen of Tuscany bear the arms of that order in chief over their personal arms. Fig. 959 represents the manner in which a "Bailli-profès" (Grand Cross) of the real Catholic and Celibate Order of St. John of Malta places the chief of the order on his shield, the latter being imposed upon a

FIG. 957.—From the tomb of Sir Thomas Tresham, last Grand Prior in England of the Knights Hospitallers.

which are taken from the effigy of Sir Thomas Tresham, Last Grand Prior in England of the Knights Hospitallers, now in All Hallows Church, Rushton, Northamptonshire, represents the method in which the arms of the *ancient* Order of St. John of Jerusalem were worn and borne.

Maltese star (this being white) and the badge of the order depending below. The "Knight-profès" does not use the chief of the order. In the German Protestant Order of Malta (formerly Bailiwick of Brandenburg) the Commendatories place the shield of their arms upon the Cross of Malta, the Knights of Justice ("Richtsritter") on the contrary assume the cross upon the shield itself (see Plate LXV. Fig. 4), whilst the Knights of Grace suspend it from the bottom of the shield. Other examples concerning the German use of heraldic insignia of knighthood will be found on Plate CXXXIX. Figs. 4 and 16. Anciently the heraldic emblems of an order were placed in the dexter chief of the shield or simply near the escutcheon (Plate LXXXIX.); in like manner would be disposed the badges of a Society of Knights or other Fraternity (Plates LXXVIII. Fig. 1 and LXXX. Fig. 4), but in a few instances a closer connection may be observed (Plate CXXVI. Fig. 4). The members of the ancient Order of La Cordelière formerly encircled their lozenges with a representation of the Cordelière, which formed a part of their habit (Fig. 864); and the officers of the Ecclesiastical Orders frequently surround their escutcheons with rosaries from which depend crucifixes. Whether this latter practice, however, should be considered merely a piece of artistic decoration, or whether it should be regarded as an ecclesiastical matter or should be included within the purview of armory, I leave others to decide.

By a curious fiction, for the origin of which it is not easy to definitely account, unless it is a survival of the celibacy required in certain orders, a knight is not supposed to share the insignia of any order of knighthood with his wife. There is not the slightest doubt that his own knighthood does confer upon her both precedence and titular rank, and why there should be any necessity for the statement to be made as to the theoretical position has long been a puzzle to me. Such a theory, however, is considered to be correct, and as a consequence in modern times it has become a rigid rule that the arms of the wife of a knight must not be impaled upon a shield which is displayed within the circlet of an order. No such rule existed in ancient times, and many instances can be found in which impaled

shields, or the shields of the wife only, are met with inside a representation of the Garter. Nevertheless, the modern idea is that when a Knight of any Order impales the arms of his wife, he must use two shields placed accollé, the dexter surmounting the sinister (Figs. 1, 251, and 358). Upon the dexter shield is represented the arms of the knight within the circlet, or the circlet and collar, as the case may be, of his order; on the sinister shield the arms of the knight are impaled with those of his wife, and this shield, for the purpose of artistic balance, is usually surrounded with a meaningless and inartistic floral or laurel wreath to make its size similar to the dimensions of the dexter shield.

The widow of a knight is required at present to immediately discontinue the use of the ensigns of the order, and to revert to the plain impaled lozenge which she would be entitled to as the widow of an undecorated gentleman. As she retains her titular rank, such a regulation seems absurd, but it undoubtedly exists, and until it is altered must be conformed to.

Knights Grand Cross (Figs. 1 and 117) and Knight Commanders (Figs. 333 and 501), as also Knights Bachelors, use the open affronté helmet of a knight. Companions of any order, and members of those orders which do not confer any precedence or title of knighthood, use only the close profile helmet of a gentleman (Figs. 243 and 558, and see the arms of Colonel Man Stuart, Plate XVIII. Fig. 1). A Knight Bachelor, of course, is at liberty to impale the arms of his wife upon his escutcheon without employing the double form (Fig. 396). It only makes the use of the double escutcheon for Knights of Orders the more incomprehensible.

Reference should also be made to the subject of impalement, which will be found in the chapter upon Marshalling, and to Fig. 811, which shows the simultaneous heraldic use of several decorations. Baronetcies are not of course knighthood, but it may be convenient here to refer to Figs. 350 and 523 as examples of the use of the badge of Ulster for a Baronet of England, Ireland, Great Britain, or the United Kingdom, and to Fig. 194, where the badge of Baronet of Nova Scotia will be found.

A. C. F-D.

CHAPTER XXXIX

THE ARMORIAL BEARINGS OF A LADY

BEARING in mind that armory was so deeply interwoven with all that was best in chivalry, it is curious that the armorial status of a woman should have been left so undefined. A query as to how a lady may bear arms will be glibly answered for her as maid (Fig. 483) and as widow (Fig. 597) by the most elementary heraldic text-book. But a little consideration will show how far short our knowledge falls of a complete or uniform set of rules.

Let what is definitely known be first stated. In the first place, no woman (save the Sovereign) can inherit or transmit crest or motto, and no woman may use a helmet or mantling. All daughters, if unmarried, bear *upon a lozenge* the paternal arms and quarterings of their father, with his difference marks. If their mother were an heiress, they quarter her arms with those of their father. In England (save in the Royal Family, and in this case even it is a matter of presumption only) there is no seniority amongst daughters, and the difference marks of all daughters are those borne by the father, and none other. There are no marks of distinction as between

daughters. In Scotland, however, seniority does exist, according to priority of birth; and, though Scottish heraldic law provides no marks of cadency as between sister and sister, the laws of arms north of the Tweed recognise seniority of birth in the event of a certain set of circumstances arising.

In Scotland, as doubtless many are aware, certain untitled Scottish families, for reasons which may or may not be known, have been permitted to use supporters to their arms. When the line vests in coheirs, the eldest born daughter, as heir of line, assumes the supporters, unless some other limitation has been attached to them. Scottish supporters are peculiar things to deal with, unless the exact terms of the patent of grant or matriculation are known.

The lozenge of an unmarried lady is frequently surmounted by a true lover's knot of ribbon, usually painted blue (Fig. 483). It has no particular meaning and no official recognition, though plenty of official use, and practically its status is no more than a piece of supposedly artistic ornament.

Concerning the law for unmarried ladies, therefore, there is neither doubt nor dispute. A widow bears arms upon a lozenge, this showing the arms of her late husband impaled with those of her own family (Fig. 597), or with these latter displayed on an escutcheon of pretence if she be an heir or coheir.

The other state in the progress of life in which a lady may hope or expect to find herself is that of married life. Now, how should a married lady display arms? Echo and the text-books alike answer, "How?" Does *anybody* know? This "fault," for such it undoubtedly is, is due to the fact that the laws of arms evolved themselves in that period when a married woman was little accounted of. As an unmarried heiress she undoubtedly was a somebody; as a widowed and richly-jointured dowager she was likewise of account, but as a wedded wife her identity was lost, for the Married Women's Property Act was not in existence, nor was it thought of. So completely was it recognised that all rights and inheritance of the wife devolved of right upon the husband, that formerly the husband enjoyed any peerage honours which had descended to the wife, and was summoned to Parliament as a peer in his wife's peerage. Small wonder, then, that the same ideas dominated the rules of armory. These only provide ways and methods for the husband to bear the wife's arms. This is curious, because there can be no doubt that at a still earlier period the practice of impalement was entirely confined to women, and that, unless the wife happened to be an heiress, the husband did not trouble to impale her arms. But a little thought will show that the two are not at variance, for if monuments and other matters of *record* are ignored, the earliest examples of impalement which have come down to us are all, almost without exception, examples of arms borne by widows. One cannot get over the fact that a wife during coverture had practically no legal status at all. The rules governing impalement, and the conjunction of the arms of man and wife, as they are to be borne by the husband, are recited in the chapter upon Marshalling, which also details the ways in which a widow bears arms in the different ranks of life. Nothing would be gained by repeating them here.

It may be noted, however, that it is not considered correct for a widow to make use of the true lover's knot of blue ribbon, which is sometimes used in the case of an unmarried lady. A divorce puts matters in *statu quo ante*.

There still remains, however, the question of the bearing of arms in her own right by a married woman under coverture at the present day.

The earliest grant of arms that I can put my hands upon to a woman is one dated 1558. It is, moreover, the only grant of which I know to one single person, that person being a *wife*. The grant is decidedly interesting, so I print it in full:—

"To ALL AND SINGULAR as well kinges heraldes and officers of armes as nobles gentlemen and others which these presents shall see or here Wyllyam Hervye Esquire otherwise called Clarencieux principall heralde and kinge of armes of the south-east and west parties of England findith due comendaçons and greting fforasmuch as auncientlye ffrom the beginnynge the valyant and vertuous actes off excellent parsons have ben comended to the worlde with sondry monumentes and remembrances off theyr good desertes among the which one of the chefist and most usuall hath ben the beringe of figures and tokens in shildes called armes beinge none other thinges then Evidences and demonstraçons of prowes and valoure diverselye distributed according to the quallyties and desertes of the parsons. And for that Dame Marye Mathew daughter and heyre of Thomas Mathew of Colchester in the counte of Essex esquire hath longe contynued in

nobylyte she and her auncestors bearinge armes, yet she notwithstandinge being ignorant of the same and ffor the advoydinge of all inconvenyences and troubles that dayleye happeneth in suche cases and not wyllinge to preiudyce anye person hath instantlye requyred me The sayde Clarencieux kinge of armes accordinge to my registers and recordes To assigne and sett forthe ffor her and her posterite The armes belonging and descendinge To her ffrom her saide auncesters. In consideraçon whereof I have at her ientle request assigned geven and granted unto her and her posterite The owlde and auncient armes of her said auncesters as followeth. That is to saye—partye per cheveron sables and argent a Lyon passant in chefe off the second the poynt goutey [a] of the firste as more plainly aperith depicted in this margent. Which armes The Saide Clarencieux kinge of Armes by powre and authorite to myne office ar nexed and grannted By the Queenes Majesties Letters patentes under The great Seale of England have ratefyed and confirmed and By These presentes do ratefye and confyrme unto and for the saide dame marye Mathew otherwise called dame Mary Jude wiffe to Sir Andrew Jude Knight late Mayor and Alderman off London and to her posterite To use bear and shew for evermore in all places of honnor to her and theyr wourshipes at theyr Lybertie and pleasur without impediment lett or interupçon of any person or persons.

"IN WITNESS WHEREOF the saide Clarencieux Kinge of Armes have signed these presentes with my hand and sett thereunto The Seale off myne office and The Seale of myne armes geven at London The xth daye off October in the Yeare of owre Lord Godd 1558 and in the ffourth and ffifth yeares off the reignes off owre Souereignes Lorde and Layde Phellip and Marye by the grace of God Kinge and Queene of England france both cycles Jerusalem Irland deffendors of the faythe Archedukes of Austrya Dukes of Burgoyne myllain & braband erles of haspurgie, Flanders and Tyrrell.

"W. HERVEY ALS CLARENCIEUX
"King of Armes.

"Confirmation of Arms to Dame Mary Mathew, 'otherwise called Dame Marye Jude, wyffe to Sir Andrew Jude, Knight, Late Lord Mayor and Alderman off London,' 1558."

In this grant the arms are painted upon a *shield*. The grant was made in her husband's lifetime, but his arms are not impaled therewith. Evidently, therefore, the lady bears arms *in her own right*, and the presumption would seem to be that a married lady bears her arms without reference to her husband, and bears them upon a shield. On the other hand, the grant to Lady Pearce, referred to at an earlier page, whilst not blazoning the Pearce arms, shows the painting upon the patent to have been a lozenge of the arms of Pearce, charged with a baronet's hand impaled with the arms then granted for the maiden name of Lady Pearce. On the other hand, a grant is printed in vol. i. of the Notes to the "Visitation of England and Wales." The grant is to Dame Judith Diggs, widow of Sir Maurice Diggs, Bart., now wife of Daniel Sheldon, and to Dame Margaret Sheldon, her sister, relict of Sir Joseph Sheldon, Knight, late Alderman, and sometime Lord Mayor of the City of London, daughters and coheirs of Mr. George Rose, of Eastergate. The operative clause of the grant is: " do by these Presents grant and assign to ye said Dame Judith and Dame Margaret the Armes hereafter mentioned Viz[t]; Ermine, an Eagle displayed Sable, membered and beaked Gules, debruised with a Bendlet Componè Or and Azure, as in the margin hereof more plainly appears depicted. To be borne and used for ever hereafter by them ye said

[a] Gutté-de-poix.

Dame Judith Diggs and Dame Margaret Sheldon and the descendants of their bodies respectively, lawfully begotten, according to the Laws, Rules and practice of Armes."

In each case it will be noted that the sisters were respectively wife and widow of some one of the name of Sheldon; and it might possibly be supposed that these were arms granted for the name of Sheldon. There seems, however, to be very little doubt that these are the arms for Rose. The painting is, however, of the single coat of Rose, and one is puzzled to know why the arms are not painted in conjunction with those of Sheldon. The same practice was followed in the patent which was granted to Nelson's Lady Hamilton. This patent, which both heraldically and historically is excessively interesting, was printed in full on p. 168, vol. i. of the *Genealogical Magazine.* The arms which in the grant are specifically said to be the arms of Lyons (not of Hamilton) are painted upon a lozenge, with no reference to the arms of Hamilton. In each of these cases, however, the grantee of arms has been an heiress, so that the clause by which the arms are limited to the descendants does not help. An instance of a grant to a man and his wife, where the wife was not an heiress, is printed in "The Right to Bear Arms"; and in this case the painting shows the arms impaled with those of the husband. The grant to the wife has no hereditary limitations, and presumably her descendants would never be able to quarter the arms of the wife, no matter even if by the extinction of the other issue she eventually became a coheir. The fact that the arms of man and wife are herein granted together prevents any one making any deduction as to what is the position of the wife alone.

There was a patent issued in the year 1784 to a Mrs. Sarah Lax, widow of John Lax, to take the name and arms of Maynard, such name and arms to be borne by herself and her issue. The painting in this case is of the arms of Maynard alone upon a lozenge, and the crest which was to be borne by her male descendants is quite a separate painting in the body of the grant, and not in conjunction with the lozenge. Now, Mrs. Maynard was a widow, and it is manifestly wrong that she should bear the arms as if she were unmarried, yet how was she to bear them? She was bearing the name of Lax because that had been her husband's name, and she took the name of Maynard, which presumably her husband would have taken had he been alive; she herself was a Miss Jefferson, so would she have been entitled to have placed the arms of Jefferson upon an escutcheon of pretence, in the centre of the arms of Maynard? Presumably she would, because suppose the husband had assumed the name and arms of Maynard in his lifetime, he certainly would have been entitled to place his wife's arms of Jefferson on an escutcheon of pretence. On March 9, 1878, Francis Culling Carr, and his second wife, Emily Blanche, daughter of Andrew Morton Carr, and niece of the late Field-Marshal Sir William Maynard Gomm, G.C.B., both assumed by Royal Licence the additional surname and arms of Gomm. Neither Mr. nor Mrs. Carr-Gomm appear to have had any blood descent from the Gomm family; consequently the Gomm arms were granted to both husband and wife, and the curious part is that they were not identical, the marks (showing that there was no blood relationship) being a canton for the husband and a cross crosslet for the wife. In this case the arms were impaled. One is puzzled to know why the grant to the wife was necessary as well as the grant to the husband.

In 1865 Mrs. Massy, widow of Hugh Massy, assumed the name and arms of Richardson in lieu of Massy. Mrs. Massy was the only child of Major Richardson Brady, who had previously assumed by Royal Licence the arms of Brady only. The painting upon the patent is a lozenge, bearing the arms of Massy, and upon an escutcheon of pretence the arms of Richardson. Of course, the arms of Mrs. Massy, as a widow, previously to the issue of the Royal Licence were a lozenge of the arms of Massy, and on an escutcheon of pretence the arms of Brady.

A few years ago a Grant of Arms was issued to a Mrs. Sharpe, widow of Major Sharpe. The arms were *to be borne by herself* and the descendants of her late husband, and by the other descendants of her husband's father, so that there is no doubt whatever that these were the arms of Sharpe. I have no idea who Mrs. Sharpe was, and I do not know that she possessed any arms of her own. Let us presume she did not. Now, unless a widow may bear the arms of her late husband on a lozenge, whether she has arms to impale with them or not, how on earth is she to bear arms at all? And yet the grant most distinctly was primarily to Mrs. Sharpe.

After the death of General Ross, the victor of Bladensburg, a grant of an augmentation was made to be placed upon the monument to the memory of the General (Fig. 776). It will be seen that the grant also was for the augmentation to be borne by his widow during her widowhood. But no mention appears of the arms of Mrs. Ross, nor, as far as I can ascertain, was proof officially made that Mrs. Ross was in her own right entitled to arms; consequently, whether she really was or was not, we may assume that as far as the official authorities officially knew she was not, and the same query formulated with regard to the Sharpe patent holds good in this case. The painting on the patent shows the arms upon a shield, and placed above is a helmet surmounted by the crest of augmentation and the family crest of Ross.

So that from the cases we have mentioned instances can be found of the arms of a wife upon a shield alone, and of a widow having arms depicted upon a lozenge, such arms being on different occasions the impaled arms of her husband and herself, or the arms of herself alone or of her husband alone; and we have arms granted to a wife, and depicted as an impalement or upon a lozenge. So that from grants it seems almost impossible to deduce any decided and unquestionable rule as to how wife or widow should bear a coat of arms. There is, however, one other source from which profitable instruction may be drawn. I refer to the methods of depicting arms upon hatchments, and more particularly to the hatchment of a married woman. Now a hatchment is strictly and purely personal, and in the days when the use of such an article was an everyday matter, the greatest attention was paid to the proper marshalling of the arms thereupon. There are so many varying circumstances that we have here only space to refer to the three simple rules, and these uncomplicated by any exceptional circumstances, which governed the hatchments of maid, wife, and widow. In the first case, the hatchment of an unmarried lady showed the whole of the background black, the paternal arms on a lozenge, and this suspended by a knot of blue ribbon. In the hatchment of a widow the background again was all black, the arms were upon a lozenge (but without the knot of ribbon), and the lozenge showed the arms of husband and wife impaled, or with the wife's in pretence, as circumstances might dictate. The hatchment of a wife was entirely different. Like the foregoing, it was devoid, of course, of helmet, mantling, crest, or motto; but the background was white on the dexter side (to show that the husband was still alive), and black on the sinister (to show the wife was dead). But the impaled arms were not depicted upon a lozenge, but upon a shield, and the shield was surmounted by the true lover's knot of blue ribbon.

I have already stated that when the rules of arms were in the making the possibility of a married woman bearing arms in her own right was quite ignored, and theoretically even now the husband bears his wife's arms for her upon his shield. But the arms of a man are never depicted suspended from a true lover's knot. Such a display is distinctly feminine, and I verily believe that the correct way for a married woman to use arms, if she desires the display thereof to be personal to herself rather than to her husband, is her husband's arms impaled with her own upon a shield suspended from a true lover's knot, and without helmet, mantling, crest, or motto. At any rate such a method of display is a correct one, it is in no way open to criticism on the score of inaccuracy, it has precedent in its favour, and it affords a very desirable means of distinction. My only hesitation is that one cannot say it is the only way, or that it would be "incorrect" for the husband. At any rate it is the only way of drawing a distinction between the "married" achievements of the husband and the wife.

The limitations attached to a lady's heraldic display being what they are, it has long been felt, and keenly felt, by every one attempting heraldic design, that artistic treatment of a lady's arms savoured almost of the impossible. What delicacy of treatment can possibly be added to the hard outline of the lozenge? The substitution of curvilinear for straight lines in the outline, and even the foliation of the outline, goes but a little way as an equivalent to the extensive artistic opportunities which the mantling affords to a designer when depicting the arms of a man.

To a certain extent, two attempts have been made towards providing a remedy. Neither can properly claim *official* recognition, though both have been employed in a quasi-official manner. The one consists of the knot of ribbon; the other consists of the use of the cordelière. In their present usage the former is meaningless and practically senseless, whilst the use of the latter is radically wrong, and in my opinion, little short of imposture. The knot of ribbon, when employed, is usually in the form of a thin streamer of blue ribbon tied in the conventional true lover's knot (Fig. 453). But the imbecility and inconsistency of its use lies in the fact that except upon a hatchment it has been denied by custom to married women and widows, who have gained their lovers; whilst its use is sanctioned for the unmarried lady, who, unless she be affianced, neither has nor ought to have anything whatever to do with lovers or with their knot. The women who are fancy-free display the tied-up knot; women whom love has fast tied up, unless the foregoing opinion as to the correct way to display the arms of a married lady which I have expressed be correct, must leave the knot alone. But as matters stand heraldically at the moment the ribbon is used with the lozenge of an unmarried lady, and its artistic advantages are manifest

in Fig. 960, specially designed by Miss C. Helard. With reference to the cordelière some writers assert that its use is optional, others that its use is confined to widow ladies. Now as a matter of fact it is nothing whatever of the kind. It is really the insignia of the old French Order of the

FIG. 960.—Armorial bearings of the late Miss Emily Paynter: Upon a lozenge, quarterly, 1. azure, three blocks argent, each charged with an annulet sable (for Paynter); 2. azure, three faggots argent (for Antron); 3. argent, three bends gules (for Bodrugan); 4. argent, two chevronels nebuly gules, between three sheaves of as many arrows sable, banded of the second (for Best).

Cordelière, which was founded by Anne of Bretagne, widow of Charles VIII., in 1498, its membership being confined to widow ladies of noble family. The cordelière was the waist girdle which formed a part of the insignia of the Order, and it took its place around the lozenges of the arms of the members in a manner similar to the armorial use of the Garter for Knights of that Order. Though the Order of the Cordelière is long since extinct, it is neither right nor proper that any part of its insignia should be adopted unaltered by those who can show no connection with it or membership of it.   A. C. F-D.

CHAPTER XL

OFFICIAL HERALDIC INSIGNIA

THE armory of all other nations than our own is rich in heraldic emblems of office. In France this was particularly the case, and France undoubtedly for many centuries gave the example, to be followed by other civilised countries, in all matters of honour and etiquette.

If English heraldry were entirely destitute of official heraldic ensigns, perhaps the development elsewhere of this branch of armory might be dismissed as an entirely foreign growth. But this is far from being the case, as there are some number of cases in which these official emblems do exist. In England, however, the instances are governed by no scale of comparative importance, and the appearance of such tokens can only be described as capricious. That a more extended usage might with advantage be made no one can deny, for usage of this character would teach the

general public that armory had a meaning and a value, it would increase the interest in heraldry, and also assist greatly in the rapidly increasing revival of heraldic knowledge. The existence of these heraldic emblems would manifestly tend towards a revival of the old and interestingly excellent custom of regularly setting up in appropriate public places the arms of those who have successively held various offices. The Inns of Court, St. George's Chapel, the Public Office at the College of Arms, and the halls of some of the Livery Companies are amongst the few places of importance where the custom still obtains. And yet what an interesting memorial such a series always becomes! The following list may not be entirely complete, but it is fairly so as far as France is concerned, and I think also complete as to England.

The following are from the Royal French Court:—

The High Constable of France: Two swords held on each side of the shield by two hands in armour issuing from the clouds.

The Chancellor: In saltire behind his arms two great maces, and over his helmet a mortier or cap sable crossed by two bands of gold lace and turned up ermine; thereon the figure of a demi-queen as an emblem of France, holding a sceptre in her right hand and the great seal of the kingdom in her left.

The Marshal: Two batons in saltire behind the arms azure, semé-de-lis or.

The Admiral: Two anchors in saltire behind the arms, the stocks of the anchors in chief azure, semé-de-lis or.

The General of the Galleys: Two anchors in saltire behind the arms.

Vice-Admiral: One anchor in pale behind the arms.

Colonel-General of the Infantry: Under his arms in saltire six flags, three on each side, white, crimson, and blue.

Colonel of the Cavalry: Over the arms four banners of the arms of France, fringed, &c., two to the dexter and two to the sinister.

Grand Master of the Artillery: Two field-pieces of ordnance under the arms, one pointing to the dexter and one to the sinister.

The Superintendent of the Finance: Two keys imperially crowned and endorsed in pale, one on each side of the arms, the dexter or, the sinister argent.

Grand Master of the Household to the King: Two grand batons of silver gilt in saltire behind the arms.

Grand Almoner: Under his arms a blue book, on the cover the arms of France and Navarre within the Orders of St. Michael and the Holy Ghost, over the Orders the Crown.

Grand Chamberlain: Two keys, both imperially crowned or, in saltire behind the arms endorsed, the wards-in-chief.

Grand Esquire: On each side of the shield a royal sword erect, the scabbard azure, semé-de-lis, hilt and pommel or, the belts folded round the scabbard azure, semé-de-lis or.

Grand Pannetier, who by virtue of his office had all the bakers of Paris under his jurisdiction, and had to lay the king's cover at his table, bore under his arms a rich cover and a knife and fork in saltire.

Grand Butler or Cupbearer: On each side of the base of the shield, a grand silver flagon gilt, with the arms of the King thereon.

Gamekeeper to the King: Two bugle-horns appending from the ends of the mantling.

Grand Falconer: Two lures appending from the ends of the mantling.

Grand Wolf-hunter: On each side of the shield a wolf's head caboshed.

Captain of the King's Guards: Two small batons sable, headed gold, like a walking-cane.

Captain of the Hundred Swiss Guards: Two batons in saltire sable, headed argent, and under the arms two black velvet caps with feathers.

First Master of the Household: Under his arms two batons in saltire.

Grand Carver to His Majesty: Under his arms a knife and fork in saltire proper, the handles azure, semé-de-lis or.

Grand Provost of the Household: Under his arms two Roman fasces or, corded azure.

Grand Quartermaster: A mace and battle-axe in saltire.

Captain of the Guards of the Gate: Two keys in pale, crowned argent, one on each side the arms.

The President of the Parliament: On his helmet a black cap with two bands of gold lace.

Under the Empire (of France) the Vice-Connétable used arms holding swords, as had been the case with the Constable of the Kingdom, but the swords were sheathed and semé of golden bees. The Grand Chamberlain had two golden keys in saltire, the bows thereof enclosing the imperial eagle, and the batons of the Maréchaux de France were semé of bees instead of fleurs-de-lis.

The Pope bears a cross with three arms, an archbishop one with two arms, a bishop one with a single arm. Besides this, two crossed keys appertain to the Pope, the golden key to bind, in bend dexter, the silver key to loose, in sinister bend (see Plate CXIII. Fig. 1, and Plate CXI. Fig. 1). British archbishops and bishops will be presently referred to. Ecclesiastical princes, who were at the same time sovereign territorial princes, bore behind their shield a pedum or pastorale (crosier), crossed with the sword of penal judicature (Plate CXIII. Fig. 4). A bishop bears the crosier with an outward bend, an abbot with an inward bend, thus symbolising the range of their activity or dominion. The arch and hereditary offices of the old German Empire had also their own attributes: thus the "Erztruchsess," Lord High Steward (Palatinate-Bavaria), bore a golden Imperial globe, which arose from a misinterpretation of the double dish, the original attribute of this dignity. The Lord High Marshal of the Empire (Saxony) expressed his office by a shield divided "per fess argent and sable," bearing two crossed swords gules. The Hereditary Standard-Bearer (Würtemberg) bore: Azure, a banner or, charged with an eagle sable, the Lord High Chamberlain (Brandenburg): Azure, a sceptre or, while the Hereditary Chamberlain (Hohenzollern) used: Gules, two crossed sceptres or, as a distinction, &c.

In Italy the Duca de Savelli, as Marshal of the Conclave, hangs on either side of his shield a key, the cords of which are knotted beneath his coronet.

In Holland Admirals used the naval Crown, and added two anchors in saltire behind the shield.

In Spain the Admirals of Castile and of the Indies placed an anchor in bend behind the shield.

The instances I am aware of which have official sanction already in this country are as stated in the list which follows:—

I have purposely (to make the list absolutely complete) included insignia which may possibly be more properly considered ensigns of rank, because it is not particularly easy always to distinguish offices from honours and from rank.

The Kings of England (George I. to William IV.), as Arch Treasurers of the Holy Roman Empire, bore: Upon an inescutcheon gules, in the centre of the arms of Hanover, a representation of the Crown of Charlemagne.

An Archbishop has: (1) His official coat of arms, which he impales (placing it on the dexter side) with his personal arms; (2) his mitre, which, it should be noted, is the same as the mitre of a Bishop, and *not* having a coronet encircling its band; (3) his archiepiscopal staff (of gold, and with two transverse arms), which is placed in pale behind his escutcheon: (4) two crosiers in saltire behind the escutcheon. It is curious to note that the pallium which occurs in all archiepiscopal coats of arms (save that of York) is now very generally conceded to have been more in the nature of an emblem of the *rank* of Archbishop (it being a part of his ecclesiastical costume) than a charge in a concrete impersonal coat of arms for a defined area of archiepiscopal jurisdiction. In this connection it is interesting to note that the Archbishops of York anciently used the pallium in lieu of the official arms now regularly employed.

A Bishop has: (1) His official coat of arms, (2) his mitre, (3) two crosiers in saltire behind his escutcheon.

The Bishop of Durham has: (1) His official coat of arms, (2) his coronetted mitre, *which is peculiar to himself,* and (which is another privilege also peculiar to himself alone) he places a *sword* and a crosier in saltire behind his arms. Reference should also be made to the chapter upon Ecclesiastical Heraldry.

A Peer has: (1) His coronet, (2) his helmet of rank, (3) his supporters, (4) his robe of estate.

THE ART OF HERALDRY

A Scottish Peer has, in addition, the ermine lining to his mantling.

A Baronet of England, of Ireland, of Great Britain, or of the United Kingdom has: (1) His helmet of rank, (2) his badge of Ulster upon an inescutcheon or canton (argent, a sinister hand erect, couped at the wrist gules).

A Baronet of Nova Scotia has: (1) His helmet of rank, (2) his badge (an orange-tawny ribbon, whereon shall hang pendent in an escutcheon argent, a saltire azure, thereon an inescutcheon of the arms of Scotland, with an imperial crown over the escutcheon, and encircled with this motto, "Fax Mentis Honestæ Gloria," pendent below the escutcheon).

A Knight of the Garter has: (1) His Garter to encircle the shield, (2) his collar and badge, (3) supporters. The Prelate of the Order of the Garter (an office held by the Bishops of Winchester) is entitled to encircle his arms with the Garter. The Chancellor of the Order of the Garter encircles his arms with the Garter. Formerly the Bishops of Salisbury always held this office, but in 1836 when the county of Berks (which of course includes Windsor, and therefore the chapel of the order) was removed from the Diocese of Salisbury to the Diocese of Oxford, the office of Chancellor passed to the Bishops of Oxford. The Dean of Windsor, as Registrar of the Order, displays below his shield the ribbon and badge of his office.

A Knight of the Thistle has: (1) The ribbon or circlet of the order, (2) his collar and badge, (3) supporters. The Dean of the Chapels Royal in Scotland, as Dean of the Order, used the badge and ribbon of his office.

A Knight of St. Patrick has: (1) The ribbon or circlet of the order, (2) his collar and badge, (3) supporters. The Prelate of the Order of St. Patrick was as such entitled to encircle his escutcheon with the ribbon or circlet of that order, from which his official badge depends. The office, of course, came to an end with the disestablishment of the Irish Church. It was held by the Archbishops of Armagh. The Chancellor of the Order of St. Patrick is as such entitled to encircle his escutcheon with the ribbon or circlet of that order, from which his official badge depends. This office, formerly held by the Archbishops of Dublin, has since the disestablishment been enjoyed by the Chief Secretaries for Ireland. The Deans of St. Patrick's were similarly Registrars of the Order, and as such used the badge and ribbon of their office.

Knights Grand Cross or *Knights Grand Commanders* of the Orders of the Bath, the Star of India, St. Michael and St. George, the Indian Empire, or the Victorian Order, have: (1) The circlets or ribbons of their respective orders, (2) their collars and badges, (3) their helmets of degree, (4) supporters.

Knights Commanders of the aforesaid Orders have: (1) The circlets or ribbons of their respective Orders, (2) their badges pendent below the shield, (3) their helmets of degree.

Companions of the aforesaid Orders, and Commanders and members of the Victorian Order, as also members of the Distinguished Service Order, the Imperial Service Order, the Order of Merit, the Order of Victoria and Albert, the Order of the Crown of India, and those entitled to the Victoria Cross, the Albert Medal, the Conspicuous Service Cross, the Kaisar-i-Hind medal, the Royal Red Cross, the Volunteer Officers' Decoration, and the Decoration of the League of Mercy, are entitled to suspend their respective decorations below their escutcheons. The officers of these orders of knighthood are of course entitled to display their badges of office. The Dean of Westminster is always Dean of the Order of the Bath.

Knights Grand Cross and *Knights Commanders of the*

Bath, if of the Military Division, are also entitled to place a wreath of laurel round their escutcheons.

Knights of Justice of the Order of the Hospital of St. John of Jerusalem in England are entitled to place upon their escutcheons a chief of the arms of the Order (gules, a cross throughout argent, embellished in the angles with a lion guardant and a unicorn, both passant or).

Knights of Grace and other Members of the Order suspend whatever badge they are entitled to wear below their shield from a black watered-silk ribbon.

[Some members of the Order display their arms upon the Cross of the Order, as was done by Knights of the original Order, from which the present Order is copied, but how far the practice is sanctioned by the Royal Charter, or in what manner it is controlled by the rules of the Order, I am not aware.]

The Lord High Constable of England is entitled to place behind his escutcheon two batons in saltire similar to the one which is delivered to him for use at the Coronation, which is now the only occasion when the office is enjoyed. As the office is only held temporarily, the existing privilege does not amount to much.

The Lord High Constable of Scotland is entitled to place behind his escutcheon, in saltire, two silver batons tipped with gold at either end. The arms of the Earl of Errol (Hereditary Lord High Constable of Scotland) have only once, at an early period, been matriculated in Lyon Register, and then without any official insignia, but there can be no doubt of the right to the crossed batons.

The Lord High Chamberlain of Scotland (I am not sure this office still exists): Two golden keys in saltire behind the escutcheon.

The Earl Marshal and Hereditary Marshal of England places two batons of gold tipped with sable in saltire behind his arms (Fig. 809).

[*A Deputy Earl Marshal* places one similar baton in bend behind his shield.]

The Earl Marischal of Scotland (until the office was extinguished by attainder) placed behind his shield two batons gules, semé of thistles, each ensigned on the top with an Imperial Crown or placed saltirewise.

The Hereditary Marshal of Ireland (an office long in abeyance) used two batons in saltire behind his arms. According to MS. Harl. 6589, f. 39: "Les armes des office du Mareschall d'Ireland sont de Goulz et cinque fucelles bendes d'Argent." These certainly do not appear to be the personal arms of those who held the office, but there is other record that some such coat was used (Fig. 961).

The Hereditary Lord Great Seneschal of Ireland (the Earl of Shrewsbury) places a white wand in pale behind his escutcheon.

FIG. 961.—Arms of John Marshal, Earl of Warwick, Hereditary Marshal of Ireland. (From Charles' Roll, f. 20.)

The Duke of Argyll places in saltire behind his arms: (1) In bend dexter, a baton gules, semé of thistles or, ensigned with an Imperial Crown proper, thereon the crest of Scotland (as Hereditary Great Master of the Household in Scotland); (2) in bend sinister, a sword proper, hilt and pommel or (as Hereditary Justice-General of Scotland).

The Master-General of the Ordnance (by Warrant of King Charles II.) bears on each side of his arms a field-piece.

The Lord Justice-Clerk of Scotland places two swords in saltire behind his shield.

The Lord Chief-Justice of England encircles his arms with his Collar of SS.

The Walker Trustees place behind their shield two

THE ART OF HERALDRY

batons in saltire, each ensigned with a unicorn salient supporting a shield argent, the unicorn horned or, and gorged with an antique crown, to which is affixed a chain passing between the fore-legs and reflexed over the back of the last, for the office of Heritable Usher of the White Rod of Scotland, now vested in the said Trustees. Before the recent Court of Claims the claim was made to exercise the office by deputy, and such claim was allowed.

The Master of the Revels in Scotland has an official coat of arms : Argent, a lady rising out of a cloud in the nombril point, richly apparelled, on her head a garland of ivy, holding in her right hand a poignard crowned, in her left a vizard all proper, standing under a veil or canopy azure garnished or, in base a thistle vert.

Serjeants-at-Arms encircle their arms with their Collars of SS.

Garter King of Arms has : (1) His official coat of arms (argent, a cross gules, on a chief azure, a ducal coronet encircled with a Garter, between a lion passant guardant on the dexter, and a fleur-de-lis on the sinister, all or) : (2) his crown ; (3) his Collar of SS (the collar of a King of Arms differs from that of a Herald, inasmuch as it is of *silver-gilt*, and on each shoulder a portcullis is inserted) ; (4) his badge as Garter pendent below his shield. His sceptre of silver-gilt has been sometimes (and doubtless correctly) placed in bend behind his escutcheon, but this has not been regularly done, nor is it adopted by the present Garter.

Lyon King of Arms has : (1) His official coat of arms (argent, a lion sejant, erect and affronté gules, holding in his dexter paw a thistle slipped vert, and in the sinister a shield of the second, on a chief azure a St. Andrew's cross—*ie*. a saltire—of the field) ; (2) his crown ; (3) two batons, representing that of his office in saltire behind his shield, these being azure semé of thistles and fleurs-de-lis or, tipped at either end with gold ; (4) his Collar of SS. ; (5) his triple chain of gold, from which depends his badge as Lyon King of Arms.

Ulster King of Arms has : (1) His official coat of arms (or, a cross gules, on a chief of the last a lion of England between a harp and a portcullis, all of the first) ; (2) his crown ; (3) his Collar of SS ; (4) his two staves in saltire behind the shield ; (5) his chain and badge as Ulster King of arms ; (6) his badge as Registrar of the Order of St. Patrick.

Clarenceux King of Arms has : (1) His official coat of arms (argent, a cross gules, on a chief of the second a lion passant guardant or, crowned of the last) ; (2) his crown ; (3) his Collar of SS.

Norroy King of Arms has : (1) His official coat of arms (argent, a cross gules, on a chief of the second a lion of England passant guardant or, crowned with an open crown, between a fleur-de-lis on the dexter and a key on the sinister of the last) ; (2) his crown ; (3) his Collar of SS.

Bath King of Arms has : (1) His crown ; (2) his Collar of SS.

I am not aware that any official arms have been assigned to Bath up to the present time ; but if none exist, there would not be the slightest difficulty in obtaining these.

An English Herald encircles his shield with his Collar of SS.

A Scottish Herald is entitled to do the same, and has also his badge, which he places below the escutcheon pendent from a ribbon of blue and white.

The English Heralds and Pursuivants in some instances use badges, but it is difficult to decide the exact status of these. They are all royal badges, but it is not clear to me whether they are used on the same footing as the Royal Arms are in other Government offices, or whether they are considered to be specifically allocated to the various offices. Those now in use will be found on page 22.

The Regius Professors (or " Readers ") in the University of Cambridge, for " Phisicke," " Lawe," " Devinity," " Hebrew," and " Greke," have official arms as follows (see grant by Robert Cooke, Clarenceux, 1590, *Genealogical Magazine*, vol. ii. p. 125) :—

Of Phisicke : Azure, a fess ermines (? ermine) between three lozenges or, on a chief gules a lion passant guardant of the third, charged on the side with the letter M sable. Crest : on a wreath or and azure, a quinquangle silver, called " simbolum sanitatis." Mantling gules and argent.

Of Lawe : Purpure, a cross moline or, on a chief gules, a lion passant guardant of the second, charged on the side with the letter L sable. Crest : on a wreath " purple and gold," a bee volant or. Mantling gules and argent.

Of Devinity : Gules, on a cross ermine, between four doves argent, a book of the first, the leaves or, charged in the midst with the Greek letter θ (Theta) sable. Crest : on a wreath " silver and gules," a dove volant argent, with an olive-branch vert in his beak. Mantling gules, double argent.

Of Hebrew : Argent, the Hebrew letter ת (Tawe) sable, on a chief gules, a lion passant guardant or, charged on the side with the letter H sable. Crest : on a wreath " silver and sables," a turtle-dove azure. Mantling gules, double argent.

Of Greke : Per chevron argent and sable, in chief the two Greek letters A (Alpha) and Ω (Omega) of the second, and in base a " cicado " or grasshopper of the first, on a chief gules, a lion passant guardant or, charged on the side with the letter G sable. Crest : on a wreath " silver and sables," an owl argent, legs, beak, and ears or. Mantling gules and argent.

The following insignia of office I quote subject to the reservation that I am doubtful how far they enjoy official sanction :—

The Lord High Chancellor of England : Two maces in saltire or, one in pale behind the shield and the purse containing the Great Seal below it.

The Lord High Chamberlain of England : Two golden keys in saltire ; and

The Lord Chamberlain of the Household : A golden key in pale behind the shield.

At Exeter the Dean, Precentor, Chancellor, and Treasurer have used official arms impaled with their own insignia. These were :—

The Dean : Azure, a stag's head caboshed and between the horns a cross patée fitchée argent.

The Precentor : Argent, on a saltire azure a fleur-de-lis or.

The Chancellor : Gules, a saltire argent between four crosslets or.

The Treasurer : Gules, a saltire between four leopards' heads or.

The Dean of the Chapel Royal, Savoy, may perhaps employ the complicated coat of the chapel to impale his personal arms, placing the escutcheon on the breast of an eagle sable, crowned or.

Many English Deaneries claim to possess arms which presumably the occupant may use to impale his own coat withal, after the example of the Dean of Exeter. Such are London, Winchester, Lincoln, Salisbury, Lichfield, Durham, which all difference the arms of the see with a letter D of gold or sable.

St. David's reverses the tinctures of the arms of the see.

Norwich and Carlisle carry : Argent, a cross sable.

Canterbury : Azure, on a cross argent the monogram **X** sable.

York differences the arms of the see by changing the crown into a mitre, and adding three plates in flanks and base.

A. C. F-D.

THE ART OF HERALDRY

CHAPTER XLI

AUGMENTATIONS OF HONOUR

OF all heraldic distinctions the possession of an augmentation of honour is the one most prized. The Sovereign is of course the fountain of honour, and though ordinary grants of arms are made by Letters Patent under the hands and seals of the Kings of Arms, by virtue of the powers expressly and specifically conferred upon them in the Letters Patent respectively appointing them to their offices, a grant of arms is theoretically a grant from the Crown. The privilege of the possession of arms in the ordinary event is left in the discretion of the Earl Marshal, whose warrant is a condition precedent to the issue of a Grant. Providing a person is palpably living in that style and condition of life in which the use of arms is usual, subject always to the Earl Marshal's pleasure and discretion, a Grant of Arms can ordinarily be obtained upon payment of the usual fees. The social status of present-day grantees of arms is considerably in advance of the status of grantees in the Tudor period. An augmentation of arms, however, is on a totally and entirely different footing. It is an especial mark of favour from the Sovereign, and the effective grant is a Royal Warrant under the hand and Privy Seal of the Sovereign. No fees are paid by the recipient. The warrant, however, recites and requires that the augmentation granted shall be exemplified and recorded in the College of Arms. Augmentations have been less frequently conferred in recent years than was formerly the case. Technically speaking, a gift of arms by the Sovereign direct where none previously existed is not an augmentation, though one is naturally inclined to include such grants in the category. Such an example is met with in the shield granted to Colonel Carlos by King Charles to commemorate their mutual adventures in the oak tree (" Or, issuing from a mount in base vert, an oak-tree proper, over all on a fess gules, three Imperial crowns also proper)."

There are many gorgeous legends relating to augmentations and arms which are said to have been granted by William the Conqueror as rewards after the Battle of Hastings. Personally I do not believe in a single one. There was a certain augmentation borne by the Dodge family, which, if it be correct, dates from the thirty-fourth year of Edward I., but whether this be authentic it is impossible to say. Most people consider the alleged *deed of grant* a forgery, and if this be so, the arms only exist by right of subsequent record and the question of augmentation rests upon tradition. The curious charge of the woman's breast distilling drops of milk to typify the nourishment afforded to the king's army is at any rate most interesting. The earliest undoubted one in this country that I am aware of dates from the reign of Edward III. Sir John de Pelham shared in the glory of the Battle of Poictiers, and in the capture of the French King John. To commemorate this he was granted two round buckles with thongs. The Pelham family arms were " Azure, three pelicans argent," and, as will be seen, these family arms were quartered with the buckles and thongs on a field gules as an augmentation. The quarterly coat forms a part of the arms both of Lord Chichester and of Lord Yarborough (Fig. 920) at the present day, and " the Pelham buckle " has been the badge of the Pelham family for centuries.

Piers Legh (Fig. 47) fought with the Black Prince and

took the Count de Tanquervil prisoner at the Battle of Crecy, " and did valiantly rere and advance the said princes Banner att the bataile of Cressy to the noe little encouragement of the English army," but it was not until the reign of Queen Elizabeth that the augmentation to commemorate this was granted. The Patent will be found on page 40.

The Battle of Flodden was won by the Earl of Surrey, afterwards the Duke of Norfolk, and amongst the many rewards which the King showered upon his successful Marshal was the augmentation to his arms of " a demi-

FIG. 962.—Armorial bearings of Ross, now borne by Rev. J. Coulman Ross, Vicar of Loversal, co. York : Gules, three estoiles in chevron between as many lions rampant argent ; and for an honourable augmentation a chief or, thereon a portion of the terrestrial globe proper, the true meridian described thereon by a line passing from north to south sable, with the Arctic circle azure within the place of the magnetic pole in latitude 70° 5' 17" and longitude 96° 46' 45" west, designated by an inescutcheon gules, charged with a lion passant guardant of the first ; the magnetic meridian shown by a line of the fourth passing through the inescutcheon with a correspondent circle, also gules, to denote more particularly the said place of the magnetic pole ; the words following inscribed on the chief, viz. " Arctæos Numine Fines." Mantling gules and argent. Crests : 1. on a wreath of the colours, on a rock a flagstaff erect, thereon hoisted the Union Jack, inscribed with the date June 1, 1831 (being that of discovering the place of the magnetic pole), and at foot, and on the sinister side of the flagstaff, the dipping needle, showing its almost vertical position, all proper ; 2. on a wreath of the colours, a fox's head erased proper. Motto : " Spes aspera levat."

lion pierced in the mouth with an arrow, depicted on the colours for the arms of the Kingdom of Scotland, which the said James, late King of Scots, bore." According to the Act of Parliament under which it was granted this augmentation would seem now to belong exclusively to Lord Mowbray and Stourton and Lord Petre, but it is borne with official sanction by the Duke of Norfolk and the rest of the Howard family.

The Battle of Agincourt is referred to by Shakespeare,

who puts these words into King Henry's mouth on the eve of that great battle (Act iv. sc. 3):—

> " We few, we happy few, we band of brothers;
> For he to-day that sheds his blood with me
> Shall be my brother; be he ne'er so vile,
> This day shall gentle his condition."

There is actual foundation in fact for these lines. For in a writ couched in very stringent and severe terms issued by the same king in after years decreeing penalties for the improper assumption and use of false arms, specific exception is made in favour of those " who bore arms with us at the Battle of Agincourt." Evidently this formed a very extensive kind of augmentation.

The reign of Queen Elizabeth furnishes an interesting example of the gift of a complete coat in the case of Sir Francis Drake, who had been using the arms of another family of the same name. The representative of that family complained to the Queen that Sir Francis, whom he styled an upstart, should take such liberties with his arms; whereupon the Queen said she would give Sir Francis arms which should outrival those of his namesake. At least, such is the legend, and though the arms themselves were granted by Clarenceux King of Arms, and I have not yet found any Royal Warrant indicating that the grant was made by specific Royal command, it is possible the story is correct. The arms are: " Sable, a fess wavy between two stars argent. Crest: a ship under reef, drawn round a terrestrial globe with a cable by a hand issuing from clouds all proper." The stars upon the shield are the two pole stars, and the wavy band between them typifies Drake's voyage round the world, as does also the peculiar crest in which the Divine hand is shown guiding his ship around the globe.

At the battle of Naseby Dr. Edward Lake fought bravely for the King, and in the service of his majesty received no less than sixteen wounds. At the end of the battle, when his left arm was useless, he put the bridle of his horse between his teeth and still fought on. The quartering of augmentation given to him was: " Gules, a dexter arm embowed in armour holding in the hand a sword erect all proper, thereto affixed a banner argent charged with a cross between sixteen escutcheons of the field, on the crest a lion of England." The sixteen shields upon the banner typify his sixteen wounds.

After the Commonwealth was established in England, Charles II. made a desperate effort to regain his crown, an effort which culminated in his disastrous defeat at the battle of Worcester. The King escaped through the gate of the city solely through the heroic efforts of Colonel Newman, and this is kept in remembrance by the inescutcheon of augmentation, viz.: " Gules, a portcullis imperially crowned or." Every one has heard how the King was accompanied in his wanderings by Colonel Carlos, who hid with him in the oak tree at Boscobel. Afterwards the King accompanied Mistress Jane Lane on horseback as her servant to the coast, whence he fled to the Continent. The reward of Colonel Carlos was the gift of the entire coat of arms already referred to. The Lanes (Fig. 57), though not until after some years had passed and the King had come back to his own again, were granted two remarkable additions to their family arms. First of all " the canton of England" (that is, the arms of England upon a canton) was added to their shield. They are the *only* family to whom such an honour has been given, and a most curious result has happened. When the use of armorial bearings was taxed by Act of Parliament the Royal Arms were specially exempted, and on account of this canton the Lane family claimed and obtained exemption from the tax. A few years later a crest was granted to them, namely, a strawberry-roan horse, " couped at the flanks," holding in its feet the

Royal crown. It was upon a horse of this colour that the King and Mistress Lane had escaped and thereby saved the crown. Mr. Francis Wolfe, of Madeley, who also was a party to the escape, received the grant of an inescutcheon

FIG. 963.—Armorial bearings of Sir Lepel Griffin, K.C.S.I: Argent, on a chevron gules, between in chief two griffins segreant, and in base a bull's head caboshed between two wings, a plate between two ostrich feathers erect argent, the escutcheon being surrounded by the circlet, and below the badge of a K.C.S.I. Crest: a griffin segreant or, between two ostrich feathers argent. Motto: " Judge not."

gules charged with a lion of England. Another family which bears an augmentation to commemorate King Charles' escape is Whitgreave (Fig. 594).

The reign of Queen Anne produced in the Duke of Marlborough one of the finest generals the world has ever seen; and in the Battle of Blenheim one of its greatest victories. The augmentation which commemorates this is a shield bearing the cross of St. George and in the centre a smaller shield with the golden lilies of France.

In the year 1797 the Battle of Camperdown was fought, when Admiral Duncan defeated the Dutch Fleet and was created Lord Camperdown. To his family arms were added a naval crown and a representation of the gold medal given by George III. to Lord Camperdown to commemorate his victory.

The arms of Nelson are most interesting, inasmuch as one version of the arms carries two separate and distinct augmentations. It is not, however, the coat as it was granted to and borne by the great Admiral himself. After the Battle of the Nile he received the augmentation on the chief, a landscape showing the palm-tree, the disabled ship, and the battery in ruins. The one crest was the plume of triumph given to the Admiral by the Sultan Selim III., and his second crest, which, however, is not a crest of augmentation, was the stern of the Spanish ship *San Josef*. After his death at the Battle of Trafalgar his brother was created Earl Nelson, and a second augmentation, namely, a fess wavy sable with the word "Trafalgar" upon it in gold letters, was added to the arms. This, however, has since been discontinued, except by Lord Bridport, who quarters it, whilst the Nelson family has reverted to the arms as they were borne by the great Admiral.

After the death of Nelson at the Battle of Trafalgar, Lord Collingwood took command, and though naval experts think that the action of Collingwood greatly

FIG. 964.—Armorial bearings of General Robert Harvey, C.B., D.S.O.: Gules, on a bend erminois, three trefoils slipped vert, on a chief argent, an eagle's head erased azure between two mullets of the field. Upon the escutcheon is placed a helmet befitting his degree, with a mantling gules and or; and upon a wreath of his liveries is set for crest, a cubit arm proper, issuing from a crescent or, charged with an eagle's head as on the chief, the hand holding a trefoil slipped vert.

minimised the number of prizes which would have resulted from the victory, Lord Collingwood received for an augmentation a chief wavy gules, thereon the lion of England, navally crowned with the word "Trafalgar" above the lion. He also received an additional crest, namely, the stern of his ship, the *Royal Sovereign*, between a wreath of oak on the one side and a wreath of laurel on the other.

The heroic story of the famous fight between the *Shannon* and the *Chesapeake* has been often told. Captain Broke sent in a challenge to the *Chesapeake* to come out and fight him, and, though a banquet was prepared by the Mayor of Boston for that evening "to meet the English officers," Captain Broke defeated the *Chesapeake* in an engagement which only lasted a very short time. He was granted an additional crest (Fig. 778), namely, an arm holding a trident and issuing from a naval crown, together with the motto, "Sævumque tridentem servamus." General Ross fought and won the Battle of Bladensburg, and took the city of Washington, dying a few days afterwards. The story is that the family were offered their choice of a baronetcy or an augmentation, and they chose the latter. The augmentation, which was specially granted

with permission for it to be placed upon the monument to the memory of General Ross (Fig. 776), consists of the arm holding the flag of the United States with a broken flag-staff which will be seen both on the shield itself, and as an additional crest. The shield also shows the gold cross for previous services at Corunna and in the Peninsula. The family were also given the surname of "Ross-of-Bladens-burg."

The capture of Curaçoa by Admiral Sir Charles Brisbane, K.C.B. (Fig. 553), is commemorated by the representation of his ship passing between the two Dutch forts; and by the additional crest of an arm in a naval officer's uniform grasping a cutlass. Admiral Sir Robert Otway, for his distinguished services, was granted: "On a chief azure an anchor between two branches of oak or, and on the dexter side a demi-Neptune and on the sinister a mermaid proper," to add to his shield. Admiral Sir George Pocock, who captured Havannah, was given for an augmentation: "On a chief wavy azure a sea-horse" (to typify his naval career), between two Eastern crowns (to typify his services in the East Indies), with the word "Havanna," the scene of his greatest victory.

Sir Edward Pellew, who was created Viscount Exmouth for bombarding and destroying the fort and arsenal of Algiers, was given upon a chief a representation of that fort, with an English man-of-war in front of it, to add to his arms. It is interesting to note that one of his supporters, though not a part of his augmentation, represents a Christian slave, in memory of those in captivity at Algiers when he captured the city. A famous augmentation occurs on the arms of Cochrane (Plate LXVIII.), to which reference was made in a previous chapter.

There were several augmentations won at the Battle of Waterloo, and the Waterloo medal figures upon many coats of arms of Waterloo officers. Colonel Alexander Clark-Kennedy, with his own hand, captured the French Eagle of the 105th French Regiment. For this he bears a representation of it and a sword crossed upon a chief over his arms, and his crest of augmentation is a demi-dragoon holding the same flag. Of the multitude of honours which were showered upon the Duke of Wellington, not the least was his augmentation. This was a smaller shield to be superimposed upon his own, and charged with those crosses of St. George, St. Andrew, and St. Patrick, which we term "the Union Jack." Sir Edward Kerrison, who distinguished himself so greatly in the Peninsula and at Waterloo, was granted a sword with a wreath of laurel and representations of his medals for Orthes and Waterloo, and, for an additional crest, an arm in armour holding a banner inscribed "Peninsula."

Sir Thomas Munro, who will be long remembered as the Governor of Madras, was rewarded for his capture of Badamy by a representation of that hill-fort in India. The augmentation of Lord Keane is very similar, being a representation of the Fortress of Ghuznee in Afghanistan, which he captured. Other instances of a similar character are to be found in the arms of Cockburn-Campbell (Fig. 966) and Hamilton-Grace.

The arms of Lord Gough are most remarkable, inasmuch as they show no less than two distinct and different augmentations both earned by the same man. In 1816, for his services in the Peninsula, he received a representation of the Spanish Order of Charles III., and on a chief the representation of the Fortress of Tarifa, with the crest of the arm holding the colours of his own regiment, the 87th, and a French eagle reversed and depressed. After his victories in the East, particularly at Goojerat, and for the subjugation and annexation of the Punjab, he was granted, in 1843, an additional quartering to add to his shield. This has the Lion of England holding up the Union Jack below the words "China" and "India." The third crest, which was then granted to him, shows a similar lion holding the Union Jack and a Chinese flag. The Durban augmentation has been already illustrated (Fig. 538).

FIG. 966.—Armorial bearings of Sir Alexander Thomas Cockburn-Campbell, Bart. : Quarterly, 1 and 4, quarterly, i. and iiii., gyronny of eight or and sable ; ii., argent, a galley sable, sails furled and oars in action ; iii., or a fess chequy azure and argent ; over all on a chief argent a rock proper, superinscribed " Gibraltar," between two medals pendent by a ribbon gules, fimbriated, for Seringapatam and Talavera (for Campbell) ; 2 and 3, quarterly, i. and iiii., argent, an ostrich feather ensigned with an imperial crown proper, between two cocks in chief and a lion's head erased in base gules ; ii. and iii., gules, six mascles, three, two and one or (for Cockburn), the escutcheon being charged with his badge of Ulster as a Baronet. Mantling sable and or. Crest : on a wreath of the colours, a dexter hand holding a scimitar proper. Mottoes : " Without fear ; " " Forward."

Sir George Pollock, " of the Khyber Pass," Bart., earned everlasting fame for himself in the first Afghan War, by forcing the Khyber Pass and by the capture of Cabul. For this he was given an Eastern crown and the word " Khyber " on a chief as well as three cannon upon a canton, and at the same time he was granted an additional crest—a lion holding an Afghan banner with the staff thereof broken. With him it seemed as if the practice of granting augmentations for military services had ceased. Lord Roberts has none, neither has Lord Wolseley. But recently the old practice was reverted to in favour of Lord Kitchener. His family arms were : " Azure, a chevron cottised between three bustards," and in the centre chief point a bezant ; with a stag's head for a crest ; but for " smashing the Khalifa " he has been given the Union Jack and the Egyptian flag with the staves encircled by a coronet bearing the word " Khartoum," all on a pile superimposed over his family arms. He also received a second crest of an elephant's head holding a sword in its trunk issuing from a mural crown.

Two other very interesting instances of augmentation of arms are worthy of mention.

Sir Ralph Abercromby, after a distinguished career, fought and won the Battle of Aboukir Bay, only to die a few days later on board H.M.S. *Foudroyant* of his wounds received in the battle. But long before he had fought and conquered the French at Valenciennes, and in 1795 had been made a Knight of the Bath. The arms which are upon his Stall plate in Westminster Abbey include his augmentation, which is an arm in armour encircled by a wreath of laurel supporting the French Standard.

Sir William Hoste gained the celebrated victory over the French fleet off the Island of Lissa in 1811, and the augmentation which was granted was a representation of

his gold medal hanging from a naval crown, and an additional crest, an arm holding a flag inscribed with the word " Cattaro," the scene of another of his victories.

Peace has its victories no less than war, but there is generally very much less fuss made about them. Consequently, the augmentations to commemorate entirely pacific actions are considerably fewer in number. The Speke augmentation has been elsewhere referred to (Plate XXXIX.), and reference may be made to the Ross augmentation (Fig. 962) to commemorate the Arctic exploits of Sir John Ross.

It is a very common idea that arms were formerly to be obtained by conquest in battle. Like many other heraldic ideas, there is a certain amount of truth in the idea, from which very erroneous generalisations have been made. The old legend as to the acquisition of the plume of ostrich feathers by the Black Prince no doubt largely accounts for the idea. That legend, as has been already shown, lacks foundation. Territorial or sovereign arms doubtless would be subject to conquest, but I do not believe that because in battle or in a tournament *à l'outrance* one person defeated another, he therefore became entitled to assume, of his own motion, the arms of the man he had vanquished. The proposition is too absurd. But there is no doubt that in some number of historic cases his Sovereign has subsequently conferred upon the victor an augmentation which has closely approximated to the arms of his victim. Such cases occur in the arms of the Clerkes, Barts., of Hitcham, Bucks, who bear : " On a sinister canton azure, a demi-ram salient of the first, and in chief two fleurs-de-lis or, debruised by a baton," to commemorate the action of Sir John Clerke of Weston, who captured Louis D'Orleans, Duke of Longueville, at Borny, near Terouenne, 5 Henry VIII. The augmentation conferred upon the Duke of Norfolk at the battle of Flodden has been already referred to, but Lloyd of Stockton (Fig. 325) carry a remarkable augmentation, inasmuch as they are permitted to bear the arms of Sir John Oldcastle, Lord Cobham, to commemorate his recapture at Bromarth after his escape from the Tower.

Augmentations which have no other basis than mere favour of kings, or consanguinity to the Royal Family, are not uncommon. Richard II., who himself adopted the arms of St. Edward the Confessor, bestowed the right to bear them also upon Thomas Mowbray, Duke of Norfolk (Fig. 823). No difference was added to them in his case, which is the more remarkable as they were borne by the Duke impaled with the arms of England. In 1397 the King conferred the same arms upon John de Holland, Duke of Exeter, differenced by a label argent, and upon Thomas de Holland, Duke of Surrey, within a bordure ermine (Fig. 201). Richard II. seems to have been inclined to the granting of augmentations, for in 1386, when he created the Earl of Oxford (Robert de Vere) Duke of Ireland, he granted him as an augmentation the arms of Ireland (" Azure, three crowns or ") within a bordure argent (Fig. 967). The Manners family, who were of Royal

FIG. 967.—Arms of Robert De Vere, Duke of Ireland and Earl of Oxford : Quarterly, 1 and 4 (of augmentation), azure, three crowns or, within a bordure argent ; 2 and 3, quarterly gules and or, in the first quarter a mullet argent.

descent, but who, not being descended from an heiress, had no right to quarter the Royal Arms, received the grant of a chief "quarterly azure and gules, in the first and fourth quarters two fleurs-de-lis, and in the second and third a lion passant guardant or." This precedent might well be followed at the present day in the case of the daughters of the Duke and Duchess of Fife. The canton in Fig. 219, and the similar canton in the arms of Caulfield, are doubtless augmentations. The Waller family, of Groombridge, co. Kent, one of whom, Richard Waller, captured Charles, Duke of Orleans, at the battle of Agincourt, received as an augmentation the right to suspend from the crest ("On a mount a walnut-tree proper") an escutcheon of the arms of that Prince, viz.: "Azure, three fleurs-de-lis or, a label of three points argent." Lord Polwarth bears one of the few augmentations granted by William III., viz.: "An inescutcheon azure charged with an orange ensigned with an Imperial crown all proper," whilst the titular King James III. and VIII. granted to John Græme, Earl of Alford, a coat of augmentation, viz.: "The Royal Arms of Scotland on the field and cross of St. Andrew counterchanged," the date of the grant being 20th January 1734. Sir John Keith, Earl of Kintore, Knight Marischal of Scotland, saved the regalia of Scotland from falling into the hands of Cromwell, and in return the Keith arms (now quartered by Lord Kintore) were augmented with "an inescutcheon gules, a sword in bend sinister surmounted by a sceptre in bend dexter, in chief an Imperial crown, the whole within an orle of eight thistles."

The well-known augmentation of the Seymour family: "Or, on a pile gules, between six fleurs-de-lis azure," is borne to commemorate the marriage of Jane Seymour to Henry VIII., who granted augmentations to all his wives except Catherine of Arragon and Anne of Cleves. The Seymour family is, however, the only one in which the use of the augmentation has been continued. The same practice was followed by granting the arms of England to the Consort of the Princess Caroline and to the late Prince Consort. See page 350.

The frequent grant of the Royal tressure in Scotland, probably usually as an augmentation, has been already referred to. King Charles I. granted to the Earl of Kinnoull as a quartering of augmentation: "Azure, a unicorn salient argent, armed, maned, and unguled or, within a bordure of the last charged with thistles of Scotland and roses gules of England dimidiated." The well-known augmentation of the Medicis family, viz.: "A roundle azure, charged with three fleur-de-lis or" (Plate XVII. Fig. 25), was granted by Louis XII. to Pietro de Medicis. The Prussian Officers, ennobled on the 18th of January 1896, the twenty-fifth anniversary of the foundation of the new German Empire, bears as a device a chief purpure, and thereupon the Prussian sceptre and

FIG. 968.—Device from the chief of the " Prussian Sword Nobility."

a sword in saltire interlaced by two oak-branches vert (Fig 968). The arms of Smyth (Fig. 501) show a curious augmentation, and the late Right Hon. Sir Thomas Thornton, G.C.B., received a Royal Licence to accept the

Portuguese title of Conde de Cassilhas and an augmentation. This was an inescutcheon (ensigned by his coronet as a Conde) " or, thereon an arm embowed vested azure, the cuff gold, the hand supporting a flagstaff therefrom flowing the Royal Standard of Portugal." The same device issuing from his coronet was also granted to him as a crest of augmentation. Sir Woodbine Parish, K.C.H., by legislative act of the Argentine Republic received in 1839 a grant of the arms of that country, which was subsequently incorporated in the arms granted to him and registered in the Heralds' College in this country (Plate XXIII.). He had been Consul-General and Chargé d'Affaires at Buenos Ayres, 1823–1832 ; he was appointed in 1824 Plenipotentiary, and concluded the first treaty by which the Argentine Republic was formally recognised. Reference has been already made (page 306) to the frequent grants of supporters as augmentations, and perhaps mention should also be made of the inescutcheons for the Dukedom of Aubigny, borne by the Duke of Richmond and Gordon, and for the Duchy of Chatelherault, borne by the Duke of Abercorn. Possibly these should more properly be ranked as territorial arms and not as augmentations. A similar coat is the inescutcheon borne by the Earl of Mar and Kellie (Fig. 813) for his Earldom of Kellie. This, however, is stated by Woodward to be an augmentation granted by James VI. to Sir Thomas Erskine, one of several granted by that King to commemorate the frustration of the Gowrie Plot in 1600.

The Marquess of Westminster, for some utterly inexplicable reason, was granted as an augmentation the right to bear the arms of the city of Westminster in the first quarter of his arms. Those who have rendered very great personal service to the Crown have been sometimes so favoured. The Halford and Gull (see page 182) augmentations commemorate medical services to the Royal Family, and it is a matter of general surprise that no augmentations have been conferred upon Sir Frederick Treves or Sir Francis Laking in connection with His Majesty's illness at the time of the Coronation.

The badges of Ulster and Nova Scotia borne as such upon their shields by Baronets are, of course, augmentations.

Two cases are known of augmentations to the arms of towns. The arms of Derry were augmented by the arms of the city of London in chief, when, after its fearful siege, the name of Derry was changed to Londonderry to commemorate the help given by the city of London. The arms of the city of Hereford had an azure bordure semé of saltires couped argent added to its arms after it had successfully withstood its Scottish siege, and this, by the way, is a striking example of colour upon colour, the field of the coat being gules.

There are many grants in the later part of the eighteenth and the beginning of the nineteenth centuries recorded in Lyon Register which at first sight appear to be augmentations. Perhaps they are rightly so termed, but as the additions usually appear to be granted by the Lyon without specific Royal Warrants, they are hardly equivalent to the English ones issued during the same period. Many ordinary grants made in England which have borne direct reference to particular achievements of the grantee have been (by the grantees and their descendants) wrongly termed augmentations. A rough and ready (though not a certain) test is to imagine the coat if the augmentation be removed, and see whether it remains a properly balanced design. Few of such coats will survive the test. The additions made to a coat to make it a different design, when a new grant is founded upon arms improperly used theretofore, are not augmentations, although departures from the truth on this detail are by no means rare. A. C. F-D.

THE ART OF HERALDRY

CHAPTER XLII

THE UNION JACK

By Rev. J. R. CRAWFORD

NOMENCLATURE

ORDERS in Council and other official documents refer to this flag as The Union Flag, The Union Jack, Our Jack, The King's Colours, and The Union Banner, which last title precise Heraldry usually adopts. In patriotic songs it is toasted as "The Red, White, and Blue," whilst in the Services men affectionately allude to it as "the dear old duster." But Britons at large cling to the title which heads this chapter; to them it is "*The Union Jack.*"

MEANING OF THIS TITLE

Why Union? Obviously because it unites three emblems of tutelar saints on one flag, and thereby denotes the union of three peoples under one Sovereign. It is the motto "*Tria juncta in Uno*" rendered in bunting.

Why Jack? Two theories are propounded, one fanciful, the other probable. Some say "Jack" is the anglicised form of "Jacques," which is the French signature of James I., in whose reign and by whose command the first Union Flag was called into being. Against this at least three reasons may justly be urged: (1) The term "*Jack*" does not appear—so far as we can discover—in any warrant referring to the Jacobean Flag of 1606. It is rather in later documents that this term occurs. (2) If the earliest Union Flag be a "*Jack*" just because it is the creation of James, then surely it follows that, to be consistent, later Union Flags, the creations of later sovereigns, should have borne those Sovereigns' names; for example *The Union Anne, The Union George!* (3) The English way of pronouncing "Jacques" is not, and probably never was *Jack*, but *Jaikes*. The other, and more feasible theory, is as follows: The term "Jaque" (e.g. *jaque de mailles*) was borrowed from the French and referred to any jacket or coat on which, especially, heraldic emblems were blazoned. In days long prior to those of the first Stuart king, mention is made of "𝔴𝔥𝔶𝔱𝔱𝔢 𝔠𝔬𝔱𝔢𝔰 𝔴𝔦𝔱𝔥 𝔯𝔢𝔡 𝔠𝔯𝔬𝔰𝔰𝔢𝔰 𝔴𝔬𝔯𝔫 𝔟𝔶 𝔰𝔥𝔶𝔭𝔭𝔢𝔰𝔪𝔢𝔫 𝔞𝔫𝔡 𝔪𝔢𝔫 𝔬𝔣 𝔱𝔥𝔢 𝔠𝔢𝔱𝔱𝔢 𝔬𝔣 𝔏𝔬𝔫𝔡𝔬𝔫," from which sentence we learn that the emblem of the nation's tutelar saint was (as in yet earlier Crusaders' days) a *fighter's* emblem. When such emblem or emblems were transferred to a flag, the term *Jaque* may well, in course of time, have been also applied to that flag, as previously to the jacket.

THE FLAG'S OFFICIAL HISTORY

Glance now at the story of those Orders in Council which created the various Union flags. The very union of the two kingdoms of England and Scotland seems to have accentuated the pettier national jealousies, so that Southrons annoyed Northerners by hoisting the St. George above the St. Andrew, and the Scotchmen retaliated by a species of *tu quoque*. The King sought to allay these quarrels by creating a British, as other than a purely English or Scottish, flag. But let the Proclamation speak for itself.

"*By the King.*

"*Whereas, some differences hath arisen between Our subjects of South and North Britaine travelling by Seas, about the bearing of their Flagges: For the avoiding of all* contentions hereafter, Wee have, with the advice of our Councill, ordered: That from henceforth all our Subjects of this Isle and Kingdome of Great Britaine, and all our members thereof, shall beare in their main-toppe the Red Crosse, commonly called St. George's Crosse, and the White Crosse, commonly called St. Andrew's Crosse, joyned together according to the forme made by our heralds, and sent by Us to our Admerall to be published to our Subjects: and in their fore-toppe our Subjects of South Britaine shall weare the Red Crosse onely as they were wont, and our Subjects of North Britaine in their fore-toppe the White Crosse onely as they were accustomed.*"—1606.

This attempt at conciliating differences deserved but did not win success. "The King's Owne Shipps" deemed themselves slighted, since all vessels were treated alike in this matter, and so persistent was the agitation that at last, in Charles I.'s reign (1634), another Proclamation was issued "*for the honour of Oure Shipps in Oure Navie Royall,*" whereby those ships alone had the right of hoisting "*the Union Flagge.*" The days of the Commonwealth brought another change, for with the King the King's Flag disappeared. The Protector caused two new flags to be made, viz. *The Great Union* (a flag little used, however, although it figured at his funeral obsequies), and which may be thus blazoned: *Quarterly, 1 and·4, The St. George; 2. The St. Andrew; 3. azure, a harp or, for Ireland; over all on an inescutcheon of pretence, sable, a lion rampant or,* for the Protector's personal arms, and *The Commonwealth Ensign,* which latter Parliament treated as the paramount flag. The most interesting features of this flag are that it was of three kinds, one red, one white, one blue, and that Ireland (but not Scotland) had a place on its folds. When the King came to his own again yet another change was witnessed. By this Proclamation ships in the Navy were to carry *The Union,* and all merchantmen *The St. George,* whilst these latter vessels were also to wear "*The Red Ensign with the St. George on a Canton.*" Passing on, we reach the days of Queen Anne, who as soon as the union of the two Parliaments was accomplished, issued a famous Proclamation often quoted. Suffice it here to outline its effect.

The two crosses of *St. George* and *St. Andrew* were—as the Treaty of Union had agreed should be—"*conjoyned in such a manner as we should think fit*"; and what that manner was is "*described on the margent*" in the shape of a sketch. But further, in place of the *St. George* being placed on the canton of the *Red Ensign* of Charles II. (itself *The Commonwealth Ensign, minus* the harp) the Proclamation ordered the "*Union*" as a canton, and finally this new Red Ensign was confined to the merchant ships, whilst "*Our Jack*" was reserved for the use of the Navy, unless by particular warrant. Thus things continued until the union of Ireland with England and Scotland. The Proclamation referring to this Act of Union closes with the Herald's verbal blazon of the full Union Flag:—"*The Union Flag shall be Azure, the Crosses Saltire of St. Andrew and St. Patrick, Quarterly per saltire, countercharged Argent and Gules, the latter fimbriated of the second, surmounted by the Cross of St. George of the third, fimbriated as the Saltire.*" Thus the Union, as displayed in bunting, was perfected.

THE ART OF HERALDRY

THE FLAG VIEWED HERALDICALLY

Our *Union Flag* is very remarkable, even amongst the flags of Christendom, both as a blending of crosses, and crosses only, and also as an emblem of the union of two or more countries. Yet it is not unique, for the flags of Denmark, Sweden, and Norway have a somewhat similar story to tell. The last two countries separated at different dates from Denmark, and then together formed a United Scandinavian Kingdom. In separating, they each took to themselves a separate flag, and again, in uniting, they called into being a Union Banner. How they treated these changes Fig. 969

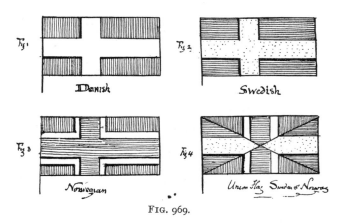

FIG. 969.

will illustrate. Notwithstanding these acts of union both Scandinavians and Britons have had, and still have, their differences over these Union Flags. Whilst, however, they base their protests on the sentiment of independence, we ground our grumblings on questions of heraldic precedence, and of the interpretation of verbal blazons. Leaving our neighbours to settle their differences, let us examine our own. Take the subject of precedence. Very early in the flag's history, Scotchmen were indignant because the St. Andrew was not placed over the St. George. All kinds of variations have been suggested to lessen this crux of precedence, but such attempts must plainly be in vain. Do what you will, some kind of precedence is unavoidable. The *St. George*, then, as representing the paramount partner, occupies the centre of the flag, whilst the *St. Andrew*, as senior in partnership to the *St. Patrick*, is placed *above the St. Patrick in the first quarter*, although throughout it is counterchanged. The words underlined are important, for when the order is reversed, then that particular flag is flying upside down.

THE VERBAL BLAZON

The mode of procedure in creating flags has been much the same from one reign to another. Briefly it is this: The Sovereign seeks the advice of, and receives a report from, the Lords of the Privy Council. These councillors are "*attended by the King of Arms and Heralds, with diverse drafts prepared by them.*" A decision being arrived at, an Order in Council, followed by a Royal Proclamation, makes known the character of the flag. In both Order and Proclamation it is usual to make reference to the verbal blazon, and to "*the form made by our heralds.*" Thus there are three agents recognised—(1) the Sovereign, the fountain of all honours; (2) the heralds, who authoritatively blazon, outline, and register all achievements; and (3) the naval authority, as that in which are vested the duty and the power of seeing the actual bunting properly made up and properly flown. In keeping with this, the general mode of procedure, the Proclamations demand our attention.

The Proclamation of James (1606). A high official of the College of Arms informs us that neither verbal blazon nor drawing of the first Union Flag is extant. On the other hand, in the Proclamations of 1707 and 1801 we have both blazon and drawing. The blazon has already been given of the 1801 flag (which is the one most needing a verbal blazon), and the drawings of both flags we here produce (Figs. 970 and 971). These drawings

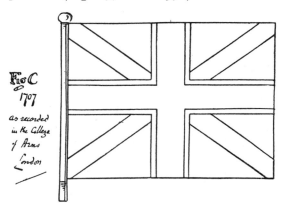

FIG. 970.—The Union Flag of 1707.

—though slightly reduced in these pages—are most careful copies of the *signed* copies supplied to us by the official already alluded to. In forwarding them he writes: "*They are not drawn to scale;*" and he adds, further on, "*they are exactly the same size as recorded in our books.*" So then we have, in these two drawings, the heralds' interpretation, *at the time*, of their own verbal blazon. Now comes the Admiralty part of the work. In the Admiralty

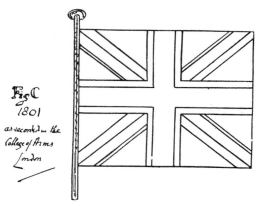

FIG. 971.—The Union Flag of 1801.

Regulations we have a "*Memorandum relative to the origin of the Union Flag in its present form.*" In this there is a brief history of the changes made in the flag from time to time, with quotations from the warrants, together with the verbal blazon AND two coloured drawings (Figs. 972 and 973). The Admiralty has also appended to the Memorandum the following interesting and ingeniously worked out *Table of Proportions, adapted for a flag* 15 *feet by* 7½ *feet*. Presumably this table forms the basis upon which all Union Flags are made up under Admiralty supervision:—

			ft.	in.	
The + of {	St. George . . . . . $\frac{1}{5}$	} together $\frac{1}{3}$ {	1	6	} $\frac{1}{3}$
	Two borders $\frac{1}{15}$ each . $\frac{2}{15}$		1	0	
The × of {	St. Patrick . . . . . $\frac{1}{15}$	} together $\frac{1}{10}$ {	0	6	} $\frac{1}{5}$
	Its border . . . . . $\frac{1}{30}$		0	3	
	St. Andrew . . . . . $\frac{1}{10}$	. . . . .	0	9	

The student of heraldry will observe that this table is based on the proportions of the Ordinaries and Sub-Ordinaries figuring on the flag, as those proportions are regulated by English Rules of Armory. These rules give a cross as $\frac{1}{3}$, a saltire as $\frac{1}{5}$, a fimbriation about $\frac{1}{20}$, of the flag's width. By the way, we notice here, yet only to

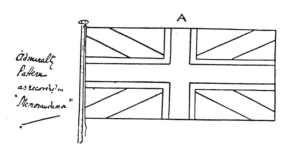

FIG. 972.—Admiralty Pattern of 1707 Flag.

dismiss it as hypercritical, the objection taken to the employment (in the verbal blazon of 1801) of the term "*fimbriated*." To our mind this objection seems a storm in a teacup. Further, it is always admissible in armory to lessen the size of charges when these crowd a field, and although we are fully aware that the laws of armory are not always nor all of them applied to flags, yet there is sufficient evidence to show that the heralds and the Admiralty did recognise the cases of shields and flags to be

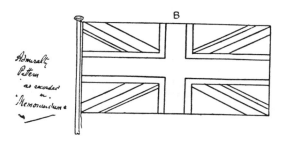

FIG. 973.—Admiralty Pattern of 1801 Flag.

somewhat analogous. But there are two features in *The Admiralty pattern* which cannot but arrest the attention of all those who have made a study of armory. The one is that the sub-ordinaries, *i.e.* the fimbriations, have different proportions given to them, although they are repetitions of the same sub-ordinary, and also seem guarded against such treatment by the very wording of the blazon, and by the practice usual in such cases. And the other is that, after counterchanging the saltires, the St. Patrick is attenuated by having its fimbriation taken off its own field, instead (as the common custom is) off the field of the flag.

THE UNION JACK'S PLACE AMONGST FLAGS

All Warrants dealing with flags provide for their being flown *at sea* (Queen Anne's Proclamation is apparently the first that adds "*and land*"), and gradually reserve for the Royal Navy—or fighting ships—the honour of alone bearing the Union Jack. The accompanying diagram shows at a glance the changes made by the several Proclamations. The latest word on this subject is "The Merchant Shipping (Colours) Act of Queen Victoria, 1894." This Act sets forth among other things that—(1) "*The red ensign usually worn by merchant ships, without any defacement or modification whatsoever, is hereby declared to be the*

proper national colours for all ships and boats belonging to any British subject, except in the case of Her Majesty's ships or boats, or in the case of any other ship or boat for the time being allowed to wear any other national colours in pursuance of a warrant from Her Majesty or from the Admiralty. (2) *If any distinctive national colours except such red ensign, or except the Union Jack with a white border, or if any colours usually worn by Her Majesty's ships, &c. are or is hoisted on board any ship . . . without warrant . . . for each offence . . . a fine not exceeding five hundred pounds.*

SUMMARY AND REFLECTIONS

From all we have considered, we arrive at certain clear conclusions. (1) Sentiment and Custom, when speaking of The Union Flag as *The* National Flag, are in error. (2) In common with *The Red Ensign, The Union Flag* is a National Flag. And (3) It is "*the fighting emblem of the Sovereign.*"

What remains to be said? Have we then no flag which we can fly as individual Sons of the Empire? Have we no flag (we speak not of private and local banners) which, as a loyal Corporation, or a king-revering Parish, we can hoist over Town Hall or Church Tower and say: "This we have a Royal Warrant for flying. It is *our* flag as Britishers." The answer, *at present*, is plainly in the negative. We have no such flag. That all kinds of flags *are* hoisted, on all kinds of occasions, over all kinds of places, gives not the least satisfaction to that increasingly growing portion of the community who are really interested in the story and meaning of flags. Many of us want things done "decently and in order" (legally, consistently, heraldically), and the Sovereign—following in the footsteps of ancestors—would do great service if by Order in Council and Royal Proclamation *He* should grant to us, *His* subjects, *a Warrant* to fly *a National colour*, which each one of us can proudly point to as "OUR JACK."

J. R. C.

POSTSCRIPT

Since going to press, much keen controversy has been continued in the public papers—notably the *Times*—on the right to fly flags, and on the heraldic character of the Admiralty pattern of 1801. This latter subject directly concerns us here, and hence this postscript. In the Heralds' Office drawing, illustrating their verbal blazon, the counterchanged saltires are represented as of equal width, the Irish fimbriation being taken off the field and *not* off the saltire. This is assuredly in keeping with the general rule and the very *raison d'être* of counterchanging. Again: there is no heraldic reason, quite the reverse, why the English and Irish charges should not be fimbriated alike, both as to metal *and* width. The present extreme width of the Admiralty St. George's edging makes the centre of the flag look as if it consisted of "*a white cross with a red cross super-induced.*" For such it has been frequently mistaken. Appended is a flag whose proportions strictly follow the verbal blazon of 1801, and also satisfy all heraldic rules. Worked into bunting it is an exceedingly handsome flag.

Flag 7½ by 15.

St. George	.	21 ins.	}	30 ins., or ⅓.
2 Fimbriations, each 4½ .	.	9 „		
St. Andrew and St. Patrick, each 6¾ .	13½ ins.	}	18 ins., or ⅕.
St. Patrick's Fimbriations . . .	4½ „		

CHAPTER XLIII

THE ARTISTIC DEVELOPMENT OF HERALDRY

IN the foregoing pages the attempt has been to trace the evolution of armory from its scientific side, and, though naturally it is impossible, even if it were desirable, to wholly divorce the scientific point of view from the artistic, in first treating of the subject in its scientific aspect, nevertheless, there yet remains to be considered the purely artistic development of armory. This can best be traced by an examination of carefully selected and typical examples of heraldic art. With few exceptions, the selection has been entirely the work of Herrn Ströhl; in fact the various examples which follow comprise the bulk of the *Heraldischer Atlas*, which is the foundation of the present work. To Herrn Ströhl's selection I have added some number of additional English examples which appeared well worthy of reproduction. In looking through the chronologically arranged series of heraldic examples which follows, it will be found, as would be the case in examining any other chronological selection, that heraldic art gradually and strikingly develops to a very high degree of artistic excellence and merit, and then as strikingly deteriorates.

With the exception of seals and effigies and occasional examples of sculpture, each of which has of necessity an isolated character, one of the earliest collections of arms, or the earliest heraldic monument of that nature on the Continent, is, or rather was—for unfortunately since 1861 the original has no longer been in existence—the decoration in the House "Zum Loch" (Fig. 974), in what was formerly called the Kilchgasse, but now the Römergasse in Zürich, a building which was probably originally erected at the end of the twelfth, or at latest at the beginning of the thirteenth century.

About 1306 the house was in the possession of the family of Wisso, nobles of Zürich. On the oak beams of the ceiling of the lower rooms were painted in water-colour, on the upright sides, coats of arms from 24 to 30 centimetres high (roughly, from 9½ to 12 inches), which, if somewhat roughly done, are of vast interest in the

History of Heraldry. Fortunately, before its demolition, careful records were taken which rendered it possible to place a copy of this ceiling in the new Swiss Museum of Zürich. For this reproduction we are indebted to the kindness of Herrn K. Bührer, editor of the newspaper *Die Schweiz* (Switzerland).

From the fact of the presence of the arms of the Bishopric of Eichstätt (red, a white crosier), and their position near the Imperial eagle, and the Habsbourg lion, the date of the decoration may be determined with some degree of certainty. In the year 1306 King Albrecht (Albert) was in Zürich, where he was celebrating the Karlstag (28th January) (Charles' Day—Charlemagne?), at which festival many noble gentlemen had presented themselves. Albert's Chancellor and friend was Johann, prefect of the canonry of the Grand Cathedral at Zürich, who in 1305 was also Bishop of Eichstätt, which bishopric, however, in 1306 he exchanged for that of Strasbourg. The paintings, therefore, would appear to have been placed there during the presence of the King and his Chancellor. Figs. 975–979 give examples of the designs.

Fig. 975. Arms of the *Roman Kingdom:* Or, an eagle displayed sable.

Fig. 976. Arms of *Von Schönenwerd*, a family which belonged to the Zürich nobility (their ancestral seat was near Dietikon on the Limmat): Per pale argent and gules, on the dexter side a lion rampant sable.

Fig. 977. Arms of the *Freiherren* (Barons) *von Rüssegg*, of Lucerne: Argent—perhaps originally "or," as they later used this colour also (see Plate XXXI. Fig. 6)—a unicorn rampant sable.

Fig. 978. Arms of *Maness von Manegg*, Zürich nobles: Gules, two warriors fighting. (See Plate XX. Fig. 4.)

Fig. 979. Arms of the *Freiherren von Tüffen*, of Zürich: Gules, a helmet, and thereupon a demi-eagle issuant argent.

Equally ancient are the shields on the brick friezes of

FIG. 974.—Copy of the ceiling of the Armorial Room in the House "Zum Loch." (Swiss Museum at Zurich).

FIG. 975.—Römisches Reich.   FIG. 976.—Schönenwerd.   FIG. 977.—Rüssegg.   FIG. 978.—Manesse.   FIG. 979.—Tüffen.

(a) Froburg.   (b) Strassberg-Nidau.   (c) Bechburg.   (d) Balm.   (e) Grünenberg.   (f) Kien.   (g) Utzingen.

FIG. 980.—The St. Urban Brick Frieze.

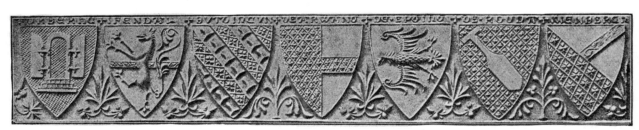

(a) Thorberg.   (b) Iffenthal.   (c) Büttikon.   (d) Aarwangen.   (e) Eptingen.   (f) Rud.   (g) Kienberg.

FIG. 981.—The St. Urban Brick Frieze.

THE ART OF HERALDRY

St. Urban, a former Cistercian monastery, near Zofingen, in the canton of Lucerne, which have now been similarly placed under the protection of the Zürich Museum. These exceedingly delicately executed terra-cotta examples would seem to have been made at St. Urban's itself, as no

FIG. 982.—Arms of the Duke of Bavaria.

FIG 983.—Arms of the Landgrave of Hesse.

FIG. 984.—Arms of the Count Von der Mark.

other examples are to be found except in the near neighbourhood of the monastery. The two friezes, Figs. 980

FIG. 985.—Arms of the Count of Holstein.

and 981, are examples of this unique and highly-developed work. The arms illustrated are :—

Fig. 980. *a.* Arms of the *Counts von Froburg :* Or, an eagle displayed ermine.
 b. Arms of the *Strassberg-Niddau* family : Gules, on a pale sable, three chevrons or.
 c. Arms of the *Barons von Bechburg* (Solothurn) : Tierced in fess gules, argent, and sable. The last of this family fell at the battle of Sempach in 1386.
 d. Arms of the *Barons von Balm* (Solothurn) : Per pale azure and argent, a lion rampant gules. The colours of the field are sometimes reversed, and a modern form of the arms shows the field paly of six.
 e. Arms of the *Barons von Grünenberg,* Burggraves of Rheinfelden.

f. Arms of the *Barons von Kien :* Azure, two eagles' claws in saltire argent, armed sable.
g. Arms of *Utzingen :* Argent, a quatrefoil vert.

Fig. 981. *a.* Arms of *Thorberg :* Gules, an open door argent.
 b. Arms of *Iffenthal :* Or, a fess azure, debruised by a lion rampant gules.
 c. Arms of the *von Buttikons,* Lords of Schenkow : Bendy of six gules and ermine.
 d. Arms of *Aarwangen :* Per pale sable and argent, on the sinister side a fess of the first.
 e. Arms of *Eptingen* of Basel : Or, an eagle displayed fesswise sable, armed gules.
 f. Arms of *Rud.* (Rued), servants of the Habsbourgs : Azure, a rudder in bend argent.
 g. Arms of *Kienberg* (Solothurn) : Per bend sable and gules, in chief a bend sinister sable ; argent, six mounds in pyramid and couped. This family became extinct in 1450.

Other early examples of arms from German sources will be found in Figs. 982–985.

PLATE LXXI

EARLY ENGLISH ROLLS OF ARMS

On the next page reference will be made to a collection of armorial drawings by Matthew Paris, and to another early roll of arms now in the possession of the Society of Antiquaries in London. There is, however, in the custody of the College of Arms a fragment of a roll which some have considered to be the oldest collected armorial record in existence. Doubtless a critical examination of the names might enable one to arrive at an approximately accurate date ; but I have had no such opportunity of examination, though there can be little doubt the fragment belongs to the early part of the thirteenth century.

THE ART OF HERALDRY

The roll, which was originally emblazoned upon parchment, has been cut up at some period. The shields, which are conjoined, appear to have been originally painted conjoined in rows of six. Each row has been cut out, the outline of the shields being carefully followed, and the rows are now fastened upon leaves of thick paper, these being bound up with other matters in volume form. The leaves to which these rows of shields are attached are preceded by a painting or illumination, doubtless belonging thereto, of some beauty in its execution and of an ecclesiastical character. This would seem to suggest that, like the paintings of Matthew Paris, these shields represent the arms of the benefactors of some religious foundation. Beyond the name which surmounts each shield no writing or other descriptive matter remains with the roll. Through the courtesy of Mr. C. H. Athill, Richmond Herald, who has had paintings made which he has certified for me, I am enabled to reproduce some of the shields from this roll. Though these reproductions are joined together, as are the shields in the original, it should be noticed that the examples selected for reproduction do not consecutively follow each other in their present order upon the original. Many—in fact a large proportion—of the shields are badly damaged, some nearly wholly obliterated. One very noticeable detail, however, at once becomes apparent. Though identically in keeping with the other heraldic work of the period, the paintings seem to have been finished in a more careful manner, and the shields lack much of the crudity of design and draughtsmanship so often met with.

The following are the particulars of those selected. It will be noticed that lines of division are wholly absent :—

1. Argent, a lion rampant sable (Count de Flandres).

2. Per pale argent and gules, an eagle displayed with two heads per pale sable and of the first (Count de B'goyns).

3. Sable, a cross engrailed argent (Robert de Ufford.)

4. Sable, a cross flory argent (Richard Syward).

5. Argent, a bear sable, muzzled argent (Reginald Fitzurse).

6. Argent, six eagles displayed, three, two, and one (Richard Tany).

7. Argent, three fleurs-de-lis sable (Willem Peiferer).

8. Argent, a manuch gules (Henry de Hastings).

9. Argent, two lions passant in pale azure (Roger de Somery).

10. Argent, three stockings, two and one gules (Nicholas de la Hese).

11. Argent, a lion rampant gules, crowned (Ibew D'Urberville).

12. Argent, two chevrons gules, a canton (or quarter) of the last (Novreram de Oriel).

13. Argent, a sun in splendour gules (unnamed).

14. Vair (The Count of Gynes [Guisnes]).

15. Argent, a cross moline sable (the Prince of Moree).

16. Gules, a saltire vair (Rauf de Wiltun).

17. Argent, a griffin segreant azure, armed gules (the King of).

18. Argent, two ravens in pale sable (Roberd Corbet).

19. Argent, six lions rampant 3, 2, and 1 sable (Roger de Leyburne).

20. Gyronny of twelve argent and azure (. . . de Bresum).

21. Per pale dancetté argent and gules (the Earl of Leicester).

22. Chequy argent and azure, a bordure ingrailed gules, a quarter (or canton) ermine (the Earl of Richmond).

23. Gules, a cross patonce argent (the Earl of Albemarle).

24. Gules, a fleur-de-lis argent (Robert de Agulum).

25. Barry nebuly argent and gules (Philip Basser).

A. C. F-D.

PLATE LXXII

EXAMPLES OF HERALDIC DRAWINGS BY MATHÆUS PARISIENSIS (MATTHEW PARIS)

(1244)

Some of the earliest drawings of arms, and possibly the earliest example of anything in the nature of a collection or roll of arms, is that of Matthew Paris.

Matthew Paris, one of the Lincolnshire family of that surname, entered the Benedictine Monastery of St. Albans in 1217, and soon began to play a very conspicuous part, not only as a scholar and historian (*Historia Anglorum, Chronica Major*, &c.), but also as the confidant and adviser of high personages, amongst whom were Henry III. of England, Louis IX. of France, Hakon IV. of Norway, and others.

The heraldic representations in his historical works are for the most part by himself, and, on account of their great age, are highly interesting. His teacher in the art of drawing was perhaps the celebrated painter and sculptor, Walter of Colchester, sexton of St. Albans, who worked in the cathedral in the time of the Abbot William of Trumpington (1214-1235). Matthew Paris died at an advanced age in the year 1259.

Plate XVIII. shows some of the most interesting coats of arms on a sheet now in the British Museum, on which the arms are painted on both sides. The work was probably done about the year 1244. (They are reproduced from *Wappen aus den Werken des Matthias von Paris* by Pusikan, Berlin, 1881.) According to Pusikan, the arms depicted on the sheet from which the reproductions were made were most probably those of the benefactors of the Cathedral of St. Albans. The first side contains thirty-three shields, some of which are unfinished, the other side seven rows of six each, thus forty-two shields.

Above the shields stand the names of the respective owners of the arms, and at the side of the blazoning of the shields. Those reproduced on Plate LXXII. are as follows :—

Fig. 1. *Scutum imperatoris Romæ* (Frederick II., Roman Emperor): Scutum aureum, aquila biceps nigra vel moniceps (Or, a double eagle displayed sable with one or two heads).

Fig. 2. *Scutum regis Francorum* (St. Louis IX., King of France): Scutum azureum VI gladioli floris aurei (Azure, six fleurs-de-lis, three, two, and one).

Fig. 3. *Scutum regis Scotiæ* (Alexander II., King of Scotland, son of William the Lion, 1214-1249. Under Alexander II. the tressure flory, which is also painted double by Matthew Paris in other places, was introduced into the arms of the kingdom): Or, a lion rampant within a tressure flory.

Fig. 4. *Scutum Nichol-de-Moles.* The name has been inserted incorrectly, and put right by a note on the upper edge of the sheet: *Hug de Baucei pictavensis.* Hugo (or Hugh) de Baucey of Poitou. Scutum aureum, ferrum molendinum de gules (Or, a cross moline [or a fer-de-moline] gules).

Fig. 5. *Scutum N. de Kenetz.:* Scutum de gules, caniculi de argento. The painting of the shield is not finished. (Gules, three talbots argent, two and one.)

On the first side, the following coat of arms also appears in the bottom row (Fig. 986): Scutum regis Castellæ et Leonum videlicet

FIG. 986.—Arms of the King of Castile and Leon.

moderni sed non partis, pater enim portavit scutum tale quale comes Provinciæ Raimundus (King Ferdinand III. of Spain): 1 and 4, Campus huius quarteri rubeus, castrum de auro-campus rubeus, castrum de auro; 2 and 3, Campus huius quarteri albus, leo de purpura-campus iste albus, leo de purpura (Quarterly, 1 and 4, gules, a castle or [for Castile]; 2 and 3, argent, a lion purpure [for Leon]).

Alphonso IX., the father of King Ferdinand, bore the arms of Aragon, like Count Raimund of Provence, because both were descended from the Princes of Aragon.   H. S.

THE ART OF HERALDRY

The Spanish coat of arms just given not only proves that in the middle of the thirteenth century the quartering of a shield was already customary in Spain, but also that purpure was an old heraldic tincture, even if seldom made use of.

Fig. 6. *Willelmi Longaspata* (William de Longespee, Earl of Salisbury), died 1257: Scutum azureum, leones aurei (Azure, [six] lions or).

Fig. 7. *Johanis de Bellocampo* (Beauchamp): Scutum album, aquila nigra (Argent, an eagle [displayed] sable, armed or).

Fig. 8. *Comitis Ricardi*, comitis scilicet Pictavii (Earl Richard of Cornwall and Poitou, died 1272, brother-in-law of the Emperor Frederic II., elected King of the Romans in 1257): Scutum album leo gules, bordura nigra, besantes d'or (Argent, a lion gules [crowned or], within a bordure sable bezantee). The arms of the Duchy of Cornwall are still sable, fifteen bezants, five, four, three, two, and one, and the family of Cornwall, baronets, still bear arms very similar to those of the ancestor from whom they (illegitimately) derive, namely: Argent, a lion rampant gules, ducally crowned or, within a bordure engrailed sable.

Fig. 9. *Comitis de Legrecestria* (Simon de Montfort, Earl of Leicester, High Steward of England, died 1265 at the Battle of Evesham in Worcestershire): Scutum album leo gules (Argent, a lion rampant [double-queued] gules) (see Plate LXXI. Fig. 21).

Fig. 10. *Ricardi de Munfichet.* (The Montfichets came over from Normandy with William the Conqueror, but died out as early as 1268. Richard was, in 1215, one of the twenty-five barons appointed to enforce the provisions of Magna Charta): Scutum d'or, III. chevrons de gules, rastel d'azure, V lambel (Or, three chevrons gules, surmounted by a label of five points azure).

Fig. 11. *Hugonis de Novilli* (Hugh de Neville of Essex, who was one of the favourites of King John, 1211): Anterior quartena cum suo pari. . . (Quarterly indented gules and vert, a bend or).

Fig. 12. *Johanis de Bassingeburne* (John, Lord Bassingbourne, was also one of the advisers of King John): Scutum superius de gules leo aureus, inferius scutum de albo fesse de gules, aves de gules (Argent, a bend between six martlets gules, on a chief of the last, a lion [passant guardant] or).

Fig. 13. *Radulfi filii Nicholai* (Ralph Fitz Nicholas appears in 1250 as "domini regis senescallus"): Scutum de gules, pentafolium d'or, bordura escal d'argent (Gules, a cinquefoil or). Of the silver border nothing is to be seen.

Fig. 14. *Comitis Cestriæ* (Earl of Chester): Scutum d'azuro garbe d'or (Azure [three] garbs or).

These are still the arms used for and attributed to the Earldom of Chester.

Fig. 15. *Comitis Tholosiæ* (Count Raimund of Toulouse, who was brother-in-law to King John): Scutum de gules crux aurea (Gules, a cross of Toulouse, voided or). The town of Toulouse still bears the cross of Toulouse, with other figures, in her arms.

SPECIMENS FROM AN ENGLISH ROLL OF ARMS

(About the Year 1300)

The remaining examples on Plate LXXII. are taken from a roll of English origin, and of but little later date. It is in the possession of the Society of Antiquaries in London, and is a parchment roll of 78 feet 6 inches long by 11 inches broad, with 486 shields upon it, which are arranged in fifty-four rows of nine shields each. The superscriptions are of later date, and the work of different hands.

The following specimens, which are taken therefrom, are reproduced from the Catalogue of the Heraldic Exhibition in London in 1894, edited by Mr. St. John Hope, Assistant Secretary to the Society of Antiquaries.

Fig. 16. *Wat de Gey* (Walter de Gey): Argent, a bend gules, surmounted by a lion rampant sable. The dexter forepaw is missing.

Fig. 17. *Jon de Brūton* (Jon de Brumton): "Or, a bend sable, surmounted by two lions passant gules.

Fig. 18. *Jon de Herondi:* Gules, billettée d'or, three lions rampant of the last.

Fig. 19. *Gile Fisshman:* Gules, a dolphin embowed or (? argent).

Fig. 20. *Henry de Mortimer:* Argent, a cross azure charged with five escallops or.

Fig. 21. *Joh' le Fitz Marmanduc:* Gules, a fess between three popinjays argent.

Fig. 22. *Will' Corbet* (William Corbet): Or, three ravens sable.

Fig. 23. *Will' de Estokes* (William de Estokes): Vair, a chief gules.

Fig. 24. *Joh' de Beneshale* (Johan de Reveshale): Or, a cross gules surmounted by a label of five points azure, each file charged with three fleurs-de-lis or.

Fig. 25. *Will' de Stephewe:* Azure, a cross or, fretty gules.

H. S.

PLATE LXXIII

EXAMPLES OF ARMS REPRODUCED FROM THE "WEINGARTNER" AND THE "HEIDELBERGER" MINNESÄNGER-LIEDERHANDSCHRIFT

(THE NOS. 1-18 REFER TO THE FIGURES ON THE PLATE)

The Minnesingers anciently were wandering minstrels who sang more especially of love—*minne*—but this word is not now used except in this or similar connections.

WEINGARTNER BOOK OF SONGS (FIGS. 1-10).

This manuscript, now consisting of 158 sheets of parchment (about 15.3 cm. high by 11.7 broad), was in the sixteenth century in the possession of the Marx magistrate at Constance, who relinquished it to the Benedictine Abbey of Weingarten (hence its name), who still owned it in 1613. Since 1810 this valuable manuscript has been in the possession of the Royal Select Library (deposited in the Public Library) of Stuttgart (*Poet.*, germ. 1). It contains verses by thirty-one Minnesingers, with twenty-five coloured pictures, of which twenty show coats of arms. The style of these coats of arms (height of shield about 3 cm.), in none of which is gold used at all, and silver only in Figs. 1 and 2, corresponds to the closing years of the thirteenth century.

The shields and helmets, which are not always united in the original, have been put together in heraldic manner in all the cases here illustrated. The examples chosen are as follows :—

Fig. 1. *Burgrave v[on] Riete[n]burg.* Arms: or, on a bend argent, three roses gules, seeded or. Crest: a rose gules, the stem between two fish-hooks or, adorned with peacock's feathers. (The Heidelberg manuscript has these arms: Or, on a bend gules, three roses argent.) The ancestral seat of the Counts von Rietenberg was over the Riedenburg market an der Altmühl, in Bavaria.

Fig 2. *Grave [Graf] Otte v[on] Botenlauben.* Arms: per fess or and chequy argent and gules, in chief a demi-double-headed eagle issuing sable. Crest: an eagle's claw erect or (Otto von Henneberg, 1175?-1245, called himself after his estate, Bodenlaube bei Kissingen, which, however, he sold again in 1234).

Fig. 3. *H. Bliger v[on] Sainach* (Herr Bligger von Stainach). Arms: gules, a harp argent. Crest: two peacock's heads and necks addorsed proper. (The Heidelberg manuscript has these arms: Azure, a harp or.) The ancestral castle was at Neckar-steinach, above Heidelberg.

Fig. 4. *H. Volrich v[on] Munegur.* Arms: per fess gules and gyronny of six argent and sable. Crest: a thing similar to a wolf's claw, or a harpoon, of gold, set round with peacock's feathers. The Heidelberg MS. gives the tinctures of these arms as per fess or, and gyronny argent and azure.

Fig 5. *H. Hiltebolt v[on] Swanegou* (Schwangau). Arms: gules, a swan argent, armed sable. Crest: a swan as in the arms. (The Heidelberg MS. makes the swan beaked and legged or.) The ancestral seat of this Swabian family stood where is now Hohenschwangau, in Upper Bavaria.

Fig. 6. *H. Uolrich v[on] Guote[n]burg.* Arms: or, a lion sable, debruised by a fess gules. Crest: a lily stalked gules, between two buffalo's horns or, each adorned with seven black reeds or bulrushes. (The Heidelberg MS. shows the crest without the lily being stalked, and makes the reeds like leaves.)

Fig. 7. *Der Truhsoeze v[on] Singe[n]b[er]g* (Ulrich von Singenberg 1219, *Truchsess* or High Steward to *St. Gall*). Arms: azure, a demi-stag argent. Crest: a star of eight rays gules, each ray adorned with a peacock's feather. (The star is divided in half, to facilitate the fastening of it to the helmet. The Heidelberg MS. has a golden star.) The seat of the Singenberg family lay on the right bank of the Sitter, above Bischofszell, in Thurgau.

Fig. 8. *H. Bernger v[on] Horheim.* Arms: gules, four lilies argent, issuing from the edge of the shield and conjoined in the centre, forming a cross. Crest: a circular hat barry of six or and gules, on the points three peacock's feathers, the quills gules. (The Heidelberg MS. makes the field azure with the same cross of lilies in gold ; and the hat there is also gold.)

Fig. 9. *H. Hartwig Raute.* Arms: chequy or and sable, a cross gules. Crest: a snail-shaped bouquetin's horn, alternately sable and or, rising out of a helmet "bandeau" (fillet or wreath), counter-company argent and azure (Heidelberg MS.: blue and gold striped horn).

Fig. 10. *Herr Walther von Mezze* (Metz). Through a mistake of the artist of the MS. this coat of arms was ascribed to *Herre Rubin* (Schloss Rubein bei Meran), who, however, according to the Heidelberg MS., bears as arms : Azure, a ruby ring. The arms depicted are : Gules, two bars chequy sable and or. Crest: a pair of wings proper (with red wing-bones) bordered with a gold curve ; issuing from a helmet bandeau company counter-company sable and or. (The Heidelberg MS. has the bars chequy argent and azure, the wings azure, and the bones covered with two rows of red and yellow feathers.) The ancestral castle of the *Metz* family stood in the Etschthale (Valley of the Etsch), between Botzen and Trient.

Two other armorial pictures from the Weingartner MS. are given on Plate V.

GREAT HEIDELBERG SONG-BOOK (FIGS. 11–18)

(Formerly called the "Parisian" and also the "Maness" MS.)

This manuscript, consisting of 246 sheets of parchment (height 35.5 cm., breadth 2.5 cm.), was found at the end of the sixteenth century among the effects of the deceased Freiherr von Hohensax auf Forsteck, who had borrowed it from the Elector of the Palatinate. In 1607 the Register came back to Heidelberg. In 1622, after the conquest of the town by Tilly, it was carried off and was found at last among the effects of the Royal Librarian, J. Dupuy, in Paris, who bequeathed it to the Royal Library in spite of frequent attempts (1815, 1823, 1871) to win the Register for Germany once more. It was only in 1888 that the Strassburg bookseller, K. Trübner, succeeded in obtaining the manuscript in exchange for valuable old French manuscripts, which he had acquired from Lord Ashburnham for £26,000 sterling. It came back to Heidelberg on April 10, 1888, and was entered in the Library catalogue as "*Codex Palatinus*, germ. No. 848." The MS. contains poems by 140 minnesingers, 137 coloured pictures, and a pen-and-ink drawing. One hundred and twenty pages show coats of arms, and ten, helmet-ornaments only. (Height of shields about 5-6 cm.). The claim that Rüdiger (Roger) Manesse of Zürich was the author of this collection of songs, is somewhat questionable.

The shield and helmets, which are emblazoned with gold and silver in the original, have here been placed in conjunction, whereas

FIG. 987.

in the original they mostly appear separated, the helmets being provided with hanging red cords (see Fig. 987). The lettering of the names was copied from the original Register.

Fig. 11. *Herr Reinmar von Zweter.* Arms: gules, an eagle displayed argent, armed or, the wing-bones terminating in eagles' heads respecting each other. Crest: a demi-eagle as in the arms. He belonged to the Palatinate family of the *Herren von Zuitern* (Zeutern, between Bruchsal and Heidelberg).

Fig. 12. *Herr Walther von der Vogelweide.* Arms: gules, a bird-cage or, and within it a bird vert. Crest: a bird-cage and bird as in the arms.

This celebrated minnesinger came of a family in the Southern Tyrol, and lived from about 1187–1227.

Fig. 13. *Meister Heinrich Frauenlob.* Arms: azure (in the Register this has turned a greenish tint), a woman's bust, crowned and vested or, wearing a veil argent. Crest: a woman's bust as in the arms, the habit continued to serve as the mantling. He died on the 29th of November 1318, at Mayence, and was carried to his grave by women (*Frauenlob* = Women's praise.)

Fig. 14. *Heinrich von Tettingen.* Arms: or, a sickle argent, the handle gules. Crest: two sickles as in the arms. His home must have been Döttigen, above Klingnau, in Aargau.

Fig. 15. *Endilhart* (Orendilhart) *von Adelburg.* Arms: or, two crab's claws in pale gules. Crest: two crab's claws erect gules. His ancestral seat was *Adelburg*, on the *Laber*, to the north of Parsburg (Bavarian Upper Palatinate).

Fig. 16. *Herr Reinmar der Alte.* Arms: barry of eight or and azure, a pale gules. Crest: a long pointed cap of the arms, surmounted with a tassel of peacock's feathers. The Weingartner MS. has the arms barry or and sable.

Fig. 17. *Herr Heinrich von Morungen.* Arms: azure, three crescents argent, each horn terminating in a star of eight rays or. Crest: a crescent as in the arms, resting on a cushion azure. The ancestral seat was the castle of Morungen, near Sangershausen.

Fig. 18. *Herr Hesse von Rinach.* Arms: or, a lion gules, the head azure, collared or. Crest: a lion's head azure, adorned with a comb

or fin gules, terminating in peacock's feathers. The family was domiciled in Aargau, and was an offshoot of the Habsbourgs of the thirteenth century, hence the arms, which, except as to the tincture of the head, were exactly the same as those of the Habsbourgs who had borne : Or, a lion gules.

Herr Wolfram von Eschenbach. (See Fig. 988.) Arms: gules, two

her wolfran von Eschilbach.

FIG. 988.

Der Tanhuser.

FIG. 989.

axes (?) argent. Crest: the charges as in the arms. Eschenbach is situated near Ansbach, and there the poet, who died about 1220,

PLATE CXXX.

EXAMPLES OF ITALIAN ARMORIAL SCULPTURE.

PLATE CXXXI.

Philippino de altavilla

Armorum melioratioq fratriby de Turricellis

EXAMPLES OF ITALIAN AND PORTUGUESE HERALDRY

PLATE CXXXII.

EXAMPLES OF ENGLISH HERALDRY, XV. AND XVI. CENTURIES.

PLATE CXXXIII.

THE ARMS OF MAGDALENE OF FRANCE AND OF MARY OF LORRAINE.
FROM THE MS. OF SIR DAVID LINDSAY OF THE MOUNT.

PLATE CXXXIV.

THE ARMS OF HAMILTON.
FROM THE HAMILTON MS.

PLATE CXXXV.

FIGURES OF KING ROBERT BRUCE AND HIS SECOND QUEEN.
FROM A MS. IN THE ADVOCATES' LIBRARY IN EDINBURGH.

PLATE CXXXVI.

PLATE CXXXVII.

PLATE CXXXVIII.

HERALDIC AND OTHER SEALS.

PLATE CXXXIX.

CONTEMPORARY SEALS.
By German Seal Engravers.

PLATE CXL.

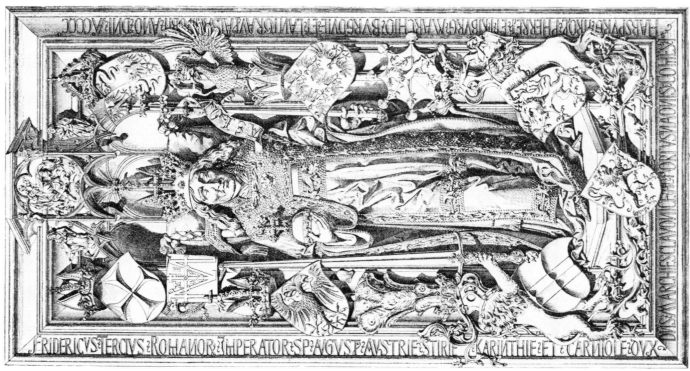

EXAMPLES OF HERALDIC MEMORIAL SLABS.

PLATE CXLI.

EXAMPLES OF HERALDIC MEMORIALS.

PLATE CXLII.

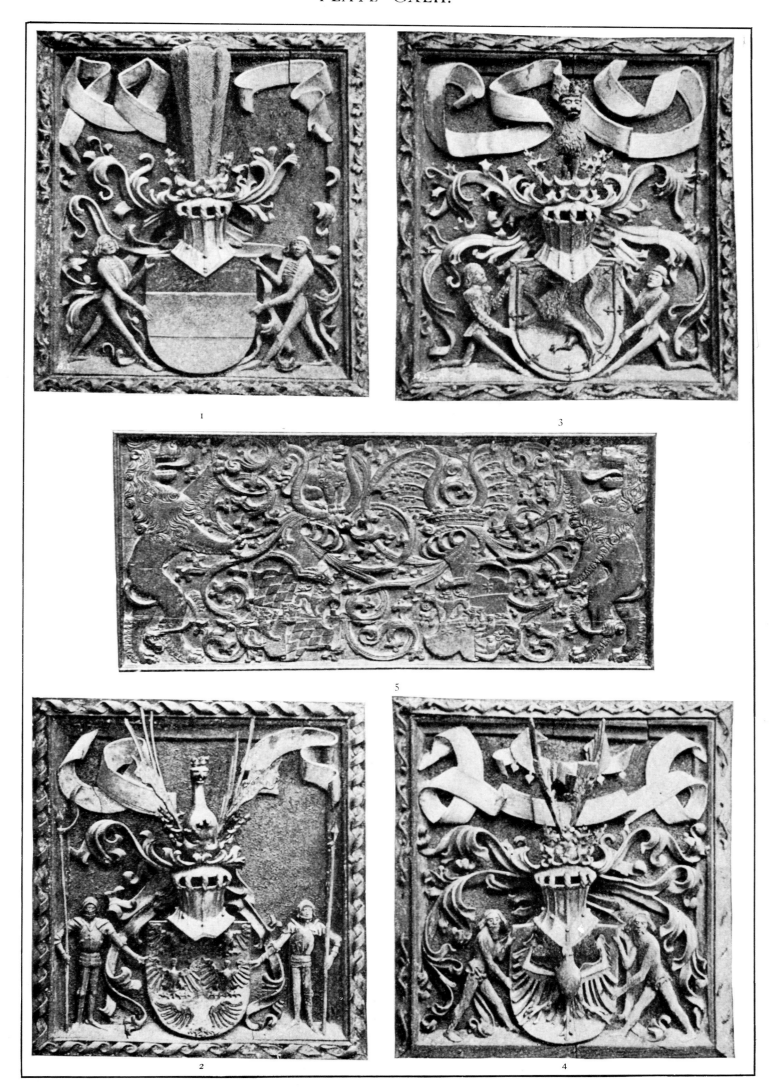

EXAMPLES OF ARMORIAL WOOD CARVINGS.

PLATE CXLIII.

EXAMPLES OF ARMORIAL WOOD CARVINGS.

PLATE CXLIV.

AN OAK CARVING FROM KING'S COLLEGE, ABERDEEN, WITH THE ARMS OF BISHOP ELPHINSTON.

PLATE CXLV.

EXAMPLES OF HERALDIC CRAFTSMANSHIP.

was buried. The Eschenbachs of the Upper Palatinate bore : Gules, three knives argent.

Every one must be familiar with the name of *Tannhäuser*, whose arms will be found in Fig. 989. Shield : per fess sable and or. Crest : two buffalo's horns conjoined to combs, the whole also per fess as in the arms. Tannhäuser's family is unknown.

Many of the coats of arms in both manuscripts were most likely not real family arms, but merely fanciful inventions adopted by or attributed to the Minnesingers. For instance, for those of Walther von der Vogelweide, Frauenlob, Tannhäuser, &c.

It is, of course, known that the first mentioned won, or assumed, his surname, "Von der Vogelweide" ("Of the bird-meadow"— only in its German form a little more poetic-sounding than when Anglicised), because he sang of birds and fields and such things of nature. H. S.

PLATE LXXIV

EXAMPLES TAKEN FROM THE "ZÜRICHER WAPPEN-ROLLE" (ZÜRICH ROLL OF ARMS)

(First half of the Fourteenth Century)

FIGS. 1-20 BELOW RELATE TO THE PLATE.

" He who has not studied thoroughly this oldest German Collection of Arms has no idea at all of the heraldry of the Middle Ages," writes Prince Frederick Karl of Hohenlohe-Waldenburg, in his "History of the Fürstenberg Arms," and these words best denote the value of this Register.

In the first half of the eighteenth century this Roll of Arms was in the possession of the well-known naturalist, and lover of armory, Joh. Jak. (Johann Jakob) Scheuchzer, of Zürich, and was merely known under the name of *Membrana Heraldica ;* after his death in the year 1733, it came into the possession of the Zürich Town Library. The Roll is at the present time 400.5 centimetres long, 12.5 centimetres broad, and consists of thirteen pieces of parchment fastened together with thread. The Roll, which is painted with coats of arms in two rows on both sides, was originally longer, but fortunately the missing piece is available in the form of a copy. The Roll, including this piece, contains five hundred and fifty-nine coats of arms and twenty-eight episcopal banners. In the year 1860 the pictures of the Roll were published in colours on twenty-five Plates by the Antiquarian Society of Zürich, from which publication the reproductions herein have been taken.

Fig. 1. *Bregenz* (No. 127 in the Roll) : "Kürsch" a pale ermine ; on the helmet, a fur cap "turned inside out" and stuck round with peacock's feathers. This is the coat of arms of the old Counts of Bregenz, who died out in 1157. Their crest appears here somewhat peculiarly drawn, a copy of the "Rolle," of the sixteenth century, in the Library of Count Königsegg at Aulendorf, shows the fur cap more distinctly apparent. (The name seems to have been preserved in the name of the town and lake of Bregenz (Ger.)—usually called Brienz in French and English, in Switzerland).

Fig. 2. (?) (No. 248) : Gules, three pieces of fur two and one ; on the helmet as crest a youth's body gules charged with a fess vair, the hood also gules edged with vair, the point of the hood adorned with a bunch of black cock's feathers.

Fig. 3. *Rötelen* (No. 143) : Vair, on a chief or, a demi-lion issuant gules. Crest : a lion's head adorned with a comb or fan vair.

Fig. 4. *Maness von Manegg* (No. 234) : Gules, two knights combatant argent. On the helmet as crest the head of a knight habited in mail and in a bassinet all proper.

The Zürich Knight, Rüdiger Maness von Manegg (died 1304), was, according to the opinion of some historians, the author both of the *Heidelberger Liederhandschrift* (see Plate LXXIII.) and also of this Roll, but the presumption that Constance was the birthplace of the Roll seems to be more probable.

Fig. 5. *Betler* (Betler von Herderen in Thurgau)—No. 420— (*Betler*=beggar in old-fashioned spelling) : Argent, a beggar habited in sable, his shoes or, on his shoulder a bag or knapsack argent, suspended by a cord gules and a pilgrim's staff in his sinister hand, and in his dexter hand a dish, both gules. On the helmet as crest a demi-beggar vested argent, the bag suspended from his shoulders sable, the cord gules, and holding in both hands a bowl sable.

Fig. 6. *Habspvrg* (No. 34) : Or, a lion rampant gules : on the helmet as crest a demi-lion gules, with a comb argent, adorned with peacock's feathers.

This is the earliest coat of arms of the Counts von Habsbourg, and can be found on the seal of a document as far back as 1186. The crest, however, occurs only in 1259. Since about 1500 the lion has been borne crowned.

Fig. 7. *Rehberg* (Rechberg of Swabia) (No. 403) : Argent, two lions rampant and addorsed gules. Crest : a demi-lion gules. The tails of the lions are usually depicted intertwined, but they do not so occur in the present instance.

Fig. 990. *Geroldseck am Wasichen* (No. 453) : Argent, billettée azure, a lion rampant gules, crowned or. Crest : a hat covered with

peacock's feathers proper, surmounted by a ball argent, ornamented with a plume of peacock's feathers, also proper.

Fig. 8. *Bienbvrg* (No. 95) : Azure, a leopard or, armed gules. Crest : two buffalo's horns gules, adorned with peacock's feathers proper.

Fig. 9. *Walbvrg* (No. 176) : Or, three leopards (lions passant guardant) in pale sable. Crest : a cushion or, with tassels gules, and thereupon a plume of peacock's feathers proper issuing from a case or.

Fig. 10. *Helfenstain* in Swabia (from *helfant*=elephant) (No. 40) : Gules, on a quadruple mount couped or, an elephant statant argent. Crest : two "combs" or "fans" argent, adorned with fan-crests of peacock's feathers.

Fig. 11. *Wvlfingen* (Wülflingen of Zürich) (No. 399) : Argent, on two linden-leaves the stalks conjoined and issuing from the base, a wolf azure. Crest : a demi-wolf azure.

FIG. 990.—Geroldseck.   FIG. 991.—Wolfurt.

Fig. 991. *Wolfvrt* (No. 298) : Argent, in base water (*furt*=a ford), two wolves current in pale azure. Crest : the head and neck of a wolf azure. In the thirteenth century the Wolfurts bore : Or, a wolf azure.

Fig. 12. *Rischach* (Reischach in Swabia) (No. 181) : Or, a boar's head couped at the neck sable, armed of the field, crined at the neck argent. Crest : a boar's head and neck couped or, armed and crined at the neck argent.

Fig. 13. (*Rechberg* im Entlebuch ?) (*Reh*=roe ; *berg*=mountain) (No. 249) : Azure, a roe-buck or, climbing up the face of a rock issuing from the dexter side of the escutcheon. Crest : the head and neck of a stag or.

Fig. 14. *Tierberg* in Swabia (No. 165) : Azure, on a quadruple mount couped argent, a hind statant or. Crest : the head and neck of a hind or.

Fig. 15. *Obaerloh* (No. 114) : Argent, a "bouquetin" sable. Crest : a demi-bouquetin sable.

Fig. 16. (?) (No. 519) : Gules, a bull sable, the nose-ring argent. Crest : a cushion argent with tassels gules, and thereupon a bull as in the arms.

Fig. 17. *Rosnow* (No. 47) : Or, a ram sable. Crest : the head and neck of a ram or.

Fig. 18. *Haimenhoven* in Swabia (No. 205) : Gules, a horse salient argent, the saddle or, the bridle gules. Crest : the head and neck of a horse argent, bridled gules.

Fig. 19. (?) (No. 375) : Argent, a mastiff [or hound] gules, gorged with a spiked dog-collar sable. Crest : a conical hat gules, and thereupon an annulet sable adorned around the outer edge with leaves argent.

Fig. 20. *Pfirt* (No. 30) : Gules, two fish hauriant and addorsed or. Crest : two fish as in the arms. H. S.

PLATE LXXV

FURTHER EXAMPLES TAKEN FROM THE "ZÜRICHER WAPPENROLLE" (ZÜRICH ROLL OF ARMS)

(First half of the Fourteenth Century)

FIGS. 1-20 BELOW RELATE TO THE PLATE.

Fig. 1. *Hvn* (Hün) (No. 404 of the Roll) : Or, an eagle's head erased sable. Crest : an eagle's head sable, armed or.

Fig. 2. *Arbon* in Thurgau (No. 48) : Argent, an eagle displayed gules, armed or. Crest : a demi-eagle displayed as in the arms.

Fig. 3. (*Heidegk* in Swabia) (No. 527): Gules, an ostrich [so described in the German blazon] azure, armed or, holding in the beak a horseshoe argent. Crest: an ostrich as in the arms. Without the horseshoe the ostrich could hardly be recognised in this parrot-like bird.

Fig. 4. *Hvnrhvsen* in Thurgau (No. 334): Argent, a double-headed cock sable, the feet, combs, and wattles gules. Crest: two cock's heads and necks conjoined or, combed and wattled gules.

Fig. 5. (*Freiherren von Hohenteufen* in Züricher Gebiet) (No. 369, Barons von Hohenteufen, in Zürich): Gules, a swan argent, beaked and legged sable. Crest: a swan's head and neck gules, adorned with a fan-comb argent.

Fig. 6. *Slat* (Slatt of Zürich) (No. 318): Argent, a double-headed eagle displayed azure, the claws gules. Crest: an eagle's head argent, the head surmounted by a plume of cock's feathers sable.

Fig. 7. *Oltinger* of Basle (No. 449): Gules, a griffin segreant argent. Crest: a demi-griffin as in the arms.

Fig. 8. *Tengen* in Switzerland (No. 149): Gules, a unicorn rampant argent. Crest: a demi-unicorn as in the arms.

Fig. 9. (*Hochenberg*) (No. 492): Sable, a "panther" argent, armed gules. Crest: a demi-"panther" as in the arms.

Fig. 10. *Kilchain* (No. 445): Argent, a wyvern gules. Crest: a demi-wyvern as in the arms.

Fig. 11. (*Obrahoven in Switzerland*) (No. 442): Argent, a fleur-de-lis gules. Crest: a demi-fleur-de-lis argent, and issuing from the point thereof a plume of cock's feathers sable.

Fig. 12. *Gvtingen* (Güttingen in Thurgau) (No. 142): Argent, a rose gules, seeded or, barbed and slipped vert. Crest: (this defies any attempt to render it in English blazon. The literal translation is "a white Mitra, on the two side-edges of which are laid a red rose with green stalk and yellow centre"). No. 213 of the Roll also shows a coat of arms of the Guttingens, the same shield device, but another crest.

Fig. 13. *Roschach* (Rorschach and Rosenberg in St. Gall) (No. 190): Argent, issuing from a triple mount in base or, a "rose-bush" vert, flowered gules. Crest: a plume of cock's feathers sable in a case argent. The arms of the Rorschach family, which became extinct in 1470, appear in a MS. of the St. Gall Cathedral Library (1520) in the same form, only the triple mount is there represented vert, which would seem a more likely rendering.

Fig. 14. *Ot a dem Rand* (*Rande*=turnip) (No. 427): Sable, a turnip proper, leaved vert. Crest: a turnip as in the arms.

Fig. 15. *Clingen* in Thurgau (No. 139): Or, an oak-tree issuing from the base azure. Crest: an annulet gules, the outer edge adorned with leaves argent. (Similar to the crest on Plate LXXIV. Fig. 19.) No. 138 on the Roll also shows a coat of arms of the Clingens, but with quite different charges.

Fig. 16. *Blattenberg* (=Leaf-mountain) (No. 311): Argent, a fess gules, from which issue three "Blätterberge" [or mountains of leaves] vert. Crest: a linden-tree vert.

Fig. 17. *Cem Tvrn* (Cem Thurn in Wallis) (No. 92): Or, a battlemented tower sable. Crest: a pointed cap or, having a ball sable on the point, and two others one on either side thereof.

Fig. 18. *Helmshoven* (No. 106): Gules, a helmet or. Crest: a helmet as in the arms.

Fig. 19. *Phlegelberg* (No. 299): Gules, on a triple mount in base vert, two threshing flails proper, the handles or. Crest: two flails as in the arms. (*Flegel*=flail; *berg*=mount.)

Fig. 20. *Grassower* (No. 309): Gules, a "steel" [for striking fire] argent. Crest: a devil's head with large ears sable, the crest enclosing the helmet. (See Plate LXXX. Fig. 2.) The devil's head seems later not to have been pleasing to the family, inasmuch as later it gave place to a bear's head.

Fig. 992. *Hennenberg* in Thuringia (No. 43): Or, on a triple mount

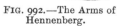

FIG. 992.—The Arms of Hennenberg.

FIG. 993.—The Arms of Werdenberg.

in base couped or, a hen sable, with feet, comb, and wattles gules. Crest: a fan-like object composed of white linden-twigs. (*Henne*= hen). The Counts von Henneberg originally bore another device

(see Ströhl's *Deutsche Wappenrolle*, p. 35); the hen appears for the first time on a seal of the year 1300.

Fig. 993. *Werdenberg* (No. 128): Argent, an ecclesiastical banner sable. Crest: a wing or. The Werdenbergs belonged to the powerful dynastic family of the Herren von der Fahne, a family which in its many branches all bore the ecclesiastical banner, but this and the field in varying colours. H. S.

PLATE LXXVI

SPECIMENS OUT OF GELRE'S "WAPENBOECK"
(1334-1372)

FIGS. 1-16 BELOW RELATE TO THE FIGURES ON THE PLATE.

The *Wapenboeck ou armorial*, of the herald von Geldren Heynen, surnamed "Gelre" (Geldern), who was born about 1315 and died about 1372 (see Plate I. Fig. 1), is now in the possession of the Royal Library at Brussels, and was reproduced in a really excellent manner by the French heraldic author Victor Bouton of Paris. The first volume of the work appeared in 1881, the third volume in 1883, the fourth volume in 1897. The second volume has not yet appeared. Altogether the *Wappenbuch* is supposed to contain over 1800 hand-coloured representations of coats of arms. Monsieur V. Bouton (who died 1901) has been good enough to allow the reproduction of some of the arms from his copy of the work.

Fig. 1. *Die Coninc van Spaengen*. (Arms of the Spanish king Don Pedro II. (the Cruel), *d.* 1369): Quarterly, 1 and 4, gules, a triple-towered castle or, the port and windows azure (Castile); 2 and 3, argent, a lion rampant purpure, crowned or (Leon). Crest: a demi-dragon (a demi-griffin) continuing into the mantling. (The metals are mostly replaced by yellow and white in this armorial register.)

Fig. 2. *Gasto de Moncada*. (Arms of Don Gaston de Moncada, Herren von Aytona, of a family in Aragon): Gules, eight bezants, two, two, two, and two. Crest: a demi-swan argent rising out of the helmet crown, armed gules, the wings or. Mantling gules.

Fig. 3. *G. t. de Morret*. (Arms of the Earl of Moray): Argent, within a double tressure flory and counterflory, three cushions lozengewise gules. Crest: issuing from a ducal coronet a stag's head and neck argent, collared and armed or. Mantling argent.

Fig. 4. (Arms of the Kingdom of Man): Gules, three legs conjoined in triangle at the thigh in chain-mail argent, spurred and buckled at the knee or. Crest: issuing from a coronet, a leg erect as in the arms. The chain-mail is continued as the mantling.

Fig. 5. *Die Coninc van [N]avaerne*. (Arms of King Charles II. (the Bad) of Navarre, *d.* 1387): Quarterly, 1 and 4, gules, an interwoven orle of coins or (Kingdom of Navarre); 2 and 3, azure, semé-de-lis or, a bend company argent and gules (Countship of Evreux). Crest: issuing from a coronet ermine a peacock's tail proper in a "quiver" or "case," this and the mantling repeating the device of the shield.

Fig. 6. *G. van Tyroel*. (Banner of the countship of Tyrol): Argent, an eagle displayed gules, armed and crowned, and charged upon the wings with "buckles" or.

Fig. 7. *Crayn*. (Arms of the duchy of Krain): Or, an eagle displayed azure, charged on the breast with a crescent (?a "buckle") counter-compony gules and argent.

Fig. 8. *Die He. v. Busseel*. (Arms of the Lords Bourchier): Argent, a cross engrailed gules between four water-budgets [or "bouses"] sable. Crest: a grey-bearded man's head with a golden crown, inside of which is a pointed cap gules, striped with gold and with a gold ball or tassel on the point. The mantling is gules. [The blazon of this crest according to English authorities is a man's head in profile proper with a pointed cap gules, and ducally crowned or.]

Fig. 9. *G. van Ceely*. (Arms of the Counts von Cilly): Azure, three six-pointed mullets or. Crest: a wing charged with the arms. Mantling azure, semé of mullets as in the arms.

Fig 10. *Sijr Alexander Stuwart*. (Arms of Sir Alexander Stewart of Buchan and Badenoch, *d.* 1404): Or, a fess chequy azure and argent. Crest: a brown (probably black) demi-lion, issuing from a crown gules and between two wings argent. Mantling brown (the continuation of the lion's skin).

Fig. 11. *Luert a Seton*. (Arms of Lord Seton): Or, within a double tressure flory and counterflory, three crescents gules. Crest: a goat's head ermine, armed and bearded or, the neck being continued into the mantling.

Fig. 12. *Avanderdeel*. (Arms of Annandale, properly the arms of Bruce, Lords of Annandale, Scotland): Or, a saltire and a chief gules. Crest: issuing from clouds proper, an arm embowed, habited gules, the thumb and first two fingers raised in benediction. On the mantling the device of the shield is repeated. (It is not unlikely that the "clouds" are an attempt to represent the wreath, which is a British development, and might have been unfamiliar to a foreign herald.)

THE ART OF HERALDRY

Fig. 13. *Sijr Joon Abb'natny.* (Arms of Sir John Abernethy of Balgony, Scotland): Argent [properly or] a lion rampant gules, debruised by a ribbon in bend engrailed sable. Crest: the head and neck of a grey camel proper, bridled vert, belled or, collared [vair?]. Mantling per pale vert and sable.

Fig. 14. *Die Coninc van Cipers.* (Arms of the King of Cyprus): Quarterly, 1 and 4, argent, a Jerusalem cross or (Jerusalem); 2 and 3, barry of ten azure and argent, a lion rampant gules, crowned and armed or (Lusignan). Crest: issuing from a mural crown or, a conical hat argent, semé of crosses couped and surmounted by a plume of cock's feathers also or. On the mantling the quarterly device of the shield is repeated.

Fig. 15. *Die G. v. Oesewoert.* (Arms of De Vere, Earls of Oxford): Quarterly gules and or, in the first quarter a mullet argent. Crest: on a chapeau gules, turned up ermine, a boar azure, armed and bristled or. Mantling gules.

Fig. 16. *Die He. van Graestoc.* (Arms of Fitz-William, Lord of Greystock): Barruly argent and azure, three chaplets [garlands of flowers] gules. Crest: a flame gules, issuing out of a crown or. On the mantling the device of the shield is repeated.

In conclusion we give the arms of the Austrian dukes (Fig. 994), those of Bohemia (Fig. 995), as also of Mecklenburg (Fig. 996) and Holstein (Fig. 997), of which the illustrations will be found here in

the eagles (Figs. 6 and 7) show a form differing from the German model. The arms of Tyrol and Krain are of great interest, especially for those interested in Austrian heraldry, on account of the early appearance of the crown of the Tyrol eagle, and the gold field on the arms of Krain.

It would be interesting to know from what sources Gelre obtained

die hroge vã mebe lenborch

FIG. 996.—The Arms of Mecklenburg.

the text. For Austria, Gelre gives the silver fess on a field of gules, and for crest the peacock's tail as it has been borne since 1231. Bohemia is represented by the well-known double-queued lion, and as crest the old black wings, semé of golden linden-leaves. The Mecklenburg arms are shown as the gold-crowned black bull's head, with the skin of the neck erased on a gold field. The crest shown is a screen in the colours of Schwerin (gules and or), striped palewise, behind which rises a peacock's feather fan. Between this and the screen a small escutcheon bearing the bull's head is placed. Judging from the tinctures of the screen, the drawing must have been made after 1358, because in December of that year the countship of Schwerin was bought back by Mecklenburg. The Holstein coat of arms shows the much-misunderstood charge, the so-called "Nesselblatt" (nettle-leaf).

If Gelre's armorial drawings be minutely examined, it will be noticed that a few striking differences occur between these coats of arms and those from the almost contemporary Zürich Roll of Arms (Plates LXXIV. and LXXV.). First and foremost, the dominating position of the crest, which occasionally exhibits a quite unusual development (see, for instance, Fig. 13, the camel's head, with the bell dangling in front of the knight's nose). The helmet-mantlings are short, the greater number simply cut with a plain outline.

The eagles' wings without wing-bones (Figs. 1, 2, and 10) drawn by Gelre are characteristic of the style of West European arms. In East European arms (Fig. 9), on the contrary, he draws the wings in their native conventional style; but, opposed to this, the tails of

FIG. 994.—The Arms of the Austrian Dukes.

FIG. 995.—The Arms of Bohemia.

the details of his arms. As concerns some of the British examples, one is surprised at the accuracy of the detail when this is compared with other earlier records of the achievements here shown. On the

FIG. 997.—The Arms of Holstein.

other hand, surely this roll must be the only authority for the flame as the crest of Greystock, the arm as the crest of Bruce, or the leg as the crest of Man.   H. S.

THE ART OF HERALDRY

PLATE LXXVII

EXAMPLES TAKEN FROM THE "SANCTI CHRISTO-PHORI AM ARLBERG BRUDERSCHAFTS BUCHE" (THE BOOK OF THE BROTHERHOOD OR FRATER-NITY OF ST. CHRISTOPHER AM ARLBERG)

(On the Arlberg Mt.)

The *Sancti Christophori am Arlberg Bruderschaft Buches*, a Register of Arms of the very highest value, is now amongst the Imperial Archives in Vienna, and contains on its 306 parchment leaves

FIG. 998.—Hospice of St. Christopher on the Arlberg.

(mostly painted on both sides) representations of arms ranging through four centuries. (The pages are 24 cm. high and 16 cm. broad.) From page 5 to page 248 are found ancient, authentic, and occasionally magnificently emblazoned coats of arms, but the remaining pages give representations in the general style and the usual heraldic calibre of the seventeenth and eighteenth centuries.

The brotherhood at St. Christopher am Arlberg, under the Bishopric of Brixen, was called into existence in the second half of the fourteenth century by a poor shepherd, Heinrich der Findling (Henry the foundling), also called Heinrich von Kempten, to provide and support a hospice for the protection of travellers on the top of the Arlberg pass. The date of the pious establishment can no longer be exactly determined, but the entry on page 109/2 gives us a clue, though a weak one, which assists in the determination of the time. *Wolf von Zillenhart*, who in 1375 became Landcomther of the German orders of Ballei an der Etsch and im Gebirge, appears registered as a simple knight of the order. The confirmation of the

FIG. 999.—The Arms of the Brotherhood. (From the *Bruderschafts Buche*.)

establishment by Duke Leopold III. of Austria followed on the 27th December 1386.

Herr Georg von Zwingenstein was the first who thought of recording coats of arms in the book. In the course of the sixteenth century the brotherhood lost its attraction, and would probably have died away altogether had not the invasion of the Swedes in 1647 brought the hospice on the Arlberg, where many of the Vorarlberg fugitives had found shelter, once more into remembrance. Christoph Reitterer, pastor at Zams, stood at that time at the head of the pious society, and he succeeded in bringing the matter once more into the right course. The whole of the archducal family, the town council of Innsbruck in a body, and many nobles and burgesses enrolled themselves in the brotherhood, but it was not long before interest in it died out once more, until at last the year 1786 brought its official dissolution.

The building with the little chapel still stands on the now isolated highway, which, owing to the Arlberg tunnel, has lost all of its ancient importance.

In 1647, at the time of the resuscitation of the brotherhood, the leaves, which were then certainly loose, were bound into a volume, the binding being of red velvet with silver fastenings; but unfortunately the leaves were very much trimmed by the binder, quite without regard to the writing or the emblazonments. Moreover, the trouble had not been taken to arrange the leaves according to the order in which they had been made, the sheets being bound up without any attempt at chronological order.

Fig. 1 (page 69/2). *Ott von Meissaw* (Meissau): Or, a unicorn rampant sable. Crest: a mastiff's head and neck per pale chequy azure and argent and or, these tinctures being continued into the mantling. The mastiff is not the original crest of the Meissau family, but that of the Burgrave von Gars. "Her Ott von Meissaw geit all Jar einen halbn guldein vnd nach seinē tod einen guldein" (Herr Otto v. Meissau gives every year half a gulden, and after his death a gulden).

Fig. 2 (page. 49). *Hertneyd von Potendorff*: Azure, a demi-lion argent, armed gules, rising out of the base gules. Crest: on the dexter side a buffalo's horn argent, and on the sinister another gules, each adorned with seven small flags of the same colours. Mantling: dexter, argent, lined gules; sinister, counterchanged. The device of some society of nobles, viz. a white pike or sturgeon twined round the neck of the helmet, is visible.

Fig. 3 (page 19/2). *Pernhart von Pettaw:* Gules, an anchor reversed argent. Crest: a wyvern sable, winged argent, each "rib" of the wings garnished with a tuft of peacock's feathers. Mantling azure and argent. (The shield is derived from the arms of the Marshals von Treun, the crest from the arms of the Holenburgs.) "Pernhart von Pettau in Steyr geit all Jar j g . . . seim tod vir guldein . . . tag Anno etc. cccc. pmo." (1401) (Bernhart von Pettau in Styria gives every year a groschen, after his death four guldens . . . day Anno, etc.).

Fig. 4 (page 41). *Ewstach von Scherffenberg* (Schärfenberg): Azure, a crown or. Crest: a crown as in the arms, and issuing from each leaf a peacock's tail proper. Mantling azure lined gules. "Ewstach von Scherffenberg geit all iar vier Grozz, vnd nach seinem tod ainen guldein auf den Arlperge" (Eustace von Schärffenberg gives every year four Groschen, and after his death a gulden to the Arlberg).

H. S.

PLATE LXXVIII

FURTHER EXAMPLES OUT OF THE "STI. CHRISTO-PHORI AM ARLBERG BRUDERSCHAFTS BUCHE"

Fig. 1 (page 86/2). *Hans Lawn* (Laun): Gules, a bend chevronny of six argent and sable. Crest: a grey-bearded man's head and neck proper, habited in sable turned up or, and continuing into the mantling of sable lined or, wreathed about the temples, the ends flotant also or and sable, crowned or, and with a pointed cap sable, surmounted by an ostrich feather argent. Accompanying this achievement is the device of some society, viz. a silver loop fringed with silver and threaded with a green ribbon, ending in a twisted knot, which is connected by means of a gold ring to a similar knot, from which a black, white, and green tassel hangs.

Fig. 2 (page 53). *Dorothe von totznbach* (Totzenbach): Gules, an eagle displayed per pale azure and or, armed and crowned of the last. Crest: an eagle rising, crowned and per pale as in the arms. Mantling: on the dexter side azure, gules, and or; on the sinister side or and azure. "Dorothe von totznpach geit aljag ain halbn guldn vnd nach seim tod ain gantzn, &c." (Dorothe von Totzenbach gives yearly half a gulden and after his death a whole one.) Dorothe appears to have been a man.

Fig. 3 (page 17). *Her. Johannes. des. reichs. reichs. Bvrggraf ze. maidburg vnd Graf ze Hardegk* (Herr Johannes, Imperial Burgrave of Magdeburg and Count of Hardegk). Arms: per pale dexter, gules, an eagle displayed, armed and crowned or, dimidiated with, on the sinister side, barry of eight argent and gules. Crest: a wing barry as in the arms, and issuing from a coronet or. Mantling gules and argent.

Fig. 4. *Grafen von Mätsch* (Vögte von Matsch): Argent, three wings azure. Crest: two buffalo horns, the dexter argent, the sinister gules, banded and tied counterchanged. The horns and their tinctures are continued into the mantling. The inscription accompanying this shield is "vnd Fraw Methild sein gemehl gebent all Jar ain guldein vnd nach irm tod zwen guldein" (And Mistress Methild [Matilda] his wife gives every year a gulden, and after her death two guldens). Both these last coats of arms are joined to one another by a gold chain (as indicated), and appear on a green ground; the writing is laid on in gold with the exception of the name "Grafen von Mätsch," which was inserted much later.

The arms of *Andre Gruener ze pazzaw* (Andrew Grüner of Passau) (Fig. 1000) also belong to the oldest entries. They are: Per fess

412

argent and sable, a fess of the last, in chief issuing from the fess two points reversed of the second. The wings on the helmet which form the crest repeat the arms. The complete inscription runs:

FIG. 1000.—Arms of Andrew Gruener.

"Andre Gruener ze pazzaw geit alle iar vier grozz : nach seinem tod einen guldein ze sand Christoffen auf den arelperkch vnd die vier . . . (Andrew Gruner of Passau gives every year four groschen : after his death a gulden to St. Christopher on the Arlberg and the four . . .). H. S.

PLATE LXXIX

FURTHER EXAMPLES FROM THE "STI. CHRISTOPHORI AM ARLBERG BRUDERSCHAFTS BUCHE"

Fig. 1 (page 139/2). *Jacob reinachher* (Reinacher): Argent, an annulet gules, adorned with six plumes of cock's feathers sable. Crest: the device as in the arms, but without the undermost plume of feathers. Mantling argent, lined gules. "Jacob reinachher git alle iar ij gros nach sim dot ein guldin" (James Reinacher gives every year two groschen, after his death a gulden").

Fig. 2 (page 60). *Rapold von Rosenhart :* Argent, three roses gules, barbed and seeded or. Crest: a cock's head and neck argent, armed and eyed or, combed and wattled gules. Mantling argent and gules. Traces of a gold helmet crown painted over it are apparent. "Rapold von Rosenhart git alle iar iij groffs nach seine dot j guldein" (Rapold von Rosenhart gives every year 3 groschen, after his death 1 gulden). In the Lower Austrian Land-Archives is to be found a grant of arms from King Wenceslaus, dated at Prague, December 23, 1411, to Rappen (Rapold) von Rosenhart, which conferred on him the right to bear a *helmet crown*. From that it follows that the coat of arms in the *Bruderschafts Buche* was painted before 1411, and in 1411, or later, the crown was added, but the gold-leaf used in making the additions did not properly adhere to the silver. The Rosenharts were an old Swabian family whose ancestral seat of the same name lay not far from Ravensburg, in Würtemberg. Rapold died between 1444 and 1445 *Jahrbuch*, "*Adler*," 1875.

Fig. 3 (page 127/2). *Steffan* (Stephen) *pielaher* (Pielacher): Or, a "miller's thumb" [a kind of fish,] in bend proper. Crest: the fish as in the arms, pierced by a staff erect gules, and issuing from the point thereof a plume of cock's feathers sable. Mantling gules and or. The shield, which in the original has been cut away in the binding at the bottom, is here completed. "Steffan pielaher git all jar ij gross vnd nach sinem dot ain gvldin" (Stephen Pielaher gives every year 2 groschen, and after his death a gulden).

Fig. 4 (page 174). *Hanns Johling* (Jochling): Sable, a cross-bow or ox-yoke in bend or. Upon the shield are placed two helmets

side by side. The dexter bears as crest wings charged with the device as in the arms, and issuing from a wreath or and sable. Mantling sable and or. The second helmet bears, issuing from a coronet gules, a pyramid of lilies with yellow filaments, in three rows of seven, six, and five. The red helmet-mantling ends in two yellow tassels. With this coat of arms is connected a small shield by a ring inserted through a corner of each shield. The arms upon the smaller shield are: Azure, a patriarchal cross between an increscent and a decrescent or. (This is probably the shield of Frau Anna Jochling.) The badge of a society, viz.: Under a crown the conjoined initials *a* and *h* (?) appear, but these are unpainted. Besides this, there will be noticed the motto "*Ich hoff*" ("I hope"). The shield, which in the original is cut away, is here shown completed. The inscription is "Hanns Johling ann sein Hawsfraw gebnt all Jar iiii g auf den adelsperkeh nach Jrem tod" (here the entry lacks), "Anno Octam" (1408) (Hans Jochling and his wife [*lit.* housekeeper] give every year 4 g. to the Arlberg, after their death . . .).

Fig. 1001 shows the coat of arms of an Anhalt prince, probably Woldemar (Vlman) V. (*d.* 1436), viz.: Party per pale, dexter, argent, an eagle displayed gules, crowned and armed or, and charged upon the wings with a golden clover-leaf buckle (Brandenburg), dimidiated with, on the sinister side, barry of ten or

FIG. 1001.—Arms of the Prince of Anhalt.

and sable (Ballenstedt). Crest: two peacocks' tails in saltire issuing from a coronet. Mantling sable and or. Inscription : "Graff Ulman, furst ze anhalt geytt ain halben guldein nach seine tod ain gulden" (Count Ulman, Prince of Anhalt, gives a half-gulden, after his death a gulden). H. S.

PLATE LXXX

FURTHER EXAMPLES FROM THE "STI. CHRISTOPHORI AM ARLBERG BRUDERSCHAFTS BUCHE"

Fig. 1 (page 106/2). *Hans von hahenwerchk* (Hohenberg): Sable, a panther argent, horned or, vomiting flames out of the nostrils gules. Crest: two wings gules, each charged with a bend or. Mantling gules.

On page 40 the same arms appear (Herr Friedrich von Hohenwerg), but the panther is there armed or.

Fig. 2 (page 30). *Fridreich tumritczer* : Gules, a "a fire-steel" in bend argent. Crest: a bear's head sable, the neck continuing into the mantling sable, lined gules. (Height of shield, 8.3 cm.) The crest is here depicted as containing the helmet, the visor being visible in the open mouth of the crest. "Fridreich tumritezer geit all iar ij gss nach seim tod ain gulden" (Friedrich tumritezer gives every year 2 groschen, after his death a guldein.) The same armorial bearings are also entered on page 292 of the Register for Albrech Grassawer. (See also Plate LXXV. Fig. 20.)

Fig. 3 (page 34/2). *Jorig Stokcharn* (Stockhorner von Starein); Or, a crescent sable. Crest: a fox sejant or. Mantling gules and

FIG. 1002.

argent. (Height of shield, 5.2 cm.) The arms appear joined with those of the wife, which, however, have not been reproduced here. The complete inscription runs: "Jorig Stokcharn vnd sain Hawsfraw gebnt all jar (o/4) grozz vnd nach yrn tod ij guldein" (Jorig Stokcharn and his wife give every year 4 groschen, and after their death 2 guldens).

Fig. 4 (page 42/2). *v. Dachsperg* (the name appeared in a later handwriting): Gules, a badger rampant argent, armed or. Crest: a demi-badger as in the arms, the back adorned with a gold comb ornamented with cock's feathers sable. Attached to the helmet by a gold chain appears the badge of the Order of the Dragon (founded by the Emperor Sigismund when King of Hungary). Another badge of some society, depicted in conjunction with these armorial bearings, consists of two arms descending from clouds or, the hands clasped vested or, the sleeves having pendent scalloped edges, of which the dexter has a white border. (Height of shield, 9 cm.) The inscription, not given here, runs: " . . . perig geit all iar ain halben guldein vnd nach sein tod ain guldein" (. . . perg gives every year a half-gulden, and after his death a gulden).

Fig. 5 (page 191). *Steffel prenner*: Or, above flames issuing in base gules, a salamander sable (? gules, in flames issuing from the chief

or, a salamandar sable). Crest: two dragon's wings or, each charged with a bend gules, and thereupon three inescutcheons argent. Mantling gules, lined or. (Height of shield, 6 cm.) The complete inscription runs: "Steffel prenner maler geit all jar ayn grozz nch seinem tott iiii grozz" (Steffel Prenner (or Brenner), artist (or painter), gives every year a groschen, after his death 4 groschen). Gules, three escutcheons argent are the arms supposed to belong to the craft of shield-workers, painters, &c.

Fig. 6 (page 26). *Wichart durr*: Argent, a dragon's head and neck issuing out of the base gules. Crest: a dragon's head and neck as in the arms, continuing into the mantling, and on the head a plume of cock's feathers sable, in a "case" or. (Height of shield, 6.5 cm.) The inscription is: "Wichart durr all jar zwen gross nach seinem tod ainen guldein" (Wichart Durr, every year 2 groschen, after his death a gulden).

An interesting drawing, two knights, full length, appears on page 63 in the Brotherhood book. One of the two, Herr Jan von Strolenburg, is shown in Fig. 1002. He is clad in silver armour and a red tunic, and on his helmet, which has a mantling gules, is a golden coronet, out of which rise two wings or. Round the neck he bears the badge of the Order of the "Fürspänger" (founded by Charles IV. at Nürnberg), viz. a golden buckle-wreath. The shield (6 cm. high) shows the arms: Or, a pheon azure, the staff gules, flighted argent. The banner shows the same arms. The inscription is: "Her Jan von Strolenburg gibt alle jar ein halben guldn zu dem Gotes Haus der weil er lebt gen arlberg den ersten suntag in der fasten" (Herr Jan (Johann) von Strolenburg gives every year a half-gulden to the God's House the while he lives on the Arlberg, the first Sunday in the fast). H. S.

PLATE LXXXI

THE EARLY ENGLISH GARTER PLATES

One of the most important series of English armorial designs is to be found in the Stall plates of the Knights of the Garter, set up in St. George's Chapel in Windsor Castle, which is the Sanctuary of the Order. Nowhere else in Europe is an equivalent series to be found, and these Garter Stall plates are both most excellent examples of contemporary heraldry, and in a large proportion most superb pieces of workmanship and design. The Order of the Garter was founded in the year 1348, and at this date one of the chapels of Windsor Castle was fitted up as the chapel of the order, and therein has been placed the helmet, crest, and sword of every knight. The actual dates at which the practice of setting up plates of the arms of the knights commenced cannot be definitely fixed, but there is good reason to believe that the practice was contemplated at the foundation of the order, for the earliest copies of the statutes extant require that as soon as one of the founder knights should die a shield of his arms, made of metal, together with his helmet, were to be fixed in the back of his stall, and it was ordained that similar plates should be set up for all other knights, though these were to be of a smaller size than the plates of the founders. Many of the plates of the founder knights still remain, and of the 800 or more knights who have since been appointed to the order very nearly 600 Stall plates remain. It is difficult to account for the missing ones, but in all probability attainder, with its penalties of defacement of arms, will account for most of those lacking. In the early part of the fifteenth century it became customary to set up the Stall plates during the lifetime of the knights; and during the same century it became a matter of rule that the plates should be set up within twelve months of the ceremony of installation. The plates are of very diverse sizes, ranging from a height of 4 to 15 inches; the majority of the early ones, however, are from 6 to 8 inches. The method of depicting the arms is equally varied; a few consist simply of the device upon the shield occupying the whole quadrangular space of the plate, but the majority show shield, helmet, crest, and mantling, and, with the exception of the earliest, the name and style of the knight. The shields are not found surrounded with the garter until the reign of Henry VII., though one example (the plate of Charles, Duke of Burgundy) is earlier than this. This is curious, because elsewhere the armorial use of the garter had come into vogue somewhat earlier. The conservatism with regard to matters of design is further illustrated by the fact that long after the use of supporters had become universal in the peerage, the arms are depicted on the Stall plates without these ornaments. The earliest Garter plate to show supporters is that of John Beaufort, Duke of Somerset, the grandfather of Henry VII. (Plate CXXXII.). The early plates are almost without exception enamelled upon gilded plates of copper, but the modern plates are first engraved and then painted. The uniformity of design to a certain extent robs the plates of scientific value as contemporary evidence of armorial art, and in using these plates as evidence it needs to be borne in mind that in many points developments of heraldic law or practice are of an earlier date than would be judged to be the case from an examination of the plates. But allowance being made of a sufficient margin to balance this, the value of the plates as scientific evidence and as examples of art is extreme. After the close of the Tudor period, in fact rather earlier than this, the plates, in common with all other heraldic art, deteriorate sadly both in boldness of design and in beauty of execution, partaking entirely since that date of the stereotyped lines adopted in official emblazonments.

The arms on Plate LXXXI. are as they are depicted on the Stall plate of Sir Gilbert Talbot, Lord Talbot, K.G. (d. 1419). The arms are: "Gules, a lion rampant, within a bordure engrailed or. Mantling gules, lined ermine. Crest: on a chapeau gules, turned up ermine, a lion statant tail extended or."

Fig. 1003 shows the arms of Stafford as they appear on

FIG. 1003.—From the Garter Stall Plate of Humphrey Stafford, Earl of Stafford, K.G., and (later) Duke of Buckingham.

the Stall plate of Sir Humphrey Stafford, Earl of Stafford and Buckingham, and subsequently Duke of Buckingham, K.G. (1429 to 1460). The arms are: "Or, a chevron gules. Mantling: on the dexter side sable, and on the sinister gules, both lined ermine. Crest: out of a coronet gules, a swan's head and neck between two wings argent, beaked gules.

Fig. 1004 represents the achievement on the plate of Sir John Grey, K.G. (1436-1439), the eldest son and heir-apparent of Reginald, Lord Grey de Ruthyn. The arms in question are: "Quarterly, 1 and 4, barry of six argent and azure, in chief three torteaux (for Grey); 2 and 3, quarterly i. and iiii., or, a maunch gules (for Hastings);

ii. and iii., barry of eight argent and azure, an orle of martlets gules (for De Valence); over all a label of three

FIG. 1004.—From the Garter Stall Plate of Sir John Grey, K.G.

points throughout argent. Mantling: or, lined ermine. Crest: on a chapeau gules, turned up ermine, a wyvern or, gorged with a label as in the arms.

Fig. 1005 shows the arms of John Mowbray, Duke of Norfolk, K.G. These are: "Gules, three lions passant guardant in pale or, a label of three points argent.

FIG. 1005.—From the Garter Stall Plate of John Mowbray, Duke of Norfolk, K.G.

Mantling gules and ermine. Crest: on a chapeau, a lion statant guardant or, crowned and gorged with a label argent."

The Garter plates of the Knights between the years 1348 and 1485 have been recently reproduced in facsimile with very valuable notes, and an introduction by Mr. W.

H. St. John Hope. However much one may disagree with Mr. Hope's curious ideas on the subject of blazon, one cannot with justice withhold from his book the high praise which the admirable reproduction of this series of plates richly deserves. A. C. F-D.

PLATES LXXXII. AND LXXXIII.

ENGLISH ARMORIAL PAINTINGS

(Early Fifteenth Century)

Bound up in the same volume with the early English roll of arms in the custody of the College of Arms described in Plate LXXI. are a few armorial paintings which, being depicted not upon shields, but in a square form, are probably designs for banners.

They very evidently have no connection whatever with the armorial roll with which they are now bound up, nor does it very plainly appear why they have been preserved. The Talbot arms appear in all the paintings, which probably are a series of banner designs prepared for the Talbot family, Earls of Shrewsbury. From the quarterings exhibited, and from the date at which these accrued in the Talbot family, it is evident that these paintings cannot belong to a period earlier in date than the end of the fourteenth century or possibly the beginning of the fifteenth century. They are probably even later. They are palpably all the work of the same artist. From the point of design, but hardly of execution, they may justly be considered as typical of the very highest range of excellence reached by heraldic art in this country. Executed in transparent water-colour over a visible outline which has been allowed to remain, the roughness of their execution, together with the smallness of their number, gives them somewhat of the appearance of trial sketches, preparatory to a more elaborate piece of work, but there can be no question of the ability of the artist or of the surpassing beauty of his work. Their reproduction gives the opportunity for a remark that modern artists might with advantage prefer these paintings as models rather than older and cruder forms. The name of the artist is unfortunately quite unknown. The examples reproduced on Plates LXXXII. and LXXXIII. are taken from certified copies which Mr. C. H. Athill, Richmond Herald, has very kindly supplied to me. The heraldic description is as follows :—

Plate LXXXII. : Quarterly, 1 and 4, gules, a lion rampant within a bordure engrailed or (for Talbot); 2 and 3, or, a chief azure, over all a hand fesswise in chief vested in a maunch argent, lined ermine.

Plate LXXXIII. : Quarterly, 1 and 4, gules, a lion rampant within a bordure engrailed or (for Talbot); 2 and 3, gules, a lion statant guardant argent, crowned or (for Lisle; see page 370). A. C. F-D.

PLATE LXXXIV

SPECIMENS OUT OF THE "SCHEIBLERSCHEN WAPPENBUCHE" (SCHEIBLER BOOK OF ARMS)

(First half of the Fifteenth Century)

There is in the possession of the baronial family of Scheibler-Hülhoven at Aix-la-Chapelle a paper register with 343 leaves (25 cm. high, 17 cm. broad) of which 225 exhibit 450 paintings of arms by a distinguished South German artist. The remaining leaves contain armorial representations of less value and of much later date. The specimens on Plate LXXXIV. are reproduced from copies made by the Court Heraldic Artist, E. Krahl.

Fig. 1. *Die Winter* (Winter of Bohlanden): Sable, billetté or, a violin in bend of the last, stringed gules. Crest: On a chapeau argent, semé of linden-leaves or, a wing sable also semé of linden-leaves or, and charged with two violins as in the arms. Mantling sable, semé of linden-leaves or.

Fig 2. *Von Gūch. Franckhen:* Argent, two pairs of sheep-shears palewise in fess. Crest: a demi-swan argent, beaked gules, the wings each charged with a pair of sheep-shears as in the arms. Mantling gules and argent.

Fig. 3. *Specht von Bubenhain* (Specht von Bubenheim, Rheinland). Or, a fess sable, fretty argent, in the sinister chief point a woodpecker gules (Specht). Crest: a "player" seated upon the helmet, the legs one on either side, habited in ragged clothes, tearing his hair with the dexter hand and holding in the sinister a board or and thereupon three dice argent. Mantling gules and argent.

Fig. 4. *Annenberg, Tyrol:* Argent, a branch in bend throughout gules, and issuing therefrom in chief three roses of the last, seeded or. Crest: two wings proper, bound with a fillet gules, tied in a knot, the ends pendent. Mantling gules and argent.

Fig. 5. *Herzoge v. Lothringen* (Dukes of Lorraine): Or, on a bend gules, three alerions volant argent, the wings expanded and inverted. Crest: out of a coronet or, an eagle rising argent. Mantling gules and argent. It was Planché who first pointed out that the word "alerion" is a perfect anagram for the name "Lorraine."

Fig. 6. *Graffen v. Nassau* (Counts of Nassau): Azure, semé of seven diagonal billets or, a lion rampant of the last. Crest: two wings argent, the pinion feathers sable, through which a yellow cord is interwoven. Mantling azure and argent.

Fig. 7. *Die Trauner . Bavaria:* Quarterly, 1 and 4, gules a "bouquetin" rampant argent, unguled or; 2 and 3, sable, two chevrons conjoined in the fess point, one reversed issuing in chief and one in base argent. Crest: a demi-bouquetin as in the arms. Mantling gules and argent.

Fig. 8. *Die Kröpfner . Tyrol.* (Kropfer): Sable, the bust of a man in profile couped proper, habited argent, banded about the temple with a ribbon argent, the ends flotant, the beard or and afflicted with a large goitre. Crest: the bust of a man as in the arms, the habit continued into the mantling and lined sable. H. S.

PLATES LXXXV. AND LXXXVI.

AN ENGLISH ROLL OF ARMS

Temp. Henry VI.

There is in the possession of the College of Arms a MS. volume of drawings of shields in trick which, from the artistic point of view, must always remain one of the most remarkable and at the same time one of the most curious and noteworthy examples of heraldic design. The MS. takes the form of a Roll of Arms, but is unaccompanied by any explanation. As an armorial record it would be readily possible to exaggerate its value, for some number of the shields are plainly quite mythical, and it is not an " official record " by which proof of arms can be made. There is nothing to show why it was compiled, nor that it ever had any official character, nor is it known how it came into the possession of the College of Arms. Its chief value is artistic, and for that reason it is a great pity that the name of the artist is lost to us. One would hesitate to put forward the examples in this roll as copies for repetition in modern heraldic art. As a whole they are out of keeping with any type of design outside the volume in which they occur. But as examples of virile work, as examples of the artistic capabilities of a coat of arms, and as specimens of design exhibiting " grip " and " go," they have never been surpassed and probably never will. The forceful exuberance of their design compels one's admiration. Mr. G. W. Eve in his " Decorative Heraldry " places the date of this manuscript as between 1540 and 1560, and adds that it was " probably a copy, with additions, of an earlier work." He writes concerning it: " The lions are distinctly extraordinary, such as are rampant having the thrown-back pose of the head exaggerated to eccentricity. The guardant lions, both rampant and passant, are without this peculiarity, but, like the rest, are unsatisfactory in the way they fail to occupy their field; having indeed every appearance of being removed from their original surroundings to be placed on shields which were not designed to contain them. So that the fault that may be said to characterise Stuart and most subsequent heraldry, was not unknown in the decorative Tudor time."

Mr. C. H. Athill, Richmond Herald, has very kindly

THE ART OF HERALDRY

certified for me various selected examples which are typical of the work of the master hand which drew them. Unfortunately the artist's name is unknown. These are reproduced herein.

These examples, though arranged in the style and form of page adopted in the original, of which they are faithful reproductions, are selected examples, and do not follow each other in the original in the order here given. The arms chosen are as follows:—

PLATE LXXXV

1. Gules, three piles wavy in point argent, a bordure engrailed of the last (Thomas Pyke).
2. Per chevron sable and argent, three stags rampant counterchanged (Francis Herston).
3. (Gules), three legs in armour conjoined at the thigh and flexed at the knees (proper, garnished and spurred or). [The arms of the Isle of Man.]
4. Azure, three hares in triangle, their ears conjoined in the fess point (Harewell).
5. Azure, three arms in armour embowed, conjoined at the shoulders in the fess point, the hands in gauntlets, each holding a sword all argent (Sir Thomas Fyndarne).
6. Or, three hose palewise in fess sable (Thomas House).
7. Gules, a wyvern argent (Sir Robert Brentle).
8. Gules, a chief azure, a lion passant double-queued over all or (Sir Robert Hastinges). [A commentator has added that the lion should be rampant over all.]
9. Argent, a lion rampant double-queued and interlaced gules (unnamed).

PLATE LXXXVI

1. Gules, a unicorn rampant chequy argent and sable (Clare).
2. Argent, three toads sable ("Pharamond"). [This is the mythical coat invented and attributed to Pharamond, in which some old writers sought to find the origin of the arms of France.]
3. Per pale gules and azure, a double-headed eagle displayed per pale argent and or (Wantleyes).
4. Barry wavy azure and argent (Wesnan).
5. Azure, three horse-barnacles or, on a chief ermine, a demi-lion issuant gules (Earl Genewyle).
6. Vert, three griffins passant or (Sir Gawayne, the good knight).
7. Azure, semé-de-lis and a lion rampant guardant argent (Sir Thomas Holland of Thropwater).
8. Azure, a lion rampant or (Sir Edmond Darell).
9. Sable, a saltire flory argent, between four lions passant guardant or (William de Ayne). A. C. F-D.

PLATE LXXXVII

SPECIMENS OF ARMORIAL ART TAKEN FROM HERALDIC BOOKS

(Fifteenth Century)

Fig. 1 is a representation of the arms of the Holy Roman-German Empire, the arms depicted being: Or, an eagle displayed sable. The tilting-helmet, which is surmounted by the crown of the sovereignty, bears as crest a black eagle, ready for flight, crowned with a similar crown. The mantling, which has a gold lining, is of black semé of yellow linden-leaves. Over the coat of arms, which is placed on a background of red damask, framed with white pearls, appear the golden letters A E I O V, and the date 1446. The five letters form a kind of riddle-motto of King Friedrich IV.'s, and allow of different readings. For instance, "Austriæ Est Imperare Orbi Universo," or "Aller Ehren Ist Oesterreich Voll" ("Of-all-Honours-is-Austria-full"), &c.

This reproduction is from the *Handregistratur* of King Frederick IV. in the possession of the Royal and Imperial House Court and State Archives in Vienna.

This register shows four magnificent paintings of arms, each occupying a full page.

Fig. 2.—*Auffenstain* (Aufenstein, a family originally Tyrolese, but at a later date possessing large estates in Kärnten): Or, standing on a stone sable, an owl proper armed or (*auf* = owl; *stein* = stone). The tilting-helmet, which has a black and gold mantling, bears as crest a yellow broad-brimmed hat, with two yellow tassels, and thereon an owl as in the arms.

Fig. 3 is a nameless coat of arms, which, however, may be not uninteresting on account of the curious crest, and the drawing of the mantling.

Fig. 4.—*Pomerania* (?): Argent, a griffin segreant gules, armed or. The crowned helmet has a mantling of argent and gules, and the crest a wing sable, semé of linden-leaves or.

Figs. 2–4 are taken from the *Oesterreichische Wappenbuch* (Austrian Book of Arms) in the possession of the Royal Family Court and State Archives in Vienna. The volume is also known as the *Wappenbuch für die oesterreichischen Herzoge* (Book of Arms for the Austrian Dukes), and is a parchment register (50 cm. high by 33 cm. broad) bearing the date 1445 on the first page.

FIG. 1006.

The greater number of the rather luxuriantly designed arms herein are quite imaginary, attributed to fabulous Austrian lords supposed to have existed in primitive times. (Compare Plate XCII.) Amongst them, despite the sketchy handling of the drawing, there is to be found much that is heraldically worthy of notice; see, for instance, Figs. 1006 and 1007, and especially the beautifully conventionalised style in which the oak garland is rendered in the latter.

Fig. 5.—*Libr d͞m. petri de Crawar* alias *de Straznycz* (Libris (?)

FIG. 1007.

of Peter de Crawar, *alias* de Strasnycz). The family of Krawar were Moravian, later calling themselves Tworkovsky, after the estate of Tworkov. Gules, an arrowhead tied by a floating kerchief argent. The silver tilting-helmet, with red mantling, lined with ermine, bears as crest, two black on the outside and gold on the inside, the wing-bones charged on the outside with gold linden-leaves, in rows.

This coat of arms is interesting inasmuch as it explains a device which appears in quite a series of arms (for the house of Odrowaz), and is repeatedly and erroneously drawn and blazoned as an "upper-lip and moustache, struck with an arrow" (refer to the arms of the Counts Sedlnitzky and others). According to Professor Dr. F. Piekosinski, the device may be traced back to the very old flag-device (Stannize) of the Polish dynastic race of the Odrowaze, composed of two Scandinavian runes—↑. (See more in detail when treating the subject under Plate CXXVI.)

The coat of arms as given in Fig. 4 is taken from a volume of the Moravian Land-Register Books. The eighth book of the Olmütz Landtafel Quaterne for the years 1412 to 1416, bears the coat of arms given here, on the front side of the cover of the book. On the covers of the registers the coat of arms of the head of the provincial board of finance for the time being always appears; thus, the first book (commenced in 1348), and the second, third, fourth, seventh, and eighth books all show the arms of Krawar.

FIG. 1008.—Sickingen.

FIG. 1009.—Honberg.

FIG. 1010.— Habsburg-Laufenburg.

FIG. 1011.—Habsburg.

Other characteristic coats of arms of this period, taken from German sources, will be found in Figs. 1008, 1009, 1010, and 1011.   H. S.

PLATE LXXXVIII

REPRESENTATIONS OF ARMORIAL BEARINGS TAKEN FROM THE WORK OF GERMAN MASTERS

(Fifteenth Century)

Figs. 1–5.—Arms with supporters, engraved by *Martin Schongauer*, also called "Schön," from his own designation of himself on a drawing: "Hipsch Martin Schongauer Maler, 1453." He was a painter, engraver, and goldsmith; born at Colmar in 1420 (?), died there in 1488.

Fig. 1 is probably the escutcheon of the family of *Stein-Kallenfels*: Per fess vert and or, in chief a lion passant argent;

but the remaining shields on the plate cannot be more exactly determined, on account of the lack of tinctures. In Figs. 4 and 5 the supporters have been omitted. Below is an exquisitely drawn figure of a lion, the symbol of St. Mark, which was designed by the same master (Fig. 1012).

FIG. 1012.—The Lion of St. Mark.

Fig. 6 is a representation of the arms of the Prince-Bishop *Rudolph II.* of Würzburg (1466–95), of the family of Scherenberg. The engraver was probably *Albrecht Glockenton* (born 1432 at Nürnberg), who worked for a long time in Würzburg.

This figure shows the arms: Quarterly, 1. argent, a chief dancetté gules (Franconia); 2 and 3, or, a pair of shears extended gules (Scherenberg) (*schere* = scissors); 4. azure, on a lance in bend or, a banner quarterly gules and argent (Würzburg). The crowned helmet with the Franconian horns, from the ends of each of which the Würzburg banner is issuant, bears the Scherenberg crest, a lion's head affronté argent, crowned with a like coronet, from which rises the three ostrich feathers azure, argent, and gules, belonging to the Würzburg crest. The helmet mantling here really deserves special attention, being exquisitely drawn.

Fig. 7.—Arms of the patrician family of *Goldast* (Gold branch), of Constance, engraved by *Bartholomæus Zeitblom* at Ulm, born 1440 (?), died between 1516 and 1521. The arms are: Azure, the branch of a tree or (Goldast). The helmet, which has a mantling of azure and or, bears as crest a griffin, the upper part azure, armed or, the hindquarters of the last. (Taken from a housekeeping book of 1470 in the possession of Prince Waldburg-Wolfegg-Waldsee.) (Compare Fig. 18, Plate XCVIII.)

The sallet or helmet which is here shown is of a form very

FIG. 1013.

seldom met with in heraldic representations, although it is heraldically correct. The mantling of the helmet is well drawn, but the crest is somewhat large in proportion to the size of the helmet.

Fig. 8 shows arms, though to what family these may belong is unknown. The design was engraved by *Israel van Meckenen*, engraver and goldsmith at Bocholt on the Aa, in Westphalia, who died 1503. The helmet is rather small in proportion to the shield, but the mantling is very beautifully designed. By the same master is the amusing heraldic device which is here reproduced (Fig. 1013).

Fig. 1014 shows the mark of the celebrated printer, *Erhard Ratdolt*, of Augsburg, in the year 1491 (14 cm. high). The escutcheon is printed in two colours, black and red, and is one of the oldest

examples of printing in colour. The arms are: Gules, the young Hercules holding in his dexter hand the two snakes intertwined, and with his sinister a six-rayed star gules in front of the lower part of his body. The helmet, which has a mantling of gules and argent, bears as crest: between two buffalo's horns gules, a star as in the arms. This beautiful escutcheon was designed by Ratdolt himself, as appears from the distich over an impression of this coat of arms:—

"Erhardi Ratdolt fœlicia conspice signa
Testata artificem qua valet ipse manum."

H. S.

PLATE LXXXIX

EXAMPLES REPRODUCED FROM CONRAD GRÜNENBERG'S "WAPPENBUCH"

(1483)

One of the finest emblazoned books of arms is Conrad Grünenberg's *Wappenbuch*, which, according to a notice in Grünenberg's own hand, was completed in 1483. "Das buch ist volbrach am Nunden tag des Abrellen Do man zalt Tusent vier hunder dru vnd Achtzig Jar." Grünenberg belonged to a well-to-do burgher family in Constance; his father was burgomaster of the town (1466–70), and filled from 1441 till his death in 1494 the office of architect to the parish church of St. Stephen at Constance. He belonged, as a burgher, to the guilds, but, by a patent from the Emperor, dated Saturday before vocem jucunditatis (May 19th) 1465, he was released from the guild and admitted into an association of noble families called "Zur Katze" (see Plate XCVIII.). He appears as a knight after his return from Jerusalem in 1486.

On the title-page of his Book of Arms (which consists of 190 paper leaves) his own coat of arms is introduced (Fig. 1015): Sable, three mounds or, and issuant therefrom a like number. The crowned helmet, with a mantling of black and gold, the former semé of golden linden-leaves, bears as crest a plume of ostrich feathers sable. By the side of the arms appear: on the dexter, the insignia of the *Order of the Holy Grave* (a cross of Jerusalem gules), and of the Aragonese *Order of the Pitcher* (a golden pitcher with three blue-bells, over a golden griffin, which bears a ribbon with the inscription: "Por. Los. Amor"); on the sinister, the insignia of the *Order of St. Katherine of Mount Sion* (a golden rose over a sword with a handle gules, round this entwined a gold ribbon with the inscription: "Por. Loyaltad Mantenir"), and of the *Society of St. George's Shield* (a shield of St. George, argent, a cross gules ornamented with gold, from which is suspended the golden figure of St. George slaying the dragon. The Grünenberg Book of Arms was purchased by the Heroldsant (Heralds' Office) of Berlin for 300 Friedrichs d'or. It was formerly in the possession of Dr. Stanz of Bern, who had at an earlier date been settled in Constance.

Besides the paper register there also exists a parchment register

(178 leaves), a more amplified but, at the same time, a not quite complete copy of the first, without either date or the name of the painter, which passed from the old Landshuter Library into the Royal Library at München. This has been published, appearing in the year 1875, after an unsuccessful attempt made as early as 1840. It is printed in colours, and was edited by the Count of Stillfried-Alcantara and M. Hildebrandt. The three specimen plates here reproduced have been copied, on a reduced scale, from this publication.

Fig. 1.—*Der Kung von Behem des hailgen Romischen Richs ertzschen vnd Kürfurst, &c.* (The King of Bohemia, of the Holy Roman Empire, Chief Cup-bearer and Elector, &c.). The arms are: Gules, a lion rampant doubled-queued, crowned, armed, and langued or. The crowned helmet, which has a mantling of black and gold, both semé of spots counterchanged, bears as crest a wing sable, semé of linden-leaves or. On both the dexter and the sinister sides of the escutcheon, but unattached, is a symbolical device or badge, namely: issuing from clouds an arm, vested, holding in the hand a rod, and hanging from the sleeve an eagle displayed and crowned, holding in its claws a motto scroll, thereon "Duo Recht." The badge is entirely of gold.

FIG. 1015.—The Arms of Conrad Grünenberg.

Fig. 2 has the following inscription above it: "Der Kaiser von Trappesod stost an Kriechen vnd an das Kaissertum von Athen Hat yetzn der turgisch Kaiser gewunnen vnd den Kaiser geköpft" (The Emperor of Trebizond, next to Greece: the Empire of Athens has now overthrown the Turkish Emperor, and beheaded him). David Komnenos, Emperor of Trebizond, died 1462. The arms are: Argent, a cockatrice or, armed, combed, and wattled gules. The crowned helmet, which has a mantling of gules and argent, bears as crest the charge of the shield, i.e. a cockatrice as in the arms. By the side of the achievement, an arched crown of gold is depicted as a symbolical badge or device.

H. S.

PLATE XC

FURTHER EXAMPLES FROM CONRAD GRÜNENBERG'S "WAPPENBUCH"

(1483. *Height of Shields, 6–6.5 cm.*)

Fig. 1. *Fry (Freiherren) von Trimberg:* Gules, a panther vomiting flames of fire azure, armed of the last, the horns or. It is here shown with divided hoofs on the hind feet, a peculiarity which is only to be met with in the neighbourhood of Lake Constance. (See also Fig. 1017 below.) Crest: a demi-figure as in the arms. Mantling gules and argent. The foregoing is practically a literal translation of the German version, but the creature is most certainly not a panther either of a heraldic or natural variety. It apparently had better be left for some one to discover and name an animal with the horns and hind feet of the domestic cow and the claws of an eagle. The coat is not included in Rietstap. Attention may be directed to a monograph on the panther, "Das Ladeswappen der Steiermark," by A. V. Siegenfeld (Graz, 1900).

FIG. 1016.

Fig. 2. *Fry vom Joch*: Argent, three crossbow yokes fessewise in pale sable (*Joch* = yoke). Crest: two buffalo's horns or, and issuing from the ends plumes of cock's feathers sable. Mantling sable and argent.

FIG. 1017.

Fig. 3. *Fry von Liebsperg*: Gules, a leopard or, armed and langued azure. Crest: a leopard's head affronté, crowned and langued azure. Mantling gules and or.

Fig. 4. *Von Schopffla das zu der richen ow litt* (Isle of Reichenau :) Argent, a cock sable with wings expanded, armed, crested, and wattled gules. Crest: two cocks' heads and necks conjoined or, armed, crested, and wattled gules. Mantling sable and or.

Fig. 5. *Heren von Parwis* in Brabant (Parwyss, an old family in the bishopric of Liège): Or, a lion gules, debruised by a label of three points azure. Crest: issuant from a pointed cap ermine, a peacock's tail. Mantling gules and or.

Fig. 6. *Fry von Russeg im aergoe* (Russeck in Aargau): Or, a unicorn sable. Crest: a swan's head and neck or, beaked argent. Mantling or and argent.

Fig. 1016 gives a capital representation of a so-called "klauflügel" (claw-wing), *i.e.* an eagle's wing conjoined to an eagle's talon, and represents the arms of the "Grafen von Canisse" (Kanisay de genere Ost) in Hungary (founder of an alleged bishopric of Kanisse or Kanisa). The arms are blazoned: "Argent, a klauflügel sable, armed or," this being in English terms: Argent, an eagle's wing expanded, conjoined to an eagle's claw sable, armed or. Crest: the same figure. Mantling sable and argent.

Fig. 1017. *Hern von Bernegk vom Wasen Jm Land Steir* (Herr von Berneck of Wasa in Styria): Or, a panther sable, vomiting flames of fire gules. Crest: a demi-figure as in the arms, continuing into a mantling of sable and or. Note remarks above as to the panther.

Fig. 1018. *Von Ramsperg vn von Rossno*: Or, a ram trippant sable. Crest: issuing from a wreath gules and argent, a demi-ram or. Mantling or and sable (see Plate LXXIV. Fig. 17). It will be noticed that this crest alone amongst all the examples given issues from a wreath or torse, this being an ornament seldom met with

FIG. 1018.

in German armory. The arms are evidently intended to pun upon the name: "ram" in Middle High German having the same meaning as in English. H. S.

PLATE XCI

FURTHER EXAMPLES FROM CONRAD GRÜNENBERG'S "WAPPENBUCH"

(1483. *Height of Shields, 6–6.5 cm.*)

Fig. 1. *Hern von Bergo*: Gules, a winged fish in bend argent. Crest: a winged fish argent, head downwards, continuing into a mantling gules and argent.

Fig. 2. *Fryher von Zimern vnd Here zuo möskirch* (Belonging to the Tournament Society "Falk und Fisch"—Falcon and Fish): Azure, a lion or, armed gules, holding in its paws a battle-axe argent, the handle gules. Crest: a stag's head and neck gules, attired or. Mantling red.

Fig. 3. *Heren vo Hassendoff* (Hassendorf): Or, a serpent sable. Crest: a demi-snake or, combed or finned sable, the body continued into a mantling of or and sable.

THE ART OF HERALDRY

Fig. 4. *Von Langenstain, Stiffter des tutschen* (deutschen) *Huses der Maiyno* (Meinau) (Och Stiffter ze sant Urban. Von Langenstain, founder of the German House of Meinau, also founder of St.

Fig. 6. *Rud von Buttinen* (Rudt von Collenberg): Gules, a mastiff's head couped argent, gorged with a spiked collar sable, the spikes argent. Crest: a mastiff's head as in the arms, continuing into the white and red mantling.

Fig. 7. *Von Frankenstain:* Or, a throwing axe (?) in bend gules, the edge upwards. Crest: two wings or, each charged with the figure in the arms. Mantling gules and or.

Fig. 1019. *Fry von Wildenfels* in Bairn: Argent, a rose sable, seeded or. Crest: on a pointed cap argent, a rose as in the arms, the cap continuing into the mantling, which is argent and sable.

Fig. 1020. *Berner von Bernnekg* (Perner von Perneck in der Elsenau): Argent, a bear rampant sable, armed or, collared and chained of the last. Crest: a demi-bear as in the arms, continued into a mantling of sable and argent. The Perners of Perneck sometimes, though probably only later, bore their arms with the field or. The Perners zum Schachen (at Schachen), who were akin to them, reversed the tinctures, *i.e.* on a field sable a bear or, collared and chained argent.

[FIG. 1019.

FIG. 1021.

Urban's): Argent, an eagle displayed gules, armed azure, the claws supporting a triple mound of the last. Crest: issuing from a wreath gules and argent, five swords sable, hilts and pommels or, points downwards. Mantling gules and argent.

FIG. 1020.

Fig. 5. *Von Rottenstain:* Argent, a bend gules, fimbriated and fretty or. Crest: upon a circular peasant's hat sable, the brim fimbriated or, a snowball proper. Mantling gules and or.

Fig. 1021. *Fuchs von Fuchsberg* (Tyrol): Or, a fox salient gules. Crest: on a cap or chapeau, turned up ermine, a fox sejant gules. Mantling gules and or. This coat of arms is not depicted in colour by Grünenberg. H. S.

PLATE XCII

HERALDIC DRAWINGS FROM CONRAD GRÜNENBERG'S "OESTERREICHISCHER CHRONIK"

(1452 *to about* 1484)

Among the MSS. in the k.u.k. Haus-, Hof- und Staats-Archives in Vienna, there is a paper volume, a kind of Chronicle of Austria, compiled by Conrad Grünenberg and emblazoned with coats of arms. In the preface he says:—

"So hab Ich Cunrat Grünemberg Riter mir fürgesetzt, Etwas ze arbaiten vnd zesamen zuo fassen, als ain Anhanger des stegraiffs, dem Hochstamendesten adel Kaiser, Kung, Ertzhertzogen vnd Fürsten Oesterreich geblütz damit Ich . . . och willen Erzöge, vermainende hie mit der gedächtnuss der aller eltesten allerdurchluchtigeste milt vnd güttigisten Herschafft ain wenig zu geschürt haben. Bittende solich werkli lesend zu besichtigen, datu Sebastyani Im LII (20 Januar 1452)."

("So I, Conrad Grünenberg, knight, have determined to make and put together something, as an Esquire to the most lofty, noble Emperor, King, Archdukes and Princes of Austria, of blood, that I . . . also the dukes, thinking here of the oldest and most serene, mild and kind government may have helped to advance it a little. Begging that such work may be looked at and read, dated St. Sebastian's in 52 (20th January 1452)").

421

Grünenberg depicts the arms of the rulers of Austria from about the year 850 after the Flood up to about 1484 A.D. The greater part of these arms (11 single coats of arms, 70 double or impaled escutcheons, and 14 triple shields) are naturally quite mythical, which he must either have taken from a book of arms (*Oesterreichisches Wappenbuch*, see page 417), likewise in the possession of the Staats-Archives, or which come from the same source as that from which the artist of the older Book of Arms derived his own. He pandered in this book to the fashion much favoured in his time, and even later, of carrying the histories of families back into remote antiquity, and supplying the place of what was lacking in historical truth by perfectly absurd imaginary tales, often childishly naif.

Grünenberg relates that in the land of Terra Amiratorum a Count Sattan von Algänianas was established, against whom a knight of "discreet" family, Abraham von Demonaria, rebelled, but got the worst of it. Abraham was consequently obliged to wander away and settle down elsewhere. On the 12th June 850 after the Flood he established himself in a country which a Jew had possessed before him and called "Judeisapta." Abraham built himself a dwelling-place, and called it Arattim, which place was later called Stockerau. Himself he signed "Abraham, a heathen (or Gentile), Margrave of Judeisapta." He bore as arms a shield striped vertically fifteen times black and white (one hesitates to heraldically blazon it paly of fifteen sable and argent), and as a crest on the helmet a bearded giant's head per pale sable and argent. The arms of his wife Susanna, daughter of Tereman von Riet, show a shield vert, within a bordure argent, and as crest, a ball gules (or torteau) (Fig. 1). Abraham conferred arms upon the country: Sable, an eagle or. Crest: an eagle, the body or, the wings sable. Mantling sable and or. It is not uninteresting to notice that the original arms of the Austrian land, which he here gives to the land of Judeisapta, were very well known to Grünenberg.

Abraham's son called the country, later on, after the dwelling-place, *Arattim*, but in course of time the name of the country was rather frequently changed (Sauritz, Sannas, Pannans, Tantanio, Mittenau, Fannau, Auarrata, Filia, Rattasama, Corodantia, Anara, Osterland, Oesterreich). The armorial bearings were also altered. Under the twentieth ruler, named Nonas, Duke of Pannans, the device of the country was changed for the first time; it then appears: Sable, an eagle displayed argent; and as crest, between two wings argent, a naked youth per fess argent and gules, seated on the helmet (Fig. 2. Here given as belonging to the twenty-second ruler.) While Fig. 1 does not appear in the 1445 register, the coat with the youth as crest may be found as the arms of Pannans, but the youth is standing, and clothed, and the mantling is dark red and white.

Fig. 3 shows the arms under the twenty-seventh Lord Manay, Duke of Tantanio. His wife was Sinna, Duchess of Bohemia, whose coat is likewise duly given in the 1445 register, but in this case not merely a woman's head but a woman's body, clothed in red, appears between the wings.

Fig. 4 gives the arms in the reign of Rolans "ain Jud Hertzog zuo Rattasma." His wife was Sana, a princess of Hungary. The older Register gives the same arms for "Rarasma," only the two crowns are placed one above another; the arms with the scorpion also appear, but the helmet has a black and white mantling.

Fig. 5 shows the arms of the country under the fifty-second ruler, likewise the hereditary arms of Sapton, a prince of Bohemia, husband of the Duchess Rachaim of Rattasma. The 1445 Register, as may be seen from Fig. 1022, exhibits the same device (Arms of Rattasma). The second coat of arms with the raven as crest is also in the older register, but certainly not so well drawn as in Grünenberg's book.

Fig. 6—Gules, an eagle quarterly argent and sable—is the coat of Duke Ludwig of Austria; his wife Ellena being a princess of Hungary. The older book does not give the eagle quarterly, but simply per pale argent and sable, the eagle of the crest being there continued in the yellow and white helmet mantling. The second coat of arms with the dragon also appears to have been copied.

The princes of the country whose existence can really be historically substantiated prior to Grünenberg's day, form the conclusion of the chronicle.

Unfortunately the last leaves of the book are very defective, of many of them only a few small pieces are preserved, but we can recognise which other alliances Grünenberg had emblazoned. The last emblazonment but one seems to have represented the Alliance of the Emperor Friedrich IV. with Eleonora of Portugal (1452), whilst the final page of the volume represents the Alliance of Sigmund of Tyrol with Eleonora of Scotland (1469), and (as it is probable that a triple shield was on the page) doubtless also for his alliance with Katharine of Saxony (1484). Of the coat of arms, there is certainly only a small portion of the Scottish tressure flory preserved.

The unheraldic conjunction of tinctures in the imaginary arms, as black and green, green and red, &c., was probably purposely selected by Grünenburg to characterise the pagan age. One peculiarity of

German heraldic art should be noticed. When the two shields are placed accollé, not only is the dexter crest helmet placed to face the sinister, but the whole shield itself with its charges is reversed. Thus in the dexter shield in Fig. 5 the bend is not a bend sinister, and the eagle in No. 6 is really quarterly argent and sable, and not

FIG. 1022.

sable and argent, as might at first sight appear. This peculiarity was not a feature of British armory at any period, though something of the same nature occurs in a few of the early Garter plates in St. George's Chapel, which, as originally set up, were arranged to face the High Altar. Consequently those on the one side of the chapel are turned to the sinister. H. S.

PLATE XCIII

THE WORK OF ALBRECHT DÜRER

(*First quarter of the Sixteenth Century*)

Albrecht Dürer, the great painter, who was born at Nürnberg, May 21, 1471, and died April 6, 1528. He was the son of a father of many children, the goldsmith Albrecht Dürer the elder, by his marriage with Barbara Holper. (The Holpers bore for arms: Azure, a ram argent.) Dürer the elder came originally from Ajtos, near Grosswardein, in Hungary (*Ajto = Thure* (doors), hence Dürer). Dürer is not only one of the greatest painters, but admittedly occupies the very first rank as an heraldic artist.

Fig. 1. The well-known "coat of arms with the cock" (perhaps *De Berghes* in Holland): Or, a lion rampant gules, armed and tongued azure. Crest: a cock with outstretched wings or, combed and wattled gules. This is one of the most beautiful of Dürer's heraldic designs. It was executed about the year 1511.

Fig. 2. A fanciful shield to represent the arms of death, 1503. On the shield appears a skull, which is treated naturally, as are the helmet wings which form the crest. The helmets in Figs. 1 and 2 both correspond exactly to the helmets 8 and 9 on Plate LI. A lady in Nürnberg bridal costume who is being attacked by a wild man is placed as a supporter to the shield.

Fig. 3. Arms of *Dürer*, 1523 (height, 35.5 cm.): Gules, on three mountains or (according to others vert), an open golden door (according to some, with a silver roof). The tilting-helmet, with mantling of gules and or and with a wreath of the same, bears as crest between two wings or (some say argent) a demi-negro without arms, habited gules, faced with or, and wearing a pointed cap gules, the brim turned up or. The assertion that the Emperor Maximilian I. made a grant of these arms to Dürer in 1512 lacks historical proof.

Fig. 4. Arms of the *Herren von Rogendorf*, 1520 (height, 62.5 cm.): Quarterly, 1 and 4, azure, on an embattled wall a star of six points or (Rogendorf); 2 and 3, argent, on three mounds vert, superimposed in bend a lion mounting gules, crowned or (Wildhaus. Margaretha v. Wildhaus, died 1492, was the wife of Kaspar v. Rogendorf, died

FIG. 1023.—From Dürer's *Ehrenpforte des Kaisers Maximilian I.*

1506). The family came originally from Marburg in Styria. Crest: a demi-lion as in the arms, between two horns per fess embattled azure and or, and issuant therefrom peacock's feathers.

H. S.

PLATE XCIV

ALBRECHT DÜRER AND HIS SCHOOL

Fig. 1. Arms of *Hector Pömer*, the last prefect of St. Lawrence's, in Nürnberg. (Died January 7, 1541.) By A. Dürer; engraved by R[ösch Hieronymus] A[nno] 1525. (Height, 29.5 cm.) This engraving was used as a bookplate (*ex libris*). The arms are: Quarterly, 1 and 4 (St. Lawrence), gules, a gridiron argent; 2 and 3 (Pömer), per bend in chief bendy gules and argent, in base sable. Crest: a demi-moor without arms, habited in gules, the hood argent, and wreathed gules and argent. St. Lawrence appears as a supporter with the instrument of his martyrdom, the gridiron. In the four corners various ancestral arms are introduced; at the top to the dexter *Pömer*, and to the sinister *Rummel*: Or, two hens addorsed sable, combed and wattled gules. At the base are the following arms: on the dexter side, *Schmidmair*: Per bend or and gules, three roses in bend countercharged. On the sinister side *Ferkmaister*: Azure, the heads and necks of two geese conjoined and addorsed argent.

Fig. 2. Arms of *Johann Stabius* (Imperial Historian, Poet and Mathematician). He was born in Austria, and taught mathematics in Vienna. He was living in 1512 at Nürnberg, and died 1522. By A. Dürer, 1521 (27.5 cm. high): Or, an eagle gules. The helmet, which has a mantling of gules and or, bears as crest upon an archducal crown an eagle as in the arms.

Fig. 3. A coat of arms with lions' heads (family unknown) by

A. Dürer, 1520 (25.5 cm. high). The shield shows a fess between three lions' (or leopards') heads crowned. Crest: a demi-lion crowned. Near the coat of arms, moreover, is the badge of some society or order, viz. a flower-pot, held by two hands, within a border of clouds.

Fig. 4. Arms of *Stephan Rosinus*, Canon (or prebendary) of Passau. School of A. Dürer, 1520–1525 (height about 25 cm.): Dimidiated per bend in chief an eagle displayed, and in base on a fess one (or more) roses. Above the helmet is the crest, viz.: on a crown an eagle displayed, charged on each of the wings with a fess and rose as in the arms.

Fig. 1024 at the side shows the "Alliance Escutcheon" of the Nürnberg families of *Scheurl* and *Tucher*, and this also is a piece of work which belongs to the school of Albrecht Dürer. To the dexter appear the arms of *Scheurl*, viz.: Gules, a panther argent, and for the crest a demi-animal as in the arms. On the sinister are

FIG. 1024.

the arms of *Tucher*, which are: Per fess in chief bendy of six sable and argent, and in base or, the head and shoulders of a negro. Crest: a demi-negro habited or, the habit continuing into the helmet mantling of or and sable, and in place of arms two buffalo's horns erect, each tierced in fess or, sable, and argent.

H. S.

PLATE XCV

ALBRECHT DÜRER AND HIS SCHOOL

Fig. 1. represents the arms of the Nürnberg councillor *Michael Behaim*, and is by A. Dürer, being executed about 1509. The Behaims of Schwarzbach (who were a Bavarian family) bore: On a field per pale argent and gules, a bend sinister wavy sable. Crest: on a wreath an eagle or sparrow-hawk rising argent, ducally gorged. Mantling gules and argent.

Fig. 2. Arms of *Johann Tschertte* (Imperial Architect and Bridge-builder at Vienna), by A. Dürer, 1521: A satyr blowing a horn (in Bohemian, *Cert or Czert*), with two hounds in leash: in the dexter canton a waning moon (or a decrescent) enclosing a human face. The tilting-helm bears as crest a demi-satyr, with horn and leash, between two buffalo's horns.

THE ART OF HERALDRY

Fig. 3. Arms of *Kress von Kressenstein*. (The family came from Kressenstein, between Eger and Asch.) (Dürer's school): Gules, a sword in bend or, hilt downwards. Mantling gules and argent. Crest: out of a crown, a bearded man's head, shoulders, and body, without arms, habited in gules, fastened at the neck with two buttons argent, wearing a cap sable, the brim turned up ermine. The man holds with two fangs of the lower jaw a sword in fess, point to the dexter or, and behind the leaves of the crest coronet, and above the brim of the cap are placed five peacock's feathers alternately large and small, which the Kress family received as an armorial augmentation from Charles V. at Augsburg, July 15, 1530.

Fig. 4. Arms of *Johann Segker*. (His seat·was at Messenbach, near Lambrechten, in Upper Austria.) (School of Dürer): Azure, a ship or, without masts. Mantling azure and or. Crest: issuing from a crown on a mast azure, a sail argent, distended by the wind to the sinister, and flying from the mast a streamer or pennon argent, charged with a saltire gules.

Fig. 5. "Alliance" coat of arms of the *Scheurl* and *Geuder* families (Christopher Scheurl married Sabine Geuder in 1560). Dürer's school, probably dating between 1513 and 1535. On a quatrefoil design are the two shields placed accollé, and in the four outer interstices are shields for the arms of the four grandparents, though three of these are blank. *Scheurl*: Gules, a panther argent. Crest: a demi-panther as in the arms. (See Plate XXXV. Fig. 5.) *Geuder*: Azure, a triangular facetted stone argent, at each corner a six-pointed star argent.

Fig. 6. represents the arms of the *Archduke Charles of Austria* (afterwards Charles V.). Dürer's school (24 cm. high). The many-quartered shield is surrounded by the collar of the Order of the Golden Fleece, and surmounted by the old Archducal cap. The shield-quarterings as here given are marshalled in a peculiar manner. On the honour point is an inescutcheon quartered with the arms of Austria, Burgundy, Tyrol, and Flanders. The shield behind is divided per pale and again per pale, in each case a point being introduced at the base. Field I. contains the old Hungarian coat; II. Bohemia; III. Quartered, Castile, Leon, Styria, and Carinthia; IV. Quartered, Arragon with Granada, Sicily, Carniola, and Görz introduced; V. Burgau and Swabia in the curved point Pfirt; VI. Upper Alsatia (Alsace) and Kyburg, in the curved point Cilli. The point is divided twice, and shows the arms of Upper and Lower (Old) Austria and the Wend March territory.

H. S.

PLATE XCVI

COATS OF ARMS BY GERMAN ARTISTS

(First half of the Sixteenth Century)

Fig. 1. Arms of *Johann Vergenhans* (alias *Nauclerus*), first Rector of the University of Tübingen (died about 1510), printed in his *Memorabilium omnis ætatis chronica commentarii*, 1516. Artist unknown. The arms show the chronicler seated at the rudder, two negroes working the ship. As crest we have a negro issuing from a coronet adorned with a fillet, and holding oars in his hands.

Fig. 2. Arms of *Sebastian* (?) *von Fegersheim*, of an old Strassburg family. This example is by *Hans Baldung* or "Grien," who was born about 1475 at Weyersheim, near Strassburg, and died in 1545 at Strassburg. He made many sketches for the heraldic decoration of glass windows. The shield shows the arms: Gules, a fess or, within a bordure argent. As crest: the crowned helmet bears a red pointed hat, ending in a golden knob. Mantling gules and or. (The golden fess on the hat, and the peacock's tail issuing out of the knob on the hat, with which in other cases the arms of the Fegersheims are always depicted, are not shown in this sketch.) In 1627, with Caspar von Fegersheim, the family became extinct. They were of the same stock and bore the same arms as the Herren von Rathsamhausen and the Weissbrötlins, who are also extinct. The Weissbrötlins bore the same shield; the Rathsamhausens had other tinctures, bearing: Argent, a fess vert, within a bordure gules.

Fig. 3. Arms of *Beatus von Dunzenheim*, Magistrate of Strassburg. The sketch bears under the arms the inscription: "Bath von Duntzenheim, 1542. Drawn by *Hans Baldung*, called Grien." The shield shows the arms following, namely: Sable, a fess between three roses argent, seeded or. The helmet has a mantling of sable and argent, and the crest is two ass's ears sable. The architectural setting of the arms which appears in the original is here omitted. One branch of this family, which became extinct in the last years of the sixteenth century, bore these arms with different tinctures, viz.: Gules, a fess between three roses argent, and in the crest the ears were one argent and one gules. The mantling was gules and argent.

Fig. 4. Arms of *Dr. Peter Apianus* (properly *Bennewitz*), Geographer and Astronomer, and also an Imperial Count Palatine, 1540. This was drawn by *Michael Ostendorfer*, draughtsman and painter at Regensburg, who died 1559. The shield shows the

arms: Or, within a circular wreath nebuly argent and azure (probably an orle of clouds), a double-headed eagle sable, with each head adorned with a nimbus. The helmet, which is crowned and accompanied with a mantling sable and or, has thereupon as the crest the device of the shield.

Fig. 5. Arms of King *Siegmund August* (Sigismund Augustus) *of Poland* (1548-1572), the last of the Jagiellos. By an unknown artist. The illustration is taken from a woodcut in a Mainz book printed about 1550. The arms are as follows: Argent, the Royal eagle of Poland displayed gules, armed and crowned or, interlaced round its body with the king's monogram. The curious arrangement also found its way into the arms of the Duchy of Prussia, in vassalage to Poland, and may still be seen in a similar form in the Royal Arms of Prussia.

Fig. 6. Arms of *O. Brunfels*, author of the *Contrafayt Kræuterbuch*, which was issued at Strassburg in 1532 (25.6 cm. high). This design was probably drawn by *Hans Weyditz* (Guiditius) of whom nothing further is known than his co-operation in the work of Brunfels. The shield shows a bend, and for the crest a pair of wings each charged with the arms.

Fig. 7—arms of *Hans Wilhelm von Loubembergk* (Laubenberg) *of Wagegg*—is from an engraved portrait from Apianus' *Instrumentenbuch*, 1533, which the author dedicated to Laubenberg. The drawing must have been by *Hans Brosamer*, who was born at Fulda 1506, and died at Erfurt 1552. The arms are: Gules, three linden-leaves in bend argent. The barred helmet has as crest between two wings, the one gules and the other argent, a pointed hat gules, with a turned-up brim argent, and on the top a golden button. The mantling is gules and argent. The shield is covered with a magnificent Renaissance diapering.

H. S.

PLATE XCVII

COATS OF ARMS BY GERMAN ARTISTS

(First half of the Sixteenth Century)

Fig. 1. Arms of the *Visconti*, Dukes of Milan. These were drawn and engraved by *Jeronymus* (Hieronymus) *Hopfer*, a copperplate engraver at Augsburg, in 1520. The shield shows the arms: Argent, a snake azure, crowned or, devouring a human figure gules.

Fig. 2. A shield with a horse bridled and salient to the sinister. This also was drawn and engraved by *J. Hopfer*. Both these coats are to be found engraved (with twenty-two others) on one plate.

Fig. 3. Arms of *Wolfstein*, engraved by *J. Hopfer*. The arms are: Or, two lions passant in pale gules. The mantling is of sable and or, and the crest is a wolf's head and neck sable continuing into the mantling, and holding in its jaws a lamb or.

Fig. 4. Arms of *Göler von Ravensburg* (Rabensberg) of Frankfurt-on-Maine, engraved by *J. Hopfer*. The shield shows the arms to be: Argent, a raven rising sable. The crest is a demi-swan issuant, the wings addorsed and semé of linden-leaves. (In Siebmacher's Book of Arms, on the other hand, the raven is crowned, and the crest is a demi-raven issuant sable, crowned and with a gold comb on the back, this having peacock's feathers.) The mantling is sable and argent.

Fig. 5 shows an imaginary coat of arms engraved by *Hans Sebald Beham* in 1544. He was a painter and copperplate engraver, was born in 1500 (?) at Nürnberg, and died at Frankfurt-on-Maine in 1550. The coat of arms bears a bantering inscription which signifies, "By God's Grace Herr von Know not where settled in a mean village." On the shield appears a lion rampant, and on the helmet, wings.

Fig. 6. Arms of *Hans Sebald Beham*, 1544, engraved by himself. The shield shows a chevron in point embowed between three inescutcheons. Crest: two buffalo's horns, each charged with a fess. The inescutcheons represent the badge of an artist (see Plate CXXII.). The inscription runs: "Seboldt Beham von Nvrmberg Maler iecz wonhafter Burger zu Frankfurt" (Seboldt Beham of Nürnberg, Painter, now resident Burgher of Frankfurt).

Figs. 7 and 8 are imaginary arms devised by *Hans Sebald Beham*, 1543. The one bears the inscription: "Wer mich will hon, der nem mich on" ("Who will have me, let him take me"), and shows an eagle on the shield; and as crest, an ostrich feather between two bouquetin's horns. The other bears the inscription: "A coat of arms for a seal" ("Ein Wapen zv einem Sigel"), and shows a cock on the shield; and for crest, a cock between two buffalo's horns. Both coats of arms are exquisitely finished examples of heraldic engraving.

Fig. 9. Arms of *Johannes Saganta* (1550), by *Hans Burgkmair* the younger, of Augsburg, born in 1500, died 1559. The shield is: Party per fess in chief or, a demi-double headed eagle displayed sable, with the nimbus of the German Empire; and the base, argent, a bend gules, between in chief three birds vert and in base three toothed sickles azure. Crest: the heads and necks of two demi-snakes, entwined and addorsed and issuing from a crown. The mantling is hung with bells at the ends.

Fig. 10. Arms of the *Altensteigs* in Swabia, by *Hans Burgkmair* the younger : Or, a saltire gules, over all an eagle displayed sable, crowned or. The mantling is sable and or, and the crest, out of a crown, a demi-eagle as in the arms, charged with a saltire gules.

Fig. 1025, which follows, was drawn by *Hans Burgkmair* the elder, 1473–1531, the father of the preceding. It shows Maximilian I.

·MAXIMILIANVS·

FIG. 1025.

seated on a throne, and at his feet an armorial shield, and thereupon the Imperial eagle (with one head), bearing on its breast a shield containing the arms of Old Hungary, Dalmatia, Croatia, New Austria, Old Burgundy, Styria, and Carinthia. Over the throne is suspended Maximilian's badge or pictorial device ; between an Imperial globe and a pomegranate, a wheel, with many knives attached to it, referring to the many dangers to which he was exposed during his life. (Usually this device will be found accompanied by the motto : " Per tot discrimina.") The design is taken from a series of pages on the " Genealogy of Maximilian." If the eagle in the coat of arms of the Altensteigs is compared with that in Fig. 13, it will be easily recognised that it is hardly possible to distinguish the work of the two Burgkmairs.

Fig. 11. Arms of *Leonhard Beckh von Bechstein* (Beckenstein) of Augsburg, 1544. Artist unknown. The shield is quarterly :

FIG. 1026.—The Arms of the Freiherren von Rindscheit.

1 and 4, or, a goat sable, crowned ; 2 and 3, gules, a point throughout argent, three roses counterchanged. The dexter helmet has for the crest, issuing from a crown, a demi-goat as in the arms, whilst

the crest upon the sinister helmet is a pair of wings issuing from a crown, and each charged with the arms as in the second and third quarters. The mantlings are sable and or, and gules and argent respectively.

Fig. 12. Arms of *Wolf Rechlinger* of Augsburg. Artist unknown. The shield is quarterly, the arms being : 1 and 4, azure, two points in base argent, each surmounted by a rose, and another rose similarly placed in base, all counterchanged ; 2 and 3, per pale argent and sable, a fess dancetté counterchanged. The shield is surmounted by two helmets, each crowned. The crest upon the dexter is a peacock's tail between two buffalo's horns azure, each showing a point argent, surmounted by a rose, the dexter mantling being azure and

FIG. 1027.—The Arms of the Freiherren von Pögel of Reiffenstein and Aarberg.

argent. The crest upon the sinister helmet is a pair of wings, each charged with the arms as in the 2nd and 3rd quarters. The sinister mantling is sable and argent.

Figs. 1026 and 1027 are other very excellent and characteristic examples of arms by German artists at about this period.

H. S.

PLATE XCVIII

EXAMPLES FROM THE ROLL OF ARMS OF THE GESCHLECHTERGESELLSCHAFT "ZUR KATZE" IN CONSTANCE

(1547)

The Meetings of the Patricians (the so-called honourable burghers, *probi cives*) of the old, free city of Constance, on the Bodensee (Lake of Constance), in whose hands was the government of the town, were held in the old " Amlungsgasse," in the house " Zur Katze " (*i.e.* at the sign of the Cat). Hence also the name of the Society. In the year 1424 the Society sold their house to the Jew Abraham, and purchased a new one in the Munstergasse (now Katzgasse No. 3), to which the old name was transferred.

When in the year 1548 the town lost its freedom, the privileges of the " Katze " also vanished. But when in the years immediately following, the " Katze " brotherhood gradually resuscitated itself once more, its political rôle had for ever finished. In course of time the greater number of the families were ennobled, a part of them died out, the other part was merged amongst the burghers, till, at the end of the eighteenth century, the Society had completely disappeared. In 1821 the house came into the possession of the firm of *Pecht*, whose lithographic establishment is now settled in the " Katze " house.

Two parchment rolls are in existence (both 63 cm. high by 75 cm. broad), on which 153 coats of arms of the families belonging to the " Katze " in 1547 have been recorded, and both are now in the possession of the town of Constance (Rosgartenmuseum). The contours of the shields, the helmets, and the mantlings are drawn as if from the same pattern, but only the first roll is completely finished ; on the second only a few coats of arms are entered. The historian Christopher Schultheiss asserts that in the year 1546 Michael von Schwarzach (Fig. 1028) (Schwarzach in Vorarlberg) collected the

FIG. 1028.

arms of the Herren of the Katze, and entered them in a book, which collection probably served as a model for the rolls. The first roll also shows the device of the Society (Fig. 1029): Azure, a

FIG. 1029.

cat argent, armed and crowned gold. On the white banner of the supporter the black cross of Constance appears.

Fig. 1. *Schwartzen*: Or, a cock's head erased sable, combed and

wattled gules, the ears argent. Crest: a cock's head and neck as in the arms, pierced by a yoke or, this being crowned on both sides, and within the crowns bunches of cock's feathers sable. Mantling sable and or.

Fig. 2. *Von Niederwyle*: Argent, on a mount in front of a tree vert, an ass passant argent. Crest: the same device. Mantling vert and argent.

Fig. 3. *Von Krützlingen*: Party per fess gules and or, in chief a star of six points or, and in base a point sable. Crest: a bird's head and neck argent, habited in a red cloth and gorged with a belled collar or, on the head yellow curly hair bound round with a red kerchief. Mantling gules and argent.

Fig. 4. *Specker*: Argent, a wyvern sable, vomiting fire, the feet, legs, and underpart of the ear gules. Crest: a demi-wyvern as in the arms, but without wings. Mantling sable and argent. (On a seal of "Cunrat Speker" of 1382 the same device appears.)

Fig. 5. *Schwartzen unter den Sulen*: Sable, an eagle displayed or. Crest: a wing-shaped screen or fan sable charged with an eagle as in the arms. Mantling sable and or.

Fig. 6. *Bettwinger*: Party per pale "Kursch" and gules. Crest: a man's head and shoulders argent, crined or, habited and with a cap per pale as the field, crined or. Mantling gules and argent.

Fig. 7. *Hafen*: Or, an earthen vessel (*grapen*) azure. Crest: an earthen vessel as in the arms. Mantling or and azure. (Hug der Hafen, Stadtamman [Magistrate] of Constance, bore the same figure on his shield in 1350.)

Fig. 8. *Von Hof*: Argent, a devil's (?) head sable, armed and langued gules, crowned or. Crest: a devil's head as in the arms, and shoulders habited argent. (Heinrich von Hoff bore the same arms on his seal in 1411.) Possibly the head may be that of a bull.

Fig. 9. *Von Roggwyl*: Gyronny of eight argent and gules. Crest: a bolster or cushion of the arms, the two corners ending in a ball or tassel or, and issuing from each a cock's feather sable. Mantling gules and argent. (Ulrich von Roggwile bore the same shield upon his seal in 1372.)

Fig. 10. *Ueberlinger*: Party per bend nebuly, in chief argent and in base per fess gules and azure. Crest: the head and neck of a greyhound argent, about the neck a hood, gules and azure. Mantling argent. (In Siebmacher's old *Wappenbuch* V. Bd. fol. 192, two shields of the Ueberlingers are given, the one party nebuly azure and argent, and argent and gules.)

Fig. 11. *Schanfigg* (Schanfingen): Argent, six mounts vert, inflamed proper and embrassé. Crest: the device as in the arms. Mantling argent.

Fig. 12. *Magugg*: Argent, on three mounds issuing in base or, two "f"-shaped twigs gules. Crest: a demi-man habited gules, crined or, holding his eyes wide open with his hands. Mantling gules and argent.

Fig. 13. *Ruhe*: Argent, a lion rampant azure. Crest: attached to the ears and scalp gules, two stag's attires argent, each tine adorned with bunches of cock's feathers sable. Mantling gules and argent.

Fig. 14. *Im Turn*: Party per bend or and gules, a bend counterchanged. Crest: a dog's head and shoulders argent, habited as the arms, the hood or, the face surrounded by a fringed border gules. Mantling or and gules.

Fig. 15. *Appentegger*: Argent, the head of a stag-beetle couped gules. Crest: the same device. Mantling argent.

Fig. 16. *Fryg*: Party per pale sable and argent, two scythe-blades counterchanged, points downwards. Crest: an indented scythe-blade argent, adorned on the back with three cock's feathers sable. Mantling sable and argent.

Fig. 17. *Blaurer* (Blarer): Argent, a cock gules. Crest: a cock's head and neck gules. Mantling gules and argent. (Konrad Blaurer, Platzvogt, of Constance, displayed this device on his seal in 1538. The Blaurers played an important part in the history of Constance.)

Fig. 18. *Goldast*: Azure, a branch with leaves or. Crest: issuing from a crown azure, a twig as in the arms argent. (Compare Plate LXXXVIII. Fig. 7.)

Fig. 19. *Ravensburg*: Gules, two bends argent, within a bordure or, masoned compony and counter-compony. [The bordure may be intended to represent a chain.] Crest: a bearded man's head proper, crined or, habited bendy as the arms; on his head a cap argent and issuing therefrom ostrich feathers gules, or, and argent; a chain terminating in a ring hangs from the neck.

Fig. 20. *Sina*: Argent, a garland vert, adorned with roses gules. Crest: a wing-shaped screen or fan argent, charged with a garland as in the arms. Mantling argent.

Fig. 21. *Hinter Sant Johans* (this curious name is literally "Behind St. John"): Gules, a unicorn's head couped argent and horned sable. Crest: a unicorn's head as in the arms. Mantling argent and sable.

Fig. 1028. *Von Schwarzach*: Argent, on a pale wavy sable, three fishes naiant of the field. Crest: on a wing-shaped screen the same device. (On seals of 1514 and 1563 the same device occurs, but instead of the wing-shaped screen, real wings are made use of to carry the device.)

The arms from both parchment rolls have been reproduced on a scale of four-fifths their natural size.

H. S.

PLATES XCIX., C., AND CI.

"PRINCE ARTHUR'S BOOK"

Amongst the manuscripts in the English College of Arms, which is peculiarly rich in examples of heraldic art of the Tudor period, is a book which is always known as "Prince Arthur's Book." The tradition is that it was expressly made for the purpose of teaching the laws of armory, together with the arms in use in England, to Arthur, Prince of Wales, the eldest son of King Henry VII. It is a large folio volume on vellum, partaking somewhat of the character of an "ordinary." The arms of most families of importance in England and of many of the principal personages of Europe are duly emblazoned in the volume. In speaking of the tradition connected with this MS., Mr. G. W. Eve remarks in his "Decorative Heraldry": "Prepared for so distinguished a purpose under the direction, perhaps by the hand of, Sir Thomas Wriothesley, Wallingford Pursuivant to Prince Arthur, and afterwards Garter King of Arms and Secretary to Henry VIII., it is of exceptional interest as a fine and careful work." Mr. Eve further remarks that "the Prince's own arms impaled with those of Katharine of Arragon fittingly appear on its first page, and these fix the date of its production as 1501–2. It is not, however, all of that period, for it is clear from internal evidence that it was added to from time to time during the first half of the century, but the style throughout is to a large extent the same." Whilst the accuracy of the tradition concerning the MS. in no way affects any estimate of its value from an artistic point of view (upon which basis it is properly judged to be one of the finest pieces of heraldic emblazonment now in existence), I am by no means certain that this tradition of its origin, which is generally accepted and which Mr. Eve repeats, is the correct one. The MS., as a note inside the cover states, was given and bequeathed to the Heralds' College by Ralph Sheldon in 1684. That, of course, definitely settles the point that it is not an official MS., and it leaves its origin a matter open for speculation; for it must be very evident that it had been in private custody for some considerable period before it passed into the possession of the College of Arms. Its name "Prince Arthur's Book" is probably a modern description taken from the fact that the painting on the first page bears the name "Prince Arthur." This, however, needs some little consideration.

The painting as it at present stands exhibits the Royal Arms of France and England quarterly, differenced by a plain label of three points argent impaled with the coat of Katharine of Arragon. The dexter supporter is the guardant lion of England (here represented as proper and not gold, as later it is more frequently found) with a similar label, the sinister supporter being an eagle sable. The name which is written above it is very evidently no part of the original design, and is manifestly a later insertion, as are many other manuscript notes which are to be met with throughout the volume. For instance the mottoes of some number of the peers are added to their supporters. These mottoes are palpably later additions, and are in the same handwriting as is the name "Prince Arthur."

If the painting upon the first page be carefully scrutinised, it becomes clearly apparent that the shield *was originally surmounted by the Royal crown of England.* The cap and the arches of the crown have been deliberately *painted out,* so as to leave remaining no more than the simple circlet of crosses patée and fleurs-de-lis which at the present day we should term the coronet of a younger son of the Sovereign. I know of no other instances where this coronet is heraldically assigned as a coronet of rank at that period to the Prince of Wales,

though it is not unlikely that it was the one used by him. It certainly appears in connection with the ostrich feather badge. Therefore the original appearance of the cap and arches of the crown shows clearly that the painting was originally made as an emblazonment of the arms of King Henry VIII. and Queen Katharine. Throughout the book there are various little instances, for example the defacement of the cardinals' hats in some cases, which lead one to the certain conclusion that the book has been "gone over" at a later period by some one "with views," and corrected in accordance therewith.

There are two reasons which may account for the alteration having been made. It may have been a conscientious protest against what many did and do consider to have been the incestuous marriage of King Henry, and that some one for that reason has deliberately tried to convert the impaled arms of Henry VIII. and Queen Katharine into the achievement of Prince Arthur, of the legality of whose marriage with Katharine of Arragon there never was any doubt. But there is another reason, which perhaps is the more likely to have been correct. Accusations of treason were lightly made but ruthlessly punished in King Henry's reign, and the execution of Sir Henry Howard, Earl of Surrey, for the treason contained in the use of those arms of St. Edward the Confessor the right to bear which had been granted to his ancestor, must have come to many people as a sharp reminder of the possibilities of treason which might lie hidden in a coat of arms. After the divorce of Queen Katharine it is quite possible that the owner of the manuscript, fearing he might lose his head by the ownership or exhibition of the painting, altered the coat so that it would suit Prince Arthur, for the same brush which painted out the arches and the cap in the Royal crown over the shield also painted out the arches and cap in the crown on the lion supporter, and added to that supporter and to the quarterly coat of France and England a white label. Having painted out the distinctive portions of the crowns and painted in the labels, the same hand perhaps has written in "Prince Arthur," so that there should be no doubt on the point. But had the book been originally intended for Prince Arthur, and had it been the intention to put his name at the beginning, we should not have found it scribbled in in small letters, but properly illuminated, and the fact that the coat of arms has been *cut out from a larger sheet* and pasted on to another only adds to the probability that the original inscription bore the name of King Henry. Prince Arthur, who was born in 1486, was created Prince of Wales in 1489, so that he would never have been known as "Prince Arthur" except in his early infancy; certainly not during the period after his marriage to Katharine of Arragon. We should have found his name as Arthur, Prince of Wales, and the description of the arms as those of "Prince Arthur" was simply intended to emphasise the fact that they belonged to *him* and not to the next Prince of Wales, who eventually succeeded as Henry VIII. If the foregoing conclusions of mine are correct, the volume must date between the years 1509 and 1533. This point, however, has little concern with the value of the MS. as a most valuable artistic monument of Tudor armorial handicraft. As such it will be difficult ever to rival, though it should be added that an appreciable proportion of the emblazonment is by no means of equal value with the finer work of the remainder, upon which a judgment of the MS. is usually founded. As is so often found to be the case in these early Rolls of Arms, many of the coats of arms in it are purely fictitious, and it should be noted that the MS. is not an official "record." But the better portion of the work is a superlative example of that high type of excellence both in design and execution which characterised so much of the heraldic art of the

Tudor period. Mr. C. H. Athill, F.S.A., Richmond Herald, has been kind enough to have certain of the arms and other paintings copied, and has certified these copies for me, and it is through his kindness that they are reproduced in this volume.

On Plate XCIX. are reproduced a series of shields selected as typical from those throughout the volume. These are:—

1. Argent, a lion rampant azure, "Monsr water Faucon-

10. Gules, three lions passant guardant in pale or, over all an escarbuncle azure. ("The brother to the King." This is probably intended for a bastardised version of the Royal Arms, but it has not been possible to identify the owner.)

11. Sable, a saltire flory argent, between four lions passant guardant or. (Here this coat is ascribed to Pykot, but elsewhere [see Plate LXXXVI.] it appears as the arms of Ayne.)

FIG. 1030.

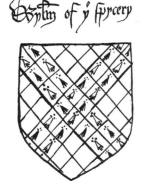
FIG. 1031.

FIG. 1032.

FIG. 1033.

berge." The ownership of these arms is somewhat of a mystery. Walter, Lord Fauconberg (the last lord of his name) died in 1407. These are not the real arms of Fauconberg, but the coat of Bruce, a quartering which the Lords Fauconberg had inherited, and which they appear to have frequently substituted for their own.

2. Or, a lion rampant double-queued sable (the Lord de Welles).

3. Vert, a lion rampant guardant argent (Monsr Richard de Shirburne).

4. Sable, two lions passant in pale paly of six argent and gules (Sir James Strangwayes).

12. Argent, a fess nebuly sable, between three lozenges gules, in the centre chief point a lion passant azure (Robert Thorne).

13. Or, a double-headed eagle displayed sable ("The Emperor.")

14. Gules, an eagle displayed barry of six or and vert, langued azure (Coche).

15. Gules, on a fess engrailed or, between three boars' heads couped argent, a mullet sable (Judde).

16. Azure, five fusils conjoined in fess argent, in chief a label of as many points gules, and on the centre fusil a crescent for difference sable (Dautrey).

FIG. 1034.

FIG. 1035.

FIG. 1036.

5. Gules, a lion statant argent (le S. de Shasta de halghton).

6. Argent, a lion statant guardant gules (le S. de Querleton).

7. Gules, a lion rampant guardant double-queued or (Earl of Teyne).

8. Barry of ten argent and azure, a gryphon segreant or (Sir John Ryseley).

9. Vert, a bicorporated lion sejant guardant within a bordure engrailed argent (Attewater).

Fig. 1030. Barry wavy of six ermine and gules, on a chevron between three "crevices" (crayfish) or, a rose between two lilies stalked and leaved (William Attwater, Dean of the Chapel Royal and of Sarum).

Fig. 1031. (William of the Spicery.)

Fig. 1032. (Monsr Amand Routhe.)

Fig. 1033. (Lucas.)

Figs. 1034, 1035, and 1036 are reproductions of crests taken from a series depicted in the volume, these being, however, strikingly fewer in number than the shields.

Fig. 1034. On a wreath argent and gules, a demi-eagle displayed vert, armed gules (Monthermer, Earl of Gloucester). The mantling is vert, lined with argent.

Fig. 1035. Out of a coronet or, an ostrich's head and wings proper, holding in the beak gules (?) a carpenter's brace and bit. The real crest holds a horse-shoe. The mantling is azure lined with ermine (the King of Hungary).

Fig. 1036. On a wreath argent and sable, a dexter arm embowed, habited in fur and tied with a ribbon argent, holding in the hand proper a lion's gamb erased sable, armed gules. The mantling is gules, lined argent (Dunstanville, Lord and Baron of Castlecombe).

Plate C. represents a curious decorative development of heraldry in Tudor times. In such designs the supporters, which are represented singly, are each depicted supporting a banner. It was exceptional at that period for the two supporters to differ. The instances chosen for reproduction are as follows :—

1. "Azure, three fleurs-de-lis or," the arms on a banner surmounted by a crown and supported by "a stag argent,

singular interest, though it would be of much advantage if it were known whether the supporter belongs to the princely rank of a cardinal, to the Archiepiscopal See of York, or was personal to Cardinal Wolsey. The supporter in question is a griffin per fess gules and argent, armed and winged or, holding in the dexter claw a mace or (presumably that of the Lord Chancellor).

4. The fourth figure upon this plate is even yet more quaint. The arms upon the banner are : Sable, a chevron engrailed argent between three plates, each charged with a pallet gules. The arms are surmounted by the chief of the Order of St. John, and the staff carries the double ecclesiastical cross. The crest (on a wreath argent and azure, a demi-lion rampant double-queued sable, gutté-d'or, holding in the dexter paw a pallet as in the arms) is made to answer the purpose of a supporter, although it had no such intrinsic character. It is nevertheless a quaint and pleasing example of artistic design. It will be noticed that the wreath is not of the livery colours, but that the banner is fringed with them—a very usual practice.

FIG. 1037.

FIG. 1038.

gorged with a coronet and winged, the inside of the wings azure, semé-de-lis or" (the arms of the Realm of France). The supporters of France are usually stated to be angels, and it would be of no little interest to ascertain the authority for this variation.

2. A banner per pale of blue and murrey (the livery colours of the Duke of York—Edward IV.), charged with his badge of a silver falcon within an open fetterlock of gold. The banner is supported by the white lion of March.

3. A banner per pale, the dexter gules, two keys in saltire argent, surmounted by a Royal crown or (the arms of the See of York) ; the sinister sable, on a cross engrailed argent, a lion passant guardant gules, between four leopards' faces azure, on a chief or, a rose of the third, between two Cornish choughs of the first, armed also of the third. The banner-staff is surmounted by a cross, and the banner by a scarlet cardinal's hat, though it may be noticed that the tassels are fewer in number than would now be the case. (Refer to the chapter on Episcopal Heraldry.) The arms are, of course, those of Cardinal Wolsey ("the lord thomas Wulcy"), Legate of the Lateran, Archbishop of York, and Chancellor of England. The fact that they are accompanied by a supporter is of

The arms and crest are those of Sir Thomas Dockwra, the last English Prior of the Knights of St. John.

The next figure (Fig. 1037) is a banner of the arms of the Duke of Suffolk (Sir Charles Brandon, K.G.), viz.: Quarterly, i. and iiii., barry of ten argent and gules, a lion rampant (sometimes represented queue-fourché) or, crowned per pale of the second and first (for Brandon); ii. and iii., quarterly 1 and 4, azure, a cross moline or (for Bruyn); 2 and 3, lozengy gules and ermine (for Rokeley). The banner is surmounted by a coronet of rank, an unusual circumstance at this period, and is supported by a falcon with wings displayed and inverted argent, standing on a small bird of the same. As will be seen from Fig. 931, which represents the arms of the Duke as they appear on his seal, this drawing in "Prince Arthur's book" differs from the usually accepted version of the Brandon arms, which makes the lion queue-fourché, and which makes the dexter supporter a lion or, crowned per pale argent and gules, gorged with a plain collar azure, the studs and chain of the last.

Fig. 1038 is a banner showing the badge of the sun in splendour of King Richard II., supported by another of his badges, the hart ducally gorged and chained.

Plate CI. and Figs. 1039 and 1040 in the text are also reproduced from " Prince Arthur's Book," and are from a series of heraldic drawings illustrative of the successive Royal badges. It should be carefully noted that these do not represent either arms or banners, but are merely drawings of badges arranged (presumably for artistic reasons) within parallelograms, each badge presumably depicted on the livery colours with which it was displayed. The one

penbuchlein of Virgil Solis, Nürnberg, 1555. [Recently republished by Georg Hirth in his *Liebhaberbibliothek alter Illustratoren* (Münich, 1886)]. The tinctures are indicated by letters inserted by Virgil Solis himself. *Kingdom of Germania :* Or, an eagle displayed sable, with the head set in a nimbus. Crest : an Imperial orb resting in the coronet. Mantling sable and or. *Kingdom of Hungary :* Party per pale, the dexter barry of eight argent and gules (old Hungarian coat of arms), the sinister gules, on three mounds vert a patriarchal cross argent (new Hungarian coat of arms). Crest : a demi-ostrich with a horse-shoe in its beak issuing from the helmet crown (com-

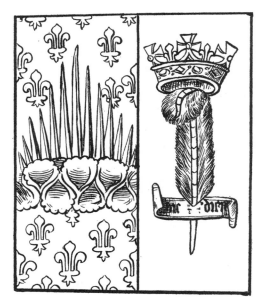

FIG. 1039.

FIG. 1040.

figure on Plate CI. shows the white rose of York *en soleil*, the fleurs-de-lis from the Royal Arms, the white lion of March, and the suns in splendour, all these being badges used by King Edward IV. The blue and murrey upon which the badges are depicted were his livery colours.

The other figure on the same Plate shows the cross of St. George and the Swan, the latter being a badge derived from the Bohun family, the wife of Henry IV. being the heiress of that family.

Fig. 1039 represents on the dexter side the well-known "sunburst" badge, and the badge of the ostrich feather.

Fig. 1040 shows the cross of St. George, the crowned rose of York and Lancaster, the red dragon (of Wales), the greyhound, the sunburst, and the crowned portcullis —all these being badges used by Henry VII. The form of the dragon should be carefully noted. As here depicted it may be taken to be the oldest and best form. The shape of the head and tail and of the claws has not gained artistically in later developments.

A. C. F-D.

PLATE CII

ARMORIAL BEARINGS BY GERMAN ARTISTS

(Second half of the Sixteenth Century)

Fig. 1. Coat of arms of the year 1579. The bearer of the arms and the artist are alike unknown. The mantling and helmet are peculiarly graceful.

Figs. 2 and 3. Imaginary arms by *Virgil Solis.* Virgil Solis, painter and copperplate engraver, was born at Nürnberg 1514, and died there on August 1, 1562. He was a very prolific artist, executing much heraldic work of noticeable beauty.

Figs. 4 and 5. *"Germania"* and *"Hungern"* (Hungary) from the *Wap-*

pare the crest in Fig. 1035). Mantling gules and argent. In both these achievements the escutcheon is surrounded by the collar of the Order of the Golden Fleece.

Fig. 6. Arms of " *Erasmvs Rauchschnabel* " (1562), by *Virgil Solis.* The arms are : Gules, issuing from a crown or, a demi-wild man proper, the face showing the beak (*schnabel*) of a bird in place of the nose and mouth, crowned also or, and carrying a club over his dexter shoulder. The helmet, which has a mantling of gules and or, bears the same figure as the crest. As supporters : dexter, a wild man ; and sinister, a wild woman proper.

Fig. 7. Arms of *Bernhard Wurmser von Schafftolsheim*, drawn by *Tobias Stimmer.* (Taken from the second part of the book *Liber practicar. observationum H. Hartmanni ab Eppingen*, printed by Thom. Gwarin, Basel, 1570.) Tobias Stimmer, painter and designer, was born at Schaffhausen 1534, and died at Strasburg in the last years of the sixteenth century. The shield is party per fess sable and or, in chief two crescents argent. The helmet, which has a mantling of sable and or, bears for crest, out of a coronet or, a maiden's body, crowned with a like coronet, habited with the device as in the arms, and in place of her arms two buffalo's horns erect or. The original coat of arms (granted to Bernhard Wormser of Strasburg by the Emperor Friedrich IV., Rome, April 8, 1452) shows the maiden dressed in black only. The *Schaddtolsheim* line became extinct in 1643.

Fig. 8. Arms of *Duke Ulrich II. of Mecklenburg*, 1552, drawn by *Lucas Cranach* the younger (properly " Muller," born at Wittenberg 1515, died there 1586), a pupil of his celebrated father, *Lucas Cranach* the elder. The shield is quartered, and charged with an inescutcheon. The inescutcheon shows the arms of the *Countship of Schwerin*, and is here party per fess or and gules (properly, gules and or). The arms are : Quarterly, 1. or, a bull's head sable, crowned or, with the skin of the neck erased, and in the nose a nose-ring argent (for the *Dukedom of Mecklenburg*) ; 2. azure, a griffin segreant or (for the *Lordship of Rostock*) ; 3. gules, a woman's arm argent, a cloth tied round it of the same and floating, the hand holding up a gem-ring or, set with a diamond (for the *Lordship of Stargard*) ; 4. or, a bull's head caboshed in bend sable, crowned or (for the *Principality of Wend*, Lordship of Werle). The shield is surmounted by three crowned helmets ; the centre one shows the crest of the Duchy of Mecklenburg, viz. a fan of peacock's feathers behind five pointed pales respectively sable, gules, or, azure, and argent, and within the pales a bull's head sable fesswise. Mantling sable and or. (Compare Plate XXII. Fig. 19.) The helmet on the dexter side bears the Schwerin crest—two buffalo's horns party per fess or and gules. Mantling gules and or. The helmet on the sinister side carries the Rostock crest, namely : two wings respectively or and azure. Mantling azure and or. H. S.

THE ART OF HERALDRY

PLATE CIII

SPECIMENS OF ARMORIAL PAINTINGS IN THE SIXTEENTH CENTURY

(Taken from an old Collection in the Adelsarchives at Vienna)

The "Adelsarchiv" in the office of the Royal and Imperial Minister for the Interior contain two volumes of a collection, in which projected armorial designs from old Government documents no longer in existence have been cut out and pasted. The first volume, entitled *Wappenbuch I.*, 39 cm. wide by 41 cm. high, and containing 335 pages, consists of paintings of the sixteenth century. The coats of arms are those submitted for approval, and the remarks annexed to the proposed arms emanate from the most widely different sources. They appertained in most cases to bourgeois people, who received only a simple *Wappenbrief ohne Nobilitation* (*i.e.* grant of arms without nobility), and as such were *Wappenbürger*. Consequently we find that the projected crowns on the helmets, animals' heads, &c., were mercilessly vetoed by the censor.

Fig. 1. *Hendelmayr* (page 175): Party per pale gules and or, a grey-bearded demi-man issuing from the base, and crowned with red roses, habited and the collar and cuffs counterchanged of the field, resting the sinister hand on his hip and holding in the dexter a pair of stag's attires proper. The helmet has a mantling or and gules on the dexter side, counterchanged on the sinister. The crest is a demi-man as in the arms, issuing from a wreath gules and or, "Hannss Hendelmayr Burg von Krainburg ussen landt." "Allowed 18th Jan. Ao. 61" ("Hans Hendelmayr, burger of Krainburg").

Fig. 2. *Geroldt* (page 44): Or, standing on a rock in base argent, a white-bearded wild man proper habited round the waist by a band also or, the ends flowing therefrom or and sable, the head adorned with three cock's feathers, the outer ones sable, the interior one or, holding in bend sinister, points downwards, a three-pronged iron fork or trident, the shaft also or. The helmet in this case is crowned, and has a mantling of sable and or. Crest: a demi-man holding a trident in bend all as in the arms. "Balthaser Gerolt, des Raths vnd Pawmaist munchen pith vndthenigst vmt diss Wapp vnd Klainat mit dem Leh." (Lehen) "ist bewilliget mit der Cron vnd lechenarticl zuo Prag den 3 januarii Anno 58." ("Balthasar Geroldt, Councillor and master builder at Münich, begs humbly for this coat of arms and crest, with the investiture." "Is allowed, with the crown and articles of investiture, at Prague the 3rd January 1558.")

Fig. 3. *Degier* (page 89): Party per fess sable and or, in chief a demi-lion issuant of the second, holding in his dexter paw an iron, Dietrich (pick-lock) and in base, over three mounds sable, issuant from the base a falcon volant proper. Mantling sable and or. Crest: on a wreath or and sable, a demi-lion as in the arms. "Ist bewilliget sampt der Cron vnd lechenartikel zuo Prag den letzten Dece'bris '58." "Is allowed, together with the crown and the appurtenances, at Prague the last of December '58." "Sol ain Cron gestelt werd." "Dietrich Degier sambt dem Lehenartiel" ("A crown shall be added. Dietrich [pick-lock] Degier, together with the appurtenances" [or investiture ?].)

This man, who reproduced his baptismal name of Dietrich in a "canting" form in his arms, also had the helmet crown "allowed" to him, although he, judging from the coat of arms drawn up, had not thought of it.

Fig. 4. *Leublin* (page 172): Per fess sable and or, over all, and standing upon three mounds in base vert, a lion rampant counterchanged, holding in the dexter paw a linden slip of three leaves vert. Mantling sable and or. Crest: on a wreath or and sable, a demi-lion rampant or, holding a slip of linden-leaves as in the arms. "Jacob leublin Gerichtschreiber zu Memmingen pittet vndthenigist Im vnd seinen prueder Georg dises Wapp Gmain zuverleih,"—"14ten Dec. Ao. 67." ("James Leublin, Clerk of the Court of Memmingen, begs humbly that this coat of arms may be granted to him and his brother George in common. 14th Dec. 1567.")

Fig. 5. *Khuen* (page 296): Party per pale gules and argent, a double rose counterchanged, seeded or. Mantling and wreath gules and argent. Crest: a pair of wings displayed, the dexter per bend and the sinister per bend sinister gules and argent, each charged with a rose as in the arms. "Georg Khuen ain Landtman in Tyrol" —"ist bewilligt den 8 Januarii Ao. 46 Zu Wien" ("George Khuon, a countryman in Tyrol"—"is allowed the 8th January 1546 at Vienna").

Fig. 6. *Mittbürger* (page 176): Gules, on a base vert, a town-gate open and provided with a portcullis, flanked by two round towers battlemented argent, and on each a cupola purpure. On the battlements above the gateway a stork's nest, and therein a stork and two young ones proper, the stork holding in its beak gules a snake, also purpure. Mantling gules and argent. Crest: the stork and nest as in the arms. "Hannss Mittbürger, Bürger zu Morspurg, bitt Allervndterthenigst vmb diss Wapen vnd Klainot.—One lehen." "Bewilligt 11. July '65" ("Hans Mittbürger, Bürger of Morspurg,

begs most humbly for this coat of arms and crest—without appurtenances."—"Allowed July 11, '65").

The stork on the town door is in a measure "Mittbürger" (coburgher) of the town.

Fig. 1041. *Trautwein* (page 321): Azure, a bunch of grapes or. Mantling azure and or. Crest: out of a crown or, a woman's body

FIG. 1041.—Trautwein.

without arms proper, vested azure, the dress cut very low, and adorned with a gold border, crined also or, and about the head a riband also azure. (Height, 13 cm.) "Hainrichen Trautweins von houen Schofens zu Hagenaw vnderthenigst bitt ist Inre obbemelt sein alt wappen mit der Cron zu verbessern sambt ainen Adelsbrieff zu vertigen"—"bewilligt die bösserung der chron sambt der Nobilitation, doch ausserhalb des Thurnirhelms" ("Heinrich Trautwein of hohen Schofen at Hagenau begs humbly to augment his old arms with the crown and a letter of nobility."—"Allowed the augmentation of the crown, and the grant of the nobility in addition to the tilting-helmet.")   H. S.

PLATE CIV

EXAMPLES FROM JOST AMMAN'S "WAPPEN- UND STAMMBUCH"

(1579 *and* 1589)

Jost (Jobst, Jodoc, Justu-) Amman (Amann, Aman), who was born at Zürich 1539, and died at Nürnberg in March 1591, in which town he had been occupied since 1560, was one of the most prolific artists of the second half of the sixteenth century. He was a master in the designing of helmet mantlings. The *Wapen- vnd Stammbuch darinnen der Keys. Maiests. Chur vnd Fürsten Graffen Freyherrn deren vom Adel, &c.* (Book of Arms and Genealogy, in it His Imperial Majesty [Electors and Princes] Counts [Barons] those of noble rank, &c.) was published by Sigmund Feyrabend, Frankfurt a. M., 1579 and 1589. F. Warnecke republished the work in phototype in 1877, and Georg Hirth the same in 1881 in his *Liebhaber-Bibliothek alter Illustratoren.* In Figs. 1, 4, 6, and 7 the supporters, which Amman so lavishly added to most of the arms, have been ignored.

Fig. 1. "*Die Greyffen*": Azure, a griffin segreant or, resting its dexter claw on an inescutcheon gules. Crest: on a wreath azure and or, a demi-griffin or. Mantling azure and or.

Fig. 2. "*Die Haller von Hallerstein*" (Nürnberg family): Quarterly, 1 and 4, party per point issuing from the dexter side of the escutcheon gules and sable, a chevron fesswise issuing from the dexter side argent; 2 and 3, per fess gules and argent, in chief a point reversed of the last, and in base a lion passant sable. The escutcheon is surmounted by two helmets, the mantling of the dexter being gules and argent, and the sinister gules and or. The dexter crest is: issuing from a coronet a demi-negress proper, habited in gules, the hair bound with a plait also gules and with a band argent, all between two buffalo's horns gules, and issuing from each a peacock's feather. The sinister crest is: on a wreath gules and or, a stag's attire on the dexter side, and on the sinister side a wing as the field of the arms (*i.e.* of the second and third quarterings).

Fig. 3. "*Die Ritter*" (Rieter, Nürnberg family): Quarterly, 1 and 4, per fess sable and or, a crowned melusine (*i.e.* a mermaid with two tails) proper, habited gules; 2 and 3, party per pale or and gules, a fleur-de-lis counterchanged, over all on an inescutcheon argent, a calf's head caboshed azure. The escutcheon is surmounted by two helmets, the dexter mantling being argent and gules, the sinister being gules and or. The dexter crest is: on a coronet a crowned melusine as in the arms; and the sinister crest is two wings displayed, each charged with the arms (*i.e.* the second quartering) continued directly into the red and gold mantling. (See Plate LXVIII. Fig. 7.)

Fig. 4. "*D. Gremp*" (Gremp of Freudenstein): Gules, from three mounds issuing in base vert a swan rising or, holding in its beak a gem-ring or, set with a stone azure. Crest: on a coronet a swan rising and issuant as in the arms.

Fig. 4. "*Die Rideseln*" (Riedesel of Eisenbach): Or, an ass's head sable, holding in its mouth three thistle-leaves vert. Crest: a pair of wings expanded sable, continuing into the mantling of sable and or, each wing charged with an escutcheon of the arms.

Fig. 6. "*Monesse*": Bendy of six gules and or, a dexter quarter azure charged with a pigeon rising argent. Crest: on a wreath gules and or, a pigeon as in the arms between two buffalo's horns, the dexter gules, the sinister or.

Fig. 7. "*Die im Hoff*" (Imhof): Gules, a sea-lion passant or, armed and langued azure, the tail erected in arch. Mantling gules and or. Crest: a sea-lion as in the arms.

Fig. 8. "*Die Stainheymer*" (Steinheimer of Frankfurt-on-the-Main): Party per fess or and argent, in chief a demi-eagle displayed sable, and in base three mounds issuing in base charged with a bar wavy, and from the summits of each mound a clover-leaf issuing vert. Mantling sable and or. Crest: on a wreath sable and or, between two buffalo's horns per fess, the dexter or and sable and the sinister sable and or, and issuing from the orifice of each a clover-leaf vert, three mounds vert, charged with a bar wavy, and issuing from the centre mount a clover-leaf or trefoil, also vert.

In the *Wappen-und Stammbuch* appears also the Imperial coat of arms, with the inscription over it, " Römische Keyserliche Maiestet " (Fig. :042). It shows, within two branches of laurel, the double eagle

with the nimbus, surmounted by the Imperial crown, and bearing a crowned " breast-shield " (*i.e.* on its breast an escutcheon) charged with the inescutcheon of Austria. The breast-shield shows the arms of Hungary, Bohemia, Castile, and Leon, as also Old Burgundy, Tyrol, and Flanders. H. S.

PLATE CV

EXAMPLES FROM JOST AMMAN'S "WAPPEN-UND STAMMBUCH"

(1579 *and* 1589 : *with other Armorial Designs by the same Master*)

Fig. 1. " *Die Stallberger* " (Stallburger, a Frankfurt family): Azure, three escallops argent. Mantling azure and argent. Crest: two wings displayed, each charged with the arms.

Fig. 2. "*Die Martorff*" (Martorf, a Frankfurt family): Party per fess argent and azure, in chief a lion passant guardant gules, in base a

bend wavy of the first. Crest: out of a coronet between two wings argent, each charged with a fleur-de-lis gules, a demi-lion affronté gules. Mantling gules and argent.

Fig. 3. "*Die Neuwhassen*" (Neuenhaus, a Frankfurt family): Argent, a chevron gules, terminating in a cross patté between three lozenges sable. (In the German blazon these are described as three black dice, placed on the points.) Mantling argent and gules. Crest: two wings displayed, each charged with the arms.

Fig. 4. "*Die von Hessenburg*" (Hessberg, a Franconian family): Party per pale argent and gules, on the dexter side three roses in pale gules, seeded or, and on the sinister as many bars argent. Crest: a bearded demi-man proper without arms, habited gules, the habit continuing into the mantling, with two reed-mace (bulrushes) issuing from his head. (This crest is also occasionally met with having black ass's ears.)

Fig. 1043 is also taken from the *Wappen- und Stammbuch*, and

shows within a cartouche, surmounted by a beautifully designed crown, the arms of Bohemia, viz.: Gules, a lion rampant double-queued argent, armed and crowned or. This concludes the specimens taken from this book.

Fig. 5. Arms of the *Dr. jur.* (Doctor of Laws) *Nikolaus Reussner*, Rector and Professor of the University of Lauingen. (From P. Ovidii Metamorphosis, hg. v. (*i.e.* published by) Gerardium Lorichium, Frankfurt-on-Main, 1581 : Party per pale, the dexter side argent, on three mounds in base vert a lion rampant gules (according to Siebmacher's Book of Arms, the lion holds a star in the dexter paw); the sinister sable two bends or. Mantling: on the dexter side gules and argent; on the sinister, sable and or. Crest: issuant from a coronet a demi-lion gules, holding in its dexter paw a six-pointed star (or ?). Two swans gorged with coronets serve as supporters.

Fig. 6. Arms of the *Bishop of Augsburg, Johann Egenolph von Knöringen* (1573–1575), designed in the year 1573. Arms: quarterly, 1 and 4, party per pale gules and argent (Bishopric of Augsburg); 2 and 3, sable, an annulet argent (Knöringen). The escutcheon is surmounted by three helmets. The centre one bears on a cushion the episcopal mitre with the head of a crosier issuing from it; the dexter helmet, which has a mantling of gules and argent, is surmounted by a coronet out of which issues a lozenge-shaped escutcheon party per pale of the Augsburg colours (*i.e.* gules and argent), adorned along its edges with peacock's feathers. The sinister helmet, which has a mantling sable and argent, bears the crest of the Knöringens, viz.: on a cushion an annulet argent, surmounted by a coronet or, from which issues a plume of ostrich feathers sable. The crown and the ostrich feathers were an augmentation by the Roman king Rupert of the Palatinate, dated "Heidelberg off den sampsstag vor unsers Herren lichnamstag" (on the Saturday before our Lord's Corpus Christi Day, 29th May 1404). In the four corners of the engraving the arms of the bishop's grandparents are introduced, viz. in the dexter upper corner Knöringen as already blazoned; in the dexter lower corner Schwendi: Azure, a fess or, between in chief and base three lozenges conjoined argent; in the sinister upper corner Westerstetten: Per fess, the chief per pale argent and gules, the base azure; and in the sinister lower Freiberg von Eisenberg: Per fess argent and azure, in base three bezants. The connection is explained by the following table:

Ulrich von Knöringen =		Wolf von Westerstetten =
Susanna von Schwendi.		Catharina von Freiberg.
Ulrich von Knöringen	=	Anna von Westerstetten.
	Johann Egenolph von Knöringen.	H. S.

THE ART OF HERALDRY

PLATE CVI

EXAMPLES FROM THE "ARCHITECTVRA" OF WENDEL DIETTERLIN

(End of the Sixteenth Century)

Wendel Dietterlin (or Dietterlein), born at Strassburg in 1550, was an architect, but was at the same time a painter, goldsmith, and engraver, and enjoyed a great repute on account of his brilliant imagination and the versatility of his accomplishments. He died in his native town in 1599. The heraldic decorations (25 cm. high by 18 broad) drawn by him in his book *Architectvra vnd Ausstheilung der V Seúlen* show the early and quaint style of his work, which is specially remarkable for the unduly exaggerated freedom of the supporters which he embodied in his designs. If the artist occasionally allowed himself to be led away by his too luxuriant imagination into grotesque designs, at any rate, despite all his failings, they are evidence of the great and original genius the possession of which cannot be denied to him. Considered from a purely heraldic standpoint his compositions are, however, both interesting and instructive. The connection between arms and architecture is nearly always happily introduced, everything has life, movement, and action, though occasionally perhaps too much exuberance ; but none of the examples of his work result in being either weak or wearisome. One cannot help regretting that in Fig. 1 the shield has been merged into a mere architectural device, and that the pose of the two lions in Fig. 3 is quite too theatrical for armorial use ; but Fig. 2, on the other hand, is a very successful piece of work, and the arrangement of the three helmets in Fig. 4 is very cleverly carried out, in a manner worthy of imitation. Karl Klimsoh, in his Collection of Designs, *Die Ornamentik* (Ornamentation), book vi. (publishers, Klimsoh & Co., Frankfurt-on-Main), gives a heraldic

FIG. 1044.—Armorial design by K. Klimsoh.

composition (Fig. 1044) drawn exactly in Dietterlin's manner, only the artist might quite easily have avoided the unnatural position of the lion's feet standing on the floating ends of the mantling.

H. S.

PLATE CVII

SPECIMENS OF ARMORIAL PAINTINGS OF THE SIXTEENTH AND SEVENTEENTH CENTURIES

(Taken from an old Collection in a Volume in the Adelsarchives in Vienna)

The arms here given are taken from an old book (*Wappenbuch II.*) in the possession of the Adelsarchiv (Nobility Archives) in Vienna. These armorial paintings are pasted in the book (16 cm. wide by 20 high), and belong chiefly to the seventeenth century, but they show no critical remarks, as is the case with the arms in

Wappenbuch I. Here and there, however, dates of patents are noted, such, for instance, as will be found on the arms of *Herkomber* (Fig. 4).

Fig. 1. *Heldt* (folio 61): Azure, a demi wild man, couped and crined or, the face proper, his sinister hand resting on his hip, and the dexter brandishing a club proper. The helmet, which is barred and has a mantling of azure and or, bears as crest a demi-man as in the arms, but the figure is continued into the mantling. The Helds were an old burgher family (mentioned as early as 1322) of Strassburg. Magistrate Abraham Held, who was born 1524, was magistrate at Strassburg after 1569, and died 25th September 1594, received on the 25th January 1581 the rank of nobility from the Emperor, with an armorial augmentation.

Fig. 2. *Faber* (folio 50): Argent, on three mounds issuing in base vert, a negro proper, a cloth gules bound round his head, flowing therefrom and entwining itself round his body, holding in his dexter hand a hammer-shaped branch of wood or, and in his left a clover-leaf slipped vert, his dexter foot entwined by a serpent proper. The tilting-helmet has a curious mantling and wreath. The former is sable, lined with or on the dexter side, and gules lined with argent on the sinister. The wreath accords with the tinctures of the mantling, and is of six coils, respectively sable, or, sable argent, gules and argent. The crest is a demi-negro as in the arms.

Fig. 3. *Schaff* (folio 141): Sable, an increscent and a decrescent interlaced argent. The tilting-helmet has a mantling of sable lined argent. Crest : a demi-wolf sable continuing into the mantling, on his shoulders a cowl, also sable, and carrying in the hood thereof three geese argent, beaked gules, the heads looking backwards.

Fig. 4. *Herkomber* (folio 72): Quarterly, 1 and 4, sable, on a mount vert, a mastiff passant argent, collared gules ; 2 and 3, argent, a chess-rook sable. (See Plate X. Fig. 71.) The helmet, which is affronté, with grills and a mantling sable and argent, bears as crest, on a wreath argent and sable, between two buffalo's horns per fess sable and argent, a chess-rook as in the arms, in front of and supported by a demi-mastiff affronté argent, collared gules, rimmed and studded or. Near the coat of arms is the date, " Regensberg, 25th June 1641."

Fig. 5. *Reitmohr* (folio 150): Or, a stag salient gules, on its back a negro à cheval proper, crowned and girdled or, grasping the attires of the stag. (*Reitmohr—reit* = ride ; and *mohr* = moor.) The helmet and crest, as in the two next coats of arms, were not shown. The Reitmohrs (originally Reitmaier) were ennobled in 1588.

Fig. 6. *Rotta* (folio 142): Or, a double-headed eagle displayed sable, the head in a nimbus argent, and superimposed thereupon in the second and third quarters of the escutcheon dimidiating the above coat the coat following, viz.: Azure, a wheel of six spokes argent. The crest, which is not reproduced here because of the decidedly sketchy treatment of the mantling in the original, is a demi-lion argent with three heads gules, each crowned or.

Fig. 7. *Bruner* (folio 2): Or, a bear rampant sable, holding in its fore-paws a battle-axe proper, with a long handle sable.

Fig. 8. *Knoblacher* (folio 140) : Per fess or and sable, two leeks in saltire proper, roots downwards, surmounted by a leek in pale root upwards, all proper, and over all an inescutcheon argent, charged with a cross patée gules. The tilting-helmet is crowned, and the mantling is, on the dexter side sable and or, and on the sinister gules and argent. The crest is, between two wings displayed, the dexter per fess gules and argent, and the sinister per fess or and sable, three leeks disposed as in the arms, and charged with a cross patée gules. (*Garlic* = Knoblauch.)

H. S.

PLATE CVIII

HERALDIC WOOD-CARVINGS IN THE POSSESSION OF THE AUSTRIAN IMPERIAL FAMILY

Contained in the second group of the Art Historical Collection of the Austrian Imperial Family are thirty-four wood models in the style of the German Renaissance, amongst them twenty-six with lozenge-shaped fields for the arms — Bohemia, Burgau, Burgundy, Castile Cilly, Dalmatia, Alsace, Görz, Granada, Hoch- und Deutschmeister des Deutschen Ritterordens (Grand Master of the Teutonic Order), Carinthia, Carniola, Kyburg, Moravia, Austria above and below the Enns), Pfyrt, Portenau, Swabia, Servia, Sicily, Slavonia, Styria, Tyrol, Hungary, Windische Mark (Wend Territory)—63 cm. high and 53 cm. broad. Unfortunately it is not definitely known for what purpose or place they were originally destined, but it has been conjectured that these models were intended for printing or stamping tapestry. In the inventory of the collection at Schloss Ambras, near Innsbruck, the first intimation of their existence occurs in 1730. The models, according to Dr. A. Ilg, who published them in 1878 by order of the Lord High Chamberlain, were made by the engraver Andreas Spängler, who worked in the first quarter of the seventeenth century. The person who commissioned him was certainly the Archduke Maximilian III., Governor of Tyrol and Grand Master of the Teutonic Order, because the arms of the Grand Master are to be found amongst the models. The models, therefore, originated sometime between the years 1602 and 1618. The figures on the plate show the following coats of arms, the blazonings of which we here append :—

Fig. 1. *Dukedom of Swabia :* Or, three lions passant in pale sable.

Fig. 2. *Kingdom of Bohemia :* Gules, a lion rampant double-queued argent, crowned, armed, and langued or.

Fig. 3. *County of Tyrol,* raised to the rank of a *Principality :* Argent, an eagle displayed gules. armed and crowned or, with trefoil "buckles" on the wings or.

Fig. 4. *Old Servia :* Gules, a boar's head sable, armed argent, with

SPECIMENS OF LETTERING

The first and second lines show an alphabet of capitals in the style of the fourteenth century, while the third line furnishes Arabic cyphers showing how they had developed in the course of the fourteenth and fifteenth centuries.   H. S.

PLATE CIX

EXAMPLES OF MANTLINGS OF THE SIXTEENTH AND SEVENTEENTH CENTURIES

Figs. 1–10 and 1046 and 1047 are from the hand of the goldsmith, designer, and copperplate engraver, *Theodor de Bry,* who was born at

FIG. 1045.—Arms of the Grand Master of the Teutonic Order.

an arrow of the last in its mouth. Thus in the great State coat of arms of Austria, 1806 and 1836. According to other representations the boar's head appears on an argent field, the arrow with the shaft being gules.

Fig. 1045. *Arms of the Grand Master of the Teutonic Order :* Argent, a cross sable charged with a cross fleuretty or, in the centre a small inescutcheon or, charged with an eagle displayed sable. It would be more correct to substitute a cross potent or (see Plate X. Fig. 31), the crutches charged with demi-fleurs-de-lis. The Grand Masters received the cross potent (Jerusalem cross) from King John of Jerusalem (1219), the lilies from King Louis IX. of France, and the Emperor Frederic II. granted the escutcheon with the eagle, the old arms of the German realm. The drawing of the lion in the Swabian coat of arms, as well as the heraldic rendering of the Servian animal, must be regarded as particularly representative examples ; the boar's head, in particular, being one of the finest heraldic representations known.

Liége 1528. As an adherent of Luther's teachings, he was obliged to leave that town in 1570, and settled at Frankfurt-on-the-Main, where he carried on a book and fine-art repository, dying in 1598.

Figs. 3 and 6, likewise Fig. 1047, are taken from the book *Emblemata Nobilitatis, Stam- vnd Wapenbüchlein* (Frankfurt, 1592). The last-mentioned figure (Fig. 1047) shows a lozenge such as has always been used for ladies' arms in British and Western-European heraldry, and which are nowadays frequently employed in Germany.

Figs. 1, 2, 4, 7–10 are from the book *Emblemata Secularia* (Frankfurt, 1596).

Figs. 11–15 are to be found in the copperplate engraving from the book " *Nieu Wapen Boexken van M. le Blon,* 1649. J. C. Vischer excudit."

Michel le Blon (Blond) was likewise a goldsmith and copperplate-engraver, and also a plenipotentiary of Queen Christine of Sweden in England. He was born at Frankfurt-on-the-Main in

1590 (1587 ?), and died at Amsterdam in 1656. (He bore for arms : Azure, a saltire argent. Crest : a phœnix.)

The designs for arms by Theodor de Bry were copied from the two above-mentioned works in the possession of the Public Library

FIG. 1046.

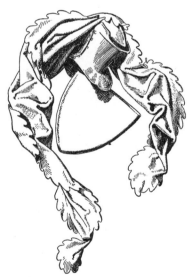

FIG. 1047.

FIG. 1048.—Model in the Late Gothic style of K. Klimsoh.

at Stuttgart, the patterns of Le Blond from single sheets in the possession of the collection of engravings of the k. k. Austrian Museum for Art and Industry in Vienna.   H. S.

PLATE CX

EXAMPLES OF HERALDIC DESIGNS OF THE SEVEN-TEENTH AND EIGHTEENTH CENTURIES

Fig. 1. Arms of the *Marquis J. L. de Beringhen* (Comte de Chateauneuf), Governor of the Citadel of Marseilles : Argent, three pallets gules, a chief azure charged with two roses argent. The shield is surmounted by the coronet of a marquess and a barred

helmet, and thereupon a similar coronet. This helmet shows, presumably as a crest, a pair of wings each charged with the arms. Round the shield are the collars of the Orders of St. Michael and La Saint Esprit. Supporters : two griffins.

Fig. 2. Arms of *Jean Bapt. Colbert* (Marquis de Seignelay), Louis XIV.'s celebrated Minister of Finance (born 1619, died 1683) : Or, a serpent azure. The coronet, helmet, and the collar of the orders are the same as in the last-mentioned arms. The crest, which in this case issues from the coronet, is a demi-unicorn. The supporters are two unicorns. The casket resting on the compartment is a reference to the office of the owner of the arms. Both coats of arms are the work of the French engraver *Sébastien le Clerc,* who was born at Metz in 1637 and died in Paris 1714.

Fig. 1049 shows the arms of *Duke Charles Leopold* of Lorraine (died

FIG. 1049.—Arms of Duke Charles of Lorraine.

1690), and was designed by the same artist. The shield, which is surrounded by the collar of the Order of the Golden Fleece, contains the arms of Lorraine, Hungary, Naples, Jerusalem, Arragon, Anjou, Guelders, Jülich, and Bar, and bears the ducal crown of Lorraine, which may be recognised by the Lorraine cross (compare Plate VII. Fig. 25). Two silver eagles, likewise adorned with the gold cross of Lorraine, act as supporters.

A charming drawing is that given in Fig. 1050, which gives the

FIG. 1050.—Arms of Cardinal Richelieu.

arms of *Cardinal Armand Jean Duplessis*, Duc de Richelieu (born 1585, died 1642), engraved by the French painter *Claude Mellan* (born at Abbeville in 1621, died 1688 in Paris), who was noted for the careful way in which he avoided the use of any crossed lines in his engravings. The arms upon the shield are : Argent, three chevronels gules.

The next engraving (Fig. 1051) represents a German piece of work of the first half of the seventeenth century, the arms of the *Landgrave of Hesse*, as used from 1500 to 1648. On the inescutcheon in the centre are the arms of the Landgraviate of Hesse, here : Azure, a lion rampant double-queued, barry of seven argent and gules, crowned or. The shield itself is quarterly, and shows in the first quarter the arms of the Countship of Katzeneln-bogen : Or, a lion rampant guardant, double-queued gules, crowned azure ; the second quarter shows the arms of the Countship of Ziegenhain : Per fess sable and or, in chief a star of six points argent ; the third quarter contains the arms of the Countship of Nidda : Per fess sable and or, in chief two stars of eight points in fess argent. The fourth quarter has the arms of the Countship of Dietz : Or, two leopards passant double-queued in pale gules. The centre helmet bears the crest of Hesse, viz. : Out of a crown two buffalo's horns argent, adorned with slips of leaves. The dexter helmet, likewise crowned, bears the crest of Katzenelnbogen : A pair of wings sable, each charged with a bezant of the arms. The helmet on the sinister side, which is not crowned, displays the Ziegenhain crest: A demi-he-goat sable, armed and unguled argent, between two wings, each of the arms. The tinctures of the mantlings correspond to those of the respective fields of the quarterings.

Fig. 3 on Plate CX. shows an English piece of work, the arms of

FIG. 1051.—Arms of the Landgrave of Hesse.

Sir Harry Pope Blount of Tittenhanger, Bart., engraved by *G. Vertue*, 1735. The arms are quarterly. 1. *Blount:* Barry nebuly of six or and sable. 2. *Sutton:* Or, a lion rampant double-queued vert, charged on the shoulder with a mullet argent. 3. *Wichard:* Azure, a chevron argent, between three martlets or. 4. *Wase:* Barry of six argent and gules, in the fess point the escutcheon of Ulster as a baronet. The helmet, which is affronté and with an open visor, has for crest, on a ducal coronet or, a wolf statant sable between two horns also or.

The two following coats of arms, Figs. 1052 and 1053, are in the style of a still later period; they afford an illustration of the decadence of heraldic art in England, from which unfortunately it is only now slowly recovering. They are by no means, however, the worst examples which might be found.

Fig. 1052. *Sackvile* (Duke of Dorset), as here depicted: Quarterly gules and argent, a bend vair. (The arms of Sackvile are really: Quarterly or and gules, a bend vair.) The crest as shown is: On a ducal coronet, a star of eight points argent. (The crest should be: Out of a coronet composed of fleurs-de-lis or, an estoile of eight rays argent.) Supporters: two leopards argent.

Fig. 11. *Watson-Wentworth* (Marquess of Rockingham): 1 and 4, argent, on a chevron engrailed azure between three martlets sable, as many crescents or (for Watson); 2 and 3, sable, a chevron between three leopards' faces or (for Wentworth). Crest: a griffin passant argent, armed and ducally gorged or. Supporters: dexter, a griffin argent, armed and ducally gorged or; sinister, a lion or. The griffin, however, is not the crest of the Watson family but that of Wentworth; the supporters are similarly taken from the arms of the Wentworths. The Watsons (Earls of Rockingham) originally used for supporters: Two griffins argent, ducally gorged or, and for crest a griffin's head erased argent, ducally gorged or. The Wentworths (Earls of Strafford), had used for supporters: Dexter, a griffin argent, sinister a lion or; and when the Watson family assumed the additional surname of Wentworth they appear to have adopted the Wentworth crest, and to have modified the supporters.

Fig. 4, Plate CX., shows the arms of *King Louis XV.* of France (1730): Azure, three fleurs-de-lis or. The shield, which is surmounted by the Royal crown of fleurs-de-lis, is surrounded by the collars of the Orders of St. Michael and of the Holy Ghost. This design was prepared for a gold frame for the portrait of the King by Juste Aurèle Meisonnier of Piermont (died 1750), and was engraved by Huquier.

Fig. 5. Arms of *Freiherren von Widmann* (Barons von Widmann),

FIG. 1052.—Arms of Sackville, Duke of Dorset.

originally from the Palatinate-Neuberg. The arms are: Quarterly, 1 and 4, or, a fleur-de-lis azure; 2 and 3, azure, a decrescent or adorned with a human face turned to the centre of the escutcheon. The

FIG. 1053.—Arms of Watson-Wentworth, Marquess of Rockingham.

arms upon the inescutcheon are: Per bend sinister gules and azure, an arm in armour brandishing a sword and issuing from the sinister side within a bordure compony or and sable. These arms, without the inescutcheon, are as borne by the Widmann-Rezzonicos (from Villach in Corinthia).

Fig. 6. Arms of *J. Heinrich Hess* (a member of a Zürich family, their name before 1602 being Schmidth): Per fess sable and argent, a fleur-de-lis counterchanged (*Ex Libris*, from the Collection of Herrn K. E. Graf zu Leiningen-Westerburg). H. S.

CHAPTER XLIV

ECCLESIASTICAL HERALDRY

ECCLESIASTICAL heraldry has nothing like the importance in British armory that it possesses elsewhere. It may be said to consist in this country exclusively of the official arms assigned to and recorded for the archiepiscopal and episcopal sees, and the mitres and crosiers which are added to the shields, and a certain number of ecclesiastical symbols which occur as charges. In Pre-Reformation days there were, of course, the many religious houses which used armorial emblems, but with the suppression of the monasteries these vanished. The cardinal's hat was recognised in former days, and would still be officially certified in England as admittedly correctly displayed above the arms of a Roman cardinal. But the curious and intricate development of other varieties of the ecclesiastical hat which will be found in use in all other European countries is not known to British armory. Nor has the English College of Arms recognised the impersonal arms of the Catholic communities. Those arms, with and without the ecclesiastical hats, play a conspicuous part in Continental heraldry.

It is difficult to assign a proper value or a definite status to the arms of the abbeys and other religious houses in this country in Pre-Reformation times. The principal, in fact the only important sources of information concerning them are the impressions of seals which have come down to us. Many of these seals show the effigies of saints or patrons, some show the impersonal arms of the religious order to whose rule the community conformed, some the personal arms of the official of the moment, others the personal arms of the founder. In other cases arms presumably those of the particular foundation or community occur, but in such cases the variations in design are so marked, and so often we find that two, three, or more devices are used indifferently and indiscriminately, that one is forced to arrive at the conclusion that a large proportion of the devices in use, though armorial in character, had no greater status than a temporary existence as seal designs. They distinctly lack the unchanging continuity one associates with armorial bearings. But whatever their status may once have been, they have now completely passed out of being and may well be allowed to rest in the uncertainty which exists concerning them. The interest attaching to them can never be more than academic in character and limited in extent. The larger abbeys, the abbots of which were anciently summoned to Parliament as Lords of Parliament, appear to have adhered rather more consistently to a fixed device in each case, though the variations of design are very noticeable even in these instances. A list of them will be found in the *Genealogical Magazine* (vol. ii. p. 3).

The suppression of the monasteries in this country was so thorough and so ruthless, that the contemporary instances of abbatical arms remaining to us from which deduction as to armorial rules and precedents can be made are singularly few in number, but it would appear that the abbot impaled the arms of his abbey on the dexter side of his personal arms, and placed his mitre above the shield.

The mitre of an abbot differed from that of a bishop, inasmuch as it had no labels—or *infulæ*—depending from within it. The abbot used a crosier, which doubtless was correctly added to his armorial bearings, but it is found in pale behind the shield, in bend, and also two in saltire, and it is difficult to assert which was the most correct form.

The crosier of an abbot was also represented with the crook at its head curved inwards, the terminal point of the crook being entirely contained within the hook. The point of a bishop's, on the other hand, was turned outwards at the bottom of the crook. The difference is said to typify the distinction between the confined jurisdiction of the abbot—which was limited to the abbey and the community under his charge—and the more open, and wider, jurisdiction of the bishop. Although this distinction has been much disputed as regards its recognition for the actual crosiers employed, there can be no doubt that it is very generally adhered to in heraldic representations, though one hesitates to assert it as an absolute rule. The official arms for the archiepiscopal and episcopal sees are of some interest. With the single exception of York, the archiepiscopal coats of arms all have, in some form or another, the pallium which forms part of an archbishop's vestments or insignia of rank, but it is now very generally recognised and conceded that the pallium is not merely a charge in the official coat for any specified jurisdiction, but is itself the sign of the rank of an archbishop of the same character and status as is the mitre, the pallium being displayed upon a shield as a matter of convenience for artistic representation. This view of the case has been much strengthened by the fact that in ancient instances of the archiepiscopal arms of York the pallium is found, and not the more modern coat of the crown and keys; but whether the pallium is to be still so considered, or whether under English armorial law it must now be merely ranked as a charge in an ordinary coat of arms, in general practice it is accepted as the latter; but it nevertheless remains a point of very considerable interest (which has not yet been elucidated) why the pallium should have been discarded for York, and another coat of arms substituted.

The various coats used by the archbishops of England and Ireland are as follows:—

Canterbury.—Azure, an episcopal staff in pale or, and ensigned with a cross pateé argent surmounted of a pall of the last, charged with four crosses formée fitchée sable, edged and fringed or.

York.—Gules, two keys in saltire argent, in chief a Royal crown or.

Armagh.—Azure, an episcopal staff argent, ensigned with a cross pateé or, surmounted by a pallium of the second, edged and fringed or, charged with four crosses formeé fitcheé sable.

Dublin.—The arms of this archbishopric are the same as those of Armagh, only with five crosses charged on the pallium instead of four.

The arms of the episcopal sees have no attribute at all similar to the charge of the pallium in the coat of an archbishop, and are merely so many different coats of arms. The shield of every bishop and archbishop is surmounted by his mitre, and it is now customary to admit the use of the mitre to all persons holding the title of bishop who are recognised as bishops by the English law.

This, of course, includes Colonial and Suffragan bishops, retired bishops, and bishops of the Episcopal Church in Scotland and in Ireland. It is a moot point whether the bishops of the Episcopal Church in Ireland and in Scotland are entitled to make use of the official arms formerly assigned to their sees at a period when those Churches were State-established; but, looking at the matter from a strictly official point of view, it would not appear that they are any longer entitled to make use of them.

The mitres of an archbishop and of a bishop—in spite of many statements to the contrary—are exactly identical, and the mistaken idea which has of late years (the practice is really quite a modern one) encircled the rim of an archbishop's mitre with the circlet of a coronet is absolutely incorrect.

There are several forms of mitre which, when looked upon as an ecclesiastical ornament, can be said to exist; but from the heraldic point of view only one mitre is recognised, and that is of gold, the labels being of the same colour. The jewelled variety is incorrect in armorial representations, though the science of armory does not appear to have enforced any particular *shape* of mitre.

The "several forms" of the mitre—to which allusion has just been made—refer to the use in actual practice which prevailed in Pre-Reformation England, and still holds amongst Roman Catholic bishops at the present day. These are three in number, *i.e.* the "precious" (*pretiosa*), the gold (*auriferata*), and the simple (*simplex*). The two former are both employed at a Pontifical Mass (being alternately assumed at different parts of the service); the second only is worn at such rites as Confirmation, &c.; while the third (which is purely of white linen) is confined to Services for the Dead, and on Good Friday. As its name implies, the first of these is of cloth of gold, ornamented to a greater or less degree with jewels, while the second—though likewise of cloth of gold—is without any design or ornament. The short Gothic mitre of Norman days has now given place to the modern Roman one, an alteration which, with its great height and arched sides, can hardly perhaps be considered an artistic improvement. Some individual Roman Catholic bishops at the present day, however (in England at any rate), wear mitres more allied to the Norman and Gothic shape.

The past fifteen or so years have seen a revival—though in a purely eclectic and unofficial manner—of the *wearing* of the mitre by Church of England bishops. Where this has been (and is being) done, the older form of mitre has been adhered to, though from the informal and unofficial nature of the revival no rules as to its use have been followed, but only individual choice.

At the recent Coronation, mitres were *not* worn; which they undoubtedly would have been had this revival now alluded to been made authoritatively.

All bishops and archbishops are entitled to place two crosiers in saltire behind their shields. Archbishops of the Roman Catholic Church have continuously placed in pale behind their shields what is known as the archbishop's cross. In actual practice, the cross carried before an archbishop is an ordinary one with one arm, but the heraldic archiepiscopal cross is always represented as a double cross, *i.e.* having two transverse pieces one above the other. In the Established Church of England the archiepiscopal cross—as in the Roman Catholic Church—is the plain two-armed variety, and though the cross is never officially recognised as an armorial attribute and is not very frequently met with in heraldic representations, there can be no doubt that if this cross is used to typify archiepiscopal rank, it should be heraldically represented with the double arms. The actual cross borne before archbishops is termed the provincial cross, and it may be of interest to here state that the Bishops of Rochester are the official cross-bearers to the Archbishops of Canterbury.

To the foregoing rules there is one notable exception, *i.e.* the Bishop of Durham. The Bishopric of Durham until the earlier part of the nineteenth century was a Palatinate, and in earlier times the Bishops of Durham, who had their own parliament and Barons of the Palatinate, exercised a jurisdiction and regality, limited in extent certainly, but little short in fact or effect of the power of the Crown. If ever any ecclesiastic can be correctly said to have enjoyed temporal power, the Bishops of Durham can be so described. The Prince-Bishops of the Continent had no such attributes of regality vested in themselves as were enjoyed by the Bishops of Durham. These were in truth kings within their bishoprics, and even to the

present day—though modern geographies and modern social legislation have divided the bishopric into other divisions—one still hears the term employed of "within" or "without" the bishopric.

The result of this temporal power enjoyed by the Bishops of Durham is seen in their heraldic achievement. In place of the two crosiers in saltire behind the shield, as used by the other bishops, the Bishops of Durham place a sword and a crosier in saltire behind their shield to signify both their temporal and spiritual jurisdiction.

The mitre of the Bishop of Durham is heraldically represented with the rim encircled by a ducal coronet, and it has thereby become usual to speak of the coronetted mitre of the Bishop of Durham; but it should be clearly borne in mind that the coronet formed no part of the actual mitre, and probably no mitre has ever existed in which the rim has been encircled by a coronet. But the Bishops of Durham, by virtue of their temporal status, used a coronet, and by virtue of their ecclesiastical status used a mitre, and the representation of both of these at one and the same time has resulted in the coronet being placed to encircle the rim of the mitre. The result has been that, heraldically, they are now always represented as one and the same article.

It is, of course, from this coronetted mitre of Durham that the wholly inaccurate idea of the existence of coronet on the mitre of an archbishop has originated. Apparently the humility of these Princes of the Church has not been sufficient to prevent their appropriating the peculiar privileges of their ecclesiastical brother of lesser rank.

A crest is never used with a mitre or ecclesiastical hat. Many writers deny the right of any ecclesiastic to a crest. Some deny the right also to use a motto, but this restriction has no general acceptance.

Therefore ecclesiastical heraldry in Britain is summed up in (1) its recognition of the cardinal's hat, (2) the official coats of arms for ecclesiastical purposes, (3) the ensigns of ecclesiastical rank above alluded to, viz. mitre, cross, and crosier.

Ecclesiastical heraldry—notably in connection with the Roman Church—in other countries has, on the contrary, a very important place in armorial matters. In addition to the emblems officially recognised for English heraldry, the ecclesiastical hat is in constant use.

The use of the ecclesiastical hat is very general outside Great Britain, and affords one of the few instances where the rules governing heraldic usages are identical throughout the Continent.

This curious unanimity is the more remarkable because it was not until the seventeenth century that the rather intricate rules concerning the colours of the hats used for different ranks and the number of tassels came into vogue.

Other than the occasional recognition of the cardinal's hat in former days, the only British official instance of the use of the ecclesiastical hat is met with in the case of the very recent matriculation of arms in Lyon Register to Right Rev. Æneas Chisholm, the present Roman Catholic Bishop of Aberdeen. The arms as matriculated to him are reproduced in facsimile on Plate CXII., but I frankly admit I am unaware why the ecclesiastical hat assigned to the bishop has ten tassels on either side. The Continental usage would assign him but six, and English armory has no rules of its own which can be quoted in opposition thereto. Save as an acceptance of Roman regulations (Roman Holy Orders, it should not be forgotten, are recognised by the English Common Law to the extent that a Roman Catholic priest is not re-ordained if he becomes an Anglican clergyman), the heraldic ecclesiastical hat of a bishop has no existence with us, and the Roman regulations would give him but six tassels. The arms as upon the Plate are: "Gules, a boar's head couped, within a bordure engrailed argent, charged with three mitres."

The use of the ecclesiastical hat, though not officially theretofore sanctioned, has however had a certain amount

FIG. 1054.—Bookplate of the Rev. George Angus, Priest in Holy Orders of the Roman Catholic Church: Argent, a lion passant guardant gules, on a chief of the last, two mullets of the field.

of unofficial use, and Fig. 1054, which is a reproduction of a bookplate, affords an example.   A. C. F-D.

The regulations which govern the use of the ecclesiastical hat, &c., outside Great Britain, will be apparent from the examples illustrated on Plates CXI. and CXIII.

The details of the arms therein represented are as follows :—

PLATE CXI

Fig. 1. Arms of *His Holiness* the late *Pope Leo XIII.* (Joachim Pecci), born March 2, 1810, at Carpineto, in the diocese of Anagni; elected on February 20th, crowned March 3, 1878, died July 20, 1903 : Over the shield is suspended the tiara, and behind the shield, in saltire, are the gold and silver keys, to bind and to unloose. (These two keys are frequently attached by a gold cord.)

Fig. 2. Arms of the *Cardinal Cammerlengo* of the Roman Church during the "Sedisvacanz" (vacancy of seat). (From the death of one Pope until his successor ascends the throne, the Holy "Conopœum" (canopy) and the crossed keys appear behind the arms of the cardinal in question.

FIG. 1055.

In Ulrich Reichenthal's *Concilium von Constanz* (Augsburg, 1483) may be found an illustration of the Papal canopy (Fig. 1055),

and it is there remarked : " Nun ist czewissen das man einem bapst so ner überland reiten will ein sölichen Hut vorfürt vñ fürt in ein starker gewappeter man auff einem weissen ross verdeckt mit einem rotten Auch gesprengt mit göld, vnd der ist rot vnd gel . . ." (Now the man is certainly a pope, so he will ride over the country with such a hat carried before him ; a strong man in armour carries it, riding on a white horse covered with a red cloth sprinkled with gold, and the canopy is red and yellow . . .").

Fig. 3. *Cardinals* use a red hat with fifteen tassels on each side. It is seldom actually worn, but has considerable processional and ceremonial use. The red hat was granted to cardinals in 1245 by

FIG. 1056.—From a drawing by Antony of Worms, *c.* 1530 (Peter Quentell's printing office, Cologne). Arms of Cardinal Bernhard von Cless, Bishop of Trient, 1514-1539 : Quarterly, 1 and 4, argent, an eagle displayed sable (for his Bishopric) ; 2 and 3, per pale argent and gules, two lions rampant counterchanged (for Cless).

Pope Innocent IV. All cardinals place it above their arms. If the cardinal is at the same time an archbishop, he places a double-armed cross behind his shield ; if a bishop, a single cross.

Fig. 4. *Patriarchs* use a green hat with fifteen green fiocci (tassels) on each side, the cords and fiocci interwoven with gold. (Edict of the Holy Congr. Ceremo. of November 3, 1826.) This is placed above the shield, and behind appears a double-armed cross. Fig. 4 shows the coat of arms of the Patriarch of Jerusalem, Luigi Piavi. The chief contains the coat of arms of the Franciscan Order, the present Patriarch belonging to that order. The Patriarch of Jerusalem, moreover, as Grand Master of the Order of the Holy Grave of Jerusalem, places his shield on a red cross of Jerusalem. (See Plate X. Fig. 32.)

Fig. 5. *Patriarch and Archbishop of Lisbon.* The Patriarchs of Lisbon bear a special heraldic distinction (granted by Pope Clement XII., 1730-1740). This consists of the Papal tiara placed over their shields. Behind the shield a palm-branch and a branch of laurel are crossed in saltire. On the shield illustrated appear the arms of Cardinal Giuseppe Sebastiano Neto, Patriarch of Lisbon since March 24, 1884. The Patriarch's motto is : " Soli Deo omnis honor et gloria."

Fig. 6. *Archbishops:* Green hat with ten green fiocci on each side. Behind the shield a two-armed cross in pale and a pastoral staff in bend sinister. A bishop's mitre (*mitra*) is placed on the shield at the right. The shield illustrated shows the arms of the Archbishopric of Cologne.

Fig. 7. *Prince-Archbishops.* The prince-archbishops and *prince-bishops* who are still in existence in Austria have no ecclesiastical rank higher than other archbishops or bishops respectively. The rank of prince is a purely temporal rank, which receives expression in the arms by means of the prince's hat and the mantle. The shield illustrated shows the official arms of the Archbishopric of Vienna.

Fig. 8. *Armenian Archbishops* use a green hat with ten green fiocci on each side. They also use the double cross and the Latin and Greek pastoral staves behind the shield, the mitre in the centre, resting on the top of the shield. *Bishops* bear the plain cross in place of the double one. On the shield appear the arms of the titular Archbishop of Salamina, *Arsenius Aïdymion*, Abbot-General of the Armenian Mechitharists. The arms, which are tierced in pairle, show in chief the arms of the *Mechitharists:* Or, a cross botonny azure, the ends charged with four Armenian letters, and in the cantons four emblems, namely : the bell of obedience, the flame of purity, the staff of poverty, and the gospel, referring to the apostolic office of the mission amongst the Armenian nation.

Fig. 9. *Greek Archbishops* (of the Union) use a green hat with ten fiocci on each side, also the double cross and a bishop's crosier in bend sinister. Resting upon the dexter side of the escutcheon is placed the Greek mitre. *Bishops* bear a plain cross. On the shield illustrated are the official arms of the Archbishopric of *Lemberg*, viz. the device of St. George slaying the dragon. The present archbishop and metropolitan, Dr. Sylvester Sembratowicz, is a cardinal, and as such bears the red cardinal's hat. The use of a prince's hat and mantle, which may occasionally be noticed, dates from the time when Poland was still a ruling kingdom, but this is not now authorised, inasmuch as the Archbishop of Lemberg no longer possesses the title of prince.

Fig. 10. *Bishops* (of the Roman Church) wear a green hat with six green fiocci on either side. They use a simple cross in pale and a crosier in bend sinister behind the shield, the mitre resting on the dexter upper edge of the shield. On the shield here given appear the arms of the Bishopric of Mayence. (A prince-bishop bears the prince's hat and mantle, as in Fig. 7.)

Fig. 11. *Archabbots* use a green hat with six green fiocci on either side, a mitre, and crosier. Archabbots possess episcopal rank. On the shield appears the arms of the Archabbacy of *Monte Cassino*, in the province of Caserta, which are identical with the arms of the Benedictine Order.

Fig. 12. Amongst the *Prelates* (of the Papal Chamber) are the Vice-Camerlengo, the Auditor, the Lord Chancellor of the Roman Exchequer, and the Lord High Steward of His Holiness. These dignitaries wear a *violet* hat with ten *red* fiocci on either side, which they are entitled to place above their arms. The Lord Chamberlain also bears the same hat, and possesses, like the Lord High Steward, the right of placing the arms of the Pope in the (honour point) upon his own as soon as he becomes a cardinal. The shield here illustrated shows the arms of the Lord Chamberlain, Mons. Francesco della Volpe: Azure, a fox or, and in chief a count's coronet of the last.

Fig. 13. *Apostolic Protonotaries* are entitled to a violet hat with six red fiocci. His Excellency Count Pettenegg informed Herr Ströhl that the apostolic protonotaries are likewise authorised to bear the Papal arms on their shields. Fig. 13 shows the arms of the Papal House-Prelate, and mitred Provost of the Votive Church at Vienna, *Dr. Gottfried Marschall*. (The arms show the Imperial eagle conjoined with the arms of the Austrian Imperial family, the three crowns being symbolical of the three archdukes, sons of the Archduke Carl Ludwig, whose education was conducted by Dr. Marschall.) Provost Marschall also bears, as a mitred provost, the mitre and crosier.

The arms of His Excellency Count *Dr. E. Gaston Pöttickh von Pettenegg*, Grand Capitulary and Commander, also until 1897 Adviser to the Council, and Director of the Central Chancery of the High Teutonic Order (President of the k. k. "Adler" Heraldic Society in Vienna), shows the shield of the Teutonic Order (Fig. 1057): Argent, a cross sable charged with a shield per pale,

FIG. 1057.

containing on the dexter side the Papal arms, and on the sinister, those of the count. Upon the shield rests the old count's crown, over the whole is suspended the hat of the Apostolic Protonotary.

Fig. 14. *House Prelates, Privy Chamberlains,* and *Privy Chaplains of His Holiness* have a violet hat with six violet fiocci. The shield shows the arms of *Mons. Luigi Francesco Fé d'Ostiani*, House-Prelate since 1873.

Fig. 15. *Honorary Chamberlains* and *Honorary Chaplains of His Holiness* are entitled to a violet hat with three violet fiocci. The shield contains the arms of *Mons. Luigi Coccettí-Vanzi*, Honorary Chamberlain since 1882. The Lauretanian Canons bear the same hat.

Fig. 16. *Generals of Orders* use a black hat with six black tassels. On the shield here illustrated appear the arms of the Cistercian Order, viz.: Azure, semé-de-lis or (France), charged with an inescutcheon bendy of six or and azure, a bordure gules (Old Burgundy). The General of the Order of the Premonstrants uses a hat and cords of white, corresponding to the habit of the Order. (This is an order of regular canons, also called white canons, founded by St. Norbert in 1120, and having their principal abbey at Prémontré, near Laon.)

Fig. 17. *Provincial Superiors of Orders* use a black hat with three black fiocci. The shield given here shows the arms of the Carmelite Order. The *Protonotare titulares* bear the same hat.

Fig. 18. *Mitred Abbots and Provosts* use a black hat with three black fiocci. Behind the shield, the crosier lies diagonally in bend sinister, and above, and on the dexter side of the shield, is the mitre. On the shield figured upon the plate appear the arms of the Benedictine monastery at *Melk* in Lower Austria, viz.: Azure, two keys in saltire or, issuing from the same bow. The keys, the attribute of St. Peter, the first patron of the monastery's church, are to be met with for the first time in the seal of the Abbot Ottokar von Streitwiesen (1324–1329). The arms used in olden times represented silver keys on a sable ground, and only in the eighteenth century did the present tinctures become permanent.

Fig. 19. *Local Superiors* (Prior, Guardian, and Rector) use a black hat with two black tassels. The shield shows the arms of the Order of the Hospitallers (Brothers of Mercy). In Austria, besides the bishops and abbots, the canons of St. Stephen in Vienna are specially entitled to bear arms. They receive a grant of shield, crowned tilting-helmet, and crest, according to their own design, if they are not previously noble.

Fig. 1058 shows the form of arms for an *Abbess*. Behind the

FIG. 1058. FIG. 1059.

shield appears the crosier, upright, with a floating "velum" (veil). The shield contains the arms of the Benedictine convent of *Nonnberg* at Salzburg. About the middle of the present century the bearing of three lilies on the upper field came into use, but these are now no longer employed. As an "abbatia regalis," for Nonnberg, the crosier is held by a crowned angel standing behind the shield.

Fig. 20 shows the arms of the *Bishopric of Durham*. These, and the peculiar mitre of Durham, have been already referred to. Fig. 21. Arms of the *Bishopric of Hereford*. In both these cases the mitres are wrongly depicted. They should be of plain gold, though the designs are admissible.

Fig. 1059, annexed, shows the arms of the *Greek Oriental Archbishops* (not of the Union). The shield is surmounted by the Greek mitre, and behind it are crossed in saltire the Greek crosier and the double cross. The *Bishops* bear a plain cross. On the shield here shown appear the arms of the *Archbishopric of Czernowitz*, viz. the device of St. John of Succowa (a town on the south boundary of Bukowina, the former seat of the Moldavian princes), patron saint of Bukowina, standing on a sabre.

For many of these notes Herr Ströhl was indebted to the kindness of His Reverence Herrn. J. E. Kirchberger, "Propsteikaplan" at the Votive Church, and Librarian of the k. k. "Adler" Heraldic Society in Vienna. H. S.

PLATE CXIII

The examples on Plate CXIII. are as follows:—

Fig. 1. Arms of *Pope Alexander VII.* (1655–1667), from an engraving by *Joseph Testana*, Italian school, eighteenth century. The quartered shield shows: 1 and 4, the arms of the family of *Rovere*, viz.: Azure, a tree (evergreen oak) eradicated or. (This tree in Italian is termed *rovere*, of which the English is "male-oak"); 2 and 3, the arms of the *Chigi* family: gules, six mounds couped in pyramid argent, surmounted by a star of eight points or. *Fabio Chigi*, a Sienese (Pope Alexander VII., elected April 7, 1655), bore in his arms those of the family of *La Rovere* (properly of the Counts Vinovo of Turin), in consequence of a grant of Julian della Rovere, Pope Julius II. (1503–1513), who gave the Rovere arms to Agostino Chigi, whose family has since continued to bear them. The heraldic rendering of the evergreen oak in the arms of Rovere affords an example of one of the most typical forms of Italian heraldry in the fifteenth century. See also Fig. 1060, which is a representation of the coat of arms on a monument over the grave of the Cardinal Bishop of Palestrina, Hieronymus Basso della Rovere, a nephew of Francis della Rovere (Pope Sixtus IV.), who died September 1, 1507. The monument is in the Church of the St. Maria del Popolo in Rome. He united the names and the arms of both families, the arms of Basso being: Per saltire argent and azure.

FIG. 1060.—Arms of Basso della Rovere.

Fig. 2. Arms of *Bishop Christopher of Brixen*, of the family of *Schroffenstein*. From Dr. Joh. Eck's "Commentary on Aristotle," Augsburg, 1520. Drawn by *Hans Burgkmair* the elder. The shield is: Quarterly, 1. the arms of the *Bishopric of Brixen*, viz.: gules, a Paschal lamb regardant argent; 4, the arms of the *Chapter of the Brixen Cathedral*: argent, an eagle displayed gules, armed and crowned or (Tyrol), surmounted by a crosier fesswise or; 2 and 3, the arms of the *Schroffensteins of Tyrol*, viz.: argent, a demi-"bouquetin" rampant sable, distilling blood. (Hans von Schroffenstein received the castle above Landeck in the Inn Valley, and derived his arms from those of the Bishop of Chur zu Lehen. The arms of Chur were: Argent, a bouquetin sable.)

Fig. 3. Arms of the *Prince-Bishop George III. of Bamberg*, of the family of *Schenken von Limburg* (1505-1522). Taken from *Aristotelis Stagyritæ*, by Dr. Joh. Eck, Augsburg, 1520. Drawn by *Hans Burgkmair* the elder. The shield is quartered, and shows in the first and fourth quarters the arms of the *Prince-Bishopric of Bamberg*: or, a lion rampant sable, debruised by a riband argent; 2 and 3, the arms of the *Limburgs*, viz.: 2. per fess dancetté gules and argent (Franconia); 3. azure, five clubs argent (for Limburg).

Fig. 4. Arms of *Cardinal Albrecht von Brandenburg* (Archbishop of Magdeburg and Bishop of Halberstadt 1513, Archbishop of Mayence 1514), with the date 1525. From a woodcut on parchment. This is an exquisite production, but unfortunately by an unknown artist, of Dürer's school. The Brandenburg shield is charged on the fess point with the shields of the Bishoprics of Magdeburg (per fess gules and argent), Mayence (gules, a wheel argent), and Halberstadt (per pale argent and gules).

Fig. 5. Arms of *Hyppolyt Aldobrandini* of Florence, Cardinal, 1585; Pope Clement VIII., 1605, engraved by *Agostino Carracci*, born at Bologna 1558, died at Parma 1601. The coat of arms is: Azure, a bend embattled and counter-embattled between six six-pointed stars in bend, three and three or.

Fig. 6. Arms of the *Redeemer of the World*: This is a curious heraldic fancy rather frequently represented abroad. The steel engraving here reproduced is to be found in a French "Horarium" of 1522. The drawing, however, was certainly done by a German hand. The mantling is one of the best designs of its class to be met with.

The mitre is to be met with as a charge and as a crest, for instance, in the case of Barclay and Barclay-Allardyce [" 1. a naked man from the middle, holding in his dexter hand a scimitar proper (for Allardyce); 2. a bishop's mitre or (for Barclay). Mottoes: 'In defence of the distressed,' 'In cruce spero'"]; and Berkeley ["A mitre gules, labelled and garnished or, charged with a chevron between ten crosses patée, six and four argent. Motto: 'Dieu avec nous'"]; and also in the case of Sir Edmund Hardinge, Bart., whose crests are curious [" 1. of honourable augmentation, a hand fesswise couped above the wrist habited in naval uniform, holding a sword erect, surmounting a Dutch and a French flag in saltire, on the former inscribed "Atalanta," on the latter "Piedmontaise," the blade of the sword passing through a wreath of laurel near the point and a little below through another of cypress, with the motto, 'Postera laude recens;' 2. a mitre gules, charged with a chevron argent, fimbriated or, thereon three escallops sable."]

The cross can hardly be termed exclusively ecclesiastical, but a curious figure of this nature is to be met with in the arms recently granted to the Borough of Southwark (Fig. 1062). It was undoubtedly taken from the device used in Southwark before its incorporation, though as there were many bodies who adopted it in that neighbourhood, it is difficult to assign it to a specific origin.

Pastoral staves and passion-nails are elsewhere referred to, and the figures of saints and ecclesiastics are mentioned in the chapter on "The Human Figure."

The emblems of the saints, which appear to have received a certain amount of official recognition—both ecclesiastical and heraldic—supply the origin of many

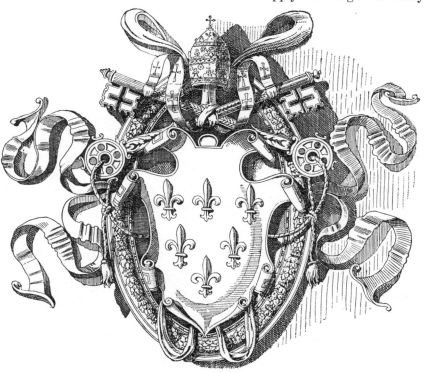

FIG. 1061.—Arms of Pope Paul III. (Alex. Farnese), from a design by Antonio de Sangallo (1482-1546): Or, six fleurs-de-lis azure.

other charges not in themselves heraldic. An instance of this kind will be found in the sword of St. Paul, which

3 K

figures on the shield of London. The cross of St. Cuthbert, which has been adopted in the unauthorised coat for the See of Newcastle-on-Tyne, and the keys of St.

Henry III., Edward I., and Edward II. The quartering for France was introduced by Edward III., as explained on page 200, and the Royal shield, as shown in Fig. 295,

FIG. 1062.—Arms of Southwark : Quarterly argent and azure, a cross quarterly gules and of the first ; between a rose of the third, barbed and seeded proper, in the first quarter a lily also of the first, slipped proper ; in the second quarter an annulet ensigned with a cross patée and interlaced with a saltire conjoined in base all or, in the third quarter ; and a stag's head caboshed also of the third in the fourth quarter.

Peter, which figure in many ecclesiastical coats, are other examples. The lilies of the Virgin are, of course, constantly to be met with in the form of fleurs-de-lis and natural flowers ; and the list might be extended indefinitely. H. S. AND A. C. F-D.

CHAPTER XLV

ARMS OF DOMINION AND SOVEREIGNTY : PLATES CXIV. AND CXV.

ROYAL arms in many respects differ from ordinary armorial bearings, and it should be carefully borne in mind that they stand, not for any particular area of land, but for the intangible sovereignty vested in the rulers thereof. They are not necessarily, nor are they in fact, hereditary. They pass by conquest. A dynastic change which introduces new sovereignties introduces new quarterings, as when the Hanoverian dynasty came to the throne of this country the quartering of Hanover was introduced, but purely personal arms in British heraldry are never introduced. The personal arms of Tudor and Stewart were never added to the Royal Arms of this country.

The origin of the English Royal Arms was dealt with on page 121. "Gules, three lions passant guardant in pale or," as the arms of England, were used by Kings John,

was in use in the reigns of Edward III., Richard II. (who, however, impaled his arms with those of St. Edward the Confessor), and Henry IV. The last-mentioned king about 1411 reduced the number of fleurs-de-lis to *three*, and the shield remained without further change till the end of the reign of Edward VI. Queen Mary did not alter the arms of this country, but during the time of her marriage with Philip of Spain they were always borne impaled with the arms of Spain. Queen Elizabeth bore the same shield as her predecessors. But when James I. came to the throne the arms were : " Quarterly, 1 and 4, quarterly, i. and iiii. France, ii. and iii. England ; 2. Scotland (or, a lion rampant within a double tressure flory and counterflory gules) ; 3. Ireland (azure, a harp or, stringed argent)." The shield was so borne by James I., Charles I., Charles II., and James II.

When William III. and Mary came to the throne an inescutcheon of the arms of Nassau (" Azure, billetty and a lion rampant or ") was superimposed upon the Royal Arms as previously borne, for William III., and he impaled the same coat without the inescutcheon for his wife. At her death the impalement was dropped. After the union with Scotland in 1707 the arms of England (" Gules, three lions," &c.) were *impaled* with those of Scotland (the tressure not being continued down the palar line), and the impaled coat of England and Scotland was placed in the first and fourth quarters, France in the second, Ireland in the third.

At the accession of George I. the arms of Hanover were introduced in the fourth quarter. These were: "Tierced in pairle reversed, 1. Brunswick, gules, two lions passant guardant in pale or; 2. Luneberg, or, semé of hearts gules, a lion rampant azure; 3. (in point), Westphalia, gules, a horse courant argent, and on an inescutcheon (over the fourth quarter) gules, the crown of Charlemagne (as Arch Treasurer of the Holy Roman Empire).

At the union with Ireland in 1801 the opportunity was taken to revise the Royal Arms, and those of France were then discontinued. The escutcheon decided upon at that date was: "Quarterly, 1 and 4, England; 2. Scotland; 3. Ireland with Hanover upon an inescutcheon." This inescutcheon was surmounted by the Electoral cap, for which a crown was substituted later when Hanover became a kingdom.

At the death of William IV., by the operation of the Salic Law, the crowns of England and Hanover were separated, and the inescutcheon of Hanover disappeared from the Royal Arms of this country, and by Royal Warrant issued at the beginning of the reign of Queen Victoria the Royal Arms and badges were declared to be as they are shown on Plate CXIV. The necessary alteration of the cyphers are the only alterations made by his present Majesty.

The supporters date from the accession of James I. Before that date there had been much variety. Some of the Royal badges have been already alluded to in the chapter on that subject.

The differences used by various junior members of the Royal Family will be found in the chapter on Marks of Cadency.

The arms of some other countries, and also some territorial arms, are illustrated on Plate CXV., and are as follows:—

Fig. 1. Arms of the *German Empire.* The German Imperial eagle sable, armed gules, bearing upon its breast the escutcheon of *Prussia*, namely: argent, an eagle displayed sable, &c., which is again charged with the shield of Hohenzollern, namely: quarterly argent and sable. The escutcheon of Prussia is surrounded by the collar of the "High Order of the Black Eagle." Above the head of the German eagle is placed the German Imperial crown (compare Plate LII. Fig. 2). The final official confirmation of this escutcheon was given August 3, 1871. (See Ströhl's, *Deutsche Wappenrolle*, 1897).

Fig. 2. Arms of the *Kingdom of Greece.* The escutcheon has the following arms, viz.: Azure, a cross couped argent (for the Kingdom of Greece), charged with the inescutcheon of the reigning dynasty. (Prince George of Holstein-Glucksburg, second son of the successor to the Danish throne, ascended the Hellenic throne March 30, 1863, as Georgios I.) This inescutcheon is quarterly, namely: or, three lions passant azure, crowned, and between nine hearts gules (Denmark); 2. or, two lions passant azure (Schleswig); 3. gules, the so-called "nettle-leaf" (Holstein); 4. gules, a horse's head couped or (Lauenburg). Superimposed upon the escutcheon is another inescutcheon party per pale: dexter, or, two bars gules (for Oldenburg); sinister, azure, a cross or (for Delmenhorst). The shield of Greece, which is surmounted by the Royal crown of that country, is surrounded by the white-edged blue ribbon of the *Erlöscrordens* (Order of the Redeemer). Supporters: on either side a figure of Hercules, standing on a compartment and holding a club in the exterior hand. Under Otto of Bavaria, 1832 to 1862, the supporters were on either side a lion crowned or. The whole is beneath a pavilion azure, lined ermine, which, bordered with silver tracery, bears a dome, semé of small crosses couped argent, and surmounted by the Royal crown.

Fig. 3. Arms of the *Grand Duchy of Luxemburg.* Argent, five bars azure, a lion rampant double-queued gules, crowned or, charged upon the breast of the lion with an escutcheon of the arms of *Nassau.* (The ruling dynasty since December 8, 1890, being of the House of Nassau, viz.: azure, billetté and a lion rampant or, armed and crowned gules.) A literal translation of the German blazon would make the field barry of eleven argent and azure. The shield is surmounted by the Grand-Ducal crown and surrounded by the green and orange-striped ribbon of the Order of the Oak-crown. The supporters are two lions or, each crowned with the Grand-Ducal crown and standing on a gold compartment. The whole of the foregoing is within a crimson pavilion lined with ermine, the canopy surmounted with the Grand-Ducal crown.

Fig. 4. Arms of the *Kingdom of Ireland*: Azure, a harp or, stringed argent. The crest: on a wreath of the colours, a tower triple-towered or, and from the gateway a stag springing argent, attired and unguled or.

Fig. 5. Arms of the *Swedish District of Gestrikland*, belonging to Gefleborg-Lan: Argent, semé of hurts, a reindeer proper. The shield is surmounted by a Swedish Ducal crown.

Fig. 6. Arms of the *Duchy of Salzburg*: Party per pale, dexter, or, a lion rampant sable; sinister, gules, a fess argent. The shield is surmounted by an old Ducal cap of the form now claimed as a Prince's cap. The old archbishopric (since January 1, 1850, forming an independent crown land) has borne since the time of Archbishop Aberchard II. (1200-1246) the Hohenstauff and Austrian armorial bearings combined in its shield.

Fig. 7. Arms of the *Hungarian Komitates Pozsony* (Pressburg): Azure, a demi-wheel or, issuing from behind three mounds in base vert, and thereupon a demi-stag salient proper. The shield is surmounted by a coronet. The device is taken from the arms of the Palffys (properly Bakocz), to whom the castle of Pressburg was presented by the Emperor Rudolph II. in 1599, and who enjoyed the dignity of Principal Count Palatine, by hereditary right. The Palffys bear the stag or.

Fig. 8. Arms of the *Spanish province of Jaen* (Andalusia): Quarterly or and gules, within a border compony of the arms of *Leon* (argent, a lion rampant purpure, crowned or), and of *Castile* (gules, a castle or, the port azure). The escutcheon is surmounted by an arched crown, containing the cap.

Fig. 9. Arms of the *Swiss Canton of Uri*: Or, a bull's head caboshed sable, langued and ringed through the nostrils gules. The device is met with for the first time—but in this case with the head turned to the sinister—on a seal of the year 1249. The outstretched tongue occurs for the first time on a seal of the year 1489. The old banners of Uri show the same device.

Fig. 10. Arms used by the *English county of Hampshire*: Per fess argent and gules, three roses counterchanged, seeded or. These are in reality the arms of the town of Southampton.

Fig. 11. Arms of the *Russian Government of Tiflis* (Transcaucasus): Or, on a cross sable, between four lions' heads erased gules, eyed and langued of the second, a Russian cross (botonny and with double arms) grasped by two naked arms, couped argent, the cross charged in base with a crescent reversed of the last. (This device is to typify the victory of the Greek Church over the crescent.) Upon the shield rests the crown of the Tsar, the labels (*i.e.* the ribbons issuing from the crown) azure. On either side of the escutcheon is an oak branch or, conjoined in saltire, below the escutcheon and intertwined with the blue ribbon of the Order of St. Andrew.

Fig. 12. Arms of the *Russian territory of Uralsk* (General Governorship of Kirkisensteppe in Central Asia): Vert, three mountains argent, rising out of water in base azure. From the centre mountain issues a Hetmann's staff (Bulawa) or, and from each of the exterior mountains issue "horse-tail lances." The water in base is charged with a fish of the second. The shield is surrounded by an ancient Tsar's crown, and is, like Fig. 11, adorned with gold oak-foliage, in this case the branches being intertwined with the dark-red ribbon of the Order of St. Alexander Newsky. Both of these Russian coats of arms were sanctioned on July 5, 1878.

Fig. 13. Arms of the *Empire of Japan.* The Imperial coat of arms is composed of a heraldically conventionalised chrysanthemum. The petals, which are sixteen in number, are of gold, edged with silver, and connected with each other at the outer edge by "barbs" of a similar design.

Fig. 14. Arms of the *Empire of Corea* (Ko-rai or Teô-sen): A blue and a red snake, intertwined and confined within a circle. The red snake typifies the male, and the blue the female idea or principle, in other words, Heaven and Earth.

Fig. 15. Arms of the *Kingdom of Siam.* These partake somewhat of a European character, but are hardly capable of a European blazon throughout. The gold-edged shield is tierced in pairle, the partition lines being of gold. The upper field is of *yellow* and on a gold pedestal three white elephants in a group, adorned with gold. In base, on the dexter side, gules, an elephant passant argent, the trappings or; on the sinister side, *pink*, two daggers (Kris) in saltire. At the sides of the shield are two Royal umbrellas, with seven red-lined canopies (? of seven degrees) supported by two Siamese dragons. At the base of the umbrellas appear the golden Royal shoes. Round the shield is entwined the collar of the "Holy Order," or the "Order of the New Gem," and of the Family Order of "Chülah Chaum Klow," the ornament of which hangs down over the gold-edged blue compartment. Over the shield is suspended the Royal crown, the point of which is surrounded by a circle of rays, and from both sides of which a pink ribbon flutters. The white mantle, richly embroidered with gold, is tied to two sceptres which are in saltire behind the shield and round which the motto-ribbon is entwined at the base.

Fig. 16. Arms of the former *South African Republic* (Transvaal). The arms, which were enclosed in a golden cartouche, were: Party per fess in chief per pale, the dexter side gules, on a mount vert, a lion couchant to the sinister or ; the sinister side, azure, on a mount a Boer habited all proper, wearing a bandolier and carrying in his sinister hand a rifle ; the base vert, on a mount proper, a transport waggon or ; over all on an inescutcheon argent an anchor cabled proper. On the cartouche, behind which the "vieurkleur" (green, red, white, and blue) flags of the country are crossed in a trophy, is perched an eagle with outstretched wings proper. The white motto-ribbon, which is twisted round two spades, bears in gold letters the inscription : "Eendract Maakt Magt." From the heraldic point of view it cannot be regretted that such a coat of arms no longer exists.

Fig. 17. Arms of the *State of Maine* (United States of North America). The "Pine-tree State" bears on its shield a wapiti-deer resting before a pine-tree, all in natural colours upon a landscape background. Supporters : dexter, a reaper with a scythe ; and sinister, a seaman with a sextant, both habited proper. Above, from behind the shield, arises a crimson motto-ribbon with the device "Dirigo" in letters of gold, over which is suspended a five-rayed golden star within a circle of rays. At the base of the shield, on the natural compartment on which the supporters stand, lies a blue ribbon inscribed with the name of the State in gold letters. The name was given to the country in 1635 in honour of the Queen Henrietta Maria, Consort of Charles I., and daughter of Henry IV. of France, Duchess of Maine. Since 1820 Maine has been a separate State.

Fig. 18. Arms of the *United Republic of Brazil* (Estados Unidos de Brazil). The arms of the State, converted into a Republic in the year 1889, shows a star surrounded by golden rays. The five points of the star are fimbriated throughout with gules and or, and each ray of the star is party of vert and or, *i.e.* of the national colours. The star is charged with a circular disc of azure, the disc being surrounded by a gilt-edged blue border, containing twenty silver stars for the twenty provinces. Within this border, likewise on a blue ground, appears the constellation of the "Southern Cross." Under the star are placed a branch of the coffee-plant and one of the tobacco-plant, arranged in orle, and over these, but behind the star, a sword in pale proper, pommel and hilt or, the hilt surmounted by a blue ribbon, which bears in gold letters the name of the confederated State and the date of its establishment.

Other territorial or sovereign arms occur in the present volume, viz. : The Earldom of Chester, Fig. 514 ; the County of Shropshire, Fig. 309 ; the Province of Brandenburg, Fig. 404 ; the Republic of Porto Rico, Fig. 589 ; and the Duchy of Saxe-Altenburg, Fig. 836.

H. S. AND A. C. F-D.

CHAPTER XLVI

EXAMPLES OF THE ARMS OF TOWNS : PLATES CXVI., CXVII., AND CXVIII.

PLATES CXVI. and CXVII. represent the arms of some number of the most important towns in these countries. It should be noted that the arms of a town belong to the mayor, aldermen, and burgesses of the town for the time being. The official blazons are as follows. :—

London (city of): Argent, a cross gules, in the first quarter a sword in pale point upwards of the last. Crest : a dragon's sinister wing argent, charged with a cross gules. Supporters : on either side a dragon with wings elevated and endorsed argent, and charged on the wing with a cross gules. Motto : "Domine dirige nos."

Birmingham (Warwickshire): Quarterly, 1 and 4, azure, a bend of five lozenges or ; 2 and 3, per pale indented of the last and gules, over all a fess ermine, thereon a mural crown of the second ; and for the crest, on a wreath of the colours, a mural crown, issuant therefrom a dexter arm embowed, the hand holding a hammer all proper, together with the motto, "Forward." Supporters : on the dexter side a man habited as a smith (representing industry) holding in the dexter hand a hammer resting on an anvil all proper ; and on the sinister side a female figure (representing Art) proper, vested argent, wreathed round the temples with laurel vert, tied by a riband gules, holding in the dexter hand resting on the shield a book bound also gules, and in the sinister a painter's palette or, with two brushes proper.

Manchester (Lancashire): Gules, three bendlets enhanced or, a chief argent, thereon on waves of the sea a ship under sail proper ; and for the crest, upon a wreath of the colours, a terrestrial globe, semé of bees volant all proper. Supporters : on the dexter side an heraldic antelope argent, attired, collared, and chain reflexed over the back or ; and on the sinister side a lion guardant or, murally crowned gules, each charged on the shoulder with a rose of the last. Motto : "Concilio et labore."

Liverpool (Lancashire) : Argent, a cormorant, in the beak a branch of seaweed called laver all proper ; and for the crest, on a wreath of the colours, a cormorant, the wings elevated, in the beak a branch of laver proper. Supporters : the dexter, Neptune, with

his sea-green mantle flowing, the waist wreathed with laver, on his head an Eastern crown gold, in the right hand his trident sable, the left supporting a banner of the arms of Liverpool ; on the sinister a Triton, wreathed as the dexter and blowing his shell, the right hand supporting a banner, thereon a ship under sail in prospective all proper, the banner staves or. Motto : "Deus nobis hæc otia fecit."

Newcastle-upon-Tyne (Northumberland) : Gules, three towers triple-towered argent. Crest : on a wreath of the colours, a tower argent, therefrom issuant a demi-lion rampant guardant or, holding a flagstaff sable, therefrom flowing a split banner of St. George. Supporters : on either side a sea-horse argent, crined and finned or. Motto : "Fortiter defendit triumphans."

Edinburgh : Argent, a castle triple-towered and embattled sable, masoned of the first and topped with three fans gules, windows and portcullis shut of the last, situate on a rock proper. On the wreath is set for crest, an anchor wreathed about with a cable all proper. Motto : "Nisi Dominus frustra." Supported on the dexter by a woman, richly attired, with her hair hanging down over her shoulders ; and on the sinister by a doe proper.

Glasgow : Argent, on a mount in base vert an oak-tree proper, the stem at the base thereof surmounted by a salmon on its back also proper, with a signet-ring in its mouth or, on the top of the tree a redbreast, and in the sinister fess point an ancient handbell, both also proper. Crest : the half-length figure of St. Kentigern affronté, vested and mitred, his right hand raised in the act of benediction, and having in his left hand a crosier all proper. Supporters : two salmon proper, each holding in its mouth a signet-ring or, and in an escroll entwined with the compartment this motto, "Let Glasgow flourish."

Leeds (Yorkshire) : Azure, a fleece or, on a chief sable three mullets argent. Crest : an owl argent ; and supporters, on either side an owl argent, ducally crowned or.

Sheffield (Yorkshire) : Per fess azure and vert, in chief eight arrows in saltire banded argent, and in base three garbs or. Crest : upon a wreath of the colours, a lion rampant argent, collared gemel azure, thereon eight arrows as in the arms. Supporters : on the dexter side a figure habited as Thor, resting his exterior hand on a hammer all proper ; and on the sinister side a figure habited as Vulcan standing in front of an anvil, and in the dexter hand a pair of pincers all also proper. Motto : "Deo adjuvante labor proficit."

Bristol (Gloucestershire) : Gules, on the sinister side a castle with two towers domed all argent, on each dome a banner charged with the cross of St. George, the castle on a mount vert, the dexter base water proper, thereon a ship of three masts or, sailing from a port in the dexter tower, her fore and main masts being visible sable, the rigging of the last, and on each round-top of the fifth, on the fore-mast a sail set, and on the main-mast a sail furled of the second. Crest : upon a wreath of the colours, two arms embowed and interlaced in saltire issuing from clouds, the dexter hand holding a snake all proper, and the sinister holding a pair of scales or. Supporters : on either side, on a mount vert, a unicorn sejant or, armed, maned, and unguled sable. Motto : "Virtute et industria."

Other town arms will be found throughout the present volume, as follows : Warrington (Fig. 51), Inverness (Fig. 239), Marylebone (Fig. 240), Dover (Fig. 241), Abergavenny (Fig. 348), Biberach (Fig. 378), Schweidnitz (Fig. 386), Oldham (Fig. 450), Bermondsey (Fig. 522), Eccles (Fig. 528), Wolverhampton (Fig. 533a), Ealing (Fig. 545), Leigh (Fig. 556), Pudsey (Fig. 557), Todmorden (Fig. 573), Camberwell (Fig. 575), Oban (Fig. 580), Alloa (Fig. 581), Wandsworth (Fig. 582), Blackpool (Fig. 584), Kensington (Fig. 593), Islington (Fig. 602), Hammersmith (Fig. 607), Swindon (Fig. 608), Hove (Fig. 610), Dukinfield (Fig. 782), Dublin (Fig. 787), Arbroath (Fig. 807), Nürnberg (Fig. 817), Calcutta (Fig. 818), Cape Town (Fig. 820), Tangermünde (Fig. 838), Southwark (Fig. 1062).

The arms on Plate CXVIII. are as follows :—

Fig. 1. *Amsterdam* (old form, Amstelledamme = Dam on the Amstell), the capital, but not (Royal) residential, town of the Kingdom of Holland : Gules, on a pale sable, three saltires couped. (Since 1508 the shield has been surmounted by the Roman-German Imperial crown, in accordance with the patent granted by the Roman king Maximilian I., February 11, 1489.) Supporters : two lions guardant or.

Fig. 2. *Oxford* (England) : Argent, an ox gules, passing over a ford of water in base barry wavy azure and argent. Crest : on a wreath of the colours, a demi-lion rampant guardant azure, crowned with an Imperial crown, holding between the paws a rose gules, charged with another argent. Supporters : on the dexter side an elephant ermine, eared, collared, and lined argent, and on the sinister side a beaver vert, its tail azure and argent, ducally gorged and lined or. Motto : "Fortis est veritas."

Fig. 3. *Brussels* (province of Brabant), capital and (Royal) residential town of Belgium : Gules, St. Michael or, overthrowing the devil sable. Upon the escutcheon is placed a coronet of pearls and behind the shield, which is supported by two lions or, standing on a natural compartment vert, two lances in saltire or, on each a flag fringed of the last, the dexter charged with the arms of *Brabant* (sable, a lion rampant or), and the sinister with the same arms of *Brussels*.

Fig. 4. *Schaffhausen* (principal town of the canton of Schaffhausen, Switzerland) : Or, on a mount in base vert, a city gateway issuing from the sinister side of the escutcheon argent, and therefrom a ram springing sable, horned and crowned or. In the first seal of the town (*c*. 1275) the ram is not springing, but standing, and is without the crown. After the Austrian rule was shaken off, the ram is found depicted springing, so appearing on an "Urfehde" (solemn oath not to take vengeance) of the year 1415, but it is not unlikely the change is one resulting merely from artistic licence. The crowning of the animal followed in 1512, in which year Pope Julius II. presented banners to the Confederates for services rendered, and attested various augmentations upon them to the animals on the shields. The arms of the canton show the ram only.

Fig. 5. *Le Havre* ("chef-lieu d'arrondissement" in the French department of Nieder-Seine) : Gules, a salamander argent, crowned and in golden flames, a chief of France (*i.e.* azure, three fleurs-de-lis or). The chief, with the Royal lilies, is to be found in the arms of most of the French towns ; but the salamander was the badge of Francis I., who founded the town in 1517.

Fig. 6. *Murlo* (province of Siena, Tuscany) : Gules, on a mount in base vert a castle argent, and on either side thereof a mouse climbing proper. The castle bears a reference to the former feudal possession of the Bishops of Siena ; the mice probably have some connection with the name of the place. Old books of arms show the two mice, but in later times these, without any authority, have been superseded by two fierce lions which appear to have taken their place.

Fig. 7. *Sorbano* (province of Florence) : Or, a mountain ash-tree (*sorbus*) proper, fructed gules, issuing from a mount in base vert, supported by two lions, the dexter vert and the sinister gules (the charges of the families of Ordelaffi and Ubertini) ; over all, on a chief argent, a fleur-de-lis gules (from the arms of Florence).

FIG. 1063.—Crest of the Town of Leipzig.

Fig. 8. *Leipzig* (kingdom of Saxony) : Party per pale, the dexter side or, a lion rampant sable (the arms of *Margrave von Meissen*) ; the sinister side or, two pallets azure (the family arms of *Wettmer*, assumed by the district of Landsberg). Crest : a conical hat striped in broad vertical bands of or and azure, and adorned in front with a plume of three ostrich feathers, the centre one azure, the exterior ones or, inserted behind the turned-up brim. Fig. 1063 gives the side view of this crest. Mantling azure and or.

Fig. 9. *Hannover* (the capital and former Royal residence of the kingdom of Hanover, now the capital of the Prussian province of Hannover) : Gules, upon a battlemented wall surmounted by two towers argent, a lion passant or, armed and langued azure. In the open portway of the wall below the raised portcullis an inescutcheon or, charged with a clover-leaf vert, the point of the leaf turned towards the base, seeded and veined also or. The crest is : upon a wreath gules and or, between two buffalo's horns, the dexter per fess gules and or, the sinister counterchanged, a clover-leaf as in the arms. Mantling gules and or. (Two gold lions are used as supporters.) In the oldest seals of the town (1266) the wall is found, together with the Brunswick lion, but without the clover-leaf, which is met with for the first time in the seal of 1534. But on coins the clover-leaf may be found as early as the first half of the fourteenth century.

Fig. 10. *Caslav* (Czaslau), a town in East Bohemia : Gules, a battlemented town-wall argent, the port ouvert. Behind the wall rise three battlemented towers, and issuing from each of the exterior towers a watchman, habited in azure, with black hat and feathers, blowing a horn or. In the centre chief point is an inescutcheon of the arms of the Kingdom of Bohemia. Upon the shield rests a mural coronet, which will be found on a seal of the town as early as 1532. The arms were granted to the town by King Wladislaw II., May 22, 1472.

Fig. 11. *Maros Vasarhely*, a Royal free town in the Hungarian Komitate (Countship) Maros-Torda (Transylvania) : Azure, an arm in armour embowed fesswise and couped at the shoulder, brandishing a sword on which are impaled the heart gules and the head erased sable of a bear. This peculiar device is taken from the old escutcheon of the Szekler-Nation, which above the bear's heart also shows a golden crown. The shield is surmounted by a golden crown.

Fig. 12. *Bombay*, capital of the Presidency of Bombay : Azure, three ships under sail lateen-rigged proper, a chief or, thereon a lion passant guardant gules, between two pallets sable, each charged with an ostrich feather erect argent ; and for a crest, upon a wreath of the colours, a lion passant guardant gules, crowned with an Eastern crown gold, supporting with the dexter forepaw an escutcheon or, charged with a sprig of the cotton-tree slipped and fructed proper. Supporters : on the dexter side a lion or, and on the sinister side a leopard proper, each gorged with an Eastern crown, and pendent therefrom an escutcheon azure, charged with a mullet argent. Motto : "Urbs prima in India."

FIG. 1064.—Arms of Breslau.
(From a drawing by Jost Amman.)

Fig. 1064 shows the arms of *Breslau*, the capital of the Prussian province of Silesia : Quarterly, 1. Bohemia ; 2. Silesia ; 3. or, a W sable (Wratislavia) ; 4. Gules, issuing from a reversed coronet, the bust of St. John the Evangelist (supposed to have been originally the bust of St. Dorothea) ; and over all the symbol of St. John the Baptist, viz. the head proper in a charger argent. Crest : between two flags barry of gules and argent, and issuing from a coronet, the bust of St. John the Evangelist. Mantling gules and argent. (Granted in 1530.)

FIG. 1065.—Arms of Augsburg.
(From a drawing by Jost Amman, 1566.)

An interesting and much-discussed heraldic figure is borne by the town of *Augsburg* (the ancient *Augusta Vindelicorum*) on its shield : Party per pale gules and silver (arms of the Bishopric of Augsburg), on the capital of a pillar or, a pine-cone (or a cembra nut) vert, also termed by some a bunch of grapes (Fig. 1065). The so-called "Stadtpyr" of Augsburg appears as early as the beginning of the fourteenth century on the seals of the town, and probably owed its origin to some excavated decorative figure from a Roman grave. The pine-cones, with their many seed-pods, were to the Romans a symbol of the inexhaustible abundance in the life of nature, and were frequently employed, in their grave-monuments especially.

These arms of Cologne ["Argent, on a chief gules, three crowns or"] will be found on Plate CXXIV. (refer to page 231).

A. C. F-D. AND H. S.

THE ART OF HERALDRY

CHAPTER XLVII

COATS OF ARMS OF SOCIETIES AND CORPORATIONS: PLATES CXIX. TO CXXV.

INTERESTING as the arms of such bodies always are, and curious and strange as is the heraldry to be deduced therefrom, the arms comprised in this category largely lack value to the heraldic student from the fact that so large a proportion are mere arms of adventure. The result is that their weird perversions of heraldic law, and their strange menagerie of charges, are but too often the perpetuation of the ignorance of their original inventors. As to this chapter particularly, I would repeat that I cannot guarantee that any particular coat of arms which follows possesses the requisite authority. Those where the date of grant is appended are of course authoritative, as are some others.

The arms on Plate CXIX. are as follows:—

Carpenters' Company, London (granted 6 Edward VI.): Argent, a chevron engrailed between three pairs of compasses extended sable.

Masons' Company, London (granted 12 Edward IV.): Sable, on a chevron engrailed between three quadrilateral castles argent, a pair of compasses extended of the field. Crest: a castle as in the arms.

Marblers, Gateshead: Gules, a chevron between two chipping axes in chief argent, and a mallet in base or. Crest: an arm embowed, vested azure, cuffed argent, holding in the hand proper an engraving chisel or.

Freemasons, Gateshead: Sable, on a chevron argent, between three towers or, a pair of compasses extended azure. Crest: a tower with a cupola or.

The arms on Plate CXXI. are as follows:—

Drapers' Company, London. Arms: Azure, three clouds proper, radiated in base or, each surmounted with a triple crown or, caps gules. Crest: a mount vert, thereon a ram couchant or, attired sable. Supporters: two lions argent, pelletté. Motto: "Unto God only be honour and glory."

Goldsmiths' Company, London. Arms: Quarterly gules and azure, in the first and fourth a leopard's head or; in the second and third a covered cup, and in chief two round buckles, the tongues fesswise, points to the dexter, all of the third. Crest: a demi-lady, her arms extended proper, issuing out of clouds of the last, vested gules, garnished or, cuffed argent, round her neck a ruff of the last; in her dexter hand a pair of scales of the third, in her sinister hand a touchstone sable. Supporters: two unicorns or, armed, crined, and hoofed argent. Motto: "Justitia virtutum regina." Another motto occasionally used by the Company was: "To God only be all glory." [*Note.*—The crest is vested in the dress of the reign of Elizabeth.]

Institute of Chartered Accountants. Arms: Argent, on a mount in base, in front of a rudder in bend sinister, a female figure proper, representing "Economy," habited gules, mantled azure, about the temples a wreath of olive, in the dexter hand a rod, and in the sinister a pair of compasses also proper; a chief of the second, thereon a balance suspended also or. Motto: "Recte numerare."

The Bank of Scotland (granted 1701): Azure, a saltire argent between four bezants.

The Mercers' Company (confirmed by St. George, *Richmond Herald*, 1634). Arms: Gules, a demi-virgin couped below the shoulders, issuing from clouds all proper, vested or, crowned with an Eastern crown of the last, her hair dishevelled, and wreathed round the temples with roses of the second, all within an orle of clouds proper. Motto: "Honor Deo."

The arms on Plate CXXIII. are as follows:—

The Trinity House. Arms: Azure, a cross gules, between four ships of three masts, each under full sail all proper, on each sail, pennant, and ensign a cross gules, and each quarter representing a sea-piece. Crest: a demi-lion rampant guardant and regally crowned or, holding in the dexter paw a sword erect argent, hilted and pommelled of the first. Motto: "Trinitas in unitate."

The Stationers' Company. Arms: Azure, on a chevron or, between three Bibles lying fesswise gules, garnished, leaved, and clasped of the second (clasps downwards), an eagle rising proper, enclosed by two roses gules, seeded or, barbed vert, from the top of the chief a demi-circle of glory edged with clouds proper, therein a dove displayed argent, over the head a circle of the last. Motto: "Verbum domini manet in æternum."

The Central London Railway (granted February 25, 1898). Arms: Argent, on a cross gules, voided of the field, between two wings in

chief sable and as many daggers erect in base of the second, in the fess point a morion winged of the third, on a chief also of the second, a pale of the first, thereon eight arrows saltirewise, banded also of the third, between, on the dexter side three bendlets enhanced, and on the sinister a fleur-de-lis or. Crest: a representation of the front of a locomotive engine proper, between two wings or. Motto: "Forward."

The Fishmongers' Company. Arms: Azure, three dolphins naiant in pale argent, finned and ducally crowned or, between two pairs of lucies in saltire (the sinister surmounting the dexter) proper, over the nose of each lucy a ducal crown of the third, on a chief gules three ducal pairs of keys endorsed in saltire or. Crest: two cubit arms erect, the dexter vested or, the sinister azure, both cuffed argent, holding in the hands proper a regal crown of the last. Supporters: dexter, a merman proper, on his head a helmet, the body only covered in armour, in his dexter hand a sabre, all of the first; sinister, a mermaid proper, crined or, in her sinister hand a mirror of the last. Motto: "All worship be to God only."

The North Borneo Company. Arms: Azure, in base on waves of the sea a native boat of North Borneo with sails, manned and oars in action proper, a chief or, thereon a lion passant guardant gules. Crest: two arms embowed, that on the dexter side being the arm of a native of North Borneo proper; that on the sinister being an arm vested azure, cuffed argent, the hand grasping a staff proper, thereon hoisted a flag flowing to the sinister or, charged with a lion guardant gules.

The Carpenters' Company. Arms: Argent, a chevron engrailed between three pairs of compasses expanded at the points sable.

Cutlers' Company of Sheffield. Arms: Argent, on a fess indented vert, between three pairs of swords in saltire proper, pommels and hilts, sable, eight arrows interlaced saltirewise, banded of the field, between two garbs or. Crest: in front of an elephant's head couped or, two swords in saltire as in the arms.

The grant depicted on Plate CXX. is the coat of

Tallow Chandlers' Company. Arms: Per fess azure and argent, a pale counterchanged, three doves of the last, each holding in the beak an olive branch or. Crests (both the following are used, but really No. 2 was substituted for No. 1): 1. a demi-angel issuing from clouds proper, vested azure, wings expanded or, crined of the last, on his head a cap, thereon a cross patée of the third, holding a dish argent, glorified or, thereon the head of St. John Baptist proper; 2. a dish argent, glorified proper, thereon the head of St. John Baptist proper. Supporters: two angels proper, vested gold, crined and ducally crowned or, the coronet surmounted with an estoile of the last, each standing on a mount vert. Mottoes: "Ecce Agnus Dei, qui tollit peccata mundi"; "Quæ arguuntur, a lumine manifestantur." (See Plate CXXXII. Fig. 2.)

Plates CXXIV. and CXXV. show some interesting variations of the arms adopted by different masonic lodges and kindred bodies, which, however, all sufficiently explain themselves.

The arms illustrated on Plate CXXII. are as follows:—

Fig. 1. Arms of the *Shoemakers' Guild* at Winterthur (Canton Zürich), 1583: Gules, above a pointed shoe sable, a draw-knife argent, the handle or.

Fig. 2. Arms of the *Bakers' Guild* at Liége: Azure, between two rolls a saw-blade in pale point downwards or. (The Bakers' Guild in Brussels also bore a saw in their arms, presumably as a sign of their right to cut anything, even wood. It is to be hoped that it was not indicative of the difficulty in dealing with the bread they baked.)

Fig. 3. Arms of the *Furriers' Guild* at Bâle: Gules, a bend composed of three rows of *Kürsch*.

Fig. 4. Arms of the *Fishermen's Guild* in the Jurisdiction of *Benfeld* (Alsace-Lorraine), seventeenth century: Azure, an oar in pale or, surmounted by two fish in saltire heads downwards argent.

Fig. 5. Arms of the *Printers' Guild*: Or, the double-headed eagle of the Roman-German Realm sable, the heads each within a nimbus, armed gules, holding in its dexter claw a leaf-holder, and in its sinister a composing-stick. The helmet, which is crowned, and has a mantling of gules and argent, has for crest a demi-griffin argent, armed gules, holding in its claws two printing-balls, one above the other, the heads conjoined. This coat of arms was not granted by the Emperor Friedrich III., as has been hitherto universally stated, but in the course of the sixteenth, seventeenth, and eighteenth centuries gradually developed itself into its present form. (For fuller details refer to Ströhl's *Wappen der Buchgewerbe*, Vienna, 1891.)

Fig. 6. Seal of the *Guild of Coppersmiths* of Vienna. This shows a copper kettle held by two griffins standing on a mount. The legend is: "Der Bvrgerlichen Kvpferschmit. Sigill in der Key res. stat. Wien." 1650.

Fig. 7. The seal of the *Guild of Blacksmiths* of Vienna. This shows, below the Imperial double eagle, a richly foliated and ornamented cartouche, bearing as a charge a horse leaping over a horseshoe. The legend is: "Sigill deren. Burgh. Hvef-Schmiden. in. Wienn." (On a document from the Burgher Master Blacksmiths of Vienna to the Master of Pulkau, 19th October 1751.)

Fig. 8. Arms of the *Cheesemongers' Guild* at Ghent: Gules, above a cheese-knife proper, the handle or, a pair of scales of the last, the weighing slabs argent, and in chief two circular cheeses proper.

Fig. 9. Arms of the *Gardeners' Guild* at Strassburg, seventeenth century : Argent, a bend gules (arms of Strassburg) between two roses of the last, seeded or, barbed, leaved, and slipped vert.

Fig. 10. Arms of the *Painters* : Gules, three inescutcheons argent. The helmet, which is crowned, and has a mantling of gules and argent, bears as crest a demi-maiden proper, richly habited per pale gules and argent, between two fallow-deer's palmated attires proper. The three shields as charges were the "canting" sign of the old-shieldworkers, by whom the pageant and battle-shields were made. In Germany the field was originally gules, in France and in the Netherlands azure, the escutcheons being argent and occasionally or. The crest consisted of dragon's wings, stag's antlers, fallow-deer's horns, and the figure was always a feminine one, though very often it is a negress which is placed between the horns. The crest was supposed to be an imitation of the so-called *Lusterweibchen* (figures of women, to hold lamps or lustres ?), which were also made by the shieldworkers. (Details of this coat of arms may be found in F. Warnecke's *Monographie über das Kunstlerwappen*, Berlin, 1887. See also Plate XXVI. Fig. 5.)

Crafts and professions which recent times have produced have of course no guild coats of arms, but the decorator occasionally attempts to symbolise heraldically these modern handicrafts, and two specimens of such symbolical designs are here added. They have not, of course, any authority.

Fig. 11. Device of the *German Gymnasts* : Or, four figures of the letter "F" addorsed in cross sable. This device was proposed at the Swabian Gymnastic Festival at Heilbron on 2nd and 3rd August 1846, by the copperplate engraver Johann Heinrich Felsing (born 1780, died 29th March 1875), of Darmstadt, and was universally adopted as the device. The four F's are taken from a rhyme of the sixteenth century : " Frisch, frei Frohlich und frumb, ist der Studenten Reichtum." " Fresh, free, Joyous, and good, is the realm of the Students."

Fig. 12. Device of the *German School Union* in Austria : Per fess sable and or, a fess gules, in chief a demi-sun in splendour issuant from the fess, and issuant from the base and surmounting the fess an oak-branch vert with two acorns or. This device was designed by Herr Ströhl in 1888. The sun on the black field is intended to denote intellectual enlightenment resulting from the schools, her illuminating rays being poured out over the fruitful oak-branch, typifying the growing German race.

Fig. 13. Device of the *Austrian Leo-Society* : Sable, a lion rampant or, armed gules, charged on the shoulder with an escutcheon of the arms of the Austrian Royal Family (gules, a fess argent), and holding in its forepaws the triple papal silver cross. These armorial bearings of this Catholic Literary Society were also designed by Herr Ströhl in 1892.

Fig. 14. Device of the *Literary Union* of Stuttgart : Party per fess or and azure, in chief a demi-mare issuant sable (half of the arms of Stuttgart), and in base a closed book gules.

Fig. 15. Seal of the *Royal Institute of British Architects* (1834) in London. The mural crown, above the circle, as also the motto ribbon, with the inscription " VSVI CIVIVM DECORI VRBIVM," which occurs below the circle, have been omitted on account of lack of space. The device shows a pillar, supported by two English lions imperially crowned, the shaft of the pillar semé of the badges of England (rose), Scotland (thistle), and Ireland (trefoil). The capital supports the globe and a rudder.

Fig. 16. Seal of the *Society of Antiquaries* in London. This seal shows the shield of St. George, charged in the centre with the Royal crown of England. Over the shield, as crest, is shown a four-armed burning lamp. Motto : " NON EXTINGVETVR." Legend : " Sigillum . Societatis . Antiquariorum . Londinensis." It should be remarked that these arms do not in any way belong to the Society. They were granted as a quartering of augmentation in 1649 by King Charles to Sir Edward Nicholas, secretary to King Charles II., and the Society might well display a better example to students of armory. The crest, of course, is a mere matter of invention. No criticism can be too strong for the dishonest action of the Society of Antiquaries, which purports to be the chief antiquarian authority in this country. The arms used by the assistant secretary and many of the fellows are equally lacking authority.

Fig. 17. Arms of the *University of Cambridge* (1573) : Gules, on a cross ermine, between four lions passant guardant or, a book gules. The *Konqilienbuch* (Council Book) of Constance (1483) shows other armorial bearings for the University, namely : France and England quarterly (the then Royal Arms of England), charged in the centre with a book gules. The arms of the University of Birmingham (Fig. 293) and of the University of Madras (Fig. 308) will also be found herein.

Fig. 18. Arms of *Eton College* (according to the patent of King Henry VI., January 1, 1449) : Sable, three (natural) lilies argent, a chief party per pale azure and gules, charged on the dexter side with a fleur-de-lis and on the sinister with a lion passant guardant or.

Fig. 19. Arms of the *Students' Association* ("Teutonia") at Jena. The arms of the Students' Associations at the German Universities are all devised upon one pattern, which, however, cannot lay claim

to any special heraldic value. (See "Arms of the German Students' Association," by Nic. Müller, 1878-79, Frankfort-on-the-Maine.)

The arms of the University Extension College at Reading (Fig. 606) and of Clifton College (Fig. 550) are other examples, and I am permitted to reproduce the bookplate of Cheltenham College (Fig. 1066).

Fig 1066.—The Bookplate of Cheltenham College : Per bend gules and sable, on a bend or, between in chief two swords in saltire proper, pommels and hilts of the third, and in base a fasces palewise of the last, a mullet of the first between two fleurs-de-lis of the second. (From the original block.)

In conclusion we give two copies from Ströhl's *Die Wappen der Buchgewerbe* (Vienna, 1891), representing the arms of the *Photochemigraphists* (Fig. 1067) and those of the *Bookbinders* (Fig. 1068).

FIG. 1067.—Arms of the Guild of Photochemigraphists.

The shield in the arms of the Photochemigraphists, invented by Franz Stuck, of Munich, in 1884, is : Party per fess, in chief sable a demi-sun in splendour issuant, the base per pale, on the dexter side, gules, an acid flask, and on the sinister argent, a printing-roller sable. The helmet has for crest, on a wreath or and sable, mantling being the same, three sunflowers proper. Motto: "In luce mundus." The arms of the bookbinders are: Gules, a bookbinding press or, and above it a bound book of the last. The helmet bears as crest

FIG. 1068.—Arms of the Guild of Bookbinders.

an arm brandishing a hammer or mallet sable, the handle or. The arm is habited in a sleeve gules, cuffed or, and continuing into the mantling of gules and or.　　　　　　H. S. AND A. C. F-D.

PLATE CXXVI

EXAMPLES OF HUNGARIAN AND POLISH ARMS

While Hungarian heraldry rests more or less on a German foundation, and only makes itself noticeable by its occasional extravagances, and, since the Turkish war, by a special predilection for devices having some reference to that struggle, ancient Polish heraldry would seem to be of an independent origin, possessing very little in common with German and West European heraldic art. The crest and the mantling and even the tinctures of the charges play a very small part, and the number of heraldic charges is comparatively limited. Modern Polish heraldry has enriched itself with many devices from the neighbouring heraldic art of Germany, but has, by so doing, as will be readily understood, lost rather than gained both in national character and in the peculiarities of its armory.

HUNGARIAN COATS OF ARMS

Fig. 1. Arms of *Martin Pethnehazy*, granted by King Sigismund at Constance, July 25, 1417: Gules, a demi-lion argent, issuing out of a coronet or, enriched with gems gules and azure, holding in its paws and shooting from a bow or, stringed argent, an arrow also gold, the pheon argent. The crowned tilting-helmet, with its mantling of gules and or, bears as crest the demi-lion as in the arms. Later, the Pethnehazys received a grant of a new coat of arms from King Mathias Corvinus at Ofen, January 9, 1462, viz.: Azure, a unicorn argent, armed or (from *Turul*, 1888).

Figs. 2 and 3. Arms of *Nikolaus Gara II.*, Royal Counsellor of King Charles VI. of France, who "besserte" (augmented) for him the old arms of Gara by a patent dated March 16, 1415. The confirmation of this augmentation by King Sigismund followed in the succeeding year. The old coat (Fig. 2) was: Azure, a snake crowned or, holding an Imperial orb in its mouth. The crowned silver tilting-helmet has a mantling of ostrich feathers azure, and as crest a plume of ostrich feathers azure, disposed in the shape of a wing, and charged with the device of the shield. The augmented coat of arms (Fig. 3) is the same shield and the same helmet, but the mantling and crest are composed of golden sun-rays. Above the rays appear two flag-cloths (perhaps ailettes; compare Plate CXXXVII. Fig. 2), each charged with the Gara arms.

Fig. 4. Arms of *Andreas Chapi*, granted to him and his relatives by King Sigismund at Constance, March 19, 1418: Azure, a lion rampant or, the dexter forepaw grasping and endeavouring to withdraw an arrow argent, pierced through both its eyes, which are embrued. Crest: a lion statant or, removing an arrow as in the arms. The silver tilting-helmet has a mantling of azure and or. The shield is surrounded by the emblem of the Order of the Dragon, a golden dragon, charged with a cross gules (compare Plate LXXX. Fig. 4). (From *Turul*, 1885.)

Fig. 5. Arms of *Nikolaus Sovari Soos*, granted by King Sigismund at Constance, March 6, 1418, to him, his son, and to other relations: Azure, issuing from a coronet or, the bust of a woman proper, crined also or, and issuing from her head two ram's horns of the last. The silver tilting-helmet has a mantling of azure and gules. Crest: out of a coronet a woman's bust as in the arms. The Chapie and the Soos are of one family. (From *Turul*, 1885.)

Fig. 6. Arms of *Count Johann Hunyadi* (until 1452 "Gubernator' of the Hungarian Realm, Father of King Mathias Corvinus, who died 1456). These arms were granted at Pressburg, February 1, 1453, by King Ladislaus V. Posthumus: Quarterly, 1 and 4, argent, a lion rampant gules, the eye or, holding in its paw a coronet of the last (this device was not borne afterwards by the family); 2 and 3, the old family arms of the Hunyadi (Corvinus), azure, a raven rising proper, the eye or, and holding in its beak a gemring or, set with a diamond. The partition lines of the shield in this painting are indicated in gold. The crowned, golden tilting-helmet has a mantling of silver lined with gold. Crest: a pair of wings addorsed or. Figs. 2 and 3, as also Fig. 6, are taken from A. Nyary's book, *Heraldika Vegerfonala*, Budapest, 1886.

Instances of arms containing reference to battles with the Turks are shown in Figs. 1069 and 1070.

Fig. 1069. Armorial shield of *Michael Mohorai Vid*, a travelling companion of King Sigismund, who distinguished him at Strass-

FIG. 1069.—Mohorai Vid (1418).

burg (1418) by the gift of a patent of arms: Gules, between two Turkish sabres addorsed argent, the bust of a Turk habited in azure, and with a white turban. The same bust of a Turk, but

FIG. 1070.—Dévay (1538).

habited in gules, is also the crest, the habit continuing into the mantling of gules and argent. The Vidffys were inhabitants of the Comitate Nograd and Hont.

Fig. 1070. Arms of *Peter Devay de Deva* (granted by King Johann

Zapolya at Schässburg, July 13, 1538: Gules, a Turk running, habited in azure, the trousers or, and with high boots proper, holding in his dexter hand a sword, and with the sinister endeavouring to draw a broken spear out of his breast, and pierced in the upper part of his body by an arrow embedded to its head. (Reproduced from the *Jahrbuch Adler*, 1892.)

Amputated bleeding Turks' heads, Turkish sabres, sword-brandishing arms in armour, sword-brandishing lions, and griffins, pandours, hussars, &c., chiefly constitute the heraldic charges of the Magyars, and lend to the armory of that nation a warlike and Tartar wildness, and often something of an even comical character.

POLISH COATS OF ARMS

The old Polish armorial devices are mostly the flag-devices—"Stannizan"—of the families of old dynasties, originating exclusively in the Runic characters of the Scandinavians, the neighbours of the Poles, in their old home Drevinenland (Holstein). To such signs, taken from the runes, belong, for instance, the

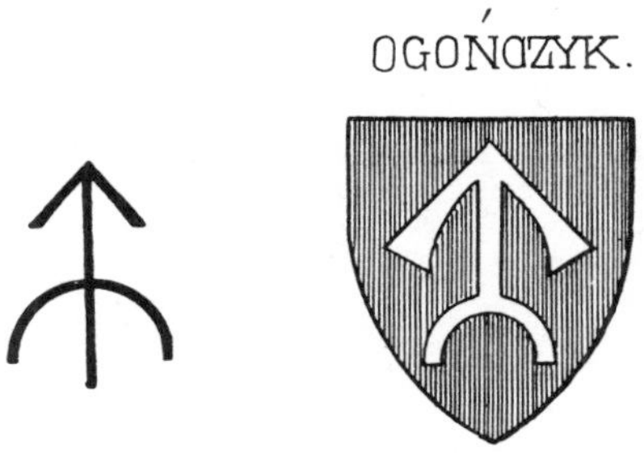

OGOŃCZYK.

FIG. 1071.

devices of (Herb) of the Ogony family (Ogoncyzk; Fig. 1071); of Odrowaz (Fig. 1072; see Plate LXXXVII. Fig. 5); and of

FIG. 1072.

Natçez (Fig. 1073), from which, later on, a bow of material was developed. Frequently occurring devices are, moreover: *Pobog*

NAŁĘCZ.

FIG. 1073.

(Fig. 1074) and *Dabrowa* (Fig. 1075), both composed of horse-shoes surmounted by small crosses, as is also a bend wavy couped, sur-

POBÓG   DĄBROWA.

FIG. 1074.    FIG. 1075.

mounted by a cross (Szreniawa; Fig. 1076). The crescent and star are the arms of Leliva (Fig. 1077), and "the two and a half armed cross" the arms of Pilawa (Fig. 1078).

These separate coats of arms were not borne by one family only, but in each case by a whole group of families, who, however, without doubt would all originate in the same dynasty. Thus, for instance, Counts Czapski, Goluchowski, Wodzicke bear, amongst others

the arms of Leliva (Fig. 1077). The arms of Natçez (Fig. 1073) are used by about one hundred and fifty families, &c.

SZRENIAWA   LELIWA.   PILAWA.

FIG. 1076.   FIG. 1077.    FIG. 1078.

Plate CXXVI. shows emblazonments of the arms of two old Polish noble families in the style of the second half of the fifteenth century, the figures of which show, and may perhaps explain, the development of the Polish armorial charges.

Fig. 7. Arms of *Count von Miączyn-Miączynski*, belonging to the arms of Suchekownaty: Gules, a hunting-horn sable, viroled and stringed or, the string surmounted by a cross of the same. The crowned buckled helmet, with its mantling of sable and gules, bears as crest a plume of three ostrich feathers sable, or, and gules (Athanasius von Miączynski Wojewode von Wolhynien, who died 1723, was ennobled December 2, 1688, by the Emperor Leopold I., on account of his services at the relief of Vienna). The figure originated in the "Stannitze" of the Madrostki (Fig. 1079) composed of the rune tyr (Fig. 1080), the symbol of sovereignty and of the rune madr (Fig. 1081), identical with the idea of "man."

When the pagan families were converted to Christianity most of the "Stannitzen" were altered by the insertion of crossed lines (Fig. 1082) in order to express also the new belief in the Cross. This device, after the death of the original ancestor, only continued to be borne by his eldest son; the younger sons were obliged to put aside

FIG. 1079.    FIG. 1080.    FIG. 1081.

the sign of the Wojewoden dignity—the rune tyr—and bore the "Stannitzen," as shown in Fig. 1083.

When, in the beginning of the fourteenth century, Central and West European heraldry penetrated to Poland, that nation endeavoured to replace the signs of the "Stannitzen," then already become incomprehensible, by objects corresponding in shape as much as possible, and in this manner arose, out of Fig. 1083, the reversed horse-shoe surrounding a cross (Arms: Zastrzembiec), the waxing half-moon containing a cross (Arms: Szeliga), and, amongst many others, also the hunting-horn surmounted by the cross (Arms: Suchekownaty), the arms of Count Miączynski.

Fig. 8. Arms of *Count von Mycielen-Mycielski*, belonging to the arms of Dolęga: Azure, a horse-shoe argent, surmounted by a small cross or, surmounting an arrow point downwards, flighted or. The crowned helmet, with a mantling azure and argent, bears as crest a wing argent, pierced by an arrow in fess, flighted or. (The family, one of the most highly esteemed of Great Poland, owning large estates in Posen, received the rank of count, in both its branches, in 1816 and 1842 respectively.)

FIG. 1082.   FIG. 1083.    FIG. 1084.    FIG. 1085.

The "Stannitze" of seniority (Fig. 1082) was always borne by the eldest son; the other members of the senior line either used the sign of the senior reversed (Fig. 1084), or, in addition, altered the place of the cross (Fig. 1085). The armorial device of Dolęga was gradually developed out of Fig. 1085 (in the way explained in Fig. 1083), as it is shown on Fig. 8. (See Professor Dr. F. Pickosin'ski, *Rycerstwo polskie wickow 'srednich*, Krakau, 1897.)

H. S.

[The same idea seems largely to underlie much of the native heraldry of Hindustan, *e.g.* in the device of the Chakra claimed and used by all chieftains tracing descent from the Chauhan clan of Rajputs.—A. C. F-D.]

THE ART OF HERALDRY

PLATE CXXVII

SPECIMENS OF FRENCH HERALDRY OF THE FIFTEENTH CENTURY

(Reproduced by Noël Bouton of Paris)

To France has always been conceded considerable importance in matters of armory. French, and particularly Burgundian heralds and Pursuivants had the reputation of being especially proficient in the Science of Armory. They transplanted French armorial usages and many of their technical words into German soil without, however, thereby stemming the national development of German Heraldic Art. In English terms of blazon the influence of France is apparent, though it is not unlikely that to the general usage of the Norman-French language, the "French" terms should be more correctly attributed. Plates CXXVII., CXXVIII., and CXXIX. give specimens of French heraldic emblazonment from the fifteenth century until the time when armory and heraldry together became decadent.

Fig. 1. Equestrian figure of one of the family of *Montmorency-Laval*, a younger branch of the House of Montmorency, one of the oldest noble families in France. The arms upon the shield are : Or, on a cross gules, between four eagles azure, five escallops argent. On the horse clothing the device of the shield is repeated. The helmet and the horse's headpiece are adorned with ostrich feathers gules. The shells are the mark of cadency borne by the Laval branch of the family.

Fig. 2. Armorial shield of the *Connétable* (Constable) *Artus de Bretagne*. The shield shows the arms of Bretagne, an ermine field upon which is placed a red label of three points, each point charged with three lions passant guardant in pale.

Fig. 3. Armorial shield of *Lieutenant-General le Comte de Donnois, Bastard d'Orleans :* The arms of Orleans (see Plate LXVII. Fig. 2), over which a bend sinister is placed.

Fig. 4. Armorial shield of *Potors de Saintrailles, Marechal] de France :* Quarterly, 1 and 4, argent, a cross couped gules ; 2 and 3, gules, a lion rampant argent. Figs. 1 to 4 are from a celebrated MS. in the National Library in Paris, the Roll of Arms by "Heroldes Berry," which contains a genealogy of the Kings of France from the time of St. Louis until Charles VII. (born 1403, died 1461).

Fig. 5. Arms of *Loys du Breuil :* Quarterly, 1 and 4, argent, two bars gules between nine lozenges azure ; 2. azure, a bend or, between six escallops argent ; 3. or, ten lozenges, five and five, conjoined in fess azure. Mantling azure and argent. Wreath gules and azure. Crest : a demi-maiden with floating hair, vested azure, her sinister hand resting on her breast. The inscription on the ribbon runs : "Loys du breulh barō dorlhac crie corcelles."

Fig. 6. Arms of *Blanche de Latour, Abbesse de Cusset :* Quarterly, 1 and 4, or, an ecclesiastical banner gules ; 2 and 3, azure, a tower argent, between four fleurs-de-lis or (the arms of Latour). The shield is placed in front of a crosier. The ribbon bears the inscription : "Blanche de latour abenesse de cusset."

Fig. 7. Arms of *Jehan de Langhat :* Or, three pallets "contre vair," "*Sturz pfahl feh.*" The tilting-helmet, with its mantling azure and argent, and the wreath of gules and argent, bears as crest, between two wings argent, the head of a dolphin azure, the gills gules. On the ribbon is the inscription : "Jehā de lāghat, cri langhat."

Fig. 8. Arms of the *Prior of Ris* (Brother Jehan de la Liere) : Argent, a lion rampant azure. The shield is placed upon an abbot's staff. The ribbon bears the inscription : "Fre ich de la liere peur de ris." Figs. 5 to 8 are taken from the *Armorial d'Auvergne et Forest*, the author of which, Guillaume Revel, was one of the heralds of King Charles VII. of France.　　　　　　H. S.

PLATE CXXVIII

EXAMPLES OF FRENCH HERALDRY OF THE SIXTEENTH CENTURY

(Copied by Noël Bouton of Paris)

Fig. 1. Arms of the *Dauphin of France*, afterwards King Henry II. (1547). The shield is quarterly, 1 and 4, quarterly i. and iiii., azure, three fleurs-de-lis or ; ii. and iii., or, a dolphin embowed azure, langued, and the gills azure (for the title of Dauphin ; see Plate LXVII. Fig. 1) ; 2 and 3, quarterly i. and iiii., azure, three fleurs-de-lis or (France) ; ii. and iii., ermine (Bretagne). The shield, which is surmounted by a coronet, is encircled by the collar of the Order of St. Michael, founded by King Louis XI. in 1469. The coat of arms is taken from a MS. in the possession of the Bibliothèque de l'Arsenal in Paris (*Traité d'Armoiries*, by Johann le Feron of Compiègne, avocat du Parlament, 1520).

Fig. 2. Arms of *Princesse Marguerite d'Angoulême, Reine de Navarre* (Duchesse de Berri et d'Alençon), sister of King Francis I. (1492–1549). The shield is dimidiated, and shows on the dexter side the arms of the kingdom of Navarre, and on the sinister side those of France. The escutcheon of Navarre is divided palewise into three, the two last fields charged with an inescutcheon showing : Or, two lions passant gules (Lordships of Biggore), the first field party per fess and the chief party per pale, and contains in chief on the dexter side, gules a cross saltire and double orle of chains linked together or (for Navarre), the tradition being that it was assumed by Sancho in memory of a successful attack in 1212 on the camp of the Moorish army under Miramomelin, which was defended by a barricade of chains ; on the sinister side or, three pallets gules (Comté de Foix) ; in base or, two cows gules, belled azure (Comté de Bearn). The second field is per fess and shows in chief, quarterly, France (azure, three fleurs-de-lis or) and gules (House of Albert) in base the arms of France surmounted by a bend compony argent and gules (Comté d'Evreux ; see Plate LXXVII. Fig. 5, and Plate LXVII. Fig. 12). The third field is party per saltire in chief and base paly of six or and gules, *Aragon* ; in the dexter flank *Castile*, and in the sinister *Leon*. This coat of arms appears in the MS. entitled "L'Epistre de Sainct Augustin a Dame Probe," by Guillaume Renouf.

Fig. 3. Arms of the *Regente Louise de Savoie, Duchesse d'Angoulème*, mother of Francois I. The shield, supported by two kneeling angels, shows two coats of arms dimidiated, namely : on the dexter side the arms of France (azure, three fleurs-de-lis or), and on the sinister the arms of Savoy (gules, a cross argent). The MS. from which the arms are taken bears the title : "Livre des douze perils d'enfer," and is to be found in the National Library, Paris.

Fig. 4. Arms of the *Abbé de Bonnevaux et Saint Pierre de Vienne* (Louis de Grolée). The shield quarterly of six (three and three), viz. : 1 and 6, gyronny of eight argent and sable ; 2 and 4, barry of six gules and argent, the silver stripes charged with six little morions, three, two, and one. (It can be seen quite plainly that this arrangement was originally that of a three-cornered Gothic shield in which the arms were probably barry of gules and vair, from which, owing to a misapprehension, the arms have been misinterpreted) ; 3 and 5 (the following is a literal translation of the German blazon) : "twice divided above, split gold and red ; in front a red carriage frame and wheels" (see Plate X. Fig. 59 and see Fig. 81) ; "in the centre, checked gold and black, in three rows ; below gold." The tilting-helmet, with its mantling sable and or on the dexter side, and gules and argent on the sinister, bears as crest a demi-lion or, issuing from a wreath gules, sable, and or. Supporters : two lions or, the tails cowarded. Motto : "Espoir de-Mywlx" (Espoir de mieux). This coat of arms is taken from a MS. "Les Commentaires de Cesar," translated into French by Robert Gaguin (beginning of the sixteenth century), in the possession of the Arsenal Library in Paris.

Fig. 5. Arms of *Jaques II. d'Amboise* 43 (Abbé de Cluny, brother of the Cardinal and Minister d'Amboise). Arms : Barry of six or and gules, and behind the escutcheon a crosier in pale or. A pilgrim's staff is introduced in the background, the staff being entwined with a motto-ribbon. The background is charged with golden pilgrim's shells. The coat of arms, carved and painted, is placed as an ornament on a battlement over the entrance-gate of the Hôtel de Cluny, rue de Sommerard, Paris. Jaques d'Amboise built, between the years 1510–1585, the palace which now contains the collection of the Musée de Cluny.　　　　　　H. S.

PLATE CXXIX

EXAMPLES OF FRENCH HERALDRY IN THE SEVENTEENTH, EIGHTEENTH, AND THE FIRST YEARS OF THE NINETEENTH CENTURIES

(Copied by Noël Bouton, Paris)

Fig. 1. Achievement representing the alliance of *King Henry IV. of France* and *Marie de Medici* in the chapel of the Château de Fontainebleau, of the time of Louis XIII. (1610-1643). Side by side with the shield of France appears the coat of Queen Marie, who was a daughter of Francis I. of Tuscany and Johanna of Austria. The well-known arms of the Medicis, in connection with the fess-shield of Austria, indicates the parentage of the Queen. The silver fess here appears enclosed within broad gold stripes, which are not really any part of the actual arms. The arms in each case depicted on an oval cartouche are placed accollée upon a larger oval of silver which is surmounted by the French regal crown, and surrounded by the collar of the Order of St. Michael.

Fig. 2. Arms of *Marie de la Tremoille* (Tremouille), from a manuscript decorated with heraldic emblems of about the time of Louis XIII. (1601-1643), now in the Bibliothèque de l'Arsenal in Paris. The arms, which are depicted on a crowned lozenge, are quartered with a point in base and charged with an inescutcheon which is party per pale ; on the dexter side, or, a chevron gules, between three eagles azure (Tremoille) ; on the sinister side, azure, semé-de-lis or, a

THE ART OF HERALDRY

tower argent (De la Tour-Turenne). The lozenge itself is quarterly: 1. of the arms of Naples (argent, an eagle displayed azure), and of Aragon (paly or and gules), dimidiated per bend ; 2. France (azure, three fleurs-de-lis or) ; 3. Bourbon-Condé (azure, a baton couped gules, between three fleurs-de-lis or ; see Plate LXVII. Fig. 7) ; in the 4th *Montmorency Laval* (see Plate CXXVII. Fig. 1) ; in point Xaintrailles (gules, a cross couped argent). On the mantle of estate, which is lined and edged with ermine, the devices of the shield are repeated. Louis I. de la Tremoille, by his marriage with Marguerite d'Amboise, came into the countship (duchy 1563) of Thouars and the Principality of Talmond. The grandson of his son Louis II., Francis, Prince de Talmond, married in 1521 Anne de Laval, daughter of Count Gui de Laval, and Charlotte of Aragon, Princess de Tarent, from which marriage the family of La Tremoille traced their claim to the throne of Naples.

Fig. 3. Arms of *Maitre Francois Elie de Voyer de Paulmy d'Argenson*, at first Bishop of Dol, then Archbishop and Prince of Embrun, Count of Guillestre and of Beaufort. He was a brother of the well-known Marc Réné, Marquis d'Argenson, Lieutenant-General of the Parisian Police, who is best known as having introduced the use of "Lettres de Cachet." This example is from a manuscript "Genealogie des Marquis d'Argenson," by Du Pratt, 1698, now in the Bibliothèque de l'Arsenal in Paris. The crowned shield is quarterly, and superimposed thereupon is an inescutcheon, surmounted by a regal crown. The arms are : Quarterly, 1 and 4, azure, two lions passant guardant in pale and crowned or (Voyer) ; 2 and 3, argent, a fess sable (D'Argenson). The inescutcheon is gules, on a mount in base vert, the lion of St. Mark passant or, holding in his dexter paw a sword. The Lion of St. Mark was really the crest of the family. Réné, the father of the two brothers, had been the French Ambassador in Venice. Behind the shield appears the double cross of his archiepiscopal rank, which is also expressed in the green hat with ten "fiocci" or tassels on either side. The mantle, lined with ermine, shows on the outside the heraldic device of the shield.

PLATE CXXX

EXAMPLES OF HERALDIC SCULPTURE AND CARVING IN ITALY

Italian heraldry, fostered chiefly by the aristocratic governing bodies of the larger towns (Venice, Genoa, Florence, &c.), and by the splendour-loving popes and cardinals of Rome, reached a very high point of development, especially in the field of sculpture and carving. The shields were generally somewhat long in shape, this doubtless resulting from the frequent horizontal partition of the shield. This development rendered possible the much-loved insertion of a chief with the Guelph or Ghibelline party-badges. The square *Tartsche*, a shield with a spear-rest at the side (Figs. 3, 4, 7, 8, and 9 upon the Plate), may be noticed in use at a very early date, as early indeed as the beginning of the fourteenth century, whereas, in Germany, this particular form of shield did not make its appearance until a much later period. The art of heraldic decoration in the sixteenth century brought into use in Italy, as was also the case in Germany, many different-shaped shields most unsuitable for the purpose of armorial display and often most unheraldic. These forms of the escutcheon were deeply slit, and with the edges curled, developing into figures which were really more of the nature of decorated cartouches than shields. A few of these from Sebastian Serlio's *Architettura*, 1551, are here produced (Fig. 1086, *a* to *f*.)

The animals found in Italian heraldry are more naturally and less conventionally treated. But for that reason they were less accommodating and elastic when applied to heraldic design than those of German armory. Eagles are always shown with inverted wings, the crowns of animals are detached, as are usually the "triple mounds," the separate heads of which are found cylindrically shaped. They are not usually represented as conjoined, but are drawn side by side.

    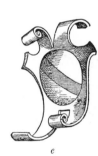 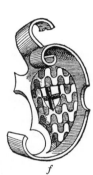

a   b   c   d   e   f

FIG. 1086.—Shields from Serlio's *Architettura*.

Fig. 4. Arms of the *Nicolay* family, domiciled in the Isle de France and Vivaris (May 15, 1645, Marquis de Goussainville, 1817 Marquis de Nicolay). This example is taken from a heraldic book of the Chambre de Comptes, 1768, a manuscript now in the possession of the Bibliothèque de l'Arsenal, Paris. The arms are : Azure, a greyhound courant proper, collared gules, ringed and rimmed or. Supporters : two greyhounds regardant proper, collared, as in the arms. A marquis's coronet rests upon the cartouche, and upon it again a helmet surmounted by a like coronet and with a mantling of or, argent, and azure. The crest of the Nicolays, a negro's head, is omitted in this representation, as is also the motto, "Laissez-Dire."

Fig. 5. Design of regimental flag, with the arms of France and the arms of the Count de Noyon : Argent, a fess gules. This flag dates from the period of Louis XVI. (1789), and is now preserved in the Museum Carnavalet in Paris.

Fig. 6. Arms of *Jean Domenique* (Baron Larry), Inspector-General of the Military Medicinal Staff (born in 1766 at Beaudeau, near Bagneres de Bigorre, died 1842 at Lyons). He was one of the greatest surgeons of his time, and served as such in the army of Napoleon I., who created him a baron January 31, 1810. The shield exhibits the following devices : Quarterly, 1. or, on a mount in base vert a dromedary passant azure, towards a palm-tree vert (in reference to the Egyptian Campaign of 1798) ; 2. gules, a sword in bend sinister point downwards argent ; 3. azure, three chevronels or ; 4. per fess in chief argent, a bend sinister wavy (? a river) gules, charged with a skate in fess counterchanged, and the base or, a pyramid sable. The shield is superimposed upon the cross of the Legion of Honour, the red ribbon of which with the Jewel of the Order is visible at the lower edge of the shield. A baron's coronet is placed on the upper edge of the shield. (This illustration and the accompanying details are from documents in the Lazaret des Val-de-Grace in Paris, and from information supplied by the family.)   H. S.

Helmets play a far less important *rôle* than is the case in German heraldry, and consequently are but seldom met with. In the few cases where, however, they do occur, they are most pleasing in appearance, with their light, elegantly draped mantlings hanging as if of material, and usually terminating in tassels. The foliation of the mantlings and sometimes even the coils of the wreath are derived from the conventionalised "acanthus" foliage, without, apparently, losing their textile effect. (See Figs. 3, 4, 7, 8, and 9.)

Fig. 1. Arms of the town of *Florence* : Argent, a fleur-de-lis gules. The representation here given is taken from a carving at the Palazzo Ferroni in Florence (*circa* 1400), and this is probably one of the most beautiful and ornate representations of a fleur-de-lis to be met with. English heraldry differentiates between the conventional form of the fleur-de-lis and the form here given, which shows smaller foliage and flowers introduced in the upper interstices, by terming this form a "fleur-de-lis flowered," and occasionally a "fleur-de-lis florenced"; but some artists, especially Mr. Eve, have followed the Continental usage, ignoring any technical distinction. The Florentine fleur-de-lis is used as their arms by many other towns in Tuscany, *e.g.* by Castelfiorentino and Dovadola, in both of which cases the arms are identical with those of Florence ; by Foviano (gules, a fleur-de-lis or), Laterina (azure, a fleur-de-lis or), Marciano (vert, a fleur-de-lis or), Pian de Sco (gules, a fleur-de-lis argent). Laterina and the two last-named towns do not appear to use the form illustrated, adopting the conventional form only.

Fig. 2. Arms of the *Guelph Party*. This example also is taken from one at the Palazzo Ferroni : An eagle displayed with wings inverted and holding a fleur-de-lis in its beak standing on a dragon overthrown. The party name "Guelphs" was borne by the Italian National Party, the adherents of the Papacy, and the enemies of the Imperial Party (the Ghibellines). In later times the name was borne by the party of the people, whilst the party of the nobles was then termed Ghibelline. The seal of the Guelphs is shown in Fig. 1087, the legend being, "✠ Sigillum Partis Gvelfe. Civitatis. Florentie."

Fig. 3. Arms of *Matteo Ferrillo* (Conte de Muro), from his monument in the Monastery S.M. la Nuova in Naples (end of fifteenth century) : Argent, a chevron, and in chief three mullets gules. Crest : a dragon's head and neck, with wings addorsed.

Fig. 4. Arms of *Troilo Boncompagni*, in the old Palace of the Bargello in Florence : Party per pale, on the dexter side a lion rampant, and on the sinister three bends. Upon the shield rest two helmets, the dexter one bearing as crest on a wreath a lion sejant, and the sinister helmet on a wreath a unicorn sejant.

FIG. 1087.—Seal of the Guelph Party.

Fig. 5. Arms of the *Altoviti of Benedetto de Rovezzano* (from the Piazzetta dei SS. Apostolo in Florence), fifteenth century : Sable, a wolf rampant argent, armed gules.

Fig. 6. Arms of the *Doge of Venice* (Agostino Barberino), 1485–1501, in the Doge's Palace in Venice : Argent, on a bend azure, between six black "mask-beards" (*Barba*), three leopards passant or. Upon the shield rests a Doge's cap with the crowned circlet.

FIG. 1088.—Davanzati.

Fig. 7. Arms of *Buffardo Cicinello*, 1451 and 1452, Podesta (Governor) of Florence. The Cicinelli, a Neapolitan family, bore : Gules, a swan argent, a bordure engrailed or. Crest : on a wreath a dragon's head and neck adorned with a comb of feathers.

Fig. 8. Arms of *Ludovico de Caccialupo*, 1451, Podesta of Florence, by birth a Bolognese. The Caccialupi came originally from Fano, in the district of Pesaro, but migrated to Bologna as early as 1288.

They bore : Azure, a wolf rampant argent, eyed and collared gules, a chief of the party-badge, viz. : azure, three fleurs-de-lis or, surmounted by a label of four points gules. Crest : on a wreath a dragon's neck, terminating in a human head and face, bearded and bridled.

Fig. 9. Heraldic sculpture in Istrian stone in the Palace at Cesena (about 1500). The arms show, on a mound in base, three nude women affronté in fess all enclosed within a coronet about their waists. The crowned helmet bears as crest a phœnix issuing from flames of fire, gorged with two coronets. I am indebted for the negative of this to Messrs. George Bell & Sons in London, publishers of Mr. G. W. Eve's " Decorative Heraldry."

Fig. 1088. Arms of the *Davanzati*, in the palace of this family at Florence (*via* Porta Rossa), end of sixteenth century. The back and upper part of the cartouche are here omitted, as also the crown. The Davanzati bore : Azure, a lion or.

FIG. 1089.—Stone Mosaic (St. Croce, Florence).

A beautiful piece of work in marble, of the Renaissance period, although not sculpture, is shown in Fig. 1089. It is a stone mosaic in the church of St. Croce, Florence (1.30 metres high). The shield is party per pale, dexter a lion rampant, sinister " vair-undy."

H. S.

PLATE CXXXI

EXAMPLES OF ITALIAN HERALDRY OF THE FIF-TEENTH CENTURY, WITH A PORTUGUESE COAT OF ARMS OF THE SIXTEENTH CENTURY

Fig. 1. Arms of the *Capodilista* in Padua, from a family MS. of the Transelgardi-Forzate-Capodilista of the year 1435, in the town library at Padua. (See *Jahrbuch* "*Adler*," 1881). The arms shown are : Or, a lion rampant azure, crowned and armed gules, collared and ringed or, and hanging from the collar over the back a white fur cloak, fimbriated vert, the fimbriations bezanté, on a chief also or, a double-headed Imperial eagle displayed sable. Crest :

FIG. 1090.—Arms of a Bishop. (Engraved by O. Gatti, 1619.)

FIG. 1091.—Arms of the Duchy of Mantua.

out of a coronet or a demi-lion azure, crowned and armed gules, with a white comb or fan on its back adorned with peacock's feathers or. The mantling, which is lined with white fur, is azure, diapered with a design in white stitching and semé of spurs or.

Fig. 2. Arms of *Philippino de Alta villa* of Alba, from an augmentation granted by King Maximilian I. at Antwerp, December 20, 1494. (Imperial Registration Book (G.G.) of King Maximilian I., in the k.u.k. Haus-, Hof- und Staats archiv Vienna.) The sketch shows the arms : Per fess azure and argent, in chief a demi-eagle displayed or, and in base on a rock proper, embrassé (detached) a fortress gules, port ouvert, and at either end of the fortress a tower, each tower bearing a so-called "Walsch" battlement. Crest : on a wreath or, argent, vert, gules, and azure, an eagle displayed or. The mantling is of blue and red on the outside, and is lined on the inside with yellow, white, and grey. This curious mantling, if not heraldically excellent, is nevertheless interesting and somewhat unique.

Fig. 3. Arms of *Andreas de Aura de Pino*, burgess of Casale, and secretary to the Marchesa Maria de Montferrat, according to a patent granted by Maximilian I. at Worms, May 20, 1495 (*Reichs-registrarbuch* = Imperial Book of Registration). The escutcheon is : Quarterly gules and argent, on a mount in base vert a laurel tree eradicated, supported on the dexter side by a lion rampant gules, and on the sinister by a lion rampant argent. This is a very favourite device in Italian heraldry. (See Plate LII. Fig. 7.)

Fig. 4. Arms of the *Torricelli*, who belonged to the ancient nobility of Upper Italy. The arms, as here given, contain an augmentation (granted by Maximilian I. at Amsterdam, December

FIG. 1092.—Reverse of the Golden Seal of King Charles III. of Spain, 1707.

20, 1494, to the brothers "de Turricelli"), and are : Party per pale vert and argent, on three mounds issuant in base or, a round tower gules, battlemented, the gateway and loopholes sable, surrounded by a gallery with "Walsch" battlements, and issuing from the tower a cock sable, combed and wattled gules, between in chief two stars of six points counterchanged. (In place of the newly-granted cock, there formerly appeared in the old coat, on the line of impalement, a third star counterchanged.) In the seventeenth century the arms were again altered, and a flag gules, with two points, bearing a double eagle displayed sable, made to issue from the dexter upper loophole. The family became extinct in 1839 with Nobile Torricella de Balbiani. (This copy is likewise taken from the *Reichsregistraturbuch G.G.*)

Fig. 5. Arms of the *Chigi* of Siena, on a "Tartsche" in the National Bavarian Museum at Munich. This example belongs to the second half of the fifteenth century. The shield is : Party per bend argent and gules, in chief six mounds conjoined in pyramid 1, 2, and 3, and in base a like device both counterchanged of the field, each pyramid surmounted by a star of eight points or. The mantling is argent, lined azure, and the wreath is azure. In this instance the peculiar drawing of the wreath may possibly be intended to represent clouds or perhaps water. The crest is a swan's head and neck argent, beaked or. (See Plate L. Fig. 1.)

Fig. 6. Arms of a Portuguese prince, perhaps the *Infant Ferdinando* (born 1507, died 1534), from a richly illustrated Genealogy of the House of Portugal in the British Museum, which came into their possession in 1840. The coat, judging from the manner in which the helmet and shield are attached, is most probably the work of a Flemish artist. The arms of Portugal, which are : Argent, five inescutcheons in cross azure, each charged with five plates in saltire, the whole within a bordure gules, charged with seven castles or (for Castile), and over all a label of three points argent, the exterior

points (which are depicted of a greater width) being each charged with the arms of Spain (Castile and Leon quartered). The helmet is barred and of gold and lined with blue. The mantling is or, lined gules, and the crest, out of a coronet or, a dragon's head and neck, the wings addorsed gules. (From Shaw's "Dresses and Decorations of the Middle Ages.")

The two following figures belong to the seventeenth century :—

Fig. 1090 shows the arms of a bishop, the charge upon the shield being a lion rampant. The engraving is by Oliviero Gatti, a pupil of Agostino Carracei and Valesio. He worked at Bologna between 1602–1648.

Fig. 1091. Arms of the *Duchy of Mantua*. The large shield shows the official arms of the Marquisate, granted to the House of Gonzaga by the Emperor Sigismund in 1432 : Argent, a cross patée throughout gules, between four eagles displayed sable (arms of the later Duchy of Guastalla). These arms are surmounted by an inescutcheon quarterly of nine, which contains successively the arms of the Grecian Empire, of the House of Gonzaga, of the Kingdom of Jerusalem, of the Kingdom of Aragon, of the Duchy of Montferrat, Gonzaga once more, the Duchy of Bar, and the town of Constantinople. (The Oriental arms came in with the Montferrat succession.) Behind the cartouche upon which the arms are depicted a golden mount arises, on which the word "Fides" may be read. Under the escutcheon appears the collar of the Order of the Golden Fleece, and the cartouche is surmounted by a coronet.

In conclusion, one more interesting coat of arms (Fig. 1092) may be noted. This appears on the Golden Seal of King Charles III. of Spain (Emperor Charles VI.), which hangs from the Royal Warrant, dated at Barcelona, August 12, 1707, authorising his brother, the Emperor Joseph I., to arrange the contract of marriage in his name with the Princess Elizabeth Christina of Brunswick-Luneberg. The seal shows strangely enough the arms of *Sardinia :* Argent, a cross gules, between four negroes' heads crowned with Eastern crowns, the faces disposed towards the centre of the shield.   H. S.

PLATE CXXXII

EXAMPLES OF ENGLISH HERALDRY

(Fifteenth and Sixteenth Centuries)

Early examples of British heraldry have been already alluded to in various chapters which I think comprise some instances of a rather more typical character, but the following are the selection made by Herr Ströhl, who remarks :—"English heraldry of the fifteenth century is in the main pretty much identical with the German in the sixteenth century. However, there come more and more to the front those stiff, inflexible forms which are still only too piously adhered to by some present-day artists, official and unofficial."

Fig. 1. Arms of *John Beaufort*, Duke of Somerset, grandson of John of Gaunt, Duke of Lancaster, from his Garter plate in St. George's Chapel at Windsor, first half of the fifteenth century : The then Royal Arms of England (*i.e.* quarterly, 1 and 4 ; France, 2 and 3, England), within a bordure compony argent and azure. The mantling, which has a scalloped edge, is of gules and or. The crest is : on a chapeau gules, turned up ermine, a lion of England statant guardant and crowned or, gorged with a collar compony as in the arms. Supporters : dexter, an eagle, crowned and with wings inverted or ; sinister, an antelope argent, armed and crined or and bezanté. As badge, on either side of the coat of arms is the badge of an ostrich feather argent, the quill compony argent and azure. This is taken from Planché's "Pursuivant of Arms," London, 1873, but in that book the background of the livery colours, as in the Garter plate, is fully reproduced.

Fig. 2. Arms of the *Tallow Chandlers' Company* of the City of London, taken from the patent of September 24, 1456. The same was drawn up by John Smert, Garter King of Arms, whose signature is appended to the arms. Party per fess azure and argent, a pale counterchanged, three doves rising of the last, beaked and legged gules, and each holding in its beak an olive branch or. The helmet, which belongs to the transition stage between the grilled and the tilting, has a mantling of gules lined with ermine. Crest : a demi-angel issuing from clouds proper, vested azure, the wings expanded or, crined of the last, holding in the hands a dish or, therein the bleeding head of John the Baptist. On January 29, 1602, William Camden, Clarencieux King of Arms (1597–1623), granted an augmentation to the arms by the addition of supporters, viz. : on a mount vert, two angels proper, vested or, crined and ducally crowned or, the coronet surmounted by an estoile of the last. At the same time the crest was altered, and was, as then granted : a dish argent, glorified by rays or, thereon the head of St. John the Baptist proper. Motto : "Quæ arguuntur a lumine manifestantur" (Catalogue of the Heraldic Exhibition in

Edinburgh, 1891.) The later grant was undoubtedly intended to supersede the former crest, but the Tallow Chandlers' Company appear to still make use of both (see page 446 and Plate CXX.).

Fig. 3. Arms of *Sir John Say*, in Broxburn Church, Hertfordshire, 1473 : Per pale azure and gules, three chevrons or, voided, counterchanged of the field. (An alternative and perhaps a better blazon is : per pale azure and gules, three chevrons or, each charged with a chevron couped of the field, counterchanged. Crest : on a wreath

a mural coronet, a plume of five ostrich feathers alternately argent and gules.

Fig. 6. Arms of *George Avelin* (alias *Evelin*), of Long Ditton, Surrey, from a patent of August 1572 by Robert Cooke, Clarencieux : Quarterly, 1 and 4, azure, a griffin passant or, on a chief of the last three mullets sable (Evelin) ; 2 and 3, argent, two bars between nine martlets vert, three, three, and three (Ailard). Crest : a demi-hind ermine, vulned in the shoulder gules.

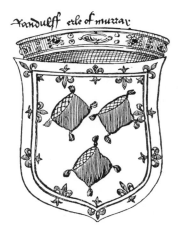

FIG. 1093.

FIG. 1094.

FIG. 1095.

of thorns, a buck's head couped or. The mantling is curious, being of gules lined with erminois. (From Waller, "Monumental Brasses from the Thirteenth to the Sixteenth Century," London, 1864.)

Fig. 4. Armorial shield of *John Wylkynton* (Wilkinson, *alias* Harlyn), of London, according to a patent dated August 3, 1519, and granted by Sir Thomas Wryotesley, Garter King of Arms (1506–1534), and Thomas Benolt, Clarencieux (1516–1534) : Gules, a fess vair, in chief a unicorn courant, between two mullets or, a bordure engrailed of the last.

Fig. 5. Arms of *Rowland Phillipson* (alias *Therwall*), of Callyarth (Colegarth, county Westmoreland), from a patent dated May 18, 1581, by Robert Cooke, Clarencieux (1567–1592) : Gules, a chevron between three boars' heads couped ermine, armed or. Crest : out of

Fig. 7. Arms of *Thomas Fleetwood*, of London, according to a patent dated 1st June 1545, by Thomas Hawley, Clarencieux (1536–1537) : Azure, a chevron engrailed lozengy or and gules between three plates, each charged with a martlet sable. Mantling gules and argent. Crest : a demi-squirrel proper, collared and chained or, holding in its paws a hazel branch vert, cracking the nut or.

Fig. 8. Arms of *William Fleetwood*, Recorder of London, taken from his book on the City of London : Quarterly, 1 and 4, per pale nebuly azure and or, six martlets, two, two, and two counterchanged ; 2 and 3, barry wavy of six ermine and sable. Mantling gules and argent. Crest : a wolf statant regardant argent.

Fig. 9. Arms of *Richard Brownlow* of the Middle Temple, Esquire according to a patent dated October 12, 1602, granted by Sir William Segar, Norroy King of Arms (1593–1603): Quarterly, 1 and 4, or, an inescutcheon within eight martlets in orle sable (Brownlow); 2 and

flory gules. (Compare the arms given by Gelre, Plate LXXVI. Fig. 3.)

Figs. 1094. Arms of *Dunbar, Earl of March* : Gules, a lion rampant

FIG. 1096.

3, azure, a cross pate fleuretté or (Panelly). Mantling sable and or. Crest : on a chapeau gules, turned up ermine, a greyhound passant or, collared, also gules.

The following two drawings of arms are from a Scottish MS. Book of Arms, which was compiled by Sir David Lindsay of the Mount, Lyon King of Arms (1529–1555), between 1538 and 1542.

Fig. 1093. Arms of *Randolph, Earl of Moray:* Argent, three cushions lozengewise within a double tressure flory counter-

argent, within a bordure of the last, within a bordure of ten roses of the last. (Gelre has the same device in his *Wappenbuch*.)

H. S.

A delightfully composed engraving (Fig. 1095) by *H. Gravelot*, engraved by *C. Grignion*, may serve to indicate the transition to modern English heraldry. But to Herr Ströhl's selection I will add an illustration of the arms of the Earl of Lauderdale, as to which (Fig. 1096) I am afraid I must add the remark that from the artistic point of view it is typically British.

CHAPTER XLVIII

THE ARMORIAL MANUSCRIPTS OF SCOTLAND

By Sir JAMES BALFOUR PAUL

Lyon King of Arms

THE armorial manuscripts of Scotland are of some value, and cannot be overlooked. In November 1898 Sir James Balfour Paul, F.S.A. (Scot.), Lyon King of Arms, delivered the Rhind Lectures on Archæology for that year, dealing with "Heraldry in Relation to Scottish History and Art." These lectures have since been republished under that title (Edinburgh : David Douglas. 1900). The sixth lecture was chiefly devoted to "Armorial Manuscripts." I could not hope to rival the intimate knowledge of Lyon upon the subject, and I therefore asked, and received, his permission to publish without alteration such parts of his lecture as dealt with the subject.

"Coming to the consideration of the armorial manuscripts of Scotland, we must at once confess that we have not any which can boast of the antiquity of several English Rolls of Arms. The MSS. known as Glover's Roll, from the name of the herald who copied it in 1586, dates from about 1240, and contains two hundred and eighteen coats

of the English knights of the period, and there are several fourteenth-century rolls which have been published. We have nothing, however, in Scotland earlier than Sir David Lindsay's MSS. This is not only the earliest, but also the most important of all the Scottish Rolls of Arms, being, as it is, the work of one of the most distinguished holders of the office of Lyon. That is to say, there can be no doubt the work was executed under his supervision, a supervision which was occasionally slack, as there are mistakes in the representation of some of the shields ; but of course it is not likely that Lindsay executed the work with his own hand. From an inscription over the arms of Sir David, at the end of the book, we learn that its date was 1542, and though this inscription is evidently a later addition, and was probably put there by Sir James Balfour in 1630, the internal evidence corroborates the assertion. But although we depend for the date upon later authority, the authorship of the book was indicated clearly enough at the time it was compiled, as the words

PLATE CXLVI.

EXAMPLES OF HERALDIC EMBROIDERY.

PLATE CXLVII.

EXAMPLES OF SWISS HERALDIC WINDOWS.

PLATE CXLVIII.

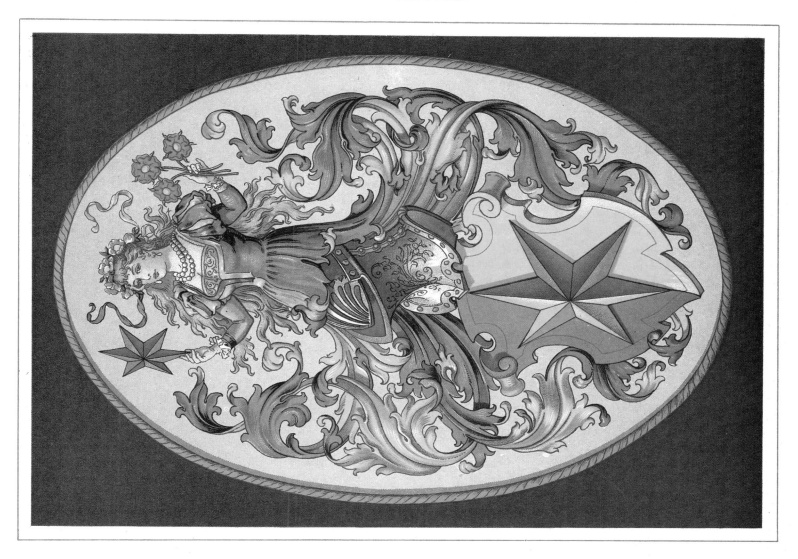

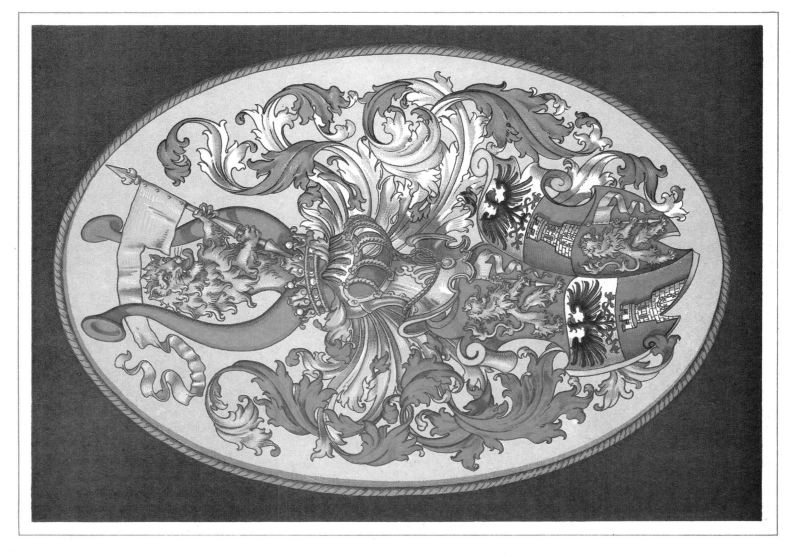

PLATE CXLIX.

EXAMPLES OF GERMAN "ALLIANCE" ACHIEVEMENTS.

PLATE CL.

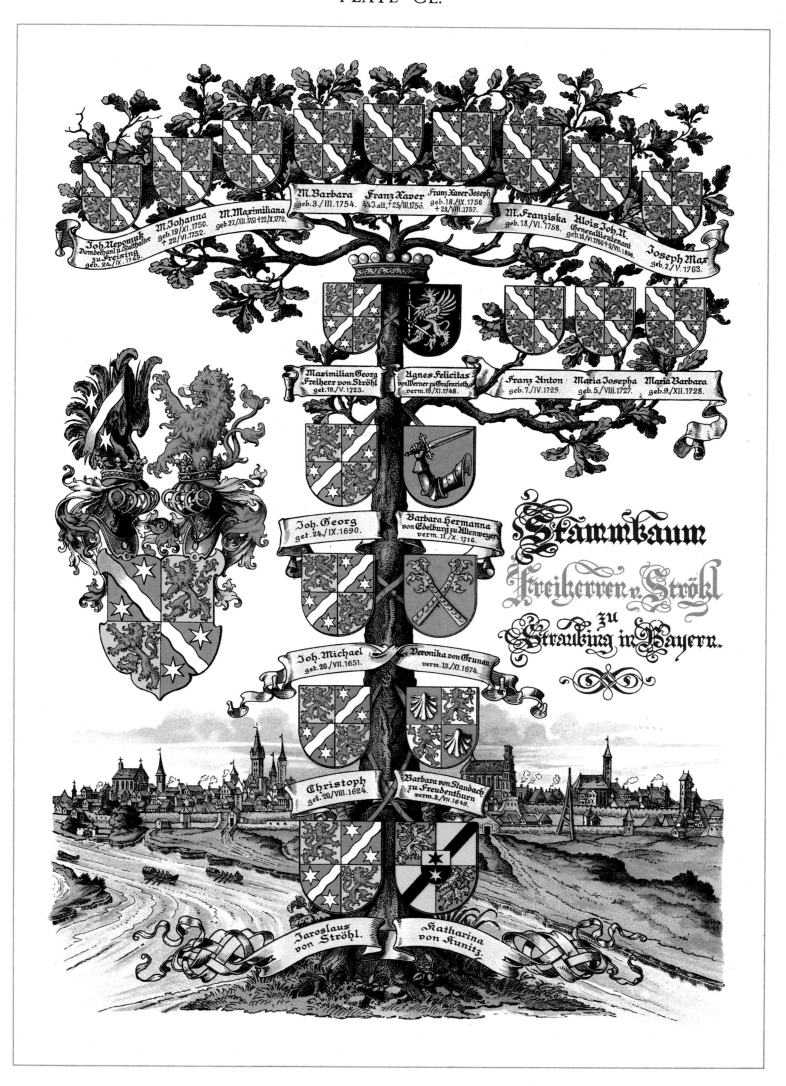

AN EXAMPLE OF AN ILLUMINATED GENEALOGICAL TREE.

PLATE CLI.

AN ILLUMINATED PEDIGREE OF THE FAMILY OF SETON.
Now in the possession of Sir Alan H. Seton Steuart, Bart.

PLATE CLII.

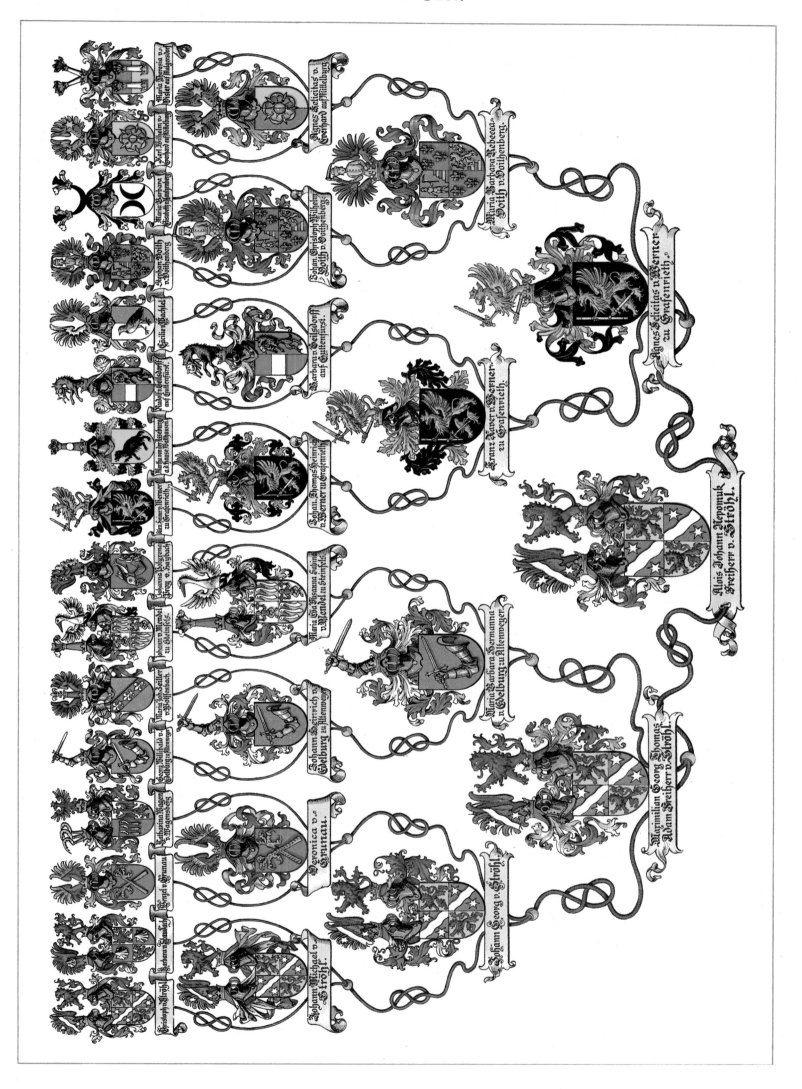

AN EXAMPLE OF AN ILLUMINATED PROOF OF SEIZE QUARTIERS.

PLATE CLIII.

EXAMPLES OF BOOKPLATES.

By Mr G. W. Eve, R.E., Mr C. W. Sherborn, R.E., and Miss Helard.

"Lyndesay of the movnth the auctor of yis present buke" were originally written above his own arms on folio 60. These have been subsequently painted over with the name and arms of Lyndesay of Crocebaskat, so that the former inscription is not found in the reproductions of the manuscripts which have been published.

The collections of arms thus made by Lindsay formed in all probability the official Register of Arms, and remained in the custody of the successive Lyons (as we find the arms of five holders of the office added at the end) till the time of Sir James Balfour, who had it formally recognised by the Privy Council, as appears from a docquet that "this booke and register of Armes done by Sir David Lindsay of the Month, Lyone King of Armes regn, Ja : 5. contenes 106 leaves, which register was approvine be the Lordes of his Majesties most honourable Privie Counsale at Haleruidehous 9 December 1630, James Balfour, Lyon : Thomas Drysdale, Islay Herald, register." When Balfour was deprived of office about 1654 by Cromwell, he appears to have carried this and other MSS. with him to Denmiln, where they remained till the Faculty of Advocates, on 14th December 1698, secured his MSS. for £150, although the heraldic MSS. (probably for reasons) are not mentioned in the catalogue. The workmanship of this manuscript deserves a few words of notice. In artistic excellence it cannot compare with some of the English armorials, or even with some of the Scottish manuscripts of late date ; the drawing is carefully finished, though rather lacking in spirit, and the colours employed are good, but often somewhat thick and heavy, in this respect markedly in contrast with some of the succeeding armorials of the century. The book begins, after the fashion of all such works of the period, with a whole series of mythical arms, such as those of John, Prince of the Great Inde ; the three Kings of Cologne ; David, King of Irsael ; Joshua and Judeus Maccabeus, Charlemagne, Arthur and Godfrey of Boulogne, Julius Cæsar, Alexander the Great, and Hector, Prince of Troy. These are followed by the kings of Europe ; and then the Scottish series opens, oddly enough, with John Baliol, the crown above whose shield is represented as broken in two. Then we have the arms of Queen Margaret, followed by those of the Stewart Queens of Scotland, down to Mary of Guise, all on lozenge-shaped shields, with crowns above (Plate CXXXIII.). After them come the nobility of Scotland, and then a large array of commoners. There are generally four shields on a page, with peaked base, and hollowed and bulged sides. Those of the dukes and earls are surmounted by jewelled circlets. Additions have been made from time to time by the insertion of arms, sometimes in the middle of the page between the four shields, and sometimes on the verso of the folio. It is desirable that these additions should be clearly distinguished from the original coats, as, though a large proportion were probably added not long after the execution of the manuscripts, yet several are of even later date than those added in blank leaves at the end, one group of which dates c. 1580–84, and another 1587–91.

The display of the arms of the queens, with corresponding tablets containing inscriptions, is the most vigorous work in the MS., and is excellent. The writing, both in these tablets and in others, which, after five separate pages and in the inscriptions above the different shields, is good throughout, there being at least three different hands in the original part of the work, the first writer being quite a skilled caligraphist.

From the undoubted fact that Sir David Lindsay was responsible for this armorial, and from the *imprimatur* of the Privy Council having been obtained for it by Sir James Balfour, it may be looked upon as practically an official record. Of course this does not make it infallible, but wonderfully few errors have crept into it. Some-

times he adopts a system of blazoning which does not commend itself to the modern herald, accustomed as he is to precision in all heraldic details. Lindsay, for instance, makes all coats which bear pallets of bars paly or barry of six, probably because it is easier to divide a shield into six rather than into seven parts.

We have to pass over a good many years before we meet with the next Scottish armorial. It is one which seems to have been executed for some member of the House of Hamilton, probably James, Lord Hamilton, second Earl of Arran and Duke of Chatelherault, as from internal evidence we may presume that its date is between the period of the death of Queen Mary's first husband, the Dauphin of France, and that of her marriage to Darnley, 1561 and 1564. The MS. is now in the Heralds' College, London, and on the title-page is the autograph of S. Morganus Colman, and on folio 90, S. Math. (*sic*) Colman. Morgan Colman was a writer who published, in 1608, "The Genealogies of King James and his Wife, Queen Anne, from the Conquest." He is said to have been steward to the Lord Keeper Egerton, and we know that he petitioned unsuccessfully for the office of herald. How the armorial came into his possession we do not know, nor have we any information as to who actually compiled or executed it. It is unlikely that it is done by any of the officials of the Lyon Court. It is more probably English work ; the execution is particularly free and vigorous, a slight pencil outline with washes of colour being employed. There are quaint rhymes given relative to the Royal alliances, similar to those which occur in the Forman MS., to be mentioned immediately. The noteworthy feature in the armorial is the almost equal footing on which the House of Hamilton is placed with the Royal House. The MS. commences with the Royal Arms, fully emblazoned with all the exterior ornaments of the shield, including supporters, each holding a flag. This is followed by a series of crowned lozenges, on which are displayed the arms denoting Royal alliances. Similarly, on page 18, the Hamilton arms are emblazoned, with supporters also holding spears with flags, and followed by a like series of crowned lozenges showing the Hamilton alliances (Plate CXXXIV.). The arms of the nobility and a few Highland coats follow. They have all the exterior ornaments of the shield, but there are some curious variations from the other sixteenth-century MSS. in the mottoes, crests, and supporters. Thus, Lord Oliphant's supporters (elephants) are represented as camels, the dogs of Lord Somerville as field-mice ; and in the case of the Lord of the Isles, his supporters are given as two hairy savages without heads, which are lying with closed eyes on the ground at the feet of their former possessors ; the crest, also, is given as a centaur, instead of a raven and rock. A free copy of this MS., probably executed in England at the end of the sixteenth century (James VI. being described as "Carolus Jacobus that now liveth beinge Kinge of Skotes ") was shown at the Edinburgh Heraldic Exhibition. It is in the collection of Mr. Scott Plummer, at Sunderland Hall. There is also another copy of the MS. in the Lyon Office, which belonged to my predecessor, Dr. Burnett.

There is an armorial in the Advocates' Library of very much the same date as the one of which I have been speaking. It is believed to have been executed under the supervision of Sir Robert Forman of Luthrie, who was Lyon from 1555 to 1567. It consists of two parts, the first twenty leaves commencing on the verso of folio 2, with the full achievement of the Royal Arms, and these are again repeated on folio 22, followed by "the armes of alliance betwix the Dolphin of France and Marie Quene of Scotland." This seems the original portion of the work, and was probably executed at the time of Mary's marriage with Francis, and may very likely be the original referred to by Sir James Balfour in his MS. roll of arms in the Advocates' Library (34 . 4 . 16), entitled "Scottish Cotts of Armes . . . ye cotts of 267 knights, landed gentlemen of ye kingdome of Scotland as they were presented to our Soverane Lady Marie by the Grace of God Quene of Scotland and douager of france, by Sir . . . Forman, Lyone Kinge of Armes in Anno 1532," for, though the arms do not altogether agree, Sir James was not very accurate; as, for example, when he gives the above date as 1532, ten years before Mary's birth. This part of the MS. contains the arms of earls, lords, and commoners, differing from the Lindsay MS. in giving the full achievement of the noblemen, namely, helmet, wreath, crest, mantling, motto, and supporters, and also in limiting them to the then existing peers, so that it is an armorial for its own date only. The shields of the commoners are represented *couché*, somewhat oblong in shape, with peaked base, and surmounted by helmet, wreath, and mantling, but no crests.

The part of the MS. which is later in date, though occurring first in the volume, begins, as I mentioned, with the Royal achievement, followed by a series of effigies of kings and queens, with the arms of the former displayed on their surcoats, and the paternal arms of the latter on their skirts. They stand on grass, below which are ornamental tablets containing quaint rhymes or legends describing who they are (Plate CXXXV.). The series differs from that of the Lindsay crowned lozenges in containing the alliance of the Bruce kings. The drawing, though somewhat rude and sketchy, is effective, the expression on the faces of the kings and queens being cleverly got, though the artist's idea of beauty of feature has not been high. The colouring is put on in washes, and is generally good, the use of a different tint to produce a shaded pattern on the mantlings and elsewhere giving a lightness wanting in Lindsay. There are certain peculiarities in the treatment of the charges; thus the chief always occupies half the field. In the Menteith coat the chevron is drawn like the couples of a house; in the Rothes coat the bend is depicted like a sleeve; the elephants of Lord Oliphant resemble rhinoceroses, &c. The names are in Roman capitals, and are coarsely done.

There is a MS. very similar to this in the British Museum (Harleian MS., No. 115), its emblazonment being evidently by the same hand. It contains (1) effigies of the kings and queens as in Forman; (2) the Hamilton arms on shields derived from the Hamilton MS.; (3) the earls and barons as in Forman, but without the commoners' arms. In subject, design, and treatment, even to minute particulars, the emblazonments of this MS. corresponding to those in the one which we assign to Forman are practically identical, so that its independent value is not great. In the written part, however, this close resemblance ceases, the inscriptions under the effigies being quite different, the family names being added in the case of earls and lords, and the spelling and form of expression in the mottoes, &c., being altered to the English form, thus showing that the writing, at all events, was probably done in the South.

The next armorial to which I would direct your attention is, perhaps, after Sir David Lindsay's, the most important MS. of the kind. Most unfortunately it is generally known by a name which ought never to have been conferred on it. Alexander Nisbet, in an evil hour, called it Workman's MS. from the fact that it was once the property of James Workman, who was Marchmont Herald and Herald Painter in 1597, and who wrote his name on it. But this was written more than thirty years after the execution of the book, and not only so, but Workman himself was the author of an armorial which should bear his name, and which has critical notes in it by Sir James Balfour. As a matter of fact, it was probably prepared

as a book of everyday reference for the Lyon Office by Sir Robert Forman, and should therefore be styled the Forman Lyon Office MS. It has on the verso of one of the leaves the date 1566 in large red figures, and there is every reason to accept this as the date of its execution. It is founded on the Forman (Advocates' Library) MS., supplemented from Lindsay, containing the effigies of the kings and queens as in the former, and the mythical coats and the arms of European sovereigns as in the latter, with additions. It is a small, thick, quarto volume, the original size of the leaves having been $6\frac{1}{2} \times 5\frac{1}{2}$, but they have, at a comparatively recent period, been carefully inlaid, and the whole volume substantially bound. It contains several obsolete peers' coats taken from Lindsay, the Hamilton alliances taken from the Hamilton MS., and many coats unrecorded in it at the period of its inception were added from time to time, so that it forms a general register of arms—though with many omissions—down to the institution of the Lyon Register in 1672, or even later. In quoting this MS. as an authority for arms it is important, therefore, that the original coats should be distinguished from those added to or altered in it. As regards execution, the original coats are apparently by the same hand and in much the same style as those in the Advocates' Library Forman, so that the remarks on the latter apply equally to this, the main difference being that everything is on a smaller scale, the Advocates' Library MS. being a folio while this is a quarto. The writing in this is, however, in a distinct current hand of the period and not in Roman capitals; but in many cases the names have been altered, written over, and in various ways obliterated, so as, in some cases, to be quite undecipherable. Many emblazonments have been painted out, and other coats substituted on the top of them, and not only have additions been made on the versos, but at least half-a-dozen leaves have been inserted in different places. It can hardly be called a tidy or very artistic MS., but the number of coats actually given is very great, no less than 741 coats of the minor barons and gentlemen being portrayed in addition to those of the royalties and peers. MS. blazons of the latter are given at the beginning of the volume, and of the former at the end, but this is probably an addition of a later date.

There is a MS. in the Lyon Office which is entitled on the back "Kings' and Nobilities' Arms, vol. i.," and which is thought to have been executed under the supervision of Sir David Lindsay of Rathillet soon after he entered in office in 1568; but there are really few or no indications which help us to fix its precise date, but from a comparison of it with the Forman (Lyon Office) MS., there seems little doubt that it is of later date than that volume, which was executed in 1566, and, as Forman died in 1568, it is unlikely that he had compiled another armorial so similar, yet dissimilar. Again, two other MSS. derived from it, the Le Breton MS. and the Dunvegan MS., afterwards referred to, were undoubtedly made during Lindsay of Rathillet's term of office, and were copied from this MS. and not from any of Forman's, so that there is a strong probability that its period is contemporaneous with that of Lindsay. It is largely founded on the Forman (Lyon Office) MS., but with important additions to the commoners' arms. Many of these additions appear in the latter MS., but whether they were copied into it from this one, or *vice versâ*, it is difficult to say; perhaps some the one way and some the other. The mythical arms, those of European sovereigns, and the effigies of the kings and queens are omitted; but in their place we have a series of crowned lozenges containing the arms of the queens similar to those in Lindsay the first. The execution of the work is extremely rude, but at the same time effects are most cleverly got, with apparently the most inadequate means; thus, with a few seemingly careless dashes of the pen and a little touch of colour a most spirited lion rampant is produced. The colours used are very inferior, as in many cases the yellows have almost—indeed altogether —disappeared, and the blue has changed to a purple or lake tint; the writing, however, is very bold and distinct. This is the earliest of a group of three armorials successively derived from one another.

The second of this group is a MS. which belongs to the Heralds' College in London, and is usually known as the le Breton Armorial. It is handsomely bound in dark red morocco, with the arms and name of "Hector le Breton, Sieur de la Doinaterie, Roy d'Armes de France," stamped on it. It was presented to the Heralds' College by George Holman of Warkworth, at the instance of Gregory King, Rouge Dragon, on the 6th of July 1686. Throughout the volume there are occasional notes in French, no doubt by its original owner, and many subsequently added in English. From internal evidence it appears to have been executed between 1581 and 1584. The arms of the peers and commoners (though the former have been brought up to date) have evidently been taken directly from the Rathillet MS., the arms do so to a great extent. Instead of the crowned lozenges, however, of that armorial, there have been substituted the series of effigies of the kings and queens from the Forman (Lyon Office) MS. The workmanship is in the quaint and vigorous style of the Rathillet armorial, but there are many points of resemblance to the Forman MS., though it is not likely by the same hand. It has, besides, two youthful portraits of King James VI. as a boy of about fourteen, one on horseback, the other seated on a throne. It has also a crowned thistle with initials I. R. Both the drawing and the colouring are ruder than the Forman MS. but better than the Rathillet MS., though not quite so spirited as either. Most of the writing is in the uniform current hand of the period, but the names to the commoners' arms are in a peculiar small Gothic printing letter, and have evidently not been written by one who was acquainted with Scottish names of families or places, as they appear in the most extraordinary disguises. Thus the name Cairns of Orchardtown is metamorphosed into Lairme of Othartown, and there are many similar mistakes. Some of the inscriptions are from Lindsay, possibly through the Rathillet or Forman MS. One of these has been considerably mangled in altering it to suit to King James instead of Queen Mary. In it he is styled a king "prudent, of young yeres wys as salamone, and to wse young Joseas."

The latest of the group of the three armorials above mentioned is one in the possession of MacLeod of Dunvegan; its date may be set down as between 1582 and 1584. Besides the peers' arms, it contains 241 commoners' coats. The pages at the end of the volume are used as a *Liber Amicoram* containing autographs of several envoys of rank to the court of James VI. One entry by Du Bartas the poet and French Ambassador to Scotland, who died in 1590, is inscribed to " William Shaw, Master of the King's Work," who was in all likelihood the possessor of the book. He was a man of varied accomplishments, and is chiefly remembered as the restorer of Dunfermline Abbey, in which edifice there was a monument erected to his memory by Queen Anne, the wife of James VI., with a highly eulogistic inscription. The armorial is, from an artistic point of view, one of the finest we have; the drawing and finishing are extremely minute, involving an amount of labour, however, scarcely commensurate with the result. The animal supporters are rather plethoric in habit, and have not the vivacity and character of those in the earlier and older armorials. The tinctures are in opaque colours, and the metals are laid on in gold and silver, remarkable

for their perfect condition. No names or mottoes were appended to the coats at the time of their execution; those which now appear must have been added long after by an unskilled hand, as they are often wrong, and many coats are still unnamed.

But the most artistic of all our Scottish armorials is one in the possession of Mrs. Hamilton of Ogilvie, called the Seton MS. from its having its binding—which is apparently the original calf—stamped with the arms of George, 5th Lord Seton. While the arms on the cover are his, it is most likely that the MS. was commissioned by his son Robert, the 6th Lord, as on the title-page there is a small panel inscribed "R. L. Seton, 1591," and in a design above, within an interlaced circle, is a monogram composed of the initials R. L. S. and M. M., the latter being those of his wife Margaret Montgomery, daughter of Hugh, 3rd Earl of Eglinton. At the top of this page the name of "James Espleine (Marchmont *alias*), Roxburgh Herald," is written, and the MS. is often alluded to by Nisbet in his "Heraldry" as Espleine's MS. There is a fine series of effigies of sixteen kings and fourteen queens, from Fergus I. to James VI., with their arms, the faces being finished with great delicacy. A curious drawing occurs entitled "The Habit of a Herald," representing a habit which no herald ever wore; but this is probably a later addition. This is followed by the arms of 53 of the nobility, 4 Highland chiefs, 280 lesser barons, 34 foreign and royal coats, and 18 miscellaneous arms. The whole execution of the work is exceedingly good, the animal supporters being drawn with character and energy; the drawing is refined, and the colouring rich and harmonious. The writing is of a later date from the rest of the work, and some coats are still unnamed.

There is in the splendid library at Haigh Hall a MS., acquired by purchase by the late Earl of Crawford, which contains an interesting collection of Scottish arms. Mr. Stoddart calls this MS. "Lindsay II.," because it is believed to have been executed for Sir David Lindsay of the Mount, Lyon from 1591 to 1621, the nephew of the great Sir David. The arms of the nobility and the gentry of Scotland are given as at the close of the seventeenth century, with a few additions of later date. The volume is bound in vellum, stamped in black on the front board with a foreign coat of arms. On page 1 there is an autograph resembling "Fraunz Kunz," and on page 4 is the inscription "Ex Libris Dr. Macniven." It contains 151 leaves, but 15 of them are blank. The peers' arms still occupy a full page, and the supporters stand on a compartment of green grass (Fig. 799). The dukes, marquises, and earls have all coronets, but the barons have simply wreaths resting on their helmets. A distinguishing feature of this MS. is that on the verso of the leaf preceding that bearing the arms of the head of a noble house, there is generally emblazoned a small shield without exterior ornaments, bearing the paternal coat of arms, and below is given a list of the principal cadets of the family. While the execution of the MS. displayed bold, vigorous work, and is superior in draughtsmanship to most of the earlier MSS., it has neither the artistic feeling and refinement in drawing, nor the sense for harmonious colour which we find in the Seton MS. The writing is beautifully done, and the ornamental flourishes and embellishments show great freedom and command of the pen. The names are, on the whole, distinctly written, the formation of the letters being very modern in style, except in the lists of cadets, where an older form is employed.

These are the more important illuminated MSS. which deal with Scottish arms. They do not exhaust the list, but I must not weary you by an enumeration which has been already too long. It serves to show, however, that the interest taken in the subject of heraldry in Scotland

THE ART OF HERALDRY

was very great, and that the skill of the artists who executed these works was in itself of quite a respectable standard, and in some cases very good indeed. They do not as a whole, I must admit, reach that brilliancy of colour and precision of line which we find in some of the English armorials and MSS., but they have a certain character of their own and a vigour of expression which redeems them at once from the commonplace, and stamps them as a very critical product of the country. What is more peculiar about them is the extraordinary variety of renderings which the different MSS. give of the same coat, and which often betoken great carelessness, if not ignorance, on the part of the workmen. Even Sir David Lindsay's MS. itself is not free from those mistakes which we can hardly conceive occurring had we personally exercised a careful supervision over the work, but these mistakes detract very slightly from the interest which every student of Scottish heraldry must feel in perusing those contemporary records of bygone times.

Besides these illuminated armorials of which I have been treating there is in existence a considerable number of MSS. dealing with Scottish arms which do not exhibit them in colour. Some of these have the different coats "tricked"—that is, simply drawn in outline in pen and ink—while many more merely give a list of names with the verbal blazon of the arms pertaining to each appended. None of these, however, are so old as the earliest of the illuminated MSS., and I need not detain you by giving you a list of them. The two most important are, perhaps, one by Sir James Balfour, which contains a description of considerably over a thousand coats, and one by James Pont, brother of Timothy Pont, the topographer and son of the minister of St. Cuthbert's, Edinburgh, of which frequent mention is made by Nisbet in his "Treatise on Heraldry."

I should like, before leaving the subject of armorial records, to say a word as to a very important branch of the subject, that is, how arms are originally constituted, and the evidence of their being authorised. Of course, in the first instance, there were no such things as grants of arms. Families gradually got into the practice of bearing as cognisances and for all practical purposes, as we have seen, those emblems or devices which their ancestors had been in the habit of using. But when such devices came to be considered as peculiarly military and knightly possessions, and not likely to be assumed, the king (as the fountain of all honour) took the bestowal of armorial bearings into his own hands—though occasionally a knight granted arms to his esquire. No formal documentary grants were, however, at first made, though the bearings of the different knights were carefully noted down by the heralds of the period. In England the earliest of these rolls in which the arms were quoted was, as I have previously mentioned, one of a date between 1240 and 1245, of which a copy made by Glover, Somerset Herald, is still in existence, with the arms blazoned but not drawn. There is also a copy of another thirteenth-century roll, and there is the great Caerlaverock Roll of 1300, containing a list of the arms of all the knights who accompanied Edward I. to the siege of that castle; it has been printed several times. In addition to these there are six or seven other English rolls of the fourteenth century. It is difficult to say exactly when the Heralds' College, which was incorporated by Richard III., first began to issue grants of arms. Dallaway, in his "Heraldic Enquiries," certainly mentions a grant long before the incorporation of the College. It is alleged to be by James Heddingley, Guyen King of Arms, to Peter Dodge, Gentleman, and to be dated the 8th day of April in the 34th year of "Edward le premier;" but although this is in a collection made by Glover, it is unlikely to be genuine. Documents written

in the reign of a sovereign who has had no predecessor of the same name do not usually describe him as "the first." Not only so, but it is stated by Austen that Guyen King of Arms was not created till the time of Henry VI.

The earliest authentic grant which I have been able to meet with is that one of the Company of the Tallow Chandlers of the City of London. It is written in the official French of the period, dated on the 24th day of September, in the year of grace 1456, and is signed by John Smart, Garter King of Arms, and is sealed with his seal bearing his own coat of arms, not an official coat. He signs like a bishop, "J. Garter." The execution of the grant is most artistic. The initial letter represents Garter himself clad in his "coat of arms" and with his official crown on his head. The company's arms are placed in the margin surmounted by a helmet, which, though vigorous enough in its own way, hardly possesses that effectiveness of design which the large cylindrical tilting-helmet has. The crest is an angel in a blue coat with a gold collar and a white neck-cloth, holding John the Baptist's head on a charger. Note the very elegant disposition of the lambrequin, which is gules, doubled ermine, after the fashion of the peers, and not the livery colours. Besides the mantling, opportunity has been taken to introduce, both in the margin and along the top of the patent, a very dainty floral pattern, somewhat in the style of the ancient missals. This, besides being the oldest, is one of the most beautiful patents of arms known to exist. As time went on they rapidly deteriorated in artistic excellence, though, of course, the individual documents varied in that respect. There is, for instance, a grant to the Carpenters' Company of London, of date 1467, or only eleven years after that to the Tallow Chandlers; but it is a miserably inferior production to the former. This, however, must have been the mere chance of a second or third rate draftsman having been employed, because we have quite good work in the charter (not a patent of arms) by Richard III. in 1483 to the Wax Chandlers. The patent to the Barber Surgeons of London in 1569 has certainly an endeavour after artistic excellence, but it wants the spontaneity and grace of the older patents. They were granted the crest of an opinacus, a monster but rarely encountered even in heraldry.

I have as yet only alluded to English patents, because, unfortunately, we have no Scottish examples of such early date. One of the earliest of the latter with which I am acquainted is of date 1567, and is by Sir Robert Forman, of Luthrie, Lyon, in favour of Lord Maxwell of Herries. The wording is rather quaint: "Till all and sundrie quhome it effeirs (unto) quhais knawlege thir presentis sal cum greting in God evirlesting, we, Schir Robert Forman of Luthrie, Knicht Lyoun King of Armes with our brethir Herauldis of the Honerable Johnne Lord Maxwell of Hereiss to assign and gif unto him sick armes in mettaill coulore as maist deulie suld appertene to him and his posteritie as become us of our office to do: Quehairfore We having respect to thais thyngis that appertenit hes assignit and assignis to him quarterlie the first and thrid (sic) silver ane saulter sable with ane lambeall of thre feitt gulis, secund ane ferde selver thre hurtcheounis sable with the beraris of the shield helme tymmerall and detoun as heir under is depainted, quhilk he and his posteritie may lefullie beir without reproofe. Quhilk we testifie be thir presents subscrivit be Marchemont Hairauld oure clerk of office quhairunto oure seile of office is appensit. At Edinburgh, the secund day of Aprile the zeir of God ane thowsand fyve hundreth thre score sevin zeiris."

I need not allude to any other old Scottish patents, as none that I know present any points of artistic excellence. I can hardly say that things much improved during the eighteenth or even during the first half of the nineteenth century. Latterly the actual writing of the patents was much better, and they were really beautiful specimens of caligraphy, but the painting of the arms left much to be desired. It is only within the last few years that this has been remedied, and as I remarked before, I think I may safely say that as regards draftsmanship the Lyon Office leads the way in heraldic records.

I have left myself but small space to speak of armorially decorated charts or trees, as they are often called. Many of these are remarkable for their design and delicacy of execution.

The most beautiful family tree in Scotland is that in the possession of Sir Allen Seton Steuart (Plate CLI.). It is not large, being only 17½ by 14½ inches; it is executed on parchment, the background being black, and the leafage of a delicate green. Over seventy shields, generally barron and femme, or in other words impaled, appeared illuminated in golden tinctures, argent being represented by the white parchment. The flowers—carnations, lilies, roses, &c.—introduced at foot, and the

figures of an ape and various words that appear above, are executed with great minuteness and beauty of colouring, while the portraits of Robert Lord Seton (afterwards 1st Earl of Winton) and his father George and their respective wives have the finish of fine miniatures. You will find a detailed account of it and a photograph of the tree itself in the illustrated edition of the Catalogue of the Edinburgh Heraldic Exhibition. Its date is 1583. Another very interesting tree, not only on account of its subject, but also on account of its author, is that of the Campbells of Glenurquhy, with portraits of the various members of the House, executed in 1635 by George Jameson, the celebrated Scottish portrait-painter. There is also a magnificent Douglas pedigree of larger size, done by James Ewing, Rothesay Herald, in 1661, in the possession of the Earl of Home at Bothwell Castle, and there is another somewhat similar one at Douglas Castle. The former is fully described in the Heraldic Exhibition Catalogue to which I previously referred.

J. B. P.

CHAPTER XLIX

MODERN ENGLISH HERALDIC ART

IT is one of the curious anomalies of heraldic art that, at a period when all that is noisiest in the great world of art in general is shouting for realism, the greatest authorities in armory are equally vehement in the advocacy of the distorted but possibly more artistic and undoubtedly more pleasing conventionalism of early heraldic examples—or, at least, whilst we are to be realistic in the shape of our shields, our helmets, and our wreaths, we are advised to go to the farthest limits of conventionalism in our lions, eagles, and other charges. Some of us are getting there slowly and by degrees, but I for my part decline to see the beauty in an eagle merely because it is copied from an ancient example, and when it is difficult to distinguish the bird from a double-headed duck. The world of heraldic art sadly needs the exercise of a little discrimination in the teachings of its prophets and patriarchs. I have referred to this point elsewhere herein at some length. The armorial art of the Plantagenet and Tudor periods has been exemplified in relation to the Garter plates, "Prince Arthur's Book," &c.

The most noticeable manifestation of heraldry and heraldic art which the Stuart Period produced is undoubtedly "A Display of Heraldry," by John Guillim, a large folio volume of several hundred pages. It is an intimate and detailed account of practically everything within the scope of the word "heraldry," and though much that Guillim wrote we now admit to be mythical, his work, nevertheless, will remain for all time one of the standard works upon the subject. The best illustrations in the book are the woodcuts, but these reach no very high level of excellence. The copperplate engravings are not of great merit, but they are highly characteristic of the period.

It is customary to observe that at the beginning of the eighteenth century heraldic art in this country was steadily on the downward grade. It has been remarked elsewhere in these pages that it would seem to be questionable how far any one is justified in comparing or "ranking" in the same fixed scale of merit the manifestations of art in any particular period with those of another, or in judging different periods with the aid of the particular yard-tape and foot-rule affected as

the standards in our own particular period. We are always inclined to do so, forgetting that the taste of one man varies from that of another, and that the general taste of one period is never in accord with that of a different period. We can rest comfortably and calmly, assured that our little tin immortals of the artistic world, by whose opinions we swear at the moment, will be certainly succeeded by others (equally immortal, but equally of the little and the tin variety) who will preach the things we now are advised to condemn. Art is long, but no particular artistic canon is eternal. Far more important to armory than the present revival in heraldic art is the greater revival in armorial truth. The art is a fashion which will change, the truth must in the end prevail. However, whether the art be adjudged good or bad, there is no doubt that the bold and free draughtsmanship of the Plantagenet and Tudor days had began to lose some of these characteristics before we first borrowed our Sovereign from Scotland. Through the Stuart and early Georgian periods the heraldic art of this country slowly but steadily developed in its floral and other accessories a wealth of detail and minutiæ, the highest development being considered a shield crowded with unnecessary quarterings, the whole painted in the latest period with the care and intricate and minute detail properly belonging to the province of the miniature-painter. This subject has been treated under the chapter upon Lambrequins, which really chiefly mark the artistic nature of heraldic painting and design. But the same feeling is noticeable in the design itself of so many of the coats of arms granted. This development of the miniature culminated in the reign of Sir Isaac Heard, Garter King of Arms, and the curious "landscape" augmentations of Lord Exmouth, Lord Nelson, and Brisbane (Fig. 553) are examples of the extreme point reached by official heraldry. These coats are simply typical of the art of the period. There is a class of mind which is always "agin the Government," and which (like the missionary who disagreed with everybody —even with the natives who ate him) must always be carping at anything official. The "landscape" augmentations to which allusion has been made are a ready opportunity to the pen of the objector, who forgets that the whole of European heraldry has passed through a similar period, and that coats of this character are being *officially granted at the present time* both in Russia and Germany.

The coats themselves have since in recent grants somewhat improved, and with Scottish and Irish grants at the present day no fault can be found, either in their composition or emblazonment. But English coats—the result of so much differencing on stock models (there must be fifty or more coats for the name of Wilson, all modelled upon the original: Sable, a wolf salient, and in chief three estoiles or)—when considered *en masse* are overcrowded with detail and with the same stereotyped details used over and over again for the purposes of differentiation. The emblazonment, like so much official work, though excellent in execution, is stereotyped in design—all of it executed in the careful style of the "miniaturist" type of herald-painting.

Far be it from me to decry the work of the "miniaturist" type of herald-painter, although under the cloak of that school there has been an enormous amount of "stationer's-shop" work turned out, good, bad, and indifferent—chiefly the last named. For work of the "miniaturist" character, the illuminated pedigree of the Royal Family, formally "recorded" under the statutes of the Order of the Bath, and now remaining in the custody of the College of Arms, is probably the finest piece of work which has ever been executed. The name of the artist responsible for it does not, however, appear to be known. The pedigree is in the form of a bound volume, the value of which is enormously enhanced by the large number of Royal autographs which it contains.

But the greater freedom from stereotyped models which outside artists enjoyed, lead one to unofficial work for evidence of the progress of heraldic art. But most outside work was equally formal and stereotyped in its character.

Figs. 1052 and 1053, which represent the arms of the Duke of Dorset and the Marquess of Rockingham, and which are included in the European series arranged by Herr Ströhl, are taken from a series of engravings of the arms of peers which, with their pedigrees, were published in the *Universal Magazine*, 1790–1800 or thereabouts. Soon after this date Berry published his well-known *Encyclopædia Heraldica*, the most important heraldic work which had been issued since Gwillim's "Display of Heraldry." This book was and still remains one of the most charming and valuable heraldic books, and has always been one of my favourites. It was in three volumes, the first a volume of heraldic terms, containing an immensity of information, far more accurate than much which has since been issued; the second a list of armorial bearings; and the third a volume of illustrations, all from engraved plates. Of the style in which they are executed the engravings are very excellent examples; but they are no more than good engravings of the "miniaturist" type of thought.

No other heraldic work of such a monumental character was issued in this country until towards the close of the century which has just ended. Heraldic interest and armorial art were kept alive by the coach-painter, the seal engraver, and the Peerage books. Seals of any size had long since gone out of general use—heraldry flourished for such purposes in the cheaper and more devious paths of embossed heraldic stationery, one of the fashionable cults being the collection of these embossed designs—all, monograms included, generally known as "crests"—which were pasted in albums or upon ladies' fans. With every desire for kindly impartiality, one cannot find anything good to say for the "cuts" of arms from the Peerage books published before the last few years.

The coach-painter we are accustomed to turn up our noses at. His heraldry, from the point of view of science

and an understanding adherence to rules, was frequently contemptible, but there is no denying the fact that in the finer examples of his work upon State carriages, &c., the execution reached, in the "miniaturist" type, a very high and very unusual pitch of excellence. Fig. 793 is a fair though by no means a superfine example of the work of a coachbuilder's herald-painter. Mr. Manley, who must now be of advanced age, is probably the greatest herald-painter of that class. Sir Bernard Burke, Ulster King of Arms, thought highly of his work, and for a long period many of the patents issued under the hand and seal of Ulster were painted by Mr. Manley.

Many heraldic books, of more or less limited scope, of course, contained illustrations of arms, amongst which reference should be made to Burke's "Extinct Peerage" and Burke's "Heraldic Illustrations." The illustrations for these works were copperplate engravings, which, however, differed little if anything in design or quality from the crowd of inartistic bookplates which were being poured out broadcast from the shops of heraldic stationers. In the seventies and eighties Mr. J. B. Payen-Payne was engaged in the production of various works, the chief of which were his Jersey Armorial and his Roll of High Sheriffs. As heraldic and genealogical works it must be admitted they merited and obtained universal condemnation, but there can equally be no doubt that the execution of the heraldic plates (for which the Messrs. Baker, father and son, were responsible) was of a high standard for work of that character.

But other forces and other ideas were being brought into play. The first to break away from the miniaturist type of heraldic design was Pugin, whose heraldic decoration of the Houses of Parliament is beyond all praise. To Pugin must the honour belong of being the first in the praiseworthy list of heraldic artists to whom we owe the happier position to which heraldic art has been raised in this country. But Pugin was not a herald-painter by profession, and his heraldic work was—if one may so describe it—a by-product of his ordinary professional practice as an architect.

Another architect by profession is Mr. Charles Alban Buckler, Surrey Herald Extraordinary. Studiously remote from the "propagation" of heraldic ideas (and the objectionable tone of personal controversy amongst themselves into which so many now writing upon heraldic subjects have fallen), the work of Mr. Buckler is but little known as of his creation, and his name will be unfamiliar to many even of those interested in heraldry. But when it is stated that he alone is responsible for the armorial decoration in the modern additions and restoration of Arundel Castle, and for the heraldic decoration upon and in Mowbray House, on the London estate of the Duke of Norfolk, his claim to be ranked as one of the foremost heraldic artists of his day will be readily conceded. A few, but a very few, bookplates have been executed from his designs for different personal friends of his. Fig. 1097 is a reproduction of one of these. Mr. Buckler was also responsible for the heraldic part of the decoration of the hall, staircase, gallery, and dining-room of Allerton Park, the seat of Lord Mowbray and Stourton. These contain several hundred carved and painted shields, and modern though this decoration is, it would be difficult to surpass its beauty of design. The execution is equally good.

The premier position, however, is generally conceded to Père Anselm, who, in the quiet seclusion of his monastic home, executed a large number of the drawings for Foster's "Peerage," a work which, after a brief career, became defunct. This was the first book ever issued in recent times, the illustrations of which were a reversion to the mediæval type of heraldic art. Whilst ungrudgingly conceding the high position merited by the illustrations

THE ART OF HERALDRY

in that work, the credit must entirely belong to the artists employed by Mr. Foster, and though this credit would nowadays appear to be somewhat usurped by him, many of the illustrations in later books which have been issued under the name of Mr. Foster fall very far short of the high standard set by Père Anselm and Mr. Forbes Nixon, who were responsible for practically the whole of the illustrations for the Peerage. Père Anselm is best known to the public by his illustrations for that book.

To hark back a little, reference should be made to a book little known to the public, but which had a very marked influence on the heraldic art of the period. The book referred to, Knight and Rumley's "Heraldic Illustrations," appears to be undated, but it is inscribed to Edmund Lodge, Esquire, Norroy King of Arms, which in a measure supplies the omission. As stated in the preface,

FIG. 1097.—Bookplate of Arthur Herbert, Esq., of Coldbrook, Aber-gavenny. Arms : Per pale azure and gules, three lions rampant argent; a crescent for difference. Mantling azure and argent. Crest : A Saracen woman's head affronté, couped at the shoulders, with long hair sable, from the ears double rings pendent or, veil azure, doubled argent, encircled with a wreath of the same ; with the motto, "Asgre an Diogell ei Pherchen."

the book was "not intended as a work of general reference, but merely for the use of artists." It contained specimen engravings of crests, shields, and supporters, and a careful study of the plates in the book will show what an extremely large proportion of the finest work of the herald-painter and engraver must have been executed with the aid of these specimen plates. They are all executed, however, in the "miniaturist" type and in the most naturalistic form, and though they will no longer appeal to the devotees of the latest ideas in heraldic art, they certainly, of their kind and for their excellence of execution, have never been surpassed. Some number of examples from Knight and Rumley have been included in these pages. (See Plates VIII. and XLII. and Figs. 48, 49, and 50.) The book was published by Mr. T. C. Jack, the founder of the firm responsible for the publication of this volume. When Fairbairn's "Book of Crests" was revised under my editorship, the specimen crests from the plates in Knight and Rumley were transferred to that volume, these illustrations being a prominent feature of the new edition.

At the conclusion of my work upon the revised edition of Fairbairn's "Book of Crests" I commenced the compilation of "Armorial Families." It would be childish to pretend that I am not aware of the position and reputation that book has attained to, when one considers the amount of space in the public prints which my disappointed rivals think it worth while to occupy with futile denunciations. Few people, I think, will deny that "Armorial Families" has done more than any other book to promote

the revived interest in the science of heraldry which the last ten or twelve years have witnessed. Whilst the responsibility for the book has always remained my own, I am ready enough and very desirous to acknowledge the large share of credit due to the artists who have worked with me, and to Messrs. T. C. & E. C. Jack, who have found the necessary capital and lent their ready co-operation to bring out its successive editions. From that work Herr Ströhl selected many examples to illustrate his "Heraldischer Atlas."

No other heraldic work of a similar size or importance has since issued from the Press, though Mr. Eve's "Decorative Heraldry" should be brought into notice. The pity of that book was that there was so little of Mr. Eve's own work in the illustrations to his volume. It was an extremely clever though necessarily somewhat brief and limited history of heraldic art illustrated by carefully chosen examples. The "Treatise on Heraldry" by Woodward and Burnett was, of course, a valuable and important work, but the artistic aspect of the matter was very largely ignored.

Two, and the most important, of the manifestations of modern heraldic art will be found in the present Lyon Register and in the many heraldic bookplates which have been executed in recent years. To these one must now turn one's attention.

THE LYON REGISTER

Dr. George Burnett, the late Lyon King of Arms, was admitted in his own lifetime to be one of the foremost and most learned heralds of his period, and since his death this judgment has in no way diminished, but, like many other distinguished heralds, his artistic judgment was defective, and the emblazonments in the Lyon Register in Scotland (and, of course, the contemporary paintings upon the patents issued from Lyon Office) were of the same (or of a worse) stereotyped form still adhered to in the Heralds' College, whilst upon the score of execution the less said the better. Ill execution of emblazonments is not a charge which can be laid at the doors of the College of Arms. At the death of Dr. Burnett in 1890, Mr. James Balfour Paul (now Sir James) was appointed Lyon King of Arms, and to his strength of mind in breaking away from the artistic "ruts" and the ill execution of former days, and in initiating the emblazonment of arms in a nearer approach to ancient Gothic examples, armory and heraldic art owe much. His example has been one of the greatest, if not the greatest, influence at work for the betterment of heraldic art. He, unlike many reformers, happily has lived to see a large measure of the results of his efforts, and he himself has had a larger share of responsibility than as a non-executant he would be likely to be credited with. Whilst training his own artist (Mr. Graham Johnston, to whose work further reference will presently be made), much of the handicraft upon the patents was entrusted to Mr. Forbes Nixon, to whom due credit should be allotted, but the whole of the work is now in the hands of Mr. Graham Johnston. Reproductions of arms from the Lyon Register since the present Lyon King of Arms initiated the new departure, will be found in Plates LVIII. and LX., and in the arms of the Marquess of Ailsa (Fig. 206), Swinton of that Ilk (Plate LXIII.), Arbroath (Fig. 807), Inverness (Fig. 239), Oban (Fig. 580), Alloa (Fig. 581), Bishop Chisholm (Plate CXII.), Wallace (Fig. 804), and Sir Robert Sutherland Duff-Dunbar (Fig. 812), which have all been reproduced by photography or other means from the Lyon Register.

A. C. F-D.

THE ART OF HERALDRY

CHAPTER L

LIVING HERALDIC ARTISTS AND BOOKPLATE DESIGNERS
IN GREAT BRITAIN

Mr. G. W. EVE, R.E.

FOREMOST amongst those whose names are at present before the public, and a head and shoulders above most of his competitors, is Mr. G. W. Eve, R.E., who certainly was the first to raise armorial emblazonment from the trade of the herald-painter to the standard of a high art. Mr. George W. Eve, born in the year 1855, is the son of another heraldic artist, of some reputation amongst the miniaturist school, which in his day

present high reputation. The selection of Mr. Eve to design and execute the series of bookplates for Windsor

FIG. 1099.—Windsor Castle Bookplate. (By Mr. G. W. Eve, R.E.)

FIG. 1098.—Windsor Castle Bookplate. (By Mr. G. W. Eve, R.E.)

FIG. 1100.—Windsor Castle Bookplate. (By Mr. G. W. Eve, R.E.

was the only accepted form in use. Mr. Eve commenced his professional career as one of the official herald-painters at the College of Arms, and though working for several of the officers of that corporation, was, whilst at the Heralds' College, principally associated with the work of the present Richmond Herald. The opportunities his position there afforded him did not satisfy his ambitions, and relinquishing his engagement under official auspices he commenced executing the marvellous etched bookplates which have been the chief means of establishing his

Castle (Figs. 1098, 1099, and 1100), to design the King's Garter banner to hang in St. George's Chapel at Windsor, and to design and execute the invitation card to the ceremony of the Coronation of King Edward VII. are ample testimony, were such needed, to the reputation his work has obtained.

Concerning the reproduction of his work, Mr. Eve expresses himself strongly as to the undesirability of reproducing any artistic work in a different medium or by a different process than that for which it was originally designed and intended. This must be admitted to the fullest degree, and to obviate this objection Plate CLIII. has been prepared, and shows examples of his work printed from the original plates. By such examples, and such only, should the executive quality of Mr. Eve's work be properly judged. But however much, from the executive point of view, artistic examples may lose in the course of reproduction, there must always remain the beauty of draughtsmanship and design, the greatest charm of all in the many excellences of his work.

Doubtless the high level which the work of Mr. Eve has reached is due to his profound knowledge of the science of heraldry, of which his recently published work, "Decorative Heraldry," will remain a proof. He was elected an Associate of the Royal Society of Painter-Etchers in the year 1894 and Fellow in 1903. Typical examples of Mr. Eve's work will be found herein by reference to Figs. 74, 100, 224, 251, 276, 277, 278, 293, 388, 406, 446, 453, 532, 823, and 1105. The genius of Mr. Eve is very versatile, and has found expression in designs for stained glass, seals, and embroidery: he has also turned his attention to modelling in jesso and enamelling.

Mr. CHARLES W. SHERBORN, R.E.

After the work of Mr. G. W. Eve, the bookplates of Mr. Charles Sherborn are most in demand. If bookplates only were to be considered, it must be admitted that there are some who rank his productions as highly as those of Mr. Eve. Whilst Mr. Eve's plates are always etched, those of Mr. Sherborn are engraved. Commencing as an engraver, Mr. Sherborn, who is a much older man than Mr. Eve, had made his reputation in that handicraft many years ago, and his work has certainly increased in excellence. Its charm lies in the beauty of its execution, and in this character Mr. Sherborn has no rival. In originality and beauty of design, and in knowledge of the laws of armory, he falls short of Mr. Eve's accomplishments, but in execution a comparison is between engraving as opposed to etching, and personal taste and predilection must come into play in any attempt to form a judgment. Where reputation depends upon excellence of handicraft, the remarks made when referring to the reproduction of Mr. Eve's plates again apply. Plate CLIII., however, shows an example of the work of Mr. Sherborn from an original plate. His fine work in the engraving of portraits (particularly after paintings by the late Mr. Wells, R.A.) is well known, but is perhaps rather outside the scope of the present volume.

Process reproductions of other plates by him will be found in Figs. 21, 313, 383, 413, 810.

Mr. FORBES NIXON

Mr. Forbes Nixon is one of the most prolific heraldic artists of the present day, and though he has been engaged in work of this character over a long period of years, in no degree has his hand lost its cunning. Though he had well and deservedly established his reputation at a much earlier period, his great opportunity came with the publication of Foster's "Peerage," he being responsible for a large number of the illustrations in that book. Figs. 131, 187, 415, and 816 are examples of his work, as are the lions in Fig. 272, specially drawn by him as typical of, and for the purpose of showing, his own

peculiar style. He did many of the illustrations for the first edition of "Armorial Families," and of these Figs. 53 and 54 are good instances of the work he executed under the limitations I imposed upon him. In the designing of book-covers, a speciality of his, he has produced most excellent work, and enjoys a widespread reputation. The cover of this book, which he designed, is, in his own estimation, one of the finest he has ever produced.

Mr. GRAHAM JOHNSTON

Mr. Graham Johnston, who was born in 1869, is now by appointment Herald-Painter to the Lyon Office, where he has been exclusively engaged for some years past. Though he has not executed very many bookplates, he has made his mark in the world of heraldic art by his characteristic emblazonments upon Scottish patents and in the official Register of Lyon Office. To a certain extent Mr. Graham Johnston's reputation is due to the careful training and advice of Lyon King of Arms; in fact, one might almost consider his abilities the direct product of the teaching of Sir James Balfour Paul. The credit must, however, necessarily remain with Mr. Johnston himself, for no teaching could produce an artist if the artistic abilities of execution were lacking, or if artistic ideas could not be assimilated. Examples of his work will be found in Figs. 58, 134, 136, 142, 150, 239, 334, 361, 411, 435, 469, 503, 508, 518, 580, 581, and 811. He stands pre-eminently at the head of those artists who have adopted the bold outline type of work which carries one's mind back to the days of Tudor heraldry, and who seek to gain their effect by boldness and strength of design and execution. Like Mr. Eve, there are few handicrafts for which he has not produced heraldic designs.

Mr. G. SCRUBY

Though comparatively few bookplates have been designed or executed by Mr. Scruby, he is rapidly becoming recognised as one of the most prominent heraldic artists of the present day. Regularly employed at the College of Arms as one of the official herald-painters, he has profited by the knowledge and assistance of those with whom he has been brought into contact. His work, executed for official purposes in the official style, which still clings to the "miniaturist" type, is of marked excellence, but no doubt his artistic capabilities can better be evidenced by some of the illustrations he has designed for "Armorial Families," or by the heraldic paintings he has been responsible for when not controlled within the stereotyped official regulations. Many of the illustrations herein are from his drawings, but perhaps special attention may be directed to Figs. 165, 169, 240, 273, 274, 275, 409, and 686. As an executive artist he will rank high.

"C. HELARD"

"C. Helard" (the name is a pseudonym) is one of many ladies who have dabbled with heraldic painting or armorial design, but amongst the large number who have attempted none have reached the reputation which Miss Helard has made as a designer of bookplates. Her openly expressed admiration for the work of Mr. Eve undoubtedly influenced her style at the time she commenced heraldic designing, but as she has pursued her course and gained more confidence in her own powers her ideas have widened, and her work is gradually acquiring a strength and originality considerably in advance of her early attempts. Plate XII., which shows the arms of Harley, is from a design by Miss Helard, as is also Plate XLVIII., and as examples of her work reference may be directed to Figs. 281, 282, 283, 299, 330, 384, 392, 397, 428, 494, and 521. Fig. 384 is a remarkably fine piece of designing.

THE ART OF HERALDRY

FIG. 1101.—Designed by Mr. J. Vinycomb, M.R.I.A.

FIG. 1102.—Designed by Mr. J. Vinycomb, M.R.I.A.

FIG. 1103.—Designed by Mr. J. Vinycomb. M.R.I.A.

FIG. 1104.—The Royal Arms, from a design
by Mr. J. Vinycomb, M.R.I.A.

But Miss Helard has many interests in life, and her output of work is not very large. The bookplates of Miss Helard, like those of Mr. Eve and Mr. Sherborn, suffer sadly in reproduction, but that on Plate CLIII. is from the original plate.

FIG. 1105.—Reproduced from an etched plate by Mr. G. W. Eve, R.E.

MR. JOHN VINYCOMB, M.R.I.A.

Mr. John Vinycomb, M.R.I.A., the author of the chapter herein upon the art of heraldic illumination, is well known as a skilful heraldic artist. Originally from the north of England, where he served his apprenticeship as an engraver, he has long been a resident in Belfast, where he held the position of chief of the artistic staff of the great printing firm of Marcus Ward & Co., Limited. On the failure of that firm, Mr. Vinycomb continued to carry on the artistic work which had been so ably pursued under his management by the old firm, devoting himself chiefly to heraldic painting and designing in conjunction with the beautiful art of illuminating.

Mr. Vinycomb has devoted his attention with no little success to most branches of decorative and pictorial art. He is also an original investigator and facile writer on archæology, heraldry, and kindred subjects, being the author of several published works and articles bearing on the artistic side of these subjects. His work "On the Processes for the Production of Ex Libris," which originally appeared in the pages of the *Ex Libris Journal*, was subsequently republished in a volume with numerous examples, forms an admirable exposition of the various means by which book illustrations and pictures are produced. Mr. Vinycomb is a vice-president of the Ex Libris Society and a frequent exhibitor. He is also a member of the Royal Irish Academy, and a fellow of the Royal Society of Antiquaries of Ireland. Mr. Vinycomb's bookplates, executed in wash and reproduced by the half-tone process, stand in a category by themselves and are very effective. They are of considerable artistic merit, as may be seen from Figs. 1101, 1102, and 1103, whilst Fig. 1104 is a very excellent treatment of the Royal Arms.

MR. W. P. BARRETT

Mr. W. P. Barrett is a bookplate designer whose work has in the last few years obtained considerable reputation.

FIG. 1106.—Bookplate executed by J. & E. Bumpus, Ltd., from a design by Mr. W. P. Barrett.

FIG. 1107.—Bookplate executed by J. & E. Bumpus, Ltd., from a design by Mr. W. P. Barrett.

467

Working under the auspices of Messrs. J. & E. Bumpus, Limited, he has designed a large number of bookplates for prominent people of the moment. The bookplates are all executed upon copper, the engraving being of a high order. The designs, which are very varied in character, appear singularly suitable to the process employed, and the bulk of his plates are of no little excellence. Messrs. Bumpus recently issued, in an Edition-de-Luxe, a series of fifty-five reproductions of Mr. Barrett's designs from the original plates. The quality of Mr. Barrett's work can perhaps be judged from Figs. 1106 and 1107, though of course the beauty and delicacy of the engraving is in a large degree lost in the process of reproduction. A. C. F-D.

PLATE CXXXVI

EQUESTRIAN SEALS OF THE THIRTEENTH TO FIFTEENTH CENTURIES

(From a Collection of Seals in the k. and k. Haus-, Hof- und Staats-Archiv in Vienna)

Fig. 1. Reverse side of the seal of *King Przemist Ottoker II. of Bohemia*, 1273. (Diameter, 11.8 cm.) The legend runs : "✠ S Otakari . Dei . Gracia . Docis . Austrie . Stirie . Domini . Carniole . 7 Marchie . Portos . Naonis." On the shield appear the arms of *Austria* (gules, a fess argent), on the flag the arms of *Bohemia* (gules, a lion rampant doubled-queued argent, crowned). On the horse-cloth are several shields; at the neck an escutcheon of the arms of *Carniola* (per pale, dexter or, three lions passant in pale sable ; sinister, the fess of Austria) ; lower down an escutcheon of *Moravia* (azure, an eagle chequy gules and argent) ; above on the haunches *Styria* (vert, a panther argent, vomiting flames of fire) ; and below an escutcheon of *Carinthia* (argent, an eagle displayed azure, charged on the breast with a crescent chequy gules and argent), or perhaps the ancient arms of *Eger* (gules, an eagle displayed sable). The pot-shaped helmet of the rider carries the crest of *Bohemia*, two eagle's wings sable.

Fig. 2. Seal of *Guido, Count of Flanders*, 1277. (Diameter, 9.5 cm.) The legend runs : "✠ S Goidonis : Comitis : Flandrie : et Marchionis : Namvcen (Namur)." The shield and the horse-cloth in places show the arms of *Flanders :* Or, a lion rampant sable.

Fig. 3. Seal of *Friedrich, Count Palatine of Saxony*, 1291.

FIG. 1108.—Pilgrim von Puchheim (1377).

(Diameter, 8.5 cm.) The legend runs : "Fridericus Dei Gracia Comes Saxonie Palatinus." The shield, banner, and horse-cloth all display the arms of the Palatinate of *Saxony* (azure, an eagle displayed or). The helmet has two buffalo's horns as crest. The original of this seal, the authenticity of which is not free from doubt, is in possession of the Staats Archiv.

Fig. 4. Seal of *John, King of Bohemia* (1311–1346). (Diameter, 9.5 cm.) The legend runs : "Johannes . Dei . Gratia . Rex . Boemic. Ac . Locemborgensis . Comes." On the shield, on the shoulder-pieces (ailettes), and on the horse-cloth appear the arms of *Bohemia* quartered with those of *Luxembourg* (barry of ten argent and azure, a lion rampant gules). The crest is that of *Bohemia*.

Fig. 5. Seal of *Duke Rudolph IV.*, the founder of Austria (1363). (Diameter, 13.3 cm.:) "✠ rudolphus : quartus : dei :gracia :archydux .

austrie : stirie : et : karinthie : dominus : carmiole : marchie : ac : portus : naonis :(Portenau) comes : in : habspurg : ferretis : et : kiburg : marcia : burgonis : ac : lantgravius : alsacie." The shield and the flag show the fess of *Austria*. Above, on the dexter side, appears the shield of *Carinthia*, and on the sinister of *Styria*. Then follows,

FIG. 1109.—Henry de Percy (1301).

on the dexter side, an escutcheon of the arms of the Countship of *Pfirt* (Fürth) (gules, two fishes haurient and addorsed heads upwards) ; on the sinister the Countship of *Habsburg* (or, a lion rampant gules). Under the horse appear the shields of the Lordship of *Portenau* (Pordenone) in the Austrian shield of union (an open gold door on three green mounds) ; of *Carniola* and the *Wend Territory* (or, a black Wend hat lined gules, and strings of the last). The crowned helmet bears the Austrian crest, viz. the peacock's tail. The horse's head is adorned with the eagle-crest. When in the year 1363 Tyrol fell to Austria, Rudolph IV. had the eagle of Tyrol substituted for the Austrian fess on the flag. Before this seal, Duke Rudolph used another seal, which brought him troubles. He attributed to himself dignities and titles which did not belong to him, and as a consequence was called to account by his father-in-law, the Emperor Charles IV. In the legend he had styled himself " Phalzerzherzog von Oesterreich, Steyrmark, Kärnten, Schwaben und im Elsass." After long hesitation he was at last obliged to give in, and discontinue the use of the seal (1361). Fig. 7 shows the obverse side of this seal. The legend runs : " ✠ Rvdolphos : Qvartos : Dei : Gracia : Palatinos : Archidox : Avstrie : Stirie : Karinthie : Suevie : Et : Alsacie : Dominos : Carniole : Marchye : Ac : Portos : Naonis : Natus : Anno : Domini : NI : CCC : XXXIX." On the shield of the rider appears the fess of *Austria*, on the flag, *Styria* ; whilst the horse-cloth shows the shields of *Carinthia*, *Habsburg* (here the lion is crowned for the first time), and *Pfirt*. As crest, the duke bears the Austrian peacock's tail issuing from the crown upon his helmet.

Fig. 6. Seal of *Frederick, Duke of Austria* (1438). (Diameter, 13.4 cm.) " S Friderici . Dei . Gracia . Docis . Austrie . Stirie . Carinthie . Et . Carniole . Dominus . Marchie . Sclavonice . Ac . Portos . Naonis . Comes . In . Habsburg . Tirolis . Ferretis . Et . Kiborg . Marchio . Borgowie . Ac . Lantgravios . Alsacie." On the " Tartsche "-shaped shield is the *Austrian* fess, and on the flag are the arms of *Styria* ; on the horse-cloth are the five eagles of the so-called *East Austrian* coat of arms. The crowned tilting-helmet bears the peacock's tail ; and on the horse's head, issuing out of a coronet, is a demi-eagle.

Fig. 8. Seal of *Pilgrim von Puchheim, Erb-Truehsessen von Oesterreich* (Hereditary Lord High Steward of Austria), 1377. The inscription round it is as follows : " ✠ S Pilgrini . Depœchhaim . Dapiferi . Avstrie." The Lord High Steward bears in his raised right hand a dish containing a fish. The horse-cloth is ornamented with the shield of Puchheim (argent, a fess gules). The office of Hereditary Lord High Steward came into the family in the year 1276.

Another interesting equestrian seal is shown in Fig. 1109. It is the seal of *Henry de Percy* (Baron Percy) in the year 1301. Shield, saddle, and horse-cloth are adorned with the blue lion on a gold field, the arms borne by the Percy family as the ancient arms of the Dukes of Brabant, from whom the Barons Percy were descended in the male line. The helmet and horse's head are both adorned with a fan-crest. The legend runs : " Sigillvm . He . . . De Perci." H. S.

THE ART OF HERALDRY

PLATE CXXXVII

EQUESTRIAN SEALS OF THE FIFTEENTH CENTURY

(From the Collection of Seals in the k. and k. Haus-, Hof-, und Staats-Archiv at Vienna)

Fig. 1. Seal of *Antony, Duke of Lorraine, Brabant, and Limburg* (1407). (Diameter, 10 cm.) The legend runs: " ss. Antonii dei . gracia . lothar . brabancie et lumburgens . ducis . sacri imperii .

Fig. 2. Seal of *Reinhold IV.* (died 1423), *Duke of Geldern and Jülich* (1407). (Diameter, 9.7 cm.) The legend runs: "✠ Sigillum Re (in) alde Dei . Gracia . Dvcis . Ghellensis." The arms of *Geldern* (azure, a lion rampant, double-queued and crowned) appear both on the shield and on the flag, and also on the shoulder-pieces (ailettes), and the horse-cloth. As crest on both the helmet and on the horse's head is a semi-circular screen adorned with the device of the shield, and with peacock's feathers on the edges.

Fig. 3. Seal of *Duke Albert V.* (when Emperor II.) *of Austria and Margrave of Moravia* (died 1439). (Diameter, 9.5 cm.) The legend runs: "Sigillum Alberti . dei . gracia . docis . Austrie . et . marchiöis . moranie." The flag and the shield placed in the field of the seal show the arms of *Austria*, but the shield of the rider bears the arms

FIG. 1110.—Séal of Rudolf IV. of Austria.

In use from 1359–1361.

marchionis." The shield of the rider is: Quarterly, 1 and 4, the arms of *France*, azure, three fleurs-de-lis or ; 2. *Brabant*, sable, a lion rampant or ; 3. *Limburg*, argent, a lion rampant double-queued gules (crowned). The horse-cloth displays the same devices. The helmet bears the French crest, of the fleur-de-lis.

of *Moravia*. The helmet is surmounted by the (old) crest of *Moravia*, the eagle's wings, gyronny (here of three) or and sable.

Fig. 4. Seal of *King Stephan Tvrtko II. of Bosnia*, 1443. (Diameter, 11 cm.) The inscription, so far as it is legible, runs: " S. Maius Stephi Turtconis Dei Gra . Rascie . Bossne Maritimarum. . . . ."

The only device upon the shield is a coronet throughout fesswise of fleurs-de-lis. On the flag and on the horse-cloth appear, as armorial bearings, a bend on a field semé of "Gleven" (i.e. lily-shaped lance-points, equivalent to our "cronels"). The same figure appears in the design of the background of the shield. These two coats of arms bear a striking resemblance to the arms of the Schärffenbergs and the Rohitsch. The former claim to be descended from the kings of Bosnia; but probably this is not the case. The Schärffenbergs bore originally: Argent, a crown sable; and later on: Azure, a crown or (Plate LXXVII. Fig. 4). The Rohitsch family bore: Azure, semé of "gleven" or, a bend argent, which they later on (misunderstanding a diapering of the same) charged with annulets gules. The crest of the rider, if one takes other representations into account, would seem to have been a long-shafted tassel of peacock's feathers, in which case this would prove another connecting link with the Schärffenberg arms.

Fig. 5. Reverse side of the ducal seal of *Frederick of Austria* (Frederick III.), 1479. (Diameter, 12.3 cm.) The legend here is the continuation of the title on the obverse side, and reads: "Domini Marchie Sclavonice . Et . Portos Naonis . Comitis in Habsburg . Tirolis . Pherretis . Et . In . Kybvrg . Marchionis . Bvrgovie . Et . Landtgravi . Alsacie." The figure wears the Austrian ducal hat. (See Plate XV. Fig. 17.) On the shields appear the following coats of arms: Landgraviate of *Upper Alsace*: Gules, a bend between six coronets or; Countship of *Kyburg*: Gules, a bend between two lions or; Countship of *Tyrol*: Argent, an eagle displayed gules, crowned and armed and charged upon the wings with the trefoil bars or; *Portenau, Habsburg, Pfirt*, Margraviate of *Burgau*: Bendy of six argent and gules, a pale or; and *Upper Austria*: Party per pale, on the dexter side an eagle displayed or; sinister, paly of four argent and gules. On the dexter side of the seal, in front of the horse, is the monogram and the well-known letter device A E I O V (see Plate LXXXVII. Fig. 1), with the date 1479.

Fig. 6. Seal of *Duke Albert der Beherzte* (the Brave) *von Sachsen* (of Saxony), died 1500, founder of the Albertine line, the present Royal Family of Saxony. (Diameter, 10.5 cm.) The inscription runs: "S. Alberti dei grā ducis saxonie lãtgrany thuringie march. misne oriētalis et landsperg comitis in orlamund." On the shield of the rider are the arms of the Duchy of *Saxony*: Barry of ten sable and or, a crown of rue in bend vert. The flag and two other shields each display a lion rampant as the arms, which are probably the armorial bearings respectively of the Landgraviate of *Thuringia* (azure, a lion rampant barry of eight argent and gules, crowned or); of the Margraviate of *Meissen* (or, a lion rampant sable); and of the Countship of *Orlamünde* (or, semé of hearts gules, a lion rampant sable). At the horse's feet are the arms of the Margraviate, properly of the Lordship of *Landsberg* (or, two pallets azure); the arms of the *Wettin* family, and of the County Palatine of *Saxony* (azure, an eagle displayed or). On his crowned tilting-helmet the rider bears the crest of Thuringia, viz.: Two buffalo's horns argent, adorned with green (or more correctly, golden) leaves, slipped.

H. S.

PLATE CXXXVIII
SPECIMENS OF ARMORIAL AND OTHER SEALS

Fig. 1. Seal of *Ferdinand I.*, as King of Hungary, 1526–1564. (Diameter, 14 cm.) Obverse: The king is represented in his coronation-robes, seated on a throne, holding his sceptre in his right hand, and the Imperial globe in his left. Above him, supported by griffins, is the crowned escutcheon of the Roman Kingdom, the Imperial eagle with one head (Ferdinand was elected King of the Romans at Cologne in 1531, and crowned at Aix-la-Chapelle). At his feet is a shield: Quarterly, 1 and 4, Austria; 2 and 3, Burgundy. At the side of the throne, each supported by an angel or cherub, follow the shields of: 1. New and Old Hungary; 2. Castille, Leon, Aragon, Sicily, and Granada; 3. Bohemia, 4; Dalmatia. The inscription is as follows: "Ferdinandvs. D. E. Cle. Rom. Rex. Semp. Avgvst. Ac. German. Hong. Boem. Dalm. Croat. Bosn. Lodomerie. Bolgarie. Sclavon. Rame. Servieo.

The reverse side (Fig. 1111) contains as the central figure a magnificently designed example of the Imperial eagle with one head, as an attribute of the King of the Romans, the breast charged with the escutcheon of Hungary. In the circle surrounding it appear the shields of most of the countries mentioned in the inscription following from right to left: Croatia, Bosnia, Galicia, Moravia, Lausitz, Habsburg, Alsace, Tyrol, Wurtemberg-Teck, Silesia, Slavonia, Lodormeria. The inscription on the reverse side, a continuation of the obverse, runs: "Rex. Infans Hispan. Arched. Avst. Dvx. Bvrgvn. Marchio. Mora. Etc. Dvx. Slesie. Wurtemb. .Ec. Comes.-Hassp. Fland. Tirol. Ec."

An equally beautifully engraved administrative seal is shown in Fig. 1112. It is the seal which the Emperor Leopold I. caused to be engraved for himself, as Elector of Bohemia, on the election of his son, the Archduke Joseph, as King of the Romans, which took place

on January 24, 1690. (Diameter, 11 cm.) The much-foliated and ornate cartouche with the Bohemian lion is surrounded by the collar of the Golden Fleece, and is surmounted by the elector's hat, and placed upon and above that is a Royal crown. The seal inscription runs: "Leopoldvs I.D.G. Hongariæ. et. Bohemiæ Rex. Hæreditarivs. Archdivx. Avstriæ. Zc." Inside the circlet of the Royal crown the date "MDCXC" is introduced. The original seal in silver is preserved in the "K. and K. Haus-, Hof- und Staats archiv, Vienna."

Fig. 2. This is the seal of *Albert Baron* (Freiherr) *von Winkel*, Bishop of Passau (1363–1380), about the date 1378. (Height, 8 cm.) Under a canopy of Gothic architecture, the seated figure of the bishop is introduced. The background of the seal on both sides of the architectural design is occupied by the figure of a wolf, taken from the arms of the bishopric (argent, a wolf gules). At the bishop's feet appear the arms of the Freiherren Winkel von Winkelberg of Lower Austria ("argent an unicorn rampant sable"). The inscription runs: Albertvs. Dei. Gracia. Pataviensis Eccl. Epis."

Fig. 3 represents the seal of *Lancelot Blackbourne*, Bishop of Exeter, 1716–1724. (Height, 9.5 cm.) The shield shows the arms of the See (gules, a sword in pale proper, the hilt or, and two keys in saltire of the last) impaling the personal arms of the bishop (namely, argent, a fess nebuly between three mullets sable). The inscription runs: "Sigillvm Lancelotti Blackbvrne Episcopi Exon AD 1716." Lancelot Blackburn, from 1724 Archbishop of York, "the gay old Archbishop" as Walpole called him, was baptized at Oxford October 20, 1676, and in his younger days was chaplain on a freebooter's ship, of which his rough manners were reminiscent. He died March 23, 1743.

Fig. 4. Seal of the notorious *Lazar Brankovies* of Servia reproduced from a document dated August 12, 1457. (Diameter, 7 cm.) Lazar was the youngest son of the Prince of Servia, Georg Brankovies, and died January 20, 1458. The coat of arms on the seal is interesting, in so far as the entire crest is repeated on the shield (argent, between two buffalo's horns azure, a lion rampant, crowned or).

Fig. 5. Seal of the *Archbishop of Salzburg*, Leonhhard v. Keutschach (1495–1519), on a document dated May 10, 1498. (Diameter, 4.5 cm.) Inside a rich Gothic architectural canopy appears the bust of the bishop, the figure being repeated below in a kneeling posture; on the dexter side are the arms of the *archbishopric* (party per pale, the dexter side or, a lion rampant sable; the sinister side gules, a fess argent). On the sinister side of the seal is the shield of Keutschach, a Carinthian family (sable, a turnip argent, leaved vert). The legend runs: " S. leonh. dei. gra. sancte. saltzburg. ecclie. archiepi. aplici. sedis. legati."

Fig. 6. Seal of the *Archbishop of Salzburg*, Maximilian Gandolf, Count von Khuenburg (1668 to 1687), engraved in 1668. (Diameter, 4 cm.) The arms, which are placed upon a cartouche, show in chief the arms of the archbishopric; below, the quartered arms of the Khuenburgs, who belonged to the old Carinthian nobility, viz.: 1 and 4, party per pale gules and argent, a roundel counterchanged (family arms); 2 and 3, party per fess sable and argent, a ——counterchanged (Steyerberg). The Steyerberg arms were bequeathed in 1468 by the last of the family to the Khuenburgs, who were related to them by marriage. In 1669 the Khuenburgs were raised to the rank of Count. Behind the shield appear an archiepiscopal cross, a crosier, and a sword, the former in pale and the latter in saltire, the last bearing a reference to the temporal jurisdiction of the sovereign archbishopric. (A similar use of the sword is found in the case of the Bishop of Durham.) Over the whole is suspended the archbishop's hat with six fiocci (tassels) on each side (see Plate LI.). The seal inscription runs: "✠ Maximil : Gand. D.G. Archiep. & Prps. Salisb. S. Sed. Ap. Leg." At the sides of the cartouche appears the date 1668.

Fig. 7. Great seal of the Swiss *Canton of Berne*. (Diameter, 8.5 cm.) This charming Rococo cartouche shows the armorial bearings of the canton (and at the same time of the town) of Berne: Gules, on a bend or, a bear passant sable. The seal inscription runs: "Sig. Maius Reip. Bernensis." The name of the seal-cutter "Mörikofer F.C." is introduced under the cartouche. The bear of Berne is to be found, for the first time, on the seal of the year 1224. The bear was originally borne sable, but after the battle of Schlosshalden, 1289, in which the banner of the Bernese was dyed with blood, the bear was placed in a bend argent, upon a field of gules. Shortly afterwards the present tincture (or) was adopted for the bend.

A very attractive disposition of arms and motto scroll and mantling is shown in the seal of the Bohemian town of Schlan) (Bohemian, Slana). (Fig. 1113, diameter, 5.2 cm.) This town, which is very ancient, bears for arms the Bohemian lion, and as a crest a pair of closed wings, one of which is gules, and the other argent. The mantling is gules and argent. The inscription runs: "Secretvm civitatis Slanensis." Interesting from its device is the old seal of the Styrian town of *Levben* (Fig. 1114), principal seat of the trade in Styrian iron. This seal is found on documents of 1298, 1328, &c. (Diameter, 6 cm.) The legend is: "✠ Sigillvm Civitatis, In. Levben." It shows the ostrich (on a red field) with a horseshoe in its beak, holding up a second in its right foot. (Compare Plate

FIG. 1111. "Reverse" side of the seal of Ferdinand I.

FIG. 1112. Seal of Leopold I. as King and Elector of Bohemia.

LXXV. Fig. 3). Konrad von Megenberg says of the ostrich : "Er izt eisen und verdäut daz, wan or ist gar haizer nâtûr." "Er hazzet diu pfärd von natur und laidigt si wo er mag." The horseshoe symbolises both these qualities in the bird, and brought it into

FIG. 1113. Seal of "Schlan," in Bohemia.

relation with iron-working, and all that has anything to do with iron.

Fig. 1115 shows the old seal of *Karl Ferdinand's University of*

FIG. 1114. Seal of Leuben, in Styria.

Prague, founded in 1348 by Charles IV., and completed and enlarged by Ferdinand III. (Diameter, 6 cm.) The legend is : "✠ Sigillvm Vniversitatis . Scolarivm . Stvdii . Pragensis." In

FIG. 1115. Seal of Prague University.

the centre of the seal, between the old and the new escutcheons of Bohemia, appears a figure of Charles IV. kneeling in front of St. Wenceslaus, to whom he offers the foundation charter.

King Wenzel's shield and flag show the eagle, the old arms of Bohemia.

In conclusion are inserted two interesting examples of rose seals, as they are called, such as were usual in East Alpine countries in the time of Ulrich von Lichtenstein, the Minnesinger from about 1227 to the turn of the century. They are considered to be a symbolic mark of Lady's service. The petals of the rose were charged with the armorial shield, or sometimes with the charge therefrom only (see Jubiläums, *Jahrbuch des "Adler,"* 1895). "Innerösterr Rosensiegel v. Alfred Ritter Antony von Siegenfeld."

Fig. 1116 shows the rose seal of *Ulrich von Lichtenstein*, which is taken from a document of the year 1241, in the k.u.k. Haus,- Hof- und Staats archiv, Vienna. (Diameter, 5.4 cm.)

FIG. 1116. Rose Seal of Ulrich von Lichtenstein.

The rose petals bear the shield of the Lichtensteins of Murau in Styria (argent, two bendlets sable), and carry also the inscription : "✠ S. Vlrici De. Lichtenstein."

Fig. 1117 is the rose seal of *Heinrich von Kranichberg*, taken from

FIG. 1117. Rose Seal of Heinrich v. Kranichberg.

a document, dated February 23, 1280, in the Archives of the Monastery of the Holy Cross, Lower Austria. (Diameter, 3.7 cm.) The leaves bear the armorial device of the Kranichbergs (gules, a crane argent. The crane is sometimes found crowned). The inscription runs : "✠ S . Dni . Hanrici . De . Chra . . . Ch."

H. S.

PLATE CXXXIX

SEAL ENGRAVING BY MODERN GERMAN ARTISTS

EXAMPLES OF THE WORK OF GUSTAV SCHUPPAN, ENGRAVER BY APPOINTMENT TO HIS HIGHNESS THE DUKE OF ANHALT, BERLIN

Fig. 1. Seal of *Sir Albert William Woods*, Garter King of Arms (born 1816, Garter 1869) : Argent, a cross of St. George gules, on a chief azure, a ducal coronet within a garter, between a lion of England passant guardant and a fleur-de-lis all or, and impaling his family arms of Woods, namely : or, on a mount vert, a lion statant guardant in front of an oak-tree proper, fructed of the first, a chief azure, thereon on a pale argent, between two circlets of the crown of a King of Arms also of the first, a cross of St. George gules, the escutcheon surrounded by the ribbon of the Order of St. Michael and St. George. (Sir Albert Woods is now K.C.B. and G.C.V.O., and the circlet of the Bath might be substituted, but no alteration has been made in the seal.) Above the escutcheon is placed the crown of his office.

Fig. 2. Seal of the *Right Hon. Sir Hercules George Robert Robinson, Baron Rosmead, and a Baronet:* Vert, a chevron engrailed between three stags at gaze or, and on an inescutcheon the Badge of Ulster. Over his coronet as a baron, which rests on the shield, appears the crest, namely : out of a crown vallery or, on a mount vert, a stag as in the arms. As supporters : on the dexter side an ostrich and on the sinister a kangaroo both regardant proper. Motto : "Legi Regi fidus."

Fig. 3. Seal of *Henry, Baron Aldenham:* Argent, three battle-axes erect within a bordure nebuly sable. The baron's coronet resting on the shield is surmounted by a peer's helmet with a mantling sable and argent, which bears as crest : on a wreath of the colours, in front of a rock a dexter arm in armour embowed, the hand in a gauntlet proper, brandishing a battle-axe in bend sinister sable. Supporters : on either side a man habited in a buff leather jerkin, gloves, and boots, armed with a three-barred helmet, long gorget and sword all proper, and holding in his exterior hand over his shoulder a battle-axe sable. Motto : "Tenax propositi."

Fig. 4. Seal of *Freiherr Curt Seutter von Loetzen,* Royal Chamberlain to Her Imperial Highness the Duchess Vera of Wurttemberg, "Rechtsritter" of the Order of Malta. The shield, which is surmounted by a coronet, is quarterly, and shows : 1 and 4, the silver cross of the Order of Malta on a field gules ; 2 and 3, his family arms : or, a horse's muzzle sable (blazoned by other authorities as a fish-basket).

Fig. 5. Seal of the Prussian Lieutenant-General *Karl Friedrich Ferdinand-Julius von Bumke* (ennobled, Berlin, January 18, 1896) : Or, issuing from a tower gules, an arm in armour brandishing a sword proper, on a chief purpure a sceptre and sword in saltire interlaced with an oak-garland vert. (See explanation of this chief in the chapter upon Augmentations.) The crowned helmet, with its mantling gules and or, bears as crest a plume of three ostrich feathers, the centre one gules, the exterior ones or.

Fig. 6. Seal of *Herrn Heinrich Warnecke* of Batum, Southern Russia : Azure, on a bend argent, three roses gules. Mantling azure and argent, crest on a wreath, a demi-stag gules. Legend : "sigill henrici warnecke, 1893."

Fig. 7. Seal of *Herr von Schoenebeck:* Azure, a fess wavy between three roses argent. The crowned helmet has a mantling azure and argent, and bears as crest a rose as in the arms, between two wings, the dexter argent, the sinister azure.

Fig. 8. Seal of *Freiherr Armin von Foelkersahm* (proprietor of an estate at Warwen, near Windau, in Courland) : Argent, a broken carriage-wheel gules. The crowned helmet has a mantling gules and argent, and the crest is a demi-wild man holding an uprooted fir-tree over his dexter shoulder. Legend : "Sig. Arminii lib. bar. de Foelkersam."

EXAMPLES OF SEALS BY KARL VOIGT, COURT ENGRAVER IN BERLIN

Fig. 9. Seal of *Graf Erbach:* Per fess gules and argent, three mullets of six points counterchanged. Mantling gules and argent. Crest : two buffalo's horns per fess, the dexter argent and gules, the sinister counterchanged. Legend : "✠ Sigill Archivi Erbacensis."

Fig. 10. Seal of *Freiherr Armin von der Osten gen. Sacken,* a captain in the Prussian Army : Quarterly, 1 and 4, per pale argent and gules, on the dexter side a bend wavy azure, on the sinister a key erect argent ; 2 and 3, azure, three roses or. The crowned helmet bears as crest, between two wings displayed, the dexter argent, the sinister gules, a pillar of the last, and issuant therefrom three peacock's feathers, the feathers charged with a rose or, and superimposed upon the pillar two keys in saltire argent.

Fig. 11. Seal of *Herr von Levetzow:* Argent, a turnstile gules. The crowned helmet has a mantling gules and argent, and bears as crest, in front of a double plume of peacock's feathers, a demi-turnstile as in the arms.

Fig. 12. Seal of *Prince Radolin-Radolunski* (of the House of Leszezy'c) : Gules, a thatched roof or, supported by four pillars argent (Polish device, *Brog*). The crowned helmet, with its mantling gules and or, bears as crest a peacock's tail charged with the device of the arms in bend. Two Prussian eagles serve as supporters. Above appears a motto scroll with the inscription : "A Lechis. Leszezyc" ; underneath, "Cœlestum in Ira. Tueor." The whole is beneath an ermine-lined purple mantle, which falls from a Prince's crown.

Fig. 13. Seal of *Heinrich von Stephen,* State Secretary to the German Imperial Post-Office (ennobled March 9, 1885). The shield is per fess, and the base per pale. In chief sable, issuing from clouds argent, two clasped hands proper, in the dexter base argent, a terrestrial globe azure ; in the sinister base gules, a post-horn or, with cords and tassels sable, argent, and gules ; over all, on an inescutcheon azure, an anchor or. The crowned helmet has a mantling of azure and or, and bears as crest an arm embowed proper, hurling a bundle of lightning-flashes. Motto : "Fest."

Fig. 14 is the seal of the well-known heraldic authority, *Professor Emil Doepler.* The shield is divided by a curved point reversed, and shows in chief gules, three inescutcheons argent (the so-called "artist's" coat of arms) ; on the dexter side, argent, a

dice sable, with five spots argent ; on the sinister, sable, a dice argent, with six spots sable, and below three mounds issuing in base conjoined to the point reversed and counterchanged of the field. Supporter : a lion, its head within a tilting-helmet with a mantling sable and argent, upon which is the crest, two arms embowed, habited respectively in argent and sable, the hands throwing a dice argent with six spots sable.

Fig. 15. Seal of *Admiralitatsrates Hugo Domeier* (a member of Patrician family at Embeck, Hanover) : Per pale or and gules, a chamois springing up against the side of a rock issuing from the dexter side of the escutcheon. The helmet has a mantling gules and or, and bears as crest, between two scythes erect, the blades meeting in saltire, a chamois as in the arms. Motto : "Allzeit Trew, Allzeit mit Hut."

EXAMPLES OF SEALS BY JOHANN SCHWERDTNER, ENGRAVER

Fig. 16. Seal of *Freiherr Ferdinand de Fin,* Landkomtur der Pallei Oesterreich des Hohen Deutschen Ritterordens. The shield is : Quarterly, 1 and 4, the arms of the Teutonic Order, argent, a cross sable ; 2 and 3, the arms of De Fin, viz. : quarterly, i. and iiii., sable, a lion rampant or, holding in its mouth a clover leaf vert ; ii. and iii., gules, a fess between three fleurs-de-lis argent (for Mirandola) ; in base, on a curved point dividing the third and fourth quarters of the second and third grand quarters, azure, an anchor argent, the beam or, over the second and third grand quarters on an inescutcheon or, a double-headed Imperial eagle sable. The shield bears three crowned and barred helmets. The centre helmet, which has a mantling sable and argent, has for crest two wings displayed argent, each charged with the cross sable of the Teutonic Order. The dexter helmet has as crest the Imperial eagle as in the escutcheon, and a mantling sable and or. The sinister helmet has a mantling gules and argent, and as crest a peacock's tail. The "profess-ritter" of the Teutonic Order charge the shield of the Order with that of their own arms, but Knights Commanders quarter the arms of the Order with their family arms, and also place the helmet with the wings upon their shield.

Fig. 17. Seal of the *Emperor Franz Joseph Suchen-Fond-Curatoriums* in the Polit. District of Oberhollabrunn, in Lower Austria. Placed together within a quatrefoil are four shields : I. *Market of Oberhollabrun:* Per fess, in chief azure a "wolf's claw" (forest sign) in bend between two mullets of six points or, in base in water, a rock on the dexter side, with a water-pipe or, towards which a swan proper is swimming. II. *Town of Retz:* Azure, a lion rampant, crowned or. This should be more correctly "guardant." III. *Market of Hangsdorf.* A translation of the German blazon would be as follows : " On a light blue ground, standing on three brown mountains, a battlemented tower with an open, rounded door, and pointed roof, adorned with a blue flag ; on the side, a tied-up vine with green leaves and blue bunches of grapes." IV. *Market Ravelsbach:* Azure, a lion rampant holding in its dexter forepaw a key all or.

SEALS BY WILHELM LENTHE, COURT ENGRAVER OF SCHWERIN

Fig. 18. Seal of *Freiherr von Hammerstein:* Party per pale, on the dexter side argent, three ecclesiastical banners gules, fringed and ornamented or (relating to the Hereditary Office as Treves Electoral Standard-bearer appertaining to the Burgrave von Hammerstein) ; on the sinister side, gules, three hammers bendwise, two and one argent, the handles or. The helmet on the dexter side is surmounted by a cap gules, turned up ermine, with an arch or, and issuing therefrom three ecclesiastical banners gules, mounted on gold standards, each terminating in a cross ; the sinister helmet is surmounted by a hat sable, turned up argent, and thereupon two wings addorsed sable, charged with a hammer bendwise as in the arms. Mantling gules and argent. Between the helmets the coronet of a Count rests on the shield, in accordance with a Royal Warrant of March 5, 1816, after the descent from the Burgraves von Hammerstein (of Andermach on the Rhine) had been officially proved. Supporters : two lions or. Motto : "Spectemur agendo."

Fig. 19. Seal of *Freiherr von Maltzahn:* Party per pale, on the dexter side two hares' heads couped in pale argent ; on the sinister side, or, a vine issuing from the partition line, having two leaves, and a bunch of purple grapes proper. Mantling azure and or. Crest : on a wreath azure and or, behind a palisade or, a fan of peacock's feathers.

SEAL BY KARL OEHRING, SEAL ENGRAVER BY APPOINTMENT IN MUNICH

Fig. 20. Seal of the *Town of Munich.* Under an open town door, flanked by two roofed and battlemented towers, appears a monk, the "canting" device of Munich (Munchen), the arms being argent, a monk sable, holding in his sinister hand a book gules, and from behind the battlements of the wall the Bavarian lion issuant.

H. S.

PLATE CXL

MEMORIAL SLABS WITH HERALDIC DECORATION

(Fifteenth Century)

Fig. 1. Memorial slab to *Martin Reuter von Klebing* (died 1416), originally in St. Andrews Church, but removed in 1862 to the south exterior of the Chapel of St. Margaret, in St. Peter's, Salzburg. The stone, which is cut from red Salzburg marble, and which is about 2 metres 30 cm. high, bears on the bevelled outer edge the following inscription : "Anno . dñi . millesimo . Quadringentesimo . XVI . obiit . Martinus . dict . Rawter . Salezburgensis . fundato . huius . Capelle . Qui . diem . suu . clausit . extremu . die . Quinto . Mens . January . Anni . eiusdem ." The inner edge of the stone received more than a hundred years later the following additional inscription : "Hie ligt begraben der edl vnd fest Hanns, Reitter der lest des namens der gestorbñ ist am sambstag nach sand Alextag 1528 iar dem gott gnadig well sun." The *Reuters of Klebing*, an old Salzburg theological family, bore : Sable, a sinister arm embowed, the first clenched, habited in an under sleeve azure, within an outer sleeve (compare our maunch) argent, and as crest the same arm, but erect and holding up a tree eradicated, the branches lopped. The sleeve here is continued into the mantling. The arms of the grandparents

Avgvst' . Avstrie . Stirie . Karinthie . Et . Carniole . Dox . Dñs . Marchie . Sclavonice Ac . Portvs . Naonis . Comes J. Habspurg . Tirol . Pherret . Et . I . Kibvrg . Marchio . Bvrgovie . Et . Lantgravi . Alsacie . Obii . Ano . Dñi . MCCCC . . . ." At the sides of the Emperor, who is represented in his coronation robes, are introduced on the dexter side the cross of St. George, the monogram of the Emperor, the arms of the Roman-German Empire, and the fess-shield of Austria, with the crest. On the sinister side are the arms of the Duchy of Milan (quarterly or and argent, in the first and fourth quarters a black eagle—Imperial vicariate ; 2 and 3, a snake azure, devouring a human figure gules—Visconti), Ancient Austria (azure, five eagles displayed or), with the archducal hat, and the crest (a crowned eagle displayed or, with wings sable, semé of linden-leaves also or), as also Styria, likewise with its crest. At the Emperor's feet the shield of the Habsburgs is laid. A ribbon with the well-known letter-device A E I O V encircles the top of the sceptre.

The admirable sculptures shown in Figs. 1118, 1119, and 1120 in the text date from the same period. The two first are of red marble, and are now the one on the north and the other on the south side of the Cathedral in the Wiener-Neustadt (Vienna—New Town), but before 1871 they were in the Chapel of St. Michael, which formerly stood near the Cathedral. (See *Zeitschrift* "*Adler*," 1873.)

Fig. 1118. Gravestone of *Anna Roll*, wife of Johann Roll, Burgomaster of the Neu-Stadt from 1467–1471. (Height, 1.93 metres.) The inscription reads : "1471" die . ascēsiosis . dñi . obiit . hoësta . dña . aña . vxor . Johīs . roll . de . argētina." Hans Roll (according

in the four corners of the stone, unfortunately, cannot be identified, with the exception of the arms of *Nussdorfer* (sable, a unicorn rampant argent, armed or).

Fig. 2. Memorial slab to *Georg Aigl zu Lind* (died 1487), also brought to the St. Margaret's Chapel of St. Peter's. The stone, also of red Salzburg marble, and about 2 metres high, bears the following inscription : "Hie ist begrabñ Gorg Aigl zu lind der gestorbñ ist am Suntag nach Scolastice Anno dñi MCCCC LXXX VII dem gott genad." The *Aigl zu Lind*, originally a Bavarian family, bore : Gules, two axes in saltire argent, the handles or, a device which is repeated on the wings of the crest, which are gules. The mantling is gules and or. At the base of the principal shield are two shields, of which only the dexter one can be identified. It belongs to the old Salzburg burgher family of the *Elsenheims* (at a later date ennobled). Their arms were : Party per pale or and sable, two buffalo's horns transfixed by an arrow fesswise, all counterchanged. Georg Aigl married Margaretha Elsenheim.

Fig. 3. *Tumbadeckel* of *Kaiser Friedrichs III. (IV.)*. This represents the effigy from the tomb of the Emperor Frederick, which was executed by Niclas Lerch, and is in St. Stephen's Cathedral, Vienna. (The reproduction is from a copy by Franz Jobst and Joseph Mocker, made under the direction of Professor Friedrich Schmidt.) The magnificent sculpture, done in red Salzburg marble, was executed during the lifetime of the Emperor, for which reason the year of his death (1493) was not inserted in its entirety, and it was never afterwards completed. The monument was only finished in 1513. The inscription runs : "Fridericus . Tercius . Romanor' . Imperator . Sp .

to a copy in the Adelsarchiv at Vienna) received from the Emperor Frederick III. at Aix-la-Chapelle, on Sunday Misericorda 1486, a patent of nobility with the following arms : Party per fess, in chief or, two mullets of six points gules ; in base sable, a crescent or. As crest, wings charged with the arms. The mantling is sable and or. In the patent a helmet-crown is also granted, with which the arms previously borne, as shown on the gravestone, appear to have been augmented. The same arms were granted by the Emperor Rudolph II., August 20, 1586, to the Court official Maximilian Kemptner. The Rolls would appear from this circumstance to have died out by that time. The Kemptners became extinct in 1663. The Rolls, it may be concluded from the inscription, originally came from Strassburg.

Fig. 1119. Gravestone of *Margaretha Kelbel*, wife of Jakob Kelbel, Burgomaster of the Neu-Stadt, 1483–1489, it being at that time the residence of Frederick III., just at the time of the downfall of Hungary, under Mathias Corvinus. The slab is 227 metres high, and bears the inscription : "Anno dñi 1474 an sand . Alban . tag . starb . Margareth . Jacoben . Kelbel . Hausfrau . . . . (remainder illegible). The shield shows half a calf as "canting" arms (calf = Kalb, and the diminutive in *Austrian* German is Kalbel, pronounced Kelbel). The tinctures are unfortunately unknown.

Fig. 1120 shows a memorial slab to *Johann Baumgartner* (died August 22, 1493) at Kufstein, in Tyrol. (From a photograph by A. Karg of Kufstein.) The stone, made of blackish marble, and 237 metres high, bears the following inscription : "Hic ligt begraben der edel vnd vest Hanns Bawmgartner zu Kuefstain ist gestorben an sand Bartholomais abent do man zelet nach der geburd Christi

MDCCC. in dem LXXXXIII. iar dem gott genedig sey amen." The Baumgardens bore : Azure, a lion rampant or, issuing from behind lattice-work or (in English heraldry this would be termed a weir).

FIG. 1120.—Memorial Slab to Johann Baumgartner.

Crest : a bearded man, habited azure turned back with or, and with a cap of the last, holding over his shoulder with both hands a battle-axe. Mantling azure and or.   H. S.

CHAPTER LI

PLATE CXLI.: FUNERAL HATCHMENTS AND MEMORIAL SLABS

IT was formerly customary upon the Continent, in remembrance of deceased persons, to hang up their arms—carved in wood or painted on circular shields—in the churches. These armories formed at the same time interesting and gorgeously coloured ornaments to the church walls (see Figs. 1 and 2). The institution of masses, and the like, were kept in the minds of posterity through these heraldic devices of the founders (see Fig. 4), a custom which, unfortunately, has entirely fallen into disuse. The more elaborate English system will be presently referred to.

Fig. 1. Arms of *Achaz Wisbeck, Erbkammermeister, des Erzstifte, Salzburg,* died 1481. (Diameter, 130 cm.) The circular shield now preserved in the Town Museum Carolino-Augusteum of Salzburg, was formerly in the chapel-of-ease at Oberalm, near Hallein, over the monument of the Wisbecks. Unfortunately an unscientific hand repainted the arms (? in 1858) so that the tinctures now appearing are for the most part incorrect. This circumstance renders it very much more difficult to identify the separate coats. The inscription runs : " Hie . ligt . der . edl . und . vest . achatz . Wispick . erib . Kamermaister . des . ertzpistub . zu . saltzpurg . der gestorben . ist . am . samstag . vor . allerheillingentag . ono . dmi 1 . 4 . 81 . i. Below on the right appear the arms of the *Wisbecks* (Wiesbech, the ancestral castle of the same name, is in the Wiesthal, near Hallein) : Argent, a bend and chief gules. (Now painted over in black and white.) The barred-helmet, with white and red mantling, bears as crest a man's bust, habited in an ermine hood, on the head a high conical cap argent (probably turned

up with red). The shield on the left shows the arms of his wife, *Luneta v. Gumppenberg* (died 1517), whom Achaz Wisbeck married in 1466 : Gules, a bend argent, charged with three "sea-leaves" vert. (It is now painted with a red bend and gold sea-leaves.) Above, to the dexter, is the shield of *Helene von Rechberg,* Luneta's mother : Or, two lions rampant and addorsed gules, with tails intertwined. (Now red on a white ground.) Above, to the sinister, appears the shield of the Bavarian *Freibergs* : Per fess argent and azure, in base three mullets of six points (2, 1). Below, on the dexter side, is the shield of the *Weissbriach* family : Per pale, the dexter side sable, three points to the dexter argent, the sinister side sable. The shield in the centre on the left belongs to the *Notthafts* : Or, a fess azure (here, however, on red). The shields (azure, a chief argent and per pale, the dexter sable, the sinister sable, two points to the sinister argent, with a smaller point or) issuing between them it is impossible to identify. The latter may perhaps be a badly repainted Weissbriach coat. (For the copies of these memorial shields we are indebted to the kindness of Herrn Museumderektors kais. Rat. Dr. Petter, of Salzburg.)

Fig. 2. Memorial shield of *Sebald Lang,* Benefactor of Munich, died 1575. The shield is at present in the Munich National Museum, and was reproduced in M. Gerlach's *Totenschilder und Grabsteine.* The inscription runs : " Anno domini . 1575 Jar . den . 3 Juni . verschid . der Erber . Sebald . Lanng . Pfleger . allhic . dem . Gott . genadt." The shield is : Party per fess, in chief argent, a demi-man issuant habited in azure, holding in his dexter hand an arrow of the last, and in his sinister a branch vert, both curved in orle, in base barry of four azure and argent. The helmet has a mantling azure and argent, and bears as crest a demi-man as in the arms.

Similar in shape is the following, Fig. 1121 here in the text :—

Fig. 1121. Memorial shield of Ludwig von Prenzenau, 1405 (diameter, 88 cm.), now in the possession of F. Warnecke, reproduced in the *Herold,* 1881, No. 10. The inscription runs : " Als ma hat gezalt M. CCCC. un . v. jar . an . sastag . nach . martini . hat . de edl . gestreg . her lvdwig . pientzeave zv . Wildenholtze gestift disc . mess . dem got genad." The coat of arms, painted on a red background and encircled by a gold cord, shows the arms : Argent, on a bend sable, three bezants. The barred helmet is of gold, with a mantling argent lined with sable, and bears as crest a man's bust with a pointed beard, the habit continuing into the mantling. On the head is a pointed conical hat surmounted by a coronet or, from which issues a plume of five ostrich feathers sable. The hat has a turned-up brim sable, charged with three bezants as on the bend.

FIG. 1121.—Memorial Shield of Ludwig von Prenzenau, 1405.

The design of the ribbon-like mantling is carried out in a most free and graceful and a very effective manner.

Fig. 3. Engraved memorial slab from the Marienkirche (Church of the Virgin Mary) at Lübeck, dating from the second half of the sixteenth century. This excessively ornate piece of work shows, besides the figures of *Tydemann Berck,* Burgomaster of Lübeck (died 1521), and his wife Elizabeth Mölres (died 1530), the arms of their families, over the heads of the two effigies. The *Berck* or *Berk* family, originating from *Berk* (otherwise Rheinberg) in Westphalia bore : Or, a cinquefoil vert, in chief a crescent azure. On the slab the crest also appears, this being the cinquefoil and crescent as in the arms, between two wings sable. Mantling azure and or and vert and or. The wife must have belonged to the Müllers of Frankfort-on-Main. Arms : Party per pale, the dexter gules, a fleur-de-lis argent ; the sinister or, a mill-wheel gules, the two coats dimidiated and the charges conjoined.

Of the same period is Fig. 5, memorial slab to *Kaspar von Thurn* of Neunbeuern (died 8th May 1510), at Küfstein, in Tyrol. (From a photograph by A. Harg at Küfstein.) The stone, of red Salzburg marble, 226 metres high, bears the following inscription : " Anno domi 1510 iar an dem heilign auffart abent starb der Edl vnd vest Caspar vom turn zw newnpeirn erbschegck, des schift Saltzburg, dem got geadig vnd parmhertzig sey." In the centre appear the arms of *Thurn*, an old Salzburg family : Gules, a chevron argent,

HATCHMENTS

A somewhat analogous custom prevailed in England, which at one time was of very considerable importance. This was the setting up of a hatchment after a death. No instances of hatchments of a very early date, as far as I am aware, are to be met with, and it is probably a correct conclusion that the custom, originating rather earlier, came into vogue in England during the seventeenth century and reached its height in the early part of the eighteenth. It doubtless originated in the carrying of

FIG. 1122.—Gravestone of Kaspar von Thurn, 1510.

FIG. 1123.—Gravestone of Konrad von Hael, 1348.

charged with two lozenges sable. As crest : a mastiff's head and neck argent. Mantling gules and argent. The Emperor Charles IV. granted a mastiff's head argent, crowned gules, on a field of sable, as arms to Jakob Thurn in 1347, but the Thurns appear only to have adopted it as the crest, and to have retained their old device for the shield. Above, on the dexter side, is the shield of his paternal grandmother, *Barbara von Waldeck* (argent, a saltire depressed gules, and issuant therefrom an eagle displayed of the last). On the sinister side are the arms of his paternal great-grandmother, whose maiden name was *von Trauenhofen* (gules, a pale argent). Below, on the dexter side, is the coat of his maternal grandfather, *Bartholo-mäus von Gufidaun* (tierced in fess gules, argent and sable). On the sinister side is the shield of his maternal grandmother, who was a *von Welsperg* (quarterly argent and sable). These arms were also borne with the tinctures reversed (see *Jahrbuch des " Adler,"* 1874). In conclusion will be found an interesting memorial slab (Fig. 1123) from the first half of the fourteenth century. It is to the memory of *Konrad von Hel* (Hael), and since 1856 has been placed in the new churchyard wall of St. John's, in the village of Tyrol. (From a photograph by Peter Moosbruger, Meraw.) The inscription on the sandstone slab runs : " Anno Domini . Millesimo cccxl Obiit . Strenu (Us . Miles . Chunra) Del . Hel . In . Die . Fabiani . M."

The *Hels* or *Haels* bore : Argent, two eagle's claws in saltire, couped gules. Crest : a " buffelgrind " (*i.e.* the scalp or skin of the head with the ears and horns of a buffalo) argent, the horns each charged with a fess gules.

ceremonial shields and helmets (afterwards left in the church) at funerals in the sixteenth century, and in the earlier practice of setting up in the church the actual shield of a deceased person. The cessation of the ceremonial funeral, no doubt, led to the cult of the hatchment. Hatchments cannot be said even yet to have come entirely to an end, but instances of their use are nowadays extremely rare, and since the early part of the nineteenth century the practice has been steadily declining, and at the present time it is seldom indeed that one sees a hatchment *in use.* The word " hatchment " is, of course, a corruption of the term " achievement," this being the heraldic term implying an emblazonment of the full armorial bearings of any person.

The manner of use was as follows. Immediately upon the death of a person of any social position a hatchment of his arms was set up over the entrance to his house, which remained there for twelve months, during the period of mourning. It was then taken down from the house and removed to the church, where it was set up in perpetuity. There are few churches of any age in this country which do not boast one or more of these hatchments, and some are rich in their possession. Those now remaining—for example, in St. Chad's Church in Shrewsbury—must number, I imagine, over a hundred. There does not appear to have been any obligation upon a clergyman either to permit their erection, or to allow them to remain for any specified period. In some churches they have been discarded and relegated to the vestry, to the coal-house, or to the rubbish-heap, whilst in others they have been carefully preserved.

The hatchment was a diamond-shaped frame, painted black, and enclosing a painting in oils upon wood, or more frequently canvas, of the full armorial bearings of the de-

PLATE CXLII

WOOD-CARVINGS OF ARMS

(Second half of the Fifteenth Century)

In the Royal Exchequer (building) of the princely family of Thurn and Taxis, the so-called "Kelamt" (Kelleramt) at Meran, the former residence of the Counts of Tyrol, there are four, unfortunately somewhat defective, armorial designs carved in wood and painted, of the time of Duke Sigismund of Austria and Tyrol (1439–90). (The copies of these arms here reproduced were made

FIG. 1124. Fragment of the Burgo-master's Chair in the Marienkirche at Lübeck.

ceased person. The frame was usually about five feet six in height, and the rules for the display of arms upon hatchments afford an interesting set of regulations which may be applied to other heraldic emblazonments. The chief point, however, concerning a hatchment, and also the one in which it differs from an ordinary armorial emblazonment, lay in the colour of the groundwork upon which the armorial bearings were painted. For an unmarried person the whole of the groundwork was black, but for a husband or wife half was black and half white, the groundwork behind the arms of the deceased person being black, and of the surviving partner in matrimony white. The background for a widow or widower was entirely black.   H. S. AND A. C. F-D.

from photographs from the studio of the Bavarian Court Photographer, Peter Moosbrugger, in Meran).

Fig. 1. The *New-Austrian Arms:* The fess-shield with the peacock's tail as crest.

Fig. 2. The *Old-Austrian Arms* (now borne as the arms of Lower Austria): Azure, five eagles displayed or. As crest an eagle's body crowned or, within wings sable, semé of linden-leaves or.

Fig. 3. Arms of the *Kingdom of Scotland:* Or, a lion rampant gules, within a double tressure flory and counterflory of the last. As crest a lion sejant affronté gules, crowned or. (Duke Sigismund's wife, 1469–1480, was Eleanora, daughter of King James I. of Scotland; hence the insertion, in the series, of this Scottish coat of arms.)

Fig. 4. Arms of the *Countship of Tyrol:* Argent, an eagle gules, armed or, charged on the wing with triple clover-leaf clasps or. As crest two wings sable, round which is twined a ribbon or, with linden-leaves of the same hanging therefrom.

THE ART OF HERALDRY

Fig. 5 shows the decoration on the lid of a small chest, in the possession of the Royal Kunstgewerbe Museum in Berlin. (Reproduced from " Wood-Carvings of the Fifteenth and Sixteenth Centuries in the Kunstgewerbe Museum of Berlin," published by J. Lessing, 1881.) The carving represents the conjoined arms of the *Bavarian-Palatinate* and *Hesse*.

The *Palatinate of Bavaria* is represented by quarterings for the following, viz. :—*County Palatine on the Rhine* (sable, a lion rampant or, crowned gules) ; *Duchy of Bavaria* (bendy paly argent and azure) ; and the *County of Veldenz* (argent, a lion rampant azure, crowned or). The barred helmet bears for crest a lion sejant gules, crowned or, between two buffalo's horns bendy paly argent and azure. Mantlings sable and gules (more correctly sable and or).

The shield of *Hesse* is also quarterly. In the first quarter appear the arms of the *Countship of Katzenelnbogen* (or, a lion rampant gules, crowned azure) ; 2. the *Countship of Ziegenhain* (per fess sable and or, in chief a six-pointed star argent) ; 3. the *Countship of Nidda* (per fess sable and or, in chief two stars argent, here six-pointed, otherwise eight-pointed) ; and 4. the *Countship of Dietz* (gules, two leopards passant guardant in pale or), over all on an inescutcheon the arms of *Hesse* : Azure, a lion rampant barry of ten argent and gules, crowned or. As crest, the crowned, barred helmet bears two buffalo's horns argent, adorned with linden-twigs or (sometimes vert). Mantling gules and argent. Supporters : two lions or, corresponding to the Bavarian and Hessian arms. Elizabeth (died 1522), daughter of the Elector Philip the Honourable (Philip der Aufrichtige) of the Palatinate, was married on July 10, 1498, to the Landgrave of Hesse, Wilhelm III. (died 1500), and the chest was probably one of the wedding presents.

Fig. 1124 shows a portion of the Burgomaster's chair in the Marienkirche at Lübeck. This unfortunately much-mutilated but magnificent piece of German wood-carving shows the arms of the Hanse-town as an Imperial free city (or, the double eagle displayed sable). Later on, the breast of the eagle was charged with the old flag-device of the town, an inescutcheon per fess argent and gules. (End of the fifteenth century.) In the " great " state coat of arms at

FIG. 1125.—Mould for a kind of gingerbread cake, belonging to the Pirkheimer family in Nürnberg.

the present day, the crowned barred helmet, with the mantling of gules and argent, and as crest the demi-eagle sable, as they are here depicted, still appear.

Fig. 1125 is a model taken from a gingerbread mould carved in wood, belonging to the Pirkheimer family in Nürnberg, and offers a striking example of heraldic craftsmanship. *Willibald Pirkheimer*, the celebrated wealthy Nürnberg councillor, the friend of Dürer and of other prominent men of his day, the last of his race (born 1470, died 1530), was married to Crescentia Rieter (died 1504), and the arms of these two Nürnberg patrician families were united on the gingerbread as below. The arms were—*Pirkheimer :* Per fess or and gules, a birch-tree eradicated vert, the trunk argent (the tree was often emblazoned all in gold). Crest : a bearded man, habited gules, wreathed about the head or and gules, and issuing from the wreath three birch-leaves vert (sometimes argent). Mantling gules and or. *Rieter :* Party per fess sable and or, a melasine (*i.e.* a mermaid with two tails) vested gules and crowned. The same figure also serves as crest. Mantling sable and or (see Plate CIV. Fig. 3). On the gingerbread mould above, the shield of the *Pirkheimers* is united to the crest of the *Rieters*, the latter, however, placed between two buffalo's horns, probably divided or and gules, adorned with birch-leaves, because a conjunction of the above-described crests of the two families on one helmet was not very possible. The buffalo's horns were either adopted by themselves for this purpose, or were

perhaps a second ancient crest of the Pirkheimers, otherwise discontinued. Plate CXLIV. represents the arms (argent, a chevron sable, between three boars' heads erased gules) of William Elphinstone, Bishop of Aberdeen (1484–1514), as existing on an oak carving in the possession of King's College, Aberdeen.   H. S.

PLATE CXLIII

WOOD-CARVINGS OF ARMS

(Second half of Sixteenth Century)

These two coats, the descriptions of which follow, are to be seen in the Chapter Hall of Münster, and are of a typical Rhineland style. The helmet does not rest upon the shield. The cord hanging from it is not in this case, as is usual in Rhineland arms, connected with the shield, but with the scroll bearing the name of the owner of the arms. The crests, especially in Fig. 1, have been executed by the artist somewhat too small in size in proportion to the helmets.

Fig. 1. *D. Gottfrid 'Araes-Elt* (Raesfeld or Rasfeld). An old, noble family of Westphalia. Arms : Or, a fess azure. Crest : two wings, each charged with the arms. Mantling azure and or.

Fig. 2. *D. Frederic, De Keppel.* An old, noble family of Münster, in Westphalia. Arms : Or, a bend of lozenges conjoined and couped gules. Crest : a ball (or screen) charged with the device upon the shield, and issuing therefrom, in the form of a trefoil, three fans of peacock's feathers, each confined in a holder. Mantling gules and or.

As a further example of the Rhineland manner of connecting the shield and helmet, Fig. 1126, the arms of *Duke Johann I.* (the

FIG. 1126.—Cleve-Mark.

Beautiful) *of Cleves* (d. 1481) may serve. It is taken from a rubbing of a bronze plate on his monument. (See "Decorative Heraldry," by G. W. Eve, 1897.) The arms are : Party per pale, dexter, gules, an inescutcheon argent, surmounted by an escarbuncle or (for *Duchy of Cleves*), and on the sinister side (for *Countship of March*, or Mark), or, a fess chequy gules and argent. The crest of the Duchy of Cleves is a bull's head gules, crowned or, armed argent, the skin of the *head* being here drawn down, in regular heraldic fashion, to form the mantling, the crest itself containing the helmet. Through the marriage of Count Adolf II. von der Mark (d. 1347) with Margareta, heiress of the Countship of Cleves, the two coats of arms were united under their son, Adolf III., 1368. The father of Johann I., Adolf IV., received the ducal title in 1417.

Fig. 3 is a carved wooden chest, now in the Teutonic National Museum (Germanisches Nationalmuseum) at Nürnberg, and is reproduced from a photograph by Christoph Müller. The coats of arms belong to the following families : 1. *Hane* (von Haen zu Sonnenschein in Dortmund) : Azure, a cock argent, crowned or (Hahn). Crest : a cock as in the arms, between two wings displayed azure. 2. *Svarte* (Schwarte I.) : Argent, two chevronels sable, between three negroes' heads proper, banded with silver fillets.

THE ART OF HERALDRY

Crest: a negro's (or Moor's) head and shoulders proper, habited sable. 3. *Prume*: Argent, a tree or. It is here shown to be eradicated, but elsewhere it appears issuing from a mount in base vert. Crest (as given here): an eagle's head and neck argent (elsewhere with outspread wings). 4. *Svarte* (Schwarte II.): Gules, on a bend sinister argent, three negroes' heads. Crest: a negro's head and shoulders, vested sable. 5. *Lemgaw* (Lemgo, Lemgau): Gules, the head of a he-goat argent, armed or. The same figure here serves as crest (but elsewhere the crest of this family is found as two horns, the one charged with a double horizontal band of red and gold, and the other similarly gold and red). 6. *Schedinge* (Scheidingen): Argent, a bend sinister chequy sable and or. Crest: two wings displayed, charged with the device of the shield. 7. *Bersvort* (von der Berswordt): Gules, a boar rampant argent. Crest: a demi-boar rampant argent, between two wings gules. 8. *Vnna*: Party per pale, the dexter side or, an eagle displayed sable, dimidiated, and issuing from the partition line; the sinister side argent, an oak branch bendwise, with three leaves proper. As crest, a bearded man's head and shoulders, habited sable. The mantlings of the barred helmets are entirely carried out in elegant foliated ornamentation in the Aldegrevers style. *Haen* and *Scheidingenare* are families of knightly descent; *Lemgau*, a family belonging to the patricians of Hamm, whilst all the other families belong to the old Town-nobility of Dortmund. (From Notes by M. von Spiessen of Münster.)

H. S.

PLATE CXLV

"HERALDIC CRAFTSMANSHIP"

There is hardly a branch of art, there is scarcely a handicraft, in which heraldry has not played its part. In wood and stone, in metal and iron, on glass and porcelain, the time-honoured armorial

Fig. 1 shows the side of the lid of the shrine of gilded silver containing the corpse of St. Simeon, in the Church of San Simeone at Zara, in Dalmatia. It was made by the Milanese Master Francesco d'Antonio, to the order of Queen Elizabeth, wife of Ludwig the Great of Hungary, and completed in the year 1380. In the pediment appear the Hungarian arms of that period: Party per pale, on the dexter side Hungary (ancient), and on the sinister France (Anjou). The crowned helmet bears as crest, between two ostrich feathers, an ostrich's head and neck, holding in its beak a horseshoe. The mantling, which is semé of fleurs-de-lis on the outside, is lined with vair.

Fig. 2 is the keystone in the nave of the cathedral at Stuttgart, and bears the arms of Württemberg, supported by four angels, and dates from about the fifteenth century. The three stags' attires fesswise in pale sable are upon a field of black on a gold ground. The helmet bears as crest a hunting-horn (gules, stringed or). (For further details concerning these arms reference should be made to the *Deutsche Wappenrolle*, page 76.)

Fig. 3 is a coat of arms in wrought iron, painted and partially gilt (79 cm. high), from a gate at Salzburg. The date of it is about the beginning of the seventeenth century. It is now in the Royal Art Museum in Berlin. The arms are those of the *Cardinal and Archbishop of Salzburg, Marcus Sitticus, Graf von Hohenems* (Hohenembs), born 1574, died 1619. He belonged to the well-known noble family from the Vorarlberg, which gave to the Church some of her high dignitaries. The shield is divided per fess, and shows the arms of the Archbishopric of *Salzburg*, viz.: Per pale or and gules, on the dexter side a lion rampant sable, and on the sinister side a fess argent. (See Plate CXV. Fig. 6.) In base are the arms of Hohenems: Azure, a "bouquetin" or, armed sable. (See Plate V. Fig. 9.) Behind the cartouche are placed a crosier and a sword in saltire, the latter as a sign of the temporal sovereignty attaching to the princely rank of the Archbishop of Salzburg.

Fig. 4. *Ornament for the cover of a book*, with the armorial shield of the town of Nürnberg, now in the German National Museum at Nürnberg.

The door-knocker in bronze on the vestry door of St. Peter's

FIG. 1127.—Door-knocker with the arms of Mecklenburg (St. Peter's Church, Lübeck).

decoration is represented, instances being met with in all directions.

Plate CXLV. shows a few examples of the heraldic decoration met with in different crafts, and adapted to different purposes and opportunities.

Church at Lübeck is composed of the armorial device of Mecklenburg, the crowned bull's head (Fig. 1127). It is a good example of how, by quite simple means, and even in a somewhat crude treatment of the materials, through utilising a heraldic suggestion, a really effective and artistic result can be achieved.

H. S.

PLATE CXLVI

EXAMPLES OF HERALDIC EMBROIDERY

(Sixteenth and Seventeenth Centuries)

Fig. 1. Arms of the *Swedish Realm and Swedish Arms of Pretension* of the time of King Eric XIV. (1560-1568), in the Royal Armoury at Stockholm. The shield is divided by a cross or, the resulting cantons being occupied by the arms as follows : 1. Azure, three crowns or (*Kingdom of Sweden*) ; 2. azure, three bends sinister wavy argent, over all, a lion rampant crowned or (*King of the Goths*) ; 3. gules, a lion rampant and crowned or, holding with all four paws a battle-axe argent, with a curved handle, called an "Olaf spear" (*Kingdom of Norway*); 4. or, semé of hearts gules, three lions passant guardant in pale azure, crowned or (*Kingdom of Denmark*). On the oval inescutcheon appear the family arms of the *Wasas* (who occupied the Swedish throne from 1523-1654), tierced in bend azure, argent, and gules, over this a sheaf of corn (or faschine) or.

FIG. 1128.—Eggenberg (XVII. Jahrh.)

Fig. 2. The achievement of *Georg Borzita von Martiniz*, 1598, in the Cathedral Treasury of St. Veit's, Prague (height, 80 cm.). 'Georgivs . Borzita . De . Martiniz . In . Smetzna . S[acrae] C[æsarea] M[ajestatis] Consiliarivs Et . Svpremvs . Regni . Bohemiæ . Cancellar [i]vs." Gules, two long-stalked, eradicated "sea-leaves" argent, curved inwards. The crowned barred helmet, with its mantling gules and argent, bears as crest : two wings displayed gules, each charged with a sea-leaf as in the arms. The Martiniz, with the Kaunitz and others, belong to the old Bohemian nobility. (The name is mentioned in documents as early as 1261.) They were in the beginning of the fifteenth century overlords of Smetzna, in the Prague district. Borzita von Martiniz (died 1479) filled the dignity of Lord High Steward to the wife of King Georg Podiebrad of Bohemia, and in honour of him his posterity have all borne the name of Borzita.

Fig. 3. The memorial arms of *Christoph. Popel, Freiherr von Lobkowitz*, 1609, in the Cathedral Treasury of St. Veit's, Prague (75 cm. high). "Christopho[rus] Popeli[us] Baro. A. Lobko[vitz]

D[omi]n[v]s In Patek . Et . Diwitz . S[acræ] C[æsarea] M[ajestatis] Rvd[olphi] II Consi[larivs] Intim[os] Svp[re]m[vs] P[ræ]fect[vs] Curi[æ] R[egiæ] Boh[emiæ.]" Quarterly, 1 and 4, per fess gules and argent (Lobkowitz) ; 2 and 3, argent, an eagle displayed in bend sable (*Zerotin*). The crowned helmet, with its mantling gules and argent, bears as crest a quiver gules, and issuing therefrom an ostrich feather argent.

Figs. 2 and 3 are taken from a publication of the Kunstgewerblichen Museum at Prague, 1891.

Figs. 4, 5, and 6—the figures of the eagle, lion, and griffin arranged for cross-stitch—are copied from the patterns in the *Stick-und Spitzenmusterbuche* (Embroidery and Lace Pattern-Book), by Hans Siebmacher, 1601. Siebmacher, the famous author of a well-known Book of Arms, lived in Nürnberg, and died in 1611.

On page 19 (Fig. 15) likewise appears an interesting piece of heraldic embroidery, to which attention may here be directed.

As a final example of embroidery, a magnificent piece of raised work (Fig. 1128) is added.

This is taken from the silk mule-trappings of *Prince Johann Christian von Eggenberg*, which were used when, in October 1673, the Emperor Leopold I. celebrated his wedding with his second wife, Claudia Felicitas of Tyrol, at the Schloss Eggenberg, near Graz. (See *Jahrbuch "Adler,"* 1881.) The shield is : Quarterly, 1. party per pale gules and azure, an eagle displayed argent, crowned or (*Adelsberg*) ; 2. argent, five roses in saltire gules (*Krumau*) ; 3. gules, a wheel argent (*Radkersburg*) 4. azure, an anchor or (*Pettau*), over all, on an inescutcheon argent, a crown or, supported by three crowned ravens in triangle, their heads to the centre. Over the arms, which are enclosed in an ornate cartouche, is a prince's hat. The whole is surrounded by a broad rectilinear ornamental border, which is not shown here. The Eggenbergs, a Graz burgher family, were singled out for distinction several times by the princes of the country, and in 1598 were raised to the rank of Baron. As early as 1467 Balthasar received a grant of Hungarian nobility with the arms, as described above, from King Mathias Corvinus. His great-grandson, Hans Ulrich, was raised to the rank of Prince in 1623, and in 1628 was created Duke of Krumau. The armorial device of the first field, but uncrowned, forms the arms of Adelsberg, in Carinthia, which then was likewise in the possession of the Eggenbergs. Radkersburg, in Styria, also belonged to this family, but nowadays the town uses gules, a wheel or. The arms of the *Pettauer*, the anchor (really the arms of the Marshals von Treun), were not quite correctly used, as regards shape and tincture, by the Eggenbergs. (See Plate LXXVII. Fig. 3.) H. S.

PLATE CXLVII

SPECIMENS OF SWISS ARMORIAL WINDOWS

The essentially Swiss custom of presenting windows, which, commencing in the fifteenth century, continued in vogue until the seventeenth, was the principal reason why the art of glass painting (or staining) attained such a high point of technical perfection in Switzerland, which at that time was unequalled elsewhere. The cantons kept painted glass in store, presenting windows to each other whenever any new building, restoration, or other occasion offered an opportunity for such a gift. In this manner arose a mutual giving and receiving, and the town-hall, guild-halls, shooting-galleries, monasteries, and churches, and even many of the inns, which at that time were regarded as public buildings, rejoiced in the adornment of glass panes depicting the armorial bearings of the thirteen confederated cantons. The custom of presenting painted glass, first practised by the cantons, spread more and more. One town presented another with glass windows, and in its turn received other windows in repayment. Guilds, societies, the rich burghers, and even the peasants took part in this favourite custom, and decorated the town-halls, monasteries, places of pilgrimage, and the houses of the burgess and the farmer. This custom afforded a productive soil for the growth of art. Many artists occupied themselves with glass-painting, and there were, for instance, in Zürich, about the year 1516, ten glass-painters, and in 1568, indeed, twenty-one. In Schaffhausen, in 1610, twelve glass-painters were domiciled. Amongst these were many celebrated masters of the art, such as Karl von Ægeri, Christoph and Josias Mürer, Nikolaus Bluntschli, and many others.

Plate CXLVII. gives illustrations of two of these glass windows, which have been reproduced from the work *Meisterwerke Schweizerischer, Glasmalerie*, published by the Historical Antiquarian Society of Winterthur (Ch. Claesen & Co., Berlin).

The first window shows the arms of the *von Lüttishofen*, a noble family resident in the cantons of Zürich and Lucerne. The arms are : Gules, a flying-fish erect, head upwards. The helmet bears as crest a demi-negress habited sable, banded about the head with fillets gules and argent, and in place of arms the paws of a lion also sable. The crest is continued into the mantling of sable and argent.

THE ART OF HERALDRY

The second glass window shows the arms of *Peter Ritter von Engelsberg*—Peter, King of Engelsbers (the castle and village of Englisberg is in the district of Seftingen, near Bern), "Comthur" of the Order of Malta. The glass, 32.5 cm. high, is in the Museum at Bern. The shield is : Party per fess or and gules, in chief a demi-lion issuing azure. The helmet is of gold, with a mantling gules and or. Crest : a high conical tournament hat surmounted by a bezant (or golden ball), with a turned-up brim ermine, and on either side of the hat is a sword erect proper. Above, on the dexter

at Erbach 1525, and died at Morsee 1571. On the motto scroll appears the date 1549, and the initials of the artist, R.M.D. (13.8 cm. high).

H. S.

FIG. 1130. Arms of the town of Speier, in the Palatinate (1549).

FIG. 1129.—Medallion from the Chancel Windows at Hindelbank (1521).

side, is suspended the coat of arms of the Order of Malta, viz. : gules, a cross argent. The date of the making of the window, 1510, is introduced in the upper part of the background. Below, on a ribbon, appears the inscription : " Fr. (frator) Peter ; vo. engelsperg . komedur. diss . huss . 1 . 5. 10."

From the same publication has been reproduced a medallion with the arms of *von Erlach*, from the chancel windows at Hindelbank, 1521 (Fig. 1129). The medallion (27 cm. in diameter), belonging to the German Early Renaissance period, shows in the centre, on a blue ground, and surrounded by green leaves, the armorial shield : Gules, on a pale argent, a chevron sable. In the border, which is decorated with tiny medallions and foliated ornament, can be seen above the shield the name and the date, which are inserted on a ribbon.

H. S.

PLATE CXLVIII

TWO DESIGNS FOR ARMORIAL PAINTINGS ON PORCELAIN

Fig. 1. Arms of *Anthony von Adlersfeld und Siegenfeld* (Reichsritter) ; Quarterly, 1 and 4, gules, a lion rampant or, holding in its paws a banner of the same ; 2 and 3, party per fess, in chief argent, an eagle displayed sable, and in base azure, a tower argent, the port closed. Crest : issuing from a coronet, and between two buffalo's horns gules, a demi-lion holding a banner as in the arms.

Fig. 2. Arms of the *Pscherer* : Party per pale azure and or, a facetted star of six points counterchanged. Mantling azure and or ; crest : a maiden crowned with roses, and with long flowing fair hair proper, habited per pale or and azure, purfled counterchanged, holding in her dexter hand a star of six points azure, and in her sinister hand three roses gules, slipped and barbed vert, seeded or. In the designing of both coats of arms, which are the work of Herr Ströhl, the first object in view was to endeavour to get a richly expanded mantling, so as to suitably fill the elliptical space at disposal. These arms are introduced here mainly as models of the artistic disposition of mantlings.

A very pleasing design of a mantling is shown in Fig. 1130, which is a drawing of the arms of the town of *Speier* (argent, a representation of the old Cathedral of Speier gules). This design is by the painter and designer Rudolf Manuel, called *Deutsch*, who was born

PLATE CXLIX

"ALLIANCE ACHIEVEMENTS"

Whilst these examples should more properly, when treating of armory from the British point of view, be considered as included within the rules for marshalling one coat of arms with another, the matter obtains in German heraldry rather different consideration from the fact that our method and meaning of impalement is practically unknown in that country. At the same time the customary German method of employing two or more separate shields contained within one achievement is not, with the exception of the impalements of arms in the cases of Knights of any Order, a method of marshalling which finds favour with us. There are one or two other exceptional cases in which with us a second shield is necessitated, but speaking generally these "Verbindungs-Wappen" or "Alliance Shields" have no place in British armory, and for British rules and examples reference should be made to the chapter on Marshalling. From the remarks of Herr Ströhl, it is not easy to determine to what extent these "Alliance Shields" are governed by accepted laws of arms or, on the other hand, to what extent they are merely separate arms placed in conjunction from some reason outside of armorial necessity, such method of conjunction being dictated and controlled simply by reasons of artistic design. Fig. 4, for example, depicts the arms of two partners, and whilst there is no rule or law in this country to prevent two partners from placing their shields close together, and from interlacing the mantlings, such a "conjunction" with us remains purely a piece of design from which no precedent or rule can be deduced. And as far as this particular instance is considered the real fact is probably that the status of the matter in Germany is the same as it would be with us, and that the example before us is on a par with the peculiarly startling practice of the Great Western Railway Company, who similarly on their coaches ally the arms of the cities of London and Bristol. The ribbons of steel laid down by the company between these two cities may be bonds akin to fetters matrimonial, but the laws of heraldry give no sanction to and take no cognisance of such a conjunction. That the Great Western Railway Company have nothing to do with the arms of London or of Bristol, and, were that possible, rather less with the robe of estate upon which the shields are carried is, by the way, one of the little peculiarities of so much of the "impersonal" armory of the present day. Another example which comes to mind, which is equally objectionable, is the "achievement" appropriated by the London County Council, which has appropriated to its use the arms of the cities of London and Westminster, which are the symbols of the very jurisdiction it has tried and failed to usurp.

To revert, however, to the German examples, Figs. 1, 2, 3, and 5 take the place of our impaled shields, resulting from marriage, the rule being in Germany that marriage is denoted by the conjunction of the two separate shields under the helmet and crest of the man.

Figs. 6 and 7 show the conjunction of ecclesiastical arms of office with personal arms. The component parts of Fig. 7 can be seen separately in Figs. 1131 and 1132. The arms illustrated on this plate are as follows :—

Fig. 1. Conjoined arms of *Löffelholz-Stromer*. (Reduced copy from a bookplate with the superscription "1493, Wolff Loffelholz," reproduced in Warnecke's *Heraldischen Kunstblättern*, B. III.) Arms of the husband : Gules, a lamb passant argent. Mantling gules and argent. Crest : on a chapeau gules, turned up ermine, in front of wings gules, semé of linden-leaves or, a lamb as in the arms (Löffelholz). Arms of the wife : Gules, three fleurs-de-lis conjoined to the corners of a triangle argent (Stromer). The shield and its figures, together with the helmet of the man, are turned towards the shield of the wife.

Fig. 2. Conjoined arms of *Behaim*, by an unknown artist of the sixteenth century (12 cm. high). Arms : Party per pale argent and gules, a bend wavy sinister sable. Crest : an eagle with wings outstretched argent, ducally gorged sable. Mantling gules and argent

(see Plate XCV. Fig. 1). The arms of the husband are turned towards those of the wife (here left blank), and both shields are held by a naked, kneeling man, wearing the Behaim helmet, which supports the crest over his head.

Fig. 3. Conjoined arms of *Rohrbach-Holzhausen*. (Perhaps by Barthol. Zeitblom.) Arms of the husband : Azure, two arms issuing from the sides of the shield, vested or, holding in the hands proper a chain-link conjoined in pale to another depending from it. Crest : issuing from a coronet two arms embowed, vested, and holding two links of chain as in the arms (Bernhard von Rohrbach, 1482). Arms

of the wife : Sable, three roses argent, seeded gules (Eilchen von Holzhausen, 1501). Supporters : a man and a woman in fifteenth-century costume. (I question if these supporters are intended to be heraldic.)

Fig. 4. Conjoined arms of *Grimm-Würsing*. (Printer's signet by Hans Burgkmair, Augsburg, 1519.) Arms of the Dr. of Med. *Sigismund Grimm* : Or, a wild man brandishing a club proper. Crest : a wild man as in the arms. Arms of *Markus Würsing* or *Wirsung* : Party per pale or and sable, in base three mounds, and above a tree eradicated, the branches ending in three clover-leaves all counterchanged. Mantling sable and or. Crest : a wing on which the device of the shield is repeated. (According to a patent, received from Georg Wirsung, May 16, 1474.) The two coats are

FIG. 1132.—Arms of Schöllingen.

turned towards one another, and the mantlings intertwined. The partnership of the two firms was dissolved in the year 1523 ; Dr. Grimm, who tried to continue printing by himself, came to grief in the following year (see Fig. 1135).

Fig. 5. Alliance arms of *Harrach-Falkenhain*. Arms of the husband : Gules, a bezant, and issuing therefrom three ostrich feathers argent. (*Franz Anton, Graf von Harrach*, died 1768.) Arms of the wife : Quarterly, 1 and 4, azure, three bezants in bend ; 2. gules, a lion rampant double-queued argent ; 3. divided per fess argent and sable, a sea unicorn counterchanged ; and on an inescutcheon argent, a hunting-horn gules (Antonie, Countess von Falkenhain). Both shields are turned towards each other, and are together surmounted by an old Count's crown. The alliance arms are here surrounded by a Liebesseil (cordelière), which is introduced here to show that the achievement is that of a widow as borne after the death of Graf von Harrach.

Fig. 6. Conjoined arms of the *Abbot Michael of Geras*. (From Ströhl's *Die Wappen der Aebte der Prämonstratenserstifte Geras und Pernegg*, 1895.) Arms of the Abbey of Geras, in Lower Austria : Chequy vert and gules. This peculiar device was granted to the Canons by King Ferdinand I., Vienna, June 22, 1542. Arms of the *Abbot Michael Wallner* (1713–1729) : Gules, on a bend vert, between two crosses patée, three mullets of six points.

Fig. 7. Conjoined arms of the *Abbott Franz of Pernegg*. (From the book mentioned above.) Arms of the *Abbey of Pernegg* (dissolved in 1783). The literal translation of the German blazon is : "On a light-blue field, a palm-tree, with a bear drawing itself up it." (This would seem to indicate arms of the landscape type.) Arms of the *Abbot Franz von Schöllingen* (1677–1707) : Quarterly, 1 and 4, argent, a leopard double-queued proper, collared gules, ringed or ; 2 and 3, sable, a griffin segreant gules, on an inescutcheon sable, a heart gules, inflamed proper. The arms of the Abbey, which appear for the first time on a seal (Fig. 1131) of the *Abbot Johann IV.*, 1593, show originally a field party per pale, and instead of the palm a leafy tree. Fig. 1132 gives a representation of the family arms of Schöllingens. The family were originally called "Schöllinger," but received in 1650, with a Patent of Nobility and a confirmation of their arms, the right to call themselves "Schöllingen." Figs. 6 and 7 both show a crosier in bend behind the arms, and it should be noted that in both instances the crook is turned inwards, thereby typifying the confined jurisdiction of the Abbot in distinction to the more open jurisdiction of a Bishop.

THE ART OF HERALDRY

PLATE CL

AN EXAMPLE OF A GENEALOGICAL TREE

The Pedigree of Ströhl

This family, which became extinct on the death of the Bavarian Lieutenant-General Alois, Freiherr von Ströhl, in the year 1836, were supposed to have originally owned estates in Silesia and in Lausitz, and to have borne the name of *Strela*, or *Strel*.

In spite of considerable research, Herr von Ströhl has not been able to prove any connection between the Strelas and Strels occurring in Silesia and Lausitz, and the Bavarian family of Ströhl; neither do the arms of these families show the least similarity.

In the interdict laid upon the Margrave of Brandenburg, Ludwig the Bavarian, May 14, 1350, a Johann von Streel is mentioned amongst the adherents of the Margrave. The migration of one or several of the Strels to Bavaria may perhaps have taken place at this time, if in reality any connection between the two families exists.

At the foot of the family tree appears, as the first authentically proved bearer of the noble name of Ströhl, *Jaroslaus*, married to *Katharina von Kunitz*, daughter of Christoph von Kunitz and Margaretha von Clam. *The Kunitz*, originally Kuttner, from Breisgau, bore : Quarterly, 1 and 4, azure, a lion rampant double-queued and crowned or; 2 and 3, or, a bend sinister sable, on an inescutcheon party per fess or and sable, two mullets of six points counterchanged. (The later Freiherren Kunitz von Weissenburg bear a more elaborate coat of arms. The son of Jaroslaus was named *Christoph*, and was baptized August 20, 1624, at St. Jacob's (St. James's), Straubing. The grandparents were godparents to the child.) He was married July 9, 1649, at Amberg, to *Barbara*, daughter of Johann Georg *von Staudach zu Freudenthurn* and of Maria Francisca Juliana von Lampfrizheim. She was baptized at Amberg July 6, 1623.

The *Staudach*, a Styrian family (at a later date Barons), bore for arms : Quarterly, 1 and 4, gules, an escallop argent ; 2 and 3, a lion rampant to the sinister gules, holding a trefoil vert in its sinister forepaw.

From this marriage resulted a son, *Johann Michael*, who was baptized in St. John's Church, at Auerbach, July 20, 1651. He bore the nickname of "von Rockenbruck" (Rosenbruck ?) He married November 13, 1674, at Auerbach, *Veronika von Grunau*, daughter of Wenzel von Grunau and *Katharina Wagen von Wagensberg*. She was baptized April 4, 1648, at Waldmünchen.

The *Grunaus*, a Silesian family, bore : Gules, two eagle's claws couped in saltire, the talons upwards.

The pair had as far as can be proved only one son, *Johann Georg*, who was baptized at Auerbach September 24, 1690, and on February 10, 1723, became Kurfürstlicher Hofkammerrat and Mautkommissär zu München (Electoral Councillor of the Exchequer, and Commissioner of Customs for Munich). He married October 11, 1716, in the Castle Chapel at Stainach, near Straubing, *Maria Barbara Hermanna von Edelburg zu Altenweyer*, daughter of Johann Georg von Edelburg and Maria Eva Susanna Sabina, Mendlin von Steinsfels. She was baptized March 21, 1696, at Neukirchen hl. Blut, and died at Kötzting May 4, 1730.

The arms of *Edelburg zu Altenweyer* are : Azure, an arm in armour embowed fesswise, couped at the shoulder, brandishing a sword all proper.

There were four children by this marriage, namely :—

1. Maximilian Georg Thomas Adam, baptized at Munich May 10, 1723.
2. Franz Anton, born April 7, 1725.
3. Maria Josepha, born August 5, 1727, and
4. Maria Barbara, born December 9, 1728.

Maximilian was married on November 19, 1748, in the Grafenrieth Castle Chapel, to *Agnes Felicitas*, daughter of Franz Zaver *von Werner auf Grafenrieth*, and of his wife Maria Barbara Rebecca voit von Voithenberg. She was born December 17, 1725, at Grafenrieth, in the Parish (Pfarrei) at Waldmünchen.

The *Werner von Grafenrieth* bore : Sable, a griffin segreant, crowned or, holding in the dexter claw a baton, in the sinister a sword.

Maximilian, Kämmerer und Kaiserlicher Landvogt der Markgrafschäft, Burgau, 1749; Kurfürstlich bayrischer Regierungsrat, 1756-1779, Regierungskanzler und Lehenprobst zu Straubing, received March 3, 1769, *patent* as a Baron, from the Elector Max Joseph III. He had previously received *knightly rank* for himself and his relatives from the Court of the Count Palatine, Graf Zeil, at Zeil, November 6, 1758, and on November 24, 1758, he was officially declared to have established his nobility by patent produced.

On February 1, 1772, he received the title of Privy Councillor, and on August 22, 1775, he really became an acting Privy Councillor. Agnes Felicitas was made Dame of the Order of the Star and Cross Order in 1782. There were nine children by this marriage :—

1. Johann Nepomuk Franz Xaver, born September 24, 1749, at Straubing. He was Canon of the Cathedral and actual Ecclesiastical Councillor, later Dean of the Cathedral and Vicar (or Governor) of Freising ; as also, on July 14, 1792, actual Imperial Privy Councillor.
2. Maria Johanna Nepom. Barbara Ludw. Elisabeth, born November 19, 1750, died June 22, 1752, at Straubing ; buried at St. Peter's.
3. Maria Maximiliana Josepha Felicitas Johanna Nepom., born December 27, 1751, died October 22, 1770; buried at St. James's, Straubing.
4. Maria Barbara Josepha Felicitas Johanna Nepom., born March 3, 1754, at Straubing.
5. Franz Xaver, ¾ year old, died March 25, 1756, at Straubing ; buried at St. Peter's.
6. Franz Xaver Joseph Johann Nepom. Maximilian, born September 18, 1756, died August 29, 1757, at Straubing.
7. Maria Franziska Xav. Johanna Nep. Josepha Felicitas Max, born June 18, 1758, at Straubing.
8. Aloys Johann Nep. Franz Xaver Joseph Max, born June 10, 1760, at Straubing, died July 9, 1836, at Munich, and was buried in the Southern Old Friedhof (Cemetery). From September 1, 1777, to May 5, 1790, he was an officer in the service of France, but then transferred his services to the Bavarian Army, in which he soon held an important position. He died as *Lieutenant-General und Kommandant der Haupt- und Residenzstadt München* k.k. Kämmerer. He had received the Military Badge of Honour, and was Knight of the Military Order of Max and Joseph, of the French Legion of Honour, of the Order of Merit of the Bavarian Crown, and of the Cross of Honour of the Order of St. Louis.

(See E. Wimmer's *Sammelblätter zur Geschichte der Stadt Straubing*, No. 124, 1884.)

9. Joseph Maximilian Franz Xaver Johann Nep., born May 2, 1763, at Straubing.

The arms of the Ströhls are : Quarterly, azure, a bend wavy between two mullets of six points argent ; 2 and 3, or, a lion rampant double-queued gules. The dexter helmet bears as crest a pair of wings addorsed, charged with the arms as in the first quarter, and the sinister helmet has as crest a demi-lion as in the second quarter. The mantlings are, dexter, azure and argent ; sinister, gules and or. (On a seal of Maximilian's appears as supporters two lions regardant double-queued and crowned.) Below in the background is a view of the Bavarian town of Straubing on the Danube, in the time of Jaroslaus von Ströhl. (Bruin and Hogenberg's *Städtebach*, about 1580.)

The surname of Ströhl did not die out in Bavaria when the baronial family became extinct, for there still exist in that country a few burgher families of the name. For instance, Herr Ströhl belongs to a family originally domiciled at Erichstätt, which, however, in spite of the birth of many children in the previous generation, will die out with himself.

CHAPTER LII

"SEIZE-QUARTIERS" : PLATE CLI

Proof of Ancestry

IF any heraldic term has been misunderstood in this country, "Seize-Quartiers" is that term. One hears "Seize-Quartiers" claimed right and left, whereas in British armory it is only on the very rarest occasions that proof of it can be made. In England there is not, and never has been, for any purpose a "test" of blood. By the statutes of various Orders of Knighthood, esquires of knights of those orders are required to show that their grandparents were of gentle birth and entitled to bear arms, and a popular belief exists that Knights of Justice of the Order of the Hospital of St. John of Jerusalem in England need to establish some test of birth. The wording of the statute, however, is very loose and vague, and in fact, judging from the names and arms of some of the knights, must be pretty generally ignored. But Peer, K.G., or C.B., alike need pass no test of birth. The present state of affairs in this country is the natural outcome of the custom of society, which always recognises the wife as of the husband's status, whatever may have been her antecedents, unless the discrepancy is too glaring to be overlooked. In England few indeed care or question whether this person or that person has even a coat of arms ; and in the decision of Society upon a given question as to whether this person or the other has "married beneath himself," the judgment results solely from the circle in which the wife and her people move. By many this curious result is claimed as an example of, and as a telling instance to demonstrate, the broad-minded superiority of the English race, as evidenced by the equality which this country concedes between titled and untitled classes, between official and unofficial personages, between the land-owning and the mercantile communities. But such a conclusion is most superficial. We draw no distinction, and rightly so, between titled and untitled amongst the few remaining families who have held and owned their lands for many generations; but outside this class the confusion is great, and to a close observer it is plainly enough apparent that great distinctions are drawn. But they are often mistaken ones. That the rigid and definite dividing-line between patrician and plebeian, which still exists so much more markedly upon the Continent, can only be traced most sketchily in this country is due to two causes—(1) the fact that in earlier days, when Society was slowly evolving itself, many younger sons of gentle families embarked upon commercial careers, natural family affection, because of such action, preventing a rigid exclusion from the ranks of Society of every one tainted by commerce; (2) the absence in this country of any equivalent of the patent distinguishing marks "de," "van," or "von," which exist amongst our neighbours in Europe.

The result has been that in England there is no possible way (short of specific genealogical investigation) in which it can be ascertained whether any given person is of gentle birth, and the corollary of this last-mentioned

fact is that any real test is ignored. There are few families in this country, outside the Roman Catholic aristocracy (whose marriages are not quite so haphazard as are those of other people), who can show that all their sixteen great-great-grandparents were in their own right entitled to bear arms. That is the true definition of the "Proof of Seize-Quartiers."

In other words, to prove Seize-Quartiers you must show this right to have existed for

	Self.	Parents.	Grand-parents.	Gt.-grand-parents.	Gt.-gt.-grand-parents.
1.	Your	Father's	Father's	Father's	Father.
2.	Your	Father's	Father's	Father's	Mother.
3.	Your	Father's	Father's	Mother's	Father.
4.	Your	Father's	Father's	Mother's	Mother.
5.	Your	Father's	Mother's	Father's	Father.
6.	Your	Father's	Mother's	Father's	Mother.
7.	Your	Father's	Mother's	Mother's	Father.
8.	Your	Father's	Mother's	Mother's	Mother.
9.	Your	Mother's	Father's	Father's	Father.
10.	Your	Mother's	Father's	Father's	Mother.
11.	Your	Mother's	Father's	Mother's	Father.
12.	Your	Mother's	Father's	Mother's	Mother.
13.	Your	Mother's	Mother's	Father's	Father.
14.	Your	Mother's	Mother's	Father's	Mother.
15.	Your	Mother's	Mother's	Mother's	Father.
16.	Your	Mother's	Mother's	Mother's	Mother.

It should be distinctly understood that there is no connection whatever between the list of quarterings which may have been inherited, which it is permissible to display, and "Seize-Quartiers," which should never be marshalled together or displayed as quarterings. In order to give a better idea of "Seize-Quartiers," and to show the comparison between a genealogical tree of a family and a proof of "Seize-Quartiers," Herr Ströhl selected the same family of von Ströhl, which appeared on

Genealogical Chart

Generation 1 (Great-great-grandparents):
- Jaroslaus von Ströhl = Katharina von Kunitz.
- Johann Georg von Staudach = Maria Franc. Juliana von Lampfritzheim.
- Friedrich von Grunau = Maria Joh. von Aheim.
- Sigismund Wagen von Wagensberg = Elisabeth von Hirnheim.
- Johann von Edelburg zu Altenweyer = Margaretha von Blankenfels.
- Johanna Zeiller von Wolffenbach = Maria Joh. von Wildenstein.
- Hermann von Mendel = Maria Cordula von Westach zu Armstorf.
- Georg Albert Proy von Hagbach = Regina von Dumberg.
- Christoph Heinrich von Werner = Barbara von Ponickau, a. d. Hause Kreischa.
- Johann Bernhard von der Asseburg zu Wallhausen und Heinenburg = Veronica von Schönberg, a. d. Hause Lichtenstein.
- Georg von Geilsdorff auf Guttenfürst = Benigna von Einsiedel, a. d. Hause Gnandstein.
- Heinrich von Wachtel auf Herzogswalde und Rochinitz. Anna Barbara von Schleinitz, a. d. Hause Salheim.
- Johann Albert Voith von Voithenberg = Maria Katharina von Grumbach.
- Georg von Hautzenberg = Katharine von der Wensf.
- Johann Alb. Heinr. Everhard auf Mittelburg = Maria Anna von Blankenfels.
- Johann von Visler auf Malgersdorf, Lichtenhag, und Rütting = Maria von Lattorff.

Generation 2 (Great-grandparents):
- Christoph von Ströhl =
- Barbara von Staudach in Freudenthurn.
- Wenzel von Grunau =
- Katharina Wagen von Wagensburg.
- Georg Willibald von Edelburg zu Altenweyer =
- Maria Joh. Zeiller von Wolffenbach.
- Johann von Mendel zu Steinfels =
- Johanna Polyxena Proy von Hagbach.
- Heinrich von Werner zu Grafenreith =
- Martha von der Asseburg, a. d. Hause Wallhausen.
- Rudolf von Geilsdorff auf Guttenfürst =
- Cäcilie von Wachtel.
- Stephan Voith von Voithenberg auf Vordern Langau =
- Maria Barbara Elisabeth von Hautzenberg.
- Karl Wilhelm von Everhard auf Mittelburg =
- Maria Theresia von Visler auf Malgersdorf, Lichtenhag, und Rütten.

Generation 3 (Grandparents):
- Joh. Michael von Ströhl = Veronica von Grunau.
  - Johann Georg von Ströhl.
- Johann Heinrich von Edelburg zu Altenweyer = Maria Eva Susanna Sabina von Mendel zu Steinfels.
  - Maria Barbara Hermanna von Edelburg zu Altenweyer.
- Johann Thomas Heinrich von Werner zu Grafenreith = Barbara von Geilsdorff auf Guttenfürst.
  - Franz Xaver von Werner zu Grafenreith =
- Johann Christoph Wilhelm Voith von Voithenberg = Agnes Felicitas von Everhard auf Mittelburg.
  - Maria Barbara Rebecca Voith von Voithenberg.

Generation 4 (Parents):
- Maximilian Georg Thomas Adam Freiherr von Ströhl = Agnes Felicitas von Werner zu Grafenreith.

Generation 5 (Self):
- Aloys Johann Nepomuk Freiherr von Ströhl.

the previous plate, for repetition in a proof of "Seize-Quartiers." The space at his disposal only permitted an emblazonment indicative of "Seize-Quartiers," which, however, is amply sufficient, and all that is required by the statutes of the Teutonic Order and the Order of Malta. Above, however, we give the particulars, which comprise a proof of "Trente Deux Quartiers," which, owing to the appointment in 1782 of Agnes, Baroness von Ströhl, as "Sternkreuzordensdame" (Dame of the Order of the Star and Cross), are preserved and recorded in the archives of that order. (Fasc. 41, No. 410.)

Few people indeed in this country can prove the more coveted distinction of "Trente Deux Quartiers," the only case that has ever come under my notice being that of the late Albert Joseph, Baron Mowbray, Segrave, and Stourton, for whom an emblazonment of his thirty-two quarters was prepared under the direction of Stephen Tucker, Esq., Somerset Herald.

After many trials (in order to add an existing English example), which have only too surely confirmed one's opinion as to the rarity of "Seize-Quartiers" in this country, it has been found possible in the case of the Duke of Leinster, and details of the "proof" follow :—

1. *Duke's Coronet* (Ribbon of St. Patrick): Argent, a saltire gules (Fitz Gerald).

2. *Lozenge:* Argent, a chief azure, over all a lion rampant gules, ducally crowned or (St. George).

3. *Earl's Coronet* (Ribbon of Hanoverian Guelphic Order): Quarterly ermine and gules, in the centre a crescent on a crescent for cadency (Stanhope).

4. *Lozenge:* Argent, a chevron gules, a double tressure flory and counter-flory of the last (Fleming).

5. *Duke's Coronet* (Garter): Quarterly, 1 and 4, barry of eight or and gules, over all a cross flory sable ; 2 and 3, azure, three laurel leaves or (Leveson-Gower).

6. *Lozenge* (surmounted by Earl's coronet): Gules, three mullets or, on a bordure of the second a tressure flory-counterflory of the first (Sutherland).

7. *Earl's Coronet* (Garter): Quarterly of six, 1. gules, on a bend between six cross crosslets fitchée argent, an inescutcheon or, charged with a demi-lion rampant, pierced through the mouth with an arrow, within a double tressure flory counterflory of the first ; 2. gules, three lions passant guardant in pale or, in chief a label of three points argent ; 3. chequy or and azure ; 4. Gules, a lion rampant argent ; 5. gules, three escallops argent ; 6. barry of six argent and azure, three chaplets gules, in the centre of the quarters a mullet for difference (Howard).

8. *Lozenge:* Sable, three bucks' heads caboshed argent (Cavendish).

9. *Baron's Coronet:* Per chevron engrailed gules and argent, three talbots' heads erased counterchanged (Duncombe).

10. *Lozenge:* Azure, a buck's head caboshed argent (Legge).

11. *Earl's Coronet* (Ribbon of Thistle): Or, a fess chequy argent

(1)	(2)	(3)	(4)	(5)	(6)	(7)	(8)	(9)	(10)	(11)	(12)	(13)	(14)	(15)	(16)
Augustus Frederick (Fitz Gerald), 3rd Duke of Leinster, born 21st August 1791, married 16th June 1818, died 10th October	William Robert (Fitz Gerald) K.P., born 13th March 1749, married 7th November 1775, died 20th October 1804.=	Hon. Emilia Olivia St. George, dau. of Usher (St. George), Baron St. George of Hatley St. George.	Lady Charlotte Augusta (Stanhope), born 15th February 1793, died 15th February 1859.	Charles (Stanhope), 3rd Earl of Harrington, G.C.H., born 17th March 1853, married 23rd May 1779, died 5th September 1859.=	Jane, dau. and co-heir of Sir John Fleming, Bart., of Brompton Park.	George Granville (Sutherland - Leveson - Gower, formerly Leveson-Gower), 2nd Duke of Sutherland, K.G., born 8th August 1786, married 28th May 1823, died 28th February 1861=	George Granville (Leveson-Gower), 1st Duke of Sutherland, K.G., born 9th January 1758, married 4th September 1785, died 5th July 1833.=	Elizabeth, *suo jure* Countess of Sutherland, born 24th May 1765, died 29th January 1839.	Lady Harriet Elizabeth Georgiana Howard, born 21st May 1806, died 27th October 1868.	George (Howard), 6th Earl of Carlisle, K.G., born 17th September 1773, married 11th March 1801, died 7th October 1848.=	Lady Georgiana Cavendish, eldest dau. and co-heir of William, 5th Duke of Devonshire, K.G.	William (Duncombe), 2nd Baron Feversham, born 14th January 1798, married 18th December 1823, died 11th February 1867=	Charles (Duncombe), 1st Baron Feversham, born 5th December 1764, married 24th September 1795, died 16th July 1841.=	Lady Charlotte Legge, only dau. of William, 2nd Earl of Dartmouth, died 5th November 1848.	George (Stewart), 8th Earl of Galloway, K.T., born 24th March 1768, married 18th April 1797, died 27th March 1834=	Lady Louisa Stewart, died 5th March 1889=	Lady Jane Paget, dau. of Henry, 1st Earl of Uxbridge, died 30th June 1842.	Right Hon. Sir James Robert George Graham, 2nd Bart., P.C., G.C.B., born 1st June 1792, died 25th October 1861=	Sir James Graham, 1st Bart., of Netherby, born April 1761, married 28th September 1782, died 13th April 1824.=	Lady Catherine Stewart, dau. of John, 7th Earl of Galloway, died 20th September 1836.	Fanny Callander, married 8th July 1819, died 25th October 1857.	Colonel James Callander of Craigforth, born 1774, died ——, married (as his 3rd wife) 1776=	Lady Elizabeth MacDonnel, dau. of Alexander, 5th Earl of Antrim, died 1796.

Charles William (Fitz Gerald), 4th Duke of Leinster, born 30th March 1819, married 30th October 1847, died 10th February 1887=			Lady Caroline Sutherland-Leveson-Gower, born 15th April 1827, died 13th May 1887.		William Ernest (Duncombe), 1st Earl of Feversham (created 1868), born 28th January 1829, married 7th August 1851=		Mabel Violet Graham.

Gerald (Fitz Gerald), 5th Duke of Leinster, born 16th August 1851, married 17th January 1884, died 1st December 1893=   Lady Hermione Wilhelmina Duncombe, born 30th March 1864, died 19th March 1895.

The Most Noble Maurice (Fitz Gerald), Duke of Leinster, Marquess and Earl of Kildare, co. Kildare, Earl and Baron of Offaly, all in the Peerage of Ireland ; Viscount Leinster of Taplow, co. Bucks, in the Peerage of Great Britain ; and Baron Kildare of Kildare in the Peerage of the United Kingdom ; Premier Duke, Marquess, and Earl of Ireland ; born 1st March 1887.

The following are the heraldic particulars of the shields which would occur were this proof of "Seize-Quartiers" similarly emblazoned. The arms are numbered across from left to right in rows of 16, 8, 4, 2, and 1.

and azure, surmounted of a bend engrailed gules, within a tressure flory counterflory of the last (Stewart).

12. *Lozenge:* Sable, on a cross engrailed between four eagles displayed argent, five lions passant guardant of the field (Paget).

13. *Baronet's Badge:* Or, on a chief sable, three escallops of the field (Graham).

14. *Lozenge:* Arms as on No. 11 (Stewart).

15. *Shield:* Quarterly, 1 and 4, sable, a bend chequy or and gules between six billets of the second; 2. azure, a stag's head caboshed or ; 3. gules, three legs armed proper, conjoined in the fess point and flexed in triangle, garnished and spurred or (Callander).

16. *Lozenge:* Quarterly, 1. or, a lion rampant gules ; 2. or, a dexter arm issuant from the sinister fess point out of a cloud proper, the hand holding a cross crosslet fitcheé erect azure; 3. argent, a ship with sails furled sable ; 4. per fess azure and vert, a dolphin naiant in fess proper (Macdonell).

17. As 1, but no ribbon of K.P.

18. *Lozenge:* Arms as 3.

19. *Duke's Coronet* (Garter) : Quarterly, 1 and 4, as in 5 ; 2. as in 5 ; 3. as in No. 6.

20. *Lozenge:* As No. 7.

21. *Baron's Coronet:* As No. 9.

22. *Lozenge:* As No. 14.

23. As No. 13, but with ribbon of a G.C.B.

FIG. 1133.—Gravestone of Aloys Freiherr von Ströhl.

24. *Lozenge:* As No. 15.

25. As 17.

26. *Lozenge:* As No. 19.

27. As 21, but Earl's coronet.

28. *Lozenge:* As No. 13, but no Baronet's badge.

29. As 17.

30. *Lozenge:* As No. 9.

31. *Arms:* Argent, a saltire gules. Crest: a monkey statant proper, environed about the middle with a plain collar, and chained or. Supporters : two monkeys (as the crest). Mantling gules and argent. Coronet of a duke. Motto : "Crom a boo."

In many "Proofs of Ancestry," of old and recent date, there will be found, as connecting links between the separate shields, branches ornamented with leaves, symbolising the genealogical tree.

These would seem more rightly to belong to a genealogical tree, and *not* to a "Proof of Ancestry," because the growth of the former is in directly the opposite direction to that of a "Proof of Ancestry" in which the *youngest* member of the family stands at the foot of the entire "Proof."

The arms of the four grandparents are very frequently to be met with on the gravestones of nobles subsidiary to the arms of the deceased : on the top dexter side the arms of the father, that is, the same as those of the person to whom the gravestone is a memorial ; on the bottom dexter the arms of the grandmother on the father's side ; on the top sinister side the arms of the mother, and underneath those of the grandmother on the mother's side. In order to

FIG. 1134.—Arms of Johanns von Heringen (1487).

avoid a repetition of the central coat of arms, occasionally, instead of the father's arms, the arms of the great-grandmother on the father's side are inserted.

According to this scheme, a gravestone of Aloys, Freiherr von Ströhl (compare "Proof" on the plate) would be grouped as follows : in the centre, *Ströhl;* at the top right-hand *Grunaw;* on the left *Werner;* on the bottom right-hand *Edelburg;* and on the left *Voith,* the charges of the arms on the dexter side being always in Germany turned towards those in the centre (Fig. 1133).

Not only on gravestones, but also in other representations of arms, the adorning of the outer framework with ancestral arms is very popular. As an example of this method of decoration, reference should be made to Fig. 1134.   H. S. AND A. C. F-D.

CHAPTER LIII

HERALDIC ILLUMINATION

BY JOHN VINYCOMB, M.R.I.A.

THE art of illuminating, when allied with heraldry, forms at once the most brilliant and effective of all the decorative arts, and its practice the most fascinating and delightful. The wide range of styles or periods of art, as well as of subjects, gives the fullest scope

and play of fancy in the treatment of the work both as to design and colouring.

It must however be kept in mind, while it is admitted that heraldry may be truly and fitly introduced with all its brilliant tinctures in conjunction with illuminating, regard must be paid to the congruity of style or period of both, so that no apparent anachronism may be made in the work. In this the knowledge and good taste of the artist will frequently be put to a severe test, so to reconcile the heraldic treatment of the shield and its accessories with the style of decoration and printing used in illuminated MSS. of a given period in the past, or with the semi-natural ornament of the present day.

The artistic treatment of heraldic subjects has for many years past been a somewhat neglected subject, a crude formality being the prevailing idea of its capabilities. A revival in this respect has taken place, and in the works of many of our leading designers heraldry is assuming its rightful place in the decorative arts of the present day.

First Principle of Heraldic Art

The leading principles adopted by the old heralds of the fourteenth century may be briefly noted. That the devices and charges upon the shields and banners of the warriors might be recognisable at a distance, they must be clearly defined, which would not be the case if painted naturally as a picture. To attain this end the first principle was the contrasting of tinctures, light upon dark and dark upon light; the metals (*or* and *argent*) partaking of light, and the furs, as opposed to the heraldic colours proper, pertaining to darkness—that is, metal may not be upon metal, nor colour upon colour, but only colour upon metal, and *vice versâ*, and the furs by contrast with either or both colours and metals.

Second Principle

A severe conventionalism and somewhat exaggerated forms of animals and things served best the purpose intended; each object being of its special tincture was outlined for greater clearness and precision, shading being but slightly made use of.

Another rule has grown into use from early times in heraldic emblazonment. The shield, helmet, mantling, crest, supporters, and all adjuncts of an achievement of arms must be painted with the light coming from the dexter side, with the shadows on the sinister.

Good Drawing Essential

Good heraldry does not, as some people imagine, imply bad drawing, quite the contrary; a certain amount of conventionalism is necessary, and the better and more characteristic the drawing, the more effective will be the result.

Proper or Natural Colour

The above remarks apply especially to those parts of an achievement tinctured of the heraldic colours. Those animate and inanimate charges which appear in heraldry termed *proper*—that is, in their proper or natural colour—the artist will naturally so conventionalise their forms as to adapt them to heraldic conditions, tincturing them in their own true and proper colours in such a way as they may show clearly and distinctly, and in harmony with the rest of the work.

It may here be stated that while the various forms of shields and helmets, the quaint and often fantastic forms of the mantling, and other accessories afford the artist exercise for his originality and taste, it is advisable in most cases to maintain a modest reticence rather than display an exuberant fancy. A simple dignity of treatment, combined with true heraldic feeling, will be found generally preferable.

PRACTICAL NOTES ON EMBLAZONING AND ILLUMINATING

It is presumed the student understands the rules and principles of heraldry, and has acquired the habit of care-ful and accurate drawing, as well as some practice in the use of the brush, &c. Heraldry and illuminating are so intimately related in practice, the same materials and methods of work are applicable to both branches of art. The following practical notes, it is hoped, will be of assistance in putting the student in a fair way of working.

APPLIANCES AND MATERIALS

At first the student need only provide those most needful at the start, and which can be added to as required, from the artist-colourman, or a complete outfit for heraldic illuminating may at once be procured. The following list includes only the most necessary. A few hints on the colours to be used and their qualities will be of service.

Materials

Vellum, Paper, &c.—Vellum, Bristol board, card-board, or paper, as may be preferred. Bristol board is perhaps the most suitable and pleasant to work upon by the beginner. Vellum is only required for important works of permanent value, and would be needless expense to practise upon.

Implements required.—Pencils, compasses with pen and pencil legs, draw-pen, tracing point, agate burnisher, small parallel rulers, several small sable brushes, tracing paper, and a limited stock of moist water-colours in tubes, are about all that are required by the beginner.

The Tinctures : Colours to be Used

Gules = *Red.*—The best colour to use is *vermilion.* It is a bright red opaque body, and for the local colour may be used pure and without any admixture. It may be shaded with carmine or crimson lake, and also for the markings. For the high lights mix a little Chinese white with the vermilion; the reflect lights may be pure orange or strong yellow.

Azure = *Blue.*—Use *French blue.* This brilliant colour is only semi-opaque, and too deep in tone to be used pure. A little Chinese white is therefore to be mixed with it, so as to reduce it to the proper strength. For the high lights a little more of the Chinese white is to be added to the local colour, while for the shadows and markings more of the pure colour is to be added.

Vert = *Green.*—Hooker's green, modified with Chinese white, answers very well. *Green oxide of chromium,* a low-toned velvety green of opaque body, may sometimes be advantageously used instead of the brighter greens. Brighten and shade as above by lighter and darker hues. Emerald green, extremely vivid in colour, though very useful for small charges, is not suitable for larger surfaces of the shield and ordinaries, being overpoweringly bright and staring.

Sable = *Black.*—*Lamp black* is the most useful colour for this, being very opaque. It is best to mix a little Chinese white to reduce the intense blackness, using the pure colour for the shadows and markings. It is well to add to the black a very little yellow with the Chinese white for the high lights, to obviate the chalky effect it is otherwise apt to have. Reflected lights to be yellow or orange. Lamp black is used in *outlining* (for which see later).

Purpure = *Purple.*—A tincture seldom used in heraldry, for which *purple lake* answers very well when modified with Chinese white, and perhaps a little French blue if found too red; shaded and brightened as the preceding.

Tenne, Tawny, or *Brusk.*—A tincture early used in British heraldry. For this orangy hue, *orange chrome* may be used.

Sanguine or *Murray* is a dark brown. This and tenne are more frequently used for liveries.

THE ART OF HERALDRY

Extra Colours.—A few supplementary colours for general use, at the discretion of the artist, will be necessary, as *chrome yellow, cadmium, yellow ochre, burnt umbre, sepia, Prussian blue, indigo, olive green, &c.*, in addition to those mentioned under tinctures.

No Regulation Standard of Strength of Tinctures.—It may be remarked that there is no regulation standard as to strength of colour for heraldic tinctures. Each artist may have his own ideas in that respect, but the following rules are generally understood and acted upon : First, that the tinctures should as nearly as possible be all of relatively equal depth or intensity of hue, so that one should not appear to be more forcible than another ; second, that high pictorial relief should never be attempted. In banners especially everything should appear even with the surface, and not as if projecting from it. Upon shields, however, the appearance of a low relief is permissible, and the colours painted firmly, producing a solid, even tint, without streaks or mottling.

How to Lay On the Tinctures.—This is generally a great difficulty with beginners, from their previous practice in water-colours, where the tints are put on in washes. Some little practice will therefore be necessary to surmount this technical difficulty ; the chief thing to keep in mind in painting with *body colour*, as all the tinctures are, is not to lay on the colour either too thick or too thin, but in a happy medium of consistency which will be understood by a little practice, painting evenly over the surface with a not too full brush, avoiding getting it thicker at one place than another, beginning at one part, and continuing gradually over the entire surface. A second coat will sometimes be found necessary to obtain an even tone of colour.

MODE OF WORKING

The Drawing Ready for Tracing.—As so much depends upon the correct drawing and disposition of the parts for the effective display of a heraldic design, it is advisable always to make a first sketch in outline upon thin writing-paper, which may be traced down to the material to be worked upon. In copying an existing drawing it is then necessary to make a tracing of it in outline in pencil.

To Reduce or Enlarge a Design.—Should a drawing or design require to be reduced from a larger to a smaller size, or *vice versâ*, the method of reducing or enlarging by squares will be found most helpful, that is, dividing the space occupied by the design in either case into the same number of squares by light pencil lines, then with the pencil follow the outline through the corresponding spaces in the altered size.

FIG. 1134*a.*—Method of reducing or enlarging by squares.

Tracing Down : Transfer Paper.—It is the most convenient way of tracing down the design to use what may be called the *transfer paper*, which is prepared as follows : Upon one side of a piece of tissue paper (6 or 8 inches square is sufficient for most purposes) rub very sparingly with black-lead, using a small pad of cotton-wool to get an evenly dark surface, dusting off the superfluous black lead before using. This paper, if preserved, will always be handy to use when required for similar purposes.

Tracing Down.—Place the sketch or tracing in its proper position on the paper, and holding it in its place with one hand or with drawing-pins or small weights, slip the transfer paper under it with the blackened side down, then with a tracing-point or a sharp, hard pencil carefully go over the outlines of the sketch, looking occasionally to see that the traced lines are not too heavy or too faint, and to make sure that no part has been omitted. We have now a clear and precise outline ready for painting. The outline having been traced down, perfect any parts with the pencil that may be defective. If the sides of the shield are proper curves, and can be made with the compasses, see that the centre points are accurately marked and the curves drawn with the pencil compasses, and the straight lines or divisions of the shield drawn with the parallel rulers, making sure always that your vertical and horizontal lines are true before using the colours. When *or* and *argent* in metals are used they should be painted first.

Brushes : Outlining Brush.—It is necessary to have several in use for flat tints, but for *outlining* it is necessary to prepare a special small sable brush by cutting a lot of the outside hairs away ; run a sharp penknife round the roots of the hair close to the quill so that only about one-third of the hair remains, then with small scissors snip off the extreme fine point, so that you will have an extremely pliant implement capable of making continuous lines of an equal thickness for the outlining. The pen compasses and the draw-pen are useful mechanical aids in outlining all regular curves and for straight lines.

Lamp Black with Gum for Outlining.—A little gum added to the lamp black is useful in outlining, as it keeps the colour from running, and produces a glossy and more decisive outline than the dull black used alone. The fine outlining brush is the best and most useful implement for outlining all parts after the tinctures are painted in, and with a little practice will be found most reliable for producing a free and even line. The writing-pen is not suitable for this purpose, as the ink from the pen is apt to spread upon the absorbent colour.

Indelible Ink for Outlining.—Some artists prefer to outline all parts with the pen before beginning the painting. When this is done it is well to use *indelible ink* (to be had from the artist's colourman) so that the colour may not wash up in painting. If a clear pencil outline is at first made the pen outline may be dispensed with.

Text-writing : Inks, Pens.—In doing *text* characters for inscriptions, &c., when of large size, the draw-pen may be used for the vertical strokes ; for smaller characters it is best to use a writing-pen with the point cut off, according to the width of stroke desired, the fine lines of the letters to be added after with an ordinary pen. Engrossing characters are best executed with a flexible crow-quill barrel steel pen. The indelible ink may be used for writing, Arnold's Japan writing ink, or similar black permanent ink. When coloured lettering is done, the paint, of proper consistency, is to be put into the pen with the brush.

Flat Painting necessary : Order of Painting the Tinctures and Shading.—It is important that each of the tinctures, particularly when the spaces are large, should be very flatly painted, of a fair regulation strength ; then paint in the shadows, after which the drawing should be outlined and the lights added. For simple work not more than three shades of any one colour need be used (unless a high degree of finish is required). First, the local colour ; second, shadings and markings; and third, the high lights and reflected lights, and finally, after the outline a general finish up.

Finishing: Light and Shade, &c.: A Simple Example.— In finishing up the shield shapes and honourable ordinaries, as well as the common charges borne thereon, a certain appearance of relief must to some extent be given of one thing being placed upon another, as *azure, a bend or*. After the tinctures are put in the *bend* must be outlined with a dark line, thicker on the sinister side. A line of white or pale gold colour within the outline on the lighted side should be drawn with the draw-pen and parallel ruler, and a similar line of *orange* on the shadow side, the shield itself being finished in same way, while upon the tincture of the field itself should be drawn a deeper shadow line of its own blue colour. This principle should be carried out in all parts, no matter how complicated, so as to give the appearance of slight relief from the groundwork.

*Or and Argent: Painting.—*When the metals *or* and *argent* are used instead of yellow and white, which represent the two metals, it is always best to paint these in first of all, so as to be able to burnish them without injuring the adjoining colours.

*Shell Gold: Aluminium.—*Shell gold and aluminium (for argent) are the most convenient forms in which the metals can be employed for small works, while for larger works gold-leaf must be employed. Shell silver should not be used, as it soon tarnishes. Aluminium has quite the same appearance, and does not tarnish. The gold and aluminium as supplied in mussel-shells is very easy of application. With a clean sable brush dipped in water mix up the gold in the shell to a proper consistency for painting, and apply very evenly, taking care that no lumps are formed, as these would blister off when the burnisher is applied. If not sufficiently well covered go over it again to equalise. When this is quite dry, it is next to be burnished to have either a *dull* or a *bright* surface.

*A Dull or Mat Surface.—*A dull or "mat" surface, as it is termed, is first produced by laying a piece of smooth writing-paper over the gold, and with the agate rub the paper briskly until the desired effect is produced.

*A Bright Metallic Surface.—*Should a bright burnished gold surface be desired, gently rub the finger lightly over the dull gold surface and burnish again without using the paper between the gold and the agate burnisher. (The slight moisture of the finger makes the burnisher glide freely over the gold without scraping or scratching.)

*Gold Colour = Or.—*When gold itself is not used, yellow, its colour symbol, is employed instead. *Cadmium*, a deep-toned yellow, slightly reduced with Chinese white, or *chrome yellow*, modified with a little yellow ochre or similar low-toned colour, answers very well for this, with shades of pure yellow ochre, deepened where needful with burnt umber.

*White = Argent.—*For this the white ground is left plain, the field or charges to be shaded with warm grey, and having yellow reflected lights.

IN CONCLUSION

With the foregoing hints the student will be in possession of the chief points to be observed and acted upon, and should he pursue the study with patience and the exercise of a true heraldic spirit, besides the consequent pleasure which the exercise affords, each successive work thus executed will be an upward step towards a higher degree of excellence.

As an employment to the artist or as a recreation and accomplishment for persons of taste and leisure, heraldic illumination possesses attractions beyond most other studies. The result is tangible and enduring, and when well executed will always be highly prized.

J. V.

FIG. 1135.

SYNOPTICAL INDEX

SYNOPTICAL INDEX

INDEX OF PROPER NAMES

INDEX OF PROPER NAMES

496

INDEX OF PROPER NAMES

INDEX OF PROPER NAMES

INDEX OF PROPER NAMES

INDEX OF PROPER NAMES

INDEX OF PROPER NAMES

INDEX OF PROPER NAMES

THE END